THE OXFORD HANDBOOK OF

EVIDENCE-BASED CRIME AND JUSTICE POLICY

THE OXFORD HANDBOOK OF

EVIDENCE-BASED CRIME AND JUSTICE POLICY

Edited by

BRANDON C. WELSH
STEVEN N. ZANE
and
DANIEL P. MEARS

OXFORD
UNIVERSITY PRESS

Oxford University Press is a department of the University of Oxford. It furthers the University's objective of excellence in research, scholarship, and education by publishing worldwide. Oxford is a registered trade mark of Oxford University Press in the UK and certain other countries.

Published in the United States of America by Oxford University Press
198 Madison Avenue, New York, NY 10016, United States of America.

© Oxford University Press 2024

All rights reserved. No part of this publication may be reproduced, stored in a retrieval system, or transmitted, in any form or by any means, without the prior permission in writing of Oxford University Press, or as expressly permitted by law, by license, or under terms agreed with the appropriate reproduction rights organization. Inquiries concerning reproduction outside the scope of the above should be sent to the Rights Department, Oxford University Press, at the address above.

You must not circulate this work in any other form
and you must impose this same condition on any acquirer.

Library of Congress Cataloging-in-Publication Data
Names: Welsh, Brandon, 1969– author. | Zane, Steven N., author. |
Mears, Daniel P., 1966– author.
Title: The Oxford handbook of evidence-based crime and justice policy /
Brandon C. Welsh, Steven N. Zane, Daniel P. Mears.
Description: New York, NY : Oxford University Press, [2024] |
Includes index.
Identifiers: LCCN 2023025331 | ISBN 9780197618110 (hardback) |
ISBN 9780197618134 (epub) | ISBN 9780197618141
Subjects: LCSH: Evidence. | Justice, Administration of.
Classification: LCC BC171 .W457 2024 | DDC 121—dc23/eng/20230720
LC record available at https://lccn.loc.gov/2023025331

DOI: 10.1093/oxfordhb/9780197618110.001.0001

Printed by Sheridan Books, Inc., United States of America

Contents

Preface ix
Contributors xi

1. Evidence-Based Crime and Justice Policy 1
   BRANDON C. WELSH, STEVEN N. ZANE, AND DANIEL P. MEARS

PART I: CONCEPTS, METHODS, AND CRITICAL PERSPECTIVES

2. Evaluating Research and Assessing Research Evidence 21
   BRANDON C. WELSH AND DANIEL P. MEARS

3. Translational Criminology and Evidence-Based Policy and Practice 37
   CODY W. TELEP

4. Implementation Science for Evidence-Based Policy 58
   DEAN L. FIXSEN, MELISSA K. VAN DYKE, AND KAREN A. BLASE

5. Toward System-Level Change, Population Impacts, and Equity 76
   HOLLY S. SCHINDLER

PART II: JUVENILE JUSTICE

6. Advancing the Evidence-Based Era: Twenty-Five Years of Lessons Learned in Washington State's Juvenile Justice System 91
   ELIZABETH K. DRAKE AND LAUREN KNOTH-PETERSON

7. Systems of Change: The Pennsylvania Model 117
   SHAWN PECK, JANET A. WELSH, KRISTOPHER T. GLUNT, AND ROGER SPAW

8. Diversion: What Do We Know? 140
   ROGER S. SMITH

9. Evidence-Based Innovations in Juvenile Probation 159
   DAVID L. MYERS AND KELLY ORTS

10. Using Evidence-Based Practices to Improve Juvenile Drug
    Treatment Courts   179
    CHRISTOPHER J. SULLIVAN, VITOR GONÇALVES, AND
    NICOLE MCKENNA

11. Evidence-Oriented Youth Justice   198
    JEFFREY A. BUTTS, JOHN K. ROMAN, AND KATHERYNE PUGLIESE

PART III: CRIMINAL JUSTICE

12. Legitimacy and Evidence-Based Policy   223
    JUSTICE TANKEBE AND ANTHONY BOTTOMS

13. Evidence-Based Policing   245
    CYNTHIA LUM AND CHRISTOPHER S. KOPER

14. CCTV Video Surveillance and Crime Control: The Current
    Evidence and Important Next Steps   265
    ERIC L. PIZA

15. Rehabilitation for Enduring Change: Toward Evidence-Based
    Corrections   286
    MICHAEL ROCQUE

16. Incarceration-Based Drug Treatment   309
    OJMARRH MITCHELL

17. Making Prisoner Re-entry Evidence-Based   326
    HELEN KOSC AND DAVID S. KIRK

18. Evidence-Based Policy for Diverse Criminal Justice Populations   349
    KAELYN SANDERS, JENNIFER COBBINA-DUNGY,
    AND HENRIKA MCCOY

PART IV: ALTERNATIVES TO SYSTEM RESPONSES

19. Early Prevention as an Alternative to Imprisonment: The Research
    Evidence on Monetary Costs and Benefits   373
    BRANDON C. WELSH, HEATHER PATERSON, AND
    DAVID P. FARRINGTON

20. Evidence-Based Intervention Programs Targeting Antisocial Children and Youth in Norway: Parent Management Training—Oregon Model (PMTO)   391
Terje Ogden, Elisabeth Askeland, and Kristine Amlund-Hagen

21. Systems of Change: Communities That Care   407
Abigail A. Fagan

22. Reducing School Crime and Student Misbehavior: An Evidence-Based Analysis   424
Allison Ann Payne

23. Evidence-Based Strategies for Preventing Urban Youth Violence   444
Katherine M. Ross, Colleen S. Walsh, Angela G. Angulo, Carine E. Leslie, and Patrick H. Tolan

24. A Place Management Approach to Promote Evidence-Based Crime Prevention   466
Tamara D. Herold

25. Using Research to Inform Services for Victims of Crime   484
Jillian J. Turanovic, Julie L. Kuper, and Mackenzie Masters

PART V: PROMOTING GREATER USE OF EVIDENCE-BASED POLICY

26. Social Inequality and Evidence-Based Policy: An Agenda for Change   509
Nancy Rodriguez

27. Applying What We Know and Building an Evidence Base: Reducing Disproportionate Minority Contact   525
Steven N. Zane

28. Applying What We Know and Building an Evidence Base: Reducing Gun Violence   550
John J. Donohue

29. Mass Evidence-Based Policy as an Alternative to Mass Incarceration   580
Daniel P. Mears and Joshua C. Cochran

30. "Big Data" and Evidence-Based Policy and Practice: The Advantages, Challenges, and Long-Term Potential of Naturally Occurring Data 598
    DANIEL T. O'BRIEN

31. Imposed Use: A New Route to Evidence-Based Policy 621
    STEVEN N. ZANE

32. The Role of Policymakers, Criminal Justice Administrators and Practitioners, and Citizens in Creating, Evaluating, and Using Evidence-Based Policy 645
    DANIEL P. MEARS AND NATASHA A. FROST

Index 667

Preface

In recent decades, calls for "evidence-based" policies in crime and justice have become commonplace. That bodes well for policy and creates innumerable opportunities and roles for researchers. But there remains a marked disjuncture between calls for evidence-based policy and an understanding of what it means for policy to be evidence-based. Matters of crime and justice seem particularly susceptible to this disconnect, one to which scholars and researchers—not just elected officials—have contributed. Regardless, these calls for evidence-based policy provide a powerful foundation for bringing about rational, cost-effective, and humane policies for the betterment of society.

The threats to—and the need for—improved policy are acute. This includes contending with crime policy agendas that continue to be driven by anecdotal evidence, program "favorites of the month," and political ideology. An evidence-based approach can help to address this state of affairs by promoting the use of the best available research evidence to inform decisions that affect the public good. Put another way, it is about making sure that research evidence stands at center stage in political and policy decisions.

This *Handbook* showcases much of what is right with evidence-based crime and justice policy and identifies the critical challenges that confront it today and in the years to come. It is intended to serve as the most authoritative and scholarly source on research and experience on evidence-based policy as it applies to crime and justice in the United States and across the Western world. The volume is guided by three core objectives: (1) to promote new and productive ways to think about evidence-based policy; (2) to show how research can contribute to and guide evidence-based policy in the domains of juvenile justice, criminal justice, and alternatives to system responses; and (3) to identify strategies that can increase reliance on evidence-based policy and, in particular, policy that is well designed, implemented, monitored, and evaluated.

The volume is divided into five parts. Part I addresses a particular question: How can we think about evidence-based policy? Chapters deal with core concepts, research methodologies, and critical perspectives. Parts II and III are organized around the two major systems in which research evidence is being used to inform policy: juvenile justice and criminal justice, respectively. Both parts include chapters that focus on key stages of processing and leading programs and practices. Part IV examines how research evidence is being used to inform policy alternatives to more punitive system responses. It includes chapters that focus on micro-level and macro-level efforts taking place outside of the system and that respond to the needs of neglected groups. Part V, which includes several crosscutting chapters, profiles efforts to promote greater use of evidence-based policy and ways to improve the knowledge base for evidence-based policymaking, especially in critical underdeveloped areas.

Writing and editing chapters for this book was immensely rewarding and great fun. Going into the project, the three of us were fairly confident that we would enjoy collaborating with one another. What we did not fully appreciate was how working with the invited chapter authors would not only produce an outstanding volume but also make this experience far more enriching for us than we ever could have imagined. This was due to the authors—from initial conversations about their chapters, to thorough and timely revisions to drafts, to producing high-quality content and brilliant writing. We thank each and every chapter author—all 53 of them—for contributing their expertise to this project, as well as for putting up with our tireless questions and requests to clarify key points that would be important for helping readers. Not least, we wish to single out for special appreciation three people who made this project possible and were indispensable from start to finish: Michael Tonry and Sandra Bucerius, the general editors of the Oxford Handbooks in Criminology and Criminal Justice, and Meredith Keffer, acquisition editor at Oxford University Press. Thank you!

Brandon C. Welsh
Steven N. Zane
Daniel P. Mears

Contributors

KRISTINE AMLUND-HAGEN is the General Director of the Norwegian Center for Child Behavioral Development.

ANGELA G. ANGULO is a former student at Virginia Commonwealth University.

ELISABETH ASKELAND is a Department Director in the Norwegian Center for Child Behavioral Development.

KAREN A. BLASE is an Implementation Scientist and Co-director of the Active Implementation Research Network.

ANTHONY BOTTOMS is the Emeritus Wolfson Professor of Criminology in the Institute of Criminology at the University of Cambridge.

JEFFREY A. BUTTS is a Research Professor and the Director of the Research and Evaluation Center at John Jay College of Criminal Justice, City University of New York.

JENNIFER COBBINA-DUNGY is an Associate Professor in the School of Criminal Justice at Michigan State University.

JOSHUA C. COCHRAN is an Associate Professor in the School of Criminal Justice at the University of Cincinnati.

JOHN J. DONOHUE is the C. Wendell and Edith M. Carlsmith Professor of Law at Stanford University Law School and a Research Associate at the National Bureau of Economic Research.

ELIZABETH K. DRAKE is a Manager at the Dispute Resolution Center of Thurston County in Washington State.

ABIGAIL A. FAGAN is the Research Foundation Professor in the Department of Sociology and Criminology and Law at the University of Florida.

DAVID P. FARRINGTON is the Emeritus Professor of Psychological Criminology in the Institute of Criminology at the University of Cambridge and Director of the Cambridge Study in Delinquent Development.

DEAN L. FIXSEN is an Implementation Scientist at the Active Implementation Research Network.

NATASHA A. FROST is a Professor in the School of Criminology and Criminal Justice at Northeastern University.

KRISTOPHER T. GLUNT is the Standardized Program Evaluation Protocol Project Manager with the Edna Bennett Pierce Prevention Research Center at Pennsylvania State University.

VITOR GONÇALVES is a doctoral student in the School of Criminology and Criminal Justice at Texas State University at San Marcos.

TAMARA D. HEROLD is an Associate Professor and the Director of the Crowd Management Research Council in the Department of Criminal Justice at the University of Nevada, Las Vegas.

DAVID S. KIRK is a Professor in the Department of Sociology and a Professorial Fellow of Nuffield College at the University of Oxford.

LAUREN KNOTH-PETERSON is a Senior Research Associate at the Washington State Institute for Public Policy.

CHRISTOPHER S. KOPER is a Professor in the Department of Criminology, Law, and Society at George Mason University.

HELEN KOSC is a doctoral student in the Department of Sociology at the University of Oxford.

JULIE L. KUPER is a doctoral student in the College of Criminology and Criminal Justice at Florida State University.

CARINE E. LESLIE is a doctoral student in the Clark-Hill Institute for Positive Youth Development at Virginia Commonwealth University.

CYNTHIA LUM is a University Professor in the Department of Criminology, Law, and Society and the Director of the Center for Evidence-Based Crime Policy at George Mason University.

MACKENZIE MASTERS is a doctoral student in the College of Criminology and Criminal Justice at Florida State University.

HENRIKA MCCOY is a Professor in the School of Social Work at the University of Texas at Austin.

NICOLE MCKENNA is a doctoral student in the School of Criminal Justice at Rutgers University.

DANIEL P. MEARS is a Distinguished Research Professor and the Mark C. Stafford Professor of Criminology in the College of Criminology and Criminal Justice at Florida State University.

OJMARRH MITCHELL is a Professor in the Department of Criminology, Law, and Society at the University of California, Irvine.

DAVID L. MYERS is a Professor of Criminal Justice and the Chair of the Department of Criminal Justice at the University of New Haven.

DANIEL T. O'BRIEN is a Professor of Public Policy and Urban Affairs and Criminology and the Director of the Boston Area Research Initiative at Northeastern University.

TERJE OGDEN is the former General Director of the Norwegian Center for Child Behavioral Development.

KELLY ORTS is employed at the State of Connecticut Judicial Branch Court Support Services Division.

HEATHER PATERSON is a doctoral student in the School of Criminology and Criminal Justice at Northeastern University.

ALLISON ANN PAYNE is a Professor in the Department of Sociology and Criminology at Villanova University.

SHAWN PECK is a doctoral student in the School of Public Affairs at Pennsylvania State University.

ERIC L. PIZA is a Professor in the School of Criminology and Criminal Justice at Northeastern University.

KATHERYNE PUGLIESE is a doctoral student at John Jay College of Criminal Justice, City University of New York.

MICHAEL ROCQUE is an Associate Professor and the Chair of the Department of Sociology at Bates College.

NANCY RODRIGUEZ is a Professor in the Department of Criminology, Law, and Society at the University of California, Irvine.

JOHN K. ROMAN is a Senior Fellow in the Economics, Justice, and Society Group at the National Opinion Research Center at the University of Chicago.

KATHERINE M. ROSS is a Postdoctoral Research Fellow in the Clark-Hill Institute for Positive Youth Development at Virginia Commonwealth University.

KAELYN SANDERS is a doctoral student in the School of Criminal Justice at Michigan State University.

HOLLY S. SCHINDLER is an Associate Professor in the College of Education at the University of Washington.

ROGER S. SMITH is the Professor of Social Work in the Department of Sociology at Durham University.

ROGER SPAW is the Evidence-Based Practices Project Manager with the Edna Bennett Pierce Prevention Research Center at Pennsylvania State University.

CHRISTOPHER J. SULLIVAN is the E. Desmond Lee Professor of Youth Crime and Violence and Chair of the Department of Criminology and Criminal Justice at the University of Missouri-St. Louis.

JUSTICE TANKEBE is an Associate Professor in the Institute of Criminology at the University of Cambridge.

CODY W. TELEP is an Associate Professor and Associate Director in the School of Criminology and Criminal Justice at Arizona State University.

PATRICK H. TOLAN is the Charles S. Robb Professor of Education in the School of Education and Human Development and a Professor in the Department of Psychiatry and Neurobehavioral Sciences in the School of Medicine at the University of Virginia.

JILLIAN J. TURANOVIC is an Associate Professor in the College of Criminology and Criminal Justice at Florida State University.

MELISSA K. VAN DYKE is an Implementation Scientist-Practitioner and Co-director of the Active Implementation Research Network.

COLLEEN S. WALSH is a doctoral student in the Clark-Hill Institute for Positive Youth Development at Virginia Commonwealth University.

BRANDON C. WELSH is a Professor of Criminology at Northeastern University, the Visiting Professor of Global Health and Social Medicine at Harvard Medical School, and the Director of the Cambridge-Somerville Youth Study.

JANET A. WELSH is a Research Professor with the Edna Bennett Pierce Prevention Research Center at Pennsylvania State University.

STEVEN N. ZANE is an Assistant Professor in the College of Criminology and Criminal Justice at Florida State University.

CHAPTER 1

EVIDENCE-BASED CRIME AND JUSTICE POLICY

BRANDON C. WELSH, STEVEN N. ZANE, AND DANIEL P. MEARS

In recent decades, calls for "evidence-based" policies in crime and justice have become commonplace. That bodes well for policy and creates innumerable opportunities and roles for researchers. As Tonry (2009, 18) has emphasized, "[e]vidence-based policies for dealing with crime, coupled with a sense of human frailty and the transience of life, may be a romantic aspiration, but it is the right aspiration."

However, the term "evidence-based" is characterized by a great deal of rhetoric. Indeed, there remains a marked disjuncture between calls for evidence-based policy and an understanding of what it means for policy to be evidence-based. Matters of crime and justice seem particularly susceptible to this situation, one to which scholars and researchers—not just elected officials—have contributed. The calls for evidence-based policy nonetheless provide a powerful foundation for propelling a movement toward bringing about rational, cost-effective, and humane policies for the betterment of society.

The need for and the threats to improved policy are acute. We must, for example, contend with a crime policy agenda that continues to be driven by anecdotal evidence, program favorites of the month, "correctional quackery," as Latessa and colleagues (2014) have highlighted, and political ideology. The end result is a questionable patchwork of programs, policies, and practices. All too frequently, the need for them is uncertain, they rest on unclear theoretical foundations, they are implemented poorly, and their effectiveness in preventing or controlling crime, or furthering justice, is unknown. Moreover, many of the approaches may make matters worse, whether through adverse effects on outcomes (McCord 2003), wasting scarce public resources (Washington State Institute for Public Policy 2019), diverting policy attention away from the most important crime priorities of the day (Mears 2010), failing to address the needs of victims (Herman 2010), or leading to inequities and unfairness in how the system treats different groups of people (Beckett and Sasson 2000; Unnever and Gabbidon 2011).

An evidence-based approach can go a long way to helping to address this array of problems by ensuring that the best available research is considered in decisions that bear on the public good. Put another way, it is about making sure that research evidence is at center stage in political and policy decisions (Welsh and Farrington 2011). As noted by Petrosino (2000, 636) in the context of efforts to reduce crime, "[a]n evidence-based approach requires that the results of rigorous evaluation be rationally integrated into decisions about interventions by policymakers and practitioners alike."

This *Handbook* sets out to showcase much of what is right with evidence-based crime and justice policy as well as to confront the challenges that it faces today and in the years to come. Specifically, the *Handbook* is guided by three core objectives: (1) to promote new and productive ways to think about evidence-based policy; (2) to show how research can contribute to and guide evidence-based policy in the domains of juvenile justice, criminal justice, and alternatives to system responses; and (3) to identify strategies that can increase reliance on evidence-based policy, and, in particular, policy that is well designed, implemented, monitored, and evaluated. (These objectives are discussed in more detail in the next section.) "Policy" throughout the volume refers broadly to laws, programs, rules, regulations, and practices.

The current chapter is designed to set the stage for this larger, more comprehensive project. Here, we provide readers with an overview of evidence-based policy as it applies to crime and justice in the United States and across the Western world. We also introduce and discuss key findings or conclusions of the 31 other chapters included in the volume. In the first section of this chapter, we discuss a "framework for action" to help guide thinking about evidence-based crime and justice policy. The second section covers core concepts, research methodologies, and critical perspectives pertinent to the evidence-based approach. Sections III and IV are organized around the two major systems in which research evidence is being used to inform policy: juvenile justice and criminal justice, respectively. Both sections focus on key stages of processing and leading programs and practices. Section V examines how research evidence is being used to inform policy alternatives to punitive-focused system responses. It includes both micro and macro efforts taking place outside of the system and responding to the needs of neglected groups. Section VI focuses on efforts to promote greater use of evidence-based policy and ways to improve the knowledge base for evidence-based policymaking, especially in critical underdeveloped areas.

I. A Framework for Action

A central starting point in advancing efforts to increase knowledge about and use of evidence-based policy is recognizing that an evidence-based approach to crime and justice goes well beyond an intervention focus. Efforts to prevent and reduce crime and to improve justice include laws, programs, rules, regulations, and practices; they also include entire criminal justice systems and their parts, including the police, courts, and corrections. We refer to all of these under the shorthand rubric of "policy."

An important—but also too-narrow—approach to defining "evidence-based" policy is to say that it is any intervention for which credible evidence, using some scientific criterion, exists to suggest that it effectively produces some outcome. This has the advantage of turning our focus to "what works" in the sense of achieving certain impacts. But it has the disadvantage of turning our attention away from other critical policy dimensions that can play an equal or greater role in the ultimate effectiveness of efforts to promote public safety and justice.

The alternative is not to dispense with a focus on effectiveness. To the contrary, that criterion should be central to any useful definition of evidence-based policy. But effectiveness is only one relevant dimension. A broader and more useful approach entails consideration of additional criteria. Specifically, "evidence-based" policy can be said to exist when it is guided by credible scientific research that answers the following questions: (1) To what extent does a social problem exist that warrants being addressed? How large is the problem? Where is it located? (2) What is the theoretical foundation of a policy? For example, does it draw on a defensible logic or one that pulls from well-evaluated theories? Does it target the causes of the problem? And does it target not just the general causes that a research literature says may exist, but also the specific causes particular to a community or population? (3) How well implemented is the policy? Are all parts of it implemented with fidelity to the policy design? What are the opportunities to improve implementation? (4) What impacts does the policy have, and across how many outcomes? What, if any, unintended effects exist? How can the former be amplified and the latter minimized? (5) How cost-efficient is the policy relative to other policies or a failure to intervene at all? How does investing in the policy affect investment in, or the implementation of, policies that target other or related outcomes?

Collectively, these sets of questions comprise what Rossi, Lipsey, and Freeman (2004) called the evaluation hierarchy, or what are termed needs, theory, implementation, impact, and cost-efficiency evaluations. The guiding logic of the hierarchy is straightforward: We should not invest in a policy that is not needed; we should ensure that a policy is grounded in sound theory, else why expect an impact; we should ensure that we implement it well, else why expect an impact; we should assess impact, else why anticipate that we will produce a net benefit for society; and, not least, we should quantify the benefit relative to alternatives so that we can invest where we will obtain the greatest return.

It would be odd to view policy as evidence-based if we ignored four of these five policy questions and only zeroed in on policies that have been shown to create at least some amount of impact. Precisely for that reason, Mears (2010) argued that the five types of evaluations provide a foundation for identifying evidence-based policy. Under this approach, "evidence-based" refers to "effectiveness" in achieving impacts (and minimizing or entirely avoiding harmful unintended impacts). But it also refers to credible research that documents the need for particular types of policy responses, establishes the theory (or the credibility of a theory) for these responses, demonstrates implementation that accords with the policy's theory, and determines whether the policy is cost-efficient relative to other approaches.

As we enter the fourth decade of this incremental yet consequential movement in crime and justice, there is much to celebrate and there is much work to do in advancing knowledge about evidence-based policy (Weisburd, Farrington, and Gill 2016; Haskins 2018). This *Handbook* seeks to contribute to this work and to stimulate efforts to propel it to new heights. Accordingly, our first goal is to promote new and productive ways to think about evidence-based policy. For example, recent calls to focus on "translational criminology" reflect an understanding that part of creating a safer and more just world involves identifying ways to take research—whether it is research on effectiveness or other dimensions—and translate it in a practical manner that takes into account real-world conditions and constraints.

Our second goal is to show how research can contribute to and guide evidence-based policy in the context of juvenile justice, criminal justice, and alternatives to system responses. There is no substitute for illustrations of how evidence-based policy can be generated and what it can look like. This volume seeks to do just that by drawing on insights from a diverse array of crime and justice domains that consider local, state, and national perspectives.

Finally, our third goal is to identify ways to increase reliance on evidence-based policy and, in particular, policy that is well designed, implemented, monitored, and evaluated. This goal stems from recognizing that policy that contributes to the public good cannot flow only from knowledge about interventions or practices that can improve outcomes (e.g., reduced crime). It also requires information that can contribute to better-designed policies that build on credible research into the causes of the problems that the policies seek to address; it requires knowledge about ways to ensure implementation that demonstrates fidelity to policy design; it requires ongoing monitoring to improve implementation; and it requires evaluation to demonstrate impacts that are substantively meaningful and cost-efficient.

To achieve these goals, the volume is guided by several strategies. One consists of drawing on leading scholars to illuminate different ways of thinking about evidence-based policy and to help readers appreciate how far we have come in particular policy areas—and just how far we have to go. Another strategy consists of recognizing that many routes to policy influence exist (Weiss et al. 2008). Critical insights come from transcending silos and drawing upon the expertise and experiences of fields outside of criminology and criminal justice. Heeding this lesson is an important feature of the volume, with authors drawn from sociology, psychology, law, economics, education, public health, and public policy and administration.

A third strategy that the *Handbook* takes is to recognize that juvenile justice and criminal justice constitute parallel yet distinct systems. There are insights that may be specific to each, and for that reason we include separate discussions of them. Fourth, the *Handbook* draws attention to ways to improve research on, and identification of, evidence-based policies at "micro levels" (e.g., programs that may be needed and are effective with certain populations) and at "macro levels" (e.g., organizational arrangements that may create greater cost-efficiency). As part of that focus, the *Handbook* introduces a series of chapters that focus on alternatives to criminal justice system responses to crime. Not least, the *Handbook* attends to the critical question of how to generate more knowledge about—and greater use of—evidence-based policy. For example, how can we increase the likelihood that policymakers, criminal justice administrators and practitioners, and citizens will understand and support the development and use of science-based policies?

Evidence-based policy ultimately comes down to research. A strength of the present volume is its attention to unpacking the complexity of research and the relevance of this complexity for informing policy. Across almost all the chapters, this point repeatedly arises. For example, Chapter 2, by Welsh and Mears, explicitly details a range of dimensions—such as the role of theory in generating hypotheses and explanations, ways in which samples affect the generalizability of results, measurement, analytical, or other factors that may bear on the accuracy or policy relevance of findings—that go into research and its evaluation. It distinguishes each of the types of evaluations that collectively constitute the evaluation hierarchy. It also points to factors that go into assessing, through systematic reviews or meta-analyses, entire bodies of work. Unique considerations go into interpreting such reviews or analyses and directly bear on discussions of evidence-based policy.

Similarly, in the *Handbook*'s final chapter (Chapter 32), Mears and Natasha Frost revisit some of these issues to illustrate their importance for how policymakers, criminal justice administrators and practitioners, and citizens might be faced with challenges in making informed judgments about what is, or is not, evidence-based policy. They do so to highlight that these groups must understand research to make informed judgments about, among other things, the risk that the research base may consist of only a few select, though perhaps well-designed, studies. It may not include studies that evaluate policy implementation or impacts in areas with social or economic conditions similar to those on which these groups are focused. Or it may not include assessments of all relevant outcomes. Awareness of what goes into research, as well as what makes it complicated, is essential for guiding and evaluating research. It also is essential for increasing the likelihood that evidence-based policy will be used and that it will be used appropriately (e.g., with fidelity to policy design).

The complexity of research to any discussion of evidence-based policy surfaces in different ways in all of the chapters. Discussions about diversion, for example, entail a need to understand the importance of counterfactuals (i.e., what state of affairs would have happened in the absence of the policy). Before undertaking a study, and interpreting the results, it is important to answer the question, "Diversion from what?" If it is diversion from dismissal from juvenile court, then an evaluation should compare outcomes from participating in a diversion program with outcomes from dismissal. If, though, it is diversion from probation, then a study should compare outcomes between diverted youth and those placed on probation. This distinction is important for interpreting work in Chapter 8, by Roger Smith, but it has broader relevance for interpreting the results of many studies.

One of the most common complexities in research is the fact that average effects are just that—average. This means that a program might reduce recidivism for the "average" person. Yet the program's effects might be much greater for some groups, and might even worsen recidivism for others. In other words, the effects may be heterogeneous. Many of the chapters identify precisely this possibility as a critical research gap. In some instances, we may have strong science to back up a claim about policy effectiveness, but we may not have strong science for knowing whether the effect is greater or lesser, or even harmful, for certain groups. That complicates policy discussions, true. But it also reflects reality, and it may offer opportunities for policy to be more targeted and effective.

Still another complexity centers on implementation. Here, again, many of the chapters emphasize this issue as a critical research gap. We may have a robust literature that identifies that a program *can* be effective but also lack systematic knowledge about factors that influence implementation. This situation has real-world impacts, because poorly implementing an evidence-based policy will not result in improved outcomes.

Not all chapters discuss the same types of research issues or discuss evidence on each dimension of the evaluation hierarchy. Similarly, they do not all cover the same types of research complexity that attends to research in particular policy areas. However, they all underscore that better research is necessary for creating more evidence-based policy. Taken as a whole, the chapters emphasize the critical need for policies that are grounded in credible research (and spanning all dimensions of the evaluation hierarchy), that address critical research gaps, and that fully acknowledge the limitations of what extant research can do to inform policy decisions.

II. Concepts, Methods, and Critical Perspectives

For many, the raison d'être of evidence-based crime and justice policy is to make society a safer and more just place to live, work, and play. This can take many forms, including reducing gun violence in communities, upholding justice for victims of crime, ensuring fair treatment for young men of color who are arrested by the police, and lowering the financial burden to families with incarcerated parents. These are the desired outcomes and outputs, the intended results that policymakers, practitioners, and citizens are striving to achieve, not to mention to sustain over time.

Important to this orientation are a number of considerations that provide guideposts that are useful for differentiating evidence-based policy from the status quo, as well as for improving policy effectiveness. High-quality research designs, translational research, implementation science, population impact, and social equity are some examples. These considerations are foundational to productive ways of thinking about evidence-based policy. This is the chief focus of Part I of the volume, which includes four chapters.

In Chapter 2, Welsh and Mears introduce general considerations that go into evaluating specific research studies and assessing bodies of research. This involves profiling critical dimensions, such as internal validity and external validity, and types of policy-relevant questions—beyond those solely focused on "what works"—that research can answer. The stakes are high. What this means is that for crime and justice policy to be evidence-based, it needs to be firmly grounded in scientific evidence. At the same time, it is important to recognize that what goes into establishing credible evidence can be complicated. And throughout this process, it is crucial that all stakeholders and other consumers of research (not just researchers) understand the complexities so that they can make more informed judgments about policy and practice.

In Chapter 3, Cody Telep takes on translational criminology and its applicability to evidence-based policy and practice. As noted by Laub (2016, 631), an important "goal of translational criminology is to address the gaps between scientific discovery, program delivery, and effective crime policy. This is the knowledge application process." In attending to what is known about translational criminology, the chapter begins with a focus on practitioner receptivity to research and then moves on to discuss what has been learned about increasing research utilization by practitioners and policymakers. According to Telep, "[t]hese prior findings suggest a number of key mechanisms that can assist in translational efforts, including dissemination work, partnerships, influential peers, facilitators for learning about research, and rewards and incentives." The chapter also profiles important case studies—with a special focus on policing and corrections—that are drawing on these mechanisms to translate research findings.

The science of implementation and its connection to evidence-based policy is the subject of Chapter 4, by Dean Fixsen, Melissa Van Dyke, and Karen Blase. Implementation science is so vital to evidence-based policy and practice that failure to use a sound implementation plan—one that relies on tested implementation methods—will undermine the whole enterprise. At the heart of this most important topic is "active implementation," which the authors describe as "an evidence-based approach to assuring the full and effective use of evidence-based programs and other innovations in practice." In many respects, active implementation is the "missing link" in the policy-administration-service chain, and it offers a more purposeful and hopeful approach to public policy designed to improve enactment in practice. The chapter offers examples of and recommendations for the critical step of including knowledge about implementation practice and science in legislation and policy, departmental administration, and service sectors.

In Chapter 5, Holly Schindler addresses another pressing challenge facing evidence-based policy: how to reproduce positive impacts of programs when the programs are scaled up for wider dissemination. At issue is not just concern about attenuation of program effects, but also about some unintended consequences of the evidence-based policy movement, including incentivizing statistical significance over meaningful change, prioritizing average impacts over subpopulation impacts, and allowing for rigidity in implementation over flexibility and cultural relevance. Schindler argues that "these and other threats to scaling have impeded progress toward achieving equitable population impacts." Drawing on lessons from diverse fields (e.g., early childhood, implementation science, collective impact, human-centered design research), the chapter discusses how social sciences can make progress toward achieving such impacts.

III. Juvenile Justice

The juvenile justice system can be thought of as a less criminogenic alternative to the criminal justice system for youth, and indeed this diversionary role is part of its mission. But it also includes a special mandate to intervene on behalf of youth and to provide a dispositional plan—rather than a criminal sentence—that is attendant to their individualized needs. Unlike the criminal justice system, a special emphasis is thus placed upon delinquency prevention through rehabilitation. Juvenile court dispositions are thought to involve individualized consideration of each juvenile offender with an eye toward their particular needs and risks.

What is unique about the juvenile justice system is that it consists of a dual mandate that is diversionary (with respect to the criminal justice system) and interventionist (with respect to the child). This makes juvenile justice an especially promising area for evidence-based programs, practices, and policies. In Part II of the *Handbook*, six chapters examine the role of evidence-based policy in the juvenile justice system. In addition to profiles of two states that have engaged in comprehensive efforts at evidence-based reforms, Washington and Pennsylvania, this part includes chapters that critically examine a commonplace intervention, juvenile drug treatment courts; examine the role of evidence-based policy in juvenile diversion and probation; and reflect on the promises and limitations of the "evidence-based" framework for youth justice.

In Chapter 6, Elizabeth Drake and Lauren Knoth-Peterson profile Washington State's experience in developing one of the most comprehensive approaches to evidence-based juvenile justice to date. As the authors relate, the Washington State Legislature has made significant investments to develop an "evidence-based" juvenile justice system since the 1990s, and for more than two decades Washington has required juvenile courts to use evidence-based programs to address the needs of youth involved in the juvenile justice system. The Washington State Institute for Public Policy (WSIPP) has been central to this focus, conducting reviews of research and cost-benefit analyses that have now been adopted by 26 US states as well as other countries. The authors discuss the policymaking context of Washington State's juvenile justice system, the corresponding interactions between research and policymaking, and the successes, challenges, and lessons learned in Washington over this 25-year endeavor.

Similarly, in Chapter 7, Shawn Peck, Janet Welsh, Kristopher Glunt, and Roger Spaw profile Pennsylvania's evidence-based approach to juvenile justice. As the authors note, Pennsylvania has been viewed by many as a "success story" regarding the implementation of evidence-based programs and practices for juvenile justice interventions and practices. Their chapter identifies emerging and ongoing challenges, including concerns regarding disproportionate engagement of minority youth in the juvenile justice system, better understanding of the needs of gender minority youth, the need for effective interventions addressing the comorbidity of youth crime and mental health disorders, and the role of social media and other online platforms. They also highlight the importance of strong partnerships at the community level, and emphasize the practical concern that continued demonstration of program impact is necessary for sustaining future funding for evidence-based programs.

In Chapter 8, Roger Smith takes a step back and considers the need for and theoretical basis of a central institution in juvenile justice: diversion from formal processing. Building on the history of diversion in the United Kingdom, Smith reviews the emergence and development of youth diversion and addresses the question of how we define and measure its achievements. The chapter then examines the best evidence for the positive impact of diversion in terms of reduced recidivism, but also develops a critique of evaluation models that concentrate primarily on reoffending as the principal success criterion for diversionary initiatives. By focusing on the broader meaning and impact of diversion within juvenile justice, the chapter provokes critical thinking about the systemic effects and wider consequences of diversion, such as net widening.

While diversion is a central component of juvenile justice, probation is the workhorse of the system, constituting the final disposition for approximately 34% of all US referrals (and 50% of formally processed referrals) in 2019 (Hockenberry and Puzzanchera 2021). In Chapter 9, David Myers and Kelly Orts examine the use of evidence-based programs and practices by juvenile probation departments in recent decades. They report that an increasing number of juvenile programs have been determined through research to be "effective" or "promising," and that validated risk assessment tools have become more effective and commonplace, allowing juvenile probation officers to better address criminogenic needs and reduce the likelihood of future offending. Despite these advances, the authors note that many ineffectual or harmful juvenile programs and practices persist. They argue that continued and strengthened research is necessary in order to improve the implementation and effectiveness of risk and needs assessment, enhance understanding and use of evidence-based programs and practices, and reduce inequities in juvenile justice. They also suggest that an organizational culture that embraces learning and change, guided by research and strengthened by collaboration, provides the optimal setting for innovation and experimentation with evidence-based programs.

One particular example of evidence-based policy in juvenile justice that targets a specific and persistent problem is juvenile drug treatment courts (JDTCs). As Christopher Sullivan,

Vitor Gonçalves, and Nicole McKenna describe in Chapter 10, despite JDTCs' implementation since the 1990s, the evidence base for their effectiveness and courts' adherence to the underlying JDTC theory of change remains limited. According to the authors, the equivocal nature of evidence to date suggests that there are some circumstances where youth may be negatively affected by the intensity of the process, and others where the JDTCs are not sufficiently tailored to meet their needs. This means that the question of which policies or practices should be supported will depend on the circumstances of individual cases, as well as the resources available to deliver JDTCs with fidelity. At present, the authors argue, JDTCs are not as well understood as they should be relative to the frequency with which they have been adopted, and their widespread use necessitates further informed research and refinement to ensure JDTCs are effective and equitable for youth and efficient and manageable for juvenile justice agencies.

Wrapping up the section is an important reflection on the concept of evidence-based juvenile justice, which the authors suggest may better be conceived as "evidence-oriented youth justice." In Chapter 11, Jeffrey Butts, John Roman, and Katheryne Pugliese examine how the term "evidence-based" is used in youth justice, including possible misuse as a marketing slogan. They posit that while promoting interventions with a rigorous evidence base is an important and valuable goal for youth justice, adhering rigidly to the existing evidence base can also hinder effective policy innovations. Instead of defensively claiming to be evidence-based, they argue, youth justice officials should be "evidence-oriented," meaning that they utilize credible evaluation findings to identify effective programs, as well as develop innovative and promising approaches to be tested by future evaluations.

IV. Criminal Justice

The criminal justice system is wide-ranging, encompassing enforcement activities and a variety of crime prevention and intervention efforts. Viewed more broadly, it includes correctional system activities, including rehabilitation programming aimed at improving reentry outcomes. Across all aspects of criminal justice, there is a need for evidence-based policy. What, though, is the state of evidence? In Part III of the *Handbook*, seven chapters tackle this question in different ways. Collectively, they illuminate critical issues that bear on evidence-based policy and what is known about what works and what does not work in particular policy areas. They illuminate major research gaps as well. While a volume that covers every function of the criminal justice system is not possible, these chapters provide a useful template for thinking about the system more broadly. Each of the chapters suggests grounds for optimism and concern. There have been tremendous advances in knowledge, but, at the same time, much remains unknown.

Many of us tend to think of policy as something that stands on its own, almost like a device that can be taken off the shelf and used to good effect. However, policy does not work that way. To be designed and implemented well—and, thus, to be effective—certain conditions must be met. It is not just policy, though. For agencies to operate as intended, a variety of conditions also must be in place. The same observation holds for citizens. For example, their support for these agencies or compliance with the law requires certain conditions to exist as well. Perhaps the most critical of these is legitimacy. Taking heed of this idea, in Chapter 12, Justice Tankebe and Anthony Bottoms present a compelling case for the centrality of citizen legitimation expectations to the legitimacy, as well as the operations and effectiveness, of the criminal justice system. The legitimacy of the criminal justice system matters for crime prevention, they emphasize, but also for citizens to achieve such goals as having a meaningful role in their communities. It is not something, though, that just happens. Legitimacy of any kind must be produced, and a variety of forces can shape it. Tankebe and Bottoms illuminate these and other considerations, and suggest ways to create micro-, meso-, and macro-level policies, practices, and agencies that have greater legitimacy.

Policing stands at center stage in the criminal justice system, and for that reason alone has led to calls to make it evidence-based. In Chapter 13, as Cynthia Lum and Christopher Koper highlight how knowledge about, and the use of, evidence-based approaches to policing have increased over the past two decades. Their chapter is replete with examples of substantial progress in the production of this knowledge and its translation into policy and practice. It is replete, too, with examples of the complicated nature of policing. For example, policing has greatly evolved over time and there can be disagreement about the precise goals that the police should be expected to achieve. That can generate differences in how the police address crime or how they consider community members in what they prioritize. More broadly, among police agencies and officers there can be varying levels of support for, or awareness or acceptance of, evidence-based approaches. Lum and Koper discuss these and other issues, such as ways to increase the use of evidence-based policing as well as the challenge of implementing it during an era in which calls for reforming policing have been ubiquitous.

Closed-circuit television (CCTV) video surveillance cameras have become a core part of the toolbox of crime prevention strategies used by the police. In Chapter 14, Eric Piza reviews the literature and finds that this technology can create a modest reduction in crime, but emphasizes that any beneficial effect is highly contingent. It can vary depending on social context and local geographic conditions. Further, the benefits may not always exceed the costs. The chapter highlights what is known about CCTV effects, in addition to the critical research gaps that should be addressed to improve knowledge about when and where CCTV can be effective and how to improve impacts and cost-effectiveness. At a broader level, Piza's chapter provides a cautionary tale about almost all criminal justice policy—there are few, if any, simple policy fixes for improving the operations or impacts of the criminal justice system. Effective adoption and use of CCTV technology requires attending to a great many considerations, including acting on knowledge about the precise conditions under which CCTV effects arise.

Whether rehabilitation can effectively reduce recidivism may be one of the most contentious and misunderstood issues in all of criminal justice and corrections. That stems, in part, from critiques in the 1970s that intersected with the politicization of crime control to create a view that rehabilitation does not "work." In Chapter 15, Michael Rocque shows that this appraisal was incorrect—evidence-based rehabilitative programs can be effective in reducing recidivism, and they may be more effective than punitive measures. But we learn that this generalization is accompanied by substantial complexity. The literature is not always consistent in how it defines "evidence-based." Some studies might view evidence of any statistically significant effect as sufficing, while others might emphasize a particular threshold of effect. Effectiveness can be diminished by poor implementation. It may vary greatly across populations or contexts. Individual characteristics may moderate intervention effectiveness. And, not least, effectiveness may look quite different if we use longer time frames when comparing outcomes among those who participated in a rehabilitative program and those who did not.

Concern about drug-related crime featured prominently as one of the primary drivers of mass incarceration. For that reason, support for drug treatment has, to some extent, garnered bipartisan support and contributed to investment in drug treatment programs. In Chapter 16, Ojmarrh Mitchell introduces us to this issue, and identifies what is, and is not, known about the effectiveness of correctional system drug treatment. He finds that medication-assisted treatment (MAT) can reduce drug relapse but does not appear to reduce recidivism; group-based counseling programs do not appear to be effective in reducing recidivism; and therapeutic community (TC) programs can be effective in reducing recidivism but may not be (as) effective in reducing drug relapse. Mitchell points to straightforward reasons for these findings, namely that interventions are more likely to reduce recidivism when they address the causes of crime and are provided at a sufficient dose for a sufficient period of time. The lesson for criminal justice policy is also straightforward: policies will be more likely to be effective when they target the causes of the social problems that they seek to address. Relying on science rather than intuition or ideology for identifying these causes can help to ensure that policies do just that.

The rapid and large-scale growth in incarceration that occurred beginning in the 1980s has led to an attendant problem—a substantial increase in the numbers of individuals returning to society after being incarcerated. Many of these individuals have characteristics that may increase their risk of offending, the prison experience itself may be criminogenic, and the challenges that they face during re-entry may also be criminogenic (Mears and Cochran 2015). In Chapter 17, Helen Kosc and David Kirk discuss these challenges, which include collateral consequences of punishment, difficulties securing gainful employment, and barriers to finding housing and reunifying with family and friends. Limited education and work experiences, along with a greater likelihood of having a mental illness or drug problem, can amplify the effects of these challenges. Kosc and Kirk note that, unfortunately, few re-entry policies or programs are evaluated using strong research designs. They emphasize the need for more and stronger research approaches, including randomized controlled trials (RCTs), to identify effective approaches to re-entry. And they emphasize the importance of identifying the precise conditions under which, and the populations for whom, such approaches can be most effective.

As many of the chapters highlight, interventions can be more effective when they target the causes of a problem. They also highlight that interventions may vary in their effects among different groups. For that reason, we want to know not only whether, on average, an intervention can be effective, but also for which groups it has stronger effects. We also want to know why. In many cases, an intervention may be less effective—or entirely ineffective or even harmful—because it does not address the unique causes among a given group of people or the contexts from which they come or to which they may return. In Chapter 18, Kaelyn Sanders, Jennifer Cobbina-Dungy, and Henrika McCoy highlight the salience of these observations (and others) for understanding the need for policies that address the unique experiences, backgrounds, and contexts of marginalized populations—such as minoritized individuals, women, and juveniles—in the criminal justice system. They highlight that some research exists to support certain policies and programs for these populations. At the same time, they highlight the need for much more research, for interventions that are designed specifically for these populations, and for structural changes in society and in the way criminal justice systems operate.

V. Alternatives to System Responses

Efforts to reduce crime and uphold justice for crime victims also take place outside of the formal juvenile and criminal justice systems. So vital are these alternative approaches that they have come to play an increasingly important role in evidence-based crime and justice policy. As one example, almost half of the crime and justice systematic reviews published by the Campbell Collaboration (a total of 55 at the time of writing) focus on interventions delivered outside of the formal justice systems. This is impressive for many reasons, not least of which is that formal justice system responses to crime account for the overwhelming share of federal, state, and local expenditures on crime in the United States. This is also the case in other Western industrialized countries; the gap is even more pronounced in developing countries.

The evidence-based movement is drawing greater attention to this issue and the attendant need for governments to strike a balance between formal justice system responses to crime and alternative approaches. This trend is happening as a result of many factors, including substantial evidence of the cost-efficiency of social and situational prevention measures (compared to "after-the-fact" responses to criminal activity), the ability of alternative approaches to mitigate the development (the "supply") of offenders and their subsequent flow into the justice systems, the ability of alternative approaches to reduce the burden of victimization as well as lower the total number of crime victims, and an awaking to the political reality of the need to denounce the futile "get on tough on crime" approach and replace it with "get smart on crime."

Part IV of the volume brings together seven chapters on alternatives to system responses. In Chapter 19, Welsh, Heather Paterson, and David Farrington examine the extent to which early prevention provides economic returns to society and whether the returns make it a more worthwhile policy alternative to imprisonment. To address this question the chapter reviews (a) the latest cost-benefit analyses of early prevention programs; (b) the first generation of studies that have examined the economics of early prevention compared to imprisonment, including Washington State's ongoing comparative cost-benefit model (see also Chapter 6); and (c) a wide range of other economic studies. Based on the highest-quality research evidence, the authors find clear and substantial support for policy options that emphasize early prevention and limit the use of imprisonment. As the authors report, the findings also demonstrate that the economic returns of early prevention compared to imprisonment are sizable, wide-ranging (i.e., cascading over multiple domains), and long-lasting, with some studies showing economic benefits accruing well into midlife.

Chapter 20, by Terje Ogden, Elisabeth Askeland, and Kristine Amlund-Hagen, profiles Norway's experience in adopting, implementing, and scaling-up the evidence-based early prevention intervention known as Parent Management Training—Oregon Model (or PMTO). Designed for at-risk children (ages 3–12 years) and their parents and tested through a series of randomized controlled trials, the authors report that PMTO has produced significant and sustained improvements in parenting and child externalizing behavior for a wide range of groups across all regions of Norway. Key to the intervention's effectiveness has been the maintenance of high treatment fidelity across generations of therapists.

In Chapter 21, Abigail Fagan reports on Communities That Care (CTC), an empirically based approach (also referred to as an "operating system") that aids communities in implementing evidence-based interventions targeting risk and protective factors to prevent delinquency, substance abuse, and violence. The scope of interventions is wide-ranging, from early developmental prevention programs for children to community interventions with high-risk youth. CTC provides community coalitions with a structured process, training, and consultation to improve their knowledge, adoption, and high-quality implementation of evidence-based interventions. Importantly, as Fagan describes, CTC is itself an evidence-based system. It arose as a product of a RCT and multiple quasi-experimental evaluations demonstrating its ability to increase the use of evidence-based interventions and reduce youth problem behaviors across the United States and in other countries.

In Chapter 22, Allison Ann Payne reviews the state of evidence-based interventions to prevent delinquency and criminal activity by young people in the context of schools. Interventions with a particular focus on improving school climate and building students' cognitive, social, and emotional skills are shown to be the most effective in reducing school crime and student misbehavior. The chapter also draws attention to the growing trend among schools in the United States to implement restrictive security and punitive disciplinary measures, which can have the effect of doing more harm than good for students, as well as countering gains made by evidence-based interventions.

In Chapter 23, Katherine Ross, Colleen Walsh, Angela Angulo, Carine Leslie, and Patrick Tolan examine evidence-based strategies for preventing youth violence in urban settings, with a special focus on contexts that experience the most violence: low-resource urban communities. The larger field of youth violence prevention provides substantial guidance in the form of risk and protective factors to be targeted (also reviewed in the chapter) and more general programs for preventing youth violence, but much less is known for this specific context. The focus on this subject is timely, and the authors draw attention to what we still need to learn for urban communities experiencing high levels of youth violence.

In Chapter 24, Tamara Herold reports on the emerging evidence base on place management strategies to prevent crime and violence. Informed by routine activity and rational choice theories, such strategies involve relying on individuals known as "place managers" (e.g., bus drivers, parking lot attendants, train conductors) exercising control over a physical place for which they have legal authority. Preventing crime is often a secondary function to their employment duties. The chapter reports that efforts to improve place management can prevent crime, but the practice is largely underutilized. The author proposes ways to advance the practice of improving place management to prevent crime. The discussion includes a focus on the context of crime place networks, which sustain crime hot spots, and one strategy that shows promise for reducing violence in them.

Chapter 25, by Jillian Turanovic, Julie Kuper, and Mackenzie Masters, focuses on victims of crime. It covers some of the difficulties victims experience in coping with trauma and navigating the criminal justice system and service programs developed to help mitigate these challenges and deliver justice to crime victims. As with some other chapters in the volume, the authors are confronted with a paucity of research knowledge about what works in the field. Accordingly, the authors discuss principles of effective victim services and evidence-based programs and practices for responding to crime victims, as well as set out some priorities for future research to help contribute to evidence-base policy in this important area.

VI. Promoting Greater Use of Evidence-Based Policy

One of the central goals of this *Handbook* is to promote new and productive ways to think about evidence-based crime and justice policy. This includes ways to improve the current knowledge base for evidence-based policymaking, especially in critical underdeveloped areas. Part V concludes the *Handbook* with seven chapters aimed at promoting greater use of evidence-based policy in areas where it is most needed. The chapters focus on specific goals, such as reducing gun violence and reducing persistent racial disproportionality in the juvenile justice system, two critical areas where rigorous evidence is limited. The chapters also focus on broader goals such as growing the research infrastructure necessary for generating credible research that can ground all aspects of policy, as well as leveraging the evidence-based framework to address the daunting subject of social inequality. Additionally, the chapters discuss possible opportunities for building a more substantial evidence base and promoting greater use of evidence-based policy, including the use of naturally occurring or "big data," the use of legal mandates to promote evidence-based policy at the state level, and the education of policymakers, criminal justice administrators and practitioners, and citizens.

In Chapter 26, Nancy Rodriguez presents an agenda for criminal justice policy that directly considers and addresses social inequality. Arguments have been advanced about ways that social inequality contributes to crime, the groups that are most likely to enter the criminal justice system, and differences and disparities in how that system responds to them (see, e.g., Mears, Cochran, and Lindsey 2016). Arguments have been advanced as well about ways that the criminal justice system, in turn, contributes to social inequality (see, e.g., Western and Sirois 2019). In short, inequality and the criminal justice system are intertwined in complicated ways, as the chapter by Sanders and colleagues in this volume (Chapter 18) attests. There is not, though, as Rodriguez's chapter underscores, a robust literature on evidence-based ways to reduce the role of social inequality in contributing to justice system involvement or how such involvement can lead to disparate impacts on groups that are socially or economically disadvantaged. Her chapter provides a critical corrective to this situation by describing strategies both in the criminal justice system and outside of it that might help to reduce social inequality.

One of the most pressing inequalities in the juvenile justice system is persistent racial and ethnic disproportionalities, often referred to as disproportionate minority contact (DMC). In Chapter 27, Zane examines the evidence basis for the scope of the DMC problem, the potential theoretical grounds for interventions to reduce DMC, and whether extant interventions have reduced DMC. In the spirit of evidence-based crime and justice policy, the chapter is guided by an evaluation framework for thinking about persistent racial disproportionalities in juvenile justice in terms of needs, theory, and promising avenues for impact. Zane argues that most research to date does not answer fundamental questions about what causes DMC and how it can be reduced. It is also argued that building an evidence base for reducing DMC will require better data, better methods, and a more concerted focus on the front end of the system, especially police contact with youth.

Another pressing issue is the reduction of gun violence. In Chapter 28, John Donohue describes the latest and best-quality evidence of efforts to reduce gun violence, as well as the challenges to provide high-quality research that can generate sound evidence-based policy in this area. Donohue argues that an increasing number of empirical studies indicate that restrictions on assault weapons and high-capacity magazines, as well as restrictions on carrying guns outside the home and on access to guns (along with determined efforts to enforce these restrictions), can provide meaningful benefits and save lives. The chapter also acknowledges that the recent, expanded interpretation of the Second Amendment adopted by the US Supreme Court may take many policy measures off the table. In light of this broader legal, cultural, and political context, Donahue argues that having the strongest possible empirical basis to establish the contours of effective gun policy is more important than ever.

A great deal of work on evidence-based policy focuses on specific laws and interventions. In Chapter 29, Mears and Joshua Cochran argue that this focus is important but that it should be augmented by a commitment to what they term "mass evidence-based policy." They highlight that mass incarceration itself is not in any clear way evidence-based. Yet it arguably has been and remains the primary policy response to crime. During a period when increasing calls for evidence-based policy emerged, states and the country as a whole invested in mass non-evidence-based policy. Mears and Cochran argue that lawmakers and criminal justice and correctional systems would, therefore, do well to systematically align practice with rhetoric. This shift will require a political and economic commitment to creating the research infrastructure necessary for generating credible research that can ground all aspects of policy. Taking evidence-based policy to scale requires the capacity to undertake need, theory, implementation, impact, and efficiency evaluations of existing and proposed policies.

One of the tools for achieving this goal of taking evidence-based policy to scale involves leveraging the advantages of "big data." In Chapter 30, Daniel O'Brien aims to demystify big data, with specific attention to its value for evidence-based policy pertaining to crime prevention and law enforcement in local communities. Using six case studies from the study and management of crime in communities, O'Brien argues that that we should focus not on the size of big data but on their "naturally occurring" origins, arising from nonresearch processes and systems. These origins create specific advantages and challenges, O'Brien observes, but if handled properly, naturally occurring data can be a boon for advancing policy, both indirectly through the advancement of research and directly through its incorporation into the evaluation, refinement, and even moment-to-moment operation of our public systems.

Central to the evidence-based paradigm is the explicit goal to increase the influence of scientific research on public policy. One direct way of accomplishing this is throughout legal mandate, or "imposed use." In Chapter 31, Zane examines state laws that require evidence-based crime and justice policy, including how such laws have been implemented and the limitations of this approach. One limitation, Zane observes, is that imposed use as it is most currently applied—namely, toward intervention programs with established impact on some desired outcomes (e.g., recidivism)—is quite narrow in scope. Another limitation is that normative considerations still drive policymaking, such that imposed use will be most appropriate in areas where policy ends are not in dispute. Zane utilizes the example of imposed use to reflect on evidence-based crime and justice policy in general and, returning to a theme of this *Handbook*, argues that it is best conceived as something broader than evidence of impact from rigorous program evaluations. Like evidence-based policy more broadly, Zane argues, imposed use represents a powerful strategy for making the means of agreed-upon policy goals more evidence-based, but is not a panacea and is not without pitfalls.

Evidence-based policy is not something that can willy-nilly be taken off a shelf and effectively be applied anywhere or everywhere. Among other things, the policy may not be relevant to certain jurisdictions, or it may not be easily implemented. In addition, evidence-based policy is not something that only researchers can help to identify. In the volume's concluding chapter (Chapter 32), Mears and Frost focus on the role that policymakers, criminal justice administrators and practitioners, and citizens can play in developing evidence-based policy, shaping its implementation, and evaluating its intended and unintended impacts. They highlight the role of these groups in determining when to adopt, change, or eliminate policies. The authors argue that any systematic creation and use of evidence-based policy requires the involvement of these groups. It also requires that these groups have sufficient knowledge about research so that they can both inform and critically evaluate research. Mears and Frost, therefore, identify strategies that might help to increase research knowledge among the groups.

References

Beckett, Katherine, and Theodore Sasson. 2000. *The politics of injustice: Crime and punishment in America*. Thousand Oaks, CA: Pine Forge Press.

Haskins, Ron. 2018. Evidence-based policy: The movement, the goals, the issues, the promise. *Annals of the American Academy of Political and Social Science*, 678:8–37.

Herman, Susan. 2010. *Parallel justice for victims of crime*. Washington, DC: National Center for Victims of Crime.

Hockenberry, Sarah, and Charles Puzzanchera. 2021. *Juvenile court statistics, 2019*. Pittsburgh: National Center for Juvenile Justice.

Latessa, Edward J., Shelley J. Listwan, and Deborah Koetzle. 2014. *What works (and doesn't) in reducing recidivism*. Waltham, MA: Anderson.

Laub, John H. 2016. Life course research and the shaping of public policy. In *Handbook of the life course*. Vol. 2, edited by Michael Shanahan, Jeylan T. Mortimer, and Monica Kirkpatrick Johnson, 623–637. New York: Springer.

McCord, Joan. 2003. Cures that harm: Unanticipated outcomes of crime prevention programs. *Annals of the American Academy of Political and Social Science*, 587:16–30.

Mears, Daniel P. 2010. *American criminal justice policy: An evaluation approach to increasing accountability and effectiveness*. New York: Cambridge University Press.

Mears, Daniel P., and Joshua C. Cochran. 2015. *Prisoner reentry in the era of mass incarceration*. Thousand Oaks, CA: SAGE.

Mears, Daniel P., Joshua C. Cochran, and Andrea M. Lindsey. 2016. Offending and racial and ethnic disparities in criminal justice: A conceptual framework for guiding theory and research and informing policy. *Journal of Contemporary Criminal Justice*, 32:78–103.

Petrosino, Anthony. 2000. How can we respond effectively to juvenile crime? *Pediatrics*, 105:635–637.

Rossi, Peter H., Mark W. Lipsey, and Howard E. Freeman. 2004. *Evaluation: A systematic approach.* 7th ed. Thousand Oaks, CA: SAGE.

Tonry, Michael. 2009. Crime and public policy. In *The Oxford handbook of crime and public policy*, edited by Michael Tonry, 3–21. New York: Oxford University Press.

Unnever, James D., and Shaun L. Gabbidon. 2011. *A theory of African American offending: Race, racism, and crime.* New York: Routledge.

Washington State Institute for Public Policy. 2019. *Updated inventory of evidence-based, research-based, and promising practices for prevention and intervention services for children and juveniles in the child welfare, juvenile justice, and mental health systems.* Olympia: Washington State Institute for Public Policy.

Weisburd, David, David P. Farrington, and Charlotte E. Gill, eds. 2016. *What works in crime prevention and rehabilitation: Lessons from systematic reviews.* New York: Springer.

Weiss, Carol H., Erin Murphy-Graham, Anthony Petrosino, and Allison G. Gandhi. 2008. The fairy godmother—and her warts: Making the dream of evidence-based policy come true. *American Journal of Evaluation*, 29:29–47.

Welsh, Brandon C., and David P. Farrington. 2011. Evidence-based crime policy. In *The Oxford handbook of crime and criminal justice*, edited by Michael Tonry, 60–92. New York: Oxford University Press.

Western, Bruce, and Catherine Sirois. 2019. Racialized re-entry: Labor market inequality after incarceration. *Social Forces*, 97:1517–1542.

PART I

CONCEPTS, METHODS, AND CRITICAL PERSPECTIVES

This part covers core concepts, research methodologies, and critical perspectives pertinent to the evidence-based approach. It includes four chapters.

CHAPTER 2

EVALUATING RESEARCH AND ASSESSING RESEARCH EVIDENCE

BRANDON C. WELSH AND DANIEL P. MEARS

CRIME and justice policy should be rational and based on the best available research evidence. Of course, getting there can be anything but straightforward. At one level, there is the need to parse out the rhetoric from the reality. Many programs, practices, and policies that claim to be "evidence-based" are far, far from it, whether due to the influence of politics or special interests. At another level, there is the need to ensure that we are using (a) the highest-quality research studies and (b) the most rigorous methods for assessing or taking stock of the available research evidence. That is the focus of this chapter.

In particular, the chapter aims to describe and discuss the fundamental roles of evaluating research (with a focus on internal, construct, and statistical conclusion validity) and assessing research evidence (with a focus on external validity) in contributing to the development of evidence-based crime and justice policy. Another aim of the chapter is to help orient—in a clear and understandable way—stakeholders and other consumers of research to key parameters that they should consider as they seek to advance evidence-based crime and justice policy.

The first section examines the role of evaluating research. A discussion of general considerations is followed by a description of types of policy-relevant questions and issues. It also explores key distinguishing features of intervention versus nonintervention research and describes the importance of context in research. The second section focuses on the role of assessing research evidence. It begins with a general discussion of external validity. Study replication and literature reviews are profiled as ways to achieve a measure of external validity. The third and final section builds on these discussions and offers concluding remarks.

I. Evaluating Research

When reviewing research studies, we generally want to know what they found and, importantly, whether what they found is an accurate representation of reality. How do we make such a determination? Doing so is, in fact, difficult. It entails reference to a multitude of factors, but it also entails judgment calls about how much any given factor, or set of factors, may matter (Mears and Cochran 2019). This point bears emphasis because there can be a tendency among policymakers, the public, and researchers to reduce research summaries to core findings, as if these findings represent reality, or "Truth" with a capital "T." Almost all research findings, though, come with a host of caveats. They at best *possibly* capture reality, which is to say under a best-case scenario they may capture "truth" with a lower-case "t." We often may not know the true state of reality until a large number of studies have been conducted. Here, then, we discuss a number of dimensions that should be considered when evaluating specific research studies.

A. General Considerations When Evaluating Research

Media and research accounts frequently equate "evidence-based" with "X factor improves a given outcome" or "X policy effectively improves a given outcome." But this take sidesteps clearly defining what "evidence-based" can mean. One view is that a study is evidence-based when it is conducted in ways that align with scientific practices. These practices are not fully codified, but they can be found in many research textbooks and in the requirements that peer-review journals sometimes explicitly request. In this chapter, we identify some of the most common types of considerations that go into making a study "evidence-based," such as internal validity, construct validity, and statistical conclusion validity (Farrington 2003). For researchers, many of the considerations will be obvious, but they are no less important.

1. Peer-Review Venues

Science builds on judgments that researchers make about studies. The traditional approach to institutionalizing reliance on scientific judgment has been reliance on peer-review journals or conference proceedings. Journal editors typically identify three or more research experts who can evaluate a manuscript to determine its credibility. The reviewers receive a "blinded" copy of the manuscript so as to remove the potential for personal biases to affect reviews. This step does not actually remove all bias, but it may help. The editor then arrives at a decision after weighing and balancing the anonymous reviews, and may decide to reject the paper, accept it, or allow a "revise-and-resubmit" that will be subject to further review. This process is far from perfect, but when it works well it provides a more systematic appraisal (based on consideration of the scientific merits of a study) than would occur if researchers published their own work with no review or assessments by their friends or nonscientists.

2. *Accuracy in Representing Prior Research*

A given study should accurately characterize the state of prior research. This information is essential for putting into context how the study differs from, compliments, and advances the larger body of science on the topic. It will not be surprising that scholars may disagree about the state of research in a given area. One illustration can be seen in narrative reviews. Conclusions from them may differ from those identified in meta-analyses or systematic reviews, in part because the latter rely on a more explicit and formal set of criteria for evaluating and summarizing prior studies (Lipsey and Wilson 2001; Pantole 2021). It may not always be evident to readers when a given study provides an unbiased, representative appraisal of existing research. Nonetheless, accuracy is critical to determining how well a given study advances science, if at all. Objectivity in the tone of the writing, reference to meta-analyses, and description of nuances in studies all can serve as cues about how accurately prior work is being presented.

3. *Reliance on Theory to Guide Questions, Hypotheses, and Explanations*

It is a truism to say that facts do not speak for themselves. We need frameworks to help interpret facts and to identify what facts may be relevant for a given question. Consider the age-crime curve. It is a fact that, in general, offending increases among individuals in mid-adolescence and rapidly declines thereafter. Why? What anticipates or explains this relationship? For that, theories are needed. Ideally, these theories not only can explain these facts but are supported by empirical studies. Absent theoretical guidance, a "finding"—such as X policy reduced recidivism by 10%—may not tell us much. It does not, for example, tell us how that relationship arose. What particular mechanism or constellation of factors created it? Well-tested theory is necessary for providing explanations of "facts."

4. *Relevance of Samples to Question or Issue*

Studies can be conducted with different types of samples. We might randomly sample individuals who leave a particular prison to assess their probability of recidivism. That sample may be useful for different purposes, but it is not relevant to understanding the causes of crime among, say, high school youth. Studies may rely on samples that are highly relevant or sometimes barely relevant to a particular question. Obviously, the former will generate more credible information. There is no substitute here for thinking carefully about what samples and questions would be relevant. That determination cannot be made through statistics. It requires judgment.

5. *Random versus Nonrandom Samples*

A critical problem with relying on everyday personal experiences is that we may not rub elbows with or see a representative slice of the public. This problem extends to reliance on nonrandom samples of a given group. For example, we may interview a small number of individuals who have had extremely favorable or unfavorable responses to a particular intervention. They would provide an unrepresentative perspective on the program. By contrast, a random sample can ensure that we have a representative view of the program and of findings that may result from our study. Studies that rely on nonrandom samples can be informative, but they can create distorted pictures of phenomena as well.

6. *Sample Size*

There is no magical sample size that best contributes to credible research. Much depends on the particular questions and hypotheses, the magnitude of expected effects, and what effect sizes would be viewed as meaningful or important. In general, larger samples will give us more confidence in results. Extremely large samples, though, can lead to a situation where virtually any comparison yields a statistically significant effect. In evaluating results, then, we want to be focused on whether a given sample is sufficiently large to be able to detect statistically significant differences, but we should simultaneously consider the substantive significance of a given magnitude of difference or association.

7. *Multiple Sources of Data*

All data sources have strengths and limitations. Administrative records data from the courts, for example, can be used to shed light on the types of cases that enter the criminal justice system and how they are processed. But they do not provide much information relevant to assessing the use of plea bargaining. Survey data can augment administrative records data, but their utility and validity may rest heavily on whether we can obtain sufficient response rates and accurate responses to questions. Interview and focus group data can reveal intricacies and the meaning of different patterns or events, but may not accurately represent what exists among a larger, more representative sample of individuals, groups, settings, and so on. Reliance on multiple sources of data can strengthen the credibility of any given finding, such as when analysis of different data sources points to the same general pattern.

8. *Measures of Constructs*

All studies rely on measures of key constructs; that is, the things, like self-control or improved cognitive functioning, that we think may affect behavior. These measures can range from lousy to outstanding. Construct validity involves whether we think our measures accurately capture the aspect of reality in which we are interested. Indices tend to be useful because they allow one to rely on multiple measures, which collectively may better tap an underlying but not directly observable construct. Studies that rely on established measures and indices—which we only know when a larger literature exists that has identified them—will generally produce more valid results.

9. *Ability to Address Causal Order*

When examining cause-and-effect, we want data over time; that is, information that has been collected on individuals, programs, prisons, etc., at multiple points over days, weeks, months, and even years, so that we can determine if a hypothesized cause, X, indeed contributes to an outcome, Y—what is called "internal validity." Many studies rely on cross-sectional data—one-time snapshots of individuals at a particular point in time—and thus cannot establish causal order. In such cases, it may be that Y actually causes X rather than that X causes Y. A correlation from cross-sectional data would accord with either possibility. For this reason, studies that rely on data over time, such as "before vs. after" treatment impact evaluations, tend to generate more credible information about cause and effect, including how a given cause produces that effect.

10. *Confounding*

Experiments allow us to isolate whether an intervention actually produces a given effect (Welsh, Braga, and Bruinsma 2013). Even so, it may be that certain factors, such as unobserved enrollment patterns that slightly shape the sample, may bias study results. The issue is even more problematic with nonexperimental research. A typical solution is for statistical analyses to control for potential confounders. Unfortunately, there is no magical number of control variables that can solve the problem (Lieberson 1985). The best one can do is to rely on prior work and theory and identify the potential confounders that may be most relevant. Credible research studies are more evidence-based when they take this approach and acknowledge the potential biasing impact that omitted confounders may have on the findings.

11. *Analytic Approach*

There are a number of approaches available for analyzing data. Sometimes one approach will be best, but in many instances several options may exist. Whatever the analytic approach, the goal is to identify a potential relationship and, typically, to address potential confounding that may bias results. Intervention studies that rely on more relevant analytic approaches will generate, in general, more accurate results.

12. *Adequate Description of Data, Measures, Analyses, and Findings*

Appraising a study requires information about exactly what went into it. Credible studies provide clear descriptions of the data (including how they were collected), the measures, how and why analyses were undertaken, study findings, and more. This—it should be said—can be quite challenging. Most journals impose page limits on studies. Some relevant information therefore may not be included. Not all reviewers will agree, though, on what is relevant. Clarity about all aspects of the study nonetheless remains a hallmark of a credible study, and is thus valuable for establishing results that we might view as evidence-based.

13. *Description of Limitations, Including Inconsistent Results*

One of the unfortunate aspects of science is that rewards—in the form of publication, prestige, or media coverage—may be more likely to occur when studies have statistically significant results. Studies instead should present results even when they do not support hypotheses or are inconsistent. Doing so enables other researchers to evaluate the veracity of the findings and to identify potential questions that may exist. For example, inconsistent results might arise from diverse factors, such as the type of sample, measures, or analytic approaches being used. Credible studies highlight such possibilities and any limitations that might be relevant for putting study results in context. This includes acknowledging when study results might simply be incorrect or might differ for a variety of populations or in different contexts. For example, "efficacy" studies assess interventions under ideal conditions and might generate positive results that one might not find in "effectiveness" studies, which examine interventions as they unfold in the "real world" (Mears 2010). Such information is critical for informing policy deliberations about "evidence-based" approaches.

B. Types of Policy-Relevant Questions and Issues When Evaluating Research

In evaluating research, we should distinguish studies that assess the evidence for a given policy dimension, such as (a) the need for a policy, (b) the underlying theoretical assumptions, (c) its implementation (and what influences implementation), (d) its impact (and what influences impact), and (e) its cost-efficiency (Rossi, Lipsey, and Freeman 2004; Mears 2010). An all-too-narrow view is to focus on whether a study demonstrates that a particular intervention "works" (e.g., reduces crime or improves public trust in the police). Policymakers and criminal justice administrators face a wide array of policy-relevant problems that go beyond that focus. Evaluating research requires, in part, assessing the particular type of questions and issues that a study addresses or for which a given study might be relevant.

1. Needs Evaluations

Prior to allocating funds for a new program, we typically would want to know if the program is actually needed. For example, research might show that a particular program can be highly effective at preventing gang violence. But if gang violence occurs rarely, expending resources on the program would be unnecessary and a waste of scarce resources. We therefore need credible research studies that assess the need for interventions.

2. Theory Evaluations

An evidence-based program can be one that relies on well-evaluated theory. All else being equal, a program that relies on such theory should be more effective than one that does not. The only way to make such a determination, however, is to conduct a study that evaluates existing theory and how well the theory guides a policy.

3. Implementation Evaluations

Even the most potentially effective interventions will fail if poorly implemented. If they target the wrong populations or do not deliver appropriate services, failure can be expected. Assessing implementation is thus critical in its own right. Indeed, government accountability requires credible research evidence demonstrating appropriate and quality implementation. Well-conducted studies, not anecdotal accounts, provide such evidence.

4. Impact Evaluations

Many seemingly good ideas or common-sense ideas that underlie interventions may produce favorable social outcomes, such as reductions in instances of excessive police use of force. But many such ideas turn out to be incorrect. Impact evaluations are needed to adjudicate whether interventions effectively achieve their outcomes. They can consist of any of a wide variety of research designs, with experiments and high-quality quasi-experiments constituting the highest standard (Welsh, Braga, and Bruinsma 2013). Evidence of impact is not alone solely relevant. We also want to identify the magnitude of the impact, what produced it, and how the impact may vary for different populations. Studies that present only a quantitative estimate of impact without putting it in context typically are not as credible as those that do.

5. Efficiency Evaluations

Evidence of intervention effectiveness does not automatically translate into evidence of efficiency. For example, two interventions might reduce hate crimes, but one may do so more cost-efficiently. Cost-effectiveness studies compare interventions that target the same outcome; cost-benefit studies compare interventions that target different outcomes, and they do so by monetizing all aspects of the interventions and outcomes. Science cannot adjudicate moral or political debates about interventions, but it can provide evidence about the potentially greater monetary returns that may accrue to certain policies. Credible efficiency studies should report on the uncertainties and assumptions that can underlie estimates, and on their inability to weigh moral or political considerations that might bear on policy decisions.

C. Distinguishing Intervention versus Nonintervention Research When Evaluating Research

Assessing an intervention generates different insights than does assessing a nonintervention. This distinction warrants emphasis because social science frequently involves the study of noninterventions, and because it produces results that might have relevance for policy. Yet these results may actually have little direct bearing on whether a particular intervention would be effective.

Consider a study of prosecutors. We identify a random sample and send questionnaires to the prosecutors, asking them their views about crime and their approach to processing individuals who have been arrested. Perhaps we find that prosecutors with fewer years of experience tend to be more aggressive in pursuing formal charges and tougher sentences. We could surmise that an intervention that focuses on prosecutors with fewer years of experience could reduce this tendency. We might surmise, too, that the explanation lies with a tendency among newer prosecutors to want to establish their get-tough credentials. Yet we really would have no systematic foundation for the intervention. Is the association actually "real"? (It may not be.) What explains the association? What might influence the factors that contribute to the association? The study might be "evidence-based" in the sense of relying on sound social science practices, and it may identify intriguing possibilities that could be relevant for policy, but it may not provide any foundation for credibly asserting that a particular policy is evidence-based.

By contrast, an intervention study—where one evaluates a particular social policy, program, or practice—provides direct information on whether the intervention effectively improved some outcome. There is no speculation about the relevance of a social science finding. We instead examine a policy and identify its impacts. As discussed in this chapter, a policy study could be quite limited in what it can tell us. For example, we might credibly assess a drug court's impact on recidivism but not know much about whether drug treatment, intensive supervision, or some other aspect of drug court operations produced the result (see Gottfredson, Najaka, and Kearley 2003). Knowledge of the potential impact can inform deliberations about whether to continue with the drug court, but the lack of knowledge about how the impact arises inhibits our ability to know what aspect of the court to emphasize. Awareness of the two types of research, as well as their respective strengths and limitations, is crucial to evaluating research studies.

D. Contextualizing Studies When Evaluating Research

Context is everything—that axiom holds true in science as well as in life. Credible studies make it easy for us to appreciate their relevance and limitations by providing contextual information. They can do so through clear description of samples, measures, analytic approach, and more. Most importantly, they can do so in describing their potential limitations.

Consider a study of the impact of time served in prison on recidivism. Researchers might find that more time increases recidivism, at least up to a point, and that, past that point, more time may decrease recidivism (Mears et al. 2016). Perhaps this finding constitutes a contribution to science. Even so, it does not explain what produced this particular relationship. And it may be that the effects hold only in the state in which the study occurred. Prison systems can and do vary in their conditions of confinement, the programming and services they offer, their professionalism, and more, all of which might influence recidivism (Mears, Cochran, and Cullen 2015). The same observation holds for juvenile justice incarceration and various sanctions (Mears et al. 2011). In fact, for any particular study, there may be all manner of specific details or idiosyncrasies of a policy—or the research—that could contribute to the study findings.

Ideally, studies would report on these details and idiosyncrasies (Farrington 2003). And, ideally, those who read or summarize the studies would report on them. Doing so would provide a more accurate representation of the significance of a particular finding and how much confidence we can have in the finding. There currently is no requirement for studies to extensively report potentially relevant details, idiosyncrasies, and other contextual information. Journals and reviewers expect some discussion of study limitations, but no consistent "checklist" of dimensions exists or is used. That elevates the importance of research for consumers considering the potential contextual factors that might shape the significance, meaning, accuracy, or generalizability of study findings.

When thinking about the importance of a particular study for policy, it is important to appreciate what the study does *not* capture. For example, a juvenile delinquency intervention evaluation might assess how well the intervention reduces offending. It might, though, say nothing about beneficial or harmful impacts on participant education, mental health, or family functioning. Studies should, ideally, emphasize this point.

Consider an equally important and related issue: program evaluations typically entail a focus on an observable intervention. They shed light on that intervention and, in so doing, may divert attention from factors that may be more relevant for achieving our goals. For example, poor intake procedures might result in too few youth being diverted. Assessing this possibility may be tricky, in part, because the procedures may consist of both informal and formal policies and practices. That makes studying the impacts of intake procedures more difficult than studying the impacts of an intervention that has clearly defined parameters. Yet the reality is that a great deal of juvenile and criminal justice consists of diverse decision-making and a wide variety of programs, systems dynamics, and outcomes relevant to specific parts of justice systems (Mears and Butts 2008; Mears and Bacon 2009; Mears and Barnes 2010; Mears 2017). Program evaluations are essential, but they do not illuminate a variety of forces that collectively contribute to safety, justice, and other outcomes. This consideration constitutes another way of putting studies into context and for evaluating their policy relevance.

II. Assessing Research Evidence

Just as it is crucial to use the highest standards to evaluate individual research studies, it is also important that equally rigorous standards be used to assess the totality of available research evidence. This involves a "taking stock" of a group of research studies. Undergirding this view is the need for a robust measure of external validity.

In intervention research, external validity refers to how well the effect of an intervention on an outcome is generalizable or replicable in different conditions, different operational definitions of the intervention and various outcomes, different persons, different environments, and so on. It can also be thought of as the "generalizability of internally valid results" (Sherman et al. 2006, 8). More generally, external validity has to do with the ability to reproduce or replicate the findings of a prior study.

External validity can be established through a number of different approaches. In the field or laboratory setting, external validity can be produced through replication studies. This is likely the approach that is most familiar to researchers, practitioners, and policymakers, harking back to undergraduate and graduate courses on research methods. External validity can also be established through reviews of the literature, especially by systematic and meta-analytic review methods. They seek to provide an approximation of external validity in the "real world." Each of these approaches is discussed in the following subsections. We begin with a brief exposition of some key issues related to external validity.

A. Conceptualizing and Operationalizing External Validity

It is often taken as a truism that having more than one research study on a specific topic is not only favorable but also needed for a program, practice, or policy to be eligible to be classified as "evidence-based." For example, in Fagan and Buchanan's (2016) review of crime prevention registries, the authors argue that a core criterion for a program to be rated as evidence-based is that the (desirable) results have been replicated or reproduced by at least one other research study (based on a unique sample of participants). This is the case with the Blueprints for Healthy Youth Development registry, which uses the term "Model program" to designate evidence-based interventions. Fagan and Buchanan (2016, 625) summarize the criterion as follows: "To be designated as a model program requires at least two high-quality RCTs [randomized controlled trials] or one RCT and one QED [quasi-experimental design].... All interventions designated as effective by Blueprints must have been replicated at least once in a well-conducted study."

Similarly, proponents of the meta-analytic review method claim that all that is needed is for two research studies to conduct a proper meta-analysis (see Wilson 2001). The same claim, that only two studies are needed, could be applied to the systematic review method. It is, though, a questionable one. The current authors have never seen a published meta-analysis or systematic review with $N = 2$. Moreover, it would be inappropriate. Having a small number of studies in these reviews (like having a small number of participants in a primary research study) limits the ability to establish external validity. We return to this point in subsection C.

Of greater concern in establishing a measure of external validity is that the research studies being compared (i.e., through replication or literature review) need to adhere to or come awfully close to approximating the principle of "like-with-like." In intervention research, this means that the nature of the intervention, target population, context, and outcome should be similar across studies, such as a comparison of a community-based mentoring program for youths to prevent delinquency with another community-based mentoring program for youths to prevent delinquency. This may seem obvious, but comparing "apples" to "apples" is essential for a valid comparison; comparing "apples" to "oranges" produces inappropriate comparisons that undermine the validity of any observed differences or similarities in the study results. Of course, there are bound to be some differences in key study characteristics (e.g., duration of intervention, risk level of sample, delivery format), and this is especially the case in large-scale systematic reviews and meta-analyses (see, e.g., Tolan et al. 2014). They should be similar in essential ways, though, such as core services thought to be critical to intervention success (Bardach 2004).

Potentially upending the view about the need for a measure of external validity—at least in the form of replication studies in the field—is when a research study has (a) an especially large number of units (i.e., participants or places) or (b) been carried out under conditions that approximate the real world (see Baron 2018; Dodge 2020). It is often the case that these two factors go hand-in-hand, but it is worthwhile to consider them separately. A study involving thousands of participants, drawn from a large geographical area (e.g., state, region, country) or setting (e.g., courts, prisons), could be representative of the target population.

In the case of real-world studies in intervention research, we can think of these as "effectiveness" or routine practice studies, with the contrast being "efficacy" or research and demonstration studies, respectively (Fagan et al. 2019; Gottfredson et al. 2015; Lipsey 2005). It needs to be noted that, in the parlance of prevention science, the aim of an effectiveness study is to increase the generalizability of findings from an efficacy study, which is "most often met through one or more replication studies" (Gottfredson et al. 2015, 910). In the present scenario, there is no prior efficacy study. Instead, researchers are starting at the effectiveness study stage, and they are doing so, presumably, with a sound theoretical and empirical foundation. This also applies to studies with large sample sizes. Nevertheless, a measure of external validity—in the form of a replication study—is a highly valued commodity in trying to bring about evidence-based policy in crime and justice. This is the focus of the next subsection.

B. Study Replication

The replication of research studies offers a powerful means of establishing a measure of external validity. It so important that researchers consider it to be one of the chief hallmarks of the scientific enterprise (Lösel 2018). Its significance is captured by the following:

> Scientists generally assume that no one study typically should be trusted. Rather, only through repeated study, and only when the additional studies consistently agree with one another, do we begin to trust that maybe an identified pattern exists or that some posited explanation is "true." In science, replication is critical. The more studies that accumulate and come to the same conclusion, the more that we can trust that the conclusion approximates "truth." (Mears and Cochran 2019, 22)

In a field setting, the process of replication often follows one of two main approaches. The classic or traditional approach to replication involves a research study in one site being replicated at another site at a later point in time and with the expressed aim of investigating whether the original study results can be reproduced. Here, a distinction can be made between direct and conceptual replication. The former involves the use of the "same type of data and methods as the original study to assess the veracity of its findings," while the latter involves the use of "different data or methods, purposely altering some component to test the generalizability of the original results" (Pridemore et al. 2018, 21).

The other approach to replication in the field involves a multisite research study. Two or more research studies (using similar protocols for recruitment, treatment, and measurement) are carried out simultaneously at different sites with the two-fold aim of investigating (a) the research hypothesis and (b) whether the results are reproduced among the multiple sites. In the case of multisite randomized controlled trials of interventions, MacKenzie, Umamaheswar, and Lin (2013, 163) outline several key reasons for their use, including the desire to replicate results from "initial single-site studies," to produce a large sample size that has sufficient statistical power to detect effects, and to discern small or moderate effect sizes.

It is also the case that replications can be considered complete or partial. The latter may be the best that can be achieved under the conditions at the time, or it is designed to serve as a first step toward a more complete replication (see Welsh et al. 2011).

C. Reviews of the Literature

In the same way that not all primary research studies are equal, some methods of reviewing the literature are far more rigorous, thus allowing for a higher degree of confidence in their findings and conclusions. Two such methods are the systematic review and meta-analytic (or meta-analysis) review. At the heart of these review methods are several principles that distinguish them from other, less rigorous literature review methods—namely, the traditional narrative review (see Petticrew and Roberts 2006; Welsh and Farrington 2007) and the less well-known vote-count review (see Sherman et al. 1997, 2006). The first principle, and by far the most important, is the need to mitigate or, better yet, eliminate researcher bias. Whether intentional or not, researcher bias is typically introduced right at the beginning of the process through the adoption of a less than comprehensive methodology for searching for studies. More often than not, the researcher will limit their search to published sources or even self-select studies to be included, based on the researcher's familiarity with them, quite possibly leaving many studies out of the review. This filtering process can lead to an incorrect conclusion based on a nonrepresentative set of studies and based on possible biases in the interpretation of these studies.

Another principle has to do with overcoming bias that exists in the research itself. In large measure this has to do with publication bias, the well-known phenomenon of scientific journals being more inclined to publish studies with statistically significant findings (Wilson 2009). Bias in research can also exist when there are geographical or language constraints placed on the studies that are eligible for inclusion in the review. Efforts need to be taken (and documented) to identify studies from across the world and reported in languages other than English. A third principle concerns the matter of transparency in the reporting of reviews. Consumers of reviews need to have access to all of the methods used, all of the decisions taken and justifications for them (e.g., why some studies are excluded), and all of the data available from the included studies. Such transparency allows other researchers to replicate reviews.

1. *Systematic Review Method*

Systematic reviews use rigorous methods for locating, appraising, and synthesizing evidence from prior studies. They are reported with the same level of detail that characterizes high-quality reports of primary research. Many features distinguish systematic reviews from less rigorous review methods; we highlight a number of these features here. One is that they have explicit objectives. This includes making clear the rationale for carrying out the review. Another is that they have explicit eligibility criteria—the researchers specify in detail why certain studies are included and other studies are excluded. This includes all of the variables of interest, including sample, context, methodological design, and outcome data.

A third feature is the use of a comprehensive set of search strategies to identify studies that meet the criteria for inclusion in the review. Examples of search strategies include electronic bibliographic databases, prior reviews of the literature, bibliographies of included and excluded studies, forward citations of studies that meet the inclusion criteria, and contacts with leading experts in the field (Petticrew and Roberts 2006). Each of these search strategies need to be used, in addition to others that may be relevant to a specific topic (e.g., searches of specific government or nongovernment websites). Importantly, searches need to be focused on identifying both published and unpublished studies, as well as studies from across the world and reported in languages other than English.

A fourth feature is that each study is screened according to eligibility criteria, with exclusions justified. The searches will undoubtedly locate many citations and abstracts to potentially relevant studies, and each of the reports of these potentially relevant studies must be screened to determine if the study meets the eligibility criteria for the review. A full listing of all excluded studies and the justifications for exclusion should be made available to readers.

A fifth feature involves assembling the most complete data possible. The researcher needs to make every effort to obtain all studies that meet the eligibility criteria. In addition, all data relevant to the review's objectives need to be carefully extracted from each included study and coded and computerized. Sometimes, original study documents lack important information, which can be characterized as poor descriptive validity (Farrington 2003). Whenever possible, the researcher needs to attempt to obtain these data from the authors of the primary studies.

2. *Meta-Analytic Review Method*

A meta-analysis involves the statistical or quantitative analysis of the results of prior research studies (Lipsey and Wilson 2001). One major product of a meta-analysis is a weighted average effect size, denoting the magnitude of the association between an independent variable and a dependent variable (e.g., the effect of an intervention on an outcome) across studies. There is usually also an attempt to investigate factors (moderators) that predict larger or smaller effect sizes in different studies. In intervention research, this is to establish whether an intervention has greater benefits in certain contexts and which characteristics of the intervention are most related to a successful outcome (Lipsey 2003).

In addition to its quantitative techniques, the meta-analytic review method should include all of the key features of the systematic review method. A systematic review may or may not include a meta-analysis. The use of meta-analysis may not be appropriate due to a small number of studies, heterogeneity across studies, or different units of analysis of the studies. But when suitable, meta-analytic techniques should be conducted as part of systematic reviews.

III. Discussion and Conclusions

Calls for evidence-based policy are all to the good, but their usefulness requires an understanding of what it means to call policy "evidence-based." No universal agreement about how best to define "evidence-based" policy exists. In this chapter, we have identified two distinct sets of considerations that go into thinking about evidence-based policy.

One consists of how we go about evaluating research. When viewed from the perspective of science, "evidence-based" can mean findings that emanate from studies that align with what might be viewed as the "canons" of good science. They rely on theory, defensible sampling techniques, appropriate and sufficiently large samples, valid measures, rigorous analytic approaches, and so on. They also provide sufficient details for placing the studies in context. That includes articulating the kinds of questions or issues that the studies can address, and those that they cannot. For example, some studies may be useful for establishing whether a sizable gang violence problem exists that may warrant attention. Others may identify the factors that impeded quality program implementation, or disjunctures between the theory and practice of a given program. Still others may assess the extent to which a given intervention improves some outcomes, and how cost-effective it is relative to other policies. Awareness of such possibilities is part and parcel of evaluating not only the validity of study findings but also their relevance.

Another distinct consideration has to do with how we make sense of a large body of research studies to arrive at what might be a closer approximation of the "truth" than what we can obtain from any one study. This activity requires different, though related, considerations. For example, one must be careful to compare "like" studies and to take steps to mitigate bias that might intentionally or unintentionally influence studies or the review. There also are different tasks that can be involved, such as synthesizing the results of many studies or seeking to replicate study findings (e.g., repeat a study with a different study population or in a different site) or reproduce them (e.g., determine if the original study results can be obtained through re-analysis of a given study's original data). Still other tasks involve the creation of registries to provide an organizational framework for classifying types or categories of programs and interventions.

In short, "evidence-based" can cover a multitude of possibilities. The common denominator is a reliance on theoretically informed and methodologically rigorous studies. These, though, do not vitiate the fact that judgment goes into assessments of particular studies or of entire bodies of research. Or that disagreements may exist about the best way to define "evidence-based" or, for a given definition, what standards to apply in determining when a given program, policy, practice—or general approach—to addressing crime and justice is evidence-based. In our view, the best path forward lies with awareness of these issues and direct engagement with them.

REFERENCES

Bardach, Eugene. 2004. Presidential address—the extrapolation problem: How can we learn from the experience of others? *Journal of Policy Analysis and Management*, 23:205–220.

Baron, Jon. 2018. A brief history of evidence-based policy. *Annals of the American Academy of Political and Social Science*, 678:40–50.

Dodge, Kenneth A. 2020. Annual research review: Universal and targeted strategies for assigning interventions to achieve population impact. *Journal of Child Psychology and Psychiatry*, 61:255–267.

Fagan, Abigail A., and Molly Buchanan. 2016. What works in crime prevention? Comparison and critical review of three crime prevention registries. *Criminology & Public Policy*, 15:617–649.

Fagan, Abigail A., Brian K. Bumbarger, Richard P. Barth, Catherine P. Bradshaw, Brittany Rhoades Cooper, Lauren H. Supplee, et al. 2019. Scaling up evidence-based interventions in US public health systems to prevent behavioral health problems: Challenges and opportunities. *Prevention Science*, 20:1147–1168.

Farrington, David P. 2003. Methodological quality standards for evaluation research. *Annals of the American Academy of Political and Social Science*, 587:49–68.

Gottfredson, Denise C., Thomas D. Cook, Frances E. M. Gardner, Deborah Gorman-Smith, George W. Howe, Irwin N. Sandler, et al. 2015. Standards of evidence for efficacy, effectiveness, and scale-up research in prevention science: Next generation. *Prevention Science*, 16:893–926.

Gottfredson, Denise C., Stacy S. Najaka, and Brook Kearley. 2003. Effectiveness of drug treatment courts: Evidence from a randomized trial. *Criminology & Public Policy*, 2:171–196.

Lieberson, Stanley. 1985. *Making it count: The improvement of social research and theory*. Los Angeles: University of California Press.

Lipsey, Mark W. 2003. Those confounded moderators in meta-analysis: Good, bad, and ugly. *Annals of the American Academy of Political and Social Science*, 587:69–81.

Lipsey, Mark W., ed. 2005. *Improving evaluation of anticrime programs*. Washington, DC: National Academies Press.

Lipsey, Mark W., and David B. Wilson. 2001. *Practical meta-analysis*. Thousand Oaks, CA: SAGE.

Lösel, Friedrich. 2018. Evidence comes by replication, but needs differentiation: The reproducibility issue in science and its relevance for criminology. *Journal of Experimental Criminology*, 14:257–278.

MacKenzie, Doris Layton, Janani Umamaheswar, and Li-Chen Lin. 2013. Multisite randomized trials in criminology. In *Experimental criminology: Prospects for advancing science and public policy*, edited by Brandon C. Welsh, Anthony A. Braga, and Gerben J. N. Bruinsma, 163–193. New York: Cambridge University Press.

Mears, Daniel P. 2010. *American criminal justice policy: An evaluation approach to increasing accountability and effectiveness*. New York: Cambridge University Press.

Mears, Daniel P. 2017. *Out-of-control criminal justice: The systems improvement solution for more safety, justice, accountability, and efficiency*. New York: Cambridge University Press.

Mears, Daniel P., and Sarah Bacon. 2009. Improving criminal justice through better decision making: Lessons from the medical system. *Journal of Criminal Justice*, 37:142–154.

Mears, Daniel P., and James C. Barnes. 2010. Toward a systematic foundation for identifying evidence-based criminal justice sanctions and their relative effectiveness. *Journal of Criminal Justice*, 38:702–710.

Mears, Daniel P., and Jeffrey A. Butts. 2008. Using performance monitoring to improve the accountability, operations, and effectiveness of juvenile justice. *Criminal Justice Policy Review*, 19:264–284.

Mears, Daniel P., and Joshua C. Cochran. 2019. *Fundamentals of criminological and criminal justice inquiry: The science and art of conducting, evaluating, and using research*. New York: Cambridge University Press.

Mears, Daniel P., Joshua C. Cochran, William D. Bales, and Avinash S. Bhati. 2016. Recidivism and time served in prison. *Journal of Criminal Law and Criminology*, 106:83–124.

Mears, Daniel P., Joshua C. Cochran, and Francis T. Cullen. 2015. Incarceration heterogeneity and its implications for assessing the effectiveness of imprisonment on recidivism. *Criminal Justice Policy Review*, 26:691–712.

Mears, Daniel P., Joshua C. Cochran, Sarah J. Greenman, Avinash S. Bhati, and Mark A. Greenwald. 2011. Evidence on the effectiveness of juvenile court sanctions. *Journal of Criminal Justice*, 39:509–520.

Pantole, Sanjay, ed. 2021. *Principles and practice of systematic reviews and meta-analysis*. New York: Springer.

Petticrew, Mark, and Helen Roberts. 2006. *Systematic reviews in the social sciences: A practical guide*. Oxford: Blackwell.

Pridemore, William Alex, Matthew C. Makel, and Jonathan A. Plucker. 2018. Replication in criminology and the social sciences. *Annual Review of Criminology*, 1:19–38.

Rossi, Peter H., Mark W. Lipsey, and Howard E. Freeman. 2004. *Evaluation: A systematic approach*. 7th ed. Thousand Oaks, CA: SAGE.

Sherman, Lawrence W., David P. Farrington, Brandon C. Welsh, and Doris Layton MacKenzie. 2006. Preventing crime. In *Evidence-based crime prevention*. Rev. ed., edited by Lawrence W. Sherman, David P. Farrington, Brandon C. Welsh, and Doris Layton MacKenzie, 1–12. New York: Routledge.

Sherman, Lawrence W., Denise C. Gottfredson, Doris Layton MacKenzie, John E. Eck, Peter Reuter, and Shawn D. Bushway. 1997. *Preventing crime: What works, what doesn't, what's promising*. Washington, DC: US Department of Justice, Office of Justice Programs.

Tolan, Patrick H., David B. Henry, Michael S. Schoeny, Peter Lovegrove, and Emily Nichols. 2014. Mentoring programs to affect delinquency and associated outcomes of youth at risk: A comprehensive meta-analytic review. *Journal of Experimental Criminology*, 10:179–206.

Welsh, Brandon C., Anthony A. Braga, and Gerben J. N. Bruinsma, eds. 2013. *Experimental criminology: Prospects for advancing science and public policy*. New York: Cambridge University Press.

Welsh, Brandon C., and David P. Farrington, eds. 2007. *Preventing crime: What works for children, offenders, victims, and places*. New York: Springer.

Welsh, Brandon C., Meghan E. Peel, David P. Farrington, Henk Elffers, and Anthony A. Braga. 2011. Research design influence on study outcomes in crime and justice: A partial replication with public area surveillance. *Journal of Experimental Criminology*, 7:183–198.

Wilson, David B. 2001. Meta-analytic methods for criminology. *Annals of the American Academy of Political and Social Science*, 578:71–89.

Wilson, David B. 2009. Missing a critical piece of the pie: Simple document search strategies inadequate for systematic reviews. *Journal of Experimental Criminology*, 5:429–440.

CHAPTER 3

TRANSLATIONAL CRIMINOLOGY AND EVIDENCE-BASED POLICY AND PRACTICE

CODY W. TELEP

EVIDENCE-BASED crime policy requires both a sufficient body of research to guide policy and practice decisions and mechanisms for policymakers and practitioners to access and act upon this empirical evidence. As much as scholars might hope that publishing their work in an academic journal or government report will have large impacts on social policy, there is little evidence that the journey from research findings to new policies or practices is an easy one (Nutley, Walter, and Davies 2007). Instead, a body of research suggests sustained work is needed to achieve policymaker or practitioner research utilization. The failure to engage in this work contributes to continued gaps between research findings and criminal justice practice (Mears 2022).

In the last decade, translational criminology has emerged as one approach to help address these gaps. John Laub (2011), then director of the National Institute of Justice (NIJ) first wrote about translational criminology in describing his strategic approach at NIJ. In some sense, the idea of translational criminology is simple and straightforward. In keeping with Sherman's (1998, 3) contention that "police practices should be based on scientific evidence about what works best," Laub (2011, 17) argues that "if we want to reduce and manage crime, we must be able to translate scientific discoveries into policy and practice." Thus, translational criminology focuses on how science can impact policy and practice decisions. But behind this seemingly simple notion is a great deal of complexity. Laub (2011, 2021) notes that translational criminology is focused on not only bringing research into practice, but also systematically studying how dissemination occurs and what techniques and strategies are effective. This involves better understanding the policy implementation process and why research has often failed to play much of a role in crime and justice policy development.

This chapter engages with that complexity in exploring what we know about translational criminology to date, what strategies are likely to be most effective for increasing utilization of research findings, and gaps and areas where future research is needed to advance our understanding of effective translational work. While the evidence base itself is the topic of other chapters in this volume, this chapter focuses on those mechanisms designed to help translate research findings in ways that make them more accessible and usable for policymakers and practitioners. I note at the outset, though, that the evidence base is a limitation in translational work. While knowledge about the effectiveness of a number of criminal justice strategies has grown rapidly in recent years, most programs are not evaluated (Mears 2022). For many practices and policies, there is little or no research to guide decision-making.

In the sections that follow, I first examine definitions of translational criminology and describe what the concept entails and how it connects to evidence-based policy and practice. I then turn to a brief review of what we know about practitioner openness to using research evidence to guide decision-making. I next summarize work from a number of policy fields to better understand the ways research can have impacts and effective mechanisms for translating research into practice. I extend that discussion by applying insights from this work to the criminal justice system, highlighting recent examples of translational efforts to improve evidence-based practice in crime and justice. I conclude by discussing gaps in our current understanding of translational work and the need for future research, particularly surrounding the implementation of evidence-based policy and practice.

I. What Is Translational Criminology?

Laub's conception of translational criminology focuses on efforts to translate research findings into policy and practice settings in ways that can improve crime control (or other) outcomes. As Laub and Frisch (2016, 53) note, "translational criminology serves as a vehicle to move beyond the rhetoric regarding the lack of research influence on policy by devising innovative dissemination strategies and developing an understanding of the processes underlying program implementation."

In recent years, other scholars have defined the term similarly. Lum and Koper (2017, 266) define translational criminology as "the theory and study of how the products of criminological and criminal justice research turn into outputs, tools, programs, interventions, and actions in criminal justice practice." Pesta and colleagues (2019, 50) describe translational criminology as "the process of knowledge creation through scientific research and its subsequent use to inform policy and practice in criminal justice," and they note that this process can include "research dissemination, policy implementation, and research translation." Across these definitions are two important points. First, dissemination is a key part of the translation process. But second, translation is not just another word for dissemination. Translational criminology entails more than disseminating research findings and includes a deep dive into the policy implementation process and an ongoing dialogue and collaboration between researchers and policymakers.

Similar to evidence-based policing and evidence-based crime policy more generally, translational criminology has its roots in medicine and efforts to translate basic scientific findings from laboratories to clinical settings (Laub 2021). More than three decades of published work has focused on translation in medical contexts, as reflected in the establishment in 2003 of the *Journal of Translational Medicine*. In the journal's initial issue, founding editor Francesco Marincola (2003) argued that translational medicine should be considered a "two-way road." By this he means that translational work should consider not only how to move from laboratory discoveries to clinical testing and eventually clinical practice in humans (or, in medical terminology, from bench to bedside), but also how clinical findings match up with basic research and how findings from clinical settings can inform the next generation of basic research (or, from bedside to bench). More recently, Cohrs et al. (2015) describe a third pillar for translational medicine—the community. They suggest that patients, medical practitioners, and healthy medical trial participants can provide valuable insights into evidence-based medicine. In their model, the benchside, bedside, and community all work collaboratively to improve medical care.

Thus, the translational process is not simply about how research can be translated into practice. There should also be a feedback loop where, in the case of medicine, knowledge gained from clinical trials, doctors, or patients informs the next stage of basic research, particularly when promising treatments are not found to be successful in human trials. Laub (2021) adopts these ideas in considering what translational criminology should look like in practice. His vision of a "two-way street" entails a process where "scientists discover new tools and idea for use in the field and evaluate their impact. In turn, practitioners offer novel observations from the field setting that stimulate basic research investigation" (Laub 2021, 169).

In the remaining sections, I describe what we know about existing translational efforts and what we have learned about translational research more generally from other fields. There is little empirical research to date directly on the key concepts surrounding translational criminology. We have little systematic research, for example, on dissemination efforts and their effectiveness (Laub 2021). But, for a concept that was introduced just more than 10 years ago, we have seen quick progress in adding to the evidence base for translation. We do have some knowledge about what works for increasing the use of research in practice, and while there is no journal focused on translation in criminology, the topic has generated journal special issues (e.g., Nichols et al. 2019), a book series from Springer,[1] and the George Mason University Center for Evidence-Based Crime Policy's (CEBCP) magazine, *Translational Criminology*.[2] The magazine started in 2011, and CEBCP had published 22 issues at the end of the 2022, all of which highlight examples of efforts to integrate research findings into police and practice.

II. How Open Are Criminal Justice Practitioners to Using Research?

One key question for translational criminology is the extent to which practitioners and policymakers are open to incorporating research evidence into their work. Prior survey-based work on receptivity to research overall suggests general openness to research evidence. But there are also gaps in practitioner understanding and use of research that translational efforts could ideally help to address. In a survey of police officers from three agencies, Telep and Lum (2014) found that respondents were rarely reading academic publications, and when they did learn about research, it was most commonly from their own agency. This suggests the importance of translational efforts that target departmental information-sharing mechanisms (e.g., training). Officers, though, generally see the value of working with researchers; more than 70% of respondents agreed that collaboration with researchers is necessary for an agency to improve its ability to reduce crime. While there is openness to researcher partnerships, officers also felt experience should guide their day-to-day work far more than scientific knowledge.

There is generally greater receptivity and openness among agency leaders, but there are still gaps that can impede the use of research in practice. Light and Newman (1992) conducted a national survey of state-level corrections administrators and researchers to assess whether respondents had access to and were aware of social science research. Nearly all respondents believed being aware of social science research was at least somewhat important. Research use, however, was generally low, and respondents were much more likely to make use of nonscholarly research than academic articles. Both research and nonresearch corrections staff rated practical experience and staff expertise as more useful in day-to-day work.

In policing, Rojek and colleagues (2012) found in a national survey of agencies (generally completed by chief executives) that research was most commonly used "sometimes" in policy decisions, with larger agencies more likely to use research. About one-third of agencies had recently engaged in a partnership with a researcher, with large agencies more likely to work with a researcher. When nonpartnership agencies were asked why they had not worked with researchers, the most common response (56%) was insufficient funding or staff resources. Only 15% of agencies said they did not think partnership with a researcher would be useful to the agency. Agencies also tended to view the partnerships as beneficial, with 83% of agencies with a partnership rating that partnership as successful or somewhat successful. These partnerships are also an important mechanism by which practitioners both learn about research findings and enhance their understanding of the research process (Hansen, Alpert, and Rojek 2014).

In a similar survey of community corrections leaders in Pennsylvania, Kim and Lee (2022) found somewhat higher levels of researcher partnership participation than among police. Probation and parole leaders generally also saw partnerships as successful, though at somewhat lower levels than police leaders. Similar to policing, just 8.6% of community corrections leaders disagreed that partnerships with researchers are necessary.

In a survey of policing chief executives in Oregon, Telep and Winegar (2016) found general openness to partnering with researchers and using research in practice, but also general support for more traditional tactics that do not have strong evidence of effectiveness. Despite little empirical support for rapid response to 911 calls as a crime control strategy, more than half of respondents described the approach as effective or very effective for reducing crime and disorder. Importantly, Telep and Winegar (2016) found that chiefs are more likely than officers to report reading about research from sources like the International Association of Chiefs of Police (IACP). Similar to Rojek and colleagues (2012), Telep and Winegar (2016) found that 90% of chiefs reported reading *The Police Chief*, while less than 5% reported reading any academic publications.

The finding that practitioners are rarely reading academic publications is consistent across public service fields (Nutley et al. 2007), suggesting the importance of other forms of dissemination, an issue I revisit in the next two sections. Even for practitioners interested in research published in academic publications, they would likely face challenges in accessing this work. Ashby (2020) found that only 22% of more than 12,000 articles published in criminology journals between 2017 and 2019 were available to nonsubscribers. Unless they are current students, practitioners rarely have access to the library subscriptions necessary to access most peer-reviewed publications. Ashby (2020) notes that researchers could do more to make this work accessible. Even though most journals allow authors to share versions of their work freely (often the submitted version), most scholars do not do so.

III. What Works in Translating Research into Practice?

Before turning to specific examples of translational work in criminology, I first examine what empirical research on the social sciences more broadly suggests about research utilization. There is much overlap in studies of research utilization and translational criminology. Importantly, such work gives guidance on the translation strategies most likely to be effective (see Giacomantonio et al. 2022; Lum and Koper 2017). Here I highlight key findings on two important areas for translation: how research is used in policy and practice, and strategies for increasing this use. For both, I draw from a larger review of the research utilization literature (Telep 2013).

Carol Weiss's (1979) foundational work on the topic makes clear that the term "research utilization" does not have a simple definition. Practitioners can use research in instrumental ways; specific research is used to provide a clear change in policy or practice. However, this is uncommon, particularly in the social sciences, where findings may be ambiguous and research rarely leads to the creation of a new product. Noninstrumental uses of research are more common. In Weiss's enlightenment model, for example, specific research findings from a single study do not affect policy as much as decision-makers saying that "social science research has given them a backdrop of ideas and orientations that has had important consequences" (Weiss 1979, 430). Conducting evaluation research in an agency, particularly when the agency takes the lead, can provide valuable skills and knowledge to individuals within the agency on what good science looks like (Weisburd and Neyroud 2011). Similarly, the interactive model considers research as one input into a complicated policymaking context, where findings interact with lobbying and viewpoints from interest groups, the public, and politicians.

Conceptual utilization can be important in developing the baseline knowledge necessary for instrumental use to occur. As Nutley, Walter, and Davies (2007, 307) note, "conceptual uses of research, which contribute to subtle but potentially weighty shifts in knowledge, understanding and discourse, can be hugely significant in policy and practice." Translational criminology can at times include a clear, rational path from study findings to a new policy or practice. But the absence of such an outcome does not imply translational work has failed. Bringing research into the conversation and the policymaking process is important, and it can slowly shift viewpoints of leaders about the value of research evidence (Lum 2009). In their interviews with juvenile court judges, prosecutors, and attorneys, for example, Murphy, Hickman, and Jones (2021) find an openness to research that was most commonly conceptual. Though judges sometimes directly applied research findings to a case, more commonly practitioners, and especially judges, described how research on brain development or the effects of trauma affected their overall approach to utilizing incarceration for juveniles.

Studies of research utilization have a long history in the social sciences. Williams's (1946) pioneering work examined military research utilization during World War II and highlighted four important issues. First, researchers must be aware of the organization's needs to ensure the research will be useful. Second, communication between the researcher and agency is important throughout the process. Ideally, practitioners are involved in planning and research design to increase buy-in. Third, there should be a direct acknowledgement of the need for translation: "[R]esearch findings are not utilized to the extent warranted by their intrinsic merit if sole reliance is placed upon dissemination by the printed page . . . the best immediate results in translating research into action came through repeated contacts with persons in positions of authority and influence . . . leaders and administrators simply will not take the time or expend the effort to digest and apply our studies to their problems unless the research sociologist or some intermediary helps" (Williams 1946, 577). Fourth, once an agency decides to act on research, there should be further research to assess what happens. This in in line with Laub's (2021) call for more research on the implementation process of innovative policies and practices to understand the effects of changes guided by prior research.

More recent studies echo many of the conclusions of Williams. Nutley et al. (2007) point to four key factors increasing the likelihood of research utilization. First, research must be well done and rigorous, but practitioners also are concerned with timeliness and findings they can comprehend and apply. Second, personal characteristics of researchers and users also do play some role. Better-educated practitioners and those with more experience in research tend to use it more, although the research in this area is not conclusive. This is consistent with receptivity to research work in policing, which generally suggests more knowledge and interest about research from more highly educated practitioners (Telep 2017b). Third, researchers need to interact with practitioners on a regular basis for research to influence practice. Nutley et al. (2007) point to the importance of repeated interactions and two-way communication to maximize the likelihood that research will be used (Rojek, Martin, and Alpert 2015). Finally, the context for the use of research is very important (Tseng 2012; Sampson, Winship, and Knight 2013). Research is most likely to be used when the findings align well with the agency environment and with the interests of frontline workers and management.

These factors suggest translational efforts can incorporate multiple strategies. I present five mechanisms here, identified by Nutley and colleagues (2007), to increase research utilization (see Lum and Koper 2017). All assume a genuine interest and dedication to translational work from researchers. Most of these strategies require sustained effort and close collaboration between researchers and practitioners. Such efforts are challenging, in part because of differing priorities and interests of researchers and practitioners, and in part because researchers sometimes come across as arrogant, condescending, or uninterested in working directly with policy and practice leaders (Engel and Whalen 2010; Petersilia 2008). In the next section, I turn to recent examples from crime and justice work that draw on these mechanisms in translational efforts.

A. Dissemination

Dissemination strategies are important for increasing awareness, but they usually are not enough on their own to ensure policymakers or practitioners will use research findings. Still, they are an important first step in exposing practitioners and policymakers to evidence-based approaches. Practitioners are more apt to listen to research findings that provide them evidence on what works, but also guidance on how to implement and adopt what works (Nutley et al. 2007). Researchers should avoid obscuring their main points with lots of jargon and complicated statistics. Dissemination products do not have to be exclusively written briefs. Burruss and Lu (2021), for example, suggest the value of data visualization approaches to make research findings more relatable and often less overwhelming than complicated tables.

Written materials (e.g., policy briefs, summary documents) can increase awareness, but dissemination is more effective when it is tailored to specific audiences (see Petersilia 2008). Nutley et al. (2007) suggest researchers should focus dissemination efforts on multiple sources, targeting different levels of the agency, as well as other key stakeholder groups for the agency (e.g. community partners, government agencies). This multifaceted effort can mean that successes in achieving research utilization in one agency will have beneficial spillover effects. Of course, such work takes time, and the creation of tailored products can make dissemination work overwhelming for researchers. This is a particular challenge, as there are rarely incentives for researchers to engage in dissemination work (Pesta et al. 2019). Funded projects often include no funds set aside for dissemination work, and for researchers in faculty positions, there may be little institutional advantage to focusing on tailored policy briefs or summary documents.

B. Partnerships

Stronger collaborations between researchers and practitioners or policymakers can also make translational efforts more effective. Partnerships can increase research use through two-way communication and a sustained co-production of knowledge (Nichols et al. 2019). Such efforts though can also be time-consuming, and they require buy-in from both researchers and practitioners. In addition, long-term partnerships have not always been common in criminal justice (Weisburd and Neyroud 2011). Rojek, Martin, and Alpert (2015) detail a number of characteristics of successful police-researcher partnerships. These include structural and logistical considerations, such as the value of external funding and grant support, geographic proximity, and lack of turnover in personnel from both the researcher and practitioner side. They also describe the importance of sustained communication to build trust and rapport. Importantly, successful partnerships require practitioners that are receptive to research and researchers, as well as researchers open to putting in the work to generate projects and findings that are of benefit to the agency. The same challenge noted earlier with researcher priorities, particularly for those in university positions, can be an issue for partnerships as well. Putting in the hours to build a strong partnership without the guarantee of a journal publication can be a challenging commitment for a researcher to make, particularly an untenured faculty member.

C. Influence

A third mechanism described by Nutley et al. (2007) is the role of social influence. Here, the focus is on influential peers or experts to push the value of research. These opinion leaders can promote the value of research findings in their networks and are likely to have greater credibility than researchers. This is consistent with the diffusion of innovation literature (Rogers 2003) and the importance of well-respected champions in pushing an innovation toward wider adoption. A challenge here can be identifying appropriate influencers in both policy and practice contexts.

D. Facilitation

Facilitation strategies focus on providing the resources necessary to adapt research findings. This may include training and technical assistance, financial resources, and clear guidelines and protocols for research use. A focus on facilitation or the nuts and bolts of implementation has been a recognized gap in evaluation work in crime and justice. Even rigorous evaluations that might provide clear guidance on "what works" frequently give little insight into how it works (Telep 2017a). Randomized experiments in criminal justice, for example, rarely collect detailed process data on treatment or intervention implementation, making it challenging to assess why a particular program was or was not effective. This "black box" frequently leaves practitioners with little guidance on how to adopt research findings into practice (Famega, Hinkle, and Weisburd 2017). Sampson, Winship, and Knight (2013) also call for going beyond average effects from rigorous studies to further consideration of the mechanisms involved in causal claims, and how these causal pathways may differ for different subgroups or in different contexts.

E. Reinforcement and Incentives

A final mechanism is the use of incentives and reinforcement to reward the use of research. This approach has been studied the least in other fields, but Nutley and colleagues (2007) suggest that there is promise for efforts to reinforce research utilization, whether that be financially or through positive recognition for implementing agencies.

These efforts to increase research utilization can be incorporated into the three main models for improving research use in practice discussed by Nutley and colleagues (2007). In the research-based practitioner model, individual practitioners bear much of the responsibility for understanding and using research. In some contexts, this may make sense (e.g., the discussion of "pracademics" in section IV.C below, and Weisburd and Neyroud's 2011 call for police ownership of science), but in most cases practitioners will not have the resources or background to take the lead on understanding and applying research. In the embedded research model, research is implanted into systems and processes throughout the organization, be it official policies and procedures, or tools the agency uses. As discussed further in the next section, this could include, for example, collaborations between researchers and practitioners to integrate research evidence into existing training models. Finally, in the organizational excellence model, the agency's structure and processes emphasize the importance of research and achieving excellence through evidence-based strategies. The organizational excellence model requires strong leadership, as a well as a "research-minded organizational culture" (Nutley et al. 2007, 204). Partnerships with academics can be especially important in developing this culture.

IV. Translational Efforts in Crime and Justice

In this section, I review recent examples of translational work, using the categories of mechanisms described by Nutley et al. (2007) in the previous section. I have tried to incorporate examples from across the criminal justice system, though I note that much of the work presented here comes from policing.

A. Dissemination

There are now a number of translation tools and dissemination strategies used to better reach policy and practice audiences. These include government websites like CrimeSolutions,[3] which rates the effectiveness of programs and practices across the criminal justice system. Expert reviewers code studies or meta-analyses and reach conclusions about whether programs and practices have evidence of effectiveness. The site provides guidance to practitioners on what works on a range of topics across the criminal justice system. The What Works Centre for Crime Reduction in the College of Policing in the UK maintains a similar crime reduction toolkit,[4] reviewing the evidence base for interventions on policing and other criminal justice topics. The toolkit also considers evidence related to program implementation and cost-effectiveness. The Center for Problem-Oriented Policing (POP Center)[5] was originally funded by the Office of Community Oriented Policing Services, but it now operates at Arizona State University. The center has a large library of guides for police agencies on particular types of problems, types of responses, and analysis and assessment tools.

Outside of government-funded pages, a number of research centers and think tanks have created translation tools and resources designed to help practitioners and policymakers understand and make sense of research. In the area of policing, the CEBCP houses multiple translation tools. These include the Evidence-Based Policing Matrix[6] (Lum, Koper, and Telep 2011), an interactive visual display of the policing crime control evidence base that plots studies on a three-dimensional diagram based on their effectiveness in reducing crime, scope of target, level of specificity, and level of proactivity. The Matrix not only provides knowledge on specific studies, but also helps agencies synthesize the crime control evidence base and develop strategies that take advantage of lessons from existing policing research.

CEBCP also hosts a What Works in Policing? site[7] that uses systematic reviews and the Matrix to provide guidance to practitioners on what is and is not effective in policing and resources and recommendations on how agencies can best implement evidence-based approaches. Telep and Gross Shader (2019) describe the innovative university-city government partnership that led to the creation of the site, originally as a way to help the Seattle Police Department assess the extent to which its strategies and policies aligned with research.

The work of the Campbell Collaboration is also designed to translate research findings into practice through supporting and publishing systematic reviews. The Campbell Crime and Justice Coordinating Group (CJCG)[8] now includes 59 completed or in-progress reviews on a variety of crime and justice topics. All reviews are published open-access through a new *Campbell Systematic Reviews* journal, and they include a plain-language summary designed for policymakers.

B. Partnerships

There are a number of examples of researcher-practitioner partnerships, particularly in policing and corrections (e.g., Burkhardt et al. 2017; Drawbridge, Taheri, and Frost 2018; Rudes et al. 2014). While partnerships are often temporary and develop around a particular grant or project (Weisburd and Neyroud 2011), some are far longer-lasting and offer opportunities for sustained collaboration between researchers and practitioners, making translation far more feasible. Participatory action research (PAR, or community-based participatory research) may be an especially useful framework for encouraging research translation and longer-term partnerships (Haverkate et al. 2020). The goal in PAR is for all participants to be equal partners in every phase of research, from defining the problem, to collecting data, to interpreting and disseminating findings. Ideally, this creates more useful and usable findings for agency partners that can more easily be incorporated into practice (Telep et al. 2020).

The benefits of collaboration in all phases of research are reinforced by Pesta et al. (2019), who describe successes and challenges in partnerships with adult and juvenile corrections agencies in Florida. They draw from interviews with researchers, policymakers, and practitioners in corrections to understand how to best translate research into practice. While participants recognized challenges in using research, particularly when findings are difficult to understand or leadership does not support research, they also noted research use facilitators, with relationships mentioned most frequently. Interviewees thus identified partnerships as a key mechanism for bringing research into practice. Pesta et al. (2019) note that these correctional partnerships benefitted from a long-standing relationship with high trust from both sides, as well as collaboration on carrying out research, which made practitioners less skeptical of the findings.

In some cases, these partnerships can develop into "embedded criminologist" models (Petersilia 2008) where academics work inside the organization, directly influencing the translation of research into practice. Petersilia describes her various roles in Governor Arnold Schwarzenegger's administration that allowed her to be deeply engaged in California prison reforms. She describes success in increasing the role of research (and number of researchers) in juvenile and adult corrections, as well as focusing agencies more on rehabilitation and re-entry. Petersilia's "lessons learned" about making research more relevant echo the findings in the previous section. These include making sure research is delivered in jargon-free ways that have clear policy relevance and recognizing the context and constraints that practitioners and policymakers are operating within. Petersilia (2008, 350) also laments the lack of research in the field on implementation, and the challenge that creates for institutionalizing evidence-based practice: "I could tell them what types of programs to develop and to whom those programs should be targeted, but I had no comparable science to offer them on program implementation. I had no research studies on how to select the right staff, how to train them appropriately, or how to change the overall culture of an organization to support such programs."

Braga and Davis (2014) describe the value of an embedded criminologist model in the policing context. After becoming commissioner of the Boston Police Department, Davis appointed Braga as chief policy advisor. While Braga had partnered with the Boston Police previously on research projects, in his new role he spent much of his time at the agency and was involved not only in evaluation work, but also in helping day-to-day to translate research findings on particular policy issues of interest. Sometimes this was as part of scheduled strategy meetings, but other times this might be a casual conversation in the cafeteria. Braga and Davis note that the embedded criminologist model allows a researcher to both lead rigorous evaluation efforts while also gaining an understanding of the agency's culture and organizational context.

Brancale and colleagues (2021) detail a rarer occurrence in crime and justice—a researcher-policymaker partnership. They describe a partnership between Florida State University and the Florida State Senate that centered around efforts to assess the impacts of pending legislation on disparities in the system. This was a large-scale effort involving a team of researchers and graduate students, who reviewed and synthesized research and legislation in other states in preparation for a very demanding legislative session, when senators wanted disparity impact assessments for 10 bills in a matter of days. While they did provide timely analyses to senators, they could not always fully assess disparities with available data. Brancale et al. (2021) conclude that a more effective approach would be trying to use evidence to influence the policy agenda, rather than coming in so late in the process once bills were drafted and about to be voted on.

C. Influence

Influence strategies in criminal justice generally rely on opinion leaders within an organization advocating for the use (and increasing creation) of research to their colleagues and other practitioners. Innovative chief executives can play an important role here. The embedded criminologist model described earlier, for example, was only possible because top leaders supported bringing in a criminologist to work directly on research and translation efforts. A challenge here, though, is that police executives have relatively short tenures, particularly in large cities. Still, innovative leaders can help promote the use of research in practice, and given the structure of most criminal justice agencies, the leader has at least some power to push ideas downward in the hierarchy (Santos and Santos 2019).

This influence need not come just from top executives, however. Increasingly, in policing in particular, advocates for research at all levels of the organization have pushed for greater engagement between researchers and practitioners. In some cases, these "pracademics" also have advanced education and training in conducting research (Huey and Mitchell

2016). Thus, they have one foot in policing and one foot in academia, and ideally can serve as effective brokers between research and practice communities. As Huey and Mitchell (2016) argue, pracademics can successfully push their agency toward more innovation and evidence-based practice through translating research within and between practice and research settings.

In a survey of authors of studies in the Matrix, Piza, Szkola, and Blount-Hill (2021) find that pracademics and embedded criminologists assist in promoting police-led projects and translational work. They also point to the benefits of crime analysts in both assisting with evaluation efforts and helping to translate research evidence to sworn personnel. They suggest that pracademics may also play an important role in bolstering the status of analysts in the agency and championing the importance of crime analysts in making an agency more evidence-based. Stanko and Dawson (2016) similarly highlight the benefits of having in-house research capacity in the London Metropolitan Police. They describe their work in the Evidence and Insight Unit (now part of the Mayor's Office for Policing and Crime[9]), pointing to their ability to both carry out internal evaluations to add to the evidence base and to ensure that programs adopted based on evidence were properly implemented with integrity.

This work is not easy, and because of the hierarchical structure of many agencies, it can be difficult for a nonleader to successfully push scientific research internally (Willis 2016). However, the creation of societies for evidence-based policing, led by practitioners, in the United States, Canada, the United Kingdom, and Australia and New Zealand makes clear that practitioners are taking more of a leadership role in translational work. Additionally, since 2014 the US National Institute of Justice has supported the Law Enforcement Advancing Data and Science (LEADS) Scholars Program (McGough 2019). The program offers resources and training, as well as funding for conferences, for mid-level managers and civilians interesting in developing their capacity for research. In 2019 the program expanded to include early-career academics to further promote collaboration between researchers and practitioners.

This influence work does not have to take place only at the agency level. The societies of evidence-based policing and the LEADS program both suggest a more national- or international-level commitment to translational work. Another example in policing comes from the Research Advisory Committee (RAC) in the IACP (see Davis and Robinson 2014). The RAC began in 2004 and is a 30-member committee made up of half practitioners and half researchers. The RAC helps push research into the field, and it has the backing of the world's largest professional association of police leaders. One key dissemination mechanism the RAC helped develop was the Research in Brief column in *The Police Chief* magazine that gives researchers an opportunity to summarize research findings with a clear emphasis on accessible language and policy and practice relevance.

D. Facilitation

Facilitation strategies in criminal justice include a variety of approaches, from training and tools to make implementing research findings more successful to assistance with protocols and operational guidelines. The involvement of researchers in training programs is a particularly promising route to give practitioners direct access to research findings.

Lum, for example, coordinated multiple CEBCP evidence-based policing workshops and leadership trainings[10] that brought together police managers and researchers for a day of presentations on the latest evidence and how to apply that evidence in practice settings. Koetzle and colleagues (2021) detail the important impacts Ed Latessa had on the field of corrections and note that this came in part from his dedicating a great deal of time to trainings and discussions with practitioners and policymakers. This commitment to training practitioners on risk assessment tools and evidence-based practice gave the University of Cincinnati Corrections Institute a wide reach and significant impact on the field. Koetzle and colleagues estimate trainings from Latessa and colleagues have reached more than 39,000 practitioners since 2011.

Facilitation approaches to translation are not limited to training efforts. Lum and Koper (2017) detail a number of facilitation projects implemented as part of the Matrix Demonstration Project[11] and designed to help translate and institutionalize research into practice. This includes an Evidence-Based Policing Playbook, a series of ideas designed to help agencies operationalize lessons from policing research into patrol deployments. Another example is evidence assessments. These are similar to translation tools, but with a more focused assessment of the crime prevention portfolio of a particular agency. Lum and colleagues (2018) examine the deployment strategies of the Federal Protective Service and provide recommendations, based on the extent to which existing programs are guided by theories linked to crime prevention and mechanisms of prevention that align with research. This provides specific guidance to an agency on their current strategies. Importantly, such work not only helps bring more research evidence into decisions about deployment strategies, but also sets up an agency for future collaborations with researchers for outcome evaluations.

Groff and Taniguchi (2019) use a software program to help translate research findings into practice and provide clear guidance on when these findings might be most useful. There is strong evidence of near-repeat patterns in burglary, an important finding for agencies interested in preventing subsequent nearby burglaries after an initial incident occurs. But Groff and Taniguchi recognize that the crime prevention benefits of focusing on preventing near-repeat incidents may be limited in instances where base rates are low or a repeat burglary occurs too quickly for police to have developed a response plan. They developed a software tool, the Near Repeat Crime Prevention Potential Calculator, to better guide agencies on how much future burglary can reasonably be prevented. This is a good example of a tool designed to more easily facilitate the use of research in practice, and to help guide agencies on when focusing resources based on prior research may be less efficient.

E. Reinforcement and Incentives

Just as Nutley et al. (2007) noted that the research on the role of incentives is more limited, I identified fewer examples of translational work incentivizing research use through reinforcement in criminal justice. One challenge here is that there is often little pressure for practitioners to be more evidence-based. As Santos and Santos (2019, 598) note in reference to policing, a "potential barrier, also intrinsic to policing is there is not often pressure on police leaders to innovative and/or incorporate research into their operations." Thus, translational work focused on policymakers and legislators may be especially important (Davis

2017) if these groups can then incentivize practitioners to be more evidence-based. The work of Brancale et al. (2019) was an important example of educating elected officials about research, which could in turn lead to increased pressure on practitioner leaders to utilize research findings.

Financial incentives, through grant funding, can be one way to encourage partnerships. Programs at the federal level include the Smart Policing Initiative,[12] funded by the Bureau of Justice Assistance (BJA). While the program has changed its focus (and name) a few times since its creation in 2009, the goal is to provide funds to both agencies and researchers to assist in implementing and evaluating evidence-based strategies. There are a number of examples across the close to 100 funded projects of these partnerships leading to effective crime reduction initiatives that add to the policing evidence base (see Coldren, Huntoon, and Medaris 2013). While federal support for partnerships has been most common, particularly through BJA "Smart Justice" initiatives, given that states and localities have greater direct control over criminal justice operations, a more localized approach to facilitating evidence-based practice would be useful (Davis 2017). As one example, Oregon's Center for Policing Excellence in the Department of Public Safety Standards and Training[13] has resources and staffing to help integrate research findings into training statewide. To push this work to the local level, the center also funded a micro grant program to incentivize cities across the state to adopt evidence-based policing approaches.

There is a small number of current awards that honor excellence in utilizing research. The RAC oversees the IACP's Leadership in Law Enforcement Research Award, which honors an agency for making policy or practice changes based on a partnership with an external researcher. CEBCP annually inducts innovative policing leaders into their Evidence-Based Policing Hall of Fame. The Hall of Fame[14] celebrates the achievements of officers or civilians who have shown a dedication to evaluating police tactics and promoting evidence-based policing in their agencies. Such recognition would ideally also occur at the agency level. Police departments typically give out annual awards for categories like bravery or investigatory success, but I do not know of any agencies recognizing outstanding achievements in evidence-based practice or research utilization.

V. THE FUTURE OF TRANSLATIONAL CRIMINOLOGY

For a term that has only been used for about a decade, there has been an impressive body of work examining translational criminology in the field. But I also recognize that work in this area is in its infancy. I have drawn here from prior reviews to explore effective mechanisms for translating research into policy and practice. But I also think the conclusions of the National Research Council (2012, 3) in a review of the use of science in public policy remain true today: "[A]lthough the relatively recent approach known as evidence-based policy and practice, focusing on improving understanding of 'what works,' has influenced the *production* of scientific knowledge, it has made little contribution to understanding the *use* of that knowledge." As a result, we know little about what works best in translating research into practice, and, importantly, we have no knowledge of whether some approaches or strategies may cause harm instead of their intended effects. Nutley et al. (2007, 2) reach a similar conclusion in their review: "[T]he irony here is that the evidence base confirming any benefits (or indeed, dysfunctions) of an evidence-based approach to public policy and service delivery is actually rather thin."

The work reviewed in this chapter is largely a collection of case studies on particular partnerships or programs designed to facilitate and increase the translation of research into policy or practice contexts. I hope the future of translational criminology brings even more of these case studies and further efforts to understand the impacts of these efforts. This can be particularly challenging, for reasons I have discussed. It is not always clear how policymakers and practitioners use research, so assessing whether a translational effort is successful may be much more challenging than evaluating whether a program reduced crime or recidivism. Indeed, it is not even evident to what extent these end users fully understand research (Mears 2022). The work on receptivity reviewed earlier suggests general practitioner openness to working with researchers, particularly among leaders, but there is less assessment of the extent to which practitioners have the background in research design and statistics that would best facilitate using research. Telep and Gross Shader (2019) discuss the challenge of assessing the impact of translational efforts in their attempts to evaluate the What Works in Policing? site. While media reports on policing effectiveness frequently mention the site, and site analytic data suggest many visitors, these sources provide little insight into whether practitioners are comprehending the site and the research findings summarized and integrating this knowledge into their strategies and tactics.

Moving forward, researchers should also take a broader perspective on evaluation evidence in considering translational efforts. Most of the work discussed in this chapter focuses on translating outcome evidence into policy and practice. This is, of course, a crucial component of ensuring greater adoption of evidence-based practices. But a focus on outcomes alone ignores other crucial evaluation questions, as well as other opportunities for translational work. Building on work of Rossi and colleagues (2019), Mears (2010) offers an evaluation research hierarchy, where outcome evaluations are but one of five types of evaluation. Needs evaluations examine whether a program or policy is necessary, theory evaluations assess whether an intervention has mechanisms for intended impacts that are grounded in theory, and process evaluations (or implementation evaluations) consider whether the program was implemented as intended. These steps should all precede examining effectiveness. And if the outcome evaluation suggests positive effects, then there should also be an evaluation of cost-efficiency or cost-effectiveness. There is a lack of research on cost-effectiveness for most evidence-based strategies (Willis and Toronjo 2019). Simply telling an agency that a program or strategy works is insufficient without additional guidance on the resources needed for successful implementation.

In many cases, there is not attention to all five types of evaluation. There is often limited attention to the role of theory in criminal justice interventions. Telep (2017a) notes that in most hot spots policing studies, for example, the mechanisms linking the program to crime reduction are not clearly specified. Deterrence is thought to underlie the program's effectiveness, but without much consideration or measurement of how that operates in practice. But even for process evaluations, which are more common, there tends to be little connection between implementation evaluations and translational work. As Gill and colleagues (2021) describe in their assessment of implantation of the Transportation Security Administration's security strategy "Playbook," there is a growing body of "first generation" research that gives guidance on "what works." But what is now needed is a larger body of "second generation" research that provides more guidance on implementing what works.

Future translational work should strive to better incorporate all types of evaluation. This should improve the quality of translational efforts. Telling an agency that something works, for example, is less useful than explaining the need for the program and the mechanisms at work in driving effectiveness and providing guidance on implementing the program as well as its implications for agency costs. Thinking more broadly about evaluation also offers additional opportunities for close collaboration between researchers and practitioners. A joint effort to map out a logic model for a program at the outset is likely to lead to a better program that combines researcher and field experience, and one that practitioners are more likely to utilize if effects are found because they understand the theory guiding it. The embedded criminologist models described earlier offer perhaps the best opportunity for this multifaceted approach to evaluation, because researchers are engaged with an agency or organization long enough to fully assess a policy or practice and then, if appropriate, apply those findings to further implementation work.

I leave a fuller discussion of implementation science to the next chapter in this volume, but emphasize that a lack of clear guidance on implementation makes translational efforts more challenging (see Santos and Santos 2019). This is also in line with recommendations by Green and colleagues (2009) in their review of knowledge utilization in public health. They suggest more collaboration between practitioners and researchers in developing research agendas, so that research addresses key issues surrounding implementation and context (see Sampson, Winship, and Knight 2013). These collaborations can lead to the creation of programs that use knowledge from prior implementation evaluations to improve design and comprehensive evaluations that maximize knowledge about program effects.

Criminal justice practice would also benefit from a sustained focus on translation at the federal level. Following Laub's (2011) initial push for translational criminology, NIJ funded eight social science projects on implementation, dissemination, and translation.[15] Some of the projects described previously developed out of awards from these solicitations. But a solicitation on translation last appeared in 2015. Funding specifically dedicated to translation would incentivize researchers to invest time and resources into this work. In contrast, in health and medicine, there has been a much greater focus on funding translational efforts. The National Institutes of Health created a National Center for Advancing Translational Sciences in 2011 to promote the use of innovative ways to more efficiently bring medical research into practice. President Biden's fiscal year 2023 budget request for the center was $873.7 million.[16] Criminologists should also pursue other funding sources for translational work. The William T. Grant Foundation, for example, has invested heavily in research to better understand how research evidence related to improving outcomes for youth influences policy and practice (Tseng 2012). The National Science Foundation also funds scientific communication projects through their Science of Science: Discovery, Communication, and Impact program, which could be a source for future translational criminology projects.

Finally, I note that future work should consider the implications of translational efforts for moving beyond a focus solely on effectiveness. Much of evidence-based crime policy focuses on what works for reducing crime or recidivism (Telep 2016). While this is a key outcome in crime and justice, it is also clear that other outcomes, such as fairness and lawfulness, are equally if not more important. Kerrison et al. (2019), for example, describe work in the Center for Policing Equity on the National Justice Database Partnership designed to reduce racial bias and discrimination through partnerships with police agencies. They recognize these are challenging issues to partner with police on, but also note the value of clear benchmarks and longitudinal data analyses that can help police leaders and the public better understand data on disparities and whether agency efforts address these disparities. We need more translational work on issues like this, to assess not just whether policy reflects "what works" but also whether such policies are implemented in ways that increase fairness and reduce inequality.

VI. Conclusions

Translational criminology focuses on efforts to bring research knowledge into policy and practice. I reviewed prior studies of research utilization to suggest mechanisms that might aid in translational work and highlighted recent efforts in criminology and criminal justice designed to make it easier and more appealing for practitioners and policymakers to utilize research findings in their work. This work is not easy, and this chapter demonstrates the complexity of research utilization and the need for further study of translational efforts, particularly surrounding the implementation of evidence-based programs. Overall, I conclude that while there has been much progress on translational work in the past decade, there is still much work to be done to understand what works best in translating evidence of what works to practitioners and policymakers.

I began this chapter by noting how translational criminology grows out of translational work in medicine, where there is both a larger evidence base and a longer-term focus on translation. But I close in noting that, even in medicine, bringing research into practice has been difficult. McGlynn and colleagues (2003) surveyed adults about the medical treatment they received and examined their medical charts to determine if they received appropriate care for a number of conditions. Overall, patients received only 54.9% of the care and treatment recommended by research. Adherence to quality indicators did not exceed 80% for any of the 25 conditions examined. In reflecting on these findings more recently, McGlynn (2020) notes that the current state of medicine is almost the same. I do not mean to end the chapter on a somber note with this example, but instead want to highlight translation challenges, even in a field where evidence-based practice is more established. This reinforces the need for continued collaborative efforts bringing together researchers, practitioners, policymakers, and communities to enable translational criminology to occur. This sustained work can help ensure that research evidence informs policy and practice and contributes to a fairer and more effective criminal justice system.

Notes

1. See more on the Springer Briefs in Translational Criminology series at https://www.springer.com/series/11178.
2. See https://cebcp.org/tcmagazine/.
3. https://crimesolutions.ojp.gov/.
4. See https://www.college.police.uk/research/crime-reduction-toolkit.
5. See https://popcenter.asu.edu/.

6. See https://cebcp.org/evidence-based-policing/the-matrix/.
7. See https://cebcp.org/evidence-based-policing/what-works-in-policing/.
8. See https://www.campbellcollaboration.org/contact/coordinating-groups/crime-and-justice.html.
9. See https://www.london.gov.uk/what-we-do/mayors-office-policing-and-crime-mopac/data-and-statistics/academic-research.
10. See https://cebcp.org/evidence-based-policing/resources-tools/.
11. See https://cebcp.org/evidence-based-policing/the-matrix/matrix-demonstration-project/.
12. See https://www.smart-policing.com/.
13. See https://www.oregon.gov/dpsst/cpe/Pages/default.aspx.
14. See https://cebcp.org/hall-of-fame/.
15. See https://nij.ojp.gov/funding/opportunities/nij-2014-3759 and https://nij.ojp.gov/funding/opportunities/nij-2015-4027.
16. See http://www.ncats.nih.gov/about/budget/budget.html.

References

Ashby, Matthew P. J. 2020. The open-access availability of criminological research to practitioners and policy makers. *Journal of Criminal Justice Education*, 32:1–21.

Braga, Anthony A., and Edward F. Davis. 2014. Implementing science in police agencies: The embedded research model. *Policing: A Journal of Policy and Practice*, 8:294–306.

Brancale, Julie, Thomas G. Blomberg, Sonja Siennick, George B. Pesta, Nic Swagar, Kaylee Noorman, Jonathan Caswell, and Cecilia Chouhy. 2021. Building collaborative evidence-based frameworks for criminal justice policy. *Criminal Justice Policy Review*, 32:795–815.

Burkhardt, Brett C., Scott Akins, Jon Sassaman, Scott Jackson, Ken Elwer, Charles Lanfear, Mariana Amorim, and Katelyn Stevens. 2017. University researcher and law enforcement collaboration: Lessons from a study of justice-involved persons with suspected mental illness. *International Journal of Offender Therapy and Comparative Criminology*, 61:508–525.

Burruss, George W., and Yunmei Lu. 2021. The value of data visualization for translational criminology. In *Visual criminology: From history and methods to critique and policy translation*, edited by Johannes Wheeldon, 251–269. New York: Routledge.

Cohrs, Randall J., Tyler Martin, Parviz Ghahramani, Luc Bidaut, Paul J. Higgins, and Aamir Shahzad. 2015. Translational medicine definition by the European Society for Translational Medicine. *New Horizons in Translational Medicine*, 2:86–88.

Coldren, James R., Alissa Huntoon, and Michael Medaris. 2013. Introducing Smart Policing: Foundations, principles, and practice. *Police Quarterly*, 16:275–286.

Davis, Ed, and Laurie Robinson. 2014. Modeling successful research-practitioner partnerships: The International Association of Chiefs of Policy Research Advisory Committee. *Translational Criminology*, 7:4–5, 8.

Davis, Mark S. 2017. *The role of state agencies in translational criminology: Connecting research to policy*. New York: Springer.

Drawbridge, Dara C., Sema A. Taheri, and Natasha A. Frost. 2018. Building and sustaining academic researcher and criminal justice practitioner partnerships: A corrections example. *American Journal of Criminal Justice*, 43:627–640.

Engel, Robin S., and James L. Whalen. 2010. Police-academic partnerships: Ending the dialogue of the deaf, the Cincinnati experience. *Police Practice and Research*, 11:105–116.

Famega, Christine, Joshua C. Hinkle, and David Weisburd. 2017. Why getting inside the "black box" is important: Examining treatment implementation and outputs in policing experiments. *Police Quarterly*, 20:106–132.

Giacomantonio, Chris, Yael Litmanovitz, Craig Bennell, and Daniel J. Jones. 2022. Expressing uncertainty in criminology: Applying insights from scientific communication to evidence-based policing. *Criminology & Criminal Justice*, June 28, 2022.

Gill, Charlotte, Julie Hibdon, Cynthia Lum, Devon Johnson, Linda Merola, David Weisburd, Breanne Cave, and Jaspreet Chahal. 2021. "Translational criminology" in action: A national survey of TSA's Playbook implementation at US airports. *Security Journal* 34:319–339.

Green, Lawrence W., Judith M. Ottoson, Cesar Garcia, and Robert A. Hiatt. 2009. Diffusion theory and knowledge dissemination, utilization, and integration in public health. *Annual Review of Public Health* 30:151–174.

Groff, Elizabeth, and Travis Taniguchi. 2019. Quantifying crime prevention potential of near-repeat burglary. *Police Quarterly*, 22:330–359.

Hansen, J. Andrew, Geoffrey P. Alpert, and Jeffrey J. Rojek. 2014. The benefits of police practitioner–researcher partnerships to participating agencies. *Policing: A Journal of Policy and Practice*, 8:307–320.

Haverkate, Danielle L., Travis J. Meyers, Cody W. Telep, and Kevin A. Wright. 2020. On PAR with the yard: Participatory action research to advance knowledge in corrections. *Corrections: Policy, Practice and Research*, 5:28–43.

Huey, Laura, and Renee J. Mitchell. 2016. Unearthing hidden keys: Why pracademics are an invaluable (if underutilized) resource in policing research. *Policing: A Journal of Policy and Practice*, 10:300–307.

Kerrison, Erin M., Phillip Atiba Goff, Chris Burbank, and Jordan M. Hyatt. 2019. On creating ethical, productive, and durable research partnerships with police officers and their departments: A case study of the National Justice Database. *Police Practice and Research*, 20:567–584.

Kim, Bitna, and Daniel Lee. 2022. Partnerships between community corrections and researchers: The view from the probation/parole chiefs. *Journal of Crime and Justice*, 45:207–227.

Koetzle, Deborah, Mirlinda Ndrecka, and Shelley Johnson. 2021. On the road: The challenges and benefits of agency research. *Victims & Offenders*, 16:939–949.

Laub, John H. 2011. Strengthening NIJ: Mission, science and process. *NIJ Journal*, 268:16–21.

Laub, John H. 2021. Moving the National Institute of Justice forward: July 2010 through December 2012. *Journal of Contemporary Criminal Justice*, 37:166–174.

Laub, John H., and Nicole E. Frisch. 2016. Translational criminology: A new path forward. In *Advancing criminology and criminal justice policy*, edited by Thomas G. Blomberg, Julie M. Brancale, Kevin M. Beaver, and William D. Bales, 52–62. New York: Routledge.

Light, Stephen C., and Theresa Kemble Newman. 1992. Awareness and use of social science research among executive and administrative staff members of state correctional agencies. *Justice Quarterly*, 9:299–324.

Lum, Cynthia. 2009. *Translating police research into practice*. Washington, DC: Police Foundation.

Lum, Cynthia, Breanne Cave, and Jordan Nichols. 2018. Are federal security efforts evidence-based? *Security Journal*, 31:139–162.

Lum, Cynthia, and Christopher S. Koper. 2017. *Evidence-based policing: Translating research into practice*. New York: Oxford University Press.

Lum, Cynthia, Christopher S. Koper, and Cody W. Telep. 2011. The Evidence-Based Policing Matrix. *Journal of Experimental Criminology*, 7:3–26.

Marincola, Francesco M. 2003. Translational medicine: A two-way road. *Journal of Translational Medicine*, 1:1–2.

McGlynn, Elizabeth A. 2020. "Improving the quality of U.S. health care—What will it take?" *New England Journal of Medicine*, 383:801–803.

McGlynn, Elizabeth A., Steven M. Asch, John Adams, Joan Keesey, Jennifer Hicks, Alison DeCristofaro, and Eve A. Kerr. 2003. The quality of health care delivered to adults in the United States. *New England Journal of Medicine*, 348:2635–245.

Mears, Daniel P. 2010. *American criminal justice policy: An evaluation approach to increasing accountability and effectiveness*. New York: Cambridge University Press.

Mears, Daniel. 2022. Bridging the research-policy divide to advance science and policy: The 2022 Bruce Smith, Sr. Award address to the Academy of Criminal Justice Sciences. *Justice Evaluation Journal*, 5:163–185.

McGough, Maureen Q. 2019. Research in the ranks: Empowering law enforcement to drive their own scientific inquiry. *NIJ Journal*, 280:31–32.

Murphy, Kelly, Shelby Hickman, and Rebecca M. Jones. 2021. Looking up at the ivory tower: Juvenile court judges' and attorneys' perceptions of research use. *Journal of Research in Crime and Delinquency*, 58:591–630.

National Research Council. 2012. *Using science as evidence in public policy*. Washington, DC: National Academies Press.

Nichols, Jordan, Sean Wire, Xiaoyun Wu, Madeline Sloan, and Amber Scherer. 2019. Translational criminology and its importance in policing: A review. *Police Practice and Research*, 20:537–551.

Nutley, Sandra M., Isabel Walter, and Huw T. O. Davies. 2007. *Using evidence: How research can inform public services*. Bristol, UK: Policy Press.

Petersilia, Joan. 2008. Influencing public policy: An embedded criminologist reflects on California prison reform. *Journal of Experimental Criminology*, 4:335–356.

Pesta, George B., Thomas G. Blomberg, Javier Ramos, and J. W. Ranson. 2019. Translational criminology: Toward best practice. *American Journal of Criminal Justice*, 44:499–518.

Piza, Eric L., Jason Szkola, and Kwan-Lamar Blount-Hill. 2021. How can embedded criminologists, police pracademics, and crime analysts help increase police-led program evaluations? A survey of authors cited in the Evidence-Based Policing Matrix. *Policing: A Journal of Policy and Practice*, 15:1217–1231.

Rogers, Everett M. 2003. *Diffusion of innovations*. 5th ed. New York: Free Press.

Rojek, Jeff, Peter Martin, and Geoffrey P. Alpert. 2015. *Developing and maintaining police-researcher partnerships to facilitate research use: A comparative analysis*. New York: Springer.

Rojek, Jeff, Hayden P. Smith, and Geoffrey P. Alpert. 2012. The prevalence and characteristics of police practitioner–researcher partnerships. *Police Quarterly*, 15:241–261.

Rossi, Peter H., Mark W. Lipsey, and Howard E. Freeman. 2019. *Evaluation: A systematic approach*. 8th ed. Thousand Oaks, CA: SAGE.

Rudes, Danielle S., Jill Viglione, Jennifer Lerch, Courtney Porter, and Faye S. Taxman. 2014. Build to sustain: Collaborative partnerships between university researchers and criminal justice practitioners. *Criminal Justice Studies*, 27:249–263.

Sampson, Robert J., Christopher Winship, and Carly Knight. 2013. Translating causal claims: Principles and strategies for policy-relevant criminology. *Criminology & Public Policy*, 12:587–616.

Santos, Roberto G., and Rachel B. Santos. 2019. A four-phase process for translating research into police practice. *Police Practice and Research*, 20:585–602.

Sherman, Lawrence W. 1998. *Evidence-based policing*. Washington, DC: Police Foundation.

Stanko, Elizabeth A., and Paul Dawson. 2016. *Police use of research evidence: Recommendations for improvement*. New York: Springer.

Telep, Cody W. 2013. *Moving forward with evidence-based policing: What should police be doing and can we get them to do it?* Doctoral dissertation, George Mason University.

Telep, Cody W. 2016. Expanding the scope of evidence-based policing. *Criminology & Public Policy*, 15:243–252.

Telep, Cody W. 2017a. Not just what works, but *how* it works: Mechanisms and context in the effectiveness of place-based policing. In *Unraveling the crime-place connection: New directions in theory and practice*, edited by David Weisburd and John E. Eck, 237–259. New York: Routledge.

Telep, Cody W. 2017b. Police officer receptivity to research and evidence-based policing: Examining variability within and across agencies. *Crime & Delinquency*, 63:976–999.

Telep, Cody W., and Claudia Gross Shader. 2019. Creating a "what works" translational tool for police: A researcher-city government partnership. *Police Practice and Research*, 20:603–616.

Telep, Cody W., and Cynthia Lum. 2014. The receptivity of officers to empirical research and evidence-based policing: An examination of survey data from three agencies. *Police Quarterly*, 17:359–385.

Telep, Cody W., and Steve Winegar. 2016. Police executive receptivity to research: A survey of chiefs and sheriffs in Oregon. *Policing: A Journal of Policy and Practice*, 10:241–249.

Telep, Cody W., Kevin A. Wright, Danielle L. Haverkate, and Travis J. Meyers. 2020. The value of participatory action research in corrections: Introduction to the special issue. *Corrections: Policy, Practice and Research*, 5:1–5.

Tseng, Vivian. 2012. The uses of research in policy and practice. *Social Policy Report*, 26:1–24.

Weisburd, David, and Peter Neyroud. 2011. *Police science: Toward a new paradigm*. Harvard Executive Session in Policing. Washington, DC: National Institute of Justice.

Weiss, Carol H. 1979. The many meanings of research utilization. *Public Administration Review*, 39:426–431.

Williams, Robin M. 1946. Some observations on sociological research in government during World War II. *American Sociological Review*, 11:573–577.

Willis, James J. 2016. The romance of police pracademics. *Policing: A Journal of Policy and Practice*, 10:315–321.

Willis, James, and Heather Toronjo. 2019. Translating police research into policy: Some implications of the National Academies report on proactive policing for policymakers and researchers. *Police Practice and Research*, 20:617–631.

CHAPTER 4

IMPLEMENTATION SCIENCE FOR EVIDENCE-BASED POLICY

DEAN L. FIXSEN, MELISSA K. VAN DYKE, AND KAREN A. BLASE

THE policy to impact gap has been noted for many years, and the issue has not been resolved (Van Meter and Van Horn 1975; Sabatier 1999; Perl 2011; Kruk et al. 2018). Federal and state legislation is passed each year that is intended to impact public services such as corrections, child welfare, education, health, mental health, public health, and substance abuse prevention and treatment (collectively called "human services" in this chapter). Though the intentions of legislators are good, the outcomes in practice rarely live up to expectations.

Unlike other policy interests where methods to enact policy goals and measure policy impact are well established, policies in human services continue to rely on diffusion (Rogers 1995) and dissemination (Greenhalgh et al. 2004) strategies that are necessary but insufficient for producing impact. It is not enough for policymakers to learn about, be able to identify, or even nominally support evidence-based programs or other innovations. They also must provide resources to support effective real-world action that achieves intended results. Keeping in mind that "in general, current crime policies are not in any obvious way rational from an evaluation research perspective" (Mears 2007, 668), we will describe a rational approach to policymaking and policy execution in this chapter.

There are three major components that connect public policy to intended benefits: legislation, administration, and services. Governments develop policy and approve legislation. Legislation is administered by departments (e.g., Department of Labor, Department of Education) at the federal level and by similar departments in states, provinces, and municipalities. Services are provided either directly by federal or state agency staff or by organizations that contract with federal and state departments to meet the goals of legislation and departmental regulations.

Implementation has never been a strong component of legislation or administration in human services (Schofield 2004; Pressman and Wildavsky 1973). Consequently, implementation supports for effective services typically are missing (Perl 2011, Kessler and Glasgow 2011). The lack of attention to and investment in implementation capacity directly impacts the quality of services delivered. Given the policy-to-impact gap, "public managers have to learn a range of often new and detailed techniques in order to implement . . . policy directives" (Schofield 2004, 283). Active Implementation practice and science provide "a range of often new and detailed techniques" that can help to enact legislative intent in the form of improved services and improved outcomes for children, families, individuals, and society (Schofield 2004, 283).

Advances in implementation science in the past few decades provide a sound basis for changing legislation and administration to achieve public policy goals more fully and reliably. Significant advances in implementation science are the results of comprehensive reviews of the diffusion and dissemination literature (Greenhalgh et al. 2004; Brownson, Colditz, and Proctor 2012) and of the implementation evaluation literature (Fixsen et al. 2005). These reviews are supplemented by intensive work with leaders of major evidence-based programs who are attempting to scale individual innovations (Blase et al. 2005, Glennan et al. 2004; Blase and Fixsen 2003; Forgatch, Patterson, and DeGarmo 2005; Spoth et al. 2004). Guidance from the growing number of implementation frameworks has been documented and summarized (Meyers, Durlak, and Wandersman 2012; Tabak et al. 2012; Nilsen and Birken 2020).

The interest in implementation has resulted in a growing profusion of concepts and descriptions. Reporting the findings from an extensive review of the literature, Allen et al. (2017, 591) concluded that "[t]he lack of clarity associated with construct definitions, inconsistent use of theory, absence of standardized reporting criteria for implementation research, and the fact that few measures have demonstrated reliability or validity were among the limitations highlighted in our review." In another review, McKibbon et al. (2010, 5) concluded that, like the Tower of Babel, "[t]he use of multiple terms across disciplines pose barriers to communication and progress for applying research findings."

Based on the literature and evaluations of long-term experience in implementation practice (Fixsen and Blase 2018; Fixsen et al. 2007), the Active Implementation Frameworks have been developed to incorporate and organize evidence-based implementation factors (Fixsen and Fixsen 2016) and provide guidance to assure the full, effective, and sustained use of effective innovations in practice (Fixsen, Blase, and Van Dyke 2019). The Active Implementation Frameworks provide common concepts, common language, and common measures to promote clear communication within and across disciplines. Thus, while this chapter focuses on criminology and corrections, the concepts are universal and draw on many disciplines.

The importance of Active Implementation cannot be stressed enough. High-fidelity use of innovations is the outcome of implementation variables done well. High fidelity is the input for achieving intended innovation outcomes (Bond and Drake 2020; Fixsen et al. 2009). Scaling to achieve population benefits depends on developing and replicating implementation capacity in the form of competent implementation teams in corrections (Fixsen, Blase, and Fixsen 2017) and in business (Harnish 2014), among others. Implementation is the active ingredient, the yeast in the dough, that supports the attainment of policy goals and societal goals.

This chapter describes effective innovation, effective implementation, and enabling contexts as key factors leading to socially significant outcomes. The implications for policymakers and policy administrators are explored, with recommendations for using new approaches to contracting for services and monitoring implementation-related processes and outcomes along with innovation-related processes and outcomes. The chapter concludes with a plea to include effective implementation in policymaking and administration so that societal goals can be realized.

I. Formula for Success

The central role of implementation science in realizing policy goals is evident in the formula for success (Fixsen, Blase, and Van Dyke 2012):

Effective Innovations X Effective Implementation X Enabling Contexts
= Socially Significant Outcomes

Note that the factors in the formula are multiplied to produce the intended outcome. Thus, if any factor is weak (a value approaching zero) then the product will be poor.

The formula for success predicts that an emphasis on any one or two factors will not appreciably improve socially significant outcomes. For example, since the 1990s the evidence-based movement has emphasized the development of effective innovations (e.g., evidence-based programs), but there have been no noticeable population improvements in outcomes in criminal behavior, education, mental health, substance abuse, and so on. While increasing the supply of effective innovations is a welcome development, it is, by itself, not enough. The widespread diffusion and dissemination of information about evidence-based programs has not necessarily led to widespread improvements in the human condition.

With social significance in mind, it is not enough to do something well one time or even a few times. "Bright spots" and "islands of excellence" and "promising results" are important and signify what is possible to achieve. These interesting experiments may benefit a few people, but not whole populations—and not society. As represented in the formula for success, populations benefit when effective innovations are supported by effective implementation in enabling contexts that facilitate realizing benefits on a socially significant scale.

In human services, the effective implementation factor continues to be weak and, as predicted by the formula for success, socially significant outcomes have therefore been difficult to achieve (Rossi and Wright 1984; Watkins 1995; National Center for Education Statistics 2013; Kruk et al. 2018; Lipsey 2009). These outcomes are not the fault of legislation or administration or service providers. The problems lay with implementation knowledge that has been poorly organized and therefore not very helpful to policymakers and administrators and not very supportive of effective services. That is now changing.

Active Implementation has defined common methods and uses common language to inform policymaking, administering policy, and providing services to achieve intended benefits. Active Implementation incorporates all the key variables identified in a variety of implementation frameworks, and has operationalized the common variables so they are doable and assessable in practice (Fixsen, Blase, and Van Dyke 2019). Based on the best available evidence, Active Implementation has defined strong implementation variables that have been tested in practice and produce consequential outcomes in terms of implementation capacity, innovation outcomes, and enabling systems (Fixsen, Blase, and Van Dyke 2019). Strong implementation variables include implementation drivers (competency development, organization change, leadership support), implementation stages (exploration, installation, initial implementation, full implementation), and implementation teams. Strong variables produce meaningful change in complex environments. For example, in treatment programs for youths referred from juvenile courts, evidence-based program sustainability for six years or more increased from about 20% to 80% when implementation teams using the implementation drivers were established in organizations using an evidence-based program (Fixsen et al. 2007). And 84% of the programs associated with high-functioning implementation teams were sustained for at least two years compared to 57% of those associated with low-functioning implementation teams (Brunk, Chapman, and Schoenwald 2014).

The formula for success makes it clear that enabling contexts are needed to help assure effective implementation supports for effective innovations to benefit whole populations. While progress has been made to include the effective innovation factor in policymaking (Haskins and Baron 2011), legislators and administrators have not had adequate guidance from implementation practice and science to include the effective implementation factor in legislation and administrative guidelines and funding methods. Two federal agencies in the United States that have emphasized and funded effective implementation are the Office of Special Education Programs (OSEP, since 2007) in the US Department of Education, and the Administrative Office of the Courts (AO, since 2021) in the US Federal Court system.

In the following subsections, the factors in the formula for success are explained and the relationships among the factors are noted.

A. Effective Innovation

The current evidence-based program movement began with seminal publications in the 1990s (Roberts 1996; Sackett et al. 1996). While the initial definition of "evidence-based programs" concerned the quality of "evidence" (Elliott and Mihalic 2004), attention soon turned to defining the quality of "programs" (Fixsen et al. 2010, Blase and Fixsen 2013, Fraser and Galinsky 2010).

In Active Implementation, an evidence-based program must meet four criteria to be considered a usable innovation (Fixsen et al. 2010). First, there is a clear *description* of the innovation, in which the philosophy, values, and principles that underlie the innovation are described. This provides guidance for all innovation-related decisions and evaluations. The philosophy, values, and principles are used to promote consistency, integrity, and sustainable effort across all organization units. In addition, the description specifies the inclusion and exclusion criteria that define the population for which the innovation is intended. The criteria define who is most likely to benefit when the innovation is used as intended, and who is not likely to benefit or may be harmed.

Second, there is a clear description of the *essential components* that define the innovation. The essential components are the features that must be present to say that an innovation exists in a given application (sometimes called core intervention components, active ingredients, or practice elements). Third, each essential component is *operationally defined*. Operational definitions are detailed descriptions of the essential functions in terms of activities (what to do and say) that allow an innovation to be used in practice and promote consistency across practitioners at the level of actual service delivery (also known as innovation configurations; Horsley and Loucks-Horsley 1998).

Finally, a usable innovation must have a practical assessment of *fidelity*. A fidelity assessment relates to the innovation philosophy, values, and principles; essential components; and core activities specified in the operational definition. A fidelity assessment is practical and can be done repeatedly in the context of typical human service systems. A fidelity assessment provides evidence that the innovation is effective when used as intended; that is, the fidelity assessment scores are highly correlated with intended outcomes. The "evidence" for an evidence-based program must inform this criterion.

Policymakers can take note of the four criteria for a usable innovation and include the requirements in legislation and administration. As a caution, appearing on a curated list of "evidence-based programs" should not be taken as an indication of meeting the four criteria for a usable innovation. For example, in an examination of programs rated on the California Evidence-Based Clearinghouse, "[n]o relationship was found between the level of scientific rating and the existence of fidelity measures. Overall, a range of fidelity strategies were used, including those considered gold standard (e.g., live or video observation). However, rarely are these strategies required" (Rolls Reutz et al. 2020). Current definitions of "evidence" typically do not include the necessary program/innovation/intervention/practice information to satisfy the usable innovation criteria.

B. Effective Implementation

As the evidence-based program movement grew, the field quickly identified a "research to practice gap" (Glasgow, Lichtenstein, and Marcus 2003) and described the "quality chasm" (Institute of Medicine 2001) between science and service outcomes. Effective implementation, the second factor in the formula for success, has been a concern for many years (Pressman and Wildavsky 1973; Van Meter and Van Horn 1975) and its importance has been noted again in the current evidence-based program movement (Kessler and Glasgow 2011; Gendreau, Goggin, and Smith 1999; Landenberger and Lipsey 2005).

An evidence-based approach to implementation practice describes the essential components of producing reliable benefits for recipients of human services (Fixsen, Blase, and Van Dyke 2019, Fixsen et al. 2005). Any innovation is a new way of work that must be learned by those who will do the work (practitioners). As shown in Figure 4.1, the competency drivers summarize how practitioners are introduced to an innovation and are supported in their efforts to use it as intended (i.e., with fidelity) with good outcomes. Information related to the usable innovation criteria informs the content for the competency drivers, such as selection, training, coaching, and fidelity assessment.

To be repeatable and sustainable, the uses of an innovation by practitioners and the uses of the competency drivers always require changes in existing organization roles, functions, and structures. As the saying goes, "If you keep doing what you've always done. . ." The organization drivers describe how administrators and managers sense the need for change (decision support data system) and make changes (facilitative administration, system intervention) to fully support practitioners' uses of innovations with fidelity. The base of the triangle refers to the leadership drivers required to initiate the uses of innovations, support the constant changes required to continually align organization components with intended outcomes, and constructively cope with unintended outcomes, adaptive challenges, and

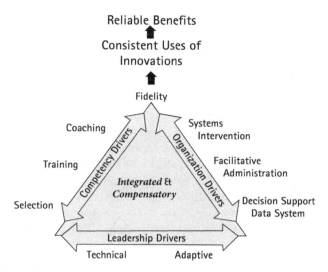

FIGURE 4.1. The Implementation Drivers that outline the essential supports for the full and effective use of innovations in practice. © 2008 Dean L. Fixsen and Karen A. Blase, used with permission of the copyright owners.

"wicked problems" that arise. The result of the leadership drivers is sustained high-fidelity use of the innovation and reliably good outcomes for recipients.

The competency, organization, and leadership drivers shown in Figure 4.1 need to be in place and fully functioning to produce and sustain consistent uses of innovations by practitioners and reliable outcomes for the intended recipients of an innovation. After a few years, the implementation drivers and the innovation practices become the new ways of work in an organization, and they eventually become the standard ways of work (Fixsen and Blase 2018). Using innovations as intended is the work of competent practitioners. Using implementation drivers as intended is the work of competent implementation teams.

In addition to usable innovations and implementation drivers, Active Implementation includes implementation teams, implementation stages, improvement cycles, and systemic change. Thus, the effective implementation factor in the formula for success includes components that interact with the other factors that contribute to socially significant outcomes (Fixsen, Blase, and Van Dyke 2019).

C. Enabling Context

Human services "operate in an unforgiving social and political environment, an environment rich with the potential for error, where the scale of consequences precludes learning through experimentation, and where to avoid failures in the face of shifting sources of vulnerability, complex processes are used to manage complex technology" (Weick, Sutcliffe, and Obstfeld 1999, 82). Systems are large and complex, powered by the inertia of legacy decisions and "ghostly" ways of work where workarounds and informal communication patterns (aspects of "ghost systems") keep things going in spite of—not because of—the formal system structures, policies, and procedures (Fixsen, Blase, and Van Dyke 2012; Behrens 2009). In ghost systems, "everyone practices a little bit of ignorance . . . to maintain the status quo" (Von Krogh, Ichijo, and Nonaka 2000, 212).

In contrast, in an enabling context, the components of a system are aligned so they support one another in coherent and purposeful ways that produce improved system performance and improved outcomes year after year. The staff are able to learn from their own experience and modify their structure, roles, and functions to reflect what they have learned. The staff and organizational units are multiskilled and are able to systematically detect and correct errors arising in other parts of the system.

An enabling context is an "ongoing accomplishment" (Weick 1987) and requires continual attention. Each component of the system continues to search for errors and faulty operating assumptions and continually makes changes needed to defragment and align functions within the system (Morgan and Ramirez 1983). Thus, "enabling contexts are the product of purposefully making changes in systems so that innovations are used as intended and their effectiveness is sustained over time" (Fixsen, Blase, and Van Dyke 2019, 271). The benefits of an enabling context have been outlined by Dooley (1997, 92–93), who states that enabling contexts:

> (a) create a shared purpose, (b) cultivate inquiry, learning, experimentation, and divergent thinking, (c) enhance external and internal interconnections via communication and technology, (d) instill rapid feedback loops for self-reference and self-control, (e) cultivate diversity, specialization, differentiation, and integration, (f) create shared values and principles of action, and (g) make explicit a few but essential structural and behavioral boundaries.

The few "boundaries" specify in advance no more than is absolutely necessary ("enabling conditions") for a system to begin operation so that a system can find its own design (Morgan and Ramirez 1983). In that process, "[t]he resources needed to perform institutional work are created through the enactment of practice" (Svensson, Tomson, and Rindzeviciute 2017). Regarding the formula for success, an enabling context promotes the use of effective innovations and effective implementation and uses the attainment of socially significant outcomes as the measure of success and the reason to improve.

D. Socially Significant Outcomes

Socially significant outcomes are outcomes that make a meaningful difference for the population of interest. The magnitude of change and the extent to which a population is positively affected are dimensions of social significance. A 10-point change in reading scores may be statistically significant; reaching a benchmark reading score that indicates a young child has "learned to read" with comprehension so she can "read to learn" for the rest of her life is socially significant. Teaching all children to read with comprehension by age nine is a socially significant outcome.

Figure 4.2 shows the factors in the formula success interacting to produce socially significant outcomes. Notice that the implementation drivers are at the center of the image. The drivers are the way to change behavior, change organizations, and sustain desired

FIGURE 4.2. The formula for success as it relates to policy, capacity, and fidelity. Fixsen, Blase, and Van Dyke (2019), used with permission of the authors.

outcomes. The content of the drivers is informed by information about the effective innovation, the capacity to use the drivers is supported by the enabling context, and the sustained and improved use of the drivers depends on the components of effective implementation.

II. Formula for Success and Implications for Policymakers

This chapter is focused on the implications of implementation science for evidence-based policy. First, legislators and other policymakers need to require evidence that the selected innovations produce intended outcomes in practice. Policymakers should keep the four criteria of a usable innovation in mind when writing legislation, especially the requirement to have data demonstrating the correlation between using an innovation with fidelity and the intended outcomes (Fixsen, Blase, and Van Dyke 2019, Chapter 6, "Usable Innovations"). Second, legislators and other policymakers need to require the use of implementation methods supported by evidence that the methods produce intended outcomes in practice. For example, require annual reports of best practices assessments for implementation drivers (Fixsen, Blase, and Van Dyke 2019; Chapter 8: Implementation Drivers Overview). Third, legislators and other policymakers need to set aside 20% of the initiative's funding for implementation supports for the use of innovations in practice. For example, they must require the use of funds to establish implementation teams that use the implementation drivers to support behavior change and organization change (Fixsen, Blase, and Van Dyke

2019, Chapter 14, Implementation Teams). Fourth, legislators and other policymakers need to set aside 10% of the initiative's funding specifically to fund quarterly assessments of the use of innovations and the use of implementation supports in practice. Additionally, they must require quarterly reports of fidelity of the use of the innovation (Fixsen, Blase, and Van Dyke 2019, Chapter 9, Implementation Competency Drivers) so that corrections can be made as needed.

These requirements would set in motion efforts to establish effective innovations and effective implementation as outlined in this chapter. The funding for implementation supports would assure the efforts, and the funding for quarterly assessments would provide the information for funding agencies and service providers to improve the initial efforts to produce socially significant outcomes.

III. Formula for Success and Implications for Administration

As Mears (2007, 671) notes, "To be effective, a policy must be implemented in the way it was intended to be carried out—that is, the specific activities and services envisioned for the policy must actually occur." The work to connect policy with new "activities and services" and improved outcomes is the responsibility of *administration*. The federal, state, and provincial departments that manage funds, provide services, contract for services, and monitor outcomes are critical to the process of realizing socially significant outcomes. Active Implementation informs how to establish, within the bureaucracy and within contracted services, the ability to accomplish the goals of legislation and monitor progress toward those goals.

The role of administration was central to the processes for realizing, in just 10 years, aspirational goals like sending astronauts to the moon and returning them safely (Dicht 2009), and for completing half of the intended 41,000-mile "National System of Interstate and Defense Highways" (McNichol 2006). In each case, the mission-driven administration of an aspirational policy made all the difference for accomplishing the goals in the 1960s.

Similar gains have not been made in corrections, education, social services, housing, employment, and other aspirational policies that also were enacted in the 1960s. Human services are interaction-based and more complex than atom-based innovations like rockets and roadways (Fixsen, Blase, and Fixsen 2017). The mutual influences that arise from interactions between and among individuals add difficulty to the task of administration of policies intended to improve human service outcomes. Administrators in human service departments need to understand implementation practice and science so that they can develop and monitor contracts accordingly.

For example, education outcomes in the United States have not changed appreciably since the 1960s (National Commission on Excellence in Education 1983; Grigg et al. 2003), even though major policies and substantial new funding ($40–50 billion each year since 2002) have been made available in the No Child Left Behind (2002) and Every Student Succeeds (2014) initiatives by the federal government. The administration of the policies did not include funds for implementation supports for education innovations. For example,

Vernez et al. (2006) studied 8,000 schools that received over $2 billion to support the use of one of four evidence-based approaches to education in grades K–8. The analysis of student outcomes showed no difference between those schools and comparison schools that did not receive federal support. The RAND evaluators included assessments of implementation supports—unusual for the early 2000s, and still unusual today. They found that teachers received about half of the recommended initial training and about one-quarter of the recommended ongoing professional development (Vernez et al. 2006).

Thus, in the near absence of implementation support (i.e., implementation drivers), the evidence-based approaches were not used as intended. Therefore, it is not surprising that the schools using "evidence-based programs" were no better than the comparison schools. The lack of improved outcomes reflected an implementation failure. The evidence-based programs themselves were effective innovations before and after their attempted use in 8,000 schools. If evidence-based programs and other effective innovations are not used fully and effectively (i.e., with fidelity) in practice, the intended benefits to students cannot be realized (National Center for Education Statistics 2013). Since the 1960s, literacy scores for nine-year-old children continue to hover around a mediocre average of 215 on a 500-point scale. Is funding important? Of course it is. Equally important is how the funds are used.

A. Road Building

Think about roads for a moment. Legislators decide where a road is to be built (start here, end there), set a time frame, and allocate the funds. The Department of Transportation then contracts with a general contractor that subcontracts with various road construction companies that have the capacity to accomplish the goals of the legislation (Kogler, Brydl, and Highsmith 1999). The subcontractors (companies) have capacity in the form of engineers, surveyors, earth-moving crews, concrete and asphalt specialists, painters, sign makers, and others to actually build a sturdy road and prepare it for use by the public.

After decades of successful road building, the infrastructure for road building exists, and policymakers, administrators, and contractors understand the time frames and costs for building a road. Legislators set the goals and the general parameters, such as timing and funding. The Transportation Department administers contracts with competent contractors and does quality assurance checks during each stage of construction. The competent contractors (road construction companies) have the capacity to do the work skillfully—they know what to do and how to do it. A few years after making the decision, the legislators can visit the completed road and enjoy a smooth ride.

Policymakers and administrators recognize that building roads in the mountains is more difficult than building roads across the plains. Yet both pale in comparison to achieving the significant changes in human services called for by legislation. Implementation capacity is not readily available in human services at this time. Administrators are not prepared to turn policy goals and parameters into relevant specifications for contracting for effective innovations and effective implementation and enabling contexts (the factors in the formula for success). There are very few general contractors and subcontractors that have the expertise to function as implementation teams. Implementation teams need to be created and become proficient in order to carry out the goals embedded in legislation (Blase, Fixsen, and Phillips 1984; Klein 2004; Nzinga et al. 2009; Spoth et al. 2004).

Investing in the development of skilled implementation teams provides an effective link for realizing policy goals. Implementation team members include experts in various roles of engaged execution of policy-relevant interventions with fidelity and at scale, and also bring with them historical knowledge of past implementation efforts that can inform current and future initiatives (Fixsen and Blase 2018). Implementation teams know the intent of the legislation, are expert users of Active Implementation science and best practices, and make disciplined use of improvement cycles that keep the entire enterprise focused on achieving the intentions of the legislation. Implementation team members are expert "adaptive leaders" (Stacey 2002; Marzano, Waters, and McNulty 2005; Heifetz, Grashow, and Linsky 2009) who can work with the legislature, leaders of government departments, and contractors to resolve "wicked problems" (Rittel and Webber 1973) that arise in practice, organization, and system change processes associated with using effective innovations in human services.

Implementation teams are like the general contractors for road building: they keep everything integrated and moving expeditiously toward effective outcomes. As such, they have value at the administrative/policymaking level, as well as within organizations that provide services (e.g., child, family, adult-serving organizations). Their expertise can help administrators reliably translate legislative goals into policy-supported service user guidance. They can also create infrastructures that support development of implementation teams within and across provider agencies to assure self-sustaining supports for the full and effective use of innovations in practice (Fixsen et al. 2005, 33–34; Fixsen, Blase, and Van Dyke 2019, Chapter 14; Fixsen, Blase, and Fixsen 2017).

Many implementation team members can be drawn from current department staff whose positions are repurposed. Other team members will need to be hired as implementation specialists. Any implementation team member will need to acquire the specialized knowledge, skills, and abilities required to use implementation science and implementation best practices effectively and efficiently.

B. New Approach to Contracting

Administering legislation to achieve intended outcomes in human services will require developing an infrastructure for implementation. Specifically, this involves the link between legislation and administrative action, on one side, and the link between administrative action and actual localized service change, on the other.

Many government agencies do not provide policy-related services directly; rather, they contract for those services. In human service departments, a typical contracting process involves a "paper exchange"—send out a request for proposals, review the proposals, and fund the ones that look the best on paper. In an implementation-informed human service department, the paper exchange is replaced by an "information exchange" that is based on the exploration stage of implementation (Romney, Israel, and Zlatevski 2014; Fixsen et al. 2005).

In an implementation-informed administration, many of the exploration stage activities are carried out prior to granting funds. In a paper exchange, good grant writers can write a fundable application. However, written words are no substitute for the engaging discussion and informed agreements by leaders that are the result of exploration activities prior to making funding decisions. Implementation-informed administrators can help create readiness by conducting contracting meetings in new ways to help potential applicants prepare to use an innovation with fidelity and socially significant outcomes.

Jim Wotring and colleagues in the Michigan Department of Community Health pioneered the use of implementation-informed methods for administering Michigan state government policies to improve children's mental health (Wotring et al. 2005). A statewide evaluation provided evidence that children with the most pervasive problems (mood disorders, behavior problems at home and school, delinquency) had the poorest mental health outcomes (Hodges, Xue, and Wotring 2004). This finding led to a search for an evidence-based program best suited for children with pervasive problems. Wotring and colleagues selected the Parent Management Training–Oregon (PMTO) program (Forgatch, Patterson, and DeGarmo 2005). PMTO had evidence of good outcomes and had established skill-based training, coaching, and fidelity assessments for practitioners.

Wotring and colleagues used the Active Implementation stages (Fixsen et al. 2005) as a guide for an implementation-informed process for selecting grantees to use PMTO in Michigan. Instead of a paper exchange, the process consisted of a series of meetings to exchange information. The request for proposals (RFP) consisted of an announcement of a meeting to explain the innovation (PMTO) and the supports (implementation drivers) that an organization would need to provide to use the innovation with fidelity and produce good outcomes. The provider agencies that were interested attended two subsequent meetings where the requirements were reviewed in detail. In the introductory meeting it was clear that this was a new process requiring decisions to commit resources and organize staff. Grant writers were replaced by organization leaders in the subsequent meetings, where each requirement was reviewed in detail. The application from an agency consisted of the list of requirements that had been reviewed and discussed during the meetings and a space for the agency to commit fully, partially, or not at all to each requirement. For example: "We agree that training will not just be an add-on to the trainee's current job when training is completed. Upon completion, we agree to develop a new job description for the trainee to allow them to function as a trainer at least half the time" (J. Wotring, personal communication, January 2005). The contracting process has continued, and by 2022, Michigan had established the implementation infrastructure to offer PMTO in 41 of the 83 counties in the state (M. Ludkte, personal communication, March 2022).

C. Administration: Implementation Progress Monitoring

Immediate access to relevant information is critical to implementation processes as well as to department administration and monitoring processes. Information to support data-based decision-making is a critical component of implementation. Moreover, we recommend that policymakers use feedback loops to enhance implementation in the service of outcomes. It is not sufficient to know what happened last year. It is critical to know what happened yesterday and last week and last month to guide decision-making. Thus, implementation best practices and the need for legislative and departmental monitoring merge.

Think back on the earlier analogy about building a road. When a road is being built, members of the transportation department and its contractors can monitor the progress being made and can test the quality of work with known methods (Petroski 1982). The monitoring goes on during the three or four years required to build a new bridge, build a few more miles of interstate highway, or build a road to open a new subdivision. Monitoring is based on the stage of work, from planning, to surveying, to grading the land, to laying asphalt, to painting stripes and installing signs. The final outcome—a completed road that is part of the public transportation system—is years away, so monitoring is based on the stages of development toward that goal. It does not make sense to measure road usage and traffic patterns before the road is built. Similarly, administering progress toward human service goals requires assessments of fidelity, outcomes, and processes at each stage of implementation (Fixsen, Blase, and Van Dyke 2019).

IV. Implementation Practice and Science

The call for implementation capacity development in human services is not new (Brown and Flynn 2002; Clancy 2006). What *is* new is the development of implementation science and practice (Fixsen, Blase, and Van Dyke 2019; Nilsen and Birken 2020). For the first time, social science data are available to guide and support effective implementation in human service systems. It now is possible for groups to implement legislation in human services with the same reliability and success that legislators have come to expect in road construction and other "bricks and mortar" enterprises.

Key outcomes for implementation teams are greater alignment and coherence in human service systems. Fragmentation, layering, and disintegrated approaches are typical in human services. Legislation is passed, state agencies appoint a director of each legislated initiative, and each initiative works fairly independently of other initiatives. This profusion of layers of initiatives results in confusion and inaction as local service entities try to incorporate the myriad legislated mandates and "innovations" and make changes in service delivery and outcomes. The errors within and across initiatives compound and soon outweigh all the efforts that go into well-intended and often passionate attempts to carry out the intentions of legislation. Thus, defragmenting the system (i.e., removing the "silos" or "fiefdoms") and uniting components for systematic, resource-efficient, and evidence-informed action is best achieved through expert implementation teams guiding those efforts.

V. Conclusion

Human services in the United States are in need of improvement. Legislators recognize this, and each year they pass new legislation intended to improve the health, education, and well-being of the people in the country. The problem is not the good intentions of legislators or the good intentions of those attempting to meet the requirements of legislation. The problem is not lack of knowledge per se. The problem is lack of implementation capacity to affect change in service delivery and the organizations and systems that manage service delivery. The solution is evidence-based policymaking that includes investment in implementation and the development of skillful human resources—implementation teams—that have the capacity to overcome the inertia built into human service systems, manage the change processes, and establish the foundations for success (i.e., what to do and how to do it).

We ardently encourage policy analysts to include strong implementation variables in their theories and their assessments of policy impact. Inclusion of implementation variables is required to realize the intentions of legislation in human service practices to improve outcomes for citizens across the nation. Ignoring implementation variables is ignoring an essential factor in the formula for success and invites continuing to churn around a mediocre mean in corrections and human services in general. With advances in implementation science, it is now becoming more possible to establish evidence-based policies to achieve the goals of legislation and policy in human services. A modest investment in the development of an infrastructure to support implementation—the new general contractors and road builders in the world of human services—will lead to systems supportive of adaptive changes in response to emerging knowledge, policy needs, service user needs, professional needs, economic challenges, and so on. Active Implementation that attends to effective innovations, effective implementation, and enabling contexts is vital to produce socially significant outcomes for the benefit of society for decades to come.

References

Allen, Jennifer D., Samuel D. Towne, Annette E. Maxwell, Lisa DiMartino, Bryan Leyva, Deborah J. Bowen, Laura Linnan, and Bryan J. Weiner. 2017. Measures of organizational characteristics associated with adoption and/or implementation of innovations: A systematic review. *BMC Health Services Research*, 17 (1): 591. doi:10.1186/s12913-017-2459-x.

Behrens, Sandy. 2009. Shadow systems: the good, the bad and the ugly. *Communications of the ACM*, 52 (2): 124–129. doi:10.1145/1461928.1461960.

Blase, Karen A., and Dean L. Fixsen. 2003. *Evidence-based programs and cultural competence.* Tampa: National Implementation Research Network, University of South Florida.

Blase, Karen A., and Dean L. Fixsen. 2013. *Core intervention components: Identifying and operationalizing what makes programs work.* Edited by US Department of Health and Human Services. Washington, DC: Office of the Assistant Secretary for Planning and Evaluation, Office of Human Services Policy, US Department of Health and Human Services.

Blase, Karen A., Dean L. Fixsen, Sandra F. Naoom, and Frances Wallace. 2005. *Operationalizing implementation: Strategies and methods.* Tampa: National Implementation Research Network, University of South Florida.

Blase, Karen A., Dean L. Fixsen, and Elery L. Phillips. 1984. Residential treatment for troubled children: Developing service delivery systems. In *Human services that work: From innovation to standard practice*, edited by S. C. Paine, G. T. Bellamy and B. Wilcox, 149–165. Baltimore, MD: Paul H. Brookes.

Bond, Gary R., and Robert E. Drake. 2020. Assessing the fidelity of evidence-based practices: History and current status of a standardized measurement methodology. *Administration and Policy in Mental Health and Mental Health Services Research*, 47 (6): 874–884. doi:10.1007/s10488-019-00991-6.

Brown, Barry S., and Patrick M. Flynn. 2002. The federal role in drug abuse technology transfer: A history and perspective. *Journal of Substance Abuse Treatment*, 22 (4): 245–257.

Brownson, Ross C., Graham A. Colditz, and Enola K. Proctor, eds. 2012. *Dissemination and implementation research in health.* New York: Oxford University Press.

Brunk, Molly, J. E. Chapman, and Sonja K. Schoenwald. 2014. Defining and evaluating fidelity at the program level: A preliminary investigation. *Zeitschrift für Psychologie*, 222:22–29. doi:10.1027/2151-2604/a000162.

Clancy, Carolyn M. 2006. The $1.6 trillion question: If we're spending so much on healthcare, why so little improvement in quality? *Medscape General Medicine*, 8 (2): 58.

Dicht, Burton. 2009. The most hazardous and dangerous and greatest adventure on which man has ever embarked. *Mechanical Engineering*, 131 (7): 28–35.

Dooley, Kevin J. 1997. A complex adaptive systems model of organization change. *Nonlinear Dynamics, Psychology, and Life Sciences*, 1 (1): 69–97.

Elliott, Delbert S., and Sharon Mihalic. 2004. Issues in disseminating and replicating effective prevention programs. *Prevention Science*, 5 (1): 47–53.

Fixsen, Dean L., and Karen A. Blase. 2018. The Teaching-Family Model: The first 50 years. *Perspectives on Behavior Science*, 42:189–211. doi:10.1007/s40614-018-0168-3.

Fixsen, Dean L., Karen A. Blase, Michelle Duda, Sandra Naoom, and Melissa K. Van Dyke. 2010. Implementation of evidence-based treatments for children and adolescents: Research findings and their implications for the future. In *Implementation and dissemination: Extending treatments to new populations and new settings*, edited by John Weisz and Alan Kazdin, 435–450. New York: Guilford Press.

Fixsen, Dean L., Karen A. Blase, and Amanda A. M. Fixsen. 2017. Scaling effective innovations. *Criminology & Public Policy*, 16 (2): 487–499. doi:10.1111/1745-9133.12288.

Fixsen, Dean L., Karen A. Blase, Sandra F. Naoom, and Frances Wallace. 2009. Core implementation components. *Research on Social Work Practice*, 19 (5): 531–540. doi:10.1177/1049731509335549.

Fixsen, Dean L., Karen A. Blase, Gary D. Timbers, and Montrose M. Wolf. 2007. In search of program implementation: 792 replications of the Teaching-Family Model. *Behavior Analyst Today*, 8 (1): 96–110. doi:10.1037/h0100104.

Fixsen, Dean L., Karen A. Blase, and Melissa K. Van Dyke. 2012. From ghost systems to host systems via transformation zones. Washington, DC: US Department of Education, Office of Vocational and Adult Education.

Fixsen, Dean L., Karen A. Blase, and Melissa K. Van Dyke. 2019. *Implementation practice and science*. Chapel Hill, NC: Active Implementation Research Network.

Fixsen, Dean L., and Amanda A.M. Fixsen. 2016. An integration and synthesis of current implementation frameworks. Chapel Hill, NC: Active Implementation Research Network.

Fixsen, Dean L., Sandra F. Naoom, Karen A. Blase, Robert M. Friedman, and Frances Wallace. 2005. *Implementation research: A synthesis of the literature*. Tampa: National Implementation Research Network, University of South Florida. www.activeimplementation.org.

Forgatch, M. S., Gerald R. Patterson, and David S. DeGarmo. 2005. Evaluating fidelity: Predictive validity for a measure of competent adherence to the Oregon Model of Parent Management Training. *Behavior Therapy*, 36 (1): 3–13.

Fraser, Mark W., and Maeda J. Galinsky. 2010. Steps in intervention research: Designing and developing social programs. *Research on Social Work Practice*, 20 (5): 459–466. doi:10.1177/1049731509358424.

Gendreau, P., C. Goggin, and P. Smith. 1999. The forgotten issue in effective correctional treatment: Program implementation. *International Journal of Offender Therapy and Comparative Criminology*, 43 (2): 180–187.

Glasgow, Russell E., E. Lichtenstein, and A. C. Marcus. 2003. Why don't we see more translation of health promotion research to practice? Rethinking the efficacy-to-effectiveness transition. *American Journal of Public Health*, 93 (8): 1261–1267.

Glennan, Thomas K., Jr., S. J. Bodilly, J. R. Galegher, and K. A. Kerr. 2004. *Expanding the reach of education reforms*. Santa Monica, CA: RAND Corporation.

Greenhalgh, Trisha, Glenn Robert, Fraser MacFarlane, Paul Bate, and Olivia Kyriakidou. 2004. Diffusion of innovations in service organizations: Systematic review and recommendations. *Milbank Quarterly*, 82 (4): 581–629.

Grigg, Wendy S., M. C. Daane, Y. Jin, and J. R. Campbell. 2003. *The nation's report card: Reading 2002*. Washington, DC: US Department of Education, Institute of Education Sciences.

Harnish, Verne. 2014. *Scaling up: How a few companies make it . . . and why the rest don't*. New York: Gazelles, Inc.

Haskins, Ron, and Jon Baron. 2011. Building the connection between policy and evidence: The Obama evidence-based initiatives. London: National Endowment for Science, Technology and the Arts (UK).

Heifetz, Ronald A., Alexander Grashow, and Marty Linsky. 2009. *The practice of adaptive leadership*. Boston, MA: Harvard Business Press.

Hodges, Kay, Yange Xue, and Jim Wotring. 2004. Outcomes for children with problematic behavior in school and at home served by public mental health. *Journal of Emotional and Behavioral Disorders*, 12 (2): 109–119.

Horsley, Donald L., and S. Loucks-Horsley. 1998. CBAM brings order to the tornado of change. *Journal of Staff Development*, 19 (4): 17–20.

Institute of Medicine. 2001. *Crossing the quality chasm: A new health system for the 21st century*. Washington, DC: National Academy Press.

Kessler, Rodger C., and Russ E. Glasgow. 2011. A proposal to speed translation of healthcare research into practice: Dramatic change is needed. *American Journal of Preventive Medicine*, 40 (6): 637–644.

Klein, Janice A. 2004. *True change: How outsiders on the inside get things done in organizations*. New York: Jossey-Bass.

Kogler, Robert A., D. Brydl, and C. Highsmith. 1999. Recent FHWA experience with metallized coatings for steel bridges. *Materials Performance*, 38 (4): 43–45.

Kruk, Margaret E., Anna D. Gage, Catherine Arsenault, Keely Jordan, Hannah H. Leslie, Sanam Roder-DeWan, Olusoji Adeyi, et al. 2018. High-quality health systems in the Sustainable Development Goals era: Time for a revolution. *Lancet Global Health*, 6:e1196–1252. doi:https://doi.org/10.1016/S2214-109X(18)30386-3.

Landenberger, Nana A., and Mark W. Lipsey. 2005. The positive effects of cognitive-behavioral programs for offenders: A meta-analysis of factors associated with effective treatment. *Journal of Experimental Criminology*, 1 (4): 451–476.

Lipsey, Mark W. 2009. The primary factors that characterize effective interventions with juvenile offenders: A meta-analytic overview. *Victims and Offenders*, 4:124–147. doi:10.1080/15564880802612573.

Marzano, Robert, Tim Waters, and Brian McNulty. 2005. *School leadership that works: From research to results*. Alexandria, VA: Association for Supervision and Curriculum Development (ASCD).

McKibbon, K. Ann, Cynthia Lokker, Nancy L. Wilczynski, Donna Ciliska, Maureen Dobbins, David A. Davis, R. Brian Haynes, and Sharon E. Straus. 2010. A cross-sectional study of the number and frequency of terms used to refer to knowledge translation in a body of health literature in 2006: A Tower of Babel? *Implementation Science*, 5 (1): 1–11. doi:10.1186/1748-5908-5-16.

McNichol, Dan. 2006. *The roads that built America*. New York: Sterling.

Mears, Daniel. 2007. Towards rational and evidence-based crime policy. *Journal of Criminal Justice*, 35:667–682. doi:10.1016/j.jcrimjus.2007.09.003.

Meyers, Duncan C., Joseph A. Durlak, and Abraham Wandersman. 2012. The quality implementation framework: A synthesis of critical steps in the implementation process. *American Journal of Community Psychology*, 50 (3–4): 462–480. doi:10.1007/s10464-012-9522-x.

Morgan, Gareth, and Raphael Ramirez. 1983. Action learning: A holographic metaphor for guiding social change. *Human Relations*, 37 (1): 1–28.

National Center for Education Statistics. 2013. *The nation's report card: Trends in academic progress 2012.* Washington, DC: Institute of Education Sciences, US Department of Education. http://nces.ed.gov/nationsreportcard/subject/publications/main2012/pdf/2013456.pdf.

National Commission on Excellence in Education. 1983. *A nation at risk: The imperative for educational reform.* Washington, DC: US Government Printing Office.

Nilsen, Per, and Sarah A. Birken, eds. 2020. *Handbook on Implementation Science.* Cheltenham, UK: Edward Elgar.

Nzinga, Jacinta, P. Mbindyo, L. Mbaabu, A. Warira, and M. English. 2009. Documenting the experiences of health workers expected to implement guidelines during an intervention study in Kenyan hospitals. *Implementation Science*, 4 (1): 44.

Perl, Harold I. 2011. Addicted to discovery: Does the quest for new knowledge hinder practice improvement? *Addictive Behaviors*, 36 (6): 590–596. doi:10.1016/j.addbeh.2011.01.027.

Petroski, Henry. 1982. *To engineer is human: The role of failure in successful design.* Vintage ed. New York: Random House.

Pressman, Jeffrey L., and A. Wildavsky. 1973. *Implementation: How great expectations in Washington are dashed in Oakland: or, why it's amazing that federal programs work at all, this being a saga of the economic development administration as told by two sympathetic observers who seek to build morals on a foundation of ruined hopes.* Berkeley: University of California Press.

Rittel, Horst W. J., and Melvin M. Webber. 1973. Dilemmas in a general theory of planning. *Policy Sciences*, 4:155–169.

Roberts, Michael C., ed. 1996. *Model programs in child and family mental health.* Mahwah, NJ: Lawrence Erlbaum Associates.

Rogers, Everett M. 1995. *Diffusion of innovations.* 4th ed. New York: The Free Press.

Rolls Reutz, Jennifer A., Suzanne E. U. Kerns, Jennifer A. Sedivy, and Cricket Mitchell. 2020. Documenting the implementation gap, part 1: Use of fidelity supports in programs indexed in the California evidence-based clearinghouse. *Journal of Family Social Work*, 23 (2): 114–132. doi:10.1080/10522158.2019.1694342.

Romney, Stephanie, Nathaniel Israel, and Danijela Zlatevski. 2014. Effect of exploration-stage implementation variation on the cost-effectiveness of an evidence-based parenting program. *Zeitschrift für Psychologie*, 222 (1): 37–48. doi:10.1027/2151-2604/a000164.

Rossi, Peter H., and James D. Wright. 1984. Evaluation research: An assessment. *Annual Review of Sociology*, 10:331–352.

Sabatier, Paul A. 1999. *Theories of the policy process*: Boulder, CO: Westview Press.

Sackett, David L., W. M. C. Rosenberg, J. A. M. Gray, R. B. Haynes, and W. S. Richardson. 1996. Evidence-based medicine: What it is and what it isn't. *British Medical Journal*, 312:71–72.

Schofield, Jill. 2004. A model of learned implementation. *Public Administration*, 82 (2): 283–308.

Spoth, Richard, Mark Greenberg, Karen Bierman, and Cleve Redmond. 2004. PROSPER community–university partnership model for public education systems: Capacity-building for evidence-based, competence-building prevention. *Prevention Science*, 5 (1): 31–39.

Stacey, Ralph D. 2002. *Strategic management and organisational dynamics: The challenge of complexity*. 3rd ed. Harlow, UK: Prentice Hall.

Svensson, Jenny, Klara Tomson, and Egle Rindzeviciute. 2017. Policy change as institutional work: Introducing cultural and creative industries into cultural policy. *Qualitative Research in Organizations and Management: An International Journal*, 12 (2): 149–168. doi:10.1108/QROM-05-2016-1380.

Tabak, Rachel G., Elaine C. Khoong, David A. Chambers, and Ross C. Brownson. 2012. Bridging research and practice: Models for dissemination and implementation research. *American Journal of Preventive Medicine*, 43 (3): 337–350.

Van Meter, Donald S., and C. E. Van Horn. 1975. The policy implementation process: A conceptual framework. *Administration & Society*, 6:445–488.

Vernez, Georges, Rita Karam, Louis T. Mariano, and Christine DeMartini. 2006. *Evaluating comprehensive school reform models at scale: Focus on implementation*. Santa Monica, CA: RAND Corporation.

Von Krogh, Georg, Kazuo Ichijo, and Ikujiro Nonaka. 2000. *Enabling knowledge creation*. New York: Oxford University Press.

Watkins, Cathy L. 1995. Follow through: Why didn't we? *Effective School Practices*, 15 (1): 57–66.

Weick, Karl E. 1987. Organizational culture as a source of high reliability. *California Management Review*, 29 (2): 112–128.

Weick, Karl E., Kathleen M. Sutcliffe, and David Obstfeld. 1999. Organizing for high reliability: Processes of collective mindfulness. In *Research in organizational behavior*, edited by R. S. Sutton and B. M. Staw, 81–123. Stanford, CA: Jai Press.

Wotring, Jim, Kay Hodges, Yange Xue, and Marion Forgatch. 2005. Critical ingredients for improving mental health services: Use of outcome data, stakeholder involvement, and evidence-based practices. *Behavior Therapist*, 28 (7): 150, 152, 154–158.

CHAPTER 5

TOWARD SYSTEM-LEVEL CHANGE, POPULATION IMPACTS, AND EQUITY

HOLLY S. SCHINDLER

EVIDENCE-BASED policymaking in the social sciences has garnered increased interest from both the public and lawmakers dating back to the 1960s (Baron 2018). The motivations behind this movement have centered on making good use of scarce resources while working to achieve population outcomes for children, families, and communities. While noble in its pursuits, evidence-based policymaking has yet to realize these goals fully. Instead, the movement has spurred a number of promising programs that have faced challenges in reproducing positive impacts when brought to scale.

One sector that this has been particularly evident is in early childhood (Gupta et al. 2021). The early childhood field was an early adopter of randomized controlled trials (RCTs) and using evidence from RCTs to inform policy. For example, the Perry Preschool Project was a demonstration project implemented in the 1960s with 123 children and their families and evaluated through random assignment. This seminal study is best known for its long-term effects for child participants who have been tracked by researchers since the start of the program (Schweinhart 2005). The Abecedarian Program was similarly evaluated through an RCT with 111 children between 1972 and 1977, with numerous positive outcomes reported for children into adulthood (Campbell et al. 2002, 2012). These two flagship studies remain the most-cited examples of evidenced-based programs for improving outcomes of young children, including lower rates of adult crime and arrest rates (Shonkoff and Fisher 2013). Their evaluations, along with others that followed, laid a foundation of support for public investment in early childhood programs (Karoly et al. 2005).

In the decades after the Perry Preschool Project and the Abecedarian Program, additional developments accelerated the focus on evidence-based policy in early childhood and other areas of education. Namely, funders such as the Institute of Education Sciences and the US Department of Health and Human Services began using rigorous evidence as the primary metric for awarding intervention funding (Baron 2018). A high-profile example is the Maternal, Infant, and Childhood Home Visiting (MIECHV) program, which funds early childhood home visiting services for 150,000 families in the United States every year

(US Department of Health and Human Services 2019). The MIECHV program continues to reserve the largest grants for programs with existing evidence of effectiveness.

These efforts have ultimately produced a large body of evidence on the potential for early childhood programs to support children and families worldwide. Yet it has proven difficult to achieve and sustain benefits as programs have attempted to scale, a problem that has been called "the scale-up effect" (List, Suskind, and Supplee 2021). Further, the evidence-based policy movement in early childhood has resulted in some unintended consequences that are orthogonal to achieving population impacts, such as incentivizing statistical significance over meaningful change, average impacts over discovering subpopulation impacts, and rigidity in implementation over flexibility and cultural relevance. Indeed, the science of scaling and early childhood have been described as "two of the greatest policy issues of our time" (Gupta et al. 2021, 1).

Given this history, the early childhood field can serve as a rich case study for other areas of social policy, including crime and justice policy. The crime and justice field shares some characteristics with the early childhood field that may make it particularly susceptible to the challenges of scaling, including complex fragmented systems and a history of inequities in design, implementation, and outcomes. This chapter aims to take a closer look at how social sciences can further work toward system level change, population impacts, and equity. It draws on lessons learned from the early childhood field, as well as concepts from implementation science, collective impact, and human centered design.

The first section explores definitions of scale and threats to successfully scaling programs. The second and third sections examine ways to address those challenges through explicitly designing programs and evaluations for scale and equity. The fourth section makes a case for moving from designing programs to changing systems. The chapter ends with concluding remarks and calls to action.

I. Defining Scale and Threats to Achieving It

There is not one agreed-upon definition of scale; however, in the most basic sense, to "scale up" means to increase the availability of successfully tested programs or policies to benefit a larger number of people. This can occur through two different types of scaling. The first is horizontal scaling, or the expansion of pilot programs to cover broader populations. This is the most common form of scaling in many social sciences, in which programs are first evaluated as small-scale pilots and eventually move through more rigorous evaluations and widespread implementation. Yoshikawa et al. (2018) term this the "small to bigger" approach to scaling.

The second type of scaling is vertical scaling, or the improvement of policy, regulatory, or other system changes. These changes may be in service of institutionalizing program innovations at a policy level or improving systems already at scale. This is sometimes referred to as the "big to better" approach (Yoshikawa et al. 2018). Though much of this chapter focuses on horizontal scaling, there is also a section dedicated to systems improvement as an important mechanism to achieving population impacts.

Why is it that so many programs successfully implemented on a small scale fail to reap the same rewards when moving from "small to bigger"? Part of the challenge is that many touch points occur from the initial program development to full-scale implementation, and threats to scaling can occur at any point along that pathway. Three key areas with common pitfalls are program design, program evaluation, and policy systems. In what follows, I briefly discuss potential threats in each of these areas.

A. Threats in Program Design

1. *Unclear Theories of Change (TOC)*

A theory of change (TOC) is a detailed set of beliefs about specific changes that are expected to result from a program. It has long been argued that TOCs can "improve decision making, lead to the planning of better programs, and so serve program participants in more relevant, more beneficial, and more efficient ways" (Weiss 1972, 3). They can also be a tool for supporting equitable outcomes. They do this through creating a framework for moving beyond the question of whether a program is effective, to consider how, why, and for whom a program does or does not work (Schindler, Fisher, and Shonkoff 2017).

In spite of these benefits, TOCs remain underutilized in fields such as early childhood. For example, in a study examining a systematically developed archived database of early childhood education studies, causal mechanisms (i.e., mediators) were rarely articulated (Schindler et al. 2019). Identifying the predicted causal mechanisms of programs is a critical aspect of TOCs and necessary for unpacking the "black box" of program strategies. When programs are not linked to specific outcomes based on explicit causal hypotheses, the variability of later effects on multiple measures becomes difficult to interpret and programs are more challenging to be scaled effectively (Schindler et al. 2019). TOCs have also been underutilized in a number of other fields, including public health, community psychology, and medicine (Coryn et al. 2011).

2. *Overly Complex Program Designs*

There is a tendency in social sciences to create programs that are overly complex and layer multiple services into one package in pursuit of larger effects. For example, in early childhood, many programs have combined early care and education with additional services, such as health screening, nutrition, and parenting education (Camilli et al. 2010). While combining multiple components into one program may seem intuitive, the provision of additional services on top of core strategies has been associated with null or even negative additional gains (Camilli et al. 2010; Grindal et al. 2016), perhaps due to the challenges of maintaining the quality of each individual component as complexity increases. Indeed, principles of human-centered design theorize that design complexity has an inverse relationship with scalability (Lyon 2021).

3. *Failing to Consider Equity*

One of the greatest threats to achieving population impacts is that many initiatives have neglected to center equity in program development, implementation, and scaling (Kania et al. 2022; Loper,

Woo, and Metz 2021). Programs have typically been developed by people who do not represent the community in which the programs are implemented. Loper and colleagues (2021, 3) note that "while an intervention needs a strong evidence base to succeed, the program and manner of implementation also need to fit the culture, values, and daily lives of the community and the people affected by the intervention." Without a deep understanding of the local community and context, programs are unlikely to be meaningful or effective. Further, programs that are developed and implemented by outsiders are less likely to acknowledge or address the ways that systemic racism and other power dynamics influence the contexts in which programs operate.

B. Threats in Program Evaluation

1. *Focus Solely on Average Impacts*

In program evaluation, an emphasis solely on whether or not a program works may mask important differences and disparities in effectiveness. In other words, focusing on mean effects conceals what strategies may be working under particular conditions (which should inform targeted scaling) and what may be working less well or not at all under other conditions (which may catalyze new ideas) (Shonkoff 2017). Instead, the common practice has been to scale programs based on average impacts without fully understanding the nuances of how and under what conditions programs may be generalizable, often leading to less favorable results when programs are offered to a broader population.

2. *Lack of Scalable Measures of Quality and Fidelity*

Another hypothesis about the scale-up effect is that quality and fidelity are difficult to maintain as programs are offered more broadly. Quality often includes both the structural and process quality of the program. Fidelity is the extent to which the planned activities match the actual activities delivered. Reliable information about both quality and fidelity is critical as programs are developed and scaled. Such data can inform aspects of the program that are easier or harder to scale in particular contexts. However, measures of quality and fidelity are typically resource- and time-intensive, making it difficult for programs to continue to collect such data, particularly as they expand (Gupta et al. 2021). For example, only one-third of high-quality early childhood evaluation studies between the 1960s and 2000s reported that they implemented measures of fidelity (Schindler et al. 2019). Reviews of the broader educational literature have also shown that the average study does not report information on fidelity (Mooney et al. 2003; Smith, Daunic, and Taylor 2007). This often leaves program implementers and policymakers without the crucial data needed to understand where things are working well and where they may be going off track.

C. Threats in Policy and Funding Systems

1. *Lack of Coordination across Systems*

Programs serving children, youth, and families are situated across numerous systems, including education, health, child welfare, and justice. These systems typically are not designed in coordination, creating a number of additional barriers to achieving population impacts. For example, the lack of coordination makes it difficult for families to navigate to appropriate services in their communities. It also makes it challenging to collect reliable data on what services families need, how they are engaging with services, and what outcomes those services are producing.

2. *Misalignment between Systems and Lived Experiences*

Similar to program development, people who do not represent impacted communities have made many of the existing policy and funding decisions. This has resulted in a disconnection between those decisions and the lived experiences of communities. The power dynamics at play have also prioritized the ideas of those in decision-making positions. This includes the very definition of "evidence-based," which relies heavily on evidence as defined by historically marginalizing institutions that often fail to consider community-defined evidence. Similarly, funding requirements may be overly prescriptive, which in turn creates challenges for communities to enact the changes they believe are needed. These types of misalignment are continuous threats to equitable population impacts.

II. Designing Programs and Evaluations for Scale

The threats to scaling described in the preceding section are sizeable and real challenges to the field in obtaining population impacts. Fortunately, we have also learned numerous lessons about how to better design programs and evaluations for scale and equity. The goal of this section is to highlight some of the most promising principles in designing programs and evaluations for scale. The subsequent section focuses specifically on designing for equity.

A. Prioritize Parsimony and Flexibility in Design

Programs have the potential to be more easily taken up by a broader population and sustained over time if they are both parsimonious and flexible in design. Parsimonious designs can be more difficult to develop and achieve than complex designs because developing something efficient yet effective requires knowledge about what aspects of a program may be most important. Flexibility is also critical for ensuring that programs can be adapted to meet local needs and can shift in response to changing needs over time. Designing program components that can be mixed and matched as needed or taken up by existing systems is one approach to flexibility. Another approach is identifying aspects of programs that are essential versus ones that can be altered or eliminated based on community needs. The development and evaluation of theories of change (TOCs), as described in the next two subsections, can aid in implementing these approaches.

B. Develop a Clear, Concise, and Community-Driven TOC

There have been numerous writings on TOCs over the past 40 years, leading to many variations in TOC definitions and descriptions (e.g., Chen 1990; Chen and Rossi 1992; Weiss 1995, 1997). While there is no one way to create a TOC, they have the best chance of fulfilling their promise when they are clear, concise, and community-driven. When a TOC clearly and concisely describes how an innovation intends to work, it can better act as a tool for reflection, evaluation, and decision-making. Key components often include some combination of program strategies, program targets/mediators, expected outcomes, and program moderators (Schindler, Fisher, and Shonkoff 2017). Importantly, TOCs may also include the values underlying the program and facilitate the sharing of the core story of the program with others. Community-driven TOCs can come to fruition through authentic community-researcher partnerships in which collaborators jointly formulate TOCs to address unmet needs, or through community-led initiatives.

C. Identify Active Ingredients, Causal Mechanisms, and Contexts

The primary goal of evaluation plans should be to investigate TOCs. In order to inform scaling and population impacts, evaluations should go beyond measuring outcomes. For example, evaluations should be designed to ask additional questions, including the following: Are our program strategies feasible and acceptable? Which program strategies are leading to expected changes in outcomes? Which causal mechanisms help explain impacts? For whom and under which conditions are program strategies operating or not operating as expected?

Identifying the strategies that drive changes is critical for making programs more efficient and scalable. In the field of prevention science, these specific strategies have been called "kernels" (Embry and Biglan 2008) or "active ingredients" (Center on the Developing Child 2016). Similarly, evaluations should aim to understand the underlying causal mechanisms that explain connections between strategies and outcomes. For example, in early childhood education programs, a common approach is to provide services to parents as a means to improving child outcomes. In a systematic analysis of early childhood education evaluations across 40 years, a majority of studies (N = 151) stated that improving parenting was a hypothesized causal mechanism. Yet only 18.5% of those studies actually included a measure of parenting in their evaluation (Schindler et al. 2019). This lack of information on causal mechanisms reduces our ability to understand *why* programs may work or not work as intended.

Lastly, it is critical for evaluations to shed light on for whom and under what conditions a program is likely to produce results (i.e., moderators). Although moderated program effects have historically been viewed as disappointing based on the hope that a single program will affect all participants, there is now greater acceptance that there is no "silver bullet." Instead, the larger goal of the field should be to offer a variety of programs and strategies that can be flexibly and appropriately matched with community needs, values, and contexts.

Understanding moderated impacts can help to inform this approach to achieving population impacts. Realizing when and why a program may benefit some children and not others (and at what costs) is also critical for identifying and responding to inequities in access, quality, and/or outcomes (Nores 2020).

Progress in this area is already underway. As the demand for evidence-based programs and policies has increased, there has been a renewed focus on TOCs, with some funders (e.g., Institute of Education Sciences) now requiring grantees to demonstrate alignment between TOCs and measures. Further, a new generation of early childhood programs has begun to utilize more fine-grained TOCs and evaluations to better understand mechanisms of change (Jones, Bub, and Raver 2013; McCormick et al. 2015; Bierman et al. 2008).

D. Employ Usable Measures of Quality and Fidelity

Fidelity and quality measures need not measure every aspect of a program; rather, they should focus on the core components or "active ingredients." This approach can help result in a streamlined measure that is more usable and continues to be applicable even as programs are scaled and adapted. Caron Bernard, and Metz (2021) detail three considerations in creating scalable measures of fidelity. First, it is important to consider the fidelity rater. While the standard has been to use independent raters, this is often impractical at scale. Instead, measures could be developed that can be implemented by practitioners. Second, brief fidelity measures (e.g., those that are valid even with partial observations) are more scalable than time-consuming measures. Third, when implemented at scale, it may be beneficial to streamline measures across programs with similar goals in order to fit into existing public systems. An example of this in early childhood is the use of statewide quality ratings of early childhood education programs. Though they have also had notable challenges, such ratings have proved useful in supporting cross-system comparisons and helping to identify differences in strengths and areas of improvement across programs (Weiland 2018). While more research is needed on the trade-offs of these approaches, they are worth strong consideration as potential ways to counteract existing challenges in scaling programs.

III. Designing Programs and Evaluations for Equity

The previous section delineates principles to aid programs in considering scale as an important design goal from the initial phases of development. Another pressing question is how to design programs and evaluations for equity. Designing programs and evaluations for equity requires viewing current systems and incentives focused on evidence-based programs and policies with a critical lens and a willingness to consider alternative processes and structures. In this section, I summarize three key ways to shift this work toward the pursuit of equitable outcomes.

A. Act on Inequities within Contexts

When working to better understand what programs work, for whom, and under what conditions, it is important to pay particular attention to the historical and present social, political, and cultural contexts in which the program is being implemented (Loper, Woo, and Metz 2021). For example, what are the ways that groups may have been oppressed based on race and ethnicity, immigration status, gender identity, or other characteristics? How do these conditions shape the implementation context? In what ways can the program attend to related micro and macro issues, such as structural racism? Turning attention to these questions may lead to different processes in the design and scaling of programs. For example, understanding the historical inequities within a context may lead to changes in who leads program development, who implements the program, where the program is located, how active ingredients are designed, and how program success is defined.

B. Center Relationships

From program design to taking a program to scale, there are often multiple stakeholders involved. These stakeholders may include program developers, researchers, policymakers, and/or affected community members. In order to shift power from traditional stakeholders to community members, centering relationships should be central throughout the work. This idea is not new; researcher-community partnerships have been written about for many years (Tseng, Easton, and Supplee 2017; Tikunoff and Ward 1983; Wagner 1997), and examples of instances in which strong relationships have grounded the development and implementation of programs are growing (e.g., see special issues of *Stanford Social Innovation Review* [Summer 2021 Supplement] and *Child Development* [Golinkoff, Hirsh-Pasek, Grob, and Schlesinger (eds.) 2017]).

Building authentic relationships requires community outsiders to consistently show up, be good listeners, create spaces for and act upon feedback, and lift up the expertise and experiences of community. These relationships are not built overnight; rather, they are built through frequent and lasting interactions that form a foundation of trust. The types of authentic relationships that can lead to equitable program development, implementation, and scaling is part of the "heart work" that is often left out of frameworks for implementation science and evidence-based policymaking, particularly as programs go to scale. It is important to recognize that the relationships built and decisions made in initial development of a program may not be applicable in new contexts or communities. New relationships need to be nurtured as programs expand and adapt over time.

C. Build Community-Defined Evidence

Evidence-based policymaking has typically relied on RCTs and standardized assessments as the gold standards for deeming a program "evidence-based." Alternatively, community-defined evidence "supports the notion that credible and useful evidence is not the exclusive purview of randomized controlled trials" (Loper, Woo, and Metz 2021, 4).

Community-defined evidence focuses on outcomes and successes as defined by the community and may take on other forms and functions that draw upon the community's assets, desires, and history. A shift toward community-defined evidence requires program developers, policymakers, and funders to see as valid other forms of evidence, including but not limited to qualitative interviews, storytelling, and community-led listening sessions (Ryan 2020). These forms of evidence can be critical not just in the early stages of development, but also in addressing evaluation questions related to a program's TOC. For example, key questions include the following: Are our program strategies feasible and acceptable? Which program strategies are leading to expected changes in outcomes? For whom and under which conditions are program strategies operating or not operating as expected?

IV. From Designing Programs to Changing Systems

Designing programs with an eye toward scaling and equity is necessary but not sufficient to achieve equitable population outcomes. Changes in policy and funding systems are also needed. This will require the development and testing of innovative approaches to multisystem collaboration and public and private funding (Dodge 2022; Yoshikawa et al. 2018). As referenced earlier in this chapter, multiple sectors influence the services and programs that touch the lives of children, youth, and families. Reducing silos through coordination at local and national levels requires regular interactions among leadership pertaining to a particular area of policy. Such interactions can be coordinated by a specific planning agency or independent convener (Yoshikawa et al. 2018). A more transformative approach that has been proposed is to move away from separate programs housed in different systems toward a more universal system of care and support for children and families (Dodge 2022).

Funding systems should also be critically examined to ensure that funding processes center principles of equity and attend to problematic power dynamics. While policymakers should continue to invest in programs with promising impacts, we should also expand funding beyond existing evidence-based programs so that more culturally responsive and community-developed programs are appropriately resourced and made more widely available. Indeed, it is becoming increasingly recognized that many evidence-based programs are decades old and may not fit the diversity of cultures, experiences, and needs of present-day society.

One promising example of a local government initiative working to expand the definition of evidence-based programming through community-based funding is Best Starts for Kids of King County (an initiative that I have been involved with). This levy-funded initiative includes a prenatal to age five years innovation fund in which community-based organizations receive direct funding and supports to develop, implement, evaluate, and scale community-driven innovations that respond to community-identified strengths and challenges (King County Best Starts for Kids 2019). This initiative has worked to implement values of equity and social justice, co-creation, clarity, shared learning, and responsive adaptation. Strode and Morris (2021) also emphasize the importance of centering equity in funder-grantee relationships through developing trust and intentionally shifting power. They suggest trust-building activities that include providing adequate resources, funding ecosystems that support the work, reducing burdensome administrative requirements, and relying on the grantee's vision.

V. Discussion and Conclusions

Evidence-based policymaking is at a crossroads. Its progress over the past several decades has brought a greater focus on evaluation and using data to inform the allocation of resources. It has also created more opportunities for dialogue and collaboration between researchers and policymakers. Yet it has fallen short of its primary goal of realizing population outcomes for children, families, and communities. We have since learned that early evidence from rigorous evaluations is not sufficient for predicting benefits to expanded populations. Further, the reliance on a narrow definition of "evidence-based" that is tied to funding has had the unintended consequences of overemphasizing statistical significance and average impacts, as well as underemphasizing the value of community voice and equity-focused implementation. How should evidence-based policymaking move forward? What new directions should it take as we learn about its strengths and shortcomings? In this chapter, I summarize a number of threats to achieving impacts at scale and identify multiple ways that programs and systems might attend to those threats. I also call for an expanded definition and use of "evidence."

The recommendations outlined aim to move us away from the long-standing debates about whether programs work or not. This false dichotomy negatively affects evaluation research and decisions about what programs receive public support and investment. Take preschool as an example. In an effort to make decisions about funding, policymakers have long asked whether or not preschool "works," and for decades evaluations have been designed in an attempt to answer that question. As it turns out, the answer is quite nuanced and depends on a number of factors that have yet to be fully identified, including variation in access, content, implementation, and populations. Evidence-based policymaking should shift to incentivize a greater articulation and evaluation of programmatic TOCs, so that we can move toward identifying active ingredients, causal mechanisms, and contexts. At the same time, programs with intentions to scale should be developed with parsimony and flexibility in mind.

Population outcomes will also require greater attention to equity and systems-level changes. When outsiders to impacted communities are involved in program development, evaluation, policymaking, and/or other decisions, there should be more consideration of social, political, and cultural contexts. Authentic, enduring relationships that intentionally elevate power within communities should be prioritized. We should also critically examine the definition of "evidence-based" through an equity lens. Whose definition is currently prioritized? Whose voices are left out? What disparities exist in terms of who receives funding based on the current definition? How might we move toward a greater focus on community-defined evidence? Attending to these questions is vital to making policy and funding systems more equitable.

The road ahead is not an easy one. There will inevitably be challenges in addressing these issues and working toward system-level change, population impacts, and equity. As we continue to grapple with how to scale from "small to bigger" and "big to better," we will surely learn new lessons that can inform future directions. The way forward will necessitate that we continuously examine evidence-based policymaking, its intended purpose, and how it can best achieve its goals. Further, new ways of working together and funding programs are needed to shift more power into the hands of communities to lead program development, while also providing supports in leveraging resources to implement, evaluate, and scale community-driven innovations.

References

Baron, Jon. 2018. A brief history of evidence-based policy. *Annals of the American Academy of Political and Social Sciences*, 678:40–50.

Bierman, Karen L., Celene E. Domitrovich, Robert L. Nix, Scott D. Gest, Janet A. Welsh, Mark T. Greenberg, Clancy Blair, Keith E. Nelson, and Sukhdeep Gill. 2008. Promoting academic and social-emotional school readiness: The Head Start REDI program. *Child Development*, 79:1802–1817.

Camilli, Gregory, Sadako Vargas, Sharon Ryan, and W. Steven Barnett. 2010. Meta-analysis of the effects of early education interventions on cognitive and social development. *Teachers College Record*, 112:579–620.

Campbell, Frances A., Elizabeth P. Pungello, Margaret Burchinal, Kirsten Kainz, Yi Pan, Barbara H. Wasik, Oscar A. Barbarin, Joseph J. Sparling, and Craig T. Ramey. 2012. Adult outcomes as a function of an early childhood educational program: An Abecedarian Project follow-up. *Developmental Psychology*, 48:1033–1043.

Campbell, Frances A., Craig T. Ramey, Elizabeth Pungello, Joseph Sparling, and Shari Miller-Johnson. 2002. Early childhood education: Young adult outcomes from the Abecedarian Project. *Applied Developmental Science*, 6:42–57.

Caron, Eb, Kristin Bernard, and Allison Metz. 2021. Fidelity and properties of the situation: Challenges and recommendations. In *The scale-up effect in early childhood and public policy: Why interventions lose impact at scale and what we can do about it*, edited by John A. List, Dana Suskind, and Lauren H. Supplee, 16–183. New York: Routledge.

Center on the Developing Child. 2016. *From best practices to breakthrough impacts: A science based approach to building a more promising future for young children and families.* Cambridge, MA: Center on the Developing Child. www.developingchild.harvard.edu.

Chen, Huey T. 1990. *Theory-driven evaluations*. Newbury Park, CA: SAGE.

Chen, Huey T., and Peter H. Rossi, eds. 1992. *Using theory to improve program and policy evaluations*. Contributions in Political Science, no. 290. New York: Greenwood.

Coryn, Chris L.S., Lindsay A. Noakes, Carl D. Westine, and Daniela C. Schröter. 2011. A systematic review of theory-driven evaluation practice from 1990 to 2009. *American Journal of Evaluation*, 32:199–226.

Dodge, Kenneth A. 2022. Presidential address: Forging a developmental science mission to improve population outcomes and eliminate disparities for young children. *Child Development*, 93:313–325.

Embry, Dennis D., and Anthony Biglan. 2008. Evidence-based kernels: Fundamental units of behavioral influence. *Clinical Child and Family Psychology Review*, 11:75–113.

Grindal, Todd, Jocelyn Bonnes Bowne, Hirokazu Yoshikawa, Holly S. Schindler, Greg J. Duncan, Katherine Magnuson, and Jack P. Shonkoff. 2016. The added impact of parenting education in early childhood education programs: A meta-analysis. *Children and Youth Services Review* 70:238–249.

Gupta, Snigdha, Lauren H. Supplee, Dana Suskind, and John A. List. 2021. Failed to scale: Embracing the challenge of scaling in early childhood. In *The scale-up effect in early childhood and public policy: Why interventions lose impact at scale and what we can do about it*, edited by John A. List, Dana Suskind, and Lauren H. Supplee, 1–21. New York: Routledge.

Jones, Stephanie M., Kristen L. Bub, and C. Cybele Raver. 2013. Unpacking the black box of the CSRP intervention: The mediating roles of teacher-child relationship quality and self-regulation. *Early Education and Development*, 24:1043–1064.

Kania, John, Junious Williams, Paul Schmitz, Sheri Brady, Mark Kramer, and Jennifer Splansky Juster. 2022. Centering equity in collective impact. *Stanford Social Innovation Review*, Winter: 38–45. https://ssir.org/articles/entry/centering_equity_in_collective_impact.

Karoly, Lynn A., M. Rebecca Kilburn, and Jill S. Cannon. 2005. *Early childhood interventions: Proven results, future promise*. Santa Monica, CA: RAND Corporation.

King County Best Starts for Kids. 2019. *Annual report: Communities building impact*. King County, WA: King County Best Starts for Kids. https://www.kingcounty.gov/~/media/depts/community-human-services/best-starts-kids/documents/BSK_2019_AnnualReport.ashx?la=en.

List, John A., Dana Suskind, and Lauren H. Supplee, eds. 2021. *The scale-up effect in early childhood and public policy: Why interventions lose impact at scale and what we can do about it*. New York: Routledge.

Loper, Audrey, Beadsie Woo, and Allison Metz. 2021. Equity is fundamental to implementation science. *Stanford Social Innovation Review*, Supplement: 3–5.

Lyon, Aaron. 2021. Designing programs with an eye toward scaling. In *The scale-up effect in early childhood and public policy: Why interventions lose impact at scale and what we can do about it*, edited by John A. List, Dana Suskind, and Lauren H. Supplee, 251–264. New York: Routledge.

McCormick, Meghan P., Elise Cappella, Erin E. O'Connor, and Sandee G. McClowry. 2015. Social-emotional learning and academic achievement: Using causal methods to explore classroom-level mechanisms. *AERA Open*, 1:1–26.

Mooney, Paul, Michael H. Epstein, Robert Reid, and J. Ron Nelson. 2003. Status of and trends in academic intervention research for students with emotional disturbance. *Remedial and Special Education*, 24:273–287.

Nores, Milagros. 2020. *Equity as a perspective for implementation research in the early childhood field*. New York: Foundation for Child Development.

Ryan, Sharon. 2020. *The contributions of qualitative research to understanding implementation of early childhood policies and programs*. New York: Foundation for Child Development.

Schindler, Holly, Philip A. Fisher, and Jack P. Shonkoff. 2017. From innovation to impact at scale: Lessons learned from a cluster of research-community partnerships. *Child Development*, 88:1435–1446.

Schindler, Holly S., Dana Charles McCoy, Philip A. Fisher, and Jack P. Shonkoff. 2019. A historical look at theories of change in early childhood research. *Early Childhood Research Quarterly*, 48:146–154.

Schweinhart, Larry. 2005. *Lifetime effects: The High/Scope Perry Preschool Study through age 40*. Ypsilanti, MI: High/Scope Press.

Shonkoff, Jack P. 2017. Rethinking the definition of evidence-based interventions to promote early childhood development. *Pediatrics*, 140:1–2.

Shonkoff, Jack P., and Philip A. Fisher. 2013. Rethinking evidence-based practice and two-generation programs to create the future of early childhood policy. *Developmental Psychopathology*, 25:1635–1653.

Smith, Stephen W., Ann P. Daunic, and Gregory G. Taylor. 2007. Treatment fidelity in applied educational research: Expanding the adoption and application of measures to ensure evidence-based practice. *Education and Treatment of Children*, 30:121–134.

Strode, Blake, and Amy Morris. 2021. Trust the people. *Stanford Social Innovation Review*, 19 (3): A5–A8.

Tikunoff, William J., and Beatrice A. Ward. 1983. Collaborative research on teaching. *Elementary School Journal*, 83:453–468.

Tseng, Vivian, John Q. Easton, and Lauren H. Supplee. 2017. Practice partnerships: Building two-way streets of engagement. *Social Policy Report*, 30:1–17.

US Department of Health and Human Services. 2019. *Maternal, infant, and early childhood home visiting*. Rockville, MD: Health Resources and Services Administration. http://mchb.hrsa.gov/programs/homevisiting/.

Wagner, Jon. 1997. The unavoidable intervention of educational research: A framework for reconsidering researcher-practitioner cooperation. *Educational Researcher*, 26:13–22.

Weiland, Chris. 2018. Commentary: Pivoting to the "how": Moving preschool policy, practice, and research forward. *Early Childhood Research Quarterly*, 45:188–192.

Weiss, Carol H. 1972. *Methods for assessing program effectiveness*. Englewood Cliffs, NJ: Prentice Hall.

Weiss, Carol H. 1995. Nothing as practical as good theory: Exploring theory-based evaluation for comprehensive community initiatives for children and families. *New Approaches to Evaluating Community Initiatives: Concepts, Methods, and Contexts*, 1:65–92.

Weiss, Carol H. 1997. Theory-based evaluation: Past, present, and future. *New Directions for Evaluation*, 76:41–55.

Yoshikawa, Hirokazu, Alice J. Wuermli, Abbie Raikes, Sharon Kim, and Sarah B. Kabay. 2018. Toward high-quality early childhood development programs and policies at national scale: Directions for research in global contexts. *Social Policy Report*, 31:1–36.

PART II

JUVENILE JUSTICE

This part examines the role of evidence-based policy in the juvenile justice system. It includes chapters that focus on key stages of processing and leading programs and practices, as well as reflections on the promises and limitations of the evidence-based framework for youth justice. There are six chapters.

CHAPTER 6

ADVANCING THE EVIDENCE-BASED ERA
Twenty-Five Years of Lessons Learned in Washington State's Juvenile Justice System

ELIZABETH K. DRAKE AND
LAUREN KNOTH-PETERSON

MORE than two decades ago, Washington became the first state to require juvenile courts to use evidence-based programs (EBPs) to address the needs of youth involved in the juvenile justice system.[1] Since then, Washington State has been a national leader, developing and implementing a standardized research approach for evidence-based policymaking (Drake, Aos, and Miller 2009; Elliott et al. 2020; Pew Center on the States 2012; Welsh and Farrington 2015; Welsh, Farrington, and Gowar 2015; VanLandingham and Drake 2012). Through the Results First Initiative, the Washington State Institute for Public Policy's (WSIPP) research and benefit-cost approach has been used in 26 US states and various counties in at least five states (Pew Center on the States 2012), and its work has been used in other countries, including the United Kingdom (Dartington Social Research Unit, n.d.) and Australia (New South Wales Government 2018).

Since the initial evidence-based policy efforts began in 1997, Washington State's juvenile justice system has undergone significant changes through reforms of local court practices, increased coordination between state agencies and juvenile court administrators, and early investments in research. From these changes, the number of youths involved in the juvenile justice system (arrested) has declined by 72% over 30 years. Courts have reduced local confinement sentences by 55% during this same period, opting to treat youth with evidence-based programs in the community. Despite these statewide gains, recent research has revealed that some of the programs and policies implemented 20 years ago may not be effective for the current population of court-involved youth. For example, WSIPP found that the Washington State Aggression Replacement Training (WSART) program was effective at reducing recidivism for youth in the early 2000s (Barnoski 2002; Barnoski 2004b). A more recent evaluation, however, found that WSART may increase recidivism rates for some court-involved youth (Knoth, Wanner, and He 2019a).[2] These findings suggest that as the characteristics of court-involved youth and associated structures change, the subsequent effectiveness of programs or practices may also change. Program outcome evaluations are typically conducted in isolation (Hsieh et al. 2021), without consideration or discussion of systemic or structural factors. Rarely has research assessed the system as a whole for court-involved youth to understand how different policy changes or changes in populations affect each other or other aspects of the juvenile and adult justice systems over time.

In this chapter, we describe the policymaking context of Washington State's juvenile justice system, the corresponding interactions between research and policymaking, and the successes, challenges, and lessons learned in Washington over this 25-year endeavor.[3] In the first section, we define the basic structure, key players, and major legislative changes in the juvenile justice system relevant to implementing evidence-based public policies over this time period. Second, we describe WSIPP's research on the juvenile justice system and how this research has been incorporated into practice. Third, we discuss changes in Washington State's justice-involved youth populations over time and describe some of the current challenges when conducting research in a court setting. Finally, we suggest pathways for a new wave of research required for evidence-based policymaking to address the complex needs of the juvenile justice population.

I. Washington State Juvenile Justice System

A. Juvenile Courts

In Washington State, 33 juvenile courts serve as the administrative authority for youth (under the age of 18) who come into contact with the justice system (Revised Code of Washington [RCW] 13.40). Broadly, the juvenile courts process cases for youth who engage in nondelinquent[4] or criminal behaviors (RCW Title 9A). Local prosecutors have the discretion to determine whether to prosecute the accused for a crime.[5] Youth adjudicated and found guilty by the juvenile court receive a disposition according to Washington's juvenile sentencing standards (RCW 13.40.0357). Based on the seriousness of the current offense and the youth's prior adjudications, judges impose a disposition of either local sanctions or a term of confinement in a state facility. The vast majority of adjudicated youth receive local sanctions (Luu 2018), which can include a period of confinement, probation, fines, community service, or other sanctions carried out by the local probation department. Youth whose dispositions include more than 30 days of confinement (RCW 13.40.020) are within the legal jurisdiction of Juvenile Rehabilitation within the Washington State Department of Children, Youth, and Families (DCYF).

Some youth may enter into a formal diversion agreement or receive a deferred disposition. For diversion, youth sign a formal agreement with the local probation department, which provides local services in lieu of formal prosecution (RCW 13.40.080). For deferred disposition, youth are prosecuted under a stipulated agreement after admitting guilt, and the court imposes a term of local supervision that may include conditions such as mandatory participation in treatment (RCW 13.40.127). Youth who successfully complete the terms of a diversion agreement or deferred disposition have the charges dismissed and removed from the youth's record, or they are permanently sealed.

B. Major Juvenile Justice Legislation

Each year, the Washington State Legislature passes numerous bills that impact the juvenile justice system (Washington State Caseload Forecast Council 2019). Typically, these changes are minor modifications in the criminal code; however, the legislature has periodically undertaken major legislative reforms. Two major historical reforms serve as the statutory foundation of Washington's current juvenile justice system. More recent legislative reforms have also impacted the juvenile justice system in terms of who is included, and what and how court-involved youth receive services.

In the 1970s, increasing juvenile arrest rates in Washington and across the nation led to growing concerns about serious and violent juvenile crime (Aos 2002; Feld 2017). In response, the legislature passed the bipartisan Juvenile Justice Act of 1977, which changed the statewide juvenile justice system to a determinate sentencing system (Boerner and Lieb 2001; Lieb and Brown 1999). The 1977 act marked a historical turning point in the juvenile justice system (Feld 2017). Washington was the first state to adopt sentencing guidelines for juveniles, and the same basic structure exists today (Aos 2002; Lieb and Brown 1999; RCW 13.40.010). The 1977 act shifted the decision to intervene with youth from probation staff to the local prosecuting attorney's office. The goals of the legislation included increased consistency through sentencing standards, increased accountability for youth who committed criminal offenses, and increased responses to the treatment needs of youth (RCW 13.40.010). The sentencing standards are based on the youth's age, the seriousness of the current offense, and the youth's prior adjudications (RCW 13.40.0357). Judges may depart from the presumptive sentencing guidelines and impose sentences above or below the standard range in limited and explicit circumstances (Lieb and Brown 1999; RCW 13.40.160; RCW 13.40.0357). Ninety-five percent of all sentences in 2018 fell within the standard range (Luu 2018).

The second major legislative reform occurred when the legislature passed the Community Juvenile Accountability Act (CJAA) in 1997 with bipartisan support (RCW 13.40.500–540).[6] The law recognized the importance that local entities (e.g., government, community groups) play in impacting crime rates. The purpose of CJAA was to "provide a continuum of community-based" care (RCW 13.40.500–540) to improve youth skills so they can function crime-free in the community (RCW 13.40.500). The CJAA modified sentencing standards, giving judges more options for youth who need treatment for substance abuse, mental health, or sexual offending in the community in lieu of confinement in a residential facility with Juvenile Rehabilitation (RCW 13.40.0357).

With the passage of the CJAA, Washington State became the first state to mandate the development of an evidence-based juvenile justice system and to fund collaborative efforts between researchers and practitioners to support efforts to rehabilitate court-involved youth. The CJAA required that state-funded programs delivered by the local courts must "cost-effectively reduce recidivism" (RCW 13.40.500; RCW 13.40.530). WSIPP was directed to develop standards for measuring the effectiveness of programs (Barnoski 1997; RCW 13.40.530) and to evaluate the costs and benefits of programs funded under the CJAA (RCW 13.40.500). A statewide advisory committee was created to oversee the continuum of care between state and local governments.

Since the passage of the CJAA, a new wave of recent legislation has modified the structure of the juvenile justice system in several ways. First, legislation has integrated developmental science related to the culpability of youth. Neuroscientists have demonstrated that adolescent brains are not fully developed until the age of 25 (Feld 2017; Scott and Steinberg 2008). The United States Supreme Court (*Graham v. Florida*, 560 U.S. 48 [2010]; *Miller v. Alabama*, 132 U.S. 2455 [2012]; *Roper v. Simmons*, 542 U.S. 551 [2005]) and the Washington State Supreme Court (*State v. Bassett*, 192 Wn.2d 67 [2018]) have also issued rulings that the use of capital punishment and life sentences without parole are unconstitutional for youth who commit crime before the age of 18. Drawing on the same developmental science research and court rulings, legislation in 2018 marked a formal shift in the contemporary juvenile justice system based on the culpability of youth and the responsibility of care for those youth (Washington State 65th Legislature 2018). The law changed the jurisdiction for youth, allowing certain youth to be retained in the juvenile justice system rather than be transferred to the adult court system. This legislation also raised the age of juvenile court jurisdiction from age 21 to age 25 for individuals convicted of a serious offense committed prior to the age of 18, allowing youth to serve their confinement sentence in a residential facility with the Washington State Juvenile Rehabilitation until age 25 before transferring to the Washington State Department of Corrections (Drake 2013a).

The second recent legislative change expanded access to evidence-based treatment for referred and diverted youth. A 2019 law gave courts the ability to receive state EBP funds for any youth referred to the prosecutor's office (Washington State 66th Legislature 2019). The law now includes youth referred to a program who have not been formally diverted or charged with an offense, or youth who would have been formally diverted or charged with an offense in the absence of the program to which the youth was referred.

In summary, the juvenile justice system in Washington State has changed significantly since 1977. Early legislative reforms focused initially on consistency in sentencing and the prioritization of criminal justice resources for youth convicted of more serious offenses or with longer criminal histories. The late 1990s brought legislative changes to prioritize the use of evidence-based policies, shifting from a juvenile justice model based on punishment to a model focused on rehabilitation and recidivism. In recent years, the legislature has acknowledged the need for reforms based on adolescent developmental science and the complex needs of youth involved in multiple systems. For example, the legislature created the DCYF, a new executive agency with the goal of improving services for youth and families, by combining several state agencies into one agency to deliver services for early learning, child welfare, and juvenile justice.[7] These larger structural changes reflect the legislature's acknowledgment that youth in the juvenile justice system have complex needs that are best attended to in a system designed for youth. These legislative reforms have impacted Washington State's justice-involved youth populations substantially, including changes in who becomes involved in the system, at what point they become involved, and what services those youth are offered.

II. EVIDENCE-BASED PUBLIC POLICYMAKING

Since the 1990s, the Washington State Legislature has taken a number of steps to develop an evidence-based juvenile justice system (Knoth et al. 2019c).[8] The central concept has been to identify and implement strategies shown through rigorous research to reduce crime in a cost-effective manner. This section provides an overview of WSIPP's role in juvenile justice research and discusses WSIPP's approach to operationalizing evidence-based requirements in Washington.

A. Washington State Institute for Public Policy

As defined in its bylaws, "The mission of the Washington State Institute for Public Policy is to assist policymakers, particularly those in the legislature, in making informed judgments about important, long-term issues facing Washington State" (WSIPP 2016, 1). WSIPP carries out its mission as an interdisciplinary research team committed to the values of "nonpartisanship, quality, and impartiality" (WSIPP, n.d.a). Since its establishment in 1983, WSIPP has operated primarily as a project-funded organization and has received its assignments from the legislature through enacted policy or budget bills or studies approved by its board of directors. Fields of study for WSIPP include juvenile and adult criminal justice as well as issues related to behavioral health, child welfare, healthcare, public health, education, workforce training, transportation, and other issues of public importance.

WSIPP occupies a unique space between academic institutions and policymaking agencies. Like academics, WSIPP conducts rigorous statistical research aimed at identifying causal relationships and isolating the unique effects of different policy or program interventions. WSIPP's research must be easily accessible and understood by policymakers and practitioners who use these findings for decision-making. WSIPP frequently serves as a bridge between policymakers and the academic research that provides the evidence for policy decisions. WSIPP's unique role at the nexus of academic research, policymaking, and practitioner implementation has fostered decades of policy decisions that are directly related to research findings (Drake et al. 2009; Vanlandingham and Drake 2012).

At the direction of the legislature, WSIPP has written 82 reports examining the juvenile justice system since the passage of the 1997 CJAA.[9] More than three-quarters of these reports were legislatively mandated. Nearly half of the reports originated from four major pieces of juvenile justice legislation, in 1994, 1997, 1999, and 2012. These major study assignments allocated ongoing research funds for a distinct period of time (e.g., CJAA), but WSIPP has not received ongoing assignments in juvenile justice to evaluate the effectiveness of the implementation of evidence-based programs in Washington. Of the 82 reports written, the most common (45%) were outcome evaluations of a specific juvenile justice program or policy in Washington, followed by systematic reviews/meta-analysis (22%). Prior to 2008, WSIPP conducted more outcome evaluations of programs operating in Washington, whereas later assignments were systematic reviews of the external research literature (Knoth et al. 2019c). Both types of research evidence offer important information, and Washington has relied on both for decision-making. The remaining studies were descriptive or for the development of the juvenile court risk assessment required for determining eligibility into EBPs (Barnoski 2004a, 2004b).

B. CJAA EBPs

As a part of the 1997 CJAA, the legislature directed WSIPP to identify cost-effective programs that reduce recidivism for youth involved in the juvenile justice system. Through systematic reviews of the literature, WSIPP identified several programs chosen for implementation in Washington's juvenile courts, including Functional Family Therapy (FFT), Coordination of Services (COS), and Multisystemic Therapy (MST) and WSART (Aos, Barnoski, and Lieb 1998; Barnoski 1999; Barnoski 2002; Fumia, Drake, and He 2015). Follow-up outcome evaluations of the implemented programs concluded that, for the most part, these programs were effective at reducing recidivism (Barnoski 2004b). Additional CJAA EBPs were added later as a part of the CJAA promising programs protocol (Drake 2010), including Education and Employment Training (EET) (Miller, Fumia, and He 2015) and Family Integrated Transitions (FIT) (Aos 2004). All CJAA EBPs meet the criteria for state funds disseminated to the local courts (Drake 2010).

WSIPP was also required to examine risk factors associated with criminal recidivism (Washington State 53rd Legislature 1994), and it developed and validated the Washington State Juvenile Court Assessment to determine a youth's risk for reoffense and guide case management (Barnoski 1999, 2004b). This seminal work served as the foundation (Barnoski 2004a) for future risk instruments that evolved to include risk, needs, and responsivity factors (Andrews and Bonta 2010) called the Positive Achievement Change Tool (Hamilton et al. 2019). Washington's risk assessment became the cornerstone for assessing and referring youth into CJAA EBPs aimed at reducing recidivism (Barnoski 2004a).

WSIPP has conducted numerous outcome evaluations of juvenile justice policies and programs in Washington to examine what programs reduce recidivism. Outcome evaluations allow researchers to examine the effectiveness of a program at improving certain outcomes (e.g., reducing recidivism). Following the initial implementation and evaluation of CJAA EBPs in the juvenile courts, a key finding demonstrated that WSART and FFT were effective only when delivered competently (Barnoski 2004b). Subsequently, WSIPP recommended quality control standards for juvenile court programs, highlighting the importance of developing a quality assurance system (Barnoski, Aos, and Lieb 2003) later implemented by the courts statewide. The quality assurance standards also highlighted the importance of data and research to monitor changes in court practices to ensure that legislative reforms maintained long-term effectiveness. The recommendations included (a) rigorous outcome evaluations of programs in Washington, (b) establishment of benchmarks to monitor program effectiveness annually, (c) establishment of completion rate standards for juvenile court EBPs, and (d) evaluations of interim outcomes (such as changes in dynamic risk characteristics) in addition to recidivism.

In 2019, WSIPP conducted a second follow-up evaluation and found that WSART participants from 2005 through 2015 were more likely to recidivate than similar youth who did not participate (Knoth et al. 2019a). Unlike previous findings (Barnoski 2004b), effectiveness did not vary based on the competence of trainers. However, youth who completed the curriculum were significantly less likely to recidivate than youth who participated in, but did not complete, the WSART program. This study raised the question of whether trainer competence was measured accurately by the WSART quality assurance protocols. The quality assurance protocols that were developed to assess program and trainer fidelity have not been validated through empirical research to ensure that they reliably measure trainer competency.

Initial legislative reforms in Washington included significant investments in research to assist with policymaking decisions. Following the implementation of these changes, however, investments in large-scale research in the juvenile justice system declined—most notably after the initial outcome evaluations for CJAA programs. Most of WSIPP's early reports were tied to major pieces of legislation (i.e., CJAA) and fewer outcome evaluations have been conducted by WSIPP since.

C. EBP Inventories

One core part of WSIPP's work has been to answer legislative questions about "what works" to impact outcomes. To answer this question, WSIPP implements a rigorous research approach with standardized procedures (WSIPP 2019b). These procedures establish a high standard of rigor and allow for a standardized comparison of different programs. First, researchers identify what works (and what does not) through outcome evaluations or systematic meta-analytic reviews. WSIPP includes studies that meet minimum standards of rigor and codes all outcomes of interest. When conducting outcome evaluations, WSIPP attempts to meet our own minimum standards of rigor (WSIPP 2019b) for systematic reviews to reach causal conclusions about a program's effectiveness. When it is not possible to use a research design that meets our own minimum standards, we indicate that the study is descriptive. WSIPP's outcome evaluations must meet the same minimum standards of rigor for inclusion in the meta-analysis.

When directed and possible, WSIPP conducts a benefit-cost analysis to assess the program's return on investment using its benefit-cost model (WSIPP 2019b). WSIPP built its first benefit-cost model in 1997 to determine whether prevention and juvenile justice programs shown to reduce crime were also cost-beneficial (Aos 1999; Aos, Barnoski, and Lieb 1998; Aos et al. 1999; Aos et al. 2004). The economic model provides a standardized, internally consistent monetary valuation of the benefits and costs of each program, per participant (WSIPP 2019b). WSIPP continues to develop and improve this model and has applied this approach to more than 400 programs and policies across different public policy areas (WSIPP 2019). For juvenile justice programs, WSIPP examines the monetary benefits of programs to taxpayers and victims of crime from reduced recidivism (Drake et al. 2009). Effect sizes are combined from step one with information about base populations in Washington and costs of criminal justice system resources (e.g., police, courts, corrections). Although any outcome can be systematically coded for the meta-analysis, not all outcomes have been monetized for WSIPP's benefit-cost analysis. Further, many outcome evaluations do not measure or report outcomes that could be monetized using the benefit-cost model. As a final step, WSIPP also assesses the risk of investing in a program by exploring the chances that the program will at least break even. Through a Monte Carlo risk simulation, the benefit-cost model runs 10,000 times, varying key inputs randomly to determine the proportion of time that a program's benefits are projected to exceed its costs.

When required by the legislature, WSIPP also classifies and defines programs as evidence-based, research-based, or promising, and produces an "inventory" list of programs by classification using the results from meta-analysis/benefit-cost analyses. Inventories that guide funding (Welsh and Greenwood 2015) are produced for juvenile justice, child welfare, and children's behavioral health services (Wanner et al. 2020) and adult corrections (Drake 2013a; Drake et al. 2009; WSIPP and EBPI 2019).[10] The first inventory came from the 2012 legislature, which required that prevention and intervention services delivered to children and youth in the mental health, child welfare, and juvenile justice systems should be increasingly "evidence-based" or "research-based" programs (Washington State 62nd Legislature 2012). The legislature directed WSIPP to use its methods for systematic reviews to classify programs based on the available evidence of effectiveness and associated benefits and costs. WSIPP's standardized meta-analysis and benefit-cost analysis provide the foundation for these inventory classifications. WSIPP's analyses and program classifications can change across iterations of the inventory due to updates in research evidence or methods. In 2019, WSIPP updated its juvenile justice analyses, including literature reviews, meta-analysis, benefit-cost analysis, and inventory classification (Knoth et al. 2019c; Wanner et al. 2020; WSIPP and EBPI 2019). In the 2019 iteration (Wanner et al. 2020), the classifications for several juvenile justice programs changed after incorporating the results from more recent studies and improvements to the benefit-cost estimates of programs, including the downgrading of WSART from evidence-based to null.

III. The Evolution of Populations and Complications of Practical Research

WSIPP has played a key role in producing research to help practitioners and policymakers incorporate evidence into public policies. Although Washington has experienced many successes over several decades, recent research also shows the importance of ongoing outcome evaluations (Barnoski et al. 2003) and monitoring to ensure that programs are successful in achieving their intended outcomes (Knoth et al. 2019a). Broader changes in the juvenile justice population may impact program effectiveness and create new research challenges.

A. Youth Involved in the Juvenile Justice System

Since the passage of major juvenile justice legislation in the 1990s, the number of youth involved in the juvenile justice system in Washington has substantially declined.[11] The number of youth arrested and adjudicated in Washington State has declined since 2003 by 59% and 69%, respectively. The juvenile courts are required to submit information on juvenile case adjudications resulting in only a guilty plea, meaning these figures do not include statewide data on youth adjudicated with a diversion or deferred disposition (Luu 2018). Thus, we cannot know from the publicly available cross-sectional data whether the observed decline in dispositions represents a decline in youth being charged with a criminal offense or if it represents an increase in the courts' use of diversion dispositions instead of conviction dispositions.

Along with a decrease in formally disposed youth, the average prior adjudication score has also decreased for justice-involved youth. Over the last 14 years, the age of court-involved youth adjudicated for their first offense increased by 8%. These changes do not necessarily mean that youth have fewer previous contacts with the justice system. Decreases in the prior adjudication score of court-involved youth may be due to increases in the use of pre-filing and post-filing diversion programs. Consequently, it may be inappropriate to compare youth with no prior adjudication score in 2020 to youth with no prior adjudication score in 2000. As reforms seek to divert youth prior to formal adjudication, we expect that the average prior adjudication score would also decrease.

Washington's juvenile justice population has declined over the past few decades, but data limitations impact our understanding of the complex factors that have impacted this change. Juvenile confinement sanctions range from up to 30 days in a local detention center to up to 260 weeks in confinement at a state-operated facility with Juvenile Rehabilitation (RCW 13.40.0357). The rate of youth admitted in local detention facilities and the average daily population of youth confined in state residential facilities has declined by 68% and 62%, respectively, over the last 10 years. The majority of court-involved youth receive local sanctions, which are served while supervised by a juvenile probation counselor (JPC) in the community. Youth sanctioned with community supervision must complete a juvenile court risk assessment to determine the level of risk, need for treatment, and eligibility for CJAA-EBPs. Although risk assessments results are accessible, there are no annual reports that track the risk-level classifications of youth adjudicated in juvenile courts. Thus, we do not know at the state population level whether there have been changes in the distribution of risk or needs, as the number of court-involved youth has also declined, as has the recidivism rate for court-involved youth. In 2019, WSIPP published a report examining changes in the recidivism rate for nearly 20 years of various court-involved populations (Knoth et al. 2019b). Overall, the decline in recidivism rates was evident across all demographic subpopulations and among youth who were adjudicated for all types of delinquent offenses.

Although these descriptive statistics indicate that the juvenile justice population has changed, we lack a comprehensive understanding of how the characteristics of the population and case outcomes have changed during this time. Information published by various state agencies suggests that the populations of justice-involved youth have changed significantly over the last two decades, and far fewer youth are involved in the juvenile justice system now compared to the late 1990s. Fewer youth are being detained in local detention facilities or in residential state facilities, and the proportion of youth convicted of a criminal offense who were sentenced to confinement has remained relatively stable over time.[12] Court-involved youth have fewer prior adjudications and are less likely to recidivate than court-involved youth in the early 2000s.

These annual reports published by state agencies provide critical information about various aspects of the juvenile justice system, and many are used to inform resource allocations to juvenile courts. However, these independent reports do not allow for a holistic understanding of how the system has changed over time. Data comes from different state agencies that have reported on characteristics of youth involved in the juvenile justice system at different time periods using varying methods, which make it impossible to establish a comprehensive understanding of how Washington's juvenile justice population has changed over time. To our knowledge, no comprehensive report has analyzed how characteristics of justice-involved youth in Washington have changed over the last 20 years. Further, few direct evaluations of Washington State's populations have been requested by the legislature to examine these systemic and population characteristics.

B. Current Research Challenges

Just as the populations of court-involved youth and the types of programs necessary to treat those youth have changed over time, so too have the approaches to research and our understanding of what works for justice-involved youth populations. WSIPP's original quality assurance recommendations acknowledged that the effectiveness of programs or practices may also change as the system changes over time (Barnoski, Lieb, and Aos 2003). WSIPP's work has highlighted several challenges from these systemic changes when producing public policy research.

1. *Treatment as Usual versus No Treatment*

To isolate the unique effect of participating in an EBP, rigorous evaluations require identifying a group of youth who participated in a program and a comparable group of youth who did not participate in the program (Shadish, Cook, and Campbell 2002). Random assignment studies that are well-implemented can help isolate a treatment effect, but in the absence of randomization, researchers must rely on quasi-experimental designs that use statistical methods to approximate random assignment.[13] For example, in the initial evaluations of CJAA EBPs programs, WSIPP took advantage of the gradual implementation and approximated random assignment by using a waitlist approach, since most programs had limited capacity during the first few years of implementation. Consequently, the selection into an EBP was essentially random, and any differences in outcomes for the youth receiving the program and the youth not receiving the program could be attributed to participation in the program.

However, as juvenile courts have expanded their use of EBPs (Drake 2010; Drake et al. 2009), selection into different treatment programs is no longer based on availability, and most adjudicated youth now receive some programming. At a minimum, youth work with a JPC who oversees the Case Management and Assessment Process, which integrates components of the risk, needs, and responsivity principles with motivational interviewing and skills-based EBPs (Andrews and Bonta 2010). That is, even youth who do not participate in EBPs still receive probation services as usual from JPCs who are trained in evidence-based principles (Drake 2018). With the expanded availability of treatment in today's court environment, it is more difficult to isolate treatment effectiveness, and it may not be possible to identify a group of youth who receive no treatment. These changes complicate the ability to evaluate program effectiveness by fundamentally changing treatment as usual in juvenile courts, and the makeup of the control condition matters (Drake 2018). WSIPP's meta-analytic research (WSIPP 2019b) in the mental health field and others (Watts et al. 2015) have shown, for example, that the size of the effect depends upon the control condition. Thus, it may become more difficult for EBPs to prove their effectiveness when the treatment as usual in the current court environment also incorporates evidence-based principles. Researchers and policymakers must take caution when distinguishing between programs that demonstrate iatrogenic effects and programs exhibiting null effects (WSIPP and EBPI 2019). Concluding that programs have not met the criteria for "what works" is not the same as concluding that programs are ineffective; doing so runs the risk of ruling out effective interventions.

2. *Selection Bias*

The development and use of dynamic, comprehensive risk and needs assessments have increased the amount of observable information that can be included in these statistical models. Nonetheless, additional information remains unobserved and many factors may influence whether or not a youth is placed in a particular type of EBP. Two important factors are the availability of alternative treatment programs and the perceived need for a particular treatment. For example, youth in juvenile courts are often eligible for both WSART and FFT. If a youth does not start WSART, it may be because the JPC thought that the youth would benefit more from FFT, or it may be that the JPC placed the youth into FFT because the court did not have a WSART group available. When evaluating the impact of a program, quasi-experimental methods must account for the complex selection decisions that may lead to systematic differences in the characteristics of youth in the treatment and comparison groups (Shadish, Cook, and Campbell 2002). Even when quasi-experimental methods can address selection bias, most statistical methods capture only observed characteristics, and bias can still remain from unobserved characteristics (Drake and Fumia 2017). Most importantly, researcher decisions can affect quasi-experimental methods, and sensitivity of these choices should be tested to be more confident in conclusions about program effectiveness.

Statistical methods must account for alternative treatments received by youth in the comparison group. For example, an evaluation of a CJAA EBP requires a comparison group of youth who did not participate in the EBP. In some cases, however, the youth in the comparison group may have participated in local programs unknown to the researchers. If the EBP of interest successfully reduces recidivism but the alternative program used for youth in the comparison group also reduces recidivism, research may not detect a difference between the two groups. This finding does not indicate that the treatment program is ineffective; rather, it indicates that the treatment program is no more effective than alternative options available to youth in the comparison group.

3. *Availability and Quality of Data*

The use of quasi-experimental methods requires consideration of characteristics that may influence the outcomes of recidivism. Research on the juvenile justice system in Washington often relies on a combination of data from multiple sources. However, because each database is maintained independently, differences exist in the type of information that is available to accurately link records from different agencies. Over the last two decades, agencies have worked together to identify areas of improvement for data related to the juvenile justice system. The CJAA advisory committee worked with local juvenile courts to develop databases to track the juvenile risk assessment data and information regarding participation in CJAA EBPs. WSIPP worked with various state agencies and partners to construct the first state unified research Criminal History Database, developed to measure recidivism and track individuals through the criminal justice system over time (Barnoski 1997) and evaluate programs efficiently (Barnoski 2004b).[14] This database has been used, for example, to analyze recidivism trends over time for various criminal justice populations in Washington (Knoth et al. 2019b), and to examine the impacts of COVID-19 on various points and locales within the criminal justice system (Hirsch 2021). These analyses illustrate the more complex, longitudinal information that cannot be gleaned from cross-sectional, annual reports.

The availability and scope of the information reported to a unified, statewide database is still limited, especially as the population of youth in the juvenile justice system shifts. Youth are increasingly diverting from the justice system by using pre-charge diversion programs. These diversion programs for referred youth motivated the recent passage of legislative reforms expanding the use of CJAA-funds to support EBPs for youth who are not formally charged (Washington State 66th Legislature 2019). Specifically, Washington lacks statewide police data on youth arrested or data from prosecutors' offices regarding youth who are referred to pre-charge diversion programs rather than formal court agreements. As such, researchers cannot examine differences in the youth who are referred but sent to treatment without filing charges and youth who are formally charged. For youth who are processed through the juvenile justice system, comprehensive data are collected only for participation in CJAA EBPs. Local juvenile courts may also rely on locally funded and operated treatment programs, or youth may be referred to mental health or substance use treatment. Currently, there is no statewide criminal justice database that tracks youths' participation in local programs. In the absence of these data, researchers cannot account fully for differences in treatment that may influence recidivism outcomes.

IV. ADVANCING A NEW EVIDENCE-BASED ERA

The evidence-based era supplanted the "nothing works" era (Martinson 1974), contributing a vast knowledge base that demonstrates that many prevention and intervention programs are effective at reducing crime (Drake et al. 2009; Knoth et al. 2019c; Lipsey 2009). For more than two decades, WSIPP has been at the forefront of this era (Aos et al. 1998; MacKenzie 2000; Sherman et al. 1997) with its standardized research approach. To date, WSIPP has updated and reported effects for more than 400 programs and policies across many public policy areas (e.g., child welfare, education, behavioral health), including more than 130 effects for adult and juvenile justice populations (WSIPP, n.d.b). WSIPP has written more than 80 nonpartisan reports on juvenile justice issues during this same time period, many of which have been used to shape public policy. Current WSIPP findings show that a variety of programs for youth in the juvenile justice system are effective at reducing recidivism (Wanner et al. 2020). WSIPP has conducted many outcome evaluations of programs offered in Washington, but the majority of programs being delivered remain unevaluated (Aos 2002; Drake 2022; Goodvin and Miller 2021; Lipsey 2018).

The Washington State Legislature began investing in significant changes to the juvenile justice system based on evidence that certain programs and strategies may effectively reduce recidivism for court-involved youth. Several "model programs" were adopted in the late 1990s to early 2000s in Washington and in other states across the nation (Elliott et al. 2020).[15] These programs demonstrated effectiveness based on systematic reviews of the research evidence and a pilot evaluation (Barnoski 2004b). However, more recent research on at least one implemented program (WSART) illustrates that the initial positive impacts from the pilot were not maintained after the program was scaled up statewide (Knoth et al. 2019a) or as the population has changed over time (Knoth et al. 2019c). Additional evaluations are necessary to identify whether quality assurance and trainer competence were related to the decline in program effectiveness over time (Barnoski, Aos, and Lieb 2003). Follow-up evaluations in other states have also demonstrated the ineffectiveness of some of these programs, calling into question the feasibility of broader-scale implementation (Lipsey 2018; Sullivan, Welsh, and Ilchi 2017).

When WSIPP's standard research approach was first developed in the 1990s, it sought to answer the question of "what works" to reduce recidivism and improve crime rates.[16] Early evaluations of court programs focused on the *overall* effectiveness on recidivism. Further, early legislation focused primarily on the goal of reducing recidivism as a specific outcome. Through this lens, WSIPP's meta-analyses and benefit-cost analyses aimed to describe "what works" to reduce crime through an *average* effect for an *average* program implementation for the *average* population (Drake et al. 2009). The landscape of evidence-based policy has changed over two decades, however, particularly in juvenile justice research. Expanded access to data after years of implementation can allow researchers to move beyond these average estimates. Thus, rather than broadly asking "what works" to improve outcomes, the policy question has evolved to "What works, and for whom?" (Knoth et al. 2019c; see also Farrington et al. 2019, 379). In this section, we discuss the key lessons learned in Washington over the past two decades that are necessary to support an EBP policy framework. We also describe the gaps to advance future research into a new era of evidence-based policymaking.

A. EBP Infrastructure and Policy Framework

A key lesson learned in Washington has been to involve key stakeholders early and throughout with full implementation support (Barnoski 2004a, 2004b). Jurisdictions must involve stakeholders, identify EBP champions, and develop local expertise as key components that are necessary for successful EBP implementation (Welsh and Greenwood 2015). The CJAA advisory committee has served as the main conduit for stakeholder engagement and development of local expertise. The CJAA committee embodies and promotes a "culture of using research to improve practice" (Welsh and Greenwood 2015, 252). For example, when the state expanded its EBP investments heavily in 2007 in the adult corrections system (Campbell et al. 2018; Drake 2013b; Drake et al. 2009), staff from the Department of Corrections sought out the CJAA advisory committee to draw upon their depth and breadth of experience supporting the evidence-based endeavor. The CJAA advisory committee has played a key role as EBP champions in Washington State, accomplishing its work within an oversight role with limited funds to achieve its objectives. The evidence-based policy process requires decision-making that is grounded in the best available research and data available at every stage of program implementation (Drake 2022; Miller and Miller 2015). EBP champions and local stakeholders are needed at all levels of the process to support a culture that integrates research into policy and practice (Welsh and Greenwood 2015).

Involving stakeholders with specialized expertise and roles is also critical to supporting a culture and infrastructure in the evidence-based policymaking process (Drake 2022; Goodvin and Miller 2021; Welsh and Greenwood 2015). For a decade, EBPI has played an increased role as a partner in the evidence-based process necessary to sustain the longer-term infrastructure with the juvenile courts. At the front end of the policy process, EBPI reviews programs nominated for the inventory by local practitioners. EBPI assesses whether these nominated programs have an underlying (a) logic model of operations and (b) theory of change (Drake 2010) to determine whether the program has the longer-term potential to raise in its evidence rating (WSIPP and EBPI 2019). The nomination process requires a foundation for the program by grounding its key components in research evidence (Drake 2010; Drake 2022; Miller and Miller 2015).[17] For nominated programs, WSIPP reviews the empirical research evidence and applies its standardized research approach to classify programs on the inventory based on the results. Notably, not all nominated programs have outcome evaluations that meet WSIPP's minimum standards of rigor.[18] At the back end of the evidence-based policy process, the Washington State Center for Court Research plays a central role in providing essential research and data functions for the state's 33 decentralized courts, including program monitoring, risk assessment, and case management practices. These essential monitoring and data functions did not exist prior to the establishment of this court research center in the mid-2000s.

Collaborative partnerships provide the local and specialized expertise necessary at each stage of the evidence-based policy process to support an EBP infrastructure that aims to (a) ground promising programs in theoretical and empirical research (Drake 2010; Drake 2022), (b) incorporate evidence into decision-making wherever possible, (c) and monitor the programs implemented (Barnoski, Aos, and Lieb 2003; Drake 2022; Welsh and Greenwood 2015). These collaborative researcher-practitioner partnerships in Washington emerged and developed slowly, and they continue to play a crucial role to support a culture and infrastructure that incorporates evidence into practice for the juvenile courts.

The EBP mission must be practically feasible for practitioners to implement, but translating research into practice to improve public policy has not been free of challenges. Similar to other research that has examined the efficacy of EBP implementation (Campbell et al. 2018; Walker et al. 2017), WSIPP interviewed stakeholders in Washington who use the evidence-based inventories to understand its benefits, drawbacks, and lessons learned (Goodvin and Miller 2021). Stakeholders reported finding value in the rigor of the inventory, noting that it helped to advance the state's progress toward evidence (Goodvin and Miller 2021), especially when state funds are tied to EBPs (Drake 2010; Drake et al. 2009; Welsh and Greenwood 2015). However, stakeholders also identified many opportunities for improvements (Goodvin and Miller 2021). Inventory users primarily cited the need for more information and technical assistance (Goodvin and Miller 2021; Pew Center on the States 2012; Welsh and Greenwood 2015; WSIPP and EBPI 2019). One user said, "The legislation that called on the child serving agencies in the State to implement evidence-based practice was well intentioned, and this is a good direction for the state to go, but [it] did not anticipate the implementation supports that are needed in order to do this well"

(Goodvin and Miller 2021, 20). While Washington has built a larger, supportive infrastructure over time, not all challenges during its implementation have been foreseen. Inventory stakeholders identified information gaps in the inventory, including lack of training, infrastructure, and limited mechanisms to identify services in communities to support promising practices with an evaluation.

Inventory stakeholders noted the important distinction between evidence-based programs and evidence-based practices (i.e., key program components) (Goodvin and Miller 2021). The inventory was designed to summarize evidence largely for full programs, a similar approach as other inventories.[19] While this information helps, stakeholders have also identified the need for a "menu" of common evidence-based characteristics to address the complex needs of the populations they serve (Goodvin and Miller 2021, p. 14; Howell and Lipsey 2012; Lipsey 2018, 2020). Further, stakeholders reported concerns about using "off-the-shelf" programs due to significant start-up and ongoing costs (Elliott et al. 2020; Goodvin and Miller 2021, 16; Lipsey 2018; Welsh, Rocque, and Greenwood 2014). They also expressed concerns about whether off-the-shelf programs could achieve the cultural adaptability needed to be responsive locally to underserved and marginalized communities (Goodvin and Miller 2021).

The policy processes for promising practices gives stakeholders the ability to address population needs at the local level and develop non-"name-brand" programs from the ground up (Drake 2010; Drake 2022; Goodvin and Miller 2021; Lipsey 2009, 145; Lipsey 2018). To illustrate the importance of developing and evaluating local non-name-brand programs and evidence-based practices in Washington, the Employment and Education Training (EET) program was developed in King County (Miller, Fumia, and He 2015).[20] EET served a local need to help youth gain important workforce skills through local employment and education opportunities. EET became the first program identified by CJAA that was approved, funded, implemented as a promising program (Drake 2010), with a follow-up evaluation that showed EET reduced recidivism cost-effectively (Miller, Fumia, and He 2015). Once local programs are approved, they are made available to other jurisdictions across the state. EET has since expanded to several other counties in Washington.

These examples in Washington highlight simultaneously both its successes and challenges with supporting a larger EBP infrastructure and framework. Although EET became a successful demonstration within CJAA's promising program framework—from evidence-informed practice to a fully developed and tested program—this effort was a substantial undertaking for numerous years for the program developers, CJAA, and others. EBP stakeholders in Washington have identified the need for more practitioner-researcher collaboration (Goodvin and Miller 2021) to fully integrate evidence and program theory into practice through grass-roots development that is responsive to local needs (Barnoski 2004b; Drake 2010; Drake 2022; Lipsey 2018; Welsh 2020). Building an evidence-based program requires a strong researcher-practitioner partnership to identify key program operations that link to a theory of change that is grounded in the empirical and theoretical research literature (Drake 2022). Further, EBP policymaking requires an ongoing technical assistance structure to help translate research into practice (Goodvin and Miller 2021; Sullivan, Welsh, and Ilchi 2017; Welsh and Greenwood 2015). A well-supported infrastructure includes funding technical assistance for implementation at all levels, as well as ongoing research and monitoring.

B. Rigorous Research to Advance the Era

As the types of treatment available for court-involved youth increase, there are additional questions about the most effective use of juvenile justice resources. Additional research could provide more useful information for evaluating the effectiveness of evidence-based programs. To further the era, EBP research must expand its current boundaries of what works (Knoth et al. 2019c) and meet the local needs of practitioners who deliver services to youth in the juvenile justice system who have complex needs. Youth involved in the juvenile justice system may have a history of trauma, family instability, and homelessness. To illustrate the complexity of this population, a recent study conducted by WSIPP examined youth involved in both the juvenile justice and child welfare systems, and this study highlights the unique challenges faced by youth who have multisystem involvement (Miller and Knoth 2019). This descriptive study found that dually involved youth had worse outcomes related to substance use, health, employment, homelessness, and subsequent criminal justice involvement compared to youth with only juvenile justice involvement. These types of analyses highlight the importance of exploring the intersection of public systems that affect youth, and exploring a variety of outcomes to advance complex policy issues in juvenile justice (Goodvin and Miller 2021).

Researchers must examine outcomes beyond recidivism (Goodvin and Miller 2021), such as employment, risk/needs scores, substance abuse, and education outcomes. The outcomes expected from a program should be rooted in its theoretical and logic model of operations (Drake 2010; Drake 2022; Miller and Miller 2015), and researchers should evaluate and report on all outcomes expected to be impacted. Measuring recidivism is ubiquitous, and it is relatively easy for researchers to obtain administrative data on an outcome that has wide stakeholder agreement. However, the narrow focus on recidivism limits the potential for practitioners to rely on evidence-based programs to meet the needs of local populations (Goodvin and Miller 2021). Policymakers should move beyond the importance of recidivism as the sole measure of program success, and consider all outcomes in accordance with the program's underlying logic, values, and objectives (Drake 2022).

The field must better understand for *whom* programs are effective (Farrington et al. 2019; Knoth et al. 2019c). For example, findings from the WSART study illustrate how programs may be more or less effective with certain populations. Specifically, female youth who participated in WSART had lower rates of recidivism than similar female youth who did not participate in the program. Subpopulation analyses are possible but require additional data, complex methods, and sensitivity analysis. To do this, researchers must examine whether program effects vary for different demographic subgroups or certain characteristics of youth (e.g., probation and post-release youth).

The field must better understand what *program characteristics* make interventions more or less effective (Drake 2022; Goodvin and Miller 2021; Lipsey 2018). Program evaluations identify whether individual programs are effective, but comprehensive treatment research is necessary to understand whether particular combinations of interventions produce additional benefits. For example, if youth are eligible for multiple evidence-based programs, how should local courts decide which treatment program a youth receives first? Current research remains limited on the programs or characteristics that should be prioritized, and on the "sequence" that programs should be delivered to maximize the effectiveness of long-term benefits (Hseih et al. 2021, p. 4; Stephenson, Harkins and Woodhams 2013).

Trends in juvenile justice policymaking in Washington State mirror similar trends across the country toward the use of evidence-based programs. Despite a nationwide push toward a more rehabilitative juvenile justice system that addresses the individual needs of justice-involved youth, there is little research that evaluates the systemic effects of these policy reforms. As described in this chapter, the juvenile justice system has changed in ways (Knoth et al. 2019a) beyond simply implementing a few specific evidence-based programs and policies (Drake et al. 2009). Over several decades, changes have occurred on how the system responds to criminal behavior as well changes in the characteristics of youth involved in the system today (Knoth et al. 2019c). The policy changes affecting Washington's juvenile justice system, and the changing populations observed over several decades, have introduced new complications to conducting research (Knoth et al. 2019a).

Research methods must account for structural conditions in the current court environment that may influence outcomes examined in evaluations of different areas of the juvenile justice system (Baumer 2013; Spohn 2009; Sutton 2013). Policy changes upstream may lead to changes downstream, and researchers may inappropriately attribute changes when evaluating parts of the system in isolation. An exploration of systemic or structural factors across the justice system (Sutton 2013) and broader population-level changes (Knoth et al. 2019a) can help researchers better isolate the unique effects of policy decisions or program implementation. For example, research could examine whether increases in the use of diversion dispositions in lieu of convictions lead to decreases in the average risk levels of court-involved youth. This approach could examine whether the evidence-based programs initially implemented for low-risk youth are still appropriate for current populations of low-risk youth. Rather than focusing on one aspect of the system (e.g., increases in the use of diversion or the effectiveness of programs for low-risk youth), a comprehensive system-based policy and research approach (Mears 2017) could provide a more complete picture of different stages in the criminal justice system and how they relate to improved youth outcomes, or it could examine packages of reforms (e.g., concurrent changes in different parts of the system) (Drake et al. 2009) to maximize desirable outcomes for youth. Information from a systems-based perspective (Mears 2017) could shed light on how policy changes in the juvenile justice system over time may be related to varying outcomes for youth.

Washington State is well situated to respond to calls for continued research on juvenile justice populations and evidence-based interventions. Systems-based research is possible only if there is sufficient access to comprehensive data on different stages of the juvenile justice system, and, as the first state to implement an evidence-based juvenile justice system, Washington has a wealth of data that could be used to evaluate short-term and long-term changes in justice-involved youth populations and program outcomes. Furthermore, research methods that account for structural conditions on outcomes often rely on methods that require more high-quality data and additional analyses to check for potential areas of bias, and these more complicated research methods are often more time- and resource-intensive. WSIPP's Criminal History Database was developed to allow for this type of longitudinal research through various stages of the system. This type of comprehensive system-based review can help identify how existing policies could be modified to better address current court populations, and it could identify areas of the system that are underserved by existing policies.

Recent methodological advancements and access to data have demonstrated the necessity of studying systemic and structural factors that impact justice outcomes. For example, systemic racial disparities and racism is perhaps the most empirically identified yet ignored policy example of empirical structural effects on outcomes (Kurlychek and Johnson 2019; Kutateladze et al. 2014; Sutton 2013; Wooldredge et al. 2015). A vast empirical research literature has examined racial disparities throughout the criminal court process (Kurlychek and Johnson 2019); however, many of these studies suffer methodological limitations. Studies that examine a single step in the criminal justice system (e.g., arrest, charging, or sentencing) have dominated the research literature and are insufficient at explaining racial disproportionality because they cannot detect indirect race effects through prior stages of the criminal court process (Baumer 2013). More recent and sophisticated methods that take a more holistic research approach measure multiple outcomes over a longer period of time to detect "cumulative disadvantage," which can occur for Black defendants as they progress through the criminal court process (Baumer 2013; Spohn 2009; Wooldredge et al. 2015, 188). Research designs that do not account for earlier case processing outcomes (e.g., pretrial detention) may erroneously conclude that racial disparities do not exist (Mitchell and MacKenzie 2004) compared to more rigorous approaches that have detected stronger effects of race on court outcomes (Baumer 2013).

To illustrate, Wooldredge et al. (2015) found a 75% increase in odds of pretrial detention for Blacks (compared with Whites) using a system-based analysis, whereas the direct effect measured only a 25% increase in odds of pretrial detention for Blacks. Therefore, "a full understanding of legal outcomes thus requires consideration of a wide range of factors, including offender, victim, and contextual characteristics, and calls for assessment of the effects of these factors at multiple stages of adjudication" (Baumer, Messner, and Felson 2000, 304). The empirical evidence on racial cumulative disadvantage (Baumer 2013; Kutateladze et al. 2014; Spohn 2009; Wooldredge et al. 2015) has important methodological and policy implications for risk assessment practices. Fourth-generation risk assessments have been shown to perform better empirically than clinical judgment (Andrews, Bonta, and Wormith 2006; Drake 2014), yet substantial research examining racial disparities has found cumulative disadvantage in case-processing outcomes (i.e., convictions). Due to the correlation of race and the factors included in risk assessments themselves (e.g., prior convictions), developers have not fully addressed disproportionality that results in risk assessment classifications, and they must continue to explore options on how to both examine and mitigate structural racial bias methodologically to improve racial disparities and public policies (Knoth and Hirsch 2021).

V. CONCLUSION

Since initial efforts began in 1997, Washington State's juvenile justice system has undergone significant changes through early investments in research, reforms of local court practices, and increased coordination between state agencies and juvenile court administrators. With these changes, the number of youth involved in the juvenile justice system has declined and courts have reduced confinement sentences substantially, opting to treat youth with evidence-based programs in the community. Washington State's policymakers, practitioners, and researchers have shared the common goal of working with the juvenile justice system so that it can best serve the needs of the justice-involved youth populations. The efforts of these stakeholders have helped make Washington an early leader in evidence-based juvenile justice policies.

While research played an integral role in supporting initial legislative reforms to the juvenile justice system, WSIPP's assignments to study, monitor, and assess the effectiveness of the CJAA reforms have decreased over time. WSIPP's initial recommendations following the CJAA included a need to engage in continuous monitoring of program effectiveness (Barnoski et al. 2003). Outcome evaluations have been a critical tool for understanding what works and what does not. Findings from the most recent WSART study highlight the importance of improved program monitoring through more regular research (Knoth et al. 2019a). Strong researcher-practitioner partnerships are critical to implementing EBPs that can meet the practical needs within the community (Drake 2022; Goodvin and Miller 2021; Lipsey 2018) and also incorporate the necessary theoretical and empirical research evidence to develop the required program protocols that inform program fidelity and help monitor outcomes (Drake 2022; Miller and Miller 2015). Collaborative partnerships with other research institutions are critical to supporting the ongoing type of technical assistance and implementation infrastructure that is needed to implement evidence-based programs statewide.

By its own definition, "evidence-based" programs require research evidence, yet the greatest lesson learned from Washington State is that the research evidence was not fully integrated into the ongoing delivery and monitoring of evidence-based program fidelity. To date, many programs have not been re-evaluated since the initial implementation. The true cost to purchase an evidence-based program (Barnoski 2009) requires not only the cost for delivering and monitoring fidelity, but also the cost of an ongoing research function to monitor an evidence-based juvenile justice system. The EBP endeavor requires programs to maintain fidelity, which requires research that is not simply adjacent, ad-hoc, or an afterthought. Rather, the research needed to sustain population impacts must be a fully funded, ongoing endeavor and a collaborative effort with key stakeholders. Further, there are significant gaps in knowledge about what other types of programs are being used by local courts or other state agencies, and whether those programs are effective. New outcome evaluations would add valuable information about the specific use of evidence-based programs and can help move beyond the one-size-fits-all policies of the past. Advances in data and methods allow researchers to now investigate what works for whom.

The scientific method is a never-ending process; as questions are answered more questions arise. The knowledge that is produced helps to build a foundation from which more evidence is born. Effective evidence-based systems require ongoing evaluations to help to identify new and improved practices or gaps in treatment that could inform future decisions about the system. A better understanding of the circumstances in which previously effective programs are now deemed ineffective is essential to ensuring that the state's investments in programs are achieving outcomes as intended. Data and research were critical to guiding initial reforms to the juvenile justice system. Since these initial reforms, data show that Washington experienced a significant shift in court practices and characteristics of the populations of court-involved youth. There are far fewer youth involved in the juvenile justice system today, and youth who are involved have far more access to treatment and community-based care.

However, findings from the WSART evaluation indicates that the policies and programs implemented two decades ago may no longer be effective in the current court environment. These changes in research are part of the broader landscape of changes in court practices and corresponding changes in court-involved populations. Data and research are now critical to fully understanding how the juvenile justice system has changed over time and to inform policymakers and practitioners about new pathways forward for the juvenile justice system. The research community in Washington has demonstrated a unique approach to designing and implementing research to inform the legislature and state and local agencies about the current state of the evidence-based juvenile justice. Washington is moving forward with a new era of research to address the complex and ever-changing needs of youth involved with the system.

Notes

1. "Evidence-based" has been defined in Washington statutes and defined differently depending on the public policy area. Unless referring to a specific statute, we use the term "evidence-based program or policy" throughout this chapter to broadly imply that rigorous research evidence demonstrates a program's effectiveness on expected outcomes.
2. Court-involved youth include youth adjudicated with a conviction disposition, deferred disposition, or diversion disposition.
3. This chapter was written based largely on an earlier WSIPP report (Knoth et al. 2019c; Wanner et al. 2020). The views expressed by the authors of this chapter are based on our individual experiences as researchers within the field of criminal justice and Washington's policy context. WSIPP conducts research across many public policy areas, and WSIPP researchers and policy stakeholders in those disciplines may have different and unique experiences of the evidence-based policymaking process.
4. Nondelinquent or dependency cases include petitions related to truancy, at-risk youth, and Children in Need of Services. See RCW 13.32A and RCW 28A.225.
5. Some statutory requirements affect prosecutorial discretion, including RCW 13.40.070 and RCW 13.40.077.
6. These statutes were integrated into the Juvenile Justice Act of 1977.
7. The consolidation included the Department of Early Learning and all programs delivered by the Children's Administration from the Department of Social and Health Services. Juvenile Rehabilitation and the Office of Juvenile Justice were absorbed within DCYF in July 2019.
8. The original report that contributed to this chapter contains a detailed table and timeline of specific WSIPP study findings and policy actions taken to create Washington's evolving evidence-based juvenile justice system (Knoth et al. 2019c). See WSIPPs publications to locate specific reports: http://www.wsipp.wa.gov/Publications.
9. See Knoth et al. 2019c. This updated figure includes juvenile justice reports published from January 1, 1997, through December 31, 2021. Study directives (assignments) may result in more than one report.

10. Inventories are required legislatively for funding in specific policy areas. The definitions used for these inventories and process for evidence-based decision-making are described in WSIPP and EBPI (2019). The primary distinguishing feature between these definitions is that evidence-based programs also achieve cost-beneficial results. Inventories represent a sub-group of the total programs reviewed by WSIPP using our systematic and standardized approach (not all programs can be monetized). Benefit-cost analyses of all programs reviewed are located on the WSIPP website (https://www.wsipp.wa.gov/BenefitCost).
11. This section summarizes data reported in Knoth et al. 2019c. Data visualizations and details about the data sources and their limitations are discussed in the original report.
12. The distribution of sanctions for conviction cases suggests that the decline in the average daily population of detention and youth sentenced to the jurisdiction of Juvenile Rehabilitation is related to the overall decline in youth involved in the justice system and/or the number of youth receiving a diversion agreement rather than changes in judicial sentencing decisions.
13. While random assignment studies are ideal and the gold standard, quasi-experimental methods can estimate causality, and both research designs must be well-executed to maintain validity.
14. The database and the code to develop the database has been shared with other state agencies who also use this information for research purposes (i.e., Research Data and Analysis at the Department of Social and Health Services; the Department of Corrections; and the Washington State Center for Court Research at the Administrative Office of the Courts).
15. Model programs are those that have been found to have positive impacts on outcomes in high-quality, causal evaluations; Office of Juvenile Justice and Delinquency Prevention.
16. As shown in this chapter, the legislature has been primarily focused on recidivism outcomes.
17. There are two promising program avenues for juvenile justice programs including CJAA's promising protocol (See Drake 2010) and the inventory process (See EBPI, https://uwcolab.org/ebpi).
18. Turanovic and Pratt (2020) argue that meta-analytic studies should be broader in their inclusion criteria. There are benefits to that approach; however, WSIPP takes a more exclusive approach with its minimum standards of rigor (WSIPP 2019b). Excluding studies based on a minimum standard of rigor allows us to be more confident in the results in the applied research policy environment. This practical approach allows us to rigorously answer the question in the most efficient manner. A minimum standard of rigor should be considered and adopted by the field for meta-analytic inclusion as causal research methods evolve over time.
19. For example, see the Results First Clearinghouse Database (https://www.pewtrusts.org/en/research-and-analysis/data-visualizations/2015/results-first-clearinghouse-database), which combines information from nine clearinghouses.
20. EET operated in Washington prior to the implementation of the promising program process (Drake 2010), and the EET program developers wanted it to be eligible to receive state EBP funds as a promising program.

REFERENCES

Andrews, Donald A., and James Bonta. 2010. *The psychology of criminal conduct*. New York: Routledge.

Andrews, Donald A., James Bonta, and J. Stephen Wormith. 2006. The recent past and near future of risk and/or need assessment. *Crime & Delinquency*, 52 (1): 7–27.

Aos, Steve. 1999. Trends in felony crime in Washington State and related taxpayer costs. Olympia: Washington State Institute for Public Policy.

Aos, Steve. 2002. The 1997 revisions to Washington's juvenile offender sentencing laws: An evaluation of the effect of local detention on crime rates. Olympia: Washington State Institute for Public Policy.

Aos, Steve. 2004. Washington State's family integrated transitions program for juvenile offenders: Outcome evaluation and benefit-cost analysis. Olympia: Washington State Institute for Public Policy.

Aos, Steve, Robert Barnoski, and Roxanne Lieb. 1998. Watching the bottom line: Cost-effective interventions for reducing crime in Washington. Olympia: Washington State Institute for Public Policy.

Aos, Steve, Roxanne Lieb, Jim Mayfield, Marna Miller, and Annie Pennucci. 2004. Benefits and costs of prevention and early intervention programs for youth. Olympia: Washington State Institute for Public Policy.

Aos, Steve, Polly Phipps, Robert Barnoski, and Roxanne Lieb. 1999. The comparative costs and benefits of programs to reduce crime: A review of research findings with implications for Washington State. Olympia: Washington State Institute for Public Policy.

Barnoski, Robert. 1997. Standards for improving research effectiveness in adult and juvenile justice. Olympia: Washington State Institute for Public Policy.

Barnoski, Robert. 1999. The Community Juvenile Accountability Act: Research-proven interventions for the juvenile court. Olympia: Washington State Institute for Public Policy.

Barnoski, Robert. 2002. Washington State's implementation of aggression replacement training for juvenile offenders: Preliminary findings. Olympia: Washington State Institute for Public Policy.

Barnoski, Robert. 2004a. Assessing risk for re-offense: Validating the Washington State Juvenile Court Assessment Manual, version 2.1. Olympia: Washington State Institute for Public Policy.

Barnoski, Robert. 2004b. Outcome evaluation of Washington State's research-based programs for juvenile offenders. Olympia: Washington State Institute for Public Policy.

Barnoski, Robert. 2009. Providing evidence-based programs with fidelity in Washington state juvenile courts: cost analysis. Olympia: Washington State Institute for Public Policy.

Barnoski, Robert, Steve Aos, and Roxanne Lieb. 2003. Recommended quality control standards: Washington State research-based juvenile offender program. Olympia: Washington State Institute for Public Policy.

Baumer, Eric P. 2013. Reassessing and redirecting research on race and sentencing. *Justice Quarterly*, 30 (2): 231–261.

Baumer, Eric. P., Steven. F. Messner, and Richard. B Felson. 2000. The role of victim characteristics in the disposition of murder cases. *Justice Quarterly*, 17 (2): 281–308.

Boerner, Dave, and Roxanne Lieb. 2001. Sentencing reform in the other Washington. *Crime and Justice*, 28:71–136.

Campbell, Christopher M., Mia J. Abboud, Zachary K. Hamilton, Jacqueline vanWormer, and Brianne Posey. 2018. Evidence-based or just promising? Lessons learned in taking inventory of state correctional programming. *Justice Evaluation Journal*, 1 (2): 188–214.

Dartington Social Research Unit. n.d. Cost benefit: Investing in Children. Devon, UK: Dartington Social Research Unit. http://www.investinginchildren.org.uk/cost-benefit/.

Drake, Elizabeth K. 2010. Washington State juvenile court funding: Applying research in a public policy setting. Olympia: Washington State Institute for Public Policy.

Drake, Elizabeth K. 2013a. The effectiveness of declining juvenile court jurisdiction of youth. Olympia: Washington State Institute for Public Policy.

Drake, Elizabeth K. 2013b. Inventory of evidence-based and research-based programs for adult corrections. Olympia: Washington State Institute for Public Policy.

Drake, Elizabeth K. 2014. *Predicting criminal recidivism: A systematic review of offender risk assessments in Washington State*. Olympia: Washington State Institute for Public Policy.

Drake, Elizabeth K. 2018. The monetary benefits and costs of community supervision. *Journal of Contemporary Criminal Justice*, 34 (1): 47–68.

Drake, Elizabeth K. 2022. Restorative justice dialogues in the criminal justice setting: A grounded approach to building an evidence-based practice. PhD diss., Washington State University.

Drake, Elizabeth K., Steve Aos, and Marna Miller. 2009. Evidence-based public policy options to reduce crime and criminal justice costs: Implications in Washington State. *Victims and Offenders*, 4:170–196.

Drake, Elizabeth K., and Danielle Fumia. 2017. Evolution of correctional education evaluations and directions for future research. *Criminology and Public Policy*, 16:549–561.

Elliott, Delbert S., Pamela R. Buckley, Denise C. Gottfredson, J. David Hawkins, and Patrick H. Tolan. 2020. Evidence-based juvenile justice programs and practices: A critical review. *Criminology and Public Policy*, 19 (4): 1305–1328.

Farrington, David P., Friedrich Lösel, Robert F. Boruch, Denise C. Gottfredson, Lorraine Mazerolle, Lawrence W. Sherman, and David Weisburd. 2019. Advancing knowledge about replication in criminology. *Journal of Experimental Criminology*, 15 (3): 373–396.

Feld, B. C. 2017. *The evolution of the juvenile court*. New York: New York University Press.

Fumia, Danielle, Elizabeth K. Drake, and Lijian He. 2015. Washington's coordination of services program for juvenile offenders: outcome evaluation and benefit-cost analysis. Olympia: Washington State Institute for Public Policy.

Goodvin, Rebecca, and Marna Miller. 2021. Washington State children and youth services inventory: Investigating use by state agencies in policy and decision making. Olympia: Washington State Institute for Public Policy.

Graham v. Florida, 560 U.S. 48 (2010).

Hamilton, Zachary, Melissa A. Kowalski, Alex Kigerl, and Douglas Routh. 2019. Optimizing youth risk assessment performance: Development of the modified positive achievement change tool in Washington State. *Criminal Justice and Behavior*, 46 (8): 1106–1127.

Hirsch, Michael. 2021. *COVID-19 and adult criminal justice: A quantitative look at affected systems*. Olympia: Washington State Institute for Public Policy.

Howell James C., and Mark W. Lipsey. 2012. Research-based guildelines for juvenile justice programs. *Justice Research and Policy*, 14 (1): 17–34.

Hsieh, Ming-Li, Kuan-Ju Chen, Pak-Sing Choi, and Zachary K. Hamilton. 2021. Treatment combinations: The joint effects of multiple evidence-based interventions on recidivism reduction. *Criminal Justice and Behavior*, 49 (6). https://doi/10.1177/00938548211052584.

Knoth, Lauren, and Michael Hirsch. 2021. Washington Offender Needs Evaluation: Review and examination of reassessments. Olympia: Washington State Institute for Public Policy.

Knoth, Lauren, Paige Wanner, and Lijian He. 2019a. Washington State's aggression replacement training for juvenile court youth: Outcome evaluation. Olympia: Washington State Institute for Public Policy.

Knoth, Lauren, Paige Wanner, and Lijian He. 2019b. Washington State recidivism trends: FY 1995–FY 2014. Olympia: Washington State Institute for Public Policy.

Knoth, Lauren, Paige Wanner, Eva Westley, and Elizabeth K. Drake. 2019c. Washington State's juvenile justice system: Evolution of policies, populations, and practical research. Olympia: Washington State Institute for Public Policy.

Kutateladze, Besiki L., Nancy R. Andiloro, Brian D. Johnson, and Cassia C. Spohn. 2014. Cumulative disadvantage: Examining racial and ethnic disparity in prosecution and sentencing. *Criminology*, 52 (3): 514–551.

Kurlychek, Megan C., and Brian D. Johnson. 2019. Cumulative disadvantage in the American criminal justice system. *Annual Review of Criminology* 2 (1): 291–319.

Lieb, Roxanne, and Megan E. Brown. 1999. Washington State's solo path: Juvenile sentencing guidelines. *Federal Sentencing Reporter*, 11 (5): 273–277.

Lipsey, Mark W. 2009. The primary factors that characterize effective interventions with juvenile offenders: A meta-analytic overview. *Victims and Offenders*, 4 (2): 124–147.

Lipsey, Mark W. 2018. Effective use of the large body of research on the effectiveness of programs for juvenile offenders and the failure of the model programs approach. *Criminology and Public Policy*, 17 (1): 189–198.

Lipsey, Mark W. 2020. Revisited: Effective use of the large body of research on the effectiveness of programs for juvenile offenders and the failure of the model programs approach. *Criminology & Public Policy*, 19:1329–1345.

Luu, Duc. 2018. Juvenile disposition summary: Fiscal year 2018. Olympia: Caseload Forecast Council.

MacKenzie, D. L. 2000. Evidence-based corrections: Identifying what works. *Crime and Delinquency*, 46 (4): 457–471.

Martinson, Robert. 1974. What works? Questions and answers about prison reform. *National Affairs*, 35:22–54. https://www.nationalaffairs.com/public_interest/detail/what-works-questions-and-answers-about-prison-reform.

Mears, Daniel P. 2017. *Out-of-control criminal justice: The systems improvement solution for more safety*. New York: Cambridge University Press.

Miller v. Alabama, 132 S. Ct. 1733 (2012).

Miller, J. Mitchell, and Holly. V. Miller. 2015. Rethinking program fidelity for criminal justice. *Criminology & Public Policy*, 14 (2): 339–349.

Miller, Marna, Danielle Fumia, and Lijian He. 2015. The King County Education and Employment Training Program: Outcome evaluation and benefit-cost analysis. Olympia: Washington State Institute for Public Policy.

Miller, Marna, and Lauren Knoth. 2019. Dually involved females and Washington State: Outcomes, needs and survey of approaches to serve this population. Olympia: Washington State Institute for Public Policy.

Mitchell, Ojmarrh, and Doris. L. MacKenzie. 2004. *The relationship between race, ethnicity, and sentencing outcomes: A meta-analysis of sentencing research*. Washington DC: U.S. Department of Justice, National Institute of Justice.

New South Wales Government. 2018. Evidence based policy and evaluation in NSW. Sydney: University of Technology Sydney. https://www.uts.edu.au/sites/default/files/2018-12/Cowell%20Evidence%20Based%20Policy%20November%202018%20-%20for%20circulation.pdf.

Pew Center on the States. 2012. Results first: Helping states assess the costs and benefits of policy options and use that data to make decisions based on results. Philadelphia: Pew Charitable Trusts. http://www.pewcenteronthestates.org.

Revised Code of Washington Title 9A. Washington Criminal Code.

Revised Code of Washington 13.40. Juvenile Justice Act of 1977.

Revised Code of Washington 13.40.010. Intent—Purpose.

Revised Code of Washington 13.40.020. Definitions.

Revised Code of Washington 13.40.0357. Juvenile Offender Sentencing Standards.

Revised Code of Washington 13.40.060. Disposition Order.

Revised Code of Washington 13.40.080. Diversion Agreement.

Revised Code of Washington 13.40.127. Deferred Disposition.

Revised Code of Washington 13.40.500—540. Community Juvenile Accountability Programs.

Roper v. Simmons, 543 U.S. 551 (2005).

Scott, Elizabeth S., and Laurence Steinberg. 2008. *Rethinking juvenile justice*. Cambridge, MA: Harvard University Press.

Shadish, William R., Thomas D. Cook, and Donald Thomas Campbell. 2002. *Experimental and quasi-experimental designs for generalized causal inference*. Boston, MA: Houghton Mifflin.

Sherman, Lawrence W., Denise C. Gottfredson, Doris L. MacKenzie, John E. Eck, Peter Reuter, and Shawn Bushway. 1997. *Preventing crime: What works, what doesn't, what's promising: A report to the United States Congress*. Washington, DC: National Institute of Justice.

Spohn, Cassia. 2009. Race, sex, and pretrial detention in federal court: Indirect effects and cumulative disadvantage. *Kansas Law Review*, 57:879.

State v. Bassett, 88 Wn. App. 1054 (Wash. Ct. App. 1997).

Stephenson, Zoe, Leigh Harkins, and Jessica Woodhams. 2013. The sequencing of interventions with offenders: An addition to the responsivity principle. *Journal of Forensic Psychology Practice*, 13 (5): 429–455.

Sullivan, Christopher J., Brandon C. Welsh, and Omeed S. Ilchi. 2017. Modeling the scaling up of early crime prevention: Implementation challenges and opportunities for translational criminology. *Criminology and Public Policy*, 16 (2): 457–485.

Sutton, John R. 2013. Structural bias in the sentencing of felony defendants. *Social Science Research*, 42 (5): 1207–1221.

Turanovic, Jillian J., and Travis C. Pratt. 2021. Meta-analysis in criminology and criminal justice: Challenging the paradigm and charting a new path forward. *Justice Evaluation Journal*, 4 (1): 21–47.

Vanlandingham, Gary R., and Elizabeth K. Drake. 2012. Results first: Using evidence-based policy models in state policymaking. *Public Performance & Management Review*, 35 (3): 550–563.

Walker, Sarah Cusworth, Aaron R. Lyon, Steve Aos, and Eric W. Trupin. 2017. The consistencies and vagaries of the Washington State inventory of evidence-based practice: The definition of "evidence-based" in a policy context. *Administration and Policy in Mental Health and Mental Health Services Research*, 44 (1): 42–54.

Wanner, Paige, Eva Westley, Lauren Knoth-Peterson, and Elizabeth K. Drake. 2020. Updated evidence classifications for select juvenile justice state-funded programs in Washington State: A resource guide. Olympia: Washington State Institute for Public Policy.

Washington State Caseload Forecast Council. 2019. 2019 Washington State juvenile disposition guidelines manual. Olympia, WA.

WSIPP (Washington State Institute for Public Policy). n.d.a. Home. Olympia, WA: WSIPP. https://www.wsipp.wa.gov.

WSIPP (Washington State Institute for Public Policy). 2016. Board of directors by-laws. Olympia, WA: WSIPP. https://www.wsipp.wa.gov/ByLaws/ByLaws_Dec2016.pdf.

WSIPP (Washington State Institute for Public Policy). n.d.b. Benefit-cost results. Olympia, WA: WSIPP. https://www.wsipp.wa.gov/BenefitCost.

WSIPP (Washington State Institute for Public Policy). 2019. Benefit-cost technical documentation. Olympia, WA: WSIPP.

Washington State Institute for Public Policy) and EBPI (Evidence Based Practice Institute). 2019. Updated inventory of evidence-based, research-based, and promising practices: For prevention and intervention services for children and juveniles in the child welfare, juvenile justice, and mental health systems. Olympia, WA: WSIPP.

Washington State 53rd Legislature. 1994. Violence Reduction Programs. Engrossed Second Substitute House Bill 2319, Chapter 7, Laws of 1994.

Washington State 62nd Legislature. 2012. Children and Juvenile Services–Evidence-Based Practices. Engrossed Second Substitute House Bill 2536, Chapter 232, Laws of 2012.

Washington State 65th Legislature. 2018. Engrossed Second Substitute Senate Bill 6160, Chapter 162, Laws of 2018, Juvenile Court Jurisdiction, Section 9.

Washington State 66th Legislature. 2019. Engrossed Senate Bill 5429, Chapter 461, Laws of 2019, Community Juvenile Accountability Program—Referred and Diverted Youth.

Watts, Sarah E., Adrienne Turnell, Natalie Kladnitski, Jill M. Newby, and Gavin Andrews. 2015. Treatment-as-usual (TAU) is anything but usual: A meta-analysis of CBT versus TAU for anxiety and depression. *Journal of Affective Disorders*, 175:152–167.

Welsh, Brandon C. 2020. The case for rigorous comparative research and population impacts in a new era of evidence-based interventions for juvenile offenders. *Criminology & Public Policy*, 19 (4): 1–8.

Welsh, Brandon C., and David P. Farrington. 2015. Monetary value of early developmental crime prevention and its policy significance. *Criminology & Public Policy*, 14:673.

Welsh, Brandon C., and Peter W. Greenwood. 2015. Making it happen: State progress in implementing evidence-based programs for delinquent youth. *Youth Violence and Juvenile Justice*, 13 (3): 243–257.

Welsh, Brandon C., David P. Farrington, and B. Raffan Gowar. 2015. Benefit-cost analysis of crime prevention programs. *Crime and Justice*, 44 (1): 447–516.

Welsh, Brandon C., Michael Rocque, and Peter W. Greenwood. 2014. Translating research into evidence-based practice in juvenile justice: Brand-name programs, meta-analysis, and key issues. *Journal of Experimental Criminology*, 10 (2): 207–225.

Wooldredge, John, James Frank, Natalie Goulette, and Lawrence Travis III. 2015. Is the impact of cumulative disadvantage on sentencing greater for Black defendants? *Criminology & Public Policy*, 14 (2): 187–223.

CHAPTER 7

SYSTEMS OF CHANGE
The Pennsylvania Model

SHAWN PECK, JANET A. WELSH,
KRISTOPHER T. GLUNT, AND ROGER SPAW

STATES vary in the scope and reach of their delinquency prevention and intervention programming. For decades, Pennsylvania has stood at the forefront of juvenile justice reform and the use of evidence-based, data-driven strategies for preventing and mitigating youth crime. In Pennsylvania, a number of state-level agencies have prioritized access to evidence-based programs (EBPs) designed to prevent delinquency, substance misuse, out-of-home placement, reoffending, and other negative outcomes for youth and their families, and to promote healthy development. Through collaborations with a variety of stakeholders, including local organizations and single-county authorities (SCAs), university-based expertise in technical assistance, prevention and implementation science, and other state level systems, Pennsylvania has achieved a high level of dissemination and access to EBPs, as well as technical assistance to provide implementation and evaluation support. Additionally, Pennsylvania has adopted a statewide surveillance system and other mechanisms for collecting and analyzing data in order to determine the ongoing effectiveness of juvenile crime prevention and intervention strategies, and to make adjustments as needed. This chapter will provide an overview of the landscape, the different state-level organizations supporting juvenile crime prevention in Pennsylvania, the conceptual underpinnings and levels of care addressed by Pennsylvania's prevention strategies, the major initiatives targeting prevention of crime and other adverse outcomes for youth, and the strategic partnerships involved with the rollout and sustained support for EBPs. Ongoing and emerging challenges facing prevention initiatives in Pennsylvania will also be discussed.

I. THE PENNSYLVANIA LANDSCAPE: CHALLENGES AND OPPORTUNITIES FOR PREVENTION

By population, Pennsylvania is the fifth-largest state in the United States, with a population of approximately 13 million in 2020 (US Census 2020). The state has a number of large ethnically and culturally diverse metropolitan areas, most notably Philadelphia in the southeast and Pittsburgh in the southwest, with significant rural, ethnically homogeneous populations in between. Thus, the nature of crime and other social problems varies significantly by region and community. Like other states, Pennsylvania has become increasingly diverse over time; the Latino population in Pennsylvania increased from 719,660 in 2010 to 1,049,615 in 2020, an increase of 45.8% (Pennsylvania State Data Center 2022). Also, like much of the country, Pennsylvania was hard hit by the opioid epidemic, and it recently experienced a resurgence of gun violence, particularly in large urban areas and communities of color (Afif et al. 2022).

Pennsylvania's prevention landscape is also broad and wide-ranging, as befitting a large and diverse state. In the sections below, we describe some of the state-level organizations that serve as the key drivers of prevention initiatives across the Commonwealth. The decentralized structure of Pennsylvania can be challenging for practitioners when establishing best practices for the implementation of evidence-based programs and practices for prevention efforts and for juvenile justice interventions because of jurisdictional variation. Although the implementation time may be prolonged because of the need to collaborate with state agencies and the developers of EBPs, the finished products are not "force-fitted" and contain buy-in from local stakeholders. As a result, best-practice and reform initiatives have become county-led and state-supported.

A. State-Level Systems Supporting Juvenile Crime Prevention and Intervention in Pennsylvania

A number of state-level agencies, departments, and commissions in Pennsylvania have embraced evidence-based prevention as part of their core missions. Central among these is the Pennsylvania Commission on Crime and Delinquency (PCCD), charged with enhancing the quality of services within correctional systems (adult and juvenile), meeting the needs of crime victims, and improving community safety across the Commonwealth. Their leadership is fully aware of both the human and economic costs of crime, as well as the cost-effectiveness of evidence-based prevention programming. Additionally, they have a sophisticated understanding of the importance of evaluation and implementation science, and of their role in continuous quality improvement. For these reasons, PCCD funds numerous crime prevention and intervention strategies throughout Pennsylvania via multiple mechanisms available to a variety of community organizations. These include universal programs such as prevention education for children and youth, often implemented in collaboration with school districts, as well as higher-level strategies such as gun violence prevention and juvenile justice reform.

The Juvenile Court Judges' Commission (JCJC) comprises juvenile court judges who are nominated by the chief justice of the Pennsylvania Supreme Court and appointed by the governor for three 3-year terms (JCJC 2021). Legislative mandates in Pennsylvania require the use of EBPs in the juvenile justice system. The juvenile courts play a critical role in assuring that these mandates are followed, requiring the use of EBPs by court officials, probation departments, and providers. The JCJC staff serve the Commonwealth by providing oversight to juvenile courts, establishing standards for administrative practices and judicial procedures, dictating employment standards for juvenile probation departments, collecting data and producing juvenile court statistics, advising juvenile courts regarding proper care of delinquent and dependent children, and administering funding to improve juvenile probation departments. Additionally, JCJC staff provide training for juvenile probation in the use of evidence-based programs and strategies (JCJC 2021).

The Pennsylvania Council of Chief Juvenile Probation Officers, commonly referred to as the Chief's Council, partners with state agencies such as the Pennsylvania Commission on Crime and Delinquency and JCJC to improve the effectiveness of juvenile probation and the services provided to adjudicated delinquent youth. The decentralized structure of Pennsylvania requires collaboration among 67 juvenile courts and probation departments to establish best practices with system improvements. Additionally, state agencies need the active participation from private service providers, academic partners, and other key stakeholders to ensure that change efforts are implemented and sustained. The Chief's Council and the JCJC coordinate and facilitate quarterly meetings for collaboration regarding juvenile justice reform initiatives. Additionally, they oversee various ongoing workgroups composed of stakeholders from all sectors of the juvenile justice system and provide various resources to increase the effectiveness of the juvenile justice system, to include funding.

The Pennsylvania Department of Drug and Alcohol Programs (DDAP) leads and supports the Commonwealth in preventing and reducing substance misuse and problem gambling. DDAP has established four overarching goals: to reduce stigma, intensify primary prevention, strengthen treatment systems, and empower sustained recovery. DDAP, formerly housed under the Department of Health, made a shift to its own department in July 2012, reflecting a strong commitment by the Commonwealth to provide education, intervention, and treatment programs in order to prevent and reduce substance abuse and addiction in Pennsylvania, which are closely related to crime and other problematic outcomes. DDAP provides funding and oversight for SCAs and their contracted providers to plan and implement proven prevention strategies within their respective counties. Flexibility is provided for the SCAs to select programs and services based on the priorities within a given community, and SCAs are encouraged to collaborate with local partners in order to establish a comprehensive prevention effort. DDAP also collaborates closely with other state-level organizations, including PCCD, to initiate, support, and sustain prevention initiatives. The Pennsylvania Department of Human Services (DHS) supports a range of services, particularly in the child welfare system, designed to prevent crime by strengthening families and improving the developmental trajectories of vulnerable children, and the Pennsylvania Children's Trust Fund is dedicated to prevent child abuse and neglect, which are distal predictors of later crime (Children's Trust 2016).

Given the high rate of comorbidity between delinquency and dependency, the Office of Children, Youth, and Families (OCYF), within DHS, partners with PCCD to fund various services for dependent and delinquent youth to include the implementation of various evidence-based programs. Within OCYF, exists the Bureau of Juvenile Justice Services (BJJS), which operates residential treatment programs for various levels of care to ensure EBPs are delivered to male and female delinquent and dependent youth who were rejected by or unsuccessful within private treatment programs. Additionally, the Pennsylvania Liquor Control Board (PLCB) provides oversight and enforcement of underage drinking laws, including training for retailers and servers in establishments selling alcohol and monitoring of these businesses to prevent law violations. Because alcohol misuse is often strongly associated with crime, youth who initiate substance use early in life are at particular risk for delinquency and other poor outcomes (Prinz and Kerns 2003). PLCB promotes a zero-tolerance, no-use policy for youth under age 21, and promotes this through its media campaigns targeting parents, as well as through various alcohol education programs for high school– and college-age youth.

The Pennsylvania Department of Education (PDE), along with local school districts throughout the state, is central to the delivery of youth-focused interventions designed to prevent and remediate youth crime and other adverse outcomes, including substance misuse and school failure. Given schools' nearly universal access to youth, the importance of schools as a hub of prevention activity cannot be overstated. Schools provide universal prevention education to all students through their health curriculum, including substance misuse and character education programs, many of which have been demonstrated to reduce problematic behavior at the population level (Greenberg et al. 2017). Additionally, schools provide more targeted services to students with various risk factors, including public pre-K programs for low-income children; Student Assistance Programs for those with mental health, substance misuse, or other barriers to learning; school social workers to address complex needs of children and families; and school-based juvenile probation services for justice-involved youth. To provide these various services, schools often work closely with other local or county-level agencies, including mental health, human service, and juvenile probation departments, as well as substance misuse prevention and intervention programs.

B. Strategic Partnerships Supporting Prevention and Intervention in Pennsylvania

Prevention efforts in Pennsylvania are facilitated by key partnerships between state-level agencies and other organizations, including university-based researchers and implementation scientists and multidisciplinary nonprofits. Often, these partnerships bring specific types of expertise, such as communications, program evaluation, or technical assistance, to the state's prevention initiatives. The Commonwealth Prevention Alliance (CPA) is a long-standing nonprofit with the mission of advancing effective prevention through education, outreach, and advocacy. CPA works closely with the Pennsylvania Commission on Crime and Delinquency and Department of Drug and Alcohol Programs to provide outreach and resources to communities and organizations, including K-12 schools and higher education, local coalitions, and SCAs. CPA sponsors an annual statewide conference that provides participants with information and expertise on a range of timely issues related to prevention, such as legalization of marijuana, and also provides marketing and communication materials for communities regarding prevention principles and practices.

The Commonwealth supports a number of university-based initiatives designed to promote and support prevention efforts. University partnerships provide expertise in prevention and implementation science, evaluation, and the translation of research findings into real-world practice. Additionally, university partnerships provide technical assistance and expertise in evaluation and implementation science for communities delivering evidence-based programs (Liberman and Hussemann 2016). The Program Evaluation Research Unit at the University of Pittsburgh (Pitt-PERU) is funded by PCCD to lead a number of harm-reduction initiatives that target overdose prevention and collect overdose surveillance data through a network of local and regional Technical Assistance Centers (TACs). TAC coalitions engage key stakeholders (i.e., SCA directors, county commissioners) and support the implementation of specific initiatives such as naloxone training for first responders. The Penn State Evidence-based Prevention and Intervention Support (EPIS) is co-funded by PCCD and DDAP and provides technical assistance and evaluation support for a number of different prevention initiatives, including the dissemination of EBPs, the Standardized Program Evaluation Protocol (SPEP™) project, and the DDAP Needs Assessment, Planning, and Evaluation Project. The overarching goal of EPIS is to increase local awareness of effective practices and principles of prevention and implementation science, so that communities increasingly use EBPs and routinely evaluate their intervention impacts.

Additionally, PCCD has partnered with the National Center for Juvenile Justice (NCJJ) on various projects for several decades. In 2010, PCCD funded The NCJJ to implement the Quality Improvement Initiative (Qii), which included partnerships with service providers and juvenile probation departments to improve the quality-of-service delivery, with an emphasis on data collection, protocols, and improvement processes (Zajac et al. 2010). In 2012, the Continuous Quality Improvement Guide emerged from this project and its components were reincarnated in the SPEP™ Program Improvement Process (PIP). Pennsylvania's juvenile justice system is rich in private and public service providers who have been actively involved in reform initiatives for decades. An extensive network of service providers works collaboratively with the Chief's Council and the JCJC to promote JJSES initiatives. Service providers receive technical assistance in response to their capacity to implement EBPs, which is often determined by their ability to receive grants, organizational philosophy, and staff complement (Liberman and Hussemann 2016). The capacity of service providers to implement EBPs has been significantly enhanced over the past decade due to initiatives such as the CQI and the SPEP™. Service providers actively participate in quarterly meetings to improve the implementation of evidence-based practices and the continual quality improvement of data collection to improve data-driven decision-making.

II. Conceptual Underpinnings of the Pennsylvania Prevention Model

Pennsylvania's approach to juvenile crime prevention is guided by several conceptual frameworks developed within the fields of prevention, intervention, and implementation science. These include the Spectrum of Mental, Emotional, and Behavioral (MEB) Interventions, the Continuum of Confidence, and the Social Development Model, which are described in the following sections.

A. The Spectrum of Mental, Emotional, and Behavioral Interventions

Figure 7.1 shows the Spectrum of MEB Interventions (updated by National Academies of Sciences, Engineering, and Medicine 2019). The Spectrum of MEB Interventions begins with health promotion and universal prevention strategies, which achieve population-level improvements in health and well-being through extremely broad reach. These include strategies to promote positive parenting, early school success, and healthy pregnancy outcomes (as a few examples), with the goal of reducing crime by strengthening protective factors such as children's health, cognitive and social-emotional development, educational attainment, and positive family and peer relationships. Effective interventions at this level prevent problems from ever occurring and are typically low-intensity and low-cost. For these reasons, they are unlikely to be effective at changing the outcomes of high-risk or multi-problem individuals or groups, but they may be effective at preventing lower-risk individuals or groups from requiring higher-level interventions.

Proceeding across the continuum, interventions become increasingly intensive, intrusive, and expensive, and are increasingly targeted toward specific groups rather than the entire population. Selective interventions target youth and families with known risk factors. For example, Head Start is a preschool program that targets children from low-income families, given that poverty is a known risk factor for crime and other poor life outcomes. *Indicated* interventions are those for individuals or groups showing early indicators of a significant disorder, including substance misuse, delinquency, and mental health problems. Many interventions utilized by the juvenile justice and child welfare systems are classified as indicated, with the goal of preventing further progression through these systems and altering the developmental trajectories of youth while they are still relatively malleable.

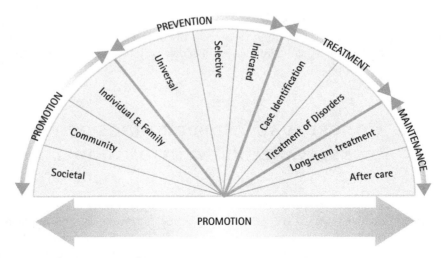

FIGURE 7.1. The Spectrum of MEB Interventions.

Source: National Academies of Sciences, Engineering, and Medicine (2019).

Once individuals have received specific diagnoses, they move from the realm of prevention to the realm of treatment, which is represented by the right side of the Spectrum of MEB Interventions and ideally involves the delivery of established and empirically validated treatments, such as medically assisted treatment (MAT) for substance use disorders or Multisystemic Therapy (MST) for juvenile offenders. Recognizing the significant risk of relapse for disorders ranging from crime to obesity, the Spectrum of MEB Interventions also includes interventions focused on aftercare and maintenance of treatment-related outcomes, including re-entry programs for individuals exiting the criminal justice system.

The Spectrum of MEB Interventions makes the compelling case for the need for well-coordinated, collaborative, multidisciplinary approaches to complex problems such as youth crime, as well as the need for a smooth transition across levels of care for individuals requiring more intensive interventions. The Spectrum of MEB Interventions has highlighted many of the challenges of the service delivery system, given that interventions at different levels on the continuum often have different stakeholder groups and little history of collaboration, sometimes resulting in individuals "falling through the cracks" as they move from one system of care to another.

B. The Continuum of Confidence

The Continuum of Confidence (Figure 7.2) reflects the strength of the research evidence supporting an intervention. Unlike the Spectrum of MEB Interventions, which classifies interventions according to their intensity and focus, the Continuum of Confidence reflects whether interventions have scientific proof that they actually achieve their intended outcomes, regardless of their level of intensity or intervention target. Although many intervention providers and policymakers understand the importance of using evidence-based interventions, they may be unaware that not all "evidence" is equally strong. The factors that determine an intervention's position on the Continuum of Confidence are related to scientific research involving the intervention and include the number and size of research evaluations conducted, the strength of the research design (e.g., use of a randomized controlled trial), the inclusion of a longitudinal follow-up to track participants' long-term

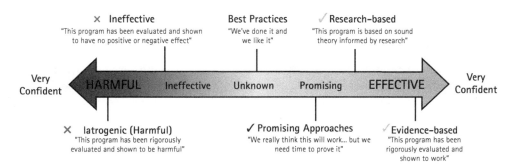

FIGURE 7.2. The Continuum of Confidence.

Source: Bumbarger (2009).

outcomes, and the use of independent replication, which reduces the possibility that study results are biased.

On the left side of the Continuum are programs that research has demonstrated to be *harmful*, meaning that program participants have more negative outcomes than those who received an alternative program or no intervention at all. Although often done with the best of intentions, harmful programs do not achieve their desired impacts and are worse than doing nothing at all. This is sometimes the case with fear-based interventions such as Scared Straight, in which participating juvenile offenders were *more likely* to reoffend than those receiving traditional probation services (Petrosino et al. 2013). *Ineffective* interventions are those that have been researched and shown to have no effects, positive or negative, while *unknown* programs (the majority actually used in applied settings today) have never undergone research evaluations and their impacts (positive or negative) are unclear. *Promising* interventions have limited research indicating that they have positive effects (e.g., one or two studies, small-scale studies, no longitudinal follow-ups, etc.), while *effective* interventions have strong research evidence (multiple studies, large-scale studies, long-term follow-ups, etc.). Whereas the Spectrum of MEB Interventions can help providers to understand their role in the prevention and treatment of problems such as crime, the Continuum of Confidence helps decision-makers to determine whether they are making responsible use of resources by utilizing the interventions most likely to yield the desired impacts.

C. The Social Development Model

Figure 7.3 shows the components of the Social Development Model (Catalano et al. 2004), a framework for delinquency prevention infused into the work of multiple state and community level organizations in Pennsylvania. The Social Development Model recognizes that youth crime is determined by multiple factors, including family, community, and peer influences. The model specifies that in order for youth to avoid becoming involved in crime, there must be opportunities for involvement in prosocial activities, as well as the opportunity to form relationships with noncriminal adults and peers. When youth have the skills to be successful in prosocial endeavors and experience these activities and relationships as positive and rewarding, they develop attachment, commitment, and beliefs in prosocial institutions (such as school or family) and are less likely to seek affiliation and engagement with criminal organizations (such as youth gangs).

The Social Development Model is most likely to be effective at preventing crime when it is embedded in community settings such as schools and youth-serving organizations, but it can also be employed by juvenile justice practitioners to prevent young people from progressing deeper into the criminal justice system. For example, interventions that target the family, including those that build strong parent-child relationships and teach parents positive and effective limit-setting, are likely to reduce delinquent behavior in youth, particularly if the reach of such interventions is facilitated by schools and other community organizations. Similarly, school-based interventions targeting the academic and social-emotional needs of vulnerable children can prevent the disengagement in school that often precedes delinquency (Catalano et al. 2004).

```
        The goal...
     HEALTHY BEHAVIOURS
   for all children and youth

         Start with...
  HEALTHY BELIEFS & CLEAR STANDARDS
 ...in families, schools, communities and peer groups

            Build...
           BONDING
    ATTACHMENT    COMMITMENT
 ...to families, schools, communities and peer groups

         By providing...
  OPPORTUNITIES   SKILLS   RECOGNITION
 ...in families, schools, communities and peer groups

       And by nurturing...
   INDIVIDUAL CHARACTERISTICS
```

FIGURE 7.3. The Social Development Model.

Source: Communities That Care, n.d.

III. Prevention and Intervention Initiatives in Pennsylvania

A major emphasis for prevention and intervention efforts has involved the collection and analysis of systematic, statewide surveillance data on youth and families engaged with various service systems. Since 1989, PCCD has collaborated with school districts throughout the state to administer the Pennsylvania Youth Survey (PAYS) to youth in 6th, 8th, 10th, and 12th grades (PCCD 2019–2020). The PAYS collects anonymous information regarding multiple domains of youth behavior, attitudes, and beliefs, including substance misuse, delinquency, mental health, community norms, peer group behaviors, and school climate. The PAYS questions are organized around known risk and protective factors associated with multiple youth outcomes. By 2020, 419 of the 500 school districts in Pennsylvania were registered to collect PAYS data, with PCCD furnishing each participating district with a report summarizing the data and providing statewide and (when available) national averages for multiple variables to allow districts to make sense of their data.

This large-scale uptake of the PAYS by school districts has been fruitful for prevention in many ways. At the state level, it provides population-level surveillance that identifies trends over time in youth problem behaviors, and allows the state to appropriately prioritize intervention funding mechanisms. For example, the PAYS has helped the leadership at DDAP and PCCD to identify emerging issues around youth vaping, bullying, depression, and anxiety, and to provide communities with resources specific to these issues. At the local level, school personnel, service providers, and parents can use the PAYS to identify specific strengths and weaknesses in their communities regarding the needs of youth, and to track over time the effectiveness of their adopted prevention strategies. The PAYS is overseen by the PAYS Advisory Group (PAYSAG), a multidisciplinary team that reviews the findings and makes periodic modifications to the survey based on stakeholder needs and input. Most recently, a fourth-grade version of the PAYS was created and piloted in a small number of districts. Additionally, the 2021 PAYS included questions regarding the impact of COVID-19 on the well-being of youth.

Another data-driven initiative in Pennsylvania includes support for the Communities That Care (CTC) model (Hawkins et al. 2008). CTC is a coalition-based approach to prevention that involves engagement of local stakeholders and systematic data collection on youth problem behaviors at the individual, family, and community levels (Figure 7.4). CTC is theoretically grounded in the Social Development Model and utilizes a risk and protective factor approach to prevention. Once information on risk and protective factors is gathered and summarized, the CTC coalition prioritizes needs (i.e., youth violence, teen pregnancy, low investment in school, etc.) and identifies evidence-based approaches to address them. Once interventions are implemented, the CTC coalition is responsible for monitoring implementation quality, providing technical assistance to program implementers, and documenting intervention outcomes through the use of sound evaluation strategies. CTC coalitions often utilize data from the PAYS, as well as other sources, to identify specific patterns of risk and protective factors for youth in particular communities. CTC is an evidence-based coalition model, shown to reduce rates of problematic youth behavior and to promote healthy youth development in communities where it is systematically implemented (Feinberg et al. 2010). In an analysis conducted specifically on CTC implementation in Pennsylvania, communities implementing CTC had higher rates of protective factors and lower rates of

FIGURE 7.4. The Communities That Care Operating System.

Source: Communities That Care, n.d.

risk factors than comparable communities that did not utilize the model, and the results were particularly strong when communities adopted evidence-based interventions to reduce risk and promote healthy development (Feinberg et al. 2010).

In order to increase overall capacity around data-driven decision-making, DDAP, in collaboration with technical assistance providers at EPIS, has led the DDAP Needs Assessment Planning and Evaluation Process with all SCAs in the Commonwealth. This project integrated aspects of CTC and the Social Development Model into training and professional development for SCA staff, as well as integrating existing data sources such as PAYS into the assessment and evaluation process. Staff members were trained to implement a data-driven approach in order to identify their county's highest priority substance use problems, as well as the underlying risk, protective, and contributing factors driving those problems. This was followed by the completion of a comprehensive resource assessment designed to identify existing services already addressing their priorities, as well as to identify current gaps in programming. SCAs then utilized their data driven priorities to develop intermediate and long-term goals and then measure their progress over time in impacting those goals. The needs assessment data, in conjunction with these measurable goals, served as the foundation for the development of a comprehensive prevention plan designed to target each county's prioritized risk, protective, and/or contributing factors.

Following the implementation of the prevention plans, SCAs complete evaluation reports to summarize the outcomes of the programs and services implemented. The needs assessment, planning, and evaluation process was designed to be cyclical and ongoing, including periodic checkpoints for evaluation and updates. It is scheduled for full rollout approximately every six years, providing counties with a fluid and data-driven process for constantly re-evaluating and prioritizing their needs and strategically implementing high-quality prevention programming, with the ultimate goal of better outcomes for citizens and more cost-effective use of taxpayer dollars. The Pennsylvania Commission on Crime and Delinquency, Department of Drug and Alcohol Programs, and Department of Education have collaborated and invested considerable resources in assisting Pennsylvania communities in the use of evidence-based interventions (EBIs) that have proven impacts on reducing risk factors such as delinquency and substance misuse, and strengthening protective factors, such as school success and positive adult-child relationships.

The EBPs eligible for state funding include model and promising programs from the University of Colorado's Blueprints for Healthy Youth Development initiative (University of Colorado, n.d.) Blueprints analyzes the research evidence behind programs and uses the Spectrum of MEB Interventions to make program designations. The most cost-effective and efficient of these are *universal* health promotion and prevention programs that target all youth regardless of risk status. When implemented with high quality and sustained over time, these programs can lead to population-level decreases in youth crime and other adverse outcomes through their broad reach and impact on foundational aspects of health youth development, such as self-control and prosocial skills (Greenberg et al. 2017). However, EBIs also include *selective* interventions for high-risk populations and *indicated* prevention programs for youth and families exhibiting signs of disorder, such as behavior problems, school difficulty, or family conflict. Because research indicates that translation of EBIs into community settings often results in reduced effectiveness due to barriers that erode implementation quality (Mihalic and Irwin 2003), Pennsylvania provides technical assistance and evaluation support for EBIs through EPIS at Penn State. EBIs currently reach more than 5,000 youth annually, and the menu includes 17 evidence-based programs, all of which have substantial empirical research supporting their effectiveness (PCCD 2020).

The EBI initiative is designed to be flexible and responsive to the changing needs of communities across the Commonwealth. In 2019, for example, PCCD added two programs to the EBI menu that were specifically focused on the mental health needs of youth, in response to PAYS data that indicated alarming increases in youth reports of depression, anxiety, and suicidal ideation. A return-on-investment analysis found that savings varied by program, but ranged from $1 to $25 savings for each dollar invested (Jones et al. 2008).

Interventions implemented through the Department of Human Services, including the Nurse-Family Partnership (NFP) program and the Children's Defense Fund, target distal factors related to crime prevention, including healthy development in infancy and early childhood and prevention of child maltreatment. NFP is an evidence-based, two-generation, nurse visitation program targeting the outcomes of young pregnant women and their infants. Longitudinal research on NFP has revealed a number of positive impacts on both mothers and children, including better pregnancy and birth outcomes; reduced abuse, neglect, and accidental injury in early childhood, and better cognitive and social-emotional development for children (Eckenrode et al. 2017). One study revealed reduced rates of delinquent behavior for children 15 years after the intervention, mediated by reduced poverty, better health and development in early childhood, and better self-regulation and school engagement (Olds et al. 1998). The Children's Defense Fund is a federal policy and advocacy organization dedicated to prevention of child abuse and neglect.

A. Evidence-Based Practices within the Juvenile Justice System

Pennsylvania's juvenile justice system radically changed in 1995 with the passing of Act 33, resulting in the establishment of Balanced and Restorative Justice (BARJ) with the following principles: Community Protection, Victim Restoration, and Youth Redemption (Pennsylvania Council of Chief Juvenile Probation Officers 2022). BARJ was based on principles of restorative justice that emphasize the importance of victim empathy and reconciling the offender to the community (Zehr 2002). Restorative justice philosophy is now evident in Pennsylvania's Juvenile Act Purpose Clause, which emphasizes the need for offenders to repair harm to the victims and community by taking accountability for their behaviors. The mission of the juvenile justice system was redefined as follows: "Consistent with the protection of the public interest, to provide for children committing delinquent acts program of supervision, care and rehabilitation which provide balanced attention to the protection of the community, the imposition of accountability for offenses and the development of competencies to enable children to become responsible and productive members of the community" (Pennsylvania Council of Chief Juvenile Probation Officers 2022).

In 2005, Pennsylvania was chosen by the John D. and Catherine T. MacArthur Foundation to be the first state to participate in its Models for Change initiative. Due to its adoption of Balanced and Restorative Justice, Pennsylvania represented a strong candidate for additional reform efforts (PCCD 2019). The three areas of focus of Pennsylvania's Models for Change reform were coordinating the mental health and juvenile justice systems, improving aftercare services and supports for youth and their families, and addressing disproportionate minority contacts within the juvenile justice system (PCCD 2012). Key juvenile justice stakeholders determined that a more permanent initiative was necessary to continue reform efforts, and strategic planning meetings were held resulting in the development of the Juvenile Justice System Enhancement Strategy (JJSES) Framework (Figure 7.5) in 2012.

JJSES was developed to achieve the mission of BARJ through evidence-based policy and practice (JCJC 2018). The JJSES committed to the philosophy to use the best empirical research available in the field and to put this research into practice (PCCD 2012). Core objectives included delinquency prevention and diversion from formal court processing (when possible), data-driven decision-making, continual quality improvement, maintaining partnerships with service providers, and involving families with all aspects of the system. The JCJC has provided state-level oversight of the JJSES since its inception. The JJSES has been a successful reform initiative that has maintained steady momentum due to the partnerships of state and local governments that meet regularly to ensure reform gains are not lost. Various evidence-based initiatives occur within the activities of the JJSES, which include Effective Practices for Community Supervision (EPICS), Motivational Interviewing, Youth Level of Service/Case Management Inventory (YLS/CMI), Massachusetts Youth Screening Instrument-Version 2 (MAYSI-2), graduated responses, and cognitive-behavioral interventions.

Another activity with the JJSES is the Standardized Program Evaluation Protocol (SPEP™), which aligns service delivery to research by systematically applying quality-related implementation factors of evidence-based programs to non-evidence-based programs via a program improvement process (Lipsey 2009). A meta-analysis of over

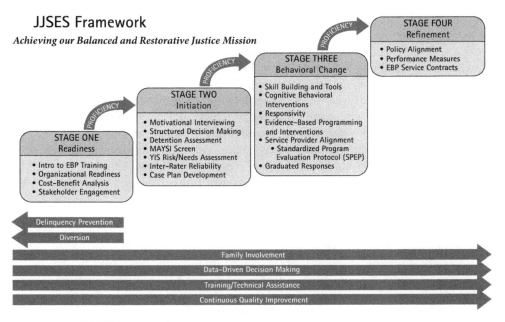

FIGURE 7.5. JJSES Framework.

Source: JJSES (2012).

740 studies was conducted to identify which factors were most closely associated with recidivism reduction in delinquent youth (Howell and Lipsey 2012). Four main factors emerged: youth risk level and aggressive/violent history, program philosophy and type, quality of service, and amount of service. The SPEP metric was developed and validated to score a service's predicted impact on recidivism reduction based on these four factors (Lipsey 2009). Because approximately 90% of programs in the US and UK are non-evidence-based (Howell and Lipsey 2012), the SPEP has the potential to significantly impact juvenile justice systems across the nation. In 2011, the Georgetown University Center for Juvenile Justice Reform selected Pennsylvania to participate in the Juvenile Justice System Improvement Project (JJSIP), which consisted of four components; the SPEP, a validated risk assessment, a dispositional matrix, and a service matrix. Since JJSIP, Penn State EPIS has served as a third-party intermediary group by providing training and technical assistance for the implementation of the SPEP, which has resulted in over 400 SPEP assessments statewide.

In 2019, the University of Pittsburgh published the findings of a validation study that examined the effectiveness of the SPEP in the Commonwealth to date (Mulvey and Shubert 2020). Key findings indicated that the SPEP score was indicative of the service's positive impact on recidivism reduction, that the performance improvement process was effective at increasing a service's positive impact on recidivism reduction, and that a service became more effective at reducing recidivism if it was improved by the SPEP process multiple times (Mulvey and Shubert 2020). Implementation of the SPEP is funded by the PCCD and guided by a SPEP Advisory Group, which is composed of juvenile justice stakeholders from various state and local governments, academic partners, and service providers.

B. Youth Diversion

PCCD and the Chief's Council have emphasized for decades the importance of diversion initiatives that bring juvenile justice stakeholders together to improve diversion services. Diversion efforts are important to juvenile justice stakeholders because they create reductions in premature involvement in the "deep end" of the juvenile delinquency system, including out-of-home placement (Dembo, Wareham, and Schmeidler 2005). Diverting youth out of the juvenile justice system provides countless benefits to youth as well as the system at large because juvenile justice stakeholders should be only focusing on higher-risk youth (Skowyra and Powell 2006). Diversion efforts also help maintain youth connectedness and engagement in the community by keeping the youth in their environment (Dembo, Wareham, and Schmeidler 2005). There has been a renewed emphasis on diversion among juvenile courts after findings from the Pennsylvania Juvenile Justice Task Force indicated that diversion efforts are proven to be effective at reducing delinquency (The Pennsylvania Juvenile Justice Task Force 2021).

Although diversion programs are typically unique to each jurisdiction within Pennsylvania, most counties have similar programs to address common needs among at-risk youth, including community service projects, victim awareness, substance misuse education and counseling, mental health treatment, crisis intervention, family counseling, recreation and organized sports programs, and educational and tutorial needs. The majority of these interventions often lack the specificity of evidence-based programs such as defined protocols or fidelity tools to monitor service delivery (Models for Change 2011). Although diversion interventions typically lack consistent implementation, evidence-based practices can be incorporated through implementing validated screening tools and needs and risk assessments, standardizing the quality of service delivery, and measuring outcomes to verify their effectiveness (Models for Change 2011).

The Commonwealth of Pennsylvania could substantially improve the effectiveness of diversion programs if these components were incorporated, resulting in improved outcomes for youth and communities. Counties could partner with state agencies to develop strategic plans to improve the quality of diversion programs and options as well as jurisdictional practices of diverting youth to ensure that lower-risk youth are diverted out of the juvenile justice system and that only higher-risk youth receive EBPs in response to their needs. Pennsylvania counties are looking into their diversion practices to increase practices of fundamental fairness when making decisions about diverting youth. Racial and ethnic disparities exist in many jurisdictions regarding the use of diversion practices (PCCD 2019). Several counties are currently working with the Georgetown University Center for Juvenile Justice Reform on the Pennsylvania Reducing Racial and Ethnic Disparities in Juvenile Justice Certificate Program (PCCD 2021). Each county will develop a capstone project to enhance their ability to improve existing practices of fundamental fairness regarding racial and ethnic disparities. Several counties will be implementing these practices with diversion youth and are developing structured decision-making tools to increase their ability to make data-driven decisions with this population.

C. Regional Distinctions

Pennsylvania is a populous and diverse state, with several large urban areas and their surrounding suburbs, as well as numerous rural and small-town communities. Although concerns about crime and violence have typically focused on urban centers such as Philadelphia and Pittsburgh, the recent opioid epidemic has highlighted the vulnerability of rural communities to substance misuse, suicide, and other "diseases of despair" often related to diminished economic opportunity (Brignone et al. 2020). The challenges to effective dissemination of evidence-based prevention are affected by regional considerations, which are also related to ethnic, cultural, and socioeconomic factors. Rural areas of the state may have limited access to services due to the resource limitations of small communities as well as factors related to distance and transportation. While some studies suggest that risk and protective factors for juvenile crime are similar across urban and rural settings, others indicate regional differences (e.g., Blackmon et al. 2016). A recent review of regional differences in juvenile crime patterns in Pennsylvania suggested that while Philadelphia and Pittsburgh had made significant progress at reducing the number of youth tried as adults from 2009 to 2018, many other counties within the state showed the opposite pattern (JCJC 2021). Pennsylvania counties also vary widely in the degree to which youth are expected to pay fines, a factor that keeps many trapped within the juvenile justice system for inappropriately long periods (JCJC 2021).

D. Ethnic and Cultural Diversity

While rural areas remain overwhelmingly White, the Latino population in Pennsylvania has grown rapidly, to nearly 8% of the population, while African Americans make up 12% of the population (US Census 2020). Pennsylvania is also home to the largest population of Old Order Amish in the nation (Elizabethtown College, Young Center 2020). This diversity raises issues regarding the cultural appropriateness and fit of prevention efforts, many of which have not been evaluated with diverse populations. Additionally, highly disadvantaged communities may be unable to provide the infrastructure support necessary for effective EBP implementation and sustainability, leading to persistent disparities in access to effective interventions (Hodge and Turner 2016). Even when interventions are available, they may fail to address specific risk and protective factors that operate within minority families or communities. For example, minority or immigrant youth frequently confront unique risk factors related to racism, discrimination, and acculturation stressors, but these factors are infrequently incorporated into prevention or intervention programs (Brody et al. 2004; Umaña-Taylor et al. 2015). Language may also pose a barrier, particularly for family-focused interventions that include parents with minimal English language proficiency, and families may be reluctant to engage in interventions due to institutional mistrust or concerns regarding immigration status. In Pennsylvania, the degree to which these barriers exist is unclear, and collecting better data in order to determine where and with whom resource gaps exist is a future goal.

E. Racial and Ethnic Disparity

Like most states, racial and ethnic minority youth are overrepresented in the juvenile justice system in Pennsylvania. In particular, minority youth, especially Black males, are much more likely than White youth to be arrested and sent to secure confinement, are less likely than White youth to be referred for diversion programs, and are more likely to be tried in adult courts for their crimes (PCCD 2019; JCJC 2021). In the juvenile realm, the federal statute mandating states to address disproportionate minority contact (DMC) was implemented in 1988 and revised in 2002, and Pennsylvania quickly became a leader in the implementation of juvenile justice reforms designed to reduce DMC (Hsia and Hamparian 1998). Figure 7.6 shows Pennsylvania's DMC reduction strategy, which was presented in PCCD's report to the governor in 2019. As a result of these efforts, racial inequities in incarceration have declined in Pennsylvania in recent years, but disparities remain. A nonexperimental analysis of the impacts of Pennsylvania's DMC reforms revealed that they reduced, but did not eliminate, disparities in Black versus White youth's experiences with the juvenile justice system (Donnelly 2019). Despite national juvenile justice reform efforts, there has not been a substantial reduction in DMC, indicating that challenges in this area remain (Peck 2018; Zane 2021). Similar problems have been observed in the child welfare system. Nationally, minority-group children are significantly more likely than White children to come under the supervision of the child welfare system and to be permanently removed from their biological families (Hill 2007; Lu et al. 2004). In Pennsylvania, minority-group children are significantly more likely than White children to be placed in foster care and to experience

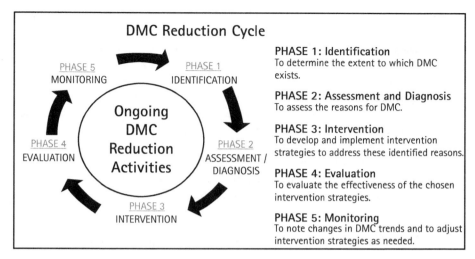

FIGURE 7.6. DMC Reduction Cycle.

multiple out-of-home placements (Pennsylvania Partnerships for Children 2020). Because child welfare involved youth are also more likely to enter the juvenile justice system (Doyle 2007), these racial disparities in child welfare involvement in Pennsylvania warrant further reform efforts.

F. Gender/Sexual Minorities

Changing social norms regarding sexual identity and orientation have presented new challenges for systems within Pennsylvania as well as other states. A recent study of youth in the juvenile justice system found that 39% of girls and 3% of boys identified as sexual minorities (lesbian/gay, nonbinary, transgender), and these youth were disproportionately likely to report experiences of sexual victimization and had lengthier out-of-home placements. Similarly, sexual minority youth are overrepresented in the child welfare system and are 2.5 times more likely than other youth to be placed outside of the home (Fish et al. 2019). The factors related to these disparities are not yet well understood, but the lack of reliable data makes it difficult for systems to know which practices and programs are most likely to be effective at meeting the needs of this population. Given the sensitivity of questions related to gender minority status, population-based data are difficult to obtain, as many communities resist inclusion of questions regarding gender identity or sexual orientation on youth surveys.

G. Mental Health Concerns and the Impact of the Online Environment

Recent trends in surveillance data in Pennsylvania (i.e., recent administrations of the PAYS) indicate high rates of depression, anxiety, and self-harm among Pennsylvania youth, with more than 40% of 10th and 12th graders indicating that they felt depressed or sad most days in 2019. Although the relations between internalizing disorders and crime are complex, the PAYS data also indicates that correlations among depression, anxiety, and substance misuse exist. School districts, as well as other state-level organizations, have endeavored to respond to this need by increasing access to resources for school-based, effective selective and indicated mental health promotion programs. Finally, research into the impacts of social media and other online platforms on crime for both youth and adults is currently scarce. Clearly, the online environment has created new opportunities for criminal networking and for the radicalization of young people (Hassan et al. 2018). The rise of near-universal social media participation by youth has greatly outpaced the development of effective strategies and programs to address its harmful effects, and this will continue to be a challenge for both Pennsylvania and society at large for the indefinite future.

IV. Summary and Recommendations

Pennsylvania has been viewed by many as a "success story" regarding the implementation of evidence-based programs and practices for prevention efforts and for juvenile justice interventions and practices. Implementation has been sustained for decades due to the strong philosophical support from practitioners and because of legislative mandates. The leadership of state agencies has demonstrated their awareness of both the human and economic costs of crime, as well as the cost-effectiveness of evidence-based prevention programming, through their ongoing, significant investments in prevention. Many local government agencies also include the implementation of EBPs for prevention efforts and for juvenile justice interventions as a standard line item in their annual budgets. Conceptual frameworks such as the Spectrum of MEB Interventions, the Continuum of Confidence, and the Social Development Model have strongly influenced the approaches taken by stakeholders within the Commonwealth.

Pennsylvania has developed strong partnerships at the community level to include universal programs for prevention education for children and youth within the public schools as well as prevention efforts for gun violence. State agencies such as the Pennsylvania Commission on Crime and Delinquency, the Juvenile Court Judges' Commission, the Department of Human Services, and the Department of Drug and Alcohol Programs have a long history of working closely together on various prevention and treatment intervention initiatives. Because many youth have cross-system involvement, such partnerships are essential to address their complex needs. Partnerships with the Commonwealth Prevention Alliance, the Pennsylvania Liquor Control Board, and the Pennsylvania Department of Education are integral to catching youth "upstream" with prevention efforts to reduce problem behavior, school failure, and substance misuse.

A number of rigorous research studies indicate the positive effects, both social and economic, of the Pennsylvania approach. For example, the Pennsylvania CTC evaluation indicated that youth in CTC communities showed less growth in delinquency over time than those in comparable non-CTC communities (Feinberg et al. 2010). Relatedly, cost-benefit research highlights the monetary savings associated with consistent implementation of high-quality prevention strategies (Jones et al. 2008). PAYS data yields a wealth of information to guide prevention efforts for mental health and substance misuse. Schools are excellent systems for the delivery of interventions to at-risk youth aimed at preventing crime because they provide universal prevention education to all students through health curriculum, including substance misuse and character development curricula, as well as services for youth that struggle with substance misuse or behavioral health issues (Domitrovich et al. 2010).

Long-term adoption of EBPs for prevention efforts and for juvenile justice interventions requires strong partnerships and engagement among local and state government agencies, service providers, academic partners, and community members. The establishment of best practices requires collaboration among these stakeholders to include the approval of developers to any adaptations. Expertise brought by academic partners has also been a key to the successful implementation of EBPs for prevention efforts and for juvenile justice interventions in the Commonwealth. In addition to providing training and technical assistance for effective implementation (Spoth et al. 2011), academic partners have established enduring relationships with developers of EBPs, which has proven invaluable for validation and for adapting the research to practice. Their expertise in translational science has also been helpful to inform policy and practice among local and state agencies. Additionally, academic partners (Brown et al. 2022; Feinberg et al. 2002; Welsh et al. 2016) coordinate community coalitions for EBP prevention initiatives, many of which have been successful at sustaining themselves beyond seed funding from state agencies. The continued demonstration of EBP impacts, including the links between early intervention and later outcomes and those between implementation quality and program effectiveness, is necessary to sustain future funding. The continued state-level investment in prevention of youth crime and problem behavior will ultimately translate to stronger youth, families, and communities throughout the Commonwealth of Pennsylvania.

REFERENCES

Afif Iman N., Ariana N. Gobaud, Christopher N. Morrison, Sara F. Jacoby, Zoë Maher, Elizabeth D. Dauer, Elinore J. Kaufman, Thomas A. Santora, Jeffrey H. Anderson, Abhijit Pathak, Lars Ola Sjoholm, Amy J. Goldberg, and Jessica H. Beard. 2022. The changing epidemiology of interpersonal firearm violence during the COVID-19 pandemic in Philadelphia, PA. *Preventive Medicine*, 158:107020. doi:10.1016/j.ypmed.2022.107020.

Blackmon, Bret J., Samuel B. Robison, and Judith L. F. Rhodes. 2016. Examining the influence of risk factors across rural and urban communities. *Journal of the Society for Social Work and Research*, 7 (4): 615–638.

Brignone, Emily, Daniel R. George, Lawrence Sinoway, Curren Katz, Charity Sauder, Andrea Murray, Robert Gladden, and Jennifer L. Kraschnewski. 2020. Trends in the diagnosis of diseases of despair in the United States, 2009–2018: A retrospective cohort study. *BMJ Open*, 10 (10): e037679.

Brody, Gene H., Velma McBride Murry, Meg Gerrard, Frederick X. Gibbons, Virginia Molgaard, Lily McNair, Anita C. Brown, et al. 2004. The Strong African American Families Program: Translating research into prevention programming. *Child Development*, 75 (3): 900–917.

Brown, C. Hendricks, Donald Hedeker, Robert D. Gibbons, Naihua Duan, Daniel Almirall, Carlos Gallo, Inger Burnett-Zeigler, Guillermo Prado, Sean D. Young, Alberto Valido, and Peter A. Wyman. 2022. Accounting for context in randomized trials after assignment. *Prevention Science*, 23 (8): 1321–1332. https://doi.org/10.1007/s11121-022-01426-9.

Bumbarger, Brian K. 2009. *Reducing delinquency and youth violence: Bridging the gap between science and practice*. Harrisburg, PA: PA Conference on Juvenile Justice.

Catalano, Richard F., Kevin P. Haggerty, Sabrina Oesterle, Charles B. Fleming, and J. David Hawkins. 2004. The importance of bonding to school for healthy development: Findings from the Social Development Research Group. *Journal of School Health*, 74:252–261.

Children's Trust. 2016. *Steps Toward Child Abuse Prevention & Creating Safe School Environments: A How-To Manual for Massachusetts Educators*. Boston: Children's Trust. https://childrenstrustma.org/uploads/files/PDFs/child_abuse_prevention_manual.pdf.

Dembo, R., J. Wareham, and J. Schmeidler. 2005. Evaluation of the impact of a policy change on diversion program recidivism. *Journal of Offender Rehabilitation*, 41 (3): 29–61.

Domitrovich, Celene, Catherine Bradshaw, Mark T. Greenberg, Dennis Embry, J. Poduska, and Nicholas Ialongo. 2010. Integrated models of school-based prevention: Logic and theory. *Psychology in the Schools*, 47 (1): 71–88.

Donnelly, E. A. 2019. Do disproportionate minority contact (DMC) mandate reforms change decision-making? Decomposing disparities in the juvenile justice system. *Youth Violence and Juvenile Justice*, 17 (3): 288–308.

Doyle, J. J. 2007. Child protection and child outcomes: Measuring the effects of foster care. *American Economic Review*, 97 (5): 1583–1610.

Eckenrode, John, Mary I. Campa, Pamela A. Morris, Charles R. Henderson Jr., Kerry E. Bolger, Harriet Kitzman, and David L. Olds. 2017. The Prevention of child maltreatment through the Nurse Family Partnership Program: Mediating effects in a long-term follow-up study. *Child Maltreatment*, 22 (2): 92–99.

Elizabethtown College, Young Center. n.d. Amish Population Profile, 2020. Elizabethtown, PA: Young Center for Anabaptist and Pietist Studies. https://groups.etown.edu/amishstudies/statistics/amish-population-profile-2020/.

Feinberg, Mark E., Mark T. Greenberg, D. Wayne Osgood, Amy Anderson, and Leslie Babinski. 2002. The effects of training community leaders in prevention science: Communities That Care in Pennsylvania. *Evaluation and Program Planning*, 25 (3): 245–259.

Feinberg Mark E., Damon Jones, Mark T. Greenberg, D. Wayne Osgood, and Daniel Bontempo. 2010. Effects of the Communities That Care model in Pennsylvania on change in adolescent risk and problem behaviors. *Prevention Science*, 11 (2): 163–171. doi:10.1007/s11121-009-0161-x.

Fish, J. N., L. Baams, A. S. Wojciak, and S. T. Russell. 2019. Are sexual minority youth overrepresented in foster care, child welfare, and out-of-home placement? Findings from nationally representative data. *Child Abuse & Neglect*, 89:203–211.

Greenberg, Mark T., Celene Domitrovich, Roger Weissberg, and Joseph Durlak. 2017. Social and emotional learning as a public health approach to education. *The Future of Children*, 27 (1): 13–32.

Hassan, G., S. Brouillette-Alarie, S. Alava, D. Frau-Meigs, L. Lavoie, A. Fetiu, and S. Sieckelinck. 2019. Exposure to extremist online content could lead to violent radicalization: A systematic review of empirical evidence. *International Journal of Developmental Science*, 12 (1–2): 71–88.

Hawkins, J. David, Richard F. Catalano, Michael W. Arthur, Elizabeth Egan, Eric C. Brown, Robert D. Abbott, and David M. Murray. 2008. Testing communities that care: The rationale, design and behavioral baseline equivalence of the Community Youth Development Study. *Prevention Science*, 9 (3): 178–190.

Hill, R. B. 2007. *An analysis of racial/ethnic disproportionality and disparity at the national, state, and county levels*. Washington, DC: Casey-CSSP Alliance for Racial Equity in Child Welfare.

Hodge, L. M., and K. M. Turner. 2016. Sustained implementation of evidence-based programs in disadvantaged communities: A conceptual framework of supporting factors. *American Journal of Community Psychology*, 58 (1–2): 192–210.

Howell, J. C., and M. W. Lipsey. 2012. Research-based guidelines for juvenile justice programs. *Journal of Criminal Justice*, 14:1–18.

Hsia, Heidi M., and Donna Hamparian. 1998. Disproportionate minority confinement: 1997 update. Washington, DC: Office of Juvenile Justice and Delinquency Prevention. https://ojjdp.ojp.gov/sites/g/files/xyckuh176/files/jjbulletin/9809/intro.html.

Jones, Damon, Brian K. Bumbarger, Mark T. Greenberg, P. Greenwood, and Sandee Kyler. 2008. *The economic return on PCCD's investment in research-based programs: A cost-benefit assessment of delinquency prevention in Pennsylvania*. State College, PA: Prevention Research Center for the Promotion of Human Development.

JCJC (Juvenile Court Judges' Commission). 2018. *Pennsylvania juvenile delinquency benchbook*. Harrisburg, PA: JCJC.

JCJC (Juvenile Court Judges' Commission). 2021. About the JCJC. Harrisburg, PA: JCJC. https://www.jcjc.pa.gov/Pages/default.aspx.

Liberman, A., and J. Hussemann. 2016. *Implementing the SPEP™: Lessons from demonstration sites in OJJDP's Juvenile Justice Reform and Reinvestment Initiative*. Washington, DC: Urban Institute. https://www.urban.org/sites/default/files/publication/86636/spep_report.pdf.

Lipsey, M. W. 2009. The primary factors that characterize effective interventions with juvenile offenders: A meta-analytic overview. *Victims and Offenders*, 4:124–147.

Lu, Y. E., J. Landsverk, E. Ellis-Macleod, R. Newton, W. Ganger, and I. Johnson. 2004. Race, ethnicity, and case outcomes in Child Protective Services. *Children and Youth Services Review*, 26 (5): 447–461.

Mihalic, S. F., and K. Irwin. 2003. Blueprints for violence prevention: From research to real-world settings-factors influencing the successful replication of model programs. *Youth Violence and Juvenile Justice*, 1 (4): 307–329.

Models for Change: Systems Reform in Juvenile Justice. 2011. *Juvenile diversion guidebook*. https://www.modelsforchange.net/publications/301/Juvenile_Diversion_Guidebook.pdf.

Mulvey, Edward and Carol Schubert. 2020. *A validation of SPEP in Pennsylvania: A brief summary*. Harrisburg, PA: Pennsylvania Commission on Crime and Delinquency.https://www.jcjc.pa.gov/Publications/Newsletters/2020/May.pdf.

National Academies of Sciences, Engineering, and Medicine. 2019. *Fostering healthy mental, emotional, and behavioral development in children and youth: A national agenda*. Washington, DC: National Library of Medicine.

New York State Department of Health. 2013. Promote mental health and prevent substance abuse. https://www.health.ny.gov/prevention/prevention_agenda/2013-2018/plan/mhsa/ebi/index.html.

Office of Juvenile Justice and Delinquency Prevention. n.d. Diversion programs. Washington, D.C.: U.S. Department of Justice. https://ojjdp.ojp.gov/sites/g/files/xyckuh176/files/mpg-iguides/topics/diversion-programs/DoYourHomework.html.

Olds, David L., C. R. Henderson Jr., R. Cole, J. Eckenrode, H. Kitzman, D. Luckey, L. Pettitt, K. Sidora, P. Morris, and J. Powers. 1998. Long-term effects of nurse home visitation on children's criminal and antisocial behavior: 15-year follow-up of a randomized controlled trial. *Journal of the American Medical Association*, 280:1238–1244.

Peck, Jennifer H. 2018 The importance of evaluation and monitoring within the disproportionate minority contact (DMC) mandate: Future directions in juvenile justice research. *Race and Justice*, 8 (4): 305–329.

Pennsylvania Chief Probation Officers Organization. n.d. President's Message. https://www.pachiefprobationofficers.org/presidents_message.php.

PCCD (Pennsylvania Commission on Crime and Delinquency). 2012. *Pennsylvania's Juvenile Justice System Enhancement Strategy: Achieving our Balanced and Restorative Justice Mission Through Evidence-Based Policy and Practice.* Harrisburg, PA: PCCD. https://www.pccd.pa.gov/Juvenile-Justice/Documents/JJSES%20Monograph%20Final%20version%20press%20ready%2005%2025%2012.pdf.

PCCD (Pennsylvania Commission on Crime and Delinquency). 2019. *2019 Pennsylvania Juvenile Justice and Delinquency Prevention Plan.* Harrisburg, PA: PCCD.

PCCD (Pennsylvania Commission on Crime and Delinquency). 2019–2020. Pennsylvania Youth Survey (PAYS). Harrisburg, PA: PCCD. https://www.pccd.pa.gov/Juvenile-Justice/Documents/2019%20PAYS/State%20of%20Pennsylvania%20Profile%20Report.Final.pdf.

PCCD (Pennsylvania Commission on Crime and Delinquency). 2020. *FY2019–2020 strategic plan and annual reports.* Harrisburg, PA: PCCD. https://www.pccd.pa.gov/AboutUs/SiteAssets/Pages/Strategic-Plan-and-Annual-Reports/FY2019-20%20PCCD%20Annual%20Report_website%20version.pdf.

PCCD (Pennsylvania Commission on Crime and Delinquency). 2021. Reducing racial and ethnic disparities in juvenile justice. Harrisburg, PA: PCCD. https://www.pccd.pa.gov/Juvenile-Justice/Documents/Georgetown/PA%20September%20RED%20Flyer.pdf.

Pennsylvania Council of Chief Juvenile Probation Officers. 2022. https://www.pachiefprobationofficers.org/barj.php.

Pennsylvania Partnerships for Children. 2020. *2020 state of child welfare: Protecting children and promoting stable families in PA.* Harrisburg: Pennsylvania Partnerships for Children. https://www.papartnerships.org/report/report-2020-state-of-child-welfare/.

Pennsylvania State Data Center. 2022. The Hispanic population in Pennsylvania. https://pasdc.hbg.psu.edu/sdc/pasdc_files/researchbriefs/RB_Hispanic_2000-2010.pdf.

Petrosino, Anthony, Carolyn Turpin-Petrosino, Meghan E. Hollis-Peel, and Julia G. Lavenberg. 2013. "Scared Straight" and other juvenile awareness programs for preventing juvenile delinquency. *Cochrane Database of Systematic Reviews*, 4: CD002796.

Prinz, R. J., and S. E. Kerns. 2003. Early substance use by juvenile offenders. *Child Psychiatry and Human Development*, 33 (4): 263–277.

Skowyra, K., and S. Powell. 2006. *Juvenile diversion: Programs for justice-involved youth with mental health disorders.* Delmar, NY: National Center for Mental Health and Juvenile Justice.

Spoth, Richard, Max Guyll, Cleve Redmond, Mark Greenberg, and Mark Feinberg. 2011. Six-year sustainability of evidence-based intervention implementation quality by community-university partnerships: The PROSPER Study. *American Journal of Community Psychology*, 48 (3–4): 412–425.

The Pennsylvania Juvenile Justice Task Force. 2021. Report & Recommendations. https://www.pacourts.us/Storage/media/pdfs/20210622/152647-pajuvenilejusticetaskforcereportandrecommendations_final.pdf.

Umaña-Taylor, Adriana J., Brendesha M. Tynes, Russell B. Toomey, David R. Williams, and Kimberly J. Mitchell. 2015. Latino adolescents' perceived discrimination in online and offline settings: An examination of cultural risk and protective factors. *Developmental Psychology*, 51 (1): 87.

US Census. 2020. 2020 survey. https://www.census.gov/programs-surveys/decennial-census/decade/2020/2020-census-main.html.

University of Colorado. n.d. Blueprints for Healthy Youth Development. http://www.blueprintsprograms.org.

Welsh, Janet A., Sarah M. Chilenski, Lesley Johnson, Mark T. Greenberg, and Richard L. Spoth. 2016. Pathways to sustainability: 8-year follow-up from the PROSPER project. *Journal of Primary Prevention*, 37 (3): 263–286.

Zajac, J., T. Deal, P. Torbet, and J. Shirey. 2010. *Quality Improvement Initiative: Improving the quality of delinquency interventions for juveniles in Pennsylvania*. Pittsburgh: National Center for Juvenile Justice and the University of Pittsburgh's Office of Child Development, Division of Applied Research and Evaluation.

Zane, Steven N. 2021. Have racial and ethnic disparities in juvenile justice reduced over time? An empirical assessment of the DMC mandate. *Youth Violence and Juvenile Justice*, 19 (2): 163–185.

Zehr, Howard. 2002. *The little book of restorative justice*. Intercourse, PA: Good Books.

CHAPTER 8

DIVERSION
What Do We Know?

ROGER S. SMITH

This chapter is dedicated to the memory of Traci Schlesinger, who was originally due to be its coauthor before her untimely death. Her commitment to social justice and to challenging racial discrimination through her academic work and beyond is recognized and applauded through this small mark of respect.

I. What Is Diversion?

The emergence of "diversion" as a specifically delineated and widely practiced form of intervention in criminal justice, particularly in youth or juvenile justice, has inevitably been accompanied by attempts to understand and analyze the structures, policies, processes, and outcomes associated with it. A considerable body of diversion-related research is now available, but while this helps to shed important light on the subject, it also highlights areas of uncertainty, incomplete knowledge, and controversy, which we must acknowledge. The first of these challenges to understanding derives from the underlying definitional problem: What, in fact, is diversion? Other key questions flow from this, notably to do with the fields and scope of activity encompassed by alternative definitions, and, in turn, how outcomes are measured, and how "success" is defined and determined.

Diversion could be conceptualized in terms of a reduction of the severity of the sanction applied in criminal justice proceedings, such as the replacement of custody with a community-based alternative, or in terms of a decision not to prosecute someone for a particular offense. In this sense, we can understand it as "diversion *from* criminal justice" as distinct from "diversion *toward* some alternative form of intervention" as a way of responding to an offense. On the one hand, then, diversion could simply mean doing nothing; that is, not taking formal action of any kind against an offender. On the other hand, it could involve substituting an alternative form of response to the reported offense to that conventionally prescribed under the criminal justice system and possibly outside of its remit altogether.

If this were the case, the type of response in question could also take different forms. It might involve restorative action to resolve the problems and possible harms associated with the offense; it might involve some form of community service; it might involve the offender accepting some form of restriction or limited measure of punishment; or it might involve a structured program of intervention to address the offender's criminogenic needs.

As well as contributing to "decriminalization," diversion can be thought of as a more positive process of "normalization" whereby individuals identified as offenders may be reintegrated into the mainstream of society, in addition to avoiding the stigmatization and disadvantage associated with acquiring a criminal record. The risk of "labeling" (Lemert 1951) may be avoided, offenders might be reintegrated into mainstream education, or they might be directed toward prosocial rather than antisocial activities. Increasingly, too, with the emergence of restorative justice as a more central feature of many justice systems, diversion can be viewed in terms of an alternative problem-solving model, focused more on resolving the issues arising from the offense than intervening with the offender in isolation (Wong et al. 2016).

Diversion might also be considered in terms of its contribution toward achieving a reduced likelihood of reoffending. Criminal justice interventions (or noninterventions) are typically judged in terms of their effect on future levels of criminality, and this is certainly a central focus of much evaluation work in the context of diversion (Wilson and Hoge 2013).

If we turn now to think of a proposed "evaluation hierarchy" (Mears 2010), alternative ways of framing "diversion" and its purposes lead to differing background assumptions about (1) the need for diversion, (2) the problem(s) we are trying to solve, (3) the mechanisms and practices that are likely to help us to solve the problem, and (4) how to establish whether they are successful in doing so. In order to consider how these issues have been addressed in policy and practice in more detail, this chapter will first discuss the purposes and objectives of diversion, before moving on to reflect on its development as a discrete area of practice, principally in the United Kingdom (specifically England and Wales),[1] but also more widely. Following this is a critical discussion of the evidence base, and some concluding thoughts on what this tells us up to now and what gaps need to be filled to provide a fuller picture.

II. Purposes and Possibilities

Alternative ways of thinking about diversion align with different assumptions about the purposes and effects of intervention and competing models of practice. In particular, there appears to be a substantial divergence between those who would identify a diversionary approach with minimum (or no) intervention, on the one hand, and those who would associate it with a more proactive, change-oriented perspective, on the other. In the former case, diversion might involve an early decision to take no (or at least minimal) action in response to apparent offending behavior. This may be associated with a nostalgic view of former policing practices, whereby young miscreants would be given a stern talking to and sent home with a (perhaps metaphorical) "clip round the ear" (Davis, Boucherat, and Watson 1989).

Nothing would be recorded and, to all intents and purposes, no crime would be deemed to have taken place. However, this approach could become problematic if it appears that young offenders have "got away with it," and are free to continue to offend with impunity.

By contrast, a more interventionist approach would assume that the detection of an offense by a child or young person requires a response—whether to assuage public expectations, to resolve the hurt caused, or to discourage reoffending. In this case, "diversion" could take a wider range of forms, with additional questions to consider. Should victims be involved, and in what ways? Should the final decision on whether or not to pursue criminal proceedings be conditional on the outcome of the diversionary intervention? If so, how should we determine what counts as satisfactory compliance? Should our focus be on resolving the offense, or on changing the offender? Should diversion be based on voluntarist principles or rely on an element of compulsion? Should diversion take place prior to any formal action (pre-prosecution), or should it be retained as an option at a later stage of the judicial process (pre-court, in-court, or even post-sentencing)? According to Zimring (2000), for example, the US juvenile court itself was originally introduced as a "diversionary" measure, sparing young people the rigors of adult judicial processes—although this objective was subsequently compromised, Feld (2017) has concluded.

Responses to such questions are played out in the form of alternative "models" of diversion, with differing objectives and success criteria, posing inevitable challenges for any attempt at evaluating them. Kelly and Armitage (2015, 130) have suggested that there has emerged a "*diversity of practice*" in juvenile diversion. They observe, nonetheless, that there remains an implicit elision between the underlying goals of "diversion from the youth justice system" and "diversion from youth crime." The present author's review of diversionary practices (Smith 2018) suggests four different but not entirely distinct approaches, grounded in notions of welfare, rights, risk management, and "responsibilization."

Under a welfarist model of diversion, the cessation of criminal proceedings is explicitly associated with a program of intervention to promote children's well-being and the capacity of families to provide effective support and moral guidance. This model has been highly influential at certain points in the development of diversion (Pratt 1986), inviting us to assume a reversible causal link between a failure to meet welfare needs and offending.

A more explicit rights-based approach draws attention to the essential "normality" of children's offending behavior, and to the criminalizing effects of being drawn into the justice system. Diversion from the justice system is therefore viewed as sufficient in itself to reduce the likelihood of further offending (Davis, Boucherat, and Watson 1989).

Risk-based approaches adopt a more systematic and individualized approach to assessing the risk associated with offending behavior and tailoring responses accordingly (Case and Haines 2009). This approach makes certain contestable assumptions about the reliability of assessment tools and intervention strategies, but it has established a degree of credibility nonetheless (in the case of the Asset assessment tool, for instance; see Baker 2014).

The fourth category, which I have termed "responsibilizing" diversion (Smith 2018), tends to be associated with problem-solving approaches, including restorative interventions. Here, the focus is on adopting informal mechanisms for resolving the harms and associated problems that might arise on the commission of an offense, typified by the youth conferencing scheme introduced in Northern Ireland (Doak and O'Mahoney 2011).

In numerical terms, diversion has certainly become more central to many juvenile justice systems. In the United States, national estimates for 2018 suggest that of those juvenile offenders referred for court proceedings, 46% were not "petitioned" and did not go to court. Of these, 59% were dealt with by way of some form of "informal" intervention, albeit these may be subject to conditions (Hockenberry and Puzzanchera 2021, 52). By comparison, Bateman (2020, 83) estimated that the proportion of reported young offenders dealt with formally by way of a "pre-court disposal" in the United Kingdom was "just under 33%" in 2018. It is likely, too, that a substantial number of young people are the subject of informal "diversionary" police responses, precise evidence of which is understandably difficult to obtain. On grounds of both scale and complexity, straightforward or uniform measures and comparisons of "what works" in diversion are unlikely to present themselves. Diversion is, indeed, "diverse" (Kelly and Armitage 2015), and we should, in consequence, seek to understand its achievements (or shortcomings) according to a range of possible criteria and potential measures of "success."

III. Looking Back at Diversion in the United Kingdom: Early Evidence of "Success"?

Informal diversionary practices have a lengthy history (Home Office 1927; Shore 1999; Smith 2018), but possibly the earliest documented (and evaluated) diversion scheme was the Juvenile Liaison Officer initiative in Liverpool (England) established in 1949 (Mays 1965), at least partially informed by concerns about "labeling." The avoidance of a court appearance was intended to prevent the young offender coming to accept "himself as a delinquent" (Mays 1965, 186). A waiver of prosecution would, however, be accompanied by provision of family support and community liaison with the aim of preventing reoffending. Fewer than 10% of male young offenders dealt with in this way by the Liverpool scheme were reported to be reconvicted subsequently (Mays 1965, 196). As the preventive element of the scheme developed, though, to include a wider group of "near delinquents and potential offenders" (Mays 1965, 187), it risked "widening the net" (Austin and Krisberg 2002), and problematizing children and young people who might not otherwise have come to official notice. The proportion of those dealt with as identified offenders by the Liverpool scheme declined from 93% in 1952 to 58% in 1960, while the equivalent figure for "potential" offenders saw an increase from 7 to 42% (Mays 1965, 187).

Notwithstanding these signs of "mission creep," by the mid-1960s, similar schemes had been initiated in at least eight other police areas in England and Scotland.

A. Emerging Questions: Diversion, Net-Widening, and Discrimination

The number of diversion programs was increasing, and reoffending or reconviction rates were low. Police cautions administered to juvenile offenders rose from 13,000 to 28,000 between 1955 and 1965 (McClintock and Avison 1968). The official crime rate was also going up, however, and the cautioning rate remained stable at around 11% of formal disposals (Smith 2018, 38). It would thus be difficult to determine whether young offenders were being diverted *from* the justice system in greater numbers, or, by contrast, were increasingly drawn *in* to face formal interventions rather than informal responses (Farrington and Bennett 1981). Similarly, the impact of juvenile liaison schemes on reoffending rates remained unclear. Farrington and Bennett (1981, 134) observed that "little [was] known about the effects of police cautions . . . on juvenile delinquency," and that "there should be more adequate research."

This period of diversionary expansionism within the United Kingdom culminated in the welfarist Children and Young Persons Act 1969. This act attempted to establish a presumption against criminalizing juvenile offenders. Juvenile cautions more than doubled between 1968 and 1971 (Ditchfield 1976), supported by an extensive network of police-run juvenile bureaus (Steer 1970). Ditchfield, however, observed the emergence of "justice by geography," with varying cautioning rates between police areas (Ditchfield 1976, 7); and "displacement." In some areas, cautions appeared to be taking the place of both low-level court outcomes (absolute or conditional discharges) and informal warnings (24). This period coincidentally provided explicit evidence of discrimination on the grounds of race in the operation of cautioning procedures. Analysis of police decisions regarding 1,146 reported juvenile offenders revealed that those classified as "Black" were more likely to be prosecuted for certain types of offenses, and "bias on the part of the police against blacks involved in these offences cannot be ruled out" (Landau and Nathan 1983, 142).

B. The Decade of Diversion: A New Rationale for the 1980s?

Following the election of the neoliberal Thatcher government in 1979, juvenile diversion was reframed. The political climate came into alignment with key critics of the welfare-led interventionist boom of the previous decade (Thorpe et al. 1980; Morris and Giller 1987), and a new consensus emerged, recognizing evidence of "net-widening." Children should accordingly be diverted *from* both justice and welfare "systems" (Morris et al. 1980), rather than *into* stigmatizing intervention programs.

Diversion in England and Wales came to be reset in the 1980s, typified by the informal model of diversion developed by the Northamptonshire Juvenile Liaison Bureaux. This county moved rapidly from a juvenile (aged 10–17) cautioning rate of approximately 35% to over 80% (Smith 2003), with no evidence of displacement or net-widening (Blagg et al. 1986). The higher rate of cautioning appeared to feed through to a reduction in the use of custody (Smith 2018). Low reoffending rates were also associated with this intensive increase in the use of diversion (Smith 1989; see also Kemp et al. 2002).

This pattern was replicated elsewhere. Between 1977 and 1991 in England and Wales, the number of young offenders between the ages of 10 and 17 processed for offenses declined from 184,000 to 115,000, and the proportion of these receiving a caution increased from just over half to four out of five. Between 1981 and 1991, the proportion of 14–16-year-olds processed who were sent to custody declined from 6.8% to 1.8%, as the impact of front-end diversion worked through the system (Smith 2007, 13–14).

C. Diversion as an Emerging "Field" of Practice and Inquiry

Perhaps because diversion does pose a challenge to much conventional wisdom or "common sense," views about crime and punishment it has become a field of considerable research interest. The Northamptonshire initiative was the subject of at least nine separate studies or evaluations (Smith 2018), despite its relatively small scale. These studies were largely qualitative, or reliant on descriptive statistical evidence, ranging from enthusiastic endorsement (Blagg et al. 1986) to the critical and dismissive (Davis, Boucherat, and Watson 1989). The focus of inquiry often extended beyond individual outcomes to consider "system" change, such as the use of restorative interventions in place of criminal proceedings (Blagg 1985).

D. Twists and Turns in the Road

In the early 1990s, with the emergence of the "punitive turn" in England and Wales, diversion was called into question (Goldson 1999). As the political and popular view of youth crime appeared increasingly punitive (Rutherford 2002; Bottoms and Dignan 2004), those who came to the notice of the justice system were less likely to be diverted from it. The contested nature of the available "evidence," and its potential for political exploitation, became clear (Smith 2018, 83). On the basis of one unpublished report from a regional police force, and in the face of contrary findings (Kemp et al. 2002), the Audit Commission (1996) and the incoming Labour government (Home Office 1997) decided that much closer constraints should be placed on pre-prosecution decision-making. The introduction of the highly structured and tariff-based framework of Reprimands and Final Warnings represented a substantial shift in the conceptualization, organization, and delivery of diversion. Each of these disposals was to be administered only once, with an inexorable tariff-based progression toward formal court proceedings for those who continued to offend. Previous police practices of administering informal warnings were to be discouraged, and at the final warning stage, the expectation was that intervention programs would routinely be implemented to prevent reoffending (Goldson 1999, 38).

Subsequent research suggested that there had been a reduction in reoffending rates following the introduction of the new arrangements (Hine and Celnick 2001). However, this study also argued that "intervening too early could be a waste of resources" (Hine and Celnick 2001, 35). Despite this, the Youth Justice Board (2002, 10) claimed that "an intervention programme at the Final Warning stage is one of the most effective ways of diverting an individual from criminality." If this provides evidence of anything, it is the tendency for politically driven claims concerning youth justice to be less than open-minded in their use (or misuse) of evidence. One government-funded researcher was quite explicit, stating that "such comments were not only highly selective, but could not be said to be based on reliable evidence" (Wilcox 2003, 30).

The reforms of the late 1990s and early 2000s coincided with falling juvenile crime rates in general (Bateman 2015), which would probably have affected reoffending rates. The pattern of disposals also changed with cautioning (Reprimand/Final Warning) rates falling relative to convictions (Smith 2018, 97), with these changing trends indicating obvious challenges for comparative studies that do not utilize contemporaneous samples. Clearly, evaluators need to be mindful of systemic changes, albeit while assessing the behavioral impacts of diversionary measures.

A further system-wide shift resulted from a government-initiated change in police detection targets (Offences Brought to Justice) in 2002, which led to a sudden rise in the number of criminal cases formally processed (Smith 2018, 101). A perverse incentive now led the police to seek out "low hanging fruit," minor and easily detected offenses typically associated with children and young people. Between 2002/03 and 2006/07, the number of disposals (pre- and post-court) administered to young offenders (10–18) increased from 168,673 to 216,011 (Solomon and Garside 2008, 40), the number of "first time entrants" to the justice system rose by almost a third (Bateman 2015, 11), and the number of "out of court" disposals went up by 135% (Kemp 2014, 2). Increased diversion rates were a consequence rather than a cause of net-widening. According to the frustrated outgoing head of the Youth Justice Board,

"The government boasts that the current achievement... is well ahead of target.... The... increase has almost entirely been achieved by handing out on-the-spot fines or cautions for relatively minor offenses" (Morgan 2007).

E. Reversal and Reinvention

In the face of criticism, government policy was amended in 2008, so as to reduce the number of "first time entrants" (FTEs) to the justice system. The doors were opened to a range of diversionary options, such as the "Youth Restorative Disposal," which restored police discretion to deal with offenses informally (Bateman 2015). Policy remained relatively stable from that point until at least the early 2020s, re-legitimizing the role of diversion at the threshold of the youth justice system (Smith 2021). A wider range of options encouraged greater flexibility in police decision-making at the local level (Bateman 2020, 79). Bateman (2020, 64), however, observes that inequalities and discrimination persisted, with young Black people remaining disproportionately susceptible to criminalization, from the point of arrest onward (Lammy 2017).

A less interventionist state left space for local creativity and the emergence of a range of "models" of diversion and wider youth justice practices (Kelly and Armitage 2015; Smith and Gray 2019). In addition to the Youth Restorative Disposal (Rix et al. 2011), evaluated initiatives have included a "Triage" scheme (Institute for Criminal Policy Research 2012), a series of Youth Justice Liaison and Diversion projects (Haines et al. 2012) and the Swansea Bureau, operating under the strapline of "children first, offenders second" (Haines et al. 2013, 5).

The Youth Restorative Disposal, for example, was made available to deal with "low-level, antisocial and nuisance offending" (Rix et al. 2011, 2), incorporating offender-victim reparation, such as an apology, or compensation. Practitioners saw it as "a good mechanism for dealing with young people and reducing FTEs [first time entrants] to the justice system" (27).

Other initiatives utilized a more diagnostic approach (Institute for Criminal Policy Research 2012; Haines et al. 2012). The Triage model, for instance, was intended to determine at which of three "levels" intervention should be pitched. Level 1 disposals would see an end to criminal proceedings, with the option of restorative measures; Level 3 disposals would involve "fast-tracked progression through" the criminal justice system (by way of prosecution); while Level 2 would involve "referral to supportive interventions" (Institute for Criminal Policy Research 2012, 5).

The Youth Justice Liaison and Diversion model aimed to divert "vulnerable" children and young people with learning difficulties or mental health needs "towards mental health, emotional support and welfare systems" (Haines et al. 2012, 24). Local implementation of these particular schemes was inconsistent, however, and no strong evidence of their achievements could be identified (Institute for Criminal Policy Research 2012, 7; Haines et al. 2012, 60).

The model developed in one Welsh city (the Swansea Bureau) was grounded in the principle of "children first." Diversion would aim to avoid the risks of both further criminalization and social exclusion. Early evidence recorded 70% fewer "first time entrants" into the formal justice system in 2011–2012 compared to 2008–2009 (Haines et al. 2013, 9). The aim of providing "supportive intervention to young people and parents" had also seemingly begun to bear fruit: "Parents appear to have been responding to the behaviour of their children without external provocation" (Haines et al. 2013, 184).

IV. A Wider View: Diversion Beyond The United Kingdom

A. Diversion in the United States

Diversion is clearly now well established in the United States (Mears et al. 2016). Palmer and Lewis (1980), for example, reported on three initiatives in California operating in 1974. According to Cressey and McDermott (1973) diversionary programs were inspired by the recommendation of the President's Commission on Law Enforcement and Administration of Justice (1967, 2) that the "formal sanctioning system . . . should only be used as a last resort." By the early 1970s, diversion projects were widespread across the United States. Klein's (1979) review of "deinstitutionalization and diversion," though, recognized considerable diversity amongst early programs. A limited number of schemes (in Baltimore, Michigan, Los Angeles, and the state of Washington) were targeted at "populations which would consistently have been inserted further into the [justice] system but for the activities of the program" (Klein 1979, 163). However, a more extensive body of activity was seemingly concentrating on delivering prevention programs "characterized by referrals from schools, welfare agencies and parents" rather than "the police or courts." Klein also suggested that areas "with adequate referral resources" tended to be skewed toward the better off, with obvious implications for disadvantaged and minority populations.

More recent accounts suggest that program heterogeneity has not diminished (NeMoyer et al. 2020, 605), as "requirements often include community service, restitution, restorative justice procedures, and mental health and substance use treatment services." Many programs operate on a conditional basis, with failure to comply with contractual requirements potentially leading to a further formal adjudication. The well-established Youth Aid Panel scheme in Philadelphia, for example, appears to operate quite a rigorous three-month program requiring both compliance (including weekly contact) and a six-month period without further arrests in order to avoid further formal proceedings. Similarly, the conditional diversion program in a "large Midwestern city" is reported to operate an elaborate selection process based on the Risk-Need-Responsivity (RNR) intervention model, with more than 70 discrete services available, although "there may still be gaps" (Wylie et al. 2019, 1140). Under the Colorado model, "first-time" young offender may be invited to enter a "restorative justice program.... Upon satisfactory completion ... no charges would be filed" (Sliva and Plassmeyer 2021, 22).

By contrast, in Maine a substantial proportion (28%) of those cases where young offenders are diverted from formal proceedings involve "no further action" (Dumont and King 2017, 10). Here, too, additional interventions and program requirements are associated with relatively more serious offenses such as burglary and criminal damage (Dumont and King 2017, 11). The Cambridge, Massachusetts, model does not rely on compliance, but involves police "handoff to behavioral health/youth service providers with no further officer outreach" (Barrett et al. 2019, 128). This program appears to be distinctive in accepting young people who have committed multiple and relatively more serious offenses, rather than "youth who have not committed an offense or who otherwise would not have been in contact with the legal system" (Barrett et al. 2019, 128). This program (Safety Net) targets "fragmentation of services through cross-system alignment and collaboration and intentionally links police, schools, after-school programs and mental health resources" (Barrett et al. 2019, 128), in much the same way as the Swansea Bureau described earlier.

B. An Even Wider View: Diversion beyond the United Kingdom and United States

Models of juvenile diversion are now widely reported internationally. These often exhibit quite similar characteristics, despite variations in judicial systems. Li and Su (2020), however, argue that the Chinese model of juvenile diversion can be distinguished from the approach taken in the United States:

> Chinese juvenile diversion does not operate according to welfarist or restorative models. Rather, juvenile diversion in China is a managerialism-driven scheme that rests on two key pillars: institutional diversion, which imposes punishment and control on juvenile offenders pursuant to their level of offending and dangerousness, and noninstitutional diversion, which revolves around risk-based management and correction through community-level interventions. (Li and Su 2020, 372)

Cautions are available for minor offenses committed by juveniles over the age of 14 following arrest (Li and Shu 2020, 381), but "diversion" can also involve a period of "administrative detention," ostensibly operating "outside the criminal justice system" and imposed at the discretion of the police. "Noninstitutional" diversion, on the other hand, involves referral to correctional programs. In common with the prevailing approach in the United States, though, these programs are conditional, with prosecution the consequence of noncompliance.

Yunita (2018) describes a restorative model introduced in Indonesia in 2012, applied in less serious cases, and which draws on "local wisdom" to inform communal decisions about how to resolve offenses. This diversion model remains subordinate to the requirements of the wider criminal justice system—applying only to relatively minor offenses, and subject to court referral in the event of failure to find a solution acceptable to the victim (Yunita 2018). Implementation of this model has also reportedly been hampered by the reluctance of law enforcement agencies to adapt to it (Darmika 2019).

Examples of restorative practice in the context of juvenile diversion exist elsewhere (Wong et al. 2016; McMahon and Pedersen 2020), in Canada and Aotearoa/New Zealand. In Aotearoa/New Zealand there is an emphasis on engagement and effective involvement of young people in mutual problem-solving, essentially by means of the Family Group Conference. Nonetheless, there remain unresolved issues in terms of effective engagement and communication (Parosanu and Lynch 2021). Tensions evident elsewhere are also apparent here: "The purpose of the youth justice system explicitly recognises the rights and interests of victims and the aim of preventing and reducing offending—indicating a more 'crime control' focused approach. But, consideration of best interests and protection of rights are required, indicating a child-centred lens" (Parosanu and Lynch 2021, 197).

V. Reviewing the Evidence

Juvenile diversion has been the subject of inquiry and evaluation more or less from the point of its recognition as a distinctive form of intervention (e.g., Mays 1965). Much of what has been discovered has led to positive conclusions about its value, and perhaps we should be content with this. However, given the range and diversity of contemporary practices associated with the term internationally, it might still be wise to reflect critically on what we know, what we don't know, what we need to know and why, and what we may never know.

A. The Impact of Diversion on Recidivism

With the passage of time and the growth in interest, a number of meta-analyses of diversion have been conducted, including those by Petrosino, Turpin-Petrosino, and Guckenberg (2010), Schwalbe et al. (2012), Wilson and Hoge (2013), Wong et al. (2016), and Wilson, Brennan, and Olaghere (2018). A further re-evaluation of several of these studies has been conducted (Gaffney, Farrington, and White 2021).

Petrosino and colleagues' (2010) study reviewed the effects and consequences of "juvenile system processing," rather than of diversion per se. Their conclusion was that formal processing "appears not to have a crime control effect, and across all measures appears to increase delinquency " (6). "Processing" was compared to either "diversion with services" (15) or "diversion alone" (14) in the 29 studies covered by their review, carried out between 1973 and 2008. It appeared that "effect sizes were more negative for processing in studies that compared it to a diversion program or provision of services than in those trials that compared processing to simple release (doing nothing)" (35). That is to say, there seemed to be some support for more active interventionist models of diversion as opposed to simply taking no further action, although none of these studies compared these alternatives directly.

Wilson and Hoge (2013) carried out a wider-ranging review of the relationship between diversion and recidivism, encompassing 45 studies. These studies were reported between 1972 and 2010, and involved 73 diversion programs (Wilson and Hoge 2013, 504). In this instance, the review included programs initiated both before and after the decision to charge the reported offender. Programs appeared to be more effective in reducing recidivism at the pre- rather than post-charge stage (506), although there was "no significant difference found between intervention and cautions programs in their effectiveness" (505). Significantly, programs "with a high prevalence of Caucasian offenders showed a greater reduction in recidivism than programs with a high prevalence of African American youth" (507). While concluding that diversion programs appear to have a substantial impact in terms of reducing recidivism, the authors also acknowledged the "considerable variability found among studies" (512), and the need for caution in drawing conclusions from the evidence under consideration.

Wilson, Brennan, and Olaghere (2018, 6) have reported on a review of "police-led diversion," covering 19 studies from 1973 to 2011, using "randomized control" or "quasi-experimental" research designs. They have concluded that diversion results in a 6% lower reoffending rate than "traditional processing." The authors of this review classified "diversion" into three categories: "diversion only (often called counsel and release), diversion with referral to services, and diversion with police-led restorative justice" (28). However, according to them, "there is no basis for concluding that there are meaningful differences across the diversion types," nor could they distinguish between "different types of youth" in terms of outcomes. Overall, though, their conclusion is that these findings are consistent with the earlier studies carried out by Petrosino, Turpin-Petrosino, and Guckenberg (2010) and Wilson and Hoge (2013), in demonstrating "the preventive effects of pre-charge diversion" (Wilson, Brennan, and Olaghere 2018, 29).

Wong et al. (2016) have also provided qualified support for diversionary interventions in the form of restorative programs, in their meta-analysis of 21 studies carried out over a 25-year period. They argue that "restorative approaches are a promising way to combat recidivism among youth and should continue to be implemented and evaluated," on the basis that 15 of these studies identified positive restorative program effects, and only six found evidence of negative outcomes in this respect. However, they have also suggested that "the quality of the literature on these programs is for the most part relatively weak," and that heterogeneity is a problem in terms of providing a consistent basis for comparative analysis (Wong et al. 2016, 1322). They, too, note a distinct ethnic bias, with those programs "serving a predominantly Caucasian sample of at-risk youths" demonstrating "a significant effect of treatment," while those whose clients "were predominantly ethnic minorities or a mix" did not (1323).

Schwalbe et al. (2012), in reviewing 28 studies undertaken between 1980 and 2011, have suggested that there is no discernible effect of diversionary programs on recidivism, apart from family "treatment" and possibly restorative interventions. Interpreting these findings is complicated, however, by the variable employment of "minimal intervention" as a comparison group (Schwalbe et al. 2012, 29) and by the "high levels of heterogeneity" that permeate "all aspects of this literature including research design, program design and the quality of program monitoring and implementation" (30). Schwalbe and colleagues (2012) conclude that whilst it might appear that "the best intervention for most diverted youths is no intervention," which minimizes the risks of "net-widening" (30), there also appears to be some positive benefit associated with well-designed "family-based interventions" (31).

Gaffney, Farrington, and White (2021) have carried out a "review of reviews," revisiting the Petrosino et al. (2010), Wilson and Hoge (2013), and Wilson et al. (2018) studies, concluding that the latter offers the most robust evidence. They conclude that "[o]verall, pre-court diversion programmes are effective in reducing reoffending, compared to formal processing" (Gaffney, Farrington, and White 2021, 3). Indeed, they appear less willing to qualify this conclusion than the meta-analyses on which they comment, including Wilson, Brennan, and Olagher (2018, 31), who observe that it is not possible to distinguish between the effects of a "*referral* to services" and "the services themselves."

There are clearly limitations in trying to pool a wide range of disparate studies undertaken over a considerable period of time, where there may well also be questions about key issues such as randomization (Petrosino, Turpin-Petrosino, and Guckenberg 2010), comparability (Wilson and Hoge 2013), and "system" effects—changing practices and political moods, for instance—which are not easily accounted for in evaluation design (Smith 2003). It would appear important to be relatively cautious about drawing strong conclusions about the benefits and outcomes of diversion programs based on the current state of knowledge revealed by this series of reviews, despite their overall encouraging tone.

B. Widening the Net—Beyond Recidivism Studies

For those such as the present author who are committed supporters of diversionary principles, it would be tempting to stop here and take what appears to be a broadly positive picture at face value, accepting that the evidence in support of "diversion" is persuasive and encouraging. Nonetheless, there is sufficient lack of clarity and room for doubt to indicate that we need to retain a critical and enquiring approach, and indeed a scope of inquiry extends beyond an apparent preoccupation with recidivism as the preeminent outcome measure.

Mears et al. (2016) have identified a number of concerns and "challenges" for diversion. These focus on key areas such as the selective exercise of police discretion, the inconsistent implementation of diversion programs, and the risk of net-widening (Mears et al. 2016, 959). They argue that systemic problems of this kind create difficulties for meta-analyses of individualized "treatment" conditions, which struggle to assess "exactly what the treatment is being compared to" (Petrosino, Turpin-Petrosino, and Guckenberg 2010, 37, quoted in Mears et al. 2016, 960). Beyond this, they highlight the uncertainty generated by differing responses to the definitional question: "What do we mean by 'diversion'"? Following this, it becomes increasingly difficult to identify common factors or characteristics in the populations targeted, the point of intervention, program content, or intended outcomes. These problems culminate in fundamental "challenges associated with estimating a system-wide impact of diversion" (Mears et al. 2016, 972). At the very least:

> Such an assessment requires information about how resources across the juvenile justice system otherwise would have been expended, how youth who engage in misdemeanors otherwise would have been processed, the magnitude of any diversion benefits or harms, and the magnitude of any benefits or harms to all other youths processed in juvenile court. (Mears et al. 2016, 972)

Mears et al. (2016, 975) observe that while "[r]ecidivism studies are important," these are insufficient to resolve the question of whether "diversion" has a proper place in youth justice, and if so, what form it should take. Aside from "impact evaluations" of other beneficial or problematic outcomes than simply recidivism, they argue that research should incorporate "process evaluations" as well as addressing the issues of net-widening, wider justice system costs and benefits, and unintended consequences. These questions could and should be extended further, to include victim and community benefits (and costs) of diversion, the advantages and disadvantages of restorative models of offense resolution, and the contribution of diversion to achieving wider goals of human rights and social justice.

This would also encompass the crucial question of whether or not diversion is capable of addressing embedded inequalities and racial discrimination (Lammy 2017); or whether it is just another mechanism for perpetuating systemic injustice. Schlesinger (2018), for example, has identified some of the mechanisms (such as the use of "dynamic" risk factors to inform decision-making) which problematize minority ethnic young people disproportionately, and result in them being less likely to be diverted from court than their white counterparts (Schlesinger 2018, 69).

A wider scope of inquiry for juvenile diversion research was indeed signposted much earlier (Dunford et al. 1982; Blomberg 1983), along with the need for methodological variation (Lipsey, Cordray, and Berger 1981). Dunford et al. (1982), for example, distinguished between "process," "impact on youth," "system," and cost-based evaluations, while giving consideration to the perceptions and experiences of providers and "clients" (to which list we would now add victims, too). Although their national (US) evaluation found little evidence of diversion programs affecting subsequent patterns of offending, this study did conclude that diversion is capable of reducing "at least one form of stigma" by limiting the "reach of the justice system" (Osgood and Weichselbaum 1984, 54). On the other hand, early studies also found substantive evidence of "net-widening" (Blomberg 1980; Decker 1985). Program implementation may not have been reflecting the "theoretical" underpinnings (Osgood and Weichselbaum 1984) of diversion, with therapeutic intervention models actually sucking in young people who would not otherwise be identified as (potential) offenders (Thorpe et al. 1980; Fuller and Morton 1993).

In rejecting a concentration on "narrowly defined outcome variables," Blomberg (1983, 32) proposed a "multi-goal" model of evaluation of juvenile diversion schemes that prefigures a more robust and rounded approach to understanding just what is happening when young people are diverted, how it impacts on them and others concerned, and what the consequences are in terms of "system" effects, such as net-widening, community involvement, and public perceptions.

C. Diversion and Social Justice: Where Is the Evidence to Be Found?

Diversion in youth justice is riddled with ambiguity,; and this, if nothing else, holds true both for diversionary practice and research into those practices. The history and development of diversion have been informed by the parallel desire to find less harmful and intrusive ways of responding to the reported crimes of the young, and at the same time to develop interventions that will reduce their propensity to offend in future. There also appears to be a broad consensus that diversion is most appropriately targeted at early and minor young offenders, preempting more serious offending (Smith 2018, 41). Diversion seems to have a fairly well-defined place at the front end of the justice system, with an identifiable target population. Following from this, it might be assumed that specific research questions and methods of evaluation could be readily mapped out (Gaffney, Farrington, and White 2021). However, operationalizing these objectives, both in terms of practice and its evaluation, has been problematic from the early days (Smith 2018, 33) and remains so today (Mears et al. 2016).

Diversion is a contested and multidimensional, concept, and it is overly simplistic to reduce the question of what it achieves or whether it works to that of comparative reoffending rates, irrespective of the demonstrable challenges in answering this convincingly. Instead, we must recognize its wider scope and ambitions—to achieve system change, to reduce the harms caused by the criminal justice system, to improve approaches to offense resolution, to enhance communities' capacity for problem-solving, to promote social justice—and then consider what we need to know to evaluate its achievements, and how we might go about finding this out. If diversion cannot satisfactorily demonstrate that it meets fundamental standards of fair, equitable, and "just" treatment of those who are subject to it, then arguably other questions are of less importance. Schlesinger (2018), for example, maps out some of the features that might be important to diversionary mechanisms that are capable of responding to offenses without incorporating intrinsic racist assumptions, such as dispensing with consideration of dynamic risk factors and minimizing the influence of prior system contact in reaching decisions. As Mears et al. (2016) imply, this could point toward prioritizing *process* (Dunford et al. 1982, 2) rather than *outcome* evaluations: "[D]iversion efforts should be coupled with process evaluations to ensure that any given effort targets the intended population, that it is used in an appropriate and equitable manner, and that programs are implemented as designed" (Mears et al. 2016, 974).

Some investigators have adopted a systemic approach to researching diversion programs. These are perhaps less prominent than pure "outcome" studies, and systematic reviews, but they do offer richer and more analytically powerful accounts of just what happens when we "divert" reported young offenders (Fischer and Jeune 1987; Mason 1995; Boden 2019; Wainwright et al. 2022). These include the studies of the Swansea Bureau (Haines et al. 2013) and the Northamptonshire Juvenile Liaison Bureaux (Blagg et al. 1986) mentioned earlier. Whilst acknowledging the possible effect of the program in reducing reconviction (rather than reoffending) rates, the mixed-methods evaluation of the Swansea Bureau also emphasizes its role in developing a "children first" model of intervention, and offering "supportive intervention to young people and parents . . . focused on engagement and promoting opportunity and positive behaviour through inter-agency working" (Haines et al. 2013, 184). At the same time, no evidence of net-widening was found to be associated with the establishment of the program (176).

In Northamptonshire, not only was there a focus on system change (Blagg et al. 1986), but there was also an opportunity to develop an early form of restorative practice and incorporate the victim perspective (Blagg 1985). As in the case of the Swansea Bureau (Haines et al. 2013), the findings from this earlier study provided the evidential impetus for progressive change in policy and practice (Smith 2018; Case and Browning 2021).

VI. Diversion, Knowledge, and Progress

In this chapter, I have sought firstly to map the development of diversion, its achievements, and associated challenges and criticisms. In seeking out a place for itself on the terrain of juvenile/youth justice, diversion has continually worked hard to justify itself in the face of resistance—ironically so, in the context of a "formal" justice system that demonstrably criminalizes young people (McAra and McVie 2007; Petrosino, Turpin-Petrosino, and Guckenberg 2010). It is perhaps understandable in light of this that so much attention has been given to the question of whether or not diversion in any of its manifestations encourages or discourages reoffending. However, the validity and strength of this evidence may ultimately be less important than the wider test of whether and to what extent diversion can and does contribute to the achievement of social justice and the reduction of social harm (Case 2021; Smith 2021). Realist methods are arguably better suited to this more ambitious task than those grounded in conventional empiricist models of inquiry (Sutton et al. 2022). These should therefore be adopted as the default mode of investigation if we want to be able to answer the core question of the social value of juvenile diversion fully and effectively.

Note

1. In this chapter, references to the United Kingdom should not obscure the fact that there is no single criminal jurisdiction covering the UK, and that most of the relevant material included here relates to England and/or Wales, rather than the separate jurisdictions of Scotland and Northern Ireland.

References

Audit Commission. 1996. *Misspent youth?* Abingdon, UK: Audit Commission.
Austin, James, and Barry Krisberg. 2002. Wider, stronger and different nets: the dialectics of criminal justice reform. *Journal of Crime & Delinquency*, 18 (1): 165–196.
Baker, Kerry 2014. *AssetPlus Rationale*. London: Youth Justice Board.
Barrett, James G, Elizabeth Janopaul-Naylor, Jacquelyn Rose, Ana M Progovac, Sherry Shu-Yeu Ho, and B. Lê Cook. 2019. Do diverted kids stay out of trouble?: A longitudinal analysis of recidivism outcomes in diversion. *Journal of Applied Juvenile Justice Services*, 125–137. https://static1.squarespace.com/static/59511c45c534a573ac245515/t/5da4adaf1610a16ec8f5dce0/1571073457274/Do-Diverted-Kids-Barrett-Final.pdf.
Bateman, Tim. 2015. *The state of youth justice 2015*. London: National Association for Youth Justice.
Bateman, Tim. 2020. *The state of youth justice 2020*. London: National Association for Youth Justice.
Blagg, Harry. 1985. Reparation and justice for juveniles. *British Journal of Criminology*, 25 (3): 267–279.
Blagg, H., N. Derricourt, J. Finch, and D. Thrpe. 1986. *The final report on the Juvenile Liaison Bureau Corby*. Lancaster, UK: University of Lancaster.

Blomberg, Thomas G. 1980. Widening the net—An anomaly in the evaluation of diversion programs. In *Handbook of criminal justice evaluation*, edited by M. Klein and K. Teilmann, 572–592. Beverly Hills, CA: SAGE.

Blomberg, Thomas G. 1983. Diversion's disparate results and unresolved questions: An integrative evaluation perspective. *Journal of Research in Crime and Delinquency*, 20 (1): 24–38.

Boden, Thomas. 2019. A realistic inquiry of welfare-orientated diversionary practice within a Youth Offending Team in supporting the wellbeing of young people within the community. Phd diss., University of Birmingham.

Bottoms, Anthony, and James Dignan. 2004. Youth justice in Great Britain. *Crime and Justice*, 31:21–183.

Case, Stephen. 2021. *Youth justice*. Abingdon, UK: Routledge.

Case, Stephen, and Ann Browning. 2021. Child first justice: The research evidence-base. Loughborough, UK: Loughborough University. https://repository.lboro.ac.uk/articles/report/Child_First_Justice_the_research_evidence-base_Full_report_/14152040.

Cressey, Donald R, and R.A. McDermott. 1973. *Diversion from the juvenile justice system*. Ann Arbor: University of Michigan.

Darmika, Ika. 2019. Diversion and restorative justice implementation In Indonesia's juvenile court system. *UNTAG Law Review (ULREV)*, 3 (2): 131–144.

Davis, Gwynn, Jacky Boucherat, and David Watson. 1989. Pre-court decision-making in juvenile justice. *British Journal of Criminology*, 29 (3): 219–235.

Decker, Scott H. 1985. A systematic analysis of diversion: Net widening and beyond. *Journal of Criminal Justice*, 13 (3): 207–216.

Ditchfield, J.A. 1976. *Police cautioning in England and Wales*. Home Office Research Study No. 37. London: HMSO.

Doak, Jonathan, and David O'Mahony. 2011. In search of legitimacy: Restorative youth conferencing in Northern Ireland. *Legal Studies*, 31 (2): 305–325.

Dumont, Robyn, and Erica King. 2017. Youth recidivism: Diversion to discharge in Maine's juvenile justice system. Portland, ME: Maine Statistical Analysis Center. http://muskie.usm.maine.edu/justiceresearch.

Dunford, Franklyn W., D. Wayne Osgood, Hart F. Weichselbaum, J. Jacobs, L. Hill, F-A. Esbensen, and E. Royal. 1982. *National evaluation of diversion projects: Final report*. Washington, DC: United States Department of Justice.

Farrington, David, and Trevor Bennett. 1981. Police cautioning of juveniles in London. *British Journal of Criminology*, 21 (2): 123–135.

Feld, Barry C. 2017. My life in crime: An intellectual history of the juvenile court. *Nevada Law Journal*, 17 (2): 299–330.

Fischer, Donald G., and Richard Jeune. 1987. Juvenile diversion: A process analysis. *Canadian Psychology/Psychologie canadienne*, 28 (1): 60–70.

Fuller, John R., and William M. Morton. 1993. Juvenile diversion: The impact of program philosophy on net widening. *Journal of Crime and Justice*, 16 (1): 29–45.

Gaffney, Hannah, David P. Farrington, and Howard White. 2021. *Pre-court diversion: Toolkit technical report*. London: Youth Endowment Fund. https://youthendowmentfund.org.uk/wp-content/uploads/2021/06/Pre-Court-Diversion-technical-report-.pdf.

Goldson, Barry. 1999. Wither diversion? Interventionism and the new youth justice. In *The New Youth Justice*, edited by B. Goldson, 111–130. Lyme Regis, UK: Russell House.

Haines, Kevin, Stephen Case, Katie Davies, and Anthony Charles. 2013. The Swansea Bureau: A model of diversion from the youth justice system. *International Journal of Law, Crime and Justice*, 41:167–187.

Haines, A., B. Goldson, A. Haycox, R. Houten, S. Lane, J. McGuire, T. Nathan, E. Perkins, S. Richards, and R. Whittington. 2012. *Evaluation of the Youth Justice Liaison and Diversion (YJLD) Pilot Scheme: Final report*. Liverpool: University of Liverpool.

Hine, Jean, and Anne Celnick. 2001. *A one year reconviction study of final warnings*. Sheffield, UK: University of Sheffield.

Hockenberry, Sarah, and Charles Puzzanchera. 2021. *Juvenile court statistics 2019*. Pittsburgh: National Center for Juvenile Justice.

Home Office. 1927. *Report of the Departmental Committee on the Care and Treatment of Young Offenders (Molony Report), Cmnd 2831*. London: HMSO.

Home Office. 1997. *No more excuses: A new approach to tackling youth crime*. London: The Stationery Office.

Institute for Criminal Policy Research. 2012. *Assessing young people in police custody: An Examination of the operation of Triage schemes*. London: Home Office.

Kelly, Laura, and Vici Armitage. 2015. Diverse diversions: Youth justice reform, localized practices, and a "new interventionist diversion"? *Youth Justice*, 15 (2): 117–133.

Kemp, Vicky. 2014. PACE, performance targets and legal protections. *Criminal Law Review*, 4:278–297.

Kemp, Vicky, Angela Sorsby, Mark Liddle, and S. Merrington. 2002. Assessing responses to youth offending in Northamptonshire. Nacro Research Briefing 2. London: Nacro.

Klein, Malcolm W. 1979. Deinstitutionalization and diversion of juvenile offenders: A litany of impediments. Crime and Justice, 1:145–201.

Lammy, David. 2017. *The Lammy Review*. London: The Stationery Office.

Landau, Simha F., and Gad Nathan. 1983. Selecting delinquents for cautioning in the London Metropolitan Area. *British Journal of Criminology*, 23 (2): 128–149.

Lemert, Edwin M. 1951. *Social pathology: A systematic approach to the theory of sociopathic behavior*. New York: McGraw-Hill.

Li, Enshen, and Mingyue Su. 2020. From punishment to control: Assessing juvenile diversion in China. *Law & Social Inquiry*, 45 (2): 372–397.

Lipsey, Mark W., David S. Cordray, and Dale E. Berger. 1981. Evaluation of a juvenile diversion program: Using multiple lines of evidence. *Evaluation Review*, 5 (3): 283–306.

Mason, Mitchell D. 1995. A qualitative evaluation of four juvenile diversion programs conducted by the University of Nebraska Cooperative Extension. M.A. diss., University of Nebraska-Lincoln.

Mays, J.B. 1965. The Liverpool Police Juvenile Liaison Officer Scheme. *Sociological Review*, 9 (S1): 185–200.

McAra, Lesley, and Susan McVie. 2007. Youth justice? The impact of system contact on patterns of desistance from offending. *European Journal of Criminology*, 4 (3): 315–345.

McClintock, Frederick H., and N. Howard Avison. 1968. *Crime in England and Wales*. London: Heinemann.

McMahon, Sheila M., and Shelby Pederson. 2020. "Love and compassion not found elsewhere": A photovoice exploration of restorative justice and nonviolent communication in a community-based juvenile justice diversion program. *Children and Youth Services Review*, 117:105306. https://www.sciencedirect.com/science/article/pii/S0190740920304540?via%3Dihub.

Mears, Daniel P. 2010. *American criminal justice policy: An evaluation approach to increasing accountability and effectiveness*. New York: Cambridge University Press.

Mears, Daniel P., Joshua J. Kuch, Andrea M. Lindsey, Sonja E. Siennick, George B. Pesta, Mark A. Greenwald, and Thomas G. Blomberg. 2016. Juvenile court and contemporary diversion: Helpful, harmful, or both? *Criminology and Public Policy*, 15 (3): 953–981.

Morgan, Rod. 2007. What's the problem? *New Law Journal*, 157.
Morris, Allison and Henri Giller. 1987. *Understanding juvenile justice*. London: Croom Helm.
Morris, Allison, Henri Giller, Elizabeth Szwed, and Hugh Geach. 1980. *Justice for children*. London: Macmillan.
NeMoyer, Amanda, Elizabeth Gale-Bentz, Naomi E.S. Goldstein, and Lisa Pema Harvey. 2020. Factors associated with successful completion of a community-based, post-arrest juvenile diversion program and subsequent rearrest. *Crime & Delinquency*, 66 (5): 603–626.
Osgood, D. Wayne, and Hart F. Weichselbaum. 1984. Juvenile diversion: When practice matches theory. *Journal of Research in Crime and Delinquency*, 21 (1): 33–56.
Palmer, Ted B., and Roy V. Lewis. 1980. A differentiated approach to juvenile diversion. *Journal of Research in Crime and Delinquency*, 17 (2): 209–229.
Parosanu, Andrea, and Nessa Lynch. 2021. Restorative justice and children's rights in Aotearoa New Zealand—Convergence and divergence. In *Restorative justice from a children's rights perspective*, edited by Annemmieke Wolthuis and Tim Chapman, 195–210. The Hague: Eleven International.
Petrosino, Anthony, Carolyn Turpin-Petrosino, and Sarah Guckenberg. 2010. Formal system processing of juveniles: Effects on delinquency. *Campbell Systematic Reviews*, 6 (1): 1–88.
Pratt, John. 1986. Diversion from the Juvenile Court. *British Journal of Criminology*, 29 (3): 212–233.
President's Commission on Law Enforcement and Administration of Justice. 1967. *The challenge of crime in a free society*. Washington DC: US Government Printing Office.
Rix, Andrew, Katy Skidmore, Richard Self, Tom Holt, and Steve Raybould. 2011. *Youth restorative disposal process evaluation*. London: Youth Justice Board.
Rutherford, Andrew. 2002. *Growing out of crime*. Hook, UK: Waterside Press.
Schlesinger, Traci. 2018. Decriminalizing racialized youth through juvenile diversion. *Future of Children*, 28 (1): 59–81.
Schwalbe, Craig S., Robin E. Gearing, Michael J. MacKenzie, Kathryne B. Brewer, and Rawan Ibrahim. 2012. A meta-analysis of experimental studies of diversion programs for juvenile offenders. *Clinical Psychology Review*, 32 (1): 26–33.
Shore, Heather. 1999. *Artful dodgers*. Woodbridge, UK: Boydell Press.
Sliva, Shannon M. and Mark Plassmeyer. 2021. Effects of restorative justice pre-file diversion legislation on juvenile filing rates: An interrupted time-series analysis. *Criminology & Public Policy*, 20:19–40.
Smith, Roger. 1989. Diversion in practice. MPhil diss., University of Leicester.
Smith, Roger. 2003. *Youth justice: Ideas, policy, practice*. 2nd ed. Cullompton, UK: Willan.
Smith, Roger. 2007. *Youth justice: Ideas, policy, practice*. Cullompton, UK: Willan.
Smith, Roger. 2018. *Diversion in youth justice*. New York: Routledge.
Smith, Roger. 2021. Diversion, rights and social justice. *Youth Justice*, 21 (1): 18–32.
Smith, Roger, and Patricia Gray. 2019. The changing shape of youth justice: Models of practice. *Criminology & Criminal Justice*, 19 (5): 554–571.
Solomon, Enver, and Richard Garside. 2008. *Ten years of Labour's youth justice reforms: An independent audit*. London: Centre for Crime and Justice Studies.
Steer, David. 1970. *Police Cautions: A Study in the Exercise of Police Discretion*. Oxford: Basil Blackwell.
Sutton, Charlie E., Mark Monaghan, Stephen Case, Joanne Greenhalgh, and Judy Wright. 2022. Contextualising youth justice interventions: Making the case for realist synthesis. *Sustainability*, 14 (2): 854.
Thorpe, David H., Dave Smith, C.J. Green, and John H. Paley. 1980. *Out of care: The community support of juvenile offenders*. London: George Allen & Unwin.

Wainwright, John Peter, Rebecca Nowland, Zoe O'Riordan, and Cath Larkins. 2022. "if you feel like you're being respected you're gonna respect them back." Lancaster, UK: The Center for Children and Young People's Participation. https://yjresourcehub.uk/images/Lancashire_YOT/Child_First_Pathfinder_Preliminary_Evaluation_Lancashire_2021.pdf.

Wilcox, Aidan. 2003. Evidence-based youth justice? Some valuable lessons from an evaluation for the Youth Justice Board. *Youth Justice*, 3 (1): 21–35.

Wilson, David B., Iain Brennan, and Ajima Olaghere. 2018. Police-initiated diversion for youth to prevent future delinquent behavior: A systematic review. *Campbell Systematic Reviews*, 14 (1): 1–88.

Wilson, Holly A., and Robert D. Hoge. 2013. The effect of youth diversion programs on recidivism: A meta-analytic review. *Criminal Justice and Behavior*, 40 (5): 497–518.

Wong, Jennifer S., Jessica Bouchard, Jason Gravel, Martin Bouchard, and Carlo Morselli. 2016. Can at-risk youth be diverted from crime?: A meta-analysis of restorative diversion programs. *Criminal Justice and Behavior*, 43 (10): 1310–1329.

Wylie, Lindsey E., Samantha S. Clinkinbeard, and Anne Hobbs. 2019. The application of risk-needs programming in a juvenile diversion program. *Criminal Justice and Behavior*, 46 (8): 1128–1147.

Youth Justice Board. 2002. *Building on success: Youth Justice Board annual review 2001/02*. London: Youth Justice Board.

Yunita, Rahmi. 2018. Diversion and local wisdom in constructivism paradigm (study on the implementation of Diversionat Konawe of Southeast Sulawesi). https://iopscience.iop.org/article/10.1088/1755-1315/175/1/012143.

Zimring, Franklin E. 2000. The common thread: Diversion in juvenile justice. *California Law Review*, 88 (6): 2477–2495.

CHAPTER 9

EVIDENCE-BASED INNOVATIONS IN JUVENILE PROBATION

DAVID L. MYERS AND KELLY ORTS

From the juvenile court's inception, probation officers and the services they provide have played a central role. Today, virtually all youth who enter the juvenile justice system interact with probation staff while progressing through the stages of intake, adjudication, and disposition of their cases. In 2019, juvenile courts nationwide handled approximately 723,000 delinquency cases, of which more than half (386,000) were petitioned formally to juvenile court (Hockenberry and Puzzanchera 2021). About 203,000 of these youth were adjudicated delinquent, of which 55,000 (27%) received an out-of-home placement and 132,000 (65%) were placed on probation. Tens of thousands of other nonadjudicated youth are placed on periods of informal probation, and probation officers are also responsible for diverting less serious and frequent offenders out of the juvenile system and into various community-based programs, along with supervising youth who return to the community following confinement (Esthappan et al. 2020; Henggler and Schoenwald 2011; Viglione et al. 2018).

Juvenile probation has the potential to be helpful, harmful, or ineffectual for youth. Many juvenile probation officers start their careers in this profession, while others have a work history in law enforcement or corrections, and the role of juvenile probation officers is often unclear (Esthappan et al. 2020; Haqanee, Peterson-Badali, and Skilling 2015; Viglione et al. 2018). Probation officers can potentially serve as change agents who intervene directly with youth through mentoring and motivating children and their families. They can also play a more distant role as a case manager who simply coordinates court proceedings and makes referrals to various types of services. A more holistic and evidence-based model of juvenile probation focuses on individualized case planning; engagement of youth, families, and communities; and enhancing racial equity and inclusion. This strategy employs multiple resources and services supported by research to minimize risk and influence behavior (Esthappan et al. 2020; Henggler and Schoenwald 2011; Howell and Lipsey 2012; Howell et al. 2019). To guide this process, juvenile probation officers are typically responsible for conducting risk and needs assessments, as well as subsequently utilizing the results to match youth with appropriate programs and supervision (Haqanee, Peterson-Badali, and Skilling 2015; Lipsey et al. 2017; Miller and Palmer 2020; Sullivan and Childs 2022; Vincent et al. 2018).

Our aim in this chapter is to evaluate the utilization of evidenced-based approaches in juvenile probation during the past several decades and to identify areas for further improvement. Being evidence-based in juvenile probation typically begins with the assessment of risk and needs, followed by using assessment results to guide supervision and treatment programming. This strategy seeks to reduce the likelihood of future offending and improve other behavioral outcomes. In addition, we will examine the implementation and effectiveness of juvenile probation programs and practices, with a goal of improving knowledge, promoting strategies and methods supported by research, and limiting or eliminating harmful practices and inequalities. Finally, organizational factors will be discussed, with an eye toward increasing fidelity in program implementation, enhancing the culture of juvenile probation departments, and strengthening the impact of services provided.

I. Evidence-Based Approaches in Juvenile Probation

For delinquency cases initially referred to juvenile court, probation officers are typically involved with detention decisions and hearings, as well as processing youth through intake procedures. Close to half (roughly 340,000 annually) of all referred cases are handled informally (Hockenberry and Puzzanchera 2021), which can involve periods of probation supervision, diversionary programs, referrals to social services, or case dismissal. More serious offenders, older juveniles, males, and minority youth are more likely to experience formal court processing and adjudication proceedings, and probation is the most common disposition regardless of offense type (Hockenberry and Puzzanchera 2021).

Effective juvenile probation requires evidence-based approaches to assessment, program-matching, and case management. Standardized risk and needs assessment instruments are typically used as the foundation of this process (Baglivio et al. 2017a, 2017b, 2018, 2019; Howell et al. 2019; Lipsey et al. 2017; Sullivan and Childs 2022; Vincent et al. 2018). By identifying the presence and/or absence of risk and protective factors, juvenile probation officers can potentially use the results to guide supervision and service referrals. If properly completed and implemented, risk and needs assessments can be used to reduce risk, enhance strengths, facilitate research-supported programming, and improve behavioral outcomes. More broadly, proponents of the Risk-Need-Responsivity (RNR) model of supervision and treatment assert that effective services and programming requires systematic assessment as a first step (Howell et al. 2019; Lipsey et al. 2017; Sullivan and Childs 2022; Vincent et al. 2018).

A. Risk, Needs, and Protection

Risk and protective factors are characteristics that have been shown through research to influence the likelihood of delinquent or criminal behavior (Baglivio et al. 2017b,

2019; Sullivan and Childs 2022; Vincent et al. 2018; Walters 2018). The presence of risk factors, and at higher levels, increases the likelihood of an individual engaging in delinquent or criminal behavior. The presence of protective factors, and at higher levels, lowers the likelihood of an individual engaging in delinquent or criminal behavior. Protective factors can also mediate or buffer the relationship between risk factors and delinquency, while building resiliency against delinquency and youth violence (Baglivio et al. 2017b, 2019; Sullivan and Childs 2022; Vincent et al. 2018; Walters 2018). In the first decades of the 21st century, a great deal of research has established the importance of considering risk and protective factors in predicting the likelihood of future delinquent and violent behavior. A goal is to use these findings to facilitate data-driven and structured decision-making to improve the delivery and effectiveness of juvenile justice services (Howell et al. 2019; Lipsey et al. 2017; Sullivan and Childs 2022; Vincent et al. 2018).

Both risk and protective factors can exist at the individual, family, peer, and community levels (Baglivio et al. 2017b, 2019; Sullivan and Childs 2022; Walters 2018). In addition, some of these factors are static, meaning they cannot be changed or influenced, while others are dynamic, meaning they are malleable and can potentially be changed through treatment or other services (Howell et al. 2019; Sullivan and Childs 2022). Due to their potential for change, including through juvenile justice system programming and referrals, some literature refers to dynamic risk factors as "criminogenic needs." In other words, "the dynamic risk factor and criminogenic need labels are often used interchangeably" (Sullivan and Childs 2022, 24). This interchangeable use of terminology can cause confusion in the field of juvenile probation (and others), which should be recognized by researchers in disseminating research findings and working collaboratively with practitioners.

Because the best predictor of future behavior is past behavior, risk assessment instruments include static factors (such as age on onset, previous arrests, and offense seriousness) in estimating the likelihood of future offending (Howell et al. 2019; Sullivan and Childs 2022). In contrast to static factors, dynamic risk factors (or criminogenic needs) include such things as substance use, poor school performance, parental abuse or neglect, family dysfunction, and association with delinquent peers (Howell et al. 2019; Sullivan and Childs 2022). In general, a combination of both types of risk factors will produce the most reliable and valid estimates of the likelihood of future offending, with the potential for targeting medium- and higher-risk juveniles with supervision and treatment services that are supported by research as being effective. Furthermore, possible protective factors that can be included in risk and needs assessments include higher neurological and cognitive functioning, positive self-esteem, quality parenting, prosocial peers, lower community crime rates, higher graduation rates, and availability of school activities and community programming (Baglivio et al. 2017b, 2019; Sullivan and Childs 2022; Walters 2018).

B. Risk-Need-Responsivity (RNR) Model

In recent decades, the most popular supervision and treatment model used in the criminal and juvenile justice systems is the RNR framework (Baglivio et al. 2017b, 2018, Haqanee, Peterson-Badali, and Skilling 2015; Howell et al. 2019; Miller and Palmer 2020; Sullivan and

Childs 2022; Viglione et al. 2018). Under RNR, the risk principle identifies who should be treated and at what level, taking into consideration their risk of recidivism and violating conditions of probation. The need principle identifies which criminogenic areas should be addressed; this can include individual, family, peers, school, and neighborhood risk factors. Finally, the responsivity principle emphasizes cognitive/social learning interventions and assessing individualized factors that influence treatment response, including a youth's motivation, strengths, and learning style. With the responsivity principle in mind, motivational interviewing is a contemporary and evidence-based technique used by many juvenile probation departments to improve youth compliance with probation conditions and enhance their engagement in recommended programming (Blasko et al. 2019; Hartzler and Espinosa 2011; Schwartz et al. 2017).

Although predominantly nonexperimental in research design, a number of studies suggest that youth interventions are more effective when guided by the RNR model (Baglivio et al. 2014, 2017a, 2017b, 2018, 2019; Henggler and Schoenwald 2011; Howell et al. 2019; Lipsey et al. 2017; Van der Put et al. 2012; Vincent et al. 2018), with recidivism reduction of 30% or more when case planning and treatment properly follows all three RNR principles (Haqanee, Peterson-Badali, and Skilling 2015; Howell et al. 2019; Lipsey 2009). To illustrate, extensive research by Baglivio and colleagues utilized administrative data pertaining to large samples of Florida youth to assess the implementation and impact of using risk and needs assessment to guide juvenile probation decision-making and services. Initial findings indicated significantly lower recidivism (19% versus 39 %) when dispositions were in line with the recommendations of the Community Positive Achievement Change Tool (C-PACT; Baglivio, Greenwald, and Russell 2014). Separate predictive research revealed reductions in dynamic risk factors and increases in promotive (i.e., protective) factors led to significantly better recidivism outcomes for youth returning to the community from residential placement (Baglivio et al. 2017a, 2017b). These findings correspond with the conclusions of Lipsey's (2009) meta-analysis and several reviews of the literature that support the utility of the RNR framework (e.g., Henggler and Schoenwald 2011; Howell et al. 2019; Lipsey et al. 2017; Vincent et al. 2018).

Juvenile probation officers are typically trained to administer risk and needs assessments, apply RNR principles, create individualized case management plans, and refer youth to appropriate programming. However, contemporary research also indicates that implementation and adherence to this framework is uneven, with practitioner uncertainty, resistance, and even manipulation of assessment results being revealed (Baglivio, Greenwald, and Russell 2014; Haqanee, Peterson-Badali, and Skilling 2015; Miller and Maloney 2013; Viglione et al. 2018). This points to the need for continued focus and research-based efforts to improve application of the RNR model with regard to the consistency of administering risk and needs assessment instruments, targeting dynamic risk and protective factors, and engaging youth in appropriately matched supervision and evidence-based programs (Early, Hand, and Blankenship 2012; Lipsey et al. 2017; Miller and Palmer 2020; Nelson and Vincent 2018; Peterson-Badali, Skilling, and Haqanee 2015; Vincent et al. 2018, 2021). In addition, there is longitudinal evidence indicating the importance of various dynamic risk-factor changes over time, suggesting that interventions guided by RNR principles need to be attuned to the ages of youth to achieve the maximum potential effect on recidivism (Van der Put et al. 2012).

C. Specific Assessment Tools

A large majority of juvenile courts nationwide have adopted a structured decision-making tool, and at least 34 states have adopted a uniform risk-assessment instrument to guide case planning (Lipsey et al. 2017; Howell et al. 2019; Sullivan and Childs 2022; Vincent et al. 2018). There are a variety of specific RNR tools that have been evaluated for their efficiency and accuracy with delinquent youths (Howell et al. 2019; Lipsey et al. 2017; Sullivan and Childs 2022; Vincent et al. 2018). These instruments and studies cannot be compared easily to one another, as the use of one tool with a certain population may not produce comparable results as another RNR tool with a different population (McCafferty 2018). However, Baird and colleagues (2013) conducted a multistate comparative study of risk assessment instruments that included nine tools and identified the Juvenile Sanctions Center (JSC) Risk Assessment Instrument as being the most valid at the time. The JSC tool contains four static items and six dynamic items, and it has been empirically validated in a number of individual studies (Howell et al. 2019).

Other risk and needs assessment instruments receiving empirical support for their predictive validity include the North Carolina Assessment of Risk (NCAR), the Ohio Youth Assessment System (OYAS), the Washington State Juvenile Court Assessment (WSJCA), the Positive Achievement Change Tool (PACT), and the Structured Assessment of Violence Risk in Youth (SAVRY) (Baglivio and Wolf 2019; Early, Hand, and Blankenship 2012; Howell et al. 2019; Sullivan and Childs 2022; Vincent et al. 2021). Early and colleagues (2012), for example, provided a thorough evaluation of the PACT by studying over 80,000 assessments in Florida. The findings revealed that youth classified in the higher PACT risk levels were significantly more likely to be rearrested than those classified in the lower risk levels, regardless of gender, race/ethnicity, age, and supervision placement type. Baglivio and Wolf (2019) subsequently used a large sample of Florida youth in residential placement to assess the R-PACT. Based on one-year rearrest data, they established predictive validity slightly better than that found in other studies of juvenile risk assessments. However, criminal history (a key static factor) played a substantial role in the total R-PACT risk score, which somewhat tempers implications for juvenile justice interventions and strengthens calls for earlier delinquency prevention efforts.

As a further illustration, the SAVRY is used to assess risk in youth ages 12 to 18 (Vincent et al. 2021). This tool utilizes a semi-structured professional judgment approach used by trained juvenile probation staff. These individuals receive three months of training, including risk/need identification, practice case vignettes, semi-structured interviews with youth and families, administrative policies, data systems, and post-training follow up. The assessment measures 6 protective factors and 24 risk factors in order to identify risk level and service matching. Nelson and Vincent (2018) initially reviewed data on 385 adolescent offenders who were assessed through SAVRY and found that 86% of case plans followed proper implementation. When evaluating the feasibility and fidelity of SAVRY, Vincent et al. (2021) found solid interrater reliability and predictive validity for risk assessments among youth of different racial/ethnic backgrounds. However, the semi-structured interviews with youth and families can be concerning, due to inherent discretion and potential for false statements and misinterpretation of information. In addition, the findings revealed an overreliance on use of mental health services, and some offices did not consistently complete assessments prior to disposition, while experiencing a lack of service availability and limited buy-in from stakeholders. These findings indicate some of the key challenges and barriers that exist with using empirically supported risk and needs assessment tools.

D. Matching Supervision and Services to Risk and Needs

Once a risk and needs assessment has been completed, probation officers must identify appropriate levels of supervision and evidence-based programs for youth referral. In general, these services should target the treatment needs that are amenable to intervention efforts, with the highest-risk youth referred to more intensive and lengthier programming, while lower-risk youth receive minimal intervention (Baglivio et al. 2014, 2017a, 2017b, 2018, 2019; Howell et al. 2019; Lipsey et al. 2017; Miller and Maloney 2013; Nelson and Vincent 2018; Sullivan and Childs 2022; Vincent et al. 2018, 2021). Overall, research shows that appropriately matching youth needs with services is associated with decreased recidivism (Haqanee, Peterson-Badali, and Skilling 2015; Howell et al. 2019; Lipsey 2009; Vincent et al. 2018).

Previously mentioned research by Baglivio and colleagues (2014) indicated significantly lower recidivism when juvenile dispositions are guided by the results of risk and needs assessment. Baglivio et al. (2018) also considered whether service matching to assessed needs, with interventions provided at appropriate dosages and for adequate lengths of time, could enhance the likelihood of success for serious and chronic juvenile offenders in residential placement. Based on Florida administrative data, matching services based on measured risk and needs, combined with receiving recommended dosage (in hours) and duration (in weeks) of treatment, led to significantly better treatment outcomes in terms of both dynamic risk reduction during placement and lower recidivism. This study was also unique in its use of propensity score matching, to compare the youth who received the complete array of service delivery and recommended treatment during their residential stay with statistically similar youth who did not receive the complete array of service and treatment. In the absence of random assignment to treatment and control groups, use of propensity score matching is considered one of the strongest quasi-experimental designs for program evaluation.

Despite these positive findings, other researchers have uncovered "slippage" in the system, as not all needs can be or are matched effectively to appropriate services (Haqanee, Peterson-Badali, and Skilling 2015; Lipsey et al. 2017; Miller and Palmer 2020; Nelson and Vincent 2018; Peterson-Badali, Skilling, and Haqanee 2015). For example, it may seem obvious to match juveniles with substance abuse issues to substance abuse treatment programs, but in practice this can be difficult (Rudes et al. 2021). It can be even more challenging to match a factor such as antisocial attitude to a specific evidence-based program (Howell et al. 2019). Furthermore, many available services (such as individual and family counseling) can address a variety of needs, but prioritizing a youth's highest areas of need can be difficult to accomplish. Finally, quantitative and qualitative research suggests that probation officer perceptions and beliefs about offense characteristics, punishment and rehabilitation, and program availability all lead to uneven service matching (Haqanee, Peterson-Badali, and Skilling 2015; Miller and Palmer 2020; Nelson and Vincent 2018; Peterson-Badali, Skilling, and Haqanee 2015).

The RNR model also emphasizes minimal intervention for low-risk youth and prioritizes more intensive and lengthier programming for medium- and higher-risk youth. It is vital not only to ensure that risk is measured accurately, but also that it is appropriately matched to the right level of treatment services without overprescribing or underprescribing. If lower-risk youth enter the juvenile justice system unnecessarily, their likelihood of reoffending increases (Henggler and Schoenwald 2011; Howell et al. 2019; Mears et al. 2016; Sullivan and Childs 2022). There are few studies, however, that critically evaluate the accuracy of matching needs to services in juvenile settings (Miller and Palmer 2020; Nelson and Vincent 2018; Vincent et al. 2018). The study by Baglivio and colleagues (2018), who employed a sample of 1,678 juvenile offenders who had their criminogenic needs matched to services, illustrates the importance of this step. Their quasi-experimental findings using propensity score matching for treatment and comparison groups indicated that individuals who received more appropriate services based on risk and needs, with recommended dosages and duration, were less likely to reoffend.

E. Use of Evidence-Based Programs and Practices

Although the use of risk and needs assessment is generally considered the foundation of evidence-based juvenile justice, the evidence-based movement has been fueled by evaluation research on the impact of programs and practices on behavioral outcomes (Howell and Lipsey 2012; Howell et al. 2019; Myers 2013). In this context, *programs* can be distinguished based on their presentation of a coherent set of services guided by delivery protocols, implementation manuals, goals, objectives, and/or logic models (Elliot et al. 2020). Use of the term *practices* typically generates more ambiguity, potentially including more routine activities that are research-based (e.g., structured decision-making, comprehensive case planning, use of information management systems) and generic types of methods that have been directed at multiple target populations and are increasingly being evaluated through the use of meta-analysis (e.g., motivational interviewing, cognitive-behavioral therapy, mentoring) (Elliot et al. 2020; Howell and Lipsey 2012; Howell et al. 2019; Lipsey 2020; Welsh 2020).

Although it seems clear that evidence-based approaches in juvenile justice (and consequently in juvenile probation) have come to the forefront in the 21st century, there has been recent debate about the rigor and extent of the actual evidence base, its use in the field, and which approaches should be embraced for further system enhancement and population impacts (Elliot et al. 2020; Lipsey 2020; Welsh 2020). As a result of the growing number of direct impact evaluations being completed in recent decades, with a corresponding desire to disseminate research findings to a wider audience, three online and regularly maintained registries exist that either focus upon or include information about programs and practices directed at juveniles (Fagan and Buchanan 2016; Howell et al. 2019). These include the Blueprints for Healthy Youth Development, housed at the University of Colorado-Boulder (https://www.blueprintsprograms.org/); the Office of Juvenile Justice and Delinquency Prevention's (OJJDP's) Model Programs Guide (https://ojjdp.ojp.gov/model-programs-guide/home); and the Office of Justice Programs' (OJP's) CrimeSolutions (https://crimesolutions.ojp.gov/).

All three registries rate programs based on both the nature of the research findings produced and the scientific rigor of the study designs employed (Fagan and Buchanan 2016; Howell et al. 2019; Elliot et al. 2020). In order for a program to be placed in the "Promising" or "Model" categories of Blueprints, and the "promising" or "effective" categories of the OJJDP and OJP registries, favorable research findings must be generated through experimental and quasi-experimental research. Reaching the "model" or "effective" categories of the three registries requires researcher and reviewer attention to program theory and logic, experimental design, strength of the outcome, length of the follow-up period, and evidence of implementation fidelity. CrimeSolutions and the Model Programs Guide use similar standards for certifying a program as "effective," while the Blueprints registry appears to utilize a higher evidentiary standard for its "Model" and "Model+" ratings (Fagan and Buchanan 2016; Elliot et al. 2020). For example, the Blueprints Model rating requires one or more randomized controlled trials (RCTs) with an experimental replication, while effective interventions in the OJJDP and OJP registries only require one RCT or a study using a sound quasi-experimental design.

As reported by Elliot and colleagues (2020), the three registries contain a relatively small number of model or effective programs specifically designed for youth in the juvenile justice system, or those who potentially would be supervised and treated through juvenile probation services and referrals. Specifically, the four Blueprints Model programs serving juvenile justice youth are Multisystemic Therapy (MST), Functional Family Therapy (FFT), Treatment Foster Care Oregon (TFCO), and MST for Problem Sexual Offenders (MST-PSB). Overall, these four programs have a deep and broad evaluation evidence base, with additional evidence they can be "scaled up" and still maintain their effectiveness (seen, for example, in the states of Washington, Florida, and Pennsylvania, as well as Chile).

In comparison to the Blueprints registry, effective juvenile justice programs in the OJP and OJJDP registries include the four model Blueprints programs and six additional programs: Adolescent Diversion Project, Multisystemic Therapy-Substance Abuse, Brooklyn Treatment Court, Juveniles Breaking the Cycle, Project BUILD, and Aggression Replacement Training (Elliot et al. 2020). Of these six, the latter four were evaluated based on quasi-experimental designs, and there is little evidence on the effectiveness of these programs when they are scaled up. The limited number of juvenile justice programs certified as either model or effective has led to the much larger number of "promising" programs being included in evidence-based literature and discussions, along with ongoing calls for more scientifically rigorous impact assessments. In addition, others have argued that more generic and perhaps similarly effective juvenile programs and practices can be identified through other forms of evaluation research, including meta-analysis (Lipsey 2020; Howell and Lipsey 2012; Howell et al. 2019; Welsh 2020).

To illustrate, Lipsey (2020) estimated that about 7% of all therapeutically oriented programs provided to juvenile offenders are listed in Blueprints, the Model Programs Guide, or CrimeSolutions. Furthermore, only about 7% of all youth who receive a juvenile court sanction are placed in Blueprints programs (despite their 24-year history). These limitations have contributed to the identification of effective generic programs that are "defined broadly as those that are substantially similar with regard to the nature and focus of services provided" (Howell et al. 2019, 63). In addition to its program ratings, OJJDP's Model Program Guide includes a lengthy list of literature reviews seeking to provide practitioners and policymakers with relevant research and evaluation findings, including those pertaining to a variety of generic programs and practices (e.g., after-school programs, cognitive-behavioral treatment, diversion, juvenile re-entry, mentoring, risk and needs assessment). While these reviews are useful for identifying and assessing more generic evidence-based programs and practices, meta-analysis allows for a more systematic and quantifiable approach to achieving this goal.

Dozens of meta-analyses have been conducted to estimate the effects of programs on the recidivism of juvenile offenders (Howell et al. 2019), and in recent years, studies using meta-analysis have been used to create an expanding category of evidence-based practices within the CrimeSolutions registry. Lipsey's (2009, 2020) extensive work revealed that interventions applied to high-risk youth, those with a therapeutic philosophy (e.g., restorative, skill-building, counseling, and multimodal interventions), and those of longer duration and implementation fidelity were associated with larger recidivism reductions (see also Howell and Lipsey 2012; Howell et al. 2019). Subsequently, these findings were used to produce the Standardized Program Evaluation Protocol (SPEP), a practical rating scheme that can be used by juvenile probation officers and other service providers to guide decision-making and assess programs and practices for juvenile offenders (Lipsey 2020). As an evidence-based tool, the SPEP can be used to evaluate juvenile probation services and program referrals, designate them as evidence-based if they produce high ratings, and guide improvement efforts if the ratings are less than desirable.

Preliminary and ongoing assessments of the SPEP instrument have revealed consistent support for its predictive validity (Howell and Lipsey 2012; Howell et al. 2019), with higher-rated programs associated with lower recidivism, and with some recent evidence indicating efforts to improve SPEP scores may also improve the effects of those programs on recidivism (Lipsey 2020). It appears, then, that the pursuit of greater use of evidence-based programs and practices in juvenile justice does not need to take a "one or the other" approach (see Welsh 2020). Certified evidence-based programs can (and should) continue to be studied and identified through scientifically rigorous research, and more general practices can (and should) continue to be assessed through various forms of evaluation research, including meta-analysis and examination of tools like the SPEP. Furthermore, these types of research are perhaps equally important for identifying programs and practices that are ineffective or harmful in serving youth who experience juvenile probation supervision and treatment.

II. Avoiding Ineffectual and Harmful Approaches

Although contemporary evaluation research has focused on "what works" in juvenile justice programs and practices, it is also important to identify "what doesn't work" (Henggler and Schoenwald 2011). By identifying ineffective and counterproductive interventions, time, effort, and funding can be invested more appropriately, and harmful programs and practices can be avoided. Most importantly, some interventions can actually affect youth negatively (i.e., increase their chances of recidivism), which is referred to as a criminogenic or iatrogenic effect (Elliot et al. 2020; Howell et al. 2019). Of the three registries discussed in the previous section, Blueprints certifies programs as Promising, Model, or Model+

(avoiding an ineffective category), while the Model Programs Guide and CrimeSolutions utilize the rating categories of no effects (which includes both null and harmful effects), promising, and effective (Elliot et al. 2020; Lipsey 2020). In addition, research based on meta-analysis also has been useful in identifying ineffective or harmful practices (Lipsey 2009, 2020; Howell and Lipsey 2012; Howell et al. 2019).

A. Possible Criminogenic Effects with Lower-Risk Juveniles

Contemporary research indicates that effective interventions focused on medium- and higher-risk youth tend to produce larger recidivism reductions than for lower-risk delinquents (Lipsey 2009; Henggler and Schoenwald 2011; Howell and Lipsey 2012; Howell et al. 2019; Peterson-Badali, Skilling, and Haqanee 2015). Moreover, the juvenile justice system has a lengthy history of concern regarding the intermingling of lower risk and younger youth with higher risk and older offenders. Empirically, there is evidence of "peer contagion" when youth of varying risk levels are intermingled in more intense group interactions (Dishion, McCord, and Poulin 1999), although this is likely more of a concern in unsupervised settings (Howell et al. 2019). In addition, lower-risk and younger youth have been shown to experience and be influenced by different risk and protective factors, as compared to higher-risk and older youth (Van der Put et al. 2012; Walters 2018). This all points to the ongoing demands for improved use of risk and needs assessment for matching youth with appropriate services, as well as readministering risk and needs assessments over time (Baglivio et al. 2017a, 2017b; Lipsey at al. 2017; Nelson and Vincent 2018; Vincent et al. 2018). This strategy can not only generate improved behavioral outcomes, but also avoid possible criminogenic or iatrogenic effects for lower-risk and younger youth.

The noninterventionist model for reducing juvenile crime, based on labeling theory, generally recommends intervening as little as possible. In the 1970s, diversion programs and policies emerged as a way to achieve this goal (Mears et al. 2016; Stafford 2016). Diversion potentially allows youth to be held accountable through early community-based interventions, while avoiding formal labeling, stigmatization, and more severe sanctions (Hoge 2016). In addition to avoiding possible criminogenic effects, lessened youth involvement in the juvenile justice system can contribute to smaller caseloads and higher cost-savings.

Diversion programs are usually intended for first- or second-time, lower-risk offenders (Hoge 2016; Mears et al. 2016; Stafford 2016). Programs relevant to juvenile courts and probation include teen/peer courts, family therapy, restorative justice, treatment programs, mentoring, and community service. However, research findings on the effectiveness of diversionary programs are mixed (Butts 2016; Mears et al. 2016; Stafford 2016). As discussed by Mears et al. (2016), the experimental and quasi-experimental research that exists generally indicates that diversion fails to produce significant improvements in recidivism relative to counsel-and-release and formal processing of similar youth.

The generally null findings associated with research on diversion may stem from these programs not relying on evidence-based strategies and techniques, but the research that has uncovered criminogenic effects suggests other mechanisms at work, such as increased strain, stigmatization, or perhaps peer contagion (Dishion, McCord, and Poulin 1999; Mears et al. 2016). In addition, not all diverted youth have the same needs, again making it crucial to assess the risk and needs of individual youth. In particular, net-widening can occur when diversion includes lower-risk and lower-need juveniles who otherwise would not be referred to juvenile court (Stafford 2016). Overall, there are a variety of factors that can influence the effectiveness of various diversion programs, pointing to the need for better program logic, improved implementation, and more rigorous evaluation to clarify the evidence base (Butts 2016; Hoge 2016; Mears et al. 2016).

B. Programs and Practices Focused on Discipline and Deterrence

A great deal of research, much of it contained in available meta-analyses and literature reviews, indicates that programs and practices focused primarily on instilling discipline (e.g., paramilitary boot camps) or generating deterrence (e.g., Scared Straight) are not only ineffective, but actually increase the likelihood of recidivism (Henggler and Schoenwald 2011; Howell and Lipsey 2012; Howell et al. 2019; Lipsey 2009). Although this same research reveals that programs relying mainly on surveillance (e.g., intensive probation supervision) can reduce recidivism, the effects tend to be smaller than for therapeutic programs. Moreover, many intensive probation programs have significant counseling components and increasingly include motivational interviewing (Blasko et al. 2019; Hartzler and Espinosa 2011; Schwartz et al. 2017), meaning that effective surveillance programs generally represent a mix of control and therapeutic strategies (Howell et al. 2019).

Although programs that are effective for juveniles treated in the community are generally effective when administered to similar juveniles in secure facilities, confinement or incarceration alone can be ineffective or harmful in sanctioning youth (Henggler and Schoenwald 2011; Howell and Lipsey 2012; Howell et al. 2019; Lipsey 2009). Prior incarceration is one of the strongest predictors of future offending, and confinement potentially can exacerbate mental health problems and expose juveniles to abuse and other forms of victimization. As juvenile probation officers typically have strong input on judicial decisions regarding secure confinement, it is imperative that facilities be utilized based on assessed risk and needs, and that they offer evidence-based therapeutic services (rather than simply a philosophical belief in discipline and deterrence).

III. Inequities in Juvenile Justice

Disproportionate minority representation in the juvenile justice system has been recognized and heavily researched for many decades (Howell et al. 2019; Piquero 2008; Sullivan and Childs 2022). OJJDP offered the term "disproportionate minority contact" (DMC) to refer to the disproportionate ratio of minority youth in the justice system compared to the general population (Gann 2019). Since the 1960s, disproportionate minority contact has been a concern at every stage of juvenile justice system processing (including within juvenile probation caseloads), although a recent meta-analysis by Zane and Pupo (2021) revealed relatively small significant effects of race/ethnicity at some stages of juvenile processing (e.g., detention, placement) and insignificant effects at others (e.g., petition, waiver, and adjudication).

It also should be noted that disproportionality by itself does not equate to systematic bias or discrimination. As presented by Mears, Cochran, and Lindsey (2016), disparities constitute a subset of minority disproportionalities in offending, processing, and sanctioning, and this subset is attributable to intended or unintended discrimination (i.e., unfairness or bias in the system). Moreover, justice system practitioners, such as juvenile probation officers, could potentially engage in either malevolent discrimination (e.g., through viewing minority youth as more criminal and less amenable to rehabilitation) or benevolent discrimination (e.g., by viewing minority youth as being more likely to reside in difficult family circumstances). In addition, disproportionalities can exist for reasons other than discriminatory actions taken by justice system personnel, such as minorities experiencing a lower likelihood of being represented by private counsel. All of these factors and more, including lack of sufficient data and monitoring systems, make studying and documenting the true prevalence of minority disparities in juvenile justice both challenging and incomplete.

Nonexperimental, predictive research generally indicates legal factors, such as criminal history and offense seriousness, are the strongest and most consistent variables used in the decision-making process (Gann 2019). Although data and research design limitations temper the strength of the findings, extralegal factors, such as race, also have been found to have significant direct effects on decisions related to confinement, treatment, and diversion. To illustrate, using a sample of over 50,000 youth referred to seven juvenile courts, Gann (2019) examined the impact of race across a variety of decision-making stages. The results indicated that minority youth were more likely to be detained prior to adjudication, placed in confinement post-adjudication, and waived to adult criminal court. Additional contemporary research has revealed that minority youth are more likely to receive harsher punishments in general, and are less likely to receive rehabilitative or diversionary services, even with the use of standardized risk assessments (Cochran and Mears 2015).

It is important to note that although the predictive research discussed earlier is useful for studying disproportionalities while controlling for selected legal and extralegal variables, it is much more challenging to identify the causes of racial and ethnic disparities (Piquero 2008), which may include societal differences in wealth and unfair life experiences (Mears, Cochran, and Lindsey 2016). In addition, it has been suggested that juvenile justice decision-making may accumulate over time to cause racial bias amplification, whereby minority youth are negatively impacted continuously through compounding racial biases as they are processed deeper into the system (Rodriguez 2010). However, a recent four-state study of over 95,000 juvenile court referrals revealed limited support for this cumulative disadvantage hypothesis (Zane et al. 2022). Although racial and ethnic disparities were greatest for the most punitive pathways of case outcomes, these disparities did not show a pattern of accumulation from the least to most punitive processing pathways, and some of the least punitive pathways were actually more likely for minority youth. Detention, though, played a strong role in this process, as racial and ethnic disparities were greatest for the processing pathways that began with detention.

In response to these ongoing research findings, there have been various governmental efforts to address DMC, including a 1994 mandate from the Office of Juvenile Justice and Delinquency Prevention that specified certain actions for continuation of federal funding (Davis and Sorensen 2013). States were required to undergo detailed inspections to determine whether DMC existed, why it exists, and how to correct it. OJJDP also emphasized the importance of using "best practices" (including standardized risk assessments) to avoid racial biases and ensure objectivity, consistency, and equity (Campbell et al. 2018). In 2014, however, US Attorney General Eric Holder expressed concern regarding the impact of risk assessments on racial disparities in the criminal justice system (McCafferty 2018). This led to a variety of studies focused on the creation, implementation, and fidelity of risk assessments on minority youth, with a desire to understand whether these instruments actually exacerbate racial disparities.

It is difficult to fully assess the influence race has on the predictive validity of youth risk assessments. Munoz and colleagues (2020) assert that designing risk assessments based solely on recidivism outcomes will always result in higher proportions of minority youth being identified as high risk, while McCafferty (2018) found that the Ohio Youth Assessment System-Disposition Instrument predicts recidivism similarly for both White and Black youth. In contrast to the focus on recidivism, program referral has been one of the least studied decision-making outcomes in the juvenile justice system, yet also one of the most crucial (Campbell et al. 2018). Appropriate service matching by probation officers, based on standardized risk and needs assessment (as opposed to personal experience and biases), is vital to generating positive outcomes for minority youth. Sentencing guidelines, multicategory dispositional options, and treatment-oriented graduated sanctions all can help ensure fair and equal treatment with regard to punitive sanctions and rehabilitative programming (Cochran and Mears 2015; Howell et al. 2019).

IV. Improving Knowledge and Use of Evidence-Based Approaches

One of the key components of the evidence-based movement is its ongoing quest for scientific knowledge, with subsequent use of that knowledge for continuous system improvement (Howell et al. 2019; Lipsey et al. 2017; Myers 2013; Sullivan and Childs 2022; Vincent et al. 2018). Areas of possible juvenile probation enhancement are highlighted in the following sections. Implementation of these recommendations will require strong leadership and buy-in from front-line staff, ongoing training, internal and external collaboration, and data-driven planning and decision-making.

A. Quality Assurance and Continuous Quality Improvement

The RNR model uses instruments that evaluate risk levels, identify areas of need, and suggest appropriate intervention services for delinquent youth. The risk factors contained in these tools have been associated statistically with reoffending, and previously discussed research shows support for their potential in guiding decision-making (Baglivio et al 2017a, 2017b, 2018, 2019; Howell et al. 2019; Lipsey et al. 2017; McCafferty 2018; Sullivan and Childs 2022; Vincent et al. 2018). This model, if implemented properly, should standardize decision-making processes and remove subjective criteria and bias.

Perhaps appearing somewhat simple in concept, the quality assurance of implementing RNR is much more complicated. The RNR model requires consistent coordinating, assessing, planning, advocating, and monitoring from juvenile probation staff and leadership (Vincent et al. 2021). Unfortunately, there is limited existing research, with mixed findings, focused on the actual implementation and fidelity associated with using these tools (Haqanee, Peterson-Badali, and Skilling 2015; Miller and Maloney 2013; Miller and Palmer 2020; Nelson and Vincent 2018; Peterson-Badali, Skilling, and Haqanee 2015; Sullivan and Childs 2022).

Fidelity must be ensured on multiple levels, including completion of the instrument, use of the results, referral to appropriate services, and delivery of the services. Quality assurance on all levels must be monitored and achieved by juvenile probation officers, supervisors, and the overarching agency. Practitioner compliance with RNR tools varies, and potential problems range from noncompletion, careless completion, manipulation, and nonadherence to tool recommendations (Miller and Maloney 2013). Levels of compliance exist at both the individual level, such as with juvenile probation officers, and an organizational justice level, with regard to policies and supervision in the workplace setting. Studies of juvenile probation compliance generally indicate high compliance for completing assessment tools, but lower compliance with regard to implementation in case planning and service recommendations (Haqanee, Peterson-Badali, and Skilling 2015). In other words, practitioners are likely to complete the assessment but ignore or underutilize the results, while creating their own treatment plan.

Juvenile probation officers may either over-refer or under-refer, rather than accurately identifying service referrals based on risk and needs (Nelson and Vincent 2018). When youth are over-referred to more intensive services, they may be more likely to perform poorly and recidivate (Baglivio, Greenwald, and Russell 2014). Furthermore, when practitioner decisions override risk assessments results, this is often due to such factors as lack of service availability, limited buy-in from justice stakeholders, unclear roles of staff, and inability to prioritize multiple areas of need (Vincent et al. 2021). To illustrate, Miller and Maloney (2013) conducted a national survey of front-line staff, revealing compliance is influenced by staff beliefs and confidence in the tool, staff monitoring and training, and perceptions of procedural justice within agencies. These results point to the ongoing importance of research, training, and policy efforts to improve the implementation of assessment tools and corresponding service recommendations (Howell et al. 2019; Miller and Palmer 2020; Nelson and Vincent 2018; Peterson-Badali, Skilling, and Haqanee 2015; Sullivan and Childs 2022).

B. Monitoring Performance and Leading Change

To be effective, implementation of the RNR framework and associated evidence-based programs and practices must be monitored and strengthened by enhanced data management systems and data-driven performance measurement (Myers 2013). Some statewide information management systems are used by probation officers to track clients, maintain assessment information, organize case planning, evaluate services, and measure case outcomes (Howell et al. 2019; Lipsey et al. 2017). These systems must be both comprehensive and user-friendly in order to support juvenile probation staff, rather than becoming an extra burden to their role (Vincent et al. 2018, 2021). Furthermore, many jurisdictions and juvenile probation departments do not yet have robust data management systems, relying instead on some combination of hand-collected data from case files and limited automated court data. In these cases, significant improvements in hardware, software, staffing, and analytical capabilities are necessary, but these enhancements might take several years and substantial resources to accomplish.

Leadership and organizational culture also have important influences on juvenile probation performance and use of evidence-based approaches (Collins-Camargo and Royse 2010; Debus-Sherrill, Breno, and Taxman 2021; Viglione et al. 2018). Leaders and an organizational culture that value evidence-based rehabilitative approaches to juvenile case management have the best chance of influencing appropriate service matching and reductions in recidivism (Esthappan et al. 2020). Agency leaders (including directors, supervisors, and judges) who support and promote the use of risk and needs assessment are most likely to influence front-line staff to implement assessment instruments and utilize the results with fidelity (Miller and Maloney 2013). Directly involving front-line staff in important decisions, such as choosing, developing, and implementing tools, can also increase engagement and commitment to the use of evidence-based approaches (Vincent et al. 2018, 2021).

C. Training and Researcher-Practitioner Partnerships

Consistent and ongoing evidence-based training for juvenile probation officers can increase adherence to RNR tools and evidence-based programs and practices (Hartzler and Espinosa 2011; Peterson-Badali, Skilling, and Haqanee 2015). Training should focus on such topics as completion of assessment tools, fidelity of decision-making, and service matching (Miller and Maloney 2013). Not only should trainings focus on the technical aspects of using risk assessment instruments and data management systems, but also the local services and resources available for youth and families. Research also suggests that trainings on the responsivity principle of RNR model can improve tool implementation, and juvenile probation officer trainings focused on criminogenic needs is effective in reducing recidivism (Haqanee, Peterson-Badali, and Skilling 2015).

To minimize racial bias, probation officers should also receive regular diversity training (Campbell et al. 2018; Esthappan et al. 2020). Results of meta-analyses indicate significant positive effects of diversity training on affective-based, cognitive-based, and skill-based outcomes, with greater effects when diversity training is complemented by other diversity initiatives, targeted to both awareness and skills development, and conducted over a significant period of time (Bezrukova et al. 2016; Kalinoski et al. 2013). Criminal and juvenile justice practitioners may be at heightened need for this type of training, and suggestive evidence indicates juvenile probation officers can benefit from training and focused reform efforts in this area (Campbell et al. 2018; Esthappan et al. 2020). In addition, any structured decision-making tool that utilizes motivational interviewing techniques should ensure that interviewers are properly trained to conduct and score them without bias (Blasko et al. 2019; Early, Hand, and Blankenship 2012; Hartzler and Espinosa 2011). Finally, supervisor trainings should focus on promoting adherence to the RNR model, monitoring staff performance, and identifying and reducing bias in case processing (Vincent et al. 2018, 2021).

As the modern evidence-based movement strengthened in recent years, researcher-practitioner partnerships became more common and are vital to generating new knowledge about evidence-based approaches and innovations. Early on, governmental and private funders encouraged applicant agencies to collaborate with a researcher, as a way to both increase the likelihood of implementation funding being awarded and generate new data and scientific findings. More recently, requirements for researcher-practitioner partnerships have been strengthened, with funder stipulations for documented researcher commitment and adequate funding levels for evaluation built into proposed budgets. At the same time, there has been growing recognition among academics that research should be relevant and useful to the "real world," leading to greater amounts of funded and published evaluation research.

Despite these developments, the systematic examination and understanding of researcher-practitioner partnerships and practitioner use of research have received relatively little attention in scholarly research. Existing research does indicate that the strength and productivity of researcher-practitioner collaborations can be influenced by such factors as the unique aspects of the research setting, sensitivity and complexity of the data, the number and types of agencies and individuals involved, research funding (or lack thereof), and researcher focus on quantifying behavioral outcomes (Clodfelter et al. 2014; Johnson, Lebold, and Paul Elam 2016; Worden, McLean, and Bonner. 2014). As criminal and juvenile justice agencies (including juvenile probation) continue to be called upon to demonstrate their efficiency in meeting their goals, researchers and practitioners will continue to be encouraged to work together to utilize existing research evidence, enhance the quality of services provided, and produce new evidence of "what works" (Esthappan et al. 2020; Howell et al. 2019; Johnson, Lebold, and Elam 2016; Lipsey et al. 2017; Vincent et al. 2018).

V. Conclusions

Although programs and practices relevant to juvenile probation have been a focal point in the evidence-based movement, there is still much to learn. Juvenile probation officers nationwide encounter roughly 700,000 youth per year, with over 30 million young people currently under some form of juvenile court custody or supervision (Hockenberry and Puzzanchera 2021). This provides both great opportunity and many challenges associated with changing the lives of young people and setting them up for future success. With this goal in mind, research has identified characteristics of effective and ineffective juvenile programs. The RNR model proposes that lower-risk youth should receive minimal intervention or be diverted from the system, and medium- and higher-risk youth should receive more intensive services supported by research and matched based on risk and needs. Existing research reviewed in this chapter generally supports these assertions. Validated risk assessment tools can help to identify risk and protective factors that are critical to treatment success and behavioral outcomes. By utilizing evidence-based programs and practices, juvenile probation officers can potentially address criminogenic needs and reduce the likelihood of future offending.

Despite these evidence-based advancements, many ineffectual or harmful juvenile programs and practices continue to exist, along with inequities and disproportionate minority representation across the juvenile justice system. Continued and strengthened research is necessary across all areas discussed in this chapter to improve the implementation and effectiveness of risk and needs assessment, enhance understanding and use of evidence-based programs and practices, and reduce inequities in juvenile justice. To achieve these goals, more scientifically rigorous experimental and quasi-experimental research is needed, such as the evaluation produced by Baglivio and colleagues (2018) that utilized propensity score matching to assess the efficacy of matching criminogenic needs to interventions and consider corresponding reductions in risk and recidivism. Further studies using stronger research designs also will expand the knowledge base contained in current online registries of programs and practices; clarify what is known about specific juvenile justice strategies (e.g., diversion, motivational interviewing); shed light on how risks and needs change over time as a result of aging, program participation, or both; and evaluate disparities in juvenile justice that potentially could be influenced by evidence-based programs and practices, as well as other societal factors.

Addressing these research and policy issues, while improving the implementation and outcomes associated with evidence-based approaches, will require internal and external collaboration by juvenile probation departments and other relevant stakeholders, along with structured monitoring of services and measurement of outcomes. Leadership will play a key role in further evidence-based advancements by promoting greater use of data, facilitating appropriate training opportunities, and developing productive relationships with researchers. An organizational culture that embraces learning and change, guided by research and strengthened by collaboration, provides the optimal setting for innovation and experimentation. Although there have been a variety of evidence-based advancements in juvenile probation, there remains much room for growth and improvement.

References

Baglivio, Michael T., Mark A. Greenwald, and Mark Russell. 2014. Assessing the implications of a structured decision-making tool for recidivism in a statewide analysis: Disposition matrix for court recommendations made by juvenile probation officers. *Criminology and Public Policy*, 14:5–49.

Baglivio, Michael T., and Kevin T. Wolff. 2019. Predicting juvenile reentry success: Developing a global risk score and risk classification levels using the residential positive achievement change tool. *Youth Violence and Juvenile Justice*, 17:241–268.

Baglivio, Michael T., Kevin T. Wolff, James C. Howell, Katherine Jackowski, and Mark A. Greenwald. 2018. The search for the Holy Grail: Criminogenic needs matching, intervention dosage, and subsequent recidivism among serious juvenile offenders in residential placement. *Journal of Criminal Justice*, 55:46–57.

Baglivio, Michael T., Kevin T. Wolff, Katherine Jackowski, and Mark A. Greenwald. 2017a. A multilevel examination of risk/needs change scores, community context, and successful reentry of committed juvenile offenders. *Youth Violence and Juvenile Justice*, 15:38–61.

Baglivio, Michael T., Kevin T. Wolff, Alex R. Piquero, James C. Howell, and Mark A. Greenwald. 2017b. Risk assessment trajectories of youth during juvenile justice residential placement: Examining risk, promotive, and "buffer" scores. *Criminal Justice and Behavior*, 44:360–94.

Baird, Chris, Theresa Healy, Kristen Johnson, Andrea Bogie, Erin Wicke Dankert, and Chris Scharenbroch. 2013. *A comparison of risk assessment instruments in juvenile justice*. Oakland, CA: National Council on Crime and Delinquency.

Bezrukova, Katerina, Chester S. Spell, Jamie L. Perry, and Karen A. Jehn. 2016. A meta-analytical integration of over 40 years of research on diversity training evaluation. *Psychological Bulletin*, 142:1227–1274.

Blasko, Brandy L., Jill Viglione, Heather Toronjo, and Faye S. Taxman. 2019. Probation officer-probation agency fit: Understanding disparities in the use of motivational interviewing techniques. *Corrections: Policy, Practice and Research*, 4:39–57.

Butts, Jeffrey. 2016. Critical diversion. *Criminology & Public Policy*, 15:983–989.

Campbell, Nordia A., Ashlee R. Barnes, Amber Mandalari, Eyitayo Onifade, Christina A. Campbell, Valerie R. Anderson, Deborah A. Kashy, and William S. Davidson. 2018. Disproportionate minority contact in the juvenile justice system: An investigation of ethnic disparity in program referral at disposition. *Journal of Ethnicity in Criminal Justice*, 16:77–98.

Clodfelter, Tammatha A., Melissa A. Alexander, Jefferson E. Holcomb, Catherine D. Marcum, and Tara N. Richards. 2014. Improving probation officer effectiveness through agency-university collaboration. *Criminal Justice Studies*, 27:308–322.

Cochran, Joshua C., and Daniel P. Mears. 2015. Race, ethnic, and gender divides in juvenile court sanctioning and rehabilitative intervention. *Journal of Research in Crime and Delinquency*, 52:181–212.

Collins-Camargo, Crystal, and David Royse. 2010. A study of the relationships among effective supervision, organizational culture promoting evidence-based practice, and worker self-efficacy in public child welfare. *Journal of Public Child Welfare*, 4:1–24.

Davis, Jaya, and Jon R. Sorensen. 2013. Disproportionate minority confinement of juveniles: A national examination of Black-White disparity in placements, 1997–2006. *Crime and Delinquency*, 59:115–139.

Debus-Sherrill, Sara, Alex Breno, and Faye S. Taxman. 2021. What makes or breaks evidence-based supervision? Staff and organizational predictors of evidence-based practice in probation. *International Journal of Offender Therapy and Comparative Criminology*, 67:662–686. https://doi.org/10.1177/0306624X211049182.

Dishion, Thomas J., Joan McCord, and Francois Poulin. 1999. When interventions harm: Peer groups and problem behavior. *American Psychologist*, 54:755–764.

Early, Kristin Parsons, Gregory A. Hand, and Julia L. Blankenship. 2012. Validity and reliability of the Florida Positive Achievement Change Tool (PACT) risk and needs assessment instrument: A three-phase evaluation. Tallahassee, FL: Justice Research Center.

Elliot, Delbert S., Pamela R. Buckley, Denise C. Gottfredson, J. David Hawkins, and Patrick H. Tolan. 2020. Evidence-based juvenile justice programs and practices: A critical review. *Criminology & Public Policy*, 19:1305–1328.

Esthappan, Sino, Johanna Lacoe, Janine M. Zweig, and Douglas W. Young. 2020. Transforming practice through culture change: Probation staff perspectives on juvenile justice reform. *Youth Violence and Juvenile Justice*, 18:274–293.

Fagan, Abigail A., and Molly Buchanan. 2016. What works in crime prevention? Comparison and critical review of three crime prevention registries. *Criminology & Public Policy*, 15:617–649.

Gann, Shaun M. 2019. Examining the relationship between race and juvenile court decision-making: A counterfactual approach. *Youth Violence and Juvenile Justice*, 17:269–287.

Hartzler, Bryan, and Erin M. Espinosa. 2011. Moving criminal justice organizations toward adoption of evidence-based practice via advanced workshop training in motivational interviewing: A research note. *Criminal Justice Policy Review*, 22:235–253.

Haqanee, Zohrah, Michele Peterson-Badali, and Tracey A. Skilling. 2015. Making "what works" work: Examining probation officers' experiences addressing the criminogenic needs of juvenile offenders. *Journal of Offender Rehabilitation*, 54:37–59.

Henggler, Scott W., and Sonja K. Schoenwald. 2011. Evidence-based interventions for juvenile offenders and policies that support them. *Social Policy Report*, 25:3–26.

Hockenberry, Sarah, and Charles Puzzanchera. 2021. *Juvenile court statistics 2019*. Pittsburgh, PA: National Center for Juvenile Justice.

Hoge, Robert D. 2016. Application of precharge diversion programs. *Criminology & Public Policy*, 15:991–99.

Howell, James C., and Mark W. Lipsey. 2012. Research-based guidelines for juvenile justice programs. *Justice Research and Policy*, 14:17–34.

Howell, James C., Mark W. Lipsey, John J. Wilson, Megan Q. Howell, and Nancy J. Hodges. 2019. *A handbook for evidence-based juvenile justice systems*. Rev. ed. Lanham, MD: Rowman & Littlefield.

Johnson, Lee Michael, Susan M. Lebold, and Paul Elam. 2016. Use of research evidence by juvenile justice and youth service professionals: A research note. *Criminal Justice Policy Review*, 27:402–419.

Kalinoski, Zachary T., Debra Steele-Johnson, Elizabeth J. Peyton, Keith A. Leas, Julie Steinke, and Nathan A. Bowling. 2013. A meta-analytic evaluation of diversity training outcomes. *Journal of Organizational Behavior*, 34:1076–1104.

Lipsey, Mark W. 2009. The primary factors that characterize effective interventions with juvenile offenders: A meta-analytic overview. *Victims and Offenders*, 4:124–147.

Lipsey, Mark W. 2020. Revisited: Effective use of the large body of research on the effectiveness of programs for juvenile offenders and the failure of the model programs approach. *Criminology & Public Policy*, 19:1329–1345.

Lipsey, Mark W., Catherine H. Conly, Gabrielle Chapman, and Shay Bilchik. 2017. *Juvenile justice system improvement: Implementing an evidence-based decision-making platform*. Washington, DC: Center for Juvenile Justice Reform.

McCafferty, James T. 2018. Unjust disparities? The impact of race on juvenile risk assessment outcomes. *Criminal Justice Policy Review*, 29:423–442.

Mears, Daniel P., Joshua C. Cochran, and Andrea M. Lindsey. 2016. Offending and racial and ethnic disparities in criminal justice: A conceptual framework for guiding theory and research and informing policy. *Journal of Contemporary Criminal Justice*, 32:78–103.

Mears, Daniel, Joshua Kuch, Andrea Lindsey, Sonja Siennick, George Pesta, Mark Greenwald, and Thomas Blomberg. 2016. Juvenile court and contemporary diversion: Helpful, harmful, or both? *Criminology & Public Policy*, 15:953–981.

Miller, Joel, and Carrie Maloney. 2013. Practitioner compliance with risk/needs assessment tools: A theoretical and empirical assessment. *Criminal Justice and Behavior*, 40:716–736.

Miller, Joel, and Krissinda Palmer. 2020. Juvenile probation officer decision-making in a reforming state: Assessing the application of evidence-based principles. *Criminal Justice and Behavior*, 47:1136–1155.

Munoz, Carla G., Rachel T. Perrault, and Gina M. Vincent. 2020. Probation officer assessments of risk when the youth look different: Contributions of structured professional judgment to concerns about racial bias. *Youth Violence and Juvenile Justice*, 19:206–226.

Myers, David L. 2013. Accountability and evidence-based approaches: Theory and research for juvenile justice. *Criminal Justice Studies*, 26:197–212.

Nelson, Rebecca J., and Gina M. Vincent. 2018. Matching services to criminogenic needs following comprehensive risk assessment implementation in juvenile probation. *Criminal Justice and Behavior*, 45:1136–1153.

Peterson-Badali, Michele, Tracey Skilling, and Zohrah Haqanee. 2015. Examining implementation of risk assessment in case management for youth in the justice system. *Criminal Justice and Behavior*, 42:304–320.

Piquero, Alex R. 2008. Disproportionate minority contact. *The Future of Children*, 18:59–79.

Rodriguez, Nancy. 2010. The cumulative effect of race and ethnicity in juvenile court outcomes and why preadjudication detention matters. *Journal of Research in Crime and Delinquency*, 47:391–413.

Rudes, Danielle S., Jill Viglione, Ashli J. Sheidow, Michael R. McCart, Jason E. Chapman, and Faye S. Taxman. 2021. Juvenile probation officers perceptions on youth substance use varies from task-shifting to family-based contingency management. *Journal of Substance Abuse Treatment*, 120:108144.

Schwartz, Katherine, Andrew O. Alexander, Katherine S. L. Lau, Evan D. Holloway, and Matthew C. Aalsma. 2017. Motivating compliance: Juvenile probation officer strategies and skills. *Journal of Offender Rehabilitation*, 56:20–37.

Stafford, Mark C. 2016. New call for assessing the effects of 21st century juvenile diversion. Criminology & Public Policy, 15:949–952.

Sullivan, Christopher J., and Kristina K. Childs. 2022. *Juvenile risk and needs assessment: Theory, research, policy, and practice*. New York: Routledge.

Van der Put, Claudia E., Geert J. Stams, Machteld Hoeve, Maja Dekovic, Han J. M. Spanjaard, Peter H. Van Der Laan, and R. P. Barnoski. 2012. Changes in the relative importance of dynamic risk factors on recidivism during adolescence. *International Journal of Offender Therapy and Comparative Criminology*, 56:296–316.

Viglione, Jill, Danielle Rudes, Vienna Nightingale, Carolyn Watson, and Faye Taxman. 2018. The many hats of juvenile probation officers: Class analysis of word-related activities. *Criminal Justice Review*, 43:252–269.

Vincent, Gina M., Rachel T. Perrault, Dara C. Drawbridge, Gretchen O. Landry, and Thomas Grisso. 2021. Risk-Need-Responsivity meets mental health: Implementation challenges in probation case planning. *Criminal Justice and Behavior*, 48:1187–1207.

Vincent, Gina M., Christopher J. Sullivan, Carrie Sullivan, Laura Guy, Edward Latessa, Jennifer Tyson, and Benjamin Adams. 2018. *Studying drivers of risk and needs assessment instrument implementation in juvenile justice*. Washington, DC: Office of Juvenile Justice and Delinquency Prevention.

Walters, Glenn D. 2018. Positive and negative social influences and crime acceleration during the transition from childhood to adolescence: The interplay of risk and protective factors. *Criminal Behaviour and Mental Health*, 28:414–423.

Welsh, Brandon C. 2020. The case for rigorous comparative research and population impacts in a new era of evidence-based interventions for juvenile offenders. *Criminology & Public Policy*, 19:1347–1354.

Worden, Robert E., Sarah J. McLean, and Heidi S. Bonner. 2014. Research partners in criminal justice: Notes from Syracuse. *Criminal Justice Studies*, 27:278–293.

Zane, Steven N., and Jhon A. Pupo. 2021. Disproportionate minority contact in the juvenile justice system: A systematic review and meta-analysis. *Justice Quarterly*, 38:1293–1318.

Zane, Steven N., Brandon C. Welsh, Daniel P. Mears, and Gregory M. Zimmerman. 2022. Pathways through juvenile justice: A system-level assessment of cumulative disadvantage in the processing of juvenile offenders. *Journal of Quantitative Criminology*, 38:483–514.

CHAPTER 10

USING EVIDENCE-BASED PRACTICES TO IMPROVE JUVENILE DRUG TREATMENT COURTS

CHRISTOPHER J. SULLIVAN, VITOR GONÇALVES, AND NICOLE MCKENNA

JUVENILE court referral trends have declined since the late 1990s and are at their lowest point in decades, as of this writing (Hockenberry 2020). Cases reaching the juvenile court declined by 55% between 2005 and 2018 and, concurrently, youth with drug-related offenses declined by 45%, but still made up a nontrivial proportion of the total (13.6% or 100,000 cases). Substance use frequently co-occurs with delinquency (Huizinga 2000; White, Conway, and Ward 2019) and may exacerbate or prolong contact with the juvenile or criminal justice systems (Hussong et al. 2004).

The juvenile justice system has embraced intervention strategies that appropriately respond to that set of problems, promote abstinence from drugs, reduce recidivism, and redirect youth developmental pathways. Juvenile drug treatment courts (JDTCs) are the most prominent practice adopted in response to this set of cases. First established in the 1990s, JDTCs were founded on principles of therapeutic jurisprudence that theorize that courts can be a catalyst for change (Ledgerwood and Cunningham 2019). In juvenile courts, this suggests that by engaging youth (and families) in appropriate treatment programs using the leverage and oversight of a specialized court docket, it is possible to reduce substance use problems to prevent later system involvement. This is inherent in the intervention logic model outlined in Figure 10.1.

Evaluation results for juvenile drug treatment courts (JDTCs) have been mixed so far. Given that the use of JDTCs has continued since their initial development, it is important to carefully interrogate all aspects of the empirical research and the underlying logic model. This includes evaluating whether they work in reducing substance use and recidivism as well as questions about variation in effects based on youth characteristics, treatment practices, and implementation fidelity. To date, there is little research on a fully specified theoretical model of how the juvenile drug treatment court is meant to promote

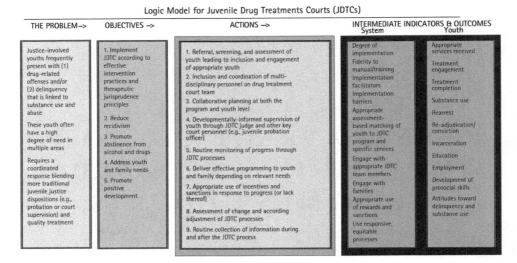

FIGURE 10.1. The Logic Model for Juvenile Drug Treatment Courts.

change in youth behavior. Similarly, little is known about adherence to key elements of a theoretically informed intervention model. This chapter comprises six sections. First, we briefly review the prevalence and nature of adolescent substance use and identify how juvenile drug courts are meant to fit as a response to those behaviors. Second, we describe the features of juvenile drug treatment courts before taking stock of the findings from that body of research in the third section of the chapter. This informs the fourth section of the chapter, which identifies ways in which JDTCs might be improved via greater fidelity to the underlying logic model. The fifth section of the chapter evaluates what researchers and evaluators could do to enhance the evidence-base around JDTCs to better inform practice. The final section reiterates key takeaway points from our review and analysis of the evidence base for JDTCs.

I. Adolescent Substance Use and Juvenile Justice Response

According to national estimates, alcohol and marijuana are the two drugs most commonly used by adolescents in the United States (National Institute on Drug Abuse 2021). The 2020 results of the Monitoring the Future (MTF) study show that approximately 18% of 12th graders, 10% of 10th graders, and 6% of 8th graders report binge drinking (five or more drinks in the past two weeks). Similarly, approximately 30% of 12th graders, 18% of 10th graders, and 7% of 8th graders reported using marijuana in the past year in the 2021 MTF. Thirty-two percent of 12th graders, 18.7% of 10th graders, and 10.2% of 8th graders reported substance use in the past year (National Institute on Drug Abuse 2021). Harder drug use is comparatively rare, with less than 1% of youth ages 12 to 17 reporting cocaine, methamphetamine, or heroin use, and 2.5% using pain killers without a prescription in the past year (National Center for Drug Abuse Statistics 2022).

The terms "addiction" and "substance dependence" are often used interchangeably in the substance use literature and typically refer to compulsive drug-seeking despite negative consequences (Stanford Medicine Children's Health 2022). For teens, substance abuse may be related to missing school or using substances in dangerous situations (e.g., driving a car), and it may interfere with relationships with friends and family. In recent years, among teenagers aged 12–17 years old, 401,000 youth met the criteria for alcohol use disorder and 681,000 met the criteria for illicit drug use disorder (Substance Use and Mental Health Services Administration 2019).

Substance use and delinquency frequently co-occur, offering an impetus for juvenile justice responses that address drugs as a means of reducing recidivism and promoting positive youth outcomes. Multiple characteristics, including individual and family factors, explain trends in adolescent substance use and therefore are relevant in responding to it. Greater parental monitoring and engaged parenting is related to less substance use (DiIorio, Pluhar, and Belcher 2003; Huebner and Howell 2003). When parents model prosocial behavior, youth are less likely to use substances (Perrino et al. 2000). Additionally, youth with parents who abuse substances are more likely to use substances and be involved in other delinquent behaviors (Barylnik 2003). In contrast, more family conflict is predictive of substance use in adolescents (Rowe et al. 2008). Trauma also impacts both substance use and delinquency. Wolff and colleagues (2020), for example, found that substance use mediates the relationship between cumulative trauma and antisocial behavior and delinquency.

In adolescence, substance use could be part of an enduring pattern of antisocial behavior across settings or may be socially structured experimentation (Moffitt 1993). Those different mechanisms in turn suggest unique responses to the problem. So, for example, if adolescent drug use is driven by individual choices about peers who also use substances, the response to the problem might require more intensive intervention than if it is a byproduct of a socialization or opportunity perspective (Sullivan, Childs, and Gann 2018; Warr 2012). Much adolescent substance use is sanctioned as status offenses, but some traditional approaches to delinquency, such as detention, residential programs, placement in group homes, and intensive supervision, are still common responses to adolescent substance use. JDTCs are one of multiple potential responses to adolescent substance use and related delinquent behavior.

II. The Evolution and Nature of Juvenile Drug Treatment Courts

Drug courts have been widely implemented, with over 1,750 adult drug courts and 308 juvenile drug courts in place across the United States (National Drug Court Resource Center 2021). The first juvenile drug courts, which were established in 1995 in Alabama, California, Florida, Nevada, and Utah, targeted substance-abusing youth charged with delinquent and/or status offenses (Sloan, Smykla, and Rush 2004). JDTCs are based on the rehabilitative ideals of the juvenile justice system but were also driven by the introduction of drug courts into the criminal justice system. The first drug court was established in 1989 with the goal of using sanctions and rewards in addition to treatment services to gain compliance and reduce the substance use and delinquency of participants (Goldkamp 1999). Drug courts were viewed as a more intensive response to substance-using offenders compared to traditional probation, but less restrictive than incarceration (Goldkamp 1999). These courts were built on principles of effective intervention and therapeutic jurisprudence, which focuses in part on how the law can be used as a tool to effectively treat those under court jurisdiction (Rottman and Casey 1999; Wexler 2000).

A. The Juvenile Drug Court Model

Juvenile drug courts comprise treatment teams, drug testing, phases, treatment, and sanctions for positive drug tests and failing to follow through with treatment (Latessa et al. 2013). As seen in Figure 10.1, youth are typically referred to JDTCs after intake screenings "flag" their substance use behavior, they are charged with substance-related offenses, or they return a positive urine sample while under probation supervision (Sloan, Smykla, and Rush 2004). While illicit drugs are considered delinquent or criminal for both adults and juveniles, there are important distinctions in how substance use is treated in the courts, given developmental and legal considerations. For example, youth in drug courts are often still enrolled in school, and thus treatment teams may include, or coordinate with, their schools and teachers. Many youth also reside with a parent or guardian, who ideally work with the drug court team, supporting the youth in treatment, providing transportation, and potentially receiving services themselves (Gilmore, Rodriguez, and Webb 2005).

The drug court model provides a collaborative treatment framework that emphasizes relationship-building between the judge, program participants, and the treatment team (Rottman and Casey 1999). JDTCs are voluntary in nature and provide services aimed at treatment for participants, all of which are in line with therapeutic jurisprudence (Fulton Hora 2002). In addition to therapeutic jurisprudence, drug courts are meant to follow effective intervention principles, such as determining the types of services that should be delivered, who they should be delivered to, the behaviors and relationships that should be targeted for change, and how those interventions will be delivered (Shaffer 2011). Research has shown that justice interventions that adhere to the Risk-Need-Responsivity (RNR) model are comparatively more successful in reducing recidivism among youth and adults. Some research on JDTCs advocates for combining multiple treatments that target youth needs (see, e.g., Tripodi and Bender 2011), meaning that in addition to targeting substance use, JDTCs address risk and protective factors such as family, peers, school, work, housing, thoughts, and behaviors.

A drug court team generally includes the judge, the probation officer, a prosecutor and defense attorney, and treatment staff (Cooper 2001; Latessa et al. 2013). In juvenile drug courts, membership could also be extended to school personnel and other community representatives. These individuals work collaboratively to support youth and provide multidisciplinary perspectives on the best approaches to success. The treatment team reviews the each youth's case prior to court sessions, with each member of the team providing input from their respective area (Cooper 2001; Latessa et al. 2013). Probation officers provide insight into supervision compliance and drug testing, while treatment providers will have more input on how participants are progressing through programming (Latessa et al. 2013). Legal actors work together to ensure public safety, consider the youth's history, and advocate for their success. The judge plays a vital role in guiding the team and encouraging and supervising participants within the therapeutic jurisprudence lens (Latessa et al. 2013).

While involved in a drug court, participants attend regular status hearings (usually weekly) with the treatment team and judge (Latessa et al. 2013). Programs are often phased, with certain expectations and restrictions specified for each point in the process (Nissen and Pearce 2011). Participants are generally required to engage in substance use treatment, submit urine analysis tests on a regular basis, participate in support groups, attend school or work, and engage with other services (Cooper 2001; Rossman et al. 2004). When participants comply with conditions, they are given incentives such as less frequent check-ins or drug testing (Cooper 2001). When they fail to meet expectations, sanctions, such as warnings, increased drug testing, or periods of detention, are triggered (Cooper 2001; Latessa et al. 2013).

B. Developmental Considerations in JDTCs

It is crucial for a drug court to be a voluntary program for youth, so as to provide a sense of choice and empowerment. Yet while JDTCs are intended to be voluntary, youth are encouraged to participate in treatment by authority figures such as parents and courts. Motivation is a key element in the success of substance abuse treatment programs (Hiller et al. 2002; Longshore and Teruya 2006), but youth tend to be less motivated than adults to engage in these interventions (Melnick et al. 1997). Generally, youth have not experienced the same long-term negative consequences of substance abuse as adults (Battjes et al. 2003). Adolescents may also lack fully developed cognitive capacities, which impedes self-control and decision-making (Griffin et al. 2011; Olver, Stockdale, and Wormith 2011). This impulsivity, coupled with peer influence, plays an important role in their delinquency and drug use (Scott and Steinberg 2009). Therefore, youth may stop using drugs without any intervention as they get older—consistent with the age-crime curve that identifies desistance as normative (Farrington 1986; Piquero, Farrington, and Blumstein 2003). These challenges lead some scholars to question whether JDTCs are appropriate for most juveniles (Butts and Roman 2004).

C. Gender and Juvenile Drug Treatment Courts

In recent decades, the proportion of girls involved in the juvenile justice system has increased (Ehrmann, Hyland, and Puzzanchera 2019; Javdani, Sadeh, and Verona 2011; Stevens, Morash, and Chesney-Linda 2011). As such, juvenile drug courts are likely to have also seen an influx of girls in their programs. In general, girls are less likely to be terminated from drug court programs (Carey, Waller, and Marchand 2006; Polakowski, Hartley, and Bates 2008), less likely to test positive for marijuana or cocaine (Gilmore, Rodriguez, and Webb 2005), more likely to graduate or complete drug court programs (Stein, Homan, and DeBerard 2015), and less likely to be arrested after graduation (Hickert, Becker, and Prospero 2010; Sloan, Smykla, and Rush 2004). In one study, boys were eight times more likely to be terminated from drug court and four times more likely to receive a new referral while participating in the drug court program compared to girls (Polakowski, Hartley, and Bates 2008). In a quasi-experiment examining the 12-year effects of juvenile drug courts, Belisle and Thompson (2020) found that participation in juvenile drug courts was related to an increased frequency in adulthood arrests and convictions for boys but not girls.

Some studies, however, have found similar completion rates of juvenile drug court programs for boys and girls (Fradella et al. 2009), and similar scores on scales measuring substance use problems, substance dependence, substance abuse, and substance frequency (Ruiz et al. 2009). In a meta-analysis of juvenile drug courts, Stein and colleagues (2015) found that a greater proportion of boys participating in the program was linked to lower recidivism rates. While the authors posit that this finding may be driven by the courts' general leniency toward girls across decision points, they claim there is "no compelling evidence ... suggesting that programs need to be designed differently for boys than girls" (Stein, Homan, and DeBerard 2015, 91). Given these mixed findings and recommendations, gender must be considered when examining juvenile drug court effectiveness, especially concerning drug use, treatment needs, use of services, and effectiveness of programs (Pelisser and Jones 2005). Specifically, girls experience high rates of traumatic experiences and have higher rates of mental health diagnoses compared to boys (Belisle and Salisbury 2021; Saar et al. 2015). These gendered factors may contribute to differential success rates in boys and girls, leading scholars, practitioners, and policymakers to advocate for gender-responsive and trauma-informed programming that takes these unique factors into consideration (Somers and Holtfreter 2018; Tripodi and Bender 2011).

D. Race/Ethnicity and Juvenile Drug Treatment Courts

Given the context of the "war on drugs" and, specifically, the fear of the "superpredator," or drug-using and drug-selling youth that inspired drug laws in the 1980s and 1990s, there is still a long-held belief that youth of color use substances at higher rates than White youth. Kakade et al. (2012) found support for the opposite trend: White youth reported higher levels of substance use and other drug-related offenses than Black youth. However, race was still a significant predictor of single and multiple arrests regardless of using and selling trends. This means that although Black youth use drugs and alcohol at lower rates, they are more likely to be brought into the justice system compared to their White counterparts (Kakade et al. 2012).

A national (US) survey conducted in 2008 with drug court coordinators showed that Black and Latino/a/x youth are underrepresented in JDTCs compared to other justice-involved populations (Huddleston and Marlowe 2011). In general, racial and ethnic minority youth fare worse in drug courts (e.g., recidivism, program completion) compared to White youth (Stein, Homan, and DeBerard 2015). Further, the findings from Stein et al.'s meta-analysis suggest that as the proportion of ethnic minority participants in a JDTC increases, recidivism levels are greater compared to White youth. This is evidence of potential discrepancy in the treatment of youth of color, who, despite having unequal access to drug courts, are frequently overrepresented in other parts of the juvenile justice system (Bishop and Leiber 2012). These findings call attention to the fact that these interventions need to be tailored based on race, ethnicity, and other intersectional identities that may affect responsivity to the practices and treatment used in JDTCs.

E. Mental Illness and Juvenile Drug Treatment Courts

Mental illness is common among justice-involved youth with drug issues (Colins et al. 2010). In one study, 49% of youth in drug treatment services were diagnosed with mood or anxiety disorders. For girls, this was even higher: 61%. This study found that co-occurring disorders were associated with several adverse outcomes, such as higher rates of problematic use, comorbid disorders, and poorer quality of life. Although individuals with dual diagnoses tend to have worse performance in these treatments, there is evidence that abstinence from alcohol and drug abuse is associated with improvements in psychiatric symptoms and subjective feeling of quality of life (Schaar and Öjehagen 2003). Fradella and colleagues (2009) also found that youth with another clinical diagnosis are less likely to complete juvenile drug court programs successfully. These findings call attention to the importance of detecting and treating mental health issues in parallel with substance abuse treatment.

F. Family Involvement and JDTCs

JDTCs frequently mandate, or at least strongly encourage, family involvement. Youth not only rely on parents and caregivers for transportation to court and treatment services, but they typically also reside with adults, siblings, and other family members. Parental support and family factors can influence effectiveness of juvenile drug courts (Alarid, Montemayor, and Dannhaus 2012; Fradella et al. 2009; Stanton and Shadish 1997). For example, among juvenile drug treatment court participants, more negative parent-child relationships are related to increases in marijuana use (Tolou-Shams et al. 2012). Additionally, a meta-analysis of treatments to reduce alcohol and/or marijuana use challenged these results, finding that family-based interventions, such as MST, were significantly better at reducing substance use (for both alcohol and marijuana use) as well as offending compared to individual-based interventions (Tripodi and Bender 2011).

III. What We Know about the JDTC Evidence Base

Despite the proliferation of JDTCs, especially in the United States, evidence for their effectiveness is still mixed. If meta-analyses assessing adult drug courts have shown consistent effects in reducing drug use and recidivism (Lowenkamp, Holsinger, and Latessa 2005; Shaffer 2011; Wilson, Mitchell, and Mackenzie 2006), there is less evidence of effectiveness for youth (Mitchell et al. 2012; Stein, Deberard, and Homan 2013; Tanner-Smith, Lipsey, and

Wilson 2016). In general, adult drug courts significantly reduced recidivism by about 10%. On the other hand, juvenile drug courts reduced recidivism by about 5%, suggesting adult system courts were more effective than those in the juvenile system (Shaffer 2006).

The most recent meta-analysis of JDTCs was conducted by Tanner-Smith and colleagues (2016). They synthesized the effects of 46 empirical research studies that used randomized or quasi-experimental approaches. After aggregating these studies' results, they found that JDTCs had slightly more favorable outcomes than traditional juvenile courts in terms of general recidivism, drug recidivism, and drug use. These differences, however, were not statistically significant. The authors, and other scholars, suggest treating these results with caution due to the mixed methodological rigor of the evidence base (Belenko and Logan 2003; Mitchell et al. 2012; Shaffer 2011; Stein, Deberard, and Homan 2013). Few of these experiments were randomized and most have high attrition rates, which compromises their internal validity (Tanner-Smith, Lipsey, and Wilson 2016). In cases where more rigorous designs have been used, limited research has found evidence of cost-efficiency for JDTCs with evidence-based treatment components (see, e.g., Sheidow et al. 2012).

A. Opening the "Black Box" of Juvenile Drug Treatment Courts

Exacerbating the uncertainty from the impact evaluation results, little is formally known about the features that make some drug courts work better than others. Goldkamp (2010), in fact, has used juvenile drug courts as an example of a justice intervention that has not been clearly defined and, in turn, is hard to study from the standpoint of construct validity. Considering this, some scholars have turned their attention to process studies. To unravel the elements enhancing these programs' effectiveness, Tanner-Smith and colleagues (2016) assessed the association between the 16 recommendations for JDTCs (U.S. Bureau of Justice Assistance 2003) and their outcomes. However, they failed to find clear evidence explaining the variability in effects. Earlier research by Shaffer (2011) showed that JDTC success was moderated by (1) *target population*—courts which excludes violent and noncompliant offenders performed better; (2) *leverage*—pre-adjudication was a positive feature while deferring sentence to secure facility was negative; (3) *intensity*—requirements of restitution and education were positively associated with effectiveness, while requirements of community service, fines, employment, and number of contacts were negatively associated with it; (4) and *staff characteristics*—weekly team meetings were positively associated with the success of these interventions, yet formal training, certification, and attendance in weekly meetings were negatively associated with success.

Given the absence of comparable variables regarding activities and strategies adopted in drug courts, Mei et al. (2019) created the Drug Court Collaboration Instrument. The authors conducted a national survey with administrators of juvenile and adult drug courts to explore the "black box" of these programs. They found that JDTCs have more issues with collaboration, judicial decision-making, operational infrastructure, information sharing and evaluation, and community and political support compared to adult drug courts.

Therefore, Mei and colleagues suggested that implementation/adherence problems may explain why JDTCs performed worse than courts targeting adults. Still, it is unclear whether implementation is consistently better in adult DTCs.

B. Linking Juvenile Drug Treatment Courts to Evidence-Based Policy

Although meta-analyses are insightful (see, e.g., Tanner-Smith, Lipsey, and Wilson 2016), other factors highlighted by empirical research are important in explaining JDTC (in)effectiveness. These have been introduced to the field in different studies and packages of recommendations. One example is the application of sanctions and rewards (Office of Juvenile Justice and Delinquency Prevention [OJJDP] 2016). In this vein, there is evidence that greater incentive-to-sanctions ratios are beneficial in terms of program completion, drug recidivism, and general recidivism (Long and Sullivan 2017). Further, evidence shows that youth are less internally motivated to engage in drug abuse treatment programs (Battjes et al. 2003), and what engages them is different from adults (Cooper 2001). Finally, scholars recommend the adoption of validated risk and need assessment tools (Belenko and Logan 2003; Blair et al. 2015).

The main guidelines for the operation of drug courts in the United States have not yet been fully studied to determine their relationship with JDTC outcomes (e.g., 10 Key Components of the NADCP of 1997, 16 Strategies of the Office of Juvenile Justice and Delinquency Prevention [OJJDP] of 2016). The recent OJJDP guidelines provide extensive direction in several areas. For example, they establish who should be part of the JDTC team in each court and the orientation and training that they should possess. They also establish how JDTCs can most effectively interface with youth and families to promote recovery and desistance and support transformation of parenting and family interactions. Other aspects of the JDTC guidelines focus on training and availability of services to meet youth needs and how court proceedings unfold in terms of interactions with youth.

Building on the best practices identified by OJJDP, Wilson, Olaghere, and Kimbrell (2019) conducted a meta-aggregation, synthesizing findings from qualitative and quantitative research. From that, they suggested that seven elements should be incorporated in these programs: (1) practices addressing substance use and criminogenic needs; (2) equitable treatment for all participants; (3) practices that engage the staff; (4) comprehensive needs assessment; (5) contingency management, case management, and community supervision strategies; (6) referring participants to evidence-based treatment; and (7) monitoring and qualitative and quantitative research findings tracking program completion and termination.

IV. Promoting More Evidence-Based Juvenile Drug Treatment Courts

Given the findings from existing research and the underlying mission of the juvenile justice system, it is essential to reconsider the "for whom" questions that are relevant in assessing an evidence base. The juvenile justice system encounters a variable set of offenses and youth, which it must be conscious of in program development and implementation (Sullivan 2019). First, JDTCs should target youth with severe drug issues. Intensive treatment for youth without such issues can cause harm through unnecessary labeling, in addition to being inadequate for their needs and wasteful of scarce resources (Logan and Link 2019). A lack of fit between youth needs and the mission of the court and available services can weaken JDTCs' effectiveness (Belisle and Thompson 2020; Butts and Roman 2004).

The success of juvenile drug treatment courts can also vary depending on the target population. This occurs in part based on age, gender, race and ethnicity, and youth needs, and it is necessary therefore to develop tailored strategies for these groups. Girls, for example, are more likely to have experienced physical or sexual abuse (Saar et al. 2015), which requires that JDTCs have a trauma-informed orientation. For Latino/a/x youth, language or cultural issues can be a barrier to engaging them and their families in programs (Alegría et al. 2006). Generally, community representatives should be consulted in formulating the best intervention strategies for youth. More fundamental than that, some staff should be able to speak other languages to communicate with juveniles and families who do not speak or are not fluent in English (Alegría et al. 2006; OJJDP 2016).

The quality and preparedness of the JDTC team are crucial to the success of juvenile drug courts (Blair et al. 2015; Tanner-Smith, Lipsey, and Wilson 2016). In order to be effective, staff must assimilate the mission and guidelines of JDTCs, develop skills to work with youth and families, and be prepared to deal with mental health and other co-occurring issues (OJJDP 2016). Considering this, it is essential to conduct ongoing staff training to promote evidence-based practices, as JDTCs are now at a stage where there are thorough guidelines to help guide implementation and practice (Hiller et al. 2021; Sullivan and McKenna 2021).

V. Improving Knowledge for Evidence-Based JDTC Practice

Juvenile drug treatment courts have been the subject of a great deal of research since they were first implemented. Reviews to this point show that there are still misunderstandings, inconsistencies, and implementation shortcomings to resolve in promoting evidence-based policy and practice for JDTCs. Most research to date involves quasi-experimental outcome evaluations, but the literature now includes several moderate-sized meta-analyses based on rigorous evaluation designs, like randomized controlled trials (RCTs). Nevertheless, more research would help to improve the understanding of (1) why the outcomes for JDTCs differ from their counterparts in the adult system, and (2) why those results tend to be null or run counter to the assumption that JDTCs will be effective.

Juvenile drug treatment courts are now widespread in the juvenile justice system, suggesting that the current emphasis should be on better understanding whether, when, and how they can be more effective, as well as their relative costs and benefits to inform next steps. Right now, the key question that must be answered with respect to JDTCs is whether the findings to date are reflective of theoretical or implementation shortcomings— or a combination of both (Berman and Fox 2016). Consequently, it is important that future research strongly considers three essential focal points.

A. Effect Heterogeneity and Treatment Mechanisms

The first consideration reflects the need to answer interdependent "how" and "for whom" questions more explicitly. This will shed more light on the JDTC findings to date, but it requires the collection of appropriate case and JDTC-level data on youth, system practices, recidivism, substance use, mental health symptoms, and developmental outcomes. In turn, these data must be analyzed to understand the conditional effects of program elements and youth factors as well as an ability to specify models of the processes and mechanisms underlying JDTC program theory (see Figure 10.1).

While ensuring strong inference based on research design and analytic procedures is important, understanding the variability of estimates in those studies is equally important (Sampson, Winship, and Knight 2013). For example, screening and enrollment processes might require further consideration to ensure appropriate cases are targeted. Research has considered the degree to which youth risk and needs, motivation, sex, and race/ethnicity play a role in youth success in JDTCs. Further understanding the expected and actual beneficiaries of JDTCs is accessible through studies of such "moderating" effects. More studies are needed that assume treatment heterogeneity, plan for it, and study it to determine what youth characteristics and need profiles will benefit most from JDTCs (Ding, Feller, and Miratrix 2019). These studies should, however, consider specific design and analytic concerns related to tests of moderation and mediation (e.g., Vanderweele 2015).

Relatedly, JDTCs are adopted based on the belief that identifying appropriate participants and then engaging in therapeutic jurisprudence will reduce negative results (e.g., substance use relapse, return to juvenile court) and promote positive developmental outcomes (e.g., school engagement, staying clean). Effectiveness is, however, predicated on an extensive series of steps being followed as intended (e.g., identifying and engaging youth in suitable treatment, appropriate balance of rewards and sanctions). More research must measure the experiences of youth in JDTCs and then relate those to case outcomes that can also be aggregated to understand court-level performance. Concurrently, research must operationalize the fully intended processes of JDTCs, as opposed to distilling a multifaceted intervention to a binary indicator. This will help offer insight into whether anticipated processes are implemented as intended and allow for more understanding of the impact on heterogeneity in program effects. Informing practice and policy requires attention beyond the question of "whether" JDTCs work. Understanding how the aspects of JDTCs presumed to be its active ingredients should be further measured and analyzed to be able to answer the question of "how" the program worked through anticipated pathways (or not; i.e., mediators). This is true regardless of whether the main relationship between JDTCs and outcomes is consistent with expectations.

B. Process and Implementation Questions

Second, implementation questions must be assessed, and linked to JDTC efficacy, to better understand the degree to which adherence to best practices is related to youth and system-level outcomes. This requires a clear delineation of the elements that were important in prior research, or that are recognized as potential reasons for varied JDTC results. This ranges from general principles of effective engagement in juvenile justice intervention—like fitting program intensity to youth needs through appropriate screening and enrollment practices—to imperatives specific to JDTCs themselves. These include the availability of evidence-based substance use treatment; court engagement between judge, youth, and families; and JDTC team composition and training.

Studies like Shaffer's (2011) have moved the field toward unpacking the "Black Box" of JDTCs. At the same time, knowledge has evolved from key drug court components published by NADCP (1997) to the JDTC guidelines developed by OJJDP (2016), but adherence levels for active JDTCs are still unclear. Clearer operationalization and measurement of those guidelines in practice will facilitate a better understanding of JDTC fidelity and intended youth outcomes (Hiller et al. 2021; Sullivan and McKenna 2021). Certainly, there are challenges in precisely and thoroughly measuring JDTC implementation inputs, but there has been growth in this area that can improve knowledge of the relationships between process and outcomes. Implementation of JDTCs can also be considered alongside other characteristics of juvenile justice systems, as elements of best practice guidelines (e.g., stakeholder cooperation, sound assessment) are part of a set of broader areas for effective performance (Sullivan 2019).

C. Research Design and Measurement

Third, in considering both fidelity to the JDTC model and mediation and moderation analysis, it is important that researchers, practitioners, and policymakers pay attention to the strength and appropriateness of the evidence. This is not simply a call for more randomized controlled trials, although those can help with strengthening interval validity of inferences, but rather a consideration of the variety of questions that must be answered to enhance the understanding and evidence base for JDTCs. Key steps include (1) general conceptualization and precise component-level measurement of what constitutes a JDTC (see e.g., Goldkamp 2010); (2) distilling and capturing key aspects of intended practices, youth experiences, intermediate changes and outcome measures (e.g., Long and Sullivan 2017; Tanner-Smith, Lipsey, and Wilson 2016); and (3) considering questions of cross-site variation and scaling up of programs based on key points of variability in the target population or implementation sites (e.g., Sampson, Winship, and Knight 2013; Walsh 2011).

Studies suggest that initial positive change often wanes over time and some relapse is common over the long term (Chassin et al. 2009; Tripodi and Bender 2011). As such, long-term aftercare is imperative to youth success (Chassin et al. 2009; Tripodi and Bender 2011), but this also means that longer follow-up is needed to best estimate the effects of JDTCs. A good deal of research on JDTC elements and youth outcomes is based on available official records. This is evident in the fact that Tanner-Smith and colleagues' (2016) data points (N = 46) were frequently based on official records of general recidivism. In turn, findings for JDTC recidivism may be influenced by a surveillance effect where youth in drug courts generally are supervised and monitored more than nonparticipating peers, making it easier to identify violations (Gilmore, Rodriguez, and Webb 2005). Place is another potential moderator of JDTC performance. Most drug court research takes place in the United States, but these courts have expanded to Canada, Australia, Europe, and, more recently, Latin American countries such as Chile (Inter-American Drug Abuse Control Commission 2013; Vîlcică et al. 2010). Therefore, it is necessary to investigate the effectiveness of this type of intervention—and identify potential strategic adaptations—for adolescents in other cultural and legal contexts.

VI. Conclusion: Evidence-Based Policy in Responding to Youth Drug Use and Delinquency

Though this chapter has predominately focused on juvenile drug treatment courts, it is important to step back and acknowledge that JDTCs are but one possible response to substance use problems in justice-involved youth. The equivocal nature of evidence to date suggests that there are some circumstances where youth may be negatively affected by the intensity of the process, and others where the JDTCs are not sufficiently tailored to meet their needs. This means that the question of which policies or practices should be supported will depend on the circumstances of individual cases as well as the resources available to deliver JDTCs with fidelity.

While it is advisable that these initiatives follow the guidelines developed by OJJDP (2016) and advocated in rigorous research on JDTCs, programs may struggle more in some areas than others. Sullivan and McKenna (2021), for example, described adherence to the OJJDP guidelines across a multistate sample of JDTC courts (N = 35) and found that, although most of the sample showed fidelity, areas like treatment and technical assistance, data collection, and collaboration with community partners were adhered to less often compared to other guideline areas. That study also found relatively lower adherence scores for eligibility and diversion standards, incentive-to-sanctions ratios, and equity in inclusion and outcomes. This suggests that JDTCs and other juvenile justice interventions must ensure quality screening, assessment, and inclusion practices as a necessary first step (Mears 2004; Sullivan et al. 2016), followed by nonpunitive incentives, in working with substance-using justice-involved youth (Long and Sullivan 2017; Schwalbe 2019). Disparities may arise depending on available resources and decisions about placement. Therefore, screening and outreach for JDTC and other substance use interventions should consider factors such as race and ethnicity, gender, and LGBTQ+ status in ensuring equal opportunities for participation. From there, JDTCs should be responsive to cultural barriers and facilitators to ensure better outcomes for diverse populations of youth.

The pattern of findings for JDTC studies—including meta-analyses with dozens of effect sizes—suggests at best very small average treatment effects. That is not uncommon in research on juvenile and criminal justice interventions, but there is evidence to suggest why this might be happening in JDTCs. This includes screening practices, implementation challenges, and balance between incentives and sanctions. Previous sections describe the general history, purpose, and operations of JDTCs. As the research to date is mixed, this review also analyzed the evidence for their effectiveness across multiple dimensions, including average treatment effects, potential moderators, and implementation practices. Future development and evaluation of JDTCs would help to answer more precise questions about the conditions under which JDTCs are appropriate for moderate-to-severe substance-using youth who encounter the juvenile justice system. At present, JDTCs are not as well understood as they should be relative to the frequency with which they have been adopted. Nevertheless, their widespread use necessitates further informed research and refinement to ensure JDTCs are effective and equitable for youth and efficient and manageable for juvenile justice agencies.

References

Alarid, Leanne Fiftal, Carlos D. Montemayor, and Summer Dannhaus. 2012. The effect of parental support on juvenile drug court completion and postprogram recidivism. *Youth Violence and Juvenile Justice*, 10 (4): 354–369.

Alegría, Margarita, J. Bryan Page, Helena Hansen, Ana Mari Cauce, Rafaela Robles, Carlos Blanco, Dharma E. Cortes, Hortensia Amaro, Armando Morales, and Paige Berry. 2006. Improving drug treatment services for Hispanics: Research gaps and scientific opportunities. *Drug and Alcohol Dependence* 84:S76–S84.

Barylnik, Julia. 2003. Psychopathology, psychosocial characteristics and family environment in juvenile delinquents. *German Journal of Psychiatry*, 6 (2): 30–32.

Battjes, Robert J., Michael S. Gordon, Kevin E. O'Grady, Timothy W. Kinlock, and Melissa A. Carswell. 2003. Factors that predict adolescent motivation for substance abuse treatment. *Journal of Substance Abuse Treatment*, 24 (3): 221–232.

Belenko, Steven, and T. K. Logan. 2003. Delivering more effective treatment to adolescents: Improving the juvenile drug court model. *Journal of Substance Abuse Treatment*, 25 (3): 189–211.

Belisle, Linsey A., and Emily J. Salisbury. 2021. Starting with girls and their resilience in mind: Reconsidering risk/needs assessments for system-involved girls. *Criminal Justice and Behavior*, 48 (5): 596–616.

Belisle, Linsey, and Kevin Thompson. 2020. Sustained outcomes? An exploratory study of juvenile drug courts and long-term recidivism. *Juvenile and Family Court Journal* 71 (1): 63–83.

Berman, Greg, and Aubrey Fox. 2016. *Trial and error in criminal justice reform: Learning from failure*. New York: Rowman & Littlefield.

Bishop, Donna. M., and Michael J. Leiber. 2012. Racial and ethnic differences in delinquency and justice system responses. In *The Oxford handbook of juvenile crime and juvenile justice*, edited by Barry Feld and Donna Bishop, 444–484. New York: Oxford University Press.

Blair, Lesli, Carrie Sullivan, Edward Latessa, and Christopher J. Sullivan. 2015. Juvenile drug courts: A process, outcome, and impact evaluation. *Juvenile Justice Bulletin*, May 2015. https://ojjdp.ojp.gov/library/publications/juvenile-drug-courts-process-outcome-and-impact-evaluation.

Butts, Jeffrey A., and John Roman. 2004. Drug courts in the juvenile justice system. In *Juvenile drug courts and teen substance abuse*, edited by Jeffrey A. Butts, John Roman, 1–25. Washington, DC: Urban Institute Press.

Carey, S., M. Waller, and G. Marchand. 2006. Clackamas County Juvenile Drug Court enhancement: Process, outcome/impact and cost evaluation. Portland, OR: NCP Research. https://npcresearch.com/wp-content/uploads/CCJDC-Enhancement-Evaluation-Final-Report1.pdf.

Chassin, Laurie, George Knight, Delfino Vargas-Chanes, Sandra H. Losoya, and Diana Naranjo. 2009. Substance use treatment outcomes in a sample of male serious juvenile offenders. *Journal of Substance Abuse Treatment*, 36 (2): 183–194.

Colins, Olivier, Robert Vermeiren, Cobi Vreugdenhil C, Wim van den Brink, and Theo Doreleijers, Erik Broekaert. 2010. Psychiatric disorders in detained male adolescents: A systematic literature review. *Canadian Journal of Psychiatry*, 55 (4): 255–263.

Cooper, Caroline S. 2001. *Juvenile drug court programs.* Washington, DC: US Department of Justice, Office of Juvenile Justice and Delinquency Prevention.

Curtis, Nicola M., Kevin R. Ronan, and Charles M. Borduin. 2004. Multisystemic treatment: A meta-analysis of outcome studies. *Journal of Family Psychology,* 18 (3): 411–419.

Diiorio, Colleen, Erika Pluhar, and Lisa Belcher. 2003. Parent-child communication about sexuality: A review of the literature from 1980–2002. *Journal of HIV/AIDS Prevention and Education for Adolescents and Children,* 5 (3–4): 7–32.

Ding, Peng, Avi Feller, and Luke Miratrix. 2019. Decomposing treatment effect variation. *Journal of the American Statistical Association,* 114 (525): 304–317.

Ehrmann, Samantha, Nina Hyland, and Charles M. Puzzanchera. 2019. *Girls in the juvenile justice system.* Washington, DC: US Department of Justice, Office of Juvenile Justice and Delinquency Prevention.

Farrington, David P. 1986. Age and crime. In *Crime and justice, Vol 7,* edited by Michael Tonry and Norval Morris, 189–250. Chicago: University of Chicago Press.

Fradella, Henry F., Ryan G. Fischer, Christine Hagan Kleinpeter, and Jeffrey J. Koob. 2009. Latino youth in the Juvenile Drug Court of Orange County, California. *Journal of Ethnicity in Criminal Justice,* 7 (4): 271–292.

Fulton Hora, Hon Peggy. 2002. A dozen years of drug treatment courts: Uncovering our theoretical foundation and the construction of a mainstream paradigm. *Substance Use & Misuse* 37 (12–13): 1469–1488.

Gilmore, Amna Saddik, Nancy Rodriguez, and Vincent J. Webb. 2005. Substance abuse and drug courts: The role of social bonds in juvenile drug courts. *Youth Violence and Juvenile Justice,* 3 (4): 287–315.

Goldkamp, John S. 1999. When is a drug court not a drug court. In *The early drug courts: Case studies in judicial innovation,* edited by Clinton W. Terry, 166–177. Thousand Oaks, CA: SAGE.

Goldkamp, John S. 2010. Construct validity: The importance of understanding the nature of the intervention under study. In *Handbook of quantitative criminology,* edited by David Weisburd and Alex Piquero, 455–479. New York: Springer.

Griffin, Patrick, Sean Addie, Benjamin Adams, and Kathy Firestine. 2011. *Trying juveniles as adults: An analysis of state transfer laws and reporting.* Washington, DC: US Department of Justice, Office of Juvenile Justice and Delinquency Prevention.

Hickert, Audrey, Erin E. Becker, and Moises Prospero. 2010. *Evaluation of Utah juvenile drug courts: Final report.* Salt Lake City, UT: Utah Criminal Justice Center, College of Social Work, University of Utah.

Hiller, Matthew L., Steven Belenko, Michael Dennis, Barbara Estrada, Chelsey Cain, Juliette R. Mackin, Raanan Kagan, and Lauren Pappacena. 2021. The impact of Juvenile Drug Treatment Courts (JDTC) implementing Federal Evidence-Based Guidelines on recidivism and substance use: Multisite Randomized Controlled Trial (RCT) and Regression Discontinuity (RDD) Designs. *Health & Justice* 9 (1): 1–15.

Hiller, Matthew L., Kevin Knight, Carl Leukefeld, and D. Dwayne Simpson. 2002. Motivation as a predictor of therapeutic engagement in mandated residential substance abuse treatment. *Criminal Justice and Behavior,* 29 (1): 56–75.

Hockenberry, Sarah. 2020. *Juveniles in residential placement, 2017.* Juvenile Justice Statistics: National Report Series Bulletin. NCJ 254498. Washington, DC: US Department of Justice, Office of Juvenile Justice and Delinquency Prevention.

Huddleston, West, and Douglas B. Marlowe. 2011. *Painting the current picture: A national report on drug courts and other problem-solving court programs in the United States.* Alexandria, VA: National Drug Court Institute.

Huebner, Angela J., and Laurie W. Howell. 2003. Examining the relationship between adolescent sexual risk-taking and perceptions of monitoring, communication, and parenting styles. *Journal of Adolescent Health*, 33 (2): 71–78.

Huizinga, David. 2000. *Co-occurrence of delinquency and other problem behaviors*. Washington, DC: US Department of Justice, Office of Juvenile Justice and Delinquency Prevention.

Hussong, Andrea M., Patrick J. Curran, Terrie E. Moffitt, Avshalom Caspi, and Madeline M. Carrig. 2004. Substance abuse hinders desistance in young adults' antisocial behavior. *Development and Psychopathology*, 16 (4): 1029–1046.

Inter-American Drug Abuse Control Commission. 2013. *Drug Treatment Courts: An international response for drug dependent offenders: A practical approach to Drug Treatment Courts for policy makers*. Washington, DC: Organization of American States. http://www.cicad.oas.org/fortalecimiento_institucional/dtca/publications/DTC_FINAL_PUBLICATION.pdf.

Javdani, Shabnam, Naomi Sadeh, and Edelyn Verona. 2011. Expanding our lens: Female pathways to antisocial behavior in adolescence and adulthood. *Clinical Psychology Review*, 31 (8): 1324–1348.

Kakade, Meghana, Cristiane S. Duarte, Xinhua Liu, Cordelia J. Fuller, Ernest Drucker, Christina W. Hoven, Bin Fan, and Ping Wu. 2012. Adolescent substance use and other illegal behaviors and racial disparities in criminal justice system involvement: Findings from a US national survey. *American Journal of Public Health*, 102 (7): 1307–1310.

Latessa, Edward J., Carrie Sullivan, Lesli Blair, Christopher J. Sullivan, and Paula Smith. 2013. *Outcome and process evaluation of juvenile drug courts*. Cincinnati: Center for Criminal Justice Research, University of Cincinnati, School of Criminal Justice.

Ledgerwood, David M., and Phillipe B. Cunningham. 2019. Juvenile drug treatment court. *Pediatric Clinics*, 66 (6): 1193–1202.

Logan, Matthew W., and Link, Nathan W. 2019. Taking stock of drug courts: Do they work? *Victims & Offenders*, 14 (3): 283–298.

Long, Joshua, and Christopher J. Sullivan. 2017. Learning more from evaluation of justice interventions: Further consideration of theoretical mechanisms in juvenile drug courts. *Crime and Delinquency*, 63 (9): 1091–1115.

Longshore, Douglas, and Cheryl Teruya. 2006. Treatment motivation in drug users: A theory-based analysis. *Drug and Alcohol Dependence*, 81 (2): 179–188.

Lowenkamp, Christopher T., Alexander M. Holsinger, and Edward J. Latessa. 2005. Are drug courts effective: A meta-analytic review. *Journal of Community Corrections*, 15 (1): 5–11.

Mears, Daniel P. 2004. Identifying adolescent substance abuse. In *Juvenile drug courts and teen substance abuse*, edited by Jeffrey A. Butts and John Roman 185–220. Washington, DC: Urban Institute Press.

Mei, Xiaohan, Jacqueline G. van Wormer, Ruibin Lu, Mia J. Abboud, and Faith E. Lutze. 2019. Validating Drug Court Collaboration Instrument: Differences in model adherence between adult and juvenile drug courts. *International Journal of Offender Therapy and Comparative Criminology*, 63 (11): 1990–2017.

Melnick, Glenn, George de Leon, Josephine Hawke, Nancy Jainchill, and David Kressel. 1997. Motivation and readiness for therapeutic community treatment among adolescents and adult substance abusers. *American Journal of Drug and Alcohol Abuse*, 23 (4): 485–506.

Mitchell, Ojmarrh, David B. Wilson, Amy Eggers, and Doris L. MacKenzie. 2012. Assessing the effectiveness of drug courts on recidivism: A meta-analytic review of traditional and non-traditional drug courts. *Journal of Criminal Justice*, 40 (1): 60–71.

Moffitt, Terrie E. 1993. Life-course-persistent and adolescence-limited antisocial behavior: A developmental taxonomy. *Psychological Review*, 100 (4): 674–701.

National Center for Drug Abuse Statistics. 2022. *Youth drug abuse*. Washington, DC: National Center for Drug Abuse Statistics. https://drugabusestatistics.org/teen-drug-use/ accessed on August 23, 2023.

National Drug Court Resource Center. 2021. Interactive map: U.S. treatment courts. Wilmington, NC: National Drug Court Resource Center. https://ndcrc.org/interactive-maps/.

National Institute on Drug Abuse. 2021. Monitoring the future 2021 survey results. Washington, DC: National Institute on Drug Abuse. https://nida.nih.gov/drug-topics/trends-statistics/infographics/monitoring-future-2021-survey-results.

Nissen, Laura B., and J. Pearce. 2011. Exploring the implementation of justice-based alcohol and drug intervention strategies with juvenile offenders: Reclaiming futures, enhanced adolescent substance abuse treatment, and juvenile drug courts. *Children and Youth Services Review*, 33 (1): S60–S65.

Office of Juvenile Justice and Delinquency Prevention (OJJDP). 2016. *Juvenile drug treatment court guidelines*. Washington, DC: Office of Justice Programs, U.S. Department of Justice.

Olver, Mark E., Keira C Stockdale, and J. Stephen Wormith. 2011. A meta-analysis of predictors of offender treatment attrition and its relationship to recidivism. *Journal of Consulting & Clinical Psychology*, 79 (1): 6–21.

Pelissier, Bernadette, and Nicole Jones. 2005. A review of gender differences among substance abusers. *Crime & Delinquency*, 51 (3): 343–372.

Perrino, Tatiana, Alina González-Soldevilla, Hilda Pantin, and José Szapocznik. 2000. The role of families in adolescent HIV prevention: A review. *Clinical Child and Family Psychology Review*, 3 (2): 81–96.

Piquero, Alex R., David P. Farrington, and Alfred Blumstein. 2003. The criminal career paradigm: Background and recent developments. In *Crime and justice: A review of research*, edited by Michael Tonry, 359–506. Chicago: University of Chicago Press.

Polakowski, Michael, Roger E. Hartley, and Leigh Bates. 2008. Treating the tough cases in juvenile drug court: Individual and organizational practices leading to success or failure. *Criminal Justice Review*, 33 (3): 379–404.

Rossman, Shelli B., Jeffrey A. Butts, John Roman, Christine DeStefano, and Ruth White. 2004. *What juvenile drug courts do and how they do it: Juvenile drug courts and teen substance abuse*. Washington, DC: Urban Institute Press.

Rottman, David, and Pamela Casey. 1999. Therapeutic jurisprudence and the emergence of problem-solving courts. *National Institute of Justice Journal*, 240:12–19.

Rowe, Cynthia L., Wei Wang, Paul Greenbaum, and Howard A. Liddle. 2008. Predicting HIV/STD risk level and substance use disorders among incarcerated adolescents. *Journal of Psychoactive Drugs*, 40 (4): 503–512.

Ruiz, Bridget S., Sally J. Stevens, Janet Fuhriman, John G. Bogart, and Josephine D. Korchmaros. 2009. A juvenile drug court model in southern Arizona: Substance abuse, delinquency, and sexual risk outcomes by gender and race/ethnicity. *Journal of Offender Rehabilitation*, 48 (5): 416–438.

Saar, Malika Saada, Rebecca Epstein, Lindsay Rosenthal, and Yasmin Vafa. 2015. *The sexual abuse to prison pipeline: The girls' story*. Washington, DC: Human Rights Project for Girls, Georgetown Law Center on Poverty and Inequality. https://www.law.georgetown.edu/pove

rty-inequality-center/wp-content/uploads/sites/14/2019/02/The-Sexual-Abuse-To-Prison-Pipeline-The-Girls'-Story.pdf.

Sampson, Robert J., Christopher Winship, and Carly Knight. 2013. Translating causal claims: Principles and strategies for policy-relevant criminology. *Criminology & Public Policy*, 12 (4): 587–616.

Schaar, Ingela, and Agneta Ojehagen. 2003. Predictors of improvement in quality of life of severely mentally ill substance abusers during 18 months of co-operation between psychiatric and social services. *Social Psychiatry and Psychiatric Epidemiology*, 38 (2): 83–87.

Schwalbe, Craig. 2019 Impact of probation interventions on drug use outcomes for youths under probation supervision. *Children and Youth Services Review*, 98:58–64.

Scott, Elizabeth, and Laurence Steinberg. 2009. *Rethinking juvenile justice*. Cambridge, MA: Harvard University.

Shaffer, Deborah Koetzle. 2006. *Reconsidering drug court effectiveness: A meta-analytic review*. PhD diss., University of Cincinnati.

Shaffer, Deborah Koetzle. 2011. Looking inside the black box of drug courts: A meta-analytic review. *Justice Quarterly*, 28 (3): 493–521.

Sheidow, Ashli J., Jayani Jayawardhana, W. David Bradford, Scott W. Henggeler, and Steven B. Shapiro. 2012. Money matters: Cost-effectiveness of juvenile drug court with and without evidence-based treatments. *Journal of Child & Adolescent Substance Abuse*, 21 (1): 69–90.

Sloan, John J., John O. Smykla, and Jeffrey P. Rush. 2004. Do juvenile drug courts reduce recidivism?: Outcomes of drug court and an adolescent substance abuse program. *American Journal of Criminal Justice*, 29 (1): 95–115.

Somers, Logan J., and Kristy Holtfreter. 2018. Gender and mental health: An examination of procedural justice in a specialized court context. *Behavioral Sciences & the Law*, 36 (1): 98–115.

Stanford Medicine Children's Health. 2022. Substance abuse/chemical dependence in adolescents. Stanford, CA: Stanford Medicine Children's Health. https://www.stanfordchildrens.org/en/topic/default?id=substance-abusechemical-dependence-in-adolescents-90-P01643.

Stanton, M. Duncan, and William R. Shadish. 1997. Outcome, attrition, and family-couples treatment for drug abuse: A metaanalysis and review of the controlled, comparative studies. *Psychological Bulletin* 122:170–191.

Stein, David M., Scott Deberard, and Kendra Homan. 2013. Predicting success and failure in juvenile drug treatment court: A meta-analytic review. *Journal of Substance Abuse Treatment*, 4 (2): 159–168.

Stein, David M., Kendra J. Homan, and Scott DeBerard. 2015. The effectiveness of juvenile treatment drug courts: A meta-analytic review of literature. *Journal of Child & Adolescent Substance Abuse*, 24 (2): 80–93.

Stevens, Tia, Merry Morash, and Meda Chesney-Linda. 2011. Are girls getting tougher, or are we tougher on girls? Probability of arrest and juvenile court oversight in 1980 and 2000. *Justice Quarterly*, 28 (5), 719–744.

Substance Abuse and Mental Health Services Administration. 2019. *Key substance use and mental health indicators in the United States: Results from the 2018 National Survey on Drug Use and Health*. Rockville, MD: Center for Behavioral Health Statistics and Quality, Substance Abuse and Mental Health Services Administration. https://www.samhsa.gov/data/.

Sullivan, Christopher J. 2019. *Taking juvenile justice seriously: Developmental insights and system challenges*. Philadelphia: Temple University Press.

Sullivan, Christopher J., Lesli Blair, Edward Latessa, and Carrie C. Sullivan. 2016. Juvenile drug courts and recidivism: Results from a multisite outcome study. *Justice Quarterly*, 33 (2): 291–318.

Sullivan, Christopher J., Kristina K. Childs, and Shaun Gann. 2018. Peer influences on offending. In *The Oxford handbook of developmental and life-course criminology*, edited by David P. Farrington, Lila Kazemian, and Alex R. Piquero, 404–431. New York: Oxford University Press.

Sullivan, Christopher J., and Nicole McKenna. 2021. *Juvenile Drug Treatment Court (JDTC) guidelines: Validation study of Court Self-Assessment (CSA)*. Washington, DC: American Institutes for Research. https://www.ojp.gov/library/publications/juvenile-drug-treatment-court-jdtc-guidelines-validation-study-court-self.

Tanner-Smith, Emily E., Mark W. Lipsey, and David B. Wilson. 2016. Juvenile drug court effects on recidivism and drug use: A systematic review and meta-analysis. *Journal of Experimental Criminology*, 12 (March): 477–513.

Tolou-Shams, Marina, Wendy Hadley, Selby M. Conrad, and Larry K. Brow. 2012. The role of family affect in juvenile drug court offenders' substance use and HIV risk. *Journal of Child and Family Studies*, 21 (3), 449–456.

Tripodi, Stephen, and Kimberly Bender. 2011. Substance abuse treatment for juvenile offenders: A review of quasi-experimental and experimental research. *Journal of Criminal Justice*, 39 (3): 246–252.

U.S. Bureau of Justice Assistance. 2003. *Juvenile drug courts: Strategies in practice*. Washington, DC: U.S. Department of Justice, Office of Justice Programs.

VanderWeele, Tyler. 2015. *Explanation in causal inference: Methods for mediation and interaction*. New York: Oxford University Press.

Walsh, Nastassia. 2011. *Addicted to courts: How a growing dependence on drug courts impacts people and communities*. Washington, DC: Justice Policy Institute.

Warr, Mark. 2012. The social side of delinquent behavior. In *The Oxford handbook of juvenile crime and juvenile justice*, edited by Barry C. Feld and Donna M. Bishop, 226–245. New York: Oxford University Press.

Wexler, David B. 2000. Therapeutic jurisprudence: An overview. *Thomas M. Cooley Law Review*, 17:125–134.

White, Helene R., Fiona N. Conway, and Judit H. Ward. 2019. Comorbidity of substance use and violence. In *Handbook on crime and deviance*, edited by Marvin Krohn, Nicole Hendrix, Gina Penly Hall, and Alan J. Lizotte, 513–532. Cham, Switzerland: Springer.

Vîlcică, Rely E., Steven Belenko, Matthew Hiller, and Faye Taxman. 2010. Exporting court innovation from the United States to Continental Europe: Compatibility between the drug court model and inquisitorial justice systems. *International Journal of Comparative and Applied Criminal Justice*, 34 (1): 139–172.

Wilson, David B., Ojmarrh Mitchell, and Doris L. MacKenzie. 2006. A systematic review of drug court effects on recidivism. *Journal of Experimental Criminology*, 2 (November): 459–487.

Wilson, David B., Ajima Olaghere, and Catherine S. Kimbrell. 2019. Implementing juvenile drug treatment courts: A meta-aggregation of process evaluations. *Journal of Research in Crime and Delinquency*, 56 (4): 605–645.

Wolff, Kevin T., Michael T. Baglivio, Hannah J. Klein, Alex R. Piquero, Matt DeLisi, and James C. (Buddy) Howell. 2020. Adverse childhood experiences (ACEs) and gang involvement among juvenile offenders: Assessing the mediation effects of substance use and temperament deficits. *Youth Violence and Juvenile Justice*, 18 (1): 24–53.

CHAPTER 11

EVIDENCE-ORIENTED YOUTH JUSTICE

JEFFREY A. BUTTS, JOHN K. ROMAN, AND KATHERYNE PUGLIESE

PRACTITIONERS and policymakers exhort youth justice systems to employ evidence-based interventions, but do they understand the term? What is an evidence-based program, practice, or policy? How is that status conferred, and who decides? Does a governing body certify evidence-based youth justice interventions? Where would one apply for consideration? Equally important, if a program or practice is not evidence-based, is it inherently ineffective, wasteful, or even harmful? Should justice officials refuse to support anything that is not evidence-based?

A policy or practice is evidence-based after being proven effective with credible evaluation methods in varying places and contexts. The observable and measurable components of the intervention affect specifically designated outcomes in meaningful and replicable ways. In other words, an evidence-based intervention delivers what it promises in the manner predicted by an articulated theory of change, and it can be trusted to do so again. One study or one pre-post difference (e.g., recidivism fell 20% after the program started) is not enough to establish a program or practice as evidence-based.

The time and resources required to establish an intervention as evidence-based can be substantial. The burden increases with the scope of the intervention and the complexity of its designated outcomes. Interventions are easier to evaluate and thus easier to establish as evidence-based policies or practices when they are narrowly focused and act quickly. Some interventions associated with the youth justice system are already established as evidence-based. The work to develop other proven interventions continues and must continue.

The youth justice field cannot be divided into "what works" and "what does not work." The available research base is not comprehensive enough to make such a judgment. The best way to view current research evidence in youth justice is as an evolving, ongoing process. Research on a wide array of policies and practices continues to clarify two types of knowledge: what we know and what we do not know yet (Taxman 2018). After decades of effort, the first category is no longer empty. The second category is immense. The second category should be the target of all future research investigations.

Adhering exclusively to evidence-based interventions would be a worthy goal if the existing research literature was full and comprehensive. With enough evidence for all their components, youth justice systems could avoid strategies backed only by hope, ideology, or financial interest. In a perfect world, every aspect of youth justice and all social policies would rely on rigorous evidence from qualified researchers. The world, however, is far from perfect. Policies and practices designed with less-than-perfect evidence are unavoidable. In youth justice, many intervention models have been around for decades without reliable evidence. Policymakers are unlikely to abandon them now, which is not always unreasonable.

The resources required for rigorous evaluation research will never be sufficient to test every element and every activity in a modern youth justice system. Much of the process is *assumed* to be necessary, including many aspects of policing, prosecutions, court hearings, and even secure confinement. If today's justice leaders refused to employ any policy or practice not backed by credible research evidence, they would end up presiding over an incomplete and fragmented system.

Where is the appropriate boundary between reasonable assumption and questionable proposition? How do organizations and systems decide the difference? Evaluation research can be expensive. Which justice components deserve research scrutiny? Policymakers and managers should not spend precious resources on trivial or self-evident questions. Research investments should focus on the most pressing questions about interventions that may advance the youth justice mission and whose effectiveness is at least somewhat in doubt. In other words, research should concentrate on policies and practices that *might* reduce the incidence of law violations by young people but *might not* be funded absent rigorous evidence.

This is where things get complicated. What should researchers investigate to resolve the most important and relevant issues about the mission of youth justice? What reduces youth crime? Where do systems need stronger evidence to build effective policies and practices?

This chapter first reviews the purpose and theoretical heritage of youth justice in the United States. Next, it examines the extent of evidence-based policies and practices in the system and the challenges faced by policymakers and practitioners working to build the system with research evidence. It concludes with recommendations for future directions in policy and practice.

Throughout the chapter, we use the term "youth justice" rather than "juvenile justice" to describe the system of laws and policies governing legal responses to young people's illegal behavior. The word "juvenile" is a legislative designation that does not apply to all young people. State lawmakers often choose to expose certain young people to criminal rather than juvenile law by withdrawing their juvenile status and transferring them to the adult court process for past behaviors, current charges, based on their age, or a combination of these factors. The chapter uses "youth justice" to acknowledge the fundamental, historical goal of the separate legal system for youth and to underscore the fragile legitimacy of "juvenile justice."

I. Mission

Beginning with Chicago's launch of the first separate juvenile court in 1899, youth justice systems in the United States were designed to be different from criminal (or adult) justice systems. Many features of adult systems are essentially self-justifying. Imposing incarceration or community supervision on people convicted of criminal offenses is the very point of the process. Reducing future crime may be a secondary goal, but the immediate and primary goal is to deliver an appropriate consequence for each offense as efficiently as possible. In criminal justice, the system outcomes with the greatest political salience are controlled by and achievable within the process itself. Those outcomes include incapacitation (*keeping this person away from the public*), retribution (*delivering just desserts, an eye for an eye*), and general deterrence (*making an example of this person as a warning to others*).

The youth justice system is different. Youth justice is not supposed to be a scaled-down criminal system that delivers consequences proportionate to a youth's illegal acts. The youth system was designed to build public safety with noncriminal, quasi-civil procedures that help youth avoid unlawful behavior. Youth courts, probation agencies, and all components of the youth justice system are expected to mitigate whatever individual, family, or community factors explain a youth's illegal behavior (Mennel 1973; Rothman 1980). Juvenile and family courts are expected to prevent youth crime (or delinquency) by deploying developmentally appropriate and individualized interventions focused on the offender rather than the offense (Feld 1987).

Before the creation of youth justice, young people charged with law violations appeared in criminal courts alongside adult defendants. Judges and juries often found young people innocent or simply released them with a warning. When youth seemed immature, jurors were inclined to acquit rather than risk a conviction that could send a young person to prison. Frustrated law enforcement advocates sought a separate court process to consider youth crimes on their own terms. To help the new juvenile courts act swiftly and decisively, legislators defined their deliberations as quasi-civil, thus avoiding the constitutional provisions constraining criminal prosecutions of adults (Butts and Mitchell 2000; Zimring 2019).

Historical analyses have sometimes characterized the founding of America's juvenile courts as an act of benevolent social reform (Tanenhaus 2004), but this ignores the complex motivations of the parties involved in creating youth justice (Platt 1977; Schlossman 1977). Certainly, some early advocates were motivated by a desire to save poor and homeless children from the streets of America's growing cities. Others wanted to devise a better legal system for reducing youth crime. Limiting due process protections and expanding judicial discretion enabled the new system to intervene more broadly and efficiently with young law violators.

Lawmakers even developed a new vocabulary for the juvenile court. Young people appearing in juvenile court were called delinquents instead of criminal defendants. Prosecutors could charge an adult with the crime of robbery, but a juvenile would be the subject of a court petition alleging a delinquent act *equivalent to robbery*. Youth found responsible for alleged law violations were *adjudicated delinquent* rather than found guilty. Final court decisions about the legal consequences of adjudication were called *dispositions* rather than sentences.

The euphemisms of juvenile law reflected the lower standard of due process and the distinctive mission of youth justice. Juvenile courts were asked to guide young people away from criminal behavior, not simply punish them for past wrongdoings. The juvenile court was to identify the factors causing youth to violate the law and provide whatever services and supports would prevent new violations. Even if those services included time in a locked facility, the official purpose of confinement was to help rather than punish youth. The state was only required to prove juvenile charges based on a *preponderance* of evidence instead of the stricter criminal standard: *beyond a reasonable doubt*. Until the US Supreme Court began to regulate juvenile law in the late 1960s, youth justice systems were not even required to provide defense attorneys, appellate procedures, or many formal procedures (Scali 2019).

The idealized approach to youth justice did not survive the 20th century, assuming it ever truly existed. The youth justice system has always had a responsibility to guard public safety. Modern social reform advocates and even critics of the juvenile process may summarize the difference between juvenile and adult courts as rehabilitation versus punishment, but the most distinctive feature of youth justice remains the quasi-civil legal authority underlying its broad discretion to intervene (Butts and Harrell 1998; Feld 2011). Although current policy debates frequently omit this aspect of youth justice, it is a critical factor in explaining why the creation of the juvenile court was just as popular with prosecutors and police officers as it was with social reformers.

Criminal courts emphasize due process and proportionate responses. Their goal is to determine each offender's guilt or innocence and to impose appropriate consequences as fairly and expeditiously as possible. The mission of the criminal justice process is to express the community's disapproval of an adult's illegal behaviors with the right amount of punishment for every conviction. Youth justice was designed to be different. The youth justice process was expected to prevent delinquency and protect the public by mitigating the causes of youth crime and not simply punishing crime. State lawmakers have partially eroded the distinctive mission of the youth justice system in recent decades with increasingly punitive laws designed to hold youth "accountable," but the legal framework of youth justice still rests explicitly on a theory of crime prevention.

II. Theory

Youth justice managers must be able to draw upon rigorous findings from previous evaluation studies to develop evidence-based youth justice interventions. Evaluations must be able to establish causal relationships between an intervention's inputs (actions and resources), outputs (products and participation), and outcomes (changes in crime rates or other predicted results). The process begins with researchers reviewing the findings of previous efforts to investigate questions arising from theory. To reduce youth crime with theoretically sound evidence, researchers and system leaders collaborate to identify whatever factors are presumed to generate youth crime. Next, they take action to disrupt the chain of events. Finally, they test their hypotheses by measuring cause and effect at whatever level of measurement is required and at however many steps of the causal path are possible.

Researchers have been working to generate theoretically relevant knowledge about delinquency prevention for decades, but important questions still outnumber reliable answers (Butts and Roman 2018). The confusion is understandable. Building youth justice interventions from theory involves profound challenges. First, many schools of thought are available to explain the causes of youth crime, and they are not mutually exclusive. Some theories are compatible, even redundant, looking at different sides of the same theoretical coin. Others offer drastically contradictory views and begin with very different assumptions. Even theories sharing key assumptions may have originated within different academic disciplines, bringing different vocabularies and methodologies.

Second, youth justice systems are responsible for addressing a wide range of illegal behaviors, from truancy or "incorrigibility" to drug offenses, property crimes, and serious violence. Finding one theory to identify a common origin for all youthful violations is futile. Inevitably, discussions about evidence-based youth justice involve various contexts and theories.

Third, while it is not always necessary to separate theories of youth crime from those explaining adult crime, youth crime is more complex. It inevitably involves cultural notions of childhood, family, and adolescent development. Some aspects of delinquency theory are rightfully part of the larger crime framework. However, youth crime and the justice system's responses to youth crime involve even more political, economic, cultural, and social equity issues.

Youth justice practitioners looking for theoretical guidance would find academic discourse very challenging. Experts in crime and delinquency typically describe four or five (or a dozen) major theories about the origins of juvenile delinquency. Any description inevitably overlooks some elements considered mainstream theory by experts in a different academic discipline. Some theories may be given too much weight. Others may be combined in ways that offend their most ardent supporters. Reviews of the theoretical literature frequently portray the history of theory as a march of progress, ending triumphantly at the doorstep of the author's preferred school of thought.

Despite ongoing discussion and development, several mainstream delinquency theories have remained relevant for more than 50 years. Each school of thought offers a coherent body of theoretical concepts recognized as foundational contributions to explaining the origins and persistence of delinquent behavior. Together, they suggest many potential reasons why some youth are more likely than others to become involved in the youth justice system. If guided by evidence, youth justice systems would develop interventions that align with one or more credible theories and test their viability with rigorous evaluations.

Delinquency theory tends to divide into two major categories: (1) individual factors versus (2) social and cultural factors (Finckenauer 1984). The individual-social distinction is essentially the same micro-macro dichotomy that sociologists from Max Weber to C. Wright Mills advised scholars to disregard in favor of a dynamic whole in which individual actors and social structures are linked. As in social sciences generally, however, theories of delinquency usually focus on one and not both. They either locate the source of youth crime in problems of individual youth or go further up the causal chain to identify various socioeconomic, cultural, and even organizational factors that underlie those individual differences. The individual-versus-social lens has profound consequences for the operations of the justice system and its potential to draw on rigorous evaluation evidence (Wikström 2019).

A. Individual

The individual school dominates youth justice policy and practice. Individual-level theories locate the origins of delinquency in the psychological characteristics and emotional resources of youth and their families. Particularly during the 20th century, some experts even looked to psychoanalytic theory to explain and intervene in youthful misbehavior. Most, however, assumed a more limited orientation while still holding that psychological or psychopathological factors were the main factors producing delinquency. One version of the psychological approach viewed the instinctual drive to behave criminally as a trait common to all youth, both delinquent and nondelinquent. The key difference was how they expressed that shared tendency (Abrahamsen 1960). Other researchers relying upon a psychological view stressed the value of self-esteem and the harm caused by negative life experiences, such as academic failure (Gold 1978). Illegal activities were believed to be an alternative means of gaining self-esteem. Researchers holding this view proposed that effective prevention policies should coordinate the efforts of schools and other community organizations to provide crime-prone youth with positive experiences that could mitigate the adverse experiences in their social environments.

The psychological view of delinquency inspired decades of research and program development, and it remains a powerful school of thought for lawmakers and youth justice professionals today. A key advantage of the psychological approach to delinquency prevention is its utility for creating affordable and scalable interventions. If the source of delinquency is found in the characteristics of individual youth, interventions to reduce delinquency may focus on one person at a time with relationship-based, therapeutic services. The psychological school of thought inspired many of the most common and well-established treatment approaches in youth justice, including cognitive-behavioral therapy (Landenberger and Lipsey 2005).

Another influential theory within the individual camp viewed the source of youth crime as a process whereby youths learn to be delinquent. Like any other behavior, delinquency is the product of reinforcements (rewards and punishments) in the social environment. Reducing youth crime requires interventions to interrupt whatever forces tend to condition youth to engage in crime. This view, known as social learning theory, is appealing to practitioners because it avoids the problem of attributing the source of youth crime to a "single mechanism" (Rutter and Giller 1984, 252).

Social learning theories do not view delinquency as evidence of underlying pathology but as adaptive, even rational behavior that individuals develop over time to cope with demands and stresses in their environment. To intervene in that process, young people must learn new ways of behaving that bring greater rewards than illegal behavior. Programs subscribing to this view would use behavioral reinforcement systems to create incentives for more desirable behavior. As with other individual theories, Finckenauer (1984, 28) attributed the influence of social learning theory in the youth justice system to its "ease of translation" and direct application in programs to change youth behavior.

However, suppose delinquency is truly an outcome of lessons learned from the social environment. In that case, a key question remains: Why do *only some* youths exposed to particular environments end up "learning" to become delinquent? Moreover, if delinquency stems from influences in the social environment, why should the youth justice system put all its effort into treating recipients of those influences rather than addressing the source? What if justice officials worked to improve harmful social environments before attempting to undo their effect on a subset of youth—especially when it may be impossible to identify that subset in advance?

Psychological theories will continue to exert their influence on the youth justice field, particularly in the design and use of treatment technologies. Still, many criminologists naturally look to social causes as well. Delinquency theories focused on social factors rather than individual deficits proliferated through the 20th century and continue to evolve. Their key challenge is informing interventions amenable to rigorous evaluation designs that could eventually qualify them as evidence-based.

B. Social

Beginning with the earliest efforts to explain delinquency and youth crime, many theorists looked beyond individual differences to consider social causes, including poverty and limited opportunity. Then as now, however, the ideological appeal and interventional suitability of individually oriented theories weighed heavily against the acceptance of theories pointing to social origins. As Empey (1981, 197) observed, theories are not embraced for their scientific quality or empirical strength alone:

> Rather, [a theory's] capacity to capture and give expression to emerging cultural trends may also determine its fate. How well it conforms to emerging beliefs and delinquency control policies may determine its popularity as much, if not more, than the actual evidence that can be brought to bear upon it.

During the 1930s and 1940s, sociologists at the University of Chicago conducted landmark studies on urban social problems, including delinquency. Researchers used survey techniques and demographic analysis to explore the social-ecological distribution of crime in urban areas and its effect on social relationships. Shaw and McKay (1942) found evidence of "high delinquency areas" in specific zones around Chicago, suggesting that delinquency's origins were at least partly due to social and environmental factors, not just the characteristics and inclinations of individuals.

The social-ecological approach inspired much research and theorizing on crime and delinquency. One school of thought, known as "social disorganization," attributed delinquency to a breakdown of community-based controls (Merton 1957). According to this approach, youth become delinquent when the social environment fails to reward academic and vocational pursuits or even blocks access to success. These ideas evolved into "strain theory," or the idea that delinquency results from socially induced pressures surrounding economic goals that prevent young people from achieving those goals. An acute disjunction between goals and means produces strain, encouraging young people to deviate from conventional norms (Phillipson 2014).

These ideas influenced national policy in the 20th century. Cloward and Ohlin (1960) proposed that criminal behavior was not always indicative of pathology and disorganization. Young people blocked from conventional success will logically pursue alternative means and opportunities. The "opportunity theory" of delinquency became an "intellectual linchpin" of the Kennedy administration's social policy, including the War on Poverty (Helium et al. 1983, 27). The concepts of social disorganization, strain, and opportunity highlighted the normative quality of delinquency within a given environment, leading researchers to investigate community characteristics as the origin of delinquent values and culture. These ideas posed compelling challenges to psychological theories focused on individual pathology.

Research also showed that youth crime was a group enterprise. This observation prompted numerous studies of peer groups and eventually the "giant" of subcultural theories: "differential association" (Finckenauer 1984, 44). Social scientists proposed that delinquent youth may not be inherently bad or fundamentally different from nondelinquent youth. They may have internalized antisocial "definitions" through interactions with their social networks. Criminal behavior could be learned from contact with others engaged in illegal conduct. Individual differences would only be relevant to the extent they influence this differential association.

Some theorists, however, found differential association to be overly deterministic, suggesting instead that delinquent behavior was largely "situational" (Matza 1990). Given the right combinations of individual and environmental characteristics, many people *could* behave criminally, but those circumstances are not always predictable. Rather than focusing on how subcultural norms differ from approved social norms, Matza recommended that theorists concentrate on whatever processes lead youth to "drift" in and out of delinquency, especially when those processes include responses from "social control" institutions. This shift was a key development in delinquency theory. Researchers began to view youth crime within a social control context, analyzing how cultural, organizational, and political responses to delinquency affected crime overall (Gottfredson and Hirschi 1990).

Psychological theories attempt to explain why only some young people commit delinquent acts. Social control theories assume "everyone has a predisposition to commit delinquent acts, there is no need for special motivational postulates . . . the issue is how people learn not to offend" (Rutter and Giller 1984, 250). Factors mediating social control processes could include economic security and access to resources, attachments to family and parents, the presence of delinquent friends, commitment to peer group activities, academic achievement, vocational aspirations, the frustration of ambition, and a young person's ability to appreciate and gain from adherence to conventional social norms. Most importantly, the young people most inclined to illegal behavior are those without strong ties to normative social institutions. Policies and practices are inherently counterproductive when they attempt to reduce delinquency by weakening such ties.

III. Guidance

A youth justice system with a strong evidence orientation would be continually hunting for proven interventions. System leaders would collaborate with practitioners and researchers to create new interventions aligned with specific theoretical precepts and then evaluate the implementation and outcomes of those interventions. Developing one effective intervention would not signal an end to the hunt. Each proven approach would be added to the menu of programs and practices while system leaders searched for other effective models.

Following the proliferation of delinquency theories in the 20th century, researchers and system leaders had several decades to create a diverse array of youth justice interventions. Youth justice systems began to deploy an impressive assortment of programs and practices. Education supports and employment readiness models became increasingly common. Youth justice more frequently included arts programs, physical fitness, and community service interventions. Even some youth confinement facilities embraced adolescent development and positive youth justice as their guiding framework (Butts 2018). The menu of youth justice interventions grew to be richer than ever.

Unfortunately, research lagged behind programmatic innovations. If practitioners and system leaders today turn to evaluations for guidance about youth justice interventions, they will find a limited assortment of proven options. Family therapy and other individually focused interventions are usually the only evidence-based models endorsed by rigorous evaluations.

Of course, individual interventions are essential ingredients for modern-day youth justice. Studies should continue to identify the key components of therapeutic models for individual youth and families. However, researchers must investigate other questions. Exploring unproven possibilities is just as important as reinforcing the evidence base for established and accepted services. What untested interventions might advance the youth justice mission?

Nearly 100 years of social science demonstrated that young people engage in illegal behavior for various reasons. Some may be more inclined simply due to individual characteristics and the circumstances of families. Others act at least partly in response to social forces outside themselves and their families, particularly economic inequities and an absence of opportunities. Obstacles to conventional success, including racial, gender, and class-based discrimination, may lead some youth to see illegal behavior as acceptable or expected. Therapeutic interventions could affect marginal rates of unlawful conduct at an individual level without altering these larger social forces or changing the overall volume of youth crime.

The justice system must operate at multiple levels to respond effectively to total youth crime. At every level, policies and practices should be guided by research. First, the full array of interventions should be shaped by theoretical frameworks from the social and behavioral sciences. Second, each intervention must be tested, monitored, and improved with the most rigorous evaluation methods compatible with the program's structure and approach. Interventions focused on social and community factors are not readily amenable to randomized controlled trials, but this does not reduce their value. It calls for a more sophisticated approach to building and assessing evidence.

Practitioners and policymakers would ideally build mission-relevant evidence by collaborating directly with evaluation researchers, but few justice agencies have the resources to do so. Instead, justice system professionals typically review summaries of research literature and fashion their intervention plans after what they find. Practitioners and system administrators, however, are unlikely to peruse the research literature themselves. Evaluation research often lies hidden behind the paywalls of academic journals. Youth justice professionals rarely pay the per-article user fees charged by academic journals (often exceeding $30 per article). Furthermore, much of the evaluation literature is written in a ponderous, academic style that working professionals find impenetrable. Youth justice workers facing uninterpretable original research turn instead to online research translators.

Several tools are available for such reviews. Two of the most influential resources provide syntheses of evaluation research to help nonresearchers ascertain whether a program or practice is evidence-based. CrimeSolutions (https://crimesolutions.ojp.gov/) and Blueprints for Healthy Youth Development (https://www.blueprintsprograms.org/) are comprehensive online evaluation guides for practitioners. Each guide helps users search for research findings that identify programs and practices backed by credible evidence. The methods used to assess the quality and accuracy of research are described in detail. References are provided for each topic.

CrimeSolutions places interventions in the categories of "effective," "promising," "inconclusive," or "no effect." Users can search for programs or practices in a given field, a subset of system areas (corrections, probation, etc.), and populations (youth or adult, community-based or institutionalized, and more). Each search includes a brief profile of the interventions listed, their service populations, and organizational settings. Profiles are clear and concise and provide practitioners with detailed information about the effectiveness of each intervention.

CrimeSolutions calls programs effective when they have been evaluated several times and are ready for further replication, while promising programs require additional research. Interventions deemed effective will have been tested by several rigorous (Class 1) studies, as opposed to reasonably credible studies with limitations (Class 2). Promising programs are likely supported by a mix of Class 1 and Class 2 studies, even some with lesser effects. The CrimeSolutions site revisits intervention profiles periodically and provides updated ratings as new studies become available.

The Blueprints site is similar to CrimeSolutions, but with a different vernacular. Interventions are designated as either "Promising" programs, "Model" programs, or "Model Plus" programs—the latter category indicating the strongest evidence-based approaches. The criteria for Model and Model Plus certifications are clear. Model programs are backed by two randomized controlled trial (RCT) evaluations or one RCT and at least one credible quasi-experimental evaluation. Model certification also requires an acceptable follow-up period to ensure the durability of effects. Model Plus certification requires even more evaluations from multiple sources. Blueprints also includes more factors in its reviews. In addition to the methodological quality of evaluations, the site assesses each program's attention to knowledge dissemination and whether an intervention is designed for an identified population.

CrimeSolutions and Blueprints are helpful resources for youth justice actors seeking to implement effective programs and practices. Each site allows users to review the findings of previous evaluations with an accessible and translatable rating scheme. Both sites, however, encourage users to see program evaluation as a competition for the best statistical effects rather than a compilation of varied evidence developed in an environment of complex theoretical and practical challenges. The online tools help practitioners identify the most rigorous evaluations in various content areas. They do not guide youth justice systems in balancing their efforts across all those areas. The tools encourage practitioners to focus on the highest-ranking program and not the best mix of programs.

Programs and practices naturally rank higher in these online tools if their operations are more amenable to rigorous evaluation designs. Namely, programs are likely to earn a higher rank if they intervene with individuals rather than neighborhoods and communities. Higher ranks are also more likely for interventions designed to produce measurable results in weeks or months rather than years, even if the effects of slower-acting programs might be greater, more durable, and more affordable. In short, individual therapy programs have an advantage in these online tools. Therapy is a good way to produce quick and defensible outcomes. Comprehensive youth justice systems, however, need to rely on a broad range of strategies, including some operating at the level of neighborhoods and communities.

Practitioners seeking guidance from online research summaries are not encouraged to think comprehensively. Suppose a youth justice leader needed to identify an effective intervention for adjudicated youth. They could go to CrimeSolutions and make a series of choices in a search protocol. First, they would navigate to the "Programs" section of the website to search the full list. Next, they would select programs for youth already involved in the justice system. In other words, they would choose programs for "youth" and "offenders." To limit the search to the highest-ranking programs, they would click "effective" and then restrict the results to interventions backed by "more than one study." Based on these selections, CrimeSolutions would produce just six interventions: mentoring, family therapy, group therapy, cognitive-behavioral treatment, and drug treatment (see Table 11.1).

The Blueprints site would provide similar results. If the youth justice practitioner wanted to find effective programs, or what Blueprints calls "Model" and "Model Plus" programs, they would begin by navigating to the "program search" area and choosing "delinquency and criminal behavior" under "program outcomes." Next, they would narrow the "target population" to several age groups: "early adolescence (12–14) – middle school" and "late adolescence (15–18) – high school." To conduct the broadest search possible, they might go to the "program specifics" category and select "community and correctional facilities." As with CrimeSolutions, the search returns only a few therapeutic interventions (see Table 11.2).

Using combined information from both websites, all programs identified as evidence-based interventions for justice-involved youth would be therapeutic: cognitive-behavioral therapy, group therapy, family therapy, interpersonal skill-building, and mentoring (see Table 11.3). Is this because therapy is the *single best* intervention for youth justice, or is it because therapy is more amenable to rigorous evaluation designs?

As an analogy, imagine a personal trainer who wanted to assess the evidence for two forms of vigorous exercise: running outdoors versus treadmills in a gym. Both activities would improve patient health, but the evaluation proof for treadmills would probably be stronger, not because treadmills are inherently superior but because they are easier to evaluate. It would be cheaper and more convenient for researchers to collect treadmill data because the equipment already monitors time, speed, incline, and resistance levels during each workout. Collecting running data would be more expensive and more complicated. Researchers would have to cope with unobserved changes in terrain, road conditions, and individual effort. Studies would likely involve self-reported measures. Judging the strength of research evidence for both forms of exercise without considering their evaluation amenability would lead to biased conclusions—not to mention an increase in gym memberships.

Assessing the value of available research evidence in youth justice should begin with understanding the mission of youth justice systems and relevant theoretical knowledge about the causes of youth crime. Strategies designed to change the behavior of individuals are important components of youth justice, but they are not wholly sufficient as a general intervention plan for public safety. Drawing exclusively on the information available from online research guides could encourage practitioners to believe therapeutic mechanisms are the only method needed to address illegal behavior in young individuals.

Research with statistically significant results and strong effect size is not the only information needed to build an effective youth justice system. Youth justice professionals should understand evaluation basics to appreciate the role of research in forming effective policies and programs. They must also respect the conceptual and theoretical foundations of interventions,

Table 11.1. CrimeSolutions search identifies only six effective programs serving youth offenders that have been evaluated by more than one study

Program	Description	Change Mechanisms	Cited Sources
Adolescent Diversion Project (Michigan State University)	A strengths-based program to divert arrested youth from the formal criminal justice system	Mentoring Conflict resolution & interpersonal skills	Davidson et al. (1987) Smith et al. (2004)
Functional Family Therapy (FFT)	A family-based prevention and intervention program using clinical family practice to decrease youth risk factors	Family therapy	Gordon et al. (1988) Sexton et al. (2010) Celinska et al. (2013)
Multidimensional Treatment Foster Care-Adolescents	Behavioral treatment to address adolescent antisocial behavior and emotional disturbance	Family therapy Cognitive-behavioral treatment Mentoring	Chamberlain et al. (1998) Chamberlain et al. (2007)
Multisystemic Therapy (MST)	Family and community treatment to address adolescent antisocial behavior and delinquency	Family therapy Cognitive-behavioral treatment Individual therapy Conflict resolution & interpersonal skills	Henggeler et al. (1992) Borduin et al. (1995) Timmons-Mitchell et al. (2006)
Multisystemic Therapy—Substance Abuse	Family treatment for adolescents with substance abuse and dependency issues	Alcohol and drug therapy/treatment Cognitive-behavioral treatment Conflict resolution & interpersonal skills	Henggeler et al. (2002) Henggeler et al. (2006)
SNAP® Under 12 Outreach Project	Multisystemic intervention for males under age 12 with aggression and antisocial behavior problems	Cognitive-behavioral treatment Family therapy Group therapy	Augimeri et al. (2007) Lipman et al. (2008)

Source: CrimeSolutions (https://crimesolutions.ojp.gov/).

not only the methodological rigor of previous evaluations. For their part, researchers should do more than report their study results to other researchers. Evaluation specialists should help policymakers and practitioners interpret new evidence as it evolves, and they should collaborate in creating innovative approaches that advance the mission of youth justice. If academic and vocational success is an important component of delinquency prevention, youth justice systems must continue to develop and evaluate strategies to achieve those goals, even if it means those efforts may be less than fully evidence-based for a time.

Table 11.2. Blueprints search identifies only three "Model Plus" interventions serving youth in the community and/or correctional facilities

Program	Description	Change Mechanisms	Citations
Functional Family Therapy (FFT)	Family-based prevention and intervention using clinical family practice modality to decrease youth risk factors	Family therapy	Alexander and Parsons (1973) Gottfredson et al. (2018)
Generation PMTO	Family training to teach family management skills and reduce antisocial behavior in children	Parental training	Akin et al. (2018, 2019) Bjørknes and Manger (2013) Bjørknes et al. (2012) DeGarmo et al. (2004) Forgatch et al. (2009) Martinez and Forgatch (2001) Patterson et al. (2010) Sigmarsdóttir et al. (2015)
Multisystemic Therapy (MST)	Family and community treatment to address adolescent antisocial behavior and delinquency	Family therapy Cognitive-behavioral treatment Individual therapy Conflict resolution & interpersonal skills	Borduin et al. (1995) Ogden and Halliday-Boykins (2004)

Source: Blueprints for Healthy Youth Development (https://www.blueprintsprograms.org/).

IV. CHALLENGES

Policies and practices in the youth justice sector are fundamentally about making choices within the constraints of law, resources, and bureaucracy. Two critical elements must be aligned to facilitate the creation and management of effective systems: policy choices and budget constraints. Policymakers in youth justice will always confront limited resources. Their budgets compete with criminal (adult) justice, social services, schools, and other fields, including public health and workforce development. Even when youth justice *wins* a budget competition, that success is a temporary opportunity to improve. Many obstacles remain.

For example, youth justice advocates worked for decades to reduce the system's reliance on secure confinement by increasing evidence for community-based services. Nevertheless, communities across the United States still struggle over this basic policy choice (McCarthy, Schiraldi, and Shark 2016). It is not enough to point out the iatrogenic effects of a strategy if that strategy has been a long-standing practice (e.g., youth confinement). Before abandoning existing approaches, lawmakers need reassurance that a new approach can operate successfully, within budget, and is preferable to other alternatives. Even then, it may take years to shift the system with rigorous evidence. For example, research about the iatrogenic effects

Table 11.3. Only five individual-level intervention models shown to have strong evidence for youth justice in two resource guides: CrimeSolutions and Blueprints

Programs	Description	Evidence-Based Models
Cognitive-behavioral therapy (CBT)	Individualized treatment to change beliefs and values contributing to problematic behavior	Cognitive Behavioral Intervention for Trauma in Schools Multisystemic Therapy Multidimensional Treatment Foster Care-Adolescents Expanded Early Pathways for Young Traumatized Children Trauma-Focused Cognitive-Behavioral Therapy
Group therapy	Therapeutic program to bring individuals together to change shared problematic behaviors and discuss personal challenges	Cognitive-Behavioral Intervention for Trauma in Schools
Family therapy	Therapeutic family-based practice to bolster familial relationships and target risk factors	Multisystemic Therapy Multidimensional Treatment Foster Care-Adolescents Expanded Early Pathways for Young Traumatized Children Families and Schools Together Trauma-Focused Cognitive-Behavioral Therapy
Interpersonal skill-building	Interventions to prevent antisocial and delinquent behavior by developing individual social skills, combatting dysfunctional beliefs, and addressing self-esteem issues	Promoting Alternative Thinking Strategies LifeSkills Training Multisystemic Therapy Adults in the Making Families and Schools Together Adolescent Diversion Project
Mentoring	Relationship-based intervention to provide youth with positive, consistent adult or peer contacts, healthy development, and reduced risk factors	Big Brothers Big Sisters Multidimensional Treatment Foster Care-Adolescents Better Futures Program

Sources: CrimeSolutions and Blueprints.

of Drug Abuse Resistance Education (D.A.R.E.) began to have an impact only after years of effort (Rosenbaum and Hanson 1998).

The struggle to design effective systems is more complex than simply choosing evidence-based programs over programs without evidence. Even strong evaluation findings from randomized controlled trials or sophisticated quasi-experimental approaches may play a limited role in policymaking. Lawmakers may need to consider other factors before implementing new programs and practices, even those backed by reliable evidence. Some concerns could be political, such as a program's relationship to a key constituency or community. Others may be pragmatic. Decision-makers might be asked to choose between an existing service provider with a successful performance history but limited evidentiary support and an untested newcomer offering an evidence-based program that would require added resources and community capacity.

Consider a hypothetical example of policymakers asked to choose one of two youth programs. One program, called "Youth at Home," is well-known across the country and has been operated by an experienced community-based organization for several years. Its only evaluation evidence, however, comes from a simple pre-post design with qualitative participant interviews. Another program, called "Changing Behavior," is backed by the findings of several high-quality studies conducted by award-winning scholars. Both programs have proposed annual contracts of $1 million. The funding decision is not an easy one.

- "Youth at Home" is a mentoring program targeted at (broadly) at-risk adolescents and operated by an established provider that has worked in the same community for decades. The program serves 1,000 youth annually with a semi-structured, relationship-based intervention delivered by adult volunteers. Program costs are limited to administrative overhead. The program was designed by well-regarded experts in adolescent development and is organized with a clear logic model and theory of change, but it has not been professionally evaluated yet. At $1,000 per youth, a contract of $1 million would serve 1,000 youth.
- "Changing Behavior" is an evidence-based cognitive-behavioral therapy program backed by several rigorous evaluations. The program targets high-risk, adjudicated adolescents and delivers intensive, individualized services. Staff members would be highly credentialed therapists earning professional salaries. While the program is well known among researchers, it is less familiar to local officials and community leaders. The cost to serve one youth for a year is $15,000, which means a contract of $1 million would allow the program to help 65 to 70 youth.

Officials in this hypothetical community would have to make a difficult choice. They could provide funding for a small, professionally admired program that would serve 70 known youthful offenders with a known probability of effectiveness. Such a choice would be safe from a political perspective. Local officials could cite the program's previous evaluation success to justify their decision-making if something were to go awry. On the other hand, they would also have to defend a sizeable expenditure that served fewer than 100 young people. Alternatively, they could fund a less guaranteed prevention program that would help 1,000 young people, only some of whom may be destined to have future justice contacts. Critics could accuse the program of being wasteful without reliable evaluation findings. If any problems were to occur, the decision-makers would not have a research base to justify their actions.

Justice systems may embrace evidence-based programs and practices for various reasons but still employ less-proven approaches at times (Greenwood 2013). Evidence-based programs are readily accepted if they promise valid outcomes (causal mechanisms are well-measured while accounting for competing explanations of effects) and reliable outcomes (repeated tests yield similar results). Some long-standing, well-received community-based organizations with positive reputations make neither of those promises, yet they continue to occupy important places in youth justice systems. Policymakers must continually revisit their assumptions about programs and practices, even those with solid track records, especially as new research findings emerge. The research lens, however, can be narrow. Policymakers may have a wider perspective and a history of making good choices within the limits of their budgets and bureaucracies. In some cases, like the hypothetical "Youth at Home" program, interventions with lesser evidence may still be preferred because they help the justice system to pursue a fuller, more comprehensive set of goals.

A. Scope

Randomized controlled trials (RCTs) are often called the "gold standard" in research. Subjects are randomly selected from a population and then randomly assigned to receive either a treatment or a no-treatment (control) condition. In criminal justice settings, however, research subjects are rarely selected randomly, and there is often a voluntary component to their participation. Researchers invite participants to join a study, and those participants must choose to be included. If they later decline to continue, an RCT would be compromised. The scope of an RCT evaluation is typically quite narrow. The difference between treatment and control may be a single event. All outcome differences are attributed to that one factor.

In practice, the outcomes of evaluations can be complex. The principal outcome of a therapeutic program for justice-involved youth may be reduced delinquency. On the other hand, a mentoring program or vocational support program could produce a wider range of plausible outcomes—e.g., school attainment and attachment, physical health, reductions in family conflict, prosocial peer associations, and broader social capital accumulation. A mentoring program could even be valued for its positive effects on the volunteer mentors. An educational support program may include peer effects intentionally. The program could involve discussions about engaging with prosocial peers and limiting contact with negative peers. It could include skill-building efforts with other adolescents and adult instructors. These adjacent peer effects would add value but also make evaluation more complicated.

One particularly important peer effect of community-based programs is "collective efficacy," or the extent to which people in a shared place are willing to work together to solve common problems. As Sampson, Morenoff, and Earls (1999, 633) noted, "[t]he importance of spatial dynamics in generating collective efficacy for children is highlighted—proximity to areas high in closure, exchange, and control bestows an advantage above and beyond the structural characteristics of a given neighborhood." Community-based programs are sometimes explicitly designed to create collective efficacy, which could have benefits for levels of crime and disorder across communities in addition to their specific effects on program participants.

Crime researchers note the effects of crime prevention programs at the "intrinsic margin" (i.e., program participants commit fewer crimes) or the "extrinsic margin" (i.e., fewer people, in general, commit crimes). Most programs for high-risk adolescents focus on the intrinsic margin, but some may have demonstrable effects on the extrinsic margin. Youth exposed to program activities before ever being involved in the justice system may benefit, and programs may affect wider community dynamics in ways that prevent illegal behavior. There may also be peer effects, where program participants adopt prosocial attitudes that affect nonparticipant youth. Extrinsic effects may not be an explicit focus of youth justice, but they are reasonable considerations for policymakers. If the converse were true—that programs had iatrogenic effects on nonparticipants—those effects would certainly be addressed in policy discussions.

B. Design

Rigorous evaluation designs often narrow the range of measurable outcomes and limit the perceived value of a program. Justice-sector RCTs also tend to have relatively short follow-up periods due to the limited duration of the intervention or the short-term availability of outcome measures. For example, legal records for justice-involved youth may not be available very long after youth reach the legal age of adulthood. The "controlled" part of RCTs may also affect participants for a very short time. Once someone exits an intervention, their exposure to the randomly assigned treatment ends. Subsequent experiences are no longer controlled. As a result, the research literature in the youth justice field does not often include long-term effects. It is not always clear whether outcomes persist or attenuate (decline over time). Community-based programs may have outcomes that emerge after participation. Youth may gain skills and assets that get better with practice and experience. They may accumulate human and social capital beyond the time researchers can measure outcomes, given the typical constraints of RCT data collection protocols.

The expected effects of a program tested by several RCT evaluations are more likely to be valid and reliable than programs only tested by quasi-experimental evaluations, programs where only some components were measured, or programs never evaluated by researchers. However, randomized trials tend to enroll relatively small samples, and their result metrics may involve wide confidence intervals. For policymakers, this may increase the perceived risk of funding an intervention. Even the smaller effect sizes of evaluation results from quasi-experiments with large samples could present less risk and be more appealing to policymakers.

Evaluation research affects the competition for scarce resources. Evaluators are inclined to compare the effects of an intervention with a no-treatment counterfactual. In practice, the actual comparison is probably other programs competing for the same funding. System officials face an explicit trade-off. They could fund an RCT with strong internal validity but most likely a very narrow design, little information about externalities or long-term effects, and wide confidence intervals. Or, they could support a quasi-experimental evaluation that may involve threats to internal validity but provides greater flexibility for additional study and future policy development. Acknowledging the existence of this tension and expanding study designs to account for a wider range of outcomes would provide more meaningful information for policy and practice. Doing so would also benefit the youth justice field in ways the current evaluation literature does not.

V. Discussion

Making policy is about choices, and all the elements described above play a role in choosing the best strategies for preventing youthful offending while minimizing the potential harms of the justice process. The value gained by leveraging the stamp of approval from evaluation research is one input into these decisions, but other factors are relevant. For example, the influence of evaluation research may be stronger as policymakers learn to appreciate the value of a diverse evidence base. Randomized controlled trials are certainly valuable, but some questions of policy and practice are not amenable to RCT evaluations. The best evidence strategy is not to base all decisions on whatever is supported by the most rigorous evaluation; it is first to identify the question at hand and then seek the strongest evaluation answer to that specific question.

Direct comparisons of the value presented by prevention programs for youth at risk of justice involvement versus those offering intensive interventions for youth already in the justice process are not helpful. Programs and practices for previously adjudicated youth focus on smaller, observable samples of young people with demonstrated risks of delinquency. Prevention programs focus on reducing the probability of justice involvement for larger populations at risk of—but not yet engaged in—illegal behavior. The effects, replicability, and overall benefit of programs are properly assessed only after acknowledging their different contexts and evaluation challenges.

Policymakers, practitioners, and researchers view the quest for evidence differently. All parties, however, must appreciate the need for carefully conducted evaluations that investigate causal mechanisms with as much precision as possible *after* accounting for the circumstances of each study and each research question. Youth justice research must analyze policies and programs by accounting for all activities, components, and intended outcomes. In youth justice, this requires evaluations using varying methods and analytic designs. Seeing RCT studies as the only acceptable form of evidence for policy and practice limits the range of potential strategies and the benefit of using diverse approaches to serve youth, families, and communities.

VI. Conclusion

It is facile to characterize youth justice policymaking as choosing programs that work versus those that do not. To meet the foundational goals of youth justice—i.e., mitigating various individual, family, and community factors leading to delinquent behavior—a less polarizing framework is required. The evidence base of youth justice is growing, but researchers still know far more about what does not work than what does. These limitations are apparent in two accessible research repositories that inform justice policy—Blueprints and CrimeSolutions. Using either of these important sources of research information, practitioners would find just five youth justice interventions that qualify as evidence-based approaches: cognitive-behavioral therapy, group therapy, family therapy, interpersonal skill-building, and mentoring. All five models implicitly locate the source of youth offending in the individual deficits of youth and families. Mainstream theories of delinquency suggest a wider range of causes, including social, economic, cultural, and structural factors. As yet, however, the evaluation field has not presented system leaders with proven, ready-to-use interventions addressing those factors. Researchers have much work to do.

The youth justice field needs research to fill critical gaps in practice and theory. Without such evidence, policymakers and funding sources will continue to build evidence within a narrow theoretical range and create less-than-comprehensive youth justice strategies. The best way to understand evaluation research and the development of evidence in youth justice today is to view it as a contentious and evolving process constantly affected by theoretical differences, political ideology, financial interest, bureaucratic dysfunction, and the practical concerns of measurement and data collection. It is not a simple, unfettered accumulation of readily available knowledge about what works.

References

Abrahamsen, David. 1960. *The psychology of crime*. New York: Columbia University Press.

Akin, Becci A., Kyle Lang, Thomas P. McDonald, Yueqi Yan, and Todd Little. 2019. Randomized trial of PMTO in foster care: Six-month child well-being outcomes. *Research on Social Work Practices*, 29 (2): 206–222.

Akin, Becci A., Kyle Lang, Yueqi Yan, and Thomas P. McDonald. 2018. Randomized trial of PMTO in foster care: 12-month child well-being, parenting, and caregiver functioning outcomes. *Children and Youth Services Review*, 95:49–63.

Alexander, James F., and Bruce V. Parsons. 1973. Short-term behavioral intervention with delinquent families: Impact on family process and recidivism. *Journal of Abnormal Psychology*, 81 (3): 219–225.

Augimeri, Leena K., David P. Farrington, Christopher J. Koegl, and David M. Day. 2007. The SNAP™ Under 12 Outreach Project: Effects of a community based program for children with conduct problems. *Journal of Child and Family Studies*, 16 (6): 799–807.

Bjørknes, Ragnhild, John Kjøbli, Terje Manger, and Reidar Jakobsen. 2012. Parent training among ethnic minorities: Parenting practices as mediators of change in child conduct problems. *Family Relations: An Interdisciplinary Journal of Applied Family Studies*, 61 (1): 101–114.

Bjørknes, Ragnhild, and Terje Manger. 2013. Can parent training alter parent practice and reduce conduct problems in ethnic minority children? A randomized controlled trial. *Prevention Science*, 14:52–63.

Borduin, Charles M., Barton J. Mann, Lynn T. Cone, Scott W. Henggeler, Bethany R. Fucci, David M. Blaske, and Robert A. Williams. 1995. Multisystemic treatment of serious juvenile offenders: Long-term prevention of criminality and violence. *Journal of Consulting and Clinical Psychology*, 63 (4): 569–578.

Butts, Jeffrey A. 2018. It's not about the art; it's about the artist. Rite of Passage Magazine, 2018 Issue. Minden, NV: Rite of Passage.

Butts, Jeffrey A., and Adele V. Harrell. 1998. Delinquents or criminals: Policy options for young offenders. Crime Policy Report. Washington, DC: Urban Institute.

Butts, Jeffrey A., and Ojmarrh Mitchell. 2000. Brick by brick: Dismantling the border between juvenile and adult justice. In *Criminal Justice 2000*, Volume 2. Washington, DC: National Institute of Justice. https://www.urban.org/sites/default/files/publication/62026/1000234-Brick-by-Brick-Dismantling-the-Border-Between-Juvenile-and-Adult-Justice.PDF.

Butts, Jeffrey A., and John K. Roman. 2018. Good questions: Building evaluation evidence in a competitive policy environment. *Justice Evaluation Journal*, 1 (1): 15–31.

Celinska, Katarzyna, Susan Furrer, and Chia-Cherng Cheng. 2013. An outcome-based evaluation of functional family therapy for youth with behavioral problems. *OJJDP Journal of Juvenile Justice*, 2 (2): 23–36.

Chamberlain, Patricia, Leslie D. Leve, and David S. DeGarmo. 2007. Multidimensional treatment foster care for girls in the juvenile justice system: 2-year follow-up of a randomized clinical trial. *Journal of Consulting and Clinical Psychology*, 75 (1): 187–193.
Chamberlain, Patricia, and John B. Reid. 1998. Comparison of two community alternatives to incarceration for chronic juvenile offenders. *Journal of Consulting and Clinical Psychology*, 66 (4): 624–633.
Cloward, Richard A., and Lloyd E. Ohlin. 1960. *Delinquency and opportunity*. New York: Free Press.
Davidson, William S., Robin Redner, Craig H. Blakely, James G. Ernshoff, and Christina M. Mitchell. 1987. Diversion of juvenile offenders: An experimental comparison. *Journal of Consulting and Clinical Psychology*, 55 (1): 68–75.
Degarmo, David S., Gerald R. Patterson, and Marion S. Forgatch. 2004. How do outcomes in a specified parent training intervention maintain or wane over time? *Prevention Science*, 5 (2): 73–89.
Empey, LaMar T. 1981. Constructing crime: Evolution and implications of sociological theory. In *New directions in the rehabilitation of criminal offenders*, edited by Susan E. Martin, Lee B. Sechrest, and Robin Redner, 196–254. Washington, DC: National Academy Press.
Feld, Barry C. 1987. The juvenile court meets the principle of the offense: Legislative changes in juvenile waiver statutes. *Journal of Criminal Law & Criminology*, 78 (3): 471–533.
Feld, Barry C. 2011. Procedural rights in juvenile courts: Competence and consequences. In *The Oxford handbook of juvenile crime and juvenile justice*, edited by Barry C. Feld and Donna M. Bishop, 664–694. New York: Oxford University Press.
Finckenauer, James O. 1984. *Juvenile delinquency and corrections: The gap between theory and practice*. Orlando, FL: Academic Press.
Forgatch, Marion S., Gerald R. Patterson, David S. Degarmo, and Zintars G. Beldavs. 2009. Testing the Oregon delinquency model with 9-year follow-up of the Oregon Divorce Study. *Development and Psychopathology*, 21 (2): 637–660.
Gold, Martin. 1978. Scholastic experiences, self-esteem, and delinquent behavior: A theory for alternative schools. *Crime & Delinquency*, 24 (3): 290–308.
Gordon, Donald A., Jack Arbuthnot, Kathryn E. Gustafson, and Peter McGreen. 1988. Home-based behavioral-systems family therapy with disadvantaged juvenile delinquents. *American Journal of Family Therapy*, 16 (3): 243–255.
Gottfredson, Denise C., Brook Kearley, Terence P. Thornberry, Molly Slothower, Deanna Devlin, and Jamie J. Fader. 2018. Scaling-up evidence-based programs using a public funding stream: A randomized trial of functional family therapy for court-involved youth. *Prevention Science*, 19 (7): 939–953.
Gottfredson, Michael R., and Travis Hirschi. 1990. *A general theory of crime*. Stanford, CA: Stanford University Press.
Greenwood, Peter. 2013. *Evidence-based practice in juvenile justice: Progress, challenges, and opportunities*. New York: Springer Science & Business Media.
Helium, Frank R., Solomon Kobrin, and Malcom W. Klein. 1983. The deinstitutionalization of status offenders: The legislative mandate. In *Community treatment of juvenile offenders: The DSO experiments*, edited by Solomon Kobrin and Malcom W. Klein, 19–38. Beverly Hills, CA: SAGE.
Henggeler, Scott W., W. Glenn Clingempeel, Michael J. Brondino, and Susan G. Pickrel. 2002. Four-year follow-up of Multisystemic Therapy with substance-abusing and substance-dependent juvenile offenders. *Journal of the American Academy of Child and Adolescent Psychiatry*, 41 (7): 868–874.

Henggeler, Scott W., Colleen A. Halliday-Boykins, Phillippe B. Cunningham, Jeff Randall, Steven B. Shapiro, and Jason E. Chapman. 2006. Juvenile drug court: Enhancing outcomes by integrating evidence-based treatments. *Journal of Consulting and Clinical Psychology*, 74:42–54.

Henggeler, Scott W., Gary B. Melton, and Linda A. Smith. 1992. Family preservation using Multisystemic Therapy: An effective alternative to incarcerating serious juvenile offenders. *Journal of Consulting and Clinical Psychology*, 60:953–961.

Landenberger, Nana A., and Mark W. Lipsey. 2005. The positive effects of cognitive-behavioral programs for offenders: A meta-analysis of factors associated with effective treatment. *Journal of Experimental Criminology*, 1 (4): 451–476.

Lipman, Ellen L., Meghan Kenny, Carrie Sniderman, Susanne O'Grady, Leena Augimeri, Sarah Khayutin, and Michael H. Boyle. 2008. Evaluation of a community-based program for young boys at-risk of antisocial behavior: Results and issues. *Journal of the Canadian Academy of Child and Adolescent Psychiatry*, 17 (1): 12–19.

Martinez, Charles R., Jr., and Marion S. Forgatch. 2001. Preventing problems with boys' noncompliance: Effects of a parent training intervention for divorcing mothers. *Journal of Consulting and Clinical Psychology*, 69 (3): 416–428.

Matza, David. 1990. *Delinquency and drift*. Reprint edition. London: Routledge.

McCarthy, Patrick, Vincent N. Schiraldi, and Miriam Shark. 2016. The future of youth justice: A community-based alternative to the youth prison model. Cambridge, MA: Harvard Kennedy School.

Mennel, Robert M. 1973. *Thorns and thistles: Juvenile delinquents in the United States 1825–1940*. Hanover, NH: University Press of New England.

Merton, Robert K. 1957. *Social theory and social structure*. New York: Free Press.

Ogden, Terje, and Colleen A. Halliday-Boykins. 2004. Multisystemic treatment of antisocial adolescents in Norway: Replication of clinical outcomes outside of the US. *Child and Adolescent Mental Health*, 9 (2): 77–83.

Patterson, Gerald R., Marion S. Forgatch, and David S. DeGarmo. 2010. Cascading effects following intervention. *Development and Psychopathology*, 22 (4): 949–970.

Phillipson, Michael. 2014. *Sociological aspects of crime and delinquency*. London: Routledge.

Platt, Anthony M. 1977. *The child savers: The invention of delinquency*. Chicago: University of Chicago Press.

Rosenbaum, Dennis P., and Gordon S. Hanson. 1998. Assessing the effects of school-based drug education: A six-year multilevel analysis of Project D.A.R.E. *Journal of Research in Crime and Delinquency*, 35(4): 381–412.

Rothman, David J. 1980. *Conscience and convenience: The asylum and its alternatives in Progressive America*. Glenview, IL: Scott, Foresman.

Rutter, Michael, and Henri Giller. 1984. *Juvenile delinquency: Trends and perspectives*. New York: Guilford Press.

Sampson, Robert J., Jeffrey D. Morenoff, and Felton Earls. 1999. Beyond social capital: Spatial dynamics of collective efficacy for children. *American Sociological Review*, 64 (5): 633–660.

Scali, Mary Ann. 2019. Meeting the mandates of Gault: Automatic appointment of counsel in juvenile delinquency proceedings. *Juvenile & Family Court Journal*, 70 (3): 7–23.

Schlossman, Steven L. 1977. *Love and the American delinquent*. Chicago: University of Chicago Press.

Sexton, Thomas, and Charles W. Turner. 2010. The effectiveness of functional family therapy for youth with behavioral problems in a community practice setting. *Journal of Family Psychology*, 24 (3): 339–348.

Shaw, Clifford R., and Henry D. McKay. 1942. *Juvenile delinquency and urban areas.* Chicago: University of Chicago Press.
Sigmarsdóttir, Margrét, Örnólfur Thorlacius, Edda Vikar Guðmundsdóttir, and David S. DeGarmo. 2015. Treatment effectiveness of PMTO for children's behavior problems in Iceland: Child outcomes in a nationwide randomized controlled trial. *Family Process*, 54 (3): 498–517.
Smith, Emilie Phillips, Angela M. Wolf, Dan M. Cantillon, Oseela Thomas, and William S. Davison. 2004. The adolescent diversion project: 25 years of research on an ecological model of intervention. *Prevention & Intervention in the Community*, 27 (2): 29–47.
Tanenhaus, David S. 2004. *Juvenile justice in the making.* New York: Oxford University Press.
Taxman, Faye S. 2018. The partially clothed emperor: Evidence-based practices. *Journal of Contemporary Criminal Justice*, 34 (1): 97–114.
Timmons–Mitchell, Jane, Monica B. Bender, Maureen A. Kishna, and Clare C. Mitchell. 2006. An independent effectiveness trial of Multisystemic Therapy with juvenile justice youth. *Journal of Clinical Child and Adolescent Psychology*, 35 (2): 227–236.
Wikström, Per-Olof H. 2019. Situational action theory: Toward a dynamic theory of crime and its causes. In *Oxford research encyclopedia of criminology and criminal justice.* New York: Oxford University Press. https://oxfordre.com/criminology/.
Zimring, Franklin E. 2019. *American juvenile justice.* 2nd ed. New York: Oxford University Press.

PART III
CRIMINAL JUSTICE

This part covers evidence-based approaches in criminal justice. It includes seven chapters.

CHAPTER 12

LEGITIMACY AND EVIDENCE-BASED POLICY

JUSTICE TANKEBE AND ANTHONY BOTTOMS

I. Hedgehogs and Foxes

Building trust and nurturing legitimacy on both sides of the police/citizen divide is the foundational principle underlying the nature of relations between law enforcement agencies and the communities they serve. . . . People are more likely to obey the law when they believe those who are enforcing it have the right—the legitimate authority—to tell them what to do. Building trust and legitimacy, therefore, is not just a policing issue. It involves all components of the criminal justice system. (President's Task Force on 21st Century Policing 2015, 1, 5)

These statements by a prestigious US committee make several important points. First, they emphasize that, in a democratic society, legitimacy and trust are "foundational principles" in law enforcement. Second, they note that while such issues are perhaps of special importance for police services, their reach extends beyond policing to "all components of the criminal justice system." Third, and by implication, they offer a quiet rebuke to criminological scholars, because serious criminological interest in legitimacy did not begin until the 1990s, following the groundbreaking research contribution of Tom Tyler's (2006) *Why People Obey the Law* (first published 1990).

Yet the task force's own analysis is in one respect puzzling. It was established by President Obama following a police shooting of a Black youth in Ferguson, Missouri, that sparked widespread protests across the country. In setting up the task force, the president spoke of "the distrust that exists between too many police departments and too many communities"; he also said that too many individuals, "particularly young people of color, do not feel as if they are being treated fairly" (President's Task Force 2015, 5). In scholarly language, these comments speak to concerns about distrust arising from *distributive injustice* (i.e., the possibility that some individuals and communities are receiving less fair treatment than others). But the primary theoretical focus of the task force, as set out in its first substantive recommendation, was different:

> Law enforcement culture should embrace a guardian mindset to build public trust and legitimacy. Toward that end, police and sheriffs' departments should adopt *procedural justice* as *the guiding principle* for internal and external politics and practices to guide their interactions with the citizens they service. (15, emphasis added)

Elsewhere, the task force also said that "the public confers legitimacy only on those whom they believe are acting in procedurally just ways" (21). Its report therefore prioritizes *procedural justice* (i.e., the manner in which people are treated by officers) as the single best way for police services to acquire greater legitimacy in the eyes of citizens. But procedural justice is not the same as distributive justice, and the task force did not discuss the relationship between the two concepts, notwithstanding the president's obvious interest in the latter.[1]

In a celebrated essay, Isaiah Berlin ([1953] 2013) drew attention to a remark by the Ancient Greek poet Archilocus: "the fox knows many things, but the hedgehog knows one big thing." Applying this to the history of ideas, Berlin distinguished between thinkers with a "single, universal organizing principle in terms of which alone all that they say and are has significance" and "those who pursue many ends, often unrelated and even contradictory" (2). In the smaller world of criminal justice legitimacy, the President's Task Force essentially took the role of the hedgehog, with procedural justice (PJ) as its "one big thing." In doing so, however, it was and is certainly not alone, as can be seen in the opening words of a recent paper:

> Procedural justice theory (PJT) is arguably the dominant model for understanding police-community relations, at least in so far as such relations are conceptualized in terms of trust, legitimacy, cooperation and compliance. (Kyprianides, Stott, and Bradford 2021, 671)

Scholars standardly describe procedural justice as focusing on four aspects of the exercise of authority (Tyler and Meares 2019, 74). Two of these refer to the making of decisions by powerholders: PJ requires that when decisions need to be made, they should be made impartially, and then explained (*neutrality*); also, that everyone involved should have an opportunity to express a view before the decision is made (*voice*). The other two matters are more personal or relational: when dealing with citizens, powerholders should show *respect* for them as people, and for their rights; also, they should show that they have *trustworthy motives*, and so can be relied upon to be acting in the interests of the whole community.[2]

We have no doubt that these are normatively desirable ways for powerholders to act, and we are equally persuaded that, in many criminal justice situations, there is strong empirical evidence that PJ generates legitimacy (Bottoms and Tankebe 2021). We are nevertheless foxes rather than hedgehogs, because we believe that the evidence about the generation of legitimacy compels us to take into account not only PJ, but also other matters such as distributive justice and the lawful and effective use of authority. Moreover, these other matters are not always subordinate to PJ.

II. Understanding Legitimacy

Legitimacy is the moral affirmation of power as valid. A good formal definition has been offered by the British political theorist David Beetham, who describes legitimate power as "power that is *acknowledged as rightful* by relevant agents, who include power holders and their staff, those subject to the power and third parties whose support or recognition may help confirm it" (Beetham 2013b, 19, emphasis in original). Legitimacy is, therefore, significantly different from what has been variously described as "dull compulsion" or "fatalism" (see Carrabine 2005; Scott 1990). This occurs when people obey rules or norms only because they think they have no effective alternative, given their powerless or disadvantaged structural position.

The central concept within Beetham's definition is therefore *rightfulness*. Because "right" is a normative concept, this immediately draws attention to the inescapably *normative* character of legitimacy and the concomitant need for *shared values* between powerholders and their audience(s) (Beetham 2013a). Social scientists studying legitimacy must therefore analyze the normative values of both powerholders and audiences, and also the conditions under which power is obtained, exercised, and maintained. It is also important to note that neither "rightfulness" nor "legitimacy" is a binary concept; hence, in real social situations, researchers will usually find themselves focusing on *gradations* in legitimacy. In addition, and more fundamentally, because norms are inherently social, Reus-Smit (2007, 159) is right to emphasize that legitimacy is a "*social concept in the deepest sense—it describes a phenomenon that is inherently social*" (emphasis added).

A decade ago, we proposed a "dialogic" approach to the social-scientific study of legitimacy in criminal justice (Bottoms and Tankebe 2012). We have since refined our thinking to incorporate Bernard Williams's (2005) concept of citizens' "basic legitimation expectations" (or BLEs), which—in a nutshell—concerns how citizens *expect* powerholders to act if they are to be seen as legitimate.[3] Hence, for Williams, the difference between legitimate and illegitimate power lies in the ability of powerholders to honor citizens' BLEs, to a reasonable extent, in specific situations. With this amendment, we remain fully committed to the social-situational, relational, and dialogic approach that we initially advocated.[4] Among other things, we have argued that

> those in power (or seeking power) in a given context make a claim to be the legitimate ruler(s); then members of the audience respond to this claim; the power-holder might adjust the nature of the claim in light of the audience's response; and this process repeats itself. It follows that legitimacy should not be viewed as a single transaction; it is more like a perpetual discussion, in which the content of power-holders' later claims will be affected by the nature of the audience response. (Bottoms and Tankebe 2012, 129)

Elsewhere in the same paper, we also indicated that a claim to legitimacy can be, and often is, made simultaneously to several "audiences." For example, a director of prisons in a given state, when introducing a new operational policy, will need to consider its potential legitimacy in the eyes not only of prisoners, but also of prison staff, the courts, the director's political masters, and perhaps others. Some of these come into the category described by Beetham (2013b, 19) as "third parties whose support or recognition may help confirm" (or otherwise) the powerholder's claim to legitimacy; others have described such third parties as "sovereigns" (Worden and McLean 2017).[5] The existence of more than one "audience" can be important, because the perceptions of different audiences can differ: for example, in an analysis of survey data from Schenectady, New York, Worden and McLean (2017) report that while police misconduct weighed heavily in judgments of police legitimacy by "sovereigns," it was less of an issue for the public.

For present purposes, three main implications for social scientific study follow from a social and dialogic view of legitimacy: we shall discuss these separately.

A. The Social and Situational Contexts of Legitimacy Dialogues

A consequence of the deeply social character of legitimacy is that legitimacy dialogues do not occur in a vacuum; on the contrary, they are always social and situational, and they assume a character that is shaped by the socioeconomic, normative, and political contexts in which they occur.[6] These can be understood to occur at several levels.

At the macro-social level, the dominant normative context of power in a state or community can shape the nature of legitimacy dialogues, as will quickly be apparent if one thinks about possible dialogues in, say, the United States, Sweden, and Saudi Arabia. Mehozay and Factor (2017) have helpfully focused on issues of this kind, arguing that there are "good reasons to hypothesize that populations will differ in their perceptions of legitimacy for cultural and historical reasons," even in circumstances where the quality of (say) the policing is identical. These authors identified four "core normative value systems" (*religious–traditional*, *liberal*, *republican-communitarian*, and *ethno-national*). Using data from the 27-country European Social Survey, they found preliminary support for their hypotheses. An interesting implication of their results is that, at least in the short term, "even optimal procedural conduct or efficiency [by powerholders] may not affect the attitudes of some populations" as regards legitimacy (Mehozay and Factor 2017, 151–152).

Turning to the meso-social level, the operation of state agencies can result in some very different legitimacy-relevant experiences for different communities in the same location. A striking example of this is found in *Pulled Over*, a mixed-methods research study by Epp and colleagues (2014) of police vehicle stops in Kansas City. Vehicle stops were of two kinds—"traffic safety stops" (for speeding, etc.) and "investigatory stops" (where a minor traffic violation may be used to seek evidence of more serious offences, including perhaps searching the vehicle). Quantitatively, African American drivers were, by comparison with Whites, disproportionately subjected to investigatory stops. Members of the African American community were acutely aware of this difference, and interview data showed that they resented the intrusiveness of investigatory stops, even when these were conducted politely. In consequence, they had more negative views of the legitimacy of the police than White drivers. As Tom Tyler put it in a back-cover endorsement of *Pulled Over*, "polite and respectful police demeanor, while to some extent palliative, cannot assuage the damaging effects of the widespread and systematic use of this policing technique on the minority community."

Recently, a team of researchers at Keele University (UK), led by Clifford Stott, has extended the examination of the social aspects of legitimacy to specific micro-level situations. Radburn and Stott (2019, 421) presented a theoretical justification for this approach, arguing that much research on PJ and legitimacy "emphasizes large-scale survey data" and is therefore in danger of "portraying a reified social world divorced from the social psychological dynamics of encounters between the police and policed." Subsequent empirical projects by the Keele team include groundbreaking studies of legitimacy and PJ in (1) encounters between the police and street homeless people (Kyprianides, Stott, and Bradford 2021), and (2) work within police interrogation suites (Savigar-Shaw et al. 2022). Both studies have yielded complex and in part unexpected results, amply justifying the team's overall approach, and emphasizing the need for police managers to consider micro- as well as meso- and macro-level social contexts. Further confirmation of this point is provided in an ethnographic study by Monica Bell (2016, 326–327) of Black mothers living in a disadvantaged area of Washington, DC. Bell reports that, like most residents of that area, these mothers were "deeply wary of police," regarding them as "corrupt [and] biased on the basis of race and class." Despite this, however, the mothers fairly frequently called the police about a local incident, for example if they thought the police were more able than anyone else to handle the particular situation. Thus, despite a strong meso-level culture of suspicion of the police, they were nevertheless granted a limited degree of legitimacy in specific micro-level contexts.

B. Understanding Legitimacy as Dialogue

The second implication of a dialogic approach flows from the mundane recognition that there are parties to a dialogue, and that these parties come with their own prior experiences, values, and priorities. In broad terms, we can distinguish two main sets of parties: "powerholders" and "audiences" (Bottoms and Tankebe 2012).

In the context of criminal justice, there are many "powerholders," including government ministers and officials, police officers, prosecutors, judges, prison staff, and probation officers. But all face one similar issue in fulfilling their roles. As the historian Wilbur Miller (1978, 1172), speaking of police, succinctly put it:

> The exercise of power is not a one-way transaction. Consequently the successful policeman must be alert to the different responses his authority evokes. To maintain his authority, he has to develop flexible strategies for dealing with these responses. Different policemen react differently to this psychological side of their work.[7]

We will return to Miller's suggestion that "flexible strategies" are needed. For now, we focus on his other main point, namely that all powerholders have to come to terms with the fact that they *are* the holders of formal power, and will therefore inevitably sometimes face challenges to or criticism of their authority. Of course, nobody likes criticism, so some such challenges might partially erode a particular individual's self-confidence in fulfilling their allotted role as (say) a police officer. These "psychological" matters for powerholders have been discussed by political scientists (e.g. Weber [1922] 1978; Barker 2001), and in previous work we have referred to them as processes relating to "self-legitimacy" (Bottoms and Tankebe 2012, 2013). That concept had not previously been used in a criminological context, so the relevant literature is still sparse. However, although the findings across studies are not fully consistent, empirical analyses have suggested that, for frontline police officers, confidence in their self-legitimacy is potentially affected by a triad of relational matters: the treatment they receive from supervisors, the interpersonal trust and respect they command among their peers, and how they believe the public perceives them (Tankebe 2022; Hacin and Mesko 2022).

Important findings on the effects of self-legitimacy have also emerged from research by Trinkner, Kerrison, and Goff (2019) in a large urban police force in the United States. The focus was the officers' degree of concern that they might "confirm a racist stereotype" when interacting with community members (that is, a concern that they might act illegitimately). The study found that the officers most likely to express such concerns had lower levels of self-legitimacy, but also *higher* levels of support for coercive policing.[8] Although the study was cross-sectional, and therefore preliminary, the authors concluded from the data that the public's "negative stereotypes of police officers can potentially undermine officer morale and public safety" (Trinkner, Kerrison, and Goff 2019, 421; see also Nix and Wolfe 2017).

Turning now from powerholders to audiences, it is here that our stance as "foxes" is most salient. In previous work (Bottoms and Tankebe 2017, 2021; see also Tankebe 2013), we have identified four basic legitimation expectations (BLEs) that have been shown empirically to generate concerns about legitimacy among audiences, though we have also said that in some situations other matters might also be important. These four BLEs are distributive justice (DJ), procedural justice, effectiveness, and lawfulness. Our approach has been endorsed by a prestigious National Academies (2022) report in the United States: the committee refers to our suggested BLEs as "four pillars of legitimacy" (19), and argues that "police organizations and donors should not guess" at whether these pillars are being achieved, but instead accurately measure them, and relate them to outcomes of reforms (20).

Two of these matters—procedural justice and distributive justice—have been previously mentioned. There is now an extensive body of research showing that citizens' perceptions that criminal justice powerholders have acted with PJ generates perceived legitimacy (for reviews, see, for example, Tyler and Meares 2019; Jackson 2018; for a meta-analysis, see Walters and Bolger 2019).[9] Criminal justice managers should therefore certainly encourage their staff to act toward citizens/suspects/prisoners in ways that are procedurally just; that is, staff should be encouraged to be respectful and trustworthy, as well as ensuring that those with whom they connect are given a voice and that key decisions are made neutrally.

But, as we have seen, in some situations, such as that studied by Epp, Maynard-Moody, and Haider-Markel (2014) in Kansas City, practices of distributive injustice are so embedded in policing (or other criminal justice domains) that the use of procedural justice can be no more than "palliative." This situation points to the need for criminal justice managers to always focus on *both* distributive and procedural justice. A further, and often neglected, aspect of distributive justice concerns *underenforcement* by police—which can happen, for example, when they do not take investigations of sexual offences against women and girls seriously, or when certain communities are underpoliced, allowing violent offenders to persist in their harms to those communities. Unfortunately, too often such underenforcement is partial, with authorities' nonresponsiveness tending to ignore "the needs of the poor, racial minorities, and the otherwise politically vulnerable" (Natapoff 2006, 1719).

In addition to procedural and distributive justice, two other matters have been shown to be important in generating audience legitimacy (remembering that "legitimacy" is the moral affirmation of power as being validly exercised). The first is the *effective use of authority* to create a social order in which people feel safe and able to function—and this is so both in prisons and in the community. Thus, Alison Liebling (2015, 21) begins a summary of research on prisoners' views of factors contributing to legitimate regimes (i.e., in effect, BLEs) by saying that "prisoners need to feel that they are safe." As regards policing, there are now a number of surveys of citizens in African countries, where the state is often weak, showing that effectiveness in providing basic social order (or safety) is more important to citizens than procedural justice in generating perceptions of police legitimacy (e.g., Tankebe 2009; Bradford et al. 2014). Such findings are consistent with Bernard Williams's (2005, 3) argument that the "securing of order, protection [and] safety" is, in any society, "the first political question," because without safety, routine everyday life becomes very difficult to sustain with any comfort.[10] Where, however, there is good basic safety, other matters (such as procedural justice) can loom larger in people's expectations of powerholders.

The powers of criminal justice professionals are, of course, founded in law, so it will be no surprise that *lawfulness* is a fourth aspect of audience legitimacy often raised by citizens or prisoners. Thus, when Kearns, Ashooh, and Lowrey-Kinberg (2020) innovatively asked a sample of 1,900 US residents the open-ended question, "When thinking about the police, what does 'legitimacy' mean to you?," the most frequently offered response was that, to be legitimate, police should "follow the law."[11] A basically similar concept is that of "bounded authority," breaches of which are seen as including not only unlawful behavior, but also acts that are technically legal but are seen by citizens as an unjustifiable encroachment on their freedom. In a survey of a nationally representative sample of adults in the United States, Trinkner, Jackson, and Tyler (2019) found that not only PJ, but also bounded authority, was a significant predictor of legitimacy; as they put it, this result therefore "expands previous conceptualizations of appropriate police behavior beyond procedural justice" (280).

Finally, we should note that, while there is indeed solid evidence that PJ, DJ, effectiveness, and lawfulness are in many situations BLEs, and therefore generators of legitimacy, this does not rule out the possibility that, in particular situations, other matters might also be important. One such situation is imprisonment, where prisoners meet prison staff many times a day and are dependent upon them for many needs (food, family visits, access to telephones, etc.). Given such structured dependence, Liebling (2022) convincingly argues that staff attention to prisoners' individual welfare must be seen as an appropriate BLE in prison settings.

C. The Dynamic Character of Legitimacy

A dialogic approach to legitimacy necessarily requires that attention is paid to how dialogues develop. In this regard, an important research step is to examine simultaneously the self-legitimacy of powerholders and the perceptions of an audience; a pioneering study of this kind has recently been completed in Slovenian prisons (Hacin and Mesko 2019).

A further crucial issue is to recognize that, in a given dialogue, either a powerholder or an audience member might fail to anticipate how others will respond to their actions, which means that legitimacy dialogues can be unpredictable. One example of this might be if a powerholder takes an inflexible attitude in a confrontation, and fails to recognize that the situation is escalating, due to the distress that this inflexibility is causing to the other party.[12] More generally, a police service in a given city might fail to recognize a growth in strength of a particular BLE, such as "no racial discrimination by police" or "the streets must be safe for women." While such intensity can evolve gradually, it is often triggered by rare and unexpected incidents, or what Nassim Taleb (2007) calls "black swan events." Recent examples of such events have been the murders by police officers of George Floyd in the United States in 2020, and of Sarah Everard in England in 2021.

A further dimension of unpredictability can arise from changes in the stances of the "third-party audiences" to which powerholders are accountable. For example, in James Jacobs's (1977) longitudinal study of Stateville Penitentiary, in Illinois, the courts altered their expectations about the nature of legitimate prison regimes, adopting a more "human rights" stance. However, the prison's warden failed to recognize the salience of this changed situation, and remained inflexible, leading to serious difficulties (see summary in Bottoms and Tankebe 2012, 167–168).

III. The Importance of Legitimacy to Powerholders and Citizens

We have so far explored legitimacy and its meaning. From a policy point of view, however, a question arises as to why legitimacy is an appropriate objective for social policy. Recalling that the 2015 President's Task Force described legitimacy as a "foundational principle" relevant to "both sides of the police/citizen divide," it is appropriate to take a closer look at why it might be seen as important by powerholders and by citizens.

A. Why Legitimacy Matters to Powerholders

Undoubtedly, some powerholders take issues of legitimacy seriously simply because, like the President's Task Force, they believe that it is of foundational normative importance. Others, however, value legitimacy for more instrumental reasons, and two reasons of this kind have been identified in the research literature. The first and primary such reason is that legitimacy is often seen as a mechanism that helps powerholders to promote voluntary compliance with laws and norms.

Given the dominance of procedural justice in much of the relevant literature, a hypothesis (H1) frequently addressed by researchers is a putative causal chain: "(Perceived) PJ [leads to] Legitimacy [leads to] Compliance." Walters and Bolger (2019) conducted a meta-analysis of studies of this hypothesis, using data from 95 samples. They found, in univariate analyses, a significant path from PJ to legitimacy, a significant path from legitimacy to compliance, and a significant path directly from PJ to compliance. However, many of the included studies were cross-sectional, and—as tests of H1—such studies are open to potential problems of bicausality. When, to avoid this problem, the authors restricted the analysis to studies using longitudinal data, it was found that "legitimacy *but not procedural justice* predicted compliance" (emphasis added), which suggested the need for scholars to identify "factors other than procedural justice that may serve as antecedents to legitimacy" (Walters and Bolger 2019, 359–360). A further implication of this analysis is, of course, that the concepts of legitimacy and compliance must always be treated as separate, and not conflated.

Experimental studies are also methodologically strong, but in relation to H1 they are few in number. In a randomized controlled trial, Mazerolle et al. (2012) found that motorists who interacted with Australian police officers trained to use a "procedural justice script" self-reported greater compliance with police directives than their counterparts in the control group; however, replications of this study have produced less positive results (for details, see Weisburd and Majmudar 2018, 240–242). More recently, Tankebe (2023) conducted an experimental vignette study in Ghana in which members of the public were randomly assigned to read procedurally just and unjust police-citizen interactions. Procedural justice was found to cause greater intended cooperation with the police,[13] and this result held even in situations in which there was social pressure against cooperation with the police. However, it also emerged that the ability of procedural justice to induce cooperation was weak when the suspect was an acquaintance or a family member; in such circumstances, the effects of PJ were diminished by the competing loyalties of prior social relationships.

In H1, the hypothesized mechanism is that if person D is treated with PJ by a powerholder, this will lead to D perceiving the powerholder as legitimate, and then complying. By contrast, although the *effectiveness* of powerholders is rightly seen as a generator of legitimacy, the mechanism in play here is more complex, because judgments of effectiveness may be made by any citizen, not just those in direct or vicarious contact with the powerholder. Indeed, it is easy to imagine a situation where a powerholder improves safety in a community by acting against those running an illegal activity (and thus causing resentment among those benefitting from the illegal activity) while simultaneously enjoying enhanced legitimacy among most residents.

It can also be a mistake to view the various potential generators of legitimacy (PJ, effectiveness, etc.) as operating singly. Strong evidence of this has arisen from important recent research on "focused deterrence" strategies in the United States. Traditional policies on deterrence, such as enhancing sentence lengths, have had a broad focus and have often been unsuccessful for various reasons, notably potential offenders' belief that they will be able to avoid detection (von Hirsch et al. 1999; Nagin 2013). "Focused deterrence" strategies have, instead, been targeted on limited groups of serious offenders, such as those prepared to use serious violence and those running drug markets.

Evaluation studies have shown this approach to be generally successful in reducing crime (see Braga and Kennedy 2020 for an excellent summary of the evidence). Interestingly, two of the key reasons for this success appear to be, first, "getting deterrence right," and secondly, a focus on "promoting legitimacy" (Braga and Kennedy 2020, 39–49). Elements of "getting deterrence right" include overcoming traditional weaknesses by (1) directly communicating with a particular group, emphasizing that if they continue with their activities they will encounter a strong response from law enforcement; and (2) placing more emphasis on certainty of detection rather than on severity of the sanction, given that the research literature has found the former to be clearly more effective.

Elements of "promoting legitimacy" include enhanced PJ and DJ when communicating with offender groups, including "treating them with respect; offering them protection and support; displaying empathy and compassion; . . . [and] admitting and even apologizing for past attitudes and actions . . . [including] the role of law enforcement in racial oppression" (Braga and Kennedy 2020, 47–48). Thus, focused deterrence aims to promote legitimacy *both* among the general community, by achieving a reduction in crime and an increase in safety (effectiveness), *and* among offenders, by greatly improving on the fairness of traditional policing by actively trying to achieve better procedural and distributive justice, while simultaneously making clear that the law will be enforced.

A second main reason why legitimacy can be attractive to powerholders is that it can sometimes serve as an instrument for justifying police actions. In a democracy, the police are understood to be, to an extent, "subservient" to the public (Herbert 2006), which requires them to be responsive to public demands. Hence, in community-oriented policing, the police work with local communities to identify priorities; they then work together to resolve them. However, tensions can sometimes emerge between community needs and what police consider to be appropriate priorities. Using data from in-depth interviews with police chiefs in England, Shannon (2022) found that these senior officers often held somewhat "confused" understandings of what legitimacy meant. Of particular interest to the author was the issue of public protection, especially of the vulnerable. While lip-service was paid to this concept as an important goal for achieving improved police legitimacy, it was shown that in practice this had sometimes evolved to become synonymous with chief officers' existing priorities; in other words, it became a "rhetorical self-justification to assert that chief officers' priorities serve a noble cause, or utilitarian greater good" (Shannon 2022, 211).

Where police managers hold a "hedgehog" view of legitimacy, with procedural justice as their "one big idea," there can be similar unfortunate distortions of the concept of legitimacy. This is because procedural justice focuses on *how* police conduct themselves rather than on *what* officers do, and the structural and situational conditions that shape their actions. Consequently, it can allow police managers to avoid thinking about substantive reforms, such as when a former Chicago police chief once told his officers that "it's not what you do, it's how you do it" (Thacher 2019, 98).

B. Why Legitimacy Matters to the Public

There has been little research attention on why legitimacy matters to the public. But a good starting point is again to be found in Bernard Williams's (2005) concept of a "basic legitimation expectation." In Williams's analysis, citizens in a democracy recognize that state authorities are needed to keep the peace, but they also know that authorities, once appointed or elected, can behave badly. So citizens, he suggests, have "legitimation expectations" about how authorities should behave if they are to be regarded as legitimate. We have identified empirically at least some of these "BLEs," but can we dig deeper and find a unifying theoretical thread that will help to explain why issues of legitimacy are so often seen as important by citizens?

We propose that the well-known "human development" or "capability" theoretical approach (see Robeyns and Byskov 2021 for a valuable overview) can supply this unifying thread, although in the space available we can discuss this only briefly. The "capability approach" was first fully developed by Amartya Sen (1999, 2009, Part III). Sen worked in the field of development economics and became convinced of the case for moving beyond aggregate indicators such as gross national product (GNP) and "using instead direct indicators of the quality of life and of the well-being and freedom" of individuals' lives (Sen 2009, 225).

The two core concepts in the capability approach are "functionings" and "capabilities." *Functionings* are "states . . . and activities that a person has achieved, such as being well-nourished, getting married, being educated" (Robeyns and Byskov 2021, 8), as well as being safe and "being able to take part in life of the community and having self-respect" (Sen 1999, 75). Many people, of course, want to develop their functionings more fully, for example by getting a more interesting job than the one they have at present. This usually requires appropriate opportunities, which a person might lack because of their background or because of social-structural impediments.

In the capability approach, people have a *capability* if they have "the substantive freedom to achieve alternative functioning combinations" (Sen 1999, 75). Sen argues that we cannot judge a person's capability by focusing on what they have done; we must focus on what a person "is in fact able to do, whether or not she chooses to make use of that opportunity" (Sen 2009, 235). Capability is, therefore, about *substantive freedoms*, which for some individuals will be extensive, but for others might be severely limited by current social arrangements.[14] For example, if a person's valued functioning is to be free from racial abuse, her well-being is undermined if there are no opportunities to safely report allegations of racial abuse. Or, if women greatly value the freedom to use public spaces, but fear for their safety prevents them from doing so, they would be said to have limited capability in this domain of their lives.

This analysis raises an issue about the ways in which capabilities can be turned into functionings—what Sen (1992) called "conversion factors." In a perceptive illustration, Robeyns and Byskov (2021, 21) note that we value bicycles not primarily because of how they are made or their color; we value them because they "take us to places where we want to go, and in a faster way than if we were walking." Thus, conversion factors (in this case, a bicycle) are facilitators or enablers of improved functioning. This has important implications for how we view (for example) policing. In a human development (or capability) approach to legitimacy, the police can be seen as having the power to act as a conversion factor; that is, some of their actions can help people to achieve things or states that they have a good reason to wish to be or to achieve (Sen 2009, 232). Therefore, when the police are corrupt or ineffective, they undermine this potential conversion role. When they engage in discriminatory practices, such as overpolicing and underprotection of a minority group, and when they violate people's sense of worth through behaviors that are disrespectful and undignified to citizens, they become a threat to individual functioning.

The person-centered focus of the capability approach means that it is well suited to understanding the importance of legitimacy from the perspective of citizens. Indeed, it allows us to understand more fully why people often have a strong emotional response to illegitimate policing, or to illegitimate staff practices in prisons. Such actions are a threat to capabilities and to what people value in some deep sense in relation to their functioning—life, dignity, bodily integrity and full membership in society (Nussbaum 2011).[15] A further advantage of the capability approach, in our view, is that it "is inescapably concerned with a plurality of different features of our lives and concerns . . . [given that the] human functioning[s] that we may value are very diverse" (Sen 2009, 233). This is congruent with a fox-like approach to legitimacy theory.

We must also note, however, that there is always a potential for conflict between powerholders' focus on institutional objectives (such as crime prevention) and citizens' needs for substantive freedoms to achieve valued functionings. For example, discriminatory police practices, such as the widespread use of "investigatory stops" on Black citizens reported by Epp, Maynard-Moody, and Haider-Markel (2014), might have prevented some crimes, yet they also undermined Black citizens' need for self-respect linked to equal treatment by the state. (For a similar UK example, see the report of a senior judge [Scarman 1981] in relation to some racially discriminatory policing in an inner-city area).

IV. Interventions to Improve Legitimacy

In this section, we examine research relating to some policy and practice interventions that have been introduced with the aim of improving legitimacy. We distinguish between two levels at which such policies and practices might be implemented: micro and macro.

A. Micro-Level Policies and Practices

The unit of intervention for micro-level initiatives is the individual powerholder. One example of such a policy is the training of police officers in procedural justice, with the aim of improving the quality of policing that citizens experience. Owens and colleagues (2018) randomly assigned police officers in Seattle to meet with supervisors to review a chosen interaction with civilians. Supervisors in a treatment group conducted the review in ways that mimicked elements of procedural justice. They were trained to encourage the officers to reflect on their decision-making processes and to explain how they handled the incident the way they did. The researchers found that supervisors can contribute to building a "better cop" by "treating police officers with the respect and the patience that is expected when officers interact with citizens" (Owens et al. 2018, 72–73). Specifically, such officers made fewer arrests, choosing instead to find other ways to resolve incidents. They were also less likely to be involved in incidents that required the use of force.

More recently, Weisburd et al. (2022) randomly assigned police officers in hot spots patrols in three US cities to receive procedural justice training. They found that, first, officers trained in procedural justice were more predisposed to listen to citizens, to avoid partial policing, and to treat citizens with respect. Second, citizens in hot spots where PJ-trained officers operated were less likely to perceive police harassment and unnecessary use of force.

A second example of a micro-level intervention concerns the adoption by police services of body-worn cameras (BWCs) as a potential way to create a more accountable, and therefore more legitimate, police service—although BWCs can also have instrumental benefits such as better evidence collection. A Campbell Systematic Review (Lum et al. 2020) assessed early research on the impacts of this technology; it found that there were no clear or consistent effects on most officer or citizen behaviors, and that there was not enough research to assess whether BWCs can strengthen police accountability or police-citizen relationships. More recently, however, Ariel et al. (2020) randomly assigned traffic officers in Uruguay to use BWCs on some shifts but not on others. The researchers were especially interested in the effect of the cameras on four generators of legitimacy—lawfulness, effectiveness, DJ, and PJ. Over a period of 10 months, drivers who interacted with the officers were contacted within 30 days to complete a telephone survey on their perceptions of the officers. Analyses showed that drivers who interacted with officers wearing cameras perceived greater police effectiveness, distributive justice, and procedural justice; however, there was no statistically significant impact on perceived lawfulness of policing (Ariel et al. 2020, 68). In New York, Braga, MacDonald, and McCabe (2022), also using a randomized design, found that officers wearing cameras received fewer complaints than others. They also complied better with mandates to document all stops, although these included unlawful stops. This suggests, as the authors argue, that cameras can provide police managers with crucial information on behaviors that threaten institutional legitimacy. However, Braga, MacDonald, and Barao (2023) found no evidence that the use of cameras can improve how citizens perceived the police. Thus, cameras appear to have different effects on "objective" and "subjective" measures of legitimacy.

B. Macro-Level Policies and Practices

Typically, macro-level policies seek a wider institutional redesign in order to repair legitimacy deficits. Consequently, they are often generated in response to significant misconduct—examples are court-mandated reforms or reforms arising from committees of inquiry. The consequences of these interventions on criminal justice agencies are often ignored in studies of legitimacy, although they can sometimes be more decisive for reforms than what decades of criminological research can achieve. By their nature, however, macro-level policy changes are not easily amenable to the experimental designs commonly used to test micro-level interventions.

An example of a court-mandated reform is the "consent decree" in the United States. Under the Violent Crime Control and Law Enforcement Act of 1994, the US Department of Justice can initiate a civil action to tackle "a pattern or practice of conduct by law enforcement officers or by officials . . . that deprives persons of rights, privileges, or immunities secured or protected by the Constitution or laws of the United States." Such civil actions usually lead to an agreement between the Justice Department and the relevant police department, which a court then approves (hence the name "consent decree"). According to Goh (2020, 901), these agreements represent "a disruption of usual practice in local departments, typically requiring that departments change policies, procedures, and training methods," so as to address the specific conduct problems identified. The research evidence shows mixed findings. Using open-sourced data, Goh found that consent decrees had no effects on police killings by municipal police departments. Powell, Meitl, and Worrall (2017), however, found that police departments subjected to consent decrees had fewer civil litigation suits filed against them after the implementation of the agreed policy changes.

Commissions of inquiry are a second form of macro-level intervention that seek to improve legitimacy, based on a review of the facts of institutional failures and various recommendations for reform. An important UK example is the MacPherson Inquiry (1999), which investigated the police response to the 1993 murder of a young Black man (Stephen Lawrence) in south London. A poorly handled police investigation and prosecution failed to achieve conviction of the suspects. Sustained pressure by the Lawrence family led to a commission of inquiry to investigate, inter alia, allegations of police racism. The commission found that police incompetence and "institutional racism" were the reasons for the failed prosecutions. More crucially for current purposes, it outlined 70 recommendations that have been implemented across all police forces in England and Wales. Among these are national targets to recruit and retain minority police officers, an independent police complaints body to investigate misconduct by individual police officers, and a change in an 800-year-old double jeopardy law to allow suspects to be retried for the same offense when certain conditions are met. These interventions have, at least partially, changed "the climate of policing," including police priorities and how they pursue them, and police relations with minority communities (Foster, Newburn, and Souhami 2005).

The distinction we have drawn between micro-level and macro-level interventions to promote legitimacy does not mean that these occupy different worlds. On the contrary, macro-level interventions can sometimes provide an impetus for criminological research at the micro level, and research evidence at the micro level can feed into macro-level interventions. A prime example of the latter is the adoption of BWCs by the New York Police Department. Over a 12-month period, researchers randomly assigned police officers of the Rialto Police Department (California) to wear body-worn cameras on some shifts but not others; they then tested the effects on police use of force and complaints against officers. The results showed that using the cameras reduced the likelihood of use-of-force and of complaints (Ariel, Farrar, and Sutherland 2015). Informed partly by these findings, a New York judge ordered the police to use body cameras in all cases where the police stopped and frisked citizens. The studies by Braga and colleagues (2022, 2023) were evaluations of the effects of the police implementation of this court-ordered intervention.

V. Principles to Guide Policies and Practice

In the invitation to contribute to this edited volume, the editors encouraged us to "highlight principles that could guide different types of criminal justice policies in improving legitimacy and, in turn, its role in improving a range of outcomes." As a first conceptual step toward this goal, we draw on the distinction made by Aristotle (2009, Book VI) between science and practical wisdom. Taylor (2005, 716) deftly summarizes Aristotle's concept of "practical wisdom" as "a true conception of the good life and the deliberative excellence necessary to realize that conception in practice via choices." As Aristotle emphasizes, "practice is concerned with particulars" (1141b), so practical wisdom requires sensitivity to the specific circumstances of each situation; yet the exercise of practical wisdom also requires a "capacity to act" in that situation in a way that will be "good for mankind" (1140b). He adds that this kind of practical wisdom can only be built up over time by experience (see also Scott 1998).

These observations are of special importance in the present context because, while criminologists (and scientists in general) can provide research-based knowledge about legitimacy, legitimate policies and practices can only be delivered by agents in the criminal justice system (practitioners)—and each of these vocations has its own skill set. Accordingly, criminologists should recognize, more than is presently the case, the value of practitioners' experiential knowledge and skills, and they should also refrain from over-claiming the extent of current research-based knowledge.

With these *caveats* in mind, we believe that the existing research base suggests some principles that are of potential relevance to the development of legitimacy-related policies and practices. We suggest five such principles, applicable both to agency managers and to front-line powerholders.

First, legitimacy should be addressed with a *plural* focus. This is for three reasons: (1) because attributions of legitimacy are always social, and can be influenced by macro-, meso- and micro-social contexts; (2) because citizens have basic legitimation expectations (BLEs) about how power should be exercised, and there is now extensive research evidence that BLEs are very often plural; and (3) because attention needs to be paid not only to audience legitimacy, but also to powerholders' self-legitimacy, given that there is some evidence that low self-legitimacy can have negative outcomes.

Second, legitimacy is always dialogic, and dialogues can develop in *unexpected* ways. This is because all parties to a dialogue have agency, and it is not uncommon for one party to fail to anticipate the response of another party. Powerholders, therefore, always need to "expect the unexpected."

Third, powerholders' recognition of the importance of citizens' BLEs needs to recognize that BLEs are linked to citizens' concerns about their *functioning* as members of society. Accordingly, dealing with citizens in legitimate rather than illegitimate ways will enhance their capability to achieve improved functioning.

Fourth, because legitimacy dialogues necessarily involve "particularities," and can develop in unexpected ways, handling them well requires a degree of *flexibility* by powerholders. As Miller (1978, 1172) pointed out, different people respond to powerholders in different ways, so "to maintain his authority, [an officer] has to develop flexible strategies." Failing to do so, and adopting a "one size fits all" approach, will normally be suboptimal (see again the Sandra Bland case, described in note 12).

Fifth, provided that a true conception of the good is maintained (see Taylor 2005), practical wisdom is enhanced by learning from experience. Given this, as Taleb (2012) has pointed out, mistakes and setbacks should be viewed positively, because learning from them will enhance future performance: we can describe this as a process of *self-schooling*.[16]

We have also identified two further important issues, relevant only to managers. First, when making changes, it is best to *take small steps* and *favor reversibility* (Scott 1998). In James Scott's (1998, 345) words, policymakers should "prefer wherever possible [to] take a small step, stand back, observe, and then plan the next step." Of course, evidence-based policy encourages criminal justice professionals to ground their initiatives in the best available research evidence. However, even where the evidence is compelling, it is difficult to predict all the consequences when such policies are put into practice in a specific context (in medical language, there can be unintended side effects). A step-by-step approach, therefore, allows criminal justice managers to monitor carefully the effects of their policy interventions—and, if necessary, reverse them. As an example, although hot spots policing has, in general, been found to reduce crime, Legewie and Fagan (2019) found that "aggressive, order-maintenance policing" at hot spots in New York had the unintended consequence of reducing educational outcomes for African American boys, raising questions about the legitimacy of the policy. In such situations, where short-term crime reduction potentially threatens longer-term functioning by citizens, reversibility needs to be a policy option.

The second issue for managers concerns *organizational structures*. Lawshe (2022, 5) has recently analyzed the adoption of BWCs by local police departments in the United States using the concept of "institutional perviousness," which includes both an organization's "susceptibility to environmental influence" and its "internal alignment with [a] proposed innovation." In a multivariate analysis, the author found that police departments with a higher perviousness rating were significantly more likely to adopt BWCs, even controlling for other covariates. This study therefore establishes the important point that institutional structures are relevant matters for study when considering issues relating to criminal justice legitimacy. At a more theoretical level, that point has been emphasized by Taleb (2007) with regard to "black swan events"—that is, unexpected events with a disproportionate impact on an organization.

Drawing on further work by Taleb (2012), it is perhaps possible to identify three types of organizational systems, differentiated by how well they can respond to serious but unexpected events, such as a fatal police shooting of an unarmed civilian, or a prison escape by a high-profile offender. Some organizations will have *fragile* legitimacy, and will therefore suffer when the unexpected occurs; some will be *resilient*, neither suffering nor gaining from black swan events; but a few may develop *anti-fragile* legitimacy characteristics—that is, they will have institutionalized a culture of learning from unforeseen events, and will therefore ultimately become stronger after the setback.

How best to develop resilient and anti-fragile criminal justice agencies seems likely to become an important topic for future research, and perhaps a good starting point for such a process will be to focus on developing organizational structures and practices that fully incorporate the principle of being ready for the unexpected, and that take seriously the research evidence on pluralism, functioning, flexibility, and self-schooling.

Acknowledgement

This chapter is dedicated to the memory of David Beetham whose work, especially *The Legitimation of Power*, has been of great influence on our approach to legitimacy in the context of criminal justice. We are grateful to Ryan Davenport for his comments on an earlier version of the chapter.

Notes

1. The key difference between distributive justice and procedural justice is that procedural justice is concerned with the fairness or otherwise of *processes*, whereas distributive justice concerns the fairness of *relative outcomes* (as discussed, for example, in Roger Hood's [1992] classic English study concerning whether offenders from different ethnic groups received similar sentences for similar crimes). However, distributive justice is not the only kind of justice concerned with outcomes. As the *Oxford Companion to Philosophy* explains: "Distributive justice concerns the ethical appropriateness of which recipients get which benefits and burdens. Retributive justice concerns the ethical appropriateness of punishment for wrongdoing. Corrective justice concerns the ethical appropriateness of compensating with some good because of a loss or appropriating some good because of a gain" (Sankowski 2005, 464). In a given situation, more than one of these various kinds of justice might, of course, be in play.
2. These elements of procedural justice are arguably foreshadowed in the strategy of community policing which "concerns changing decision-making processes and creating new

cultures within police departments" (Skogan 2019, 28; see also Weisburd and Majmundar 2018). One of its foundational elements is the building of strong relationships with local communities for the co-production of social order. This involves offering these communities a "voice" in identifying and responding to crime problems. It, therefore, involves *listening* to communities, demonstrating a commitment to their well-being and safety, and acting with overall civility (Skogan 2019).

3. For fuller discussion of the concept of a "basic legitimation expectation," see Bottoms and Tankebe (2017, 2021). Williams originally used the language of "basic legitimation demand" (BLD), but we argued in our 2021 paper that "expectation" was a more appropriate word.
4. The value of a dialogic framework for the study of legitimacy has been, in part, challenged by Martin and Bradford (2019, 569–572). Their argument is based on some misunderstanding of our position, but we cannot here enter into this debate.
5. "Third party" audiences can include not only official state bodies, but also—in some circumstances—civil society groups.
6. Many of the empirical studies cited in this and subsequent sections are based on survey data. Different studies have used varied survey items to measure "legitimacy," because legitimacy's core meaning of "moral affirmation of power as valid" is very difficult to capture in survey items. It is not practicable to discuss these variations within the scope of this chapter, so we have chosen to treat all purported measurements of legitimacy at face value.
7. These comments were made in a review of the classic policing study by William Ker Muir (1977). Muir identified four main role adaptations by police officers: "avoiders," "enforcers," "reciprocators," and "good policemen." He argued that these divergent adaptations developed early in an officer's career, in response to challenging situations encountered when on patrol.
8. In this study, there were no significant differences between White and African American officers.
9. We emphasize that this well-established result concerns *perceived* PJ. A further endorsement of the result has come from a committee of the US National Academies of Sciences, Engineering and Medicine, but that committee also concluded that "the research base is currently insufficient to draw conclusions about whether procedurally just policing causally influences either perceived legitimacy or cooperation" (Weisburd and Majmundar 2018, 248, Conclusion 6-4). The committee is here consciously drawing a distinction between "procedurally just policing" and "*perceived* procedurally just policing," reflecting the facts that: (i) there is at present a relative scarcity of studies of what the committee calls "objective" (i.e., researcher-assessed) PJ behavior by powerholders, and (ii) that the only study to date that has directly compared "objective" and "subjective" (i.e., citizen-assessed) powerholder PJ found only a "small, albeit statistically significant, correlation" between the two measures (240, citing Worden and McLean 2017). These are correct statements, but in our view they should not be seen as detracting from the strength of the evidence that perceived PJ usually leads to perceived legitimacy. Additionally, and in light of important research evidence that videos of real-life police behavior can be interpreted in widely divergent ways by different observers (Waddington and colleagues 2015, 2017), the committee's simple distinction between "objective" and "subjective" PJ should perhaps also be treated with caution.
10. Such examples illustrate why, as Beetham (2013a, 137) has emphasized, effectiveness is rightly seen as a normative as well as an instrumental matter, for "how can the . . . powers

11. For some readers, this phrase might sound like a version of procedural justice, because both "following the law" and procedural justice concern the manner in which criminal justice powerholders do their jobs. However, PJ theorists emphasize that PJ is about how citizens feel that they have been treated, which might or might not have much to do with the law. Thus, a powerholder's action can be legal but not procedurally just: an example would be if an arresting officer refuses to listen to a suspect on the street (thus denying him a "voice"), and insists that nothing is said until the formal interview in the police station (which the officer is legally entitled to do). Conversely, police officers can be perceived to be procedurally just even in circumstances where their actions are illegal, as shown in a recent research study (Tankebe, Boakye, and Amagnya 2020).
12. For example: after a traffic stop with, eventually, very unfortunate consequences, the driver (Sandra Bland) posed 34 questions to the police officer, all of which were met either with silence or with the single repeated reply "I'm giving you a lawful order." The dialogue showed a "lack of alignment between audience legitimacy and powerholder legitimacy" (Lowrey-Kinberg and Buker 2017, 403).
13. Note that "cooperation with police" (e.g. by supplying information) is not the same as compliance with law. Bolger and Walters (2019) carried out a meta-analysis of studies that measured PJ, legitimacy and cooperation with police, in addition to their meta-analysis relating to compliance with law (Walters and Bolger 2019). However, in the "cooperation" paper, there was a paucity of prospective studies meeting the criteria for inclusion in the analysis, which meant that "the causal direction of [the observed] relationships could not be tested" (98).
14. This account of the capability approach restricts itself to what Sen (2009, 232) calls an "informational focus in judging and comparing overall individual advantages"; it therefore "does not, on its own, propose any specific formula about how that information may be used." For a more substantive approach to capabilities, which is also of significant interest for legitimacy theory, see Nussbaum (2011).
15. This can be seen as an extension, within the broader context of legitimacy, of Tyler's (2006,175–176) theorization of procedural justice through the "group-value model."
16. For those who find mnemonics helpful, these five principles can be rendered as PUFFS (Pluralism, Unexpectedness, Functioning, Flexibility, and Self-Schooling).

References

Ariel, Barak, William A. Farrar, and Alex Sutherland. 2015. The effect of police body-worn cameras on use of force and citizens' complaints against the police: A randomized controlled trial. *Journal of quantitative criminology*, 31:509–535.

Ariel, Barak, Renee J. Mitchell, Justice Tankebe, Maria E. Firpo, Ricardo Fraiman and Jordan M. Hyatt. 2020. Using wearable technology to increase police legitimacy in Uruguay: The case of body-worn cameras. *Law & Social Inquiry*, 45:52–80.

Aristotle. 2009. *The Nicomachean ethics*. Edited by L Brown, translated by D Ross. Oxford: Oxford University Press.

Barker, Rodney. 2001. *Legitimating identities: Self-presentation of rulers and subjects*. Cambridge: Cambridge University Press.

Beetham, David. 2013a. *The legitimation of power* 2nd ed. Basingstoke, UK: Palgrave Macmillan.

Beetham, David. 2013b. Revisiting legitimacy, twenty years on. In *Legitimacy and criminal justice: An international exploration*, edited by Justice Tankebe and Alison Liebling, 19–36. Oxford: Oxford University Press.

Bell, Monica C. 2016. Situational trust: How disadvantaged mothers reconceive legal cynicism. *Law & Society Review*, 50:314–347.

Berlin, Isaiah. (1953) 2013. *The hedgehog and the fox*.2nd ed. Edited by H. Hardy, with additional contributions. Princeton NJ: Princeton University Press.

Bolger, Colin P., and Glenn D. Walters. 2019. The relationship between police procedural justice, police legitimacy and people's willingness to co-operate with law enforcement: A meta-analysis. *Journal of Criminal Justice*, 60:93–99.

Bottoms, Anthony E., and Justice Tankebe. 2012. Beyond procedural justice: A dialogic approach to legitimacy in criminal justice. *Journal of Criminal Law and Criminology*, 102:119–70.

Bottoms, Anthony E., and Justice Tankebe. 2013. "A voice within": Power-holders' perspectives on authority and legitimacy. In *Legitimacy and criminal justice: An international exploration*, edited by Justice Tankebe and Alison Liebling, 60–82. Oxford: Oxford University Press.

Bottoms, Anthony E., and Justice Tankebe. 2017. Police legitimacy and the authority of the state. In *Criminal law and the authority of the state*, edited by Antje du Bois-Pedain, Magnus Ulväng and Petter Asp, 47–88. Oxford: Hart.

Bottoms, Anthony E., and Justice Tankebe. 2021. Procedural justice, legitimacy and social contexts. In *Procedural justice and relational theory*, edited by Denise Meyerson, Catriona Mackenzie, and Therese MacDermott, 85–110. London: Routledge.

Bradford, Ben, Aziz Huq, Jonathan Jackson, and Benjamin Roberts. 2014. What price fairness when security is at stake?: Police legitimacy in South Africa. *Regulation and Governance*, 8:246–268.

Braga, Anthony A., and David M. Kennedy. 2020. *A framework for addressing violence and serious crime: Focused deterrence, legitimacy and prevention*. Cambridge: Cambridge University Press.

Braga, Anthony A., John M MacDonald, and Lisa M. Barao. 2023. Do body-worn cameras improve community perceptions of the police? Results from a controlled experimental evaluation. *Journal of Experimental Criminology*, 19:279–310.

Braga, Anthony A., John M. MacDonald and James McCabe. 2022. Body-worn cameras, lawful police stops, and NYPD officer compliance: A cluster randomized controlled trial. *Criminology*, 60:124–158.

Carrabine, Eamonn. 2005. Prison riots, social order and the problem of legitimacy. *British Journal of Criminology*, 45:896–913.

Epp, Charles R., Steven Maynard-Moody, and Donald P. Haider-Markel. H.2014. *Pulled over: How police stops define race and citizenship*, Chicago: University of Chicago Press.

Foster Janet, Tim Newburn, and Anna Souhami. 2005. *Assessing the impact of the Stephen Lawrence Inquiry*. Home Office Research Study No. 294 London: Home Office.

Goh, Li S. 2020. Going local: Do consent decrees and other forms of federal intervention in municipal police departments reduce police killings? *Justice Quarterly*, 37:900–929.

Hacin, Rok, and Gorazd Mesko.2019. *The dual nature of legitimacy in the prison environment*. Cham, Switzerland: Springer Nature.

Hacin, Rok, and Gorazd Mesko.2022. Self-legitimacy of police officers in Slovenia. *Policing: An International Journal*, 45:693–706.

Herbert, Steve. 2006. Tangled up in blue: conflicting paths to police legitimacy. *Theoretical Criminology*, 10:481–504.

Hood, Roger. 1992. *Race and sentencing*. Oxford: Clarendon Press.
Jackson, Jonathan. 2018. Norms, normativity and the legitimacy of justice institutions. *Annual Review of Social Science*, 14:145–165.
Jacobs, James B. 1977. *Stateville: The penitentiary in mass society*. Chicago: University of Chicago Press.
Kearns, Erin M, Emma Ashooh, and Belen Lowrey-Kinberg. 2020. Racial differences in conceptualizing legitimacy and trust in police. *American Journal of Criminal Justice*, 45:190–214.
Kyprianides, Arabella, Clifford Stott, and Ben Bradford. 2021. "Playing the game": Power, authority and procedural justice in interactions between police and homeless people in London. *British Journal of Criminology*, 61:670–689.
Lawshe, Nathaniel. 2022. Investigating the influence of institutional perviousness on the adoption of body-worn cameras by United States police agencies. *Criminal Justice Studies*, 35:1–17.
Legewie, Joscha, and Jeffrey Fagan. 2019. Aggressive policing and the educational performance of minority youth. *American Sociological Review*, 84:220–247.
Liebling, Alison. 2015. Description at the edge: I-it/I-thou relations and action in prisons research. *International Journal for Crime, Justice and Social Democracy*, 4:18–32.
Liebling, Alison. 2022. Penal legitimacy, well-being and trust: The role of empirical research in "morally serious" work. In *Crime, justice and social order: Essays in honour of A. E. Bottoms*, edited by Alison Liebling, Joanna Shapland, Richard Sparks and Justice Tankebe, 273–303. Oxford: Oxford University Press.
Lowrey-Kinberg, Belen, and Grace C. Buker. 2017. "I'm giving you a lawful order": Dialogic legitimacy in Sandra Bland's traffic stop. *Law and Society Review*, 51:379–412.
Lum, Cynthia, Christopher S. Koper, David B. Wilson, Megan Stoltz, Michael Goodier, Elizabeth Eggins, Angela Higginson, and Loraine Mazerolle. 2020. Body-worn cameras' effects on police officers and citizen behavior: A systematic review. *Campbell Systematic Reviews* 16:e1112.
Macpherson Inquiry. 1999. *The Stephen Lawrence Inquiry: Report of an inquiry by Sir William Macpherson of Cluny*. Cm 4262. London: The Stationery Office.
Martin, Richard, and Ben Bradford. 2019. The anatomy of police legitimacy: Dialogue, power and procedural justice. *Theoretical Criminology*, 25:559–577.
Mazerolle, Loraine, Sarah Bennett, Emma Antrobus, and Elizabeth Eggins. 2012. Procedural justice, routine encounters and citizen perceptions of police: Main findings from the Queensland Community Engagement Trial (QCET). *Journal of Experimental Criminology*, 8:343–367.
Mehozay, Yoav, and Roni Factor. 2017. Deeply embedded core normative values and legitimacy of law enforcement authorities. *Journal of Research in Crime and Delinquency*, 54:151–180.
Miller, Wilbur R. 1978. Review of *Police: Streetcorner politicians* by W. K. Muir. *Journal of American History*, 64:1172.
Muir, William K. 1977. *Police: Streetcorner politicians*. Chicago: University of Chicago Press.
Nagin, Daniel. 2013. Deterrence in the twenty-first century. In Crime and Justice in America 1975–2005, edited by Michael Tonry. Special issue, Crime and Justice: A Review of Research, 42:199–263.
Natapoff, Alexandria. 2006. Underenforcement. *Fordham Law Review*, 75:1715–1776.
National Academies. 2022. *Developing practices that build legitimacy*. Washington, DC: National Academies Press.

Nix, Justin, and Scott E. Wolfe. 2017. The impact of negative publicity on police self-legitimacy. *Justice Quarterly*, 34:84–108.

Nussbaum, Martha C. 2011. *Creating capabilities*. Cambridge MA: Harvard University Press.

Owens, Emily, David Weisburd, Karen L. Amendola, and Geoffrey P. Alpert. 2018. Can you build a better cop? Experimental evidence on supervision, training, and policing in the community. *Criminology & Public Policy*, 17:41–87.

Powell, Zachary A., Michele B. Meitl, and John L. Worrall. 2017. Police consent decrees and Section 1983 civil rights litigation. *Criminology & Public Policy*, 16:575–605.

President's Task Force on 21st Century Policing. 2015. *Final report*. Washington DC: Office of Community Oriented Policing Services.

Radburn, Matthew, and Clifford Stott. 2018. The social psychological processes of procedural justice: Concepts, critiques and opportunities. *Criminology and Criminal Justice*, 19:421–438.

Reus-Smit, Christian. 2007. International crises of legitimacy. *International Politics*, 44:157–174.

Robeyns, Ingrid, and Morten F. Byskov. 2021. The capability approach. In *Stanford encyclopedia of philosophy*, edited by E. N. Zalta. Winter 2021 edition. Stanford, CA: Stanford University. https://plato.stanford.edu/entries/capability-approach/.

Sankowski, Edward T. 2005. Justice. In *The Oxford companion to philosophy*, edited by Ted Honderich, 463–464. 2nd ed. Oxford: Oxford University Press.

Savigar-Shaw, Leanne, Matthew Radburn, Clifford Stott, Arabella Kyprianides, and Deborah Tallent. 2022. Procedural justice as a reward to the compliant: An ethnography of police-citizen interaction in police custody. *Policing and Society*, 32:778–793.

Scarman, Lord. 1981. *The Brixton Disorders, 10–12 April 1981*. Cmnd 8427. London: Her Majesty's Stationery Office.

Scott, James C. 1990. *Domination and the arts of resistance: Hidden transcripts*. New Haven, CT: Yale University Press.

Scott, James C. 1998. *Seeing like a state: How certain schemes to improve the human condition have failed*. New Haven, CT: Yale University Press.

Sen, Amartya.1992. *Inequality re-examined*. Oxford: Clarendon Press.

Sen, Amartya.1999. *Development as freedom*. New York: Knopf Press.

Sen, Amartya.2009. *The idea of justice*. London: Allen Lane.

Shannon, Ian.2022. *Chief police officers' stories of legitimacy: Power, protection, consent and control*. Basingstoke, UK: Palgrave Macmillan.

Skogan, Wesley. 2019. Advocate: Community policing. In *Police innovation: Contrasting perspectives*, edited by David Weisburd and Anthony A. Braga, 27–44. Cambridge: Cambridge University Press.

Taleb, Nassim N. 2007. *The black swan: The impact of the highly improbable*. New York: Random House.

Taleb, Nassim N. 2012. *Antifragile: Things that gain from disorder*. New York: Random House.

Tankebe, Justice. 2009. Public cooperation with the police in Ghana: Does procedural fairness matter? *Criminology*, 47:1265–1293.

Tankebe, Justice. 2013. Doing things differently: The dimensions of public perceptions of police legitimacy. *Criminology*, 51:103–135.

Tankebe, Justice. 2023. Moral contexts of procedural (in)justice effects on public cooperation with police: A vignette experimental study. In *Exploring contemporary police challenges*, edited by Sanja K. Ivković, Jon Maskály, Christopher M. Donner, Irena C. Mraović, and Dilip Das, 19–33. New York: Routledge.

Tankebe, Justice. 2022. Rightful authority: Exploring the structure of police self-legitimacy. In *Crime, justice and social order: Essays in honour of A. E. Bottoms*, edited by Alison

Liebling, Joanna Shapland, Richard Sparks and Justice Tankebe, 335–354. Oxford: Oxford University Press.

Tankebe, Justice, Kofi E. Boakye, and Moses A. Amagnya. 2020. Traffic violations and cooperative intentions among drivers: The role of corruption and fairness. *Policing and Society*, 30:1081–1096.

Taylor, Christopher C. W. 2005. Phronesis. In *The Oxford companion to philosophy*, edited by Ted Honderich, 716. 2nd ed. Oxford: Oxford University Press.

Thacher, David. 2019. The limits of procedural justice. In *Police innovation: Contrasting perspectives*, edited by David Weisburd and Anthony A. Braga, 95–118. Cambridge: Cambridge University Press.

Trinkner, Rick, Jonathan Jackson, and Tom R. Tyler. 2019. Bounded authority: "Appropriate" police behavior beyond procedural justice. *Law and Human Behavior*, 42:280–293.

Trinkner, Rick, Erin M. Kerrison, and Phillip A. Goff. 2019. The force of fear: Police stereotype threat, self-legitimacy and support for excessive force. *Law and Human Behavior*, 43:421–435.

Tyler, Tom R. 2006. *Why people obey the law*. 2nd ed. New Haven, CT: Yale University Press. Princeton, NJ: Princeton University Press.

Tyler, Tom R., and Tracey L. Meares. 2019. Procedural justice in policing. In *Police innovation: Contrasting perspectives*, edited by David Weisburd and Anthony A. Braga, 71–94. Cambridge: Cambridge University Press.

Von Hirsch, Andrew, Anthony E. Bottoms, Elizabeth Burney, and Per-Olof H. Wikström. 1999. *Criminal deterrence and sentence severity*. Oxford: Hart.

Waddington, Peter A. J., Kate Williams, Martin Wright, and Tim Newburn. 2015. Dissension in public evaluations of the police. *Policing and Society*, 25:212–223.

Waddington, Peter A. J., Martin Wright, Kate Williams, and Tim Newburn. 2017. *How people judge policing*. Oxford: Oxford University Press.

Walters, Glenn D., and Colin P. Bolger. 2019. Procedural justice perceptions, legitimacy beliefs and compliance with the law: A meta-analysis. *Journal of Experimental Criminology*, 15:341–372.

Weber, Max. (1922) 1978. *Economy and society*. Edited by G Roth and C Wittich. Berkeley: University of California Press.

Weisburd, David, and Malay K. Majmundar, eds. 2018. *Proactive policing: Effects on crime and communities*. Washington DC: National Academies Press.

Weisburd, David, Cody W. Telep, Heather Vovak, Taryn Zastrow, Anthony A. Braga, and Brandon Turchan. 2022. Reforming the police through procedural justice training: A multicity randomized trial at crime hot spots. *Proceedings of the National Academy of Sciences*, 119:e2118780119.

Williams, Bernard. 2005. *In the beginning was the deed: Realism and moralism in political argument*. Princeton, NJ: Princeton University Press.

Worden, Robert E., and Sarah J. McLean. 2017. *Mirage of police reform: Procedural justice and police legitimacy*. Oakland, CA: University of California Press.

CHAPTER 13

EVIDENCE-BASED POLICING

CYNTHIA LUM AND CHRISTOPHER S. KOPER

NOTE: This chapter draws extensively from *Evidence-Based Policing: Translating Research into Practice* by Cynthia Lum and Christopher Koper (Oxford University Press, 2017).

IN an address to the National Police Foundation[1] in 1998, Lawrence Sherman was likely the first to articulate the principles of evidence-based policing. He asserted that "police practices should be based on scientific evidence about what works best" (Sherman 1998, 2), explaining that police should strive to use the results of scientifically rigorous evaluations of law-enforcement tactics, strategies, and policies to guide decisions. In addition, he argued that law enforcement officials should generate and apply analytical and research knowledge from internal and external sources and track and test activities for their effects (see also Sherman 2013). Evidence-based policing, Sherman argued, could improve feedback systems in police practice, thereby facilitating a dynamic learning process and ultimately progress toward the goals and mandates of police in democracies.

Since Sherman's definition was articulated, various meanings have been attributed to evidence-based policing by advocates and skeptics alike. Here, we use a broad and holistic definition: evidence-based policing includes efforts to generate and improve the supply, demand for, and use of scientific knowledge in policing, as well as the processes and techniques that link the supply of research with its implementation. These efforts include translating research knowledge into digestible and usable forms, building receptivity toward science within police agencies and the communities in which they operate, and institutionalizing knowledge and scientific processes into police practices and decision-making.

Within a democratic framework, such efforts are not owned, determined, or led only by the police. Instead, various actors, including researchers, practitioners, citizens, community groups, students of policing, philanthropists, government bureaucrats, and others engage in evidence-based policing in dynamic and varied ways, and preferably in partnership. For example, researchers may help generate knowledge through evaluations and analyses that they conduct through partnerships with police and communities. But they also might help to institutionalize the use of research through developing academy curricula or training officers in the field on specific approaches. Police officers may be trained on implementing evidence-based approaches, or they might play the researcher role in testing and evaluating strategies, as many Evidence-Based Policing Hall of Fame inductees have done.[2] Community members may provide feedback on policing interventions or help develop new programs. Government organizations might fund research efforts, create requirements for agencies to engage in evidence-based policing, or facilitate training and technical assistance associated with research findings. In this sense, evidence-based policing is neither a tactic nor a strategy, but rather a paradigm of policing that encompasses the actors and activities within its enterprise.

Some or all of these definitions might sound strange to a casual observer of policing. Wouldn't the police already use the best approaches to prevent, reduce, detect, and deter crime and disorder and maintain trust and confidence in the community? There are multiple challenges to answering this question. Significant barriers may exist to adjusting police organizations to align with knowledge about effective and legitimate policing. Most fundamentally, police officers, supervisors, detectives, and police leaders may not be aware of this research evidence, as it may not be taught in academies, field training, or in-service training. Additionally, police agencies, officers, and community members sometimes disagree about police responsibilities and mandates. Much of the research on evidence-based policing stems from a democracy-grounded view of what policing should be (e.g., protecting the public, following the rule of law, gaining legitimacy from the public). Yet some officers (or community members) may not believe that it is the job of law enforcement to prevent or reduce crime or to satisfy citizen concerns. Law enforcement agencies may also have little to no incentive to follow science, and they may believe that scientific knowledge is inferior to police experience or "craft" knowledge. Community members may also reject or ignore science in favor of advocacy or political ideologies.

These challenges also exist in fields where it may seem science would play a prominent role—including the public health and medical fields, as Sherman (1998) has detailed. Like other public service organizations, law enforcement agencies are complicated systems constrained and shaped by rules, technologies, resources, politics, emotions, incentives, mythology and traditions, and individual experiences. Adjusting the philosophy and culture of policing to embrace a more evidence-based approach may require fundamental changes in long-standing practices deeply embedded within the organization.

This chapter describes evidence-based policing and contrasts it with the standard model of policing and alternatives to the standard model, such as community- and problem-oriented policing. We then turn our attention to changes in policing necessary to institutionalize and sustain an evidence-based approach. Although we highlight several findings from research on police crime prevention strategies, our primary intent is not to survey the field of police research. Instead, we seek to highlight the more neglected but critical issue of making police practice more evidence-based by translating research for practice, building receptivity to research in policing, institutionalizing evidence-based practices, and applying evidence-based policing to current challenges in police reform.

I. A Starting Point: The "Standard" or "Traditional" Model of Policing

To understand evidence-based policing and the challenges to its implementation, one needs to understand the current approach to policing and what drives decision-making within that approach. A helpful place to begin is to describe the "standard" model of policing, sometimes referred to as the "traditional," "professional," or "reactive" model. This model continues to be the dominant model of policing in the United States and the United Kingdom (Lum and Koper 2017). Even though other models have been introduced (community policing, problem-oriented policing, intelligence-led policing, predictive policing, legitimacy policing, etc.), the standard model remains deeply ingrained in police training, deployment, supervision, management, technology, leadership, and accountability. Describing it helps to compare, contrast, and understand various challenges to reforms and innovations in policing, including evidence-based policing.

The standard model can best be described by detailing the daily activities of patrol officers, which are the primary source from which other core characteristics and cultures of police organizations emerge. Patrol officers are usually assigned to a geographic area (e.g., a beat, post, or sector) where they are responsible for handling calls for service and other responsibilities throughout their shift. Their primary responsibility is responding to calls for service from people who call both emergency (e.g., 911, 999) and nonemergency numbers to report crimes, suspicious behavior, and other complaints and concerns. To handle each call, officers apply their training, rules of criminal procedures, different technologies available to them, standard operating procedures of their organization, legally derived force and authority, past experiences, personal knowledge, and information obtained from the situation itself. It is important to note that most service requests from people do not result in a formal law enforcement action (e.g., report, arrest, citation). The vast majority of calls for police service are not reporting high-priority crimes in progress, but more mundane conflicts, disorders, suspicions, traffic problems, or minor offenses (Lum, Koper, and Wu 2022). Thus, policies, laws, and procedures are often *not* formally applied in many call responses, and officers have a great deal of discretion in handling individual calls for service. Even when a crime has been committed, officers can sometimes choose whether or not to make an arrest or invoke the law.

No matter what other tasks officers are assigned or decide to undertake during their patrol shift, the reaction to citizen calls for service is the backbone of modern policing. Therefore, a great deal of training and standard operating procedures are focused on this reactive response. In addition, detective work extends from this reactive, case-by-case response to calls for service for a small subset of these calls, selected for additional investigation (Bayley 1994). However, although responding to 911 calls dominates officer activity, it is not everything that uniformed officers do. In places with low crime rates, an officer might only receive one or two calls for service per day. However, even in the most populated and high-crime-rate jurisdictions, calls for service are separated by sometimes brief and sometimes lengthy periods of time. This "noncommitted time," as Kelling et al. (1974) referred to it in their landmark Kansas City Preventive Patrol Experiment, is the period between calls for service when an officer is not doing any business related to a particular call or other administrative duty. Empirical estimates of noncommitted time are surprisingly high. Noncommitted time can range from 25% (Weisburd et al. 2015) to as much as 80% of an officer's day, with most estimates in the range of 40% to 80% (Famega 2005; Famega, Frank, and Mazerolle 2005; Lum et al. 2020).

In the standard model of policing, officers' behaviors during both committed and noncommitted times are marked by two characteristics: high levels of discretion and low levels of supervision. Noncommitted time varies considerably from officer to officer, squad to squad, and agency to agency. Compared to officer responses to calls for service, there is even much less (if any) guidance on how officers should spend noncommitted time. At a minimum, officers may be expected to carry out preventive patrol in their areas of responsibility to create a sense of police "omnipresence" to try and deter crime. However, officers may also accompany other officers on their calls, proactively seek out criminal offending, patrol high-crime areas, talk to community members, stop suspicious people and vehicles, check in with local businesses, write reports, carry out other administrative duties, run personal errands, or do nothing and wait for the next call for service. In an empirical analysis of four agencies, Lum et al. (2020) found that officers primarily spend this noncommitted time on two activities: traffic stops and unstructured, generalized place-based patrol as they wait for the next call. The choice, frequency, and types of activities officers engage in during their noncommitted time depend almost entirely on individual officer discretion. There is also little supervision of this discretionary activity in the standard model. As Lum et al. (2020) also found, first-line supervisors play passive roles in guiding officers' everyday work, either when they are responding to calls for service or during their noncommitted time. Supervision is also reactive in the standard model and may only be activated if an officer requests help, gets into an accident, commits use of force, or does something that requires a supervisor's report.

This high level of discretion and low level of supervision in the standard model reflects and contributes to a decision-making approach that highly values individual experience, traditions, hunches, feelings, and, as it is sometimes characterized, the "craft" of policing. Scientific knowledge—that is, information derived from systematic analysis or evaluation—plays a minor role, if any, in this paradigm (outsider knowledge and information more generally is devalued in the standard model). For example, responses to 911 calls and the managing of calls through discretion are not carried out in a particular way because of a solid link to the effectiveness of such approaches in reducing calls for service, preventing crime, or apprehending offenders. Rather, they are shaped by standard operating procedures, the associated policies that dispatch officers to those events, officers' past experiences, and sometimes by citizen demands. Generalized patrol during noncommitted times is based on academy-taught beliefs of "omnipresence" and beat-level responsibility, not necessarily on scientific knowledge about how deterrence works at geographic crime concentrations. In addition, many agencies' current approach to criminal investigations is strongly tied to policy, procedures, and investigative traditions rather than scientifically derived knowledge about effective investigative practices (see Lum et al. 2023; Prince, Lum, and Koper 2021).

Because this approach to policing is so dominant and ingrained in officers who share these experiences, these characteristics of the standard and reactive model permeate and shape other systems within policing. They are, at the same time, fostered and nurtured by them. These systems include academy and post-academy "field" or "in-service" training; incentives, promotions, and rewards; management, supervision, and accountability;

technology and reporting mechanisms; and leadership. Within all of these systems, personal experience, beliefs about craft and what it means to be a "good officer," and how long officers have been in the profession are highly valued measures of competence, as is knowledge of procedures, laws, and policies related to reactive policing activities.

II. Alternatives to the Standard Model and Where Evidence-Based Policing Fits

Because of its dominance, the standard model of policing is often viewed as the "basic" model of policing—necessary at a minimum, or perhaps one that is so dominant that it would be hard to imagine policing any other way. However, in the late 1970s and into the 1980s, policing practice and research discovered limitations in the standard model. Fast response to 911 calls did not seem to help apprehend suspects or even prevent crime (Sherman and Eck 2002; Spelman and Brown 1981). Random preventive patrols by officers also did not seem to deter crime (Kelling et al. 1974; Police Foundation 1981; Trojanowicz 1986; Sherman and Weisburd 1995). Strong links between reactive arrest and crime rates were also not found (see reviews by Nagin 1998, 2013; Sherman and Eck 2002). In the case of some offenders, such as juveniles or unemployed domestic abusers, an arrest may potentially *increase* offending (Klein 1986; Sherman et al. 1991, 1992; Smith and Gartin 1989).

These limitations, as well as public protests about heavy-handed and discriminatory police activity in the 1960s and 1970s, led to the emergence of alternatives to the standard model. For example, community policing calls for the police to be responsive to community members and value their input and participation in prioritizing and directing police operations and resources (Mastrofski 1998; Mastrofski, Worden, and Snipes 1995; Skogan 2004; Skogan and Hartnett 1997; Skolnick 1999; Trojanowicz 1994). While responding to 911 calls and arresting offenders may still be necessary, community policing emphasizes that police must be accountable, transparent, open, responsive, reliable, and fair (Mastrofski 1999). Within a community-oriented policing model, officers are expected to use their noncommitted time to strengthen relationships with citizens through such activities as attending community meetings, engaging with community leaders or groups, conducting follow-up visits with victims or witnesses, or addressing quality-of-life problems.

Another alternative approach was problem-oriented policing (POP), first articulated by Herman Goldstein (1979, 1990). The POP model questions the focus on responding to individual calls for service on a case-by-case basis, arguing that these calls in combination signal broader underlying community problems. Therefore, problem-solving policing stresses analyzing calls and incidents to detect underlying problems that can be addressed proactively. Eck and Spelman (1987) explain this process through their "SARA" model—"scanning," "analysis," "response," and "assessment." Much of the "response" in POP is based on the premise that crime can be averted by changing malleable features of the social or physical environment or by changing social routines that contribute to crime opportunities (see discussions in Brantingham and Brantingham 1993; Clarke and Cornish 1985; Felson 1994). For example, these changes might include improving lighting, closing problem bars, increasing video surveillance, or even adjusting the spatial and temporal patterns of police patrol to tackle hot spots. They are also linked to what Mazerolle and Ransley (2005) describe as "third-party policing," in which police work with regulatory authorities to address problem issues in the social and physical environment (see also Buerger and Mazerolle 1998).

A more recent alternative to the standard model is intelligence-led policing. Ratcliffe (2008) states the concept was first conceived and operationalized in the United Kingdom (see HMIC 1997). He defines intelligence-led policing as efforts that focus on targeting serious offenders, triaging crime problems, making greater use of surveillance and informants, and, most importantly, making intelligence central to decision-making (see Ratcliffe 2008, 83–84). Ratcliffe argues that the meaning of intelligence-led policing has broadened over time and encompasses a managerial strategy that emphasizes information analysis, sharing, and use to develop strategies to address policing problems. Intelligence-led policing differs from the standard model in that it uses a managerial approach grounded in information and analysis rather than call and case response. Management models such as CompStat[3] or predictive policing[4] arguably fall under the broader umbrella of intelligence-led policing, with their heavy emphasis on crime analysis, computerized mapping, and data to manage police operations.

We mention these other alternatives to make three critical points. First, the standard model of policing is not the only way the police can do business. Indeed, the goal of these alternatives is to reduce calls for service and reactive arrests in the first place through preventive interventions, thereby reducing the heavy reliance on the standard model.

Second, the standard model of policing may not even be the "best" approach to policing, despite its dominance. By saying "best," we encourage the reader to think about a broad range of outcomes sought by the police and the public. These include crime prevention, improving people's trust and confidence in the police, detecting and catching offenders, protecting community members' rights, reducing disparity or mistreatment, improving clearance rates, strengthening collective police efficacy in the community, or even improving police officer job satisfaction and professional development. Several tactics in the standard model may not be the best approach to achieve these goals. As the National Academies of Sciences concluded in two ad hoc consensus committees on effective policing strategies (National Research Council 2004; National Academy of Sciences 2018), there is now empirical evidence that the mainstays of the standard model are not strongly linked either to crime control outcomes or to improving community members' trust and confidence in the police.

Finally, the third and most provocative point: despite the emergence of these alternatives, none have been able to dethrone the standard model from its dominance in policing. These alternatives became secondary to the standard model rather than replacements. They reflected new ways of thinking, valued outsider knowledge, and required institutional adjustments to policing that needed substantial resources and buy-in from police agencies and communities. Many new approaches implicated significant challenges and ideas that went against the grain of the standard model's approach and philosophy and that often did not arise from within law enforcement circles. Given the substantial weight that police in the standard model place on their own experience, discretion, and internally derived procedures, many of these alternatives were viewed suspiciously by the police and sometimes also by citizens, who did not trust the police enough to participate themselves in some of these alternatives.

Is evidence-based policing, then, just another alternative? The answer is both "yes" and "no." Yes, evidence-based policing is an alternative to the standard model because it values an alternative method of decision-making—one based on research, analysis, evaluation, and science—to inform the daily activities, tactics, internal policies, and short- and long-term strategies of policing. Further, as Sherman (1998, 5) asserts, evidence-based policing is different from other alternative models, as it is the only model that "contains the principles for its own implementation." In other words, Sherman notes that evidence-based policing "contains a principle for both changing practices and measuring the success of those changes with risk-adjusted outcomes research" (5). At the same time, evidence-based policing is not an alternative. Why? Like some models (especially community policing), evidence-based policing recognizes that there are needs, interests, input, and knowledge that police must respond to from outside the policing profession. Moreover, evidence-based policing can encompass tactics, strategies, and perspectives of community policing, problem-solving, intelligence-led policing, predictive policing, managerial innovations (e.g., CompStat), or even elements of the standard model itself. The main difference, though, is the grounding of these approaches in research to guide and evaluate them.

In short, evidence-based policing is an approach to law enforcement that suggests that if a particular policing model, action, strategy, tactic, or internal managerial approach will be used to achieve an outcome (whatever that outcome is), then those actions should be demonstrably connected to the desired outcomes. The connection should not be based on guessing, anecdotal experience, or gut feelings, as these may be wrong or biased. Instead, experience, anecdotes, and gut feelings need to be tested. Thus, determining the connection between actions and outcomes requires research, analysis, evaluation evidence, and empirical information. If, for example, we plan to use community meetings to improve police-community relationships and reduce fear of crime, we should do so because there is reliable evidence that meetings achieve these goals. If not, then resources should be spent on other community engagement activities that *do* improve police-community relationships and reduce fear. Likewise, if we believe hiring more educated officers will reduce officer use of force or citizen complaints, we should have some assurance this will happen before we limit ourselves to hiring only college-educated officers. An even more contemporary example: if we want to remove the police from specific responsibilities and give those activities to another social service to fulfill, we need to understand whether these other social services can effectively provide those services. (See Lum and Koper [2017, Chapter 2] and Mears [2010] for further discussions of the types of analyses that can support evidence-based practices in policing and criminal justice.)

More generally, evidence-based policing reflects a value in modern democracies that there must be empirical justification and evaluative and objective accountability for governmental actions and spending (Chalmers 2003; Mears 2010; National Research Council 2004; Sherman 2003; Sherman et al. 2002). As Dewey (1954) asserts, policy proposals are testable hypotheses, which should be subjected to evaluation and flexible to adjustment and learning. An evidence-based approach challenges the internal use of perceived best practices, consensus-based decision-making, traditions, and reliance on experience, emotions, hunches, and gut feelings, which have been dominant forces behind police decision-making. Not only have these approaches sometimes failed to connect actions with outcomes, but they also are susceptible to bias, nearsightedness, cronyism, or other negatives that can unintentionally harm community members and officers. These approaches also do not reflect objective accountability principles of democratic governance.

III. Achieving Evidence-Based Policing

As we emphasized at the beginning, we take the definition of evidence-based policing further: Evidence-based policing doesn't just require the generation and use of research knowledge to guide decision-making. It also includes the processes and efforts used to make that information digestible, translate it into usable forms, and incorporate and institutionalize it into regular systems of policing. Unfortunately, knowledge rarely stands on its own merits, and this is especially the case in policing. The heavy reliance on tradition and personal experience to inform decision-making challenges the legitimacy and role of science in policing. Even if scientific findings are accepted as legitimate, there are language, experience, and expectation gaps between those who generate research and those who could use that research that challenge research translation and use.

Take, for example, proactive, directed patrol. We now have a great deal of research evidence, amassed since the 1980s, which suggests that when police proactively target specific high-crime places or high-risk people with problem-solving and deterrence measures, they can reduce crime at those places or among those individuals (National Research Council 2004; National Academy of Sciences 2018). However, patrol practice is focused much more on reactive response to 911 calls for service, not proactive patrol activities in-between calls for service. Even when police agencies and their leaders accept the principles behind proactive and focused policing efforts, adjusting everyday deployment to better align with this evidence can be challenging. Patrol officers need training and supervision to carry out effective interventions and understand the negative consequences that might arise from these types of deployment approaches (i.e., disparity, use of force, ineffectiveness, increases in minor arrests that may clog the jails). Daily patrol and investigative deployments would have to be redeveloped to reflect this knowledge, requiring less emphasis on responding to calls for service and greater emphasis on activities during an officer's noncommitted time. Because training alone is rarely enough to change behavior, first-line supervisors have to consistently hold officers accountable to these deployment changes and guide them in effectively using their time in-between calls. Crime analysis has to be generated and disseminated to officers to know where and when to patrol or upon whom to carry out focused deterrence efforts. These efforts also require well-developed information technology and reporting systems so that activities during noncommitted time can be tracked and evaluated for effectiveness, an essential element of evidence-based policing (Sherman 2013). Officers and communities also have to create systematic feedback and collaboration approaches to better understand and tackle specific problems at specific places.

As this example illustrates, achieving evidence-based policing requires meeting several conditions. In particular, three essential and related activities are needed: *translation, receptivity,* and *institutionalization* (Lum and Koper 2017). Research studies are often written in forms that are not police-friendly and emphasize scientific aspects that may be of little interest to patrol commanders working on deployment operations or community members concerned about police activities. Therefore, research needs to be translated into digestible forms that are both understandable and applicable to contemporary law enforcement and community concerns. Even when research is translated, law enforcement agents need to be receptive to findings, which requires much more than winning officers' hearts and minds. Receptivity entails educational, structural, and cultural adjustments in law enforcement agencies that encourage officers and agencies to be amenable to such knowledge. Receptivity and translation are, in turn, related to institutionalization, which requires fundamental adjustments to an organization's systems and infrastructures, such as those mentioned in our directed patrol example. Each of these is described below.

A. Translation

An essential step toward evidence-based policing is translating existing research into digestible forms that law enforcement officers and community members can operationalize (Lum 2009). Research products such as peer-reviewed publications and technical reports to grant sponsors are not translations but extensive displays and explanations of research activities for academic, research, or policy audiences and purposes. To achieve translation, research has to be distilled down to its most essential descriptions and findings and then interpreted for operational activities that make sense to practitioners. Further, because several studies of a similar intervention may come to different conclusions, efforts to synthesize and generalize from multiple studies are also crucial to translation. Early forms of research synthesis in policing include the University of Maryland's "What Works" Report to Congress (Sherman et al. 1997; updated in Sherman et al. 2002) and Campbell Collaboration systematic reviews that rigorously assess and analyze the collective research evidence on particular policies or practices (Petrosino et al. 2003).

The Evidence-Based Policing Matrix (herein "the Matrix") was likely the first online translation tool specifically focused on translating research on law enforcement interventions to reduce crime.[5] Readers can find a detailed explanation and discussion of the Matrix in Lum, Koper, and Telep (2011) and updated in Chapter 3 of Lum and Koper (2017). Inspired by systematic reviews and research on childhood well-being (see Rosenberg and Knox 2005), we, along with Cody Telep, developed the Matrix as a visual systematic review and evidence map to show the field of evaluation research in policing related to crime prevention.

In a single visualization, the Matrix provides an evidence map of evaluated policing interventions according to three dimensions of those interventions: what they are targeting (individuals, groups, micro places, neighborhoods, or jurisdictions); whether they are reactive, proactive, or highly proactive; and whether they are general or more focused and tailored in nature. Mapped studies are also flagged for whether they show significant positive, mixed, null, or backfire effects. By mapping research studies according to these three dimensions and their findings, one can see groupings of studies at a particular intersection of dimensions (e.g., proactive, micro-place, and tailored interventions) and form generalizations about the effectiveness of interventions at that intersection (e.g., mostly effective, mixed findings, mostly ineffective with some backfire effects). Information about each study is also provided in one-page summaries so that users can see what specific interventions led to effective (or ineffective) outcomes. In addition, the Matrix and all of the study summaries are freely accessible.

As a translational tool, the Matrix has general and specific uses. Four generalized principles that arise from the Matrix can guide police tactical and strategic development. When these principles, stated below, are used to develop crime prevention strategies, they can increase the probability that any given strategy developed will be effective in reducing or preventing crime:

1. Officers are more effective when they are proactive, not reactive.
2. Police can be effective if they proactively patrol, investigate, and mitigate places, not just people.
3. Individual- or persons-based strategies are more effective when targeted and focused. However, an overreliance on arrest as a strategy is likely an ineffective crime deterrent.
4. Officers are more effective when they tailor their actions to particular problems.

As a specific translation tool, the Matrix's online interface includes the aforementioned one-page study summaries that translate lengthy and complicated academic articles, reports, and dissertations into simplified, plain language descriptions of the interventions and findings. These summaries go beyond the academic abstracts often found in peer-reviewed journal articles. For example, these descriptions include details of the intervention so that agencies can either replicate effective approaches or identify similar approaches in their agencies that may not be effective. The summaries also include information about how the intervention was evaluated and the level of methodological rigor to which the evaluation was conducted. Specific findings and implications from studies are also provided in plain language for law enforcement audiences. Finally, links to similar studies and approaches, including guides, are listed. In this way, the Matrix provides more specific information about successful interventions that agencies can adapt for their purposes. Because unsuccessful interventions are also included, summaries can also provide examples of the types of tactics and strategies that do not seem to work (and sometimes illuminate why).

Translation is not just the work of researchers; police personnel and community groups also have individuals that can be central translators of research evidence. These actors include crime analysts, embedded criminologists, research and planning staff, and "pracademics" (i.e., police officers with advanced training and dedication to evidence-based approaches—see Sherman 2013) who not only conduct research within their agencies but can also be the translational link between research findings and deployment strategies. Crime analysts, in particular, are at the core of successful evidence-based policing (see Lum and Koper 2017, 227–238). Although they are often underutilized or used in ways that do not facilitate evidence-based approaches, crime analysts often have the technical skills and the research and operational knowledge to support the development, application, and evaluation of evidence-based strategies.

Other important translators in police agencies are more focused on applying research findings. This group includes agency leaders who have the power to make substantive adjustments to policies, procedures, strategies, tactics, and technologies to be more aligned with evidence-based practice. Academy, field-training, and in-service instructors also play an essential translation and dissemination role as educators within the agency, provided that they are familiar with the latest knowledge on policing and police operations. Finally, closer to the field, first-line supervisors play a crucial translational role, as they can guide line-level patrol officers and investigators in the daily use of evidence-based approaches and hold them accountable for doing so.

It is important to note that any of these actors can also hinder and thwart research translation by their actions or rhetoric. For example, a first-line supervisor might say to his officers, "Look, just do this proactive activity that the chief wants; he'll be replaced in a couple of months, and we can just go back to *real* policing." This articulation doesn't benefit research translation. Another example of poor translation is the story of how broken windows theory (Wilson and Kelling 1982) was translated by some police departments and leaders. This theory was translated into operations primarily focused on aggressive policing characterized by the widespread use of misdemeanor arrests and stop and frisks (Lum and Vovak 2018). These strategies can be ineffective when indiscriminately used and generate negative consequences for police legitimacy. However, as Braga, Welsh, and Schnell (2015) have argued, policing disorder can also be done in different ways (through problem-solving, community-focused efforts, or interventions targeting opportunity structures) with more positive effects (for both crime control and police legitimacy). Unfortunately, police often translate research ideas or theories into operations that they know best (i.e., arrests or stops).

B. Receptivity

Receptivity and institutionalization go hand-in-hand in evidence-based policing. As defined in Chapter 8 of Lum and Koper (2017, 134), receptivity is "the willingness of police practitioners (civilian or sworn personnel) to not only be aware of and understand research and research processes, but also be open to the value of research and demand it." However, receptivity goes beyond winning the hearts and minds of police officers about evidence-based policing. It is inextricably linked with research implementation and institutionalization, specifically the development of agency infrastructure to facilitate receptivity and implementation of evidence-based practices.

Officers have varying views about the value of research and scientific evidence for policing. In surveys of police officers, Lum et al. (2012) show that many officers value experience more than research evidence, and many still believe in the effectiveness of tactics that have been shown with science to be ineffective (and vice versa). One example from Lum et al. (2012) that stands out is officers' skepticism in one agency about the effectiveness of directed patrols at crime hot spots. This skepticism persisted *after* that agency had implemented a large-scale hot spots effort that effectively reduced violence crime calls in those hot spots by 25%. Officers are much more likely to be exposed to and value internal rather than externally generated information and beliefs, and they continue to be suspicious of crime analysts or researchers within their agency who may be building evidence supporting operations.

C. Institutionalization

Building receptivity to research findings cannot be achieved merely through training and knowledge dissemination. Decades of training on community-oriented policing, for example, have not necessarily led to a deeper or more meaningful practice of community policing by police officers. Instead, specific parts of the policing organization that drive patrol officer and detective behaviors have to be adjusted to align with the research evidence. What we mean by "institutionalization" is that knowledge from research and research processes becomes normalized into police operations, so much so that officers view operations informed by research knowledge and analysis as "business as usual." Institutionalization of research knowledge also means that the various policing systems can be adjusted to incorporate knowledge from research and scientific methods. These systems include, but are not limited to:

- Professional development, including academy instruction, field training, in-service training, informal mentoring at the first-line supervisor level, and leadership training.
- Patrol deployment, including the activities, technologies, shift structures, and patrol operations.
- Investigative deployment, including the processes that are used for case selection and development, as well as overall strategies that link investigations to patrol deployment.
- Supervision, especially first-line supervisory systems, but all supervision at every rank.
- Accountability systems, to include supervisory and managerial systems; systems of promotions, assessments, and rewards; community-police accountability systems; and internal accountability mechanisms.
- Technology of all types, including those that support deployment, analysis, investigation, and management.
- Crime analysis, research, and planning, particularly as these capabilities are used to support evidence-based approaches.
- Leadership systems, including promotion, accountability, communications, and strategic development.

For example, at the most basic level, police academy and in-service curricula have to incorporate what we know from research about police tactics, strategies, activities, and community reactions to those activities into their curriculum, *and* in a way that facilitates learning across an officer's career (National Academy of Sciences 2022). Academies are where police officers first learn about and assimilate an understanding of police operations and police culture (Chan, Devery, and Doran 2003). Therefore, what is taught in the academy shapes an officer's early views. Institutionalization requires that various academy training modules be reexamined and then recalibrated to be more aligned with the evidence. The challenge is that academy training rarely covers the science of policing but is mostly focused on law and legal procedures, execution of legal procedures (arrest, use of force, criminal investigations, submitting evidence, etc.), and other skills and capabilities related to the physical aspects of policing (physical fitness, driver training, firearms training, etc.). Similarly, institutionalizing evidence-based policing into field training requires adjusting existing experiential exercises to align with the evidence on police tactics and strategies.[6]

Habits and traditions in policing are hard to break, and sustainable changes often have to come from adjusting policing's internal structures and systems and not just from training. Going back to our example of proactive policing in patrol, officers may need clear directives and guidance on what tactics they should carry out in patrol during their noncommitted time rather than just be told to "be proactive," which often leaves them to use limited tools like traffic and pedestrian stops or arrests (Koper et al. 2020; Lum et al. 2020). To institutionalize research findings in patrol, officers need operational guidance in the form of directives, supervision, and accountability systems.

One illustration of this approach can be seen in the *Evidence-Based Policing Playbook*[7] (herein, "the Playbook"). Modeled after a football playbook, this freely available guide provides specific operational directives for actions in the field that are based on rigorous research without going into the technical specifics of the research studies. The Playbook includes both crime prevention plays and plays to improve citizens' trust and confidence in the police. Crime prevention plays use research knowledge from the Matrix and criminological research to inform activities that officers might undertake to reduce and prevent particular conditions and problems. Examples include a "Burglary Prevention Play" based on burglary prevention research by Bowers and Johnson (2005) and Johnson and Bowers (2004), which gives officers guidance on how to strengthen target-hardening among residents and businesses in the immediate aftermath of a nearby burglary. Another example is the "Directed Koper Patrols Play," which is based on Koper's (1995) research on hot spots patrol. It encourages officers to make periodic and unpredictable stops of 10–15 minutes at hot spot street segments and intersections; it also provides suggestions for activities during those stops. A "Focused Deterrence Play" (see Braga, Weisburd, and Turchan 2019) guides officers on intervening with high-risk groups in collaboration with other government and community partners. Similarly, trust and confidence plays include guidance for improving exchanges with citizens (based on the principles of procedural justice), recruiting community partners for prevention and problem-solving, and other ways to improve customer service. Finally, the Playbook also includes several "refreshers" that provide information about the principles behind effective crime prevention strategies (i.e., those from the Matrix) and specific topics like situational crime prevention techniques and problem-oriented policing.

In these ways, the Playbook is an example of a translational tool and a strategy for institutionalizing research knowledge into everyday patrol. The point of the Playbook is that we cannot expect patrol officers to implement evidence-based approaches if they have no guidance in doing so. Further, plays (and proactivity) have to be tracked for officers to be assessed and rewarded (or corrected) for their efforts. In addition, first-line supervisors may have to mentor officers in implementing plays, and, in turn, agencies must have the necessary systems and standards, aligned for the use of plays or other proactive guides, for supervisors to monitor, track, and mentor officers in these activities (e.g., see Koper et al. 2020). In sum, institutionalization requires much more than officers just using the Playbook at their discretion.

Another example of institutionalization is the Case of Place tool[8] (see details in Chapter 12 of Lum and Koper 2017). Police spend an incredible amount of time and resources investigating individuals and crime incidents that have already occurred. However, studies show that crime is geographically concentrated at specific locations (i.e., hot spots). These concentrations are stable over time and influenced by various situational and environmental factors and routine activities. Numerous studies on which the Matrix draws have illustrated the utility of focusing police patrol and problem-solving approaches at these locations to prevent crime and disorder. As an extension of this principle, the Case of Place tool attempts to apply traditional investigative practices (e.g., locating and interviewing suspects, witnesses, and victims; gathering evidence; following leads) to a different unit of investigation (places), given what the evidence tells us about place-based policing. In addition, the tool emphasizes systematic investigation and tracking of problem places—i.e., opening case folders on these locations—to assist police in developing problem-solving prevention strategies. Examples of the use of this tool can be found in Bond and Nader (2018); Koper, Egge, and Lum (2015); and Tate et al. (2013). Others have carried out similar strategies that are also excellent examples (see Herold et al. 2020; Madensen et al. 2017).

These operational tools are not enough to institutionalize research use into practice. As mentioned, police agencies can be stubborn organizations, with several layers of infrastructure that often inhibit or reject adjustments. Thus, institutionalization also requires supervision, management, strategic planning, and leadership efforts. Implementing ideas like the Playbook, Case of Place tool, or other evidence-based tactics and strategies cannot be sustained unless performance metrics are aligned with these activities. For example, in our empirical studies of the realities of police proactivity (Koper et al. 2020; Lum et al. 2020), we discovered that while police officers are often asked to be proactive, they are rarely judged or rewarded for their efforts, providing little incentive for them to comply with such requests. However, promotions, rewards, and annual reviews and assessments can be revamped to incorporate these principles. For instance, those applying for a sergeant's position could be assessed on whether their activities in their noncommitted time align with research on the best use of this time. This would require agencies to have systems for tracking those activities (which is often not the case in practice—see Koper et al. 2020; Sherman 2013) and that agencies provide officers with evidence-based training on the best ways to prevent crime and improve police-citizen relations. Moving up the ranks, first-line supervisors would have to adjust their supervisory and mentorship styles to be more aligned with evidence on effective policing and evidence on transformational supervision and experiential learning. For purposes of strategic planning and management, higher-level commanders could also take advantage of evidence maps like the Matrix to determine whether the suite of deployment activities the agency is using is best aligned with what we know about effective policing (for an example of this activity, see Veigas and Lum 2013).

IV. Evidence-Based Policing in an Era of Reform

Progress toward evidence-based policing is a glacial, if not a vacillating and tenuous, movement in policing today. Nevertheless, optimism for the approach can be seen in the leadership exhibited by the Evidence-Based Policing Hall of Fame members and in efforts by the National Policing Institute (formerly the National Police Foundation). In the United States, fulfilling some of Sherman's (1998) initial vision, several funding agencies of the US Department of Justice have made evidence-based practices a requirement for funding local law enforcement agencies. The evidence also continues to grow, with researchers and practitioners generating research on important policing topics.

However, the movement is also tenuous. There is a strong element within some police agencies, leaders, and officers that is at worst anti-science, or at best is highly skeptical that science can help the police. Some of this skepticism also comes from academics who over-romanticize policing as a craft, arguing that the police are in the best position to determine what is "good policing" or that evidence is far too simplistic to address the complexities of policing. We have ample evidence that suggests these beliefs are incorrect and harmful to the advancement of the policing profession. But perhaps what makes evidence-based policing tenuous is not opposition to the science per se, but the many challenges, as already discussed, of institutionalizing that knowledge into the daily practices of policing.

Adding to the tenuous nature of evidence-based policing is the current reform context within which we write. The United States is experiencing one of its most profound crises in policing. This era will be most likely remembered for the killing of George Floyd by a Minneapolis Police Department officer, resulting in massive worldwide protests, calls for "defunding" the police, and extensive examinations of police policies and practices. However, several significant sentinel events during the 2000s also contributed to this reform era, including the deaths of Trayvon Martin, Michael Brown (Ferguson), and Freddie Gray in Baltimore City, and the publication of the President's Task Force on 21st Century Policing (2015) report. Coupled with the COVID-19 pandemic that began shortly before Floyd, policing has experienced profound exogenous shocks, including a declining interest in people wanting to pursue policing as a profession.

Several new ideas and questions about the police mandate also mark this reform period. These include removing police from specific public safety responsibilities, such as responding to traffic problems or being present in schools; requiring "co-response" by social service workers or mental health providers with police to certain 911 calls for service; requiring the police to divert young people away from criminal justice involvement as opposed to arresting them for delinquent behavior; asking the police to try new models of de-escalation and use-of-force-avoidance; and asking or requiring officers to wear body-worn cameras to help reduce their uses of force and improve their treatment of people. Some of these suggestions are partially supported by studies that suggest they may be promising, although many ideas remain untested. Many suggestions stem from long-standing anger and frustration of the police by people, especially Black Americans, who have historically borne the harm from police maltreatment, violation of civil rights, and discrimination.

The challenge for evidence-based policing is amplified during this era of reform (Lum 2021). We have a great deal of research on how the police can effectively reduce and prevent crime (even though the police do not regularly use this information). To a lesser extent, we also have research that points us to police practices that can improve police-community relationships and exchanges. However, we do not know if newly proposed reforms will deliver the outcomes people seek. We have little knowledge on whether changes in police use-of-force policies will reduce officer use of force (and disparities in uses of force). While there are promising suggestions for training in de-escalation, implicit bias, procedural justice, problem-solving, and body-worn cameras, we do not have much research on how these efforts change actual operations and police officer behaviors. And one critical question remains largely unanswered: What strategies can police implement to *reduce* disparities in their outputs?

While periods of reform can offer opportunities and openings for new ideas like evidence-based policing to flourish, it can also hurt such ideas if ideology and activism become more important than science-based reforms. At present, even the term "science" has been politicized, which will likely impede its use in policing. We are, however, optimistic. Society needs policing research, perhaps now more than ever, to help inform contemporary debates and efforts to reform policing. Recruitment and hiring, training, use-of-force policies, and disciplinary practices will undoubtedly be at the center of police reform efforts. Much more research is needed to understand the links between training, policies, and actual police behaviors. Communities considering reductions in police funding and responsibilities will require careful analysis of their needs to determine the scope and volume of work that can be safely and effectively transferred to other government and community entities. Crime prevention will remain critical to the police function, but police will need to work harder at preventing crime in ways that strengthen rather than harm their community relationships and that do not create or exacerbate criminal justice disparities. The philosophy of evidence-based policing provides a path forward in addressing these concerns and reforming police practices and organizations in ways that balance public safety with police lawfulness, legitimacy, and fairness.

Notes

1. Renamed the National Policing Institute in March 2022, see https://www.policinginstitute.org/.
2. See https://cebcp.org/hall-of-fame/.
3. CompStat is a managerial approach that stresses data-driven problem identification and assessment, geographic resource allocation, problem-solving, and greater accountability for managers (see Silverman 2006; Weisburd et al. 2003).
4. Predictive policing is a model that focuses police resources proactively on places, people, and times predicted to be at high risk (see Bratton and Malinowski 2008; Perry et al. 2013).
5. See http://cebcp.org/evidence-based-policing/the-matrix/.
6. For an example of institutionalizing evidence into field training, see Lum and Koper (2017), 164–176.
7. See http://cebcp.org/evidence-based-policing/the-matrix/matrix-demonstration-project/playbook/.
8. See http://cebcp.org/evidence-based-policing/the-matrix/matrix-demonstration-project/case-of-places/.

References

Bayley, David H. 1994. *Police for the future.* New York: Oxford University Press.
Bond, Brenda J., and Elias Nader. 2018. Institutionalizing place-based policing: The adoption of a case of place approach. *Policing: An International Journal*, 41 (3): 372–385.
Bowers, Kate, and Shane D. Johnson. 2005. Domestic burglary repeats and space-time clusters: The dimensions of risk. *European Journal of Criminology*, 2 (1): 67–92.
Braga, Anthony A., David Weisburd, and Brandon Turchan. 2019. Focused deterrence strategies effects on crime: A systematic review. *Campbell Systematic Reviews*, 15 (3): e1051. https://doi.org/10.1002/cl2.1051.
Braga, Anthony A., Brandon C. Welsh, and Cory Schnell. 2015. Can policing disorder reduce crime? A systematic review and meta-analysis. *Journal of Research in Crime and Delinquency*, 52 (4): 567–588.
Brantingham, Patricia L., and Paul J. Brantingham. 1993. Environment, routine and situation: Toward a pattern theory of crime. *Advances in Criminological Theory*, (5): 259–294.

Bratton, William J., and Sean W. Malinowski. 2008. Police performance management in practice: Taking COMPSTAT to the next level. *Policing*, 2 (3): 259–265.

Buerger, Michael E., and Lorraine Green Mazerolle. 1998. Third-party policing: A theoretical analysis of an emerging trend. *Justice Quarterly*, 15 (2): 301–327.

Chalmers, Iain. 2003. Trying to do more good than harm in policy and practice: The role of rigorous, transparent, up-to-date evaluations. *Annals of the American Academy of Political and Social Science*, 589 (1): 22–40.

Chan, Janet, Chris Devery, and Sally Doran. 2003. *Fair cop: Learning the art of policing*. Toronto: University of Toronto.

Clarke, Ronald V., and Derek B. Cornish. 1985. Modeling offenders' decisions: A framework for research and policy. *Crime and Justice*, 6:147–85.

Dewey, John. 1954. *The public and its problems*. Athens, OH: Swallow Press.

Eck, John E., and William Spelman. 1987. *Problem-solving: Problem-oriented policing in Newport News*. Washington, DC: National Institute of Justice.

Famega, Christine N. 2005. Variation in officer downtime: A review of the research. *Policing: An International Journal of Police Strategies & Management*, 28 (3): 388–414.

Famega, Christine N., James Frank, and Lorraine Mazerolle. 2005. Managing police patrol time: The role of supervisor directives. *Justice Quarterly*, 22 (4): 540–559.

Felson, Marcus. 1994. *Crime and everyday life: Insight and implications for society*. Thousand Oaks, CA: Pine Forge Press.

Goldstein, Herman. 1979. Improving policing: A problem-oriented approach. *Crime & Delinquency*, 25 (2): 236–258.

Goldstein, Herman. 1990. *Problem-oriented policing*. Philadelphia: Temple University Press.

Herold, Tamara D., Robin S. Engel, Nicholas Corsaro, and Stacey L. Clouse. 2020. *Place network investigations in Las Vegas, Nevada: Program review and process evaluation*. Cincinnati, OH: IACP-UC Center for Police Research and Policy. https://www.theiacp.org/sites/default/files/Research%20Center/LVMPD_PIVOT%20Program%20Review_Final.pdf.

HMIC (Her Majesty's Inspectorate of the Constabulary). 1997. *Policing with intelligence*. London: HMIC.

Johnson, Shane D., and Kate J. Bowers. 2004. The burglary as clue to the future: The beginnings of prospective hot-spotting. *European Journal of Criminology*, 1 (2): 237–255.

Kelling, George L., Anthony M. Pate, Duane Dieckman, and Charles E. Brown. 1974. *The Kansas City preventive patrol experiment: A summary report*. Washington, DC: Police Foundation.

Klein, Malcolm W. 1986. Labeling theory and delinquency policy: An experimental test. *Criminal Justice and Behavior*, 13 (1): 47–79.

Koper, Christopher S. 1995. Just enough police presence: Reducing crime and disorderly behavior by optimizing patrol time in crime hot spots. *Justice Quarterly*, 12 (4): 649–672.

Koper, Christopher S., Jeffery Egge, and Cynthia Lum. 2015. Institutionalizing place-based approaches: Opening a case on a gun crime hot spot. *Policing: A Journal of Policy and Practice*, 9 (3): 242–254.

Koper, Christopher S., Cynthia Lum, Xiaoyun Wu, and Noah Fritz. 2020. Proactive policing in the United States: A national survey. *Policing: An International Journal*, 43 (5): 861–876.

Lum, Cynthia. 2009. *Translating police research into practice*. Ideas in American Policing, No 11. Washington, DC: National Policing Institute (formerly National Police Foundation).

Lum, Cynthia. 2021. Perspectives on policing. *Annual Review of Criminology*, 4:19–25.

Lum, Cynthia, and Christopher S. Koper. 2017. *Evidence-based policing: Translating research into practice*. Oxford: Oxford University Press.

Lum, Cynthia, Christopher S. Koper, and Cody W. Telep. 2011. The Evidence-Based Policing Matrix. *Journal of Experimental Criminology*, 7 (1): 3–26.

Lum, Cynthia, Christopher S. Koper, and Xiaoyun Wu. 2022. Can we really defund the police? A nine-agency study of police response to calls for service. *Police Quarterly*, 25 (3): 255–280. https://doi.org/10.1177/10986111211035002.

Lum, Cynthia, Christopher S. Koper, Xiaoyun Wu, William Johnson, and Megan Stoltz. 2020. Examining the empirical realities of proactive policing through systematic observations and computer-aided dispatch data. *Police Quarterly*, 23 (3): 283–310.

Lum, Cynthia, Cody W. Telep, Christopher S. Koper, and Julie Grieco. 2012. Receptivity to research in policing. *Justice Research and Policy* 14 (1): 61–96.

Lum, Cynthia, and Heather Vovak. 2018. Variability in the use of misdemeanor arrests by police agencies from 1990 to 2013: An application of group-based trajectory modeling. *Criminal Justice Policy Review*, 29 (6–7): 536–560.

Lum, Cynthia, Charles Wellford, Thomas Scott, Heather Vovak, Jacqueline A. Scherer, and Michael Goodier. 2023. Differences between high and low performing police agencies in clearing robberies, aggravated assaults, and burglaries: Findings from an eight-agency case study. *Police Quarterly*. https://doi.org/10.1177/10986111231182728.

Madensen, Tamara D., Maris Herold, Matthew G. Hammer, and Blake R. Christenson. 2017. Research in brief: Place-based investigations to disrupt crime place networks. *Police Chief Magazine*, 84 (4): 14–15.

Mastrofski, Stephen D. 1998. Community policing and police organization structure. In *How to recognize good policing: Problems and issues*, edited by Jean Paul Brodeur, 161–89. Thousand Oaks, CA: SAGE.

Mastrofski, Stephen D. 1999. *Policing for people*. Ideas in American Policing. Washington, DC: Police Foundation. https://www.policinginstitute.org/wp-content/uploads/2015/06/Mastrofski-1999-Policing-For-People.pdf.

Mastrofski, Stephen D., Robert E. Worden, and Jeffrey B. Snipes. 1995. Law enforcement in a time of community policing. *Criminology*, 33 (4): 539–563.

Mazerolle, Lorraine, and Janet Ransley. 2005. *Third party policing*. Cambridge: Cambridge University Press.

Mears, Daniel P. 2010. *American criminal justice policy: An evaluation approach to increasing accountability and effectiveness*. New York: Cambridge University Press.

Nagin, Daniel S. 1998. Criminal deterrence research at the outset of the twenty-first century. *Crime and Justice*, 23:1–42.

Nagin, Daniel S. 2013. Deterrence in the twenty-first century. *Crime and Justice*, 42:199–263.

National Academy of Sciences. 2018. *Proactive policing: Effects on crime and communities*. Washington, DC: The National Academies Press.

National Academies of Sciences. 2022. *Police training to promote the rule of law and protect the population*. Washington, DC: The National Academies Press. https://doi.org/10.17226/26467.

National Research Council. 2004. *Fairness and effectiveness in policing: The evidence*. Washington, DC: National Academies Press.

Perry, Cheryl L., Kelli A. Komro, Sara Veblen-Mortenson, Linda M. Bosma, Kian Farbakhsh, Karen A. Munson, Melissa H. Stigler, and Leslie A. Lytle. 2003. A randomized controlled trial of the middle and junior high school DARE and DARE Plus programs. *Archives of Pediatrics & Adolescent Medicine*, 157 (2): 178–184.

Petrosino, Anthony, Robert F. Boruch, David P. Farrington, Lawrence W. Sherman, and David L. Weisburd. 2003. Toward evidence-based criminology and criminal justice: Systematic reviews, The Campbell Collaboration, and the Crime and Justice Group. *International Journal of Comparative Criminology*, 3 (1): 42–61.

Police Foundation. 1981. *The Newark Foot Patrol Experiment*. Washington, DC: Police Foundation.

President's Task Force on 21st Century Policing. 2015. *Final report of the President's Task Force on 21st Century Policing*. Washington, DC: Office of Community Oriented Policing Services.

Prince, Heather, Cynthia Lum, and Christopher S. Koper. 2021. Effective police investigative practices: An evidence-assessment of the research. *Policing: An International Journal (of Strategies and Management*, 44 (4): 683–707.

Ratcliffe, Jerry H. 2008. *Intelligence-led policing*. Cullompton, UK: Willan.

Rosenberg, Mark, and Lyndee M. Knox. 2005. The matrix comes to youth violence prevention: A strengths-based, ecologic and developmental framework. *American Journal of Preventive Medicine*, 29 (5, Suppl. 2): 185–190.

Sherman, Lawrence W. 1998. Evidence-based policing. Ideas in American Policing. Washington, DC: Police Foundation. https://www.policinginstitute.org/wp-content/uploads/2015/06/Sherman-1998-Evidence-Based-Policing.pdf.

Sherman, Lawrence W. 2003. Misleading evidence and evidence-led policy: Making social science more experimental. *Annals of the American Academy of Political and Social Science*, 589 (1): 6–19.

Sherman, Lawrence W. 2013. The rise of evidence-based policing: Targeting, testing, and tracking. *Crime and Justice*, 42:377–451.

Sherman, Lawrence W., and John E. Eck. 2002. Policing for crime prevention. In *Evidence-based crime prevention*, edited by Lawrence W. Sherman, David P. Farrington, Brandon C. Welsh, and Doris Layton MacKenzie, 295–329. London: Routledge.

Sherman, Lawrence W., David P. Farrington, Brandon C. Welsh, and Doris Layton MacKenzie. 2002. *Evidence-based crime prevention*. London: Routledge.

Sherman, Lawrence W., Denise Gottfredson, Doris MacKenzie, John Eck, Peter Reuter, and Shawn Bushway. 1997. *Preventing crime: What works, what doesn't, what's promising: A report to the United States Congress*. Washington, DC: National Institute of Justice.

Sherman, Lawrence W., Janell D. Schmidt, Dennis P. Rogan, and Patrick R. Gartin. 1991. From initial deterrence to long-term escalation: Short-custody arrest for poverty ghetto domestic violence. *Criminology*, 29 (4): 821–850.

Sherman, Lawrence W., Janell D. Schmidt, Dennis P. Rogan, Douglas A. Smith, Patrick R. Gartin, Ellen G. Cohn, J. Collins, and Anthony R. Bacich. 1992. The variable effects of arrest on criminal careers: The Milwaukee domestic violence experiment. *Journal of Criminal Law and Criminology*, 83 (1): 137–169.

Sherman, Lawrence W., and David Weisburd. 1995. General deterrent effects of police patrol in crime "hot spots": A randomized, controlled trial. *Justice Quarterly*, 12 (4): 625–648.

Silverman, Eli. 2006. Compstat's Innovation. In *Police innovation: Contrasting perspectives*, edited by David L. Weisburd and Anthony A. Braga, 267–283. Cambridge, MA: Cambridge University Press.

Skogan, Wesley G. 2004. *Community policing: Can it work?* Belmont, CA: Wadsworth Thomson Learning.

Skogan, Wesley G., and Susan M. Hartnett. 1997. *Community policing, Chicago style*. New York: Oxford University Press.

Skolnick, Jerome H. 1999. *On democratic policing*. Ideas in American Policing. Washington, DC: Police Foundation. https://www.policinginstitute.org/wp-content/uploads/2015/06/Skolnick-1999-On-Democratic-Policing.pdf.

Smith, Douglas A., and Patrick R. Gartin. 1989. Specifying specific deterrence: The influence of arrest on future criminal activity. *American Sociological Review*, 54 (1): 94–106.

Spelman, William, and Dale K. Brown. 1981. *Calling the police: Citizen reporting of serious crime*. Washington, DC: Police Executive Research Forum.

Tate, Renee, Thomas Neale, Cynthia Lum, and Christopher S. Koper. 2013. Case of places. *Translational Criminology*, Fall 2013: 18–21. https://cebcp.org/wp-content/uploads/2019/06/TC5-Fall2013.pdf.

Trojanowicz, Robert C. 1986. Evaluating a neighborhood foot patrol program: The Flint, Michigan project. In *Community crime prevention: Does it work?*, edited by Dennis Rosenbaum, 157–78. Beverly Hills, CA: SAGE.

Trojanowicz, Robert C. 1994. The future of community policing. In *The challenge of community policing: Testing the promises*, edited by Dennis Rosenbaum, 258–62. Thousand Oaks, CA: SAGE.

Veigas, Howard, and Cynthia Lum. 2013. Assessing the evidence base of a police service patrol portfolio. *Policing: A Journal of Policy and Practice*, 7 (3): 248–262.

Weisburd, David, Elizabeth R. Groff, Greg Jones, Breanne Cave, Karen L. Amendola, Sue-Ming Yang, and Rupert F. Emison. 2015. The Dallas Patrol Management Experiment: Can AVL technologies be used to harness unallocated patrol time for crime prevention? *Journal of Experimental Criminology*, 11 (3): 367–391.

Weisburd, David, Stephen D. Mastrofski, Ann McNally, Rosann Greenspan, and James J. Willis. 2003. Reforming to preserve: Compstat and strategic problem solving in American policing. *Criminology & Public Policy*, 2 (3): 421–456.

Wilson, James Q., and George Kelling. 1982. Broken windows: The police and neighborhood safety. *Atlantic Monthly*, 249 (3): 29–38.

CHAPTER 14

CCTV VIDEO SURVEILLANCE AND CRIME CONTROL
The Current Evidence and Important Next Steps

ERIC L. PIZA

IN the Criminal Justice Process and Policy course I taught for the John Jay College doctoral program from 2016 to 2020, I became notorious among students for frequently uttering "it's not a refrigerator" during discussions on whatever crime control technology was in vogue. This comment was meant to criticize standard operating procedure surrounding criminal justice technology deployment. The refrigerator is effective through simplicity. The user plugs the unit into an electric outlet, fills it with groceries, and never has to think about the inner workings of refrigeration to realize the goal of keeping beverages cold and food fresh. Crime prevention technology is not nearly as straightforward. Whether or not technology delivers the intended crime prevention benefits depends on a range of contextual factors, inclusive of the technological infrastructure, implementation capacity of the public safety agency, social setting in which technology interventions take place, and the manner by which officers use technology in practice (Ariel 2019; Lum, Koper, and Willis 2017; Salvemini et al. 2015). Unfortunately, criminal justice practitioners often deploy technology absent any consideration of such contextual factors needed to maximize the likelihood of success. They set up the technology and expect it to achieve the intended goals on its own.

My "it's not a refrigerator" refrain is applicable to most crime control technology, but is particularly appropriate in the case of closed-circuit television (CCTV) video surveillance cameras. Because it cannot physically block access to certain areas or safeguard individual objects or people, CCTV relies on perceptual mechanisms by which potential offenders believe camera presence substantially heightens the risk associated with crime commission (Ratcliffe 2006). While lay persons (and even some "experts") may assume conspicuous camera presence alone sufficiently communicates heightened risk, such causal mechanisms can be difficult to generate in practice (Gannoni et al. 2017; Gill and Loveday 2003; Piza, Caplan, and Kennedy 2014b). The nuanced nature of the CCTV literature reflects this reality. While the overall body of research finds CCTV can generate significant (albeit modest) crime reductions, effects are highly contextual, contingent on a range of geographic and programmatic factors (Piza et al. 2019; Welsh and Farrington 2002, 2009). The research evidence becomes further mixed when alternate outcomes such as case closure and cost-effectiveness are considered (Piza 2021).

This chapter provides a primer on the current state of research on CCTV. It begins by discussing key considerations pertaining to CCTV research methodology. A critical overview of the research evidence follows. The chapter concludes with a discussion of important knowledge gaps in the literature and key takeaways for practitioners and policymakers.

I. Methodological Considerations

A. Units of Analysis

A challenge with CCTV research is operationalizing areas receiving "treatment." As previously mentioned, CCTV effect on crime rests on a causal mechanism by which potential offenders identify cameras and view the cameras as increasing the likelihood of detection and apprehension (Ratcliffe 2006). As such, CCTV is grounded in deterrence and rational choice perspectives, and seeks to increase formal surveillance within specific areas targeted by the video cameras (Cornish and Clarke 2003). CCTV is a place-based intervention, and representing offender perceptions geographically is difficult, if not impossible. As argued by Ratcliffe, Taniguchi, and Taylor (2009, 751), "the difficulty with offender perceptions is that they are not measurable without extensive and expensive interviewing. Furthermore, the resultant offender perception will most likely vary from person to person. In other words, while the range of a CCTV camera—as perceived by a criminal—is in the eye of the beholder, finding and interviewing suitable beholders is beyond the budget of most studies, and the results are likely to be quite variable." The challenge for researchers is to operationalize CCTV target areas in a manner that maximizes the overlap between potential offenders' conception of "space" and a CCTV camera's line of sight.

CCTV target areas have been operationalized a number of different ways in the literature. Much CCTV research has considered aggregate areas containing CCTV cameras, such as neighborhoods or police districts, as target areas (e.g., Jang et al. 2018; Prenzler and Wilson 2019; Sivarajasingam, Shepherd, and Matthews 2003; Squires 1998). An alternate popular approach has been to use circular buffer areas around CCTV camera locations as the unit of analysis (Cameron et al. 2008; King, Mulligan, and Raphael 2008; Lim et al. 2016; Mazerolle, Hurley, and Chamlin 2002). Researchers have argued that both of these approaches may compromise construct validity (Caplan, Kennedy, and Petrossian 2011; Ratcliffe, Taniguchi, and Taylor 2009).

Given that CCTV cameras have the capacity to view limited distances, using areas such as "districts" or "neighborhoods" as the unit of analysis likely vastly overestimates CCTV coverage. Furthermore, preexisting administrative boundaries may make poor units of analysis for social science research because they are drawn to facilitate service delivery and are not necessarily representative of the behavior clusters that are of interest for surveillance (Piza, Caplan, and Kennedy 2014a). While buffer zones truncate the size of target areas, they inaccurately depict CCTV coverage by assuming a 360 degree, unobstructed line of sight for each camera. This is rarely, if ever, the reality of a real-word environment, with features such as street signs, trees, and buildings commonly obscuring a camera's line of sight (Piza, Caplan, and Kennedy 2014a). Buffers may be particularly susceptible to the modifiable aerial unit problem, as reflected by the wide range of radius distances prior CCTV research has used when creating buffers (see Kronkvist 2022, Table 2).

More recent CCTV research has used viewsheds to operationalize CCTV camera target areas. Viewsheds estimate the actual area within a CCTV camera's line-of-sight, incorporating natural constraints to visibility such as trees or buildings (Ratcliffe, Taniguchi, and Taylor 2009). Viewsheds can further enable researchers to readily measure micro-level factors to ensure comparability between treatment and control units. Viewsheds reflect the larger trend in crime-and-place research to incorporate more micro-level units of analysis in recognition that they better reflect the spatial patterns of variables of interest (Oberwittler and Wikstrom 2009) and account for variance more efficiently than does the use of larger units of analysis (Schnell, Braga, and Piza 2017; Steenbeek and Weisburd 2015).

To the author's knowledge, Ratcliffe and colleagues' (2009) evaluation of 18 pilot CCTV cameras in Philadelphia, Pennsylvania, was the first to use viewsheds. Ratcliffe and colleagues visited the CCTV viewing station, working with police officers to digitize individual viewsheds by panning and zooming the cameras and discussing active viewing areas with the officers. Viewshed distances were typically set as the limit where a street-sign could be read.[1] A 500-foot buffer around the viewsheds were designated as the displacement area. Control areas were designated as the surrounding police districts beyond the displacement area. Ratcliffe and Groff's (2019) longitudinal analysis of Philadelphia's fully deployed 192-camera system took a similar approach to designating viewshed, displacement, and control areas.

In their analysis of the first 73 cameras installed in Newark, New Jersey, Caplan, Kennedy, and Petrossian (2011) expanded the viewshed methodology by developing a method to operationalize viewsheds when researchers do not have access to CCTV camera feeds. Caplan and colleagues (2011) first created 582-foot (approximately the length of two city blocks in Newark) buffers around each camera location. Viewsheds were then digitized within a Geographic Information System (GIS) by drawing polygons within the 582-foot buffer and excluding areas that were blocked by obstructions visible from the aerial imagery. Caplan and colleagues operationalized control areas by randomly generating 73 points on street segments in a GIS and then repeating the aforementioned viewshed creation process for each. This differs from most other CCTV evaluation studies using viewsheds, which typically use one operationalization for target sites (i.e., viewsheds) and another for comparison sites (e.g., police districts, cameras buffers, etc.) (La Vigne and Lowry 2011; Lim and Wilcox 2017; Ratcliffe and Groff 2019; Ratcliffe, Taniguchi, and Taylor 2009).

Piza (2018) combined the direct observation (Ratcliffe and Groff 2019; Ratcliffe, Taniguchi, and Taylor 2009) and aerial imagery (Caplan, Kennedy, and Petrossian 2011) viewshed approaches in his evaluation of the fully deployed 146-camera CCTV system in Newark. Piza viewed the live feeds all CCTV cameras and digitized the viewshed of each site within a GIS. Aerial map imagery and a detailed base map (with layers depicting streets, land parcels, and building footprints) were incorporated to ensure digitized viewsheds reflected the physical landscape by accounting for visible obstructions. Catchment zones of 291 feet (approximately the median block length in Newark) were created around each viewshed to allow for a test of spatial displacement. For all street intersections falling outside of CCTV viewsheds and catchment zones (N = 961), Piza repeated the viewshed creation process to create a pool of control cases for the evaluation, with the final set of control selected through statistical matching.

Kronkvist's (2022) recent examination of CCTV in Malmö, Sweden, demonstrates how unit of analysis operationalization can influence study results. Kronkvist generated different target, displacement, and control areas to test the effect of CCTV on violent and property crime in a residential neighborhood over a five-year (2.5 years pre/post) study period. Target and control areas were operationalized as the camera's encompassing small area for market statistics (SMAS) unit (classified by Statistics Sweden), a circular buffer around camera locations, and camera viewsheds. Catchment sites were operationalized as the SAMS contiguous to the target site and a buffer surrounding the target site. Most results were nonsignificant owing to low statistical power. When results were statistically significant, the triads of treatment/control/buffer areas produced varying results. Property crime either decreased significantly at control areas compared to target areas or remained unchanged, while violent crime decreased between 6% and 34% compared to control conditions depending on the triad used. The viewshed methodology was generally associated with null effect sizes. findings suggest viewsheds may allow for more robust tests of CCTV than alternate units of analysis.

B. Experimentation and Quasi-Experimentation

Evidence-based crime prevention emphasizes the use of the best available research evidence to guide program development and implementation (Sherman et al. 1997). The strength of a given research study is largely related to its levels of internal, construct, and statistical conclusion validity (Welsh 2019). Research designs incorporating comparable control conditions—namely, experiments and quasi-experiments—are privileged for their ability to protect against threats to these types of validity. Experiments, also referred to as randomized controlled trials (RCTs), best reduce bias by randomly assigning cases to either treatment or control conditions, ensuring these groups are statically equivalent across pertinent variables (Cook and Campbell 1979; Farrington et al. 2006).

In many respects, the CCTV research literature is more robust than the research literature for crime prevention technology generally. Lum and Koper (2017) describe police technology as an example of "evidence-based policing playing catch-up," in the sense that a much smaller pool of scientific evidence is available for technological interventions than officer-driven crime prevention strategies. Conversely, case-control CCTV evaluation studies have occurred often enough for three systematic reviews to have been conducted over less than a 20-year period (Piza et al. 2019; Welsh and Farrington 2002, 2009). In other respects, CCTV research lags behind research on other contemporary police technologies. For example, the tangential video surveillance technology of police body-worn cameras has been evaluated through the frequent use of experimental and strong quasi-experimental designs (Lum et al. 2020; White and Malm 2020). Conversely, 78 of the 158 (49.4%) evaluation studies identified for potential inclusion in the CCTV systematic review and meta-analysis were excluded most commonly for not incorporating suitable control conditions (Piza et al. 2019).

Practical considerations often necessitate the post-hoc evaluation of CCTV, forgoing random assignment. Given that CCTV cameras are largely permanent fixtures, with cameras hard-wired to physical structures and wireless networks configured to stream footage to a centralized control room, changing target areas post-experimentation would incur significant financial costs (Piza 2018).[2] As such, practitioners install cameras at locations of their choosing, giving little to no thought to the implications for research design (Piza 2021). Nonetheless, researchers have incorporated RCTs in CCTV evaluations on three occasions. La Vigne and Lowry (2011) conducted a blocked randomized experiment, randomly assigning 100 parking lots operated by the Washington Metropolitan Area Transit Authority to receive digital cameras equipped with motion detectors or serve as a control case. Hayes and Downs (2011) assigned 47 large retail-store locations in the United States to receive one of three situational crime prevention treatments: in-aisle CCTV public view monitors, in-aisle CCTV domes, or polycarbonate protective safe boxes. Piza et al. (2015) incorporated a randomized block design to assign 38 clusters of CCTV viewsheds to either a treatment group receiving additional proactive CCTV monitoring and a team of directed patrol units or a control group receiving standard levels of CCTV monitoring and police patrol. While not a direct test of CCTV, because both treatment and control conditions had cameras, Piza et al.'s RCT tested the effect of better integrating CCTV with proactive policing functions.

Natural experiments are considered high-quality alternatives to RCTs when random assignment is not possible. Natural experiments provide robust checks against endogeneity due to treatment occurring in a random or as-if random process, despite falling outside the direct control of researchers (Dunning 2008). Such as-if random allocation of treatment distinguishes natural experiments from traditional quasi-experiments (Dunning 2012). Alexandrie (2017) reviewed five natural experiments alongside the RCTs conducted by Hayes and Downs (2011) and La Vigne and Lowry (2011). Selection criteria differed across the review conducted by Alexandrie (2017) and those conducted by Piza et al. (2019) and Welsh and Farrington (2002, 2009). All five of the natural experiments reviewed by Alexandrie (2017)—published between the years 2008 and 2017—were excluded by Piza and colleagues (2019) due to the lack of separate control areas in the research design. This illustrates the important role research designs play in the interpretation of evaluation study findings.

The CCTV evaluation literature is dominated by quasi-experimental designs, given the challenges associated with random assignment of treatment and capitalizing on naturally occurring as-if random processes. Of the 80 studies fitting the inclusion criteria of the most recent CCTV review, 76 (95%) used quasi-experimental designs (Thomas et al. 2022). It is important to note that quasi-experiments vary in their levels of methodological rigor and internal validity. Quasi-experiments incorporate a nonequivalent control group design when steps are not taken to ensure that treatment and control conditions are similar on potentially confounding variables. Such nonequivalent quasi-experiments have a heighted risk of bias due to the presence of extraneous variables differing across treatment and control areas (Farrington et al. 2006). Bias caused by extraneous variables can be addressed by using statistical adjustments, such as matching (Rosenbaum 2002). Matching attempts to generate equivalency between treatment and control conditions in the absence of randomization. Sixteen (20%) of the studies included in the most recent CCTV review used matching techniques to conduct quasi-experiments with near-equivalent control groups (Thomas et al. 2022). The precise nature of matching varied, from statistical algorithms such as propensity score matching (e.g., Piza 2018) to manual matching of units based on similarities across factors such as crime levels, land usage, and neighborhood sociodemographic characteristics (e.g, Farrington et al. 2007; La Vigne et al. 2011). Three-quarters of the matched quasi-experiments and all of the aforementioned RCTs were conducted in the United States from 2011 onward, reflecting a rapidly developing CCTV literature in this country (Thomas et al. 2022).

Irrespective of research design, causal analysis represents only the first step in policy analysis. The next step involves forecasting how well the evaluated program would perform in a new environment, which centers on considerations of external validity (Sampson, Winship, and Knight 2013). External validity relates to the generalizability of a study's findings. Eck (2017) distinguishes internal and external validity in terms of their differing foci. Internal validity is inherently retrospective, concerned with evaluating the quality of existing evidence, while external validity is prospective, primarily concerned with predicting what might occur in the future (i.e., if prior research findings will replicate when a practice is applied in a new jurisdiction). Systematic reviews and meta-analyses can help establish a program's external validity because these efforts include all studies fitting a specified inclusion criteria. The studies included in a systematic review typically involve a range of different environments, treated populations, and operational definitions of the intervention (Welsh and Farrington 2007). Unfortunately, while some meta-analyses provide explicit information on the contexts and causal mechanisms that undergird a program's effect, most do not (Tompson et al. 2021). When sufficient contextual information cannot be gleaned directly from a meta-analysis, agency personnel may be able to incorporate detailed observational information on the crime problem and tailor evidence-based practices to fit the nature of the problem at hand (Welsh 2019). These types of efforts are key, as strict replication of programs is oftentimes impossible in real-world situations (Bardach 2004).

II. The Research Evidence

A. CCTV and Crime Prevention

The collective knowledge of CCTV evaluation research is synthesized in the updated systematic review and meta-analysis of Piza and colleagues (2019), which updated the work of Welsh and Farrington (2002, 2009). CCTV evaluation studies were selected for inclusion according to four criteria, as per the protocol of the Campbell Collaboration: (1) CCTV was the main focus of the intervention; (2) the evaluation used an outcome measure of crime; (3) the research design involved, at a minimum, before-and-after measures of crime in treatment and comparable control areas; and (4) both treatment and control areas experienced at least 20 crimes during the pre-intervention period. Pooled effects across all studies included in the meta-analysis found crime decreased in CCTV areas by about 13% as compared to control areas. Achieved crime reductions were not negatively affected by displacement, as only 6 of the 50 studies incorporating adjacent control areas found any evidence of displacement.

Piza et al. (2019) found certain characteristics of CCTV systems were significantly associated with effect size, reflecting Welsh and Mears's (this volume) argument that "context is everything" when assessing research evidence on crime and justice policy. Findings of Piza and colleagues' (2019) meta-analysis indicate strategic considerations largely influence the effect of CCTV. Schemes incorporating active monitoring practices were associated with a significant crime reduction of approximately 15% while passively monitored systems did not generate any significant effects. Schemes incorporating multiple complementary interventions alongside CCTV were associated with a significant 34% reduction in crime, with no significant effects observed for schemes deploying no or a single complementary intervention. A follow-up meta-analysis conducted by Welsh and colleagues (2020) found CCTV schemes operated by private security personnel generated larger crime prevention effects than those operated by police or those using a mix of police and security personnel.

Piza and colleagues (2019) found the strongest effects of CCTV within car parks (37% reduction), similar to the prior reviews (Welsh and Farrington 2002, 2009). Contrary to the prior reviews, Piza and colleagues found that CCTV schemes deployed in residential areas also generated significant crime reductions of approximately 12%. CCTV had the largest effect on drug crime (approximately 20% reduction), followed by reductions of approximately 14% for both vehicle crime and property crime, with no significant effects observed for violent crime. CCTV was associated with crime reductions in the United Kingdom and South Korea, with no significant effects observed for other countries.[3] Thomas and colleagues (2022) noted that UK schemes more often incorporated contextual factors associated with increased likelihood of success—such as deployment in car parks, active camera monitoring, and the deployment of multiple complementary interventions alongside CCTV—as compared to CCTV schemes reported in other countries.

Several evaluation studies have found that CCTV effect can also vary within individual surveillance systems. Matczak et al. (2021) found overall null effects of CCTV in Poland, though 10 of the 17 treatment areas showed evidence of a prevention effect as compared to control areas. Ratcliffe, Taniguchi, and Taylor (2009) found that just as many individual cameras had no effect as those that showed a benefit in Philadelphia, despite the aggregate system generating a 13.3% reduction in overall crime. Caplan, Kennedy, and Petrossian (2011) found that while motor vehicle theft was the only crime type to experience a system-wide reduction in Newark, each crime type included in the analysis decreased at between 34 and 58 individual cameras sites. The aggregate and camera-specific findings were largely replicated in analyses of Newark's full 146-camera system (Piza 2018; Piza, Caplan, and Kennedy 2014a).

Research studies highlight specific contextual factors that may explain such intra-system variation in CCTV effect. Piza and colleagues (2014a) found the presence of certain facility types influenced CCTV effect in Newark. For example, the presence of bars was associated with reductions in violent crime and robbery. The presence of retail stores was associated with increases in property crime and theft from auto, while the presence of schools was associated with increased levels of auto theft. Piza and colleagues further uncovered significant effects of enforcement actions generated by proactive CCTV monitoring, which were associated with decreases in overall crime, violent crime, and theft from auto. Contextual effects of land usage were also found by Lim and Wilcox (2017) in Cincinnati. While Cincinnati's overall CCTV system produced minimal crime prevention benefits, many individual camera sites in residential areas experienced reductions in assault, robbery, and burglary, with diffusion of benefits observed much more often than displacement. In their evaluation of Detroit's Project Green Light—an intervention in which volunteer businesses installed a minimum of four surveillance cameras, lighting, and signage identifying their participation in the program—Circo and McGarrell (2021) found gas stations experienced the most substantial increases in disorder and property crime over the first month of the program. Over the full post-intervention period, property crime generally decreased at liquor stores and retail stories and remained stable in bars and restaurants.

B. CCTV and Case Clearance

The majority of CCTV research focuses solely on the technology's crime deterrence effects (Piza 2021), with studies typically only reporting process measures and descriptive statistics on how CCTV cameras are used by investigators (see e.g., Brookman and Jones 2022; Brown 1995; Gill et al. 2005; La Vigne et al. 2011). However, a literature on CCTV's effect on offender apprehension has emerged over the prior decade. Piza, Caplan, and Kennedy (2014b) tested the effect of CCTV on the on-scene apprehension of offenders in Newark, New Jersey. Piza and colleagues found in-progress crime incidents detected and reported by CCTV resulted in an on-scene enforcement action at a significantly higher rate than crimes reported by citizen calls to the 911 emergency line (33.1% vs. 17.0%). CCTV's increased on-scene enforcement rate over 911 calls was maintained across five of the seven disaggregate crime types included in the analysis: disorder (32.3% vs. 26.8%), drug offenses (44.5% vs. 20.4%), and incidents classified as "other crime" (26.3% vs. 14.4%), "high-priority" (42.2% vs. 8.6%) and "intermediate-priority" (30.6% vs. 18.0%).[4]

A number of additional studies have evaluated the role of CCTV in retroactive police investigations, many of which focused on crime on railway networks. Robb, Coupe, and Ariel (2015) and Sharp (2016) measured the correlation between a range of solvability factors (inclusive of CCTV) on the clearance of metal theft and pickpocketing incidents, respectively, investigated by the British Transport Police. While Robb et al. (2015) found CCTV was positively correlated with case clearance, its effect size (measured as standardized mean difference between cleared and uncleared cases) of 0.935 was lower than all but 4 of the 14 statistically significant solvability factors. Sharp (2016) found 29 of 63 variables exhibited a statistically significant relationship with case closure. CCTV had the third-highest effect size. Pickpocketing incidents were 20 times more likely to be solved when CCTV footage was available, as compared to cases without CCTV footage.

Studies using case control quasi-experimental designs have found more positive effects of CCTV on crime clearance in railroad environments. Ashby (2017) found CCTV provided video evidence of crimes occurring on the British railway network in 45% of cases, with investigators judging footage as useful in 65% of these cases (which accounted for 29.4% of all cases). Ashby (2017) found having useful CCTV evidence increased the likelihood of case closure from slightly over 20% to approximately 50% (see Figure 3 in Ashby 2017). Such investigatory benefits were maintained across all crime types except fraud, drug, and weapon offenses, with the largest effects observed for robbery (from 8.9% to 55.7%). Morgan and Dowling (2019) similarly evaluated the effect of CCTV on investigations of crime occurring within a rail network in New South Wales, Australia. They used propensity score matching to create a control group that was statistically equivalent to the CCTV group across five variables (principal offense type, day of the week, time of day, location of the incident, and incident severity). Morgan and Dowling (2019) found clearance rates of cases involving CCTV footage to be 18% higher than the control cases. Effects were particularly strong for property damage and theft/burglary, with CCTV associated with case clearance increases of 64% and 71%, respectively.

A number of recent evaluation studies have measured the investigatory benefits of CCTV within public settings. Similar to the design of Morgan and Dowling (2019), Robin, Peterson, and Lawrence (2021) incorporated propensity score matching to test the effect of CCTV on case clearance in Milwaukee. They found overall case clearances were 14% higher at CCTV-covered intersections than matched control intersections. Crime incidents classified as "Group B" offenses saw case clearances that were 25% higher in CCTV intersections than controls.[5] Petras (2018) tested the effect of CCTV on the clearance of crimes investigated by the Central Connecticut State University Police Department. Correlation coefficients demonstrated CCTV use was moderately associated with both case clearance and the time to case clearance.

Other studies focusing on public settings have found mixed results. Paine (2012) found CCTV footage being preserved at the crime scene was not significantly related to the clearance of either completed or attempted burglaries in Thames Valley, UK. Jung and Wheeler (2021) found that crime clearance rates significantly increased from the pre- to post-installation period within 500 feet of CCTV camera locations. Changes in clearance rates were insignificant at greater distances. An analysis of disaggregate crime types found theft was the only crime type demonstrating a significant increase in clearance rate within the aforementioned 500-foot CCTV area. Gerell (2021) analyzed the effect of a CCTV system covering deprived neighborhoods in Gothenburg, Sweden. While clearance rates increased for both property crime and violent crime in target areas as compared to controls, neither change achieved statistical significance.

The mixed effect observed across studies is a primary theme in the research on CCTV's role in case clearance and police investigations. Reasons for this effect heterogeneity are currently unclear. If lessons from research on the crime prevention capacity of CCTV extend to case clearance, we would expect the nature by which CCTV cameras are integrated into daily operations to influence their effect (Piza et al. 2015, 2019). However, attributing the lessons of the CCTV crime prevention literature to case clearance may be premature given the small (but growing) number of studies that have rigorously tested CCTV's effect on offender apprehension. Future research should prioritize measurement of programmatic and contextual aspects of CCTV that may influence case clearance.

C. Cost-Effectiveness of CCTV

Cost-benefit analysis has emerged as a key component of evidence-based crime prevention due to its ability to quantify the fiscal prudence of programs and practices (Welsh, van der Laan, and Hollis 2013). To the author's knowledge, three cost-benefit analyses of CCTV interventions have been conducted to date. It is important to note that these studies considered only the reduction of crime when calculating program benefits. Monetary benefits of case clearance has yet to be quantified in this body of research.

Gill and Spriggs (2005) included a cost-benefit analysis in their national evaluation of 14 CCTV schemes in the United Kingdom. Gill and Spriggs (2005) used estimates generated by Brand and Price (2000) to measure the monetary cost of crime. CCTV intervention inputs were measured from agency documents, with equipment the largest expense, accounting for an average of 78% of expenditures across the CCTV schemes. Of the four CCTV schemes to experience a significant crime reduction, two showed evidence of cost-effectiveness, with every £1 spent on CCTV generating £1.24 and £1.27 in savings, respectively. Conversely, the other two schemes were cost-prohibitive, with every £1 spent generating only £0.67 and £0.42 in savings, respectively.

La Vigne et al. (2011) conducted cost-benefit analyses of CCTV in Baltimore and Chicago. In both cities, benefits achieved from crime reductions exceeded the upfront and maintenances costs of CCTV, though results were sensitive to how crime costs were calculated. La Vigne and colleagues included both tangible (e.g., government expenditures of the criminal justice system, victim's lost wages, etc.) and intangible (e.g., fear of crime, pain and suffering, etc.) costs to reflect the full spectrum of victimization. In Chicago, every $1 spent on the CCTV system generated $4.30 in savings when both crime and victim costs were considered, and $2.81 in savings when only crime costs were considered. Lesser cost-savings were observed in Baltimore, with every $1 spent on CCTV generating $1.49 in benefits when both crime and victim costs were considered and $1.06 in savings when only tangible costs were included. The tangible-cost findings reflect, in the words of La Vigne and colleagues (2011, 22), "a more relevant ratio from a local financing perspective, as any victimization cost savings that might be attributed to the camera system are not transferred to governments' budgets."

Piza et al. (2016) conducted a cost-benefit analysis of the Newark CCTV Directed Patrol Strategy (Piza et al. 2015). They classified intervention costs according to whether they related to the intervention outputs (i.e., the additional CCTV operators, directed patrol officers, and police vehicles) or the preexisting CCTV system (i.e., camera installation, camera maintenance, existing CCTV operators and supervisors). Piza and colleagues (2016) calculated costs of crime two ways: (1) including all tangible societal and criminal justice system costs, and (2) including only criminal justice system costs. Results indicate that every $1 spent on Directed Patrol Strategy outputs generated between $19.36 and $31.62 in savings in light of the achieved crime reduction. Cost-effectiveness reduced when costs of the preexisting CCTV system were accounted for (between $1.63 and $2.04). Overall, the analysis of Piza et al. (2016) suggests that a strategy pairing directed patrol with active CCTV monitoring is cost-effective for agencies with existing (and previously paid for) CCTV systems but may be cost-prohibitive for agencies needing to first invest in CCTV.

A key challenge in interpreting these findings is clearly determining the counterfactual condition. The true value of cost-benefit analysis comes from quantifying the cost-effectiveness of a portfolio of interventions to assist policymakers in determining how to invest limited public resources (Aos 2015; Welsh and Farrington 2015). CCTV systems typically cost millions of dollars to install, with maintenance expenses requiring substantial financial commitment on a regular basis (La Vigne et al. 2011). In the spirit of cost-benefit analysis, given that money dedicated towards CCTV could instead be devoted to other programs and practices, it is important to demonstrate CCTV is worth funding over less expensive options (Piza et al. 2016). However, CCTV researchers are typically unable to determine what alternative programs an agency could have spent money on in lieu of CCTV. As such, analysis findings speak to a CCTV system's absolute cost-effectiveness rather than its relative cost-effectiveness compared to other policy options. This challenge is exacerbated by the fact that policing and situational crime prevention interventions have incorporated cost-benefit analysis less frequently than other disciplines (Piza et al. 2016). The increased use of cost-benefit analysis in the crime prevention field would allow for more in-depth comparison of the cost-effectiveness of various programs and practices competing for public funding.

III. Important Knowledge Gaps

Despite the development of a robust literature on CCTV, there remain a number of pertinent issues in need of empirical examination. For one, disparities in populations bearing the brunt of surveillance have not received sufficient empirical attention. Harms of CCTV surveillance, in terms of exacerbating racial inequalities, should be balanced against the crime control benefits (Hollis 2019). This may be accomplished by embracing an expanded research agenda that includes metrics on equal access, equal treatment, and equal impact of CCTV (Hollis 2019; Piza, Chu, and Welsh 2022). In considering this issue, it is concerning that CCTV programs have typically been developed absent the type of community involvement that has become increasingly popular in contemporary policing (see, e.g., Gimenez-Santana, Caplan, and Kennedy 2022; Katz and Huff 2020). Such an approach can be facilitated in CCTV projects through action research frameworks involving active and ongoing collaboration between researchers, practitioners, and community stakeholders—such as Community Technology Oversight Boards (Piza et al. 2022).

The CCTV knowledge base on crime control has also stalled in certain respects. While high-quality evaluation studies increased in residential areas (from 2 to 16) and the United States (from 4 to 24) between Welsh and Farrington (2009) and Piza et al. (2019), research has stagnated for certain settings. No new public transport settings met the inclusion criteria for the updated systematic review.[6] Research on the deployment of CCTV in certain countries has also been hindered by weak research designs. We do not know as much as we should about between-country variation in CCTV effect and, by extension, what lessons might be gleaned from examining such variation. While 17 evaluation studies have focused on CCTV in Australia, only one incorporated the type of quasi-experimental method required for inclusion in the systematic review. Evaluation studies from five countries were entirely excluded from the systematic review (Colombia, Germany, Japan, the Netherlands, and Uruguay) due to the universal absence of control conditions (Thomas et al. 2022). Furthermore, while research conducted in the United Kingdom dominated the early CCTV literature, no evaluation studies were conducted in the UK between 2010 and 2016, the final six years covered by the updated systematic review (Thomas et al. 2022). More research is needed to determine whether the positive effects achieved in the UK were maintained over subsequent decades. Comparative work measuring CCTV effect across countries is also important, as relevant policies, oversight, legislative restrictions, and normative values can influence variation in the adoption and effect of CCTV across the world.

CCTV has also become a component of a larger apparatus of surveillance technologies, inclusive of license plate readers, linked traffic cameras, and gunshot detection technology

(Skogan 2019). Computer vision and deep-learning technologies are also being developed to automate the detection of crime-related events, such as a weapon, fugitive vehicle, or aggressive physical behavior (Bhatti et al. 2021; Idrees, Shah, and Surette 2018). Research is needed to test whether and the level to which such a package of technological interventions improves upon stand-alone CCTV systems. Given the developed nature of the CCTV literature, there may be opportunities to use the current knowledge base to inform research and policy development relating to a range of contemporary police technologies (Piza 2021). Publicly disseminating CCTV research findings for such purposes represents an opportunity to increase research translation (Laub 2012) within the police technology realm.

More research is needed on issues other than program outcomes, as policymakers need to know more than whether a given practice "works." Program implementation is a particularly underexplored aspect of evidence-based crime prevention (Sidebottom and Tilley 2022; Weisburd, Farrington, and Gill 2017). Implementation issues are problematic in technological interventions such as CCTV, given the variety of interconnected software, hardware, and policy dimensions required for success (Piza et al. 2022; Salvemini et al. 2015). In this vein, CCTV researchers should answer recent calls for evidence-based crime prevention to move beyond focusing solely on crime outcomes in order to generate research findings that provide more practical guidance to policymakers (Sidebottom and Tilley 2022; Tompson et al. 2021; Weisburd et al. 2017).

IV. Conclusion

Should public safety agencies invest in CCTV? The honest answer is "it depends." While this answer may frustrate practitioners who need to make strategic decisions within a rapidly evolving operational environment—and look to research to help inform such decisions—it is the answer most reflective of the current research evidence.

There are some steps public safety agencies can take to help decide whether CCTV is an appropriate solution in their jurisdiction, and to help maximize the likelihood that CCTV will be effective. CCTV deployment should be preceded by an in-depth analysis of the spatial distribution and nature of crime patterns (Ratcliffe 2006; Welsh and Farrington 2002). A public safety agency wishing to combat robbery, for example, is best served by first identifying specific places experiencing disproportionate levels of robbery. Secondly, the specific incidents should be analyzed to identify whether or not the crime activity is susceptible to CCTV. For example, a street corner where a large number of robberies occurs is a more appropriate camera location than the outside of a mall where robberies occur indoors.

Initial problem analyses can be followed by a needs assessment that can determine the appropriate size, scope, and operational mission of CCTV for a given agency (Gill et al. 2006). A rigorous problem analysis may further assist implementation by identifying necessary preparations and support needed to increase the likelihood of success. Criminal justice policies, as well as social policy in general, often face challenges such as inadequate or poor staff training and lack of capacity to track process measures to the level needed to adjust program activities over time (Mears 2010; Rossi, Lipsey, and Freeman 2004; Salvemini et al. 2015). Identifying such issues before a program commences can enable the agency to remedy (or at least mediate) specific threats to program implementation.

It is important for the agency to make an honest assessment of the human capital available for surveillance purposes at the outset. Agency policies should also be drafted in a manner that's supportive of active monitoring practices. Piza, Caplan, and Kennedy (2014b) found the CCTV system in Newark became too large to be efficiently and effectively monitored, with each camera installation phase associated with up to a 47% reduction in weekly surveillance activity. This was exacerbated by the fact that financial constraints precluded additional personnel being added to surveillance functions, an issue that has been observed elsewhere (see, e.g., Priks 2015). CCTV operators in Newark further reported that the Newark Police Department's differential dispatch policy, which typically resulted in long time frames between incident reporting and officer dispatch, discouraged CCTV operators from reporting crime incidents unless they rose to the level of serious violence. In other words, the Newark PD was not taking advantage of the real-time identification of crime, despite this being an anticipated benefit of CCTV (Piza et al. 2022).

Agencies should also be mindful of a key finding of Piza and colleagues' (2019) meta-analysis: CCTV schemes incorporating multiple complementary interventions substantially outperformed other schemes. This reflects research finding CCTV effect is heighted when paired with proactive policing strategies (La Vigne et al. 2011; Piza et al. 2015)[7] and offender beliefs that CCTV presence does not guarantee increased risk of apprehension (Gannoni et al. 2017; Gill and Loveday 2003). Police agencies need to ensure their officers have the capacity to quickly address the criminogenic factors identified by CCTV operators. This can be easier said than done given the sometimes overwhelming demands placed on patrol functions by the 911 call system. However, police can identify whether spatial crime patterns indicate only a subset of cameras warrant additional resources in the form of complementary interventions. In such instances, these cameras could be prioritized for integration with other proactive interventions (Piza et al. 2015). If resource constraints prevent an agency from dedicating additional resources to CCTV operations, agency leadership should commit to installing only the number of cameras they can realistically support with proactive monitoring and policing efforts (Piza et al. 2014b, 2015).

Agencies facing such resource constraints (or that prioritize the prevention of violent crime, which CCTV has exhibited less effect on) should frankly consider whether funds would be better allocated toward other crime prevention programs. This is especially so given that the types of proactive activities associated with CCTV effect require a commitment of resources over and beyond what is needed to support stand-alone CCTV camera deployment (Circo and McGarrell 2021; Piza et al. 2015, 2019). The consideration of alternate strategies is facilitated by the amount of synthesized evidence available on a range of police and situational crime prevention interventions (Piza and Welsh 2022; Welsh 2019). When considering the cumulative findings of the CCTV cost-benefit research, CCTV schemes often fail to deliver sufficient crime reduction benefits to offset the costs of installing and operating the system (Gill and Spriggs 2005; La Vigne et al. 2011; Piza et al. 2016). Even studies finding monetary benefits likely do not speak to the true monetary cost benefits public safety agencies can expect, mainly because cost estimates typically include intangible societal costs. As argued by Ratcliffe (2015), "monetary costs to society mean little to the police as they do not recoup the costs of any crime reduction directly."

In considering operational efficiency, it is crucial that agencies remain mindful of social equity. Actively soliciting the input of community organizations can be invaluable. The City of Newark partnered with the local chapter of the American Civil Liberties Union (ACLU) when planning its CCTV program to ensure technological protections, such as ensuring the video monitoring software automatically blacked out all windows and other views into private spaces (Piza et al. 2022). Written policies should also clearly outline legal requirements for reasonable suspicion and probable cause. Prior research has documented CCTV operators relying on extra-legal factors to select individuals for surveillance (Loveday and Gill 2004; Norris and McCahill 2006) and engaging in inappropriate (e.g., commenting on the attractiveness of women involved in domestic disputes) (Norris and Armstrong 1999) or illegitimate (e.g., watching television) (Gill et al. 2005) surveillance activities. In this sense, the success of CCTV may be influenced by nontechnological factors, such as written policy, training, and performance oversight.

Notes

1. This information was gleaned from personal communication with Ratcliffe on April 13, 2022.
2. Redeployable CCTV cameras are an exception, given they can be moved quickly from place to place (Gill, Rose, and Collins 2015). In addition to potentially facilitating rigorous research designs, this could provide a general cost savings as compared to permanent, hard-wired cameras (Verga and Douglas 2008). However, redeployable CCTV does not seem to be used nearly as often as traditional CCTV. Research has also reported redeployable CCTV to commonly experience implementation failure (Gill et al. 2006).
3. Piza and colleagues (2019) noted the small number of studies conducted in South Korea (N = 3) call for caution in interpreting the magnitude of effects.
4. Piza and colleagues considered both arrests and other enforcement actions (e.g. citations and suspect record checks) in their analysis due to heterogeneous nature of crimes observed on CCTV. While arrest may be the only appropriate response for some serious offenses, police officers have discretion to take a less punitive action in most instances. Results were mostly unchanged when focusing on only arrests or other enforcement. The lone exceptions were arrest rates being significantly higher in the CCTV group for "low-priority" incidents and disorder not achieving statistical significance in the other enforcement analysis.
5. Robin and colleagues (2021) classified Group B offenses as minor offenses, such as disorderly conduct, drunkenness, driving under the influence, loitering, and trespassing.
6. However, it should be noted that Priks's (2015) evaluation of CCTV in the Stockholm subway system uses a one-group longitudinal time series design that controls for extraneous factors, which fits the selection criteria of other recent Campbell Collaboration systematic reviews (see e.g., Braga, Weisburd, and Turchan 2018).
7. However, it should be noted that Gerell (2016) found a project integrating actively monitored CCTV and foot patrols did not generate any significant effects in Malmö, Sweden.

References

Alexandrie, Gustav. 2017. Surveillance cameras and crime: A review of randomized and natural experiments. *Journal of Scandinavian Studies in Criminology and Crime Prevention*, 18 (2): 210–222. https://doi.org/10.1080/14043858.2017.1387410.

Aos, Steve. 2015. What is the bottom line? *Criminology and Public Policy*, 14 (4): 633–638.

Ariel, Barak. 2019. Technology in policing. In *Police innovation: Contrasting perspectives*. 2nd ed., Vol. 2, edited by David L. Weisburd and Anthony A. Braga, 485–516. Cambridge: Cambridge University Press. https://doi.org/10.1017/CBO9780511489334.

Ashby, Matthew P. J. 2017. The value of CCTV surveillance cameras as an investigative tool: An empirical analysis. *European Journal on Criminal Policy and Research*, 23 (3): 441–459. https://doi.org/10.1007/s10610-017-9341-6.

Bardach, Eugene. 2004. Presidential address—the extrapolation problem: How can we learn from the experience of others? *Journal of Policy Analysis and Management*, 23:205–220.

Bhatti, Muhammad Tahir, Muhammad Gufran Khan, Masood Aslam, and Muhammad Junaid Fiaz. 2021. Weapon detection in real-time CCTV videos using deep learning. *IEEE Access*, 9:34366–34382. https://doi.org/10.1109/ACCESS.2021.3059170.

Braga, Anthony A., David Weisburd, and Brandon Turchan. 2018. Focused deterrence strategies and crime control: An updated systematic review and meta-analysis of the empirical evidence. *Criminology and Public Policy*, 17 (1): 205–250. https://doi.org/10.1111/1745-9133.12353.

Brand, Sam, and Richard Price. 2000. The economic and social costs of crime. Research Study No 217. London: Home Office.

Brookman, Fiona, and Helen Jones. 2022. Capturing killers: the construction of CCTV evidence during homicide investigations. *Policing and Society*, 32 (2): 125–144. https://doi.org/10.1080/10439463.2021.1879075.

Brown, Ben. 1995. *CCTV (Closed Circuit Television) in town centres: Three case studies*. London: Home Office.

Cameron, Aundreia, Elke Kolodinski, Heather May, and Nicholas Williams. 2008. *Measuring the effects of video surveillance on crime in Los Angeles*. Los Angeles: University of Southern California, School of Policy, Planning, and Development.

Caplan, Joel M., Leslie W. Kennedy, and Gohar Petrossian. 2011. Police-monitored CCTV cameras in Newark, NJ: A quasi-experimental test of crime deterrence. *Journal of Experimental Criminology*, 7 (3): 255–274. https://doi.org/10.1007/s11292-011-9125-9.

Circo, Giovanni, and Edmund McGarrell. 2021. Estimating the impact of an integrated CCTV program on crime. *Journal of Experimental Criminology*, 17 (1): 129–150.

Cook, Thomas D., and Donald T. Campbell 1979. *Quasi-experimentation: Design and analysis issues for field settings*. Boston: Houghton Mifflin.

Cornish, Derek B., and Ronald V. Clarke. 2003. Opportunities, precipitators, and criminal decisions: A reply to Wortley's critique of situational crime prevention. In *Theory for practice in situational crime prevention*, edited by Martha J. Smith and Derek B. Cornish, 41–96. Monsey, NY: Criminal Justice Press.

Dunning, Thad. 2008. Improving causal inference: Strengths and limitations of natural experiments. *Political Research Quarterly*, 61 (2): 282–293. https://doi.org/10.1093/ije/dyt058.

Dunning, Thad. 2012. *Natural experiments in the social sciences. A design-based approach*. Cambridge: Cambridge University Press.

Eck, John E. 2017. Some solutions to the evidence-based crime prevention problem. In *Advances in evidence-based policing*, edited by Johannes Knutsson and Lisa Tompson, 45–63. New York: Routledge.

Farrington, David P., Martin Gill, Sam J. Waples, and Javier Argomaniz. 2007. The effects of closed-circuit television on crime: Meta-analysis of an English national quasi-experimental multi-site evaluation. *Journal of Experimental Criminology*, 3 (1): 21–38. https://doi.org/10.1007/s11292-007-9024-2.

Farrington, David P., Denise C. Gottfredson, Lawrence W. Sherman, and Brandon C. Welsh. 2006. The Maryland scientific methods scale. In *Evidence-based crime prevention*, edited by Lawrence W. Sherman, David P. Farrington, Brandon C. Welsh, and Doris L. MacKenzie 13–21. Rev. ed. New York: Routledge.

Gannoni, Alexandra, Matthew Willis, Emmeline Taylor, and Murray Lee. 2017. *Surveillance technologies and crime control: Understanding police detainees' perspectives on police body-worn video (BWV) and CCTV cameras*. Canberra City, Australia: Criminology Research Advisory Council.

Gerell, Manne. 2016. Hot spot policing with actively monitored CCTV cameras: Does it reduce assaults in public places? *International Criminal Justice Review*, 26 (2): 187–201. https://doi.org/10.1177/1057567716639098.

Gerell, Manne. 2021. CCTV in deprived neighbourhoods—A short-time follow-up of effects on crime and crime clearance. *Nordic Journal of Criminology*, 22 (2): 221–239. https://doi.org/10.1080/2578983X.2020.1816023.

Gill, Martin, Jenna Allen, Patricia Jessiman, Jonathan Kilworth, Daniel Swain, Angela Spriggs, Martin Hemming, Deena Kara, and Ross Little. 2005. *Control room operation: Findings from control room observations*. London: Home Office.

Gill, Martin, and Karryn Loveday. 2003. What do offenders think about CCTV? *Crime Prevention and Community Safety: An International Journal*, 5 (3): 17–25. https://doi.org/10.1057/palgrave.cpcs.8140152.

Gill, Martin, Athena Rose, and Kate Collins. 2015. *A good practice guide for the implementation of redeployable CCTV*. London: Home Office.

Gill, Martin, Athena Rose, Kate Collins, and Martin Hemming. 2006. Redeployable CCTV and drug-related crime: A case of implementation failure. *Drugs: Education, Prevention, and Policy*, 13 (5): 451–460. https://doi.org/10.1080/09687630600737188.

Gill, Martin, and Angela Spriggs. 2005. *Assessing the impact of CCTV*. Home Office Research Study No 292. London: Home Office.

Gimenez-Santana, Alejandro, Joel M. Caplan, and Leslie W. Kennedy. 2022. Data-informed community engagement: The Newark Public Safety Collaborative. In *The globalization of evidence-based policing: Innovations in bridging the research-practice divide*, edited by Eric L. Piza and Brandon C. Welsh, 191–205. Abingdon, UK: Routledge.

Hayes, Read, and Daniel M. Downs. 2011. Controlling retail theft with CCTV domes, CCTV public view monitors, and protective containers: A randomized controlled trial. *Security Journal*, 24:237–250. https://doi.org/10.1057/sj.2011.12.

Hollis, Meghan E. 2019. Security or surveillance?: Examination of CCTV camera usage in the 21st century. *Criminology and Public Policy*, 18 (1): 131–134. https://doi.org/10.1111/1745-9133.12427.

Idrees, Haroon, Mubarak Shah, and Ray Surette. 2018. Enhancing camera surveillance using computer vision: A research note. *Policing: An International Journal*, 41 (2): 292–307.

Jang, Yongseol, Dohyeong Kim, Junwi Park, and Dowoo Kim. 2018. Conditional effects of open-street closed-circuit television (CCTV) on crime: A case from Korea. *International Journal of Law, Crime and Justice*, 53 (June): 9–24. https://doi.org/10.1016/j.ijlcj.2018.02.001.

Jung, Yeondae, and Andrew P. Wheeler. 2021. The effect of public surveillance cameras on crime clearance rates. *Journal of Experimental Criminology* 40 (2): 553–571. https://doi.org/10.1002/pam.22280.

Katz, Charles M., and Jessica Huff. 2020. Implement collaborative strategic crime control initiatives. In *Transforming the police: Thirteen key reforms*, edited by Charles M. Katz and Edward R. Maguire, 31–46. Long Grove, IL: Waveland Press.

King, Jennifer, Deidre K. Mulligan, and Steven Raphael. 2008. *CITRIS Report: The San Francisco community safety camera program: An evaluation of the effectiveness of San Francisco's community safety cameras.* Berkeley: Center for Information Technology Research in the Interest of Society, University of California.

Kronkvist, Karl. 2022. The effect of target, catchment, and comparison site operationalization on CCTV impact evaluations: Methodological considerations from a case study. *Journal of Experimental Criminology* 18:765–782. https://doi.org/10.1007/s11292-021-09468-9.

La Vigne, Nancy G., and Samantha Lowry. 2011. *Evaluation of camera use to prevent crime in commuter parking facilities: A randomized controlled trial.* Washington, DC: Urban Institute Justice Policy Center.

La Vigne, Nancy G., Samantha Lowry, Joshua A. Markman, and Alison M. Dwyer. 2011. *Evaluating the use of public surveillance cameras for crime control and prevention.* Washington, DC: Urban Institute Justice Policy Center.

Laub, John H. 2012. Translational criminology. *Translational Criminology*, 3:4–5.

Lim, Hyungjin, Changjoo Kim, John E. Eck, and Jeonglim Kim. 2016. The crime-reduction effects of open-street CCTV in South Korea. *Security Journal*, 29 (2): 241–255. https://doi.org/10.1057/sj.2013.10.

Lim, Hyungjin, and Pamela Wilcox. 2017. Crime-reduction effects of open-street CCTV: Conditionality considerations. *Justice Quarterly*, 34 (4): 597–626. https://doi.org/10.1080/07418825.2016.1194449.

Loveday, Karryn, and Martin Gill. 2004. The impact of monitored CCTV in a retail environment: What CCTV operators do and why. *Crime Prevention and Community Safety*, 6:43–55.

Lum, Cynthia M., and Christopher S. Koper. 2017. *Evidence-based policing: Translating research into practice.* Oxford: Oxford University Press.

Lum, Cynthia M., Christopher S. Koper, and James Willis. 2017. Understanding the limits of technology's impact on police effectiveness. *Police Quarterly*, 20 (2): 135–163. https://doi.org/10.1177/1098611116667279.

Lum, Cynthia M., Christopher S. Koper, David B. Wilson, Megan Stoltz, Michael Goodier, Elizabeth Eggins, Angela Higginson, and Lorraine Mazerolle. 2020. Body-worn cameras' effects on police officers and citizen behavior: A systematic review. *Campbell Systematic Reviews*, 16 (3): 1–40. https://doi.org/10.1002/cl2.1112.

Matczak, Piotr, Andrzej Wójtowicz, Adam Dąbrowski, Michael Leitner, and Natalia Sypion-Dutkowska. 2021. Effectiveness of CCTV systems as a crime preventive tool: Evidence from eight Polish cities. *International Journal of Comparative and Applied Criminal Justice*, 47 (1): 37–56. https://doi.org/10.1080/01924036.2021.1976237.

Mazerolle, Lorraine, David Hurley, and Mitchell Chamlin. 2002. Social behavior in public space: An analysis of behavioral adaptations to CCTV. *Security Journal*, 15 (3): 59–75.

Mears, Daniel P. 2010. *American criminal justice policy: An evaluation approach to increasing accountability and effectiveness*. New York: Cambridge University Press.

Morgan, Anthony, and Christopher Dowling. 2019. *Does CCTV help police solve crime?* Canberra: Australian Institute of Criminology.

Norris, Clive, and Gary Armstrong. 1999. CCTV and the social structuring of surveillance. In *Surveillance of public space: CCTV, street lighting and crime prevention*, edited by Nick Tilley and Kate Painter, 157–178. Crime Prevention Studies, Vol. 10. Monsey, NY: Criminal Justice Press.

Norris, Clive, and Michael McCahill. 2006. CCTV: Beyond penal modernism? *British Journal of Criminology*, 46 (1): 97–118. https://doi.org/10.1093/bjc/azi047.

Oberwittler, Dietrich, and Per-Olof H. Wikstrom. 2009. Why small is better: Advancing the study of the role of behavioral contexts in crime causation. In *Putting crime in its place: Units of analysis in geographic criminology*, edited by David Weisburd, Wim Bernasco, and Gerben J. N. Bruinsma, 35–59. New York: Springer.

Paine, Colin. 2012. Solvability factors in dwelling burglaires in Thames Valley. MA diss., Wolfson College.

Petras, Sarah. 2018. Is closed circuit television (CCTV) an effective tool for case clearance? MA diss., Central Connecticut State University.

Piza, Eric L. 2018. The crime prevention effect of CCTV in public places: A propensity score analysis. *Journal of Crime and Justice*, 41 (1): 14–30. https://doi.org/10.1080/0735648X.2016.1226931.

Piza, Eric L. 2021. The history, policy implications, and knowledge gaps of the CCTV literature: Insights for the development of body-worn video camera research. *International Criminal Justice Review*, 31 (3): 304–324. https://doi.org/10.1177/1057567718759583.

Piza, Eric L., Joel M. Caplan, and Leslie W. Kennedy. 2014a. Analyzing the influence of micro-level factors on CCTV camera effect. *Journal of Quantitative Criminology*, 30 (2): 237–264. https://doi.org/10.1007/s10940-013-9202-5.

Piza, Eric L., Joel M. Caplan, and Leslie W. Kennedy. 2014b. Is the punishment more certain? An analysis of CCTV detections and enforcement. *Justice Quarterly*, 31 (6): 1015–1043. https://doi.org/10.1080/07418825.2012.723034.

Piza, Eric L., Joel M. Caplan, Leslie W. Kennedy, and Andrew M. Gilchrist. 2015. The effects of merging proactive CCTV monitoring with directed police patrol: A randomized controlled trial. *Journal of Experimental Criminology*, 11 (1): 43–69. https://doi.org/10.1007/s11292-014-9211-x.

Piza, Eric L., Sarah P. Chu, and Brandon C. Welsh. 2022. Surveillance, action research, and community technology oversight boards: A proposed model for police technology research. In *The globalization of evidence-based policing: Innovations in bridging the research-practice divide*, edited by Eric L. Piza and Brandon C. Welsh, 206–222. Abington, UK: Routledge.

Piza, Eric L., Andrew M. Gilchrist, Joel M. Caplan, Leslie W. Kennedy, and Brian A. O'Hara. 2016. The financial implications of merging proactive CCTV monitoring and directed police patrol: A cost-benefit analysis. *Journal of Experimental Criminology*, 12 (3): 403–429. https://doi.org/10.1007/s11292-016-9267-x.

Piza, Eric L., and Brandon C. Welsh 2022. Evidence-based policing: Research, practice, and bridging the great divide. In *The globalization of evidence-based policing: Innovations in bridging the research-practice divide*, edited by Eric L. Piza and Brandon C. Welsh, 3–20. Abington, UK: Routledge.

Piza, Eric L., Brandon C. Welsh, David P. Farrington, and Amanda L. Thomas. 2019. CCTV surveillance for crime prevention: A 40-year systematic review with meta-analysis. *Criminology and Public Policy*, 18 (1): 135–159. https://doi.org/10.1111/1745-9133.12419.

Prenzler, Tim, and Eric Wilson. 2019. The Ipswich (Queensland) safe city program: An evaluation. *Security Journal*, 32 (2): 137–152. https://doi.org/10.1057/s41284-018-0152-3.

Priks, Mikael. 2015. The effects of surveillance cameras on crime: Evidence from the Stockholm subway. *Economic Journal*, 125 (588): F289–F305. https://doi.org/10.1111/ecoj.12327.

Ratcliffe, Jerry H. 2006. *Video surveillance of public places*. Problem-Oriented Guides for Police. Response Guide Series, No. 4. Washington, DC: US Department of Justice, Office of Community Oriented Policing Services.

Ratcliffe, Jerry H. 2015. Towards an index for harm-focused policing. *Policing, A Journal of Policy and Practice*, 9 (2): 164–182. https://doi.org/10.1093/police/pau032.

Ratcliffe, Jerry H., and Elizabeth R. Groff. 2019. A longitudinal quasi-experimental study of violence and disorder impacts of urban CCTV camera clusters. *Criminal Justice Review*, 44 (2): 148–164. https://doi.org/10.1177/0734016818811917.

Ratcliffe, Jerry H., Travis Taniguchi, and Ralph B. Taylor. 2009. The crime reduction effects of public CCTV cameras: A multi-method spatial approach. *Justice Quarterly*, 26 (4): 746–770. https://doi.org/10.1080/07418820902873852.

Robb, Paul, Timothy Coupe, and Barak Ariel. 2015. "Solvability" and detection of metal theft on railway property. *European Journal on Criminal Policy and Research*, 21 (4): 463–484. https://doi.org/10.1007/s10610-014-9253-7.

Robin, Lily, Bryce E. Peterson, and Daniel S. Lawrence. 2021. How do close-circuit television cameras impact crimes and clearances? An evaluation of the Milwaukee police department's public surveillance system. *Police Practice and Research*, 22 (2): 1171–1190. https://doi.org/10.1080/15614263.2020.1772783.

Rosenbaum, Paul R. 2002. *Observational studies*. 2nd ed. New York: Springer.

Rossi, Peter H., Mark W. Lipsey, and Howard E. Freeman. 2004. *Evaluation: A systematic approach*. 7th ed. Thousand Oaks, CA: SAGE.

Salvemini, Anthony V., Eric L. Piza, Jeremy G. Carter, Eric L. Grommon, and Nancy Merritt. 2015. Integrating human factors engineering and information processing approaches to facilitate evaluations in criminal justice technology research. *Evaluation Review*, 39 (3): 308–338. https://doi.org/10.1177/0193841X15583404.

Sampson, Robert J., Christopher Winship, and Carly Knight. 2013. Translating causal claims: Principles and strategies for policy-relevant criminology. *Criminology and Public Policy*, 12 (4): 587–616.

Schnell, Cory, Anthony A. Braga, and Eric L. Piza. 2017The influence of community areas, neighborhood clusters, and street segments on the spatial variability of violent crime in Chicago. *Journal of Quantitative Criminology*, 33 (3): 469–496. https://doi.org/10.1007/s10940-016-9313-x.

Sharp, Stephanie. 2016. Pickpocketing on the railway: Targeting solvable cases. MA diss., Fitzwilliam College.

Sherman, Lawrence W., Denise C. Gottfredson, Doris L. MacKenzie, John E. Eck, Peter Reuter, and Shawn Bushway. 1997. *Preventing crime: What works, what doesn't, what's promising*. Washington, DC: Office of Justice Programs, National Institute of Justice.

Sidebottom, Aiden, and Nick Tilley. 2022. EMMIE and the What Works Centre for Crime Reduction: Progress, challenges, and future directions for evidence-based policing and crime reduction in the United Kingdom. In *The globalization of evidence-based policing: Innovations in bridging the research-practice divide*, edited by Eric L. Piza and Brandon C. Welsh, 73–91. Abingdon, UK: Routledge.

Sivarajasingam, Vaseekaran., J.P. Shepherd, and K. Matthews. 2003. Effect of urban closed circuit television on assault injury and violence detection. *Injury Prevention*, 9 (4): 312–316. https://doi.org/10.1136/ip.9.4.312.

Skogan, Wesley G. 2019. The future of CCTV. *Criminology and Public Policy*, 18 (1): 161–166. https://doi.org/10.1111/1745-9133.12422.

Squires, Peter. 1998. *CCTV and crime reduction in Crawley*. Brighton, UK: Health and Social Policy Research Center.

Steenbeek, Wouter, and David L. Weisburd. 2015. Where the action is in crime? An examination of variability of crime across different spatial units. *Journal of Quantitative Criminology*, 32 (3): 449–469. https://doi.org/10.1007/s10940-015-9276-3.

Thomas, Amanda L., Eric L. Piza, Brandon C. Welsh, and David P. Farrington. 2022. The internationalisation of CCTV surveillance: Effects on crime and implications for emerging technologies. *International Journal of Comparative and Applied Criminal Justice*, 46 (1): 81–102. https://doi.org/10.1080/01924036.2021.1879885.

Tompson, Lisa, Jyoti Belur, Amy Thornton, Kate J. Bowers, Shane D. Johnson, Aiden Sidebottom, Nick Tilley, and Gloria Laycock. 2021. How strong is the evidence-base for crime reduction professionals? *Justice Evaluation Journal*, 4 (1): 68–97. https://doi.org/10.1080/24751979.2020.1818275.

Verga, Simona, and A. J. Douglas. 2008. *Initial statistical analysis of the effects of closed-circuit surveillance on rates of crime*. Ottawa, ON: Toronto Police Service, Operational Research Team, Centre for Security Science.

Weisburd, David, David P. Farrington, and Charlotte Gill. 2017. What works in crime prevention and rehabilitation: An assessment of systematic reviews. *Criminology and Public Policy*, 16 (2): 415–449. https://doi.org/10.1111/1745-9133.12298.

Welsh, Brandon C. 2019. Evidence-based policing for crime prevention. In *Police innovation: Contrasting perspectives*, edited by David L. Weisburd and Anthony A. Braga, 439–456. Cambridge: Cambridge University Press.

Welsh, Brandon C., and David P. Farrington 2002. Crime prevention effects of closed circuit television: A systematic review. London: Home Office. https://doi.org/10.4073/csr.2008.17.

Welsh, Brandon C., and David P. Farrington 2007. *Preventing crime: What works for children, offenders, victims and places*. New York: Springer.

Welsh, Brandon C., and David P. Farrington 2009. Public area CCTV and crime prevention: An updated systematic review and meta-analysis. *Justice Quarterly*, 26 (4): 716–745. https://doi.org/10.1080/07418820802506206.

Welsh, Brandon C., and David P. Farrington 2015. Monetary value of early developmental crime prevention and its policy signifiance. *Criminology and Public Policy*, 14 (4): 673–680.

Welsh, Brandon C., Eric L. Piza, Amanda L. Thomas, and Daivd P. Farrington. 2020. Private security and closed-circuit television (CCTV) surveillance: A systematic review of function and performance. *Journal of Contemporary Criminal Justice*, 36 (1): 56–69. https://doi.org/10.1177/1043986219890192.

Welsh, Brandon C., Peter H. van der Laan, and Meghan E. Hollis. 2013. Systematic reviews and cost-benefit analysis: Toward evidence-based crime policy. In *Experimental criminology: Prospects for advancing science and public policy*, edited by Brandon C. Welsh, Anthony A. Braga, and Gerben J. N. Bruinsma, 253–276. New York: Cambridge University Press.

White, Michael D., and Aili Malm. 2020. *Cops, cameras, and crisis. The potential and the perils of police body-worn cameras.* New York: New York University Press.

CHAPTER 15

REHABILITATION FOR ENDURING CHANGE
Toward Evidence-Based Corrections

MICHAEL ROCQUE

THE purpose—whether stated or understood—of the correctional system has been in flux through time and has often been a source of disagreement among the public and policymakers alike. What happens when we convict someone of a crime? Do we provide them with the resources and support they need to become law-abiding citizens? Do we lock them up in order to prevent more harm done to the community? Are we punishing the individual to send a message to the public regarding the morality of the act for which they were convicted? The term "corrections," in fact, is relatively new. In 1947, Leon Stern published an essay in *The Prison Journal* arguing for the creation of a "State Department of Corrections," which would replace the Department of Welfare in operating the prisons in Pennsylvania. Importantly, the Department would

> classify and transfer prisoners so that each prisoner may be assigned to an appropriate institution and be given the individual program in that institution most conducive to rehabilitation or reform. The dangerous prisoner will be sent to maximum security care, the amenable adult to minimum security care, the youth to industrial training. Work and school programs, medical, psychiatric, and psychological services will be set up to assist individuals in their rehabilitation. (Stern 1947, 283–284)

Clearly then, the goal of incarcerating individuals would be to "correct" what was wrong and reduce their chances of reoffending. This is not to say, of course, that rehabilitation was absent from the philosophies of prison systems prior to the mid-20th century. After all, the term "penitentiary" implies that the purpose of incarceration was to help improve the individual. But, as Cullen (2013, 312) has written, the period from 1920 to the 1970s was the time in which "rehabilitation consolidated its hold. . . . The very use of the term 'corrections'— whether in reference to correctional institutions or community corrections—signaled the ideological dominance of the rehabilitative ideal."

Several eras, each marked by their own pithy catchphrases, have emerged in corrections. Prior to the 1970s, a period of cautious optimism reigned. The "progressive era," which spanned the beginning of the 20th century to around 1920 brought about reforms in correctional practices, with an eye toward humanitarianism and rehabilitation (Walker 1998). Not much was known about whether rehabilitation was effective or did what it was supposed to, but most believed that it was the proper approach to handling those convicted of crimes (Cullen 2013). That changed, however, in the mid-1970s, during which the "nothing works" era arose based on political dynamics as well as the famous "Martinson Report" (Cullen and Gendreau 2001). During that period, faith in rehabilitation declined and some concluded that rehabilitation as a guiding principle had failed (see, e.g., Wilson 1975). In the 1990s, the "what works" era emerged, as scholars sought to push back against the narrative that there was no solid evidence that treatment for those convicted of crimes produced positive outcomes (Cullen and Gilbert 1982). Finally, the present-day may be accurately summed up as the "evidence-based corrections" era. Evidence-based programs (EBP) or practices dominate scholarly discussions within corrections, and clearinghouses listing programs that meet certain criteria have proliferated.

A large body of literature now exists on evidence-based corrections. That said, there is controversy with respect to which strategies or approaches are most effective or cost-efficient. In large part, this is because while much progress has been made in discovering what works, there is still work to be done to improve the evidence. The purpose of this chapter is to review the state of knowledge on correctional rehabilitation, with attention to both policies and practices that are effective as well as those that are not. The focus will be on policy and practices within prisons and the community. The second section of the chapter will discuss ways to improve both the evidence and use of evidence in corrections.

I. Evidence for Correctional Rehabilitation

Since Robert Martinson's (1974) essay, interpreted widely to mean that "nothing works" in corrections to reduce recidivism, scholars have made great strides in understanding rehabilitation. The "what works" era was in no small part ushered in by a group of Canadian psychologists, who argued that there actually was strong evidence about how to reduce recidivism, and that the key was to understand risk levels, criminogenic needs, and the ways in which the client may respond to treatments (Andrews, Bonta, and Hoge 1990). This basic idea served as the framework for the "Risk-Need-Responsivity" (RNR) paradigm, which is arguably the most dominant one across North American correctional systems. Andrews and colleagues argued that a psychological view of crime, though anathema to "mainstream" criminology, provided a foundation for intervention. Mainstream criminology, they suggested was "antidifferentiation" and "antitreatment," and mistakenly took lack of "covariation" between programs and recidivism as "unthreatened evidence that we know nothing about individual criminal conduct" (21). A focus on risk, need, and responsivity, in their view, could and did lead to principles of effective intervention, such as the notion that treatment should be prioritized, and would be more effective, for high-risk individuals (e.g., those with a higher actuarial risk score indicating a greater likelihood of recidivism) (Gendreau 1996).

When programs that adhered to the RNR approach were evaluated, data indicated that they were effective in reducing recidivism. In a meta-analysis of 45 studies, Andrews and colleagues (1990) found that programs that utilized "appropriate" interventions (targeting high-risk individuals, using behavioral interventions, etc.) were more likely to reduce recidivism. This study, a reanalysis of a dataset of controlled studies that had previously been used to demonstrate the ineffectiveness of treatment (Whitehead and Lab 1989), was an important step in reversing the nothing works narrative. Since that time, the RNR approach has continued to proliferate, with several actuarial risk assessment tools designed to assess both risk and needs, such as the Level of Service Inventory-Revised (LSI-R) and a tool to assess program adherence to the approach (the Correctional Program Assessment Inventory). It is no exaggeration to say that the RNR model is the prevailing approach used by correctional agencies in the United States and other Western nations (Justice Inspectorates 2020). Meta-analyses of rigorous studies continue to show that programs adhering to the model are more effective (Hanson et al. 2009; Koehler et al. 2013).

A. Prison-Based Programs and Policies

Treatment in prisons and jails is diverse. It includes a focus on a wide range of issues such as substance use, relationship dynamics, and occupational and education deficits. Reviews of meta-analyses of correctional treatment programs consistently show that they positively influence behavior by reducing recidivism (Lipsey and Cullen 2007). Ideally, rehabilitation is tailored to the specific needs and deficits of the individual. This requires each individual to be assessed to determine the areas that are in need of improvement. In this section, programs and policies will be reviewed according to whether they address specific skills, general cognitive processes, or address a need, such as substance abuse. As a note, where possible, meta-analyses, or statistical evaluations of numerous studies on a topic, are used to distill the literature. However, this method is not without shortcomings. For example, if programs are not evaluated or if evaluations finding "null" effects are not published, they cannot be included in the meta-analyses. The method, therefore, is only as good as the literature allows.

1. Skills-Based Programming and Policies

One of the most persistent findings in the literature on recidivism is that those who are able to find meaningful employment are less likely to return to crime (Berg and Huebner 2011; Skardhamar and Telle 2012). Thus, it follows that providing job training and connecting inmates to occupational resources in the community would be effective measures to reduce reoffending. Within prisons, work- or employment-based programs seek to provide inmates with skills necessary to find meaningful employment upon release. Such programs are perhaps the most long-standing in prisons, as labor was considered fundamental to the inmate experience in the earliest American prisons, and thought to be important for rehabilitation (Rubin 2021). But work programs are also used to occupy prisoner time, and so simply having inmates perform work-related tasks may not always be done for the purpose of rehabilitation (Bushway 2003).

While there is certainly heterogeneity in terms of work programs, research tends to show that those who participate in them during incarceration are less likely to recidivate than those who do not. One meta-analysis included studies evaluating vocational, educational, and work programs in prison (Wilson, Gallagher, and MacKenzie 2000). Across 33 studies with 53 program/comparison group assessments, vocational, educational, and work programs were associated with lower recidivism. The largest effect was for postsecondary education programs, followed by vocational training programs and adult basic education/GED programs. There was no statistically significant effect for correctional work/industries. It should be noted that only 6% of the comparisons in the meta-analysis utilized randomized assignment, which limits the ability to make strong conclusions about these interventions.

Studies have also been conducted on employment programs for those who have been released into the community. In their meta-analysis, Visher, Winterfield, and Coggeshall (2005) included eight studies that utilized random assignment. Overall, the authors found that the effect size was quite small (.03) and not statistically significant. One study in the meta-analysis that did show a statistically significant effect was the re-evaluation of the National Supported Work Demonstration Project (Uggen 2000). This study is noteworthy because it illustrates heterogeneity in the effectiveness of work programs. Uggen (2000) found, for example, that the program reduced recidivism for those older than age 26 but had no impact for younger individuals. Most of the studies in the meta-analysis were also somewhat dated. Given the changes in the economy in recent years, "rigorous evaluations of contemporary employment interventions for former prisoners are sorely needed" (Visher, Winterfield, and Coggeshall 2005, 311). This appraisal remains true today.

One issue with the employment and vocational training programs is that there is variation in the type of training that is provided. In addition, at least theoretically, for these programs to "work," they must first help the individual find employment. Evaluations should examine whether the programs led to greater levels of employment post-release, and whether that is, in turn, related to recidivism. Duwe's (2017) review of employment/work programs in prison found that, overall, such programs did seem to increase employment, but had a "minimal" effect on recidivism (p. 10). Why might this be the case? The life-course literature has suggested that employment on its own will not result in a turning point in an individual's trajectory. Rather, that employment must be meaningful (Sampson and Laub 1993). To the extent that employment/work programs can help individuals find meaningful (and financially stable) employment, they may have stronger effects on recidivism. However, if the programs influence risk factors for crime other than work, they may be effective as well. Meta-analyses should consider the content of the training to determine whether certain aspects are more effective than others. Recent meta-analyses of dog-training programs, which sometimes seek to provide vocational training, have shown positive effects on internal factors like self-control as well as recidivism (Cooke and Farrington 2016; Duindam et al. 2020). In general, much more work is needed to examine the effects of work/vocational programs in prison and after release. That includes identifying the heterogeneity in these programs and which ones may be most effective in general or for certain populations.

More research has been conducted evaluating educational programs in prisons. The theoretical connection from education programs to later criminal behavior is similar to that for work programs, as increased education ostensibly creates employment opportunities. Several meta-analyses have been conducted on education programs in prisons, which are quite widespread in the United States (Latessa, Johnson, and Koetzle 2020). The RAND

Corporation (Davis et al. 2013) conducted a study meant to build on previous reviews of education programs (Aos, Miller, and Drake 2006; Lipton, Martinson, and Wilks 1975; MacKenzie 2006; Wilson, Gallagher, and MacKenzie 2000). The meta-analysis included 50 recidivism, 18 employment, and 4 test score studies, with 71, 22, and 9 effect sizes, respectively. For recidivism, the overall effect was calculated as an odds ratio of .64, which translates to a 64% reduction in the odds of recidivism for those who experienced educational programming compared to those who did not. With respect to employment outcomes, the study similarly found positive effects, with an overall odds ratio of 1.13, which means those receiving educational programming were more likely to find employment on release. A more recent meta-analysis (Bozick et al. 2018) provides an interesting update to the RAND study. While educational programming (57 studies) was found to reduce recidivism, such programs did not improve employment outcomes (21 studies) in this review. Overall, reviews tend to conclude that educational programs are effective in reducing recidivism (Latessa, Johnson, and Koetzle 2020; MacKenzie 2006), but Latessa and colleagues note that completion of the programs seems to be important in producing positive outcomes.

2. *Cognitive-Behavioral Treatments*

Cognitive-behavioral treatment, often called cognitive-behavioral therapy (CBT) is a type of approach that seeks to identify problematic thinking patterns and attitudes that lead to unwanted behaviors. Thinking patterns, sometimes called "criminal thinking," involve "distorted cognition—self-justificatory thinking, misinterpretation of social cues, displacement of blame, deficient moral reasoning, schemas of dominance and entitlement, and the like" (Lipsey, Landenberger, and Wilson 2007, 4). There have been numerous meta-analyses of CBT, for both juveniles and adults, often finding positive results (Latessa, Johnson, and Koetzle 2020; MacKenzie 2006). Latessa and colleagues (2020, 115) noted that CBT "programs that include multiple components appear to have the greatest potential for reducing antisocial and violent behavior." In Lipsey and Cullen's (2007) review, they identified five meta-analyses of specifically CBT approaches, in addition to several others that reviewed programs utilizing CBT techniques (such as Reasoning and Rehabilitation). Each study found positive effects of CBT, with recidivism reductions ranging from -32% to -8% for generic CBT for adults.

Cognitive-based approaches are used for a wide range of populations, from juveniles to adults, those convicted of sexual offenses, and those suffering from substance use disorders. With respect to those convicted of sexual offenses, meta-analyses have shown promise. Harrison and colleagues' (2020) meta-analyses of 25 studies, producing 42 effect sizes, found that CBT was effective in reducing sexual and violent recidivism, but there was quite a bit of variability in the effects. Another meta-analysis examining ten CBT evaluations for sexual offenders who were classified as moderate to high risk found that such programs are effective, with larger reductions in general recidivism. A review of the literature on CBT for criminal justice found that 63.1% of substance/drug use programs evaluated showed promise in reducing problem behavior and that effects of CBT are generally stronger for juveniles than adults (Feucht and Holt 2016). In Lipsey, Landenberger, and Wilson's (2007) Campbell Collaboration review of 58 studies, the authors found that programs that were more effective targeted anger/conflict and were operated by highly trained professionals. In a recent meta-analysis of in-prison psychological interventions, Beaudry et al. (2021) found an overall significant reduction in recidivism; however, when they excluded small sample studies (those with less than 50 participants), the effect was no longer significant.

3. *Substance Use and Abuse Programs*

Substance use and abuse is closely associated with crime and deviance (Menard, Mihalic, and Huizinga 2001). Estimates suggest that over 25% of federal and state prisoners were using alcohol, and over 30% were using drugs, when they committed the offense for which they were incarcerated (Maruschak, Bronson, and Alper 2021). Thus, treatment programs that focus on substance use and abuse should theoretically be effective in reducing later criminal behavior. Reviews of programs that treat substance abuse indicate that they do in fact reduce recidivism, but there is variation among types of programs, with some not designed appropriately to be effective (Latessa et al. 2020). According to Duwe (2017), chemical dependency programs are more effective if they are conducted within a therapeutic community and utilize CBT. Providing care upon release is also vital to help prevent relapse. One meta-analysis found that therapeutic communities were associated with reduced reoffending, whereas boot camps and counseling were not (Pearson and Lipton 1999). Therapeutic communities (TC) are immersive programs, often run by formerly addicted individuals and those who are also incarcerated, that focus on providing the individual with the resources needed to take control of their addiction (Wexler and Love 1994; Wexler 1995). In their review of psychological interventions in prisons, Beaudry and colleagues (2021) found that two randomized controlled trials of TCs reduced recidivism.

B. Community-Based Rehabilitation Programs

Correctional rehabilitation also takes place in the community, either as an alternative to incarceration or upon release. For juveniles, programs that take place in the community and for which there is strong evidence of effectiveness are listed by clearinghouses such as the Blueprints for Healthy Youth Development program (blueprintsprograms.org). Blueprints rates programs as "Model" and "Model Plus" when there is evidence of effectiveness from rigorous evaluations. Model Plus programs include "independent" evaluation, meaning the program developers were not involved in the study. Among the programs that target criminal behavior are Functional Family Therapy (FFT) and Multisystemic Therapy (MST). These programs address risk factors in the juvenile's environment, such as family interactions and school/peer relationships. For example, FFT, which is used for juveniles from age 11–18, involves clinical treatment with therapists, typically lasting about three months. The treatment focuses on enhancing self-efficacy within the family, facilitating strategies that will allow the family to function well even after therapy ends (Sexton and Alexander 2000). Meta-analyses of the program have found moderate effects on substance use and problem behavior, though not in every comparison (Baldwin et al. 2011; Hartnett et al. 2017). Overall, there are seven Model and Model Plus programs for adolescents that take place in the community listed on the Blueprints website, with another nine "Promising" programs.[1] Family interventions appear to be effective in changing behavior of youth but more research is needed on family programs for adults (Latessa et al. 2020).

Community-based treatment appears to be effective in reducing recidivism for both juveniles and adults. In Lipsey and Cullen's review of systematic reviews (2007), the authors identified seven meta-analyses of community treatment programs (some meta-analyses examined both community and residential programs), with each showing that treatment reduced recidivism, from 14% to 38%. Interestingly, some work has shown that community-based treatment is more effective than treatment that takes place within facilities. Lipsey's (2018) meta-analysis of rehabilitation programs for justice-involved adults found that compared to other settings, treatment on parole had statistically significantly higher effect sizes. Probation treatment had higher effect sizes as well, but not statistically significantly so. For young offenders (<=age 25), a meta-analysis also showed higher effect sizes for community based treatments (Koehler et al. 2013).

Certain of the types of programs discussed in the prison rehabilitation section also take place within the community. For example, community-based substance use and abuse programs for criminal justice-involved individuals appear effective as a post-release supervision approach in reducing crime, but not as effective as therapeutic communities (Holloway, Bennett, and Farrington 2006). Cognitive-behavioral therapy is also used for those on probation and parole. Little (2005) meta-analyzed nine studies evaluating a particular CBT program, Moral Reconation Therapy. His results indicated a statistically significant effect of treatment on recidivism (ES.2238). Finally, sex offender treatment programs occur in both facilities and in the community. Hanson and colleagues (2002) meta-analyzed psychological treatment evaluations for sex offenders in both the community and institutional environment. For adults, both types of treatment reduced sexual recidivism, but no effects were found for adolescents. With respect to general recidivism, only community treatment showed effects, for both adults and adolescents. Other meta-analyses have similarly suggested that sex offender treatment can reduce recidivism (Reitzel and Carbonell 2006; Schmucker and Lösel 2015), particularly when they are conducted in accordance with the principles of effective intervention (Hanson et al. 2009; Latessa, Johnson, and Koetzle 2020) or when they use CBT or chemical castration/psychotherapy (MacKenzie 2006). It is important to note, though, that a common refrain in each of these meta-analyses is that high-quality studies are rare in the literature and so caution is warranted.

An approach that bridges prison and community-based rehabilitation focuses on reintegrating the individual into society following incarceration. Re-entry issues were largely overlooked until the 1990s when then president of the National Institute of Justice Jeremy Travis began to examine best practices and strategies to reduce recidivism (Travis 2000, 2005). In an early review, Joan Petersilia (2004) argued that much more research was needed to identify effective re-entry approaches. This still appears to be the case today (Duwe 2017). Meta-analyses of program evaluations generally show inconsistent or weak effects. These programs often focus on finding employment or enhancing employability of ex-offenders. Visher, Winterfield, and Coggeshall (2005) reviewed studies of employment programs for offenders in the community, finding no effects, but noting the small number of high-quality evaluations. Berghuis (2018) meta-analyzed data from nine randomized controlled trials (RCTs) evaluating re-entry programs for adult males, finding there was a modest effect for both arrest and conviction. None of the studies showed statistically significant results.

Another meta-analysis (Bouchard and Wong 2018) of 41 supervision programs (after care and intensive supervision) for juveniles was similarly inconclusive. For aftercare programs, criminal contacts, arrests, and charges were reduced but no effects were found for convictions. For intensive supervision, there were no effects found for either offenses or convictions. A recent review argued that mixed findings of re-entry program results may be due to the quality of the evaluations but also to the quality of the programs themselves (Petrich et al. 2022). Indeed, throughout the re-entry literature, there are examples of programs with strong effects on employment and recidivism, but also many examples of programs with null or modest effects (see, e.g., Duwe 2015). Thus, program variability is likely a key to understanding mixed findings of re-entry evaluations.

II. What Does Not Work in Correctional Rehabilitation?

While the evidence on what works in correctional rehabilitation is filled with caveats and calls for more research, we do seem to have a good idea about what does *not* work to reduce reoffending and increase public safety. Punishment and supervision with little attention to programming or risk levels does not reduce recidivism, and may in some cases make things worse (Cullen, Johnson, and Nagin 2011; Latessa, Johnson, and Koetzle 2020; Loeffler and Nagin 2022; Petrich et al. 2021).

Doing something—more programming, for example—for incarcerated individuals can be key. Duwe and Clark (2017) showed that in Minnesota prisons, if individuals were "warehoused"—that is, they did not receive any programming—they had a higher rate of recidivism. Being involved in one program decreased recidivism for this sample and being involved with two programs doubled that reduction.

It is important to note that incarceration experiences are not uniform, either by geographic location or individual characteristics. These differences need to be taken into account to more fully assess the effects of incarceration and to better understand the experiences of those who report beneficial change during imprisonment (Mears, Cochran, and Cullen 2015; Kazemian 2021). It is also necessary to continue to explore how treatment effects may differ across populations and correctional settings.

Additionally, deterrence-based approaches focused on punitiveness appear to be ineffective or iatrogenic (harm-inducing). For example, one infamous intervention called "Scared Straight" initiated in the 1970s was based on the notion that exposing juveniles at risk for, or who have already engaged in, delinquency to adult prisons would be so shocking that the youth would change their course of behavior. However, systematic reviews have consistently shown that Scared Straight and other "juvenile awareness programs" significantly increase crime for juveniles (see, e.g., Petrosino, Petrosino, and Buehler 2005). Another model premised on the idea that young offenders can be shocked into a new lifestyle is the correctional boot camp. Correctional boot camps seek to provide structure and discipline in individuals' lives, much like that found in the military. Yet, despite some program variation, the results of evaluations of boot camps have been disappointing. A Campbell Collaboration systematic review by Wilson, MacKenzie, and Mitchell (2005) found virtually no effect on recidivism for this model. Thus, primarily punitive or deterrence-based approaches that do not provide skills or treatment do not seem to be effective in reducing offending.

In their book on what works (and doesn't) to reduce recidivism, Latessa and colleagues (2020) discussed examples of what they called "correctional quackery," or approaches not grounded in evidence-based theory and that are thus unlikely to work. These include acupuncture, drama therapy, yoga, and handwriting formation. They discussed a program that sought to introduce men "to their feminine side" by having the men dress as women. Aside from being offensive, this type of approach is not aligned with any theory that would lead us to expect it to change antisocial behavior.

III. Promoting and Enhancing Evidence-Based Practices in Corrections

Since Martinson's (1974) declaration, a massive body of literature has accumulated attesting to the effectiveness of particular approaches to correctional rehabilitation. Vocational and educational programs, cognitive-behavioral therapy, substance use/abuse programs, and holistic programs for at-risk youth appear generally to reduce recidivism. However, questions remain, which may impede adoption of evidence-based programs. This section reviews factors that may serve to reduce the use of programs in correctional agencies, including cost, and other factors, such as unknown variation in program effects and lack of clarity about what evidence-based means.

A. Costs of Programming

One factor that may lead to agency hesitancy to adopt programs is the sheer cost of rehabilitation (for example, Functional Family Therapy is estimated to cost around $52,000 to initiate[2]). These costs may deter some correctional agencies from investing in certain programs. Particularly at a time when the COVID-19 pandemic has led to severe staff shortages in correctional facilities (Blakinger et al. 2021), the resources needed to focus on high-quality rehabilitation approaches may be lacking. However, given the costs of crime and of traditional criminal justice responses, any strategy that reduces offending has the potential to create substantial cost savings. Existing work on this subject tends to suggest that the benefits of correctional treatment outweigh the costs (Welsh 2004). For example, while initiating Functional Family Therapy can be expensive, research on the cost savings of the program indicates that the program results in over $1 billion in saved costs due to reduced incarceration (Robbins and Turner 2018). An analysis by the Washington State Institute for Public Policy showed that FFT cost, on average, $3,358 per participant, but resulted in $37,554 in savings (Lee, Aos, and Pennucci 2015).

Again, there is variability in the benefits of programming, and more work is needed to promote the use of evidence-based practices. As Weisburd and colleagues (2017, 436) stated, "[e]conomic data from program evaluations are crucial if we want to make research more useful for policy makers." To the extent that research can offer clear recommendations with solid cost-benefit analyses to correctional agencies, evidence-based practices may be more likely to be implemented.

Costs can be saved in other ways that have shown promise in reducing recidivism. Aligned with the risk-need-responsivity model, for low-risk offenders, the best course of action may often be simply forgoing involvement in the criminal justice system. Diversion, compared to normal treatment for juveniles who have committed crimes, has been shown to reduce recidivism (Wilson, Brennan, and Olaghere 2018; Wilson and Hoge 2013) and drug use (Hayhurst et al. 2019), though this may not be the case for juveniles compared to community punishments (Koops-Geuze and Weerman 2023). However, a meta-analysis on diversion programs for juveniles found no overall effect (Schwalbe et al. 2012). Within these studies, the authors found that diversion to family treatment did significantly reduce recidivism, consistent with the community-based programming section. Other diversion programs, such as the use of specialized drug and mental health courts, appear effective in reducing offending (Fox et al. 2021; Zhang et al. 2019; but see Schucan Bird and Shemilt 2019).

Thus, given the cost savings associated with diversion (Collins, Lonczak, and Clifasefi 2019), criminal justice officials and policymakers may be open to greater utilization of such programs. More research is needed on diversion, including the ways in which programs differ and the effectiveness of diversion for adults. For example, diversion can be initiated by police, in jail settings, in courts, or even after incarceration (see Lange, Rehm, and Popova 2011). Additionally, diversion may not be appropriate in all instances. The possibility of "net-widening" or using diversion when criminal justice system involvement would not have occurred without a diversion program, however, exists for this strategy. Thus, diversion programs might end up causing harm to some individuals (see Mears et al. 2016).

B. Program Effectiveness Variability

As has been documented in this chapter, there is a large amount of variability in the literature on the effectiveness of correctional rehabilitation approaches. There are several possible reasons for this variability, including programs without strong theoretical models or those that do not align with the principles of effective correctional intervention (Duwe 2017). The principles of effective correctional intervention come from the RNR paradigm, and consist of seven core elements needed for successful programming: (1) organizational culture (the organization must be open and able to respond to challenges and is stable); (2) program implementation and maintenance (programs are initiated based on need of the clients and when the agency is stable); (3) management and staff characteristics (both are equipped and trained in treatment and rehabilitation areas); (4) risk and need practices (clients are evaluated on a routine basis); (5) program characteristics (programs focus on behavioral treatment focusing on prosocial values and behaviors); (6) core correctional practices (program staff engage in particular behaviors such as motivational interviewing); and (7) interagency communication (clients are able to be referred to relevant agencies for resources) (Gendreau, Smith, and French 2006). Scholarship shows that these principles are related to positive outcomes (Lowenkamp, Latessa, and Smith 2006; Smith, Gendreau, and Schwartz 2009).

Another issue is whether a well-designed treatment program is implemented with fidelity to the model. Fidelity is the degree to which a program is implemented and executed as it was intended. For example, a program may require a certain dosage, or time in treatment. If the program is altered in such a way that dosage is reduced, the program may not be as effective. When programs are implemented, what stakeholders often want to know is "did it work?"—however that is defined. This necessitates an outcome evaluation. However, process evaluations are arguably as important, to assess whether the program was implemented in a way that is "consistent with program theory and design" (Miller and Miller 2015, 339). Miller and Miller (2015) call for more mixed-methods research to evaluate whether programs are implemented with fidelity. Fidelity studies, however, are rare. One review of 563 Correctional Program Checklist evaluations, which assesses fidelity to the principles of effective intervention, found substantial variability. Of the four types of programs assessed, none scored higher than 51% adherence (Farringer et al. 2021). Implementation of programs with fidelity is no easy task, and it requires both support and resources. Further, as Mears (2010) notes, it is important to develop standards for process evaluations to gauge success or failure, and the lack of such standards may hinder fidelity assessments. The scholarship that exists, however, tends to show that fidelity improves program effectiveness (Duwe and Clark 2015; Landenberger and Lipsey 2005; Lipsey 2009). Additionally, a recent study found that while fidelity has increased over time, there is much to be desired (Duriez et al. 2018). It is clear that more research is needed on the degree to which programs are implemented with fidelity across correctional settings and how to improve it. Programs that require less time and fewer resources to implement will clearly be more attractive to correctional agencies.

Finally, it seems that while much work has been done to evaluate the sources of variability in terms of program effectiveness, there remains a great deal to be learned about individual heterogeneity in terms of responsivity. In other words, programs may not have the same effect for each client. The RNR approach recognizes that programs should be tailored to individual criminogenic needs and to those who present with more than minimal risk. To facilitate this matching of risk and need with programs, a suite of tools exist (such as the Level of Service Inventory-Revised, LSI-R) to assess both risk and need. However, even though it is logical that a client who scores high on substance use/abuse risk domain would benefit from substance use treatment, it is unclear whether the risk/need instruments succeed in matching clients to programs that would be most effective for them. For example, Duwe and Rocque (2016) examined recidivism rates for those who participated in programs matched to their needs as identified by the LSI-R. The results were mixed; some types of programming showed better results when participants scored high on the needs they are meant to address. Others did not, though, which suggests that the tool may not be adept at identifying certain needs.

It is a complex task to identify appropriate treatment for clients. Taxman and Caudy (2015) argued that risk assessment tools help us understand which clients need treatment but not "what or how" that treatment should be administered. Clients often have more than one need, for example, and those needs may interact with each other in determining risk. Their work identified four latent classes of offenders based on type of risk and need (such as criminal peers, employment problems, substance abuse). This grouping led to better prediction of recidivism than risk assessment, which suggests that more nuanced evaluations are needed to guide treatment decisions. More work is needed to assess how best to match client needs to programs in order to enhance and promote the use of best practices in corrections.

Additionally, clients may vary in responsivity to programs due to genetic differences. The differential susceptibility hypothesis suggests that variation in genetic profiles may result in variation in how responsive individuals are to environmental factors (Belsky and Pluess 2009). This hypothesis moves beyond the framing of genetic variants as "risk factors" and recognizes that while some individuals may be more susceptible to negative influences, they may also be more susceptible to positive ones. This knowledge could help improve the implementation of correctional rehabilitation programs by matching treatment to individual responsivity.

Certain work has shown that interventions are more effective for individuals with particular genetic alleles (Simons and Lei 2013), which is promising for future efforts to increase the effectiveness of correctional programming. Kevin Beaver and colleagues (2014, 4) argue that this could work by funneling offenders "into a number of different programs based on alleles (genetic variants) they possess for polymorphisms that have been shown to be responsivity factors." They note that this sort of work is routinely done in pharmacogenetics, where patients have their genes tested before being prescribed medication.

The use of biological factors to enhance treatment effectiveness has not been embraced by correctional agencies to date. However, Jamie Newsom and Francis Cullen (2017) illustrate how findings from biological research could be used to provide more information on risk as well as responsivity. Currently, risk factors utilized in correctional agencies are typically those related to social and behavioral indicators (e.g., substance use, unemployment, presence of prior convictions). Neurological functioning and heart rate are also risk factors that may be easily incorporated into such assessments (Newsome and Cullen 2017).

C. Clarifying "Evidence-Based"

One challenge for correctional agencies is to identify "what works" for their population. Often, programs are developed and tested on particular samples that may or may not transfer to other geographic locations and populations, lacking what researchers call "external validity." In other words, as Campbell and colleagues (2018, 4) put it, "even the most rigorous studies (i.e., randomized controlled trials [RCTs]) or well conducted meta-analyses provide evidence that the program has indeed worked somewhere. Such evidence still is not necessarily a guarantee that it will actually work here." Another issue is called "developer bias," which is the notion that when the developer of a program is involved in the evaluation of that program, the effects are likely to be stronger. This could happen for a variety of reasons, from a tendency to report positive and significant effects, to a greater degree of fidelity of implementation when the developer is involved. Petrosino and Soydan (2005) reported on previous meta-analyses as well as their own, finding that when the program developer also helped evaluate the program, the program's effect on recidivism was higher.

Additionally, the term "evidence-based" is somewhat cloudy. There is no one agreed-upon definition of evidence-based and much variation used by clearinghouses. What qualifies as evidence? There is general agreement that strong evidence requires strong evaluation methods (e.g., experimental or quasi-experimental designs). But should one rigorous evaluation be sufficient? The Blueprints for Healthy Youth Development, referred to previously in this chapter, gives more weight to "independent" evaluations, and to those "ready for scale," meaning they have clear guidelines for dissemination. The National Institute of Corrections considers evidence-based to mean that "1) there is a definable outcome; 2) it is measurable; and 3) it is defined according to practical realities (recidivism, victim satisfaction, etc.)."[3] CrimeSolutions.gov, operated by the National Institute of Justice, identifies programs as effective, promising, or no effects, and indicates whether there are one or more studies evaluating them. Effective programs are those with "strong evidence to indicate they achieve their intended outcomes when implemented with fidelity."[4] Clearly there is subjectivity in rating programs and determining when the term "evidence-based" can and should be used. Generally, the size of the effects is not even a consideration in these ratings, but rather whether the program had statistically significant effects, a factor influenced by a variety of conditions, including statistical power.

All of this variation presents a barrier to the effective adoption of evidence-based programs and practices in corrections. As Elliott (2013, 17) argues, "Multiple lists with different selection processes and scientific standards and an inconsistent application of standards present a confusing picture to both public and private agencies looking for guidance in selecting an evidence-based program." Elliott goes on to suggest that systematic reviews and meta-analyses represent one tool to help wade through the muck of the program evaluation literature. Currently, there is no gold standard for assessing whether a program or practice is evidence-based, but to the extent that systematic reviews are useful, the Campbell Collaboration project (https://www.campbellcollaboration.org/) may be a more appropriate venue to find and assess effective strategies for rehabilitation. In order to promote the use of evidence-based practices and programs in corrections, considerable attention should be paid to standardizing assessments and lists of programs to reduce confusion.

IV. What about "Enduring" Change?

The title of this chapter is "Rehabilitation for Enduring Change." This implies that the effect of the intervention or treatment is lasting and not periodic. However, for a variety of reasons, program evaluations tend to be short-term. For example, in their meta-analysis of the effects of prison education programs on recidivism, Bozick et al. (2018), found that nearly half of the studies followed subjects for one or three years post-release, though some were more long-term (e.g., 10 years). In a recent review of 29 randomized trials of prison programs, only two had a follow-up longer than five years, but 13 studies had a follow-up of a year or less (Beaudry et al. 2021). In terms of outcomes, most research attention evaluating correctional programs focuses on recidivism (Campbell et al. 2018; Duwe 2017). Recidivism is measured as the presence of an indicator of criminal behavior (usually an official measure such as arrest or conviction). If a program is shown to have a lower rate of recidivism compared to something else, scholars claim evidence of effectiveness for "rehabilitation." But short-term recidivism is a poor indicator of whether an individual is truly rehabilitated, particularly given the constraints imposed on those supervised in the community. Longer-term follow-ups are needed to assess the evidence for enduring change for correctional interventions. It does correctional agencies little good to spend money on a program that reduces one-year recidivism rates only to find recidivism thereafter rises to previous levels.

A. Desistance-Focused Rehabilitation

In order to assess whether programs promote rehabilitation, policymakers and practitioners should turn their attention toward the concept of desistance from crime. "Desistance" is a term used to describe the process of moving away from criminal behavior until the individual no longer engages in such behavior (Rocque 2017). While the literature on desistance has advanced theoretically, the use of this knowledge in corrections has lagged behind. For example, the most common metric used in correctional program evaluation is recidivism—whether the individual has committed a new crime, often measured via arrests, convictions, or new incarcerations. However, recidivism is a limited measure for evaluations of desistance; individuals may recidivate but be in the process of desisting from crime. In other words, they may be making intentional commitments to change in attitudes and behaviors but still engage in crime or misconduct (Kazemian 2021). A recent report from the National Institute of Justice argued that binary (e.g., recidivism or not) outcome measures, particularly utilizing official data (arrests, convictions, incarceration) were not ideal to capture the process of desistance. First, "recidivism is often viewed as an all or nothing type of outcome: If you recidivate, you have failed. Desistance, as a process, implies that a certain amount of failure may be expected on one's journey toward cessation of criminal conduct" (Rocque 2021, 7). Additionally, zero arrests/convictions assumes that reform occurs only if there is no risk of reoffending, yet even for the general public, there is a non-zero risk of committing crimes (see Blumstein and Nakamura 2009; Kurlycheck, Brame, and Bushway 2006). Second, measurements using official data only scratch the surface of criminal behavior, and are not optimal to measure progress toward rehabilitation.

It is imperative for evaluation researchers to expand the outcomes examined in assessments of programs and practices. Desistance is not necessarily a linear process, but one that can have fits and starts (see Piquero 2004). All-or-nothing types of assessments, which apply to noncriminal outcomes as well (e.g., housing, employment), may only be telling part of the story for these individuals (Klingele 2019). There are a variety of theoretical reasons why individuals may find themselves engaging in criminal behavior despite a program or intervention having a positive effect. Klingele (2019) argued that "markers of desistance" should be used rather than traditional recidivism measures to assess whether change has occurred. These markers include such things as the time between crimes and the severity of crimes over time (if crimes are more widely spaced and decreasing in severity, desistance may be occurring).

Additionally, rehabilitation implies that individuals have changed who they are and how they see themselves. Thus, other outcomes—such as those representing "criminality," "cognitive transformations," and personal identity (Giordano et al. 2002; Paternoster et al. 2016)—should be considered key parts of program evaluation. Programs or interventions that seek to directly engage with personal identity warrant more attention. For example, Petrich (2016) argued that restorative justice programs in prisons may be effective in helping inmates reframe their identities. To the extent that policymakers and practitioners truly want to know whether programs rehabilitate, scholars should expand and refine outcome measures in evaluation research. As Klingele (2019, 804) put it, "criminal justice system actors should resist efforts to oversimplify the effectiveness or ineffectiveness of interventions by reference to a measure as insensitive as pure recidivism rates."

B. Expanding Follow-Up Time

Longer-term evaluations, while costly, are also necessary for determining the extent to which programs and practices are effective in terms of rehabilitation. Short-term evaluations can signal whether programs have an impact on behavior, but that impact may be short-lived. In Rocque's (2021) report on the implications of desistance research for policy and practice, he recommended a follow-up of 9–10 years in order to assess whether reform has truly occurred. This recommendation is based on evidence that the probability of recidivism for those convicted of crimes approaches that of the general population after 6–10 years (Kurlychek, Brame, and Bushway 2006; Hanson 2018). Clearly, this sort of time frame will not be economically feasible for most routine evaluations of correctional programs, but investment should be made in the cases of "brand-name" programs and those at the top of clearinghouse lists that have been deemed evidence-based.

The improvements in technology and data-collection tools that have occurred in corrections in recent years should increase the ability of agencies to track outcomes in more appropriate ways. Computerized information management systems allow officials to quickly access and analyze information on inmates released from their systems. Other types of technologies, such as cell phones and Internet surveys, may help with tracking of other information that heretofore had been difficult to access. Such technology could also improve how individuals are monitored upon release and the provision of services to them as they transition back to the community (American Probation and Parole Association 2020).

C. Disparity Assessments

The correctional system, much like society in general, is reflective of numerous deeply woven inequalities. These run along gender, race, and social class lines. However, the trend in correctional rehabilitation research has been laser focused on establishing which programs work best (and which do not) and less so on whether programs work better for some rather than others. Throughout the discussion of what works (and doesn't) in this chapter, where applicable, program effects for juveniles compared to adults were discussed. With respect to gender, research has long supported the idea that females find their way to criminal behavior in distinct ways, and so the treatments that may work for women may differ (Kruttschnitt 2013). One study found that for women leaving prison, their needs on companion and financial domains were higher than for men (Heilbrun et al. 2008). In their review of risk and need factors for women in prisons, Wright and colleagues (2012) recommended the following types of programs for this population: (1) cognitive-behavioral and relational programs that also address women's strengths (e.g., empathy), (2) substance use programs, (3) trauma-informed approaches (recognizing many women who come to prison have been abused in the past), (4) mental health services, and (5) relationship programs.

Less research has examined disparities by other identities, such as race or ethnicity. One study examined whether certain factors led to more or less efficacy for Black vs. White parolees, finding that age and personality variables interacted with race (Spiropoulos et al. 2014). Interestingly, while the program (Reasoning and Rehabilitation) was found to be effective for Whites older than age 22, only Blacks aged 23–27 seemed to respond. A later study found that program factors, such as class size and number and gender of the instructor affected outcomes differently by race (Spiropoulos et al. 2018). The data used for this study were from an evaluation that had shown the program to reduce White recidivism rates, but not Black rates overall (Van Voorhis et al. 2002). Race, along with other types of identity (e.g., social class) should be examined further in the context of responsivity so that the efficacy of rehabilitation efforts can be maximized.

V. Conclusion

The history of rehabilitation in corrections is an interesting one, with twists and turns, leading up to the present moment in which it finally feels as if the field has a good grasp on what works, and what doesn't. Certain types of programs and interventions have consistently shown evidence of effectiveness compared to alternatives, as demonstrated in systematic reviews. These include education/employment programs, cognitive-behavioral therapy, substance abuse treatment, and sex offender treatment. We also have a good sense that punitive measures intended to scare individuals "straight" or supervision without therapeutic qualities are ineffective, and may to some degree be iatrogenic. There is also good evidence that evidence-based programs are cost-effective for agencies.

However, "what we know" has to be tempered by acknowledging that there is much more work to be done in correctional rehabilitation research. There is no standard definition of what "evidence-based" means, which can lead to confusion for those attempting to determine what approaches are best for their populations. Relatedly, to be classified as evidence-based, a program need only demonstrate in rigorous evaluations that it has some effect. The size of the effect in statistical and practical terms is generally not a focus of discussion. Further, we do not have a good understanding of the sources of heterogeneity in program evaluations. More work needs to be done to study the ways in which implementation as well as individual factors influence variation in program outcomes.

While much more research is needed to clarify what we do not know about evidence-based programming in corrections, the literature is consistent that some intervention is better than purely custodial sanctions. Thus, efforts should be made to encourage correctional agencies to use the best evidence available in selecting programs and interventions for their populations. A "desistance-focused" mindset may also be helpful in moving researchers and practitioners closer to evaluating, understanding, and facilitating true enduring change in the future.

Notes

1. https://www.blueprintsprograms.org/program-search/?localPageSize=5000&0_delinquencyAndCriminalBehavior=1&age%5B%5D=756&age%5B%5D=755&programSetting%5B%5D=767&programSetting%5B%5D=764&programSetting%5B%5D=770&programSetting%5B%5D=766&programSetting%5B%5D=763&programSetting%5B%5D=761&programSetting%5B%5D=771&keywords=.
2. https://www.blueprintsprograms.org/programs/28999999/functional-family-therapy-fft/.
3. https://nicic.gov/projects/evidence-based-practices-ebp.
4. https://crimesolutions.ojp.gov/about/how-we-review-and-rate-program-start-finish.

References

American Probation and Parole Association. 2020. Leveraging the power of smartphone applications to enhance community supervision. Lombard, IL: American Probation and Parole Association. https://www.appa-net.org/eweb/docs/APPA/stances/ip-LPSAECS.pdf.

Andrews, Don A., James Bonta, and Robert D. Hoge. 1990. Classification for effective rehabilitation: Rediscovering psychology. *Criminal Justice and Behavior*, 17:19–52.

Andrews, Donald A., Ivan Zinger, Robert D. Hoge, James Bonta, Paul Gendreau, and Francis T. Cullen. 1990. Does correctional treatment work? A clinically relevant and psychologically informed meta-analysis. *Criminology*, 28:369–404.

Aos, Steve, Marna Miller, and Elizabeth Drake. 2006. Evidence-based adult corrections programs: What works and what does not. Olympia: Washington State Institute for Public Policy.

Baldwin, Scott A., Sarah Christian, Arjan Berkeljon, and William R. Shadish. 2012. The effects of family therapies for adolescent delinquency and substance abuse: A meta-analysis. *Journal of Marital and Family Therapy*, 38:281–304.

Beaudry, Gabrielle, Rongqin Yu, Amanda E. Perry, and Seena Fazel. 2021. Effectiveness of psychological interventions in prison to reduce recidivism: A systematic review and meta-analysis of randomised controlled trials. *Lancet Psychiatry*, 8:759–773.

Beaver, Kevin M., Dylan B. Jackson, and Dillon Flesher. 2014. The potential use of genetics to increase the effectiveness of treatment programs for criminal offenders. *Recent Advances in DNA and Gene Sequences* (formerly *Recent Patents on DNA and Gene Sequences*), 8:113–118.

Belsky, Jay, and Michael Pluess. 2009. Beyond diathesis stress: differential susceptibility to environmental influences. *Psychological Bulletin*, 135:885–908.

Berg, Mark T., and Beth M. Huebner. 2011. Reentry and the ties that bind: An examination of social ties, employment, and recidivism. *Justice Quarterly*, 28:382–410.

Berghuis, Maria. 2018. Reentry programs for adult male offender recidivism and reintegration: A systematic review and meta-analysis. *International Journal of Offender Therapy and Comparative Criminology*, 62:4655–4676.

Blakinger, Keri, Jamiles Lartey, Beth Schwartzapfel, and Christie Thompson. 2021. US prisons face staff shortages as officers quit amid COVID. Associated Press, November 1. https://apnews.com/article/coronavirus-united-states-prisons-staff-shortages-health-dba13f1c6368392be2bc5e7375170a78.

Blumstein, Alfred, and Kiminori Nakamura. 2009. Redemption in the presence of widespread criminal background checks. *Criminology*, 47:327–359.

Bouchard, Jessica, and Jennifer S. Wong. 2018. Examining the effects of intensive supervision and aftercare programs for at-risk youth: A systematic review and meta-analysis. *International Journal of Offender Therapy and Comparative Criminology*, 62:1509–1534.

Bozick, Robert, Jennifer Steele, Lois Davis, and Susan Turner. 2018. Does providing inmates with education improve postrelease outcomes? A meta-analysis of correctional education programs in the United States. *Journal of Experimental Criminology*, 14:389–428.

Bushway, Shawn. 2003. *Reentry and prison work programs.* Urban Institute Reentry Roundtable, New York University, May, 21. https://www.urban.org/sites/default/files/publication/59406/410853-Reentry-and-Prison-Work-Programs.PDF.

Campbell, Christopher M., Mia J. Abboud, Zachary K. Hamilton, Jacqueline vanWormer, and Brianne Posey. 2018. Evidence-based or just promising? Lessons learned in taking inventory of state correctional programming. *Justice Evaluation Journal*, 1:188–214.

Collins, Susan E., Heather S. Lonczak, and Seema L. Clifasefi. 2019. Seattle's law enforcement assisted diversion (LEAD): Program effects on criminal justice and legal system utilization and costs. *Journal of Experimental Criminology*, 15:201–211.

Cooke, Barbara J., and David P. Farrington. 2016. The effectiveness of dog-training programs in prison: A systematic review and meta-analysis of the literature. *The Prison Journal*, 96:854–876.

Cullen, Francis, T. 2013. Rehabilitation: Beyond nothing works. *Crime and Justice*, 42:299–376.

Cullen, Francis T., and Paul Gendreau. 2001. From nothing works to what works: Changing professional ideology in the 21st century. *The Prison Journal*, 81:313–338.

Cullen, Francis, T., and Karen E. Gilbert. 1982. *Reaffirming rehabilitation.* Cincinnati, OH: Anderson.

Cullen, Francis T., Cheryl Lero Jonson, and Daniel S. Nagin. 2011. Prisons do not reduce recidivism: The high cost of ignoring science. *The Prison Journal*, 91 (3, suppl.): 48S–65S.

Davis, Lois M., Robert Bozick, Jennifer L. Steele, Jessica Saunders, and Jeremy N. V. Miles. 2013. *Evaluating the effectiveness of correctional education: A meta-analysis of programs that provide education to incarcerated adults.* Santa Monica, CA: Rand.

Duindam, Hanne M., Jessica J. Asscher, Machteld Hoeve, Geert Jan J. M. Stams, and Hanneke E. Creemers. 2020. Are we barking up the right tree? A meta-analysis on the effectiveness of prison-based dog programs. *Criminal Justice and Behavior*, 47:749–767.

Duriez, Stephanie A., Carrie Sullivan, Edward J. Latessa, and Lori Brusman Lovins. 2018. The evolution of correctional program assessment in the age of evidence-based practices. *Corrections*, 3:119–136.

Duwe, Grant. 2015. The benefits of keeping idle hands busy: An outcome evaluation of a prisoner reentry employment program. *Crime and Delinquency*, 61:559–586.

Duwe, Grant. 2017. *The use and impact of correctional programming for inmates on pre-and post-release outcomes.* Washington, DC: National Institute of Justice. https://www.ojp.gov/pdffiles1/nij/250476.pdf.

Duwe, Grant, and Valerie Clark. 2015. Importance of program integrity: Outcome evaluation of a gender-responsive, cognitive-behavioral program for female offenders. *Criminology and Public Policy*, 14:301–328.

Duwe, Grant, and Valerie Clark. 2017. The rehabilitative ideal versus the criminogenic reality: The consequences of warehousing prisoners. *Corrections*, 2:41–69.

Duwe, Grant, and Michael Rocque. 2016. A jack of all trades but a master of none? Evaluating the performance of the Level of Service Inventory–Revised (LSI-R) in the assessment of risk and need. *Corrections*, 1:81–106.

Elliott, Delbert, S. 2013. Crime prevention and intervention over the life course. In *Handbook of life-course criminology: Emerging trends and directions for future research*, edited by Chris L. Gibson and Marvin D. Krohn, 297–315. New York: Springer.

Farringer, Alison J., Stephanie A. Duriez, Sarah M. Manchak, and Carrie C. Sullivan. 2021. Adherence to "what works": Examining trends across 14 years of correctional program assessment. *Corrections*, 6:269–287.

Feucht, Thomas, and Tammy Holt. 2016. Does cognitive behavioral therapy work in criminal justice? A new analysis from CrimeSolutions. *NIJ Journal*, 277:10–17. https://www.ojp.gov/ncjrs/virtual-library/abstracts/does-cognitive-behavioral-therapy-work-criminal-justice-new.

Fox, Bryanna, Lauren N. Miley, Kelly E. Kortright, and Rachelle J. Wetsman. 2021. Assessing the effect of mental health courts on adult and juvenile recidivism: a meta-analysis. *American Journal of Criminal Justice*, 46:644–664.

Gendreau, Paul. 1996. Principles of effective intervention with offenders. In *Choosing correctional options that work: defining the demand and evaluating the supply*, edited by Alan T. Harland, 117–130. Thousand Oaks, CA: SAGE.

Gendreau, Paul, Paula Smith, and Sheila A. French. 2006. The theory of effective correctional intervention: Empirical status and future directions. In *Taking stock: The status of criminological theory*, edited by Francis. T. Cullen, John Paul Wright, and Kristie R. Blevins, 419–446. New Brunswick, NJ: Transaction.

Giordano, Peggy C., Stephen A. Cernkovich, and Jennifer L. Rudolph. 2002. Gender, crime, and desistance: Toward a theory of cognitive transformation. *American Journal of Sociology*, 107:990–1064.

Hanson, R. Karl. 2018. Long-term recidivism studies show that desistance is the norm. *Criminal Justice and Behavior*, 45:1340–1346.

Hanson, R. Karl, Guy Bourgon, Leslie Helmus, and Shannon Hodgson. 2009. The principles of effective correctional treatment also apply to sexual offenders: A meta-analysis. *Criminal Justice and Behavior*, 36:865–891.

Hanson, R. Karl, Arthur Gordon, Andrew J. R. Harris, Janice K. Marques, William Murphy, Vernon L. Quinsey, and Michael C. Seto. 2002. First report of the collaborative outcome data project on the effectiveness of psychological treatment for sex offenders. *Sexual Abuse: A Journal of Research and Treatment*, 14:169–194.

Harrison, Jennifer L., Siobhan K. O'Toole, Sue Ammen, Sean Ahlmeyer, Sheera N. Harrell, and Jacinda L. Hernandez. 2020. Sexual offender treatment effectiveness within cognitive-behavioral programs: A meta-analytic investigation of general, sexual, and violent recidivism. *Psychiatry, Psychology and Law*, 27:1–25.

Hartnett, Dan, Alan Carr, Elena Hamilton, and Gary O'Reilly. 2017. The effectiveness of functional family therapy for adolescent behavioral and substance misuse problems: A meta-analysis. *Family Process*, 56:607–619.

Hayhurst, Karen P., Maria Leitner, Linda Davies, Rachel Flentje, Tim Millar, Andrew Jones, Carlene King, Michael Donmall, Michael Farrell, Seena Fazel, Rocheele Harris, Matthew Hickman, Charlotte Lennox, Soraya Mayet, Jane Senior, and Jennifer Shaw. 2019. The effectiveness of diversion programmes for offenders using Class A drugs: a systematic review and meta-analysis. *Drugs: Education, Prevention and Policy*, 26 (2): 113–124.

Heilbrun, Kirk, David Dematteo, Ralph Fretz, Jacey Erickson, Kento Yasuhara, and Natalie Anumba. 2008. How "specific" are gender-specific rehabilitation needs? An empirical analysis. *Criminal Justice and Behavior*, 35:1382–1397.

Holloway, Katy R., Trevor H. Bennett, and David P. Farrington. 2006. The effectiveness of drug treatment programs in reducing criminal behavior: A meta-analysis. *Psicothema*, 18:620–629.

Justice Inspectorates. 2020. *The risk-need-responsivity model*. London: Her Majesty's Inspectorate of Probation. https://www.justiceinspectorates.gov.uk/hmiprobation/research/the-evidence-base-probation/models-and-principles/the-rnr-model/.

Kazemian, Lila. 2021. *Positive growth and redemption in prison: Finding light behind bars and beyond*. New York: Routledge.

Klingele, Cecelia. 2019. Measuring change: From rates of recidivism to markers of desistance. *Journal of Criminal Law and Criminology*, 109:769–817.

Koehler, Johann A., Friedrich Lösel, Thomas D. Akoensi, and David K. Humphreys. 2013. A systematic review and meta-analysis on the effects of young offender treatment programs in Europe. *Journal of Experimental Criminology*, 9:19–43.

Koops-Geuze, Gwendolyn J., and Frank M. Weerman. 2023. Community sanctions in youth justice compared to other youth crime responses: A meta-analysis. *European Journal of Criminology*, 20:758–781.

Kruttschnitt, Candace. 2013. Gender and crime. *Annual Review of Sociology*, 39:291–308.

Kurlychek, Megan C., Robert Brame, and Shawn D. Bushway. 2006. Scarlet letters and recidivism: Does an old criminal record predict future offending? *Criminology and Public Policy*, 5:483–504.

Landenberger, Nana A., and Mark W. Lipsey. 2005. The positive effects of cognitive–behavioral programs for offenders: A meta-analysis of factors associated with effective treatment. *Journal of Experimental Criminology*, 1:451–476.

Lange, Shannon, Jürgen Rehm, and Svetiana Popova. 2011. The effectiveness of criminal justice diversion initiatives in North America: A systematic literature review. *International Journal of Forensic Mental Health*, 10 (3): 200–214. Latessa, Edward J., Shelley L. Johnson, and Deborah Koetzle. 2020. *What works (and doesn't) in reducing recidivism*. 2nd ed. New York: Routledge.

Lee, Stephanie, Steve Aos, and Annie Pennucci. 2015. *What works and what does not? Benefit-cost findings from WSIPP*. Doc. No. 15-02-4101. Olympia: Washington State Institute for Public Policy. http://www.wsipp.wa.gov/ReportFile/1602/Wsipp_What-Works-and-What-Does-Not-Benefit-Cost-Findings-from-WSIPP_Report.pdf.

Lipsey, Mark W. 2009. The primary factors that characterize effective interventions with juvenile offenders: A meta-analytic overview. *Victims and Offenders*, 4:124–147.

Lipsey, Mark W. 2018. *Rehabilitation programs for adult offenders: A meta-analysis in support of guidelines for effective practice*. Rockville, MD: National Criminal Justice Reference Service. https://www.ojp.gov/pdffiles1/nij/grants/252504.pdf.

Lipsey, Mark W., and Francis T. Cullen. 2007. The effectiveness of correctional rehabilitation: A review of systematic reviews. *Annual Review of Law and Social Science*, 3:297–320.

Lipsey, Mark W., Nana A. Landenberger, and Sandra J. Wilson. 2007. Effects of cognitive-behavioral programs for criminal offenders. *Campbell Systematic Reviews*, 3:1–27.

Lipton, Douglas S., Robert Martinson, and Judith Wilks. 1975. *The effectiveness of correctional treatment: A survey of treatment valuation studies*. New York: Praeger.

Little, Gregory L. 2005. Meta-analysis of moral reconation therapy recidivism results from probation and parole implementations. *Cognitive-Behavioral Treatment Review*, 14:14–16.

Loeffler, Charles E., and Daniel S. Nagin. 2022. The impact of incarceration on recidivism. *Annual Review of Criminology*, 5:133–152.

Lowenkamp, Christopher T., Edward J. Latessa, and Paula Smith. 2006. Does correctional program quality really matter? The impact of adhering to the principles of effective intervention. *Criminology and Public Policy*, 5:575–594.

MacKenzie, Doris L. 2006. *What works in corrections: Reducing the criminal activities of offenders and delinquents*. New York: Cambridge University Press.

Martinson, Robert. 1974. What works? Questions and answers about prison reform. *The Public Interest*, 35:22–54.

Maruschak, Laura, Jennifer Bronson, and Mariel Alper. 2021. *Alcohol and drug use and treatment reported by prisoners: Survey of prison inmates, 2016*. Washington, DC: Bureau of Justice Statistics. https://bjs.ojp.gov/library/publications/alcohol-and-drug-use-and-treatment-reported-prisoners-survey-prison-inmates.

Mears, Daniel P. 2010. *American criminal justice policy: An evaluation approach to increasing accountability and effectiveness*. Cambridge: Cambridge University Press.

Mears, Daniel P., Joshua C. Cochran, and Francis T. Cullen. 2015. Incarceration heterogeneity and its implications for assessing the effectiveness of imprisonment on recidivism. *Criminal Justice Policy Review*, 26:691–712.

Mears, Daniel P., Joshua J. Kuch, Andrea M. Lindsey, Sonja E. Siennick, George B. Pesta, Mark A. Greenwald, and Thomas G. Blomberg. 2016. Juvenile court and contemporary diversion: Helpful, harmful, or both? *Criminology & Public Policy*, 15:953–981.

Menard, Scott, Sharon Mihalic, and David Huizinga. 2001. Drugs and crime revisited. *Justice Quarterly*, 18:269–299.

Miller, J. Mitchell, and Holly Ventura Miller. 2015. Rethinking program fidelity for criminal justice. *Criminology and Public Policy*, 14:339–349.

Newsome, Jamie, and Francis T. Cullen. 2017. The risk-need-responsivity model revisited: Using biosocial criminology to enhance offender rehabilitation. *Criminal Justice and Behavior*, 44:1030–1049.

Paternoster, Raymond, Ronet Bachman, Erin Kerrison, Daniel O'Connell, and Lionel Smith. 2016. Desistance from crime and identity: An empirical test with survival time. *Criminal Justice and Behavior*, 43:1204–1224.

Pearson, Frank S., and Douglas S. Lipton. 1999. A meta-analytic review of the effectiveness of corrections-based treatments for drug abuse. *The Prison Journal*, 79:384–410.

Petersilia, Joan. 2004. What works in prisoner reentry? Reviewing and questioning the evidence. *Federal Probation*, 68:4–8.

Petrich, Damon M. 2016. Theorising desistance-promotion in circle processes: The role of community in identity transformation. *Restorative Justice*, 4 (3): 388–409.

Petrich, Damon M., Francis T. Cullen, Heejin Lee, and Alexander L. Burton. 2022. Prisoner reentry programs. In *Handbook of issues in criminal justice reform in the United States*, edited by Elizabeth Jeglic and Cynthia Calkin, 335–363. New York: Springer.

Petrich, Damon M., Travis C. Pratt, Cheryl Lero Jonson, and Francis T. Cullen. 2021. Custodial sanctions and reoffending: A meta-analytic review. *Crime and Justice*, 50:353–424.

Petrosino, Anthony, and Haluk Soydan. 2005. The impact of program developers as evaluators on criminal recidivism: Results from meta-analyses of experimental and quasi-experimental research. *Journal of Experimental Criminology*, 1:435–450.

Petrosino, Anthony, Carolyn Turpin-Petrosino, Meghan E. Hollis-Peel, and Julia G. Lavenberg. 2005. "Scared Straight" and other juvenile awareness programs for preventing juvenile delinquency. *Campbell Systematic Reviews*, 1:1–62.

Piquero, Alex R. 2004. Somewhere between persistence and desistance: The intermittency of criminal careers. In *After crime and punishment*, edited by Shadd Maruna and Russ Immarigeon, 102–125. Cullompton, UK: Willan.

Reitzel, Lorraine R., and Joyce L. Carbonell. 2006. The effectiveness of sexual offender treatment for juveniles as measured by recidivism: A meta-analysis. *Sexual Abuse: A Journal of Research and Treatment*, 18:401–421.

Robbins, Michael S., and Charles W. Turner. 2019. Call for revision of Weisman and Montgomery's review of Functional Family Therapy. *Research on Social Work Practice*, 29 (3): 347–357.

Rocque, Michael. 2017. *Desistance from crime: New advances in research and theory*. New York: Palgrave.

Rocque, Michael. 2021. But what does it mean? Defining, measuring, and analyzing desistance from crime in criminal justice. In *Desistance from crime: Implications for research, policy, and practice*, 1–39. Washington, DC: National Institute of Justice.

Rubin, Ashley. T. 2021. *The deviant prison: Philadelphia's Eastern State Penitentiary and the origins of America's modern penal system*. New York: Cambridge University Press.

Sampson, Robert J., and John H. Laub. 1993. *Crime in the making: Pathways and turning points through life*. Cambridge, MA: Harvard University Press.

Schmucker, Martin, and Friedrich Lösel. 2015. The effects of sexual offender treatment on recidivism: An international meta-analysis of sound quality evaluations. *Journal of Experimental Criminology*, 11:597–630.

Schucan Bird, K., and I. Shemilt. 2019. The crime, mental health, and economic impacts of prearrest diversion of people with mental health problems: A systematic review. *Criminal Behaviour and Mental Health*, 29 (3): 142–156.

Schwalbe, Craig S., Robin E. Gearing, Michael J. MacKenzie, Kathryne B. Brewer, and Rawan Ibrahim. 2012. A meta-analysis of experimental studies of diversion programs for juvenile offenders. *Clinical Psychology Review*, 32 (1): 26–33.

Sexton, Thomas L., and James F. Alexander. 2000. *Functional Family Therapy*. Juvenile Justice Bulletin 184743. Washington, DC: US Department of Justice, Office of Juvenile Justice and Delinquency Prevention. https://ojjdp.ojp.gov/library/publications/functional-family-therapy.

Simons, Ronald L., and Man Kit Lei. 2013. Enhanced susceptibility to context: A promising perspective on the interplay of genes and the social environment. In *Handbook of life-course criminology*, edited by Chris L. Gibson and Marvin D. Krohn, 57–67. New York: Springer.

Skardhamar, Torbjørn, and Kjetil Telle. 2012. Post-release employment and recidivism in Norway. *Journal of Quantitative Criminology*, 28 (4): 629–649.

Smith, Paula, Paul Gendreau, and Kristin Swartz. 2009. Validating the principles of effective intervention: A systematic review of the contributions of meta-analysis in the field of corrections. *Victims and Offenders*, 4:148–169.

Spiropoulos, Georgia V., Emily J. Salisbury, and Patricia Van Voorhis. 2014. Moderators of correctional treatment success: An exploratory study of racial differences. *International Journal of Offender Therapy and Comparative Criminology*, 58:835–860.

Spiropoulos, Georgia V., Patricia Van Voorhis, and Emily J. Salisbury. 2018. Programmatic moderators of CBT correctional treatment for Whites and African Americans. *International Journal of Offender Therapy and Comparative Criminology*, 62:2236–2258.

Stern, Leon T. 1947. Why we need a State Department of Corrections. *The Prison Journal*, 27:283–285.
Taxman, Faye S., and Michael S. Caudy. 2015. Risk tells us who, but not what or how: Empirical assessment of the complexity of criminogenic needs to inform correctional programming. *Criminology and Public Policy*, 14:71–103.
Travis, Jeremy. 2000. *But they all come back: Rethinking prisoner reentry*. Sentencing and Corrections: Issues for the 21st Century, no 7. Washington, DC: National Institute of Justice. https://www.ojp.gov/pdffiles1/nij/181413.pdf.
Travis, Jeremy. 2005. *But they all come back: Facing the challenges of prisoner reentry*. Washington, DC: Urban Institute.
Uggen, Christopher. 2000. Work as a turning point in the life course of criminals: A duration model of age, employment, and recidivism. *American Sociological Review*, 65:529–546.
Van Voorhis, Patricia, Lisa M. Spruance, P. Neal Ritchie, Shelley Johnson-Listwan, Renita Seabrook, and Jennifer Pealer. 2002. The Georgia cognitive skills experiment outcome evaluation: Phase II. Unpublished Report. Cincinnati: University of Cincinnati.
Visher, Christy A., Laura Winterfield, and Mark B. Coggeshall. 2005. Ex-offender employment programs and recidivism: A meta-analysis. *Journal of Experimental Criminology*, 1:295–316.
Walker, Samuel. 1998. *Popular justice: A history of American criminal justice*. New York: Oxford.
Weisburd, David, David P. Farrington, and Charlotte Gill. 2017. What works in crime prevention and rehabilitation: An assessment of systematic reviews. *Criminology and Public Policy*, 16:415–449.
Welsh, Brandon C. 2004. Monetary costs and benefits of correctional treatment programs: Implications for offender reentry. *Federal Probation*, 68:9–13.
Wexler, Harry K. 1995. The success of therapeutic communities for substance abusers in American prisons. *Journal of Psychoactive Drugs*, 27:57–66.
Wexler, Harry K., and Craig T. Love. 1994. Therapeutic communities in prison. *NIDA Research Monograph*, 144:181–181.
Whitehead, John T., and Steven P. Lab. 1989. A meta-analysis of juvenile correctional treatment. *Journal of Research in Crime and Delinquency*, 26:276–295.
Wilson, David B., Iain Brennan, and Ajima Olaghere. 2018. Police-initiated diversion for youth to prevent future delinquent behavior: A systematic review. *Campbell Systematic Reviews*, 14 (1): 1–88.
Wilson, David B., Catherine A. Gallagher, and Doris L. MacKenzie. 2000. A meta-analysis of corrections-based education, vocation, and work programs for adult offenders. *Journal of Research in Crime and Delinquency*, 37:347–368.
Wilson, David B., Doris L. MacKenzie, and Fawn Ngo Mitchell. 2005. Effects of correctional boot camps on offending. *Campbell Systematic Reviews*, 1:1–45.
Wilson, Holly A., and Robert D. Hoge. 2013. The effect of youth diversion programs on recidivism: A meta-analytic review. *Criminal Justice and Behavior*, 40:497–518.
Wilson, James Q. 1975. *Thinking about crime*. New York: Basic Books.
Wright, Emily M., Patricia Van Voorhis, Emily J. Salisbury, and Ashley Bauman. 2012. Gender-responsive lessons learned and policy implications for women in prison: A review. *Criminal Justice and Behavior*, 39:1612–1632.
Zhang, Saijun, Hui Huang, Qi Wu, Yong Li, and Meirong Liu. 2019. The impacts of family treatment drug court on child welfare core outcomes: A meta-analysis. *Child Abuse and Neglect*, 88:1–14.

CHAPTER 16

INCARCERATION-BASED DRUG TREATMENT

OJMARRH MITCHELL

A large proportion of people confined in US prisons and jails have drug problems. The majority of individuals held in US state prisons (58%) and two-thirds (63%) of people serving post-conviction sentences in US jails meet the criteria for drug dependence or abuse (Bronson et al. 2017). Likewise, the majority of individuals with drug problems at some point in their lives have been incarcerated, and many people with drug problems have repeated contact with correctional institutions (see, e.g., March et al. 2006; Kinner et al. 2009).

Correctional settings in many regards are well-suited for the administration of drug treatment and other rehabilitation programming. The heavy clustering of individuals with drug use disorders makes the provision of drug treatment in these contexts efficient. Incarcerated individuals typically have ample unoccupied time available for engagement in treatment activities. And correctional facilities have the ability to incentivize treatment engagement by offering increased amenities or privileges to treatment participants. Taken together, correctional facilities have a conspicuous opportunity to address drug problems among incarcerated individuals.

Yet there are several barriers that complicate the administration of drug treatment successfully in correctional settings. Perhaps foremost is the general difficulty of treating drug use disorders. Most people with drug use disorders do not achieve abstinence after the first treatment episode, and even individuals who abstain from drug use for years may subsequently relapse into uncontrolled drug use. Drug relapse is part and parcel of drug dependence; that is, drug use is a chronic relapsing condition that many individuals battle for much of their lives. Another formidable challenge specific to institutional corrections is the widespread but largely implicit philosophy that prioritizes safety and security concerns, and views rehabilitative programming as ancillary to their mission. As a consequence of this philosophy, resources for rehabilitative programming are limited and only a small percentage of individuals in need actually receive treatment commensurate with their needs. Further, the concentration of drug-involved individuals in prisons and jails leads to drug markets surfacing to meet their demand for psychoactive substances. The availability of drugs behind bars may discourage treatment engagement and undermine efforts to achieve abstinence.

If these treatment barriers can be overcome, drug treatment interventions have many potential benefits. Ultimately, effective drug treatment can help to break the cycle of uncontrolled drug use, crime, and incarceration, as well as improve the social functioning of those treated (e.g., improved health and mental health, increased engagement with family, employment). It is important to note, however, that successful drug treatment also has the potential to improve correctional environments by decreasing in-prison drug use, fatal overdoses, and the disorder and violence associated with in-prison drug markets.

This chapter describes common drug treatment programs administered in correctional settings, summarizes empirical assessments of these programs' effectiveness, and scrutinizes the quality and quantity of this evidence. Before doing so, Part I provides relevant background concerning the overrepresentation of drug-involved individuals in correctional settings, the factors producing this overrepresentation, and characteristics/conditions associated with drug use disorders. This information helps understand why treating individuals with drug use problems is so challenging, and it explains why certain interventions are effective in reducing the harms of uncontrolled drug use. Part II details the key features of the six most popular drug treatment modalities available in US prisons and jails. Part III summarizes the effectiveness of these modalities in reducing post-release recidivism and drug use. The final portion, Part IV, discusses the implications of these findings.

I. Drug Use Disorders and Their Associated Characteristics

Treating drug use disorders, even under ideal conditions, is difficult. Prisons and jails clearly are not ideal contexts for such treatment, as the conditions of confinement induce stress and boredom. Psychoactive drugs, which are widely available in correctional settings but at markedly higher costs, can provide a temporary relief from these conditions. However, the heavy concentration of drug-involved individuals housed in America's correctional facilities makes providing drug treatment in such settings logical and efficient. Crafting effective incarceration-based interventions to break the cycle of uncontrolled drug use and crime requires an understanding of the relationship between drug use and offending, as well as other problems typically confronting drug-involved populations. This section discusses these important background issues.

A. Drug Use, Drug Problems, and Incarceration Risk

Most people who use psychoactive substances suffer few negative consequences of drug use and do not develop drug use disorders. In the United States, it is normative for people to experiment with these substances. Most often this experimentation occurs during adolescence or early adulthood. In fact, drug use is highly patterned. It typically begins with drugs that are legal for adults, namely tobacco or alcohol. Many people who have tried these substances progress to cannabis, hallucinogens, and prescription pills. A large share of people discontinues drug use at this stage, but a minority continue on to try harder drugs such as amphetamines, cocaine, heroin, and prescription opioids. With the possible exception of cannabis, most people discontinue illicit drug use as they move into adulthood. For these people, illicit drug use can be characterized as irregular, short-lived, and rarely leading to contact with the criminal justice system.

Drug use for a relatively small proportion of users develops into a pattern of heavy and uncontrolled drug use that has significant negative consequences. Such patterns of drug use are often referred to as drug "addiction," "dependence," or "abuse." Regardless of the nomenclature used, individuals whose drug use is characterized by these terms use drugs frequently, use multiple different drugs (i.e., polydrug use), and continue to use drugs for long periods of time. Further, many people who develop drug problems use drugs intravenously. Intravenous drug use is in itself indicative of uncontrolled drug use, as it signals that a user has developed significant drug tolerance and needs a more efficient means of administration to achieve the desired effect.

While drug use is not a strong risk factor for criminal justice contact or incarceration, drug dependence is a powerful predictor of these outcomes. One way of demonstrating the relationship between drug dependence and incarceration is to compare the proportion of incarcerated population with a drug use disorder to this proportion in the general population. For instance, 58% of state prisoners met *DSM-IV* criteria for drug dependence or abuse, in comparison to 4% of the general population who were not involved with the justice system (Bronson et al. 2017); thus, the rate of drug dependence among state prisoners is 14 times higher than in the general population.

The stark overrepresentation of people with drug dependence and drug use disorders in correctional settings is due to at least four factors. First, manufacturing, distributing, selling, and possessing of illicit drugs are criminal offenses in themselves. Second, drug law enforcement activities are designed to make the price of illicit drugs increasingly expensive. The expense of these drugs causes many people with drug dependencies to resort to income-generating criminal activities such as theft, fraud, drug distribution, and sex work to afford their habits. Third, use of certain drugs such as cocaine and amphetamines, especially when used with alcohol, can cause paranoid psychosis, increased aggression, and make users easy to provoke—all of which increase the likelihood of violent behavior. Fourth, the illicit nature of drug markets shutters legal means of dispute resolution, and, as a result, violence is often used to settle disagreements among those in the marketplace. These four factors, among others, explain the overrepresentation of individuals with drug dependencies in correctional facilities.

Individuals with addictions to psychoactive substances have always been overrepresented in US correctional institutions. The relationship between drug addiction and confinement, however, has been strengthened in the past several decades by the intensified drug enforcement activities associated with the war on drugs. Since the mid-1980s, the United States has adopted policies that extended the targets of previous drug wars from drug producers/manufacturers and high-level traffickers to now include low-level street dealers and even drug users (see, e.g., Musto 1999; Boyum and Reuter 2005; Mitchell 2009). The stated aims of these efforts were to make the United States a drug-free society; for instance, the Anti-Drug Abuse Act of 1988 declared "it to be U.S. policy to create a drug-free society by 1995" (HR 5210, 100th Congress). This goal has not been achieved; indeed, the prevalence of drug use has grown since this declaration. Yet the war on drugs has been remarkable successful in different way—it has escalated the severity of punishment for drug offenses.

The increased punitiveness of sanctions for drug crimes led to growing numbers of drug-involved individuals being detained in US correctional facilities. The National Center on Addiction and Substance Abuse (2010), for instance, estimated that the percentage of "substance-involved" people held in state prisons grew from 81% to 85% between 1996 and 2006. Surveys of US correctional populations also find evidence of increased involvement with drugs; as an example, 50% of individuals held in state prisons who were surveyed in 1991 reported using drugs in the month before their offense (Mumola 1999), in comparison to 65% in 2016 (Maruschak, Bronson, and Alper 2021). Likewise, the prevalence of drug use disorders increased among those held in state prison from 53.5% to 58.5% between 2004 and 2007–2009, when the survey items used to assess drug problems were identical (Mumola and Karberg 2004; Bronson et al. 2017).

B. Characteristics Associated with Drug Problems and Incarceration Risk

Uncontrolled drug use is just one of several problems typically facing people with drug dependencies. Mental health disorders are also strikingly common among those held in jails and prisons who have drug abuse problems. A nationally representative sample of Americans found that approximately 11% of adults had a diagnosable mental health disorder under *DSM-IV* criteria in their lifetime (Elbogen and Johnson 2009). The most common problems were major depression (8%), psychotic disorders (3%), and mania (1.8%). In stark contrast, 63% of state prisoners and 74% of jail inmates with a substance use disorder had a co-occurring mental health disorder; most frequent was mania, followed by major depression and then psychotic disorders. In total, 42% of all state prisoners and 49% of all jail inmates had *both* substance abuse and mental health problems (James and Glaze 2006).

Homelessness is another condition commonly associated with drug use disorders among incarcerated populations. In the year prior to incarceration, roughly 6% of people held in state prisons without drug use disorders experienced a bout of homelessness, but this figure among state prisoners with drug use disorders is more than twice as high at 14% (James and Glaze 2006). And if one focuses only on those inmates who reported being homeless prior to incarceration, 78% of these individuals had both substance use and mental health disorders (McNiel et al. 2005).

Moreover, homelessness and incarceration reinforce one another. Several studies have found that incarceration increases the likelihood of subsequent homelessness (see e.g., Metraux, Roman, and Cho 2007; Greenberg and Rosenheck 2008; Mogk et al. 2020; Moschion and Johnson 2019; Adler 2021), and other research has found that homelessness and housing instability increases the likelihood of recidivism (Håkansoon and Berglund 2012; Kirk et al. 2018). Still other research indicates that the risk of homelessness increases with the number of prior terms of incarceration. Individuals who have served one prior term of imprisonment have rates of homelessness that are 7 times greater than the general population, and the rate of homeless is 13 times greater than the general population among individuals who have served multiple prison terms (Couloute 2018). Overall, formerly incarcerated people have rates of homelessness nearly 10 times that of the general public. The bidirectional nature of the incarceration-homelessness relationship leads to many people experiencing homelessness to cycle in and out of correctional institutions. For instance, interviews with 101 individuals experiencing homelessness in Seattle found that 78% of the sample had been previously incarcerated and, among these interviewees, the average number of prior terms of incarceration was 7.3.

Criminal behavior and drug abuse are often thought of as male behaviors, yet drug use disorders, mental health problems, and homelessness are all substantially more common among females with a history of incarceration. Nearly 70% (69%) of females held in state prisons have drug use disorders in comparison to 57% of male detainees (Bronson et al. 2017). Similarly, just shy of three-fourths (73%) of female state prisoners displayed signs of mental health disorders, but for males this rate was 55% (James and Glaze 2006). And 9.5% of females confined in state prisons were homeless in the year prior to incarceration versus 6% for all prisoners (male and females combined), and the prevalence of homelessness for female prisoners with mental health problems was 17% in comparison to 13% for all prisoners with mental problems (male and females combined) (James and Glaze 2006).

The close connections between problems with drugs, mental health, and housing instability, all of which vary by gender, have important implications for interventions designed to ameliorate these problems. First and foremost, most effectively treating these interlinked conditions would seem to require interventions that address all of them or, alternatively, address the underlying causes producing each of them. Stated somewhat differently, treatment programs that are most likely to be most effective in achieving program goals will broadly treat the whole individual—not simply focus narrowly on any one of the problems confronting justice-involved individuals. Second, given the pervasiveness of homelessness and housing instability more generally, successful interventions may need to prioritize finding or providing stable housing upon re-entry, because providing effective treatment for the many problems facing returning citizens may be difficult to address without first addressing basic housing needs. And because females in the justice system are more likely to have multiple challenges in addition to drug problems, treatment programs may need to be gender-specific or include gender-specific components to maximize their effectiveness.

C. Implications of Undertreated Drug Problems in Correctional Settings

The causal relationships between illicit drug use and nondrug offending are inconsistent across the components of the "criminal career" (see, e.g., Piquero, Farrington, and Blumstein 2003). Drug use does not typically cause initiation into nondrug offending, as involvement in minor forms of criminal behavior usually precede or occur at the same time as first-time drug use (see, e.g., Makkai and Payne 2003). Increased drug use, however, does appear to cause the frequency of offending to intensify (Ball et al. 1981). That is, increased drug use leads to increased offending via various mechanisms, including heavy drug use/dependence, which may motivate income-generating offending to support drug habits; the pharmacological effects of some drugs, which may motivate offending (e.g., by increasing aggression) or facilitate offending (e.g., providing courage to offend, coping with sex work); and the illicit nature of drug markets, which increases the likelihood that disputes between those in the marketplace result in violence (see Bennett and Holloway 2009). Conversely, offending also increases drug use; for example, lucrative crimes are often celebrated by splurging on illicit substances (see, e.g., Bennett and Holloway 2009). Further, the lifestyles of heavy drug users bring them into frequent contact with other drug users and people engaged in criminal activities, which presents them with opportunities both to use drugs and to engage in criminal activity—creating reciprocal relationships between problematic drug use and crime. Uncontrolled drug use also elongates the length of criminal careers by delaying desistance (Jennings et al. 2016). The end result is that problem drug users often engage in crime at high rates and over long but often intermittent periods, as individuals with drug problems often experience periods of uncontrolled drug use, controlled drug use, and abstinence (i.e., drug dependence is a chronic, relapsing condition).

Given these robust relationships between drug use and offending, it should come as no surprise that individuals with drug problems who are untreated or undertreated are likely to return to drug use both while incarcerated and upon release. One dramatic demonstration of the negative implications of failing to effectively treatment drug problems is the rising rates of fatal overdoses in correctional institutions and immediately after release. Psychoactive substances are present in prisons; however, their high costs and the inconsistent availability of specific drugs lead to prisoners losing some of their drug tolerance. This reduced tolerance, in turn, makes drug overdoses common. In-custody fatal overdoses have reached new heights in recent years. State prisoners' mortality rate due to drugs increased 633% between 2001 and 2019, from 3 to 22 per 100,000 prisoners (Carson 2021b). These statistics demonstrate that many incarcerated individuals with drug problems continue to use while in custody, despite often deadly consequences.

The risk of drug relapse continues upon reentry. Rates of fatal overdose are especially high in the first two weeks after reentry, when the availability of relatively inexpensive drugs becomes pervasive. Binswanger and colleagues (2007) examined death records in Washington state and found that the risk of fatal overdose was 129 times higher in the two weeks following release among former prisoners in comparison to other state residents. This risk falls markedly thereafter but remains considerably higher than Washington state residents as a whole. Similar findings are evident in a quantitative synthesis of five other studies examining mortality in the weeks after release from prison (Merrall et al. 2010). The implication of these findings is that return to drug use is common and oftentimes almost immediate after release.

Beyond the risk of fatal drug overdose, drug relapse is concerning due to its association with other kinds of criminal activity. For instance, Western's (2018) study of re-entry in the Boston area found that drug relapse was one of three factors that distinguished individuals who returned to prison from those who did not. Reincarceration was twice as likely among individuals with a history of drug problems than the overall sample, and three times more likely for individuals with a history of drug problems who relapsed in comparison to returning citizens with similar histories but who did not return to drug use. The Boston re-entry study's findings are confirmed by a long line of research that indicates recidivism and drug relapse are strongly related (see, e.g., Gendreau, Little, and Goggin 1996; Bonta, Law, and Hanson 1998). This relationship, however, is most often confined to the use of amphetamine, cocaine, heroin, or multiple illicit substances. Håkansson and Berglund

(2012), as an example, found that only the use of these hard drugs predicted the likelihood of recidivating, while the use of marijuana, sedatives, and hallucinogens did not.

The conditions frequently associated with drug abuse further elevate the risk of recidivism. Homelessness, like drug relapse, is most acute in the period shortly after release from prison (Petersilia 2003; Hamilton and Campbell 2013) and individuals experiencing homelessness have elevated probabilities of recidivism (Baldry et al. 2004; Håkansoon and Berglund 2012; Lutze, Rosky, and Hamilton 2014). Conversely, research establishes that providing stable housing reduces the number of individuals returned to prison (Lutze et al. 2014; Kirk et al. 2018). Some research also concludes that returning citizens with a history of inpatient psychiatric treatment is an additional independent predictor of recidivism (Håkansoon and Berglund 2012). Further, the relationship between drug relapse and recidivism is stronger among formerly incarcerated females than males (Dowden and Brown 2002).

Without appropriate and effective interventions, individuals released from prison with histories of serious drug abuse are likely to reoffend. Drug relapse upon re-entry is common, quick, and sometimes deadly. Homelessness is an acute and chronic challenge confronting individuals returning to free society. Struggles to maintain mental health are rampant. Uncontrolled drug use, mental health issues, and homelessness exacerbate each other and the risk of reincarceration. And drug, mental health, and housing stability problems are all more common among females in institutional- and community-correctional settings.

II. Incarceration-Based Drug Treatment Modalities

There are six common drug treatment modalities, and a seventh, while much less common than the others, is spreading in response to the opioid epidemic. In particular, correctional settings most often include drug detoxification, drug education, 12-step self-help (e.g., AA, NA), group counseling, cognitive-behavioral, therapeutic community, and medication assisted treatment (MAT) programs. These programs vary substantially in their duration, intensity, and focus. Each is described in this section, but it is important to note that these programs are not mutually exclusive. In fact, many incarceration-based drug interventions integrate two or more of these programs.

Drug detoxification services are typically offered to individuals with drug dependencies who are experiencing withdrawal symptoms. Detoxification aims to manage these symptoms. For drugs that produce physical dependence with florid withdrawal symptoms (e.g., alcohol, heroin, opioids), healthcare providers administer medications to control these symptoms. Discontinuing the use of other drugs generally does not elicit severe withdrawal symptoms; for these drugs, withdrawal can be managed through counseling services. If drug use is completing discontinued, detoxification can be accomplished quickly—often in a matter of days; yet drug cravings persist much longer.

Second, drug education programs are ubiquitous in correctional settings. Such programs educate their students about the harms associated with drug use, the relationship between drugs and crime, signs of drug abuse, and situations that can trigger drug use. These programs are offered in groups (classes), typically are short in duration (20 hours or less), and may be required for individuals assessed as having a drug use disorder (Leukefeld and Tims 1993; US Government Accountability Office 2020). A goal of drug education programs is to get those with serious drug problems to acknowledge these problems and motivate them to participate in more intensive forms of drug treatment programming.

Third, self-help, 12-step programs in the model of Alcoholics/Narcotics Anonymous (AA/NA) are ubiquitous as well. These programs are led by incarcerated peers who are in recovery. Individuals seeking to control their drug use come together to form networks of current and recovering drug users. They meet regularly to discuss and try to resolve common challenges, provide fellowship, and support each other's efforts to achieve and maintain abstinence.

Fourth, cognitive-behavioral therapy aims to reduce uncontrolled drug use and related problems by fostering long-term thinking patterns. These programs are based on the finding that people involved in criminal behavior often exhibit short-term, impulsive thinking patterns. Thus, a goal of cognitive-behavioral therapy is to encourage long-term thinking patterns. Such programs teach participants to anticipate the consequences of their behaviors, to recognize the early signs of drug cravings and environments likely to induce cravings, and to craft techniques for managing drug cravings and steering clear of high-risk environments. Cognitive-behavioral programs are sometimes used as stand-alone drug treatment programs, but much more frequently lessons based on cognitive behavioral principles are integrated into other drug treatment modalities.

Fifth, drug counseling programs utilize a combination of group and individual counseling sessions, cognitive-behavioral and life skills training, drug education, and self-help groups. These activities are typically provided on an intensive, outpatient basis, meaning that participants are housed in the general prison population but meet regularly for counseling sessions. Less common are inpatient counseling programs that set aside separate housing units for program participants. The duration of such programs is most often 30 to 90 days. And counseling programs are led by trained substance abuse counselors.

Sixth, therapeutic communities (TCs) are intensive, long-term, inpatient (residential) drug treatment programs. Program participants are housed in separate units to create an environment conducive to treatment. TCs do not simply treat drug use disorders; instead, TCs view substance abuse as one manifestation of larger, underlying disorders. Consistent with this philosophical orientation, TC programming is multifaceted and targets problematic thinking patterns, antisocial peer associations, personality disorders, mental health problems, histories of abuse, and the trauma that is often a consequence of abuse. This holistic, multifaceted approach is ambitious and typically requires substantial time. In fact, TC programs typically have the longest duration of any incarceration-based drug treatment intervention—lasting from 6 to 12 months. Notably, program participants largely run the residential units in which TC programs are housed, while under the supervision of prison staff. Participants maintain order in the residential unit, monitor each other's behavior for compliance with program rules, and play leading roles in treatment sessions. TC programs are well known for the confrontational approach participants take toward each other, but they are also highly supportive of each other's efforts at personal reformation.

Finally, medication-assisted treatment (MAT) consists of drug treatment programs for individuals with opioid use disorders. There are three medications currently used to treat opioid addiction: methadone, buprenorphine, and naltrexone. Methadone and buprenorphine are used as opioid substitutes that prevent withdrawal symptoms and reduce cravings for opioids. Naltrexone also reduces the opioid cravings and prevents withdrawal symptoms, but it also blocks the euphoric high caused by opioid use, if one continues opioid use. Thus, MATs are designed to reduce the use of illicit opioids by reducing cravings and preventing withdrawal symptoms, which in theory should lead to reductions in drug overdose, needle sharing, and drug-related crime. MAT services in correctional settings can be a continuation of MAT services begun in the community or started in correctional settings prior to re-entry with the expectation that such services will be continued in the community upon release.

Availability and access to these seven drug treatment programs vary widely. Drug education, 12-step peer group, nonresidential group treatment, and cognitive-behavioral programs are ubiquitous in correctional settings. For example, of the 122 facilities operated by the US Bureau of Prisons, all 122 offered each of these four programs (Carson 2021a). By contrast, residential drug treatment programs were offered in 72 (64%) of these facilities, and 15 (13%) facilities offered alternative but equally intensive drug treatment programs.

A minority of drug-involved individuals participate in treatment. Roughly 33% of individuals held in state prisons and 46% of individuals held in federal prisons who met the criteria for substance use disorders participated in some form of substance abuse programming since admission (Maruschak, Bronson, and Alper 2021). Many of the individuals who chose to engage in treatment participated in multiple modalities. The vast majority of those active in drug treatment programs joined 12-step peer groups and/or drug education programs, but involvement in more intensive programs was less common. Roughly 12% and 15% of individuals detained in state and federal prisons with substance use disorders, respectively, participated in residential programs; these figures for counseling programs were 10% and 18%, respectively. And approximately 1% of drug-involved individuals confined in state and federal prisons received maintenance drugs since admission (Maruschak, Bronson, and Alper 2021).

These statistics demonstrate that there is not a dearth of drug treatment programming in US prisons, as nearly all prison systems provide some form of drug treatment programming; instead, there is large disconnect between the most accessible drug treatments programs and the needs of individuals they are intended to serve. Most of the interventions offered in institutional corrections, and those with the greatest number of participants, are low in intensity and short in duration. That makes them ill-suited for treating individuals with serious substance abuse disorders. Availability and access to treatment programs more commensurate with the needs of drug-involved individuals serving sentences in correctional institutions is more limited. Simply stated, there is a stark mismatch between drug problems facing those incarcerated and the programming typically made available in correctional facilities.

III. The Effectiveness of Incarceration-Based Drug Treatment Modalities

There are scores of evaluations of incarceration-based drug treatment programs. The bulk of these evaluations assess TCs, various iterations of group counseling programs, and less commonly MATs. Few studies evaluate the effectiveness of drug education, detoxification, 12-step, or cognitive-behavioral therapies as stand-alone programs. Instead, these treatment modalities are often components of TC, group counseling, or MAT programs. Additionally, these incarceration-based treatment programs are often combined with community-based treatment upon release. Combining drug treatment modalities and extending the duration of treatment engagement by stacking programming is a logical means to enhance treatment effectiveness, as many drug-involved individuals confront multiple problems that contribute to uncontrolled drug use and criminal activity. Yet the practice of combining and stacking programs complicates the task of evaluating the independent effects of these programs on post-release outcomes.

Most evaluations of drug treatment programs delivered in institutional settings examine the effectiveness of these programs in reducing recidivism and/or post-release drug use. The outcome measures tapping these two concepts commonly are dichotomized and therefore capture relatively blunt differences between program participants and their comparison group. A sizeable portion of these evaluations compare the relative effectiveness of different treatment modalities (i.e., utilize treatment vs. treatment designs). These studies demonstrate the *relative* effectiveness of different treatment modalities (i.e., which treatment is more effective than the other); however, such evaluations are incapable of establishing their *absolute* effectiveness in affecting the outcomes of interest (e.g., does a specific treatment modality reduce recidivism in comparison to no treatment). Another set of evaluations assesses program effects by comparing program graduates to participants who did not successfully complete the program of interest. These studies provide weak evidence of the evaluated program's absolute effect, as this research design is compromised by selection bias (i.e., unobserved but systematic differences between groups). Research that compares all program participants to similar individuals who did not participate or who received treatment as usual most clearly identify program effects on the outcomes of interest in absolute terms. Further, by estimating program effects in comparison to no treatment or treatment as usual, the relative effectiveness of treatment programs can be compared, if one is willing to assume the various treatment programs serve similar populations. Thus, this section concentrates on studies employing treatment-no treatment/treatment-as-usual designs (hereafter, "no treatment comparisons" for parsimony).

To assess the effectiveness and relative effectiveness of common drug treatment programs administered in institutional settings, this chapter reviews the *quantity* and *quality* (i.e., methodological rigor) of studies examining the impact of these programs on measures of recidivism and/or drug use. Methodological rigor is particularly important to drug treatment evaluations in correctional settings, as the potential for selection bias is high. Individuals choosing to engage in drug treatment may differ from nonparticipants on measures that are difficult to measure, such as motivation, amenability to treatment, and social support. The potential of group differences on these characteristics is problematic, as these characteristics may be associated with greater treatment success and lower recidivism, and can lead to biased estimates of program effects when employing designs most susceptible to selection bias (e.g., weak quasi-experimental designs). Thus, the findings of studies that credibly handle the possibility of selection bias—such as randomized experiments and rigorous quasi-experiments that construct highly comparable treatment and comparison groups—are given greater emphasis in this review.

Fortunately, the results of this body of research, along with assessments of their methodological rigor, have been synthesized by a series of systematic reviews and meta-analyses (Pearson and Lipton 1999; Mitchell, Wilson, and MacKenzie 2007, 2012; Doyle et al. 2019;

Strange et al. 2022). While these reviews are largely consistent with one another, this chapter primarily relies on the results of Mitchell and colleagues' (2012) meta-analysis for three reasons: (1) it is the most recent *quantitative* synthesis of the evidence base, which facilitates assessments of each program's absolute and relative effects; (2) relatively few suitable studies evaluations have been published in this area since the publication of this meta-analysis; and (3) the results of the most recent studies, which were not available at the time Mitchell et al. published their review, are consistent with these authors' findings.

MAT is the least commonly available prison-based drug treatment program, but assessment of these programs has been expanding in response to the opioid epidemic. There is a robust evidence base concerning the effects of community-based opioid maintenance programs that typically finds that participation in these programs reduce the use of illicit opioids and increase engagement in drug treatment modalities (see, e.g., Moore et al. 2019). A much smaller number of evaluations of in-prison MAT programs exists. For instance, Mitchell and associates' meta-analysis found six independent evaluations of MAT programs that used no-treatment comparison groups, including one experimental evaluation. These studies most commonly find that individuals who received a MAT were less likely to use illicit drugs than those who did not receive a MAT. Methadone was the medication most frequently administered in treatment programs, followed by buprenorphine. The finding of reduced illicit drug use among those administered MAT is confirmed in evaluations using random assignment. When the results of all individual studies are combined, collectively MAT evaluations find that such programs reduce the odds of illicit drug use by 85% (1.85 [1.24, 2.76]) on average in comparison to no treatment.

The current body of research, however, indicates that MATs do not reduce recidivism. Of the six studies that measured the effects of MAT on recidivism, only the study that used experimental methods found that individuals in the MAT program had significantly reduced odds of recidivism over a three-month observation period (Kinlock et al. 2008). Overall, the combined mean effect size of MATs on recidivism outcomes was small and not statistically significant (1.09 [0.71, 1.67]), after removing a negative outlier.

The findings of two more recent systematic reviews confirm these findings. Strange and colleagues (2022) synthesized MAT evaluations made available prior to November 2020 that assessed effects on recidivism and drug overdose outcomes. MAT participation reduced the odds of nonfatal drug overdoses by approximately 60% and fatal overdoses by 20%, but the latter effect was not statistically significant. These authors also found receiving MAT did not reduce the odds of reincarceration or rearrest. Another meta-analysis of this body of research by Moore and associates (2019) adds an important nuance to the findings concerning MAT participation and recidivism. Their review found that recidivism was significantly lower among MAT participants who initiated treatment in-prison and engaged in community-based drug treatment. This finding suggests that stacking in-prison and community-based drug treatment is crucial for recidivism reduction. However, it is important to point out that this finding is susceptible to selection bias, as many individuals who participated in community-based programming did so voluntarily, which magnifies the possibility of selection bias affecting these findings.

There is a larger body of research examining incarceration-based group counseling programs. Twenty-six independent evaluations of group counseling programs were included in Mitchell et al.'s review. The overwhelming majority of these studies employed quasi-experimental methods, and only two studies were randomized experiments. The small number of experimental evaluations of incarceration-based counseling programs is notable, as the results of this body of research on recidivism outcomes vary sharply by this methodological feature. In particular, 14 of the 24 quasi-experimental evaluations (58%) found that treatment participants had significantly lower odds of continued contact with the justice system, and the overall mean odds-ratio effect size for these 24 quasi-experimental evaluations was 1.49 with a 95% confidence interval of 1.17 to 1.89—meaning that the odds of recidivism was 49% lower for participants than nonparticipants. The two experimental studies, however, found no evidence of reductions in recidivism, with a mean effect size of 1.09 and a 95% confidence interval from 0.52 to 2.31, which is neither substantively large nor statistically significant. More generally, Mitchell et al.'s synthesis of the research on counseling programs found that the estimated effect of counseling programs on recidivism declined as the methodological rigor of the evaluations increased. Thus, the effect of incarceration-based group counseling programs is equivocal, with less rigorous studies producing evidence of their effectiveness but the most methodologically rigorous research finding limited evidence of these programs' effectiveness in suppressing recidivism.

The evidence base examining the effects of counseling programs on post-release drug use is scant. Only three evaluations of this kind were included in Mitchell et al.'s meta-analysis. All of these studies were quasi-experiments. One was rated as a rigorous quasi-experiment and the two others were rated as weak quasi-experiments. The rigorous quasi-experimental study and one of the other studies found that drug relapse was statistically lower among participants than nonparticipants; however, the third study found that participants were considerably more likely to relapse. This variability in findings leads to the overall effect size having a wide confidence interval, 0.35 to 1.70, and a mean of 0.77, which indicates that on average drug relapse was higher among participants than nonparticipants, but this difference is not reliable.

The evidence base evaluating TCs is most extensive and rigorous. Thirty-five of the 66 independent evaluations compiled in Mitchell and associates' research concerned TCs. Eleven of these evaluations were rated as rigorous quasi-experiments and two other studies were randomized experiments. These studies find relatively consistent support for the effectiveness of TC programs in reducing recidivism. Mitchell et al. (2012) estimate that the odds of recidivism is 40% lower for TC participants than nonparticipants (i.e., the mean odds-ratio effect size was 1.40 [1.14, 1.71]). Further, and in contrast to the evidence concerning group counseling programs, evidence of TCs' effects on recidivism is stronger in more rigorous evaluations. In fact, the two experimental evaluations collectively found that the odds of recidivism were 90% lower among TC participants.

Additionally, the existing evidence indicates that TCs' effects on recidivism are long-lived. One experimental evaluation of a TC program based in Delaware's correctional system concluded that participants' odds of being arrest-free five years after release were 60% greater than that of nonparticipants. Another study that examined the effects of the same TC program for up to 18 years after re-entry continued to find lower rates of new arrests (Martin et al. 2011).

One important but easily neglected finding from Mitchell et al.'s meta-analysis is the effect of gender composition and the effectiveness of TC programs. In particular, TC evaluations with all female samples had larger effect sizes than all male samples. More specifically, TC participants had odds of recidivism that were 65% lower than nonparticipants in all female samples, but the corresponding odds among all male samples were 36%. These findings indicate that TC programs are effective for male and female participants; and, more softly, these findings suggest the TC programs may be more effective among female than male participants—despite the fact that drug-involved female incarcerees typically have greater personal problems than males.

Prison-based TCs appear to be particularly effective in reducing recidivism when combined with drug treatment in the community. Evaluations of TCs conducted in Delaware, Pennsylvania (Welsh 2007), and Minnesota (Duwe 2010) all find that recidivism is considerably lower among individuals who completed both in-prison TC programming and continued drug treatment in a post-release aftercare phase. For instance, Inciardi, Martin, and Butzin (2004) found that individuals who completed both treatment components had much higher probabilities of remaining arrest-free five years after release (48%) than those who only completed the in-prison program (28%). Again, it needs to be emphasized that these findings may be affected by self-selection bias because individuals who agree to participate in both programs and/or who actually complete both programs may differ systematically on unobserved variables. Consequently, research finding enhanced effectiveness when in-prison TC programming is combined with community-based after release may be biased.

The effects of TC programs on drug relapse are decidedly mixed. Of the 13 independent evaluations of TC programs, 4 found that TC participants had statistically lower rates of relapse, 5 others found nonstatistically significant reductions in drug relapse, and the 4 remaining studies found that participants had higher relapse rates than nonparticipants. The combined mean odds-ratio effect size and its confidence interval, however, find that TC participants have lower rates of drug relapse on average than nonparticipants, with a mean odds-ratio effect size of 1.33 and a 95% confidence interval from 1.00 to 1.76 ($p = 0.049$). Thus, the knowledge base indicates that TC participation decreases the odds of drug relapse by 33%.

IV. Discussion and Conclusions

Taken together, the body of knowledge concerning the effects of incarceration-based drug treatment programs on recidivism and drug relapse provides three important conclusions. First, the existing body of evaluations indicates that MATs reduce drug relapse after release from prison. Participation in MATs, however, does not lower the odds of recidivism. Given that MATs focus on salving off drug cravings and withdrawal symptoms but do not directly address the totality of underlying causes of offending, these findings are predictable.

Second, rigorous impact evaluations of group-based counseling programs do not provide evidence of these programs' effectiveness in reducing recidivism. There is some evidence to suggest that these programs do reduce reoffending, but, almost uniformly, evaluations reaching such conclusions are methodologically weak. The evidence assessing these programs' effects on drug relapse is too scant to draw firm conclusions, but the extant research most often does not find meaningfully lower rates of relapse among program participants.

Third, evaluations of TC programs find robust and long-lasting effects of participation on lowering recidivism. These evaluations also indicate, but with less confidence, that TC programs lower the likelihood of drug relapse. The positive effects of TC programming appear to be related to their intensity, long duration, and multifaceted nature; that is, TC programs attend to the multitude of challenges confronting the whole person—not just uncontrolled drug use.

None of these conclusions are surprising, given the many problems typically confronting incarcerated and drug-involved individuals. Drug use disorders are difficult to treat by themselves, but this difficulty increases when one is also ensnared in the justice system, has mental health problems, and/or faces uncertain housing situations. The existing research demonstrates that group-based counseling and MAT programs are insufficient in intensity and in duration to address these problems. By contrast, TCs are long-term, intensive interventions that target each individual's problems in a holistic fashion. Further, many TC participants continue their treatment engagement in the community, which may serve to alleviate housing instability at least temporarily and provide the kinds of stable environments conductive to personal reformation. More succinctly, in-prison TCs encompass the key features needed to effectively address the challenges facing justice-involved individuals with serious drug problems.

The implications of this research for policy and practice are straightforward. TC programs, because of their positive effects on the outcomes of interest, should continue to be supported. TC programs also need additional evaluations, particularly evaluations of these programs' effects on drug use, drug use frequency, and drug use in the long term. The current research base suggests that in order to effectively reduce drug use and recidivism, MATs need to be combined with interventions that address more holistically and intensively the host of co-occurring challenges that face individuals with substance abuse disorders. The extant literature does not support the effectiveness of group-based counseling programs as stand-alone therapies, but these programs may still be important as a bridge that links incarcerated individuals with drug problems to more intensive modalities and as a component of more intensive modalities. Finally, access to more rigorous and comprehensive drug treatment modalities such as incarceration-based TCs need to be expanded to be commensurate with the treatment needs of incarcerated populations.

References

Adler, Rachel H. 2021. The nexus of homelessness and incarceration: The case of homeless men in Trenton, NJ. *Journal of Men's Studies*, 29:335–353.

Baldry, Eileen, Desmond McDonnell, Peter Maplestone, and Manu Peeters. 2004. *The role of housing in preventing re-offending*. Melbourne, Australia: Housing and Urban Research Institute.

Ball, John C., Lawrence Rosen, John A. Flueck, and David N. Nurco. 1981. The criminality of heroin addicts: When addicted and when off opiates. In *Drugs-crime connection*, edited by J. A. Inciardi, 39–65. Beverly Hills, CA: SAGE.

Bennett, Trevor, and Katy Holloway. 2009. The causal connection between drug misuse and crime. *British Journal of Criminology* 49:513–531.

Binswanger, Ingrid A., Marc F. Stern, Richard A. Deyo, Patrick J. Heagerty, Allen Cheadle, Joann G. Elmore, and Thomas D. Koepsell. 2007. Release from prison—a high risk of death for former inmates. *New England Journal of Medicine*, 356:157–165.

Bonta, James, Moira Law, and Karl Hanson. 1998. The prediction of criminal and violent recidivism among mentally disordered offenders: A meta-analysis. *Psychological Bulletin*, 123:123–142.

Boyum, David, and Peter Reuter. 2005. *An analytic assessment of U.S. drug policy*: Washington, D.C: AEI Press.

Bronson, Jennifer, Jessica Stroop, Stephanie Zimmer, and Marcus Berzofsky. 2017. *Drug use, dependence, and abuse among state prisoners and jail inmates, 2007-2009*. Washington, DC: US Department of Justice, Bureau of Justice Statistics.

Carson, E. Ann. 2021a. Federal prisoner statistics collected under the First Step Act, 2020. Washington, DC: US Department of Justice, Bureau of Justice Statistics.

Carson, E. Ann. 2021b. *Mortality in state and federal prisons, 2001-2019: Statistical tables*. Washington, DC: US Department of Justice, Bureau of Justice Statistics.

Couloute, Lucius. 2018. *Nowhere to go: Homelessness among formerly incarcerated people*. Northampton, MA: Prison Policy Initiative.

Dowden, Craig, and Shelley L. Brown. 2002. The role of substance abuse factors in predicting recidivism: A meta-analysis. *Psychology, Crime and Law*, 8:243–264.

Doyle, Michael F., Anthony Shakeshaft, Jill Guthrie, Mieke Snijder, and Tony Butler. 2019. A systematic review of evaluations of prison-based alcohol and other drug use behavioural treatment for men. *Australian and New Zealand Journal of Public Health*, 43:120–130.

Duwe, Grant. 2010. Prison-based chemical dependency treatment in Minnesota: An outcome evaluation. *Journal of Experimental Criminology*, 6:57–81.

Elbogen, Eric B., and Sally C. Johnson. 2009. The intricate link between violence and mental disorder: Results from the National Epidemiologic Survey on Alcohol and Related Conditions. *Archives of General Psychiatry*, 66:152–161.

Gendreau, Paul, Tracy Little, and Claire Goggin. 1996. A meta-analysis of the predictors of adult offender recidivism: What works! *Criminology*, 34:575–607.

Greenberg, Greg A., and Robert A. Rosenheck. 2008. Jail incarceration, homelessness, and mental health: A national study. *Psychiatric Services*, 59:170–177.

Håkansson, Anders, and Mats Berglund. 2012. Risk factors for criminal recidivism—a prospective follow-up study in prisoners with substance abuse. *BMC Psychiatry*, 12:1–8.

Hamilton, Zachary K., and Christopher M. Campbell. 2013. A dark figure of corrections: Failure by way of participation. *Criminal Justice and Behavior*, 40:180–202.

Inciardi, James A., Steven S Martin, and Clifford A. Butzin. 2004. Five-year outcomes of therapeutic community treatment of drug-involved offenders after release from prison. *Crime & Delinquency*, 50:88–107.

James, Doris J., and Lauren E. Glaze. 2006. *Mental health problems of prison and jail inmates*. Washington, DC: Bureau of Justice Statistics.

Jennings, Wesley G., Alex R. Piquero, David P. Farrington, Maria M. Ttofi, Rebecca V. Crago, and Delphine Theobald. 2016. The intersections of drug use continuity with nonviolent offending and involvement in violence over the life course: Findings from the Cambridge Study in Delinquent Development. *Youth Violence and Juvenile Justice*, 14:95–109.

Kinlock, Timothy W., Michael S. Gordon, Robert P. Schwartz, and Kevin E. O'Grady. 2008. A study of methadone maintenance for male prisoners: 3-Month postrelease outcomes. *Criminal Justice & Behavior*, 35 (1): 34–47.

Kinner, Stuart A., Jessica George, Gabrielle Campbell, and Louisa Degenhardt. 2009. Crime, drugs and distress: Patterns of drug use and harm among criminally involved injecting drug users in Australia. *Australian and New Zealand Journal of Public Health* 33:223–227.

Kirk, David S., Geoffrey C. Barnes, Jordan M. Hyatt, and Brook W. Kearley. 2018. The impact of residential change and housing stability on recidivism: Pilot results from the Maryland Opportunities through Vouchers Experiment (MOVE). *Journal of Experimental Criminology*, 14:213–226.

Leukefeld, Carl G., and Frank R. Tims. 1993. Drug abuse treatment in prisons and jails. *Journal of Substance Abuse Treatment*, 10:77–84.

Lutze, Faith E., Jeffrey W. Rosky, and Zachary K. Hamilton. 2014. Homelessness and reentry: A multisite outcome evaluation of Washington State's reentry housing program for high risk offenders. *Criminal Justice and Behavior*, 41:471–491.

Makkai, Toni, and Jason Payne. 2003. *Key findings from the Drug Use Careers of Offenders (DUCO) study*. Canberra: Australian Institute of Criminology.

March, Joan Carles, Eugenia Oviedo-Joekes, and Manuel Romero. 2006. Drugs and social exclusion in ten European cities. *European Addiction Research* 12:33–41.

Martin, Steven S., Daniel J. O'Connell, Raymond Paternoster, and Ronet D. Bachman. 2011. The long and winding road to desistance from crime for drug-involved offenders: The long-term influence of TC Treatment on re-arrest. *Journal of Drug Issues*, 41:179–196.

Maruschak, Laura M., Jennifer Bronson, and Mariel Alper. 2021. *Alcohol and drug use and treatment reported by prisoners*. Washington, DC: Bureau of Justice Statistics.

McNiel, Dale E., Renée L. Binder, and Jo C. Robinson. 2005. Incarceration associated with homeless, mental disorder, and co-occurring substance abuse. *Psychiatric Services*, 56:840–846.

Merrall, Elizabeth L.C., Azar Kariminia, Ingrid A. Binswanger, Michael S. Hobbs, Michael Farrell, John Marsden, Sharon J. Hutchinson, and Sheila M. Bird. 2010. Meta-analysis of drug-related deaths soon after release from prison. *Addiction*, 105:1545–1554.

Metraux, Stephen, Caterina G. Roman, and Richard S. Cho. 2007. Incarceration and homelessness. Paper presented at the 2007 National Symposium on Homelessness Research, Washington, DC.

Mitchell, Ojmarrh. 2009. Ineffectiveness, financial waste, and unfairness: The legacy of the war on drugs. *Journal of Crime & Justice*, 32:1–19.

Mitchell, Ojmarrh, David B. Wilson, and Doris L. MacKenzie. 2007. Does incarceration-based drug treatment reduce recidivism? A meta-analytic synthesis of the research. *Journal of Experimental Criminology*, 3:353–375.

Mitchell, Ojmarrh, David B. Wilson, and Doris L. MacKenzie. 2012. *The effectiveness of incarceration-based drug treatment on criminal behavior: 2012 update*. Oslo, Norway: Campbell Collaboration, Crime and Justice Group.

Mogk, Jessica, Valerie Shmigol, Marvin Futrell, Bert Stover, and Amy Hagopian. 2020. Court-imposed fines as a feature of the homelessness-incarceration nexus: A cross-sectional study of the relationship between legal debt and duration of homelessness in Seattle, Washington, USA. *Journal of Public Health Policy*, 42:107–119.

Moore, Kelly E., Walter Roberts, Holly H. Reid, Kathryn M. Z. Smith, Lindsay M. S. Oberleitner, and Sherry A. McKee. 2019. Effectiveness of medication assisted treatment for opioid use in prison and jail settings: A meta-analysis and systematic review. *Journal of Substance Abuse Treatment*, 99:32–43.

Moschion, Julie, and Guy Johnson. 2019. Homelessness and incarceration: A reciprocal relationship? *Journal of Quantitative Criminology*, 35:855–887.

Mumola, Christopher J. 1999. *Substance abuse and treatment, state and federal prisoners, 1997*. Washington, DC: Bureau of Justice Statistics.

Mumola, Christopher J., and Jennifer C. Karberg. 2006. *Drug use and dependence, state and federal prisoners, 2004* Washington, DC: Bureau of Justice Statistics.

Musto, David F. 1999. *The American disease: Origins of narcotic control.* 3rd ed. New York: Oxford.

National Center on Addiction and Substance Abuse. 2010. *Behind bars II: Substance abuse and America's prison population.* New York: National Center on Addiction and Substance Abuse.

Pearson, Frank S., and Douglas S. Lipton. 1999. A meta-analytic review of the effectiveness of corrections-based treatments for drug abuse. *The Prison Journal*, 79:384–410.

Petersilia, Joan. 2003. *When prisoners come home: Parole and prisoner reentry.* New York: Oxford University Press.

Piquero, Alex R., David P. Farrington, and Alfred Blumstein. 2003. The criminal career paradigm. *Crime and Justice*, 30:359–506.

Strange, C. Clare, Sarah M. Manchak, Jordan M. Hyatt, Damon M. Petrich, Alisha Desai, and Cory P Haberman. 2022. Opioid-specific medication-assisted therapy and its impact on criminal justice and overdose outcomes. *Campbell Systematic Reviews*, 18:e1215.

US Government Accountability Office. 2020. *Bureau of Prisons: Improved planning would help BOP evaluate and manage its portfolio of drug education and treatment programs.* Washington, DC: US Government Accountability Office.

Welsh, Wayne N. 2007. A multisite evaluation of prison-based therapeutic community drug treatment. *Criminal Justice and Behavior* 34:1481–1498.

Western, Bruce. 2018. *Homeward: Life in the year after prison.* New York: Russell Sage Foundation.

CHAPTER 17

MAKING PRISONER RE-ENTRY EVIDENCE-BASED

HELEN KOSC AND DAVID S. KIRK

FIFTY years ago, Nils Christie (1971, 145) described the role of criminologists as cultural workers whose "obligation" it was to "penetrate" contemporary problems as they arise and work alongside policymakers to "keep a constant fight going against being absorbed and tamed" by the status quo of society. Christie assigned to criminologists the *capacity* to transform the way penality is understood and the *responsibility* to spread that understanding beyond the halls of academia and into wider political discourse.

While this *responsibility* of using criminology to inform social policy is certainly felt, criminologists are left skeptical of their *capacity* to do so. That *capacity* to shape public discourse and policy that Christie described is not given to criminologists freely; it must constantly be negotiated. And, as it currently stands, criminology too often finds itself rather distanced from policy discussions and debate (Fagan 2014; La Vigne 2021; Nagin 2022). Something in the negotiation is prohibiting criminologists from fulfilling their "obligations" as cultural workers.

We will argue in this chapter that one strong prohibitor is the lack of robust and replicable findings in criminological research, focusing specifically on the absence of evidence-based research pertaining to re-entry programs and policy. Realizing criminologists' *capacity* to inform public discourse and policy requires necessitates a strong effort by criminologists to incorporate evidence-based research into the study of re-entry.

I. STUDYING RE-ENTRY

Before we can make the argument in support for evidence-based re-entry research, it is important to unpack the concept of re-entry further, to better understand how it is conceptualized and measured, as well as its significance within the life course.

Despite the fact that most formerly incarcerated individuals return to the same communities in which they were sentenced (Kirk 2009; Harding, Morenoff, and Herbert 2013; Chamberlain and Wallace 2016), oftentimes the world they re-enter is drastically different. Because of the collateral consequences of punishment (Kirk and Wakefield 2018), securing a job (Pager 2003; 2008), finding somewhere to live (Gojkovic, Mills, and Meek 2012), receiving support (Rade, Desmarais, and Mitchell 2016), and building meaningful relationships (Burnett 2004; Gadd and Farrall 2004) becomes infinitely more challenging.

The collateral consequences of punishment are not the only threat to desistance from crime post-release. On average, the incarcerated population has limited education (Heitzeg 2009; Meiners and Winn 2014; Doleac 2018), limited work experience (Farrington et al. 1986; Burdett, Lagos, and Wright 2003; Doleac 2016), high rates of severe mental illness (Massoglia and Schnittker 2009; Yi, Turney, and Wildeman 2017), heightened anxiety and emotional trauma (Piel 2020), a high risk of suicide (Pratt et al. 2006), and high rates of substance use disorders (Bronson et al. 2017; Alexander et al. 2020).

But these risk factors are further intensified when accompanied by a criminal record. Researchers have put forth numerous hypotheses regarding the mechanisms responsible for producing difficulties for previously incarcerated individuals upon release. These include the disruption of social and familial ties (Sampson and Laub 2003), the broader influence on social networks upon release (Hagan 1993), the labeling effects and stigma associated with a criminal record (Schwartz and Skolnick 1962), the loss of human capital (Becker 1975), the trauma of the incarceration itself (Parenti 1999), and the legal barriers to employment that the record may cause (Dale 1976). Pager (2003) goes as far as to argue that the "negative credential" associated with a criminal record is a stratifying mechanism on its own. Inspired by the experimental audit study of Schwartz and Skolnick (1962), Pager (2003) applies an experimental design to empirically evaluate whether a causal relationship exists between a criminal record and employment outcomes. She finds that mere contact with the criminal justice system, in the absence of any transformative or selective effects, severely limits subsequent employment opportunities—with ex-offenders being half to one-third as likely as nonoffenders to be considered by employers. Other researchers have used longitudinal survey data to study the effect of a criminal record on employment probabilities and future income and have found similarly strong and negative effects (Freeman 1987; Nagin and Waldfogel 1995; Beckett and Western 2001).

Recidivism rates (or rates of repeat offending) are often used as a measure of the effectiveness of prison systems, post-release support, and management programs, and by virtue of that, quality of re-entry experience. In a country like the United States, where there are more than 1.2 million people in state and federal prisons (Carson 2021), 37% will be rearrested within one year of release and 23% will be reconvicted of a crime (Durose and Antenangeli 2021). In the United Kingdom, 42% of individuals released from custody are reconvicted of a crime within one year of release from incarceration (UK Ministry of Justice 2022). The process of re-entry, however, encapsulates other relevant outcomes beyond simply recidivism, such as those outcomes involved in the process of successfully returning to one's community, obtaining employment, accessing treatment for mental health and addiction, and restoring one's full citizenship (Petersilia 2003; Mears and Cochran 2015).

There is consensus across the literature that the quality of the re-entry experience undoubtedly influences an individual's despondency and likelihood of recall or reoffense—be it intentional or not. "Perfect" re-entry, therefore, would create the kind of conditions under which an individual is least likely to fall back into a criminal lifestyle and most likely to make a healthy transition to their community (Travis and Visher 2005). Re-entry presents the individual with a number of triggering risk factors and challenges that threaten successful reintegration. It should therefore be the role of re-entry policies and practices to recognize and moderate the impact of those stressors to encourage successful community reintegration, not just to minimize rates of reoffense (Petersilia 2003).

While government agencies and nonprofit organizations offer a number of programs intended to support and improve prisoner re-entry outcomes, relatively few have been rigorously evaluated for their effects (Doleac 2019b, 508). For this reason, we, like many other sociologists and criminologists, advocate for more evidence-based evaluations of re-entry supports as well as the strict use of evidence when designing future policy and programming.

II. Evidence-Based Study in Criminology

Evidence-based study is the use of empirically sound evidence to establish the effect of a treatment, including considerations of cost-effectiveness (Mears 2010). The fundamental problem of causal inference that evidence-based study aims to address is that for any unit of treatment we cannot observe that unit's counterfactual outcome—i.e., what would have happened if the individual had not received the treatment (Neyman 1935; Rubin 1974; Rubin 1978; Holland 1986). Experiments are able to overcome this problem through randomization of the treatment. It is through randomizing a treatment and studying the average of observations that experiments can provide an unbiased estimate of the average causal effect of the treatment (Rubin 1974, 1978; Holland 1986).

Of course, randomized experiments are not always possible or feasible with respect to criminal justice interventions. Accordingly, Farrington and colleagues (2002) developed the Maryland Scientific Methods Scale (SMS) as a tool to evaluate and communicate the methodological quality of the effects of criminological prevention programs and interventions (Farrington et al. 2002). The SMS, which is informed by the classic work of Cook and Campbell (1979), focuses particular attention on conveying the internal validity of studies. While raw correlational analyses fall at the bottom of the SMS hierarchy, it should come as no surprise that randomized controlled trials (RCTs) and natural experiments occupy the top two spots. RCTs, because of their ability to resolve issues of omitted variable bias by randomly assigning individuals to experimental groups, are often referred to as the "gold standard" of evidence-based research (Sampson et al. 2013). Similarly, natural experiments seek to avoid selection bias by dividing individuals into treatment versus control groups based on factors that are unrelated to the outcome of interest—i.e., assignment to treatment and control groups "as if" random. On the five-point SMS scale, cross-sectional designs and simple "before-and-after" designs occupy the two lowest scale positions, accordingly, since they fail to sufficiently rule out threats to internal validity. The SMS classification system, like other similar hierarchies of evidence (Petrosino et al. 2001; Doleac 2019a, 2019b), makes it possible to compare the effectiveness of programs in different settings. It is also effective at communicating to scholars, policymakers, and practitioners alike that not all research is of the same quality, and that more weight should be given to those programs with higher-quality evaluations.

Unfortunately, RCTs and natural experiments are relatively rare in criminological research, especially research pertaining to the re-entry of formerly incarcerated individuals. Sampson and colleagues (2013) argue that this is because criminology tends to adopt what they call "backward" causality—i.e., researchers often look for the causes *of* an effect, as opposed to a "forward-looking" approach, which looks for the effects of a cause (see also Holland 1986). As Lussier and Gress (2014)—whose research focuses specifically on released sex offenders—argue, while RCTs are the gold standard in evaluating the efficacy of treatment, they can be ethically difficult to navigate in research on the formerly incarcerated, particularly that involving sex offenders. Conversely, Boruch (1975; see also Weisburd 2003) makes a persuasive argument that it is actually unethical to not rigorously evaluate programs and policies. The risk in doing suboptimal evaluation of an intervention or prevention program is that we will draw incorrect conclusions about efficacy, perhaps leading to a detrimental situation where a crime occurs that could have been prevented, or the continued reliance on and dedication of finite resources to programs with minimal positive or even detrimental effects.

The absence of RCTs in re-entry research is unfortunate, because participants in re-entry programming (the treated) can be very different than nonparticipants (the untreated) in ways beyond the researcher's control, thus making it difficult to know what would have happened in the absence of treatment. For instance, re-entry programs often screen participants based on motivation to change, so the treatment group will be positively selected on qualities such as eagerness and initiative, which may improve re-entry outcomes on their own (Doleac 2019a, 2019b). Two seemingly similar participants—based on observable characteristics alone—may be very different on the unobservable, unaccounted for dimensions. These unobservable differences make it very challenging to identify the causal effect.

As a result, relatively few existing re-entry programs are supported by evidence at the natural experiment or RCT tier of the SMS or similar classification schemes. Instead, most quantitative re-entry studies use nonexperimental methods such as descriptive analyses, matched comparison groups, or statistical controls. Thus, while research pointing to the positive effects of particular treatment programs exists, these findings may not be internally valid and may not replicate.

Of course, there are trade-offs with RCTs. The controlled conditions of an experiment facilitate internal validity of inferences, but may be challenging or impossible to replicate in the real world, thereby limiting the generalizability of the findings (Sampson et al. 2013; Nagin and Sampson 2019). As a case in point, the Baltimore Living Insurance for Ex-Offenders (LIFE) experiment, which was implemented with precision by a team of dedicated researchers, found that income maintenance of $60/week to formerly incarcerated individuals decreases the likelihood of rearrest for theft (Mallar and Thornton 1978). Given the promise of the LIFE program, the US Department of Labor funded a much larger follow-up initiative called the Transitional Aid Research Project (TARP). TARP was designed to be closer to a real-world setting and was implemented by government agencies rather than researchers. The evaluation of TARP revealed that outside of the controlled, ideal research setting, income maintenance does not appear to reduce the likelihood of rearrest (Rossi, Berk, and Lenihan 1980). By implication, evidence-based re-entry should not just focus on establishing internal validity of research findings, but external validity as well.

III. THE STATE OF CURRENT PROGRAMMING AS EVALUATED USING RCTs

In Table 17.1 we present an overview of the evaluation of existing programmatic areas related to prisoner re-entry, focusing primarily on programs implemented outside of prison. Space constraints prevent a comprehensive review, so we selectively focus our discussion on the program and intervention evaluations in the table, because they are of a high potential standard per the criteria of the SMS. More comprehensive reviews can be found at the National Institute of Justice's CrimeSolutions website (http://www.crimesolutions.gov/), the What Works in Reentry Clearinghouse (https://whatworks.csgjusticecenter.org/), and the Washington State Institute for Public Policy's cost-benefit analysis of social programs (http://www.wsipp.wa.gov/BenefitCost?topicId=2).

The table covers seven categories or domains of programs: wrap-around services, intensive supervision or case management, social support, employment, housing, cognitive-behavioral therapy and mental health treatment, and substance abuse treatment. Within each category, we provide a general description of the aim or purpose of programs and interventions, a description of corresponding program evaluations, and our assessment as to whether and why a given category of re-entry services yields evidence of effectiveness. And while the vast majority of the evaluations we highlight in the table focus on outcomes related to recidivism, we would again emphasize that "re-entry" actually involves a broad range of outcomes that could be the focus of evaluations, such as employment, placement in housing, and completion of substance abuse or mental health treatment.

IV. AN EXAMPLE OF THE DEVELOPMENT OF EMPIRICALLY BASED POLICIES AND PROGRAMS

Thus far we have provided a framework for evaluating evidence related to prisoner re-entry and reintegration, and have surveyed a select number of RCTs across a number of domains of support. In this section, we provide an example of a long-term project specifically designed for the purpose of methodically increasing the rigor of evidence about the relationships between place, residential change, and successful re-entry, as well as translating research findings into tangible policy-relevant recommendations.

Our example starts with the assertion that a likely contributor to the vicious cycle of recidivism among the incarcerated and formerly incarcerated is the fact that many released prisoners often return in very close proximity to the locations where they resided prior to incarceration. These locations are often characterized by the same criminal opportunities and criminal peers that proved detrimental to their behavior in the past. Many formerly incarcerated individuals move back to former neighborhoods despite an expressed interest to avoid such places because of a lack of housing opportunities elsewhere. If desistance from crime is facilitated by separating from past situations and establishing a new set of

Table 17.1. Select Overview of Prisoner Re-entry Programs

Category of Program	Aim/Purpose	Evaluation	Verdict
"Wrap-Around" Services	Wrap-around services are those that aim to serve multiple, complementary needs at once (Doleac 2019a, 2019b). Participants are often assigned a case manager who will evaluate their needs and refer them to appropriate services. These services may begin upon release or within the prison to prepare for release.	Grommon and colleagues (2013) evaluated one such wrap-around service program and found that, despite the array of services offered, the program had no significant effects on rearrest or reincarceration. Cook et al. (2015) discovered similar findings when evaluating an employment-focused wrap-around program in Milwaukee: no beneficial effects on long-term employment or the likelihood of rearrest, and no significant effect on reincarceration. Evaluations of Reintegration of Ex-Offenders (RExO) by Wiegand and Sussell (2016) as well as the Second Chance Act (SCA) by D'Amico and Kim (2018) similarly found no significant effect of wraparound services.	As it stands, the existing evidence suggests that wrap-around services, as currently implemented, are not generally effective. Doleac (2019a, 2019b) offers a few reasons why this might be the case, such as the ineffectiveness of individual parts of the program or the very comprehensiveness of the service itself, offering too much support across too many areas.
Intense Supervision/ Case Management	Much like wrap-around services, these services cater to the participants' needs while also guaranteeing the substantial involvement of case managers.	Guydish and colleagues (2011) randomly assigned female, drug-involved probationers in San Francisco to more intensive and supportive case management (treatment), or probation as usual (control), and they found no significant difference in arrest rates after 12 months. Scott and Dennis (2012) measured the effect of Recovery Management Checkups (RMCs) for recently released women with substance abuse issues. The checkups did increase participation in substance abuse treatment, but had no significant effect on incarceration or arrest rates.	As it stands, increasing the level of supervision and/or providing intensive case management appears to have no benefits in terms of reduced criminal justice involvement and associated behavior. In some cases, it led to increases in criminal justice contact.

(continued)

Table 17.1. Continued

Category of Program	Aim/Purpose	Evaluation	Verdict
		Hennigan and colleagues (2010) measured the effects of intensive supervision randomly assigned to juvenile probationers in Los Angeles, and generally found no significant differences in outcomes between the treatment and control groups five years later. The one exception was that low-risk boys, aged 15 or younger, assigned to receive intensive supervision had a higher incarceration likelihood and a higher likelihood of continued criminal justice involvement than those unassigned to treatment. Boyle and colleagues (2013) studied high-risk parolees in New Jersey, randomly assigned to a Day Reporting Center (DRC) versus those with parole supervision as usual. Those assigned to a DRC were significantly more likely to be convicted of a new offense in the first 6 months. There were no significant differences in recidivism between the two groups after 18 months. Barnes and colleagues (2012) tested the effect of supervision levels for low- and high-risk probationers in Philadelphia. There were no significant differences in recidivism across the treatment (low-intensity supervision) and control (normal supervision) groups 18 months later. Hyatt and Barnes (2017) randomly assigned high-risk probationers to "moderate-risk" or "high-risk" labels that determined the actual level of supervision they received. One year after assignment, there was no significant difference between the two groups in new offenses or days incarcerated.	However, cost savings generated by reducing supervision levels of low-risk individuals does not appear to increase recidivism (Barnes et al. 2012). Additionally, there is a body of research that compares intensive supervision in lieu incarceration, generally finding a substantial benefit relative to cost (WSIPP 2019).

| Social Support/Positive Peer Group | Research consistently shows that a majority of formerly incarcerated individuals rely on family and friends for support and even accommodation upon immediate release. There are programs that aim to increase social support from the community and/or the participant's own social circle. These programs point to the importance of good quality social ties for desisting from crime (Berg and Huebner 2011). | Pettus-Davis and colleagues (2017) evaluated a program called "Support Matters," designed to encourage involvement in positive social support networks. Seven months after random assignment to the program versus re-entry as normal, there was no difference in rearrests rates across treatment and control groups. (Note: the study may have been underpowered given the small sample size, N=40). Pettus-Davis (2021) has proposed a new family skills training intervention, "Support4Families," that she has developed using evidence-driven, social support research, to meet the demand after evaluating other ineffective social support programs. This training intervention has yet to be rigorously evaluated.

Shamblen and colleagues (2017) considered the "Creating Lasting Family Connections Fatherhood Program (CLFCFP)," designed for individuals with a substance abuse disorder, and found no significant differences in reincarceration at the three-month follow-up.

DiZerega (2010) and Mullins and Toner (2008) evaluated two examples of parole officer–focused family engagement programs—"Engaging Offenders' Families in Reentry" and "Implementing Family Support Approach for Community Supervision." Both of these intervention programs were found to improve relationships between parole officers and the justice-involved individual, but not between the individual and their family members. | Some research still endorses the importance of social support for maintaining desistance; however, findings illustrate that the programs currently implemented are yielding little to no beneficial effect on participants.

Rather hopefully, Pettus-Davis (2021) is using her earlier empirical analyses (2017) to develop an evidence-driven support program. |

(continued)

Table 17.1. Continued

Category of Program	Aim/Purpose	Evaluation	Verdict
Employment	Economic models of crime suggest that improving post-prison labor market prospects should reduce recidivism. Some programs aim to offer those recently released from prison with transitional jobs–paid employment opportunities with the aim of helping participants transition into private sector jobs upon completion of the program.	Uggen (2000) evaluated the National Supported Work Demonstration and found that those individuals randomly assigned to the program and offered a basic supported job opportunity had increased employment and reduced recidivism, but these findings only applied for older men aged >26. (Note: outcomes were self-reported and the sample suffered from attrition). Cook et al. (2015) systematically evaluate enhanced employment opportunities and services through randomized controlled trials, observing that services that improve human capital help significantly boost employment and earnings upon release. However, whether there is a significant and sufficient impact on recidivism for the intervention to be cost-effective is more uncertain. They found that the difference of reimprisonment rates for the treatment and control groups during the first year was not significant (22% vs 26%). They also found average earnings to be quite low for both treatment and control groups, and that a temporary increase in subsidized employment does not lead to more employment in unsubsidized jobs. Other studies of similar transitional/subsidized job programs found that while participants were far more likely to be employed afterwards than those in the control group, this rate quickly dropped once the program was completed, such that there were no long-term benefits to employment (Cook et al. 2015; Valentine and Redcross 2015; Barden et al. 2018). As noted earlier, Mallar and Thornton (1978) evaluated the LIFE experiment, finding no evidence of a reduction in recidivism following job placement services, although they did find that income maintenance of $60/week decreases the likelihood of rearrest for theft. Redcross and colleagues (2010) examined the Transitional Job Reentry Demonstration (TJRP) programs and found that while the program boosted employment rates early on, the effect was limited to subsidized jobs and had no post-program effect on employment. Similarly, the evaluation of the Center of Employment Opportunities (CEO) assistance programs by Redcross and colleagues (2012) found a mixture of null and positive results on recidivism depending on the time frame and definition applied. Wright et al. (2014) investigate the effects of an employment-focused program that offers vocational training to the recently released. They found no impact on subsequent employment or recidivism.	Findings related to employment programs suggest that the training in these programs may lead to an increase in employment, at least while participants are still active in the program, yet they are ineffective with respect to reducing recidivism. It may be the case that the benefits are not strong enough to overcome the collateral consequences of a criminal record (see Pager 2003).

| Housing / Residential | Some programs offer participants a temporary residence upon release in hopes that it will serve as a temporary base and also as a positive community for them.

Some research also examines whether residential relocation to different neighborhoods and cities can be beneficial. However, it is difficult to empirically measure the effects of relocation absent random assignment to locations, as individuals will tend to self-select into locations, making it difficult to cleanly identify a causal relationship between relocation and desistance (Kirk 2020). | Lee (2019) used the random assignment of prison case managers, who recommend either halfway house release or parole release, in a quasi-experimental design to investigate the effects of residence in a halfway house (versus parole to the community). He finds that assignment to halfway houses increased reincarceration, with a higher incidence of technical violations of parole and new offenses.

Doleac and colleagues (2020) reanalyzed an experimental study of Oxford Houses (Jason, Olson, and Harvey 2015) for recently released individuals recovering from alcohol or drug dependence. They find that assignment to Oxford Houses, relative to the status quo situation for formerly incarcerated individuals, increased the likelihood of reincarceration.

Nakamura (2018) evaluated a program in which those parolees who expressed a willingness to relocate to a different county upon release from prison were randomly assigned to a halfway house either in the county where they resided prior to incarceration or in a different county. The evaluation revealed that allowing parolees to move to a different county reduces the likelihood of recidivism, particularly for those with a substance abuse problem. | Halfway houses and residential programs for individuals with substance dependence appear to increase the likelihood of recidivism.

As for residential relocation, since it is unethical to mandate that individuals sever their peer networks, it is difficult to measure the effects of residential relocation or separating from deviant peers. However, the Nakamura (2018) study provides suggestive evidence of the benefits of residential relocation. We provide further discussion of residential relocation in the next section. |

(continued)

Table 17.1. Continued

Category of Program	Aim/Purpose	Evaluation	Verdict
Mental Health Interventions/ Cognitive-Behavioral Therapy (CBT)	On average, the incarcerated population has higher rates of severe mental illness (Fisher et al. 2006; Massoglia and Schnittker 2009; Yi et al. 2017), heightened anxiety and emotional trauma (Piel 2020), and a higher risk of suicide (Pratt et al. 2006) than the general population. For this reason, academics and policymakers have long stressed the importance of mental health interventions and therapy in reintegration programming.	Research shows that many services for released individuals with severe mental health issues in the US are provided by criminal justice agencies and are deficient (Wilson and Draine 2006; Draine and Herman 2007; Baillargeon et al. 2009; Papalia et al. 2020). Programs that do exist and show some promise, such as Forensic Assertive Community Treatment (FACT), are extremely costly, laborious, and limited in range (Morrissey, Meyer, and Cuddeback 2007). An excellent exemplar of a study that conducts a rigorous scientific evaluation of a long-standing, state-wide program for the mentally ill is that of Hartwell and colleagues (2012). They examined the post-incarceration outcomes of individuals with serious mental illness enrolled in the Massachusetts Department of Mental Health (DMH) Forensic Transition Team (FTT) program while also creating a blueprint of best practices to inform future evaluations requiring administrative data and agency collaborations.	As it stands, far more research needs to be done to empirically evaluate mental health services available to individuals upon release from prison. Presently, the results are mixed and heterogeneous.

| Substance Abuse Treatment | Since, on average, the incarcerated population has high rates of substance use disorders (Bronson et al. 2017; Alexander et al. 2020), many programs hope to improve re-entry by providing treatment for those with substance abuse issues. | Substance abuse treatment is one re-entry domain where the use of rigorous research designs is more common, although many of the RCTs are implemented inside prison rather than in the community. For instance, various iterations of the Therapeutic Communities program implemented in prison settings reveal significant declines in substance use and the likelihood of reincarceration after release (Prendergast et al. 2004; Sullivan et al. 2007). While not technically a re-entry initiative, diversion programs such as the Drug Treatment Alternative to Prison (DTAP), which involve drug treatment in lieu of incarceration or in exchange for a reduced or split sentence, also show promise for reducing drug use and the risk of reoffending (Dynia and Sung 2000). A community supervision strategy worth noting is the Hawaii Opportunity Probation with Enforcement (HOPE) program. Hawken and Kleiman (2009) empirically evaluated HOPE, randomly assigning individuals with substance-abuse issues to the program and others to probation as normal, and found that those enrolled in the program were less likely to be rearrested, to have their probation revoked, or to be incarcerated. Replications of HOPE, however, found mixed results (Hawken and Kleiman 2011; Grommon et al. 2013; Hawken et al. 2016; Lattimore et al. 2016; Davidson et al. 2019). | While there is considerable heterogeneity in prison-based substance abuse programs, with many relying on 12-step programs, many show promise for reducing substance abuse and later incarceration. The mixed findings across different HOPE implementations reveal that the success of the treatment can vary depending on the individual and the program specifics. |

structured daily activities (Laub and Sampson 2003), then returning to one's old environment and routines may drastically limit an individual's chances of desisting from crime.

One of the earliest of the relatively few studies of the relationship between residential change and criminal recidivism is Buikuisen and Hoekstra's (1974) study of male juveniles in the Netherlands sentenced to prison in the 1960s. Buikuisen and Hoekstra found a significant relationship between residential patterns and recidivism, controlling for nearly two dozen background characteristics. Seventy-six percent of sample members who returned to the same address where they resided in the past were reconvicted within roughly five years of their release from prison versus 60% of individuals who moved to a different residence. More recent research buttresses the argument that residential change can lead to a reduction in recidivism (Osborn and West 1980; Sharkey and Sampson 2010).

The challenge with these various studies is that they are all observational—i.e., they fall within levels 1 to 3 on the Maryland Scientific Methods Scale. There is some possibility, perhaps a very likely possibility, that some unmeasured characteristic of individuals influences both where they live and their criminal behavior, and may therefore account for the statistical correlation between place of residence and recidivism. A more rigorous research design on the hierarchy of evidence is necessary in order to more convincingly demonstrate that there is an unbiased relationship between residential change and recidivism.

The devastation to New Orleans in the wake of Hurricane Katrina in 2005 presented Kirk (2020) an opportunity to build the rigor of evidence related to the efficacy of residential change. The hurricane was an exogenously induced tragedy that forced some recently released prisoners to move to a different parish (i.e., county) who otherwise would have returned to their home parish. The natural experiment associated with Hurricane Katrina therefore allowed Kirk to examine the relationship between residential change and recidivism at a heightened level of rigor than previous studies (i.e., level 4 on the MSM; Kirk 2020). He found substantial reductions in rates of reincarceration among the formerly incarcerated who moved away from their former parishes. Individuals who moved were 13 percentage points less likely to be reincarcerated through eight years post-release.

Even with a natural experiment, however, there is some possibility that alternative explanations may explain the findings. Hence, Kirk sought to continue to build the rigor of evidence related to residential change. Moreover, it remained to be seen whether findings from a natural experiment would translate to a real-world policy environment. This dual recognition motivated Kirk's development of the Maryland Opportunities through Vouchers Experiment (MOVE), a randomized housing mobility program for the formerly incarcerated, implemented in cooperation with the Maryland Department of Public Safety and Correctional Services.

The objective of the MOVE program was to test whether residential relocation far away from former neighborhoods, incentivized through a grant-funded housing subsidy, would yield reductions in criminal recidivism. The basic design of MOVE consisted of two randomly assigned groups, although a pilot test of the program examined slight alterations of the design (Kirk et al. 2018). The treatment group consisted of formerly incarcerated individuals who received a housing subsidy that could only be used in a jurisdiction different from the one where they resided prior to incarceration. For the pilot test, the project specified a minimum distance of 40 miles between prior and current places of residency for the treatment group. This standard was set because past housing mobility experiments like the Moving to Opportunity program had seen disappointing results related to behavioral change when people moved only a few miles away—not far enough to create a real change in circumstances (Sampson 2008; Rosenbaum and Zuberi 2010).

The control group consisted of individuals who received a housing subsidy in the jurisdiction where they resided prior to incarceration. The value of the housing subsidy provided to both treatment group and control group participants was pegged to HUD's established "fair market rent" in a given geographic area. Accordingly, both groups received an equivalent housing subsidy, with the distinction between the groups being that one group could only use the subsidy in a new jurisdiction relative to where they used to live and the other group could only use the subsidy in the home jurisdiction.

As of this writing, a full-scale implementation of MOVE has not yet been implemented, but a pilot of the MOVE program yielded results suggesting that free subsidized and stable housing, particularly if located away from a former area of residence, could substantially reduce an individual's likelihood of recidivism (Kirk et al. 2018).

While more work needs to be done to assess the effectiveness of the MOVE program and to determine if there is a causal relationship between residential change and recidivism, we used this example to illustrate an agenda designed to push progressively higher on the hierarchy of evidence in order to make convincing evidence-based recommendations about policies related to housing and place of residence for the formerly incarcerated.

V. Why We Need More Empirical Research in Re-entry and Beyond

Upon examining the current state of the literature, the question of how we can improve evidence-based policy and practice in prisoner re-entry is a very important one. Laub (2012; also Laub and Frisch 2016) describes this process as "translational criminology," which refers to bridging the gap between scientific evidence and policy, through interactive relationships between policymakers and criminologists.

As it currently stands, however, Laub's vision remains a nascent goal rather than an accomplishment. As Tseng (2012) reveals, policymakers prefer information produced by professional associations and interest groups over empirical evidence from academic journals. These findings are echoed by research done by the International Association of Chiefs of Police in 2011, showing that only one-third of police practitioners consult academic journals when making policy decisions (Lum et al. 2012; Alpert, Rojek, and Hansen 2013).

Sampson and colleagues (2013) remind us that the greater demand for criminology to influence policy comes simultaneously with an increased attention to and higher demand for causal claims brought about by the "causal revolution." Successful implementation of re-entry policies and practices, therefore, rests on a thorough understanding of the causal mechanisms that underlie those policies and practices. Laub and Frisch (2016) agree that a major challenge to translational criminology is the quality of the extant criminological research, although the necessity of effectively communicating findings and program characteristics to policymakers and practitioners, who may be disinterested in nuances and complexities, is another key challenge.

Nevertheless, some criminologists will go as far as arguing that criminologists simply do not have sufficient knowledge to responsibly inform public policy (Tittle 2004). In Wellford's (2009) provocative panel paper at the American Society of Criminology's 2009 annual meeting, titled "Criminologists Should Stop Whining about Their Impact on Policy and Practice," he argued that until criminology has sufficient knowledge and causal certainty, it cannot readily inform public policy.

And while, in recent years, criminology as a discipline has made notable progress toward informing policy with scientific evidence (Blomberg et al. 2016), unfortunately, as our overview in Section IV suggests, most re-entry interventions and practices are not rigorously evaluated or implemented, and when they are, there is often little to no evidence of a treatment effect. In some cases, there is even a detrimental effect of treatment, which needs to be understood (Welsh, Yohros, and Zane 2020). This may result because programs are poorly conceived with little connection to criminological theory, or because certain theories do not stand up to rigorous empirical scrutiny. In many instances, the community protection models currently in place are actually contributing to the marginalization and isolation of the formerly incarcerated—creating a harmful paradoxical situation whereby risk management programs are only intensifying risk by creating further barriers to healthy desistance. If scholars want evidence to be used to inform and improve policies, then more emphasis needs to be placed on the empirical quality of that evidence. Policymakers must be guided by rigorous and reliable findings, which criminological research on re-entry often lacks.

Thus, the first step to having more informed and effective programming is to design future re-entry policies and programs applying the current state of research. Using research to inform best practice will ensure better reintegration policies that offer more meaningful support.

The second step is to rigorously evaluate and identify which existent re-entry programs are effective. Beyond identifying whether a program has a positive, null, or negative effect on desistance, a thorough evaluation should also involve a cost-benefit analysis of re-entry programs. A good model for this is the comprehensive effort by the Washington State Institute for Public Policy (WSIPP) to conduct cost-benefit analyses of social programs. In one study, WSIPP compared the dollar-value costs and benefits of 54 highly appraised re-entry programs in the United States, to determine which and how many programs break even. The study found that 26% of the programs were far more costly than they were effective, and were therefore not an effective use of taxpayer dollars (Aos, Miller, and Drake 2006). This kind of research has a direct policy impact because of its empirical and practical value.

Rigorously evaluating the effectiveness of re-entry programs also implies acknowledging the importance of contextual variation and outcome heterogeneity when implementing policy across multiple diverse locations. As alluded to earlier in the chapter, Sampson and colleagues (2013) warn us that causal analyses tend to carry with them an "implicit exportability claim": the assumption that findings with internal validity must have external validity and can be applied to different contexts, when this is untrue. It is important, therefore, when evaluating specific policy strategies and practices, that researchers refrain from "transporting" causal effects from one experimental study to a new population or context (Pearl and Bareinboim 2014).

VI. Conclusions and Next Steps

We are left with what appears to be a rather dire situation on our hands. With the relatively little empirical evaluation of re-entry policies that presently exists, it is imperative that criminologists adopt experimental or quasi-experimental evaluations of existent and future re-entry programs to add valuable information to a thin empirical literature. Given the replication crisis in science (Camerer et al. 2018), as well as our previous statements about the challenges of external validity, lone and single-site RCTs are insufficient as an evidence base for broad investment of resources in a given intervention, whereas evidence of effectiveness through preregistered RCTs across multiple sites and multiple research teams provides a solid base for policymaking and programmatic design.

Some scholars believe that the potential of re-entry and reintegration schemes are severely limited by the peripheral and inevitable difficulties facing the formerly incarcerated. While Maruna (2001) rightfully calls the question of how to improve the process of prisoner re-entry "one of the most important issues facing [researchers] in the next few decades" (17), he cynically suggests that reintegration schemes "can only go so far in opening up opportunities" for individuals while "the economy is weak and prejudice is high" (70).

Other scholars, such as ourselves, take the same doubts as those facing Maruna as an urgent call to improve the knowledge and application of evidence-based policy and practice in prisoner re-entry. Because of the innumerable risk factors and challenges facing a formerly incarcerated individual during reintegration, the importance of investing in effective, particularly cost-effective re-entry practices cannot be overstated. We are left then, with one critical question: How can we improve our understanding and promote more use of evidence-based policy and practice in prisoner re-entry?

The solution lies in effective scientific communication among policymakers and practitioners. Criminologists must be collaborative rather than confrontational (McAra 2017), and collaboration requires the production of robust and replicable knowledge that can be easily utilized by practitioners in the pursuit of effective policy. Research translation involves communicating scientific knowledge directly to practitioner audiences for the purpose of institutionalizing evidence-based practice (Laub 2012). Bridging the gap between scientific evidence and policy also requires openness to evidence among practitioners—a culture that is not anti-science. It is only through this that trusting and productive relationships between criminologists and practitioners can be maintained. Since effective policy is a priority of academics and practitioners alike, we should work together to design evaluations that are rigorous while remaining feasible (Doleac 2019a, 2019b).

Finally, while we have devoted parts of our chapter to the pressing demand for more evidence-based re-entry research, we have also highlighted the meaningful work that does apply empirical standards to re-entry research, such as our own (Kirk 2020). The Campbell Collaboration is another example of scholars devoted to the systematic review of public policy and the dissemination of scientific evidence on interventions (Petrosino et al. 2001). We hope that rather than discouraging researchers, our chapter encourages them by restating the importance to add to the presently thin evaluation literature of re-entry.

References

Alexander, Caleb G., Kenneth B. Stoller, Rebecca L. Haffaiee, and Brendan Saloner. 2020. An epidemic in the midst of a pandemic: Opioid use disorder and Covid-19. *Annals of Internal Medicine*, 173:57–58.

Alpert, Geoffrey P., Jeff Rojek, and Andrew Hansen. 2013. *Building bridges between police researchers and practitioners: Agents of Change in a Complex World.* Washington, DC: US Department of Justice.

Aos, Steve, Marna G. Miller, and Elizabeth K. Drake. 2006 *Evidence-based public policy options to reduce future prison construction, criminal justice costs and crime rates.* Olympia: Washington State Institute for Public Policy.

Baillargeon, Jacques, Ingrid A. Binswanger, Joseph V. Penn, Brie A. Williams, and Owen J. Murray. 2009. Psychiatric disorders and repeat incarcerations: The revolving prison door. *American Journal of Psychiatry*, 166 (1): 103–109.

Barden, Bret, Randall Juras, Cindy Redcross, Mary Farrell, and Dan Bloom. 2018. *New perspectives on creating jobs: Final impacts of the next generation of subsidized employment programs.* Washington, DC: Employment and Training Administration, United States Department of Labor.

Barnes, Geoffrey C., Jordan M. Hyatt, Lindsay C. Ahlman, and Daniel T. L. Kent. 2012. The effects of low-intensity supervision for lower-risk probationers: Updated results from a randomized controlled trial. *Journal of Crime and Justice*, 35:200–220.

Becker, Gary S. 1975. *Human capital: A theoretical and empirical analysis, with special reference to education.* 2nd ed. Cambridge, MA: National Bureau of Economic Research.

Beckett, Katherine, and Bruce Western. 2001. Governing social marginality: Welfare, incarceration, and the transformation of state policy. *Punishment & Society*, 3 (1): 43–59.

Berg, Mark T., and Beth M. Huebner. 2011. Reentry and the ties that bind: An examination of social ties, employment, and recidivism. *Justice Quarterly*, 28:382–410.

Blomberg, Thomas G., Julie M. Brancale, Kevin M. Beaver, and William D. Bales. 2016. *Advancing criminology and criminal justice policy.* New York: Routledge.

Boruch, Robert F. 1975. On common contentions about randomized field experiments. In *Experimental testing of public policy: The proceedings of the 1974 Social Sciences Research Council Conference on Social Experimentation*, edited by R. F. Boruch and H. W. Reicken, 107–142. Boulder, CO: Westview Press.

Boyle, Douglas J., Laura M. Ragusa-Salerno, Jennifer L. Lanterman, and Andrea Fleisch Marcus. 2013. An evaluation of day reporting centers for parolees: Outcomes of a randomized trial. *Criminology & Public Policy*, 12:119–143.

Bronson, Jennifer, Jessica Stroop, Stephanie Zimmer, and Marcus Berzofsky. 2017. *Drug use, dependence, and abuse among state prisoners and jail inmates, 2007–2009.* Washington, DC: Bureau of Justice Statistics.

Buikhuisen, Wouter, and Ria H. A. Hoekstra. 1974. Factors related to recidivism. *British Journal of Criminology*, 14:63–69.

Burdett, Kenneth, Ricardo Lagos, and Randall Wright. 2003. Crime, inequality, and unemployment. *American Economic Review*, 93 (5): 1764–1777.

Burnett, Ros. 2004. To reoffend or to not reoffend? The ambivalence of convicted property offenders. In *After crime and punishment*, edited by S. Maruna and R. Immarigeon, 152–180. Cullompton, UK: Willan.

Camerer, Colin F., Anna Dreber, Felix Holzmeister, et al. 2018. Evaluating the replicability of social science experiments in *Nature* and *Science* between 2010 and 2015. *Nature Human Behaviour*, 2:637–644.

Carson, Ann E. 2021. *Prisoners in 2020—Statistical tables*. Washington, DC: Bureau of Justice Statistics.

Chamberlain, Alyssa W., and Danielle Wallace. 2016. Mass reentry, neighborhood context and recidivism: Examining how the distribution of parolees within and across neighborhoods impacts recidivism. *Justice Quarterly*, 33 (5): 912–941.

Christie, Nils. 1971. Scandinavian criminology facing the 1970s. *Scandinavian Studies in Criminology*, 43:121–149.

Cook, Philip J., Songman Kang, Anthony A. Braga, Jens Ludwig, and Mallory E. O'Brien. 2015. An experimental evaluation of a comprehensive employment-oriented prisoner re-entry program. *Journal of Quantitative Criminology*, 31:355–382.

Cook, Thomas D., and Donald T. Campbell. 1979. *Quasi-experimentation: Design and analysis issues for field settings*. Chicago: Rand McNally.

Dale, Mitchell W. 1976. Barriers to the rehabilitation of ex-offenders. *Crime & Delinquency*, 22 (3): 322–337.

D'Amico, Ronald, and Hui Kim. 2018. *Evaluation of seven Second Chance Act adult demonstration programs: Impact findings at 30 months*. Oakland, CA: Social Policy Research Associates.

Davidson, Janet, George King, Jens Ludwig, and Steven Raphael. 2019. *Managing pretrial misconduct: An experimental evaluation of HOPE pretrial*. Goldman School of Public Policy Working Paper. Berkeley: University of California at Berkeley.

DiZerega, Margaret. 2010. *Engaging offenders' families in reentry: Coaching packet*. Hatboro, PA: Center for Effective Public Policy.

Doleac, Jennifer L. 2016. *Increasing employment for individuals with criminal records*. Washington, DC: Brookings Institute, Hamilton Project.

Doleac, Jennifer L. 2018. Strategies to productively reincorporate the formerly-incarcerated into communities: A review of the literature. IZA Discussion Paper No. 11646. Bonn, Germany: Institute of Labor Economics.

Doleac, Jennifer L. 2019a. "Evidence-based policy" should reflect a hierarchy of evidence. *Journal of Policy Analysis and Management*, 38 (2): 517–519.

Doleac, Jennifer L. 2019b. Wrap-around services don't improve prisoner reentry outcomes. *Journal of Policy Analysis and Management*, 38 (2): 508–514.

Doleac, Jennifer L, Chelsea Temple, David Pritchard, and Adam Roberts. 2020. Which prisoner reentry programs work? Replicating and extending analyses of three RCTs. *International Review of Law & Economics*, 62:1–16.

Draine, Jennifer, and Daniel B. Herman. 2007. Critical time intervention for re-entry from prison for persons with mental illness. *Psychiatric Services*, 58:1577–1581.

Durose, Matthew R., and Leonardo Antenangeli. 2021. *Recidivism of prisoners released in 34 states in 2012: A 5-year follow-up period (2012–2017)*. Washington, DC: Bureau of Justice Statistics.

Dynia, Paul, and Hung-En Sung. 2000. The safety and effectiveness of diverting felony drug offenders to residential treatment as measured by recidivism. *Criminal Justice Policy Review*, 11 (4): 299–311.

Fagan, Abigail A. 2014. Criminology and public policy. In *The encyclopedia of theoretical criminology*, edited by. Mitchell Miller, 188–192. Hoboken, NJ: Wiley-Blackwell.

Farrington, David P., Bernard Gallagher, Lynda Morley, Raymond J. St. Ledger, and Donald J. West. 1986. Unemployment, school leaving, and crime. *British Journal of Criminology*, 26 (4): 335–356.

Farrington, David P., Denise C. Gottfredson, Lawrence W. Sherman, and Brandon C. Welsh. 2002. The Maryland Scientific Methods Scale. In *Evidence-based crime prevention*, edited by L. W. Sherman, D. P. Farrington, B. C. Welsh, and D. L. MacKenzie, 13–21. London: Routledge.

Fisher, William H., Eric Silver, and Nancy Wolff. 2006. Beyond criminalization: Towards a criminologically informed framework for mental health policy and services research. *Administration and Policy in Mental Health and Mental Health Services Research* 33:544–557.

Freeman, Richard B. 1987. The relation of criminal activity to Black youth employment. *Review of Black Political Economy*, 16:99–107.

Gadd, David, and Stephen Farrall. 2004. Criminal careers, desistance and subjectivity: Interpreting men's narratives of change. *Theoretical Criminology*, 8 (2): 123–156.

Gojkovic, Dina, Alice Mills, and Rosie Meek. 2012. *Accommodation for ex-offenders: Third sector housing advice and provision*. Birmingham, UK: Third Sector Research Centre.

Grommon, Eric, William S. Davidson II, and Timothy S. Bynum. 2013. A randomized trial of a multimodal community-based prisoner reentry program emphasizing substance abuse treatment. *Journal of Offender Rehabilitation*, 52:287–309.

Guydish, Joseph, Monica Chan, Alan Bostrom, Martha A. Jessup, Thomas B. Davis, and Cheryl Marsh. 2011. A randomized trial of probation case management for drug-involved women offenders. *Crime and Delinquency*, 57:167–198.

Hagan, John. 1993. The social embeddedness of crime and unemployment. *Criminology*, 31:465–491.

Hartwell, Stephanie W., Xiaogang Deng, William H. Fisher, Carl E. Fulwiler, Usha Sambamoorthi, Craig Johnson, Debra A. Pinals, Lisa Sampson, and Julianne Siegfriedt. 2012. Harmonizing databases? Developing a quasi-experimental design to evaluate a public mental health re-entry program. *Evaluation and Program Planning*, 35 (4): 461–472.

Harding, David J., Jeffrey D. Morenoff, and Claire W. Herbert. 2013. Home is hard to find: Neighborhoods, institutions, and the residential trajectories of returning prisoners. *Annals of the American Academy of Political and Social Science*, 647 (1): 214–236.

Hawken, Angela, and Mark A. R. Kleiman. 2009. *Managing drug involved probationers with swift and certain sanctions: Evaluating Hawaii's HOPE*. Washington, DC: US Department of Justice.

Hawken, Angela, and Mark A. R. Kleiman. 2011. *Washington Intensive Supervision Program: Evaluation report*. Seattle, WA: Seattle City Council.

Hawken, Angela, Jonathan Kulick, Kelly Smith, Jie Mei, Yiwen Zhang, Sara Jarman, Travis Yu, Chris Carson, and Tifanie Vial. 2016. *HOPE II: A follow-up to Hawaii's HOPE evaluation*. Washington, DC: US Department of Justice.

Hennigan, Karen, Kathy Kolnick, Tian Siva Tian, Cheryl Maxson, and John Poplawski. 2010. *Five year outcomes in a randomized trial of a community-based multi-agency intensive supervision juvenile probation program*. Washington, DC: US Department of Justice.

Heitzeg, Nancy A. 2009. Education or incarceration: Zero tolerance policies and the school to prison pipeline. *Forum on Public Policy*, 2009 (2). https://eric.ed.gov/?id=EJ870076.

Holland, Paul W. 1986. Statistics and causal inference. *Journal of the American Statistical Association*, 81 (396): 945–960.

Hyatt, Jordan M., and Geoffrey C. Barnes. 2017. An experimental evaluation of the impact of intensive supervision on the recidivism of high-risk probationers. *Crime & Delinquency*, 63:3–38.

Jason, Leonard A., Bradley D. Olson, and Ronald Harvey. 2015. Evaluating alternative aftercare models for ex-offenders. *Journal of Drug Issues*, 45 (1): 53–68.

Kirk, David S. 2009. A natural experiment on residential change and recidivism: Lessons from Hurricane Katrina. *American Sociological Review*, 74 (3): 484–505.

Kirk, David S. 2020. *Home free: Prisoner reentry and residential change after Hurricane Katrina*. New York: Oxford University Press.

Kirk, David S., Geoffrey C. Barnes, Jordan M. Hyatt, and Brook W. Kearley. 2018. The impact of residential change and housing stability on recidivism: Pilot results from the Maryland Opportunities through Vouchers Experiment (MOVE). *Journal of Experimental Criminology*, 14 (2): 213–226.

Kirk, David S., and Sara Wakefield. 2018. Collateral consequences of punishment: A critical review and path forward. *Annual Review of Criminology*, 1:171–194.

Lattimore, Pamela K., Doris Layton MacKenzie, Gary Zajac, Debbie Dawes, Elaine Arsenault, and Stephen Tueller. 2016. Outcome findings from the HOPE demonstration field experiment: Is swift, certain, and fair an effective supervision strategy? *Criminology and Public Policy*, 15:1103–1141.

Laub, John H. 2012. Translational criminology. *Translational Criminology*, 3:4–5.

Laub, John H., and Nicole E. Frisch. 2016. Translational criminology: A new path forward. In *Advancing criminology and criminal justice policy*, edited by Thomas G. Blomberg, Julie M. Brancale, Kevin Beaver, and William D. Bales, 52–62. London: Routledge.

Laub, John H., and Robert J. Sampson. 2003. *Shared beginnings, divergent lives: Delinquent boys to age 70*. Cambridge, MA: Harvard University Press.

La Vigne, Nancy G. 2021. Fits and starts: Criminology's influence on policing policy and practice. In *The globalization of evidence-based policing*, edited by Eric L. Piza and Brandon C. Welsh, 53–72. London: Routledge.

Lee, Logan M. 2019. Halfway home? Residential housing and reincarceration. Working Paper. Grinnell, IA: Grinnell University.

Lum, Cynthia, Cody W. Telep, Christopher Koper, and Julie Grieco. 2012. Receptivity to research in policing. *Justice Research and Policy*, 14 (1): 61–95.

Lussier, Patrick, and Carmen L.Z. Gress. 2014. Community re-entry and the path toward desistance: A quasi-experimental longitudinal study of dynamic factors and community risk management of adult sex offenders. *Journal of Criminal Justice*, 42 (2): 111–122.

Mallar, Charles D., and Craig V. D. Thornton. 1978. Transitional aid for released prisoners: Evidence from the LIFE experiment. *Journal of Human Resources* 13:208–236.

Maruna, Shadd. 2001. *Making good: How ex-convicts reform and rebuild their lives*. Washington, DC: American Psychological Association.

Massoglia, Michael, and Jason Schnittker. 2009. No real release. *Contexts*, 8 (1): 38–42. https://doi.org/10.1525/ctx.2009.8.1.38.

McAra, Lesley. 2017. Can criminologists change the world? Critical reflections on the politics, performance and effects of criminal justice. *British Journal of Criminology*, 57 (4): 767–788.

Mears, Daniel P. 2010. *American criminal justice policy: An evaluation approach to increasing accountability and effectiveness*. New York: Cambridge University Press.

Mears, Daniel P., and Joshua C. Cochran. 2015. *Prisoner reentry in the era of mass incarceration*. Thousand Oaks, CA: SAGE.

Meiners, Erica R., and Maisha T. Winn. 2014. *Education and Incarceration*. New York: Routledge.

Morrissey, Joseph, Piper Meyer, and Gary Cuddeback. 2007. Extending assertive community treatment to criminal justice settings: Origins, current evidence, and future directions. *Community Mental Health Journal* 43:527–544.

Mullins, Tracy G., and Christine Toner. 2008. *Implementing the family support approach for community supervision*. Lexington, VA: Family Justice and American Probation and Parole Association.

Nagin, Daniel S. 2022. Unraveling mass incarceration: Criminology's role in the policy process. *Criminology*, 60 (3): 401–405.

Nagin, Daniel S., and Robert J. Sampson. 2019. The real gold standard: Measuring counterfactual worlds that matter most to social science and policy. *Annual Review of Criminology*, 2:123–145.

Nagin, Daniel, and Joel Waldfogel. 1995. The effects of criminality and conviction on the labor market status of young British offenders. *International Review of Law and Economics*, 15 (1): 109–126.

Nakamura, Kiminori. 2018. *Residential relocation and recidivism*. Final Report to the Pennsylvania Commission on Crime and Delinquency. College Park, MD: University of Maryland.

Neyman, Jerzy. 1935. On the problem of confidence intervals. *Annals of Mathematical Statistics*, 6 (3): 111–116.

Osborn, S. G., and D. J. West. 1980. Do young delinquents really reform? *Journal of Adolescence*, 3 (2): 99–114.

Pager, Devah. 2003. The mark of a criminal record. *American Journal of Sociology*, 108 (5): 937–975.

Pager, Devah. 2008. *Marked: Race, crime, and finding work in an era of mass incarceration*. Chicago: University of Chicago Press.

Papalia, Nina, Benjamin Spivak, Michael Daffern, and James R. P. Ogloff. 2020. Are psychological treatments for adults with histories of violent offending associated with change in dynamic risk factors? A meta-analysis of intermediate treatment outcomes. *Criminal Justice and Behavior*, 47 (12): 1585–1608.

Parenti, Christian. 1999. *Lockdown America: Police and prisons in the age of crisis*. London: Verso.

Pearl, Judea, and Elias Bareinboim. 2014. External validity: From do-calculus to transportability across populations. *Statistical Science*, 29 (4): 579–595.

Petersilia, Joan. 2003. *When prisoners come home: Parole and prisoner reentry*. New York: Oxford University Press.

Petrosino, Anthony, Robert F. Boruch, Haluk Soydan, Lorna Duggan, and Julio Sanchez-Meca. 2001. Meeting the challenges of evidence-based policy: The Campbell Collaboration. *Annals of the American Academy of Political and Social Science*, 578 (1): 14–34.

Pettus-Davis, Carrie. 2021. Support4Families: A proposed intervention model to support families of individuals returning home from incarceration. *Families in Society*, 102 (3): 316–332.

Pettus-Davis, Carrie, Allison Dunnigan, Christopher A. Veeh, Matthew O. Howard, Anna M. Scheyett, and Amelia Roberts-Lewis. 2017. Enhancing social support post-incarceration: Results from a pilot randomized controlled trial. *Journal of Clinical Psychology*, 73:1226–1246.

Piel, Jennifer. 2020. Letter to the editor—Behavioral health implications of inmate release during COVID-19. *Journal of Forensic Sciences*, 65 (4): 1379–1381.

Pratt, Daniel, Mary Piper, Louis Appleby, Roger Webb, and Jenny Shaw. 2006. Suicide in recently released prisoners: A population-based cohort study. *Lancet*, 368 (9530):119–123.

Prendergast, Michael L., Elizabeth A. Hall, Harry K. Wexler, Gerald Melnick, and Yan Cao. 2004. Amity Prison-Based Therapeutic Community: 5-year outcomes. *The Prison Journal*, 84 (1): 36–60.

Rade, Candalyn B., Sarah L. Desmarais, and Roger E. Mitchell. 2016. A meta-analysis of public attitudes toward ex-offenders. *Criminal Justice and Behavior*, 43 (9): 1260–1280.

Redcross, Cindy, Dan Bloom, Erin Jacobs, Michelle Manno, Sara Muller-Ravett, Kristin Seefeldt, Jennifer Yahner, Alford A. Young Jr., and Janine Zweig. 2010. *Work after prison: One-year findings from the Transitional Jobs Reentry Demonstration.* New York: MDRC.

Redcross, Cindy, Megan Millenky, Timothy Rudd, and Valerie Levshin. 2012. *More than a Job: Final Results from the evaluation of the Center for Employment Opportunities (CEO) Transitional Jobs Program.* OPRE Report 2011-18. New York: MDRC.

Rosenbaum, James E., and Anita Zuberi. 2010. Comparing residential mobility programs: Design elements, neighborhood placements, and outcomes in MTO and Gautreaux. *Housing Policy Debate*, 20 (1): 27–41.

Rossi, Peter H., Richard A. Berk, and Kenneth J. Lenihan. 1980. *Money, work, and crime. Experimental evidence.* New York: Academic Press.

Rubin, Donald B. 1974. Estimating causal effects of treatments in randomized and nonrandomized studies. *Journal of Educational Psychology*, 66 (5): 688–701.

Rubin, Donald B. 1978. Bayesian inference for causal effects: The role of randomization. *Annals of Statistics*, 6 (1): 34–58.

Sampson, Robert J. 2008. Moving to inequality: Neighborhood effects and experiments meet social structure. *American Journal of Sociology* 114:189–231.

Sampson, Robert J, and John H. Laub. 2003. Life-course desisters? Trajectories of crime among delinquent boys followed to age 70. *Criminology*, 41 (3): 301–340.

Sampson, Robert J., Christopher Winship, and Carly Knight. 2013. Translating causal claims: Principles and strategies for policy-relevant criminology. *Criminology & Public Policy*, 12 (4): 587–616.

Schwartz, Richard D., and Jerome H. Skolnick. 1962. Two studies of legal stigma. *Social Problems*, 10 (2): 133–142.

Scott, Christy K., and Michael L. Dennis. 2012. The first 90 days following release from jail: Findings from the Recovery Management Checkups for Women Offenders (RMCWO) experiment. *Drug and Alcohol Dependence*, 125:110–118.

Shamblen, Stephen R., Christopher Kokoski, David A. Collins, Ted N. Strader, and Patrick McKiernan. 2017. Implementing Creating Lasting Family Connections with reentry fathers: A partial replication during a period of policy change. *Journal of Offender Rehabilitation*, 56 (5): 295–307.

Sharkey, Patrick, and Robert J. Sampson. 2010. Destination effects: Residential mobility and trajectories of adolescent violence in a stratified metropolis. *Criminology* 48 (3): 639–681.

Sullivan, Christopher J., Karen McKendrick, Stanley Sacks, and Steven Banks. 2007. Modified therapeutic community treatment for offenders with MICA disorders: Substance use outcomes. *American Journal of Drug and Alcohol Abuse*, 33 (6): 823–832.

Tittle, Charles R. 2004. The arrogance of public sociology. *Social Forces*, 82:1639–1643.

Travis, Jeremy, and Christy Visher, eds. 2005. *Prisoner reentry and crime in America.* New York: Cambridge University Press.

Tseng, Vivian. 2012. The uses of research in policy and practice. *Social Policy Report*, 26 (2): 1–24.

Uggen, Christopher. 2000. Work as a turning point in the life course of criminals: A duration model of age, employment, and recidivism. *American Sociological Review*, 65 (4): 529–546.

UK Ministry of Justice. 2022. *Proven reoffending statistics: April 2019 to March 2020.* London: Ministry of Justice.

Valentine, Erin J., and Cindy Redcross. 2015. Transitional jobs after release from prison: Effects on employment and recidivism. *IZA Journal of Labor Policy*, 4:1–17.

WSIPP (Washington State Institute for Public Policy). 2019. *Intensive supervision (surveillance and treatment)*. Olympia, WA: WSIPP.

Weisburd, David. 2003. Ethical practice and evaluation of interventions in crime and justice: The moral imperative for randomized trials. *Evaluation Review* 27:336–354.

Wellford, Charles F. 2009. Criminologists should stop whining about their impact on policy and practice. In *Contemporary issues in criminal justice policy: Policy proposals from the American Society of Criminology*, edited by Natasha A. Frost, Joshua D. Freilich, and Todd R. Clear, 17–23. Belmont, CA: Wadsworth.

Welsh, Brandon C., Alexis Yohros, and Steven N. Zane. 2020. Understanding iatrogenic effects for evidence-based policy: A review of crime and violence prevention programs. *Aggression and Violent Behavior*, 55:101511.

Wiegand, Andrew, and Jesse Sussell. 2016. *Evaluation of the Re-Integration of Ex-Offenders (RExO) program: Final impact reports*. Washington, DC: US Department of Labor.

Wilson, Amy B., and Jeffrey Draine. 2006. Collaborations between criminal justice and mental health systems for prisoner re-entry. *Psychiatric Services*, 57:875–878.

Wright, Benjamin J., Sheldon X. Zhang, David Farabee, and Rick Braatz. 2014. Prisoner reentry research from 2000 to 2010: Results of a narrative review. *Criminal Justice Review*, 39 (1): 37–57.

Yi, Youngmin, Kristin Turney, and Christopher Wildeman. 2017. Mental health among jail and prison inmates. *American Journal of Men's Health*, 11 (4): 900–909.

CHAPTER 18

EVIDENCE-BASED POLICY FOR DIVERSE CRIMINAL JUSTICE POPULATIONS

KAELYN SANDERS, JENNIFER COBBINA-DUNGY, AND HENRIKA MCCOY

THE US criminal legal system is vast and far-reaching. The criminal legal system encompasses individuals who have contact with law enforcement, those who are incarcerated, and those who are under some form of correctional supervision. In the United States, more than 10 million people are arrested each year (Neusteter and O'Toole 2019). Excessive surveillance and enforcement practices to arrest a staggering number of people serves as a gateway into the criminal legal system, thus contributing to mass incarceration. Currently, more than 6.3 million people are under supervision of the correctional system, including 2 million held in carceral institutions and over 4.3 million under community supervision (Minton, Beatty, and Zeng 2021). Because of its expansiveness, the criminal legal system has harmful effects for individual people, families, and communities—especially communities of color.

Additionally, research has explored the collateral consequences of justice involvement. Many face barriers to employment, housing, public assistance, education, voting, and getting a driver's license, among others (Vallas and Dietrich 2014). The consequences are compounded by an individual's social location—including race or ethnicity, gender, social class, age, sexuality, ability, and geographic location (Shih et al. 2019)—which can act as a marginalizing status. For example, justice system involvement is a marginalizing status, and for some it may be their "master status" (Hughes 1945) or most important social identity.

When thinking about social identities, it is crucial to recognize that many intersect with one another, thus creating unique individual experiences. The level of oppression or privilege experienced varies depending on whether one's social identities provide more or less privilege (Crenshaw 1989, 1990). There are a plethora of marginalized individuals in the criminal legal system (e.g., minoritized populations, women, and juveniles). However, population-specific responses are often nonexistent, and the unique experiences of these groups are not usually considered. As a result, designing and implementing evidence-based policies tailored to the experiences of each group is necessary. This chapter intends to address this gap by providing (1) a review of the criminal justice research about three diverse groups: minoritized individuals,[1] women, and juveniles; and (2) recommendations for group-specific evidence-based policies. Our primary focus will be on the correctional system; however, we will allude to the broader criminal legal system throughout.

I. Minoritized Individuals and the Criminal Legal System

Mass incarceration disproportionately impacts minoritized individuals in the United States, and they are heavily overrepresented in carceral institutions (Alexander 2012; Sawyer and Wagner 2022; Ulmer 2018). Hispanic men are 2.5 times more likely to be incarcerated than White men, and Black men are 6.5 times more likely to be incarcerated than White men (Vallas and Dietrich 2014). Racial disparities in the criminal legal system are caused by a number of factors. The most common explanations for these disparities are policies and practices, implicit bias and stereotyping, and structural disadvantages in communities of color. Likewise, racial disparities are often seen throughout the criminal legal system, not just inside institutions (Hinton, Henderson, and Reed 2018; Nellis 2016). For example, research has found that ethnicity and poverty are correlated with age of first police contact and arrest (Allen 2018; Kerley et al. 2004).

The rise in imprisonment in the United States was attributed to harsher punishment laws, which also caused racial disparities (Alexander 2012; Hinton, Henderson, and Reed 2018; Ulmer 2018). Drug laws, in particular, were one of the largest contributors to these disparities. Even though rates of drug use are similar for Black and White individuals, Black people are more likely to be arrested for a drug offense (Hinton, Henderson, and Reed 2018; Nellis 2016). Likewise, police presence is common in areas with high minority populations, and they often use practices (e.g., stop and frisk, hot spots policing) that are used to target specific types of people or areas. Moreover, pretrial detention is more likely for Black defendants due to income inequality and practitioner bias (Hinton, Henderson, and Reed 2018; Nellis 2016; Ulmer 2018). Race and ethnicity also impact sentencing, as minoritized individuals typically receive harsher sentences, especially young Black and Hispanic men (Nellis 2016; Ulmer 2018).

It is well documented that justice-involved individuals face a myriad of stigmatization experiences and challenges related to their system involvement, and that the collateral consequences of incarceration disproportionately affect people of color (Alexander 2012; Blankenship et al. 2018; Hinton, Henderson, and Reed 2018; Nellis 2016; Williams, Wilson, and Bergeson 2019). Devah Pager's (2003) landmark study on criminal records and employment illustrates this point. In this study, Pager found that Black and White individuals with criminal records were less likely to receive callbacks for jobs compared to those without a criminal record; however, Black individuals *without* a criminal record were *less* likely to receive callbacks than White individuals with a criminal record. This underscores the point that race and criminal status impact and influence one another. Other studies have found similar issues relating to criminal status, race, and employment (see Decker et al. 2015). There is also considerable research documenting the economic marginalization Black justice-involved individuals face: the marginalization is often much higher than that experienced by White justice-involved individuals (Cobbina 2009; Hoskins 2019; Lipsitz 2011).

These racial disparities and criminal stigma not only impact the individual but also their family and community (Blankenship et al. 2018; Hinton, Henderson, and Reed 2018; Williams, Willson, and Bergeson 2020). At the familial level, Black children are more likely than White children to have an incarcerated parent (Hinton, Henderson, and Reed 2018). Moreover, when structurally disadvantaged communities lose members to incarceration, they lose economic resources, and the cycle of involvement in the criminal legal system continues. Eventually, this cycle becomes normalized in these communities. The nominalization, in turn, may contribute to lasting harms in communities of color.

These racial disparities also impact the view that minoritized individuals have of the criminal legal system, especially law enforcement (Cobbina and Morash 2015; Metcalfe and Baker 2022). Mistrust is higher in communities of color, especially communities with larger numbers of Black residents (Drakulich 2013; Drakulich and Crutchfield 2013), as many believe that police as a whole treat people of color unfairly and disrespectfully (Cobbina 2019; Kane 2005). Discriminatory policing, in particular, strikes a chord among many African Americans who generally view contemporary police strategies through a historical lens. From the very beginning of American society, scholars have noted that the police, first in the form of "Slave Patrollers," and later in the form of organized police forces, have often engaged in unfair practices such as racial profiling (Del Carmen 2008). Studies show that compared to White individuals, African Americans of all social classes have greater perceptions of distributive justice (civilians are concerned about the fairness of outcomes) and procedural injustice (civilians are concerned with the fairness of the procedures used to achieve outcomes), and that their perceptions of injustice are not based solely on favorableness of traffic stop outcomes but on civilians' perceptions of inequalities and unfair procedures used in traffic stops (Engel 2005). When the police are perceived as racially/ethnically biased, it undermines trust and cooperation with the police and increases perceptions that police are ineffective at policing these communities (Drakulich and Crutchfield 2013). Perceptions of legitimacy within the criminal legal system are central to notions of justice and efforts to prevent crime, as mistrust in police underscore challenges to improving police-community relations.

II. Minoritized Individuals and Evidence-Based Policy

A common argument proffered about the relationship between Black communities and the police blames Black communities for the problems that exist and depicts them as viewing the police as illegitimate with limited effectiveness. However, that oversimplification blames those most likely to be victimized by the police, fails to acknowledge the legitimacy of their experiences, and homogenizes a group of diverse thinkers. There are many in Black communities who agree with that perception because it is based on their experience with the police. According to the President's Task Force on 21st Century Policing, many police officers have not adhered to some of the basic pillars of policing. As a group, the police have not consistently built trust and legitimacy, engaged in transparent oversight, used less lethal weapons, and increased public safety and reduced crime (Lum et al. 2016). They have also not been frequently or consistently held accountable, even when exposed as having inflicted harm, including death. There are wide-ranging demands about how to address policing, including calls for abolishment, defunding, and reformation. Accompanying those calls is pressure to use the funding that currently enables the discriminatory policing practices in communities of color to instead fund the missing and lacking services needed in those same communities. Such demands ultimately require the police to acknowledge their original history as slave patrols, because of how it influences policing practices (Durr 2015), and be held accountable. The failure to acknowledge the complex relationship between Black communities and the police, as well as the responsibility that police have in that relationship, only exacerbates and continues the harmful practices inflicted on Black communities.

Because much of the criminal legal system's racial disparities are attributed to policy and practice, it is vital that evidence-based policies target these two levels rather than solely on implicit bias training despite its importance. As noted previously, harsh punishment policies contributed to current disparities. Therefore, mandatory minimum sentencing and other determinate sentencing laws should be reviewed and revised at the federal and state level, as they have fueled prison population growth, exacerbated racial disparities, and prohibited judges from considering an individual's circumstances or showing mercy (Siegler 2021). Evidence seems to indicate that giving judges the discretion to conclude that no or a limited time in jail is an appropriate outcome will reduce racial inequalities behind bars (Gillette 2020). Similarly, it is necessary to revise policies and laws with disparate racial impact. For example, several school districts in Florida's Miami-Dade and Broward County Public Schools have enacted new school disciplinary policies to reduce racial disparities in out-of-school suspensions and police referrals. And evidence shows that the school district in Los Angeles has nearly eliminated police-issued truancy tickets and has enacted new disciplinary policies to reduce reliance on its school police departments (Watanabe 2013).

Moreover, since racial bias is inherent in risk assessment instruments, jurisdictions such as Multnomah County, Oregon, developed a new risk assessment instrument for criminal justice decision-making and examined each element through the lens of race while also eliminating known sources of bias, such as gang affiliation. The development of this new risk assessment led to a greater than 50% reduction in the number of youth detained and a near complete elimination of racial disparity in the proportion of delinquency referrals that result in detention (Ghandnoosh 2015). Likewise, a review of the risk assessment instrument in consideration of pretrial release in Minnesota's Fourth Judicial District showed three indicators were correlated with race but not significant predictors of pretrial offending or failing to appear in court. After these factors were removed from the instrument, there were reductions in sources of racial bias (Ghandnoosh 2015). Lastly, some states have also created "racial impact legislation." This legislation requires policymakers to consider outcomes of policy changes prior to passing laws. Doing so allows them to consider alternative methods that will not worsen racial disparities. Implementing more racial impact legislation may prove useful for other states as well (Nellis 2016).

Misconduct data about the use of excessive force should be regularly and systematically collected and analyzed by independent, non-law-enforcement entities who ultimately make recommendations, formulate a strategic plan, and oversee implementation (Institute for Criminal Justice Training Reform 2022). Furthermore, disparities in the prison population can be reduced through pretrial changes. Reducing or eliminating cash bail will greatly help minoritized individuals, as they are more likely to be poor than White individuals, and thus suffer more from the usage of the cash bail system (Woolridge et al. 2015). Changes in policing practices may prove fruitful as well for reducing racial disparities. Previously passed laws that prohibited racial discrimination did lessen racial disparities in traffic stops (Tomaskovic-Devey and Warren 2009). Future policy should be created to lessen investigatory stops, which often cause racial disparities. This can be done by requiring the recording of all stops, the race/ethnicity of the driver, and the result of the stop (Epp, Maynard-Moody, and Haider-Markel 2017).

The creation of policies must be coupled with addressing key problems in policing, such as those identified by the President's Task Force on 21st Century Policing. Implementing programs that can lead to positive outcomes such as successful re-entry are essential. However, implementing new programs that are simply reactive to the continuous flood of minoritized individuals into the justice system will not change the perception of illegitimacy and ineffectiveness and the ongoing harm perpetrated on minoritized communities.

III. Women in the Criminal Justice System

Women make up the fastest-growing incarcerated population, as their population has risen for decades despite lower levels of offending (Belknap 2015; Sawyer 2018). Over 200,000 women and girls are held in US carceral institutions, and close to a million are under community supervision (Kajstura 2019). Women's rising presence in the correctional system is tied to the war on drugs, the increase in "tough on crime" policies and mandatory minimum sentences, and reduced funding for community mental health care (Bloom, Owen, and Covington 2004). Prior research has identified common pathways women take into crime (see Bohmert, Galasso, and Cobbina 2018; Brennan et al. 2012; Daly 1992). Typically, justice-involved women have varying histories of victimization, trauma, abuse, mental health issues, and social or economic marginalization. The result is that the profile of women who have contact with the criminal legal system or who are under some form of correctional control is distinct from that of men.

Compared to their male counterparts, who are more likely to be imprisoned for violent offenses, women are more likely to be incarcerated for drug and property offenses (The Sentencing Project 2020). On average, women who are in prison are disproportionately persons of color, economically marginalized (Morash et al. 2017), undereducated/unskilled (Bloom, Owen, and Covington 2003), mothers of one or more minor children (Kajstura 2019), have experienced victimization and trauma (Scroggins and Malley 2010; Verona, Murphy, and Jaydani 2016), have serious health problems (Morash 2010), have mental health disorders (James and Glaze 2006; Wilmoth 2005), and have substance dependencies (Mumola and Karberg 2006). Many women who suffer from abuse struggle with anxiety, depression, and PTSD (Lynch, Fritch, and Heath 2012; Wilmoth 2005). If these mental illnesses are not treated, it can cause women to self-medicate via drugs and/or alcohol to cope with the pains of abuse (Chesney-Lind 1997; Daly 1998).

Although imprisoned men also suffer from drug problems, a larger proportion of women entering and exiting prison face substance addictions (Mumola 1999; Wilson, Gallagher, and MacKenzie 2000). However, not all women behind bars have access to prison-based drug treatment programs, and those who do often find them limited in duration and community-based programs post-release to be scarce (Harm and Phillips 2001). Drug convictions can have vital consequences post-incarceration. Individuals convicted of a felony offense are banned from receiving public assistance, which largely impacts women of color, as they are not only susceptible to poverty but disproportionately represented in the welfare system. Moreover, women who are a part of other marginalized groups (e.g., minoritized women) have experiences simultaneously compounded by other aspects of their identity. For example, Black women are the most overrepresented group in US prisons (Bloom, Owen, and Covington 2003; Williams, Spencer, and Wilson 2021), and the incarceration rate of Black women is higher than that of Black men, White women, and Latina women (Willingham 2011). The intersections of gender and race create a distinctive experience for minoritized women.

In addition, compared to men, women rely more heavily on social support post-release (Barrick, Lattimore, and Visher 2014; Clone and DeHart 2014; Cobbina, Huebner, and Berg 2012). Following release from prison, women are more likely than men to reconnect with family members and to depend on them for emotional and material assistance (Cobbina, Huebner, and Berg 2012). Such prosocial support from family and friends has proven vital for women's re-entry success (Martinez and Christian 2009). Moreover, reunifying with children is especially important for women returning home from prison, often serving as a form of inspiration (Giordano, Cernkovich, and Rudolph 2002; Richie 2001). Nevertheless, the relationship between motherhood and desistance is complicated. While childbearing can serve as an impetus for the maturation out of criminal involvement and can facilitate the development of a prosocial self-image, children can also become a source of parental stress when tied with life responsibilities (Bachman et al. 2016). Taking care of children while juggling one or two jobs can prove challenging and impact their ability to desist from crime and successfully integrate back into society.

Prior to entering the criminal legal system, many women were victimized during childhood (Bloom, Owen, and Covington 2003; Brennan et al. 2012; Hall et al. 2013; Van Voorhis et al. 2009). After release from prison, women are still vulnerable to the abuse and unsafe treatment they faced prior to their incarceration, especially if returning to the same environment. Because many community-based programs offer services to victims only, justice-involved women who have experienced victimization can have a difficult time accessing programs (Richie 2001). More generally, numerous studies have found that justice-involved women live in poverty and have low annual incomes (Bloom, Owen, and Covington 2003; Cobbina et al. 2014; Van Voorhis et al. 2009). Many also reside in areas with multiple indicators of neighborhood risk (i.e., drug activity, break-ins) (Cobbina et al. 2014; Hall et al. 2013). Because of the neighborhood conditions, it can be difficult for these women to avoid reoffending (Cobbina et al. 2014).

Poverty and economic marginalization are large and well-documented factors in women's lawbreaking behavior (Bloom, Owen, and Covington 2003; Daly 1992; Maher and Daly 1996; Heilbrun et al. 2008; Lindquist et al. 2009; Van Voorhis et al. 2009). Oftentimes, it is caused by lack of employment and education, which can hinder women's re-entry (Bloom, Owen, and Covington 2003; Allen 2018; Dodge and Pogrebin 2001; Hall et al. 2013; Richie 2001). Transportation access is another barrier affecting re-entry challenges (Bohmert and DeMaris 2018; Richie 2001). When trying to find a job, women may encounter barriers due to their criminal history (Roddy, Morash, and Hoskins 2021). Having low education and vocational skills worsens their employment barriers (Salisbury, Boppre, and Kelly 2016) and increases the likelihood of recidivism (Huebner, DeJong, and Cobbina 2010). Because the programming offered in prison tends to be inadequate, women often rely on family, public agencies, and community-based agencies for employment, education, housing, and financial support (Cobbina 2010; Dodge and Pogrebin 2001; Goodson-Miller 2022; Richie 2001). For some women, desistance from crime becomes harder due to lack of support (Cobbina 2010; Richie 2001). Regardless, justice-involved women still have few job skills (Dodge and Pogrebin 2001; Hall et al. 2013). Because of this and their criminal history, women end up with low-wage jobs with little upward mobility (Dodge and Pogrebin 2001; Hall et al. 2013).

Economic marginalization also causes women to seek out help from social service agencies and programs. However, the federal and state governments reduced access to housing, food assistance under SNAP (Supplemental Nutrition Assistance Program, formerly food stamps), and cash assistance through TANF (Temporary Assistance for Needy Families), which started with the 1996 federal reform bill and heavily impacted justice-involved individuals (Bloom, Owen, and Covington 2004). Subsisting on benefits and then losing them has been linked to higher recidivism risk for justice-involved women (Morash et al. 2017). Housing access, in particular, is a pressing issue women face (Allen 2018; Richie 2001, Hall et al. 2013) and is closely linked to employment and education struggles (Richie 2001). Many women leaving prison experience homelessness multiple times and cannot find housing with family due to spoiled relationships or simply being overburdened (Richie 2001). Even with using temporary housing, most women still must find long-term housing by themselves. There are very few community-based programs focusing on housing, and the amount of government-funded low-income housing is minuscule and often inaccessible for justice-involved women (Hall et al. 2013; Richie 2001). Altogether, justice-involved women have co-occurring needs and risks that challenge their successful re-entry. Because of this, evidence-based policy and practice must account for the gender-specific needs and risks of justice-involved women.

Traditionally, evidence-based policy discussions exclude women (Bloom, Owen, and Covington 2003; Van Voorhis 2012), which limits successful interventions (Bloom, Owen, and Covington 2003; Richie 2001). If the ultimate goal is to curb recidivism and facilitate successful re-entry, responses that focus on the individual, community, and macro-level social, economic, and political structures are vital. In addition to surmounting their individual barriers, people leaving prison have to contend with widening inequality, declining wages, lack of access to quality education, a deepening housing crisis, and the enduring effects of structural racism (Bushway and Uggen 2021). Crime rates fluctuate dramatically over time and across space, which suggests that individual factors *and* community context play a significant role in driving criminal behavior and opportunities. While much of the work on re-entry generally focuses on changing individual attitudes and behaviors, it is limited by ignoring the constraints imposed by social structure and policies (National Academies of Sciences, Engineering, and Medicine 2022). Thus, the dynamic interaction between individual and social/environmental factors must be taken into account to support the reintegration and desistance process, as both are impacted by structure and agency (Allen 2018).

Substantial literature highlights the importance of using gender-responsive programming that focuses on risk factors and needs (i.e., victimization, substance abuse, mental health, family reunification, negative relationships, trauma, and poverty) specific to women (Bloom, Owen, and Covington 2003; Van Voorhis et al. 2010; Van Voorhis 2012; Wright et al. 2007), as this has proven to reduce recidivism (Gehring, Van Voorhis, and Bell 2010; Gobeil, Blanchette, and Stewart 2016; Grella 2009; Hall et al. 2013). Justice-involved women report that access to post-release services that help with housing, employment, clothing, and other essentials aid their re-entry. While studies show that gender-neutral assessments are valid for women, they can also be improved with the addition of a number of gender-responsive factors found to be predictive of institutional misconduct and community recidivism (Van Voorhis et al. 2010; Wright, Salisbury, and Van Voorhis 2007). To further improve how women are treated, the following gender-responsive needs should be assessed: mental health history, depression/anxiety, psychosis, child abuse, adult victimization, relationship dysfunction, parental stress, and housing safety. Strengths should also be examined, including self-efficacy, parental involvement, family support, and educational assets.

Additionally, one method used by women to avoid reoffending is being preoccupied with legitimate activities (Cobbina et al. 2014). Therefore, using evidence-based policy to inform programs that are gender-responsive and provide legitimate activities may help reduce recidivism. For example, the Moving On program uses relational theory and cognitive-behavioral intervention to help women (Van Dieten and MacKenna 2001), and it has led to lower rates of rearrest, conviction, and incarceration (Gehring, Van Voorhis, and Bell 2010).

Similarly, the Female Offender Treatment and Employment Program (FOTEP) uses intensive case management to focus on substance abuse, employment, and family reunification and reduced recidivism (Grella 2009). The success of these programs illustrates how focusing on gender-specific needs and risk helps improve outcomes for justice-involved women. Likewise, another method is to treat substance abuse along with co-occurring mental health issues and trauma that so many justice-involved women suffer from (Bloom, Owen, and Covington 2003; Van Voorhis 2012). Programs like Beyond Trauma (Covington 2003) use cognitive-behavioral practices alongside mindfulness, guided imagery, art techniques, and psychoeducation to simultaneously treat women's issues and lower prison return rates (Messina et al. 2010).

Additionally, many argue for the use of wraparound services that focus on co-occurring needs (Bloom, Owen, and Covington 2003; Richie 2001). The Women Offender Case Management Model (WOCMM), one example of a wraparound service, creates comprehensive case management strategies for women (Van Dieten 2008), and it was found to decrease recidivism (Morash 2010). The use of gender-responsive drug courts has also proved helpful in reducing women's sanctioning, drug use, and arrests, and in improving psychological well-being (see Morash and Hoskins 2022).

The current research on evidence-based policy for justice-involved women demonstrates how incorporating gender-specific needs and risks can greatly improve outcomes. However, more work still needs to be done to improve the outcomes for this diverse population (Bloom, Owen, and Covington 2003; Morash and Hoskins 2022). Further, the creation and evaluation of gender-specific programs is a first step into ensuring justice-involved women receive proper treatment. Van Voorhis (2012) also recommends conducting more controlled studies of women-specific models if we want to increase women's presence in evidence-based policy. It is also important to keep in mind the qualitative difference between responsivity (i.e., needs that must be accommodated considered before addressing criminogenic need) and risk factors. Doing so has implications for what is included in evidence-based policy (Van Voorhis 2012).

IV. YOUTH AND THE JUVENILE JUSTICE SYSTEM

The US correctional population includes 49,000 youth confined in carceral institutions, with most confined for person-related offenses (Sawyer and Wagner 2022). Many are held for probation violations, and others are held for status offenses, such as truancy and running away (Sawyer and Wagner 2022). The juvenile justice system began in 1899 with the creation of the first juvenile court in Cook County, Illinois (Snyder and Sickmund 2006). At that time, children were no longer being perceived as miniature adults (Feld 1991) and instead were seen as innocent, vulnerable, and in need of rehabilitation. Those ideas were not assigned to Black youth, who despite experiencing the same challenges as White youth were labeled with the same stereotypes as all Black people: criminal, uncivil, and immoral (Agyepong 2018); thus, efforts were largely focused on White youth while predominantly excluding Black youth.

Ultimately, the Illinois Juvenile Court Act of 1899 was passed, which partially defined *dependent* as "any child who for any reason is destitute or homeless or abandoned; or dependent upon the public for support; or has not had proper parental care or guardianship." Alternatively, a *delinquent* child was classified as any child "under the age of 16 years who violates any law of the State or any city or village ordinance." The two terms were racialized and codified, with *dependent* typically applied to White youth and *delinquent* to Black youth, even though both groups experienced many of the same societal challenges (Agyepong 2018).

In practice, White youth had access to social services and support from providers, whereas Black youth were remanded to state institutions, adult prisons, workhouses, and convict-leasing (Ward 2012). Black children were disproportionately represented in institutions for delinquents, not because they committed more crimes, but because of racism and the lack of options available to provide care for Black children classified as dependent (Agyepong 2018). The impact of race, and its intersection with gender, in the early formation of the juvenile court demonstrates the disparate treatment of Black youth in the juvenile justice system as a foundational philosophy, not a recent phenomenon, as is often implied.

A. Current Levels of Racial and Ethnic Disparities

The levels of racial and ethnic disparities in the juvenile justice system were considered for the first time by the federal government with the passing of the Juvenile Justice and Delinquency Prevention Act of 1974. It sought to address the long-standing disproportionate detention and confinement of minorities in secure facilities. However, despite multiple reauthorizations—most recently as the Juvenile Justice Reform Act of 2018—and an expansion of the definition from confinement to contact, racial and ethnic disparities still exist. Since 2005, there has been a steady decline in the total number of delinquency cases—there was a drop of 48% between 2009 and 2018; moreover, for youth charged with status offenses, there was a 49% decline (Hockenberry and Puzzanchera 2020). However, Black youth continue to be seen as and categorized as criminal, and White youth are often granted the privilege of adolescent irresponsibility (Henning 2021). Consequently, racial disparities between White and Black youth continue to exist across all decision points in the juvenile justice system, despite an overall decrease in the numbers of youth in the system across racial groups. This outcome is evident when reviewing *Juvenile Court Statistics, 2018*, the most recent Office of Juvenile Justice and Delinquency Prevention report. Black youth comprised 15% of the US population, yet they were 35% of all delinquency cases, more likely to have their cases be formally processed, and most likely to have their cases be judicially waived to criminal court. In addition, they remained the smallest group to be adjudicated delinquent and were the least likely to receive probation (Hockenberry and Puzzanchera 2020).

B. Pathways to the Juvenile Justice System

Black youth are channeled into the juvenile justice system via a number of pathways, including the child welfare system, school-to-prison pipeline, and their mental health needs. It is quite common for youth who are in child welfare, versus the general population, to have contact with juvenile justice (Kim et al. 2020; Ryan and Testa 2005). Known as crossover or dual-system-involved youth (Herz et al. 2012), they are more likely when compared to youth with no child welfare involvement to experience harsher outcomes (Ryan et al. 2007) and recidivate (Herz, Ryan, and Bilchik 2010; Huang, Ryan, and Herz 2012; Ryan et al. 2007).

The school-to-prison pipeline provides easy entrée for Black youth to enter the juvenile justice system. First, the integration of police into school settings exposes youth to legal and punitive sanctions that previously would have been handled internally. Second, responses such as out-of-school suspensions or expulsions increase the likelihood that youth will be out of school, have contact with the police, and be referred to the juvenile court (Meiners and Winn 2010; Nicholson-Crotty, Birchmeier, and Valentine 2009).

Moreover, the rate of mental health needs among justice-involved youth are higher than among the general youth population (Burke, Mulvey, and Schubert 2015; Vaughn, Sattler, and Holzer 2022). Also more extensive are their histories of experiencing trauma (McCoy, Leverso, and Bowen 2016; Novak and De Francisco Lopes 2022; Pyle et al. 2016; Vaughn, Sattler, and Holzer 2022). For Black youth, there is often a failure to treat and a greater likelihood of being responded to with punitive measures (Cauffman 2004; Fader, Kurlychek, and Morgan 2014; Rodriguez 2013). Patterns of mental health service use also vary based on other factors, such as age, gender, race/ethnicity, family issues, and placement (Burke, Mulvey, and Schubert 2015; Kim et al. 2020).

Because of this, the American Academy of Child and Adolescent Psychiatry recommended youth in the justice system be screened for trauma and its impact on emotional functioning and behavior (Penn and Thomas 2005). One attempt to accomplish this goal has been the widespread adoption of the Massachusetts Youth Screen Instrument-Version 2 (MAYSI-2). This is a self-report screener used to identify youth that may need an immediate response, monitoring, or further assessment (Grisso and Barnum 2006). Unfortunately, racial differences on the MAYSI-2 have been identified using quantitative (McCoy 2011) and qualitative methods (McCoy 2014). Findings included detained Black and White males interpreting mental health symptoms, and the dimension of time, differently (McCoy 2011, 2014). These differences are an example of why there are differences in who is referred for treatment versus whose behavior is criminalized (McCoy 2014). Research has long demonstrated that Black youth are much more likely to be referred to correctional facilities and White youth to mental health services (e.g., Cauffman and Grisso 2005; Martin and Grubb 1990; Rogers and Peterson 2014). For example, this pattern was shown to be true for a Pennsylvania group of 13 to 19 juvenile offenders in residential care where, despite controlling for predisposing, enabling, and need factors, Black youth were still less likely to be referred for mental health services (Lee, Goodkind, and Shook 2017). The same was true in an examination of administrative data about youth in residential programs (N = 10,100) from the Florida Department of Juvenile Justice, which indicated that Black youth, despite histories of trauma and behavioral signs, were less likely than White youth to have been referred for psychiatric treatment (Baglivio et al. 2017).

Youth in the juvenile justice system encounter a multitude of other challenges that can hinder, or even be harmful, in their trajectory. There are factors impacting their employment access (Cavanagh, Clough, and Thomas 2021), as well as issues relating to interpretations of their personality, social and emotional behaviors, and cognition (Novak and De Francisco Lopes 2022; Pyle et al. 2016) It is not uncommon for them to experience multiple issues at one time, particularly due to their intersectionality and history of trauma and victimization (Pyle et al. 2016). Thus, it is imperative that evidence-based policies be designed to address the structural factors that impact these youth, including the connection to the child welfare system, the lack of access to accurate and responsive mental health services, the use of school environments as a gateway to the juvenile justice system, and the many other factors that unduly influence their trajectories.

C. Youth and Evidence-Based Policy

Trauma is prevalent in justice-involved youth and it is imperative that it be considered within the juvenile justice system, especially because system involvement may retraumatize or revictimize youth (Ford et al. 2007; Hennessey et al. 2004; McCoy, Leverso, and Bowen 2016). Engaging trauma-informed experts is imperative (McCoy, Leverso, and Bowen 2016). Judges need to take a holistic approach when making determinations about the youth before them. They must look beyond the crime committed and sentencing guidelines and contextualize whether the youth have a history in child welfare, their school experiences, history of mental health needs and services, and history of trauma and victimization. Since trauma can impact behaviors, using a trauma-informed lens can help provide context regarding some youth behaviors (Espinosa, Sorenson, and Lopez 2013).

In addition, systems of care should be community-based and coincide with individual need and motivation level (Novak and De Francisco Lopes 2022; Vaughn, Sattler, and Holzer 2022). Interventions should also address multiple risk factors at once (Pyle et al. 2016). Some of the current evidence-based practices that demonstrated effectiveness in youth populations are Multisystemic Therapy (MST), Functional Family Therapy

(FFT), cognitive- behavioral therapy, dialectical behavior therapy (see also Quinn and Shera 2009), and Aggression Replacement Training (Vaughn, Sattler, and Holzer 2022). Treatment should be reconceptualized to describe behavior rather than label it and minimize the role of the juvenile justice system, and it should be tailored to the individual. This approach emphasizes skill development rather than behavioral compliance (Vaughn, Sattler, and Holzer 2022).

Black Family Development in Detroit is one example of community-based service for youth. It serves as an alternative to detention and incarceration and is focused on keeping youth in the community. This program reduced out-of-home placements by 50% and reduced recidivism from 56% in 1998 to 17.5% in 2012 (Connecticut Juvenile Justice Alliance 2015). Also important is a focus on emotional well-being. Allocating more funding for counselors and social workers in detention centers would enable them to focus more on family counseling, community empowerment, and strengthening emotional well-being (Toldson et al. 2010). Finally, including in federal legislation and programs for justice-involved youth employment development and training, as well as mentoring, may help youth have access and achieve their employment and educational plans (Fields and Abrams 2010).

It is also important to keep in mind that the juvenile justice system was designed for male youth (Hoskins 2018), which has created a need for gender-responsiveness in the juvenile justice system. Although practitioners understand that trauma and relational issues are pathways to crime for girls, they are unable to connect that to system responses (Rubino, Anderson, and McKenna 2021). Additionally, their biases and ignorance about girls' social identities present opportunities for further victimization and traumatization. This need advances the support for incorporating gender-responsiveness, diverse inclusion in staff hiring, and increased diversity, equity, and inclusion training for staff (Rubino, Anderson, and McKenna 2021). Coupling those actions with a trauma-informed framework will help connect pathways to system responses and create an environment that is conducive to the diversity of system-involved girls (Rubino, Anderson, and McKenna 2021). Another essential approach is the interlocking of other institutions (e.g., housing and education) within the juvenile justice system, and creation of structural-level solutions (Singh et al. 2021).

Similarly, the high level of racial and ethnic disparities in the juvenile justice system represents another issue that evidence-based policy can resolve. Since the identification in 1974 of disproportionate minority confinement, various efforts have been tried to address the issue. Some have been federally funded, while others have been through agency programs and in collaboration with community stakeholders (see McCoy and Pearson 2019). Unfortunately, the issue remains, with little to no progress. New policies must be created, continually evaluated, and updated regularly that address the outcome of racial and ethnic disparities as well as the various feeders into the juvenile justice system (e.g., lack of access to accurate and appropriate mental health services, the criminalization of mental health needs, the school-to-prison pipeline, the significant overlap with the child welfare system, and the lack of access to employment opportunities). These policies should be created with the input of all stakeholders: community members, youth formerly involved in the juvenile justice system, justice system professionals, and experts in issues impacting system-involved youth. By including representatives of each sphere, the likelihood of success will be improved.

V. Conclusion

In conclusion, it is clear that diverse groups in the criminal legal system suffer from unique experiences, and as of now, the evidence-based policies and practices that exist have not greatly reduced the harm they have experienced. Much of the existing, evidence-based policies and practices account for the specific needs and factors that push and pull diverse individuals into the criminal and juvenile justice systems. Doing so acts as a means to stabilize noncriminogenic factors so that criminogenic factors are effectively handled. To further improve our knowledge of evidence-based policy and practice for these populations, more research of all methods must be conducted to better understand not only what these populations need but also what help they desire.

Many of the issues drawing these groups to the system are structural and occur years before they ever reach the justice system. Therefore, we must identify ways to remove personal and structural barriers (e.g., poverty or race-based discrimination) that move people closer to crime, and we must provide non-justice-system services for individuals who have been victimized or are suffering from issues relating to trauma and substance abuse. We greatly caution against supporting policies that widen the net of the criminal legal system and cause increased surveillance (e.g., electronic monitoring; see Kilgore 2015). Policies and practices that reduce the scope of the criminal legal system and its collateral consequences are the ones that deserve support and promotion.

Finally, it is essential that the knowledge base about evidence-based policy and practice for diverse criminal justice populations be strengthened. One immediate way to accomplish this goal is for the evidence to be informed by those most impacted. Questions should be created by experts—those who are members of the community and are being impacted. Embracing this strategy will automatically diversify not just the questions being asked but the needs identified and the solutions proposed. Our first and best recommendation for how to create and promote policies that address the unique risks and needs of minoritized communities: ask them.

Notes

1. We use the word *minoritized* instead of *minority* because minority is a noun that describes a person, place, or thing that is smaller, numerically, than the majority. Minoritized is a verb that refers to being forced into a group that is mistreated, discriminated against, and faces prejudices that are enforced upon them because of situations outside of their control. It captures differences in power and access. Therefore, individuals who are mistreated or discriminated against based on different identities are not minorities but are minoritized. It is possible for minoritized individuals to make up a larger share of the population numerically (to be considered the majority) and still be treated unfairly (Smith 2016). Throughout the remainder of the paper, the verb *minoritized* will be used to describe these individuals.

References

Agyepong, Tera Eva. 2018. *The criminalization of black children: Race, gender, and delinquency in Chicago's juvenile justice system, 1899-1945*. Chapel Hill: University of North Carolina Press.

Alexander, Michelle. 2012. *The new Jim Crow: Mass incarceration in the age of colorblindness*. New York: New Press.

Allen, Elizabeth Karyn. 2018. Justice-involved women: Narratives, marginalization, identity and community reintegration. *Affilia*, 33 (3): 346-362.

Bachman, Ronet, Erin M. Kerrison, Raymond Paternoster, Lionel Smith, and Daniel O'Connell. 2016. The complex relationship between motherhood and desistance. *Women & Criminal Justice*, 26 (3): 212-231.

Baglivio, Michael T., Kevin T. Wolff, Alex R. Piquero, Mark A. Greenwald, and Nathan Epps. 2017. Racial/ethnic disproportionality in psychiatric diagnoses and treatment in a sample of serious juvenile offenders. *Journal of Youth and Adolescence*, 46:1424-1451.

Barrick, Kelle, Pamela K. Lattimore, and Christy A. Visher. 2014. Reentering women: The impact of social ties on long-term recidivism. *The Prison Journal*, 94 (3): 279-304.

Belknap, Joanne. 2015. *The invisible woman: Gender, crime, and justice*. 4th ed. Belmont, CA: Thomson Wadsworth.

Blankenship, Kim M., Ana Maria del Rio Gonzalez, Danya E. Keene, Allison K. Groves, and Alana P. Rosenberg. 2018. Mass incarceration, race inequality, and health: Expanding concepts and assessing impacts on well-being. *Social Science & Medicine*, 215:45-52.

Bloom, Barbara, Barbara A. Owen, and Stephanie Covington. 2003. *Gender-responsive strategies: Research, practice, and guiding principles for women offenders*. Washington, DC: National Institute of Corrections.

Bloom, Barbara, Barbara Owen, and Stephanie Covington. 2004. Women offenders and the gendered effects of public policy. *Review of Policy Research*, 21 (1): 31-48.

Bohmert, Miriam Northcutt, and Alfred DeMaris. 2018. Cumulative disadvantage and the role of transportation in community supervision. *Crime & Delinquency*, 64 (8): 1033-1056.

Bohmert, Miriam Northcutt, Matthew Galasso, and Jennifer Cobbina. 2018. Impacts of conviction and imprisonment for women. In *Handbook on the consequences of sentencing and punishment decisions*, edited by Beth M. Huebner and Natasha A. Frost, 161-172. New York: Routledge.

Brennan, Tim, Markus Breitenbach, William Dieterich, Emily J. Salisbury, and Patricia Van Voorhis. 2012. Women's pathways to serious and habitual crime: A person-centered analysis incorporating gender responsive factors. *Criminal Justice and Behavior*, 39 (11): 1481-1508.

Burke, Jeffrey D., Edward P. Mulvey, and Carol A. Schubert. 2015. Prevalence of mental health problems and service use among first-time juvenile offenders. *Journal of Child and Family Studies*, 24 (12): 3774-3781.

Bushway, Shawn, and Christopher Uggen. 2021. Fostering desistance. *Contexts*, 20 (4): 34-39.

Cauffman, Elizabeth. 2004. A statewide screening of mental health symptoms among juvenile offenders in detention. *Journal of the American Academy of Child & Adolescent Psychiatry*, 43 (4): 430-439.

Cauffman, Elizabeth, and Thomas Grisso. 2005. Mental health issues among minority offenders in the juvenile justice system. In *Our children, their children*, edited by Darnell. F. Hawkins, 390-412. Chicago: University of Chicago Press.

Cavanagh, Caitlin, Isabelle Clough, and April Gile Thomas. 2021. Concerns about the COVID-19 pandemic among justice-involved and low-income youth. *Juvenile and Family Court Journal*, 72 (4): 5–30.

Chesney-Lind, Meda. 1997. *The female offender: Girls, women, and crime.* Thousand Oaks, CA: SAGE Publications.

Clone, Stephanie, and Dana DeHart. 2014. Social support networks of incarcerated women: Types of support, sources of support, and implications for reentry. *Journal of Offender Rehabilitation*, 53 (7): 503–521.

Cobbina, Jennifer E. 2009. *From prison to home: Women's pathways in and out of crime.* St. Louis, MO: University of Missouri- Saint Louis.

Cobbina, Jennifer E. 2010. Reintegration success and failure: Factors impacting reintegration among incarcerated and formerly incarcerated women. *Journal of Offender Rehabilitation*, 49 (3): 210–232.

Cobbina, Jennifer E. 2019. *Hands up don't shoot.* New York: New York University Press.

Cobbina, Jennifer E., Beth M. Huebner, and Mark T. Berg. 2012. Men, women, and postrelease offending: An examination of the nature of the link between relational ties and recidivism. *Crime & Delinquency*, 58 (3): 331–361.

Cobbina, Jennifer E., and Merry Morash. 2015. Women offenders' perception of treatment by police and courts. In *Lives of incarcerated women*, edited by Candace Kruttschnitt and Catrien Bijleveld, 142–157. New York: Routledge.

Cobbina, Jennifer E., Merry Morash, Deborah A. Kashy, and Sandi W. Smith. 2014. Race, neighborhood danger, and coping strategies among female probationers and parolees. *Race and Justice*, 4 (1): 3–28.

Connecticut Juvenile Justice Alliance. 2015. Juvenile Prisons: National consensus and alternatives. Bridgeport: Connecticut Juvenile Justice Alliance.

Covington, Stephanie. 2003. *Beyond trauma.* Center City, MN: Hazeldon.

Crenshaw, Kimberlé. 1989. Demarginalizing the intersection of race and sex: A black feminist critique of antidiscrimination doctrine, feminist theory, and antiracist politics. *University of Chicago Legal Forum*, 1989 (1): 8.

Crenshaw, Kimberlé. 1990. Mapping the margins: Intersectionality, identity politics, and violence against women of color. *Stanford Law Review*, 43:1241.

Daly, Kathleen. 1992. Women's pathways to felony court: Feminist theories of lawbreaking and problems of representation. *Southern California Review of Law and Women's Studies*, 2:11.

Daly, Kathleen. 1998. Gender, crime, and criminology. In *The handbook of crime and punishment*, edited by Michael Tonry, 85–108. New York: Oxford University Press.

Decker, Scott H., Natalie Ortiz, Cassia Spohn, and Eric Hedberg. 2015. Criminal stigma, race, and ethnicity: The consequences of imprisonment for employment. *Journal of Criminal Justice*, 43 (2): 108–121.

Del Carmen, Alejandro. 2008. *Racial profiling in America.* Upper Saddle River, NJ: Pearson/Prentice Hall.

Dodge, Mary, and Mark R. Pogrebin. 2001. Collateral costs of imprisonment for women: Complications of reintegration. *The Prison Journal*, 81 (1): 42–54.

Drakulich, Kevin M. 2013. Perceptions of the local danger posed by crime: Race, disorder, informal control, and the police. *Social Science Research*, 42:611–632.

Drakulich, Kevin M., and Robert D. Crutchfield. 2013. The role of perceptions of the police in informal social control: Implications for the racial stratification of crime and control. *Social Problems*, 60:383–407.

Durr, Marlese. 2015. What is the difference between slave patrols and modern day policing? Institutional violence in a community of color. *Critical Sociology*, 41:873–879.

Engel, Robin S. 2005. Citizens' perceptions of distributive and procedural injustice during traffic stops with police. *Journal of Research in Crime and Delinquency*, 42 (4): 445–481.

Epp, Charles R., Steven Maynard-Moody, and Donald Haider-Markel. 2017. Beyond profiling: The institutional sources of racial disparities in policing. *Public Administration Review*, 77 (2): 168–178.

Espinosa, Erin M., Jon R. Sorensen, and Molly A. Lopez. 2013. Youth pathways to placement: The influence of gender, mental health need and trauma on confinement in the juvenile justice system. *Journal of Youth and Adolescence*, 42 (12): 1824–1836.

Fader, Jamie J., Megan C. Kurlychek, and Kirstin A. Morgan. 2014. The color of juvenile justice: Racial disparities in dispositional decisions. *Social Science Research*, 44:126–140.

Feld, Barry C. 1991. Justice by geography: Urban, suburban, and rural variations in juvenile justice administration. *Journal of Criminal Law and Criminology*, 82 (1): 156–210.

Fields, Diane, and Laura S. Abrams. 2010. Gender differences in the perceived needs and barriers of youth offenders preparing for community reentry. *Child & Youth Care Forum*, 39 (4): 253–269.

Ford, Julian D., John F. Chapman, Josephine Hawke, and David Albert. 2007. *Trauma among youth in the juvenile justice system: Critical issues and new directions*. Delmar, NY: National Center for Mental Health and Juvenile Justice.

Gehring, Krista, Patricia Van Voorhis, and Valerie Bell. 2010. What works for female probationers? An evaluation of the Moving On program. *Women, Girls, and Criminal Justice*, 11 (1): 6–10.

Ghandnoosh, Nazgol. 2015. *Black Lives Matter: Eliminating racial inequity in the criminal justice system*. Washington, DC: The Sentencing Project.

Gillette, Caroline. 2020. Do mandatory minimums increase racial disparities in federal criminal sentencing. *Undergraduate Economic Review*, 17 (1): 9.

Giordano, Peggy C., Stephen A. Cernkovich, and Jennifer L. Rudolph. 2002. Gender, crime, and desistance: Toward a theory of cognitive transformation. *American Journal of Sociology*, 107 (4): 990–1064.

Gobeil, Renée, Kelley Blanchette, and Lynn Stewart. 2016. A meta-analytic review of correctional interventions for women offenders: Gender-neutral versus gender-informed approaches. *Criminal Justice and Behavior*, 43 (3): 301–322.

Goodson-Miller, Marva V. 2022. A first look at justice-involved women's egocentric social networks. *Social Networks*, 70:152–165.

Grella, Christine. 2009. *Female Offender Treatment and Employment Project (FOTEP): Summary of evaluation findings*. Los Angeles: UCLA Integrated Substance Abuse Programs.

Grisso, Thomas, and Richard Barnum. 2006. *Massachusetts Youth Screening Instrument, version 2: MAYSI-2: User's manual and technical report*. Sarasota, FL: Professional Resource Press.

Hall, Martin T., Seana Golder, Cynthia L. Conley, and Susan Sawning. 2013. Designing programming and interventions for women in the criminal justice system. *American Journal of Criminal Justice*, 38 (1): 27–50.

Harm, Nancy J., and Susan D. Phillips. 2001. You can't go home again: Women and criminal recidivism. *Journal of Offender Rehabilitation*, 32 (3): 3–21.

Heilbrun, Kirk, David Dematteo, Ralph Fretz, Jacey Erickson, Kento Yasuhara, and Natalie Anumba. 2008. How "specific" are gender-specific rehabilitation needs? An empirical analysis. *Criminal Justice and Behavior*, 35 (11): 1382–1397.

Hennessey, Marianne, Julian D. Ford, Karen Mahoney, Susan J. Ko, and Christine B. Siegfried. 2004. Trauma among girls in the juvenile justice system. Los Angeles: National Child Traumatic Stress Network.

Henning, Kristin. 2021. Prosecuting race and adolescence. In The Oxford *handbook of prosecutors and prosecution*, edited by Ronald F. Wright, Kay L. Levine, and Russell M. Gold, 447–474. New York: Oxford University Press.

Herz, Denise, Philip Lee, Lorrie Lutz, Macon Stewart, John Tuell, and Janet Wiig. 2012. *Addressing the needs of multi-system youth: Strengthening the connection between child welfare and juvenile justice*. Washington, DC: Center for Juvenile Justice Reform.

Herz, Denise C., Joseph P. Ryan, and Shay Bilchik. 2010. Challenges facing crossover youth: An examination of juvenile-justice decision making and recidivism. *Family Court Review*, 48 (2): 305–321.

Hinton, Elizabeth, L. Henderson, and Cindy Reed. 2018. *An unjust burden: The disparate treatment of black Americans in the criminal justice system*. New York: Vera Institute of Justice.

Hockenberry, Sarah and Charles Puzzanchera. 2020. *Juvenile court statistics 2018*. Pittsburgh: National Center for Juvenile Justice.

Hoskins, Kayla. 2018. Women, girls, and reentry. In *Oxford bibliographies in criminology*, edited by B. M. Huebner. New York: Oxford University Press.

Hoskins, Kayla M. 2019. Race and re-entry after incarceration. In *Oxford research encyclopedia of criminology and criminal justice*. Edited by Henry Pontell. New York: Oxford University Press.

Huang, Hui, Joseph P. Ryan, and Denise Herz. 2012. The journey of dually-involved youth: The description and prediction of rereporting and recidivism. *Children and Youth Services Review*, 34 (1): 254–260.

Huebner, Beth M., Christina DeJong, and Jennifer Cobbina. 2010. Women coming home: Long-term patterns of recidivism. *Justice Quarterly*, 27 (2): 225–254.

Hughes, Everett Cherrington. 1945. Dilemmas and contradictions of status. *American Journal of Sociology*, 50 (5): 353–359.

Institute for Criminal Justice Training Reform. 2022. *Vision for a path forward*. Gardena, NY: The Institute for Criminal Justice Training Reform. https://www.trainingreform.org/reimagining-police-training.

James, Doris J., and Lauren E. Glaze. 2006. *Mental health problems of prison and jail inmates*. Washington, DC: Office of Justice Programs.

Kane, Robert J. 2005. Compromised police legitimacy as a predictor of violent crime in structurally disadvantaged communities. *Criminology*, 43 (2): 469–498.

Kajstura, Aleks. 2019. *Women's mass incarceration: The whole pie 2019*. Northampton, MA: Prison Policy Initiative.

Kerley, Kent R., Michael L. Benson, Matthew R. Lee, and Francis T. Cullen. 2004. Race, criminal justice contact, and adult position in the social stratification system. *Social Problems*, 51 (4): 549–568.

Kilgore, James. 2015. *Electronic monitoring is not the answer: Critical reflections on a flawed alternative*. Urbana-Champaign Independent Media Center.

Kim, Minseop, Antonio R. Garcia, Nahri Jung, and Sheila Barnhart. 2020. Rates and predictors of mental health service use among dual system youth. *Children and Youth Services Review*, 114:105024.

Lee, Lewis H., Sara Goodkind, and Jeffrey J, Shook. 2017. Racial/ethnic disparities in prior mental health service use among incarcerated adolescents. *Children and Youth Services Review*, 78:23–31.

Lindquist, Christine H., K. Barrick, P. K. Lattimore, and Christy A. Visher. 2009. Prisoner reentry experiences of adult females: Characteristics, service receipt, and outcomes of participants in the SVORI multi-site evaluation. Washington, DC: National Institute of Justice.

Lipsitz, George. 2011. In an avalanche every snowflake pleads not guilty: The collateral consequences of mass incarceration and impediments to women's fair housing rights. *UCLA Law Review*, 59:1746.

Lum, Cynthia. Christopher S. Kopper, Charlotte Gill, Julie Hibdon, Cody Telep, and Laurie Robinson. 2016. An evidence-assessment of the recommendations of the President's Task Force on 21st Century Policing—Implementation and research priorities. Fairfax, VA: Center for Evidence-Based Crime Policy.

Lynch, Shannon M., April Fritch, and Nicole M. Heath. 2012. Looking beneath the surface: The nature of incarcerated women's experiences of interpersonal violence, treatment needs, and mental health. *Feminist Criminology*, 7 (4): 381–400.

Maher, Lisa and Kathleen Daly. 1996. Women in the street-level drug economy: Continuity or change? *Criminology*, 34 (4): 465–492.

Martin, Todd W., and Henry Jefferson Grubb. 1990. Race bias in diagnosis and treatment of juvenile offenders: Findings and suggestions. *Journal of Contemporary Psychotherapy*, 20 (4): 259–272.

Martinez, Damian and Johnna Christian. 2009. The familial relationships of former prisoners: Examining the link between residence and informal support mechanisms. *Journal of Contemporary Ethnography*, 38 (2): 201–224.

McCoy, Henrika. 2011. A path analysis of factors influencing racial differences on the Massachusetts Youth Screening Instrument–Version 2. *Journal of Offender Rehabilitation*, 50:119–141.

McCoy, Henrika. 2014. Using cognitive interviewing to explore causes for racial differences on the MAYSI-2. *Crime & Delinquency*, 60:647–666.

McCoy, Henrika, John Leverso, and Elizabeth A. Bowen. 2016. What the MAYSI-2 can tell us about anger-irritability and trauma. *International Journal of Offender Therapy and Comparative Criminology*, 60:555–574.

McCoy, Henrika, and Emalee Pearson. 2019. Racial disparities in the juvenile justice system. In *Encyclopedia of Social Work*, 1–24 (online edn).

Meiners, Erica R., and Maisha T. Winn. 2010. Resisting the school to prison pipeline: The practice to build abolition democracies. *Race Ethnicity and Education*, 13 (3): 271–276.

Metcalfe, Christi, and Thomas Baker. 2022. Race, ethnicity, justice, and self-regulating beliefs among a sample of justice-involved men and women. *Race and Justice*, 1–20.

Messina, Nena, Christine E. Grella, Jerry Cartier, and Stephanie Torres. 2010. A randomized experimental study of gender-responsive substance abuse treatment for women in prison. *Journal of Substance Abuse Treatment*, 38 (2): 97–107.

Minton, Todd D., Lauren G. Beatty, and Zhen Zeng. 2021. *Correctional populations in the United States, 2019—Statistical tables*. Washington, DC: Bureau of Justice Statistics.

Morash, Merry. 2010. *Women on probation and parole: A feminist critique of community programs & services*. Boston, MA: Northeastern University Press.

Morash, Merry, and Kayla Hoskins. 2022. Effective community interventions for girls and women in the criminal justice system. In *The Wiley handbook on what works with women and girls in conflict with the law: A critical review of theory, practice, and policy*, edited by Shelley L. Brown and Loraine Gelsthorpe, 256–266. Hoboken, NJ: Wiley-Blackwell.

Morash, Merry, Deborah A. Kashy, Miriam Northcutt Bohmert, Jennifer E. Cobbina, and Sandi W. Smith. 2017. Women at the nexus of correctional and social policies: Implications for recidivism risk. *British Journal of Criminology*, 57 (2): 441–462.

Mumola, Christopher J. 1999. *Substance abuse and treatment, state and federal prisoners, 1997*. Washington, DC: Bureau of Justice Statistics.

Mumola, Christopher J., and Jennifer C. Karberg. 2006. *Drug use and dependence, state and federal prisoners, 2004*. Washington, DC: Bureau of Justice Statistics.

National Academies of Sciences, Engineering, and Medicine. 2022. *The limits of recidivism: Measuring success after prison*. Washington, DC: National Academies Press. https://doi.org/10.17226/26459.

Nellis, Ashley. 2016. *The color of justice: Racial and ethnic disparity in state prisons*. Washington, DC: The Sentencing Project.

Neusteter, S. Rebecca, and Megan O'Toole. 2019. *Every three seconds: Unlocking police data on arrests*. Brooklyn, NY: The Vera Institute.

Nicholson-Crotty, Sean, Zachary Birchmeier, and David Valentine. 2009. Exploring the impact of school discipline on racial disproportion in the juvenile justice system. *Social Science Quarterly*, 90 (4): 1003–1018.

Novak, Abigail, and Vitoria De Francisco Lopes. 2022. Child delinquency, ACEs, and the juvenile justice system: Does exposure to ACEs affect justice system experiences for children? *Youth Violence and Juvenile Justice*, 20 (2): 113–138.

Pager, Devah. 2003. The mark of a criminal record. *American Journal of Sociology*, 108 (5): 937–975.

Penn, Joseph V., and Christopher Thomas. 2005. Practice parameter for the assessment and treatment of youth in juvenile detention and correctional facilities. *Journal of the American Academy of Child & Adolescent Psychiatry*, 44 (10): 1085–1098.

Pyle, Nicole, Andrea Flower, Anna Mari Fall, and Jacob Williams. 2016. Individual-level risk factors of incarcerated youth. *Remedial and Special Education*, 37 (3): 172–186.

Quinn, Ashley, and Wes Shera. 2009. Evidence-based practice in group work with incarcerated youth. *International Journal of Law and Psychiatry*, 32 (5): 288–293.

Richie, Beth E. 2001. Challenges incarcerated women face as they return to their communities: Findings from life history interviews. *Crime & Delinquency*, 47 (3): 368–389.

Roddy, Ariel L., Merry Morash, and Kayla M. Hoskins. 2021. An exploration of employment-related personal projects undertaken by women on probation and parole. *Feminist Criminology*, 16 (1): 3–25.

Rodriguez, Nancy. 2013. Concentrated disadvantage and the incarceration of youth: Examining how context affects juvenile justice. *Journal of Research in Crime and Delinquency*, 50 (2): 189–215.

Rogers, Kenneth M., and Eunice Peterson. 2014. Juvenile justice in the United States: Minority youth. *Adolescent Psychiatry*, 4:261–269.

Ryan, Joseph P., Denise Herz, Pedro M. Hernandez, and Jane Marie Marshall. 2007. Maltreatment and delinquency: Investigating child welfare bias in juvenile justice processing. *Children and Youth Services Review*, 29 (8): 1035–1050.

Ryan, Joseph P., and Mark F. Testa. 2005. Child maltreatment and juvenile delinquency: Investigating the role of placement and placement instability. *Children and Youth Services Review*, 27 (3): 227–249.

Rubino, Laura L., Valerie R. Anderson, and Nicole C. McKenna. 2021. Examining the disconnect in youth pathways and court responses: How bias invades across gender, race/ethnicity, and sexual orientation. *Feminist Criminology*, 16 (4): 480–503.

Salisbury, Emily J., Breanna Boppre, and Bridget Kelly. 2016. Gender-responsive risk and need assessment: Implications for the treatment of justice-involved women. In *Handbook on risk and need assessment*, edited by Faye S. Taxman, 236–259. New York: Routledge.

Sawyer, Wendy. 2018. *The gender divide: Tracking women's state prison growth*. Northampton, MA: Prison Policy Initiative.

Sawyer, Wendy, and Peter Wagner. 2022. *Mass Incarceration: The whole pie 2022*. Northampton, MA: Prison Policy Initiative.

Scroggins, Jennifer R., and Sara Malley. 2010. Reentry and the (unmet) needs of women. *Journal of Offender Rehabilitation*, 49 (2): 146–163.

The Sentencing Project. 2020. Incarcerated women and girls. Washington, DC: The Sentencing Project. https://www.sentencingproject.org/fact-sheet/incarcerated-women-and-girls/.

Siegler, Alison. 2021. *End mandatory minimums*. Washington, DC: Brennan Center for Justice.

Smith, I. E. 2016. Minority vs. minoritized: Why the noun just doesn't cut it. *The Odyssey*, September 16. https://www.theodysseyonline.com/minority-vs-minoritize.

Shih, Kristy Y., Elizabeth G. Holman, Daphne C. Hernandez, Chalandra M. Bryant, Tiffany L. Brown, and Miriam Mulsow. 2019. *Inclusion and diversity committee report: What's your social location? Highlights from the special session at the 2018 NCFR annual conference NCFR report*. Saint Paul, MN: National Council on Family Relations.

Singh, Sukhmani, Andrew Nalani, Deanna A. Ibrahim, Joshua G. Adler, Shabnam Javdani, and Erin Godfrey. 2021. When diversity is not enough: An intersectional examination of how juvenile legal system actors of color experience the system's welfare mandate for girls of color. *American Journal of Community Psychology*, 69 (1–2): 71–85.

Snyder, Howard N., and Melissa Sickmund. 2006. *Juvenile offenders and victims: 2006 national report*. Washington, DC: Office of Juvenile Justice and Delinquency Prevention.

Toldson, Ivory A., Kamilah M. Woodson, Ronald Braithwaite, Rhonda C. Holliday, and Mario De La Rosa. 2010. Academic potential among African American adolescents in juvenile detention centers: Implications for reentry to school. *Journal of Offender Rehabilitation*, 49 (8): 551–570.

Tomaskovic-Devey, Donald, and Patricia Warren. 2009. Explaining and eliminating racial profiling. *Contexts*, 8 (2): 34–39.

Ulmer, Jeffrey. 2018. Race, ethnicity, and sentencing. In *Oxford research encyclopedia of criminology and criminal justice*. Edited by Henry Pontell. New York: Oxford University Press.

Vallas, Rebecca, and Sharon Dietrich. 2014. *One strike and you're out: How we can eliminate barriers to economic security and mobility for people with criminal records*. Washington, DC: Center for American Progress.

Van Dieten, Marilyn. 2008. *Women offender case management model*. Washington DC: National Institute of Corrections.

Van Dieten, Marilyn, and Patricia MacKenna. 2001. *Moving On facilitator's guide*. Toronto: Orbis Partners.

Van Voorhis, Patricia. 2012. On behalf of women offenders: Women's place in the science of evidence-based practice. *Criminology & Public Policy*, 11:111.

Van Voorhis, Patricia, Ashley Bauman, Emily M. Wright, and Emily J. Salisbury. 2009. Implementing the women's risk/needs assessment (WRNAs): Early lessons from the field. *Women, Girls & Criminal Justice*, 10 (6): 81–96.

Van Voorhis, Patricia, Emily M. Wright, Emily Salisbury, and Ashley Bauman. 2010. Women's risk factors and their contributions to existing risk/needs assessment: The current status of a gender-responsive supplement. *Criminal Justice and Behavior*, 37 (3): 261–288.

Vaughn, Michael G., Leslie J. Sattler, and Katherine J. Holzer. 2022. Juvenile offenders. In *Clinical forensic psychology*, edited by Carlo Garofalo and Jelle J. Sijtsema, 377–395. Cham, Switzerland: Palgrave Macmillan.

Verona, Edelyn, Brett Murphy, and Shabnam Javdani. 2016. Gendered pathways: Violent childhood maltreatment, sex exchange, and drug use. *Psychology of Violence*, 6 (1): 124.

Ward, Geoff K. 2012. Birth of a juvenile court. In *The Black child-savers: Racial democracy and juvenile justice*, 77–103. Chicago: University of Chicago Press.

Watanabe, T. 2013. LAUSD issuing far fewer truancy tickets, report says. *Los Angeles Times*, November 3.

Williams, Jason M., Zoe Spencer, and Sean K. Wilson. 2021. I am not your felon: Decoding the trauma, resilience, and recovering mothering of formerly incarcerated Black women. *Crime & Delinquency*, 67 (8): 1103–1136.

Williams, Jason M., Sean K. Wilson, and Carrie Bergeson. 2019. "It's hard out here if you're a black felon": A critical examination of black male reentry. *The Prison Journal*, 99 (4): 437–458.

Williams, Jason M., Sean K. Wilson, and Carrie Bergeson. 2020. Health implications of incarceration and reentry on returning citizens: A qualitative examination of Black men's experiences in a northeastern city. *American Journal of Men's Health*, 14 (4): 1–16.

Willingham, Breea C. 2011. Black women's prison narratives and the intersection of race, gender, and sexuality in US prisons. *Critical Survey*, 23 (3): 55–66.

Wilmoth, Deborah. 2005. Mental health needs of women in prison: An international perspective with an Australian angle. *International Journal of Prisoner Health*, 1 (2–4): 249–254.

Wilson, David B., Catherine A. Gallagher, and Doris L. MacKenzie. 2000. A meta-analysis of corrections-based education, vocation, and work programs for adult offenders. *Journal of Research in Crime and Delinquency* 37 (4): 347–368.

Wooldredge, John, James Frank, Natalie Goulette, and Lawrence Travis III. 2015. Is the impact of cumulative disadvantage on sentencing greater for Black defendants? *Criminology & Public Policy*, 14 (2): 187–223.

Wright, Emily M., Patricia Van Voorhis, Ashley Bauman, and Emily Salisbury. 2007. *Gender-responsive risk/needs assessment: Final report*. Prepared for the Minnesota Department of Corrections and the Advisory Task Force on the Woman and Juvenile Female Offender in Corrections. Unpublished manuscript.

PART IV

ALTERNATIVES TO SYSTEM RESPONSES

This part examines how research evidence is being used to inform policy alternatives to more punitive system responses. It includes chapters that focus on micro- and macro-level efforts taking place outside of the system and that respond to the needs of neglected groups. There are seven chapters.

CHAPTER 19

EARLY PREVENTION AS AN ALTERNATIVE TO IMPRISONMENT
The Research Evidence on Monetary Costs and Benefits

BRANDON C. WELSH, HEATHER PATERSON, AND DAVID P. FARRINGTON

As part of a larger menu of strategies, both early prevention and imprisonment play an important role in reducing crime in society. Broadly conceived, early preventive interventions are designed to foster a wide array of prosocial life-course outcomes, as well as to help alleviate any number of negative outcomes, including criminal activity and associated consequences such as a sentence of incarceration (Farrington and Welsh 2007). In addition to the immediate protection of the public, imprisonment serves as a means of deterrence (general and specific) and also aims to rehabilitate the offender for successful reintegration to the community (MacKenzie 2006).

A large body of academic and policy research demonstrates that early prevention can be an effective and worthwhile (i.e., cost-beneficial) policy alternative to imprisonment (see e.g., Donohue and Siegelman 1998; Welsh and Farrington 2011; Drake and Knoth-Peterson, this volume). This is relevant to the larger debate on prevention versus punishment. Here, the central argument is that preventive interventions can steer children and youth away from a life of crime and, in turn, reduce society's reliance on the use of prison and other punitive sanctions (Welsh and Farrington 2012). This involves prevention in the first instance and interventions with children and adolescents who are starting to exhibit antisocial behaviors (e.g., in school, in the community, at home) and coming into conflict with the law.

Importantly, the research that is part of this debate—and which will be reviewed in this chapter—does not say that prisons cannot reduce crime or that governments at the local, state, and federal levels should let offenders out wholesale. Equally important is that early prevention does not represent a panacea or cure-all for the problems of delinquency and criminal offending. Instead, the research states in clear terms that "there are a number of worthwhile alternatives to prison that can help state [and other] governments lower their spending on prisons" (Welsh and Farrington 2011, 122S).

Hence, the question at the heart of this chapter is not so much whether early prevention can be a worthwhile policy alternative to imprisonment, but rather what is the breadth and order of magnitude of its economic returns to society? We set out to answer this question by updating, after a period of more than ten years, our prior work on the subject (Welsh and Farrington 2011). As with the previous work, this chapter focuses on the highest-quality research studies. In the case of evaluation research, this includes experimental and rigorous quasi-experimental designs. Also, we draw upon the most rigorous reviews of the literature (i.e., systematic reviews and meta-analyses) that only include high-quality studies. This ensures that our conclusions are based on the best available evidence (see Welsh and Mears, this volume).

This chapter is divided into six sections. The first section provides an overview of the economic costs of imprisonment, with a focus on the United States. This focus is due to the availability of robust cost data and as a way to capture the context of a large portion of the research reviewed in subsequent sections. The second section describes the policy tool of economic analysis, with special reference to benefit-cost analysis. The third section reports on the findings of benefit-cost analyses of early prevention programs that are targeted on delinquency and later criminal offending. Most of the programs have long-term follow-ups, spanning multiple stages of the life-course of participants, which provide a window into how economic benefits (relative to costs) change and whether they persist over time. The fourth section reviews the first generation of comprehensive studies that have examined the economic efficiency of early prevention compared to imprisonment. The fifth section is concerned with other (the next generation) research that has continued to investigate which policy option provides the best economic return for society. This section also looks at studies that are probing key economic issues central to this debate. The sixth and final section discusses implications for public policy.

I. Costs of Imprisonment

In the United States, federal, state, and local governments spent more than $89 billion on the correctional system in 2017 (latest data available; Buehler 2021). This translates to about $740 per household. During this year, approximately 1.5 million individuals were incarcerated (Bronson and Carson 2019). State and local governments accounted for a little more than 90% of these expenditures (Buehler 2021). These costs have gone up considerably in recent years; for example, in the last decade (from 2008 to 2017), spending on corrections increased by $14 billion.

The Prison Policy Initiative's 2017 report *Following the Money of Mass Incarceration* examined the financial burden of mass incarceration in the United States (Wagner and Rabuy 2017). Drawing on 2012 data from the Bureau of Justice Statistics, the report found that expenditures on public correctional agencies (prisons, jails, parole, and probation) exceeded $80 billion. Public corrections employees received the bulk of this expenditure ($38.4 billion). A substantial portion of correctional spending (approximately $16.1 billion in 2012) went toward inmate healthcare, food, and utilities. Construction costs and interest payments on past construction accounted for another $5.2 billion.

Importantly, this level of spending on prisons across the country is also causing a substantial drain on state and local government budgets, as well as diverting scarce resources from critical sectors like education, health, and social services. According to Wexler (2010), "[c]orrections expenditures compete with and diminish funding for education, public health, public safety, parks and recreation, and programs specifically designed to reduce the prison population." Not only do the high costs of incarceration divert funds away from these important endeavors, but former inmates are also more likely to have to rely on public services, such as Medicaid and Food Stamps. This is a result of high rates of unemployment and other difficulties they experience in returning to the community (Weidner and Schlutz 2020). An earlier study by Ellwood and Guetzkow (2009) found that state spending on corrections had an adverse effect on spending on welfare, but not in other areas, such as education and health.

II. Economic Analysis for Evidence-Based Policy

Economic analysis aims to provide a fair and reliable assessment of the value for money of programs, policies, and practices. It can be described as a policy tool that allows choices to be made between alternative uses of resources or alternative distributions of services (Knapp 1997, 11). It is a key component of evidence-based crime policy (Mears 2007, 2010). According to Drake and colleagues (2009, 194), "while determining whether a program reduces crime remains the necessary first condition for rational public policy making, an economic analysis constitutes the necessary additional condition for identifying viable and fiscally prudent options." Many criteria are used in economic analysis. The most common is efficiency or value for money (achieving maximum outcomes from minimum inputs). It is important to note that a focus on economic efficiency does not imply that programs should be continued only if their benefits outweigh their costs. Other non-economic criteria need to be considered, including equity in the distribution of services.

Benefit-cost and cost-effectiveness analysis are the two most widely used techniques of economic analysis. Only the former (the main focus of this chapter) allows for an assessment of both benefits and costs. A cost-effectiveness analysis can be referred to as an incomplete benefit-cost analysis. Cost-effectiveness analysis is incomplete because no attempt is made to estimate the monetary value of program effects (benefits or dis-benefits), only of program resources used (costs). Benefit-cost analysis, by contrast, monetizes both costs and benefits and compares them. Cost-effectiveness does, however, provide a point of comparison between program inputs or costs and outcomes (e.g., X dollars produced Y crimes prevented), thus permitting an assessment of which program represents the most desirable investment. Another way to think about how benefit-cost and cost-effectiveness analysis differ is that "cost-effectiveness analysis may help one decide among competing program models, but it cannot show that the total effect was worth the cost of the program" (Weinrott et al. 1982, 179), unlike benefit-cost analysis.

A benefit-cost analysis is a step-by-step process that follows a standard set of procedures. There are six steps: (a) define the scope of the analysis, (b) obtain estimates of program effects, (c) estimate the monetary value of costs and benefits, (d) calculate present value and assess profitability, (e) describe the distribution of costs and benefits (an assessment of who gains and who loses, e.g., program participants, government/taxpayer, crime victims), and (f) conduct sensitivity analyses by varying the different assumptions made. It is beyond the scope of this chapter to discuss each step. For a detailed explanation, see Barnett (1996), and for a discussion of methodological features of benefit-cost analysis, see Layard and Glaister (1994). That said, of central importance is the need to measure both the tangible costs of crime (e.g., the value of stolen goods) and the intangible costs (e.g., the distress and suffering caused to victims; see Cohen and Farrington 2021). Intangible costs can be measured by asking members of the public how much they are willing to pay to avoid being victimized.

Two other key features of benefit-cost analysis require brief mention. The first is that, in practical terms, a benefit-cost analysis is an extension of an outcome or impact evaluation, and is only as defensible as the evaluation on which it is based. Weimer and Friedman (1979, 264) recommended that benefit-cost analyses be limited to programs that have been evaluated with an "experimental or strong quasi-experimental design." (For more information on the importance of rigorous evaluation designs, see Welsh and Mears, this volume.)

The second key feature is that many perspectives can be taken in measuring program costs and benefits. Some benefit-cost analyses adopt a society-wide perspective that includes the major parties that can receive benefits or incur costs, such as the government or taxpayer, crime victim, and program participant. Other analyses may take a more narrow view, focusing on only one or two of these parties. The decision about which perspective to take has important implications for evaluating the program, particularly if it is being funded by public money. That is, if conclusions are to be drawn about the monetary value of a program to the public, the benefits and costs must be those that the public will either receive or incur (respectively). In addition, the perspective one takes can have important implications for the program's monetary value. For instance, adopting a societal perspective for a marginally effective program, and therefore increasing the number of parties to which benefits may accrue, will likely increase the chances that the program will produce a return rather than a loss on investment. On the other hand, if a benefit-cost analysis of the same program adopts a narrower perspective, the chances of producing a return rather than a loss on investment will likely decrease.

III. Early Prevention of Delinquency and Later Offending

There is a growing body of high-quality scientific evidence on the effectiveness of early childhood programs in preventing delinquency and later criminal offending (see Farrington 2021; Farrington et al. 2017; Welsh, Farrington, and Yohros 2022). Included in this evidence base are programs that have carried out benefit-cost analyses, which show that early prevention can be a worthwhile expenditure for program participants and families and society at-large (Welsh, Farrington, and Raffan Gowar 2015). We discuss several of the most prominent ones to illustrate the types of programs that have been found to be cost-beneficial.

One of the most well-known of these programs is Perry Preschool (Schweinhart et al. 2005). Carried out in the early 1960s in Ypsilanti, Michigan, 123 children were allocated (approximately at random) to treatment and control groups. The treatment children attended a daily preschool program taught by professional teachers, backed up by weekly home visits (by the teachers) usually lasting two years when children were 3 and 4 years of age. The aim of the "plan-do-review" program was to provide intellectual stimulation, to increase thinking and reasoning abilities, and to increase later school achievement.

The program had long-term benefits, extending up to age 50 (the latest follow-up). This follow-up analyzed the program's impact on criminal activity beyond adolescence (i.e., ages 20 to 50 years) or, as Heckman and Karapakula (2019, 43) call it, "life-course-persistent crime." Compared to the control group, men in the treatment group were significantly less likely to be convicted of a serious crime (7% vs. 30%). By age 50, 23% of the control group men had two or more convictions for violent misdemeanors compared to only 3% of the treatment group men.

Improvements were also found in many other important life-course outcomes. For example, between the ages of 26 and 40, treatment group participants (men and women) spent a greater amount of time employed (56% vs. 41.5%) and reported higher annual incomes. Heckman and Karapakula (2019) suggest that this is due to treatment group participants spending significantly less time incarcerated. For the first time, as part of the age-50 follow-up, participants received a number of health tests, indicating that treatment group men (compared to their control counterparts) had significantly lower levels of total cholesterol and arterial inflammation. They were also more likely to cook frequently or eat homemade meals and were less likely to be bedridden. Compared to their control counterparts, women in the treatment group exhibited lower levels of hair cortisol (indicating lower levels of long-term stress), were less likely to have diabetes or substance use disorder, and were more likely to exercise regularly. Tests to assess cognitive and noncognitive skills were also performed, concluding that treatment group males had significantly higher levels of executive functioning skills than control males.

These and other improvements over the life course translated into substantial financial benefits. A benefit-cost analysis at age 40 found that the Perry program yielded more than $17 of benefit per dollar of cost, with three-quarters (76%) of this returned to the general public—in the form of savings in crime, education, and welfare costs and increased tax revenue—and 24% benefiting program participants. Heckman and his colleagues' (2010) reanalysis found a slightly lower but still high return of $7 to $12 of benefit per dollar of cost.

For the age-50 follow-up, García and colleagues (2021) expanded the benefit-cost analysis to include intra- and intergenerational benefits, with a specific focus on siblings' and children's education, income, health, and criminal activity. It was estimated that $9 was returned to society for each $1 spent on the program. The authors speculate that the benefits from an increase in early childhood spending on treatment group participants extended beyond the individual and also impacted their families and children.

Like Perry, the Child-Parent Center (CPC) program in Chicago provided disadvantaged children, ages 3 to 4, with a high-quality, active learning preschool supplemented by family support. It also provided children with the educational enrichment component into elementary school, up to age 9. Begun in 1967, the CPC is the second oldest federal preschool program in the country (after Head Start) and the oldest "extended early intervention" program. It is located in 24 centers within high-poverty neighborhoods across Chicago.

A rigorous nonrandomized controlled design was used to evaluate the program, with a sample of more than 1,500 children. By age 26, the treatment group, compared to their control counterparts, had significantly lower rates of felony arrest (13.3% vs. 17.8%) and higher rates of school completion (79.7% vs. 72.9%) (Reynolds et al. 2011). An earlier evaluation found that the treatment group (compared to controls) also had lower rates of incarceration (21% vs. 26%) (Reynolds et al. 2007). A benefit-cost analysis of the program, which included some outcomes measured up to age 26 (crime was measured at age 18), found that, for every dollar spent on the program, the average return in benefits to society was $5.21, with a range of $2.11 to $7.20 (Reynolds et al. 2011). The majority of the monetary benefits were from reduced interaction with the criminal justice system (57%), followed by special education savings (19%), increased tax revenues (11%), reduced spending on child welfare (9%), and smaller benefits from increased grade retention and reduced depression (Reynolds et al. 2011). A more recent benefit-cost analysis, carried out when participants were 37 years old, focused on health outcomes. Based on lower rates of diabetes and smoking among treatment group participants compared to their control counterparts, it was found that, for every dollar spent on the program, between $1.35 and $3.66 was returned to society (Varshney, Temple, and Reynolds 2022).

Another program, the Carolina Abecedarian Project, targeted children born to low-income, multi-risk families. A sample of 111 children aged 3, mostly African American (98%), were randomly assigned either to receive full-time preschool child care (focusing on the development of cognitive and language skills) or not. Families of children in both the treatment and control groups received supportive social services as needed (Campbell et al. 2002). At age 21, 104 of the participants were interviewed, and it was found that fewer of the treatment group members compared to the controls (but not significantly so) reported being convicted for a misdemeanor offense (14% vs. 18%) or a felony offense (8% vs. 12%) or had been incarcerated (14% vs. 21%). Also, significantly fewer of the treatment group participants (compared to the controls) were regular marijuana users, significantly fewer had become a teenage parent, significantly more had attended college or university, and they had significantly higher-status jobs. A benefit-cost analysis found that, for every dollar spent on the program, $2.50 was saved to society (Barnett and Masse 2007).

Head Start, long considered the nation's most important early childhood program, which reaches about half of all impoverished children, has been the subject of a number of evaluations and benefit-cost analyses. A large-scale study of the long-term effects of Head Start, by Garces and colleagues (2002), found that children who attended Head Start (at ages 3 to 5) were significantly less likely to report being arrested or referred to court for a crime by ages 18 to 30 compared to their siblings who did not attend the program.

In one of the first benefit-cost analyses, Currie (2001) found that Head Start's short- and medium-term benefits could offset between 40% and 60% of its costs, and the addition of a small fraction of long-term benefits would make the program a worthwhile public investment. Ludwig and Phillips's (2008) review of the benefits and costs of Head Start, which drew upon the first report of the program's national randomized experiment and other studies, concluded that the program was a worthwhile investment of taxpayer dollars in both the short and long term. A more recent benefit-cost analysis, by Johnson and Jackson (2019), compared the efficiency of funding Head Start versus funding traditional K-12 education. The study's key finding was that, "for a district that spent $4,500 per-pupil (about 10 percent above the average K-12 spending level), the marginal dollar spent on Head Start led to between 1.5 and 2.5 times the improvement in adult outcomes as that spent on K-12 education" (Johnson and Jackson 2019, 346). The authors concluded that a transfer of funds from K-12 education toward Head Start would result in better average outcomes for youth.

Preventive interventions implemented during both prenatal and postnatal development also provide evidence of effectiveness and economic efficiency in preventing delinquency and later offending. The best example of one of these programs is the Nurse-Family Partnership (NFP). First tested in Elmira, New York, in the early 1980s, 400 first-time and disadvantaged mothers were randomly assigned to receive home visits from nurses during pregnancy, or to receive visits both during pregnancy and during the first two years of life, or to a control group who received no visits. The visits lasted about one hour and the mothers were visited on average every two weeks. The nurses gave advice about prenatal and postnatal care of the child, infant development, and the importance of proper nutrition and avoiding smoking and drinking during pregnancy.

The results of the experiment showed that prenatal plus postnatal home visits caused a significant decrease in recorded child physical abuse and neglect during the first two years of life, especially by poor, unmarried, teenage mothers; 4% of visited mothers versus 19% of nonvisited mothers of this type were guilty of child abuse or neglect (Olds et al. 1986). In a 15-year follow-up, which included 330 mothers and 315 children, significantly fewer treatment compared to control group mothers were identified as perpetrators of child abuse and neglect (29% vs. 54%; Olds et al. 1997). At the age of 15, children of the treatment mothers had incurred significantly fewer arrests than their control counterparts (20 as opposed to 45 per 100 children; Olds et al. 1998). In the latest follow-up at age 19, compared to their control counterparts, daughters of the full sample of mothers had incurred significantly fewer arrests and convictions and daughters of the higher-risk mothers had significantly fewer children of their own and less Medicaid use; few effects were observed for the sons (Eckenrode et al. 2010). Large-scale replication experiments of NFP in Memphis, Tennessee, and Denver, Colorado, have also shown desirable effects on a wide range of outcomes for both nurse-visited mothers and their children (Kitzman et al. 2010; Olds et al. 2014).

Drawing on a number of NFP sites from across the country, Miller (2013) carried out a benefit-cost analysis of the program. Analyses showed a favorable return of $2.90 for each dollar spent on the program, with monetary benefits derived from a wide range of improvements over the life course, including lower rates of youth criminal arrests and substance use, reduced use of governmental assistance programs like Medicaid and Food Stamps, and better health outcomes (Miller 2013). Miller's analysis was extensive and demonstrated that NFP also positively impacted mothers' outcomes. In addition to increasing birth spacing and reducing the number of subsequent births, some data suggested that NFP mothers experienced fewer convictions and domestic violence incidents, and had lower rates of depression (Miller 2013).

Benefit-cost analyses of a number of other early prevention programs targeted at different stages of the life-course provide further evidence of the value-for-money of this approach. These programs include the Seattle Social Development Project (SSDP; Hawkins et al. 2008), Stop Now and Plan (SNAP; Farrington and Koegl 2015), and Communities That Care (CTC; Kuklinski et al. 2021). SSDP, which aims to build social bonds among children in grades 1 through 6, yielded $2.25 for every $1 spent on the program. For SNAP, which aims to intervene and redirect negative behavioral patterns in youth, Farrington and Koegl (2015) estimated that it produced a return to society on the order of $2.05 to $3.75 per $1 spent on the program. This analysis was based on official convictions. Broadening the analysis to include self-reported offenses, the authors estimated that the benefit-to-cost ratio improved nearly eight-fold: between $17.33 and $31.77 were saved for every $1 spent. CTC is an empirically based operating system that aids communities in implementing evidence-based preventive interventions targeting risk and protective factors to improve the health of youth. Analyses based on primary outcomes found that CTC returned $12.88 to society for every $1 spent on the program. Approximately half of the monetary benefits were associated with crime reduction, 35% from increased earnings, and 16% from savings in healthcare costs (Kuklinski et al. 2021).

IV. Early Prevention versus Imprisonment

The benefit-cost analyses reviewed in the previous section provide important insights regarding the economic efficiency of early preventive interventions; these provide a key source of information for policymakers. Also important for policymakers is an understanding of the economic efficiency of *competing* policy options. That is, compared to imprisonment, as well as other forms of punishment, which one provides the best economic return for society? This section examines the first generation of studies that investigated this crucial policy question.

One of the most well known of these studies was conducted by the RAND Corporation (Greenwood et al. 1996). It assessed the cost-effectiveness (i.e., serious crimes prevented per $1 million spent, based on 1993 dollars) of California's new three-strikes law compared with four prevention and intervention strategies with demonstrated efficacy in reducing crime: a combination of home visits and day care, parent training, graduation incentives, and supervising delinquent youth. Each of these alternatives was based on well-known experiments with small to moderately large sample sizes.

The first step in the modeling process was the estimation of program costs and crime reduction effectiveness of the four alternatives. To conduct fair comparisons among these interventions and with the three-strikes law, three main "penalties" were assigned to the former. These were: (a) targeting: the proportion of the population targeted by the program who are likely to become involved in criminal behavior (e.g., children of low income, teenage mothers for the home visiting/day-care program); (b) decay: the loss of effectiveness after treatment ends; and (c) scale-up: the decrease in program effects from expanding the program statewide (Greenwood et al. 1996, 16).

Parent training and graduation incentives were the most cost-effective, while home visiting/day care was the least cost-effective. The number of serious crimes prevented per $1 million expended was estimated at 258 for graduation incentives, 157 for parent training, 72 for delinquent supervision, 60 for the three strikes law, and 11 for home visiting/day care. Crimes prevented were not calculated on a per annum basis. Instead they represent the predicted total effect produced by each program on each California cohort (an estimated 150,000 at-risk children born in California every year).

It is important to comment briefly on the poor showing of the home visiting/day care program. The small number of crimes prevented per $1 million is attributable to two key factors (a third is discussed below): first, the long-term delay in achieving an effect on crime, and second, the high cost of delivering the services, particularly the day-care component, which was estimated at $6,000 per child per year over four years.

Donohue and Siegelman (1998) carried out a thought experiment, which has some similarities to Washington State's comparative benefit-cost model. The authors set out to investigate if the "social resources that will be expended a decade or more from now on incarcerating today's youngsters could instead generate roughly comparable levels of crime *prevention* if they were spent today on the most promising social programs" (Donohue and Siegelman 1998, 31, emphasis in original). These included a range of early prevention programs and a national vocational program, and most of the estimates were based on well-known experiments or quasi-experiments with small to large sample sizes.

On the basis of a 50% increase in the US prison population over 15 years, assumed from the level in December 1993 and trends at the time, it was estimated that this policy would cost between $5.6 and $8 billion (in 1993 dollars) and result in a 5–15% reduction in crime. The next steps involved estimating the percentage of the cohort of 3-year-olds who could be served by allocating the saved prison costs (the $5.6 to $8 billion) to the different social programs and then estimating the crime reduction benefits that could be achieved by selected programs under a range of targeting conditions (i.e., the worst 6% of delinquents, males only, and young Black males only). Two early prevention programs were selected: the Perry Preschool project and the Syracuse University Family Development Research program (Lally, Mangione, and Honig 1988). It is at this stage that the authors apply a scaling-up penalty of 50% to each program. This had the result of reducing Perry's crime reduction effectiveness from 40% to 20% and Syracuse's effectiveness from 70% to 35%.

The authors found that both early prevention programs could achieve reductions in crime that were within the range of what was expected from a continuation of the prison policy of the day (5–15%), even if they were allocated the lower bound amount that would have been spent on prisons ($5.6 billion). This was considered the worst-case scenario. In the best-case scenario, which did not include the scaling-up penalty and allocated the upper bound amount of prison spending ($8 billion), the Perry and Syracuse programs produced crime reductions of 21% and 26%, respectively.

Nagin (2001) reexamined the studies by Greenwood et al. (1996) and Donohue and Siegelman (1998). One of his main concerns was that these studies failed to consider the full potential benefits of the early prevention programs. By its very nature, developmental crime prevention is designed to improve individual functioning across multiple domains. Indeed, this is precisely what evaluations of the included programs showed. But the two studies only considered the benefits from lower rates of delinquent and criminal activity. Educational, employment, family, health, and other important benefits were not taken into account, which had the effect of greatly reducing the measured economic return to society.

This point is made clear in another RAND study by Karoly and colleagues (1998). In the case of the Nurse-Family Partnership program, for example, which was used in the study by Greenwood et al. (1996), an analysis of the distribution of benefits accruing to government revealed that more than half (57%) of the benefits were caused by a reduction in welfare costs, almost one-quarter (23%) were due to tax revenue from increased employment income, 20% were caused by a reduction in juvenile and criminal justice costs, and less than

1% were due to a reduction in healthcare services. These conclusions are based on a conservative benefit-cost analysis which found that, in the home visits program, benefits exceeded costs by a ratio of 4.1:1. Another benefit-cost analysis by Donohue (2009, 308) embraced this view, concluding that "there is reason to believe that alternatives to incarceration might well be more socially attractive than our current reliance on incarceration as the predominant crime-fighting strategy."

Unquestionably, the most important body of research in this area is the Washington State Institute for Public Policy's ongoing comparative benefit-cost model (see Drake and Knoth-Peterson, this volume). In 1997, the Washington State Legislature commissioned the institute, the nonpartisan research arm of the legislature, to assess the effectiveness and economic efficiency of a range of crime prevention and criminal justice programs, with the aim to "identify interventions that reduce crime and lower total costs to taxpayers and crime victims" (Aos, Barnoski, and Lieb 1998, 1). The institute developed a comprehensive benefit-cost model along the lines of a "bottom line" financial analysis, which it considered to parallel the approach used by investors who study rates of return on financial investments (Drake, Aos, and Miller 2009).

The institute's research began with a systematic review of experimental and high-quality quasi-experimental studies, carried out in conjunction with the University of Washington's Social Development Research Group. A five-step analytical model was then used to describe each program's economic contribution. The first step of the model involved estimating each program's effectiveness, and meta-analytic techniques were used. Effect sizes were converted into numbers of crimes saved. Step two looked at whether previously measured program results could be replicated in Washington State. Step three involved an assessment of program costs, estimated on the basis of what it would cost the state government to implement a similar program (if the program was not already operating in the state). Step four involved monetizing each program's effects on crime. The final step involved calculating the economic contribution of the program, which is expressed as a benefit-cost ratio and in net present value. Programs can be judged on their independent and comparative economic efficiency.

What started out as a highly rigorous yet fairly modest policy research initiative soon turned into the most comprehensive approach to develop evidence-based crime policy in the country (Greenwood 2006). Following the institute's first set of reports, the legislature authorized a number of system-level randomized controlled trials of the most effective and cost-beneficial juvenile and adult intervention programs. The results of these trials helped to refine local practice and service delivery. By 2006, the institute had systematically reviewed and analyzed almost 600 of the highest-quality evaluations of crime prevention and criminal justice programs, estimated the costs and benefits of effective programs, and "projected the degree to which alternative 'portfolios' of these programs could affect future prison construction needs, criminal justice costs, and crime rates in Washington" (Aos, Miller, and Drake 2006, 1). This work was commissioned by the legislature to address the projected need for two new state prisons by 2020 and possibly a third by 2030.

Based on a moderate-to-aggressive portfolio of evidence-based programs (i.e., $63–$171 million expenditure in the first year), it was found that a significant proportion of future prison construction costs could be avoided, about $2 billion saved by taxpayers, and crime rates lowered slightly (Aos, Miller, and Drake 2006, 16). In the following year, the state legislature abandoned plans to build one of the two prisons and in its place approved a sizeable spending package ($48 million) on evidence-based crime prevention and intervention programs (Drake, Aos, and Miller 2009). This research showed that other strategies were more effective than prison and would generate substantial financial savings to the state government and taxpayers.

V. Other Economic Research

A wide range of other economic studies have also investigated the crucial question of which policy option provides the best economic return for society, in addition to probing key issues central to this debate. A number of benefit-cost analyses of standard prison and other sentencing alternatives demonstrate that prisons are not economically efficient (see Bierie 2009; Marsh and Fox 2008; McDougall et al. 2008). One of these studies, by Zarkin and colleagues (2012), found that diverting offenders to community-based substance abuse treatment rather than prison can be a key way to conserve financial resources. According to the authors, approximately 50% of state prisoners in the United States meet the criteria for drug abuse or dependence, but only 10% at most receive treatment during incarceration. Based on a dynamic lifetime simulation model of a nationally representative sample of 1.14 million incarcerated individuals, the study found that diverting 40% of these prisoners from incarceration to community-based treatment produced a lifetime societal net benefit of $22.5 billion. Diverting as few as 10% of eligible offenders generated a lifetime societal net benefit of $8.5 billion.

A common concern with using alternative sentences or reducing prison populations is that it will negatively impact public safety. Sundt and colleagues (2016) investigated this concern by examining crime rates in California immediately before and after the enactment of the California Public Safety Realignment Act, a law enacted to alleviate prison overcrowding and reduce the state corrections budget. In a period of 15 months, the prison population was reduced by 27,527 inmates and overcrowding declined from 181% to 150%, resulting in savings of approximately $453 million in 2012. Between 2012 and 2014, there was no change in state violent or property crime rates. The authors concluded that, "[w]ith a mixture of jail use, community corrections, law enforcement and other preventive efforts, California counties have provided a comparable level of safety to that previously achieved by state prisons" (Sundt, Salisbury, and Harmon 2016, 316).

The potential savings in incarceration costs were the focus of a simulation model, by Ebel et al. (2011), which estimated the extent to which the US homicide rate might be reduced by implementing a number of developmental and community crime prevention programs. Of particular interest were the Nurse-Family Partnership, Perry Preschool, and Multisystemic Therapy (Sawyer and Borduin 2011). The authors estimated the effects of these programs on arrests for violence, combined this information with data from the Pittsburgh Youth Study on the probability of an arrest for violence being followed by a homicide conviction, and scaled up to national US homicide figures. The effectiveness of the programs was scaled down by half to allow for attenuation of effects from demonstration projects to national implementation. Based on 2002 figures, it was estimated that these three prevention programs, implemented nationally and consecutively, could prevent one-third of all US homicides. It was also estimated that the programs could save 4,200 lives, nearly 80,000 years of potential life lost, and save almost 225,000 person-years of incarceration, which amounts to over $5 billion per year in savings in incarceration costs.

Another important line of research has involved the use of the methodology of public opinion polling known as "contingent valuation," which has many advantages over conventional polling methods. The contingent valuation approach allows for the "comparison of respondents' willingness to pay for competing policy alternatives" (Nagin et al. 2006, 629). In a large-scale study of public preferences for responses to juvenile offending in Pennsylvania, Nagin and colleagues found that the public values early prevention and offender treatment significantly more than increased incarceration. Households were willing to pay an average of $126 in additional taxes on nurse home visitation programs to prevent delinquency compared to $81 on longer sentences. Additionally, households were willing to pay more in taxes for offender treatment programs than for longer sentences: $98 versus $81. At the state level, public support for the prevention option translated into $601 million that hypothetically could be used to prevent delinquency, compared to $387 million for longer sentences for juvenile offenders.

In another contingent valuation study to gauge the public's preferences for a range of alternative responses to crime, Cohen and colleagues (2006) found that the public overwhelmingly supported increased spending of tax dollars on youth prevention programs compared to building more prisons. Public support for spending more taxes on drug treatment for nonviolent offenders as well as on police also ranked higher than support for building more prisons, but not as high as for youth prevention programs. Many other studies show public support for allocating money to early prevention rather than to building more prisons (see Cullen et al. 2007; Roberts and Hastings 2012).

Studies on the costs of crime can also make important contributions to assessing the benefits and costs of early prevention compared to prison. It is important to note that high crime costs do not themselves suggest a policy solution. For this we need to carry out an economic analysis, preferably a benefit-cost analysis (see Miller et al. 2021). What these cost studies do is provide information on the unit costs of crime as well as the order of magnitude of the problem. Cohen and Piquero (2009) estimated that the typical criminal career over the juvenile and adult years costs society between $2.1 and $3.7 million (in 2007 dollars). In 2022 dollars (and accounting for inflation), these costs are $2.9 and $5.2 million, respectively. The authors also estimated the dollar costs of the associated problem behaviors of heavy drug use and dropping out of high school, bringing the total societal cost of a high-risk youth to $3.6 to $6.2 million (in 2022 dollars).

In a follow-on study that looked at the costs of crime across offender trajectories for a real-life cohort in Philadelphia, Cohen and colleagues (2010) found that the 200 high-rate chronic offenders cost society more than $281 million (in 2022 dollars). Based on another real-life cohort of 500 Pittsburgh boys, Welsh and colleagues (2008) conservatively estimated that this group caused a substantial burden of harm to society in the form of victimization costs, ranging from $89 to $110 million (in 2000 dollars). From an early age the cohort was responsible for substantial crime victim losses, with these losses mounting in the teen years. Similar results have been obtained in other countries. For example, Raffan Gowar and Farrington (2013) estimated that the 400 males in the Cambridge Study in Delinquent Development cost £6 million (approximately $9 million) in officially recorded offending and £44 million (approximately $66 million) according to self-reported offending over 13 years (in 2012 dollars).

VI. Discussion and Conclusions

The question at the heart of this chapter is not so much whether early prevention can be a worthwhile policy option to imprisonment, but rather what is the breadth and order of magnitude of its economic returns to society? To address this question we reviewed (a) the latest benefit-cost analyses of early prevention programs, some with long-term follow-ups over the life course; (b) the first generation of studies that have examined the economics of early prevention compared to imprisonment, including Washington State's ongoing comparative benefit-cost model; and (c) a wide range of other research studies that are generating important insights on the economics of imprisonment and alternative strategies.

Based on the highest-quality research evidence, we found clear and substantial support for policy options that emphasize early prevention and limit the use of imprisonment. Importantly, the economic returns of early prevention compared to imprisonment are sizable, wide-reaching (i.e., cascading over multiple domains), and can be long-lasting, with some studies showing economic benefits accruing well into midlife. So important is the latter that one program's report is titled *Lifetime Effects* (Schweinhart et al. 2005).

It is of course naïve to think that the research evidence in support of early prevention compared to imprisonment will be the sole influence on policy. There are many considerations involved in the policymaking process, ranging from the relative importance of crime in society to particular views or biases held about one approach compared with another. Of central concern here is the importance, for rational policy, of putting research evidence at center stage in the policymaking process. But we must be mindful that the linkages between research and policy are sometimes less than clear, with evaluation influence on policy taking a number of different routes (see Weiss, Murphy-Graham, and Birkeland 2005; Zane, this volume).

Another challenge that confronts early crime prevention is the worry by politicians that they may be perceived as "soft on crime" by supporting prevention instead of punishment-oriented measures. Similarly, early prevention is sometimes equated with social welfare. Like the dismantling of federal welfare in the United States in the 1990s and concerns about the Affordable Health Care Act, early prevention could be seen as just another taxpayer-subsidized handout that is not deserved. However, supporting a policy stance to get elected while ignoring or mischaracterizing research runs counter to the public good.

The good news is that the evidence-based movement is making strides toward breaking down or tempering the soft-on-crime concern. Instead of emotions and opinions, facts and evidence are becoming the new currency in federal, state, and local debates about crime policy (Welsh, Zane, and Mears, this volume). As shown in the present chapter, there is a growing emphasis on taking account of financial costs and benefits in formulating public policies. It may take some time, but the slogan "get tough on crime" may one day be replaced with "get smart on crime," or "reduce crime in the most cost-effective way." The public should demand that their tax dollars are invested more efficiently.

Yet another challenge that confronts early prevention is that the benefits from reduced crime will not be apparent for a number of years—at least until children reach adolescence. This can conflict with the short time horizons of politicians; that is, programs that show results only in the longer term can be unappealing to those who have to face re-election every few years. One potential remedy to this situation is to educate politicians about the many other desirable effects that these preventive interventions can produce in the short term. For example, preschool intellectual enrichment and home visitation programs show improvements in school readiness and school performance on the part of the children, greater employment and educational opportunities for parents, and increased family stability. These short-term benefits alone can translate into substantial cost savings for government.

The problem of the short time horizons of politicians is not restricted to crime policy. Ludwig (2012) suggests applying ideas from other policy areas to early crime prevention. For example, in the area of government budgeting, this same problem has led to calls for "'intergenerational accounting'—the idea that we should think about government expenditure and revenues as flows over long periods of time, and make clear to the public the impact that different policy decisions will have on these long-term flows" (37). Another suggestion is to expand the definition of gross domestic product in order to account for nonmonetary considerations, such as the "value of a country's stock of environmental quality" (37). When people invest, they are not necessarily looking for quick results but for long-term benefits. Government policymakers should also be able to defer gratification, plan for the future, and think about what legacy they are leaving to the next generation.

References

Aos, Steve, Robert Barnoski, and Roxanne Lieb. 1998. Preventive programs for young offenders effective and cost-effective. *Overcrowded Times*, 9 (2): 1, 7–11.

Aos, Steve, Marna G. Miller, and Elizabeth K. Drake. 2006. *Evidence-based public policy options to reduce future prison construction, criminal justice costs, and crime rates*. Olympia: Washington State Institute for Public Policy.

Baker, Thomas, Hayley M. D. Cleary, Justin T. Pickett, and Mark G. Gertz. 2016. Crime salience and public willingness to pay for child saving and juvenile punishment. *Crime & Delinquency*, 62:645–668.

Barnett, W. Steven. 1996. *Lives in the balance: Age-27 benefit-cost analysis of the High/Scope Perry Preschool program*. Ypsilanti, MI: High/Scope Press.

Barnett, W. Steven, and Leonard N. Masse. 2007. Comparative benefit-cost analysis of the Abecedarian program and its policy implications. *Economics of Education Review*, 26:113–125.

Bierie, David. 2009. Cost matters: A randomized experiment comparing recidivism between two styles of prisons. *Journal of Experimental Criminology*, 5:371–397.

Bronson, Jennifer, and E. Ann Carson. 2019. *Prisoners in 2017*. Washington, DC: Bureau of Justice Statistics.

Buehler, Emily. 2021. *Justice expenditure and employment extracts, 2017—preliminary*. Washington, DC: Bureau of Justice Statistics.

Campbell, Francis A., Craig T. Ramey, Elizabeth Pungello, Joseph Sparling, and Shari Miller-Johnson. 2002. Early childhood education: Young adult outcomes from the Abercedarian project. *Applied Developmental Science*, 6:42–57.

Cohen, Mark A., and David P. Farrington. 2021. Appropriate measurement and use of "costs of crime" in policy analysis: Benefit-cost analysis of criminal justice policies has come of age. *Journal of Policy Analysis and Management*, 40:286–293.

Cohen, Mark A., and Alex R. Piquero. 2009. New evidence on the monetary value of saving a high risk youth. *Journal of Quantitative Criminology*, 25:25–49.

Cohen, Mark A., Alex R. Piquero, and Wesley G. Jennings. 2010. Studying the costs of crime across offender trajectories. *Criminology & Public Policy*, 9:279–305.

Cohen, Mark A., Roland T. Rust, and Sara Steen. 2006. Prevention, crime control or cash? Public preferences towards criminal justice spending priorities. *Justice Quarterly*, 23:21–39.

Cullen, Francis T., Brenda A. Vose, Cheryl N. Lero Jonson, and James P. Unnever. 2007. Public support for early intervention: Is child saving a "habit of the heart"? *Victims and Offenders*, 2:109–124.

Currie, Janet. 2001. Early childhood education programs. *Journal of Economic Perspectives*, 15:213–238.

Donohue, John J. 2009. Assessing the relative benefits of incarceration: Overall changes and the benefits on the margin. In *Do prisons make us safer? The benefits and costs of the prison boom*, edited by Steven Raphael and Michael A. Stoll, 269–341. New York: Russell Sage Foundation.

Donohue, John J., and Peter Siegelman. 1998. Allocating resources among prisons and social programs in the battle against crime. *Journal of Legal Studies*, 27:1–43.

Drake, Elizabeth K., Steve Aos, and Marna G. Miller. 2009. Evidence-based public policy options to reduce crime and criminal justice costs: Implications in Washington State. *Victims and Offenders*, 4:170–196.

Duncan, Greg J., and Katherine Magnuson. 2004. Individual and parent-based intervention strategies for promoting human capital and positive behavior. In *Human development across lives and generations*, edited by P. Lindsay Chase-Lansdale, Kathleen Kiernan, and Ruth J. Friedman, 93–135. New York: Cambridge University Press.

Ebel, Beth E., Frederick P. Rivara, Rolf Loeber, and Dustin A. Pardini. 2011. Modeling the impact of preventive interventions on the national homicide rate. In *Young homicide offenders and victims: Risk factors, prediction, and prevention from childhood*, edited by Rolf Loeber and David P. Farrington, 123–135. New York: Springer.

Eckenrode, John, Mary Campa, Dennis W. Luckey, Charles R. Henderson, Robert Cole, Harriet Kitzman, et al. 2010. Long-term effects of prenatal and infancy nurse home visitation on the life course of youths: 19-year follow-up of a randomized trial. *Archives of Pediatrics and Adolescent Medicine*, 164:9–15.

Ellwood, John W., and Joshua Guetzkow. 2009. Footing the bill: Causes and budgetary consequences of state spending on corrections. In *Do prisons make us safer? The benefits and costs of the prison boom*, edited by Steven Raphael and Michael A. Stoll, 207–238. New York: Russell Sage Foundation.

Farrington, David P. 2021. The developmental evidence base: Prevention. In *Forensic psychology*. 3rd ed., edited by David A. Crighton and Graham J. Towl, 263–293. Chichester, UK: Wiley.

Farrington, David P., Hannah Gaffney, Friedrich Lösel, and Maria M. Ttofi. 2017. Systematic reviews of the effectiveness of developmental prevention programs in reducing delinquency, aggression, and bullying. *Aggression and Violent Behavior*, 33:91–106.

Farrington, David P., and Christopher J. Koegl. 2015. Monetary benefits and costs of the Stop Now And Plan program for boys aged 6–11, based on the prevention of later offending. *Journal of Quantitative Criminology*, 31:263–287.

Farrington, David P., and Brandon C. Welsh. 2007. *Saving children from a life of crime: Early risk factors and effective interventions*. New York: Oxford University Press.

Garces, Eliana, Duncan Thomas, and Janet Currie. 2002. Longer-term effects of Head Start. *American Economic Review*, 92:999–1012.

García, Jorge L., Frederik H. Bennhoff, Duncan Ermini Leaf, and James J. Heckman. 2021. The dynastic benefits of early childhood education. Working paper. Chicago: Becker Friedman Institute for Economics, University of Chicago.

Greenwood, Peter W. 2006. *Changing lives: Delinquency prevention as crime-control policy*. Chicago: University of Chicago Press.

Greenwood, Peter W., Karyn E. Model, C. Peter Rydell, and James Chiesa. 1996. *Diverting children from a life of crime: Measuring costs and benefits*. Santa Monica, CA: RAND.

Hawkins, J. David, Rick Kosterman, Richard F. Catalano, Karl G. Hill, and Robert D. Abbott. 2008. Effects of social development intervention in childhood 15 years later. *Archives of Pediatrics and Adolescent Medicine*, 162:1133–1141.

Heckman, James J., and Ganesh Karapakula. 2019. The Perry Preschoolers at late midlife: A study in design-specific inference. Working paper. Cambridge, MA: National Bureau of Economic Research.

Heckman, James J., Seong Hyeok Moon, Rodrigo Pinto, Peter A. Savelyev, and Adam Yavitz. 2010. The rate of return to the HighScope Perry Preschool program. *Journal of Public Economics*, 94:114–128.

Johnson, Rucker C., and C. Kirabo Jackson. 2019. Reducing inequality through dynamic complementarity: Evidence from Head Start and public school spending. *American Economic Journal: Economic Policy*, 11:310–349.

Karoly, Lynn A., Peter W. Greenwood, Susan S. Everingham, Jill Houbé, M. Rebecca Kilburn, C. Peter Rydell, Matthew Sanders, and James Chiesa. 1998. *Investing in our children: What we know and don't know about the costs and benefits of early childhood interventions*. Santa Monica, CA: RAND.

Kitzman, Harriett J., David L. Olds, Robert E. Cole, Carole E. Hanks, Elizabeth A. Anson, Kimberly J. Arcoleo, et al. 2010. Enduring effects of prenatal and infancy home visiting by nurses on children: Follow-up of a randomized trial among children at age 12 years. *Archives of Pediatrics and Adolescent Medicine*, 164:412–418.

Knapp, Martin. 1997. Economic evaluations and interventions for children and adolescents with mental health problems. *Journal of Child Psychology and Psychiatry*, 38:3–25.

Kuklinski, Margaret R., Sabrina Oesterle, John S. Briney, and J. David Hawkins. 2021. Long-term impacts and benefit-cost analysis of the Communities That Care prevention system at age 23, 12 years after baseline. *Prevention Science*, 22:452–463.

Lally, J. Ronald, Peter L. Mangione, and Alice S. Honig. 1988. The Syracuse University Family Development Research Program: Long-range impact of an early intervention with low-income children and their families. In *Parent education as early childhood intervention: Emerging directions in theory, research and practice*, edited by D. R. Powell, 79–104. Norwood, NJ: Ablex.

Layard, Richard, and Stephen Glaister, eds. 1994. *Cost-benefit analysis*. 2nd ed. New York: Cambridge University Press.

Ludwig, Jens. 2012. Cost-effective crime prevention. In *Contemporary issues in criminological theory and research: The role of social institutions*, edited by Richard Rosenfeld, Kenna Quinet, and Crystal Garcia, 29–39. Belmont, CA: Wadsworth.

Ludwig, Jens, and Deborah A. Phillips. 2008. Long-term effects of Head Start on low-income children. *Annals of the New York Academy of Sciences*, 1136:257–268.

MacKenzie, Doris Layton. 2006. *What works in corrections: Reducing the criminal activities of offenders and delinquents*. New York: Cambridge University Press.

Marsh, Kevin, and Chris Fox. 2008. The benefit and cost of prisons in the UK: The results of a model of lifetime re-offending. *Journal of Experimental Criminology*, 4:403–423.

McDougall, Cynthia, Mark A. Cohen, Raymond B. Swaray, and Amanda Perry. 2008. Benefit-cost analyses of sentencing. *Campbell Systematic Reviews*, 2008:10.

Mears, Daniel P. 2007. Towards rational and evidence-based crime policy. *Journal of Criminal Justice* 35:667–682.

Mears, Daniel P. 2010. *American criminal justice policy: An evaluation approach to increasing accountability and effectiveness*. New York: Cambridge University Press.

Miller, Ted. R. 2013. *Nurse-Family Partnership home visitation: Costs, outcomes, and return on investment*. Beltsville, MD: H.B.S.A.

Miller, Ted R., Mark A. Cohen, David I. Swedler, Bina Ali, and Delia Hendrie. 2021. Incidence and costs of personal and property crimes in the USA, 2017. *Journal of Benefit-Cost Analysis*, 12:24–54.

Nagin, Daniel S. 2001. Measuring economic benefits of developmental prevention programs. In *Costs and benefits of preventing crime*, edited by Brandon C. Welsh, David P. Farrington, and Lawrence W. Sherman, 251–68. Boulder, CO: Westview Press.

Nagin, Daniel S., Alex R. Piquero, Elizabeth S. Scott, and Laurence Steinberg. 2006. Public preferences for rehabilitation versus incarceration of juvenile offenders: Evidence from a contingent valuation survey. *Criminology & Public Policy*, 5:627–652.

Olds, David L., Charles R. Henderson, Robert Chamberlin, and Robert Tatelbaum. 1986. Preventing child abuse and neglect: A randomized trial of nurse home visitation. *Pediatrics*, 78:65–78.

Olds, David L., John Eckenrode, Charles R. Henderson, Harriet Kitzman, Jane Powers, Robert Cole, Kimberly Sidora, Pamela Morris, Lisa M. Pettitt, and Dennis W. Luckey. 1997. Long-term effects of home visitation on maternal life course and child abuse and neglect: Fifteen-year follow-up of a randomized trial. *Journal of the American Medical Association*, 278:637–643.

Olds, David L., Charles R. Henderson, Robert Cole, John Eckenrode, Harriet Kitzman, Dennis W. Luckey, Lisa M. Pettitt, Kimberly Sidora, Pamela Morris, and Jane Powers. 1998. Long-term effects of nurse home visitation on children's criminal and antisocial behavior: 15-year follow-up of a randomized controlled trial. *Journal of the American Medical Association*, 280:1238–1244.

Olds, David L., John R. Holmberg, Nancy Donelan-McCall, Dennis W. Luckey, Michael D. Knudtson, and JoAnn Robinson. 2014. Effects of home visits by paraprofessionals and by nurses on children: Follow-up of a randomized trial at ages 6 and 9 years. *Journal of the American Medical Association Pediatrics*, 168:114–121.

Raffan Gowar, B., and David P. Farrington. 2013. The monetary cost of criminal careers. In *Kriminologie, kriminalpolitik, strafrecht (Criminology, crime policy, penal law)*, edited by Klaus Boers, Thomas Feltes, Joerg Kinzig, Lawrence W. Sherman, Franz Streng, and Gerson Trueg, 441–456. Tubingen, Germany: Mohr Siebeck.

Reynolds, Arthur J., Judy A. Temple, and Suh-Ruu Ou. 2003. School-based early intervention and child well-being in the Chicago Longitudinal Study. *Child Welfare*, 82:633–656.

Reynolds, Arthur J., Judy A. Temple, Suh-Ruu Ou, Dylan L. Robertson, Joshua P. Mersky, James W. Topitzes, et al. 2007. Effects of a school-based, early childhood intervention on adult health and well-being. *Archives of Pediatrics and Adolescent Medicine*, 161:730–739.

Reynolds, Arthur J., Judy A. Temple, Barry A. B. White, Suh-Ruu Ou, and Dylan L. Robertson. 2011. Age 26 cost-benefit analysis of the Child-Parent Center early education program. *Child Development*, 81:379–404.

Roberts, Julian V., and Ross Hastings. 2012. Public opinion and crime prevention: A review of international trends. In *The Oxford handbook of crime prevention*, edited by Brandon C. Welsh and David P. Farrington, 487–507. New York: Oxford University Press.

Sawyer, Aaron M., and Charles M. Borduin. 2011. Effects of Multisystemic Therapy through midlife: A 21.9-year follow-up to a randomized clinical trial with serious and violent juvenile offenders. *Journal of Consulting and Clinical Psychology*, 79:643–652.

Schweinhart, Lawrence J., Jeanne Montie, Zongping Xiang, W. Steven Barnett, Clive R. Belfield, and Milagros Nores. 2005. *Lifetime effects: The High/Scope Perry Preschool study through age 40*. Ypsilanti, MI: High/Scope Press.

Sundt, Jody, Emily J. Salisbury, and Mark G. Harmon. 2016. Is downsizing prisons dangerous? The effect of California's Realignment Act on public safety. *Criminology & Public Policy*, 15:315–341.

Varshney, Nishank, Judy A. Temple, and Arthur J. Reynolds. 2022. Early education and adult health: Age 37 impacts and economic benefits of the Child-Parent Center preschool program. *Journal of Benefit-Cost Analysis*, 13:57–90.

Wagner, Peter, and Bernadette Rabuy. 2017. *Following the money of mass incarceration*. Northampton, MA: Prison Policy Initiative. https://www.prisonpolicy.org/reports/money.html.

Weidner, Robert, and Jennifer Schultz. 2020. Examining the relationship between incarceration and population health: The roles of region and urbanicity. *Criminal Justice Policy Review*, 32:403–426.

Weimer, David L., and Lee S. Friedman. 1979. Efficiency considerations in criminal rehabilitation research: Costs and consequences. In *The rehabilitation of criminal offenders: Problems and prospects*, edited by Lee Sechrest, Susan O. White, and Elizabeth D. Brown, 251–272. Washington, DC: National Academy of Sciences.

Weinrott, Mark R., Richard R. Jones, and James R. Howard. 1982. Cost-effectiveness of teaching family programs for delinquents: Results of a national evaluation. *Evaluation Review*, 6:173–201.

Weiss, Carol H., Erin Murphy-Graham, and Sarah Birkeland. 2005. An alternative route to policy influence: How evaluations affect D.A.R.E. *American Journal of Evaluation*, 26:12–30.

Welsh, Brandon C., and David P. Farrington. 2011. The benefits and costs of early prevention compared with imprisonment: Toward evidence-based policy. *Prison Journal*, 91 (3): 120S–137S.

Welsh, Brandon C., and David P. Farrington. 2012. Science, politics, and crime prevention: Toward a new crime policy. *Journal of Criminal Justice*, 40:128–133.

Welsh, Brandon C., David P. Farrington, and B. Raffan Gowar. 2015. Benefit-cost analysis of crime prevention programs. *Crime and Justice*, 44:447–516.

Welsh, Brandon C., David P. Farrington, and Alexis Yohros. 2022. Preventing delinquency and later criminal offending. In *The Cambridge handbook of forensic psychology*, edited by Jennifer M. Brown and Miranda A. H. Horvath, 627–642. Cambridge: Cambridge University Press.

Welsh, Brandon C., Rolf Loeber, Bradley R. Stevens, Magda Stouthamer-Loeber, Mark A. Cohen, and David P. Farrington. 2008. Costs of juvenile crime in urban areas: A longitudinal perspective. *Youth Violence and Juvenile Justice*, 6:3–27.

Wexler, Harry. 2010. An opportunity to reform the criminal justice system. *Los Angeles Times*, January 20.

Zarkin, Gary A., Alexander J. Cowell, Katherine A. Hicks, Michael J. Mills, Steven Belenko, Laura J. Dunlap, and Vincent Keyes. 2012. Lifetime benefits and costs of diverting substance-abusing offenders from state prison. *Crime & Delinquency*, 61:829–850.

CHAPTER 20

EVIDENCE-BASED INTERVENTION PROGRAMS TARGETING ANTISOCIAL CHILDREN AND YOUTH IN NORWAY
Parent Management Training—Oregon Model (PMTO)

TERJE OGDEN, ELISABETH ASKELAND, AND KRISTINE AMLUND-HAGEN

The philosophies of dealing with juvenile delinquents vary between countries. While some countries have adopted a welfare philosophy, others apply a more punishment-oriented approach, emphasizing youth accountability and deterrence. Norway, as one of the Scandinavian countries, practices a mix of justice- and welfare-based principles. Norway has no formal juvenile court or juvenile justice system, and offenders under the age of 15 years are usually dealt with by the child welfare system. The age of criminal responsibility is 15 years, and even if those aged 15 to17 years are formally the responsibility of the adult criminal system, most of the adolescents in this age group are also transferred to the child welfare services or diverted to treatment community service or mediation programs. The child welfare system can provide a wide range of interventions that are stepped up gradually, according to the seriousness of the youth's situation. According to the Norwegian Welfare Act, voluntary preventive measures in the home and local community must be prioritized and child welfare services have to consider whether family-based interventions could be implemented rather than placement out of home (McCart, Ogden, and Henggeler 2013).

During the 1990s, media and public attention in Norway focused on youth violence and the disappointing outcomes of publicly funded out-of-home treatments (Kjellsberg and Dahl 1998; Ogden 2010). The media pressed for political action, and in 1997, on a request from the Ministry of Child and Family Affairs and the Ministry of Health and Care Services, the Norwegian Research Council hosted a conference on interventions targeting serious behavior problems in children and youth. A group of experts appointed by the Norwegian Research Council critically examined several candidate programs and recommended that some of the parenting programs should be systematically implemented and tested in randomized trials (Zeiner et al. 1998). The ministries decided to support the implementation and testing of Parent Management Training—Oregon model (Forgatch 1994) for children aged 3 to 12, as well as Multisystemic Therapy (MST) for adolescents aged 13 to 18 (Henggeler et al. 2009).

In Norway at the time, no epidemiological studies on serious behavior problems (also referred to as conduct disorder, conduct problems, antisocial behavior, and externalizing behavior problems) had been conducted, making it difficult to estimate the exact number of children who were in need of treatment or help. Based on prevalence numbers from smaller studies, the expert group estimated that conduct disorder occurred in 4% of a rural population, and 9% of an urban one (Wichstrøm, Skogen, and Øia 1996; Zeiner et al. 1998). Some years later an official report estimated the prevalence of conduct disorder (CD) among children and youth based on available international and Norwegian research. Conduct disorder was estimated to be 3.5% in each age cohort, with 1.8% having oppositional behavior disorder (ODD) and 1.7% having CD (Skogen and Torvik 2013). This indicated that at least 30,000 Norwegian youth between the ages of 4 and 18 had behavior problems in the clinical range. Among these, the estimated number of children receiving qualified help amounted to 0.4% (N = 4456). The official estimates and figures were supported by input from the regional specialist and municipal general services with the fact that that the interventions did not meet the youths' needs. In addition, policy discussion centered on the needs for early intervention and prevention, based on research indicating that if early onset of CD was left untreated, it might turn into life-course persistent antisocial behavior (Moffitt 1993).

Following the conference, the Ministry of Child and Family Affairs funded a project at the University of Oslo's Institute of Psychology, with the aim of increasing the research knowledge, the competence level, and the capacity of the child and adolescent service system to address the challenges of antisocial and criminal behavior. Another goal was to decrease the use of incarcerations and placements out of home due to such problems. Consequently, the Ministry of Child and Family Affairs invited representatives of all 19 county health directors in Norway to participate in the nationwide implementation of the PMTO (Ogden et al. 2005). At the turn of the century, a strategy for the large-scale implementation, evaluation, and sustainability of the programs were developed as a collaborative effort among the program developers, the two ministries, and the staff at the Behavior Project.

I. "The Behavior Project" and the National Implementation Strategy

The goal of the Behavior Project at the University of Oslo's Institute of Psychology was to secure program operations and treatment fidelity at the regional, county, and municipal level. The project was fully funded by the ministries, and over a five-year period it expanded from a small-scale activity to a rather large project with a staff of 30. The first generation of PMTO practitioners was trained from 1999, and 34 out of 44 completed the therapist training. Among these therapists some were recruited to the National Implementation Team (NIT) and given an important role in the training of the next generations of therapists. The NIT had five national consultants and six regional coordinators. Other main components of the national implementation strategy were the establishment of (a) a permanent national center for implementation and research on evidence based interventions; (b) a plan for local implementations at the county and municipal levels; (c) a comprehensive therapist recruitment, training, and maintenance program; and (d) a network for collaboration, supervision, and monitoring program fidelity (Ogden et al. 2005). In 2009 a case study of the national implementation strategy indicated that the strategy had worked as planned and that PMTO was implemented with a high degree of program sustainability over a period of 10 years (Ogden et al. 2009).

The implementation strategy used can be described as a combination of a "top-down" and a "bottom-up" approach. Top-down initiatives are centrally initiated and may easily create resistance at the practitioner level, while bottom-up initiatives are based on shared control between program purveyors and local stakeholders. The strength of the bottom-up strategy is the practitioners' sense of ownership, but it may be vulnerable due to uncertain long-term funding and support from the political and administrative level. The tension between the top-down and bottom-up strategies were handled by combining the national initiative and funding with decisions and adaptations that matched local challenges and readiness for change. And even if the implementation and evaluation of PTMO were based on a recommendation from an expert group and supported by the ministries, the municipal right of self-determination made it clear that the decision of whether or not to adopt the program was completely up to the local stakeholders. In the practice field, the decision to choose between PMTO and more traditional approaches was left to the local politicians, agencies, and practitioners.

After a five-year project period, the National Center for Child Behavioral Development (NCCBD) was established in 2003, in order to support implementation and research activities. The center has separate departments for child and youth development, both of which are responsible for the training, supervision, and quality assurance support to local sites and practitioners across Norway. A research department was also established in order to conduct research on the implementation and outcomes of the interventions.

II. Parent Management Training—Oregon Model

PMTO aims to reduce children's problem behaviors by developing and strengthening parents' parenting skills, and getting them to take advantage of their strengths (Reid, Patterson, and Snyder 2002). Targeted efforts are made for the parents to learn to identify, define, and observe the child's behavior in new ways. Although the problems parents seek help to solve vary from family to family, the treatment contains some predefined core components that are described in a handbook (Askeland, Christiansen, and Solholm

2005). How much each component is emphasized varies with the needs of the child and the family.

PMTO is based on the SIL model which stands for "social learning and interaction theory" and explains how children and parents influence each other in a mutual, negative interaction, which is referred to as "the coercive family process" (Patterson 1982). According to the SIL model, parents influence their child's behavior through their support of adapted or prosocial behavior, and by using negative parenting techniques, such as threats or coercion. If the child through escalating confrontations makes the parents give in, the parents' evasive behavior and the child's acting out behavior are confirmed, through negative and positive reinforcement, respectively. This easily leads to a spiral of aggressive and antisocial behavior.

The core components or working ingredients of PMTO are positive involvement, skill encouragement, discipline or limit setting, problem-solving, and monitoring. The first core component is positive involvement, where parents show interest in, attention to, and care for their child. This component introduces a change in the communication pattern in the family and increases the social bonding between parents and child. Skill encouragement is the second core component, and parents learn the conditional use of positive consequences and tangible rewards in order to promote the child's use of skills. Parents give the child positive feedback in the form of praise and encouragement and also use direct and indirect rewards. The third component is effective discipline and limit setting, which is the consistent and conditional use of short and moderate negative consequences in order to discourage deviant child behavior. The sanctions are used when the child breaks family rules or does not comply with reasonable requirements. Negative consequences are applied within a context of positive involvement and acceptance. The goal is to teach the child to make choices and also take responsibility for their own actions. The fourth component is problem-solving, which helps family members negotiate disagreements and establish house rules and consequences for following or not following them. The fifth core component involves the use of effective parental monitoring and involvement of the school. Effective monitoring includes the establishment of good daily routines, and that the parents keep track of where the child is, what the child is doing, who the child is with, and how the child is doing (Askeland, Apeland, and Solholm 2014). Although all parenting dimensions are central to the child's behavioral improvement, parents' skills in the use of discipline and monitoring are particularly important intervention components. Patterson (2005) reported that these two dimensions accounted for about three times as much variance in child outcomes as the other three measures of parenting. The other three being positive involvement, skill encouragement, and problem-solving.

During sessions, the parents learn positive parenting skills through role play and exercises. When succeeding in role-plays, they are encouraged to practice their skills at home. In the following session, parents' experiences are reviewed with the therapist so that any problems can be solved before new skills are introduced. The learning process requires motivation, time, and commitment from the parents. Therefore, it is important that the parents have confidence in the therapist and that a good working relationship (also referred to as a therapeutic alliance) is established and maintained (Hukkelberg and Ogden 2016).

A. The PMTO Training Program

The PMTO program was developed in order to train parents to change their child's antisocial behavior in the home (Patterson, Reid, and Dishion 1992). When the approach was introduced in Norway, few training opportunities for practitioners were available. The first regular practitioner training program of PMTO was developed as a collaborative initiative between the program developers and the Norwegian Implementation Team (NIT) (Askeland, Christiansen, and Solholm 2005; Askeland, Apeland, and Solholm 2014). Included in the training program was a PMTO handbook based on Patterson's (1982) social interaction and coercion model and on protocols from previous Oregon Social Learning Center (OSLC) clinical trials (Forgatch 1994). In the "train-the-trainers" approach, every new generation of therapists trains the next generation. Contrary to this approach, however, the Norwegian training program used NIT, which was recruited from the first generation of therapists as a permanent training team for all the next generations.

The first generation had a clinical background from the specialist child and adolescent services, and most of them had at least six years of university studies in psychology, psychiatry, or education. But then there was a shift in the professional background of the candidates. The next generations were also clinically experienced, but most of them had a background with the municipal child and adolescent services and three years of college training in social work, child welfare, nursing, or teaching. Guidelines for program participation were specified, as well as the resources that would be provided by the federal authorities and resources that would be required from the participating municipal services. Candidates were recruited through their workplaces, and their superiors had to agree that they should be allowed to apply their new competencies after completing the training. Each agency also had to agree to the candidates' participation in all training activities and ensure that they would have time to complete therapy with five families during training. In 2018, among the 491 therapists trained in PMTO, 314, or 64%, are still certified and practicing, and of the 215 recruited agencies, 164, or 76%, still have active PMTO interventionists (Askeland et al. 2019).

III. PMTO Intervention Trials: Testing for Effectiveness

Motivated by the discussion about the relevance of US-developed programs in Norway ("may work in the US, but does not work here"), a full scale replication study was carried out in order to test the transferability of the PMTO program to Norway (Ogden and Hagen 2008). A controlled effectiveness study was conducted in which 112 children aged 12 or younger and their parents were randomly assigned to PMTO (N = 59) or to regular services (N = 53). Study participants were recruited through regular child welfare and child mental health services. Among these, the retention rate was 87% (N = 97) at post-treatment assessment, approximately 11–12 months later. Analyses showed that those who were lost to post-treatment assessment were not different from the completers at intake on any of the main outcome variables or on variables like age, gender, or parent demographics, as well as recruitment site. Therapists were recruited by an open invitation to all PMTO therapists who also were asked to recruit comparison therapists from their own or neighboring agencies. A total of 33 PMTO therapists were recruited from all regions of Norway, and those who offered PMTO did so exclusively and were not involved in the control condition. The comparison group was very heterogeneous, so no common guidelines or research protocol could be summarized. The PMTO families were treated individually over the course of a mean average of 26 sessions.

The clinical outcomes showed that parents who received PMTO reported significant fewer externalizing behavior problems in their children and the teachers reported a higher level of social competence at post assessment compared to the children who had received regular services. The practical clinical significance was reported as effect sizes (Cohen's d), and these are typically smaller in effectiveness trials than in efficacy trials. It is therefore noteworthy that the effect sizes in this effectiveness study ranged from $d = .16$ and $d = .20$ for the Child Behavior Checklist (CBCL) Externalizing and Total Problem scales, respectively, to medium-sized effects for the teacher-reported Social Skills Rating Scale (SSRS) and the discipline dimension ($d = .47$ and $d = .30$, respectively). However, the 95% confidence interval did include zero for a few of these effect sizes, and so these numbers should be interpreted with some caution.

Even if PMTO proved effective for the whole age range (3–12 years), it was particularly effective in the treatment of problem behavior in children who were eight years or younger at treatment intake, evidenced by teacher ratings of externalizing and total problem behavior and by daily parent observational reports over three successive days. The families' assessment of the treatment showed that 77% of the parents in the PMTO group would recommend the treatment to others who might be in need of it, compared to 38% of the comparison families (Ogden and Hagen 2008).

In a one-year follow-up study (Hagen, Ogden, and Bjørnebekk 2011), the positive behavior changes were sustained in the PMTO group, but the comparison group had caught up with the intervention group on several of the outcome variables. Therefore, the overall effectiveness of PMTO at one-year follow-up could at best be described as modest. Two separate mediation models were tested in the follow-up study, showing that assignment to PMTO predicted improvements in several child outcomes mediated by greater effective parent discipline and improved family cohesion (Hagen et al. 2011). Among the limitations of the study was the rate of attrition. Of the 112 children and families who completed the intake assessment battery, 67% (N = 75) participated in the follow-up assessment. Of the 37 families who did not participate in the follow-up assessment, there was a nonsignificant difference in attrition rate between the intervention conditions. But the study ended up with a sample with power too low to answer questions about subgroups, and possibly also to detect real differences between groups.

In sum, the two studies presented here represented the first effectiveness trial of PMTO implemented by trained therapists working in regular community services. It was also among the few RCTs conducted by an independent research team examining the clinical outcomes of PMTO. Moreover, the studies allowed us to investigate the treatment effectiveness as it was disseminated and applied in a different country, crossing both national and language borders. But even if the mean outcomes of these studies were generally encouraging, some parents did not improve their parenting skills, and some children changed only marginally. Finding out which families drop out of treatment and why some families do not benefit from treatment are important goals for future studies. The results also point to the importance of improving the intervention model for older children. As children grow older, peers and persons outside of the family become more influential. As such, monitoring peer relations and promoting peer relational skills becomes more important. It may also be considered a limitation of the studies that so little attention was directed at what went on in school. Greater emphasis should probably be placed on collaborating with teachers and other school staff, and turning negative contingencies around in the school context.

A. Prediction Studies of PMTO

In a nonrandomized study of 331 children with clinical levels of conduct problems, child, parent, and therapy variables were entered as predictors in order to examine the relative importance of each predictor (Hagen and Ogden 2017). Outcomes were change scores in externalizing behavior and social skills as rated by parents and teachers. The children were between the ages of 3 and 12 years, and only 26% were girls. Attrition was lowest among parents whose children had the highest initial teacher rated scores on the Teacher Report Form (TRF; Achenbach 1991) and whose fathers spent more hours in treatment. Otherwise, there were no differences between families who completed or dropped out of treatment.

Overall results indicated that children with the highest scores on externalizing problems and the lowest scores on social skills at intake had the greatest gains, as reported by both parents and teachers. This could be interpreted as a tendency of those with the highest scores to have the greatest potential to change, but also as regression to the mean. As demonstrated in earlier studies, girls improved more than boys (Kjøbli and Ogden 2009). Of particular interest was the finding that therapist satisfaction with treatment was a significant predictor of teacher-rated improvements in social skills. This can mean that PMTO therapists were able to assess the outcomes of treatments even if they had little direct contact with the child. Fathers who took part in treatment spent on average 13.7 hours in treatment, and their participation predicted positive child behavioral changes. In this study, therapeutic alliance predicted parent-rated improvements in externalizing behavior, and may probably be a necessary but not sufficient ingredient for child behavioral change. Further, the outcomes indicated that PMTO may be adaptable to both single- and two-parent families. Also of interest was the finding that economic support of single-parent families did not predict outcomes, and the explanation may be that the economic support of single-parent families is relatively generous in Norway. Neither did maternal nor paternal depression predict any outcomes, probably indicating that parents with moderate mental health problems may benefit from PMTO.

1. *PMTO and Attention-Deficit/Hyperactivity Disorder (ADHD)*

A separate study examined whether ADHD predicted the effectiveness of PMTO among 253 children and families, of whom 97 children were reported to have an ADHD diagnosis (Bjørnebekk, Kjøbli, and Ogden 2015). Although different at intake, the groups had close to an equal change in behavioral status following treatment. The study indicated that reductions in conduct problems following PMTO were of the same magnitude in children with or without ADHD, except in the presence of maternal depression or low family income. But because of the nonrandomized design of the study, no conclusion could be made about the causal relationship between the intervention and the outcomes.

IV. PMTO Implementation Studies: Testing for Fidelity

Generally, effective programs are assigned scale-up penalties due to challenges in the implementation process, although this assumption has rarely been empirically tested. An exception was in a study by Welsh, Sullivan, and Olds (2010), which found that, over time, fidelity decreased with every new generation of therapists trained, and so did the child outcomes. But a Norwegian study challenged the scale-up penalty assumptions and findings by comparing fidelity scores and outcomes across several generations of PMTO therapists (Tømmerås and Ogden 2015). Central to this study was the training and supervision of subsequent generations of PMTO therapists conducted by the National Implementation Team, with numerous implementation support activities. PMTO-candidates underwent an 18-month training period during which regional groups of four candidates met regularly throughout the training period. After becoming a PMTO therapist, supervision was performed in regional groups of eight, who exchanged experiences and ideas (Ogden et al. 2005). By offering continuous training in PMTO, and by holding the implementation factors rather constant, the NIT prevented negative effects of turnover among therapists.

The study included two waves of PMTO implementation. The first wave took place in the child and adolescent specialist services (the Effect Group, or EG) and the next in the municipal welfare services (the Dissemination Group, or DG). The DG was recruited from multiple agencies that were intended to deliver PMTO, and had more diverse background training than therapists in the EG. Therefore, the DG was characterized by greater heterogeneity in workplace and background training than the EG. Even if the inclusion criteria were similar in both phases of implementation, the larger heterogeneity in the client group found in the second wave of implementation may be explained by the fact that the municipal welfare services usually target children with more differential risk levels and greater heterogeneity in behavior problems (compared to the specialist services). The PTMO fidelity scores and child behavioral outcomes were then compared in the effectiveness and dissemination phases of implementation. And despite the increasing heterogeneity of the service providers and the target group, no attenuation of program effects was detected. The absence of a scale-up penalty in Norway may be attributed to the establishment of NIT as part of a stable and sustainable implementation infrastructure. The lack of a scale-up penalty may also be related to program maturation; that is, improvement in outcomes due to increased therapist experience and competence over time. However, the study was unable to detect whether the lack of a scale-up penalty might be related to other unmeasured implementation factors. But considering the study from an applied point of view, the results emphasize the importance of having an implementation infrastructure that maintains program effects on child behavior by supporting the core implementation components at the competency as well as at the organizational level.

A next study evaluated the long-term implementation outcomes over additional generations of PMTO-trained therapists. Data was collected from 491 Norwegian practitioners across seven therapist generations, who initiated training in the PMTO model (Askeland et al. 2019). The measurement of fidelity scores across seven generations of therapist who completed training from 1999 to 2014 showed no drop in mean ratings of fidelity, with an overall mean score of 6.8 on a scale from 1 to 9 (range: 6.34–6.94). The outcomes showed sustained fidelity scores across seven generations in spite of increasing heterogeneity among therapists trained and a shift of focus in the target population from clinical to primary services. One limitation to this study was that fidelity was assessed only at certification, and it was not actually tested whether the fidelity scores predicted child outcomes. Even if the use of a fidelity measure with strong predictive validity is still somewhat rare in implementation studies, the authors recommend that regular fidelity assessments should take place to ensure sustained intervention fidelity. The conclusions from a study by Tømmerås and Ogden (2015) are strengthened by the aforementioned work, which demonstrates the sustainability of PMTO in Norway over nearly two decades. This is based on a strong infrastructure, a clear implementation strategy, and careful attention to intervention fidelity for each new generation of therapists.

A. The Relative Importance of Treatment Fidelity and Working Alliance

The discussion about the relative importance of common factors and program factors has long been of interest to researchers and clinicians. Common factors are nonspecific treatment ingredients that are unrelated to method and therapeutic orientation, such as therapeutic alliance. Contrary to common factors are program-specific factors like treatment fidelity. Among critics of evidence-based practices, the therapeutic relation is the most important ingredient in treatment, while the specific program or method means less (Wampold 2001). However, deciding the relative importance of alliance versus fidelity in the prediction of treatment outcomes cannot be answered without including both concepts in the same statistical model. The main goal of a study by Hukkelberg and Ogden (2013) was to examine the relative influence of therapeutic alliance and treatment fidelity on change in externalizing problem behavior as reported by parents. Both fidelity and alliance were measured three times during therapy for 331 participating families. The fidelity was measured with the Fidelity of Implementation Rating System (FIMP) (Knutson et al. 2009) and alliance was measured with the short Working Alliance Inventory (WAIS; Hukkelberg and Ogden 2016). The parents' alliance assessment was not seen by the therapists, but sent directly from the parents to the researchers.

Using a longitudinal design, the development and relation between treatment fidelity and parent-therapist alliance were investigated and results suggested that, statistically, treatment fidelity and working alliance seemed to be separate processes, although they were theoretically related process variables. Parents reported high and stable levels of alliance and fidelity at all three time-points. Working alliance was reported by parents, and fidelity was assessed by observers (PMTO specialists), and these seldom converge. These independent assessments made it impossible for parents to know the extent to which the treatment components were delivered as intended or not. And even if they perceived progress in therapy, they could not decide if this was due to the program factors or not. Alliance and fidelity might also be independent, as high treatment fidelity could be achieved without establishing a good working relationship, and vice versa.

It turned out that treatment fidelity predicted reductions in parent-reported externalizing behavior, over and beyond working alliance. The findings emphasize the importance of treatment fidelity as a specific program factor, and that alliance alone is not sufficient to change problem behavior in children. However, this should not be taken to mean that therapeutic alliance is unimportant. Parents who experience a good alliance with the therapist may more easily adopt new parenting skills compared to those who experience a poor alliance. But more research is needed to investigate whether these findings can be replicated and extended beyond PMTO. Among the limitations of the study was the finding of high and stable assessments of both alliance and fidelity, indicating a possible ceiling effect. It is important to note that the potential impact of therapist characteristics on alliance was not investigated, and several studies have demonstrated that therapist characteristics may influence the outcome.

V. Adaptations of the PMTO Intervention: Testing Differentiation

Experience with PMTO showed that a certain proportion of families managed with fewer sessions than prescribed in the original model, and this sparked the impetus for the further development of the model. The purpose was to give the municipalities an opportunity to gradually build up their own professional competence, so that fewer children and families needed help in the specialist services in child welfare and child and adolescent psychiatric services. Furthermore, the intention was to be able to provide an intervention as early as possible in children's development and to divide the treatment model into modules so that municipalities could build up step-by-step competence. The model was introduced in 2010 and described in a paper by Solholm, Kjøbli, and Christiansen (2013). The early interventions for children at risk program (Norwegian acronym, TIBIR) model was a structured version with a low threshold for admission to treatment in municipal services, and with shorter or alternative interventions. Three intervention modules were tested in separate trials: Brief Parent Training (BPT: Kjøbli and Ogden 2012), Individual Social Skills Training for children (ISST: Kjøbli and Ogden 2014), and Parent Group Training (Kjøbli, Hukkelberg, and Ogden 2012). Within this adapted program, the full-scale PMTO treatment is still offered, but only as a backup for those families that need more extensive help. The TIBIR program was implemented in a variety of primary care settings, including public child health clinics, school psychology services, and kindergartens. By 2018 a total of 1,313 professionals were delivering TIBIR interventions in 111 municipalities or districts.

A. Brief Parent Training

The BPT module promotes parenting skills through three to five sessions, and is provided by permanent employees in municipal children and family services. The effect of parent training was examined in a randomized controlled trial (RCT) in regular practice (N = 216). Compared with other services, BPT showed improvements in parental practice and children's behavior (Kjøbli and Ogden 2012). Significantly positive results with small to moderate effect sizes were found on 10 of 15 outcome measures. Six months after treatment, a follow-up study was conducted showing that the positive results were maintained on 6 of 14 variables for children and parents (Kjøbli and Bjørnebekk 2013). However, apart from social competence assessments at post-treatment, the teacher assessments did not favor the intervention group at any time.

B. Parent Group Training

PGT was delivered to groups of caregivers (involving up to eight children) who met weekly for 12 sessions, each lasting about 2.5 hours. Each group was led by two qualified PMTO therapists who had received group intervention training. The intervention was evaluated both immediately following and six months after termination of the intervention (Kjøbli, Hukkelberg, and Ogden 2013). Participating in the study were 137 children (3–12 years) and their parents, who were randomly assigned to group-based training or usual services. Short- and long-term beneficial effects were reported from parents, although only short-term effects and no follow-up effects were found when examining teacher assessments.

C. Parent Training for Minority Groups

To overcome the lack of participation by ethnic minorities in parent training programs, the PMTO implementation team hired bilingual "link workers" to contact Somali and Pakistani mothers, who are the most dominant immigrant groups in Norway. This approach improved their recruitment and participation in the parent groups created specifically for these ethnic groups (Bjørknes, Jakobsen, and Nærde 2011; Bjørknes et al. 2012). A RCT with wait-list control assessed the PMTO intervention effectiveness on maternal parenting practices and child behavior in a group of 96 mothers from Somalia and Pakistan and their children aged three to nine years (Bjørknes and Manger 2013). PMTO significantly enhanced positive parenting practices and reduced mother-reported child conduct problems, but once again no behavioral changes were registered in teacher reports.

D. Individual Social Skills Training

TIBIR also has a module for individual social competence training, which consists of 8 to 10 sessions for each child. The training is a cognitive-behavioral intervention that is flexible and adapted to the child's age and behavior. All the children who received the intervention were taught the "Stop, think before you act" strategy, as well as to make socially appropriate plans before they act, to cope with anger and to reduce aggressive and negative behavior (Augimeri et al. 2007). An RCT was conducted immediately after training and six months thereafter. Participants included 198 children (ages 3 to 12 years) who were randomly allocated to receive social skills training or regular practice. Results showed positive changes in most outcomes in both intervention conditions, but no significant group differences were evident. The results also indicated that individual child treatment has a limited effect and should probably be supplemented with parental interventions (Kjøbli and Ogden 2014).

The feedback from the field on early interventions for children at risk (TIBIR) has been positive and, with the exception of the social skills module, controlled evaluations have produced encouraging results. The evaluations included positive parent satisfaction with treatment and moderate effect sizes in their assessments of child behavior. However, teacher assessments have not shown the same positive trend. BPT has been the most successful of the modules, and also the one that is most in demand in the municipalities.

VI. Discussion and Conclusions

This chapter set out to examine two decades of implementing Parent Management Training—Oregon model in Norway. This has been a systematically, growing iteration process over two decades, in which seven generations of interventionists have been trained and certified in order to offer parent training to mothers and fathers with conduct disordered children (Askeland et al. 2019). A particular characteristic of both the original and the adapted Oregon versions of Parent Management Training were based on Gerald Patterson's theory about the causes of aggression. The PMTO (now rebranded GenerationPMTO; Askeland et al. 2019) is presented as an empirically supported program and the Blueprints for Healthy Youth Development (n.d.) registry has designated it as a model program.

Conducted as RCTs in real world practice across all regions of Norway, effectiveness studies have demonstrated a small to moderate but consistent impact of PMTO and adapted versions of the intervention program. The participants were representative of children and families that contacted child welfare or other community services in order to get help for their problems. Overall, the findings reported here suggest that PMTO principles and components were successfully transported from the United States to regular services in Norway with sustained positive outcomes and competent adherence. PMTO has proved to be a robust treatment model that has produced significantly positive results in studies conducted in regular practice for children aged 3 to 12 years, the short-term changes have persisted over time, and the results were as good for girls as for boys and for minority mothers and their children. The trend was also positive for families and children with ADHD, although maternal depression and low family income might moderate the outcomes.

PMTO has been tested with positive outcomes in both individual and group trainings and in high and low dosages of treatment. Across the studies, the parent-rated outcomes ranged from small to large, but the lack of improvements in child problem behavior reported by teachers in most of the studies remains a challenge.

Indicators of internal validity come from randomized controlled trials demonstrating a causal relationship between the program and child outcomes (Ogden and Hagen 2008). Effect sizes (Cohen 1992), which are usually lower in effectiveness than in efficacy studies, were moderate for the CBCL Externalizing ($d = .16$) and the CBCL Total Problems Scale ($d = .20$), medium-sized for teacher-reported social skills ($d = .47$), and large for the Parent Satisfaction Scale ($d = .83$). Evaluation of Brief Parent Training demonstrated small to moderate effect sizes in the range of $d = .21$ to $d = .65$ (Kjøbli and Ogden 2012). The group version of the PMTO intervention demonstrated effect sizes of $d = .31$ to $d = .47$ for the Eyberg Problem Behavior Scale and effect sizes of $d = .38$ for the Merrell externalizing and $d = .39$ for the Merrell Social Competence Scale (Kjøbli, Hukkelberg, and Ogden 2012). In the culturally adapted version of PMTO targeting Pakistani and Somali mothers, effect sizes were also in the small to moderate range (Bjørknes and Manger 2013).

The indicators of external validity come from effectiveness studies conducted under real-world conditions (Ogden and Hagen 2008; Bjørknes and Manger 2013), and replications based on adapted versions of the parenting model (Kjøbli, Hukkelberg, and Ogden 2012; Kjøbli and Ogden 2012). Several child and adolescent services located in different municipalities and regions across Norway have recruited participants to the studies from local parents seeking help from public services to help their children cope with acting out and aggressive behavior. The strengths of the studies are their reliance on the same theoretical SIL model, the recruitment and assessments conducted in real world practice, and the robust and positive outcomes, although with small to moderate effect sizes. The published articles demonstrate that the PMTO intervention program has proved to be sustainable in Norway over a period of more than 20 years, and new generations of interventionists have been trained with no scale-up penalty. That is, subsequent generations have maintained high fidelity scores measured by the FIMP system. The limitations of the Norwegian PMTO studies are related to the rather small groups included in the trials, the scarcity of girls among the participating children, and the lack of positive teacher-rated child outcomes. There are also indications of improvements in impact when fathers take part in the parent training (Kjøbli and Ogden 2009), and also an increased effect when children attend some of the sessions (Hagen and Ogden 2017).

Several evidence-based treatment programs have surfaced during the last decades and have proven effective in the prevention and reduction of risk factors predicting law-breaking behavior in adolescents and adults. In Norway, the intervention program PMTO was implemented from 1999 and has been sustained to this day. This parent training intervention has a solid theoretical foundation in the social interaction learning theory and the family coercion model. It also draws on ecological and transactional principles (Patterson 1982). The aim of this intervention is to promote effective parenting skills to reduce and prevent the further escalation of child problem behavior. The parent training targets coercive transactional communication processes in the family, by teaching parenting skills, including positive involvement, effective discipline, problem-solving, skill encouragement, and monitoring. Among the contextual factors that have contributed to the long-term sustainability and effectiveness of evidence-based practices in Norway, the following seems to be most important: (a) a genuine interest and commitment at the political and administrative level for the national implementation of evidence-based programs, (b) increased interest among practitioners for evidence-based practice, (c) establishing a self-sustaining national center for implementation and research, (d) the ability of the program developers to support the implementation and research efforts, and (e) positive feedback from families and the media (Ogden et al. 2009).

References

Achenbach, T. M. 1991. *Manual for the child behavioral checklist for ages 4–18.* Burlington: University of Vermont.

Askeland, E., A. Apeland, and R.Solholm, eds. 2014. *PMTO. Foreldretrening for familier med barn som har atferdsvansker.* Oslo: Gyldendal Akademisk.

Askeland, E., T. Christiansen, and R. Solholm. 2005. *PMTO håndbok.* Oslo: Atferdssenteret, Unirand.

Askeland, E., M. Forgatch, A. Apeland, M. Reer, and A. A.Grønlie. 2019. Scaling up an empirically supported intervention with long-term outcomes: The nationwide implementation of GenerationPMTO in Norway. *Prevention Science,* 20 (8):1189–1199.

Augimeri, L. K., D. P. Farrington, C. J. Koegl, and D. M. Day. 2007. The SNAP™ Under 12 Outreach Project: Effects of a community based program for children with conduct problems. *Journal of Child and Family Studies,* 16:799–807.

Bjørknes, R., R. Jakobsen, and A. Nærde. 2011. Recruiting ethnic minority groups to evidence-based parent training. Who will come and how? *Children and Youth Services Review,* 33 (2): 351–357.

Bjørknes, R., J. Kjøbli, T. Manger, and R. Jacobsen. 2012. Parent Training among ethnic minorities: Parenting practices as mediators of change in child conduct problems. *Family Relations,* 61 (1): 101–114.

Bjørknes, R., and T. Manger. 2013. Can parent training alter parent practice and reduce conduct problems in ethnic minority children? A randomized controlled trial. *Prevention Science,* 14 (1): 52–63.

Bjørnebekk, G., J. Kjøbli, and T. Ogden. 2015. Children with conduct problems and co-occurring ADHD: Behavioral improvements following parent management training. *Child & Family Behavior Therapy,* 37 (1): 1–19.

Blueprints for Healthy Youth Development. n.d. Experimentally proven programs. Boulder CO: Blueprints for Healthy Youth Development. www.blueprintsprograms.org/.

Cohen, J. 1992. Statistical power analysis. *Current Directions in Psychological Science,* 1:98–101.

Forgatch, M. S. 1994. *Parenting through change: A programmed intervention curriculum for groups of single mothers.* Report. Eugene, OR: Oregon Social Learning Center.

Hagen K. A., and T. Ogden. 2017. Predictors of changes in child behaviour following parent management training: Child, context, and therapy factors. *International Journal of Psychology,* 52 (2): 106–115.

Hagen, K., T. Ogden, and G. Bjørnebekk. 2011. Treatment outcomes and mediators of Parent Management Training: A one-year follow-up of children with conduct problems. *Journal of Clinical Child and Adolescent Psychology,* 40 (2): 1–14.

Henggeler, S. W., S. K. Schoenwald, C. M. Borduin, M. D. Rowland, and P. B. Cunningham. 2009. *Multisystemic treatment of antisocial behaviour in children and adolescents.* 2nd ed. New York: Guilford Press.

Hukkelberg, S., and T. Ogden. 2013. Working alliance and treatment fidelity as predictors of externalizing problem behaviors in parent management training. *Journal of Consulting and Clinical Psychology,* 81 (6): 1010–1020.

Hukkelberg, S., and T. Ogden. 2016. The short Working Alliance Inventory in parent training: Factor structure and longitudinal invariance. *Psychotherapy Research*, 26:719–726. doi:10.1080/10503307.2015.1119328.

Kjøbli, J., S. Hukkelberg, and T. Ogden. 2012. A randomized trial of group parent training: Reducing child conduct problems in real-world settings. *Behaviour Research and Therapy*, 51 (3): 113–121.

Kjøbli, J., and T. Ogden. 2009. Gender differences in intake characteristics and behavior change among children in families receiving parent management training. *Children and Youth Services Review*, 31:823–830.

Kjøbli, J., and T. Ogden. 2012. A randomized effectiveness trial of Brief Parent Training in primary care settings. *Prevention Science*, 13 (6): 616–626.

Kjøbli, J. and T. Ogden. 2014. A randomized effectiveness trial of individual child social skills training: Six-month follow-up. *Child and Adolescent Psychiatry and Mental Health*, 8:31. doi:10.1186/s13034-014-0031-6.

Knutson, N. M., M. S. Forgatch, L. A. Rains, and M.Sigmarsdóttir. 2009. *Fidelity of Implementation Rating System (FIMP): The manual for PMTO™*. Eugene, OR: Implementation Sciences International.

Moffitt, T. E. l993. Adolescence-limited and life-course-persistent antisocial behavior: A developmental taxonomy. *Psychological Review*, 100:674–701.

Ogden, T. 2010. *Familiebasert behandling av alvorlige atferdsproblemer blant barn og ungdom (Family-based treatment of serious behavior problems among children and youth)*. PhD dissertation, University of Bergen.

Ogden, T., and K. Amlund-Hagen. 2008. Treatment effectiveness of Parent Management Training in Norway: A randomized controlled trial of children with conduct problems. *Journal of Consulting and Clinical Psychology*, 76 (4): 607–621.

Ogden, T., K. Amlund-Hagen, E. Askeland, and B.Christensen. 2009. Implementing and evaluating evidence-based treatments of conduct problems in children and youth in Norway. *Research on Social Work Practice*, 19 (5): 582–591.

Ogden, T., M. Forgatch, E. Askeland, G.R. Patterson, and B. Bullock. 2005. Implementation of Parent Management Training at the national level: The case of Norway. *Journal of Social Work Practice*, 19 (3): 317–329.

Patterson, G. R. 1982. *Coercive family process*. Eugene, OR: Castalia.

Patterson, G. R. 2005. The next generation of PMTO models. *The Behavior Therapist*, 28 (2): 25–32.

Patterson, G. R., J. B., Reid, and T. J. Dishion. 1992. *A social interactional approach*. Vol. 4, Antisocial boys. Eugene, OR: Castalia.

Reid, J. B., G. R., Patterson, and J. J. Snyder, eds. 2002. *Antisocial behavior in children and adolescents: A developmental analysis and a model for intervention*. Washington, DC: American Psychological Association.

Skogen, J. C., and F. A. Torvik. 2013. *Atferdsforstyrrelser blant barn og unge i Norge. Beregnet forekomst og bruk av hjelpetiltak. (Conduct disorder among children and youth in Norway. Estimated incidence and use of remedial measures)*. Report 2013:4. Oslo: Norwegian Institute of Public Health.

Solholm, R., J. Kjøbli, and T.Christiansen. 2013. Early initiatives for children at risk—Development of a program for the prevention and treatment of behavior problems in primary services. *Prevention Science*, 14 (6): 535–544.

Wampold, B. E. 2001. *The greath psychotherapy debate: Models, methods and findings.* Mahwah, NJ: Erlbaum.

Welsh, B. C., C. J. Sullivan, and D. L. Olds. 2010. When early crime prevention goes to scale: A new look at the evidence. *Prevention Science,* 11 (2): 115–125.

Wichstrøm, L., K. Skogen, and T. Øia. 1996. The increased rate of conduct problems in urban areas: What is the mechanism? *Journal of American Academy of Child and Adolescent Psychiatry,* 35:471–479.

Zeiner, P., E. Backe-Hansen, S. Eskeland, T. Ogden, P. Rypdal, and H. Sommerschild. 1998. *Barn og unge med alvorlige atferdsvansker. Hva kan nyere viten fortelle oss og hva slags hjelp trenger de?* Oslo: Norges Forskningsråd.

CHAPTER 21
....

SYSTEMS OF CHANGE
Communities That Care

....

ABIGAIL A. FAGAN

POLICYMAKERS, scholars, and practitioners have increasingly called for evidence-based policies to reduce crime and improve criminal justice (National Academies of Sciences 2019; Welsh and Farrington 2012; Pew-MacArthur Results First Initiative 2015). Such policies have the potential to provide more rational, effective, and cost-effective approaches to crime and justice (Pew-MacArthur Results First Initiative 2015; Drake, Aos, and Miller 2009; Mears 2007). Accordingly, criminal justice interventions are now more likely to be subject to rigorous, scientific evaluations (Telep, Garner, and Visher 2015) that can provide credible evidence of effectiveness. As highlighted on the CrimeSolutions website (https://crimesolutions.ojp.gov/) and similar registries, many evidence-based interventions (EBIs) have now been demonstrated as effective in preventing crime and related problems (Elliott and Fagan 2017).

Despite these advances, criminal justice agencies and community organizations have been slow to adopt EBIs, and some of the most common practices used to reduce crime have never been rigorously evaluated or have been demonstrated as ineffective (e.g., "Scared Straight" programs and boot camps) (Cullen 2013; MacKenzie 2013). This chapter describes a solution to address this problem: the Communities That Care (CTC) prevention system. CTC provides community-based coalitions with materials, training, and consultation to build their capacity to prevent crime. CTC is itself an evidence-based intervention, having been demonstrated to increase the use of EBIs in communities and to prevent youth substance use, delinquency, and violence (Fagan et al. 2018).

The four sections of this chapter describe (1) the development of the CTC system, (2) its core components, (3) its evidence of effectiveness in reducing youth offending, and (4) its potential to advance evidence-based crime control policies in the United States. As discussed in the first section, CTC was endorsed decades ago by the Office of Juvenile Justice and Delinquency Prevention (OJJDP), as part of its Comprehensive Strategy for Serious, Violent and Chronic Juvenile Offenders (Office of Juvenile Justice and Delinquency Prevention 1995). Unlike OJJDP strategies taking place within the juvenile justice system, CTC is community-based and relies on community members, leaders, and organizations to work together to prevent delinquency. The involvement of community members is expected to increase local support for prevention, increase the use of EBIs, and enhance their fit for the community and impact on participants (Catalano et al. 2012; Fagan et al. 2018).

Although its creation predated the evidence-based movement in crime and justice, since its inception CTC has emphasized the use of EBIs by community organizations. Recognizing that most community members will not have extensive knowledge about EBIs or how, specifically, to prevent youth offending, CTC provides multiple, interactive trainings for community members to learn about, discuss, and practice methods to prevent offending by selecting, implementing, and evaluating EBIs. In recent years, some state governments have funded CTC coalitions in multiple communities to ensure a uniform, evidence-based approach to crime prevention. These initiatives, along with the earlier endorsement by OJJDP, suggest that CTC has the potential to contribute to a national crime prevention agenda and to substantially reduce rates of crime across the United States.

I. History of CTC

CTC was developed in the 1980s by Drs. David Hawkins and Richard Catalano when they were professors at the University of Washington. In partnership with the National Council on Crime and Delinquency, they began to summarize information about the causes and prevention of juvenile delinquency and violence (Fagan et al. 2018). They first reviewed criminological theories and data from longitudinal studies that identified risk and protective factors that preceded and influenced the onset of delinquency, violence, and substance use (Hawkins et al. 1987). They also examined evidence from evaluation studies that existed at that time to identify EBIs that could be delivered to youth of varying ages in community settings, outside of correctional facilities, to prevent delinquency (Hawkins et al. 1988). Their goal, which would take years to complete, was to translate this scientific information into a comprehensive, step-by-step process that communities could use to prevent youth delinquency and violence.

In its early stages, the CTC system provided communities with two sets of in-person trainings (Manger et al. 1992). The first, for community leaders, reviewed scientific research about risk and protective factors, the development of criminal offending over the life course, and programs shown to prevent this development. Information about these programs was provided in a user-friendly text, the *Communities That Care Prevention Strategies Guide* (Hawkins and Catalano [1996, 2000] 2004). The second training helped community coalitions to conduct local needs assessments to identify the prevalence of problem behaviors and risk and protective factors experienced by youth that contributed to these outcomes.

This early CTC model was pilot tested for feasibility and effectiveness using funding through OJJDP's Comprehensive Strategy (Office of Juvenile Justice and Delinquency Prevention 1995; Wilson and Howell 1993). The Comprehensive Strategy was one of the first federal initiatives to recognize that crime control strategies needed to include preventive as well as reactive mechanisms. It emphasized that efforts to arrest, incarcerate, and/or rehabilitate youth offenders were only part of the crime solution, and that communities also needed to promote healthy youth development and reduce the early initiation of offending.

OJJDP endorsed the CTC system and recommended that communities use CTC as the prevention component of its Comprehensive Strategy (Wilson and Howell 1993).

From 1994 to 1996, over $50 million was provided to about 400 communities in 49 states to implement CTC and specific EBIs intended to prevent delinquency (Office of Juvenile Justice and Delinquency Prevention 1996; Fagan et al. 2018). An evaluation of this initiative reported that CTC coalitions implemented 277 delinquency prevention programs, and 90% of the coalitions delivered at least two interventions identified as evidence-based in the OJJDP *Comprehensive Strategy Guide* (an expanded version of the CTC *Prevention Strategies Guide*). The evaluation also suggested that youth in CTC communities were less likely to engage in delinquency (United States Government Accountability Office 1996). However, given the lack of control communities in the study, the initiative provided only preliminary evidence of CTC's effectiveness.

A. Revisions to the CTC System

Drs. Hawkins and Catalano used information reported by communities in these and other pilot studies to further develop and expand the CTC system. For example, many communities reported challenges conducting local needs assessments and determining which interventions they should use to address risk and protective factors of concern (Fagan et al. 2018). This problem led to the development of the CTC Youth Survey (Arthur et al. 2007), one of the first youth self-report surveys to provide reliable and valid information about risk and protective factors, delinquency, violence, and substance use. After the survey was pilot tested, the CTC guidance was revised to recommend that communities administer the survey in their local schools with representative samples of middle and high school students to gather information on elevated risk factors and depressed protective factors. To address challenges related to EBI selection, the CTC developers updated the CTC *Prevention Strategies Guide* with information about new EBIs (Hawkins and Catalano [1996, 2000] 2004) and added a training workshop focused on EBI selection, implementation, and evaluation.

B. Theoretical Basis

The development of CTC not only took into account feedback from community stakeholders but also was informed by criminological theories, specifically life-course developmental and social disorganization theories. Implicit in life-course theories of criminology is the idea that criminal behavior develops over time and is affected by multiple factors located in multiple ecological domains (i.e., individual, peer, family, school, and community) (Cullen 2011; Kazemian, Farrington, and Piquero 2019). These influences are commonly referred to as risk and protective factors, as their presence elevates or suppresses, respectively, the likelihood of crime (Hawkins et al. 1998). In addition, the perspective states that most criminal behaviors have their onset (i.e., first occurrence) early in the life course, typically between ages 10 and 15 years, and that their prevalence and frequency peak in late adolescence and early adulthood (Farrington 2003; Elliott 1994). To prevent the onset of crime, therefore, interventions should be delivered during childhood and early adolescence. Based on this rationale, CTC guides communities to select developmental interventions that reduce risk factors and increase protective factors and implement them with children and adolescents (Fagan and Hawkins 2013). Interventions can also target parents/family members, teachers/schools, and communities, since delinquency is affected by risk and protective factors in multiple settings.

CTC's design was also influenced by the social development model (SDM), a life-course theory developed by Drs. Hawkins and Catalano (Catalano and Hawkins 1996; Hawkins and Weis 1985). As a life-course theory, the SDM recognizes that many risk and protective factors affect the onset, persistence, and desistance of problem behaviors, as well as the development of positive outcomes. The theory posits that children learn problem and positive behaviors during social interactions and via socialization experiences in the community, home, school, and peer group. It hypothesizes that youth who have close ties to prosocial groups and individuals, especially those that provide healthy beliefs and clear standards for positive behaviors, will be most likely to develop positive outcomes (Catalano and Hawkins 1996; Hawkins and Weis 1985). Conversely, those who lack such bonds and/or form bonds with antisocial individuals and institutions are at greatest risk for negative outcomes.

The SDM provides the basis for several aspects of the CTC system (Fagan, Hawkins, et al. 2018). First, it suggests that coalitions should conduct local needs assessments to measure levels of risk and protective factors experienced by youth in multiple social contexts. It also underlies CTC's recommendation that communities select and implement EBIs that reduce risk factors and create strong bonds between young people and their families, schools, peer groups, and communities. The SDM also provides the theoretical basis for using a community-based mobilization strategy to prevent youth problem behaviors. The involvement of a diverse and relatively large group of individuals and agencies communicates to youth that their communities care about them and should, in turn, strengthen youth's bonds to the community and encourage their adherence to community norms and laws. In addition, the use of broad-based coalitions to plan and oversee prevention activities allows community stakeholders to develop strong bonds to each other and to their communities, which should promote their collective efficacy (Sampson, Raudenbush, and Earls 1997); that is, their ability to work together to effectively prevent delinquency.

As the last point suggests, CTC is also informed by social disorganization theories (Shaw and McKay 1942; Bursik and Grasmick 1993; Sampson, Raudenbush, and Earls 1997). Based on data indicating that rates of delinquency and crime vary across regions, cities, and neighborhoods (Shaw and McKay 1942; Sampson 2012), social disorganization theory hypothesizes that certain features of ecological settings influence illegal behavior, such as community levels of poverty, residential mobility, availability of drugs or weapons, physical and social disorder, and local resources and services (Sampson, Raudenbush, and Earls 1997; Shaw and McKay 1942; Anderson 1999; Bursik and Grasmick 1993; Pratt and Cullen 2005). Collective efficacy is also important and represents the degree to which adult residents of a community trust and respect one another, share norms and values, and are willing to intervene and take informal action to address youth crime (Sampson, Raudenbush, and Earls 1997).

Social disorganization theory provides a theoretical basis for CTC's reliance on local coalitions to plan and oversee prevention activities (Fagan, Hawkins, et al. 2018). When adults participate in CTC coalitions, they learn how to engage in effective, collaborative action to prevent youth delinquency and the importance of providing a unified message to youth that positive behaviors are valued and problem behaviors are not. The involvement of multiple community members should increase collective efficacy, and, in turn, reduce youth delinquency.

Also consistent with social disorganization theory, CTC recognizes that communities differ from one another, not just in terms of their crime rates but also in the prevalence of risk and protective factors that influence criminal behaviors (Fagan, Hawkins, et al. 2018; Feinberg et al. 2012). As a result, CTC does not advocate that communities implement the same EBI or set of EBIs. Rather, it guides each coalition to conduct its own needs assessment (using the CTC Youth Survey) to identify the specific risk factors that are elevated and the specific protective factors that are suppressed. Coalitions then select EBIs that will address their risk and protective factors of concern. Before implementing EBIs, they also consider whether or not EBIs are a good fit for their local context. In this way, CTC provides a structured process that can be used by any community to prevent crime, but it also allows communities to tailor their specific prevention activities to their own unique contexts.

II. THE FIVE PHASES OF THE CTC SYSTEM

CTC's structured and science-based approach to crime prevention involves activities undertaken in five cyclical phases: (1) assessing local readiness to engage in collaborative prevention efforts; (2) activating key leaders and forming a diverse coalition of community stakeholders; (3) using local data to identify factors that contribute to youth problem behaviors (i.e., risk and protective factors) and assess current prevention services; (4) selecting EBIs that address risk and protective factors and fill gaps in services; and (5) implementing and evaluating EBIs to determine their quality, reach, and impact (Fagan et al. 2018). Information about how to enact these phases is conveyed to CTC coalitions in user-friendly materials and multiple trainings that take place over 12 to 18 months. The expectation is that this process will build provide the infrastructure needed for coalitions to sustain their efforts over time.

CTC is typically initiated by one or more community residents who believe the system may be beneficial for their community. In Phase 1 (*Getting Started*), these *catalysts* or *champions* recruit other community members and begin to assess their *readiness* to undertake a collaborative approach to preventing youth delinquency. A community is ready to undertake such an initiative when community members agree that a problem is present and needs to be addressed, believe that it can be prevented, share a sense of commitment to and responsibility for the community, have effective leaders who can facilitate collaborative action, and have sufficient resources and an organizational infrastructure to support prevention activities (Fagan, Hawkins, et al. 2018; Hawkins, Catalano, and Arthur 2002; Chilenski, Greenberg, and Feinberg 2007). In this stage and in Phase 2, community members discuss the degree to which these factors are present, and they identify additional community characteristics that may facilitate or impede CTC implementation. For example, they consider levels of trust/mistrust among community members, the success/failure of prior collaborative efforts, current community initiatives that might interfere with CTC, and the amount of human and financial resources available to support CTC. If significant barriers are identified, the community should resolve those issues before moving forward.

In Phase 2 (*Get Organized*), communities identify key leaders who will support CTC, especially governmental, law enforcement, and education leaders who control resources and have connections to important stakeholders, including organizations that may deliver EBIs. They should also hire a full-time paid coordinator and begin to form a coalition that includes representatives from all organizations and stakeholders concerned about healthy youth development and/or preventing youth crime. CTC trainers provide coaching and support to key leaders, coalitions, and the CTC coordinator in this phase about risk and protective factors related to youth crime, the existence of EBIs to address these factors, and the actions that will be required during Phases 3, 4, and 5. CTC materials also provide guidance on coalition governance (e.g., electing a chair, vice chair, treasurer, and/or secretary) and structure (e.g., establishing workgroups responsible for key activities) to ensure that coalitions are well functioning and sustainable (Fagan et al. 2018).

In Phase 3 (*Develop a Profile*), coalitions learn how to conduct needs and resource assessments. The first step in the needs assessment is for coalitions to collect data on levels of risk and protective factors and behavior problems experienced by youth in their own communities, as geographically defined by coalition members. Because it is difficult to obtain locally specific information about these outcomes from administrative data (e.g., from schools or law enforcement), CTC requires that communities administer the CTC Youth Survey in local schools. The survey was designed to collect anonymous information from middle and high school students about their exposure to risk and protective factors in multiple ecological domains, as well as their involvement in problem behaviors including substance use, violence, and nonviolent delinquency (Arthur et al. 2002). The survey can be completed in a typical class period (e.g., 50 minutes) and has been demonstrated as valid and reliable across age, gender, and race/ethnic groups (Arthur et al. 2002; Glaser et al. 2005). CTC community coalitions are directed to administer this survey with as many students as possible in grades 6 through 12 to obtain a representative sample of community youth. They can then analyze the data to identify the percentage of youth reporting elevated levels of risk factors and low levels of protective factors (Arthur et al. 2007). Based on this information, coalition members identify three to five risk and protective factors they view as most problematic and in need of intervention.

Coalitions then receive guidance and training about how to conduct a resource assessment and identify current prevention services in their communities. Although data indicating elevated risk factors and low protective factors might suggest a lack of services, it could be that agencies are not using EBIs, are not implementing EBIs according to their requirements, or are not delivering EBIs to enough individuals to significantly impact risk and protective factors (Fagan et al. 2018). The goal of the resource assessment is to identify which interventions are being used, which risk and protective factors (if any) they address, whether or not services are "evidence-based," how well they are being implemented, and the populations receiving services. Coalition members collect these data from local service providers, then review the information and identify gaps in services—specifically, the risk and protective factors that are not currently being addressed by well-implemented EBIs.

The goal of Phase 4 (*Create a Plan*) is for coalitions to create an action plan listing the EBIs that will be implemented to fill gaps in services and address risk and protective factors. These may be new interventions or EBIs identified in the resource assessment that will be expanded or improved. In this phase, the CTC materials and guidance emphasize the importance of selecting interventions with strong and credible evidence of effectiveness. As already mentioned, early iterations of CTC provided information about EBIs in written guides created by Drs. Hawkins and Catalano. Given the rapid pace of intervention development and evaluation, CTC now recommends that coalitions select interventions listed as effective on the Blueprints for Healthy Youth Development website (http://www.blueprintsprograms.com/), especially those identified as "Model" interventions. Although other EBI registries exist, CTC endorses Blueprints because it is regularly updated, focuses on interventions intended to prevent youth problem behaviors (and to promote healthy youth development), and has rigorous criteria for inclusion to ensure that recommended interventions have a strong evidence base (Fagan et al. 2018).

CTC provides coaching to help coalition members become familiar with this site and gather information about the EBIs available to target risk and protective factors of concern. Multiple EBIs may exist to target a particular risk/protective factor, and it is important that community coalitions compare their financial costs, requirements, and "fit" with the local community, as doing so should help ensure that EBIs are fully implemented and sustained over time (Fagan et al. 2018; Horner and Blitz 2014). When conducting these fit assessments, coalitions might consider the degree to which each program's content and methods align with the community's norms, are culturally relevant and appropriate, and will be supported by program providers, participants, and the broader community (Elliott and Fagan 2017). They also need to consider whether or not local human and financial resources exist to fully implement the EBI and reach a large enough percentage of the population to impact outcomes. Based on these considerations, the coalition agrees on a set of EBIs to be adopted, and also documents in their action plan how, when, and to whom the services will be delivered (e.g., the organizations charged with the delivery, staffing requirements, budgets, start dates, recruitment goals and plans, etc.).

Phase 5 (*Implement and Evaluate*) is the final step in the CTC process and the one that continues through the remainder of the CTC initiative. This phase begins when EBIs are implemented and involves the ongoing evaluation of each EBI to ensure it is implemented as intended and that it is producing its intended benefits. Much research has demonstrated that EBIs can be difficult to enact and that community providers often deviate from intervention protocols during implementation (Durlak and DuPre 2008; Fixsen et al. 2005). Although adaptations may enhance EBI delivery and impact, changes that significantly alter EBI requirements are likely to reduce effectiveness. Research also suggests that integrity is enhanced when program staff or supervisors routinely collect data about implementation and use the data to engage in continuous quality improvement when problems arise (Elliott and Fagan 2017; Walker, Bumbarger, and Phillippi 2015). During Phase 5, CTC coaches assist coalitions and local organizations to collect and analyze such data and provide feedback to implementers to ensure high-quality delivery.

Phase 5 also entails the ongoing maintenance of the CTC coalition. Over time, a coalition may lose its officers, staff, and/or volunteer members, and those who remain may need to be re-engaged. CTC recommends that coalitions create a specific workgroup responsible for coalition functioning, whose activities include recruiting and training new members, holding celebratory events to honor members, and publicizing CTC's successes to increase public support (Fagan et al. 2018). This workgroup or another will also need to engage fundraising or grant-writing activities to ensure that the coalition and EBIs have adequate financial resources. Phase 5 also involves the repetition of some activities from prior phases. For example, the CTC Youth Survey should be readministered every two years to monitor changes in risk and protective factors and problem behaviors. If coalitions identify new areas of concern, they may need to select new EBIs to address these needs. If previously selected EBIs do not seem to be working and/or implementation problems are identified that cannot be addressed, coalitions may need to discontinue these services and adopt new EBIs. The community action plan should be updated to reflect these and other changes.

III. The Evidence Base for CTC

As emphasized throughout this chapter, a key component of CTC is its requirement that communities implement EBIs to prevent youth crime. To what extent, then, can CTC be considered an evidence-based model that reduces community rates of delinquency? In fact, as described in this section, the CTC system has a strong evidence base, having been evaluated and shown to reduce youth offending in a randomized trial occurring in 24 US communities (Hawkins, Catalano, et al. 2008), a quasi-experimental trial conducted across Pennsylvania (Chilenski et al. 2019), and in some international evaluations (Jonkman et al. 2015; Rowland et al. 2022). Two independent reviews of this literature have concluded that CTC is effective (European Monitoring Centre for Drugs and Drug Addiction 2017; Hutchinson and Russell 2021), and both the Blueprints for Healthy Youth Development and CrimeSolutions registries identify CTC as a Promising (i.e., effective) intervention for reducing delinquency.

A. Findings from the Community Youth Development Study

The strongest claims of CTC's effectiveness in preventing crime come from the Community Youth Development Study (Hawkins, Catalano, et al. 2008), a randomized controlled trial that involved a detailed analysis of CTC's implementation to ensure high internal validity and an analysis of its short- and long-term effects on community processes and individual behaviors. The study began in 2002, when 24 small- to medium-sized cities in seven US states were matched in pairs within each state on size, poverty, racial/ethnic diversity, and crime rates, then randomly assigned to implement CTC (N = 12) or to serve as control communities (N = 12) in which prevention services were conducted as usual (Hawkins, Catalano, et al. 2008). Beginning in 2003, CTC communities received five years of training and technical assistance to implement CTC and four years of funding to implement EBIs (Quinby et al. 2008).

The main goal of the randomized trial was to assess the degree to which CTC reduced behavior problems (substance use, delinquency, and violence), as well as risk and protective factors, among young people living in CTC communities compared to control communities. These changes were examined using data from a longitudinal panel of 4,407 individuals from all 24 communities who completed surveys annually from grades 5 to 10, as well as every one or two years through their early 20s (Brown et al. 2009). The trial also assessed changes in community mobilization, collaboration, and adoption of EBIs (Fagan et al. 2018).

Consistent with study hypotheses, the findings indicated that CTC was effective in changing youth exposure to risk and protective factors. In Year 3 of the study, two years after EBIs had begun and when students in the longitudinal panel were in grade 7, those in the CTC communities, compared to those in control communities, reported significantly lower levels of the risk factors targeted by EBIs selected by CTC coalitions (Hawkins, Brown, et al. 2008). These differences were maintained in grade 10 (Hawkins et al. 2012). Youth in CTC communities also reported greater increases in protective factors in grade 8 compared to those in control communities (Kim, Gloppen, et al. 2015), although these differences were not sustained at grade 10 (Kim, Oesterle, et al. 2015).

Analysis of panel data also demonstrated that CTC delayed the initiation (i.e., onset) and promoted abstinence of behavior problems. When the panel was in grade 7, youth in CTC communities were less likely to report having ever engaged in delinquent behaviors compared to those in control communities (Hawkins, Brown, et al. 2008). Significant effects in delaying the initiation of alcohol and cigarettes were found beginning in Grade 8 (Hawkins et al. 2009) and continued through high school, as did effects on delinquency onset (Hawkins et al. 2012, 2014). At age 19, those in the CTC communities were significantly more likely to have refrained from committing any delinquent acts compared to those in control communities, but no differences were found for substance use abstinence (Oesterle et al. 2015). However, outcomes examined when the longitudinal panel was age 23 indicated greater abstinence from alcohol use, illicit drug use, and illegal behaviors for those in the CTC versus control communities (Kuklinski et al. 2021). For example, 33% of the CTC panel reported having never engaged in crime at age 23 compared to 28.1% of the control group.

Effects on the prevalence of substance use, delinquency, and violence were less pronounced and prolonged, evidenced only when the panel was in middle and high school. For example, when in grade 8, about 16% of CTC youth reported drinking in the past month compared to 21% of control youth, and 5.7% of CTC youth versus 9% of control youth reported binge drinking in the past two weeks. CTC youth also reported fewer delinquent acts in grade 8 (Hawkins et al. 2009). At grade 10, the odds of engaging in any delinquent or any violent behavior in the past year were 17% and 25% lower, respectively, among CTC versus comparison youth (Hawkins et al. 2012). None of these types of effects were statistically significant at grade 12 (Hawkins et al. 2014) or age 19 (Oesterle et al. 2015).

Data from the randomized trial also indicated improvements in EBI implementation and sustainability, collaboration among stakeholders, and attitudes about youth substance use in CTC compared to control communities. Data collected from CTC coalition chairpersons indicated that all CTC coalitions selected EBIs to target their prioritized risk and protective factors (Fagan et al. 2009). Reports from service providers in all 24 communities indicated that, compared to control communities, CTC communities delivered a greater number of EBIs to greater numbers of participants and were more likely to sustain their programs after study funding for EBIs had ended (Fagan et al. 2011, 2012). Interviews with key leaders (e.g., mayors and school superintendents) indicated greater increases in collaboration between residents in CTC versus control communities in the first two years of the study (Brown et al. 2007) and a greater increase in community norms discouraging youth substance use from the start of the study through 2009 (Rhew et al. 2013).

CTC has also been demonstrated to be cost-beneficial. When comparing the costs associated with CTC implementation incurred during the randomized trial to the savings realized from preventing cigarette use, alcohol use, and delinquency through grade 12, CTC was determined to save $4.23 for every dollar invested (Kuklinski et al. 2015). When updated to reflect CTC intervention effects on substance use and crime when the longitudinal panel was age 23, a benefit-cost analysis indicated that CTC returned $12.88 for every dollar invested (Kuklinski et al. 2021).

B. Evidence from a Quasi-Experimental Evaluation in Pennsylvania

CTC has not only demonstrated effectiveness in reducing crime when evaluated in a highly controlled, well-implemented randomized trial, but also when evaluated in a more naturalistic experiment conducted in Pennsylvania. Communities in this state began to implement CTC in the early 1990s as part of OJJPD's Comprehensive Strategy initiative (Office of Juvenile Justice and Delinquency Prevention 1995). Impressed by promising results seen in these communities, Pennsylvania lawmakers provided additional funds to expand CTC implementation to over 120 coalitions across the state (Fagan et al. 2018). State funding has continued through the 2000s, supporting CTC coalitions and their implementation of EBIs. The state also created the Evidence-based Prevention and Intervention Support Center (or EPISCenter) to provide training and technical assistance to CTC coalitions and other communities to build their capacity to select, implement, and sustain EBIs (Bumbarger and Campbell 2012).

Research suggests that statewide centers such as the EPISCenter are essential for increasing the dissemination and high-quality implementation of EBIs (Welsh and Greenwood 2015; Fixsen et al. 2013; Mettrick et al. 2015) and evidence from Pennsylvania supports this hypothesis. Information gathered from chairpersons in CTC communities has indicated that CTC coalitions have successfully implemented EBIs to prevent youth delinquency (Brow, Feinberg, and Greenberg 2010; Brown et al. 2015; Bumbarger and Campbell 2012). Moreover, data collected from students participating in a version of the CTC Youth Survey conducted in middle and high schools across the state have shown improvements in substance use, delinquency, and depression for those living in areas with CTC coalitions compared to those living in other areas (Feinberg et al. 2007; Chilenski et al. 2019). These outcomes also appear to be stronger when CTC coalitions implement more EBIs (Feinberg et al. 2007, 2010; Chilenski et al. 2019).

C. Other Evidence of Effectiveness

Most of the communities involved in both the randomized trial and the Pennsylvania study were located in suburban and rural areas with mostly White residents. However, CTC has also been implemented in urban, lower-income, and/or ethnically diverse communities in the United States. (Brady et al. 2018; Kingston et al. 2016; Gorman-Smith et al. 2021). Notably, the Centers for Disease Control and Prevention (CDC) has funded CTC coalitions in Chicago, Denver, and Richmond (Virginia) through its National Centers of Excellence in Youth Violence Prevention initiative (https://www.cdc.gov/violenceprevention/youthviole

nce/yvpc/index.html), which promotes partnerships between academics and communities to address structural and economic determinants of violence. Consistent with the CTC approach, coalitions in the CDC-funded communities involved diverse stakeholders who worked together to identify areas of concern and develop locally specific plans to address their specific needs. These plans have, in some cases, included attention to diversity and inclusion. For example, based on input from over 70 community partners, the CTC coalition in Chicago decided to not only implement EBIs for youth and families, but also advocate for greater equity in local schools and more employment opportunities for adults (Kingston et al. 2021).

As another example, a CTC coalition in northwestern Massachusetts made racial justice and health equity central to its mission. To do so, coalition members disaggregated CTC Youth Survey data to identify disparities according to students' race, ethnicity, LGBTQ status, and income, then implemented EBIs to address these inequalities. Analysis of subsequent survey data indicated some reductions in racial disparities in youth alcohol and cigarette use (Allen et al. 2021).

IV. Conclusions and Future Directions

In 2007, Farrington and Welsh (2007) called for the US government to create a national strategy to prevent crime, one guided by scientific evidence and locally driven approaches. They advocated that CTC be used as the overarching delivery system for prevention services, stating that "with support from a national agency, the CTC model could be implemented in all communities across the United States" (Farrington and Welsh 2007, 173). This vision has not yet been realized. However, encouraged by the evidence of CTC's effectiveness in preventing youth problem behaviors, hundreds of communities in the United States and abroad have now implemented this evidence-based prevention system.

Moreover, some states (e.g., Colorado, Montana, and Utah) have followed the Pennsylvania model and funded CTC coalitions in multiple communities across their states. Doing so allows these states to ensure a uniform and scientifically informed approach to crime prevention that emphasizes the dissemination and high-quality implementation of EBIs targeting locally specific needs. Although there is consensus that greater use of EBIs is required to significantly impact public health problems, including crime, very few models have been created to facilitate EBI dissemination, and even fewer have been rigorously evaluated to determine their ability to do so (Fagan, Bumbarger, et al. 2019). CTC is a notable exception and offers a community-based solution to this challenge. Evidence from the quasi-experimental evaluation in Pennsylvania indicated that, when implemented throughout the state, CTC increased EBI implementation and reduced rates of delinquency (Feinberg et al. 2007; Chilenski et al. 2019). The more recent statewide CTC initiatives have not yet been evaluated for impact, but evidence that they also produce statewide reductions in crime would bolster Farrington and Welsh's (2007) call to install CTC in communities across the nation.

A critical advantage of the CTC system is its ability to provide communities with a structured and evidence-based approach to crime prevention, while also allowing local coalitions to tailor the system to their particular context to ensure that EBIs are appropriate, acceptable, and effective. In doing so, the CTC system has the potential to address inequalities in youth exposure to risk and protective factors and involvement in problem behaviors. Recent efforts suggest that CTC can be successfully implemented in underserved communities (Kingston et al. 2021) and may reduce disparities in delinquency and substance use (Allen et al. 2021), though more rigorous evaluation is required to fully understand CTC's potential for doing so. Such initiatives should include in-depth examination of communities' experiences implementing the CTC system, and this information should inform revisions to the system to more systematically address issues of diversity, inclusion, and equity. These data will be especially important if CTC is scaled up across states, as communities will vary in their populations, needs, values, and resources.

Scaling-up CTC and EBIs across states and the nation will require considerable human and financial resources and stable rather than short-term investments (Fagan, Bumbarger, et al. 2019). Although funding prevention efforts at scale is challenging, states have successfully implemented CTC using a variety of funding mechanisms, including funding from marijuana legalization (in Colorado), health and human services (in Montana), and criminal justice (in Pennsylvania). Stable funding streams that support EBI implementation in public systems, including education, behavioral health, and especially juvenile justice, could also be used (Fagan, Bumbarger, et al. 2019). As mentioned, OJJDP provided one of the first large-scale investments in CTC (Office of Juvenile Justice and Delinquency Prevention 1995, 1996), and it could again endorse and fund communities to implement CTC as *the* delivery system for providing delinquency prevention programming in the United States. The fact that CTC has been demonstrated as cost-effective (Kuklinski et al. 2015, 2021) should further persuade policymakers that CTC is a rational, effective, and efficient means of crime prevention.

REFERENCES

Allen, Kat, Rachel Stoler, Keyedrya Jacobs, Ilana Gerjuoy, Sage Shea, and Leigh-Ellen Figueroa. 2021. Centering racial justice and grassroots ownership in collective impact. *Stanford Social Innovation Review*, 19:1–8

Anderson, Elijah. 1999. *Code of the street*. New York: W. W. Norton.

Arthur, Michael W., John S. Briney, J. David Hawkins, Robert D. Abbott, Blair Brooke-Weiss, and Richard F. Catalano. 2007. Measuring community risk and protection using the communities that care youth survey. *Evaluation and Program Planning*, 30:197–211.

Arthur, Michael W., J. David Hawkins, John A. Pollard, Richard F. Catalano, and Anthony J. Baglioni. 2002. Measuring risk and protective factors for substance use, delinquency, and other adolescent problem behaviors: The Communities That Care Youth Survey. *Evaluation Review*, 26:575–601.

Brady, Sonya S., Capetra J. Parker, Elijah F. Jeffries, Tina Simpson, Blair L. Brook-Weiss, and Kevin P. Haggerty. 2018. Implementing the Communities That Care prevention system: Challenges, solutions, and opportunities in an urban setting. *American Journal of Preventive Medicine*, 5S:S70–S81.

Brown, Eric C., John W. Graham, J. David Hawkins, Michael W. Arthur, Megan M. Baldwin, Sabrina Oesterle, John S. Briney, Richard F. Catalano, and Robert D. Abbott. 2009. Design and analysis of the Community Youth Development Study longitudinal cohort sample. *Evaluation Review*, 33:311–334.

Brown, Eric C., J. David Hawkins, Michael W. Arthur, John S. Briney, and Robert D. Abbott. 2007. Effects of Communities That Care on prevention services systems: Findings from the community youth development study at 1.5 years. *Prevention Science*, 8:180–191.

Brown, Louis D., Mark E. Feinberg, and Mark T. Greenberg. 2010. Determinants of community coalition ability to support evidence-based programs. *Prevention Science*, 11:287–297.

Brown, Louis D., Mark E. Feinberg, Valerie B. Shapiro, and Mark T. Greenberg. 2015. Reciprocal relations between coalition functioning and the provision of implementation support. *Prevention Science*, 16:101–109.

Bumbarger, Brian K., and Elizabeth Morey Campbell. 2012. A state agency–university partnership for translational research and dissemination of evidence-based prevention and intervention. *Administration and Policy in Mental Health*, 39:268–277.

Bursik, Robert J., Jr., and Harold G. Grasmick. 1993. *Neighborhoods and crime: The dimensions of effective community control.* New York: Lexington Books.

Catalano, Richard F., Abigail A. Fagan, Loretta E. Gavin, Mark T. Greenberg Jr., Charles E. Irwin, David A. Ross, and Daniel T. L. Shek. 2012. Worldwide application of prevention science in adolescent health. *Lancet*, 379:1653–1664.

Catalano, Richard F., and J. David Hawkins. 1996. The social development model: A theory of antisocial behavior. In *Delinquency and crime: Current theories*, edited by J. David Hawkins, 149–197. New York: Cambridge University Press.

Chilenski, Sarah M., Jennifer Frank, Nicole Summers, and Daphne Lew. 2019. Public health benefits 16 years after a statewide policy change: Communities That Care in Pennsylvania. *Prevention Science*, 20:947–958.

Chilenski, Sarah M., Mark T. Greenberg, and Mark E. Feinberg. 2007. Community readiness as a multidimensional construct. *Journal of Community Psychology*, 35:347–365.

Cullen, Francis T. 2011. Beyond adolescence-limited criminology: Choosing our future—The American Society of Criminology 2010 Sutherland Address. *Criminology*, 49:287–330.

Cullen, Francis T. 2013. Rehabilitation: Beyond nothing works. *Crime and Justice*, 42:299–376.

Drake, Elizabeth K., Steve Aos, and Marna G. Miller. 2009. Evidence-based public policy options to reduce crime and criminal justice costs: Implications in Washington State. *Victims and Offenders*, 4:170–196.

Durlak, Joseph A., and Emily P. DuPre. 2008. Implementation matters: A review of the research on the influence of implementation on program outcomes and the factors affecting implementation. *American Journal of Community Psychology*, 41:327–350.

Elliott, Delbert S. 1994. Serious violent offenders: Onset, developmental course, and termination—The American Society of Criminology 1993 Presidential Address. *Criminology*, 32:1–21.

Elliott, Delbert S., and Abigail A. Fagan. 2017. *The prevention of crime.* Malden, MA: Wiley Blackwell.

European Monitoring Centre for Drugs and Drug Addiction. 2017. Communities That Care (CTC): A comprehensive prevention approach for communities. EMCDDA Papers. Luxembourg: Publications Office of the European Union.

Fagan, Abigail A., Michael W. Arthur, Koren Hanson, John S. Briney, and J. David Hawkins. 2011. Effects of Communities That Care on the adoption and implementation fidelity of evidence-based prevention programs in communities: Results from a randomized controlled trial. *Prevention Science*, 12:223–234.

Fagan, Abigail A., Brian K. Bumbarger, Richard P. Barth, Catherine Bradshaw, Brittany R. Cooper, Lauren H. Supplee, and Deborah K. Walker. 2019. Scaling-up evidence-based interventions in U.S. public systems to prevent behavioral health problems: Challenges and opportunities. *Prevention Science*, 20:1147–1168.

Fagan, Abigail A., Koren Hanson, John S. Briney, and J. David Hawkins. 2012. Sustaining the utilization and high quality implementation of tested and effective prevention programs using the Communities That Care prevention system. *American Journal of Community Psychology*, 49:365–377.

Fagan, Abigail A., Koren Hanson, J. David Hawkins, and Michael W. Arthur. 2009. Translational research in action: Implementation of the Communities That Care prevention system in 12 communities. *Journal of Community Psychology*, 37:809–829.

Fagan, Abigail A., and J. David Hawkins. 2013. Preventing substance use, delinquency, violence, and other problem behaviors over the life-course using the Communities That Care system. In *Handbook of life-course criminology*, edited by Chris L. Gibson and Marvin D. Krohn, 277–296. New York: Springer-Verlag.

Fagan, Abigail A., J. David Hawkins, Richard F. Catalano, and David P. Farrington. 2018. *Communities That Care: Building community engagement and capacity to prevent youth behavior problems*. New York: Oxford University Press.

Farrington, David P. 2003. Developmental and life-course criminology: Key theoretical and empirical issues—The 2002 Sutherland Award Address. *Criminology*, 41:221–255.

Farrington, David P., and Brandon C. Welsh. 2007. *Saving children from a life of crime: Early risk factors and effective interventions*. New York: Oxford University Press.

Feinberg, Mark E., Mark T. Greenberg, D. Wayne Osgood, Jennifer Sartorius, and Daniel Bontempo. 2007. Effects of the Communities That Care model in Pennsylvania on youth risk and problem behaviors. *Prevention Science*, 8:261–270.

Feinberg, Mark E., Damon E. Jones, Michael J. Cleveland, and Mark T. Greenberg. 2012. The community epidemiology of underage drinking: Variation across communities in relations of risk to alcohol use. *Prevention Science*, 13:551–561.

Feinberg, Mark E., Damon Jones, Mark T. Greenberg, D. Wayne Osgood, and Daniel Bontempo. 2010. Effects of the Communities That Care model in Pennsylvania on change in adolescent risk and problem behaviors. *Prevention Science*, 11:163–171.

Fixsen, Dean L., Karen A. Blase, Allison Metz, and Melissa Van Dyke. 2013. Statewide implementation of evidence-based programs. *Exceptional Children*, 79:213–230.

Fixsen, Dean L., Sandra F. Naoom, Karen A. Blase, Robert M. Friedman, and Frances Wallace. 2005. Implementation research: A synthesis of the literature. FMHI Publication #231. Tampa, FL: National Implementation Research Network.

Glaser, Renita R, M. Lee Van Horn, Michael W. Arthur, J. David Hawkins, and Richard F. Catalano. 2005. Measurement properties of the Communities That Care Youth Survey across demographic groups. *Journal of Quantitative Criminology*, 21:73–102.

Gorman-Smith, Deborah, Dave Bechhoefer, Franklin N. Cosey-Gay, Beverly E. Kingston, Maury A. Nation, Kevin J. Vagi, Juan A. Villamar, and Marc A. Zimmerman. 2021. A model for effective community-academic partnerships for youth violence prevention. *American Journal of Public Health*, 111:S25–S27.

Hawkins, J. David, Eric C. Brown, Sabrina Oesterle, Michael W. Arthur, Robert D. Abbott, and Richard F. Catalano. 2008. Early effects of Communities That Care on targeted risks and initiation of delinquent behavior and substance use. *Journal of Adolescent Health*, 43:15–22.

Hawkins, J. David, and Richard F. Catalano. (1996, 2000) 2004. *Communities That Care prevention strategies guide*. South Deerfield, MA: Channing Bete.

Hawkins, J. David, Richard F. Catalano, and Michael W. Arthur. 2002. Promoting science-based prevention in communities. *Addictive Behaviors*, 27:951–976.

Hawkins, J. David, Richard F. Catalano, Michael W. Arthur, Elizabeth Egan, Eric C. Brown, Robert D. Abbott, and David M. Murray. 2008. Testing Communities That Care: Rationale and design of the Community Youth Development Study. *Prevention Science*, 9:178–190.

Hawkins, J. David, Todd I. Herrenkohl, David P. Farrington, Devon Brewer, Richard F. Catalano, and Tracy W. Harachi. 1998. A review of predictors of youth violence. In *Serious and violent juvenile offenders*, edited by Rolf Loeber and David P. Farrington, 106–146. Thousand Oaks, CA: SAGE.

Hawkins, J. David, Jeffrey M. Jenson, Richard F. Catalano, and Denise M. Lishner. 1988. Delinquency and drug abuse: Implications for social services. *Social Service Review*, 62:258–284.

Hawkins, J. David, Denise M. Lishner, Jeffrey M. Jenson, and Richard F. Catalano. 1987. Delinquents and drugs: What the evidence suggests about prevention and treatment programming. In *Youth at high risk for substance abuse*, edited by Barry S. Brown and A.R. Mills, 116–133. Rockville, MD: National Institute on Drug Abuse.

Hawkins, J. David, Sabrina Oesterle, Eric C. Brown, Robert D. Abbott, and Richard F. Catalano. 2014. Youth problem behaviors 8 years after implementing the Communities That Care prevention system: A community randomized trial. *JAMA Pediatrics*, 168:122–129.

Hawkins, J. David, Sabrina Oesterle, Eric C. Brown, Michael W. Arthur, Robert D. Abbott, Abigail A. Fagan, and Richard F. Catalano. 2009. Results of a type 2 translational research trial to prevent adolescent drug use and delinquency: A test of Communities That Care. *Archives of Pediatric and Adolescent Medicine*, 163:789–798.

Hawkins, J. David, Sabrina Oesterle, Eric C. Brown, Kathryn C. Monahan, Robert D. Abbott, Michael W. Arthur, and Richard F. Catalano. 2012. Sustained decreases in risk exposure and youth problem behaviors after installation of the Communities That Care prevention system in a randomized trial. *Archives of Pediatrics and Adolescent Medicine*, 166:141–148.

Hawkins, J. David, and Joseph G. Weis. 1985. The social development model: An integrated approach to delinquency prevention. *Journal of Primary Prevention*, 6:73–97.

Horner, Robert H., and Caryn Blitz. 2014. The importance of contextual fit when implementing evidence-based interventions. ASPE Research Brief. Washington, DC: Office of the Assistant Secretary for Planning and Evaluation, Office of Human Services Policy, US Department of Health and Human Services.

Hutchinson, Morica, and Beth S. Russell. 2021. Community coalition efforts to prevent adolescent substance use: A systematic review. *Journal of Drug Education*, 50:3–30.

Jonkman, Harrie B., Claire Aussems, Majone Steketee, Hans Boutellier, and Pim Cuijpers. 2015. Prevention of problem behaviours among adolescents: The impact of the Communities That Care strategy in the Netherlands (2008–2011). *International Journal of Developmental Science*, 9:37–52.

Kazemian, Lila, David P. Farrington, and Alex Piquero. 2019. Developmental and life-course criminology. In *The Oxford handbook of developmental and life-course criminology*, edited by David P. Farrington, Lila Kazemian and Alex Piquero, 3–10. New York: Oxford University Press.

Kim, B. K. Elizabeth, Kari M. Gloppen, Isaac C. Rhew, Sabrina Oesterle, and J. David Hawkins. 2015. Effects of the Communities That Care prevention system on youth reports of protective factors. *Prevention Science*, 16:652–662.

Kim, B. K. Elizabeth, Sabrina Oesterle, J. David Hawkins, and Valerie Shapiro. 2015. Assessing sustained effects of Communities That Care on youth protective factors. *Journal of the Society for Social Work and Research*, 6:565–589.

Kingston, Beverly, Martica Bacallao, Paul Smokowski, Terri N. Sullivan, and Kevin S. Sutherland. 2016. Constructing "packages" of evidence-based programs to prevent youth violence: Processes and illustrative examples from the CDC's youth violence prevention centers. *Journal of Primary Prevention*, 37:141–163.

Kingston, Beverly E., Marc A. Zimmerman, Monica L. Wendel, Deborah Gorman-Smith, Erin Wright-Kelly, Sabrina Mattson Arredondo, and Aimee-Rika T. Trudeau. 2021. Developing and implementing community-level strategies for preventing youth violence in the United States. *American Journal of Public Health*, 111:S20–S24.

Kuklinski, Margaret R., Abigail A. Fagan, J. David Hawkins, John S. Briney, and Richard F. Catalano. 2015. Benefit-cost analysis of a randomized evaluation of Communities That Care: Monetizing intervention effects on the initiation of delinquency and substance use through grade 12. *Journal of Experimental Criminology*, 11:165–192.

Kuklinski, Margaret R., Sabrina Oesterle, John S. Briney, and J. David Hawkins. 2021. Long-term impacts and benefit-cost analysis of the Communities That Care prevention system at age 23, 12 years after baseline. *Prevention Science*, 22:452–463.

MacKenzie, Doris Layton 2013. First do no harm: A look at correctional policies and programs today: The 2011 Joan McCord Prize lecture. *Journal of Experimental Criminology*, 9:1–17.

Manger, Tracy Harachi, J. David Hawkins, Kevin P. Haggerty, and Richard F. Catalano. 1992. Mobilizing communities to reduce risks for drug abuse: Lessons on using research to guide prevention practice. *Journal of Primary Prevention*, 13:3–22.

Mears, Daniel P. 2007. Towards rational and evidence-based crime policy. *Journal of Criminal Justice*, 35:667–682.

Mettrick, Jennifer, Deborah S. Harburger, Patrick J. Kanary, Rebecca Bertell Lieman, and Michelle Zabel. 2015. Building cross-system implementation centers: A roadmap for state and local child serving agencies in developing Centers of Excellence (COE). Baltimore: Institute for Innovation & Implementation, University of Maryland.

National Academies of Sciences, Engineering, and Medicine. 2019. *Fostering healthy mental, emotional, and behavioral development in children and youth: A national agenda*. Washington, DC: The National Academies Press.

Oesterle, Sabrina, J. David Hawkins, Margaret R. Kuklinski, Abigail A. Fagan, Christopher Fleming, Isaac C. Rhew, Eric C. Brown, Robert D. Abbott, and Richard F. Catalano. 2015. Effects of Communities That Care on males' and females' drug use and delinquency 9 years after baseline in a community-randomized trial. *American Journal of Community Psychology*, 56:217–228.

Office of Juvenile Justice and Delinquency Prevention. 1995. *Guide for implementing the comprehensive strategy for serious, violent, and chronic juvenile offenders*. Washington, DC: Office of Juvenile Justice and Delinquency Prevention.

Office of Juvenile Justice and Delinquency Prevention. 1996. *1996 report to Congress: Title V incentive grants for local delinquency prevention programs*. Washington, DC: Office of Juvenile Justice and Delinquency Prevention.

Pew-MacArthur Results First Initiative. 2015. Legislating evidence-based policymaking. Washington, DC: Pew Charitable Trusts, MacArthur Foundation.

Pratt, Travis C., and Francis T. Cullen. 2005. Assessing macro-level predictors and theories of crime: A meta-analysis. In *Crime and justice*, edited by Michael Tonry, 373–450. Chicago: University of Chicago Press.

Quinby, Rose, Abigail A. Fagan, Koren Hanson, Blair Brooke-Weiss, Michael W. Arthur, and J. David Hawkins. 2008. Installing the Communities That Care prevention system: Implementation progress and fidelity in a randomized controlled trial. *Journal of Community Psychology*, 36:313–332.

Rhew, Isaac C., Eric C. Brown, J. David Hawkins, and John S. Briney. 2013. Sustained effects of the Communities That Care system on prevention service system transformation. *American Journal of Public Health*, 103:529–535.

Rowland, Bosco, Adrian B. Kelly, Mohammadreza Mohebbi, Peter Kremer, Charles Abrahams, Julie Abimanyi-Ochom, Rob Carter, et al. 2022. Evaluation of Communities That Care—Effects on municipal youth crime rates in Victoria, Australia: 2010–2019. *Prevention Science*, 22:24–35.

Sampson, Robert J. 2012. *Great American city: Chicago and the enduring neighborhood effect*. Chicago: University of Chicago Press.

Sampson, Robert J., Stephen W. Raudenbush, and Felton Earls. 1997. Neighborhoods and violent crime: A multilevel study of collective efficacy. *Science*, 277:918–924.

Shaw, Clifford R. and Henry D. McKay. 1942. *Juvenile delinquency and urban areas*. Chicago: University of Chicago Press.

Telep, Cody W., Joel H. Garner, and Christy A. Visher. 2015. The production of criminological experiments revisited: The nature and extent of federal support for experimental designs, 2001–2013. *Journal of Experimental Criminology*, 11:541–563.

United States Government Accountability Office. 1996. *Report to the Committee on the Judiciary, U.S. Senate, and the Committee on Economic and Educational Opportunity, House of Representatives*. Washington, DC: United States Government Accountability Office.

Walker, Sarah Cusworth, Brian K. Bumbarger, and Stephen W. Phillippi Jr. 2015. Achieving successful evidence-based practice implementation in juvenile justice: The importance of diagnostic and evaluative capacity. *Evaluation and Program Planning*, 52:189–197.

Welsh, Brandon C., and David P. Farrington. 2012. Science, politics, and crime prevention: Toward a new crime policy. *Journal of Criminal Justice*, 40:128–133.

Welsh, Brandon C., and Peter Greenwood. 2015. Making it happen: State progress in implementing evidence-based programs for delinquent youth. *Youth Violence and Juvenile Justice*, 13:243–257.

Wilson, John J., and James C. Howell. 1993. *A comprehensive strategy for serious, violent, and chronic juvenile offenders*. Washington, DC: Office of Juvenile Justice and Delinquency Prevention.

CHAPTER 22

REDUCING SCHOOL CRIME AND STUDENT MISBEHAVIOR
An Evidence-Based Analysis

ALLISON ANN PAYNE

ALTHOUGH schools should be spaces safe from crime and victimization, this is unfortunately not the case. Even though they spend fewer waking hours there, students report similar victimization rates at school compared to those away from school. Indeed, despite declines in serious violent crime and overall school crime during the past three decades, crime and disorder in schools are still a cause for concern. During the 2017–2018 school year, 80% of public schools in the United States recorded one or more crime incidents and 47% reported these incidents to the police; in addition, 71% of public schools recorded one or more *violent* incidents and 21% recorded one or more *serious violent* incidents (Wang et al. 2020). Throughout this same year, 33% of public schools recorded one or more thefts and 13% reported that bullying occurred among students on a daily or weekly basis. Surveys of public-school students also indicate the continual presence of crime and disorder. In 2018, 33 per 1,000 students experienced violent victimizations at school, compared with 16 per 1,000 students away from school. In the previous year, 9% of students reported being in a physical fight at school, 6% reported being threatened or injured with a weapon such as a gun or knife at school, and 4% reported carrying a weapon to school. In addition, 20% of students reported being bullied at school, with 30% of bullying victims reporting being bullied between 3 and 10 days in the school year (Wang et al. 2020).

Beyond the cost of injury and property damage and loss, school crime is costly because it reduces the ability of schools to carry out their educational mission. Teachers in disorderly schools spend a large proportion of their time handling behavior problems rather than instructing students, resulting in lower levels of student academic engagement, academic performance, and eventually graduation rates. Indeed, a large portion of teachers state that student misbehavior interferes with their ability to teach (Robers et al. 2015). In addition, fear of victimization also influences students' attendance, such that students are more likely to avoid school activities or places, or even school itself, due to fear of attack or harm (Hutzell and Payne 2018).

Predictably, reducing crime has become a high priority for American schools. Guided by a crime control model, responses to school crime and disorder have become increasingly formal over the last 20 years, with greater recourse to arrest and the juvenile courts rather than informal, school-based discipline. At the same time, there has been a considerable investment in measures such as security cameras and police officers in schools. Unfortunately, there is no evidence to suggest that these responses have reduced school crime and disorder; indeed, there is evidence of severe negative consequences (Payne and Welch 2018). By contrast, there is a sizeable body of research supporting the effectiveness of interventions focused on changing risk factors for student misbehavior, delinquency, and crime. School-level strategies aimed at school climate and discipline management have been shown to be effective at preventing or reducing such behavior, as have individual-level programs targeting students' self-competence and cognitive skills.

This chapter will begin with an examination of the use of restrictive security and punitive discipline measures, including the consequences therein. An evidence-based alternative will then be presented: strategies aimed at improving school- and student-level risk factors for crime and deviance. Schoolwide risk factors for crime and disorder will be discussed, followed by strategies and example interventions aimed at improving these school characteristics. Student-level risk factors for antisocial and delinquent behavior will then be discussed, followed by strategies and example interventions focused on improving these student characteristics. Finally, recommendations for schools and research will be presented.

I. School Security and Discipline

It is widely acknowledged that American schools are supportive of strict approaches to preventing and managing student misbehavior. Schools are increasingly adopting restrictive security measures, with the majority of schools now using multiple security and surveillance strategies. Most prominent among these are hiring security personnel such as uniformed guards or law enforcement officers, installing security cameras, requiring faculty and staff identification badges, and controlling building access through locked or monitored doors. Many schools require student identification badges and uniforms or implement strict dress codes, and may also use metal detectors, perform regular locker searches, require students to carry clear book bags, and use drug-sniffing dogs. This trend in what has been referred to as "school prisonization" has increased over time. For example, the percentage of schools reporting the use of security cameras increased from 19% during the 1999–2000 school year to 83% during the 2017–2018 school year. During that same time, controlling building access increased from 75% to 95% and the use of identification badges for faculty and staff increased from 25% to 70%. Similarly, schools reporting the use of security personnel, including police officers, at least once per week, increased from 42 to 61% between the 2005–2006 school year and the 2017–2018 school year (Wang et al. 2020).

Student discipline has also grown increasingly punitive. Of the 50.5 million students enrolled in public schools during the 2015–2016 school year, 2.7 million received one or more in-school suspensions while another 3.5 million received one or more out-of-school suspensions (Rafa 2019). During the 2017–2018 school year, 35% of public schools took at least one serious disciplinary action against a student; of these, 73% were suspensions, 22% were transfers, and 5% were removals with no services provided (Wang et al. 2020).

As with security, this student criminalization trend has grown over time: exclusionary discipline increased sharply from the early 1970s through the early 2000s and continued to increase gradually for the next decade, finally leveling off over the past 10 years (Ryberg et al. 2021). This rise of punitive discipline has been furthered by zero-tolerance policies and increased hiring of police officers in schools, causing a shift from administrative discretion to mandatory penalties and from in-school discipline to increasing use of suspension or arrest.

It is also important to note that stricter security and disciplinary measures are not used equally in schools. More restrictive security is found in schools with a larger student body, a greater proportion of minority students, and a greater proportion of students receiving free or reduced lunches, as well as schools located in urban areas and in the southern part of the United States. (Finn and Servoss 2014; Mowen and Parker 2017; Steinka-Fry, Fisher, and Tanner-Smith 2016). Similarly, harsher disciplinary responses are more often used in schools with greater student enrollment, greater student disadvantage, proportionally more Black and Latinx students, and schools located in urban areas and in the South (Byrd et al. 2015; Kupchik and Ward 2014; Ramey 2015; Welch and Payne 2010, 2018). This disparity is seen at the individual level as well, particularly the fact that Black and Latinx students disproportionately experience exclusionary discipline compared to White students (Department of Education Office for Civil Rights 2014).

Although this increase in restrictive security and punitive discipline has coincided with a decrease in school crime and victimization rates, there is no evidence of a causal link; this is largely due to the lack of studies examining the effectiveness of these approaches (Gottfredson, Cook, and Na 2014). By contrast, research has indicated that there is a good chance that these strategies are having a *negative* effect on students and schools. More restrictive security is associated with higher truancy rates, lower levels of school and peer connectedness, and overall decreases in academic performance (Brady, Balmer, and Phenix 2007; Fisher and Cuellar 2021; Tanner-Smith and Fisher 2016; Theriot 2016). Schools using these measures experience increases in school crime and disorder, including weapon and drug crimes (Devlin and Fisher 2021; Devlin and Gottfredson 2018; Gottfredson et al. 2020; Servoss 2017; Tanner-Smith, Durlak, and Marx 2018). More restrictive security is also associated with increases in reporting and referrals to law enforcement for minor offenses, property offenses, and serious and nonserious violent offenses (Devlin and Gottfredson 2018; Na and Gottfredson 2013; Nance and Heise 2022; Sorensen et al. 2021).

Additionally, students who are punitively disciplined are more likely to experience poor school performance, grade retention, negative attitudes toward schools, and dropping out (Gardella 2015; Skiba and Rausch 2006). Their graduation rates are lower and subsequent professional opportunities are limited (Lasnover 2015; Vincent and Tobin 2011). These students are also more likely to engage in fighting, weapon-carrying, smoking, substance drug use, and other delinquent acts (Lasnover 2015; Welch and Payne 2014). Punitive school discipline has been associated with justice system contact, arrest, probation, and incarceration, thus confirming the school-to-prison pipeline as a tragic reality for some students (Barnes and Motz 2018; Mittleman 2018; Rosenbaum 2020; Wolf and Kupchik 2017). Thus, instead of helping students develop positive social and behavioral skills, these approaches increase the likelihood that crime and disorder will continue to occur both at school and in the greater community.

II. School Interventions Based on Risk Factors

Fortunately, a sizeable body of work demonstrates a better way: School-based programs, practices, and policies focused on changing school- and individual-level risk factors are far more effective at preventing or reducing school crime and disorder. Indeed, schools are a logical place for these types of prevention strategies (Gottfredson 2001). Students spend a large segment of their day there, and the adults who work in schools care about the development of students and have regular access to these students during their formative years. In addition, students naturally expect to learn in such a setting, and the greater community is generally supportive of school strategies. Thus, schools are a "key setting for building social, emotional, and behavioral outcomes" and provide a "socializing context . . . to learn a range of life skills" (Goldberg et al. 2019, 756). Unsurprisingly, some form of prevention program or practice can be found in nearly all schools, ranging from schoolwide initiatives to create positive supportive climates to smaller programs focusing on the behavior of higher-risk students (Flannery and Farrell 2019).

The most effective school-based interventions are those that target risk factors for crime and antisocial behavior. Risk factors are characteristics of an individual or environment that increase the likelihood of negative behavior, and a sizeable body of work has identified factors that may be targeted by school programs, policies, or practices. Indeed, much research has demonstrated the effectiveness of school-based interventions that target these risk factors (Waschbusch et al. 2019). Meta-analyses of interventions in schools find these strategies display significant impacts not only on aggressive, disruptive, and problem behavior, but on other outcomes as well, including anger and hostility, social skills and adjustment, and school performance and participation (Durlak et al. 2011; Sklad et al. 2012; Taylor et al. 2017; Wilson, Gottfredson, and Najaka 2001; Wilson and Lipsey 2007). The mean effect sizes for reductions in problem behavior range from .09 to .39, which has clear practical consequences for schools. For example, as Wilson and Lipsey (2007) detail, if 20% of a school's students engage in negative behavior, implementation of an intervention with an effect size of .29 would reduce that amount to 13% of students. This represents a 33% reduction of problem students, a meaningful decrease for schools. Importantly, these interventions have positive impacts for both higher- and lower-risk students (Healy et al. 2020).

It is common practice to discuss school-based interventions as part of a nested, tiered approach (Bottiani, Heilbrun, and Bradshaw 2019; Waschbusch et al. 2019), such as the pyramid seen in Figure 22.1. The different levels are defined by the degree of risk possessed by the individual, with students moving up the levels as needed. Universal interventions are found in the first tier, applied to all students regardless of risk status, and are generally effective at preventing problem behavior for the majority of students. Programs and practices at the universal level can be separated into schoolwide interventions, aimed at improving environmental influences, or individual-level interventions, focused on changing student characteristics. Approximately 15–20% of students do not respond to universal interventions and therefore move up to the second tier, where selective interventions target students who are at higher risk for problem behavior but are not yet displaying such behavior. A smaller

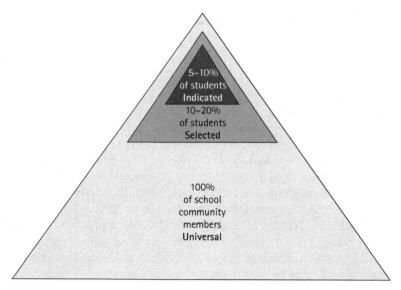

FIGURE 22.1. Intervention Tiers.

subset of students, around 5%, may already be engaged in deviant or delinquent behavior, and thus continue moving up to the third tier. At this level, indicated interventions provide struggling students with the most intensive and specialized programming.

III. SCHOOL-LEVEL UNIVERSAL INTERVENTIONS

At the school level, school climate has been highlighted as an important risk factor for crime and disorder, with studies indicating that a positive and communal school climate can improve a school's safety and foster a school's success (Payne 2016). Students in schools with a positive climate engage in fewer acts of deviance, delinquency, crime, and violence. They demonstrate lower levels of substance use and aggression, are subjected to fewer suspensions and expulsions, and display lower levels of truancy and dropping out. They are also less afraid to attend school and are less likely to be victimized. The specific components of school climate include the cultural system of norms and values, the management of school discipline, and the social system of relationships among school community members. Schools that effectively communicate clear expectations for behavior demonstrate lower rates of victimization and crime (Gottfredson, Cook, and Na 2014).

In addition, contrary to the punitive discipline discussed in Section I, clear rules and fair rule enforcement are far more effective in obtaining lower levels of school disorder. Schools that establish and maintain rules, consistently enforce rules, and provide rewards for compliance and consequences for infractions experience lower levels of crime and victimization (Gottfredson et al. 2005). Finally, students who experience supportive relationships with their teachers display less victimization, fewer bullying incidents, and decreased engagement in delinquent and violent behaviors, while those with cohesive and trusting relationships with their peers experience lower incidents of problem behaviors and victimization (Payne 2016). Ultimately, the climate of a school affects its ability to regulate students' behaviors, such that school crime and disorder will be lower when the climate is "more socially cohesive and has a shared sense of values and beliefs" (Zaykowski and Gunter 2012, 435). Thus, schoolwide interventions should be aimed at building a supportive and collaborative school community based on respect and trust by enhancing the clarification and communication of behavior expectations along with the consistency and fairness of enforcement (Gottfredson, Cook, and Na 2014; Mielke and Farrington 2021).

One effective schoolwide strategy is to implement normative change efforts aimed at clarifying and communicating what student behavior should look like; these strategies often target a specific type of behavior, such as substance use or bullying, and have been shown to be effective at reducing the intended focus (Gottfredson, Cook, and Na 2014), with effect sizes ranging from .09 to .15 (Wilson, Gottfredson, and Najaka 2001). An example of one such program is the Olweus Bullying Prevention Program (OBPP), intended to reduce and prevent bullying in elementary, middle, and high schools through school-, classroom-, and individual-level components. The overarching focus of this program is the clear message that bullying will not be tolerated in the school. The school-level component of OBPP includes the formation of a Bullying Prevention Coordinating Committee, which collects data on the prevalence of bullying in the school, conducts program trainings, and ensures adult supervision of bullying-prone areas such as playgrounds and stairwells. Strategies in the classroom reinforce the behavior expectations surrounding bullying through discussions and activities, while individual-level responses intervene with students involved in bullying, either as perpetrators or victims, and their parents (Blueprints for Healthy Youth Development 2023c).

Although self-reported bullying perpetration and victimization findings are mixed, the results from most evaluations of OBPP are positive. Indeed, in Pennsylvania, Limber et al. (2018) found decreases ranging from 13% to 29% in perpetration and victimization two and three years after the start of program participation. In addition, studies in Norway and South Carolina found reductions in other problem behavior, including truancy, vandalism, and theft; the original Norway study also found improvements in social relationships and school climate (Olweus and Alsakar 1991; Schroeder et al. 2012). Finally, studies have found improvements in attitudes surrounding bullying, such as increased empathy for victims of bullying and decreased willingness to join in ongoing bullying (Blueprints for Healthy Youth Development 2023c).

A broader schoolwide strategy to enhance school climate includes interventions designed to improve the school's capacity to regulate student behavior. These are generally comprehensive approaches focused on discipline policies and management and often use a team model to choose and implement interventions designed to improve the overall school ethos, primarily by focusing on responses to behavior (Gottfredson, Cook, and Na 2014). One meta-analysis found this strategy has an effect size of .39 for the reduction of delinquency (Wilson, Gottfredson, and Najaka 2001). The best-known intervention using this approach is Schoolwide Positive Behavioral Interventions and Support (SWPBS), designed for all levels of schooling to create a school community focused on respect, responsibility, and safety. SWPBS uses the pyramid and team structure described previously to create and maintain a positive school climate: The entire school community is involved with the basic preventive supports of the primary tier and students move up through the secondary and tertiary intervention tiers based on behavioral need. The main focus of Tier One is establishing and communicating expectations for behavior for all students through instruction in the classroom and reinforcement in other settings, such as the cafeteria and hallways. In addition, data on student behavior are collected, analyzed, and used to identify students who are not responding to the schoolwide strategies. These students move up to Tier Two, where additional support is provided. Finally, a small subset of students receives the most intensive support at Tier Three (Horner, Sugai, and Anderson 2010).

Because SWPBS is not a packaged curriculum, but rather a data-driven structure designed to help school teams make decisions on what interventions would best serve which students at each tier, it can be complicated to evaluate. However, "results from randomized control studies, . . . quasi-experimental designs, . . . and systematic evaluation designs . . . form a pattern demonstrating that SWPBS . . . is associated with improved behavior" (Horner, Sugai, and Anderson 2010, 7). Implementation of the Tier One SWPBS structure appears to produce positive outcomes: Schools in Maryland that used the SWPBS structure experienced a significant reduction in school suspensions compared with schools that did not, while schools in Illinois and Hawaii showed significant improvements in school safety perceptions compared with control schools (Bradshaw, Mitchell, and Leaf 2010; Horner et al. 2009). Additionally, a wide range of studies illustrate the effectiveness of interventions available for use in Tiers Two and Three, individual-level strategies which will be discussed further on in this chapter. Essentially, there is a range of studies supporting possible interventions at each tier (Horner, Sugai, and Lewis 2020).

Another common strategy used to create a positive communal school climate is the use of restorative approaches in the schools. Within the restorative justice model, student misbehavior is viewed as a violation of the relationships between the offender and the victim as well as between the offender and the overall school community. In order to restore the harm caused, the school facilitates an environment in which the offending student and those individuals whose trust was violated can reconcile and thereby mend their relationship (Payne and Welch 2018). Recent studies illustrate how restorative justice in schools has evolved from an incident-based strategy that focuses solely on misbehavior and discipline toward a broader approach that focuses on the overall school community. Rather than dealing mainly with specific incidents or problems between only a few individuals, this whole-school model addresses how restorative justice can be used to build a communal school climate, recognizing the importance of building and maintaining relationships among all members of the school community. The prevention of violations goes beyond each isolated incident to instead incorporate a multilevel intervention system similar to the pyramid previously described (González, Sattler, and Buth 2019; Morrison 2007). At the initial level, all school community members are engaged in the development of skills necessary to build and maintain relationships and to create a positive school climate based on restorative values. The next two levels focus on specific incidents and individuals, with the secondary level using less formal techniques to repair harm, and the tertiary level centering on those who need the most intensive intervention (Morrison 2007).

Despite the growing use of restorative justice in US schools, rigorous research on the effectiveness of this intervention is sorely lacking (Fronius et al. 2019; Zakszezki and Rutherford 2020). Initial studies of the impact of restorative justice approaches were primarily descriptive in nature, and few of the quantitative studies that are emerging are experimental or quasi-experimental (Zakszeski and Rutherford 2020). Nevertheless, findings from both early descriptive studies and newer, more rigorous, studies on restorative justice offer promising support. Results indicate improvements in various indicators of school climate and academic achievement as well as fewer episodes of student misbehavior, including bullying and fighting, with reported reductions ranging from 40% to 58% (Darling-Hammond et al. 2020; Fronius et al. 2019; Gardella 2015; González, Sattler, and Buth 2019; Gregory and Evans 2020; Morrison and Vaandering 2012). Restorative approaches also appear to reduce the use of punitive discipline responses, such as suspensions and expulsions, with some studies reporting reductions in suspensions ranging from 44% to 87% (Darling-Hammond et al 2020; Fronius et al. 2019; González, Sattler, and Buth 2019; Gregory and Evans 2020; Katic, Alba, and Johnson 2020).

IV. Student-Level Universal Interventions

Universal interventions that focus on changing student characteristics generally work to build cognitive, social, and emotional skills. Much research has established that adolescent brains are still developing these competencies necessary for a successful life (American Academy of Child and Adolescent Psychiatry 2016); helping students to build skills like conflict management and responsible decision-making can lead to positive outcomes in school and beyond (Goldberg et al. 2019). In addition, those children and adolescents who do engage in antisocial behavior often display cognitive traits such as impulsivity and hostility, which often lead them to misinterpret other's intentions as hostile, not thinking before acting, and not considering alternative solutions to problems (Gottfredson and Gottfredson 2018). Additionally, many of these students suffer from social and emotional deficiencies, which can also lead to social, academic, and behavioral problems (Durlak et al. 2011). Thus, student-level universal programs focus on building prosocial competencies. The most successful interventions generally use cognitive-behavioral delivery methods, with students learning skills using interactive methods, including role play, rehearsal, and feedback (Gottfredson and Gottfredson 2018). Meta-analyses of these strategies find overall effect sizes ranging from .10 to .21 for reductions in aggressive, disruptive, and delinquent behavior (Wilson and Lipsey 2007; Wilson, Gottfredson, and Najaka 2001).

An example of such a program is LifeSkills Training, a three-year intervention designed to reduce and prevent substance use, particularly alcohol, tobacco, and marijuana use. This program is taught by teachers in the classroom, with 15 sessions during sixth grade and 5 to 15 sessions over the next two years (Blueprints for Healthy Youth Development 2023b). There are three program components: self-management, social skills, and drug resistance. The self-management unit focuses on decision-making, problem-solving, and self-control skills, while the social skills unit centers on effective communication, including verbal and nonverbal assertiveness. The resistance skills unit contains lessons on common misconceptions about alcohol, tobacco, and drug use, as well as ways to handle social pressure to engage in substance use and other risky behavior. Studies show both short-term and long-term reductions in alcohol, tobacco, and marijuana use, including some dramatic percentage differences between program and control students. For example, some evaluations show reductions in cigarette smoking of up to 87% directly after the program (Botvin, Renick, and Baker 1983), 50% lower rates of binge drinking one and two years after the program (Botvin et al. 2001a, 2001b), and 66% less marijuana use by program students relative to control students (Botvin et al. 1990). Similarly, six years after the program, participants' weekly use of tobacco, alcohol, and marijuana was 66% lower than control students (Botvin et al. 1995). Short-term reductions in delinquency and violence were also seen, as were reductions in use of opioids, methamphetamine, and hallucinogens six years later (Blueprints for Healthy Development 2023b).

One of the most common universal student-level strategies used to build prosocial competencies is social and emotional learning (SEL). This type of programming helps students develop competencies in five core areas: self-awareness, self-management, social awareness, relationship skills, and responsible decision-making (Weissberg et al. 2015). Skills are "taught, modeled, and practiced so that children, adolescents, and adults can handle daily tasks, interactions, and challenges effectively" (Weissberg 2019, 65). Multiple meta-analyses have demonstrated that SEL interventions are effective across a range of outcomes, including effect sizes ranging from .13 to .28 for behavioral improvements and .26 to .33 for academic improvements (Bottiani, Heilbrun, and Bradshaw 2019; Goldberg et al. 2019; Mahoney, Durlak, and Weissberg 2018–2019; Weissberg 2019). Students who participate in such programming experience lower levels of disruptive behavior, fighting, bullying, verbal aggression, drug use, and disciplinary referrals when compared with control students (Mahoney, Durlak, and Weissberg 2018–2019). They also feel more connected to and perform better in school, which in turn may lead to fewer problem behaviors (Mahoney, Durlak, and Weissberg 2018–2019; Mielke and Farrington 2021; Weissberg 2019).

Promoting Alternative Thinking Strategies (PATHS) is an example of a SEL intervention shown to have positive outcomes. Elementary school teachers present between 36 and 52 lessons two to three times per week and engage students in daily activities to reinforce and generalize the material. Lessons focus on topics within five areas—self-control, emotional understanding, positive self-esteem, friendships, and problem-solving skills—and are taught using cognitive-behavioral strategies (Blueprints for Healthy Youth Development 2023d). Students who participate in PATHS demonstrate reductions in aggression, hyperactivity, delinquency, and other problem behaviors (Blueprints for Healthy Youth Development 2023d; Conduct Problems Prevention Research Group 1999). Indeed, a meta-analysis of PATHS shows effect sizes of .42 and .26 for reductions in aggressive behavior as reported by teachers and parents, respectively (Malti, Ribeaud, and Eisner 2011). Improvements are also seen in academic performance, school functioning, and social skills (Blueprints for Healthy Youth Development 2023d; Domitrovich, Cortes, and Greenberg 2007).

V. Selected and Indicated Interventions

Similar to the student-level strategies at the universal tier, interventions at the selected and indicated tiers focus on the characteristics identified by research as risk factors for antisocial, deviant, and delinquent behavior. These programs primarily aim to improve the cognitive, social, and emotional deficits that lead disruptive and aggressive children and adolescents to attribute hostility to other's intentions and to misunderstand their own responsibility for conflict and behavior (Gottfredson 2001). This programming is designed for higher-risk students who do not respond to the schoolwide universal strategies. Thus, interventions are generally more intense than the universal competency curriculum described earlier and are delivered in small groups or one-on-one by a trained facilitator. Most programs address problem behavior with behavior modification strategies, such as manipulating rewards and incentives, and/or cognitive-behavioral therapy, such as addressing maladaptive thinking (Gottfredson and Gottfredson 2018; Mielke and Farrington 2021; Waschbusch et al. 2019). Meta-analyses find effect sizes ranging from .29 to .32 for selected and indicated programs using these strategies (Wilson, Gottfredson, and Najaka 2001; Wilson and Lipsey 2007).

One cognitive-behavioral intervention supported by rigorous evaluation studies is the Coping Power Program. Aggressive and disruptive students in fifth and sixth grade attend 34 small group sessions led by a program specialist and a guidance counselor over a 16-month period, as well as 30-minute individual sessions once every two months. During the 50-minute group sessions, the students work on anger management, communication and social skills, and effective problem-solving (Blueprints for Healthy Youth Development 2023a). They establish group rules and reinforcements, learn how to generate alternate solutions and consider consequences to problem situations, and create self-statements to use as mantras when needed. They watch and model videos of other children using these skills when in such situations, then plan and make their own videos to practice what they have learned. During the same 16-month period, the parents of these students attend eleven group sessions, where they learn how to set appropriate goals and expectations for behavior, give effective instructions, apply effective reinforcements, and support the new skills and behavior their children are learning (Blueprints for Healthy Youth Development 2023a). Studies of the Coping Power Program show positive outcomes. In two different studies, students engaged in less self-reported delinquency and substance use one year after the program compared with control students; effect sizes for these outcomes ranged from .25 to .58. They also displayed improvements in aggressive behavior, as rated by their teachers, with effect sizes ranging from .25 to .38 (Lochman and Wells 2003, 2004). In addition, a third study found that students reported lower substance use five years after program participation (Zonnevylle-Bender, Matthys, and Lochman 2007).

VI. Integration and the Whole School Approach

There is some indication that a whole-school approach, which operates at multiple levels and includes multiple components, is successful at reducing deviance, delinquency, and victimization for all school community members. For example, a pivotal report on bullying prevention by the National Academies (2016) recommends taking a multi-tiered approach similar to the National Research Council's public health model of mental health intervention, and studies suggest that a whole-school model of restorative justice is likely to be more effective than an incident-based approach (Fronius et al. 2019; González, Sattler, and Buth 2019). Whole-school programs that reflect an overall school culture of respect and support would likely be the most successful in reducing school crime and disorder because a positive and communal school climate has been associated with a wide range of beneficial outcomes, including lower levels of truancy, dropping out, fear, victimization, substance use, aggression, deviance, delinquency, and violence (Payne 2016). The comprehensive nature of this approach is key, as it addresses not just student behavior but the entire school climate as well. Thus, vertical integration of interventions, as discussed by Bottiani, Heilbrun, and Bradshaw (2019), appears to be indicated as a structure that would ensure maximum exposure to a prosocial ethos, relationships, norms, and competencies for all members of the school community. Such a framework could entail using a schoolwide program like SWPBS as an umbrella structure under which an SEL program such as PATHS could be implemented at the universal student level (Bottiani, Heilbrun, and Bradshaw 2019). Students in need of greater intervention could then be placed in a selected or indicated level program such as CPP, where they would receive more intensive behavior modification training and cognitive-behavioral therapy. A similar process is used in the whole-school approach to restorative justice (as previously discussed): a multilevel structure in which all school community members work to build and maintain relationships for a positive school climate forms the foundation while informal or more intensive interventions are used as needed to repair harm (Morrison 2007).

Importantly, shared language and techniques across tiers and interventions should be integrated into daily activities and interactions. Research indicates the greatest benefits occur when the messages, norms, and themes are incorporated into the routine practices of the school, when adopted as a philosophy by the entire school community rather than implemented as one practice or program (Goldberg et al. 2019). The whole-school framework takes a comprehensive approach, addressing attitudes and behaviors of all school members, social interactions and relationships, discipline policies and procedures, and pedagogical and curricular decisions (Gregory and Evans 2020; Velez et al. 2020). In this way, this approach is not merely a program or set of practices but a core framework and set of values fundamental to the transformation not only of individual students' behavior but of a school's climate and community as well. Although the implementation of this framework will require considerable adjustments across all school levels, the potential for effective outcomes for victims, perpetrators, and the entire school community encourages the employment of such processes.

VII. Recommendations for Schools and Research

Undoubtedly the first recommendation is for schools to reduce their reliance on restrictive security and punitive discipline measures. It appears that educational policy is moving in this direction with regard to exclusionary discipline: over the past five years, state legislatures have been increasingly enacting bills restricting the use of these responses, or at least encouraging the use of alternative strategies (Rafa 2019). There is some indication of a slow decrease in the employment of punitive discipline; for example, suspension rates in secondary schools decreased from 9.6% during the 2011–2012 school year to 7.4% during the 2017–2018 school year (Ryberg et al. 2021). Unfortunately, racial disparities in exclusionary discipline continue to be seen, as does the use of restrictive security measures (Ryberg et al. 2021; Wang et al. 2020). Given the lack of evidence tying these security and disciplinary approaches to any reduction in crime or disorder, along with the clear negative consequences that ultimately end in the school-to-prison pipeline, it is not in schools' best interest to utilize their resources in this way.

Instead, schools should focus on implementing evidence-based programs, practices, and policies, or on enhancing those that are already in place. These interventions should aim to change the school and student characteristics known to increase the risk for antisocial or delinquent behavior. For example, much research supports the impact a positive school climate, as indicated by supportive and collaborative relationships and clear and fairly enforced rules and norms, can have on a school's level of crime and disorder (Payne 2016). Similarly, a strong body of work supports the building of students' social, emotional, and cognitive competencies in order to reduce engagement in deviant and delinquent behavior for both low-risk and high-risk individuals (Gottfredson and Gottfredson 2018; Wilson and Lipsey 2007). Thus, interventions that aim to improve these characteristics of schools and students are the most successful at preventing or reducing misbehavior, crime, and victimization. Fortunately, there are several sources schools and districts can turn to when looking to select an evidence-based intervention. These include University of Colorado's Blueprints for Healthy Youth Development, Substance Abuse and Mental Health Services Administration's Evidence-Based Practices Resource Center, Institute of Education Sciences' What Works Clearinghouse, and the combined CrimeSolutions/Model Program from the National Institute of Justice and Office of Juvenile Justice and Delinquency Prevention.[1] These resources continually review evaluation research to find effective interventions based on rigorous research, thus helping schools make informed program selections.

A recommended approach is to integrate school- and student-level universal, selected, and indicated interventions (Bottiani, Heilbrun, and Bradshaw 2019). Whole-school programs that reflect an overall school culture of respect and support and ensure maximum exposure to prosocial competencies and norms would appear to be the most successful in reducing crime and victimization (Bottiani, Heilbrun, and Bradshaw 2019; Fronius et al. 2019; González, Sattler, and Buth 2019). This approach could be accomplished through a process of vertical integration of programs such as SWPBS, PATHS, and CPP, or through an adoption of a whole-school restorative justice model. Either way, shared language and techniques should be incorporated into a school's daily activities, interactions, and practices.

An absolute recommendation for the implementation of any intervention, and particularly for the whole-school approach, is the strong and continuous reliance on data. These data should be used to inform both the choice of program and the selection of participants. Initially, a needs assessment should be conducted by gathering data indicating what problem behaviors are occurring as well as where and how often they occur; data should also be collected regarding who is involved, both as victims and perpetrators (Flannery and Farrell 2019). Evidence-based programs can then be implemented, relying on what the data show in terms of the problems that should be targeted and the students that should be involved. Importantly, behavior should be continually monitored in a "reliable and valid manner" (Waschbusch et al. 2019, 100) to ensure proper implementation, and adjustments should be made as needed.

SWPBS offers clear steps on the continuous use of data for the selection of interventions and for determining which students need support beyond the universal level. Indeed, one of the main advantages of SWPBS is the "active and cyclical use of data for decision-making" (Horner, Sugai, and Anderson 2010, 4). At the universal level, data are used to guide the implementation of strategies to prevent or reduce problem behavior. Examples might include determining where more adult supervision is needed to increase monitoring of student behavior or choosing a particular activity to increase student connectedness. Data are then used to select which higher-risk students would benefit from which intensive program at the selected and indicated levels. At these secondary and tertiary tiers, student behavior is monitored through data more often to ensure student progress and to make changes if needed. Reliance on data in this manner ensures success at all levels of the SWPBS structure (Horner, Sugai, and Anderson 2010).

One area in which the use of data is essential is the implementation process. Given that much research has highlighted the importance of implementation—the "practices of selecting and using interventions shown to be effective in high quality research evaluations" (Elliott and Fagan 2017, 301)—it is certainly recommended that schools and districts adhere to high-quality implementation. The positive outcomes seen in program evaluations tend to occur only when said programs are implemented well, and certainly larger impacts are seen when these interventions are implemented with higher quality (Waschbusch et al. 2019). Thus, schools should strive to achieve high implementation fidelity, following as closely as possible the evidence-based program model, as any deviations may undermine effectiveness (Elliott and Fagan 2017). Indeed, one of the first studies to document the impact implementation has on effectiveness was an evaluation of LifeSkills Training, showing that greater adherence to program information and activities led to greater reductions in substance use (Botvin et al. 1995). Beyond adherence, program dosage, quality of delivery, and participant responsiveness are all important elements to implementation quality (Elliott and Fagan 2017).

This recommendation is particularly important for comprehensive schoolwide interventions, as studies have found that these approaches often encounter problems with implementation (Goldberg et al. 2019). This is likely the reason why some studies have found a lack of effectiveness for comprehensive interventions (Wilson and Lipsey 2007). Whole-school models need extensive planning, training, and support that goes beyond an individual program's manual and specific lessons. Indeed, these "interventions may take multiple years to take hold . . . may be hampered by staff and resource limitations, as well as teachers and school leader disagreement" (Mielke and Farrington 2021, 11). Thus, conducting assessments of needs, fit, and readiness for change are all important steps in the implementation process (Elliott and Fagan 2017). In addition, several school and intervention factors influence implementation, including the local program development process, integration in school operations, organizational capacity, and administrative support (Payne, Gottfredson, and Gottfredson 2006). Strategies to achieve high-quality implementation have been identified by prevention science research, including the creation of an implementation plan and team, proper staff training and supervision, regular technical assistance from program developers, and a continual cycle of data collection and review for implementation improvements (Elliott and Fagan 2017).

Finally, and as always, more research is recommended. Evidence from randomized trials is the gold standard, and thus more of these studies would certainly be valuable, particularly ones focused on whole-school approaches. It is also important to explore moderators of intervention effectiveness to understand how outcomes vary by student and school factors. There is some indication that impact differs by the risk level and socioeconomic status of the students, with larger effects seen for higher-risk students and students from lower-income areas (Wilson and Lipsey 2007). However, there is a range of other student, classroom, school, and community factors that may have an impact, such as academic ability, teaching style, school size, and neighborhood crime (Waschbusch et al. 2019). In addition, research should fully evaluate the whole-school approach, as some research questions the effectiveness of multicomponent interventions (Wilson and Lipsey 2007). It is likely that this is a result of poor implementation fidelity (Waschbusch et al. 2019), but further examination is certainly warranted. Finally, given that a whole-school approach is recommended, it is important that future research be multilevel in nature, collecting data at the student, classroom, and school level to accurately reflect the nested nature of the educational setting.

In conclusion, although school crime and disorder are at a relatively low level, there is still much that can be done to improve the experiences of all members of the school community. It is clear that restrictive security and punitive discipline do more to harm than help students and schools. Instead, evidence-based interventions focused on improving a school's climate and building students' cognitive, social, and emotional skills have greater positive outcomes, including reductions in victimization, deviance, and delinquency. Focusing on high-quality, data-driven implementation of these approaches would go far in ensuring the safety and success of a school and the academic and behavioral success of its students.

Note

1. These resources can be found at the following websites: https://www.blueprintsprograms.org/; https://www.samhsa.gov/resource-search/ebp; https://ies.ed.gov/ncee/wwc/; https://crimesolutions.ojp.gov/; https://ojjdp.ojp.gov/model-programs-guide/home.

References

American Academy of Child and Adolescent Psychiatry. 2016. Teen brain: Behavior, problem solving, and decision making. Washington, DC: American Academy of Child and Adolescent Psychiatry. https://www.aacap.org/AACAP/Families_and_Youth/Facts_for_Families/FFF-Guide/The-Teen-Brain-Behavior-Problem-Solving-and-Decision-Making-095.aspx.

Barnes, James C., and Ryan T. Motz. 2018. Reducing racial inequalities in adulthood arrest by reducing inequalities in school discipline: Evidence from the school-to-prison pipeline. *Developmental Psychology*, 54 (12): 2328–2340. https://doi.org/10.1037/dev0000613.

Blueprints for Healthy Youth Development. 2023a. Coping Power. Boulder, CO: Blueprints for Healthy Youth Development. https://www.blueprintsprograms.org/programs/194999999/coping-power/.

Blueprints for Healthy Youth Development. 2023b. LifeSkills Training. Boulder, CO: Blueprints for Healthy Youth Development. https://www.blueprintsprograms.org/programs/5999999/lifeskills-training-lst/.

Blueprints for Healthy Youth Development. 2023c. Olweus Bullying Prevention Program. Boulder, CO: Blueprints for Healthy Youth Development. https://www.blueprintsprograms.org/programs/11999999/olweus-bullying-prevention-program/.

Blueprints for Healthy Youth Development. 2023d. Promoting Alternative Thinking Strategies (PATHS). https://www.blueprintsprograms.org/programs/33999999/promoting-alternative-thinking-strategies-paths/.

Bottiani, Jessika H., Anna Heilbrun, and Catherine P. Bradshaw. 2019. Models of health promotion and preventive intervention. In *School safety and violence prevention*, edited by Matthew J. Mayer and Shane R. Jimerson, 71–94. Washington, DC: American Psychological Association. http://dx.doi.org/10.1037/0000106-004.

Botvin, Gilbert J., Eli Baker, Linda Dusenbury, Elizabeth M. Botvin, and Tracy Diaz. 1995. Long-term follow-up results of a randomized drug abuse prevention trial in a White middle-class population. *JAMA*, 273 (14): 1106–1112. https://doi.org/10.1001/jama.1995.03520380042033.

Botvin, Gilbert J., Eli Baker, Linda Dusenbury, Stephanie Tortu, and Elizabeth M. Botvin. 1990. Preventing adolescent drug abuse through a multimodal cognitive-behavioral approach: Results of a 3-year study. *Journal of Consulting and Clinical Psychology*, 58 (4): 437–446. https://doi.org/10.1037/0022-006X.58.4.437.

Botvin, Gilbert J., Kenneth W. Griffin, Tracy Diaz, and Michelle Ifill-Williams. 2001a. Drug abuse prevention among minority adolescents: posttest and one-year follow-up of a school-based preventive intervention. *Prevention Science*, 2 (1): 1–13.

Botvin, Gilbert J., Kenneth W. Griffin, Tracy Diaz, and Michelle Ifill-Williams. 2001b. preventing binge drinking during early adolescence: One-and two-year follow-up of a school-based preventive intervention. *Psychology of Addictive Behaviors*, 15 (4): 360–65. https://doi.org/10.1037/0893-164X.15.4.360.

Botvin, Gilbert J., Nancy L. Renick, and Eli Baker. 1983. The effects of scheduling format and booster sessions on a broad-spectrum psychosocial approach to smoking prevention. *Journal of Behavioral Medicine*, 6 (4): 359–379.

Bradshaw, Catherine, Mary Mitchell, and Philip Leaf. 2010. Examining the effects of schoolwide positive behavioral interventions and supports on student outcomes. *Journal of Positive Behavior Interventions*, 12 (3): 133–148. https://doi.org/10.1177/1098300709334798.

Brady, Kevin P., Sharon Balmer, and Deinya Phenix. 2007. School-police partnership effectiveness in urban schools: An analysis of New York City's Impact Schools Initiative. *Education and Urban Society*, 39 (4): 455–478. https://doi.org/10.1177/0013124507302396.

Byrd, Kaitland M., Lindsay L. Kahle, Anthony A. Peguero, and Ann Marie Popp. 2015. Social control and intersectionality: A multilevel analysis of school misconduct, location, race, ethnicity, and sex. *Sociological Spectrum*, 35 (2): 109–135.

Conduct Problems Prevention Research Group. 1999. Initial impact of the fast track prevention trial for conduct problems: II. Classroom effects. *Journal of Consulting and Clinical Psychology*, 67 (5): 648–657. https://doi.org/10.1037/0022-006X.67.5.648.

Darling-Hammond, Sean, Trevor A. Fronius, Hannah Sutherland, Sarah Guckenburg, Anthony Petrosino, and Nancy Hurley. 2020. Effectiveness of restorative justice in US K-12 schools: A review of quantitative research. *Contemporary School Psychology*, 24 (3): 295–308. https://doi.org/10.1007/s40688-020-00290-0.

Devlin, Deanna N., and Benjamin W. Fisher. 2021. An examination of school resource officers as an approach to reduce social disturbances in schools: Evidence from a national longitudinal study. *Journal of School Violence*, 20 (2): 228–240. https://doi.org/10.1080/15388220.2021.1875843.

Devlin, Deanna N., and Denise C. Gottfredson. 2018. The roles of police officers in schools: Effects on the recording and reporting of crime. *Youth Violence and Juvenile Justice*, 16 (2): 208–223. https://doi.org/10.1177/1541204016680405.

Domitrovich, Celene E., Rebecca C. Cortes, and Mark T. Greenberg. 2007. Improving young children's social and emotional competence: A randomized trial of the preschool "PATHS" curriculum. *Journal of Primary Prevention*, 28 (2): 67–91. https://doi.org/ 10.1007/s10935-007-0081-0.

Durlak, Joseph A., Roger P. Weissberg, Allison B. Dymnicki, Rebecca D. Taylor, and Kriston B. Schellinger. 2011. The impact of enhancing students' social and emotional learning: A meta-analysis of school-based universal interventions. *Child Development*, 82 (1): 405–432. https://doi.org/10.1111/j.1467-8624.2010.01564.x.

Elliott, Delbert, and Abigail Fagan. 2017. *The prevention of crime*. Malden, MA: Wiley Blackwell.

Finn, Jeremy D., and Timothy J. Servoss. 2014. Misbehavior, suspensions, and security measures in high school: Racial/ethnic and gender differences. *Journal of Applied Research on Children*, 5 (2): Article 11.

Fisher, Benjamin W., and Matthew J. Cuellar. 2021. Missed connections: Examining the link between exposure to school security and students' sense of connectedness to school. *Journal of School Violence*, 20 (4): 581–596. https://doi.org/10.1080/15388220.2021.2007114.

Flannery, Daniel J., and Albert D. Farrell. 2019. Evaluating school-based violence prevention programs: Challenges and opportunities now and into the future. In *School safety and violence prevention: Science, practice, policy*, edited by Matthew J. Mayer and Shane R. Jimerson, 297–323. Washington, DC: American Psychological Association. https://doi.org/10.1037/0000106-013.

Fronius, Trevor, Sean Darling-Hammond, Hannah Persson, Sarah Guckenburg, Nancy Hurley, and Anthony Petrosino. 2019. *Restorative justice in US schools: An updated research review*. San Francisco: WestEd.

Gardella, Joseph H. 2015. *Restorative practices: For school administrators considering implementation*. Nashville: Vanderbilt University.

Goldberg, Jochem M., Marcin Sklad, Teuntje R. Elfrink, Karlein M. G. Schreurs, Ernst T. Bohlmeijer, and Aleisha M. Clarke. 2019. Effectiveness of interventions adopting a whole school approach to enhancing social and emotional development: A meta-analysis. *European Journal of Psychology of Education*, 34 (4): 755–782. https://doi.org/10.1007/s10 212-018-0406-9.

González, Thalia, Heather Sattler, and Annalise J. Buth. 2019. New directions in whole-school restorative justice implementation. *Conflict Resolution Quarterly*, 36 (3): 207–220. https://doi.org/10.1002/crq.21236.

Gottfredson, Denise C. 2001. *Schools and delinquency*. Cambridge: Cambridge University Press.

Gottfredson, Denise C., Philip J. Cook, and Chongmin Na. 2014. School social organization, discipline management, and crime. In *Encyclopedia of criminology and criminal justice*, edited by Gerben Bruinsma and David Weisburd, 4636–4645. New York: Springer.

Gottfredson, Denise C., Scott Crosse, Zhiqun Tang, Erin L. Bauer, Michele A. Harmon, Carol A. Hagen, and Angela D. Greene. 2020. Effects of school resource officers on school crime and responses to school crime. *Criminology & Public Policy*, 19 (3): 905–940. https://doi.org/10.1111/1745-9133.12512.

Gottfredson, Gary D., and Denise C. Gottfredson. 2018. School violence. In *The Cambridge handbook of violent behavior and aggression*, edited by Alexander T. Vazsonyi, Daniel J.

Flannery, and Matt DeLisi, 557–574. Cambridge: Cambridge University Press. https://doi.org/10.1017/9781316847992.

Gottfredson, Gary D., Denise C. Gottfredson, Allison A. Payne, and Nisha C. Gottfredson. 2005. School climate predictors of school disorder: Results from a national study of delinquency prevention in schools. *Journal of Research in Crime and Delinquency*, 42 (4): 412–444. https://doi.org/10.1177/0022427804271931.

Gregory, Anne, and Katherine R. Evans. 2020. *The starts and stumbles of restorative justice in education: Where do we go from here?* Boulder, CO: National Education Policy Center.

Healy, S. R., J. Y. Valente, S. C. Caetano, S. S. Martins, and Z. M. Sanchez. 2020. Worldwide school-based psychosocial interventions and their effect on aggression among elementary school children: A systematic review 2010–2019. *Aggression and Violent Behavior*, 55:101486. https://doi.org/10.1016/j.avb.2020.101486.

Horner, Robert H., George Sugai, and Cynthia M. Anderson. 2010. Examining the evidence base for school-wide positive behavior support. *Focus on Exceptional Children*, 42 (8): 1–14. https://doi.org/10.17161/foec.v42i8.6906.

Horner, Robert H., George Sugai, and Timothy Lewis. 2020. *Is school-wide positive behavior support an evidence-based practice?* Arlington, VA: Center on PBIS. https://www.pbis.org/resource/is-school-wide-positive-behavior-support-an-evidence-based-practice.

Horner, Robert, George Sugai, Keith Smolkowski, Lucille Eber, Jean Nakasato, Anne Todd, and Jody Esperanza. 2009. A randomized, wait-list controlled effectiveness trial assessing school-wide positive behavior support in elementary schools. *Journal of Positive Behavior Interventions*, 11 (3): 133–144. https://doi.org/10.1177/1098300709332067.

Hutzell, Kirsten L., and Allison Ann Payne. 2018. The relationship between bullying victimization and school avoidance: An examination of direct associations, protective influences, and aggravating factors. *Journal of School Violence*, 17 (2): 210–226.

Katic, Barbara, Laura A. Alba, and Austin H. Johnson. 2020. A systematic evaluation of restorative justice practices: School violence prevention and response. *Journal of School Violence*, 19 (4): 579–593. https://doi.org/10.1080/15388220.2020.1783670.

Kupchik, Aaron, and Geoff Ward. 2014. Race, poverty, and exclusionary school security: An empirical analysis of US elementary, middle, and high schools. *Youth Violence and Juvenile Justice*, 12 (4): 332–354. https://doi.org/10.1177/1541204013503890.

Lasnover, Sara. 2015. The early effects of the removal of willful defiance from the discipline policy at urban high schools. PhD diss., UCLA.

Limber, Susan P., Dan Olweus, Weijun Wang, Matthew Masiello, and Kyrre Breivik. 2018. Evaluation of the Olweus Bullying Prevention Program: A large scale study of us students in grades 3–11. *Journal of School Psychology*, 69:56–72. https://doi.org/10.1016/j.jsp.2018.04.004.

Lochman, John E., and Karen C. Wells. 2003. Effectiveness of the Coping Power Program and of classroom intervention with aggressive children: Outcomes at a 1-year follow-up. *Behavior Therapy*, 34 (4): 439–515. https://doi.org/10.1016/S0005-7894(03)80032-1.

Lochman, John E., and Karen C. Wells. 2004. The Coping Power Program for preadolescent aggressive boys and their parents: Outcome effects at the 1-year follow-up. *Journal of Consulting and Clinical Psychology*, 72 (4): 571–578. https://doi.org/10.1037/0022-006X.72.4.571.

Mahoney, Joseph L., Joseph A. Durlak, and Roger P. Weissberg. 2018–2019. An update on social and emotional learning outcome research. *Phi Delta Kappan*, 100 (4): 18–23. https://doi.org/10.1177/0031721718815668.

Malti, Tina, Denis Ribeaud, and Manuel P. Eisner. 2011. The effectiveness of two universal preventive interventions in reducing children's externalizing behavior: A cluster randomized controlled trial. *Journal of Clinical Child & Adolescent Psychology*, 40 (5): 677–692. https://doi.org/10.1080/15374416.2011.597084.

Mielke, Monica, and David P. Farrington. 2021 School-based interventions to reduce suspension and arrest: A meta-analysis. *Aggression and Violent Behavior*, 56:101518. https://doi.org/10.1016/j.avb.2020.101518.

Mittleman, Joel. 2018. A downward spiral? Childhood suspension and the path to juvenile arrest. *Sociology of Education*, 91 (3): 183–204. https://doi.org/10.1177/0038040718784603.

Morrison, Brenda. 2007. *Restoring safe school communities: A whole school response to bullying, violence and alienation*. Annandale, VA: Federation Press.

Morrison, Brenda E., and Dorothy Vaandering. 2012. Restorative justice: Pedagogy, praxis, and discipline. *Journal of School Violence*, 11 (2): 138–155. https://doi.org/10.1080/15388220.2011.653322.

Mowen, Thomas J., and Karen F. Parker. 2017. Minority threat and school security: Assessing the impact of Black and Hispanic student representation on school security measures. *Security Journal*, 30 (2): 504–522. https://doi.org/10.1057/sj.2014.42.

Na, Chongmin, and Denise C. Gottfredson. 2013. Police officers in schools: Effects on school crime and the processing of offending behaviors. *Justice Quarterly*, 30 (4): 619–650. https://doi.org/10.1080/07418825.2011.615754.

Nance, Jason P., and Michael Heise. 2022. Law enforcement officers, students, and the school-to-prison pipeline: A longitudinal perspective. *Arizona State Law Journal* 527:54. http://dx.doi.org/10.2139/ssrn.3976360.

National Academies of Sciences, Engineering, and Medicine. 2016. *Preventing bullying through science, policy, and practice*. Washington, DC: National Academies of Sciences, Engineering, and Medicine.

Olweus, Dan, and Francoise D. Alsaker. 1991. Assessing change in a cohort-longitudinal study with hierarchical data. In *Problems and methods in longitudinal research: Stability and change*, edited by David Magnusson, Lars R. Berman, Georg Rudinger, and Bertil Torestad, 107–132. New York: Cambridge University Press.

Payne, Allison A. 2016. *Creating and sustaining a positive and communal school climate: Contemporary Research, present obstacles, and future directions*. White Paper for National Institute of Justice, Comprehensive School Safety Initiative. Washington, DC: US Department of Justice. https://www.ojp.gov/pdffiles1/nij/250209.pdf.

Payne, Allison Ann, Denise C. Gottfredson, and Gary D. Gottfredson. 2006. School predictors of the intensity of implementation of school-based prevention programs: Results from a national study. *Prevention Science*, 7 (2): 225–237.

Payne, Allison A., and Kelly Welch. 2018. The effect of school conditions on the use of restorative justice in schools. *Youth Violence and Juvenile Justice*, 16 (2): 224–240. https://doi.org/10.1177/1541204016681414.

Rafa, Alyssa. 2019. Policy analysis: The status of school discipline in state policy. Demver, CO: Education Commission of the States.

Ramey, David M. 2015. The social structure of criminalized and medicalized school discipline. *Sociology of Education*, 88 (3): 181–201.

Robers, S., Zhang, A., Morgan, R., and Musu-Gillette, L. 2015. *Indicators of school crime and safety: 2014*. Washington, DC: National Center for Education Statistics and Bureau of Justice Statistics.

Rosenbaum, Janet. 2020. Educational and criminal justice outcomes 12 years after school suspension. *Youth & Society*, 52 (4): 515–547. https://doi.org/10.1177/0044118X17752208.

Ryberg, Renee, Sarah Her, Deborah Temkin, and Kristen Harper. 2021. Black students and students with disabilities remain more likely to experience suspension. Bethesda, MD: Child Trends. https://www.childtrends.org/publications/despite-reductions-black-students-and-students-with-disabilities-remain-more-likely-to-experience-suspension.

Schroeder, Betsy A., Allison Messina, Diana Schroeder, Karla Good, Shiryl Barto, Jennifer Saylor, and Matthew Masiello. 2012. The implementation of a statewide bullying prevention program: Preliminary findings from the field and the importance of coalitions. *Health Promotion Practice*, 13 (4): 489–495.

Servoss, Timorhy J. 2017. School security and student misbehavior: A multi-level examination. *Youth Society*, 49 (6): 755–778.

Skiba, Russell J., and M. Karega Rausch. 2006. Zero tolerance, suspension, and expulsion: Questions of equity and effectiveness. In *Handbook of classroom management: Research, practice, and contemporary issues*, edited by Carolyn M. Evertson and Carol S. Weinstein, 1063–1089. New York: Routledge.

Sklad, Marcin, Rene Diekstra, Monique de Ritter, Jehonathan Ben, and Carolien Gravesteijn. 2012. Effectiveness of school-based universal social, emotional, and behavioral programs: Do they enhance students' development in the area of skill, behavior, and adjustment? *Psychology in the Schools*, 49 (9): 892–909. https://doi.org/10.1002/pits.21641.

Sorensen, Lucy C., Montserrat Avila Acosta, John Engberg, and Shawn Bushway. 2021. The thin blue line in schools: New evidence on school-based policing across the US. EdWorkingPaper No. 21-476. Providence, RI: Annenberg Institute at Brown University. https://doi.org/10.26300/heqx-rc69.

Steinka-Fry, Katarzyna T., Benjamin W. Fisher, and Emily E. Tanner-Smith. 2016. Visible school security measures across diverse middle and high school settings: Typologies and predictors. *Journal of Applied Security Research*, 11 (4): 422–436. https://doi.org/10.1080/19361610.2016.1210482.

Tanner-Smith, Emily E., Joseph A. Durlak, and Robert A. Marx. 2018. Empirically based mean effect size distributions for universal prevention programs targeting school-aged youth: A review of meta-analyses. *Prevention Science*, 19 (8): 1091–1101. https://doi.org/10.1007/s11121-018-0942-1.

Tanner-Smith, Emily E., and Benjamin W. Fisher. 2016. Visible school security measures and student academic performance, attendance, and postsecondary aspirations. *Journal of Youth and Adolescence*, 45 (1): 195–210. https://doi.org/10.1007/s10964-015-0265-5.

Taylor, Rebecca D., Eva Oberle, Joseph A. Durlak, and Roger P. Weissberg. 2017. Promoting positive youth development through school-based social and emotional learning interventions: A meta-analysis of follow-up effects. *Child Development*, 88 (4): 1156–1171.

Theriot, Matthew T. 2016. The impact of school resource officer interaction on students' feelings about school and school police. *Crime & Delinquency*, 62 (4): 446–469. https://doi.org/10.1177/0011128713503526.

US Department of Education Office for Civil Rights. 2014. Civil rights data collection data snapshot: School discipline. Washington, DC: US Department of Education. http://www2.ed.gov/about/offices/list/ocr/docs/crdc-discipline-snapshot.pdf.

Velez, Gabriel, Madeline Hahn, Holly Recchia, and Cecilia Wainryb. 2020. Rethinking responses to youth rebellion: Recent growth and development of restorative practices in schools. *Current Opinion in Psychology*, 35:36–40. https://doi.org/10.1016/j.copsyc.2020.02.011.

Vincent, Claudia G., and Tary J. Tobin. 2011. The relationship between implementation of School-Wide Positive Behavior Support (SWPBS) and disciplinary exclusion of students from various ethnic backgrounds with and without disabilities. *Journal of Emotional and Behavioral Disorders*, 19 (4): 217–232. https://doi.org/10.1177/1063426610377329.

Wang, Ke, Yongqiu Chen, Jizhi Zhang, and Barbara A. Oudekerk. 2020. Indicators of School Crime and Safety: 2019. NCES 2020-063/NCJ 254485. Washington, DC: National Center for Education Statistics. https://eric.ed.gov/?id=ED606370.

Waschbusch, Daniel A., Rosanna P. Breaux, and Dara E. Babinski. 2019. School-based interventions for aggression and defiance in youth: A framework for evidence-based practice. *School Mental Health*, 11 (1): 92–105. https://doi.org/10.1007/s12310-018-9269-0.

Weissberg, Roger P. 2019. Promoting the social and emotional learning of millions of school children. *Perspectives on Psychological Science*, 14 (1): 65–69. https://doi.org/10.1177/1745691618817756.

Weissberg, Roger, Joseph A. Durlak, Celene E. Domitrovich, and Thomas P. Gullotta. 2015. social and emotional learning: Past, present, and future. In *Handbook of social and emotional learning: Research and practice*, edited by Joseph A. Durlak, Celene E. Domitrovich, Roger P. Weissberg, and Thomas P. Gullotta, 3–19. New York: Guilford Press.

Welch, Kelly, and Allison A. Payne. 2010. Racial threat and punitive school discipline. *Social Problems*, 57 (1): 25–48. https://doi.org/10.1525/sp.2010.57.1.25.

Welch, Kelly, and Allison A. Payne. 2014. Racial implications of school discipline and climate. In *Responding to school violence: Confronting the Columbine effect*, edited by Glenn W. Muschert, and Anthony A. Peguero, 125–138. Boulder, CO: Lynne Rienner.

Welch, Kelly, and Allison A. Payne. 2018. Latino student threat and the school-to-prison pipeline. *Sociology of Education*, 91 (2): 91–110. https://doi.org/10.1177/0038040718757720.

Wilson, David B., Denise C. Gottfredson, and Stacy S. Najaka. 2001 School-based prevention of problem behaviors: A meta-analysis. *Journal of Quantitative Criminology*, 17 (3): 247–272.

Wilson, Sandra Jo, and Mark W. Lipsey. 2007. School-based interventions for aggressive and disruptive behavior: Update of a meta-analysis. *American Journal of Preventive Medicine*, 33 (2): S130–S143. https://doi.org/10.1016/j.amepre.2007.04.011.

Wolf, Kerrin C., and Aaron Kupchik. 2017. School suspensions and adverse experiences in adulthood. *Justice Quarterly*, 34 (3): 407430. https://doi.org/10.1080/07418825.2016.1168475.

Zakszeski, Brittany, and Laura Rutherford. 2021. Mind the gap: A systematic review of research on restorative practices in schools. *School Psychology Review*, 50 (2–3): 371–387. https://doi.org/10.1080/2372966X.2020.1852056.

Zaykowski, Heather, and Whitney Gunter. 2012. Youth victimization: School climate or deviant lifestyles? *Journal of Interpersonal Violence*, 27 (3): 431–452. https://doi.org/10.1177/0886260511421678.

Zonnevylle-Bender, Marjo J. S., Walter Matthys, and John E. Lochman. 2007. Preventive effects of treatment of disruptive behavior disorder in middle childhood on substance use and delinquent behavior. *Journal of the American Academy of Child & Adolescent Psychiatry*, 46 (1): 33–39. https://doi.org/10.1097/01.chi.0000246051.53297.57.

CHAPTER 23

EVIDENCE-BASED STRATEGIES FOR PREVENTING URBAN YOUTH VIOLENCE

KATHERINE M. ROSS, COLLEEN S. WALSH, ANGELA G. ANGULO, CARINE E. LESLIE, AND PATRICK H. TOLAN

YOUTH violence is a widespread public health crisis: 42% of homicides worldwide involve youth (WHO 2020), and in the United States, over half of homicides involve young people between the ages of 15 and 34 (CDC 2021a). Additionally, over half a million youth are arrested annually in the United States (Children's Defense Fund 2019), and 20% of youth report experiencing bullying (CDC 2022a). Youth in urban settings and youth of color are disproportionately impacted by youth violence. For instance, while homicide is the third leading cause of death for youth overall in the United States, it is the first leading cause of death for Black youth, with the majority (86%; CDC 2016) of those deaths attributed specifically to gun violence. Additionally, of youth in the juvenile justice system, 67% are youth of color (US Department of Justice 2017). Youth in urban settings are far more likely to experience violence, with estimated rates ranging from 50% to nearly 100% of youth reporting exposure to community violence (Zimmerman and Messner 2013; Ross et al. 2022). Finally, within urban settings, underresourced and minority communities bear the majority of violence related crimes (Rowlands and Love 2022).

Experiences of violence negatively impact youth's developmental trajectory, as well as their short- and long-term mental, physical, and emotional health. Violence concentrated in urban communities of color further isolates and deprives them of city resources and contributes to a cycle of social alienation and criminalization of youth behavior. Furthermore, youth violence has profound economic impacts in terms of resources allocated to treating affected individuals and communities, and resources lost in the form of contributions and productivity from youth and communities directly impacted. A recent report from the CDC (2022b) estimates the financial loss to be upwards of $1 billion annually.

As is convention and in line with the CDC, this chapter defines youth as individuals between the ages of 10 and 25 years. Within this general category, there are notable developmental and social differences between individuals who are school aged and can legally claim minor status (ages 10–17), which we categorize as adolescents, and individuals who are beyond secondary school and are on the path to or have full independence and legal responsibility (ages 18–25), which we refer to as young adults.

The empirical literature points to some common precedents and consequences for each particular area of violence that is the focus of this chapter: aggressive behaviors, delinquency, and gun violence. Many evidence-based practices (EBPs) are developed to address one of these specific outcomes or are developed to directly target specific precedents associated with them. In order to best understand and make recommendations for selecting and implementing EBPs for youth violence prevention (YVP) in urban settings, it is important to first outline the empirical evidence for precedents (i.e., risk, protective, and promotive factors) for youth violence specific to urban settings. This is the focus of sections I and II. In the next sections, we examine EBPs for preventing urban youth violence, in addition to highlighting gaps in knowledge and making recommendations for creating a community-informed framework for YVP in urban settings. The chapter concludes with several recommendations regarding practices that should or should not be supported for urban YVP and next steps for research and practice.

I. Precedents to Youth Violence: Risk, Promotive, and Protective Factors

Prevention science aims to identify the common precedents to youth violence in order to identify targets for policy and practice. In other words, it is important to understand the factors (experiences and behaviors) that lead to violent outcomes in order to prevent violence from occurring in the first place. Precedents are grouped into risk and protective factors. In the context of youth violence, risk factors are factors that are associated with an increased likelihood of violent outcomes; decreasing risk factors is often the primary focus of violence prevention efforts. An alternative approach to targeting risk factors is to understand or cultivate protective factors, or factors that minimize the impact that risk factors have on violent outcomes. Protective factors are conceptualized as modifying or blunting the impact of risk. Finally, there are promotive factors, or positive factors that *directly* lessen the likelihood of violent outcomes. However, within the extant literature on violent outcomes, this distinction among the positive influences is not always made or recognized, grouping positive factors that have a direct and indirect impact as "protective factors."

Risk and protective factors exist and are interdependent across the developmental ecology, within and across the individual (e.g., social, emotional, behavioral skills), familial (e.g., family support and monitoring), peer/social (e.g., prosocial relationships), and community levels (e.g., positive youth development resources, community social, and behavioral norms). Once developmentally influential factors are identified, they can become the direct target of intervention and prevention efforts.

Increasingly, the field is acknowledging that it is critical to consider culture and context when identifying risk and protective factors within each level of the ecological model. Specifically, theoretical models of racial and ethnic minority identity stress the importance of considering their unique cultural experiences (in the form of unique strengths, such as racial identity, and unique risks, such as experiences with discrimination and systemic oppression) and social cognitive development when identifying risk and protective factors for violence (e.g., Spencer, Cunningham, and Swanson 1995; Coll et al. 1996). Considering the disproportionate impact that youth violence has in urban communities and in youth communities of color, a key focus of this chapter is to highlight findings specific to these populations and denote areas where further inquiry is needed.

Before delving into the empirical literature, it is important to note that the resilience framework of risk and protective factors has historically minimized or ignored the conditions and systems of oppression that have caused racial and ethnic groups of youth to experience a greater burden of risk than White youth. For instance, youth in urban neighborhoods have been categorized as "at risk" due to poverty status. However, this risk is typically rooted in systemic marginalization (e.g., redlining, racism; Benns et al. 2020) and barriers to accessing city resources. More recent studies have made an effort to move away from the language of "at risk" in an attempt to focus on *actual* behavior (i.e., presence of violence, or not) rather than *potential* for violent behavior (Scott et al. 2005).

II. Summary of Risk and Protective Factors for Youth Violence

In order to compose a set of empirically established primary precedents, or risk and protective factors, for youth violence, we reviewed the literature for the following key areas of youth violence: (1) aggressive behaviors, (2) delinquency, and (3) gun violence. For each area, we focused our search on studies examining youth living in urban communities.

A. Aggression and Bullying Perpetration

An entire subset of violence prevention literature is dedicated to aggression, sometimes termed "bullying perpetration" when occurring in school settings, which is broadly defined as an external behavior done with the intent of harming another person (Lösel and Farrington 2012).

1. Risk Factors

Previous studies have identified a general set of risk factors for aggression in youth, regardless of racial/ethnic identity or urban/rural location, which includes being male, having low socioeconomic status in childhood, low IQ, low academic achievement, exhibiting antisocial behavior, or witnessing violence (Farrington and Loeber 2000; Hawkins et al. 2012; Henry, Tolan, and Gorman-Smith 2001; Lösel and Farrington 2012).

However, other risk factors exist specifically for youth of color in urban neighborhoods, including low emotion regulation, fear of negative evaluation by peers, or experiencing violence victimization or racial discrimination (Caldwell et al. 2004; Taylor, Sullivan, and Kliewer 2013; Ozer and Weinstein 2004; Yule, Houston, and Grych 2019). Several studies have highlighted the salience of *peers and social groups* as risk factors. More specifically, associating with peer groups exhibiting aggressive or antisocial behavior and/or engaging in substance use are associated with elevated rates of aggression and violence (Henry, Tolan, and Gorman-Smith2001). At the *family level*, risk factors include low family functioning, parents with supportive attitudes towards aggression, less family cohesion or involvement, and negative disciplinary practices related to aggression and violence in youth in urban contexts (Henry, Tolan, and Gorman-Smith 2001; Gorman-Smith et al. 1996). At the *community level*, low neighborhood cohesion, high rates of community violence, and social dysfunction act as risk factors for youth in these settings (Paschall and Hubbard 1998; Sheidow et al. 2001).

2. *Protective Factors*

It is critical to note that the majority of youth possessing one or more of the aforementioned risk factors do not engage in violent or aggressive behaviors. A laundry list of protective factors has been found to buffer risk for aggression and violence broadly (e.g., high IQ, low impulsivity, elevated anxiety, prosocial attitudes, positive parent-child relationship, consistent parental monitoring, middle class status, positive school climate and connectedness, good grades, prosocial peers, living in a more affluent neighborhood). Specifically for youth of color in urban communities, identity formation and positive family functioning has been found to directly relate with lower levels of community violence exposure, or buffer (indirectly effect) against community violence risk factors (Caldwell et al. 2004; Sheidow et al. 2001; Spencer, Cunningham, and Swanson 1995). For example, the development of racial identity has been identified as a psychosocial protector for mental health and behavior outcomes, such that stronger racial identity is related to lower levels of mental illness and violence (Spencer, Cunningham, and Swanson 1995).

The literature on risk and protective factors for aggressive behaviors is largely focused on adolescent populations and rarely focuses specifically on young adults. In fact, we conducted the first exploratory study of promotive and protective factors for aggressive behaviors in an urban, predominantly Black young adult sample living in a community experiencing high rates of violence. Our findings indicate that the majority of promotive effects were at the *individual level* (e.g., positive views of personal future, sense of purpose, interpersonal competence, planning and decision-making, conflict resolution, self-esteem, personal power), with one significant factor at the *school and community levels* (achievement motivation and having a religious community, respectively). In terms of protective factors, we found that having a religious and spiritual community (at the *community level*) was the only factor that was protective at high levels of community violence exposure. These findings suggest that building strengths and assets across the ecological model is important, but the onus of violence prevention should not be put on individual-level factors. Directly addressing the risk factors (e.g., the community conditions and lack of available resources) is of utmost importance (Ross et al. 2022).

B. Delinquency

Delinquency is often assessed in tandem or as an outcome of violence for youth in urban contexts. Although "delinquent behavior" does not automatically denote juvenile justice system involvement, the term does organize behaviors of concern by their illegality and potential criminal justice impact. While aggression is a component of many delinquent offenses and the risk and protective factors are largely overlapping, they are not synonymous. Examples of delinquent offenses include causing harm to others, destruction of property, theft, drug possession, drug use, and truancy (US Department of Justice 2017). With the majority of adolescents involved in the juvenile system having been referred by age 15, and primarily being youth of color from underresourced neighborhoods, the need to focus prevention efforts on late childhood and early adolescence is clear (Chapman et al. 2006).

1. Risk Factors

The research literature provides strong evidence of *community* (e.g., residing in a high poverty neighborhood), *familial* (e.g., parental mental illness), and *individual* (e.g., low intelligence, educational attainment) risk factors for delinquency (Baumgartner and Amso, n.d.; Bowes et al. 2010; Conger and Conger 2002). Despite the overrepresentation of Black and Brown youth who are system-involved, the literature on risk and protective factors for these youth, in particular those from urban communities, remains considerably underdeveloped (Chapman et al. 2006).

For Black urban youth in particular at the *individual level*, low socioeconomic status, being male, low academic grades and reading achievement, and substance use were strongly associated with delinquency (Maguin, Loeber, and Lemahieu 1993; McCord 1994; Stevens-Watkins and Graves 2011). Perhaps some of the most studied risk factors for delinquency are found at the *family level*, and include low parental education, low parental monitoring and supervision, poor family functioning, and inconsistent and harsh disciplinary practices (McCord 1994; Patterson, Reid, and Dishion 1992). Risk factors for delinquency related to *peers* include affiliation with antisocial, substance using, and delinquent peers (Paschall and Hubbard 1998; Stevens-Watkins and Graves 2011). Additionally, *community- and school-related* risks include poor school adjustment, social disorganization, poor sense of belonging to the community, community violence rates, and lack of supervision by other adults and adolescents in the community (Chapman et al. 2006; Gorman-Smith, Tolan, and Henry 2000). However, when considering urban environments, it is important to underscore the importance of *structural* barriers to community building and cohesion, which are more exaggerated in urban environments due to factors such as increased noise, lack of access to transportation, and transitory neighbors (Gorman-Smith, Tolan, and Henry 2000).

2. Protective Factors

Similar to youth who experience risk factors for violence and aggressive behavior, not all youth who possess risk factors for delinquency engage in delinquent behavior; the possession of risk factors is not an inevitable condemnation. At the *individual level*, higher levels of future certainty, expectation for college attendance, and self-concept have been identified as protective factors for delinquent behavior risk reduction (Bynum and Weiner 2002; Caldwell, Wiebe, and Cleveland 2006). At the *family level*, youth in urban environments have been found to engage in delinquent behavior less if closely monitored and supervised by parents (Paschall et al. 2003). Similarly, when family functioning is high, specifically related to successful emotional cohesion and family orientation, as well as consistent parenting and specified family roles and responsibilities, neighborhood risks related to delinquency are buffered (Gorman-Smith, Tolan, and Henry 2000). Finally at the *community level*, a buffering effect from youth involvement in religious institutions has been found for neighborhood disorder (Johnson et al. 2000).

C. Gun Violence

Gun carrying is an important behavior to discuss, as it relates to youth gun violence and is especially related to gun violence in urban settings. Youth in urban settings report various reasons for carrying a gun, including safety, protection, and status (Oliphant et al. 2019). Youth gun carrying in urban communities (about 17%) differs considerably from rates of youth in rural settings (10%). Also relevant, youth gun carrying for those with past involvement in the juvenile system is significantly higher (ranging from 50% to 100%) when compared to their non-involved peers. Youth gun carrying is established as a primary risk factor for other forms of violence (e.g., physical aggression, bullying, assault, violent injury; for a review, see Oliphant et al. 2019). Similarly, youth who carry guns put themselves and their peers at elevated risk for sustained serious injury and death.

1. Risk Factors

Risk factors for urban youth gun carrying do not vary greatly compared to risk factors discussed previously for other kinds of youth violence, with *individual-level* factors being nearly identically (e.g., male sex, older adolescent age, low SES, drug use). Youth gun carrying has been found to be positively associated with easy access to guns and violence exposure, aggression and victimization, mental health issues, juvenile system involvement, and poor academic grades. Though most studies have focused on individual risk characteristics of youth, at the *peer level*, peer gun carrying and delinquency, as well as peer positive beliefs about guns, have been identified as risks for gun carrying. *Family-level* risk factors identified include lack of family closeness, mentorship, and family discussion of gun related consequences, as well as presence of a family member who has been shot (Oliphant et al. 2019).

2. Protective Factors

Protective factors for gun carrying include elevated parental monitoring, respect for maternal caregivers, higher school attachment, exposure to drug and violence prevention programming, neighborhood collective efficacy, and strict state gun laws for youth broadly (Oliphant et al. 2019). Four recent studies have examined potential protective factors (O'Connor et al. 2023; Ross et al. 2023; Walsh et al. 2023; Sullivan et al. 2023) specifically for Black youth (ages 12–17) and young adults (ages 18–22) in urban communities. Study findings demonstrated that *individual* (beliefs against fighting and having a positive outlook), and *family* (family assets and family prosocial involvement) factors for youth and individual (ethnic identity) factors for young adults were directly associated with lower likelihood of gun carriage. Significant protective factors were also found, but findings indicated that they were only protective at low levels of risk. Protective factors for youth included *individual-level* (personal assets, positive outlook) *peer-level* (social assets), *school-level* (school assets, family prosocial involvement in school), and *community-level* (social connectedness, informal social control, and community recognition for prosocial involvement) factors. Protective factors for young adults included *individual* (positive outlook), *family* (family cohesion), *school* (currently being a student) and *community* (neighborhood attachment and community assets) factors.

D. Risk and Protective Factors Conclusions

In synthesizing the literature on aggression, delinquency, and gun violence impacting urban youth, we identified some common risk and protective factors. First, there are fewer promotive/protective factors identified for this population than there are risk factors. Many of the protective factors derive from one empirical study, whereas many of the risk factors have been identified and replicated across a wide body of work. Notably, much of the protective factor findings are drawn from exploratory work using cross-sectional designs. This means that we cannot determine the direction of the association. Further inquiry is warranted here, with multiple waves of data needed. Of the identified protective factors, positive future outlook, family support and functioning, family boundaries, involvement, and supervision have been commonly identified as significantly related to all three violent outcomes for urban youth. Additionally, substance use, peer antisocial behavior, and exposure to community violence have been identified as significant risk factors for the three violent outcomes.

III. Evidence-Based Practices for Youth Violence Prevention

What do we know about EBPs for urban YVP? To help answer this pressing question, we reviewed leading programs and practices in two violence prevention registries: (1) Blueprints for Healthy Youth Development (2022), and (2) National Centers of Excellence in YVP (CDC 2021b). We were interested in identifying programs or practices that targeted one of the outcomes identified in the three primary areas discussed earlier (aggression, delinquency, and gun violence) and are intended for use in urban settings. We examined programs in terms of outcomes targeted, risk and/or protective factors targeted, population targeted (e.g., age, race/ethnicity, geographic setting, and whether it was a universal, selected, or targeted program/practice), ecological context of delivery (e.g., individual, family, school, or community), and the empirical evidence of effectiveness. The details of our findings are included in Table 23.1 (divided into 1A and 1B for clarity). We profile some key findings here.

Table 23.1A. Summary of Evidence-Based Programs for Youth Violence Prevention

Program Details					
Program Name	Ecological Level	Universal/Targeted	Intervention Type	Target Populations	Violent Outcome(s) Targeted[a]
Offender-Focused Policing	Individual	Targeted	Policing & Community Safety	Juvenile repeated offenders	Crime & Delinquency
SafERteens	Individual	Targeted	One-on-One Counseling	Youth hospitalized for violent injuries or heavy alcohol use	General Aggressive Behaviors Crime & Delinquency
Caught in the Crossfire	Individual	Targeted	Mentorship	Youth hospitalized for violent injuries	Crime & Delinquency
Functional Family Therapy (FFT)	Family	Targeted	Family Therapy	Youth at risk for, and/or presenting with delinquency, violence, substance use, EBD	Crime & Delinquency
Parent Management Training—Oregon Model (GenerationPMTO)	Family	Targeted	Parenting Training	Youth exhibiting EBD	Aggressive Behaviors Crime & Delinquency
EFFEKT	Family	Universal	Parenting Training	Parents of middle school students	Crime & Delinquency
Group Teen Triple—Level 4	Family	Universal Targeted	Parenting Training	Parents of middle school students	Conduct Problems
Guiding Good Choices	Family	Universal	Parenting Training	Parents of middle school students	Crime & Delinquency
Multisystemic Therapy (MST)	Family Community	Targeted	Family Therapy	Juvenile offenders	Conduct Problems Crime & Delinquency General Violence
Positive Action	School	Universal	School-Based—Encourage Positive Behaviors	Youth in elementary and middle school	Bullying Crime & Delinquency General Violence
Project Towards No Drug Abuse	School	Universal	School-Based—Address Negative Behaviors	High school youth who are at risk for drug use and violence-related behavior	General Violence

(continued)

Table 23.1A. Continued

Program Details

Program Name	Ecological Level	Universal/Targeted	Intervention Type	Target Populations	Violent Outcome(s) Targeted[a]
Achievement Mentoring	School	Targeted	School-Based—Address Negative Behaviors	Youth exhibiting EBD	Crime & Delinquency
LifeSkills Training (LST)	School	Universal	School-Based—Address Negative Behaviors	Middle school students	Crime & Delinquency General Violence
Learning Together	School	Universal	School-Based—Address Negative Behaviors	Middle school students	Conduct Problems Bullying Crime & Delinquency
Olweus Bullying Prevention Program	School	Universal Targeted	School-Based—Address Negative Behaviors	Students and adults in elementary, middle, and high schools	Bullying Crime & Delinquency
Safe Streets	Community	Universal	Policing & Community Safety	Communities with high rates of youth violence	Gun Violence
Communities That Care	Community	Universal	Community–Coalition	Communities interested in implemented a community wide prevention program	General Aggressive Behaviors Crime & Delinquency
Big Brothers Big Sisters of America	Community	Targeted	Mentorship	At-risk youth and volunteer adult mentors	General Aggressive Behaviors
ThrYve	Community	Universal	Community–Coalition	Communities interested in reducing youth violence	Violence Generally

[a] Categories are based on those listed on Blueprints.
[b] Race and/or ethnicity were not focused on as criteria for sampling. Majority White and majority non-White samples were used, with varying percentages of African American, Hispanic/Latino, Native American, and/or other racial/ethnic minority group participants across studies.
[c] All studies were conducted outside the United States, including Sweden and the Netherlands (EFFEKT), New Zealand (Group Teen Triple–Level 4), and the UK (Learning Together).
[d] Virtually all study participants were White/Caucasian.

Table 23.1B. Summary of Evidence-Based Programs for Youth Violence Prevention (continued)

Program Details		Empirically Tested With					
Program Name	Protective Factors Targeted	Youth (10–17)	Young Adult (18–25)	Racial/Ethnic Minorities	Urban Setting	Ecological Settings	
Offender-Focused Policing	No Protective Factors Targeted	Yes (15–7)	Yes (18–25)	No[b]	Yes	Community	
SafERteens	Clear Behavior Standards	Yes (14–7)	Yes (18)	No[b]	Yes	Hospital	
	Developing Resiliency & Positive Coping Skills/Behaviors Social Skills & Problem-Solving Skills Interactions With Prosocial Peers Prosocial Parent Involvement & Positive Disciplinary Practices Increase Academic Self-Efficacy & Achievement Prosocial Opportunities/Involvement At School						
Caught in the Crossfire	No Protective Factors Targeted	Yes (12–17)	Yes (18–20)	No[b]	Yes	Hospital	
Functional Family Therapy (FFT)	Clear Behavior Standards Social Skills & Problem-Solving Skills Prosocial Behavior & Involvement Interactions With Prosocial Peers Improving Parent-Child Relationships Prosocial Parent Involvement & Positive Disciplinary Practices	Yes (11–17)	Yes (18)	No[b]	Yes	Transitional Contexts Social Services Correctional Facility Mental Health Center	
Parent Management Training—Oregon Model (GenerationPMTO)	Clear Behavior Standards Social Skills & Problem-Solving Skills Prosocial Behavior & Involvement Interactions With Prosocial Peers Improving Parent-Child Relationships Prosocial Parent Involvement & Positive Disciplinary Practices	Yes (10–16)	No	Yes (Hispanic/Latino)	Yes	Mental Health Center Community	
EFFEKT	No Protective Factors Targeted	Yes (13–16)	No	No[c]	Yes	School Community	
Group Teen Triple—Level 4	Prosocial Behavior & Involvement Prosocial Parent Involvement & Positive Disciplinary Practices	Yes (12–15)	No	No[c]	Yes	Community	

(continued)

Table 23.1B. Continued

Program Details		Empirically Tested With				
Program Name	Protective Factors Targeted	Youth (10-17)	Young Adult (18-25)	Racial/Ethnic Minorities	Urban Setting	Ecological Settings
Guiding Good Choices	Clear Behavior Standards Social Skills & Problem-Solving Skills Interactions With Prosocial Peers Improving Parent-Child Relationships	Yes (11-14)	No	No[d]	No	Family
Multisystemic Therapy (MST)	Clear Behavior Standards Social Skills & Problem-Solving Skills Prosocial Behavior & Involvement Interactions With Prosocial Peers Improving Parent-Child Relationships Prosocial Parent Involvement & Positive Disciplinary Practices Prosocial Opportunities/ Involvement At School Prosocial Opportunities/Involvement In The Community	Yes (4-17)	Yes (18)	No[b]	Yes	Family Community
Positive Action	Clear Behavior Standards Developing Resiliency & Positive Coping Skills/ Behaviors Social Skills & Problem-Solving Skills Prosocial Behavior & Involvement Interactions With Prosocial Peers Improving Parent-Child Relationships Increase Academic Self-Efficacy & Achievement Prosocial Opportunities/Involvement At School	Yes (5-14)	No	No[b]	Yes	Family School Community
Project Towards No Drug Abuse	Developing Resiliency & Positive Coping Skills/ Behaviors Social Skills & Problem-Solving Skills Prosocial Behavior and Involvement	Yes (13-17)	Yes (18-19)	No[b]	Yes	School
Achievement Mentoring	Clear Behavior Standards Prosocial Behavior & Involvement Improving Parent-Child Relationships Prosocial Opportunities/ Involvement At School	Yes (12-16)	No	No[b]	Yes	School
LifeSkills Training (LST)	Clear Behavior Standards Developing Resiliency & Positive Coping Skills/ Behaviors Social Skills & Problem-Solving Skills	Yes (11-16)	No	Yes (African American; Hispanic/ Latino)	Yes	School Community

Program	Protective Factors Targeted				
Learning Together	Clear Behavior Standards Developing Resiliency & Positive Coping Skills/Behaviors Social Skills & Problem-Solving Skills Prosocial Behavior & Involvement Increase Academic Self-Efficacy & Achievement Prosocial Opportunities/Involvement At School	Yes (11-12)	No	No[c]	Yes	School
Olweus Bullying Prevention Program	Clear Behavior Standards Social Skills & Problem-Solving Skills Prosocial Behavior & Involvement Interactions With Prosocial Peers Prosocial Parent Involvement & Positive Disciplinary Practices Prosocial Opportunities/Involvement At School	Yes (7-17)	Yes (18)	No[b]	Yes	School
Safe Streets	No Protective Factors Targeted	Yes (12-17)	Yes (18-24)	Yes (Unspecified)	Yes	Community
Communities That Care	Clear Behavior Standards Developing Resiliency & Positive Coping Skills/Behaviors Social Skills & Problem-Solving Skills Prosocial Behavior & Involvement Interactions With Prosocial Peers Improving Parent-Child Relationships Prosocial Opportunities/Involvement At School Prosocial Opportunities/Involvement In The Community	Yes (0-17)	Yes (18-22)	No[b]	Yes	School Community
Big Brothers Big Sisters of America	Prosocial Behavior & Involvement Improving Parent-Child Relationships Increase Academic Self-Efficacy & Achievement Prosocial Opportunities/Involvement In The Community	Yes (6-17)	Yes (18)	No[b]	No	Community
ThrYve	Social Skills & Problem Solving Skills Interactions With Prosocial Peers Prosocial Parent Involvement & Positive Disciplinary Practices Increase Academic Self-Efficacy & Achievement Prosocial Opportunities/Involvement At School Prosocial Opportunities/Involvement In The Community	Yes (12-17)	Yes (18)	Yes (African American; Hispanic/Latino)	Yes	Family School Hospital Community

Nineteen EBPs were identified. Of these 19 programs, 11 were developed for universal administration (e.g., entire school or school district) and the other 8 were developed to target a particular subgroup (e.g., offenders, hospitalized victims of violence, emotionally and behaviorally disturbed students). Some programs were developed to address more than one violent outcome (e.g., aggression and delinquency; N = 7) or violence generally (N = 5). Only one program was specifically designed to address gun violence (Safe Streets; Webster et al. 2013). In examining the ecological context in which the programs were implemented, the most common were family and school (N = 6 each), community (N = 4), and individual (N = 3). There was one program that addressed both the family and community level (Multisystemic Therapy; Van der Stouwe et al. 2014) and one program that, while primarily community-based, is intended to be multi-level (ThrYve; Watson-Thompson et al. 2020). All 19 programs were tested in adolescent (youth between 12 and 17 years old) samples, while only 6 were specifically tested in young adult (individuals between 18 and 24 years old) samples (6 programs were tested in adolescent samples that included 18-year-olds). Additionally, the majority of the EBPs included an urban sample of young people (N = 17, with 2 of these taking place outside of the US). Only a small subset of the EBPs were specifically studied for effectiveness with minority youth; 3 with Black/African American and/or Hispanic/Latino youth (GenerationPMTO, Forgatch and Kjobli 2016; LifeSkills Training, Spoth et al. 2013; and ThrYve, Watson-Thompson et al. 2020) and 1 with racial/ethnic minority youth not specified (Safe Streets, Webster et al. 2013).

We found some important limitations among the EBPs that are relevant for youth-serving agencies and organizations. For example, some programs have yet to directly evaluate violent outcomes in published studies. Of the two programs that were originally designed outside of the United States (Olweus Bullying Prevention Program, Olweus and Alsaker 1991; Learning Together, Bonell et al. 2018), Learning Together does not yet have empirical evidence for US urban youth of color. Olweus has now been adapted and widely implemented in the United States, but has shown inconsistent effectiveness for youth of color (Bauer, Lozano, and Rivara 2007).

Each program included in Table 23.1 has unique strengths and assets that merit review, and we use the remainder of this section to provide additional details of four programs. We selected one exemplar for each of the outcome foci (aggression, delinquency, and gun violence) and one that targets youth violence more generally.

A. EBP Example of Targeting Aggressive Behaviors

The Olweus Bullying Prevention Program was developed in the 1990s as part of an effort to address severe bullying in elementary, middle, and high schools across Norway. The program has universal and targeted components. At the school level, a school leadership team is formed with the intent to address school climate and develop an agreed-upon set of behavioral norms to be followed by the entire school. All adults in the school (e.g., from support staff to the principal) are charged with monitoring and reinforcing student behavior to adhere to these standards. There is a classroom curriculum component with lessons that promote social and emotional skill development. A key component of the curriculum is conducting classroom meetings that address problematic student issues and reinforce the agreed-upon school behavioral norms. Finally, at the targeted level, there are components targeting youth and their families who are involved in bullying incidents, either as victims or perpetrators.

The Olweus program, while originally designed in Norway, has been widely adopted and tested across the globe. Studies indicate that when implemented with fidelity, school climate improves, incidents of bullying decrease, and students' relationships improve. Some studies have demonstrated effects that are sustained after three years (Limber et al. 2018). Most studies are limited by their quasi-experimental designs and lack of randomization. Additionally, effects for non-White youth have not been sufficiently demonstrated (Bauer, Lozano, and Rivara 2007; Limber et al. 2018).

B. EBP Example of Targeting Delinquency

Developed in the 1970s, Functional Family Therapy (FFT) is a short-term, family-based therapy intervention designed for youth between the ages of 11 and 18 who are at risk for juvenile justice involvement and institutionalization. Through five cumulative phases (Engagement, Motivation, Assessment, Behavior Change, and Generalization), therapists work with families to help reduce conduct disorders, substance abuse, delinquency, and other maladaptive behaviors among youth. Specific risk and protective factors targeted by FFT are tailored to each family, and can include those at the individual (e.g., aggression, antisocial behavior, gang involvement; prosocial behavior and problem solving skills), peer (e.g., peer substance use, interaction with prosocial peers), and family (e.g., family history of conflict, problem behavior, violence, or neglect; positive attachment to parents, parental social support, nonviolent discipline) levels (Functional Family Therapy 2022).

FFT has been tested in a wide range of contexts, including urban, rural, and outside of the United States, and has been applied among racially diverse populations (with 10–60% of samples being representing by non-White youth). Since its formation, the program has accumulated empirical support for its effectiveness in reducing felony recidivism; instances of new drug offenses, property offenses, technical violations, and delinquent adjudications; use of drugs or alcohol; youth internalizing and externalizing behaviors; youth risk behaviors; and aggressive behaviors (e.g., Gottfredson et al. 2018).

However, there are some limitations present among the studies of FFT. For example, several studies had issues with sampling, such as small sample sizes, samples that were nonrandom or only taken from one location, or limited or with no information provided regarding sample reliability or validity (e.g., Eeren et al. 2018). Also, some studies did not test for differential attrition or baseline controls (e.g., Peterson 2017). Most glaringly, some studies showed no long-term and/or post-test effects of the FFT programming or no significant effects of the program at all (Humayun et al. 2017). Other possible limitations of FFT include the high cost of starting up and implementing the program, as well as the resources and training required for providers to properly carry out the intervention (the program is recommended to be implemented by master's level therapists and overseen by a licensed clinical therapist).

C. EBP Example of Targeting Gun Violence

Modeled after Chicago's CeaseFire program, Safe Streets is an evidence-based, public health program, developed by researchers at Johns Hopkins University (JHU) to reduce gun violence among youth ages 14–24 (Webster et al. 2013). While the program is overseen by the Baltimore (Maryland) City Health Department, it is implemented by various community-based organizations across Baltimore. While reducing youth gun violence is the primary aim, Safe Streets utilizes outreach and community mobilization strategies to interrupt the transmission of violence, change community norms regarding acceptability of violence, and increase community social cohesion (Masho et al. 2014). Safe Streets is implemented in urban neighborhoods identified as having rates of violence within the top 25% of the city. Due to systemic and other historical factors, these neighborhoods are almost exclusively racial/ethnic minoritized youth and families.

An evaluation of Safe Streets indicated that it was associated with a large reduction in homicide (26% to 56%) and nonfatal shootings (34% to 44%) across three of four intervention communities (Webster et al. 2013). Additionally, the study found a decrease in youths' overall acceptability rating towards using a gun during interpersonal conflict, for those residing in intervention neighborhoods. Lastly, the program surveyed youth to assess overall impact on their lives. Most youth reported receiving job assistance (88%), getting into a school (95%), and resolving family conflicts (100%). Overall, 80% of youth reported that their lives had improved in some way as a result of being involved in the program.

While Safe Streets was demonstrated to have a significant impact on the reduction of violence within intervention neighborhoods, there are a couple of noteworthy limitations. First, evaluations used to measure reduction in violence were based solely on administrative records, which did not include unreported incidents of violence. Second, further evaluation of these and other prevention efforts are needed to confirm and replicate these findings in other communities.

D. EBP Example of Targeting Youth Violence in General

Together Helping Reduce Youth Violence for Equity (ThrYve) is a multilevel YVP program developed out of the University of Kansas in 2017. ThrYve utilizes a comprehensive socio-ecological model to identify risk and protective factors across the individual, interpersonal, social, and community domains in urban areas of high violence. Across these domains, program staff work closely with youth and community members to provide a collaborative network of youth opportunities, including access to support networks, trainings, and outreach efforts aimed to reduce youth violence and address social determinants of health. Additionally, ThrYve strives to utilize a positive youth development approach to empower and foster resilience for youth of racial and ethnic minoritized identities.

ThrYve is embedded within the community, working closely with 40 community partners across 14 community sectors to ensure representation and collaboration throughout implementation. To ensure ongoing and continuous feedback, efforts are documented and evaluated in striving for community change. ThrYve has shown promising preliminary evidence of both community and system changes across socioecological levels (Watson-Thompson et al. 2020).

IV. Steps to Improving Evidence-Based Policy and Practice in Youth Violence Prevention

There are many ways that we can improve evidence-based policy and practice for YVP in urban contexts. Most importantly, we need to prioritize urban youth voices as a central tenant not only in research sampling, but also in research and program design and delivery. Additionally, the empirical literature is lacking in identifying the many strengths and assets that youth in these contexts possess or have access to. A focus on this can help to combat the negative perceptions and stereotypes of these populations and turn the onus of prevention work to where it belongs: addressing the history and systemic racism that has led communities to these conditions in the first place. While there is much anecdotal and newly emerging empirical evidence that identifies such strengths (e.g., Ross et al. 2022), the research is partially lagging due to the lack of strengths-based measures developed specifically for urban young people. There is a real opportunity for qualitative and mixed-methods work involving young people to develop and establish strengths-based tools that can help researchers and practitioners identify, report, and modify and/or evaluate urban youth promotive and protective factors as they relate to YVP strategies.

The empirical literature suggests that there are some key protective factors related to violent outcomes that current EBPs are not explicitly addressing. First, there is evidence to suggest that building racial and ethnic identity, as well as tools for coping with discrimination, may be a productive avenue for violence prevention. Of the programs that we identified, we could not find any that explicitly address this. Relatedly, sense of self and self-esteem also seem to be related to a decreased likelihood of violent outcomes, but have not been key targets of existing EBPs.

Another area for exploration is around future orientation and positive outlook; this seems particularly important for young people in urban settings where they are witnessing young lives cut short due to violence. There is a need to build adult capacity to acknowledge and support high, positive, future expectations with young people. This may include educational aspirations, but it needs to be expanded to more holistically encompass young people's physical and emotional health and well-being, through vocational and career mentorship and training, as well as family and financial goals. Finally, more intentional work is needed around building understanding and aiming prevention efforts at community- and policy-level changes that can improve the circumstances that youth in urban contexts are facing. We know that urban communities face unique challenges, such as resource deprivation (e.g., food deserts) and service access (e.g., transportation), as a result of historic systemic issues (e.g., redlining, poverty); thus, system-level changes must be made to amend these issues and prevent youth violence. Creating safer and equitable communities across US cities is of utmost importance for preventing youth violence and should be a public health priority.

V. Discussion and Conclusions

The empirical work that examines risk and protective factors for youth violence and the existing EBPs points out many gaps and limitations for urban populations. In the meantime, how can we promote more use of evidence-based policy and practice for urban YVP? While we wait for the empirical work to build and specify for these populations, there are approaches that we can use in real time to discover and create contextually relevant frameworks for research and practice. For instance, in a study on YVP in an urban community, we identified risk factors for youth violence by asking community stakeholders, "What in your community is leading to youth violence?" (Ross et al. 2021). While traditional quantitative measures were also used to gain a broad and representative picture of community needs, this question gave us rich and detailed information on what the most salient risk factors were for this specific community. Furthermore, we asked this question to three important community stakeholder groups: (1) community residents who identified as caregivers of youth living in the community (majority mothers), (2) community service providers who directly worked with residents, and (3) organizational leaders or heads of organizations that had influence and decision-making power over the community.

We were able to identify where community stakeholders had a unified or diverging perspective on the most pressing risk factors for youth violence in the community. Diverging perspectives pointed out gaps in knowledge for certain stakeholder groups or areas where the focus of prevention programming may be met with criticism and resistance. Conversely, areas of synergy can be leveraged to gain support and momentum across stakeholder groups for the selection and uptake of interventions. Our findings pointed out that while many of the risk factors identified were consistent with findings from other communities(e.g., drugs and alcohol), there were some community specific risk factors that needed to be addressed (e.g., parenting challenges, stress and trauma) in order to improve conditions for residents and facilitate a community-wide acceptance and adoption of EBPs. This approach could be used not only for identifying risk factors, but also for identifying strengths or protective factors in the community (e.g., by asking stakeholders, "What strengths and assets exist in the community that help to prevent or reduce youth violence?") and specific targets to consider when selecting, implementing, or modifying an existing EBP. More qualitative work is needed to inform this work and gain perspectives from individuals living and working in these communities.

There are several existing structures that may be utilized to help communities develop context-specific approaches. The Strategic Prevention Framework (SPF) developed by the Substance Abuse and Mental Health Services Administration (SAMHSA), for example, has a structure for communities to do this work. SPF consists of five phases: assessment, building capacity, planning, strategy implementation, and evaluation (SAMHSA 2019). This is similar to the phases followed in the Communities That Care (CTC) model: Get Started, Get Organized, Develop a Community Profile, Create a Plan, and Implement and Evaluate (Center for Communities That Care 2020). In both of these methodologies, the bedrock of the intervention is partnerships with the community that facilitate coalition building and trust. Taken together with an approach that tackles violence prevention across the ecological model, such as ThrYve, and incorporates emerging evidence of promising protective factors, there is a real opportunity to strengthen YVP and improve youth outcomes.

From our review of YVP interventions, we underline the need to provide more readily available EBP information, including strengths and limitations, in order to promote increased use of EBPs. In our review, we often had difficulty locating key program characteristics (e.g., sample, implementation), and we have more access than the general public due to our affiliation with a public university. For communities and adults who work with youth, there are more barriers to gaining this information. For now, we recommend consulting the Blueprints website (blueprintsprograms.org), but more work is needed to translate the scientific findings for general consumption and to properly identify those programs and practices that are developed with and tested for urban youth populations, in particular youth of color.

Finally, we cannot ignore the decades of policies and practices that led to the concentration of urban communities by race, who, as a result, experience extreme deprivation of resources while facing high rates of community violence. Broader education is needed for adults regarding the healthy development of Black youth and the unjust criminalization of youth behavior. Policies that view these communities from a strengths-based perspective will recognize the inherent strengths possessed by youth and families, as well as the resilience and perseverance that they possess. These factors should be the focus to bring about culturally and contextually specific approaches that meet the particular needs of the community. Continuing to push EBPs that were developed in predominantly White samples or nonurban communities is a waste of resources and a disservice to these communities. Though our understanding of precedents and consequences of youth violence in urban settings is still formative, from this knowledge we know these youth face unique challenges, possess unique strengths, and have unique experiences. Because of this, we know it is important to continue to build the knowledge base and develop well-informed interventions to support prevention of youth violence in urban settings.

References

Bauer, Nerissa S, Paula Lozano, and Frederick P Rivara. 2007. The effectiveness of the Olweus Bullying Prevention Program in public middle schools: A controlled trial. *Journal of Adolescent Health*, 40:266–274.

Baumgartner, H, and D Amso. n.d. Resilience in individuals and communities. Providence, RI: Developmental Cognitive Neuroscience Laboratory, Brown University.

Benns, Matthew, Matthew Ruther, Nicholas Nash, Matthew Bozeman, Brian Harbrecht, and Keith Miller. 2020. The Impact of historical racism on modern gun violence: Redlining in the City of Louisville, KY. *Injury*, 51:2192–2198.

Blueprints for Healthy Youth Development. 2022. *Providing a registry of experimentally proven practices*. Boulder CO: Blueprints for Healthy Youth Development. https://www.blueprintsprograms.org.

Bonell, Chris, Elizabeth Allen, Emily Warren, Jennifer McGowan, Leonardo Bevilacqua, Farah Jamal, Rosa Legood, et al. 2018. Effects of the Learning Together intervention on bullying and aggression in English secondary schools (INCLUSIVE): A cluster randomised controlled trial. *Lancet*, 392 (19163): P2452–2464.

Bowes, Lucy, Barbara Maughan, Avshalom Caspi, Terrie E. Moffitt, and Louise Arseneault. 2010. Families promote emotional and behavioural resilience to bullying: Evidence of an environmental effect. *Journal of Child Psychology and Psychiatry and Allied Disciplines*, 51:809–817.

Bynum, Evita G., and Ronald I. Weiner. 2002. Self-concept and violent delinquency in urban african-american adolescent males. *Psychological Reports*, 90 (2): 477–486.

Caldwell, Cleopatra Howard, Laura P. Kohn-Wood, Karen H. Schmeelk-Cone, Tabbye M. Chavous, and Marc A. Zimmerman. 2004. Racial discrimination and racial identity as risk or protective factors for violent behaviors in African American young adults. *American Journal of Community Psychology*, 33:91–105.

Caldwell, Roslyn M., Richard P. Wiebe, and H. Harrington Cleveland. 2006. The influence of future certainty and contextual factors on delinquent behavior and school adjustment among African American adolescents. *Journal of Youth and Adolescence*, 35:591–602.

CDC (Centers for Disease Control and Prevention). 2016. Fast facts: Firearm violence prevention. Atlanta: National Center for Injury Prevention and Control, Division of Violence Prevention. 2016.

CDC (Centers for Disease Control and Prevention). 2021a. Community violence prevention. Atlanta: National Center for Injury Prevention and Control, Division of Violence Prevention. 2021.

CDC (Centers for Disease Control and Prevention). 2021b. Site descriptions: Current YVPCs. Atlanta: National Center for Injury Prevention and Control, Division of Violence Prevention. 2021.

CDC (Centers for Disease Control and Prevention). 2022a. Fast fact: Preventing bullying. Washington, DC: US Department of Health and Human Services. 2022.

CDC (Centers for Disease Control and Prevention). 2022b. Preventing youth violence. Washington, DC: US Department of Health and Human Services. 2022.

Center for Communities That Care. 2023 (August 18). The Center for Communities that Care. https://www.communitiesthatcare.net.

Chapman, John F., Rani A. Desai, Paul R. Falzer, and Randy Borum. 2006. Violence risk and race in a sample of youth in juvenile detention: The potential to reduce disproportionate minority confinement. *Youth Violence and Juvenile Justice*, 4:170–184.

Children's Defense Fund. 2019. *The state of America's children: Youth justice*. Washington, DC: Children's Defense Fund.

Coll, Cynthia García, Gontran Lamberty, Renee Jenkins, Harriet Pipes McAdoo, Keith Crnic, Barbara Hanna Wasik, and Heidie Vázquez García. 1996. An integrative model for the study of developmental competencies in minority children. *Child Development*, 67 (5): 1891–1914.

Conger, Rand D., and Katherine J. Conger. 2002. Resilience in midwestern families: Selected findings from the first decade of a prospective, longitudinal study. *Journal of Marriage and Family*, 62 (2): 361–373.

Eeren, Hester v., Lucas M. A. Goossens, Ron H. J. Scholte, Jan J. V. Busschbach, and Rachel E. A. van der Rijken. 2018. Multisystemic Therapy and Functional Family Therapy compared on their effectiveness using the propensity score method. *Journal of Abnormal Child Psychology*, 46:1037–1050.

Farrington, D. P., and R. Loeber. 2000. Epidemiology of juvenile violence. *Child and Adolescent Psychiatric Clinics of North America*, 9 (4): 733–748.

Forgatch, Marion S., and John Kjøbli. 2016. Parent Management Training—Oregon Model: Adapting intervention with rigorous research. *Family Process*, 55:500–513.

Functional Family Therapy. 2022. Evidence-based interventions for youth and families. https://www.fftllc.com/.

Gorman-Smith, Deborah, Patrick H. Tolan, and David B. Henry. 2000. A developmental-ecological model of the relation of family functioning to patterns of delinquency. *Journal of Quantitative Criminology*, 16:169–198.

Gorman-Smith, Deborah, Patrick H. Tolan, Arnaldo Zelli, and L. Rowell Huesmann. 1996. The relation of family functioning to violence among inner-city minority youths. *Journal of Family Psychology*, 10 (2): 115–129.

Gottfredson, Denise C., Brook Kearley, Terence P. Thornberry, Molly Slothower, Deanna Devlin, and Jamie J. Fader. 2018. Scaling-up evidence-based programs using a public funding stream: A randomized trial of Functional Family Therapy for court-involved youth. *Prevention Science*, 19:939–53.

Hawkins, J. David, Todd Herrenkohl, David P. Farrington, Devon Brewer, Richard F. Catalano, and Tracy W. Harachi. 2012. A review of predictors of youth violence. In *Serious and violent juvenile offenders: Risk factors and successful interventions*, edited by Rolf Loeber and David P. Farrington, 106–146. Thousand Oaks, CA: Sage Publications, Inc.

Henry, David B., Patrick H. Tolan, and Deborah Gorman-Smith. 2001. Longitudinal family and peer group effects on violence and nonviolent delinquency. *Journal of Clinical Child and Adolescent Psychology*, 30 (2): 172–186.

Humayun, Sajid, Lauren Herlitz, Melanie Chesnokov, Moira Doolan, Sabine Landau, and Stephen Scott. 2017. Randomized controlled trial of Functional Family Therapy for offending and antisocial behavior in UK youth. *Journal of Child Psychology and Psychiatry and Allied Disciplines*, 58:1023–1032.

Johnson, Byron R., Sung Joon Jang, Spencer de Li, and David Larson. 2000. The "invisible institution" and Black youth crime: The church as an agency of local social control. *Journal of Youth and Adolescence*, 29:479–498.

Limber, Susan P., Dan Olweus, Weijun Wang, Matthew Masiello, and Kyrre Breivik. 2018. Evaluation of the Olweus Bullying Prevention Program: A large scale study of U.S. students in grades 3–11. *Journal of School Psychology*, 69:56–72.

Lösel, Friedrich, and David P. Farrington. 2012. Direct protective and buffering protective factors in the development of youth violence. *American Journal of Preventive Medicine*, 43:S8–S23.

Maguin, Eugene, Rolf Loeber, and Paul G. Lemahieu. 1993. Does the relationship between poor reading and delinquency hold for males of different ages and ethnic groups? *Journal of Emotional and Behavioral Disorders*, 1 (2): 88–100.

Masho, Saba W., Diane L. Bishop, Torey Edmonds, and Albert D. Farrell. 2014. Using surveillance data to inform community action: The effect of alcohol sale restrictions on intentional injury-related ambulance pickups. *Prevention Science*, 15 (1): 22–30.

McCord, J. 1994. Family socialization and antisocial behavior: Searching for causal relationships in longitudinal research. In *Cross-national longitudinal research on human development and criminal behavior*, edited by E. G. M. Weitekamp and H. J. Kerne, 177–188. Dordecht, the Netherlands: Springer.

O'Connor, Kelly E., Terri N. Sullivan, and Katherine M. Ross. 2023. Individual- and peer-level risk and protective factors for gun carriage among adolescents living in low-income urban communities. *Journal of Interpersonal Violence*, 38 (7–8): 5564–5590.

Oliphant, Stephen N., Charles A. Mouch, Ali Rowhani-Rahbar, Stephen Hargarten, Jonathan Jay, David Hemenway, Marc Zimmerman, and Patrick M. Carter. 2019. A scoping review of patterns, motives, and risk and protective factors for adolescent firearm carriage. *Journal of Behavioral Medicine*, 42 (4): 763–810 .

Olweus, Dan, and Françoise D. Alsaker. 1991. Assessing change in a cohort-longitudinal study with hierarchical data. In *Problems and methods in longitudinal research: Stability and change (European Network on Longitudinal Studies on Individual Development)*, edited by B. Torestad, D. Magnusson, L. Bergman, and G. Ridinger, 107–132. Cambridge, MA: Cambridge University Press.

Ozer, Emily J., and Rhona S. Weinstein. 2004. Urban adolescents' exposure to community violence: The role of support, school safety, and social constraints in a school-based sample of boys and girls. *Journal of Clinical Child and Adolescent Psychology*, 33 (3): 463–476.

Paschall, Mallie J., and Michael L. Hubbard. 1998. Effects of neighborhood and family stressors on African American Male adolescents' self-worth and propensity for violent behavior. *Journal of Consulting and Clinical Psychology*, 66 (5): 825–831.

Paschall, M. J., C. L. Ringwalt, and R. L. Flewelling. 2003. Effects of parenting, father absence, and affiliation with delinquent peers on delinquent behavior among African American male adolescents. *Adolescence*, 38:15–34.

Patterson, G. R., J. B. Reid, and T. J. Dishion. 1992. *A Social interactional approach*. Vol. 4, *Antisocial boys*. Eugene, OR: Castalia.

Peterson, Andrew. 2017. Functional Family Therapy in a probation setting: Outcomes for youths starting treatment January 2010–September 2012. Olympia: Washington State Center for Court Research. https://www.courts.wa.gov/subsite/wsccr/docs/FFT_Outcomes_2016.pdf.

Ross, Katherine M., Diane L. Bishop, Carine E. Leslie, Derek A. Chapman, and Terri N. Sullivan. 2022. Identification of promotive and protective factors for young adults living in concentrated disadvantage. *Youth and Society*, 55 (5): 799–823.

Ross, Katherine M., Terri Sullivan, Kelly O'Connor, Stephanie Hitti, and Manuel N. Leiva. 2021. A community-specific framework of risk factors for youth violence: A qualitative comparison of community stakeholder perspectives in a low-income, urban community. *Journal of Community Psychology*, 49 (5): 1134–1152.

Ross, Katherine M, Colleen S Walsh, Kelly E O'Connor, and Terri N Sullivan. 2023. Ecological promotive and protective factors deterring gun carriage for young adults living in communities with high rates of community violence, *Journal of Community Psychology*, 49:1164–1180.

Rowlands, D. W., and Hanna Love. 2022. Mapping gun violence: A closer look at the intersection between place and gun homicides in four cities. Washington, DC: Brookings Institution. https://www.brookings.edu/2022/04/21/mapping-gun-violence-a-closer-look-at-the-intersection-between-place-and-gun-homicides-in-four-cities/.

SAMHSA (Substance Abuse and Mental Health Services Administration). 2019. *Substance Abuse and Mental Health Services Administration: A guide to SAMHSA's Strategic Prevention Framework*. Rockville, MD: SAMHSA.

Scott, Susie, Lindsay Prior, Fiona Wood, and Jonathon Gray. 2005. Repositioning the patient: the implications of being "at risk." *Social Science & Medicine*, 60:1869–1879.

Sheidow, Ashli J., Deborah Gorman-Smith, Patrick H. Tolan, and David B. Henry. 2001. Family and community characteristics: Risk factors for violence exposure in inner-city youth. *Journal of Community Psychology*, 29:345–360.

Spencer, Margaret Beale, Michael Cunningham, and Dena Phillips Swanson. 1995. Identity as coping: Adolescent African-American males' adaptive responses to high-risk environment. In *Racial and ethnic identity: Psychological development and creative expression*, edited by H. W. Harris, H. C. Blue, and E. E. H. Griffith, 31–52. New York: Taylor & Frances/Routledge.

Spoth, Richard, Linda Trudeau, Chungyeol Shin, Ekaterina Ralston, Cleve Redmond, Mark Greenberg, and Mark Feinberg. 2013. Longitudinal effects of universal preventive intervention on prescription drug misuse: Three randomized controlled trials with late adolescents and young adults. *American Journal of Public Health*, 103 (4): 665–672.

Stevens-Watkins, Danelle, and Scott L. Graves. 2011. Risk and protective factors among African American adolescent males that predict adult involvement in the criminal justice system: Evidence from a national sample. *Journal of Ethnicity in Criminal Justice*, 9:136–151.

Sullivan, Terri N, Katherine M. Ross, Colleen S. Walsh, Kelly E. O'Connor, and Diane E. Bishop. 2023. Relations between exposure to community- and cyber-violence and gun carriage: Examining risk, promotive, and protective factors across the ecological model among Black youth living in low-income urban communities. *Youth and Society*. https://journals.sagepub.com/doi/abs/10.1177/0044118X231172531. .

Taylor, Katherine A., Terri N. Sullivan, and Wendy Kliewer. 2013. A longitudinal path analysis of peer victimization, threat appraisals to the self, and aggression, anxiety, and depression among urban African American adolescents. *Journal of Youth and Adolescence*, 42 (2): 178–189.

US Department of Justice. 2017. *OJJDP statistical briefing book*. Washington, DC: Office of Juvenile Justice and Delinquency Prevention.

Van der Stouwe, Trudy, Jessica J. Asscher, Geert Jan J. M. Stams, Maja Dekovic, and Peter H. van der Laan. 2014. The effectiveness of Multisystemic Therapy (MST): A meta-analysis. *Clinical Psychology Review*, 34:468–481.

Walsh, Colleen S, Katherine M. Ross, Diane L. Bishop, and Terri N Sullivan. 2023. Identifying protective factors that mitigate relations between experiences with violence and gun carriage for young adults living in low-income urban communities. *Journal of Interpersonal Violence*, 38:15–16.

Watson-Thompson, Jomella, Nadia Jessop, Ithar Hassaballa, Priya Vanchy, Janee Henderson, and Courtney Moore. 2020. Together Helping Reduce Youth Violence for Equity (ThrYve): Examining the development of a comprehensive multisectoral approach to youth violence prevention. *American Journal of Community Psychology*, 66 (3–4): 244–255.

Webster, Daniel W., Jennifer Mendel Whitehill, Jon S. Vernick, and Frank C. Curriero. 2013. Effects of Baltimore's Safe Streets program on gun violence: A replication of Chicago's CeaseFire program. *Journal of Urban Health*, 90:27–40.

World Health Organization. 2020. *Youth Violence*. Geneva, Switzerland: World Health Organization. https://www.who.int/news-room/fact-sheets/detail/youth-violence.

Yule, Kristen, Jessica Houston, and John Grych. 2019. Resilience in children exposed to violence: A meta-analysis of protective factors across ecological contexts. *Clinical Child and Family Psychology Review*, 22:406–431.

Zimmerman, Gregory M., and Steven F. Messner. 2013. Individual, family background, and contextual explanations of racial and ethnic disparities in youths' exposure to violence. *American Journal of Public Health*, 103 (3): 435–442.

CHAPTER 24

A PLACE MANAGEMENT APPROACH TO PROMOTE EVIDENCE-BASED CRIME PREVENTION

TAMARA D. HEROLD

THIS chapter is concerned with promoting more evidence-based practice in place-based crime prevention. One evidence-based intervention, place management, shows promising results for reducing crime at high-crime places (Douglas and Welsh 2022), but it is rarely systematically implemented or rigorously evaluated. Police tactics to improve place management, beyond serving as place managers themselves, have not been integrated into daily police activities. The reasons are twofold. First, resources needed to improve place management usually lie beyond police control. Second, crime theories have yet to fully explicate how and why hot spots persist over time and the role place management plays in sustaining these crime concentrations.

This chapter is divided into four sections. The first demonstrates that places matter. It offers a definition of place that allows us to connect crime to place management practices. Evidence showing the nonrandom distribution of crime is presented, revealing that crime is highly concentrated among a small group of places. Studies show that these high-crime places can increase risks of crime at nearby places, thus explaining why crime prevention efforts at one place often reduce crime and disorder in places beyond target locations. The second section demonstrates that place management matters. It describes place managers and how they influence crime. The process of place management is described, followed by evidence that links place managers and management practices to crime at place. Evaluations show that efforts to improve place management can reduce crime, yet some have noted that the practice is underutilized.

The third section seeks to advance the practice of improving place management to reduce crime. It presents a new theory to explain persistent violent hot spots and a strategy for addressing them. Less visible crime-involved places, included in a typology known as CS[4], are described. A theory explaining how these places form place networks to sustain crime hot spots is presented. Finally, a strategy aimed at dismantling crime place networks,

Place Network Investigations, is described, along with early evaluation evidence showing significant violence reductions. The fourth and final section offers speculation concerning environments surrounding place networks, providing new directions for research and practice.

I. Places Matter

Justice system organizations, including police, have historically focused on people. Over the past several decades, those involved in crime prevention have gradually expanded their focus to acknowledge the importance of places for understanding and responding to crime. This shift has notably impacted crime prevention theory, policy, practice, and effectiveness. This section explains both the concept and significance of place. This discussion shows that place definitions have important implications for how we study and approach crime prevention, as well as how we select and interpret evidence surrounding crime and place.

A. Defining Place

The term "place" is ambiguous. It is used to describe extraordinarily large and exceptionally small units of analysis, as well as every-sized place in between. A place can be a continent; it can also be a hotel balcony. Comparative criminologists might use the term to study differences in homicide trends between Western and non-Western societies. Those studying racial profiling might use the term to describe disparities across police jurisdictions. This chapter will not focus on larger units of analysis, like countries, states, cities, or even neighborhoods. These units of analysis represent "pooled" places (Madensen and Eck 2013).

Weisburd and colleagues (2004) were among the first to examine crime distributions across street segments. The term "street segment" typically refers to the section of a street located between two intersections or between an intersection and a dead end (e.g., a cul-de-sac). A street segment is a type of "proximal" place (Madensen and Eck 2013). Multiple property owners fall within a proximal place, but the individual locations within a proximal place influence each other. The spatial immediacy between different properties often allows crime at one property to affect conditions at another. Consider the impact of a large fraternity party on nearby residences, or what might occur at neighboring locations when intoxicated patrons leave a bar at closing. There is also evidence that proximal places are tied to unequal crime distributions (see e.g., Schnell, Braga, and Piza 2017; Weisburd, Morris, and Groff 2009).

After this section, the word place will refer to "proprietary" places (Madensen and Eck 2013). A proprietary place is a single address or property parcel. Five features define proprietary places (Eck 1994). First, a proprietary place exists in two-dimensional space, either virtual or physical. While some places move (e.g., boats, airplanes, trains, busses) and others are stationary, they are real, not conceptual, and they can be located. Second, a proprietary place has boundaries. Legal documents, including property deeds, typically codify the boundaries and bestow certain legal rights (e.g., authority to build structures or exclude others) to deed owners within their property boundaries. Third, a proprietary place often has a dominant function, and place function determines how people use the space. People shop at retail stores, live in apartments, work out at gyms, park in garages, and worship in churches. Some proprietary places serve multiple functions. People can shop and live in a single mixed-use building.

Fourth, a propriety place is usually relatively small, particularly in relation to proximal and pooled places. Pooled places contain many proximal places, and proximal places contain many proprietary places. Some propriety places are notably large, including casinos, shopping malls, hotels, and airports. Most proprietary places are much smaller. Hundreds of people may live in a single high-rise apartment, but the place's physical footprint can take up less than half a street block. Fifth, and most importantly, a proprietary place has an owner. Ownership is significant because it confers legal authority (and responsibility) to manage a place. Proximal and proprietary places have many owners, and so responsibility for crime within these types of places is diffuse. As such, a focus on proprietary places allows us to best understand how place management impacts crime.

B. Evidence Linking Crime to Place

The evidence is consistent that crime is highly concentrated. Beginning in the late 1980s, several dozen studies directly examined the link between crime and place. Each of these studies confirmed that most places experience little to no crime, while a few places experience a great deal of crime (Lee, Eck, and Martinez 2017). This finding holds true no matter the city, year, type of crime, or place examined. Early research found that crime risks across homogenous types of places (e.g., single family homes, parks, high schools, parking lots) remain relatively stable over time (Spelman 1995). Some types of places are consistently associated with higher levels of crime than others. However, even among places with higher crime risks—like bars, transit stations, check-cashing facilities, and public housing—crime still concentrates. If we examine the distribution of crime across only one type of facility (e.g., crime across all bars in a city), most are crime free and only a few are risky (Eck, Clarke, and Guerette 2007). No known study has found an exception to this rule. Consequently, this phenomenon has been labeled the "Iron Law of Troublesome Places" (Wilcox and Eck 2011) and the "Law of Crime Concentration" (Weisburd 2015).

As noted previously, a crime-generating place can negatively impact nearby properties. John Eck uses the term "purlieu" (pronounced *pearl-loo*) to describe the immediately adjacent area likely to be impacted by a high-crime place. High-crime places can radiate crime into their purlieus. Criminologists' interest in crime radiation began with a series of studies focused on the impact of bars. These studies were conducted across Canada, the United Kingdom, and the United States (see Engstad 1975; Hope 1985; Roncek and Bell 1981). This research continues, with recent studies examining the crime radiating effects of bus stops (Liu et al. 2020), vacant housing (Porter et al. 2019), casinos (Lan, Liu, and Eck 2021), and drug treatment clinics (Moyer and Ridgeway 2020). The most direct study of crime radiation found, with a high level of certainty, that crimes occurring inside of places increased incidents of crime outside those locations (see Bowers 2014).

Research findings on the diffusion of crime control benefits also demonstrate that reducing crime at high-crime places can improve conditions in purlieus. Crime diffusion is the opposite of displacement. Place-intervention skeptics maintain that blocking crime at one location will simply shift crime to another location. Yet studies find that crime does not inevitably move around the corner (see Weisburd et al. 2006). A meta-analysis examined 16 evaluations of geographically focused policing initiatives and found that these interventions were associated with significant declines in crime and disorder, and that they tended to lower crime, rather than displace it, in surrounding areas (Bowers et al. 2011).

In sum, strong evidence exists that crime is not random. Crime clusters among a small group of high-crime places. Ignoring high-crime places can increase victimization risk in their purlieus. If effectively addressed, place-based crime reductions may improve crime and disorder in places beyond targeted locations. This brings us to the practice most influential to levels of crime at place: place management.

II. Place Management Matters

To effectively reduce crime, we must first determine the party responsible for the task. Jane Jacobs asserts that accountability cannot be assigned solely to police:

> The first thing to understand is that the public peace—the sidewalk and street peace—of cities is not kept primarily by police, necessary as police are. . . . In some city areas—older public housing projects and streets with very high population turnover are often conspicuous examples—the keeping of public sidewalk law order is left almost entirely to the police and special guards. Such places are jungles. No amount of police can enforce civilization where the normal, casual enforcement of it has broken down. (Jacobs 1961, 31–32)

Jacobs advocates for conditions that will bring people together in ways that will increase surveillance through more "eyes on the street" (54) to deter crime. But who creates these conditions? Who owns crime? Ultimately, accountability lies with place managers.

A. Defining Place Management

Place managers conduct place management. A person must possess two powers to be a place manager. First, they must have the potential to exert control over a place. Second, they must have the legal authority to exercise this control (see Eck 1994). In a general sense, a place manager either owns a place or has been delegated authority to use and operate a place (e.g., a person or management company employed to operate a place, a renter/tenant of a property).

In routine activity theory (see Cohen and Felson 1979; Eck 1994), place managers are one of three crime controllers. Guardians are concerned with protecting potential targets, and handlers act to control the behavior of potential offenders. Because place managers have the legal authority to determine whether controllers (managers, guardians, and handlers) or necessary crime elements (offenders and targets) are present in any given place, they have a larger role in crime control. So, who owns crime? Place managers do. The rights and responsibilities afforded to place owners and their managers, including the authority and ability to control places, makes them accountable (and legally responsible) for crime at place.

All places have place managers. Some places have multiple place managers. A renter and a landlord both have legal authority (within limits) over what happens in an apartment unit. Public spaces have place managers. Traffic and engineering departments manage roadways. Park departments manage public parks. Public works departments manage sidewalks. Even abandoned and vacant properties have place managers. Someone owns that property—a person or corporate entity listed on the deed. In some cases, local governments seize abandoned or condemned properties and subsequently become their place manager. Since all places have managers, the decisions and actions they make or fail to make can explain why crime is highly concentrated at only a few places. These decisions and actions constitute place management.

Place management is a process controlled by place managers. It involves directing and carrying out place operations. The process of place management consists of four functions used to organize the physical and social environment of a place (Madensen 2007). These processes, used separately or in combination, include organizing space, regulating conduct, controlling access, and acquiring resources (also known as ORCA).

1. *Organizing Space*

Place managers select and control the physical settings of a place. By purchasing specific properties or selecting specific places to lease, they decide where to put the place. Homeowners decide where they want to live, entrepreneurs decide where to open their business, and local governments decide where to place schools and community centers. Selecting a location close to other high-crime places has important management implications. If located within the purlieu of a risky facility, place managers may need to work harder to frustrate would-be criminals and block opportunities for crime at their location. We see evidence of these practices when property owners install additional window security features (e.g., bars), build high perimeter walls, or offer customers surveilled off-street parking (see, e.g., Eck and Weisburd 1995).

After location selection, managers establish the physical appearance and structure of the property. This includes building floor plans, internal and external physical features (e.g., seating, cueing areas, parking facilities, public versus private space), and open space landscaping. These decisions have crime prevention implications. For example, crime-susceptibility at convenience stores has been linked to specific place features, including parking lot size, availability of gasoline service, low lighting, obstructed windows, and concealed cash register placement (see, e.g., Altizio and York 2007; D'Alessio and Stolzenberg 1990). Space organization, including its repair and upkeep, influence how people use places and whether the place provides attractive crime opportunities.

Physical place design also influences informal (and formal) social control. Crime controllers must be able to detect potential offenders before they can effectively intervene (Reynald 2010). Adequate sightlines and lighting are necessary conditions for intervention. Signage, wall placements, and other large displays and objects can obstruct vision and create appealing crime spaces. High bookshelves prevent a librarian from noticing theft. A blocked window prevents a patrol officer from noticing a burglary in progress. Poorly lit areas, regardless of sightlines, create similar conditions. Thus, how place managers organize space impacts the effectiveness of all potential crime controllers, including themselves.

2. Regulating Conduct

The organization of physical space and the behaviors that occur at a place are interdependent. This behavioral-environmental alignment is detailed in Barker's (1968) explanation of behavioral settings. Walking into a fast-food restaurant, the behavioral setting prompts users to approach and order from a counter. Visiting a fine dining establishment, the behavioral setting prompts users to wait to be ushered to a table. The themes and designs of drinking establishments determine whether patrons will be able to sit and converse with friends, dance, watch and cheer for sports teams, or play competitive games (Madensen 2007). To a notable extent, decisions concerning the physical design of a place help place managers control user behaviors. But place managers also regulate conduct at places by setting and enforcing rules.

Place rules make known the actions prohibited and activities permitted or encouraged. Place managers can discourage unwanted behaviors by posting or directly communicating rules and consequences. Signs at parks indicate operating hours and whether dogs are permitted. Printed concert tickets provide a list of items permitted and prohibited at the venue. Lifeguards can instruct people not to dive into shallow water or run near the pool. Place managers can also directly promote behaviors. Video screens at sports stadiums can direct fans to yell, shelter in place, exit, or kiss an adjacent person. Team mascots can provoke cheering in crowds. Messaging at stadiums can also encourage reporting of undesirable behavior by other place users by advertising phone or text hotlines (Madensen and Eck 2008a). Following the 80-20 rule, most problems at places tend to be caused by a small number of people. These individuals might be controlled by the owner, some other regular employee, or an employee specializing in enforcement (e.g., hired security or off-duty police). Regular place users might also engage in behavioral intervention, something Felson (1995) refers to as a general level of accountability for place management.

Like physical place design, rule setting can encourage or discourage social control. Signs suggesting that exiting patrons walk together to their vehicles might enhance guardianship, while employment policies requiring bystander intervention—for example, to reduce excessive use of force among correctional officers—can increase handling. Alternatively, a gambling establishment might discourage employees from calling police to avoid negative publicity surrounding unsavory incidents that occur at their properties. Place managers might also set rules to prevent repeat victimization. Landlords who offer tenants early lease termination without penalty can facilitate the safety of domestic violence victims who need to escape their perpetrators (Johnson 2005). Bar policies prohibiting overservice to intoxicated patrons can prevent repeated theft, assault, and robbery victimizations (Graham and Homel 2008; Madensen and Eck 2008b).

3. Controlling Access

Place managers decide who can enter and use their places. They also regulate when and under what circumstances those with permission to enter can do so. Controlling property access also overlaps with how place managers organize space and regulate conduct. Physical features can control access (e.g., gates with keycodes, doors requiring electronic key cards, license plate readers at entry points). Place rules can also determine when and where access is permitted or how it is encouraged. Businesses establish operating hours, state parks require overnight camping permits, and college administrators establish dorm visitation rules for guests. Place managers control access when they enforce these rules. Access control is associated with decreased victimization across a variety of contexts, including schools (Vagi et al. 2018).

Specific business practices and marketing can attract desired clientele, while discouraging others. Choice of nightclub music influences crowd behavior and demographics (Anderson, Daly, and Rapp 2009). Increasing meal and drink prices can shrink and alter clientele pools. Prohibiting co-sleeping could reduce sexual assaults, but also discourage unhoused couples from accessing homeless shelters (Donley and Wright 2012).

Access control practices that remove offenders, restrict target access, or deflect specific types of offenders can reduce repeat victimization. Place managers also regulate access by evicting those initially granted permission to enter. Bouncers remove violent people from bars. Tow trucks are enlisted to remove vehicles with expired permits. Landlords evict crime-involved tenants. Shopping malls prohibit gatherings of large groups of unsupervised or rowdy juveniles. Retail stores trespass known shoplifters. Place managers can also control access to targets on their properties. High-value or frequently targeted items are placed behind counters, displayed with limited stock, or otherwise secured (Hayes, Downs, and Blackwood 2012). Targets can be protected by place managers by deflecting potential offenders. Landlords screen tenants to avoid renting to individuals with extensive criminal histories, and stadiums revoke season ticket holder rights to fans who engage in violence.

4. *Acquiring Resources*

Place managers need resources to obtain and operate places. Thus, place owner decision-making is tightly linked to the pursuit of resources (Madensen 2007). Businesses require revenue to pay for merchandise and staff, upkeep facilities, and generate profits. Noncommercial place managers need to acquire resources, too. Most homeowners must work to pay for mortgages, utilities, and household repairs. City parks departments must prove budgetary needs to city officials to request continued or increased funding to maintain existing facilities or expand services. Universities must attract students to collect tuition, solicit alumni donations, and hire faculty who can secure grant funding to pay for operations. Nonprofit organizations—including those that provide food, health, and other nongovernment social services—must attract donor funding.

A place manager's ability to attract resources will influence each of the other three ORCA functions. Homeowners without resources cannot afford to fix locks broken during a burglary, install motion lighting systems to deter unwanted visitors, or install fencing to restrict property access. Business managers without resources cannot renovate places or afford training needed for staff to effectively regulate patron conduct. Underresourced managers might make decisions to offer hot products associated with theft (Clark and Webb 1999) or relax efforts to exclude problematic patrons in efforts to generate revenue. Daily decisions surrounding resource acquisition can directly affect crime.

Place managers may or may not be concerned about crime. Some place managers, particularly those with resources, might work hard to prevent crime; others might not. If the crime does not interfere with place operations, or if the place manager benefits from the crime, then they are likely to be less concerned with crime at their locations. Place managers might view crime as the cost of doing business (Zidar, Shafer, and Eck 2018), and shift the burden of dealing with the problem onto the public (e.g., by continually calling police) or simply ignore offenses occurring on their properties. Consider motel operators who ignore obvious prostitution and drug dealing activities to maintain high occupancy levels. There are many examples of place managers who benefit directly from crime, including those who own metal recycling facilities and choose to ignore and accept obviously stolen products as the cost of various metals (e.g., copper) increases (Sidebottom, Ashby, and Johnson 2014).

Place managers choose how to respond to crime events at places. There are four general types of place management styles, defined by place managers' reaction to crime: reactors, enablers, promoters, and suppressors—or REPS (Eck and Madensen-Herold 2018). Reactors want to avoid crime at their places. While they do not spend much time or effort trying to anticipate how victimization might occur, they will modify their places after experiencing crime or the threat of crime. A reactor homeowner might install a doorbell camera system after packages are stolen from their porch.

Enablers do little to address crime opportunities at their places, even after experiencing victimization, for a variety of reasons. They might not care, recognize threats, or have adequate resources to address the potential for harm at their properties. An enabler homeowner might not be able to replace a broken window or not understand the importance of yard maintenance for deterring crime (see Troy, Nunery, and Grove 2016). Enablers' inaction creates conditions conducive to criminal activity.

Promoters realize and capitalize on the potential for crime at places. These managers actively create space conducive to criminal activity: a bartender overserves well-tipping patrons, a gun store owner buys and sells stolen weapons and neglects background checks, a convenience store owner allows parking lot drug dealing in exchange for profitable kickbacks. By attracting motivated offenders, places managed by promoters are most likely to serve as crime radiators and increase crime in their purlieu, particularly if nearby locations are managed by other promoters or enablers.

Suppressors are like reactors in that they want to prevent crime, but these managers proactively address conditions that provide crime opportunities. They install burglar alarms when first purchasing their property, hire staff to manage large events, or screen backpacks to deflect offenders with weapons. Crime is least likely to occur at places with suppressor-style managers because they care, recognize the potential for harm, and actively work to block crime opportunities.

The REPS typology explains differences in place manager decision-making. It represents a continuum of practices, rather than discrete categories, and acknowledges that managers might move between different management styles over time when conditions change (e.g., after earning a large profit or filing for bankruptcy). The typology underscores variation in the use of ORCA functions and helps to explain variations in concentrations of crime across places.

The four place management functions, known as ORCA, directly or indirectly influence crime at place. The crime reduction approach featured later in this chapter will show the importance of leveraging these functions to lessen crime. First, the following summary presents evidence that links place management to crime. While it first explains how place managers create the conditions for crime, it then presents empirical evidence that crime is concentrated among few managers.

B. Evidence Linking Place Management to Crime

As discussed, there is a wealth of evidence linking crime to places. Advancements in place management theory spurred examinations of links between crime-place concentrations and property ownership. Crime aggregated to apartments owned by specific individuals or organizations shows higher concentrations of crime at the owner level than at the place level (Payne 2010). This means a few owners own most crime occurring at apartments. When examining other types of facilities, controlling for ownership reduces the relationship between crime and place (Lee, O, and Eck 2021). If place owners use similar management practices across their properties, then crime at places is associated with the management style (REPS) and processes (ORCA) used by these owners. And this evidence suggests that crime is linked to place management.

Further strengthening the crime-place management link, research finds that place crime levels change when ownership changes. Analysis of high-crime apartment buildings found that these places became problematic following purchase by a new owner (Clarke and Bichler-Robinson 1998). This finding was replicated more than a decade later. Apartment ownership changes were associated with crime increases, particularly among larger complexes with some level of past crime (Payne 2010).

In addition to evidence linking crime concentrations and fluctuations to place managers, studies reveal that improving place management reduces crime. Evaluations of interventions to improve place management show nearly consistent positive effects. Large systematic reviews of studies examining place manager implementation of situational crime prevention interventions show evidence of effectiveness (Eck 2002; Guerette 2009).

Eck and Guerette (2012) reviewed 149 evaluations of situational prevention implemented by place managers across various types of places, including residential, retail, transportation, recreation, and public places. The authors conclude that "[t]here are numerous place-based interventions that work, at least at some places against some crime" (2012, 368). Although not a representative sample of place-based interventions, and despite the relatively weak evaluation methods used in the many of the studies, the authors' findings suggest that place management practices matter. More than three-fourths (77%) of the evaluations found that a wide variety of place management interventions (e.g., CPTED, access controls, lighting, alarms, target hardening) reduced crime.

Douglas and Welsh (2022), authors of the most recent systematic review of place management studies, identified six methodologically rigorous evaluations (i.e., at minimum, these studies included before-and-after measures of crime in treatment and comparable control areas). The studies were conducted in the United Kingdom, United States, and Canada, across a variety of settings (i.e., high-rise residential building, parking garage, bar/nightclub, and neighborhood settings), and used diverse place management tactics (e.g., concierge system, opening a nearby taxi business, staff and landlord training). The authors conclude, "The generally favorable results from the six evaluations included in this updated systematic review suggest that place managers represent a promising, albeit underutilized, situational technique for preventing crime" (76).

Pressuring place managers has also reduced crime. A technique known as third-party policing (Buerger and Mazerolle 1998), where police attempt to persuade or coerce nonoffending parties—including place managers—to take responsibility for preventing crime, has reduced calls-for-service at motels (Bichler, Schmerler, and Enriquez 2013) and reported crime at other rental properties (Eck and Wartell 1998). Charging property owners fees for excessive police calls in Anchorage, Alaska, and Green Bay, Wisconsin, reduced calls by about 25% (Payne 2017).

The best available evidence demonstrates that crime is concentrated among place managers, and place managers have the capacity to control crime. Place managers have been described as the "linchpin" for crime prevention at places (Madensen and Eck 2013, 567). They have legal authority and responsibility to safely manage their properties. Although beyond this chapter's scope, any evidence concerning the effectiveness of place-based crime prevention interventions, including situational crime prevention, crime prevention through environmental design, and defensible space, offers evidence that place management changes can effectively reduce crime. These crime prevention strategies can only be enacted with place manager cooperation.

III. Place Network Investigations

Crime scientists attempt to determine why some places experience so much crime, while other similar or nearby places experience little to no crime. As repeated throughout this chapter, much of this variation is explained by place management. But despite recurring police attention and improvements in place management, hot spots tend to persist in the same locations over time (see Schnell and McManus 2020). Why?

Abt (2019) studied urban street violence and concluded that violence is "sticky." As evidence demonstrates, crime is not random. Violence, like all crime, clusters among small groups of people and places. Because violence sticks, we can predict who will commit violence and where it will occur. Predictable events can be prevented. Police have acted on this knowledge for decades. They make targeted arrests of high-risk offenders. They develop deployment strategies that put officers in high-crime locations. Police also engage in problem-solving and work with place managers to drive down crime at problematic places. Evaluations consistently show that these strategies successfully reduce crime (Braga, Weisburd, and Turchan 2018; Braga et al. 2019; Hinkel et al. 2020). Yet, violence and other forms of crime tend to re-emerge in the same places when declines in prevention impact, including "deterrence decay," occurs (Sherman 1990, 2). A recent explanation for this phenomenon focuses on crime place networks. Place networks consist of highly visible high-crime places. But they also consist of less visible crime-involved places.

A. Hidden Crime Places in Crime Hot Spots

Important evidence is often invisible. Sometimes we fail to see useful evidence because it has been, intentionally or unintentionally, hidden. A car might be backed into a parking space, hiding the rear license plate linked to a stolen vehicle. Sometimes we see key evidence, but do not understand its usefulness. A local schoolteacher calls police to report social media posts made by a distressed student, but the assigned detective is unaware that the content aligns with school shooting precursors.

Police and others interested in crime prevention largely concern themselves with visible evidence. Most of this evidence comes from public calls-for-service and crime reports. The research in this chapter is based on visible crime places. But there are four types of crime-involved places (known as CS^4) that underlie persistent hot spots (Madensen and Eck 2013), and only one is readily visible in crime data.

1. *Crime Sites*

Crime events cluster at or near specific places. Places with large numbers of crimes are called "crime sites." Crime sites represent one type of crime-involved place and are the only places visibly depicted on traditional crime maps. Accountability models, like CompStat, hold officers and their supervisors accountable for reducing victimization at repeat crime sites. Police Chief Bill Bratton famously used the CompStat model to focus officers on locations containing crime sites and drive down New York City crime in the 1990s (Bratton and Malinowski 2008). Yet offenders commonly use other locations. There are at least three other types of crime-involved places. Unlike crime sites, these places are more likely to be ignored. They do not regularly attract police attention and are often overlooked, since police have not historically recognized the importance of these places.

2. *Convergence Settings*

Convergence settings are places where potential offenders regularly meet (Felson 2003). Any public place (e.g., local bar, neighborhood park) or public space (e.g., a street corner) where people can gather can serve as a convergence setting. Offenders use convergence settings to engage in recreational activities, recruit potential accomplices, exchange information, plan future offenses, and sell stolen goods. While some of these activities are criminal (e.g., selling stolen goods), such activity is often consensual and does not attract police attention. Many of the other activities are not criminal in nature and are unlikely to be reported to police.

To the extent that police or community members are familiar with known criminals and can identify the public places regularly frequented by these offenders, they are aware of existing convergence settings. Whether or not the police or community recognize the importance of these places is another matter. Although Felson (2003) did not initially propose that convergence settings are strictly public places, they are conceptualized in this way to distinguish them from a different type of crime-involved place: comfort spaces.

3. *Comfort Spaces*

Comfort spaces are nonpublic, offender-controlled places (Hammer 2011). They are owned by offenders, their relatives and friends, or other associates. Offenders use comfort spaces to hang out privately with co-offenders and stage nearby crimes. They offer safe places for offenders to stash their tools or illicit products and belongings, including drugs, weapons, stolen goods, and—in cases of human trafficking—people. Comfort spaces can be houses or apartments. They can be situated inside of businesses. For example, a comfort space can be established in the back room of a convenience store with a permitting manager or owner.

Offenders often avoid committing observable crimes at these sites to keep them hidden. Thus, comfort spaces rarely appear in police crime data. However, specialized units covertly monitoring offender movement might discover comfort spaces associated with illicit markets and violent group activity. Watchful community members discover comfort spaces when they attract unknown persons at curious hours. Criminal activities occurring in public convergence settings and private comfort spaces are further facilitated by the last type of crime-involved place: corrupting spots.

4. *Corrupting Spots*

Corrupting spots are places, usually operating as legitimate businesses, that stimulate crime at other locations (Madensen and Eck 2013). Recycling plants buying stolen copper, websites hosting illegal pornography, pawn shops laundering money, and stores buying and selling stolen jewelry are examples of corrupting spots. These places increase crime in their purlieu as nearby offenders seek to profit from the illicit practices of these businesses.

The crimes at corrupting spots are largely consensual and rarely reported to police. Corrupting spots are sometimes known to federal agencies involved in large-scale organized crime investigations. Federal agencies are frequently accused of failing to share investigative intelligence with local authorities who have differing missions (regional/ transnational versus local crime). Information sharing can be further hindered if a high-value confidential informant, assisting with a federal regional or transnational investigation, is engaged in criminal activity at a local corrupting spot. But, again, patrol officers, specialized units, and community members who witness suspicious business transactions or talk with others who observe such behaviors can often identify local places likely to be corrupting spots.

B. Theory and Strategy for Persistent Violent Hot Spots

Repeat violent crime sites are highly visible. Police are regularly called to them, and they are prominently displayed on crime maps. While less likely to generate calls-for-service, we have explained why police (and community members) are sometimes aware of the other three "hidden" crime places: convergence settings, comfort spaces, and corrupting spots. It is proposed that violence and other crime remain sticky because we have failed to acknowledge the significance of these places.

Careful observation of offender movement within hot spots uncovers the connections between the CS^4 places. In serious violent hot spots, street violence is facilitated by these connections. Each type of place serves a function for the network. Offenders move between place network locations while carrying out daily activities. For example, moving between six places, an offender picks up product at a comfort spot, distributes the product to co-offenders in a convergent setting, drops off money and hangs out and eats at a corrupting spot, gambles with friends at a comfort space, sells a weapon and engages in a shooting at a crime site, and then seeks refuge in a comfort space. Two implications stem from this example: (1) visible crime occurred at only one of six offender-used locations, and (2) removing one crime-involved place does not disrupt the larger network.

Police drive down crime by focusing resources on crime sites in hot spots. Crime reductions are usually temporary because the rest of the crime place infrastructure remains intact. Rather than attempt to build an entirely new place network elsewhere, offenders retreat into the remaining network locations. When police shift their attention to other problematic locations, offenders return and reoccupy the crime site. The network continues to function and violence bounces back. As first discovered in Cincinnati, persistent violent hotspots—many of which had existed for decades—make up only 1.4% of land mass but account for a disproportionate number of officer injuries and crimes, including more than 40% of persons shot in the city (Herold and Eck 2020). Place Network Investigations (PNI) is a strategy used to achieve sustainable violence reductions in these locations.

The PNI strategy involves two processes. First, departments assign skilled investigators to uncover place networks. Second, city leaders assemble to review investigative findings and find ways to stop offenders from using identified place network locations. This requires heightened organization and reprioritization of existing public resources.

Officers use investigative techniques to find networked places. They identify known offenders and the places they frequent by interviewing patrol officers, specialized units, city and social service personnel, and community members. Analysts help investigators better understand crime and victimization patterns to uncover network places. Investigators identify people and place connections through covert and overt surveillance activities and identify place functions—whether specific places serve as crime sites, convergence settings, comfort spaces, corrupting spots, or some combination (e.g., a retail store that serves as a corrupting spot, but also a common crime site). Investigators use additional sources of information (e.g., business employees, security personnel) and confidential informants to build civil and criminal cases against noncooperative place owners.

A PNI Board (sometimes called an All-City Team or the Board), consisting of city department representatives and community members and organization leaders, assembles to review investigative findings, observe the crime hot spot, and use data from their respective agencies to further identify potential network places. The Board offers recommendations and prioritizes resources to dismantle the network, offering alternatives to arrest-focused strategies and traditional police crime suppression tactics, including revoking business licenses through civil remedies, legislating new management practices, mandating employee training, and requiring structural building changes or complete property abatement. City resources are prioritized to eliminate crime-facilitating conditions in a jurisdiction's most vulnerable locations. Board representatives demolish vacant buildings, alter traffic patterns, move public transit locations, repair blighted property, and increase lighting (Herold et al. 2020).

Place management practices are changed in every place identified in the network. Each intervention involves altering at least one of the four ORCA functions. Promoters are blocked from using places and enablers are provided resources and incentives (or consequences) for changing place dynamics. Place management changes build community resilience and sustained crime reductions by removing offenders' abilities to use network places for illicit activities and encouraging community control of public spaces by reactivating them in positive ways (e.g., turning an empty field into a community center; see Herold and Eck 2020). This further promotes conditions favorable for crime suppressor interventions.

Early PNI evaluations showed significant violence reductions with little to no evidence of displacement. In two initial Cincinnati pilot sites, gun violence declined by about 80%. In one site, gunshot victims decreased from 18 in 2015 to 5 in 2016, with no shooting victims reported in the last three months of the year (Madensen et al. 2017). Expansion of PNIs across the city found that shootings declined by 50% on average across five hot spots (Hammer 2020). A PNI pilot site in Las Vegas experienced a 40% reduction in gun violence within the first year (Herold et al. 2020; Herold and Prosser 2020).

More PNI evaluations are in progress. The strategy has been adopted by diverse US jurisdictions, including Dallas, Texas; Denver, Colorado; Philadelphia, Pennsylvania; Tucson, Arizona; and Wichita, Kansas. Several other cities are considering PNI adoption. Current and future evaluations will help to further assess the strategy's crime reduction sustainability and determine the contexts in which PNI is most effective.

IV. Discussion and Conclusions

This chapter summarized evidence showing that crime is highly concentrated across places. It also described the process of place management, called ORCA, and provided evidence that place management is linked to, and likely responsible for, observable crime distributions. It offered evidence that place managers can control crime. These examinations and a recent systematic review (Douglas and Welsh 2022) led to the conclusion that place management is a promising crime reduction technique, yet it remains underutilized.

In response, a new approach to improving place management in hot spots was presented. The idea of hidden crime places in crime place networks was offered as the basis for a theory of persistent violent hot spots. A new strategy, Place Network Investigations, uses this theory to uncover place networks, improve place management, and achieve sustainable crime reductions. While traditional police suppression at crime sites alone reduces crime, we continually place officers in harm's way for short-lived crime reductions with tactics that have historically damaged police-community relations. By acknowledging the role and importance of all CS[4] crime places, we can devise innovative and more impactful crime reduction strategies that lessen reliance on traditional justice system processes. Early evidence suggests that PNI offers one way to accomplish this objective.

Many of the processes referenced in this persistent hot spot theory stem from unsystematic qualitative observations and have yet to be rigorously evaluated. Further study is needed to uncover the causal mechanisms that keep offenders from establishing new sites elsewhere. Interdisciplinary theory and evidence support the hypothesis that place networks are not easily transferable to other locations because they require combinations of specific environmental conditions. When archaeologists look for lost civilizations, they select dig sites based on constellations of places and place features: possible stone excavation locations, rocks that might have supported walls, suspiciously aligned earthen mounds, all near a water source. Crime place networks might also be built in locations with conditions that allow crime to flourish, including access to transportation, economic conditions that hinder place management, in places with high concentrations of vulnerable populations. Such speculation offers promising new research directions with significant crime prevention implications.

References

Abt, Thomas. 2019. *Bleeding out: The devastating consequences of urban violence—and a bold new plan for peace in the streets*. New York: Basic Books.

Altizio, Alicia, and Diana York. 2007. *Robbery of convenience stores*. Washington, DC: Office of Community Oriented Policing Services.

Anderson, Tammy, Kevin Daly, and Laura Rapp. 2009. Clubbing masculinities and crime: A qualitative study of Philadelphia nightclub scenes. *Feminist Criminology*, 4 (4): 302–332.

Barker, Roger G. 1968. *Ecological psychology*. Stanford, CA: Stanford University Press.

Bichler, Gisela., Karin Schmerler, and Janet Enriquez. 2013. Curbing nuisance motels: an evaluation of police as place regulators. *Policing: An International Journal*, 36 (2): 437–462.

Bowers, Kate. 2014. Risky facilities: Crime radiators or crime absorbers? A comparison of internal and external levels of theft. *Journal of Quantitative Criminology*, 30 (3): 389–414.

Bowers, Kate J., Shane D. Johnson, Rob T. Guerette, Lucia Summers, and Suzanne Poynton. 2011. Spatial displacement and diffusion of benefits among geographically focused policing initiatives: A meta-analytical review. *Journal of Experimental Criminology*, 7 (4): 347–374.

Braga, Anthony A., Brandon S. Turchan, Andrew V. Papachristos, and David M. Hureau. 2019. Hot spots policing and crime reduction: An update of an ongoing systematic review and meta-analysis. *Journal of Experimental Criminology*, 15 (3): 289–311.

Braga, Anthony A., David Weisburd, and Brandon Turchan. 2018. Focused deterrence strategies and crime control: An updated systematic review and meta-analysis of the empirical evidence. *Criminology & Public Policy*, 17 (1): 205–250.

Bratton, William J., and Sean W. Malinowski. 2008. Police performance management in practice: Taking COMPSTAT to the next level. *Policing: A Journal of Policy and Practice*, 2 (3): 259–265.

Buerger, Michael E., and Lorraine Green Mazerolle. 1998. Third-party policing: A theoretical analysis of an emerging trend. *Justice Quarterly*, 15 (2): 301–327.

Clarke, Ronald V., and Gisela Bichler-Robertson. 1998. Place managers, slumlords and crime in low rent apartment buildings. *Security Journal*, 11 (1): 11–19.

Clarke, Ronald V. G., and Barry Webb. 1999. *Hot products: Understanding, anticipating and reducing demand for stolen goods*. Police Research Series no. 112. London: Home Office.

Cohen, Lawrence E., and Marcus Felson. 1979. Social change and crime rate trends: A routine activity approach. *American Sociological Review*, 44 (4): 588–608.

D'Alessio, Stewart, and Lisa StolzenBerg. 1990. A crime of convenience: The environment and convenience store robbery. *Environment and Behavior*, 22 (2): 255–271.

Donley, Amy M., and James D. Wright. 2012. Safer outside: A qualitative exploration of homeless people's resistance to homeless shelters. *Journal of Forensic Psychology Practice*, 12 (4): 288–306.

Douglas, Stephen, and Brandon C. Welsh. 2022. There has to be a better way: Place managers for crime prevention in a surveillance society. *International Journal of Comparative and Applied Criminal Justice*, 46 (1): 67–80.

Eck, John E. 1994. Drug markets and drug places: A case-control study of the spatial structure of illicit drug dealing. PhD diss., University of Maryland.

Eck, John E. 2002. Preventing crime at places. In *Evidence-based crime prevention*, edited by Lawerence W. Sherman, David P. Farrington, Brandon C. Welsh, and Doris Layton MacKenzie, 241–294. New York: Routledge.

Eck, John E., Ronald V. Clarke, and Rob T. Guerette. 2007. Risky facilities: Crime concentration in homogeneous sets of establishments and facilities. *Crime Prevention Studies*, 21:225–264.

Eck, John E., and Rob T. Guerette. 2012. Place-based crime prevention: Theory, evidence, and policy. In *The Oxford handbook of crime prevention*, edited by Brandon C. Welsh and David P. Farrington, 354–383. New York: Oxford University Press.

Eck, John E., and Tamara D. Madensen-Herold. 2018 Place management, guardianship, and the establishment of order. In *Deterrence, choice, and crime*, edited by Francis T. Cullen, Cheryl Lero Jonson, and Daniel S. Nagin, 269–307. New York: Routledge.

Eck, John E., and Julie Wartell. 1998. Improving the management of rental properties with drug problems: A randomized experiment. In *Civil remedies and crime prevention*, edited by Lorraine Green Mazerolle and Jan Roehl, 161–185. Monsey, NY: Criminal Justice Press.

Eck, John E., and David Weisburd, eds. 1995. *Crime and place*. Crime Prevention Studies, Vol. 4. Monsey, NY: Criminal Justice Press.

Engstad, Peter A. 1975. Environmental opportunities and the ecology of crime. In *Crime in Canadian society*, edited by Robert A. Silverman, James J. Teevan Jr., and Vincent F. Sacco, 193–211. Toronto: Butterworth.

Felson, Marcus. 1995. Those who discourage crime. In *Crime and place*, edited by John E. Eck and David Weisburd, 53–66. Monsey, NY: Criminal Justice Press.

Felson, Marcus. 2003. The process of co-offending. In *Theory for practice in situational crime prevention*, edited by Martha J. Smith and Derek B. Cornish, 149–168. Monsey, NY: Criminal Justice Press.

Graham, Kathryn, and Ross Homel. 2008. *Raising the bar: Preventing aggression in and around bars, pubs and clubs*. Devon, UK: Willan.

Guerette, Rob T. 2009. The push, pull, and expansion of situational crime prevention evaluation: An appraisal of thirty-seven years of research. In *Evaluating crime reduction initiatives*, edited by Johannes Knutsson and Nick Tilley, 29–58. Monsey, NY: Criminal Justice Press.

Hammer, Matthew. 2011. Crime places of comfort. Unpublished Masters Demonstration Project paper. Cincinnati, OH: University of Cincinnati, School of Criminal Justice.

Hammer, Matthew G. 2020. Place-based investigations of violent offender territories (PIVOT): An exploration and evaluation of a place network disruption violence reduction strategy in Cincinnati, Ohio. PhD diss., University of Cincinnati.

Hayes, Read, Daniel M. Downs, and Robert Blackwood. 2012. Anti-theft procedures and fixtures: A randomized controlled trial of two situational crime prevention measures. *Journal of Experimental Criminology*, 8 (1): 1–15.

Herold, Tamara D., and John E. Eck. 2020. Gun violence in Cincinnati, Ohio. In *Problem-oriented policing*, edited by Michael S. Scott and Ronald V. Clarke, 28–39. New York: Routledge.

Herold, Tamara D., Robin S. Engel, Nicolas Corsaro, and Stacey L. Clouse. 2020. *Place Network Investigations in Las Vegas, Nevada: Program review and process evaluation*. Cincinnati: University of Cincinnati, Center for Police Research and Policy.

Herold, Tamara D., and Jamie Prosser. 2020. Crime place networks in Las Vegas: A new violence reduction strategy. *Police Chief Magazine*, 87 (6): 51–57.

Hinkle, Joshua C., David Weisburd, Cody W. Telep, and Kevin Petersen. 2020. Problem-oriented policing for reducing crime and disorder: An updated systematic review and meta-analysis. *Campbell Systematic Reviews*, 16 (2): e1089.

Hope, Tim. 1985. *Implementing crime prevention measures*. London: Her Majesty's Stationery Office.

Jacobs, Jane. 1961. *The death and life of great American cities*. New York: Random House.

Johnson, Anne C. 2005. From house to home: Creating a right to early lease termination for domestic violence victims. *Minnesota Law Review*, 90 (6): 1859–1888.

Lan, Minxuan, Lin Liu, and John E. Eck. 2021. A spatial analytical approach to assess the impact of a casino on crime: An example of JACK Casino in Downtown Cincinnati. *Cities*, 111 (April): 103003. https://doi.org/10.1016/j.cities.2020.103003.

Lee, YongJei, John E. Eck, and Natalie N. Martinez. 2017. How concentrated is crime at places? A systematic review from 1970 to 2015. *Crime Science*, 6 (1): 1–16.

Lee, YongJei, SooHyun O, and John E. Eck. 2021. Why your bar has crime but not mine: Resolving the land use and crime-risky facility conflict. *Justice Quarterly*, 39 (5): 1009–1035.

Liu, Lin, Minxuan Lan, John E. Eck, and Emily Lei Kang. 2020. Assessing the effects of bus stop relocation on street robbery. *Computers, Environment and Urban Systems*, 80 (March): 101455.

Madensen, Tamara D. 2007. Bar management and crime: Toward a dynamic theory of place management and crime hotspots. PhD diss., University of Cincinnati.

Madensen, Tamara D., and John E. Eck. 2008a. *Spectator violence in stadiums*. Washington, DC: Office of Community Oriented Policing Services.

Madensen, Tamara D, and John E. Eck. 2008b. Violence in bars: Exploring the impact of place manager decision-making. *Crime Prevention and Community Safety*, 10 (2): 111–125.

Madensen, Tamara D., and John E. Eck. 2013. Crime places and place management. In *The Oxford handbook of criminological theory*, edited by Francis T. Cullen and Pamela Wilcox, 554–578. New York: Oxford University Press.

Madensen, Tamara D., Maris Herold, Matthew G. Hammer, and Blake R. Christenson. 2017. Research in brief: place-based investigations to disrupt crime place networks. *Police Chief Magazine*, 84 (4): 14–15.

Moyer, Ruth A., and Greg Ridgeway. 2020. The effect of outpatient methadone maintenance treatment facilities on place-based crime. *Journal of Experimental Criminology*, 16 (2): 227–245.

Payne, Troy C. 2010. Does changing ownership change crime? An analysis of apartment ownership and crime in Cincinnati. PhD diss., University of Cincinnati.

Payne, Troy C. 2017. Reducing excessive police incidents: Do notices to owners work? *Security Journal*, 30 (3): 922–939.

Porter, Lauren C., Alaina De Biasi, Susanne Mitchell, Andrew Curtis, and Eric Jefferis. 2019. Understanding the criminogenic properties of vacant housing: A mixed methods approach. *Journal of Research in Crime and Delinquency*, 56 (3): 378–411.

Reynald, Danielle M. 2010. Guardians on guardianship: Factors affecting the willingness to supervise, the ability to detect potential offenders, and the willingness to intervene. *Journal of Research in Crime and Delinquency*, 47 (3): 358–390.

Roncek, Dennis W., and Ralph Bell. 1981. Bars, blocks, and crimes. *Journal of Environmental Systems*, 11 (1): 35–47.

Schnell, Cory, Anthony A. Braga, and Eric L. Piza. 2017. The influence of community areas, neighborhood clusters, and street segments on the spatial variability of violent crime in Chicago. *Journal of Quantitative Criminology*, 33 (3): 469–496.

Schnell, Cory, and Hannah D. McManus. 2020. The influence of temporal specification on the identification of crime hot spots for program evaluations: A test of longitudinal stability in crime patterns. *Journal of Quantitative Criminology*, 38 (1): 51–74.

Sherman, Lawrence W. 1990. Police crackdowns: Initial and residual deterrence. In *Crime and justice*, edited by Michael Tonry and Norval Morris, 1–48. Chicago: University of Chicago Press.

Sidebottom, Aiden, Matt Ashby, and Shane D. Johnson. 2014. Copper cable theft: Revisiting the price-theft hypothesis. *Journal of Research in Crime and Delinquency*, 51 (5): 684–700.

Spelman, William. 1995. Criminal careers of public places. In *Crime and place*, edited by David Weisburd and John E. Eck, 115–144. Monsey, NY: Willow Tree Press.

Troy, Austin, Ashley Nunery, and J. Morgan Grove. 2016. The relationship between residential yard management and neighborhood crime: An analysis from Baltimore City and County. *Landscape and Urban Planning*, 147 (March): 78–87.

Vagi, Kevin J., Mark R. Stevens, Thomas R. Simon, Kathleen C. Basile, Sherry P. Carter, and Stanley L. Carter. 2018. Crime Prevention Through Environmental Design (CPTED) characteristics associated with violence and safety in middle schools. *Journal of School Health*, 88 (4): 296–305.

Weisburd, David. 2015. The law of crime concentration and the criminology of place. *Criminology*, 53 (2): 133–157.

Weisburd, David, Shawn Bushway, Cynthia Lum, and Sue-Ming Yang. 2004. Trajectories of crime at places: A longitudinal study of street segments in the city of Seattle. *Criminology*, 42 (2): 283–321.

Weisburd, David, Nancy A. Morris, and Elizabeth R. Groff. 2009. Hot spots of juvenile crime: A longitudinal study of arrest incidents at street segments in Seattle, Washington. *Journal of Quantitative Criminology*, 25 (4): 443–467.

Weisburd, David, Laura A. Wyckoff, Justin Ready, John E. Eck, Joshua C. Hinkle, and Frank Gajewski. 2006. Does crime just move around the corner? A controlled study of spatial displacement and diffusion of crime control benefits. *Criminology*, 44 (3): 549–592.

Wilcox, Pamela, and John E. Eck. 2011. Criminology of the unpopular: Implications for policy aimed at payday lending facilities. *Criminology & Public Policy*, 10 (2): 473–482.

Zidar, Michael S., Jillian G. Shafer, and John E. Eck 2018. Reframing an obvious police problem: Discovery, analysis and response to a manufactured problem in a small city. *Policing: A Journal of Policy and Practice*, 12 (3): 316–331.

CHAPTER 25

USING RESEARCH TO INFORM SERVICES FOR VICTIMS OF CRIME

JILLIAN J. TURANOVIC, JULIE L. KUPER, AND MACKENZIE MASTERS

CRIMINAL victimization can be a traumatic event that carries negative consequences over the life course. Especially when it is violent in nature, victimization has been linked to a range of health and social problems in the short and long term. Such problems include depression and anxiety, symptoms of post-traumatic stress disorder (PTSD), poor physical health, substance use, relationship strain, financial hardship, problems at school or work, and further victimization (Macmillan 2001; Turanovic and Pratt 2019; Turanovic 2019). These harmful consequences can also be felt by those indirectly affected by crime—such as secondary victims who witness serious violence or are impacted by the homicide of a loved one. These outcomes of victimization are concerning, given that millions of Americans are violently victimized each year. Indeed, recent estimates from the National Crime Victimization Survey (NCVS) suggest that in 2020 there were nearly 4.6 million violent incidents involving victims aged 12 or older (Morgan and Thompson 2021).

In an effort to mitigate the harms that victims and survivors experience, numerous victim service programs have been developed. Since the 1970s, victim service programs have received hundreds of millions of dollars from the Victims of Crime Act (VOCA) allocated for victim assistance and compensation (Doerner and Lab 2021; Newmark 2004). Today, more than 12,000 programs of various sizes operate throughout the country, providing a range of services to victims of crime (Oudekerk, Warnken, and Langton 2019). Such services can comprise referrals to community-based treatment providers, crisis interventions for victims who are struggling with post-victimization trauma, emergency aid for victims with immediate needs (e.g., shelter, clothing, food, cash), or court advocacy for victims who are overwhelmed by the complexities of the legal system (Lurigio 2014; Skogan, Davis, and Lurigio 1990; Turanovic and Biro 2023).

Despite the exponential growth of victim service programs over the past several decades, relatively little is known about "what works" in the field of victim services (Blomberg, Waldo, and Chester 2002). Compared to other areas of criminal justice inquiry that focus on the needs of offenders, much less research has been produced on the effectiveness of providing support services to victims (Xie and Lynch 2017). A review commissioned by the National Institute of Justice (Lurigio 2014) noted that the lack of data concerning the effectiveness of victim service programs is a serious obstacle to creating evidence-based policies. In addition, research shows that victims and criminal justice system personnel often lack knowledge of available victim services and perceive victim services as a low priority in a system that is designed primarily for processing offenders (Englebrecht 2011; Sims, Yost, and Abbott 2005).

With these issues in mind, the purpose of this chapter is to take stock of the research evidence on victim services. We begin by describing victim services, the forms of assistance that are typically offered, and their use. Next, we discuss principles of effective victim services and identify evidence-based programs and practices for responding to victims of crime. We conclude with a discussion of gaps and challenges in the identification of "what works" in victim services, and put forth several directions for future research.

I. Overview of Victim Services

Once considered only witnesses to a case, victims have been increasingly granted a range of rights and protections in the aftermath of a crime (Fisher, Reyns, and Sloan 2016). Spurred in part by the crime victims' rights movement and the President's Commission on Crime in 1967, experimental victim-witness programs began to emerge in the 1970s. By 1977 there were more than 100 federally funded victim-witness programs, and by 1979 the number had increased to more than 400 (Blomberg, Waldo, and Chester 2002). Most of these early programs were focused on providing witness services to assist in the prosecution of criminal cases (Blomberg, Waldo, and Bullock 1989). These services have been widely expanded over time to provide various forms of assistance expressly for victims, such as victim compensation, individual and group counseling, shelters for victims of domestic violence, rape crisis counseling, death notifications, and support for survivors of homicides (Doerner and Lab 2021; Turanovic and Pratt 2019; Turanovic et al. 2020). And though the research is limited, several studies suggest that victim service programs can help to alleviate trauma, increase perceptions of social support, and shield victims from the stress and uncertainty of criminal justice system processing (Erez, Globokar, and Ibarra 2014; Herman 2005; McDermott and Garofalo 2004; Sullivan, Bybee, and Allen 2002).

Victim service programs can be community-based or located within law enforcement agencies, prosecutors' offices, or departments of corrections. Generally, these programs are staffed with victim advocates who are trained to support crime victims and work collaboratively with other agencies to get help and information for the victims served. According to Zweig and Yahner (2013), victim service programs will generally offer some forms of (1) safety and crisis intervention (e.g., safety planning, danger assessment, emergency housing), (2) individual advocacy and case management (e.g., individual treatment plans, needs assessment, referral to specialized treatment providers), (3) emotional support (e.g., crisis hotlines, counseling, active listening, individual or group-based therapy), (4) legal advocacy (e.g., criminal justice education and information sharing, court accompaniment, preparation of the victim impact statement), or (5) financial compensation (e.g., assistance with filing compensation or requesting restitution).

Many victim service programs across the United States receive support from the Crime Victims Fund, established by VOCA. The Crime Victims Fund is not financed by tax dollars, but rather by the fines and penalties paid by convicted federal offenders. Forfeited bail bonds; deposits from federal courts and the Federal Bureau of Prisons; and gifts, donations, and bequests by private parties also contribute to the fund (Office for Victims of Crime 2022). Funds are distributed to states for their own victim compensation and crime victim assistance programs. States typically release funds to different service programs through a competitive application process. VOCA stipulates that a portion of funds be prioritized for programs that assist victims of certain crime types (e.g., sexual assault, intimate partner abuse, or child abuse) and underserved populations (e.g., male victims of color, non-English speaking residents, rural victims, LGBTQIA+ victims), otherwise, states are permitted to fund programs of their choosing within broad boundaries.

In addition to VOCA funding, the growth of victim service programs has been sustained by the passing of victims' rights legislation within all states, modeled after the federal Crime Victims' Rights Act of 2004 (P.L. 18 U.S.C. § 3771). Almost universally, state legislation includes victims' rights to reasonable, accurate, and timely notice of case proceedings, as well the right to participate in the criminal justice process—rights that victim advocates can help to guarantee. Despite the passing of victims' rights legislation in all states and the presence of various national organizations that represent victim services (e.g., the National Organization for Victim Assistance, the National Association of VOCA Assistance Administrators, the National Center for Victims of Crime), programs can vary extensively in their scope and features. Even within smaller communities, there is widespread variability in victim services in terms of the clients they serve, the types of services offered, their organizational capacity, and the quality and sustainability of services provided.

Despite the increased availability of programming, victim services are often underused. Recent statistics from the NCVS suggest that only 8% of victims of violent crime receive victim services (Morgan and Truman 2020). Similarly, Sims, Yost, and Abbott (2005) found that, in their survey of victims in Pennsylvania, fewer than 1 in 25 (3%) reported ever using victim services or a victim-witness program. The authors found several reasons for the low usage rate, including that the majority of victims surveyed (57%) were not notified that such programs existed. Other victims reported not using these services because they thought it would be a hassle or because they could receive assistance from friends or family instead.

In general, victims whose crimes go unreported or undetected by law enforcement are less likely to receive services. Some victims may not feel comfortable disclosing their trauma to police or they may be fearful of the consequences of reporting, especially if they are involved with the perpetrator, either economically or romantically (Albanesi, Tomasetto, and Guardabassi 2021). Police referrals are one of the most common sources through which victims are connected to programs (Langton 2011; Roman et al. 2022; Zaykowski 2014). In some instances, victims may even be ineligible for services if a police report is not filed (Evans 2014; Newmark 2004). Prosecutors' offices represent another key linkage to victim service programs, but these offices often do not have contact with victims until a case reaches the prosecution or court processing phase—typically, several months after the crime occurred, beyond when immediate support, advocacy, and interventions are most needed (Turanovic et al. 2020).

Research has revealed distinct knowledge gaps about victim services among helping professionals in different areas, such as legal services, law enforcement, public health, and mental health (Vinton and Wilke 2014). Victims who seek support from professionals who are unaware or misinformed about victim services in their broader community may face additional hardships and unnecessary delays in service delivery. These issues are troubling given that they do not affect victims of crime equally. Rather, underserved victims are more likely to include already vulnerable populations, including immigrant and ethnic/racial minority groups, people with substance use or mental health disorders, individuals with physical disabilities, victims with criminal histories, and members of the LGBTQIA+ community (Taylor 2014; Zaykowski 2017).

Depending on the type of crime experienced, victims may also require a unique set of services and specialized forms of assistance that are not always offered in a single centralized location. For example, victims of intimate partner violence may need help securing temporary housing, assistance with safety planning, or require a danger assessment (Campbell 2006; Kolb 2014; Maier 2012a; Ullman 2010). Secondary victims of homicide, alternatively, may require emotional support and grief counseling, or assistance filing compensation requests for funeral expenses (Turanovic et al. 2020). Sexual assault victims may require examinations by specialized nurses and medical attention in addition to crisis support (Campbell et al. 2006). For those who are traumatized or dealing with severe crimes, a greater dosage of services may also be required. Little research has been conducted to determine how the needs of victims of various crime types differ or how their experiences with victim services vary. Navigating between different service providers and case managers without interagency communication can create additional distress for victims, and few victim service programs are comprehensive enough to provide ongoing services to victims of different crimes with a range of service needs (Lurigio 2014; Taylor 2014).

II. Principles of Effective Victim Services

Despite such widespread variability in the clientele served, organizational capacity, and scope of different victim service programs, victim services should still be governed by a set of common principles. In such a growing and heterogeneous field, even the development of unified standards of professionalism has been a point of discourse and contention (DeHart 2014). And though the research evidence is not definitive, here we draw from a series of best-practice resources and model standards put forth by the Office for Victims of Crime (2016) to identify six principles of effective victim services. Specifically, based on the literature, we argue that victim services should be (1) responsive early on after a crime incident, (2) coordinated in their response, (3) collaborative and communicative with individual victims, (4) trauma-informed and victim-centered, (5) culturally competent, and (6) confidential. These six principles are discussed in more detail in the following sections.

A. Principle 1: Be Responsive Early On

Victim service programs must be responsive to the specific needs of crime victims soon after a crime occurs. The effectiveness of services is likely to be undermined if too much time passes between when a crime happens and when victims are connected to service providers, or if the services offered are not well tailored to the needs of individual victims. Early contact can be beneficial, with victim services providing key information on next steps to follow, financial compensation, and necessary referrals. Early connections to supportive services in the aftermath of trauma can help put survivors on a healthier path to recovery (Doerner and Lab 2021; Fisher, Reyns, and Sloan 2016; Turanovic and Pratt 2019). Especially for victimization that occurs in the home—such as among family members or intimate partners—the abuse may be prolonged if victims are not connected with supportive resources that can assist with safety planning, programming, and relocation (Bostock, Plumpton, and Pratt 2009; Camacho and Alarid 2008).

Ideally, response protocols should be in place to make prompt, around-the-clock referrals to victim services. Some victim service agencies offer hotlines staffed with crisis responders 24 hours per day to provide immediate assistance and dispatch victim advocates. Such a process can be beneficial in cases of death or homicide, in which victim advocates can accompany law enforcement to provide compassionate death notification and support for next of kin (Turanovic et al. 2020). Early contact with service providers can also help ensure the timely collection and preservation of forensic evidence. In cases of sexual assault, victim advocates can support and accompany victims through obtaining a sexual assault nurse exam and help to minimize its traumatic impact (Whitman 2013). Emergency needs should be attended to first, ensuring physical safety until the next meeting with the service provider.

B. Principle 2: Provide a Coordinated Response

Relatedly, to ensure a timely and coordinated response, victim service providers must be well connected to other helping professionals, law enforcement agencies, and first responders (Gibel, Carter, and Ramirez 2015; Larsen, Tax, and Botuck 2009; Newmark 2004). Some victim service organizations have worked to establish protocols where investigators or other law enforcement notify victim services when they respond to certain forms of violent criminal incidents. For example, police officers will call a violent crime helpline staffed by a victim advocate to (1) notify victim services that a crime occurred, (2) provide case details, and, if necessary, (3) request an advocate on scene to provide a crisis response. Once victim service organizations are notified of a crime, they can assign an advocate to provide support and follow-up to the victim(s). Response protocols of this kind have been successful in connecting victims with needed resources early on (Turanovic et al. 2020). This type of coordinated response can also help to free up law enforcement officers' time for investigations and evidence gathering, as victim advocates can come to represent the primary point of contact for victims' case updates and information (Blomberg, Waldo, and Chester 2002).

Coordination between victim services and other helping professionals is also important, as victims of crime may experience an assortment of safety, security, economic, psychological, and physical health needs (Bennett et al. 2004). Because victims may be unaware of available programs or feel overwhelmed by the prospects of seeking assistance from other organizations, it is important that victim advocates facilitate access for victims to a network of social and community resources (Albanesi, Tomasetto, and Guardabassi 2021; Hullenaar and Frisco 2020). These coordinated response efforts can be enhanced through interdisciplinary trainings with victim advocates, or presentations and outreach activities by service organizations. For certain crimes, the formal establishment of a multidisciplinary taskforce may also help to ensure a coordinated response among victim services, law enforcement, and other community-based organizations (Turanovic et al. 2020). Research shows that survivors are more likely to feel empowered when various agencies establish operational partnerships (Albanesi, Tomasetto, and Guardabassi 2021).

C. Principle 3: Be Collaborative and Communicative with Victims

While responsivity and coordination across service providers is imperative, of equal importance is collaboration and communication with victims themselves. Victim service workers must effectively communicate and collaborate with victims on a given course of action. Victim advocates should discuss their qualifications, availability of services, and experiences to clarify the role they can play in the lives of survivors (Office for Victims of Crime 2016). It is critical to set an appropriate tone during initial meetings with victims. For example, advocates should begin with a warm welcome, inform victims of how long the meeting will last and remind them that they are in control, have documents on hand that outline available services and victims' rights, review common responses to trauma, clarify the concept of confidentiality, and, if necessary, discuss any policies on mandatory reporting (Office for Victims of Crime 2022).

Conducting a needs assessment can allow advocates to convey relevant information to victims so that they can make informed choices about the services they wish to obtain. To avoid overwhelming victims, however, a thorough needs assessment is rarely conducted during the initial meeting. Rather, a thorough assessment tends to take place over several meetings, after more rapport is built, allowing victims to prioritize their needs and become more comfortable sharing details of their life circumstances (Office for Victims of Crime 2016). A thorough assessment involves information-gathering on short- and long-term needs for housing, food, clothing, child care, public benefits, immigration support, criminal or legal support, court accompaniment and advocacy, transportation assistance, medical care, substance use treatment, mental health services, crime victim compensation, culturally specific or faith communities, language or educational programs, and employment training or assistance (Office for Victims of Crime 2022). Assessments should also be ongoing to identify victims' accomplishments and strengths, and to collaboratively identify new service needs.

Case management is a central component in the provision of effective victim services, where service providers must perform multiple roles as a point person and facilitator of communication to help victims navigate complex social and legal systems (Blomberg, Waldo, and Chester 2002; Office for Victims of Crime 2022). To enhance collaboration and communication, victim service workers should create a case management plan with victims and review it at each meeting. Additionally, service providers must offer opportunities for contact beyond in-person meetings (e.g., availability by email, phone, and text), and check in regularly. Victim advocates should also spend time, if case processing is imminent, to help victims understand the complexities of the legal system and detail how cases of their nature are typically handled by investigators and the courts. Taking time to coach victims on the court process can reduce stress and uncertainty, and help victims be better prepared and willing to assist prosecutors and provide testimony (Camacho and Alarid 2008; Parsons and Bergin 2010).

D. Principle 4: Be Trauma-Informed and Victim-Centered

Effective victim services are those that are both trauma-informed and victim-centered. First, trauma-informed approaches are mindful of the vulnerability of crime victims, and recognize that having to repeatedly recount details of the crime and its aftermath throughout the criminal justice process can feel like a form of revictimization (Englebrecht, Mason, and Adams 2014; Maier 2012b; Spencer et al. 2018). Trauma-informed services prioritize the restoration of a survivor's feelings of safety, choice, and control, which are often compromised in a victimization event (Office for Victims of Crime 2016). Second, victim-centered approaches are those that prioritize victims' wishes, needs, and concerns, and empower them as engaged participants in the legal process. Victim-centered approaches aim to support victims' rights, dignity, autonomy, and self-determination above all (Office for Victims of Crime 2022). Empowerment and human agency are dynamic qualities that facilitate resilience and an ability to cope with distress (Brown and Westaway 2011). As such, restoring victims' abilities to feel like they are in control of their own lives may help them to overcome adversity and recover from trauma.

E. Principle 5: Be Culturally Competent

Cultural competency is another hallmark of effective victim services. Culturally competent services are mindful of the unique spiritual practices, gender roles, healing rituals, and linguistic and behavioral scripts of specific groups, including those defined by race, ethnicity, immigrant status, religion, sexual orientation, or gender identity (Carleton 2021; Turanovic and Biro 2023). Crime victims may refrain from reporting or seeking out services because they are not sure that victim assistance providers will understand their experiences or their cultural practices (Bell and Mattis 2000; Bui 2003). For example, some victims may experience discrimination or microaggressions that dissuade them from connecting with service providers (Becerra et al. 2017; Camacho and Alarid 2008; Fussell 2011). Culturally competent approaches thus use language and techniques that do not evoke harmful stereotypes that erode trust and service engagement (Pyles and Kim 2006). Immigrant victims of crime must also be able to engage with service providers in a language they understand,

and be guided through a potentially foreign criminal justice process (Gibel, Carter, and Ramirez 2015).

It is recommended that victim service providers employ individuals who match the diversity of the populations that they serve, including multicultural and multiethnic spokespeople—in short, to ensure representation in their workforce (Sawrikar 2020). Another method of ensuring cultural sensitivity might entail establishing relationships with community leaders in multicultural places and within (traditional and nontraditional) immigrant destinations. Education and training on promoting cultural awareness is a logical step in bolstering cultural competency. As history has shown, an absence of cultural sensitivity in victim assistance risks systematically disadvantaging survivors of certain groups and wastes energy and resources attempting to apply an unproductive "one-size-fits-all" intervention (Edwards 2012). To be sure, evidence suggests that trauma-informed, culturally competent services contribute positively to victims' well-being (Serrata et al. 2020).

F. Principle 6: Be Confidential

Finally, confidentiality is a core element of effective victim services. Rules of confidentiality in victim services usually (1) limit the disclosure of information without the victim's consent, and (2) require victim service providers to disclose any limits to confidentiality to the victim. Sharing personal information without informed consent can be a violation of professional ethics for the provider and further traumatize the victim (Cole 2011). Confidentiality helps the victim feel safe when reporting crimes to police, receiving medical attention, or working with a service provider. It encourages victims to disclose information that may make them uncomfortable or fearful (Logan et al. 2004). Still, laws designed to protect confidentiality and/or establish privilege are complex. Victim advocates must be knowledgeable about relevant privacy rules and regulations, evidentiary privileges, state and federal statutes and constitutional rights (including crime victims' rights legislation). They must also be aware of the unique status of minors, persons with disabilities, or other protected classes (Office for Victims of Crime 2022).

III. Evidence-Based Victim Service Programs

In addition to identifying broad principles of effective victim services, it is important to discuss the state of the literature on evidence-based programming in victim services. However, a key challenge in synthesizing this collection of research is that it tends to be scattered across numerous academic journals, individual agency or government office publications, victim advocate training materials, and funding organization archives. The research also varies widely in its methodological quality and rigor. Many evaluations of victim service programs lack an experimental design or are based on convenience samples that exclude hard-to-reach populations (Lurigio 2014; Xie and Lynch 2017). As such, generalizability (or external validity) has been a limiting factor in the victim service evaluation literature for some time (Sullivan 2011; Wathen and MacMillan 2003).

A. What Works and What Is Promising

In light of these issues, here we present an overview of evidence-based programs and practices in victim services that have been rated as effective or promising by CrimeSolutions (see CrimeSolutions.ojp.gov). CrimeSolutions is a web-based resource housed by the National Institute of Justice that details programs and practices in criminal justice that have undergone rigorous evaluation (e.g., randomized controlled trials) and meta-analyses. The programs are rated on both effectiveness and strength of the available evidence and classified into one of four categories: "effective," "promising," "inconclusive," or "no effects." CrimeSolutions provides information on dozens of programs and practices related to victimization, although most are intended to help individuals avoid becoming a victim of crime (e.g., prevention programs), or are focused on reductions in recidivism for offenders (e.g., victim and offender mediation). Of course, CrimeSolutions is not a comprehensive resource, nor was it developed specifically for dissemination of victim services research. Still, several effective and promising programs and practices relevant to victim services are detailed. A summary of these is provided in Table 25.1, along with each program/practice's CrimeSolutions rating. The main difference between the "promising" and "effective" ratings is that the evaluation outcomes of the promising programs/practices were based on just one or two studies, rather than a meta-analysis or multisite randomized controlled trial (which is usually required for the rating to be "effective").

As seen in Table 25.1, most evidence-based programs and practices are tailored to treating traumatized youth and young adults, or female victims of intimate partner violence and sexual assault. The aims of some programs and practices, such as the Community Advocacy Project and the Children's Advocacy Center Model, are to help connect victims to available community resources. Most are focused on treatment and are rooted in cognitive-behavioral therapy—a type of psychotherapy in which negative patterns of thought about the self and the world are challenged to reduce unwanted behaviors and mood disorders. Many of the effective and promising programs follow a structured curriculum and take place over the duration of several weeks. These programs tend to be led by a trained victim advocate or therapist, with common goals of managing and improving trauma reactions and social and emotional adjustment. Several of these programs also incorporate trauma narration (e.g., writing and retelling the traumatic event), eye movement desensitization and reprocessing (EMDR; e.g., using therapist directed rapid eye movements to alleviate distress), education about trauma symptoms and trauma reactions, and support groups with other victims.

There are a handful of comprehensive victim service organizations around the country that offer several of these evidence-based treatment services in-house, as they employ both victim advocates and licensed counselors or psychotherapists (Blomberg, Waldo, and Chester 2002; Turanovic et al. 2020). For victim service organizations that are not as large or comprehensive, it is important that referrals are made to community service providers that offer evidence-based treatment services.

Table 25.1. CrimeSolutions Rated Effective and Promising Programs in Victim Services

Program	Victims Served	Description	Evaluation Outcome	Rating
Psychotherapies for Victims of Sexual Assault	Sexual assault victims	Psychotherapeutic interventions are designed to reduce psychological distress, symptoms of PTSD, and rape trauma through counseling, structured or unstructured interaction, training programs, or predetermined treatment plans. Most treatments include cognitive-behavioral therapy or insight/experiential therapy. Characteristics of treatment (duration, number of sessions, treatment setting, therapist experience) will vary depending on the type of therapy.	Meta-analytic results show that psychotherapeutic approaches reduce symptoms of PTSD for sexual assault victims.	Effective
Cognitive-Processing Therapy for Female Victims of Sexual Assault	Female victims of sexual assault	A manualized, 12-session cognitive therapy program designed to alleviate symptoms of PTSD. Therapy sessions focus on distorted and over-generalized beliefs about oneself and the world. Female victims of sexual assault are exposed to their traumatic experience through writing and reading out loud detailed accounts of the incident. Therapists encourage the expression of emotions in this process to determine areas of conflicting beliefs, logic, or assumptions in relation to the trauma.	Randomized controlled trial results indicated that women in the treatment group demonstrated reduced symptoms of both PTSD and depression, compared with women in the control group.	Effective
Prolonged Exposure Therapy	Victims of violence with PTSD or subdiagnosis of PTSD	A cognitive-behavioral treatment program to reduce symptoms of PTSD, depression, anger, guilt, and general anxiety. The program consists of 8-15 once- or twice-weekly sessions, each lasting 70-90 minutes. There are four components: (1) imaginal exposure (revisiting of the traumatic memories), (2) in-vivo exposure (gradually approaching trauma reminders), (3) psychoeducation about causes and reactions to trauma, and (4) breathing retraining to manage anxiety.	Randomized controlled trial results indicated that women in the treatment group experienced reductions in the severity of PTSD, depression, and anxiety symptoms, and an improvement in social functioning and trauma-related guilt, compared with women in the control group.	Effective

(continued)

Table 25.1. Continued

Program	Victims Served	Description	Evaluation Outcome	Rating
Children's Advocacy Center Model	Youth victims of abuse, violence, and maltreatment	A multidisciplinary, victim-centered program that delivers comprehensive, culturally competent care to diagnose and provide treatment for all types of child maltreatment cases. Coordination with local child-friendly facilities enable professionals from victim advocacy, child protective services, law enforcement, prosecution, and the medical and mental health fields to work together to investigate, prosecute, and treat child abuse. The team approach improves interagency communication, increases the effectiveness of investigations and prosecutions, and results in fewer traumatic interviews with victims.	The program showed a statistically significant increase in the receipt of physical health examinations and counseling referrals for treatment group youth, compared with youth in the community comparison group.	Effective
Trauma-Focused Cognitive-Behavioral Therapy	Youth victims of sexual or physical abuse and their parents	This treatment is designed to help 3- to 18-year-olds and their parents overcome the negative effects of trauma, such as child sexual or physical abuse. Treatment consists of 12–18 weekly sessions. The aim is to treat serious emotional problems such as PTSD, fear, anxiety, and depression. Parental treatment components and child-parent sessions are aimed at developing new skills to process thoughts and feelings stemming from traumatic events.	Treatment group children demonstrated lower PTSD and depressive symptoms and fewer problematic behaviors, compared with children in the control group. Parents in the treatment group also had lower depressive symptoms, compared with parents in the control group.	Effective
Trauma-Focused Treatment for Juveniles and Young Adults with Trauma Symptoms and Externalizing Behaviors	Youth and young adults exposed to traumatic events	Treatment consists of trauma-focused cognitive-behavioral therapy for 12–18 weeks and eye movement desensitization and reprocessing (EMDR). The goal of EDMR is to alleviate distress through accessing and processing traumatic memories in brief doses while focusing on therapist-directed eye movements. EMDR takes place in eight phases: history taking, treatment planning, preparation, reprocessing, installation of a positive cognition, checking for and processing residual disturbing body sensations, positive closure, and evaluation.	Meta-analytic results found that juveniles and young adults who received trauma-focused treatment exhibited fewer trauma symptoms and fewer externalizing behaviors.	Effective

Therapeutic Approaches for Sexually Abused Children and Adolescents	Youth victims of sexual abuse	A variety of therapeutic approaches are designed to treat the negative impacts of child sexual abuse, such as cognitive-behavioral therapy for sexually abused preschoolers, trauma-focused cognitive-behavioral therapy, child-centered therapy, EMDR, imagery rehearsal therapy, a recovering from abuse program, supportive counseling, and stress inoculation training. Such therapeutic approaches aim to reduce the developmental consequences that result from sexual maltreatment.	Meta-analytic results show that therapeutic approaches for child and adolescent sexual abuse reduce symptoms of PTSD, externalizing behaviors, and internalizing behaviors.	Effective
Trauma Affect Regulation: Guide for Education and Therapy (TARGET)	Youth and adults suffering from PTSD	A manualized, trauma-focused psychotherapy that teaches skills for processing and managing trauma-related reactions to stressful situations, such as PTSD symptoms, traumatic grief, survivor guilt, and shame. The goal of treatment is to help individuals regulate intense emotions and gain control of PTSD reactions. In the brief therapy form, individuals receive counseling in 12 weekly sessions.	Treated adults showed lower PTSD symptoms, depression, and anxiety than comparison group adults. Treated youth showed higher levels of hope and lower levels of the PTSD criterion of intrusive re-experiencing than comparison group youth. There were no impacts on other mental health outcomes.	Effective
Sexual Assault Nurse Examiner (SANE) Program	Victims of sexual assault	The program aims to provide specialized and coordinated services to victims of sexual assault during their first contact with the healthcare environment. The program guides patients through services including medical treatment, treatment for sexually transmitted infections (STIs), emergency contraception, contact with law enforcement, collection of forensic samples, and referrals to other services in a secure and private manner.	Treatment group patients had a greater number of referrals to victim services and greater likelihood of consenting to evidence collection, pregnancy tests, and STI treatment, compared with patients treated in the standard emergency room. Across multiple sites, results showed an increased likelihood of guilty plea and conviction.	Promising

(continued)

Table 25.1. Continued

Program	Victims Served	Description	Evaluation Outcome	Rating
Moms' Empowerment Program	Mothers who have been victims of intimate partner violence	A 10-session support group program in which two therapists are assigned to groups of 5–7 women. The program provides psychoeducation about violence and its impacts, assists with advocacy needs, and teaches skills that promote good mental health. Goals are to enhance mothers' parenting and disciplinary skills, increase their social and emotional adjustment, and reduce their children's behavioral and adjustment difficulties.	Results showed an improvement in children's externalizing behaviors and attitudes about family violence, although there was no effect on children's internalizing behaviors. Mothers in the program experienced greater reductions in intimate partner violence over time.	Promising
Meditation for Female Trauma Intimate Partner Violence Survivors with Co-occurring Disorders	Female victims of intimate partner violence with co-occurring disorders	A 6-week Tibetan meditation curriculum for treating the problems associated with trauma and co-occurring disorders (e.g., substance abuse, depression) in female survivors of intimate partner violence. The group meets for 1 hour, twice a day, 5 days a week for a total of 60 hours of meditation. Sessions focus on breathing and training for mindfulness and calmness, empathy skills, and compassion for oneself and others.	Women who participated in the meditation curriculum had fewer mental health and trauma symptoms, and a higher level of change in mental health and trauma symptoms, compared with women in the control group who received services as usual.	Promising
Community Advocacy Project	Female victims of intimate partner violence	A community-based advocacy intervention for female victims of intimate partner violence who are leaving a domestic violence shelter program. The program uses a strengths-based model and provides free safety planning and community-based advocacy services. Over 10 weeks, women meet weekly with an advocate for 4–6 hours.	Participants were more likely to access community resources, engage in activities to meet their needs, have an improved quality of life, and experience a reduction in re-abuse. There were no impacts on continued involvement with assailants or perceived social support.	Promising
Lethality Assessment Program (Oklahoma)	Female victims of intimate partner violence	A crisis-response program in which police connect female victims of intimate partner violence with a social service provider at the scene of a dispute. The social service provider advises the victim on safety precautions and encourages her to come into the social service office to receive more information and services.	Relative to women in the control group, women in the program reported less victimization/violent encounters, were more likely to apply for an order of protection, and were more likely to receive domestic violence services at the 7-month follow up.	Promising

B. What Does Not Work

CrimeSolutions also details various programs and practices in victim services that are rated as having "no effects." What these programs tend to have in common is that they do not involve a great deal of consistent contact or follow-up with victims of crime. Other programs, however, tend only to be evaluated in terms of their impact on offender recidivism or revictimization—not outcomes related to victims' connection with support services, counseling, or well-being—which may mask some potential benefits of victim service programs.

One practice rated as having "no effects" is the Second Responder Program for victims of family violence. Second responder programs were developed in the 1980s to assist victims of repeat intimate partner violence or household abuse (Davis et al. 2021). Second responders visit homes where family violence incidents were reported to the police and provide victims with information on their legal rights and options, the cyclical nature of family violence, obtaining orders of protection, developing a safety plan, and seeking shelter. Second responders may also try to connect victims to social services, such as counseling, job training, public assistance, or civil legal assistance. The response time of second responders varies by program. Some responses occur while police officers are still at the scene of the incident; some may occur within 72 hours of a report to the police; and others may occur 7–14 days after the incident. The amount of time that second responders work with victims also varies by program, and usually depends on the victim's receptiveness. Meta-analytic findings show that second responder programs neither reduce official reports of abuse to the police nor victims' self-reports of abuse (Davis et al. 2006; Davis, Weisburd, and Taylor 2008). What is unclear, however, is whether such a program could have benefits for victims that were not assessed—such as their connection to treatment providers or willingness to participate in the criminal justice process. Davis and colleagues (2008), for example, found that second responder programs increased (slightly) victims' willingness to report incidents to the police.

Another practice with a "no effects" rating is the Advocacy Intervention for Women Who Experience Intimate Partner Violence. Advocacy interventions focus on preventing further abuse and mitigating the consequences of abuse once it has ceased. The core activities of advocacy interventions may include providing legal, housing, and financial advice; facilitating access to community resources (e.g., shelters, emergency housing, psychological interventions); and providing safety planning and advice. Short-term crisis advocacy may also be provided, where advocates work with victims for a short period of time, ranging from 1 hour to about 12 hours. A meta-analysis found advocacy interventions to have no impact on incidences of subsequent physical abuse (Rivas et al. 2016), hence the "no effects" rating. But the meta-analysis also indicated some potential benefits for advocacy interventions, including somewhat improved overall quality of life among women recruited from shelters or primary care clinics, and reduced depression among pregnant women (Rivas et al. 2016). Though the methodological quality of the studies assessed was not strong, these findings suggest that it is important to use metrics to assess the effectiveness of victim service programs that are not only focused on offender recidivism or revictimization.

IV. Challenges and New Directions to Providing Evidence-Based Services to Victims of Crime

Victim service agencies and practitioners experience myriad challenges when seeking to find and implement evidence-based practices. Even though victim services research has been ongoing since the 1970s, the salient findings and evidence are often not communicated to the practitioner community (Orchowsky et al. 2015). Consequently, practitioners who are engaged in direct client services are often unaware of research findings that may improve their practice. Even if they are aware of the results, they may not have the ability or resources to interpret relevant findings and adopt new programs into their practice, especially if they are lacking technical support and adequate supervision. Chief concerns for victim service agencies often include a lack of financial support, adequate staffing, training, and other resources (Blomberg, Waldo, and Chester 2002; Office for Victims of Crime 2016). Indeed, the successful implementation of evidence-based practice hinges upon the ability of agencies to hire, train, and support practitioners to ensure they are providing the service as intended.

A common criticism of victim services is that they lack comprehensive and accessible supports (Blomberg, Waldo, and Chester 2002). Survivors of crime have a variety of needs, and siloed service systems make it incredibly difficult for survivors and victim service professionals to determine what services are available, who is eligible, and ensure adequate connection and follow-up with the available supports (Office for Victims of Crime 2016). There is often a disconnect between criminal justice and victim service agencies, which complicates the collaborative efforts required to meet the needs of survivors and their families. Moreover, victims often report negative experiences with criminal justice and victim service practitioners. They may feel judged, blamed, stigmatized, dismissed, unimportant, or disrespected when seeking support from agencies designed to help them (Greeson, Campbell, and Fehler-Cabral 2016; Wolf et al. 2003). Even the most effective practice or program cannot succeed if the implementation is tarnished by unpleasant interpersonal experiences with practitioners.

Furthermore, beyond CrimeSolutions, it is difficult to easily identify evidence-based practices in victim services. Various webinars and trainings are offered by the Center for Victim Research and the National Center for Victims of Crime in attempts to bridge the gaps between research and practice. These efforts can be tremendously helpful, but knowledge will remain hindered unless the strength of research evidence improves. The lack of methodological rigor in the victim services literature remains a serious challenge. Researchers conducting meta-analyses often find considerable heterogeneity in studies on victim services with respect to the specific types of services provided, modes and dosage of service delivery, and the reliability and validity of outcome measures assessed (Rivas et al. 2016). Many evaluations are also statistically underpowered or lack an appropriate comparison group (Allen, Robertson, and Patin 2021; Bates and Douglas 2020; Stefanidou et al. 2020). This combination of factors makes it difficult to determine the efficacy of specific programs and practices. It is often unknown whether the mixed findings in the literature point to the ineffectiveness of a particular program or to methodological shortcomings in the program's evaluation or implementation.

Additionally, more must be learned about how well victim service agencies function, how equipped they are to provide services, and how satisfied victims are with the services offered. Victim advocates provide a range of services to victims of crime, yet surprisingly little is known about how the demanding work they do affects them or impacts the quality of services delivered (Slattery and Goodman 2009). Risks for secondary traumatic stress are high in jobs that serve victims of crime, which can lead to issues with burnout, staff turnover, and inadequate service provision (Globokar, Erez, and Gregory 2019).

It is also important to strengthen interagency linkages to victim services (Stark 2000). Sometimes victims "fall through the cracks" of a service network due to weaknesses in communication and a breakdown in collaboration among agencies. Strong linkages are characterized by consistent communication and information sharing between agencies, a clear knowledge of services, referral mechanisms, and trust that referred clients will access services and be treated appropriately (Balaswamy 2002; Koss et al. 2004). Providing victim-centered services while developing and maintaining effective community partnerships requires organizational stability (Blomberg, Waldo, and Chester 2002). Sound management and systems of accountability are necessary to support sustainable services (DeHart 2014). Public demands for services have been voiced, particularly for comprehensive, one-stop programs that are freely accessible and serve victims of various crimes.

Tensions can arise between victim service agencies and criminal justice personnel—such as law enforcement or prosecutors—when training, values, and protocols clash (Globokar, Erez, and Gregory 2019; Johnson, McGrath, and Miller 2014; Sudderth 2006). Some investigators or prosecutors may think that advocates overstep professional boundaries if they provide legal advice or interfere with investigations or the court process (Hartman and Belknap 2003; Payne and Thompson 2008). However, victim services can help victims prepare testimony, cooperate with investigators and prosecutors, and deliver victim impact statements—thereby facilitating victims' participation in the criminal justice system (Englebrecht 2011; Erez, Ibarra, and Downes 2011; Schuster and Propin 2011).

Lastly, few systematic, credible empirical assessments exist of the beneficial impacts of victim services on a range of outcomes for victims of crime. What is especially lacking are studies that (1) rely on strong methodological research designs, such as longitudinal analysis and matching analysis; (2) assess impacts on multiple outcomes (e.g., mental and physical health, personal and social functioning, service needs, and perceptions of the criminal justice system); (3) determine how, if at all, victim services differentially impact historically underserved groups (e.g., racial and ethnic minorities, immigrant populations, older adults, LGBTQIA+ persons) and underserved crime types (e.g., elder abuse, robbery, stalking, burglary, complex homicide); and (4) draw on the insights of victim services personnel about the impacts of services and how their effectiveness can be enhanced. These are important avenues for future research that can greatly contribute to the evidence base on "what works" in victim services.

V. Conclusion

Victim services are a critical and often overlooked component of the criminal justice system. The need for victim services has grown due to improved education and outreach

(Office for Victims of Crime 2022), but changing populations, varying needs, and increasingly complex social systems continue to create challenges for service staff. Still, victim service providers have a professional responsibility to be responsive, coordinated, collaborative, trauma-informed, victim-centered, culturally engaged, and confidential in their interactions with trauma survivors. Of course, upholding these fundamental goals is no easy feat, as providers are consistently asked to do more with less (Gibel, Carter, and Ramirez 2015). Victim service programs are commonly under-resourced and understaffed, and providers are often overworked. As the evidence-base in this area continues to improve, so too will the services provided to victims. Ultimately, the desired outcomes for those dedicated to victim services are that victims have the services and resources they need, the response to victims by the criminal justice system and communities is effective and leads to a reduction in adverse outcomes, and the programs that serve victims are high quality, viable, and sustainable.

References

Albanesi, Cinzia, Carlo Tomasetto, and Veronica Guardabassi. 2021. Evaluating interventions with victims of intimate partner violence: A community psychology approach. *BMC Women's Health*, 21 (138): 1–15.

Allen, Ashley Batts, Emily Robertson, and Gail A. Patin. 2021. Improving emotional and cognitive outcomes for domestic violence survivors: The impact of shelter stay and self-compassion support groups. *Journal of Interpersonal Violence*, 36 (1–2): NP598–624.

Balaswamy, Shantha. 2002. Rating of interagency working relationship and associated factors in protective services. *Journal of Elder Abuse & Neglect*, 14 (1): 1–20.

Bates, Elizabeth A., and Emily M. Douglas. 2020. Services for domestic violence victims in the United Kingdom and United States: Where are we today? *Partner Abuse*, 11 (3): 350–382.

Becerra, David, M. Alex Wagaman, David Androff, Jill Messing, and Jason Castillo. 2017. Policing immigrants: Fear of deportations and perceptions of law enforcement and criminal justice. *Journal of Social Work*, 17 (6): 715–731.

Bell, Carl C., and Jacqueline Mattis. 2000. The importance of cultural competence in ministering to African American victims of domestic violence. *Violence Against Women*, 6 (5): 515–532.

Bennett, Larry, Stephanie Riger, Paul Schewe, April Howard, and Sharon Wasco. 2004. Effectiveness of hotline, advocacy, counseling, and shelter services for victims of domestic violence: A statewide evaluation. *Journal of Interpersonal Violence*, 19 (7): 815–829.

Blomberg, Thomas G., Gordon P. Waldo, and Carol A. Bullock. 1989. An assessment of victim service needs. *Evaluation Review*, 13 (6): 598–627.

Blomberg, Thomas G., Gordon P. Waldo, and Deborah Chester. 2002. Assessment of the program implementation of comprehensive victim services in a one-stop location. *International Review of Victimology*, 9 (2): 149–174.

Bostock, Jan, Maureen Plumpton, and Rebekah Pratt. 2009. Domestic violence against women: Understanding social processes and women's experiences. *Journal of Community & Applied Social Psychology*, 19 (2): 95–110.

Brown, Katrina, and Elizabeth Westaway. 2011. Agency, capacity, and resilience to environmental change: Lessons from human development, well-being, and disasters. *Annual Review of Environment and Resources*, 36 (1): 321–42.

Bui, Hoan N. 2003. Help-seeking behavior among abused immigrant women: A case of Vietnamese American women. *Violence Against Women*, 9 (2): 207–239.

Camacho, Christina M., and Leanne Fiftal Alarid. 2008. The significance of the victim advocate for domestic violence victims in municipal court. *Violence and Victims* 23 (3): 288–300.

Campbell, Rebecca. 2006. Rape survivors' experiences with the legal and medical systems: Do rape victim advocates make a difference? *Violence Against Women*, 12 (1): 30–45.

Campbell, Rebecca, Stephanie M. Townsend, Susan M. Long, Kelly E. Kinnison, Emily M. Pulley, S. Bibiana Adames, and Sharon M. Wasco. 2006. Responding to sexual assault victims' medical and emotional needs: A national study of the services provided by SANE programs. *Research in Nursing & Health*, 29 (5): 384–398.

Carleton, Benjamin. 2021. *One size does not fit all: Tailoring victim services for the local Native American population in Pennington County, South Dakota*. Arlington, VA: CNA.

Cole, Jennifer. 2011. Victim confidentiality on Sexual Assault Response Teams (SART). *Journal of Interpersonal Violence*, 26 (2): 360–376.

Davis, Robert C., Christopher D. Maxwell, and Bruce Taylor. 2006. Preventing repeat incidents of family violence: Analysis of data from three field experiments. *Journal of Experimental Criminology*, 2 (2): 183–210.

Davis, Robert C., Kevin Petersen, David Weisburd, and Bruce Taylor. 2021. Updated protocol: Effects of second responder programs on repeat incidents of family abuse: An updated systematic review and meta-analysis. *Campbell Systematic Reviews*, 17 (4): e1200.

Davis, Robert C., David Weisburd, and Bruce Taylor. 2008. Effects of second responder programs on repeat incidents of family abuse. *Campbell Systematic Reviews*, 4 (1): 1–38.

DeHart, Dana. 2014. A university partnership for victim service professional development: Model standards for serving victims and survivors of crime. *Journal of Criminal Justice Education*, 25 (4): 421–434.

Doerner, William G., and Steven P. Lab. 2021. *Victimology*. 9th ed. New York: Routledge.

Edwards, Frances L. 2012. Cultural competency in disasters. In *Cultural competency for public administrators*, edited by Kristen A. Norman-Major and Susan T. Gooden, 197–217. New York: Routledge.

Englebrecht, Christine M. 2011. The struggle for "ownership of conflict": An exploration of victim participation and voice in the criminal justice system. *Criminal Justice Review*, 36 (2): 129–151.

Englebrecht, Christine, Derek T. Mason, and Margaret J. Adams. 2014. The experiences of homicide victims' families with the criminal justice system: An exploratory study. *Violence and Victims* 29 (3): 407–421.

Erez, Edna, Julie L Globokar, and Peter R Ibarra. 2014. Outsiders inside: Victim management in an era of participatory reforms. *International Review of Victimology*, 20 (1): 169–188.

Erez, Edna, Peter Ibarra, and Daniel M. Downes. 2011. Victim welfare and participation reforms in the United States: A therapeutic jurisprudence perspective. In *Therapeutic jurisprudence and victim participation in justice: International perspectives*, edited by Edna Erez, Michael Kilchling, and Jo-Anne Wemmers, 15–40. Durham, NC: Carolina Academic Press.

Evans, Douglas. 2014. *Compensating victims of crime*. New York: Research & Evaluation Center, John Jay College of Criminal Justice.

Fisher, Bonnie S., Bradford W. Reyns, and John J. Sloan III. 2016. *Introduction to victimology: Contemporary theory, research, and practice*. New York: Oxford University Press.

Fussell, Elizabeth. 2011. The deportation threat dynamic and victimization of Latino Migrants: Wage theft and robbery. *Sociological Quarterly*, 52 (4): 593–615.

Gibel, Susan, Madeline M. Carter, and Rachell Ramirez. 2015. *Evidence-based decision making: A guide for victim service providers*. Washington, DC: National Institute of Corrections. https://nicic.gov/evidence-based-decision-making-victim-service-provider-users-guide.

Globokar, Julie L., Edna Erez, and Carol R. Gregory. 2019. Beyond advocacy: Mapping the contours of victim work. *Journal of Interpersonal Violence*, 34 (6): 1198–1223.

Greeson, Megan R., Rebecca Campbell, and Giannina Fehler-Cabral. 2016. Nobody deserves this: Adolescent sexual assault victims' perceptions of disbelief and victim blame from police. *Journal of Community Psychology*, 44:90–110.

Hartman, Jennifer L., and Joanne Belknap. 2003. Beyond the gatekeepers: Court professionals' self-reported attitudes about and experiences with misdemeanor domestic violence cases. *Criminal Justice and Behavior*, 30 (3): 349–73.

Herman, Judith Lewis. 2005. Justice from the victim's perspective. *Violence Against Women*, 11 (5): 571–602.

Hullenaar, Keith L., and Michelle Frisco. 2020. Understanding the barriers of violence victims' health care use. *Journal of Health and Social Behavior*, 61 (4): 470–485.

Johnson, Melencia, Shelly A. McGrath, and Michelle Hughes Miller. 2014. Effective advocacy in rural domains: Applying an ecological model to understanding advocates' relationships. *Journal of Interpersonal Violence*, 29 (12): 2192–2217.

Kolb, Kenneth H. 2014. *Moral wages: The emotional dilemmas of victim advocacy and counseling*. Berkeley: University of California Press.

Koss, Mary P., Karen J. Bachar, C. Quince Hopkins, and Carolyn Carlson. 2004. Expanding a community's justice response to sex crimes through advocacy, prosecutorial, and public health collaboration: Introducing the RESTORE program. *Journal of Interpersonal Violence*, 19 (12): 1435–1463.

Langton Lynn. 2011. *Use of victim service agencies by victims of serious violent crime, 1993–2009*. Washington, DC: US Department of Justice, Bureau of Justice Statistics. https://bjs.ojp.gov/content/pub/pdf/uvsavsvc9309.pdf.

Larsen, Mandi, Corey Tax, and Shelly Botuck. 2009. Standardizing practice at a victim services organization: A case analysis illustrating the role of evaluation. *Administration in Social Work*, 33 (4): 439–449.

Logan, T. K., Erin Stevenson, Lucy Evans, and Carl Leukefeld. 2004. Rural and urban women's perceptions of barriers to health, mental health, and criminal justice services: Implications for victim services. *Violence and Victims*, 19 (1): 37–62.

Lurigio, Arthur J. 2014. *Violent victimization in the United States: Major issues and trends*. Washington, DC: National Institute of Justice. https://www.ojp.gov/pdffiles1/nij/248746.pdf.

Macmillan, Ross. 2001. Violence and the life course: the consequences of victimization for personal and social development. *Annual Review of Sociology*, 27 (1): 1–22.

Morgan, Rachel E., and Alexandra Thompson. 2021. *Criminal victimization, 2020*. Washington, DC: US Department of Justice, Bureau of Justice Statistics. https://bjs.ojp.gov/sites/g/files/xyckuh236/files/media/document/cv20.pdf.

Morgan, Rachel E., and Jennifer L. Truman. 2020. *Criminal victimization, 2019*. Washington, DC: US Department of Justice, Bureau of Justice Statistics. https://bjs.ojp.gov/content/pub/pdf/cv19.pdf.

Maier, Shana L. 2012a. The complexity of victim-questioning attitudes by rape victim advocates: Exploring some gray areas. *Violence Against Women* 18 (12): 1413–1434.

Maier, Shana L. 2012b. Sexual assault nurse examiners' perceptions of the revictimization of rape victims. *Journal of Interpersonal Violence*, 27 (2): 287–315.

McDermott, M. Joan, and James Garofalo. 2004. When advocacy for domestic violence victims backfires: Types and sources of victim disempowerment. *Violence Against Women*, 10 (11): 1245–66.

Newmark, Lisa C. 2004. *Crime victims' needs and VOCA-funded services: Findings and recommendations from two national studies*. Washington, DC: National Institute of Justice. https://www.ojp.gov/pdffiles1/nij/grants/214263.pdf.

Office for Victims of Crime. 2016. *Achieving excellence: Model standards for serving victims and survivors of crime*. Washington, DC: US Department of Justice, Office of Justice Programs. https://ovc.ojp.gov/library/publications/achieving-excellence-model-standards-serving-victims-and-survivors-crime.

Office for Victims of Crime. 2022. *Human Trafficking Taskforce e-guide: Strengthening collaborative responses*. Washington, DC: US Department of Justice, Office for Victims of Crime Technical Training and Assistance Center. https://www.ovcttac.gov/taskforceguide/eguide/.

Orchowsky, Stan, Jennifer Yahner, Janine Zweig, Sherry Hamby, and Susan Howley. 2015. *Bridging the gap between research and practice for crime victim service*. Webinar Video, 1:09:35. Washington, DC: Justice Research and Statistics Association. https://www.youtube.com/watch?v=EMGi0caLkzY.

Oudekerk, Barbara A., Heather Warnken, and Lynn Langton. 2019. *Victim service providers in the United States, 2017*. Washington, DC: US Department of Justice, Bureau of Justice Statistics. https://bjs.ojp.gov/content/pub/pdf/vspus17.pdf.

Parsons, Jim, and Tiffany Bergin. 2010. The Impact of criminal justice involvement on victims' mental health: The impact of criminal justice involvement. *Journal of Traumatic Stress*, 23 (2): 182–188.

Payne, Brian K., and R. Alan Thompson. 2008. Sexual Assault Crisis Centre workers' perceptions of law enforcement: Defining the situation from a systems perspective. *International Journal of Police Science & Management*, 10:23–35.

Pyles, Loretta, and Kyung Mee Kim. 2006. A multilevel approach to cultural competence: A study of the community response to underserved domestic violence victims. *Families in Society*, 87 (2): 221–229.

Rivas, Carol, Jean Ramsay, Laura Sadowski, Leslie L Davidson, Danielle Dunnes, Sandra Eldridge, Kelsey Hegarty, Angela Taft, and Gene Feder. 2016. Advocacy interventions to reduce or eliminate violence and promote the physical and psychosocial well-being of women who experience intimate partner abuse: A systematic review. *Campbell Systematic Reviews*, 12 (1): 1–202.

Roman, Caterina G., Hannah J. Klein, Courtney S. Harding, Joshua M. Koehnlein, and Verishia Coaxum. 2022. Postinjury engagement with the police and access to care among victims of violent street crime: Does criminal history matter? *Journal of Interpersonal Violence*, 37 (3–4): 1637–1661.

Sawrikar, Pooja. 2020. Service organisations' cultural competency when working with ethnic minority victims/survivors of child sexual abuse: Results from a program evaluation study in Australia. *Social Sciences*, 9 (9): 152.

Schuster, Mary Lay, and Amy D. Propin. 2011. *Victim advocacy in the courtroom: Persuasive practices in domestic violence and child protection cases*. Boston: Northeastern University Press.

Skogan, Wesley G., Robert C. Davis, and Arthur J. Lurigio. 1990. *Victims' needs and victim services*. Washington, DC: National Institute of Justice. https://www.ojp.gov/pdffiles1/Digitization/145343NCJRS.pdf.

Serrata, Josephine V., Rebecca Rodriguez, Janice E. Castro, and Martha Hernandez-Martinez. 2020. Well-being of Latina survivors of intimate partner violence and sexual assault receiving trauma-informed and culturally specific services. *Journal of Family Violence*, 35:169–180.

Sims, Barbara, Berwood Yost, and Christina Abbott. 2005. Use and nonuse of victim services programs: Implications from a statewide survey of crime victims. *Criminology & Public Policy*, 4:361–384.

Slattery, Suzanne M., and Lisa A. Goodman. 2009. Secondary traumatic stress among domestic violence advocates: Workplace risk and protective factors. *Violence Against Women*, 15 (11): 1358–1379.

Spencer, Dale, Alexa Dodge, Rosemary Ricciardelli, and Dale Ballucci. 2018. "I think it's revictimizing victims almost every time": Police perceptions of criminal justice responses to sexual violence. *Critical Criminology*, 26:189–209.

Stark, Erin. 2000. *Denver victim services 2000 needs assessment*. Washington, DC: U.S. Department of Justice, Office of Justice Programs, Office for Victims of Crime. https://www.ncjrs.gov/ovc_archives/bulletins/dv_10_2000_1/files/NCJ183397.pdf.

Stefanidou, Theodora, Elizabeth Hughes, Katherine Kester, Amanda Edmondson, Rabiya Majeed-Ariss, Christine Smith, Steven Ariss, et al. 2020. The identification and treatment of mental health and substance misuse problems in sexual assault services: A systematic review. *PLOS ONE*, 15 (4): e0231260.

Sudderth, Lori K. 2006. An uneasy alliance: Law enforcement and domestic violence victim advocates in a rural area. *Feminist Criminology*, 1 (4): 329–353.

Sullivan, Cris M. 2011. Evaluating domestic violence support service programs: Waste of time, necessary evil, or opportunity for growth? *Aggression and Violent Behavior*, 16 (4): 354–360.

Sullivan, Cris M., Deborah I. Bybee, and Nicole E. Allen. 2002. Findings from a community-based program for battered women and their children. *Journal of Interpersonal Violence*, 17:915–936.

Taylor, Bruce G. 2014. *The state of victim services research*. Paper presented at the NIJ Technical Working Group Meeting on Violent Victimization Research. Washington, DC: U.S. Department of Justice, National Institute of Justice. https://www.ojp.gov/pdffiles1/nij/248746.pdf.

Turanovic, Jillian J. 2019. Heterogeneous effects of adolescent violent victimization on problematic outcomes in early adulthood. *Criminology*, 57:105–135.

Turanovic, Jillian J., and Szilvia Biro. 2023. Adult victims of violence: Outcomes and services. In *Handbook of evidence-based criminal justice practices*, edited by Bryanna Fox and Edelyn Verona, 56–64. New York: Routledge.

Turanovic, Jillian J., Thomas G. Blomberg, George B. Pesta, Julie L. Kuper, and Julie Brancale. 2020. *Palm Beach County victim services driving under the influence (DUI) related deaths demonstration project*. Washington, DC: Office for Victims of Crime.

Turanovic, Jillian J., and Travis C. Pratt. 2019. *Thinking about victimization: Context and consequences*. New York: Routledge.

Ullman, Sarah E. 2010. *Talking about sexual assault: Society's response to survivors*. Washington, DC: American Psychological Association.

Vinton, Linda, and Dina J. Wilke. 2014. Are collaborations enough? Professionals' knowledge of victim services. *Violence Against Women*, 20 (6): 716–729.

Wathen, C. Nadine, and Harriet L. MacMillan. 2003. Interventions for violence against women: Scientific review. *Journal of the American Medical Association*, 289:589–600.

Whitman, Charlene. 2013. *Presence of victim advocate during sexual assault nurse exam: Summary of state laws*. Aequitas Strategies in Brief, Issue 17. Washington, DC: Aequitas.

Wolf, Marsha E., Uyen Ly, Margaret A. Hobart, and Mary A. Kernic. 2003. Barriers to seeking police help for intimate partner violence. *Journal of Family Violence*, 18 (2): 121–129.

Xie, Min, and James P. Lynch. 2017. The effects of arrest, reporting to the police, and victim services on intimate partner violence. *Journal of Research in Crime and Delinquency*, 54 (3): 338–378.

Zaykowski, Heather. 2014. Mobilizing victim services: The role of reporting to the police. *Journal of Traumatic Stress*, 27 (3): 365–369.

Zaykowski, Heather. 2017. Issues in victim services. In *Routledge handbook on victims' issues in criminal justice*, edited by Cliff Roberson, 3–14. New York: Routledge.

Zweig, Janine, and Jennifer Yahner. 2013. Providing services to victims of crime. In *Victims of crime*, edited by Robert C. Davis, Arthur J. Lurigio, and Susan Herman, 325–348. 4th ed. Thousand Oaks, CA: Sage.

PART V

PROMOTING GREATER USE OF EVIDENCE-BASED POLICY

This part covers strategies for promoting greater use of evidence-based policy in efforts to address crime and improve justice. It includes seven chapters.

CHAPTER 26

SOCIAL INEQUALITY AND EVIDENCE-BASED POLICY
An Agenda for Change

NANCY RODRIGUEZ

THE COVID-19 pandemic brought tremendous adversity to every segment of society. As children's education and social worlds were disrupted and families adjusted to a new normal of remote living and working, a quarter of American's were laid off or lost their jobs. Two years after the start of the pandemic, families and communities continued to cope and grapple with the educational, economic, and health outcomes of the pandemic. A distinguishing feature of the pandemic is the disproportionate impact it had on segments of society, in particular lower-class Americans and people of color. The service industry workforce, overwhelmingly composed of minorities and women, was acutely impacted, resulting in disparate employment and health outcomes. The racial disparity in employment increased in 2020, and while the unemployment rate has dropped for Latinos, it remains high among Blacks (Smith, Edwards, and Duong 2021). Native American, Latinos, and Blacks experienced the highest rates of COVID-19 infection, hospitalizations, and mortality, devastating communities of color (Centers for Disease Control and Prevention 2022). Put simply, quality of life for many people has gotten worse, revealing that social inequality profoundly shapes and dictates the social, economic, and health outcomes of Americans.

Importantly, individuals most disproportionally affected by the adversities of COVID-19 also experienced changes in their communities with regard to crime. In 2020, increases in crime rates (i.e., homicide, aggravated assault, gun violence, and motor vehicle thefts) were visibly concentrated in communities characterized by racial disparity, segregation, poverty, and unemployment (Rosenfeld and Lopez 2021). Coupled with the numerous calls for racial justice, local, state, and the federal government have prioritized addressing the consequences of the pandemic and reducing disparate treatment in the justice system. As a researcher deeply committed to advancing evidence-based criminal justice policy and practice (Rodriguez 2018), and who had the privilege of serving as the director of the National Institute of Justice, I thank the editors Brandon Welsh, Daniel Mears, and Steven Zane for this timely volume on the importance of science in criminal justice policy. I appreciate the opportunity to contribute to the volume by reflecting on current times and offering my perspective on the role of social inequality and criminal justice policy in the 21st century.

Research has shown that the criminal justice system can perpetuate and exacerbate poverty, income inequality, and disadvantage for individuals, families, and communities. In this chapter, I highlight the relationship between social inequality, crime, and the criminal justice system. In the absence of massive social policy change for reducing inequality, I offer several criminal justice system strategies for reducing social inequality in the criminal justice system. I also discuss two school- and community-based efforts that can mitigate the adversities faced by marginalized populations. Collectively, these policies and practices are feasible and pragmatic, showing promise to aid in efforts to reduce social inequality. Lastly, I discuss the critical role that data metrics and data accessibility play in producing evidence-based research and, consequently, in addressing social inequality in the criminal justice system.

I. National Context, Social Inequality, and Crime

While the national conversation around criminal justice reform has been active for some time, the COVID-19 pandemic, coupled with racial strife, elevated the importance of policy for addressing racial injustice, racism, and inequalities. Never before has science been both celebrated (e.g., the rapid creation of COVID-19 vaccines) as well as rejected in favor of ideological beliefs and preferences. For criminologists dedicated to using research for addressing crime and improving criminal justice system processes and outcomes, the current context is unsettling. Crime rates are up in cities throughout the United States and gun violence has led to historically high homicide rates among racial and ethnic groups (Davis, Rose, and Crifasi 2023). An increase in prescriptions of opioid medications, fueled by pharmaceutical companies, has led to staggering statistics on drug overdose, opioid use disorder, and misuse of prescription pain relievers and opioids (US Department of Health and Human Services 2020). While considerable attention is paid to opioid use, misuse, and death among Whites and in rural communities, from 2011–2016, Blacks, relative to other groups, had the highest increase in the overdose death rate involving fentanyl and fentanyl analogs (Substance Abuse and Mental Health Services Administration 2020).

As a researcher who has devoted a significant amount of time to examining the treatment of youth in the juvenile justice system, I find the prospects for children highly worrisome. In 2020, the leading cause of death among children and adolescents was a gun-related injury (Goldstick, Cunningham, and Carter 2022). The pandemic led to substantial learning loss and educational lags for children, erasing many prior educational gains. The mental health challenges experienced by children and adolescents were particularly acute. The stresses of the pandemic, which led to increases in depression and anxiety among children and suicide attempts among young people, left parents and caregivers unable to find, afford, and access behavioral health services (Spencer et al. 2021). Again, given the additional strains that working-class families and communities of color faced during the pandemic, children from these communities were most adversely impacted.

Importantly, advancing policy that reduces the intergenerational transmission of inequality is of the highest priority. Upon assuming office, President Biden made racial equity a priority in his administration. On January 20, 2021, he released an Executive Order (EO) advancing racial equity and charging federal agencies to address inequities in policies and practices that limit and prevent equal opportunity (Biden 2021). A federal government agenda that centers and highlights inequalities in access to education, home lending, healthcare and behavioral health services, and the criminal justice system is critical and timely. Although the EO is primarily charged with addressing racial inequality, income inequality and advancing economic opportunity play a significant role in the EO, as racial and economic inequality are intrinsically tied in underserved communities. A discussion on the drivers of inequality in society is beyond the scope of this chapter, but it is worth noting that scholars highlight the role that systemic and institutional racism and unfair treatment have in inciting and exacerbating unequal access to opportunities and resources (Heimer 2019; Pager and Shepherd 2008; Rothstein 2017; Turney and Wakefield 2019).

Indeed, inequality has significant implications for crime and justice. Unequal access to education, employment, housing, and behavioral health and substance abuse treatment are key in criminal offending and criminal justice involvement (Sampson, Wilson, and Katz 2018). These circumstances may drive criminal activity among marginalized groups, like racial and ethnic minorities, women, the poor, and the disabled. Differential treatment within the criminal justice system, in the application of law via enforcement (e.g., policing practices), processing (e.g., pretrial detention) and outcomes (e.g., sentence of incarceration) may create, perpetuate, and exacerbate inequality. Importantly, the criminal justice system may not only be a driver of inequality, it may also further exacerbate inequalities faced by those who come into contact with the system (Turney and Wakefield 2019; Western and Pettit 2010).

The extent to which the criminal justice system, via processing and various system outcomes, is solely responsible for the amount of inequality individuals face versus the inequality that brought them to the attention of the criminal justice system is unknown (Mears, Cochran, and Lindsey 2016). In fact, it is likely that the criminal justice system is responsible, to varying degrees, for the overall inequality faced by justice involved individuals. Research has established that race and class are salient factors in social inequality and that criminal justice system outcomes can lead to inequality, given the differential treatment minorities and low-income individuals receive in criminal justice outcomes (Stewart et al. 2020; Western 2006). In the front end, young men of color are overrepresented in arrest rates (Beck 2021) and in the jail population (Zeng and Minton 2021). In the back end, mass incarceration led to the overrepresentation of Blacks, Latinos, and Native Americans in prison populations (National Research Council 2014). The racial and ethnic disparities that characterize juvenile court processes and outcomes can also compound inequalities for those that later engage with the criminal justice system (Feld 2017).

The criminal justice system has been shown to have cascading effects on individuals' families and communities. Although the nature and extend of collateral consequences of criminal justice system involvement is well documented, a few comments are worth noting. Criminal justice system contact can result in disruptions in housing, employment, and family responsibilities. Given their criminal record, individuals may be unable to gain lawful employment and maintain stable housing. Researchers have documented how incarceration exacerbates inequality among families and communities. Family members' incarceration has negative effects on overall family well-being above and beyond existing disadvantages prior to incarceration (Lee and Wildeman 2021). Incarceration is also associated with adverse educational outcomes and behavioral and mental health indicators among children. Physical and mental health adversities are also found among mothers of family members in prisons. At the macro level, the spatial concentration of crime, police presence, and incarceration only fuel concentrated disadvantage and social inequality.

Scholars have documented the role of cumulative disadvantage in the creation and production of social inequality by the criminal justice system. One way in which cumulative disadvantage may look and unfold is in the accumulation of district outcomes in the system, which impact outcomes further down in the system. Although there is limited adult criminal justice research that tests cumulative disadvantage in criminology (Kurlychek and Johnson 2019), researchers note that racial disparities are more pronounced in the front end of the system, contributing to the disparities in the back end of the system. For example, individuals of color are less likely to be diverted from the system and more likely to be processed formally than their White counterparts. Formal system involvement may then result in differential treatment for people of color in pretrial decisions and sentencing outcomes. Such disparities accumulate over time from one decision to another, increasing inequality and producing cumulative disadvantage. Despite the limited work that has empirically tested the cumulative disadvantage among adults in the criminal justice system, juvenile justice research offers some insight on its role in producing inequality (Bishop and Frazier 1996; Leiber and Fox 2005; Rodriguez 2010). Zane and colleagues (2021) analyzed 14 different pathways of youth processing from least to most punitive and found limited support for cumulative disadvantage in youth processing. Rather, the authors found that youth experienced two central pathways of processing: youth who are detained and youth who are not detained. The racial disparities in court outcomes were most pronounced for the detention pathways, providing empirical evidence of the harmful and unintended consequences of youth detention and consistent with findings on the impact of pretrial detention in subsequent system outcomes.

II. Policies or Practices in Addressing Social Inequality in Criminal Justice

Despite the important nexus between social inequality and the criminal justice system, there is very limited evidence-based research on policies and practices that reduce disparities and inequality. Much attention has centered on reducing the number of people who have contact with the justice system as a way to reduce harm and to avoid compounding adversities produced by the criminal justice system. In the absence of large-scale policy change for addressing the root causes of social inequality in society, there are strategies within and outside of the criminal justice system to reduce inequality that can be pursued for social change.

A. Policies in the Criminal Justice System

Below, I highlight several strategies that could be adopted or scaled throughout the United States and, subsequently, reduce inequality.

1. *Provide Language Access Services*

An often neglected component of federal law and due process protections is language accessibility. If the criminal justice system in the 21st century is committed to reducing inequality, it must ensure all individuals, either in the community or in the care and custody of the legal system, are provided language access services. Federal enforcement and oversight around language rights fall under Title VI of the Civil Rights Act of 1964, 42 U.S.C. 2000d et seq. ("Title VI"), which prohibits discrimination based on race, color, and national origin by programs and activities receiving federal financial assistance. The courts have established that primary language is an expression of national origin under Title VI (*Lau v. Nichols*, 414 U.S. 563, 1974). According to Census data, 12% of people in the United States are limited English proficient (LEP) (US Census Bureau 2018), which means they speak a non-English language and speak English less than "very well." Based on this estimate, the justice system, especially the police, as they engage with community members, must regard language accessibility as an integral part of practice. Unfortunately, the ambiguity of federal guidance on language accessibility has led to a patchwork of services. However, need assessments of community residents, leveraging the skills sets among the workforce of bilingual and multilingual employees, and the hiring of a Language Access Coordinator can lead to service access and improved outcomes for the LEP population. Ultimately, the provision of language access services throughout system processing can help to address the social inequality created by limited access to services because of language barriers.

2. *Diverting Individuals Away from Criminal Justice Systems*

Community-based services that address factors which disproportionately bring people of color to the criminal justice system, such as drug use, mental health, and homelessness, must be scaled and serve as the primary vehicles of care for individuals. As such, social inequality would be reduced through the diversion of individuals away from the justice system and into noncriminal justice systems aimed at addressing social problems. Maintaining an infrastructure that supports health and overall well-being of citizens is necessary for reducing social inequality. Social services and public health systems must serve as the key entities for responding and addressing the root causes of crime. This would include accessing the appropriate interventions and services, which may include substance abuse, medical care, mental health interventions, and/or housing for individuals. Jurisdictions throughout the country have adopted various models of diversion strategies, as well as co-responder models that serve as collaborative partnerships between law enforcement and behavioral health treatment services (Blais et al. 2022). Teams work together to provide treatment and services for individuals in need and target the problems of drug use, mental health, homelessness, and poverty that bring individuals into the justice system. While more research is needed to evaluate the cost and impact of crime of such models (Park et al. 2021), the diversion of individuals away from the system will not only reduce system involvement and collateral consequences associated with system involvement but will also directly address critical health needs.

3. *Limit Police Contact with Children and Youth*

Evidence indicates that police interactions with children and youth produce harm and lead to adverse outcomes (Geller 2021). In fact, researchers note the devastating impact that over policing and aggressive policing can have on youth, including stress and adverse mental health and educational outcomes (Ang 2021; Boyd, Ellison, and Horn 2016; Sewell et al. 2021).

In line with minimizing criminal justice system contact for those suffering from health and economic ills, law enforcement agencies must limit interactions with children and young people.

There are relatively few instances involving children and youth where a police response is warranted. Matters involving children and youth are most appropriately handled by experts in behavioral health and social services. Research shows that youth of color are far more likely than their White counterparts to have contact with the police (McGlynn-Wright et al. 2022). Further, high rates of police presence and aggressive forms of policing present in communities of color lead to trauma and health disparities, only exacerbating social inequality. Amanda Geller's (2021) work on police contact as a potential adverse childhood experience (ACE) and driver of health disparities is further evidence of the importance of having a public health response for addressing the needs children and youth.

4. *Family-Centric Interventions for Justice-Involved Youth and Families*

Since the pandemic, family life has been significantly impacted. For families engaged in the juvenile justice system, addressing youths' needs is only part of an array of family needs. Youth rehabilitation and treatment does not exist in isolation, especially in a time when families continue to endure the economic and health impacts of COVID-19.

For children, youth, and families, the juvenile justice system can play an important role in reducing the harms caused and exacerbated by the pandemic. Researchers have long established the role of family-related matters in juvenile court decisions (Feld 1999; Rodriguez, Smith, and Zatz 2009). Specifically, juvenile court actors view family functioning, including family support and cooperation as most influential in informing court outcomes (Leiber 2003; Leiber and Mack 2003). Perceptions of families as capable of supervising youth has been examined in prior work (Bridges and Steen 1998). Not surprisingly, when parents are perceived to not provide adequate supervision, the court is most likely to formally process youth (Bishop and Frazier 1996; Bortner 1982). Recent work has also noted that attributions of family supervision are shaped by family structure and race and ethnicity (Goldman and Rodriguez 2020).

In light of the significant role that family factors play in juvenile court decision-making, it is vital that family is included as a central component of youth rehabilitation and overall improved well-being. A legal system that fails to address the needs of families will, at best, be partially effective in addressing the needs of youth, and, at worst, be responsible for the neglect and possible exacerbation of poor family dynamics. Research has shown the effectiveness of Functional Family Therapy (FFT) and Multisystemic Therapy (MST) and should be supported across jurisdictions (National Research Council 2013). Family interventions that center family therapy, the development of parenting skills, and support family members struggling with income instability and stable housing will make significant impact in reducing social inequality. The juvenile justice system must prioritize family-centric treatment and ensure that access is provided to families. Prioritizing families and understanding how to support youths' families is critical for reducing juvenile justice disparities and broader social inequalities.

5. Advancing Pretrial Reform

Pretrial reform and reducing disparities in pretrial detention holds great promise in reducing both subsequent adverse outcomes in system processing and overall social inequality. In this pretrial reform discussion, I focus on initial appearance hearings and bail hearings. Pretrial processes play a key role in producing inequality via three sources: (1) pretrial detention disproportionally impacts people of color; (2) pretrial detention leads to more severe outcomes in system processing; and (3) pretrial detention produces collateral harms such as loss job, disruption in caretaking duties, and debt. The pretrial stage disproportionately impacts minorities, both in pretrial release decisions and bail amounts. Racial and ethnic minorities are less likely to be released, more likely to be denied bail, and more likely to receive higher bail amounts than their White counterparts (Dobbie and Yang 2021). Studies have found that pretrial detention is associated with more severe sentencing outcomes than those not held during the pretrial stage and leads to higher rates of recidivism (Page and Scott-Hayward 2022). The detention of a person, even if for a short period, can have significant impact on families and communities. The harms of pretrial detention are then compounded by the collateral harms set in motion by pretrial detention, including job loss and family and home instability.

The bail system has been regarded as a vehicle of punishment for the poor, as the majority of defendants held in pretrial detention are there because they are unable to pay the bail amount set by a judge. One way to reduce such disparate outcomes is by having counsel at the initial appearance, when bail and the conditions of release are set (Madhuri, Stolzenberg, and D'Alessio 2022). Although *Gideon v. Wainwright*, 372 U.S. 335 (1963) requires states to provide legal counsel to all indigent defendants accused of felony crimes at critical stages of processing, the Supreme Court has not decided on whether bail hearings qualify as a critical stage of processing (Kalb 2018). However, studies have found that the absence of an attorney at initial appearance can impact the bail amount and release decisions (Drinan 2009; Madhuri, Stolzenberg, and D'Alessio 2022). Monetary sanctions, known as legal financial obligations, produce an array of collateral consequences for individuals' families, housing, health, the labor market (State Monetary Sanctions and the Costs of the Criminal Legal System 2022). These collateral consequences directly implicate the broader patterns of justice produced inequality. Strategies that ensure that monetary sanctions are in line with what an individual can pay will have an impact in reducing social inequality.

6. Expanding Correctional Programming

In the back end of the criminal justice system, providing correctional programming and treatment for incarcerated populations, while also bridging treatment to re-entry services, can have a profound impact in reducing social inequality. Evidence indicates that correctional programming plays an important role in addressing the needs of incarcerated persons and improving post-release outcomes. Unfortunately, programs have limited capacity, often serving a fraction of those who need treatment. For example, although there is a critical need for substance abuse treatment within correctional settings, it is estimated that only 15% of individuals in state prisons receive drug-related treatment (Visher, Yahner, and La Vigne 2010). Not only can programs reduce recidivism (Bryne 2020), but they can address individuals' needs and develop skills that may improve labor market participation. Whether its educational/vocational training, cognitive-behavioral therapy, or substance abuse treatment programs, in-prison programming can lead to successful re-entry.

While all forms of correctional programming demand support, I highlight the role of programs geared toward improving employment outcomes for reducing social inequality. Studies have found that collateral harms come with having a criminal record and that they impede employment opportunities. Blacks, who are overrepresented in prison, experience higher unemployment rates once released relative to other groups (Western and Siroir 2019). Programs and policies that center job training *and* re-entry planning can yield great success. The recent collaboration between the Department of Justice (DOJ) and the Department of Labor (DOL) geared toward prerelease intervention (e.g., education, skill development) and re-entry that includes housing, healthcare, transportation, and social services will improve post-release outcomes and reduce inequality. The DOJ and DOL joint $145 million investment for the support of released persons from the Bureau of Prisons is evidence-based and will reduce social inequality among justice involved persons.

B. Schools Policies and Practice

Although there are multiple areas outside of the criminal justice system where policies could be pursued to reduce social inequality, the K-12 school system stands out as one area where policies and practices could reduce inequalities among children and youth.

Much has been written about the role of police in school, in particular the avenue in which police presence leads to system involvement for youth. Unfortunately, like other punitive responses to crime problems, police presence may not serve to prevent crime or delinquent behavior in schools (Montes et al. 2021). Although the research on the impact of school resource officers (SROs) on schools is limited, some studies have found that their presence increases youth arrests, criminal justice contact, and disciplinary actions, and reduces graduation rates and college enrollment (Gottfredson et al. 2020; King and Schindler 2021; Weisburst 2019). Reducing the contact that young people have with police on school campuses can not only reduce system involvement for young people but also de-emphasize the role of the justice system when responding to the behavioral and emotional needs of children and youth.

Broader disciplinary processes in schools can also lead to disparities and inequalities. Studies indicate that youth of color are more like to be suspended and/or be expelled from school due to a disciplinary infraction (Pearman et al. 2019). Recent work has also highlighted the interaction between race and gender in these processes (Lehmann and Meldrum 2021). Disciplinary processes can lead to juvenile justice entry and more severe treatment for school-based referrals than police-based referrals (Goldman and Rodriguez 2022). Disciplinary processes that do not serve to meet the needs of youth should be eliminated and replaced with mechanisms that improve youth well-being and school engagement and performance.

C. Community Prevention Strategy

Advocates, policymakers, and researchers have promoted the role of prevention in addressing crime and social inequality. While there is an array of community-based policies and programs for the prevention of crime and reduction of criminal justice contact, I offer one policy created in the state of California that offers tremendous impact in addressing social inequality. In light of the strong relationships between ACEs and adverse education and health outcomes, and disparities in ACEs among people color, women, and the poor (Felitti et al. 1998), in 2019 the California Department of Health Care Services (DHCS) and the California Surgeon General (CA-OSG) launched the first of its kind population screening of ACEs.

The statewide effort, known as the ACE Aware Initiative (https://www.acesaware.org), is designed to train clinicians to screen children and adults for ACEs in primary care settings and to provide treatment via trauma-informed care and evidence-based interventions. Legislative action has since followed that expands coverage for ACE screenings by providing funds to educate and serve communities with the greatest risk for toxic stress and expand networks of care for California residents. Screening of individual using trauma-informed care, as well as referring individuals to other services, will rest on the successful linking of primary care to other social services. Improving health outcomes and the well-being for all children and families by addressing traumatic events will undoubtedly serve to reduce social inequality in the state of California. Policies and efforts of this sort are highly encouraged in all other states.

It is important to share a note of caution on interventions that seek to rely on noncriminal justice systems to address the needs of marginalized communities. First, assessments of children and youth should only in exceptional circumstances lead to their entry into the child welfare system. Unfortunately, children and youth in foster care have experienced significant life adversities and often age out of foster care without any economic or social support systems (Synder 2004). The strengthening of families and the improvement of family function via holistic approaches should be a primary goal. It is also important to recognize that kinship families are a key resource for social services agencies and the justice system, which requires acknowledging the diversity of family systems across racial/ethnic communities (Beckman and Rodriguez 2021).

As previously noted, policies or practices that push people into the justice system in instances in which the roots of problems could be addressed by other sectors, or sentencing schemes that impose severe sanctions, causing harm by removing person from the community and imposing additional costs, must be curtailed. On a broader scale, any practice that disproportionately targets communities of color for generating revenue, as shown in the Ferguson Report (Shaw and United States 2015), should not be pursued, given their role in creating and exacerbating inequality.

III. Improving Knowledge for Addressing Social Inequality in Criminal Justice

Centering data-driven efforts and science will be instrumental in any effort designed to reduce social inequality. This includes acknowledging the limitations of our data metrics and doing whatever possible to ensure more accurate representation of growing subgroups. In order to expand knowledge on evidence-based policy and practice for reducing social inequality, systematic data on ethnicity and sexual orientation and gender identity will be crucial.

A. Race and Ethnicity Data Metrics

It is important to first acknowledge that most crime and justice studies compare the outcomes of Black and White individuals. While Latinos represent 20% of the total US population, there are only population estimates of Latinos in the justice system. This is due, in large part, to criminal justice data management systems that fail to capture ethnicity and routinely classify Latinos as White. The Urban Institute has documented the data limitations on Latinos across justice system points, even in states like California that have a significant Latino population (https://apps.urban.org/features/latino-criminal-justice-data/). The invisibility of Latinos in criminal justice data has significant implications for criminal justice reform and efforts designed to address racial and ethnic groups disparities. Importantly, the absence of Latino/a metrics in justice system data artificially inflates the number of "Whites" in the justice system and masks the actual White/Black disparities (Beck and Blumstein 2018).

Metrics on Native Americans who enter the justice system are also incomplete. Native Americans who are concentrated in certain geographic areas and who have experienced generations of historical trauma due to colonialism are processed in three distinct justice systems: the federal, state, or tribal system. Researchers of Indigenous rights have raised awareness on how these multiple legal jurisdictions problematize effective responses to the needs of tribal community members (Rolnick 2016). The documented disparities experienced by these racial and ethnic group in criminal justice outcomes emphasize the need for metrics and research on the experiences of these two subpopulations. In the absence of systematic criminal justice data that includes Latinos and Native Americans, we are limited in our ability to both document the scope of inequality as experienced by these groups and target responses to reduce such inequality. Ultimately, these consequences problematize all criminal justice data-driven efforts.

B. Sexual Orientation and Gender Identity Data Metrics

The growth and changing nature of sexual orientation and gender identity demands that such identities be included in data metrics in crime and justice (National Academies of Sciences, Engineering, and Medicine 2022). While there is great heterogeneity within the

LGBTQ population, studies have found that members of this community experience health and mental health disparities, stigma, and discrimination at high rates. Researchers have also found that LGBTQ youth are disproportionately represented in the foster care system and juvenile justice system, and that they experience high rates of harassment and sexual victimization (Conron and Wilson 2019). Without data on transgender, nonbinary, and intersex individuals, addressing the complex needs of this population as well as providing for their safety, given the heightened risk of harassment for this group both in the justice system and in the community, will be impossible.

C. Promoting Evidence-Based Policy and Practice in Social Inequality in Criminal Justice

This volume is dedicated to elevating and expanding the use of evidence-based research in criminal justice policy and practice. I encourage the continued support of placing rigorous science at the forefront of criminal justice policy. Along with the various perspectives shared by the chapter authors, there are two dimensions that I believe are crucial in promoting research in the policy space. These are the collaborations we engage in as researchers and the accessibility of research.

Within the research community, it is important to work across disciplines and truly foster interdisciplinary work. Unfortunately, to date, the work around criminal justice policy remains heavily guided by a few disciplines and perspectives. Policy informed by science to address social inequality requires expertise from a host of disciplines. Research in medicine, education, psychology, and economics, to name a few, has much to offer regarding ways to curb social inequality. Scientific collaborations that draw from scientists across disciplines will not only lead to innovation but also to a more comprehensive approach to addressing social inequality. It will also provide access to policy spaces in other sectors (e.g., education, public health).

I encourage researchers to seek collaborations with practitioners and policymakers as a way to increase access to research findings. Criminal justice professionals and policymakers have a deeper understanding of the practical and financial constraints that may impede the implementation of policies and programs for reducing inequality. Collaborations with these stakeholders can expedite policy change and remove bureaucratic barriers that may exist in advancing policy. In many ways, practitioners and policymakers serve as agents of change, and working with researcher collaborators they can more effectively implement policies rooted in evidence.

Much has been written about public criminology. My point here is not to promote the publication of work to the general public, which of course plays a role in the translation of research, but rather to highlight vehicles for increasing access beyond general dissemination strategies like op-eds and news articles. As I noted at the beginning of this chapter, current times, in which anti-intellectualism is prominent, reinforce the importance of the translation of scientific findings to the general public. I encourage researchers to work with criminal justice agencies and community organizations to present and share findings via different sources (e.g., public and private engagements) (Rodriguez 2018b). Also, the development of policy briefs for various audiences, which can be shared widely and to various stakeholders, increases access and the opportunity to scale evidence-based policy. Lastly, I encourage researchers to regard justice-involved individuals as a key resource and audience of scientific work. Their perspectives and advocacy can lead to policy change in ways that engages communities dedicated to reducing social inequality. This may include expanding researcher-practitioner partnerships to ensure they are inclusive of justice-involved persons, as well as ensuring that community-based participatory research teams include justice-involved or justice impacted persons.

IV. Conclusion

Reducing social inequality has become a national policy priority. In this chapter, I set out to discuss the relationship between social inequality, crime, and justice and offer strategies for reducing inequality in society. Research has established that the criminal justice system plays a role in creating and exacerbating social inequality. Despite the lack of evidence-based policies for reducing inequality in the criminal justice system, there are strategies that justice actors can adopt to reduce inequality. While the criminal justice system can do its part to reduce inequality, schools and community-based efforts will also need to assume an active role in reducing the use of criminal justice responses for noncriminal justice matters. Improving the well-being of residents by providing access to services (e.g., medical care, mental health treatment, and substance abuse treatment) and reducing economic strain should be cornerstones of all efforts designed to address inequality. Importantly, the implementation of any policy will require filling existing gaps on key demographic indicators (i.e., ethnicity and gender identity), creating diverse researcher-practitioner collaborations, and making research findings accessible via various methods.

While reducing social inequality is a long-term endeavor, there are several action steps researchers can implement in their work. First, review your past and current work with an eye toward inequality, as a driver of crime and violence, victimization, and criminal justice outcomes. Expose it and explore vehicles to reduce it. Second, ensure data contain the representation of various subgroups (e.g., across race, gender, ethnicity, and gender identity), and when they don't, note that in your work, alongside the implications of such absence. Relatedly, move away from prescribed categories of identity and allow subjects to self-identify as they wish. Third, lean on community organizations for innovative responses for addressing inequality and leverage resources in social services, education, and the labor sector to improve the well-being of marginalized populations and justice-involved individuals. Lastly, researchers must be strong advocates of mental health treatment as a fundamental piece of crime prevention and criminal justice reform efforts. Any strategy to improve quality of life and promote public safety in the 21st century will be incomplete without a behavioral health component.

References

Ang, Desmond. 2021. The effects of police violence on inner-city students. *The Quarterly Journal of Economics*, 136:115–168.

Beck, Alan. 2021. *Race and ethnicity of violent crime offenders and arrestees, 2018.* Washington DC: US Department of Justice, Office of Justice Programs, Bureau of Justice Statistics.

Beck, Alan, and Alfred Blumstein. 2018. Racial disproportionality in U.S. state prisons: Accounting for the effects of racial and ethnic differences in criminal involvement, arrests, sentencing, and time served. *Journal of Quantitative Criminology*, 34:853–883.

Beckman, Laura, and Nancy Rodriguez. 2021. Race, ethnicity, and official perceptions in the juvenile justice system: Extending the role of negative attributional stereotypes. *Criminal Justice and Behavior*, 48:1536–1556.

Biden, Joseph R. 2021. Executive Order on Advancing Racial Equity and Support for Underserved Communities through the Federal Government. Washington, DC: White House https://www.whitehouse.gov/briefing-room/presidential-actions/2021/01/20/executive-order-advancing-racial-equity-and-support-for-underserved-communities-through-the-federal-government/.

Bishop, Donna. M., and Charles Frazier. 1996. Race effects in juvenile justice decision-making: Findings of a statewide analysis. *Journal of Criminal Law & Criminology*, 86:392–414.

Blais, Etienne, Jacinthe Brisson, François Gagnon, and Sophie-Anne Lemay. 2022. Diverting people who use drugs from the criminal justice system: A systematic review of police-based diversion measures. *International Journal of Drug Policy*, 105:103697.

Bortner, M. A. 1982. *Inside a juvenile court.* New York: New York University Press.

Boyd, Rhea W., Angela M. Ellison, and Ivor B. Horn. 2016. Police, equity, and child health. *Pediatrics*, 137 (3): e20152711.

Bridges, George. S., and Sara Steen. 1998. Racial disparities in official assessments of juvenile offenders: Attributional stereotypes as mediating mechanisms. *American Sociological Review*, 63:554–570.

Bryne, J. 2020. *The effectiveness of prison programming: A review of the research literature examining the impact of federal, state, and local inmate programming on post-release recidivism.* Washington, DC: U.S. Courts.

Centers for Disease Control and Prevention. 2022 (August 11). *COVID Data Tracker.* Atlanta, GA: US Department of Health and Human Services, CDC.

Conron, Kerith. J., and Bianca Wilson, eds. 2019. *A research agenda to reduce system involvement and promote positive outcomes with LGBTQ youth of color impacted by the child welfare and juvenile justice systems.* Los Angeles: Williams Institute.

Davis, Ari, Rose Kim, and Cassandra Crifasi. 2023. *A year in review: 2021 gun deaths in the US.* Baltimore, MD: Johns Hopkins Center for Gun Violence Solutions, Johns Hopkins Bloomberg School of Public Health.

Dobbie, William, and Crystal S. Yang. 2021. The U.S. pretrial system. *Journal of Economic Perspectives*, 35:49–70.

Drinan. Cara. 2009. The third generation of indigent defense litigation. *New York University Review of Law & Social Change*, 33:427–478.

Feld, Barry. 1999. *Bad kids: Race and the transformation of the juvenile court.* Oxford: Oxford University Press.

Feld, Barry. 2017. *The evolution of the juvenile court: Race, politics, and the criminalizing of juvenile justice.* New York: New York University Press.

Felitti, Vincent J., Robert F. Anda, Dale Nordenberg, David F. Williamson, Alison M. Spitz, Valerie Edwards, Mary P. Koss, and James S. Marks. 1998. Relationship of childhood abuse and household dysfunction to many of the leading causes of death in adults: The Adverse Childhood Experience (ACE) Study. *American Journal of Preventative Medicine*, 14:245–258.

Geller, Amanda. 2021. Youth-police contact: Burdens and inequities in an adverse childhood experience. *American Journal of Public Health*, 111:1300–1308. doi:10.2105/AJPH.2021.306259.

Goldman, Margaret, and Nancy Rodriguez. 2020. The state as the "Ultimate Parent": The implications of family for racial and ethnic disparities in the juvenile justice system. *Race and Justice*, 12 (4): 714–735.

Goldman, Margaret, and Nancy Rodriguez. 2022. Juvenile court in the school-prison nexus: Youth punishment, schooling and structures of inequality. *Journal of Crime & Justice*, 45:270–284.

Goldstick, Jason, Rebecca Cunningham, and Patrick M. Carter. 2022. Current causes of death in children and adolescents in the United States. *New England Journal of Medicine*, 386:1995–1956.

Gottfredson, Denise C., Scott Crosse, Zhiqun Tang, Erin L. Bauer, Michele A. Harmon, Carol A. Hagen, and Angela D. Greene. 2020. Effects of school resource officers on school crime and responses to school crime. *Criminology and Public Policy*, 19:905–940.

Heimer, Karen. 2019. Inequalities and crime. *Criminology*, 57:377–394.

Kalb, Johanna. 2018. Gideon incarcerated: Access to counsel in pretrial detention. *UC Irvine Law Review*, 9:101–140.

King, Ryan, and Marc Schindler. 2021. Reconsidering police in schools. *Contexts*, 20:28–33.

Kurlychek, Megan C., and Brian D. Johnson. 2019. Cumulative Disadvantage in the American Criminal Justice System. *Annual Review of Criminology*, 2:291–319.

Lau v. Nichols, 414 U.S. 563, 1974.

Lee, Hedwig, and Christopher Wildeman. 2021. Assessing mass incarceration's effects on families. *Science*, 374:277–281.

Lehmann Peter S., and Ryan C. Meldrum. 2021. School suspension in Florida: The interactive effects of race, ethnicity, gender, and academic achievement. *Justice Quarterly*, 38:479–512.

Leiber, Mike. 2003. *The context of juvenile justice decision-making: When race matters*. Albany: State University of New York Press.

Leiber, Mike, and Kate Fox. 2005. Race and the impact of detention on juvenile justice decision making. *Crime & Delinquency*, 51:470–497.

Leiber, Mike, and Kristin Mack. 2003. The individual and joint effects of race, gender, and family status on juvenile justice decision-making. *Journal of Research in Crime and Delinquency*, 40:34–70.

Madhuri, Sharma, Lisa Stolzenberg, and Stewart J. D'Alessio. 2022. Evaluating the cumulative impact of indigent defense attorneys on criminal justice outcomes. *Journal of Criminal Justice*, 81:101927. https://doi.org/10.1016/j.jcrimjus.2022.101927.

McGlynn-Wright, Anne, Robert D. Crutchfield, Martie L. Skinner, and Kevin P Haggerty. 2022. The usual, racialized, suspects: The consequence of police contacts with Black and White youth on adult arrest. *Social Problems*, 69:299–315.

Mears, Daniel P., Joshua C. Cochran, and Andrea M. Lindsey. 2016. Offending and racial and ethnic disparities in criminal justice: A conceptual framework for guiding theory and research and informing policy. *Journal of Contemporary Criminal Justice*, 32:78–103.

Montes, Andrea N., Daniel P. Mears, Nicole L. Collier, George B. Pesta, Sonja E. Siennick, and Samantha J. Brown. 2021. Blurred and confused: The paradox of police in schools. *Policing: A Journal of Policy and Practice*, 15:1546–1564.

National Academies of Sciences, Engineering, and Medicine. 2022. *Reducing inequalities between lesbian, gay, bisexual, transgender, and queer adolescents and cisgender, heterosexual adolescents: Proceedings of a workshop*. Washington, DC: National Academies Press.

National Research Council. 2013. *Reforming juvenile justice: A developmental approach.* Washington, DC: National Academies Press.

National Research Council. 2014. *The growth of incarceration in the United States: Exploring causes and consequences.* Washington, DC: National Academies Press.

Page, Joshua, Scott Hayward, and Christine Bail. 2022. Pretrial justice in the United States: A field of possibility. *Annual Review of Criminology*, 5:91–113.

Pager, Devah, and Hana Shepherd. 2008. The sociology of discrimination: Racial discrimination in employment, housing, credit, and consumer markets. *Annual Review of Sociology*, 34:181–209.

Park, Alice, Alison Booth, Adwoa J. Parker, Arabella Scantlebury, Kath Wright, and Martin Webber. 2021. Models of mental health triage for individuals coming to the attention of the police who may be experiencing mental health crisis: A scoping review. *Policing: A Journal of Policy and Practice*, 15:859–895.

Pearman, Francis, Chris Curran, Benjamin Fisher, and Joseph Gardella. 2019. Are achievement gaps related to discipline gaps? Evidence from national data. *AERA Open*, 5:1–18. https://journals.sagepub.com/doi/full/10.1177/2332858419875440.

Rodriguez, Nancy. 2010. The cumulative effect of race and ethnicity in juvenile court outcomes and why preadjudication detention matters. *Journal of Research in Crime & Delinquency*, 47:391–413.

Rodriguez, Nancy. 2018. Expanding the evidence base in criminology and criminal justice: Barriers and opportunities to bridging research and practice. *Justice Evaluation Journal*, 1:1–14.

Rodriguez, Nancy, Hillary Smith, and Marjorie Zatz. 2009. "Youth is enmeshed in a highly dysfunctional family system": Exploring the relationship among dysfunctional families, parental incarceration, and juvenile court decision making. *Criminology*, 47:177–208.

Rolnick, Addie C. 2016. Untangling the web: Juvenile justice in Indian country. *New York University Journal of Legislation and Public Policy*, 19:49–140.

Rosenfeld, Richard, and Ernesto Lopez. 2021. *Pandemic, social unrest, and crime in U.S. cities.* Washington, DC: Council on Criminal Justice.

Rothstein, Richard. 2017. *The color of law: A Forgotten history of how our government segregated America.* New York: Liveright.

Sampson, Robert. J., William. J. Wilson, and Hanna Katz. 2018. Reassessing "Toward a Theory of Race, Crime, and Urban Inequality": Enduring and new challenges in 21st century America. *DuBois Review*, 15:13–34.

Sewell, Alyasah, Justin Feldman, Ray Rashawn, Keon Gilbert, Kevin Jefferson, and Hedwig Lee. 2021. Illness spillovers of lethal police violence: The significance of gendered marginalization. *Ethnic and Racial Studies*, 44:1089–1114.

Shaw, T. M., and United States. 2015. *The Ferguson report: Department of Justice investigation of the Ferguson Police Department.* Washington, DC: Department of Justice, Civil Rights Division.

Smith, Sean, Roxanna Edwards, and Hao C. Duong. 2021. Unemployment rises in 2020, as the country battles the COVID-19 pandemic. *Monthly Labor Review.* US Bureau of Labor Statistics, June.

Snyder, Howard N. 2004. An empirical portrait of the youth reentry population. *Youth Violence and Juvenile Justice*, 2:39–55.

Spencer, Andrea E., Rachel Oblath, Rohan Dayal, J. Krystel Loubeau, Julia Lejeune, Jennifer Sikov, and Meera Savage. 2021. Changes in psychosocial functioning among urban, school-age children during the COVID-19 pandemic. *Child and Adolescent Psychiatry and Mental Health*, 15:73.

State Monetary Sanctions and the Costs of the Criminal Legal System: The Consequences of Monetary Sanctions. 2022. Special issue, *RSF: The Russell Sage Foundation Journal of Social Sciences* 8.

Stewart, Eric A., Patricia Y. Warren, Cresean Hughes, and Rod K. Brunson. 2020. Race, ethnicity, and criminal justice contact: Reflections for future research. *Race and Justice*, 10:119–149.

Substance Abuse and Mental Health Services Administration. 2020. *The Opioid Crisis and the Black/African American population: An urgent issue.* Publication No. PEP20-05-02-001. Rockville, MD: Substance Abuse and Mental Health Services Administration, Office of Behavioral Health Equity.

Title VI of the Civil Rights Act of 1964 ("Title VI"), 42 U.S.C. 2000d et seq.

Turney, Kristin, and Sara Wakefield. 2019. Criminal justice contact and inequality. *RSF: The Russell Sage Foundation Journal of the Social Sciences* 5:1–23.

US Census Bureau. 2018. *Limited English-speaking households, 2018 American Community Survey 5-year estimates.* Washington, DC: US Census Bureau. https://data.census.gov/cedsci/table?q=Language%20Spoken%20at%20Home&tid=ACSST5Y2019.S1602.

US Department of Health and Human Services. National Survey on Drug Use and Health, 2019. 2020. Washington, DC: US Department of Health and Human Services.

Visher, Christy, Jennifer Yahner, and Nancy La Vigne. 2010. *Life after prison: Tracking the experiences of male prisoners returning to Chicago.* Washington DC: Urban Insitute.

Weisburst, Emily. 2019. Patrolling public schools: The impact of funding for school police on student discipline and long-term education outcomes. *Journal of Policy Analysis and Management*, 38:338–365.

Western, Bruce. 2006. *Punishment and inequality in America.* New York: Russell Sage Foundation.

Western, Bruce, and Becky Pettit. 2010. Incarceration and social inequality. *Daedalus*, Summer 2010. https://www.amacad.org/publication/incarceration-social-inequality.

Western, Bruce, and Catherine Sirois. 2019. Racialized re-entry: Labor market inequality after incarceration. *Social Forces*, 97:1517–1542.

Zane, Steven, Brandon. C. Welsh, Daniel P. Mears, and Gregory M. Zimmerman. 2021. Pathways through juvenile justice: A system-level assessment of cumulative disadvantage in the processing of juvenile offenders. *Journal of Quantitative Criminology*, 38:483–514.

Zeng, Zhen, and Todd D. Minton. 2021. Jail inmates in 2019. Washington DC: US Department of Justice, Office of Justice Programs, Bureau of Justice Statistics.

CHAPTER 27

APPLYING WHAT WE KNOW AND BUILDING AN EVIDENCE BASE
Reducing Disproportionate Minority Contact

STEVEN N. ZANE

RACIAL disparities in the juvenile and criminal justice systems represent one of the most pressing social issues in the United States. The continued and clearly observable overrepresentation of minority defendants in the criminal and juvenile justice systems is at odds with the country's founding ideals of freedom and equality, posing a direct threat to the perceived legitimacy and fairness of our legal system and society more generally. In the juvenile justice system, racial disproportionalities across various points of system processing, from referral to final disposition, are commonly referred to as disproportionate minority contact (DMC).[1]

The present chapter takes an evidence-based approach to the issue of DMC, guided by the evaluation hierarchy framework described by Rossi and colleagues (2004). As Mears (2010, 10, emphasis in original) discusses, when applied to the criminal justice system, such an approach responds to five sets of questions:

> First, we assess whether a need for a policy exists; this is a *needs evaluation*. Second, we then assess whether the theory underlying the policy is logical; coherent; and, ideally, supported by research; this is a *theory evaluation*. Third, we assess how well a policy is implemented; this is typically termed an *implementation* or a *process evaluation*. Fourth, we assess (1) whether the policy actually is associated with intended outcomes (this is typically termed an *outcome evaluation*) and (2) whether it likely causes the outcomes (this is typically termed an *impact evaluation*). Fifth, we assess whether the policy's benefits outweigh its costs and whether the benefits, relative to costs, are substantially greater than those of another policy; this is a *cost-efficiency* evaluation.

Attempts to reduce DMC in the juvenile justice system are not so well established or rigorously defined that we can yet speak of the implementation fidelity, causal impact, or cost-efficiency of specific programs, practices, or policies aimed at reducing racial disproportionalities in juvenile justice. Accordingly, and with the goals of applying what we know and of building an evidence base for reducing DMC, the present chapter focuses on several questions. First, what is the extent of the DMC problem? How large is it, and where is it located? Second, what are the potential theoretical grounds for interventions to reduce DMC? Third, what kind of evidence do we have that interventions have or have not reduced DMC? Finally, what are the implications for research and policy aimed at reducing DMC?

I. The DMC "Picture"

The first step, corresponding to a "needs evaluation," is to identify the current scope of the DMC problem. In 2019, there were approximately 722,600 delinquency referrals (Hockenberry and Puzzanchera 2021). Of these, 43% were White youth, 35% were Black youth, and 19% were Hispanic youth. Relative to their respective populations, then, this indicates that Black youth are substantially overrepresented among juvenile court referrals (a ratio of rates equal to 2.9) while Hispanic youth are not overrepresented at referral (a ratio of rates equal to 1.0).

Black and Hispanic youth were also overrepresented at other points of contact with the juvenile justice system, though less so than at referral. First, following referral, 20% of White youth were detained compared to 29% of Black youth (a ratio of rates equal to 1.4) and 32% of Hispanic youth (a ratio of rates equal to 1.6). Second, among referrals, 34% of White youth were diverted from formal processing compared to 20% of Black youth (a ratio of rates equal to 0.6) and 28% of Hispanic youth (a ratio of rates equal to 0.8). Third, 48% of White youth were formally petitioned compared to 60% of Black youth (a ratio of rates equal to 1.2) and 52% of Hispanic youth (a ratio of rates equal to 1.1). Fourth, among petitioned cases, 53% of White youth were adjudicated delinquent compared to 50% of Black youth (a ratio of rates equal to 0.9) and 52% of Hispanic youth (a ratio of rates equal to 1.0). Fifth, among adjudicated cases, 22% of White youth received out-of-home placement compared to 31% of Black and Hispanic youth (a ratio of rates equal to 1.4). Finally, among petitioned cases, 0.7% of White youth were waived to criminal court compared to 1.1% of Black youth (a ratio of rates equal to 1.5) and 0.6% of Hispanic youth (a ratio of rates equal to 0.9).

Figure 27.1 displays these disproportionalities as ratios of the proportion of minority youth (relative to their population) to the proportion of White youth (relative to their population) at each stage of juvenile justice processing. As noted, for Black youth, DMC is greatest at referral (2.9), while for Hispanic youth, DMC is greatest at detention (1.5). Due to the differences in initial referral, Black youth were especially overrepresented throughout the system. Specifically, since Black youth comprised 35% of referrals in 2019, they also made up 40% of youth who were detained, 40% of youth who were petitioned, 37% of youth who were adjudicated delinquent, 43% of youth who were placed out-of-home, and 52% of all youth who were waived to criminal court. Given that Black youth made up only approximately 15% of all youth, these represent quite striking disproportionalities—again, largely due to differences that emerge in rates of referral.[2]

A second question, in addressing the scope of the DMC problem, is whether these national estimates of DMC mask important variation in racial and ethnic disproportionality across states. As Piquero (2008, 69) observes, "It remains unclear whether

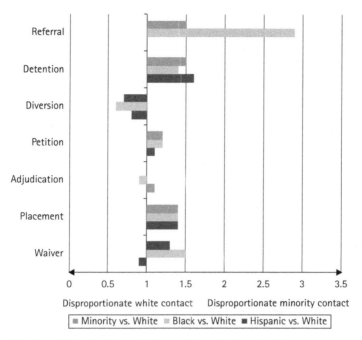

FIGURE 27.1. National Relative Rate Indices of Juvenile Justice Contact, 2019.

Source: Puzzanchera et al. (2023).

minority overrepresentation is a widespread, nationwide phenomena or a matter of certain jurisdictions and states operating in certain ways." On the one hand, it is possible that DMC is relatively uniform across states. This often appears to be the presumption in discussions of DMC and how to reduce it (see, e.g., Cabaniss et al. 2007). On the other hand, perhaps DMC is not a problem in all states. The most recent data affirms that there is substantial variation in Black-White disproportionalities across states. In 2019, for example, the Black-White ratio of placement rates ranged from 1.7:1 in New Mexico and 2.2:1 in Indiana to 11.3:1 in Wisconsin and 17.5:1 in New Jersey, while the Hispanic-White ratio of placement rates ranged from 1:1 in Florida to 4.1:1 in New Jersey and 5.7:1 in Massachusetts (Sickmund et al. 2021).[3] This would seem to indicate that, from a policy perspective, approaching DMC as a national problem may be misguided, and a localized approach may be more appropriate.

In documenting the scope and nature of the DMC problem, there is also the question of whether it has changed over time. Leiber and Fix (2019) recently assessed national trends in the relative rate index (RRI) from 2005 through 2015. They found that, at referral, the Black-White RRI had increased from 2.7 in 2005 to 3.1 in 2015, while the Hispanic-White ratio of rates remained stable around 1.1. At detention, the Black-White RRI remained constant at 1.3 while the Hispanic-White RRI increased from 1.4 to 1.5. At secure placement, the RRI has hovered around 1.3 and 1.4 for Black and Hispanic youth, respectively. The most recent national data indicates that the proportion of youth arrests who are Black and Hispanic has actually increased—for example, from 33% and 16% in 2005 to 35% and 19% in 2019, respectively. In the case of Hispanic youth, this can be attributed to an overall increase in the Hispanic population from 2005 to 2019, while in the case of Black youth, this change does not reflect a larger population (Puzzanchera et al. 2023). Notably, then, there has been no clear pattern of DMC reduction at the national level, despite "a wide range of initiatives [that] have been developed and implemented, as well as [an] enormous amount of dollars . . . spent via the Federal Title II Formula Grants and other funding by private foundations, states, and localities" (Leiber and Fix 2019, 586).

This discussion presents a bird's eye view of DMC in the juvenile justice system. It shows us that Black youth are substantially overrepresented throughout the juvenile justice system, while Hispanic youth are somewhat overrepresented at certain points (i.e., detention, placement), but not others (referral, waiver). Additionally, DMC varies substantially across states, although it has remained fairly stable over time. Of course, these disproportionalities are purely descriptive. This information tells us *that* DMC exists but they do not tell us *why*.

Another way of framing this issue is that, in the context of identifying the problem of DMC and how it might be addressed, we must move beyond identifying *disproportionalities* and attempt to identify *disparities* within the system. As Mears, Cochran, and Lindsey (2016) observe, there has been some conceptual confusion in the literature due to inconsistent (and perhaps uncritical) usage of terms such as "difference," "disproportionality," and "disparity" in research on race and criminal justice. Mears and colleagues (2016, 85, 87) note that "disproportionality" involves "racial or ethnic differences that are greater than what would be expected given the group population sizes among those for whom a given outcome is possible," while the term "disparity" seems to indicate "any disproportionality attributable to overt or covert, or intended or unintended, discrimination against minorities" since disparity "connotes 'unfairness.'"[4] Despite this apparent connotation, the term "disparity" is often used just to mean difference or disproportionality. Indeed, under the Juvenile Justice and Delinquency Prevention Act (JJDPA) of 2018, "racial and ethnic disparity means minority youth populations are involved at a decision point in the juvenile justice system at disproportionately higher rates than nonminority youth at that decision point" (Pub. L. 115–385, title I, § 102). In other words, disparity and disproportionality are used to refer to the same phenomena, despite having different connotations.

The conceptual confusion here raises an important issue, since the descriptive disproportionalities do not (alone) evidence discrimination, as may sometimes be inferred. In fact, as Mears and colleagues (2016) point out, there can be "warranted disproportionalities" that do not involve unfairness and thus are not properly considered disparities. Most obviously, disproportionalities due to differences in offending do not necessarily indicate any unfairness or inequity (although they might). This brings us to the next phase of the analysis, corresponding to "theory evaluation": what *causes* the patterns of DMC that we have so far identified?

II. What *Causes* DMC?

What causes the disproportionalities (including variation across stages and jurisdictions) highlighted above? As Baumer (2013, 236) observes, "At one extreme, they could reflect racial differences in criminal participation and no bias in the application of criminal law;

at the other, they could reflect racial equality in the prevalence, incidence, and nature of offending, yet significant racial bias in how the law is applied to those who engage in criminal activity." These two extremes are generally referred to as the "differential involvement" and "differential treatment" hypotheses, respectively (Piquero 2008). The differential involvement explanation posits that "minority youth are overrepresented in the system because they engage in more crime than white youth and/or because they engage in more serious crimes than their white counterparts," while the differential treatment explanation posits that "minority youth are subjected to more formal and more severe forms of social control than comparable white youth at all stages of juvenile justice processing" (Engen, Steen, and Bridges 2002, 96).[5]

Navigating between differential involvement and differential treatment as potential causes of DMC is especially complex in the context of juvenile justice. The juvenile justice system is not intended to be as formalistic as the criminal justice system, such that many difficult-to-measure, "extralegal" factors may be legitimately related to juvenile court outcomes. For example, the juvenile court's assessment of family situation and neighborhood connections to peer groups (e.g., gangs) may be relevant to juvenile justice decision-making outcomes but also associated with race in the aggregate, complicating the search for root causes of DMC.

A. Evidence of Differential Involvement

Operating in the background of most research on racial and ethnic disparities in the juvenile justice system is the possibility that DMC is caused by differential involvement in delinquent behavior by minority youth. Some early assessments of minority overrepresentation in the juvenile and criminal justice system failed to find considerable evidence of racial bias, supporting a differential involvement explanation for racial disparities (see Blumstein 1982; Hindelang 1978; Tittle and Curran 1988). In the context of the criminal justice system, Blumstein (1982, 1993, 2009) has argued that differential treatment cannot account for most of the racial disproportionality in system outcomes, and that differential offending behaviors in the population instead must be the root cause of such disparity (see also Beck and Blumstein 2018).

Consistent with Blumstein's observation, a separate body of research has consistently found, based on victimization and self-report data, that Black persons are significantly more likely to engage in criminal or delinquent behavior compared to White persons—especially for violent crime (see, e.g., Elliot 1994; Felson and Kreager 2015; Felson, Deane, and Armstrong 2008; Huizinga, Loeber, and Thornberry 1993; Sampson, Morenoff, and Raudenbush 2005). In an early summary of this research, Sampson and Lauritsen (1997, 330) observed that "offender and victims share a similar demographic profile—especially for violence. Both violent offenders and victims of violent offending tend to be young, male, black, and live in urban areas." This general conclusion has been confirmed by more recent reviews of the literature (see, e.g., Piquero et al. 2015).

The question, of course, is whether differential involvement explains *some*, *most*, or *all* of the racial and ethnic disproportionalities in the juvenile justice system. This motivates research on whether minority youth are treated differently than similarly situated White youth across different stages of the justice system.

B. Evidence of Differential Treatment

The most common approach to identifying racial and ethnic disparities involves what Baumer (2013) calls the "modal approach" of sentencing research. According to this approach, a regression analysis controls for factors that contribute to the variation in the outcome and that may also be associated with race or ethnicity (such as offense severity and criminal history), such that any remaining variation in outcomes can be attributable to race (i.e., a statistically significant race coefficient) and provide evidence of racial disparity (perhaps even discrimination). The vast majority of DMC research has followed this approach. In a recent meta-analysis of this literature, Zane and Pupo (2021) reviewed 67 studies (consisting of 79 independent samples) that used regression analysis to assess the relationship between race and ethnicity and major juvenile court outcomes. For Black/White differences, they found evidence of small average effects on detention (OR = 1.49, $p < .001$) and placement (OR = 1.26, $p < .001$); a very small average effect on intake (OR = 1.19, $p < .01$); and no significant average effects on petition, waiver, or adjudication. For Hispanic/White differences, they found evidence of a small average effect on detention (OR = 1.35); very small average effects on petition (OR = 1.14, $p < .01$), adjudication (OR = 1.11, $p < .001$), and placement (OR = 1.13, $p < .01$); and no average effects on intake or waiver. They concluded, "[W]e found that there are unexplained trivial-to-small effects of race and ethnicity on some, but not all, stages of juvenile justice processing" (Zane and Pupo 2021, 1310–1311). This suggests that there is little systematic evidence of differential treatment at most stages of post-referral processing.

The major exception to this assessment involves preadjudication detention, where evidence suggests that there may be some amount of differential treatment. This is important because detention is strongly associated with later punitive outcomes, such as secure placement and waiver to adult court (see Rodriguez 2007, 2010). That is, the effect of race on other juvenile justice outcomes might be mediated by detention, possibly masking direct effects and leading to lower average effects observed at subsequent stages of processing. This possibility is related to the more general concern expressed by scholars that racial discrimination in the criminal justice system is more generally masked by the "narrow focus on episodic disparity in individual outcomes at singular stages of criminal case processing" (Kurlychek and Johnson 2019, 307). As Piquero (2008, 69) emphasizes, "it may be that racial and ethnic disparities begin at the very earliest stage and that effects accumulate as youth proceed through the system."

Consistent with this observation, scholars have recently called for increased attention to cumulative disadvantage in the criminal justice system (see Kurlychek and Johnson 2019). Only one study to date has estimated cumulative disadvantage in the juvenile justice system—the authors found little evidence of cumulative disadvantage in a holistic sense (Zane et al. 2022). Rather, they found that Black and Hispanic defendants were more likely to experience pathways through the juvenile justice system that began with pretrial detention, while pathways without detention did not exhibit racial disparities. Interestingly, Sutton (2013) found the same pattern in the criminal justice system. These findings point to *detention* as the major source of post-referral racial disproportionality, but they do not necessarily demonstrate differential treatment at detention. As Zane et al. (2022, 509–510) noted:

It is possible that detention is associated with more severe dispositions for legitimate reasons rather than motivated by bias. For one, there could be other factors, such as gang involvement, not captured by control variables such as prior record and offense type. Detention may also reflect an assessment that a juvenile has a less promising prospect of returning safely to the community.

Going forward, it stands to reason that whether racial disproportionality at detention involves differential treatment or unmeasured case characteristics should constitute a primary research question for DMC scholars.

C. Limitations of the DMC Evidence Base

1. *Model Specification: Omitted Variable Bias and Overcontrol Bias*

In the context of nonexperimental research, a key limitation involves model specification and the problem of omitted variable bias (Baumer 2013). Almost a century ago, Thorstein Sellin (1935, 217) noted that racial disproportionalities in the criminal justice system "hide a number of possible variables." Since this early observation, scholars have worried that omitted variable bias may plague observational research on race and criminal justice. In his book-length criticism of research on racial discrimination in the criminal justice system, for example, Wilbanks (1987, 46–47) argued that "we cannot attribute the remaining unexplained variation [in our statistical models] to race unless all the most important control variables have been introduced. There is always the possibility that the introduction of one or more additional (and theoretically important) controls might have reduced the remaining variation to zero."

More recently, Baumer (2013) has similarly observed that since most research on race and sentencing is based on administrative data, it cannot distinguish between competing theories because some degree of omitted variable bias is inevitable. As noted, Baumer (2013) refers to the "modal" approach to studying race and sentencing as involving regression analyses of restricted samples (e.g., convicted defendants) where the association between race/ethnicity and some system outcome is estimated after controlling for possibly confounding factors such as offense type, offense severity, and prior record. The problem? We know that such analyses leave out much that might ultimately explain the association we find between race and justice system outcomes. As Baumer (2013, 255) puts it, "there are good reasons to be skeptical of the conclusions drawn from many of the existing studies."

In the juvenile justice system, omitted variable bias presents an especially difficult problem due to the court's social welfare mission (Piquero 2008). Unlike the criminal justice system, the court purports to make decisions about the best outcome for the child and the community based on myriad factors such as age, perceived culpability, dangerousness, and potential for reform, as well as environmental risk factors such as family situation and peer delinquency (Bishop and Leiber 2012). There are thus myriad unmeasured case characteristics, such as developmental maturity, substance abuse, family situation, attitudinal factors (e.g., demeanor), and victim characteristics, that may be associated with outcomes and, by extension, racial disproportionalities in outcomes. Given the court's reform-oriented mission, suspicion of peer delinquent groups may be especially salient, as juvenile court actors may feel responsible for ascertaining the youth's holistic situation, including the prospect of returning safely to the community (see Fine et al. 2017). As Clair and Winter (2016, 342–343) report, for example, one juvenile judge admitted that her detention decision for a Black defendant was motivated by extralegal concerns: "I am thinking if I let this kid go back into the community, the kid's coming back in a body bag." Many such factors are simply never accounted for in typical DMC research, yet they likely contribute to racial disproportionalities. They also illustrate the potential for disproportionalities to result from decisions that are not necessarily disparate in the sense of being due to racial bias but may arise from seemingly good intentions. That does not vitiate concerns about disparities but simply illustrates that the concept of disparity includes substantial heterogeneity.

While omitted variable bias may often lead to *overestimation* of the influence of race on juvenile justice processing, overcontrol bias can lead to an *underestimation* of the true effects of race. Here, the problem is that an analytical model may condition on a variable that is on the causal path between treatment and outcome, what is typically called a mediating variable in contrast to a confounding variable (Elwert and Winship 2014). In the case of research on racial disproportionality in the juvenile justice system, a regression model may overcontrol for certain case-level factors that are bound up with racial attributions according to the differential treatment perspective (Frase 2013). For example, as already noted, the largest disproportionality in post-arrest processing occurs at preadjudication detention (Zane and Pupo 2021), and detention is also more strongly associated with subsequent outcomes than other control variables (Zane and Pupo 2023). This raises a fundamental theoretical question: Is detention best conceived as a confounding variable—and thus controlled for to prevent confounding—or as a mediating variable on the causal pathway between race and subsequent outcomes—in which case it should *not* be controlled to prevent confounding?

The role of criminal history also nicely illustrates the difficulty posed by omitted variable bias, on the one hand, and overcontrol bias, on the other. By most accounts, prior record is a legitimate component of the punishment decision: it may signal that the defendant has not been deterred by past punishment and is more likely to offend in the future, or simply that the defendant is more culpable for failing to reform his ways (i.e., no mitigating factor for "first time offense"). If Black defendants are more likely to have a prior record, or to have a more extensive or serious record, then failing to control for criminal history will overestimate the (illegitimate) influence of race, since it is confounded with the (legitimate) influence of a prior court record. This is "omitted variable bias." But another possibility is that prior record is itself racialized, representing past differential treatment, such that is more accurate to model criminal history as *mediating* the relationship between race and punitive outcomes (Frase 2013). Here, controlling for prior record would in fact underestimate the true influence of race. This is "overcontrol bias." There is no empirical solution here, just two patterns that accord with the same observed data.

2. *Selection Bias*

Another serious limitation of most DMC research is selection bias, where reductions in sample size across different stages of processing are nonrandom (Elwert and Winship 2014).

If, for example, Black juvenile defendants are more likely to be petitioned than similarly situated White defendants due to differential treatment, the sample of *petitioned* referrals is now different from the sample of total referrals. If there are no differences in adjudication outcomes between Black and White juveniles—which happens to be the case (see Zane and Pupo 2021)—this might signal that there is no bias. But since, in our example, White and Black petitioned youth are not similarly situated due to differential treatment at petition, Black youth should in fact be less likely to be adjudicated delinquent than the (worse) White defendants—such that the equal likelihood of adjudication we observe may still reflect differential treatment (see Crutchfield, Fernandes, and Martinez 2010).

Another example involves case dismissal, where it appears that Black youth are more likely to be dismissed compared to White youth. On its face, this appears to indicate that there is anti-White bias by intake officers and prosecutors charged with determining dismissal. But another possibility is that there was differential treatment at the point of arrest, such that Black youth and White youth referrals are not similarly situated (see Kempf-Leonard 2007). If Black youth tend to be arrested in situations where there is less evidence, for example, then they would tend to represent weaker cases than White youth and be more likely to be dismissed. It is thus possible that the lower likelihood of case dismissal actually reflects anti-Black bias at an earlier decision point.

This brings us to the point where the selection bias problem is most notable: police contact with youth. Unlike other stages of processing, which can be conceptualized as closed systems, youth referrals to the juvenile court occur in an open system. In order to determine whether there is differential treatment at arrest, it is necessary to compare actual arrests to actual offending—the latter of which is *not observed*. In research on police discrimination, scholars refer to this as the "denominator problem." Neil and Winship (2019, 79) comment: "When comparing rates of contact by race it is unclear what the proper denominator should be . . . the denominator we choose reflects our assumption as to what we think the police are doing, not necessarily what they are actually doing. Choosing the wrong denominator, our inference is likely to be wrong." For example, using a population denominator assumes that police arrest people at random—which seems unlikely—while using a crime denominator assumes the police only arrest actual criminals—which is more plausible, but also seems unlikely.

With other stages of processing, the denominator is clear: For differential treatment at judicial placement, we compare youth who have been adjudicated delinquent; for differential treatment at adjudication of delinquency, we compare youth who have been petitioned; for differential treatment at petition, we compare youth who have been referred to the juvenile justice system. As mentioned, youth at each stage of processing might not be similarly situated due to selection bias, but this problem is amplified at referral. Why? To identify differential treatment at arrest, we must compare similarly situated youth who have committed offenses that would warrant a referral to the juvenile justice system—yet there is no data source for us to draw upon for our denominator.

Others have thus observed that establishing whether racial differences in arrest are due to racial bias of police officers or differential offending behaviors is nearly impossible without direct observation: "If minority youths are more often arrested in situations where similar white youths are released or handled informally, these differentials will be almost impossible to detect" (Bishop and Leiber 2012, 458). This presents a serious challenge to determining the extent to which differential involvement versus differential treatment contributes to DMC.[6]

3. *The Limits of Archival Data*

Finally, one global limitation of all research that attempts to identity differential treatment in the juvenile and criminal justice system is that most research is based on retrospective administrative data that does not capture actual decision-making. Baumer (2013, 249) observes that "few studies in the literature on race and sentencing get very close to measuring how or what judges, juries, or prosecutors actually think about defendants of different races, much less how such thoughts might shape their sanctions." Ulmer (2012, 33–34, emphasis in original) similarly remarks that "almost all the theoretical frameworks applied to sentencing . . . directly or indirectly rest on depictions of individual social psychological processes. *None of these processes can be directly observed with sentencing or even earlier case processing outcome data.*" Most recently, Mears (2022, 7) concludes that "despite decades of research on race and sentencing, basic questions about when, where, how, and why race influences punishment remain unanswered, in part because researchers continue to have to rely on administrative records databases."

Due to these data limitations, most research on racial and ethnic disproportionalities in the juvenile justice system merely *implies* differential treatment based on regression analyses that yield statistically significant race and ethnicity effects. As one leading juvenile justice scholar put it, "When racial/ethnic effects to the disadvantage of minority youth are found through multivariate statistical analyses that cannot be fully explained by legal factors, the general conclusion argues that the presence of bias and stereotyping on behalf of juvenile court actors accounts for these differences. My own studies have also included this statement" (Peck 2018, 311). Yet, as Peck acknowledges, unexplained variation in statistical models based on limited, archival data does not demonstrate differential treatment. Doing so would instead require "actual measured perceptional processes of how court actors make decisions," including clear measures of "the attitudes, beliefs, and perceptions of juvenile court workers" (312).

As a result of the three major limitations of the evidence base described here, we do not know conclusively what proportion of DMC is due to differential involvement versus differential treatment. Evidence suggests that DMC at referral is mostly attributable to differential involvement as well as the disparate impact of race-neutral policies (i.e., place-based differences in crime detection), resulting in substantially higher arrest and referral rates for Black youth compared to White and Hispanic youth. Still, research is unable to identify the proportion of DMC at referral that is due to differential treatment, and it is possible that differential treatment plays some nontrivial role in perpetuating disproportionalities. Post-referral, small disproportionalities also emerge, but these could be due to differences in offending (and other behavior, such as cooperation)[7] that are difficult to capture in typical empirical analyses. While it is possible that these disproportionalities reflect some degree of differential treatment, the best evidence indicates that post-referral DMC is not primarily attributable to differential treatment by juvenile justice system actors.

III. WHY HAS DMC PERSISTED DESPITE REFORMS?

Solutions require an understanding of causes. Otherwise, they are likely to be misguided and represent "theory failure" in the terminology of evaluation literature (see Rossi, Lipsey, and Freeman 2004). That DMC has not substantially declined over time despite much attention and reform can be understood in terms of the causes of DMC. First, if DMC is largely caused by differential treatment of minority youth by juvenile justice system actors, then reducing DMC will require reforms that change the behavior of those actors. This might include, for example, cultural sensitivity training as well as increased reliance on less subjective screening methods (e.g., standardized risk and needs assessment). Second, if DMC is largely caused by disparate impact of juvenile justice policies that place an undue burden on certain populations of youth, then reducing DMC will require system-level reform such as deinstitutionalization of status offenders, providing alternatives to secure detention, placing less emphasis on criminal history, and changing how police patrol high-risk minority neighborhoods. Third, if DMC is largely caused by differential involvement in crime by minority youth, then reducing DMC will require changes to the structural and cultural factors that produce the differences in offending behaviors in the first place. Since DMC is most likely a result of a combination of these factors, one approach would be not to worry about their relative contributions to the problem and just implement all three kinds of reform. But, given limited time and resources, it is important to attempt to evaluate what kinds of reform would be most effective in reducing DMC.

In a review of "best practices" of DMC-reduction efforts, Cabaniss and colleagues (2007, 395) enumerated the following major strategies adopted by various states: (1) decision-point mapping and data review; (2) cultural competency training; (3) adding more community-based prevention and intervention programs, most notably detention alternatives; (4) removing decision-making subjectivity through standardized screenings and protocols; (5) reducing barriers to family involvement; and (6) cultivating state leadership to legislate system-level change. These different responses appear to be guided by different theories: (2) and (4) seem guided by differential treatment, (5) and (6) seem guided by disparate impact, and (3) seems be guided by differential involvement. Overall, however, it seems fair to conclude that differential treatment is the main theory of DMC that has motivated juvenile justice system reform to date (Tracy 2005).

What, then, accounts for the failure to reduce DMC? Broadly speaking, there are two reasons. First, attempts to reduce DMC may be poorly designed or implemented, although the basic logic model behind the policy is theoretically sound. In evaluation terminology, we can think of this as implementation failure. Second, a policy can be based on an inadequate or wholly erroneous theoretical foundation, such that even well-implemented interventions will not cause the desired change. We can think of this as theory failure. It is worth considering both possible explanations for the persistence of DMC in the juvenile justice system more than 30 years after federal action was taken to address it (see Zane 2021).

A. Implementation Failure

Perhaps the most obvious explanation for the failure to reduce DMC in the juvenile justice system is that there has been no substantial effort to do so. The largest response to date is the federal "DMC mandate," introduced in 1988 as an amendment to the 1974 Juvenile Justice and Delinquency Prevention Act (JJDPA). The DMC mandate incentivizes states to identify, assess, and intervene to reduce DMC at the local level. The 1992 reauthorization of the DMC mandate included five ongoing phases of compliance: identification, assessment of causes, interventions, evaluation, and monitoring (Leiber and Peck 2013). The 1992 reauthorization also included a financial incentive: states risked losing 25% of their formula grant funding if they did not show a "good faith effort" to comply with the mandate (Leiber 2002). The DMC mandate was again reauthorized with amendment in 2002, expanding the scope of the mandate to all decision points along the juvenile justice continuum—reflected in changing the term "confinement" to "contact." Most recently, the JJDPA was reauthorized as the Juvenile Justice Reform Act of 2018 (and the term "disproportionate minority contact" was replaced by "racial and ethnic disparities").

While the DMC mandate incentivizes states to make a "good faith effort" to identify and address DMC within their jurisdictions, others have observed that "the actual implementation of such initiatives, especially those involving system change, has been slow to nonexistent" (Leiber and Rodriguez 2011, 113). Leiber (2002) observes that the DMC mandate was motivated by an effort to do something rather than nothing, but a more aggressive mandate may be necessary to produce desired outcomes. As Leiber and Fix (2019, 602) point out, the implementation of the DMC mandate has always remained "judicious" to allay states' concerns about the federal government "overreaching and meddling in state and local affairs." While this may represent prudent politics, it also limits the effectiveness of the mandate by failing to provide more specific instructions to states and provide stronger incentives to comply. Put more bluntly, "the federal government set the bar so low that today nearly anything—regardless of how attenuated or remote from actual results—done in the name of 'DMC' is still considered adequate," leading to a situation in which the mandate is nothing more than a "symbolic gesture" (Bell and Ridolfi 2008, 14). As a result, it is argued, the DMC mandate has simply not been taken seriously by most states, and not much has been accomplished beyond the identification stage. While a majority of states have implemented some kinds of interventions aimed at reducing DMC within their jurisdictions, only four states have conducted a formal evaluation of such an intervention (Peck 2018). According to this perspective, what is needed going forward is a "redoubling of commitment and carefully planned change" to reduce DMC (Leiber, Bishop, and Chamlin 2011, 487).[8]

A second possible source of implementation failure involves a focus on post-referral juvenile justice system processing. As we have seen, the major source of racial disproportionalities is the entry of youth into the system via *referral*. Yet the focus of juvenile justice reform more often involves post-referral processing—from preadjudication detention to secure confinement. Dillard (2013, 210) observes that "the focus on the backend of the system has strong historical roots," with little mention of police contact in many early assessments of racial disparities in juvenile justice. Indeed, until 2002 the DMC mandate focused exclusively on *confinement* rather than *contact*. According to this perspective, proper implementation of the DMC mandate requires a shift in focus away from juvenile court judges and toward police and intake officers (Dillard 2013, 215).

B. Theory Failure

The second explanation for persistent DMC in the juvenile justice system is theory failure. Theory failure captures the insight that "attempts to remedy are sure to fail until jurisdictions determine the cause of DMC before launching into a solution" (Nellis and Richardson 2010, 268). Most proposed efforts to reduce DMC are focused on *system* solutions, such as strengthening the DMC mandate's federal requirements for state compliance (e.g., providing cultural sensitivity and implicit bias training for juvenile justice officers), improving systematic data collection, and enacting racial impact statements that require states to assess whether pending legislation will have a disparate impact on minority youth (Nellis and Richardson 2010). But such system solutions will only reduce DMC to the extent that DMC is actually *caused* by system problems.

If attempts to reduce DMC are largely driven by the theory of differential treatment, as they have been (Tracy 2005), then they should be expected to fail to the extent that DMC is due, instead, to differential involvement. For example, one common recommendation for reducing DMC is cultural or racial sensitivity training (see, e.g., Peck 2018). Clearly, this solution assumes differential treatment by the juvenile justice officials or police that would be subject to the training. Notably, however, no research to date indicates that such training is effective at reducing DMC. There is some research that police training may reduce the use of arrests to resolve incidents (Owens et al. 2018) as well as complaints against police (Wood, Tyler, and Papachristos 2020), but no research indicating that such training actually reduces racial disproportionalities at arrest.[9]

As we have seen, DMC is largely a product of differential referrals to the juvenile justice system. If Black youth are more likely to engage in delinquent behavior (or more serious delinquent behavior) and to have more prior contact with the system, this would result in higher referrals rates. According to Davis and Sorenson (2013), about 72% of Black-White disproportionality in (national) juvenile placement in 2019 was explained by differences in arrest—leaving 28% that could be explained by other factors such as differential treatment.[10] The DMC mandate's approach, however, focuses on identifying, assessing, intervening, evaluating, and monitoring racial and ethnic disproportionalities within the juvenile justice system. This approach largely fails to consider that the main cause of disparities may be "structural factors about which state agencies can do little" (Piquero 2008, 62). While the DMC mandate calls for identifying and addressing DMC, it does not mandate identifying the *causes* of DMC. Identifying such causes is necessary for any effort to successfully reduce DMC. On this understanding, then, the failure to reduce DMC is not due to the weak implementation of the DMC mandate, but to its theoretical assumptions regarding the root causes of DMC.

One possibility is *full* theory failure: that DMC is due entirely to differential involvement rather than differential treatment. In such a case, any efforts to address minority overrepresentation by reducing system bias (whether individual or institutional) will fail to have an impact because system bias is not driving DMC (see Tracy 2005). A second possibility is *partial* theory failure, where the problem is that DMC is due to *both* differential treatment and differential involvement. Even here, reforms will encounter only limited success to the extent that they are guided by the assumption of differential treatment. Specifically, efforts to reduce DMC will likely experience diminishing returns if differential treatment is addressed but differential involvement is not—over time, the balance of disproportionality that is due to differential treatment will decrease and the balance due to differential involvement will increase (see Blumstein 1982, 1993, 2009).

IV. What Can Be Done?

Several recommendations for research and policy emerge from this discussion. First, echoing Baumer's (2013) call, more research is needed that identifies the extent to which DMC is caused by differential treatment by juvenile justice system actors. Here, two types of research are needed. The first is research that attempts to overcome omitted variable bias and possibly achieve causal identification of race effects within the juvenile justice system. The second is research that examines the actual decision-making of juvenile justice officials. Second, there is a need for research (and possibly reform) to focus on police contact with juveniles, and how this initial contact produces large Black-White disproportionalities at referral. Third, reforms must occur outside the system that address the social conditions that give rise to differential involvement in crime that may be the main contributor to DMC. Fourth, it is important to keep in mind that general juvenile justice reforms, such as alternatives to detention, benefit minority youth in an absolute sense even if they do not reduce DMC.

A. Beyond "Modal" DMC Research

First, to identify differential treatment or discrimination in juvenile justice, it is necessary to use methods capable of overcoming the omitted variable bias that plagues the vast majority of DMC research—what Baumer (2013) calls the "modal" approach to race and sentencing research. Most promising would be *experimental evidence* that circumvents the problem of omitted variable bias altogether. In the context of criminal justice, some research has exploited natural experiments in order to study whether judges treat defendants differently based on their race (see, e.g., Abrams, Bertrand, and Mullainathan 2012; Cohen and Yang 2019; Yang 2015). Generally, this research literature has found evidence of some differential treatment by judges, such that racial disproportionalities are greater among White judges than Black judges. In the context of juvenile justice, however, I am aware of only one study that has exploited the random assignment of judges to examine the role of race in judicial decision-making (Depew, Eren, and Mocan 2017). Unfortunately, the authors did not attempt to estimate differential treatment of Black and White youth. Instead, they estimated the difference in custody and sentence length according to the race of the juvenile court judge.[11] Future research should attempt to exploit natural experiments or employ other causal identification methods to arrive at robust estimates of differential treatment in juvenile court.

Even more important, however, is that future research study actual decision-making in the juvenile court. While research on actual decision-making is important for the broader race and sentencing literature as well (see Baumer 2013; Ulmer 2012), it is especially important for juvenile court. This is because, even to the extent that disproportionalities in juvenile court represent differential treatment, it may be well-intended and within the paternalistic mission of the court. As Peck (2018, 311) observes:

> [T]here are not enough details in the data to conclude if racial/ethnic differences in juvenile court outcomes are indicative of sole punishment based on racial/ethnic stereotypes or seen as efforts to rehabilitate youth in having a better chance at life outcomes through juvenile court intervention (e.g., removed from negative home environment, substance use treatment, counseling, etc.).

That is, it may be that differential treatment of minority youth does not reflect racial discrimination, but rather individualized consideration of the needs and risks of particular children—and minority children have, on average, greater needs and risks. This of course greatly complicates interpretation of quantitative findings of "race effects" in juvenile justice processing.

Very little research on DMC has actually attempted to identify whether juvenile justice officials are racially biased in their decision-making.[12] One early and oft-cited example is Bridges and Steen (1998), who evaluated 233 narrative reports written by probation officers about juvenile defendants processed in the early 1990s. These were based on school reports and interviews with the youth and youth's family, and included information on the youth's social history and the probation officer's perception of future prospects. In reviewing the reports, the authors found that "probation officers consistently portray black youths differently than white youths" such that the probation officers were more likely to attribute "blacks' delinquency to negative attitudinal and personality traits" while their "depictions of white youths more frequently stress the influence of the individual's social environment" (Bridges and Steen 1998, 567). Findings indicated that in addition to a significant association between race and negative internal attributions, there was a significant association between negative internal attributions and probation officers' sentence recommendations. (Offender race was *not* directly associated with sentence recommendations, however.) While this is an interesting study that potentially suggests evidence of racial discrimination, it also involves a small sample from more than 20 years ago. In fact, the main finding—that internal negative attributions were greater for Black youth—was only marginally statistically significant ($p < .10$ in a one-tailed test).

Surprisingly, almost no research has employed similar approaches more recently.[13] On the one hand, Harris (2009) examined 92 probation fitness reports for Black and Hispanic youth and found that probation officers had consistent "scripts" guided by focal concerns, such that there were no statistically significant differences in the attributions applied to Black and Hispanic youth. On the other hand, Beckman and Rodriguez (2021) reviewed 285 juvenile probation reports and found that the odds of negative internal attributions were significantly higher for Black and Latino youth compared to White youth. Additionally, they found that negative internalized attributions were strongly associated with lower odds of diversion. Interestingly, however—and similar to Bridges and Steen—race and ethnicity were *not* associated with likelihood of diversion after controlling for attributions, and the authors did not examine whether there were indirect race effects mediated by negative internal attributions. Future research must attempt to assess the actual perceptions of juvenile justice decision-makers. Without such research, it may be that the question of differential treatment in the juvenile justice system—and what it *means*—will remain largely unanswered.

B. Enhanced Focus on Arrests and Referrals

Second, future attempts to reduce DMC should focus almost entirely on the point of arrest or referral. As already noted, the main driver of minority overrepresentation in the juvenile justice system involves entrance into the system. While some racial and ethnic disproportionalities appear to be produced within the system, especially at detention (see Zane and Pupo 2021), overall racial disproportionality is overwhelmingly the product of differences in arrest. Relatedly, while the majority of youth referrals involve arrests by police, schools are the second leading source of referrals (Peck 2018).

What causes disproportionalities in juvenile court referrals is really *the* crucial question in understanding DMC—but it remains an underresearched one. In large part, this is due to the unique methodological challenges that are involved in assessing the causes of differences in arrests and referrals (see Neil and Winship 2019). As one scholar laments, "it is virtually impossible really to know whether youths' behavior or police officers' behavior have the greater effect on initial disparities" (Kempf-Leonard 2007, 80). More research is needed on this key decision point, especially in light of theoretical expectations that implicit cognitive biases may be greater compared to other stages of processing (Mears et al. 2017). Ultimately, this means better data and better methods for this important but difficult-to-study decision point (Neil and Winship 2019).

C. The Need for Social Reform

The third major takeaway from this chapter is that reform *within* the juvenile justice system may be limited in its ability to address the root causes of DMC. Specifically, to the extent that DMC is largely the product of broader social forces that contribute to higher levels of offending by certain historically disadvantaged groups, there is little that system reform can accomplish. To the extent that differences in offending persist, DMC will persist. It is really that simple.

The point here is not that differential involvement accounts for *all* racial disproportionality in the juvenile justice system. Indeed, most scholars agree that DMC cannot be *totally* explained by racial differences in offending. As discussed previously, there are valid reasons to suspect that differential treatment and disparate impact of neutral policies also contribute to DMC, especially involving initial contact with police. Still, it seems clear that most of the DMC problem is rooted in group differences in offending. Yet efforts to address DMC thus far seem to have assumed that racial disproportionality in the juvenile justice system is largely caused by differential treatment rather than differential involvement. To the extent that differential involvement is the primary contributor to DMC, system reforms will not address the root problem.

Successful efforts to reduce DMC must be guided by an accurate theory of crime causation. The causes of differential offending by minority youth, especially Black youth, is a "question that, surprisingly, has been ill-studied" (Piquero 2008, 64). Piquero (2015, 27) has more recently observed that "[o]f all the correlates or facts of crime, the one that in my view has been the least studied is that centered on race/ethnic differences in antisocial and criminal behavior over the life course."[14] The best explanations for differential involvement involve structural disadvantage (Sampson and Wilson 1995; Sampson, Wilson, and Katz 2018) as well as cultural adaptations to such disadvantage, such as the "code of the street" (see Anderson 1999). Additionally, there is the possibility of "disparate impact"—that even in the absence of differences in offending, some groups may be more likely to be arrested for certain crimes due to their social environments. For example, Black youth involved in drug dealing in open air street markets are more likely to be arrested than White youth involved in drug dealing out of their suburban backyards—largely because the former is more associated with violence than the latter.[15] Similarly, police may be more likely to view certain behavior as suspicious (and, for example, worthy of a *Terry* frisk for officer safety) in a high-crime area that might not be viewed as suspicious in a low-crime area. Whether due to racial differences in offending (e.g., violent crime) or disparate impact of the way the law is enforced in different social contexts (e.g., drug crime), addressing the root causes of DMC would likely involve large-scale social change rather than justice system reforms.

A host of scholars have made similar observations over the years. Bishop (2014, 246) observed that "minority overrepresentation in the juvenile justice system cannot be addressed adequately through reforms in the justice system itself. It is far more important to attend to structural conditions (poverty, unemployment, racial segregation, family disruption)." Similarly, Bishop and Leiber (2012, 475) note, "To be sure, there are some improvements that can be made within the system, but these are ancillary to the social and economic restructuring that will be required to produce lasting change." More broadly, with respect to the criminal justice system, Tonry (2011, 17) argues that "[o]f course every effort should be made to eliminate bias and stereotyping, but even their diminution will not significantly reduce racial disparities or the absolute number of black people in prisons." Mears and colleagues (2016, 100) likewise observe that "[n]o amount of fair criminal justice processing or sanctioning will compensate for unfair life chances that minorities face."

Policy reform thus needs to move beyond a myopic focus on the justice system. For one, more resources should be dedicated to primary and secondary prevention efforts (as opposed to intervention efforts for system-involved youth), especially developmental prevention aimed at early risk factors for Black children and adolescents (Peck 2018). In addition to direct prevention efforts aimed at individual risk factors, there is also a need to address the structural and cultural conditions that give rise to minority overrepresentation in offending and justice system involvement (see, e.g., Anderson 1999; Sampson 2009; Sampson and Lauritsen 1997; Sampson and Wilson 1995). While addressing these larger macro-social issues may be a slow process with no silver bullet solutions, it is probably necessary to achieve any lasting reductions in DMC.

D. Juvenile Justice System Reform Benefits Overrepresented Minority Youth

Finally, if much or most of DMC is due to factors that cannot be addressed by juvenile justice system reform alone—if such reforms will not reduce DMC without accompanying large-scale social change—does this imply that there is nothing to be done within the system? Not at all. As Zimring (2014, 174) argues, reducing disproportionate minority contact can be conceived in absolute as well as relative terms:

> [T]here are two problems that are rather different when addressing the impact of the system on minority kids, the disproportionate use of sanctions on minorities and the negative effects that these sanctions have on the largely minority kids who are captured by the system. A critic of the system will have two goals—reducing the harm to kids and reducing the proportion of minority kids in the system.

Given that these two goals may sometimes be in conflict, Zimring argues that reform efforts should prioritize overall harm reduction rather than reducing the proportion of minorities in the system. Zimring provocatively suggests that by focusing too much on "equalizing disadvantage," we may lose sight of the larger goal to have less contact with all youth—and focusing on getting the proportions "just right" can actually obscure this larger goal (173).[16] (For example, the simplest way for a cynical prosecutor to reduce minority overrepresentation would be simply to prosecute more White youth.)

While reducing DMC has proven elusive, juvenile justice reforms to date *have* reduced the number of juvenile offenders who are detained prior to adjudication, increased the number who are diverted through informal processing, and reduced the number of youths who are placed under secure confinement or transferred to criminal court. Given that minority youth continue to be overrepresented in the juvenile justice system, they also benefit disproportionately from reforms that reduce overall youth contact with the system. When we focus only on relative disparities, it appears that no progress has been made. Minority overrepresentation remains high, similar to minority overrepresentation in the criminal justice system. But in absolute terms, the rates of confinement in the criminal justice system are three times higher than the juvenile system. Zimring (2014, 184–185) makes this observation:

> The major positive reforms in juvenile justice over the past generation—deinstitutionalization of status offenders and diversion—have not had dramatic impact on the disproportionate involvement of minority youth in the deep end of the juvenile system. But the lower levels of incarceration embraced by juvenile courts mean that the harms suffered within juvenile courts by all sorts of youth are much smaller than the harms imposed on young offenders in America's criminal courts. It turns out that the entire apparatus of juvenile justice is functioning as a substantial harm-reduction program for minority delinquents.

This provides a silver lining to what can be viewed pessimistically as the failure of juvenile justice reform to reduce DMC. The juvenile justice system has dramatically reduced overall youth contact with the system over the past 20 years. While reducing relative disparities may lie beyond the reach of the juvenile justice system and implicate larger social changes, reforms that make the system less punitive and reduce harm will continue to benefit all youth—including minority youth who remain overrepresented within the system.

Notes

1. The term "disproportionate minority contact" was recently replaced by "racial and ethnic disparities" in the Juvenile Justice and Delinquency Prevention Act (JJDPA) of 2018.

2. It is worth comparing to Hispanic youth, who made up 24 percent of the youth population yet only 19 percent of referred youth, 23 percent of detained youth, 18 percent of petitioned youth, 21 percent of adjudicated youth, 24 percent of placed youth, and 12 percent of waived youth (Puzzanchera et al. 2023). While others have tended to emphasize the importance of examining Hispanic-White differences in juvenile justice in addition to Black-White differences (see, e.g., Rodriguez 2007), it is important to highlight that disproportionalities are substantially larger for Black than Hispanic youth.
3. Research indicates that variation in racial disproportionality across states remains after controlling for other factors. Most recently, for example, Zane and colleagues (2020) found significant variation in racial and ethnic disproportionalities in juvenile justice outcomes across four states (especially at detention). This suggests that disproportionalities may be related to differences at the state level as well as the court level, such as differences in organizational structure, law and policy, or even political culture.
4. Elsewhere, in the context of health outcomes, Hebert and colleagues (2008, 374) similarly ask, "When does a difference become a disparity?" The authors answer that the term *disparity* can be defined along a continuum ranging from difference (with no connotation of unfairness) to overt discrimination, stating that "there is little consensus on what constitutes a disparity, or when a difference between two groups should be given the more charged term of disparity. To many, disparity implies an inequity or an injustice rather than a simple inequality" (Hebert, Sisk, and Howell 2008, 374).
5. A third explanation is that, absent bias by individual decision-makers, racial disproportionalities may be produced by the application of seemingly neutral policies or laws—often referred to as "disparate impact." Policies emerging out of the "war on drugs" appear to fit this pattern (see, e.g., Tonry 1995, 2011; Tonry and Melewski 2015). As Tonry and Melewski (2015, 27) put it, "The reason why so many more blacks than whites are arrested for drug crimes is well known and long recognized. They are much easier to arrest." Conceptually, disparate impact can be thought of as a form of differential treatment at the levels of systems or institutions rather than individuals. In terms of policy solutions, however, disparate impact may be more similar to differential involvement in requiring structural changes outside the justice system.
6. There is also the problem that, to the extent that differential involvement exists, it makes it difficult to assess fair treatment at the aggregate level. Using the example of police stops, Neil and Winship (2019, 90) write, "If the offending rate is higher for blacks, then either innocent blacks are stopped at a higher rate or offending whites are stopped at a lower rate. Put differently, there is a trade-off between two types of fairness: differential treatment and some form of disparate impact."
7. Regarding cooperation, research indicates that Black and Latino youth have significantly more negative perceptions of police compared to White youth, even after controlling for other demographics, social bonds, criminal history, and location (see Peck 2015). Negative perceptions of police may translate into different suspect attitudes (i.e., less cooperative) that perpetuate a vicious cycle of mistrust between police and minority youth.
8. There is some evidence that more substantial reforms, such as in Pennsylvania, may have reduced DMC in those counties that funded interventions (see Donnelly 2017, 2019).
9. For example, Lamotte et al. (2010) found that police training designed to reduce DMC in Connecticut was associated with increased *knowledge* of DMC but did not evaluate whether it contributed to a *reduction* in DMC.

10. Davis and Sorenson (2013) followed Blumstein's formula for calculating the proportion of racial disproportionality in imprisonment that was attributable to differences in arrest. Blumstein (1982) initially found that 80% of disproportionality in imprisonment in 1979 was explained by differences in arrest, while Beck and Blumstein (2018, 863) found that in 2004 through 2011, "approximately 70 to 75% of the racial disproportionality among state prisoners is accounted for by black-white differences in arrests." Also, similar to Blumstein's findings, Davis and Sorenson reported that the "explained disproportionality" in placement ranged from a low of 30% for public order crimes and 56% for drug crimes, on the one hand, to 93% for robbery, 102% for sexual assault, 113% for auto theft, and 158% for homicide, on the other. This indicates that the potential post-arrest differential treatment of Black youth appears highest for minor crimes and lowest for serious, violent crimes (where they are actually underrepresented at placement relative to arrests).

11. The authors examined 12,800 cases before 105 juvenile court judges in Louisiana from 1996 to 2012. They found that same-race juvenile-judge assignment increased the odds of custody and length of sentence. That is, Black judges punished Black juveniles more harshly than White judges did, while White judges punished White youth more harshly than Black judges did. To explain this finding, the authors suggested that victims and perpetrators are typically members of the same racial group, such that "judges may be expected to punish perpetrators who cause harm to the in-group" (Depew, Eren, and Mocan 2017, 232).

12. There is also a body of research that assesses the opinions of juvenile justice officials regarding DMC and related issues (see, e.g., Leiber 2003; Mears et al. 2010; Ward et al. 2011). While certainly informative, this kind of research does not actually tell us whether differential treatment contributes to DMC through, for example, racialized attributions on the part of juvenile justice decision makers.

13. As Beckman and Rodriguez (2021, 1538) write, "To our knowledge, Bridges and Steen's (1998) analysis remains the sole empirical test of attribution theory in the context of race and court processing."

14. This reinforces an earlier observation by Sampson and Wilson (1995, 37): "[T]he discussion of race and crime is mired in an unproductive mix of controversy and silence." In their seminal theory of race, violence, and urban inequality, Sampson and Wilson criticized the "subterfuge" of "denying race-related differentials in violence and focusing instead on police bias and the alleged invalidity of official crime statistics . . . in spite of evidence not only from death records but also from survey reports showing that blacks are disproportionately victimized by, and involved in, criminal violence" (38).

15. As Moskos (2008, 76) writes, "In America, most illegal drugs are sold peacefully and privatively among middle-class suburbanites. Violence stems from the minority of drug deals that happen in urban public locales . . . defined by three basic traits: outdoor selling, profits based on high volume, and violence."

16. Zimring (2014) also points out that reforms aimed at reducing overall youth contact with the justice system can also have unanticipated effects in terms of proportional representation, the latter of which involves many complicated factors that cannot be fully controlled. For example, the deinstitutionalization of status offenders may actually *increase* racial disproportionalities to the extent that White youth are overrepresented among status offenders (see Zane 2021).

References

Abrams, David S., Marianne Bertrand, and Sendhil Mullainathan. 2012. Do judges vary in their treatment of race? *The Journal of Legal Studies*, 41 (2): 347–383.

Anderson, Elijah. 1999. *Code of the street: Decency, violence, and the moral life of the inner city*. New York: W. W. Norton.

Baumer, Eric P. 2013. Reassessing and redirecting research on race and sentencing. *Justice Quarterly*, 30 (2): 231–261.

Beck, Allen J., and Alfred Blumstein. 2018. Racial disproportionality in U.S. state prisons: Accounting for the effects of racial and ethnic differences in criminal involvement, arrests, sentencing, and time served. *Journal of Quantitative Criminology*, 34 (3): 853–883.

Beckman, Laura, and Nancy Rodriguez. 2021. Race, ethnicity, and official perceptions in the juvenile justice system: Extending the role of negative attributional stereotypes. *Criminal Justice and Behavior*, 48 (11): 1536–1556.

Bell, James, and Laura John Ridolfi. 2008. *Adoration of the question: Reflections on the failure to reduce racial and ethnic disparities in the juvenile justice system*. San Francisco: W. Haywood Burns Institute.

Blumstein, Alfred. 1982. On the racial disproportionality of United States' prison populations. *Journal of Criminal Law and Criminology*, 73 (3): 1259–1281.

Blumstein, Alfred. 1993. Racial disproportionality of U.S. prison populations revisited. *University of Colorado Law Review*, 64:743–760.

Blumstein, Alfred. 2009. Race and the criminal justice system. *Race and Social Problems*, 1 (4): 183.

Bishop, Donna M. 2014. Race, delinquency, and discrimination: Minorities in the juvenile justice system. In *Controversies in juvenile justice and delinquency*, edited by Peter J. Benekos and Alida V. Merlo, 223–252. 2nd ed. New York: Routledge.

Bishop, Donna M., and Michael J. Leiber. 2012. Racial and ethnic differences in delinquency and justice system responses. In *The Oxford handbook of juvenile crime and juvenile justice*, edited by Barry C. Feld and Donna M. Bishop, 445–484 . Oxford: Oxford University Press.

Bridges, George S., and Sara Steen. 1998. Racial disparities in official assessments of juvenile offenders: Attributional stereotypes as mediating mechanisms. *American Sociological Review*, 63 (4): 554–570.

Cabaniss, Emily R., James M. Frabutt, Mary H. Kendrick, and Margaret B. Arbuckle. 2007. Reducing disproportionate minority contact in the juvenile justice system: Promising practices. *Aggression and Violent Behavior*, 12 (4): 393–401.

Clair, Matthew, and Alix S. Winter. 2016. How judges think about racial disparities: Situational decision-making in the criminal justice system. *Criminology*, 54 (2): 332–359.

Cohen, Alma, and Crystal S. Yang. 2019. Judicial politics and sentencing decisions. *American Economic Journal: Economic Policy*, 11 (1): 160–191.

Crutchfield, Robert D., April Fernandes, and Jorge Martinez. 2010. Racial and ethnic disparity and criminal justice: How much is too much? *Journal of Criminal Law and* Criminology, 100 (3): 903–932.

Davis, Jaya, and Jon R. Sorensen. 2013. Disproportionate minority confinement of juveniles: A national examination of Black-White disparity in placements, 1997–2006. *Crime & Delinquency*, 59:115–139.

Depew, Briggs, Ozkan Eren, and Naci Mocan. 2017. Judges, juveniles, and in-group bias. *Journal of Law and Economics*, 60 (2): 209–239.

Dillard, Dorothy. 2013. Limited disproportionate minority contact discourse may explain limited progress in reducing minority over-representation in the US juvenile justice system. *Youth Justice*, 13:207–217.

Donnelly, Ellen A. 2017. The disproportionate minority contact mandate: An examination of its impacts on juvenile justice processing outcomes (1997–2011). *Criminal Justice Policy Review*, 28:347–369.

Donnelly, Ellen A. 2019. Do disproportionate minority contact (DMC) mandate reforms change decision-making? Decomposing disparities in the juvenile justice system. *Youth Violence and Juvenile Justice*, 17 (3): 288–308.

Elliott, Delbert S. 1994. Serious violent offenders: Onset, developmental course, and termination: The American Society of Criminology 1993 Presidential Address. *Criminology*, 32:1–21.

Elwert, Felix, and Christopher Winship. 2014. Endogenous selection bias: The problem of conditioning on a collider variable. *Annual Review of Sociology*, 40:31–53.

Engen, Rodney L., Sara Steen, and George S. Bridges. 2002. Racial disparities in the punishment of youth: A theoretical and empirical assessment of the literature. *Social Problems*, 49:194–220.

Frase, Richard S. 2013. Research on race and sentencing: Goals, methods, and topics. *Justice Quarterly*, 30:262–269.

Felson, Richard B., Glenn Deane, and David P. Armstrong. 2008. Do theories of crime or violence explain race differences in delinquency? *Social Science Research* 37:624–641.

Felson, Richard B., and Derek A. Kreager. 2015. Group differences in delinquency: What is there to explain? *Race and Justice*, 5:58–87.

Fine, Adam, Sachiko Donley, Caitlin Cavanagh, Sarah Miltimore, Laurence Steinberg, Paul J. Frick, and Elizabeth Cauffman. 2017. And justice for all: Determinants and effects of probation officers' processing decisions regarding first-time juvenile offenders. *Psychology, Public Policy, and Law*, 23 (1): 105–117.

Harris, Alexes. 2009. Attributions and institutional processing: How focal concerns guide decision-making in the juvenile court. *Race and Social Problems*, 1 (4): 243–256.

Hebert, Paul L., Jane E. Sisk, and Elizabeth A. Howell. 2008. When does a difference become a disparity? Conceptualizing racial and ethnic disparities in health. *Health Affairs*, 27 (2): 374–338.

Hindelang, M. J. 1978. Race and involvement in common law personal crimes. *American Sociological Review*, 43 (1): 93–109.

Hockenberry, Sarah, and Charles Puzzanchera. 2021. *Juvenile court statistics, 2019*. Pittsburgh: National Center for Juvenile Justice.

Huizinga, David, Rolf Loeber, and Terence P. Thornberry. 1993. Longitudinal study of delinquency, drug use, sexual activity, and pregnancy among children and youth in three cities. *Public Health* Reports, 108:90–96.

Kempf-Leonard, Kimberly. 2007. Minority youths and juvenile justice: Disproportionate minority contact after nearly 20 years of reform efforts. *Youth Violence and Juvenile Justice*, 5:71–87.

Kurlychek, Megan C., and Brian D. Johnson. 2019. Cumulative disadvantage in the American criminal justice system. *Annual Review of Criminology*, 2 (1): 291–319.

LaMotte, Valerie, Kelly Ouellette, Jessica Sanderson, Stephen A. Anderson, Iva Kosutic, Julie Griggs, and Marison Garcia. 2010. Effective police interactions with youth: A program evaluation. *Police Quarterly*, 13 (2): 161–179.

Leiber, Michael J. 2002. Disproportionate minority confinement (DMC) of youth: An analysis of state and federal efforts to address the issue. *Crime & Delinquency*, 48:3–45.

Leiber, Michael J. 2003. *The contexts of juvenile justice decision making: When race matters.* Albany: State University of New York Press.

Leiber, Michael, Donna Bishop, and Mitchell B. Chamlin. 2011. Juvenile justice decision making before and after the implementation of the disproportionate minority contact (DMC) mandate. *Justice Quarterly*, 28:460–492.

Leiber, Michael J., and Rebecca Fix. 2019. Reflections on the impact of race and ethnicity on juvenile court outcomes and efforts to enact change. *American Journal of Criminal Justice*, 44 (4): 581–608.

Leiber, Michael J., and Jennifer H. Peck. 2013. Race in juvenile justice and sentencing policy: An overview of research and policy recommendations. *Law & Inequality: A Journal of Theory and Practice*, 31:331–368.

Leiber, Michael, and Nancy Rodriguez. 2011. The implementation of the disproportionate minority confinement/contact (DMC) mandate: A failure or success? *Race and Justice*, 1:103–124.

Mears, Daniel. 2022. Bridging the research-policy divide to advance science and policy: The 2022 Bruce Smith, Sr. Award address to the Academy of Criminal Justice Sciences. *Justice Evaluation Journal* 5 (2): 163–185.

Mears, Daniel P. 2010. *American criminal justice policy: An evaluation approach to increasing accountability and effectiveness.* Cambridge: Cambridge University Press.

Mears, Daniel P., Joshua C. Cochran, and Andrea Lindsey. 2016. Offending and racial and ethnic disparities in criminal justice: A conceptual framework for guiding research and informing policy. *Journal of Contemporary Criminal Justice*, 32:78–103.

Mears, Daniel P., Miltonette O. Craig, Eric A. Stewart, and Patricia Y. Warren. 2017. Thinking fast, not slow: How cognitive biases may contribute to racial disparities in the use of force in police-citizen encounters. *Journal of Criminal Justice*, 53:12–24.

Mears, Daniel P., Tracey L. Shollenberger, Janeen B. Willison, Colleen E. Owens, and Jeffrey A. Butts. 2010. Practitioner views of priorities, policies, and practices in juvenile justice. *Crime & Delinquency*, 56 (4): 535–563.

Moskos, Peter. 2008. *Cop in the hood: My year policing Baltimore's eastern district.* Princeton, NJ: Princeton University Press.

Nellis, Ashley, and Brad Richardson. 2010. Getting beyond failure: Promising approaches for reducing DMC. *Youth Violence and Juvenile Justice*, 8:266–276.

Neil, Roland, and Christopher Winship. 2019. Methodological challenges and opportunities in testing for racial discrimination in policing. *Annual Review of Criminology*, 2:73–98.

Puzzanchera, Charles, Anthony Sladky, and Wei Kang. 2023. National Racial and Ethnic Disparities (R/ED) Databook. Office of Juvenile Justice and Delinquency Prevention. https://www.ojjdp.gov/ojstatbb/r-ed-databook/asp/display.asp.

Owens, Emily, David Weisburd, Karen L. Amendola, and Geoffrey P. Alpert. 2018. Can you build a better cop? Experimental evidence on supervision, training, and policing in the community. *Criminology & Public Policy*, 17 (1): 41–87.

Peck, Jennifer H. 2015. Minority perceptions of the police: A state-of-the-art review. *Policing: An International Journal of Police Strategies & Management*, 38 (1): 173–200.

Peck, Jennifer H. 2018. The importance of evaluation and monitoring within the disproportionate minority contact (DMC) mandate: Future directions in juvenile justice research. *Race and Justice*, 8 (4): 305–329.

Piquero, Alex R. 2008. Disproportionate minority contact. *The Future of Children*, 18:59–79.
Piquero, Alex R. 2015. Understanding race/ethcity differences in offending across the life course: Gaps and opportunities. *Journal of Developmental and Life-Course Criminology*, 1:21–32.
Piquero, Alex R., Wesley G. Jennings, Brie Diamond, and Jennifer M. Reingle. 2015. A systematic review of age, sex, ethnicity, and race as predictors of violent recidivism. *International Journal of Offender Therapy and Comparative Criminology*, 59:5–26.
Rodriguez, Nancy. 2007. Juvenile court context and detention decisions: Reconsidering the role of race, ethnicity, and community characteristics in juvenile court processes. *Justice Quarterly*, 24 (4): 629–656.
Rodriguez, Nancy. 2010. The cumulative effect of race and ethnicity in juvenile court outcomes and why preadjudication detention matters. *Journal of Research in Crime and Delinquency*, 47:391–413.
Rossi, Peter H., Mark W. Lipsey, and Howard E. Freeman. 2004. *Evaluation: A Systematic Approach*. 7th ed. Los Angeles: SAGE.
Sampson, Robert J. 2009. Racial stratification and the durable tangle of neighborhood inequality. *Annals of the American Academy of Political and Social Science*, 621:260–280.
Sampson, Robert J., and Janet L. Lauritsen. 1997. Racial and ethnic disparities in crime and criminal justice in the United States. *Crime and Justice*, 21:311–374.
Sampson, Robert J., Jeffrey D. Morenoff, and Stephen Raudenbush. 2005. Social anatomy of racial and ethnic disparities in violence. *American Journal of Public Health*, 95 (2): 224–232.
Sampson, Robert J., and William J. Wilson. 1995. Toward a theory of race, crime, and urban inequality. In *Crime and inequality*, edited by John Hagan and Ruth D. Peterson, 37–56. Stanford, CA: Stanford University Press.
Sampson, Robert J., William J. Wilson, and Hanna Katz. 2018. Reassessing "Toward a Theory of Race, Crime, and Urban Inequality": Enduring and new challenges in 21st century America. *Du Bois Review: Social Science Research on Race*, 15 (1): 13–34.
Sellin, Thorsten. 1935. Race prejudice in the administration of justice. *American Journal of Sociology*, 41 (2): 212–217.
Sickmund, Melissa, T. J. Sladky, Charles Puzzanchera, and Wei Kang. 2021. Easy Access to the Census of Juveniles in Residential Placement: State Comparisons. Office of Juvenile Justice and Delinquency Prevention. https://www.ojjdp.gov/ojstatbb/ezacjrp/.
Sutton, John R. 2013. Structural bias in the sentencing of felony defendants. *Social Science Research*, 42:1207–1221.
Tittle, Charles R., and Debra A. Curran. 1988. Contingencies for dispositional disparities in juvenile justice. *Social Forces*, 67:23–58.
Tonry, Michael. 1995. *Malign neglect: Race, crime, and punishment in America*. New York: Oxford University Press.
Tonry, Michael. 2011. *Punishing race: A continuing American dilemma*. New York: Oxford University Press.
Tonry, Michael, and Matthew Melewski. 2015. The malign effects of drug and crime control policies on Black Americans. *Crime and Justice* 37:1–44.
Tracy, Paul E. 2005. Race, ethnicity, and juvenile justice: Is there bias in postarrest decision making? In *Our children, their children: Confronting racial and ethnic differences in American juvenile justice*, edited by Kimberly Kempf Leonard and Darnell F. Hawkins, 245–269. Chicago: University of Chicago Press.

Ulmer, Jeffrey T. 2012. Recent developments and new directions in sentencing research. *Justice Quarterly*, 29:1–40.

Ward, Geoff, Aaron Kupchik, Laurin Parker, and Brian Chad Starks. 2011. Racial politics of juvenile justice policy support: Juvenile court worker orientations toward disproportionate minority confinement. *Race and Justice* 1 (2): 154–184.

Wilbanks, William. 1987. *The myth of a racist criminal justice system*. Belmont, CA: Brooks/Cole.

Wood, George, Tom R. Tyler, and Andrew V. Papachristos. 2020. Procedural justice training reduces police use of force and complaints against officers. *Proceedings of the National Academy of Sciences*, 117 (18): 9815–9821.

Yang, Crystal S. 2015. "Free at last? Judicial discretion and racial disparities in federal sentencing." *Journal of Legal Studies*, 44 (1): 75–111.

Zane, Steven N. 2021. Have racial and ethnic disparities in juvenile justice reduced over time? An empirical assessment of the DMC mandate. *Youth Violence and Juvenile Justice*, 19 (2): 163–185.

Zane, Steven N., Daniel P. Mears, and Brandon C. Welsh. 2020. How universal is disproportionate minority contact? An examination of racial and ethnic disparities in juvenile justice processing across four states. *Justice Quarterly*, 37 (5): 817–841.

Zane, Steven N., and Jhon A. Pupo. 2021. Disproportionate minority contact in the juvenile justice system: a systematic review and meta-analysis, 1988–2019. *Justice Quarterly*, 38 (7): 1293–1318.

Zane, Steven N., and Jhon A. Pupo. 2023. What predicts out-of-home placement in juvenile court dispositions? A systematic review and meta-analysis. *Journal of Youth and Adolescence* 52 (1): 229–244.

Zane, Steven N., Brandon C. Welsh, Daniel P. Mears, and Gregory M. Zimmerman. 2022. Pathways through juvenile justice: A holistic assessment of cumulative disadvantage in the processing of juvenile offenders. *Journal of Quantitative Criminology*, 38:483–514.

Zimring, Franklin E. 2014. Minority overrepresentation: On causes and partial cures. In *Choosing the Future for American Juvenile Justice*, edited by Franklin E. Zimring and David S. Tanenhaus, 169–186. New York: New York University Press.

CHAPTER 28

APPLYING WHAT WE KNOW AND BUILDING AN EVIDENCE BASE
Reducing Gun Violence

JOHN J. DONOHUE[1]

The 45,247 firearms deaths by all causes in the United States in 2020 was the highest level ever recorded according to data from the Centers for Disease Control and Prevention (CDC)—a 14% increase from 2019 (Ridley 2021). The toll in deaths, injuries, and psychological trauma in the United States is substantial, particularly because we stand at the top of the mountain in suffering these social costs among affluent nations. Firearm deaths now exceed motor vehicle deaths, but are still far lower than deaths attributed to smoking or COVID-19, although gun deaths do fall more heavily on younger Americans than these diseases (Azrael et al. 2018; Cummings et al. 1997; DeSimone, Markowitz, and Xu 2013).

In 2020, the two biggest components of the overall firearm death toll were 19,384 gun homicides and 24,292 gun suicides. Firearm homicides increased by nearly 5,000, or 35%, from 2019 to 2020, while non-firearm homicides only increased by 9.8%. In the United States, most murders are committed with firearms. Specifically, in 2020, 79% of homicides were committed with firearms, an increase of 10 percentage points since 2014 (CDC). The CDC defines "firearm violence" to include all deaths by firearms—which are necessarily rather violent events (CDC 2021). But since suicides are sufficiently differently motivated and often have a different social impact than assaultive crime, it can be useful to limit the discussion of "gun violence" to the criminal use of firearms. I will follow that approach in this chapter.[2]

Under this narrow definition, then, gun violence becomes a subset of violent crime more generally. Vastly more violent crimes do not involve guns than do, but the social costs of gun violence are rising as a percent of all violent crime costs, as guns are increasingly the preferred option for those seeking to murder or attempting to inflict serious bodily injury.[3] Again, one is confronted by a choice of scope: everything that reduces violent crime of any sort will likely reduce gun violence, so a chapter on reducing gun violence could discuss all anti-crime measures from policing (Chalfin and McCrary 2018)[4] and incarceration (Donohue 2009; Wagner and Sawyer 2020; Schnitzer et al. 2019) to social programs (Lyon 2019; see also Davis and Heller 2020; Donohue and Siegelman 1998; Heller 2014; Heller et al. 2017),[5] enhanced street lighting (Chalfin et al. 2022; Mitre-Becerril et al. 2022), surveillance cameras (Caplan, Kennedy, and Petrossian 2011), improved health care and drug treatment,[6] and DNA databases (Anker, Doleac, and Landersø 2021).

A reasonable approach to limit the range of policies to be analyzed would confine the discussion to policies that deal with access to and use of guns and restrictions on types and characteristics of weapons. But this approach has its own challenges, since the Supreme Court's decision in *New York State Rifle & Pistol Association v. Bruen* (2022) reveals that a majority of the Court is uninterested in empirical evidence about gun safety and has expanded the scope of the Second Amendment in a manner that could substantially restrict many aspects of gun safety regulation designed to reduce gun violence. In this event, new forms of gun safety regulation may need to be explored, and in some jurisdictions there may be a renewed interest in adopting some general anti-crime measures that do not involve any focus on firearms.

The chapter will proceed as follows. Section I will discuss the key concept of the instrumentality effect, which highlights that more lethal weapons elevate the likelihood of deaths from criminal assaults. This clearly documented effect is consistent with the general patterns of elevated homicides as well as killings by police in countries and US states with more guns. Section II examines the impact of restricting gun access for high-risk persons, and Section III illustrates the impact of restricting gun carrying outside the home. Section IV discusses the effectiveness of measures designed to limit the lethality of firearms (or make them less appealing to mass shooters), such as bans on assault weapons and large-capacity magazines. Section V explores the impact of age restrictions on gun violence, and Section VI concludes the chapter.

I. THE INSTRUMENTALITY EFFECT

Decades of research has shown that while everything from sticks to knives to firearms can be used in assaults, there is a considerable variation in the survivability of assault depending on the instrumentality employed. Since firearms are considerably more lethal, greater restrictions on access to firearms by those who are at higher risk of engaging in criminal violence is likely to reduce firearm deaths and injuries.

A half-century of consistent empirical evidence has established that there is a strong instrumentality effect in violent activity (Zimring 1972). A seminal 1972 study by UC Berkeley professor Frank Zimring found "that the outcome of gun assaults had a large random element, and that the power of the firearm was one systematic factor influencing the likelihood that an individual with a gunshot injury would survive" (Braga and Cook 2018). An inspired study by Anthony Braga and Phil Cook in 2018 confirmed the accuracy of the Zimring assessment. Braga and Cook examined the files of 511 gunshot victims kept by the Boston Police Department and found that survivability from gunshot wounds varied considerably based on attributes of the weapon and ammunition that generated the wound. The authors calculated that switching to less deadly firearm options could reduce the homicide rate substantially.

The Braga and Cook study documented that the death rate from handgun assault injuries increased substantially as the caliber of the firearm increased. Critically, the caliber was not correlated with observable indicators of the intent and determination to kill by the shooter. This finding is important because it refutes the alternative explanation for the instrumentality effect that choice of weapon simply reflects criminal intent (hence leading to more lethal outcomes). Nor did firearm caliber have any systematic association with the number or location of bullet wounds. But the shooter's use of a medium caliber handgun (.38, .380, and 9 mm) more than doubled the odds of dying compared to small caliber handguns (.22, .25, and .32).[7] Large caliber handguns (.357 magnum or greater) more than doubled the odds of dying compared to medium caliber handguns. The authors conclude:

> The results here support the view that the intrinsic power and lethality of the weapon had a direct effect on the likelihood that a victim of a criminal shooting died. For Boston, in the period studied here, simply replacing larger-caliber guns with small-caliber guns with no change in location or number of wounds would have reduced the gun homicide rate by 39.5%. It is plausible that larger reductions would be associated with replacing all types of guns with knives or clubs. (Braga and Cook 2018, 8)

Based on decades of compelling evidence and research, "it is widely accepted among medical and public health professionals that the likelihood of death in an assault increases with the power of the gun" (Braga and Cook 2018, 2). In 2020, Frank Zimring and Phil Cook shared the Stockholm Prize in Criminology based in part on their work confirming this effect (Stockholm University Department of Criminology 2020).

A. Suggestive International Evidence on Guns and Homicide

Certainly, the core insight from the instrumentality effect—that less lethal weaponry would lead to fewer overall homicides—is consistent with the international evidence that suggests that more guns lead to more homicides. The key elements of this suggestive finding is that (1) the United States does not have more criminals than other affluent nations, (2) the United States has dramatically more guns per capita than any other nation, and (3) the United States clearly has far higher rates of homicide than any other affluent nation. Figure 28.1 shows the relationship between per capita income and homicide rates across 112 countries with at least five million inhabitants, and the basic pattern is that homicide rates fall with wealth as shown by the downward sloping regression line.

Moreover, all of the 31 countries richer than Russia (GDP per capita of $27,200) are essentially at or below the regression line, except for the United States. The population-weighted GDP per capita for these 30 non-US countries is only $43,300, compared to the US value of $62,630. But these other affluent nations have homicide rates of 1.08 per 100,000 and firearm homicide rates of 0.25 per 100,000, compared to the 2019 US values of 5.4 and 4.12, respectively. Based on its wealth, you would expect the United States to have a homicide rate of 1.64 and a firearm homicide rate of 0.27. Indeed, without its massively higher incarceration rates, the outlier status of US homicide rates would be even greater. Moreover, this array of empirical facts also suggests that the notion that gun prevalence could be powerfully restraining homicidal violence through legitimate defensive gun use is unlikely. The working hypothesis that emanates from the international evidence on gun prevalence and homicide in rich countries suggests that more guns in civilian hands will lead to more homicides.

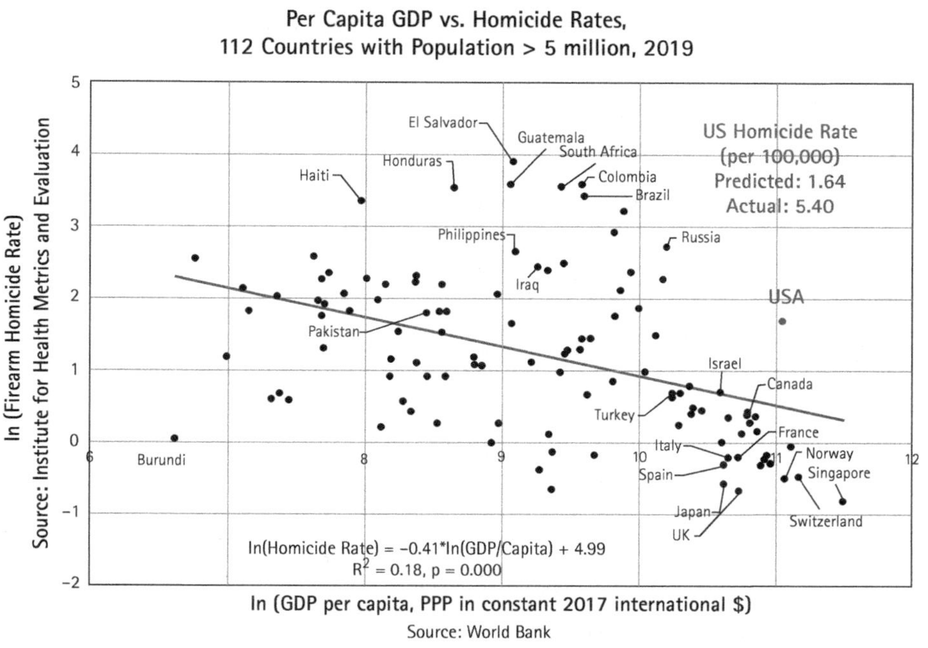

FIGURE 28.1. Per capita GDP vs. homicide rates.

B. Suggestive Evidence from the Individual US States

Figure 28.2 depicts a measure of gun prevalence (the percentage of suicides committed with a firearm) and the CDC homicide rate for all fifty US states in 2020. The regression line clearly trends up, but of course the statistically significant coefficient on gun prevalence cannot tell us whether and to what extent more guns lead to more murders or more murders lead to more guns. This point illustrates the ever-present "challenge of causality" that exists in all observational studies. Cross-sectional analyses involving comparisons across nations or US states are limited in their capacity to sort out the simultaneous relations between guns and crime, but more advanced techniques, such as panel data regression and synthetic controls, are better suited to the ultimate goal of establishing causal relationships.

The graph reveals the enormous variation in the murder rates for similar levels of the gun prevalence index: for example, compare Louisiana's rate of 18.9 per 100,000 with Idaho's rate of 2.3 per 100,000, despite their roughly equal, high levels of gun prevalence. Obviously, many factors influence a state's murder rate besides the prevalence of guns.

C. Panel Data Evidence on Gun Prevalence and Homicide

For decades, evidence has been building that firearm accessibility in the home increases rather than decreases the risk of homicide victimization and suicide (Anglemyer, Horvath, and Rutherford 2014). A new, meticulous study with extraordinarily detailed individual

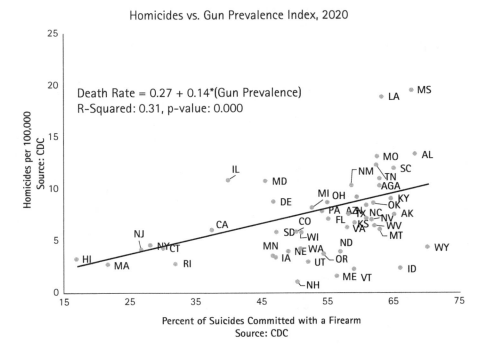

FIGURE 28.2. Homicides vs. Gun Prevalence Index, 2020.

Source: Donohue et al. (2022), depicting the impact of RTC laws on violent crime using the DAW Model, 1979–2019; 95% confidence intervals using cluster-robust standard errors and the number of states contributing to each estimate displayed.

data from 2004–2016 has shown that almost 600,000 California residents who did not own guns but lived with others who did had a considerably higher risk of dying by homicide (Studdert et al. 2022). The authors used extended Cox proportional hazard models adjusted for cohort members' gender, age, racial and ethnic group, and, partially, the presence of a long gun in the home to examine the impact of gun carrying. The models allowed the baseline hazard to vary by census tract, ensuring that people who resided with handgun owners (exposed) were compared only with people living in gun-free homes (unexposed) in the same small neighborhood. In this way, the study adjusted for local factors, such as crime rates and economic conditions, that may have confounded the relationship of interest. In other words, bringing a gun in the home elevates the risk of death, thereby undermining the view that private gun purchases on balance protect household members from homicidal victimization.

But even if the detailed information using individual data reveals that a gun purchase increases the risk of death for the purchaser and his family, greater private gun possession could still have a broader deterrent value if criminals reduce their activity because of an actual or perceived increased risk of encountering armed resistance. The combined effect of the increased risk in the home of the gun purchaser plus any deterrent umbrella generated by this possession can only be assessed with macro data that captures all of the consequences of increased gun prevalence. Cook and Ludwig (2006) provide this evidence in their attempt to sort out the causal link between gun prevalence and homicide in a county-level panel data analysis for the period 1980–1999. They summarize their primary finding as follows:

> In sum, gun prevalence is positively associated with overall homicide rates but not systematically related to assault or other types of crime. Together, these results suggest that an increase in gun prevalence causes an intensification of criminal violence—a shift toward greater lethality, and hence greater harm to the community. (387)[8]

Cook and Ludwig deem that this link is strongest for handguns, which are the preferred firearm for most gun violence. This fact would support measures that would limit access to handguns, but the options for permissible regulation of handguns has itself been restricted in the United States since the Supreme Court's controversial 5–4 *Heller* decision in 2008 struck down a handgun ban in the District of Columbia.

D. Gun Prevalence and Killings by US Police

While in recent years COVID-19 and the failure to vaccinate have been the greatest threat to police officers in terms of overall causes of work-related deaths, Zimring (2017) has shown that virtually the only assaultive threat to police officers comes from those with firearms. Since offenders may well find it easier to access a gun in the informal or underground market in jurisdictions where gun possession is common, higher overall firearm availability may increase the risks to police officers, who may in turn resort to more deadly force than might otherwise be the case. When Daniel Nagin (2020) explored this relationship, he found a clear link between gun prevalence and killings *by* police, even after controlling for the level of crime in the jurisdiction.[9] It is interesting to speculate whether and to what extent greater gun prevalence explains not only the fact that US police officers kill Americans at vastly higher rates than police in other affluent nations, but also whether these killings in turn generate feedback effects that strain community-police relations in ways that elevate overall crime in the United States.

II. Efforts to Restrict Gun Access for Those at Elevated Risk of Engaging in Criminal Activity Effectively Reduces Crime

The Braga and Cook revelation that one might be able to achieve a 40% reduction in firearm homicides simply through a reduction in the caliber of handguns—with perhaps even greater reductions through broader firearm prohibitions—is certainly intriguing, but a number of complexities must first be addressed. First, if one could eliminate higher-caliber handguns, would this diminish the effectiveness of guns as a tool of self-defense? Since the vast majority of the time that guns are used defensively they are only brandished, this would suggest that caliber reduction would not be a major impediment to defensive gun use.[10]

Second, one must consider whether any prohibition on higher-caliber weapons can effectively reduce the number of banned weapons in the hands of those who would misuse them. The claim that such prohibitions will only disarm the law-abiding is not persuasive, since the categories of those who will and will not use guns in a criminal manner are not readily identifiable. Just in the month of May 2022, "law-abiding citizens" who exercised their Second Amendment rights to legally purchase assault rifles killed 10 in a Buffalo supermarket, 21 in an elementary school in Uvalde, Texas, and 4 in a hospital in Tulsa. If they had been restricted to less lethal weapons, the death toll would likely have been lower (and the severely criticized police in Texas might have been more willing to urgently confront the shooter).

An alternative to reducing the lethality of legal weaponry is to either adopt initiatives designed to restrict firearm acquisition by those who are deemed to be at risk for violence or to punish more harshly those who do in fact use firearms to commit violent crime. A number of persuasive studies conclude that such measures can be successful.

A. California's 1991 Gun Ban for Those Convicted of a Violent Misdemeanor

In 1991, California expanded the list of conditions that prohibited an individual from legally purchasing a firearm to include the commission of a violent misdemeanor (the prohibition was for a period of 10 years). Professor Garen Wintemute and a team of researchers (Wintemute et al. 2001) did a careful study that showed that the 1991 law substantially reduced violent criminal offending for the covered group. Specifically, the researchers examined the criminal records of two groups over a three-year period: the treatment group consisted of 927 persons aged 21 to 34 years who *attempted* to purchase a handgun in California in 1991 but were denied because of prior convictions for violent misdemeanors. The control group included 787 persons who also had prior convictions for misdemeanor violence but legally purchased handguns in 1989 or 1990 (prior to the law's adoption) and were of the same age range as the group denied in 1991 (the authors also controlled for sex and criminal history). The control group, which was able to buy firearms just prior to the 1991 restrictions, had a 29% *higher* rate of future criminal offending involving guns and/or violence than the treatment group that was prohibited from purchasing weapons. Importantly, the two groups did not differ in terms of future criminal offending that did not involve firearms or violence.

This well-crafted study illustrates that when California restricted the ability of certain high-risk individuals to purchase guns, there was a documented reduction in violent crime among those individuals. By looking at roughly comparable individuals before and after California began barring individuals with convictions for misdemeanor violence from gun possession, the researchers could estimate whether the background check system curtailed the violence of the newly banned individuals. The study concluded that denying firearm purchases to this category of applicants significantly reduced "future criminal offending involving firearms and/or violence" by 22% (=29/129).

B. The 1996 Lautenberg Amendment Reduced Domestic Violence

Similar evidence that gun violence could be reduced by prohibiting gun possession by those with a conviction of misdemeanor domestic violence was also presented by Raissian (2016). In 1996, Congress adopted the Lautenberg Amendment, which for the first time disqualified those with a misdemeanor conviction for domestic violence from obtaining or possessing firearms. This federal law became operative immediately in states that had a domestic-assault statute, but it was challenged in states that lacked a distinct domestic-violence statute (as opposed to a general law of assault). These legal challenges delayed implementation in various federal circuit courts of appeals, and it took 13 years before eight of the nine US circuit courts, and finally the US Supreme Court, ruled that no distinct domestic violence statute was needed for the ban to apply as long as the crime involved a domestic victim.

Raissian (2016) was able to exploit the staggered implementation of the gun prohibition and found that the law restrained domestic violence both before a conviction (because of the threat of losing one's gun rights) and after (because there are severe federal penalties for a disqualified person who uses a gun to commit assault and because the amendment would screen out convicted batterers trying to buy a gun from a dealer). Raissian concluded that the gun ban reduced killings of female intimate partners by 17%, with no indication of substitution to other weapon types.

C. California's Universal Background Check Screens Out Felons and Reduces Violence

A second study by Professor Wintemute and his fellow researchers documents another successful effort in California to keep guns away from higher-risk individuals, thereby generating a substantial and statistically significant reduction in crime (Wright, Wintemute, and Rivara 1999). This study looked at individuals who were both arrested for felonies *and* later sought to buy guns. Of this pool of arrestees, the treatment group was composed of 177 individuals who were convicted, which then stopped them from lawfully buying a weapon, since the universal background check screened them out because of their felony convictions.

The second group of arrestees—the control group—was composed of 2,470 individuals who succeeded in buying guns because they were not convicted of any felony (despite the felony arrest). As between the two groups, one would imagine, if anything, the treatment group would be more criminally disposed than the control group, because the former group had all been convicted of a felony, while the control group had not. But the study showed the ability to buy guns was a more potent criminogenic factor: the control group had a *higher* crime rate by virtue of the ability to legally purchase and possess firearms (adjusting for the nature and extent of their prior criminal history). The law preventing the felons from buying guns led to a 19.4% (=24/124) statistically significant reduction in their future violent criminality.

D. California Goes After the Guns of Known Felons and Other Prohibited Purchasers

Ben-Michael, Feller, and Raphael (2021) assess whether the Armed and Prohibited Persons System (APPS) database launched in 2006 affected murder rates in California. APPS uses existing data to identify firearm owners among persons who have become prohibited from owning firearms as a result of a new criminal conviction or other event. Law enforcement officers then seek to recover those firearms. A special legislative appropriation funded a three-year trial to eliminate the backlog of such cases, and the California Department of Justice staged the recovery effort in a place-based randomized pattern to aid in assessing its effectiveness at reducing crime.

The authors used a synthetic control analysis to implement this assessment. This approach is designed to select a group of states that when appropriately weighted has a similar pattern of violent crime prior to California's 2006 adoption of the APPS program. This weighted group of states is the "synthetic control," which can then be used to generate a plausible counterfactual for the California in the years after adoption. Comparing the post-adoption crime path of California with its synthetic control over the same years generates an estimate of the impact on violent crime of the California program.

The authors successfully generated a good pretreatment fit for the rate of homicide for the state of California. After treatment, the homicide rates for California and its synthetic control diverge greatly and the gap widens for 11 years. Relative to California's synthetic control, California's murder rate decreased by 24% (equivalent to 1.64 per 100,000). When the authors disaggregated gun from nongun homicides and constructed the synthetic controls of those two groups, they found that the difference between the synthetic estimates and California's true rate hovered around zero for nongun homicides while gun homicides dropped by 1.22 per 100,000 population.

E. Deterring the Criminal Use of Guns with Enhanced Penalties

Abrams (2012) disentangles the deterrence and incapacitation effects of incarceration by exploiting the staggered state-level adoption of "add-on" gun laws, which impose a sentence enhancement for convicted felons found to have possessed a firearm during the commission of the felony. Using a two-way fixed-effects model that includes a variety of demographic covariates as well as a control for the presence of mandatory minimum laws over a nearly 40-year time interval, Abrams's preferred model shows that, three years after passage, add-on laws reduce gun robbery rates by about 5%. Abrams concludes that this reduction stems from a deterrent effect, because even without the add-on law, felons would still be in prison for the underlying offense in this short period after adoption. Of course, the add-on penalty would ultimately have an incapacitative effect (adding to the deterrent effect) for those who remain in prison longer because of the harsher sentencing law.

III. Restrictions on Gun Carrying Outside the Home

Gun carrying outside the home generates an array of lethal or adverse outcomes that must be carefully weighed against any possible benefits from gun carrying. New York City has been among the most active jurisdictions in trying to reduce these harmful consequences, and it has enjoyed an enviable level of success in crime reduction over the last three decades. Indeed, the violent crime reduction in the states that have resisted the move toward right-to-carry (RTC) laws dwarfs the improvements in crime rates experienced by states that have stimulated greater gun carrying by adopting RTC laws.

A. The Best Recent Empirical Evidence Supports the Value of Restricting Gun Carrying in Reducing Violent Crime

While early research suggested that RTC laws might have overall beneficial impacts on violent crime, those studies were largely dismissed by a report of the National Research Council (2005).[11] The best, modern research, which has benefited from improvements in econometric methodology as well as the increase in the number of states adopting RTC laws and the longer period of years available for study, has decidedly tipped in the direction of finding that RTC laws *increase* violent crime.

A 2019 paper by Donohue, Aneja, and Weber (hereinafter DAW) examined the impact on violent crime from the adoption of state laws granting citizens a right to carry guns outside the home (either with or without a requirement to secure a permit to do so). DAW used two empirical approaches employing data from all 50 states and the District of Columbia from 1979–2014: a panel data analysis with state- and year-fixed-effects and a synthetic controls analysis generating estimates for 33 states that adopted RTC laws over that time period. Both approaches revealed a similar pattern: the impact of RTC adoption led to an immediate increase in and worsening pattern of violent crime that was substantial and statistically significant. The panel data estimate of the average effect of RTC laws across the post-adoption period was 9%, and the synthetic control analysis indicated that the average increase in violent crime grew to 13–15% by the 10th year after adoption.

1. DAW Panel Data Analysis Links RTC Laws with Increased Violent Crime

Figure 28.3 depicts the panel data estimates of how RTC laws influence crime for each year after adoption. The figure shows that the DAW econometric model works well: *prior* to RTC law adoption, the model is predicting the law would have no effect—exactly what a researcher would want the model to predict for a law that is not yet passed. As soon as the law goes into effect, however, one sees there is a growing price to be paid in terms of increasing violent crime. This panel data model controls for a variety of criminal justice, socioeconomic, and demographic factors that could also influence violent crime, such as the lagged incarceration rate, the lagged police employee rate, real per capita personal income,

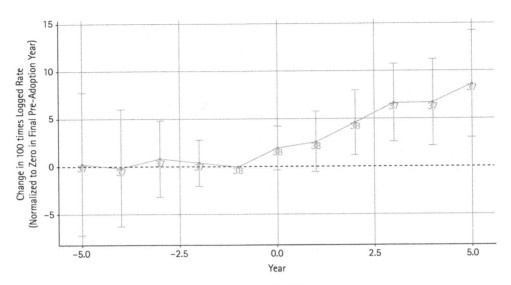

FIGURE 28.3. Violent crime rises with passage of RTC laws.

Source: Donohue et al. (2022) depicting the impact of RTC laws on violent crime using the DAW Model, 1979–2019. 95 percent confidence intervals using cluster-robust standard errors and the number of states contributing to each estimate displayed.

the unemployment rate, poverty rate, beer consumption, the percentage of the population living in MSAs, and six demographic variables (based on different age-sex-race categories). The overall estimated 9% increase in violent crime was statistically significant ($p = .002$).

2. DAW Synthetic Controls Analysis Links RTC Laws with Increased Violent Crime

DAW also generated synthetic control estimates for 33 states and probed the sensitivity of these estimates using an array of different implementation choices available for synthetic controls analyses. Across every model, the results tightly converged to a finding that RTC laws increase violent crime by 13–15% by the 10th year after adoption. Plausible estimates of the elasticity of crime with respect to incarceration are around −0.15, which implies that the average RTC state would need to approximately double its prison population to offset the increase in crime caused by RTC adoption. In other words, the social costs of allowing citizens to carry guns outside the home as a matter of right are substantial.

3. The Recent Literature Supports the Conclusion that RTC Laws Increase Violent Crime

Most recent studies, which have the advantage of access to both more complete data and improved empirical methodologies, have found that RTC laws lead to *higher* rates of violent crime and/or homicide. In January 2023, RAND released an updated version of its analysis of the literature on the impact of RTC laws, in which it concluded—at its highest level of evidentiary support—that RTC laws increase total and firearm homicides (RAND 2023). Table 28.1 describes 17 *additional* empirical papers from just the last six years linking RTC laws to higher violent crime.

Table 28.1. The Growing Evidence of the Link between RTC Laws and Higher Violent Crime

Article	Findings
1. Donohue (2017)	Notes that RTC laws increased firearm homicides by 9.5% during the 2000–2014 period.
2. Siegel et al. (2017)	Finds that RTC laws increase overall homicides rose by 6.5% and firearm homicides rose by 8.6%.
3. Crifasi et al. (2018)	Finds that "[r]ight-to-carry laws are associated with increases in firearm homicide."
4. McElroy and Wang (2018)	McElroy and Wang's model indicates that RTC laws increase violent crime and "strongly rejects Lott and Mustard (1997)'s famous deterrence hypothesis."
5. Doucette, Crifasi, and Frattaroli (2019)	Finds that from 1992 to 2017, having an RTC law was significantly associated with 29% higher rates of firearm workplace homicides.
6. Gius (2019)	Finds that "states that changed from 'prohibited' to 'shall issue' [RTC laws] experienced a 12.3% increase in gun-related murder rates and a 4.9% increase in overall murder rates."
7. Knopov et al. (2019)	After examining "the relationship between state firearm laws and homicide victimization rates . . . in 39 states during the period between 1991 and 2016, [the study found that] 'shall issue' [RTC laws] laws were associated with [5.7 percent] higher homicide rates among both white and black populations."
8. Siegel et al. (2019)	Finds that "after simultaneously controlling for . . . 10 firearm laws, . . . 'shall issue' [RTC] laws were associated with 9.0% higher homicide rates."
9. Fridel (2021a)	Finds that "more permissive concealed carry legislation was associated with a 10.8% increase in the firearms homicide incidence rate, yet had no significant effect on mass shootings."
10. Sabbath et al. (2020)	Finds that "restricting the ability to carry concealed weapons "was associated with a 5.79% reduction" in workplace homicide rates.
11. Billings (2021)	Finds "strong evidence that increases in CHPs [Concealed Handgun Permits] coincide with large increases in stolen guns, [followed by] an increase in violent crimes as well as an increase in the share of violent crime using guns. This is consistent with a mechanism of stolen guns being transferred to criminals that are using guns to commit violent crimes."
12. Van Der Wal (2022)	Finds that "RTC laws significantly increase violent crime by 7.5%."
13. Fridel (2021b)	After showing the robustness of her findings that RTC laws increase firearm homicides, Fridel concludes "it is imperative that firearms research prioritizes the use of contemporary data and methods to shape policies for contemporary problems."

(continued)

Table 28.1. Continued

Article	Findings
14. Doucette et al. (2023)	Finds that "shall-Issue CCW law adoption was associated with a 9.5% increase in rates of assaults with firearms during the first 10-years post-law adoption."
15. Doucette et al. (2022)	Finds that "permitless CCW adopting states saw a 12.9% increase in the OIS victimization rate."
16. Stansfield, Semenza, and Silver (2023)	After noting "increases in the number of CCWs in 2010–2017 were statistically associated with increases in total gun homicide in 2011–2018," the authors conclude that "far from concealed carry making people safer, our model finds acute safety risks associated with expansion of legal firearm carrying."
17. Donohue et al. (2022)	Finds that RTC laws spur large increases in violent crime, caused in part by substantial jumps in gun thefts and diminished police effectiveness.

B. Potential Victims Use Guns Defensively Less Than 0.9% of the Time They Are Confronted by a Criminal

If, as the studies outlined suggest, gun carrying outside the home for protection against violent crime *increases* overall violent crime, then permissive gun carrying cannot be socially beneficial on average, because there is no crime-reduction benefit to offset the array of other costs that gun carrying imposes. Indeed, this would be true even if RTC laws had *no* impact on violent crime, since again there would be no crime-reduction benefit to offset its other costs. Those who believe that guns are socially protective often think that there are enormous numbers of defensive gun uses each year. Unfortunately, these figures are often grotesquely exaggerated and should not be relied upon.

One federal judge striking down California's restrictions on large-capacity magazines cited the study often referenced by the gun lobby, "which estimated that there are 2.2 to 2.5 million defensive gun uses by civilians each year. Of those, 340,000 to 400,000 defensive gun uses were situations where defenders believed that they had almost certainly saved a life by using the gun" (*Duncan v. Becerra* [2019], citing Kleck and Gertz [1995]). These numbers are highly implausible. The largest number of homicides in any year since 1933 was roughly 25,000, so the idea that private gun use saved anywhere near the quoted numbers strains credulity. Of course, if guns powerfully saved lives in the aggregate, the United States would have a low rate of homicide given its extensive arsenal, but instead we have homicide rates vastly higher than other affluent nations.

Hemenway and Solnick (2015) highlight why the simple surveys that invite respondents to report if they have used a gun for self-defense are inherently unreliable, while the more professional, vastly larger, and more tailored approach of the National Crime

REDUCING GUN VIOLENCE 563

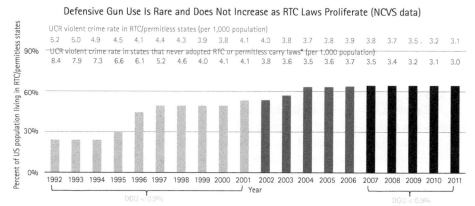

FIGURE 28.4. Defensive gun use is rare and does not increase as RTC laws proliferate (NCVS data).

Note: City-level panel data estimate of the impact of RTC laws on the share of robberies committed with a firearm, 1979–2019, controlling for lagged incarceration, lagged sworn officers per capita, percent of household led by females, percent of households consisting of an individual living alone, percent below poverty line, per capita income, and four demographic controls. 95% confidence intervals using standard errors clustered at the state level displayed.

Victimization Survey (NCVS) is far more likely to generate meaningful data on defensive gun use. The best evidence on the percentage of crimes in which a victim does use a gun defensively is less than 0.9% of the time that victims are confronted by criminals. Interestingly, as Figure 28.4 shows, the NCVS data revealed an identical but extremely low percentage of defensive gun uses for both 1992–2001 as well as for 2007–2011. This constant and low percentage is telling because it shows that as RTC laws expanded greatly across the nation, there was absolutely no increase in the likelihood that a potential victim would defend against crime with a gun. Specifically, in the first period from 1992 to 2001, 41% of the population lived in states with RTC (or permitless carry) laws. By, the second period, this percentage had jumped to 67%—a 63% increase in the proportion of the country living in RTC states. And yet this massive increase in gun carrying did nothing to elevate the overall likelihood of defensive gun use, which was at exactly the same low rate it had been in the earlier period.

Note that the period after 1992 was one of declining crime for a variety of reasons, but the growth in RTC laws does not appear to be one of them. The first two rows of Figure 28.4 highlight that the 64.3% drop in violent crime in the nine states and the District of Columbia that had no RTC law at any time over this period was vastly greater than the crime drop in RTC states.

The best evidence on the protective benefits from firearms comes from the analysis of NCVS data by Hemenway and Solnick (2015), which finds that "of over 14,000 incidents in which the victim was present, 127 (0.9%) involved a [self-defense gun use] SDGU. After any protective action, 4.2% of victims were injured; after SDGU, 4.1% of victims were injured."

The authors conclude that, "[c]ompared to other protective actions, the National Crime Victimization Surveys provide little evidence that SDGU is uniquely beneficial in reducing the likelihood of injury."

An often overlooked factor when considering the impacts of more gun carrying outside the home is that it tends to encourage more gun carrying by criminals. Figure 28.5 again depicts the results of a panel data model evaluating the impact of RTC laws, and it shows that the percentage of robberies committed with a firearm *increases* sharply after adoption of a RTC law. This obviously socially harmful response might even be worth tolerating if the increased legal arms carrying reduced rates of robbery, but there is not even the slightest evidence that it does.

Another overlooked unintended consequence of greater gun carrying is the large increase in lost and stolen guns. Indeed, guns are stolen far more frequently than they are even attempted to be used for defensive purposes, and there is considerable evidence that gun carrying outside the home leads to higher levels of gun thefts.[12] Donohue, Aneja, and Weber (2019) estimated that the increased gun carrying by roughly 16 million permit holders induced by RTC laws has increased the number of gun thefts by roughly 100,000 per year, since guns left in cars and elsewhere by permit holders are easy targets for thieves. Donohue and colleagues (2023) find that, in cities with an average population of over 250,000 between 1979 and 2019, the introduction of RTC increases violent crime by 20%, in part fueled by a 50% increase in gun theft.

The recent empirical literature on the link between stolen guns and crime highlights the importance of this pathway in elevating violent crime. Stephen Billings (2022) examines an

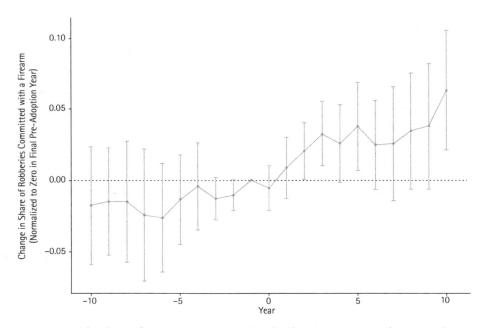

FIGURE 28.5. The share of robberies committed with a firearm increases after RTC adoption.

Note. City-level panel data estimate of the impact of RTC laws on the share of robberies committed with a firearm, 1979–2019, controlling for lagged incarceration, lagged sworn officers per capita, percent of household led by females, percent of households consisting of an individual living alone, percent below poverty line, per capita income, and four demographic controls. 95 percent confidence intervals using standard errors clustered at the state level displayed.

extraordinarily rich data set with information on individuals who have obtained a concealed handgun permit (such as name, date of birth, address, date of permit issue) linked with reported crimes and arrests from 2007–2011 in Charlotte, North Carolina. Billings finds that gun thefts rise sharply with the increase in RTC permits, which in turn leads to increased violent crime. Similarly, Khalil (2017) analyzes crime data from the National Incident-Based Reporting System (NIBRS) for over 400 jurisdictions from 34 different states from 1993–2010 and finds that the number of firearms reported stolen in each police jurisdiction leads to statistically significant increases in homicide, aggravated assault, and robbery.

IV. The Increasing Danger from the Growing Lethality of Firearms

One of the unfortunate consequences of the continuing advances in the lethality and power of modern firearms is that without appropriate government action the dangers posed by civilian weaponry will continue to outpace any legitimate benefit that firearms might provide. The lesson of the November 2017 massacre at the Sutherland Springs Baptist Church in Texas highlights the growing dangers. The killer in that case used an AR-15 rifle that was modified to include a laser scope and features that could allow large-capacity magazines (LCMs) to be more quickly reloaded to maintain a relentless barrage. The killer stood outside and fired straight through the walls of the church as he strafed along at just above the top of the levels of the church pews, allowing him to shoot 254 shots from outside the church in a matter of minutes on his way to killing 26 men, women, and children. No portable weapon in civilian hands at the time of the adoption of the Second Amendment could possibly generate this degree of destruction.

Similarly, the shooter at a Las Vegas country music concert in October 2017 took advantage of the power of assault weapons and large-capacity magazines, magnified with new bump-stock technology, to kill 60 and wound 487 others (Gomez and White 2017). New inexpensive and increasingly available technologies, such as the auto sear, can convert a semi-automatic pistol or AR-15 into a weapon that is fully automatic, able to fire off all of the rounds in a magazine with the single pull of the trigger (Stephens and Hamilton 2022).

Sadly, the capacity for mayhem extends even beyond assault weapons, as modern pistols can be powerful enough to easily penetrate walls and allow a large number of bullets to be fired in a short amount of time. No concealed weapon available to an unemployed 21-year-old in 1791 could in a few minutes fire 70 bullets, killing nine with at least five bullet holes in each victim, as Dylann Roof was able to do in a Charleston church in July 2015 (Robles and Stewart 2015). The evident social harms will likely continue to grow as gun technology increases firearm lethality.

A. Bans on Assault Weapons and Large-Capacity Magazines

The first scholar to document the beneficial effect of the federal assault weapons ban in reducing mass shooting deaths was Louis Klarevas, the author of *Rampage Nation: Securing*

America from Mass Shootings (2016). The experience from before, during, and after the 10-year period from 1994 to 2004 when the federal assault weapons ban was in effect provides important evidence that this federal law saved lives and reduced the mayhem from the deadliest mass shootings. Examining gun massacres in which at least six were killed, Klarevas found that these incidents and the number of resulting deaths fell during the decade in which the federal assault weapons ban was in place and then rebounded when the ban was lifted in 2004.

I thought it would be useful to further explore the Klarevas finding with different data, and thus turned to the *Mother Jones* database of mass shootings (Follman, Aronsen, and Pan 2022). This database limits the gun crimes to killings occurring in a public place and omits killings related to armed robbery, gang activity, or domestic violence, in accord with recent FBI practice. Based on these criteria, Figure 28.6 shows the number of incidents of such gun massacres and the deaths resulting therefrom (Donohue and Boulouta 2019a, 2019b). The figure illustrates clearly that the number and deadliness of these mass shootings dropped during the 10 years of the federal assault weapons ban from September 1994 through 2004 and rose sharply after the federal ban was lifted.[13] Although the number of incidents is too limited to highlight the 25% drop in gun massacres, the 40% drop in overall fatalities during the period of the federal ban is substantial and noteworthy.

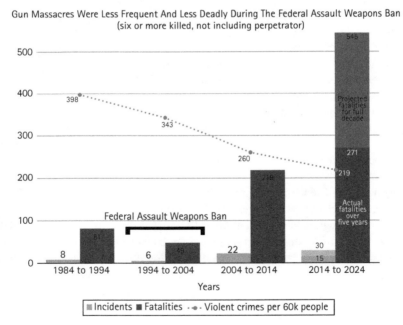

Mass shooting data from Mother Jones; dates begin and end in September to reflect the period from 9/13/1994 to 9/12/2004 when the federal assault weapons ban was in place, except for the last column, which ends in 9/2/2019. Violent crime rate data from UCR; dots mark ten-year averages, except for the last dot, which ends in 6/2018.

FIGURE 28.6. Gun massacres were less frequent and less deadly during the Federal Assault Weapons Ban.

After the federal ban lapsed in 2004, the gun market was flooded with increasingly more powerful weaponry that allowed mass killers to kill ever more quickly, with predictable results. The decade after the ban elapsed saw a 266% increase in mass shooting incidents and a 347% increase in fatalities, even as overall violent crime continued downward (reflected in the dotted line in Figure 28.6). In other words, my independent assessment confirms the pattern first revealed by Louis Klarevas: gun massacres fell during the assault weapons ban and rose sharply when it was removed in 2004.

What has happened since 2014 is even more alarming. In five years, the number of fatalities in these gun massacres has already topped the previous high that occurred during the first decade after the federal assault weapon ban was removed. This murderous leap has occurred at the same time that overall violent crime persisted on a downward trend, as the dotted line in Figure 28.6 confirms.[14] If we continue at the post-2014 pace until 2024, the last column of Figure 28.6 shows that we will have an astonishing order of magnitude increase in gun massacre deaths over a 20-year period.[15]

The evident effectiveness of the assault weapons ban in reducing mass shooting deaths should not be surprising: during the decade of the federal assault weapons ban, mass killers could not simply enter a gun store and buy an assault weapon with a large-capacity magazine, as they can do in most of the United States today.[16]

Figure 28.7 illustrates the average number of fatalities in each mass shooting for the same four periods shown in Figure 28.6. The pattern is the same: fatalities per incident fell during the federal assault weapon ban and have risen sharply thereafter. With the weaponry available to citizens getting increasingly more potent and plentiful, the average number of people who die in every incident has increased by 90% since the decade after elimination of the assault weapons ban.

Assault weapons and/or large-capacity magazines were used in all 15 gun massacres since 2014 in which at least six people were killed (other than the shooter), as shown in Figure 28.6; all 273 people who died in these 15 gun massacres were killed by weaponry prohibited under the federal assault weapons ban.[17]

B. Panel Data Evidence on the Violence-Reducing Impacts of Bans on Assault Weapons and Large-Capacity Magazines

A number of studies have evaluated the impact of bans on assault weapons and large-capacity magazines that hold more than 10 rounds. Post et al. (2021) examined data on mass shootings that killed at least four individuals from 1966 to 2019 and found that the federal assault weapons ban in place from 1994–2004 "resulted in a significant decrease in public mass shootings, number of gun deaths, and number of gun injuries."

Siegel et al. (2020) explored the impact of bans on large-capacity magazines over the period 1976–2018 and found that these bans led to "38% fewer fatalities (95% CI [12%, 57%]) and 77% fewer nonfatal injuries (95% CI [43%, 91%]) when a mass shooting occurred." Looking at the period from 1990 to 2017, Klarevas (2016) found that "states without [a large-capacity magazine] ban experienced significantly more high-fatality mass shootings and a higher death rate from such incidents."

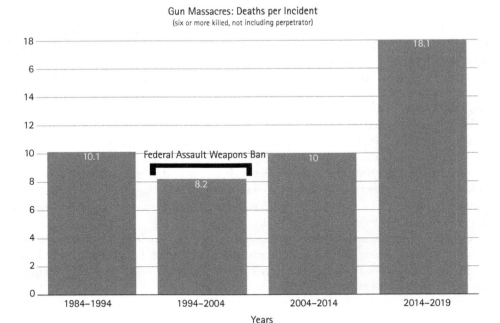

Mass shooting data from Mother Jones; dates begin and end in September to reflect the period from 9/13/1994 to 9/12/2004 when the federal assault weapons ban was in place, except for the last column, which ends in 9/2/2019.

FIGURE 28.7. Gun massacres: Deaths per incident.

Webster et al. (2020) examined fatal mass shootings over the period from 1984 to 2017 and concluded "that LCM bans were associated with significant reductions in the incidence of fatal mass shootings but that bans on assault weapons had no clear effects on either the incidence of mass shootings or on the incidence of victim fatalities from mass shootings." It is not surprising, though, that the standard errors were large in the estimated impacts of assault weapons in the Webster et al. study, since there was such a strong overlap between having a magazine ban and an assault weapon ban at the same time. This was the case for the 10 years of the federal assault weapon ban and is true for 8 of the 10 states that ban both large-capacity magazines and assault weapons (Vermont and Colorado only limit magazine size), making it difficult for a regression study to tease out the independent effect of each.

Table 28.2 addresses this concern by examining the impact of having either ban in place based on an original panel data analysis of *Mother Jones* mass shootings data from 1982 to 2019. Here, I run a population-weighted state-level two-way fixed effects regression, using the same set of control variables that were used in DAW 2019.

As Table 28.2 indicates, having an assault weapon ban (whether at the state or federal level) or large-capacity magazine ban in place in a given state causes statistically significant decreases in per capita rates of deaths and overall casualties due to mass shootings. The model also suggests that these gun safety restrictions suppress the rate of mass shooting incidents and injuries, although the evidence is statistically weaker for these dependent

Table 28.2. The Effect of Assault Weapon and Large-Capacity Magazine Bans on Mass Shootings, 1982–2019

	Mass Shooting[a] Incidents per 10,000,000 Population	Mass Shooting Deaths per 1,000,000 Population	Mass Shooting Injuries per 1,000,000 Population	Mass Shooting Casualties[b] per 1,000,000 Population
Assault Weapon or Large-Capacity Magazine Ban[c]	–.07 (0.05)	–.09** (0.04)	–.22* (0.12)	–.31** (0.15)

Notes: Outcome variables are based on *Mother Jones'* database of mass shootings in the 50 states plus Washington DC from 1982 to 2019. The OLS regressions also included the socioeconomic control variables used in DAW 2019 as well as state and year fixed effects. The coefficients on these variables were omitted from this table to conserve space. Regressions are weighted by each state's 1999 population, and standard errors are clustered at the state level.
[a] Mass shootings are defined as attacks in public places in which four or more victims were killed.
[b] Casualties are defined as people who were either injured or killed during a mass shooting.
[c] The variable "Assault Weapon or Large-Capacity Magazine Ban" is assigned a value of 1 for each state-year for which either an assault weapon ban or large-capacity magazine ban was active, and 0 for all other state-years.
* $p < 0.1$; ** $p < 0.05$; *** $p < 0.01$.

variables. Overall, this analysis serves to further reinforce and expand upon the earlier findings that bans on assault weapons and large-capacity magazines save lives.

V. AGE-BASED RESTRICTIONS ON GUN ACCESS

There is considerable evidence that a substantial number of 18- to 20-year-olds are impulsive, immature, and prone to making poor or unreasoned decisions for a number of reasons, including underdeveloped cognitive abilities and issues with mental health, such as depression, anxiety, and suicidality. Neuroscience and social science data support the conclusion that 18- to 20-year-olds pose a considerable risk of increased danger to themselves and others if they possess firearms, and the recent mass killings in Buffalo and Uvalde of May 2022 are only the most recent, dramatic confirmations of this phenomenon. The heightened risk is due to three principal factors: (1) the still-developing cognitive systems of 18- to 20-year-olds increases their risk of impulsive behavior, (2) the onset of mental illness during emerging adulthood is correlated with self-harm and suicide attempts, and (3) the frequency of binge drinking during emerging adulthood is a stimulant to violence that is obviously more dangerous when accompanied with gun possession (Webster et al. 2016).

When one considers that the majority of 18- to 20-year-olds struggle with some form of untreated mental illness, stress, and/or risky behavior with alcohol and illegal drugs,[18] greater restrictions on gun use are advisable for this age group in order to protect them from harming themselves and others. Because this is the period when so many of these pathologies first present themselves, the opportunities to identify *in advance* those who will commit suicidal and homicidal acts is far more limited than among those who are 21 or older, by which time a greater history of potential or actual pathology will have been established and observed. This information can then be used to limit all access to weapons by those whose prohibiting behavior will be entered into the national firearm background check system.

The ability to responsibly carry a gun outside the home for protection is dependent upon a complicated assessment of the likely costs and benefits of such behavior, which is beyond the capacity of a substantial number of those under 21. One reflection of the drastically inadequate competence in risk assessment for this age group was captured by the National Longitudinal Study of Youth, which asked 17- and 18-year-olds about their risk of dying in the next year. The Black youthful respondents predicted their chance of death was 22%, while White youth estimated the risk of death in the next year to be 16%. As Nobel economist James Heckman notes in commenting on these responses, "Both numbers are absurdly high" (Carneiro, Heckman, and Masterov 2005, 28). Such gross misperceptions of risk are incompatible with sensible decisions about carrying guns outside the home.

One of the most consistent facts of crime over time is that 18- to 20-year-olds commit homicide at disproportionately high rates. Therefore, legislative efforts to reduce homicides appropriately focus on this age group and are likely to generate beneficial results. Figure 28.8 presents murder arrest rates by age for the United States for 2019. The figure clearly shows that the 18 to 20-year-old age group is the most homicidal. Specifically, in 2019, the single most homicidal age group in the nation was age 19, with both 18- and 20-year-olds having higher murder arrest rates than any other age groups except for age 19.[19]

In other words, if one wants to reduce homicidal violence in a targeted fashion, it is prudent to have restrictions for firearm acquisition and use for the age groups that exhibit the highest rates of homicide—namely, 18- to 20-year-olds—as a substantial majority of states have done. Indeed, while anecdotes of instances when guns have been used for protection can perpetuate the myth that gun carrying might provide benefits sufficient to offset its

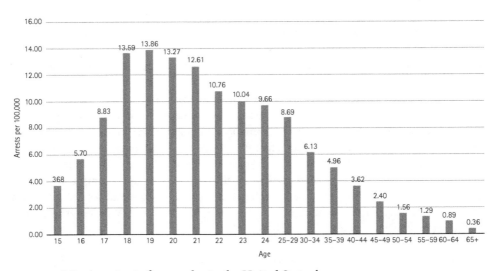

FIGURE 28.8. Arrest rate for murder in the United States by age, 2019.

large costs, the empirical evidence does not support this view. A study of gun carriers older than age 21 in Philadelphia from 2003–2006, who almost all said they carried to protect against crime, found that gun possession was associated with a significantly *increased* risk of being shot in an assault. Although successful defensive gun uses do occur, this study further challenges the view that gun carrying is on balance protective (Branas et al. 2009).

A recent study has looked at younger gun carriers in Phoenix and Philadelphia from 2000 to 2010 and found that they were at vastly higher rates of being shot when they were carrying than when they were not carrying. The authors state that "the key finding is that even among populations with chronic exposure to gun violence, gun carrying is associated with increased risk of gun violence victimization and exposure, while even the temporary cessation of gun carrying is associated with the reduction of such risks" (Hureau and Wilson 2021).

VI. Conclusion

The spike in gun violence during the COVID-19 pandemic has increased interest in ways to reduce the social costs of the criminal use of firearms. The strong instrumentality effect tells us that lives will be saved if gun possession and carrying by those at greater risk of misuse can be limited, the lethality of weaponry can be contained, and the grounds for carrying weapons is appropriately restricted. The studies discussed in this paper support the conclusion that (1) comprehensive background checks, (2) increased barriers to straw purchases designed to circumvent this screening mechanism, and (3) efforts to disarm known prohibited possessors can save lives and reduce crime.[20]

Clearly, there are challenges in the effort to provide high-quality research that can generate sound evidence-based policy to address firearm violence. Data quality is always a problem in this area, where police operate under a voluntary reporting regime to the FBI. Some states are recidivists in repeatedly failing to provide sound—or even any—data to the Uniform Crime Reports (UCR). The NIBRS system is designed to give richer data about criminal acts, but many states have not begun reporting in this fashion, and when some states cannot even keep up with the more modest burdens of UCR reporting, one wonders whether the greater demands of NIBRS will simply overwhelm them. On top of this, the gun lobby often battles to prevent the public from knowing the details of gun incidents, such as using laws that restrict information about gun permits held by criminals or that limit governmental funding of gun research.

In addition, Cook and Donohue (2017, 1261) note that "the greatest challenge is often that policy reforms are intrinsically difficult to evaluate because of a lack of a credible basis for estimating the counter-factual" and that while "it has been possible to use quasi-experimental methods to develop credible results, it is important going forward for public agencies to adopt an experimental frame of mind, recognizing that the true effect of the reform is not known, that it should be known before disseminating a reform, and that a systematic trial may help dispel uncertainty."

There is one additional problem that poses substantial challenges in the domain of gun violence. Political and economic forces are also working to move the country in the opposite direction on each of these issues, at times using motivated research to create a climate of doubt about legitimate research and at other times engineering elevated fear of crime and misleading claims about the protective benefits of firearms. The Supreme Court and many state legislatures have been dramatically shaped by these forces, and a growing literature has demonstrated that "even well-educated people . . . are quite susceptible to misleading, cherry-picked facts" (Ranney and Clark 2016, 64). Therefore, it is quite possible that some of the policy measures discussed here that can reduce mass shootings or overall gun violence will simply be taken off the table by an expansive reading of the Second Amendment or by legislative initiatives responding to gun lobby pressure and an intense displeasure among a committed minority of citizens with any regulation thought to interfere with the freedom to possess and wield increasingly lethal weaponry. Having the strongest possible empirical basis to establish the contours of effective gun policy so that wise policies can both be implemented and withstand constitutional attack is more important than ever.[21]

Notes

1. I am grateful to Matthew Bondy, Theodora Boulouta, Samuel Cai, Ammar Inayatali, Mira Korb, and Nicolas Peña Tenjo for providing excellent research assistance.
2. Of course, the categories are not entirely separate: in 2020, 570 suicides were murder-suicides that also led to 703 murders (see Mascia 2021).
3. In 2020, 79 percent of homicides were by firearm, which is the highest proportion on record (see Ridley 2021).
4. Braga (2021) notes that with enough manpower and willpower, the police could solve many more homicides and shootings, which tend to have rather low clearance rates, thereby allowing perpetrators to continue their violence.
5. For example, cognitive-behavioral therapy may be one particularly low-cost method of reducing violence (see Blattman, Jamison, and Sheridan 2017). Additionally, Kessler et al. (2021) study the New York City Summer Youth Employment Program (SYEP) using a randomized lottery and find "SYEP participation decreases arrests and convictions during the program summer, effects that are driven by the small fraction (3 percent) of SYEP youth who are at-risk, as defined by having been arrested before the start of the program."
6. Doleac (2018) discusses research showing that opening additional drug treatment facilities and expanding Medicaid cost-effectively reduces both violent and financially motivated crime. Deza, Maclean, and Solomon (2020) also provide a discussion of expanded access to mental health care.
7. For example, in 1981, 70-year-old Ronald Reagan survived a shot in the chest from a .22 caliber revolver, while his chances of survival would presumably have been less with many of the more high-powered handguns in use today.
8. Cook and Ludwig (2019) provide further discussion on the strength of this relationship in response to Hayo et al. (2019).
9. Hemenway et al. (2018) had previously found a strong relationship between rates of fatal police shootings and the prevalence of firearms across states.
10. Although the precise percentage is difficult to pin down, a careful critique of John Lott's claims that defensive gun use involved only brandishing 95–98 percent of the time concluded that "the bulk of the evidence suggests that a value in the 70 to 80 percent range in more reasonable" (McDowall 2005, 259).

11. While some early studies suggested that right-to-carry (RTC) laws might have some beneficial effects in reducing homicide (see Lott and Mustard 1997), a distinguished panel of the National Research Council examined this evidence and in 2005 issued a statement endorsed by 15 of the 16 committee members stating that "the scientific evidence does not support [t]his position" (National Research Council 2005). The sole dissenter was James Q. Wilson. Wilson's role as a dissenter from some of the top econometricians in the country on the NRC panel on the econometric evaluation of RTC laws is quite remarkable, especially since he acknowledged in the second sentence of his dissent that he was "not an econometrician."
12. Hemenway et al. (2017) found that people who carried firearms at least once in the past month were three times more likely to have a firearm stolen than other gun owners.
13. The federal assault weapons ban took effect September 13, 1994. It expired on September 13, 2004, due to a sunset provision that enabled the law to lapse.
14. This downward trend in violent crime even as mass shootings rise after 2004 is important evidence of the harmful impact of ending the federal assault weapons ban. Without that evidence, one might mistakenly think that the overall violent crime drop of roughly 14% during the decade of the federal assault weapons ban was simply part of downward crime, which itself explains the drop in mass shooting deaths. The experience after 2004 undermines that view.
15. Note that the numbers of mass shootings would be substantially larger using alternative definitions, such as the Gun Violence Archive definition of *four individuals wounded by gunfire in a single incident*. Using that more capacious definition, there were 366 mass shootings in the first 318 days of 2019, killing 408 and injuring 1,477 (see Gal and Gould 2019).
16. Only seven states and the District of Columbia ban assault weapons, and all of those states plus Colorado and Vermont restrict the permissible size of the ammunition magazines.
17. After Figure 28.6 was created, two other victims of the Las Vegas shooting died from their horrendous and agonizing injuries, which elevates to 273 the number of deaths from public gun massacres in the last five years (see CNN 2019).
18. Well over half of 18–20-year-olds suffer from mental illness, engage in illicit substance abuse, binge drinking or heavy alcohol use, or have serious thoughts of suicide. Moreover, this age group had the highest need for substance abuse treatment, and, with less than 5% of those with a substance abuse disorder receiving treatment, it had the lowest percentage receiving treatment of any age group (see SAMHSA 2021).
19. It should also be noted that the FBI violent crimes data for the nation also confirms that 18- to 20-year-olds consistently have the highest rates of rape and robbery, as well as homicides. The total number of arrests presented in the FBI Table 38 is based on data from law enforcement agencies that cover 229,735,355 people out of the 329,474,910 total US population in 2019 (see Uniform Crime Reports 2020).
20. A recent RAND review of a selection of papers on the impact of background checks did not include a number of the papers referenced in this chapter (Smart et al. 2020). Based on this more limited evaluation, the RAND review found that "[t]here is moderate evidence that background checks reduce firearm homicides. Most available studies have examined the effects of dealer background checks or the combined effects of dealer and private-seller background checks when both are required by a state." The RAND study acknowledged that "if performing background checks on a subset of firearm transfers causes reductions in homicides, then extending the practice to all firearm transfers,

including private sales, could further reduce firearm homicides." Indeed, this is close to a logical necessity.

21. While conceding that the "right to keep and bear arms . . . has controversial public safety implications," Justice Clarence Thomas writing for the Supreme Court in *Bruen* in 2022 explained that statistics about the harms from gun violence could not "justify granting States greater leeway in restricting firearm ownership and use." Nonetheless, it remains critically important to fully establish both the costs and benefits of gun ownership and carrying, and the mechanisms that underlie these effects.

References

Abrams, David S. 2012. Estimating the deterrent effect of incarceration using sentencing enhancements. *American Economic Journal: Applied Economics* 4 (4): 32–56. https://doi.org/10.1257/app.4.4.32.

Anglemyer A, T. Horvath, and G. Rutherford. 2014. The accessibility of firearms and risk for suicide and homicide victimization among household members: a systematic review and meta-analysis. *Annuals of Internal Medicine*, 160:101–110.

Anker, Anne Sofie Tegner, Jennifer L. Doleac, and Rasmus Landersø. 2021. The effects of DNA databases on the deterrence and detection of offenders. *American Economic Journal: Applied Economics* 13 (4): 194–225. https://doi.org/10.1257/app.20190207.

Azrael, Deborah, Joanna Cohen, Carmel Salhi, and Matthew Miller. 2018. Firearm storage in gun-owning households with children: Results of a 2015 national survey. *Journal of Urban Health* 95 (3): 295–304. https://doi.org/10.1007/s11524-018-0261-7.

Baron, Jason E., Joshua M. Hyman, and Brittany N. Vasquez. 2022. Public school funding, schoolquality, and adult crime. NBER Working Paper 29855. Cambridge, MA: National Bureau of Economic Research. http://www.nber.org/papers/w29855.

Ben-Michael, Eli, Avi Feller, and Steven Raphael. 2021. The effect of a targeted effort to remove firearms from prohibited persons on state murder rates. Working Paper. Berkeley: University of California, Berkeley, Goldman School of Public Policy. https://gsppi.berkeley.edu/avi-feller/papers/APPS_Draft.pdf.

Billings, Stephen B. 2022. Smoking gun? Linking gun ownership to neighborhood crime. SSRN Scholarly Paper ID 3588439. Rochester, NY: Social Science Research Network. https://doi.org/10.2139/ssrn.3588439.

Blattman, Christopher, Julian C. Jamison, and Margaret Sheridan. 2017. Reducing crime and violence: Experimental evidence from cognitive behavioral therapy in Liberia. *American Economic Review* 107 (4): 1165–1206. https://doi.org/10.1257/aer.20150503.

Braga, Anthony A. 2021. Improving police clearance rates of shootings: A review of the evidence. New York: Manhattan Institute.

Braga, Anthony A., and Philip J. Cook. 2018. The association of firearm caliber with likelihood of death from gunshot injury in criminal assaults. *JAMA Network Open* 1 (3): e180833. https://doi.org/10.1001/jamanetworkopen.2018.0833.

Branas, Charles C., Therese S. Richmond, Dennis P. Culhane, Thomas R. Ten Have, and Douglas J. Wiebe. 2009. Investigating the link between gun possession and gun assault. *American Journal of Public Health*, 99 (11): 2034–2040. https://doi.org/10.2105/AJPH.2008.143099.

Caplan, Joel M., Leslie W. Kennedy, and Gohar Petrossian. 2011. Police-monitored CCTV cameras in Newark, NJ: A quasi-experimental test of crime deterrence. *Journal of Experimental Criminology* 7 (3): 255–274.

Carneiro, Pedro, James J. Heckman, and Dimitriy Masterov. 2005. Labor market discrimination and racial differences in premarket factors. *Journal of Law and Economics*, XLVIII:1–39.

CDC (Centers for Disease Control and Prevention). 2021. Fast facts: Firearm violence prevention. Atlanta: CDC. https://www.cdc.gov/violenceprevention/firearms/fastfact.html.

Chalfin, Aaron, Benjamin Hansen, Jason Lerner, and Lucie Parker. 2022. Reducing crime through environmental design: Evidence from a randomized experiment of street lighting in New York City. *Journal of Quantitative Criminology* 38 (1): 127–157. https://doi.org/10.1007/s10940-020-09490-6.

Chalfin, Aaron, and Justin McCrary. 2018. Are U.S. cities underpoliced? Theory and evidence. *Review of Economics and Statistics* 100 (1): 167–186. https://doi.org/10.1162/REST_a_00694.

CNN. 2019. Woman says sister injured in 2017 Las Vegas shooting has died. KVIA (blog), November 18. https://kvia.com/regional-news/2019/11/18/woman-says-sister-injured-in-2017-las-vegas-shooting-has-died/.

Cook, Philip J., and Jens Ludwig. 2006. The social costs of gun ownership. *Journal of Public Economics*, 90 (1–2): 379–391. https://doi.org/10.1016/j.jpubeco.2005.02.003.

Cook, Philip J., and Jens Ludwig. 2019. The social costs of gun ownership: A reply to Hayo, Neumeier, and Westphal. *Empirical Economics* 56 (1): 13–22. https://doi.org/10.1007/s00181-018-1497-5.

Crifasi, Cassandra K., Molly Merrill-Francis, Alex McCourt, Jon S. Vernick, Garen J. Wintemute, and Daniel W. Webster. 2018. Correction to: Association between firearm laws and homicide in urban counties. *Journal of Urban Health* 95 (5): 773–776. https://doi.org/10.1007/s11524-018-0306-y.

Cummings, Peter, David C. Grossman, Frederick P. Rivara, and Thomas D. Koepsell. 1997. State gun safe storage laws and child mortality due to firearms. *JAMA: The Journal of the American Medical Association* 278 (13): 1084. https://doi.org/10.1001/jama.1997.03550130058037.

Davis, Jonathan M. V., and Sara B. Heller. 2020. Rethinking the benefits of youth employment programs: The heterogeneous effects of summer jobs. *Review of Economics and Statistics* 102 (4): 664–677. https://doi.org/10.1162/rest_a_00850.

DeSimone, Jeffrey, Sara Markowitz, and Jing Xu. 2013. Child access prevention laws and nonfatal gun injuries. *Southern Economic Journal* 80 (1): 5–25.

Deza, Monica, Johanna Catherine Maclean, and Keisha T. Solomon. 2020. Local access to mental healthcare and crime. NBER Working Paper 27619. Cambridge, MA: National Bureau of Economic Research. https://doi.org/10.3386/w27619.

District of Columbia v. Heller, 554 U.S. 570 (2008).

Doleac, Jennifer L. 2018. New evidence that access to health care reduces crime. Commentary. Washington, DC: Brookings Institution, January 3. https://www.brookings.edu/blog/up-front/2018/01/03/new-evidence-that-access-to-health-care-reduces-crime/.

Donohue, John J., III. 2009. Assessing the relative benefits of incarceration: The overall change over the previous decades and the benefits on the margin. In *Do prisons make us safer? The benefits and costs of the prison boom*, edited by Steven Raphael and Michael Stoll, 269–341. New York: Russell Sage Foundation. http://search.ebscohost.com/login.aspx?direct=true&scope=site&db=nlebk&db=nlabk&AN=1069875.

Donohue, John J., III. 2017. Laws facilitating gun carrying and homicide. *American Journal of Public Health*, 107 (12): 1864–65. https://doi.org/10.2105/AJPH.2017.304144.

Donohue, John J., III, Abhay Aneja, and Kyle D. Weber. 2019. Right-to-carry laws and violent crime: A comprehensive assessment using panel data and a state-level synthetic control analysis. *Journal of Empirical Legal Studies*, 16 (2/May): 198–247. https://doi.org/10.1111/jels.12219.

Donohue, John J., III, and Theodora Boulouta. 2019a. The assault weapon ban saved lives. *Stanford Law School Blogs: Legal Aggregate* (blog), October 15. https://law.stanford.edu/2019/10/15/the-assault-weapon-ban-saved-lives/.

Donohue, John J., III, and Theodora Boulouta. 2019b. That assault weapon ban? it really did work. *New York Times*, September 4. https://www.nytimes.com/2019/09/04/opinion/assault-weapon-ban.html.

Donohue, John J., III, Samuel V. Cai, Matthew V. Bondy, and Philip J. Cook. 2023. Why Does Right-to-Carry Cause Violent Crime to Increase? NBER Working Paper 30190. Cambridge, MA: National Bureau of Economic Research. https://www.nber.org/papers/w30190.

Donohue, John J., III, and Peter Siegelman. 1998. Allocating resources among prisons and social programs in the battle against crime. *Journal of Legal Studies*, 27 (1): 1–43. https://doi.org/10.1086/468012.

Doucette, Mitchell L., Cassandra K. Crifasi, and Shannon Frattaroli. 2019. Right-to-carry laws and firearm workplace homicides: A longitudinal analysis (1992–2017). *American Journal of Public Health*, 109 (12): 1747–53. https://doi.org/10.2105/AJPH.2019.305307.

Doucette, Mitchell L., Alex D. McCourt, Cassandra K. Crifasi, and David W. Webster. 2023. Impact of Changes to Concealed Carry Weapons Laws on Fatal and Non-Fatal Violent Crime, 1980–2019. *American Journal of Epidemiology*, 192 (3): 342–355. https://doi.org/10.1093/aje/kwac160.

Doucette, Mitchell L., Julie A. Ward, Alex D. McCourt, David W. Webster, and Cassandra K. Crifasi. 2022. Officer-involved shootings and concealed carry weapons permitting laws: Analysis of gun violence archive data, 2014–2020. *Journal of Urban Health*, 99 (3): 373–384. https://doi.org/10.1007/s11524-022-00627-5.

Duncan v. Becerra, 366 F. Supp. 3d 1131 (S.D. Cal. 2019).

Follman, Mark, Gavin Aronsen, and Deanna Pan. 2002. US mass shootings, 1982–2022: Data FROM *Mother Jones*' investigation. *Mother Jones* (blog). https://www.motherjones.com/politics/2012/12/mass-shootings-mother-jones-full-data/.

Fridel, Emma E. 2021a. Comparing the impact of household gun ownership and concealed carry legislation on the frequency of mass shootings and firearms homicide. *Justice Quarterly*, 38 (5) 1–24. https://doi.org/10.1080/07418825.2020.1789693.

Fridel, Emma E. 2021b. The futility of shooting down strawmen: A response to Kleck (2020). *Justice Quarterly*, 38 (5): 925–941. https://doi.org/10.1080/07418825.2020.1856401.

Gal, Skye, and Shayanne Gould. 2019. There have been 366 mass shootings in the US so far in 2019—Here's the full list. *Insider*, November 14. https://www.insider.com/number-of-mass-shootings-in-america-this-year-2019-8.

Gius, Mark. 2019. Using the synthetic control method to determine the effects of concealed carry laws on state-level murder rates. *International Review of Law and Economics*, 57 (March): 1–11. https://doi.org/10.1016/j.irle.2018.10.005.

Gomez, Alan, and Kaila White. 2017. Here are all the victims of the Las Vegas shooting. *USA Today*, October 6.

Hayo, Bernd, Florian Neumeier, and Christian Westphal. 2018. The social costs of gun ownership revisited. *Empirical Economics*, 56 (1): 1–12. https://doi.org/10.1007/s00181-018-1496-6.

Heller, Sara B. 2014. Summer jobs reduce violence among disadvantaged youth. *Science*, 346 (6214): 1219–1223. https://doi.org/10.1126/science.1257809.

Heller, Sara B., Anuj K. Shah, Jonathan Guryan, Jens Ludwig, Sendhil Mullainathan, and Harold A. Pollack. 2016. Thinking, fast and slow? Some field experiments to reduce crime and dropout in Chicago. *Quarterly Journal of Economics*, 132 (1): 1–54. https://doi.org/10.1093/qje/qjw033.

Hemenway, David, Deborah Azrael, Andrew Conner, and Matthew Miller. 2018. Variation in rates of fatal police shootings across US states: The role of firearm availability. *Journal of Urban Health*, 96 (1): 63–73. https://doi.org/10.1007/s11524-018-0313-z.

Hemenway, David, Deborah Azrael, and Matthew Miller. 2017. Whose guns are stolen? The epidemiology of gun theft victims. *Injury Epidemiology*, 4 (1): 11. https://doi.org/10.1186/s40 621-017-0109-8.

Hemenway, David, and Sara J. Solnick. 2015. The epidemiology of self-defense gun use: Evidence from the National Crime Victimization Surveys 2007–2011. *Preventive Medicine*, 79 (October): 22–27. https://doi.org/10.1016/j.ypmed.2015.03.029.

Hureau, David, and Theodore Wilson. 2021. The co-occurrence of illegal gun carrying and gun violence exposure: Evidence for practitioners from young people adjudicated for serious involvement in crime. *American Journal of Epidemiology*, 190 (12): 2544–2551. https://doi.org/10.1093/aje/kwab188.

Kessler, Judd B., Sarah Tahamont, Alexander M. Gelber, and Adam Isen. 2021. The effects of youth employment on crime: Evidence from New York City lotteries. NBER Working Paper 28373. Cambridge, MA: National Bureau of Economic Research. https://doi.org/10.3386/w28373.

Khalil, Umair. 2017. Do more guns lead to more crime? Understanding the role of illegal firearms. *Journal of Economic Behavior & Organization*, 133 (January): 342–361. https://doi.org/10.1016/j.jebo.2016.11.010.

Klarevas, Louis. 2016. *Rampage nation: Securing America from mass shootings*. Amherst, NY: Prometheus Books.

Klarevas, Louis, Andrew Conner, and David Hemenway. 2019. The effect of large-capacity magazine bans on high-fatality mass shootings. *American Journal of Public Health* 109 (July). https://ajph.aphapublications.org/doi/10.2105/AJPH.2019.305311.

Kleck, Gary, and Marc Gertz. 1995. Armed resistance to crime: The prevalence and nature of self-defense with a gun. *Journal of Criminal Law and Criminology* 86 (1): 150. https://scholarlycommons.law.northwestern.edu/cgi/viewcontent.cgi?article=6853&context=jclc.

Knopov, Anita, Michael Siegel, Ziming Xuan, Emily F Rothman, Shea W Cronin, and David Hemenway. 2019. The impact of state firearm laws on homicide rates among Black and White populations in the United States, 1991–2016. *Health & Social Work* 44 (4): 232–240. https://doi.org/10.1093/hsw/hlz024.

Lott, John R., Jr., and David B. Mustard. 1997. Crime, deterrence, and right-to-carry concealed handguns. *Journal of Legal Studies* 26 (1): 1–68. https://doi.org/10.1086/467988.

Lyon, Ed. 2019. Imprisoning America's mentally ill. *Prison Legal News*, February 4. https://www.prisonlegalnews.org/news/2019/feb/4/imprisoning-americas-mentally-ill/.

Mascia, Jennifer. 2021. Should suicides be considered "gun violence"? *The Trace*, December 13. https://www.thetrace.org/2021/12/gun-violence-suicide-rate-data-shooting-deaths/.

McDowall, David. 2005. Review: John R. Lott, Jr.'s *Defensive Gun Brandishing Estimates*. *Public Opinion Quarterly*, 69 (2): 246–263.

McElroy, Marjorie B., and Will Wang. 2014. Do concealed gun permits deter crime? New results from a dynamic model. SSRN Scholarly Paper ID 2469534. Rochester, NY: Social Science Research Network. https://doi.org/10.2139/ssrn.2469534.

Mitre-Becerril, David, Sarah Tahamont, Jason Lerner, and Aaron Chalfin. 2022. Can deterrence persist? long-term evidence from a randomized experiment in street lighting. *Criminology and Public Policy*, 21 (4): 865–891. http://achalfin.weebly.com/uploads/8/5/4/8/8548116/lights_followup.pdf?utm_source=The+Trace+mailing+list&utm_campa

ign=d9def82aaf-EMAIL_CAMPAIGN_2019_08_29_06_04_COPY_01&utm_medium=email&utm_term=0_f76c3ff31c-d9def82aaf-112411265.

Nagin, Daniel S. 2020. Firearm availability and fatal police shootings. *ANNALS of the American Academy of Political and Social Science*, 687 (1): 49–57. https://doi.org/10.1177/0002716219896259.

National Research Council. 2005. *Firearms and violence: A critical review*. Washington, DC: National Academies Press.

New York State Rifle & Pistol Association v. Bruen, 597 U.S. ___ (2022).

Post, Lori, Maryann Mason, Lauren Nadya Singh, Nicholas P. Wleklinski, Charles B. Moss, Hassan Mohammad, Tariq Z Issa, Adesuwa I. Akhetuamhen, Cynthia A. Brandt, Sarah B. Welch, and James Francis Oehmke. 2021. Impact of firearm surveillance on gun control policy: Regression discontinuity analysis. *JMIR Public Health and Surveillance*, 7 (April). doi:10.2196/26042.

Raissian, Kerri M. 2015. Hold your fire: Did the 1996 Federal Gun Control Act expansion reduce domestic homicides? *Journal of Policy Analysis and Management*, 35 (1): 67–93. https://onlinelibrary.wiley.com/doi/abs/10.1002/pam.21857.

RAND. 2023. Effects of Concealed-Carry Laws on Violent Crime. https://www.rand.org/research/gun-olicy/analysis/concealed-carry/violent-crime.html.

Ranney, Michael Andrew, and Dav Clark. 2016. Climate change conceptual change: Scientific information can transform attitudes. *Topics in Cognitive Science*, 8:49–75. doi:10.1111/tops.12187.

Ridley, Joi. 2021. EFSGV analysis of 2020 CDC data. Washington, DC: Educational Fund to Stop Gun Violence. https://efsgv.org/press/efsgv-analysis-of-2020-cdc-data/.

Robles, Frances, and Nikita Stewart. 2015. Dylann Roof's past reveals trouble at home and school. *New York Times*, July 16. https://www.nytimes.com/2015/07/17/us/charleston-shooting-dylann-roof-troubled-past.html.

Sabbath, Erika L., Summer Sherburne Hawkins, and Christopher F. Baum. 2020. State-level changes in firearm laws and workplace homicide rates: United States, 2011 to 2017. *American Journal of Public Health*, 110 (2): 230–236. https://doi.org/10.2105/AJPH.2019.305405.

SAMHSA (Substance Abuse and Mental Health Services Administration). 2021. *Key substance use and mental health indicators in the United States: Results from the 2020 National Survey on Drug Use and Health*. Rockville, MD: SAMHSA. https://www.samhsa.gov/data/sites/default/files/reports/rpt35325/NSDUHFFRPDFWHTMLFiles2020/2020NSDUHFFR1PDFW102121.pdf.

Schnitzer, Patricia G., Heather K. Dykstra, Theodore E. Trigylidas, and Richard Lichenstein. 2019. Firearm suicide among youth in the United States, 2004–2015. *Journal of Behavioral Medicine* 42 (4): 584–590. https://doi.org/10.1007/s10865-019-00037-0.

Siegel, Michael, Max Goder-Reiser, Grant Duwe, Michael Rocque, James Alan Fox, and Emma E. Fridel. 2020. The relation between state gun laws and the incidence and severity of mass public shootings in the United States, 1976–2018. *Law and Human Behavior*, 44 (5): 347–360 doi:10.1037/lhb0000378.

Siegel, Michael, Molly Pahn, Ziming Xuan, Eric Fleegler, and David Hemenway. 2019. The impact of state firearm laws on homicide and suicide deaths in the USA, 1991–2016: A panel study. *Journal of General Internal Medicine*, 34 (10): 2021–2028. https://doi.org/10.1007/s11606-019-04922-x.

Siegel, Michael, Ziming Xuan, Craig S. Ross, Sandro Galea, Bindu Kalesan, Eric Fleegler, and Kristin A. Goss. 2017. Easiness of legal access to concealed firearm permits and homicide rates in the United States. *American Journal of Public Health*, 107 (12): 1923–1929. https://doi.org/10.2105/AJPH.2017.304057.

Smart, Rosanna, Andrew R. Morral, Sierra Smucker, Samantha Cherney, Terry L. Schell, Samuel Peterson, Sangeeta C. Ahluwalia, et al. 2020. *The science of gun policy: A critical synthesis of research evidence on the effects of gun policies in the United States*. 2nd ed. Santa Monica, CA: RAND Corporation.

Stansfield, Richard, Daniel Semenza, and Ian Silver. 2023. The relationship between concealed carry licenses and firearm homicide in the US: A reciprocal county-level analysis. *Journal of Urban Health*, 100 (4): 657–665. https://doi.org/10.1007/s11524-023-00759-2.

Stephens, Alain, and Keegan Hamilton. 2022. The return of the machine gun. *The Trace*, March 24.

Stockholm University Department of Criminology. 2020. 2020 winners of the Stockholm Prize in Criminology. Stockholm University Department of Criminology. https://www.su.se/english/about-the-university/prizes-and-academic-ceremonies/the-stockholm-prize-in-criminology/2020-winners-of-the-stockholm-prize-in-criminology-1.515785.

Studdert, David M., Yifan Zhang, Erin E. Holsinger, and Lea Prince. 2022. Homicide deaths among adult cohabitants of handgun owners in California, 2004 to 2016. *Annals of Internal Medicine*, June. doi:10.7326/M21-3762.

Uniform Crime Reports. 2020. Crime in the U.S. 2019, Table 38. Washington, DC: FBI. https://ucr.fbi.gov/crime-in-the-u.s/2019/crime-in-the-u.s.-2019/tables/table-38/table-38.xls.

Van Der Wal, Willem M. 2022. Marginal structural models to estimate causal effects of right-to-carry laws on crime. *Statistics and Public Policy*, 9 (1): 163–174. https://doi.org/10.1080/2330443X.2022.2120136.

Wagner, Wendy, and Peter Sawyer. 2020. Mass incarceration: The whole pie. *Prison Policy Initiative*, March 24. https://www.prisonpolicy.org/reports/pie2020.html.

Webster, Daniel W., Alexander D. McCourt, Cassandra K. Crifasi, Marisa D. Booty, and Elizabeth A. Stuart. 2020. Evidence concerning the regulation of firearms design, sale, and carrying on fatal mass shootings in the United States. *Criminology and Public Policy*, 19 (1): 171–212 https://onlinelibrary-wiley-com.stanford.idm.oclc.org/doi/full/10.1111/1745-9133.12487.

Webster, Daniel W., John J. Donohue III, Louis Klarevas, Cassandra K. Crifasi, Jon S. Vernick, David Jernigan, Holly C. Wilcox, Sara B. Johnson, Sheldon Greenberg, and Emma E. McGinty. 2016. *Firearms on college campuses: Research evidence and policy implications*. Baltimore: Johns Hopkins Bloomberg School of Public Health. https://www.jhsph.edu/research/centers-and-institutes/johns-hopkins-center-for-gun-violence-prevention-and-policy/_archive-2019/_pdfs/GunsOnCampus.pdf.

Wintemute, Garen J., Mona A. Wright, Christiana M. Drake, and James J. Beaumont. 2001. Subsequent criminal activity among violent misdemeanants who seek to purchase handguns: Risk factors and effectiveness of denying handgun purchase. *JAMA*, 285 (8): 1019. https://doi.org/10.1001/jama.285.8.1019.

Wright, M. A., G. J. Wintemute, and F. P. Rivara. 1999. Effectiveness of denial of handgun purchase to persons believed to be at high risk for firearm violence. *American Journal of Public Health*, 89 (1): 88–90. https://pubmed.ncbi.nlm.nih.gov/9987473/.

Zimring, Franklin E.. 1972. The medium is the message: Firearm caliber as a determinant of death from assault. *Journal of Legal Studies*, 1 (1): 97–123. https://doi.org/10.1086/467479.

Zimring, Franklin E. 2017. *When police kill*. Cambridge, MA: Harvard University Press.

CHAPTER 29

MASS EVIDENCE-BASED POLICY AS AN ALTERNATIVE TO MASS INCARCERATION

DANIEL P. MEARS AND JOSHUA C. COCHRAN

Our goal in this chapter is to help imagine new ways of thinking about evidence-based policy (EBP) and how to increase its use. Rather than argue for adoption of specific policies that research suggests may be effective, we argue for a systemic approach, one that infuses all crime and justice policy with an evidence-based focus. Without such a focus, there will be little appreciable gain in public safety or justice (Mears 2022). As an abundance of research has established, specific interventions may provide pockets of improvement (see, for example, Sherman et al. 2002; MacKenzie 2006; Welsh and Farrington 2007; Welsh, Braga, and Bruinsma 2013; Latessa, Listwan, and Koetzle 2014; Lum and Koper 2017; Jeglic and Calkins 2018; Taxman 2018). They should be pursued. Without a concomitant and systemic commitment to EBP, however, they will remain isolated bright spots in an otherwise bleak landscape of inefficient and ineffective criminal justice practice that will worsen without a change to how policy is designed and evaluated.

We argue that illustration of this situation can be seen in the large-scale investment globally, but especially in America, in mass incarceration over the past several decades. This shift lacked any solid evidence-based foundation—despite many policymakers calling for accountability and adoption of "evidence-based" approaches—and simultaneously has precluded a comparable large-scale investment in EBP. These conditions create a vicious cycle in which non-EBP becomes institutionalized and opportunities for increased EBP diminish.

Against that backdrop, we argue for a commitment to what is needed to fulfill policymaker and public calls for government to operate with accountability and to invest in effective policy, including laws, rules, programs, interventions, and agency practices. This commitment entails institutionalizing and increasing funding for research at multiple governmental levels and creating criminal justice and corrections agency requirements to conduct need, theory, implementation, impact, and cost-efficiency evaluations of existing and proposed policies. Such an approach would be radical. But it would be consistent with calls for EBP, is necessary for substantial improvements in safety and justice, and, importantly, can be achieved.

The first section discusses the disjuncture between policymaker and criminal justice administrator rhetoric in calling for EBP and actual support for it. The second section presents several problems that result from this disjuncture. The third seeks to answer the question: What would have happened if, instead of investing in mass incarceration and corrections. the country invested in mass EBP? The fourth describes the contours of what mass EBP could have, and still could, look like. The fifth argues that mass EBP is possible and necessary. Finally, the sixth section reflects on these points and highlights the importance of investing in mass EBP.

I. Rhetoric versus Practice: Mass Incarceration and Non-EBP

The rhetoric from policymakers, since at least the 1980s, increasingly has been to call for government accountability and EBP (Mears 2010). This can been seen in part in the publication of a US Office of Justice Programs report in the mid-1990s, *Preventing Crime: What Works, What Doesn't, What's Promising* (Sherman et al. 1997), the title of which was a revisiting of the title of the famous essay, "What Works," by Robert Martinson (1974), from over two decades earlier. Martinson's report contributed to and reflected a period of research and policy that viewed rehabilitation with skepticism. It concluded that rehabilitation, by and large—at least as designed or implemented in extant studies—is ineffective. In subsequent decades, mass incarceration and a more general large-scale expansion of criminal justice and corrections occurred (Mears and Cochran 2015). Various accounts have described this period as a punitive, or "get-tough," era, one that emphasized retribution, deterrence, and incapacitation (Garland 2001, 2013; Petersilia 2003; Gottschalk 2013).

During the decades that followed the Martinson report, skepticism about rehabilitation persisted (see, e.g., Farabee 2005). However, scholars increasingly revisited, with renewed vigor and more methodological sophistication, the question of whether rehabilitation "works." The general consensus was that, under certain conditions and for certain populations, it can be effective, and that, more broadly, a variety of crime prevention efforts also can reduce crime (see, e.g., Cullen 2005; Lipsey and Cullen 2007; MacKenzie 2006; Welsh and Farrington 2007; Cullen and Gilbert 2013; Welsh, Braga, and Bruinsma 2013; Latessa, Listwan, and Koetzle 2014; MacKenzie and Farrington 2015; Jeglic and Calkins 2018; see, however, Beaudry et al. 2021).

In short, during the "get-tough" era, increasing evidence surfaced that effective criminal justice and correctional interventions exist. Phrases like "what works" and "evidence-based" became more common in accounts of legislative and criminal justice and correctional system activities. Legislators, for example, pushed for greater accountability and reliance only on "what works" (Mears 2010). This emphasis could hardly be criticized. Who could be against accountability or EBP? Notably, for conservative "get-tough" policymakers or criminal justice or correctional system administrators, this emphasis could be used as justification, if the Martinson (1974) report was to be believed, for embracing punitive policies.

The end result was a stark disjuncture between rhetoric and practice that persists today. One problem with the rhetoric has been ambiguity in what "evidence-based" means. It could refer to policies that research has shown can reduce crime. Yet this common-sense view leaves a number of problems unaddressed. For example, what exactly constitutes evidence of effectiveness? How many studies must be conducted to arrive at an assessment that some policy "works"? How large must the effects be? Do only the results of experimental-design studies count as evidence, or do results from quasi-experimental designs also count?

No objective standards exist for answering any of these questions. Researchers themselves may disagree about them. But they all would agree that strong research designs grounded in rigorous analyses of empirical data are crucial. Such results stand in contrast to ideologically grounded beliefs about what may, or may not be, effective.

Additional problems with the rhetoric also exist. One example can be seen by using the evaluation hierarchy (Rossi, Lipsey, and Freeman 2004) to define "evidence-based" policy (Mears 2010). The hierarchy is built on the logic that policies should only be implemented when needed, they should be built on a sound theoretical causal logic, they should be implemented well (or else they cannot be effective), they should be effective, and they should be cost-efficient. One needs research on all of these dimensions to have EBP. It would be, for example, ineffective and inefficient to invest in unnecessary policies. Assessing the need for a policy requires research capable of quantifying the scope and causes of a social problem.

Regardless of some of the confusion that attends the use of the term "evidence-based," policymakers and agency administrators clearly have shifted toward calls for EBP and claims that they rely on it. They have said that they want and support EBP. Yet they may not have been consistent in what they mean by "evidence-based." That is one way in which the rhetoric differs from practice. To implement EBP would require consistency in what is meant by EBP.

There is a related and larger disjuncture. To the extent that policymakers and agency administrators have intended EBP to stand for policies that research indicates are effective—based on many studies across many sites, under different contexts and conditions, and evaluated using strong research designs—the era of get-tough policies makes little sense. Mass incarceration, in particular, stands out. Since the late 1970s, the United States has embarked on a large-scale investment in mass incarceration, with incarceration rates rising from around 100 individuals in state or federal prisons per 100,000 residents to 500 per 100,000 residents in 2010 (Mears and Cochran 2015; Carson 2021). The rate has since declined to 358 incarcerated individuals per 100,000 residents in 2020; the rate for individuals age 18 or older is 459 per 100,000 residents (Carson 2021, 1).

Incarceration rates and prison populations remain at historically high levels—with the United States having an incarceration rate that exceeds that of all other countries—and have parallels in the larger correctional system. For example, in 1980, approximately two million individuals were under the supervision of probation, parole, prison, and jail systems in the United States (Glaze and Park 2012, 1); by year-end 2019, that number had grown to over six million individuals (Minton, Beatty, and Zeng 2021, 1). This correctional system expansion has been accompanied by concomitant growth in law enforcement, courts, jails, prisons, and related personnel, and, by extension, the costs associated with such growth (Mears and Cochran 2015).

The scale of the investment is not just historically unprecedented. It also locks in a commitment to this get-tough strategy. Prison and correctional populations have declined in recent years (Carson 2021; Minton, Beatty, and Zeng 2021), but they remain at levels that greatly exceed the trajectory of prison or correctional system growth throughout most of the 20th century. And, notably, policymakers continue to advocate for the opposite trend—increasing rather than decreasing prison populations (see, e.g., Austin et al. 2021; Shorman and Kuang 2022).

If this investment were grounded in a robust social science literature that clearly and unequivocally established substantial reductions in offending among sentenced individuals (perhaps through specific deterrence) or in crime rates (perhaps through general deterrence), it would be consistent with calls for EBP. But it is not. Reviews point to mixed evidence about either type of effect (see, e.g., Nagin, Cullen, and Jonson 2009; Travis, Western, and Redburn 2014; Austin et al. 2021). The mixed evidence includes studies that identify potential beneficial effects but also ones that identify potential harmful effects of incarceration and longer stays in prison (e.g., Clear 2007; Cochran, Mears, and Bales 2014; Mears et al. 2016). The state of evidence was weak at the beginning of the get-tough era, and accumulating evidence has only raised questions about the crime-reducing benefits of a tough-on-crime approach, and of its effectiveness relative to alternative or additional approaches (Travis, Western, and Redburn 2014; Mears and Cochran 2015).

That does not mean that increasing incarceration cannot reduce crime appreciably or that it cannot have specific deterrent or rehabilitative effects. It does mean that this investment in mass incarceration—really, mass corrections—constituted a policy without a foundation in evidence, a non-EBP. Indeed, when viewed from the perspective of the evaluation hierarchy, there is little evidence that any systematic empirical assessment was undertaken by state or federal lawmakers to establish (1) the need for get-tough approaches (beyond pointing to the fact of crime or any increase in it), (2) the theoretical grounds for the effectiveness of these approaches compared with others, (3) that it was implemented appropriately (e.g., targeting high-severity crimes and offenders), (4) that it achieved its intended impacts (and minimized unintended ones), and (5) that it was cost-efficient. Concerns about potential harms that could offset benefits is not an academic one. Scholars identified a range of unintended effects that could arise, including higher crime rates in disadvantaged communities, a worsening of housing and employment outcomes for released prisoners, and greater racial and ethnic disparities in the administration of justice (Clear 2007; Mears and Cochran 2015).

II. Problems Resulting from a Rhetoric-versus-Practice Disjuncture

The existence and persistence of mass corrections are rooted in practical circumstances that create resistance to broad system-level changes. They are rooted as well in a partisan political landscape that emphasizes punitiveness rather than treatment or a public health orientation (Forer 1994; Tonry 2007; Gunderson 2022; Mears 2022). These forces maintain and reinforce a correctional system largely guided by retribution, deterrence, and incapacitation. Accordingly, they loom over any discussion of reforms because they constitute barriers to the kinds of systemic changes that are necessary to infuse corrections with an evidence-based approach to punishment, public safety, and justice. Here, we discuss why, and further below we discuss that, though formidable, these barriers are surmountable.

One problem with mass incarceration—and, more broadly, mass corrections—is that the substantial investments in jails, prisons, and community supervision divert attention from alternative strategies (Mears and Cochran 2015). Jails and prisons account for the bulk of the costs, but expanded community supervision populations are costly as well (Kyckelhahn 2012; Buehler 2021). These costs amount to a chokehold that hamstrings legislatures and agencies into a myopic focus on continuing "business as usual." In jails and prisons, that translates into a near-exclusive focus on order maintenance. Other goals that typically would be associated with "effective" corrections—such as rehabilitation, lower crime, more justice, and greater cost-efficiency—get left behind. Investments in expanded correctional systems are like investments in a mortgage from which a homeowner cannot escape. With increasingly more income constantly allocated to mortgage payments, there is less and less room to move, change jobs, or prioritize anything else. So, too, with mass incarceration and corrections—states and local jurisdictions simply have less leeway to pursue large-scale alternatives.

The growth in mass corrections is not simply a financial matter. It represents a psychological investment. "Get-tough" policy is the new "normal." It creates a bar or threshold that suggests that this default mode is presumptively best unless an alternative can be shown to be demonstrably better. It also arguably creates a mindset that resists change, if only because change would require acknowledging potential past mistakes. For example, in the 2016 Democratic primary, Hillary Clinton faced criticism about her husband's role in promoting policies in the 1990s that may have contributed to racial and ethnic disparities in punishment (Williams 2016). Her choices? Defend the policies or acknowledge problems or limitations in them. The latter approach can be politically costly for any politician, and thus contributes to reinforcing the status quo.

We are left, then, with an inability to appreciably shift policy in an evidence-based direction. Some interventions might emerge for which strong evidence exists. These are laudable (see, e.g., Sherman et al. 2002; Lipsey and Cullen 2007; Welsh, Braga, and Bruinsma 2013; Latessa, Listwan, and Koetzle 2014; McKenzie and Farrington 2015). But they do not compensate for the substantial lack of strong science to support mass incarceration or corrections, or the bulk of programs, practices, and everyday decision-making throughout criminal justice (Mears and Bacon 2009; Mears 2010, 2017, 2022; Mears and Barnes 2010). Worse, small-scale investment in EBP may enable lawmakers and agency officials to illustrate their commitment to strong science while distracting from their role in perpetuating a system that is not, as a whole, evidence-based. This sleight of hand, whether intended or not, interferes with the possibility of systemic changes that place all crime and justice efforts on an evidence-based platform.

The resource and psychological constraints created by mass incarceration are self-defeating, and permit only piecemeal changes rather than systems-level, evidence-based changes (Mears 2019). They create an environment in which any improvements are limited in scope and scale. Meanwhile, agency administrators must, unavoidably, focus on proximate goals of controlling large correctional populations. They simply do not have the room or mandate to create an evidence-based system of corrections or, more broadly, criminal justice policy and practice.

Localized investment in EBP can present problems that are more subtle. For example, when correctional systems adopt an evidence-based program here or there, they may divert attention from system-wide problems. Moreover, adoption of EBPs is not necessarily a universal good. Consider Multisystemic Therapy (MST). It is generally considered to be an effective recidivism-reducing tool (van der Stouwe et al. 2014). Yet assessments of MST—as with any other intervention—generally are relative to business-as-usual practices. Failing to fully recognize this fact obscures that the answer perhaps does not lie in adopting MST or other similar programs. Rather, the more effective and cost-efficient answer might lie in systematically altering how we approach corrections entirely. Put differently, rather than improve intervention with a few individuals or one part of corrections, the better approach might be to improve the system.

There is a related problem. Just because MST or any other EBP may be helpful does not mean that it is necessary or appropriate in virtually any context. Much depends on the particular problems, populations, and contexts that a specific correctional system faces (Mears and Cochran 2015). For example, there may be a more pressing need for better staff training. To illustrate, personnel may not understand how best to interact with incarcerated persons, and might even unwittingly (or purposely) provoke them. If so, improving this problem might well constitute a higher priority, and it might even contribute to greater reductions in recidivism.

This problem is readily apparent if we adopt an evaluation perspective. From this perspective, we want policies that are needed, theoretically well-grounded, implemented appropriately, effective, and cost-efficient (Rossi, Lipsey, and Freeman 2004). Effectiveness is an important consideration. But it does not outweigh the other types of evaluation considerations. Poor implementation alone, for example, will undermine policy effectiveness, and so has to be monitored and improved if correctional systems are to achieve their goals (Mears 2010).

Unfortunately, many accounts of EBP focus primarily on effectiveness and ignore the salience of other dimensions of policy, such as the existence of credible evidence of policy need, implementation, or cost-efficiency. In addition, they shed little light on how to improve systems (Mears 2019). Focusing on micro-level changes while ignoring systems problems is self-defeating. It is an approach akin to installing a shiny new seat into a broken-down car. The seat does its job well—it is comfortable and perhaps provides good lumbar support. Installing it, though, does not alter the fact that the car is broken and will not take you where you want to go. Piecemeal approaches to EBP not only risk diverting attention from system-wide EBP, but also from identifying system reliance on *non*-EBP. The latter is, it turns out, all too common, enough so that some researchers have a name for it: correctional quackery (Latessa, Listwan, and Koetzle 2014, 85).

This situation is compounded further by a political landscape that, by and large, has rewarded tough-on-crime approaches (e.g., Simon 2007; Tonry 2007; Gunderson 2022). Lawmakers may emphasize government accountability and EBP, but the politicization of crime leads to actions that emphasize non-EBP. And it does so in ways that permeate corrections. National reliance on supermax prisons, for example, was built on little credible theoretical or empirical research on the need for or effectiveness of them, much less their cost-efficiency relative to approaches that address systemic and operational contributors to disorder and violence (Mears 2013). As with the broader get-tough movement, policymakers and corrections officials framed the problem as an individual-level one—identify a few "bad apples," punish them, and all will be well.

III. What If We Had Invested in Mass EBP?

What would corrections look like today if, beginning in 1980 and the start of the punitive era, policymakers had invested whole cloth not in mass incarceration but rather in mass EBP?

For context, it is important to recognize that the country spent hundreds of billions of dollars over several decades on mass incarceration without simultaneously investing in a research infrastructure that could support mass EBP (Blumstein and Petersilia 1995; Mears 2017; Laub 2021). It essentially institutionalized non-EBP by investing in a policy that lacked a credible research base, was expensive, and would be difficult to alter—and it failed to invest in research that could shed light on a plethora of evidence-based laws, programs, and practices.

Mass EBP would have looked different. First, it almost assuredly would have led to a more diversified portfolio of efforts to prevent and reduce crime and to ensure justice to victims and the accused alike. Why? Mass incarceration constitutes an all-in investment on deterrence and, more than that, on the severity of punishment. It ignores a range of factors that contribute, at the macro level, to crime rates or, at the individual level, to offending. And it ignores that the certainty and celerity of punishment may also play a role in deterrence (Durlauf and Nagin 2011). Let us assume that increased incarceration assuredly has some incapacitative and deterrent effects. That seems a safe assumption, but the approach taken ignores that a greater effect might have arisen through investment in more certain and perhaps less severe punishments and through reliance on a host of approaches that address the broader spectrum of factors that contribute to macro-level crime rates and micro-level offending.

Second, mass EBP would have entailed substantial investment in research infrastructure that could guide policy (Mears 2017). Policymakers and agency officials would not need to make knee-jerk decisions in response to perceived or actual emergencies. They would be less able to seek recourse in political ideology or personal beliefs. Instead, they could draw on objective and accurate information about problems and their causes and solutions. They would have information about the distribution of crime or prisoner misconduct, for example, as well as the factors contributing to them and, in turn, what policies or policy adjustments would be warranted.

Agency officials also would have information about systems operations, such as how administrative policy shifts were implemented across different prisons, and why implementation varied. Monitoring is a critical aspect of any successful business. With the investment in research infrastructure, correctional systems would have had the ability to identify and correct implementation problems. They could monitor outcomes, such as recidivism rates of individuals leaving particular prisons. In turn, they could identify why recidivism rates were lower at some prisons and higher at others, then take steps to implement changes at the latter. They also could identify impending problems.

Although some problems may arise randomly, many may not. Prison riots are illustrative. A particular incident might spark one, but a range of preexisting conditions likely would enable such a spark to matter. Surveys of personnel and incarcerated persons might identify conditions that increase the chances of riots. If monitored, officials could take steps to alleviate tensions or concerns at different prisons, and thus reduce the likelihood of riots. A system of mass EBP, then, would be accompanied by research infrastructure that could aid not only in evaluating policy impacts but also in guiding efforts to ensure that emerging needs were identified and met, and that policy implementation was improved. In that way, research infrastructure would both contribute to and reinforce the benefits of mass EBP.

Third, mass EBP would have led to the accumulation of credible evidence about what works and what does not across all of criminal justice and corrections. It also would have led to more systematic identification of policy needs and problems, their causes, and how to more effectively design and implement policies, programs, and practices. It would have led to a greater set of EBP options, such that lawmakers and administrators could make informed decisions about when one EBP might be more appropriate or possible to implement in a particular context. Not least, unnecessary or ineffective policies would be quickly identified and discarded.

Fourth, a mass EBP "ecosystem" likely would have reduced the politicization of policy choices. It would not remove politics—in a democracy, a range of factors should weigh in on policy. Research is not and should not be the final arbiter. But it would have reduced the ability of individuals or groups to make baseless claims about the need for or the effectiveness of particular policies. At the least, it would have made the baselessness of the claims more apparent and difficult to sustain. And it would have increased the expectation that policy be grounded in research that is as objective and as valid as possible.

IV. Contours of Mass EBP

What would mass EBP look like? It could mean that all of criminal justice involved reliance on effective decision-making, practices, programs and interventions, laws, informal or formal policies, what we refer to collectively as "policies." That might seem ideal, but there are problems with it. For one, reference to "effective" begs the question of what is meant by "effective." For another, it misses that effectiveness is not, in fact, the only way to view EBP. For example, EBP could be viewed as entailing investment in policies that are needed.

Mass EBP thus requires a much broader set of steps than "simply" investing in policies that research may have shown to be effective in improving outcomes. Here, then, we draw on our prior work (Mears and Cochran 2015; Mears 2017) and that of other scholars (e.g., Sherman et al. 2002; Blumstein and Petersilia 2005; Lipsey and Cullen 2007; Latessa, Listwan, and Koetzle 2014) to sketch the contours of what mass EBP could look like. We recognize that the totality of what we present may not be politically feasible. But without a vision of the ideal, it will be difficult if not impossible to make substantial progress. What, then, do the contours entail?

A. Infrastructure for EBP

There must be infrastructure at multiple governmental levels—federal, state, and local—to support the necessary research. Indeed, there can be no mass EBP without mass research infrastructure to create and guide it. Research capacity must be built into the lifeblood of lawmaking and government agencies.

That means that there must be a substantial increase in funding for research. It is, we submit, critical for policymakers and government agencies to appreciate scale here. For example, if a state expends $1 billion on corrections, but only $1 million on research, it simply cannot provide insight into much of anything that occurs in corrections. An investment of $10 million would help, yet would only amount to 1% of that budget. For reference, $1 million might be required to support a single well-conducted experimental-design study of a large-scale re-entry program. By implication, the $10 million would help, but only with judicious attention to cost-efficient data collection and analysis, and with little investment in any type of experimental-design impact evaluations given their substantial cost.

Against such a backdrop, it warrants emphasis that states typically spend relatively little of their criminal justice or corrections allocations on research. Informally, one can take stock by comparing staffing in research divisions to the staffing for entire agencies; research divisions tend to be substantially understaffed. One can, too, take stock by considering the federal government's nominal expenditures on research. For example, the National Institute of Justice, the federal agency responsible for research on crime and justice, operates with an approximately $40 million budget (Laub 2021, 167). This is, quite literally, a pittance compared to investment in other policy arenas, such as healthcare (Blumstein and Petersilia 1995). The point was made bluntly by Petersilia (1991, 6), who commented that "for every U.S. citizen, federal funders spend $32 on health research, but only 13 cents on criminal justice research." Yet no other federal or state agency has the funding to support research into the nature and causes of crime or the design, implementation, and effectiveness of responses to crime.

What about states? They invest far less than on research than the federal government. Blumstein and Petersilia (1995, 467) emphasized that "there is little question but that the locus of research on crime and criminal justice should be the responsibility of the federal government." Their emphasis here is on "basic" research; that is, investigations into the core causes of crime and various criminal justice outcomes. States cannot do such research because they simply do not have extra funding for it. Indeed, most local and state criminal justice agencies do well simply to provide descriptive information about the populations they serve and some details about processing. That is, their focus is on "applied," policy-focused studies.

How about colleges and universities? They can certainly contribute to the science of crime and justice, but not in a systematic way that provides relevant information to criminal justice stakeholders on a day-to-day basis. This same observation holds true for nongovernmental research organizations, such as foundations and research institutes.

Even if the federal government were to invest far more in crime and justice research aimed at advancing science ("basic" research), that would not substitute for creating infrastructure to conduct applied research. State and local criminal justice systems need research that they can use to guide decisions about operations and policies. That requires the building, staffing, and technology resources to create and analyze data and to provide real-time feedback to different stakeholders. The only way that can happen is to invest in this infrastructure.

A simple way of viewing the matter is to imagine flying a plane in cloudy weather over mountainous terrain. We need real-time information about the land, wind, rain, other planes, and more. Anything less means that we quite likely will crash. Most government and university reports at best provide one-time snapshots of particular programs or initiatives, not the state of system operations or the implementation or impacts of diverse policies. That is, they do not provide real-time monitoring or evaluation. And so they quietly "crash" by failing to reduce crime or improve criminal justice operations or impacts as efficiently as possible. Indeed, the impacts of our system of justice go largely unknown (Mears 2017).

The solution? Invest substantially in research infrastructure. Policymakers sometimes advocate for running government like a business. If they did, they would invest substantially more in research. Successful businesses require detailed information about markets, production, distribution, customer satisfaction, factors that contribute to all of these dimensions, and ways to address these factors to improve each dimension. It is no different for criminal justice. Lawmakers and agencies need the resources that allow for data collection, analyses, stakeholder discussions of them, and ongoing performance monitoring and policy evaluation.

B. Political Commitment to EBP

The only way that a substantial shift to create such infrastructure occurs is with political commitment to it. That commitment must go beyond calls for government accountability and reliance on EBP. And it must go beyond adoption of specific programs, practices, or policies. It must entail annual allocations of research dollars—for legislative and agency decision-making—sufficient to provide information necessary to make informed judgments about policies.

This condition may be obvious, yet the lack of research infrastructure at federal, state, and local levels can only mean two things. First, either these calls are entirely superficial, designed to gain political capital, with no intention of taking actions to follow through on them. In this view, the calls flow from the politicization of crime and are used as cover to justify particular policies or approaches. Second, the calls flow from a lack of understanding about what is necessary to create EBP. We know of no research that adjudicates between these two possibilities. Regardless, the fact remains that without lawmakers and agency officials committing to sustained investment in research, there can be no mass EBP.

Consider a state prison system that adopts a few EBPs. Perhaps the agency officials believe that their prison system is guided by EBP. It is not. Myriad decision-making protocols, rules, programs, policies, trainings, and the like will remain unexamined and, by extension, cannot be accurately characterized as "evidence-based." To rectify this situation requires research infrastructure for illuminating each of these dimensions and more. Ultimately, creating this infrastructure—for all of criminal justice—requires that lawmakers and agency officials align in supporting a lasting change to the status quo of minimal research funding.

C. The Evaluation Hierarchy: Institutionalizing Its Use to Create EBP

There must be a requirement that government agencies, and the policies, programs, and practices that they fund, conduct research that aligns with the evaluation hierarchy. This means tasking governmental research agencies with a focus on empirically based evaluations, using standard social science research methods, of the (1) need for and (2) the theory, (3) implementation, (4) impact, and (5) cost-efficiency of proposed and existing policies, programs, and practices (Rossi, Lipsey, and Freeman 2004; Mears 2010; Mears and Cochran 2015).

The logic of the hierarchy as a basis for creating EBP is straightforward. If there is a need for policy, proceed; if there is not, then do not proceed. If a policy is needed, design one based on the best available theory and empirical evidence about the size and distribution of the problem (across groups, places, or organizations), as well as its causes. Then implement the policy and monitor its implementation, making adjustments where necessary to improve implementation. Next, evaluate the policy's impact through the most rigorous, within the boundaries of what is feasible, research designs. Monitor implementation and outcomes continuously, and make adjustments to the policy's design and implementation to improve impacts (Mears and Butts 2008; Mears and Bacon 2009; Mears 2014, 2016). Finally, assess the cost-efficiency of the policy to identify the impacts of the policy using a universal metric of benefits to costs, as expressed in monetary units. The hierarchy should be augmented by efforts to identify and quantify potential policy harms.

Observe that this view of "evidence-based" goes well beyond the use of experimental or quasi-experimental research designs to assess a particular program's impact. It entails reliance on established social science methods to ground all aspects of policy on credible empirical research. That includes decisions to adopt, expand, or eliminate policies and how to design and implement policies to demonstrate accountability and to increase impacts and cost-efficiency.

For there to be any appreciable large-scale improvement in EBP, application of the hierarchy should occur across all aspects of criminal justice, including lawmaking, law enforcement, the courts, corrections (probation, jails, prisons, parole), and crime prevention efforts (Mears and Barnes 2010). For example, there have been calls recently to "defund the police." An evidence-based approach to this task would require first identifying the need to do so. What is the nature, magnitude, and distribution of the problem? What goals would be achieved? It would include identifying, on theoretical and empirical grounds a policy design that would better achieve these goals. It then would entail quantifying the policy's impact and cost-efficiency.

A central problem with criminal justice is the lack of any coherent coordination of efforts (Mears 2017). Lawmakers, law enforcement, courts, prisons, jails, and so on all operate more or less independently. There is, then, a need for a centralized agency that coordinates all aspects of criminal justice. It should oversee efforts to implement the evaluation hierarchy into all aspects of decision-making, as well as efforts to incorporate the views of those groups most likely to be affected by policies. This can be done through surveys, focus groups, and other approaches. At the same time, it should be charged with continuously updating a registry of various policies that have, or have not, been effective in a given state, county, city, or town, and with determining why this is the case. That can serve to avoid reinventing the wheel and repeating the mistakes of the past. It is almost certainly the case that creating a centralized agency would not be straightforward and would encounter resistance from criminal justice and corrections agencies. Overcoming the challenges is, we would argue, possible. And it is also necessary if we are to appreciably improve the effectiveness of the many and diverse efforts to address crime.

D. Constant Evaluation and Improvement

A commitment to EBP must necessarily entail a commitment to continuous monitoring and evaluation of criminal justice policy and to a policymaking and policy revision process that incorporates the resulting information (Mears 2017). Developing appropriate and effective policies cannot happen in a vacuum. It requires multiple sources of information and the views of diverse stakeholders (e.g., citizens, groups most likely to be affected by policies, criminal justice system groups most likely to implement the policies). As one example of the importance of such a process, Taxman (2018) has highlighted that critical components of sustained high-quality implementation include developing an organizational structure that can support implementation evaluations and a culture of change based on results of the evaluations.

V. Creating Mass EBP Is Possible and Necessary

A shift to mass EBP would be a substantial one, but there are many reasons for optimism. One is that government and politics are primed to accept EBP as a standard. The rhetoric of EBP has infused political discourse. Many criminal justice and corrections agencies use the terminology. Scholars have increasingly developed considerable bodies of research on EBP and an array of challenges in, and opportunities for, developing and implementing EBP, as the present volume attests. In addition, research capacity has been much improved. The amount and quality of data, the ready availability of so much of it in electronic form, improved computing and analytic power—these changes and more have improved in recent decades. Such developments bode well for improved EBP, so long as the will is there to invest the requisite resources and political capital to make it happen and to take steps to address inequalities and inefficiencies.

Political will is essential because there will need to be substantial investments in research infrastructure and in systemic reliance on research to guide, evaluate, and modify policy (Mears 2017). It will be essential, too, for creating systemic change. There will need to be a focus on creating entire systems that rest on EBP, not just reliance on an evidence-based program here or there. There will, in short, need to be an alignment between rhetoric and practice. We believe that such changes are possible and would result in improved public safety and justice. At the least, it would allow for greater accountability by helping to illuminate the "black box" of all that happens in criminal justice and corrections (Mears 2008).

Our sense of optimism is strengthened by already existing models from healthcare. There are, without a doubt, problems in healthcare decision-making (Mears and Bacon 2009). However, the healthcare system offers important lessons. Consider the following steps that the Food and Drug Administration (FDA) follows in developing pharmaceutical interventions. The first step entails identifying the most pressing problems. Second, there is the development of preliminary solutions that might address these problems. Third, a systematic research evaluation is undertaken to assess the effectiveness of these solutions across various populations, places, and circumstances. Fourth, this body of evidence is subjected to third-party review, independent of political, economic, or other potentially biasing forces. And, fifth, cost-effective solutions that are approved need to be supported and then monitored for continued efficacy. These steps echo those of the evaluation hierarchy (Rossi, Lipsey, and Freeman 2004), which calls for empirical assessment of need, creating a sound theoretical foundation for a policy, documenting implementation and ways to improve it, assessing effectiveness, and then evaluating a policy's cost-efficiency relative to other options. Neither the FDA process or the hierarchy are systematically woven into criminal justice or correctional system practice (Mears 2010, 2017), but they provide a clear touchstone for what to do and how to do it.

There are other examples of this kind of work that have been organized and funded within specific states that also provide grounds for optimism. For example, the Washington State Institute for Public Policy (WSIPP) conducts nonpartisan research to inform state policymaking and monitoring (see Drake and Knoth-Peterson, this volume). It focuses on any policy domain relevant to the state legislature, not just criminal justice. They operate independently to assess policies and provide cost-benefit analyses to inform legislators' and agency officials' efforts to support needed and effective policy.

Another criminal justice–specific example is the Texas Criminal Justice Policy Council (CJPC). The CJPC focused on research and policy evaluation to advise juvenile and adult correctional practices. Until then-governor Rick Perry terminated it in 2003 (Lomax 2004), the CJPC operated with a roughly $1 million annual budget and had done so under Democratic and Republican governors. Prior to CJPC's termination, the Texas Sunset Advisory Commission, in 1996, recommended—after highlighting that the state spent approximately $3.4 billion annually on law enforcement and corrections—that the council be continued for another 12 years (Texas Sunset Advisory Commission 1996, 1). The annual CJPC budget then would have amounted to less than 3% of 1% of the state's law enforcement and corrections expenditures. Mention of a now defunct institution underscores that an investment in research is fundamentally a political activity and a reflection of political priorities. If states do in fact want EBP, and want to install a research infrastructure as we have advised here, they will have to pay for it.

There exist still other grounds for optimism. The move toward "translational criminology," which was spearheaded by the former director of the National Institute of Justice (Laub 2012), suggests a movement toward federal recognition of the need for mass EBP. A greater receptivity to experimental-design approaches to evaluating policy—which typically cannot happen without the support of criminal justice and correctional system agencies—suggests a similar movement (Welsh, Braga, and Bruinsma 2013). At the same time, alongside of "correctional quackery" lies a great deal of interest from these agencies in EBP (Latessa, Listwan, and Koetzle 2014; Taxman 2018). And numerous examples exist of new ways to approach corrections, such as the use of technology to enhance treatment delivery and using financial incentives to encourage communities to create and implement effective alternatives to incarceration (Cullen, Jonson, and Mears 2017).

VI. Conclusion

It may seem like a pie-in-the-sky argument to suggest that mass EBP can happen. That is fair. Yet societal change takes time. Some changes evolve slowly, others occur rapidly. The last 100 years of US history alone is testimony to the slow but also rapid changes that can happen. We can see this phenomenon in criminal and juvenile justice. In the 1960s, for example, a series of landmark US Supreme Court cases created wide-ranging constitutional protections for juveniles accused of delinquency. Of course, the enactment of the juvenile court alone at the end of the 1800s marked a radical departure from how young people accused of crimes were treated. The next several decades witnessed a slow unfolding of the idea of a separate juvenile justice system. The "due process" revolution of the 1960s marked another tidal change. Even so, it did not instantly result in uniform protections for all youth, nor did it ameliorate disproportionalities in due process violations among different demographic and social groups (Feld 2019).

In somewhat parallel fashion, America and many countries throughout the world embarked on a historically unprecedented expansion of prisons and jails. This shift toward "mass incarceration" did not have to happen, but rather arose from a variety of causes (Garland 2013; Gottschalk 2013; Mears and Cochran 2015). Ironically, it occurred just as policymakers began to proclaim the virtues of accountability and reliance on "what works." The paradox remains striking—just as calls for EBP arose, the United States relentlessly pursued a policy (i.e., increased use of prison and reliance on longer prison terms) for which relatively little credible research evidence existed regarding its need, theory, appropriate use, impacts, or cost-efficiency. As but one example, mass incarceration proceeds from an assumption that the main cause of crime, whether at the individual or societal level, is insufficient fear of punishment. An entire field of study, criminology, counters that view, but was largely ignored.

Will investing in the infrastructure for mass EBP be costly? Absolutely. Would it require substantial and sustained political commitment to EBP? Yes. But there is really no other alternative if we are to appreciably improve public safety and justice policy. And, importantly, such change does not have to occur overnight. We have indicators that policymakers, criminal justice administrators and practitioners, and the public want government accountability and effective policy, and we have many examples of places and agencies that are pursuing EBP. Hopefully, in 25 years, people will be able to look back and refer to the era of mass EBP. If they do, the betting money is that society will be safer and there will be more justice.

References

Austin, James, Todd Clear, Richard Rosenfeld, and Joel Wallman. 2021. The danger of a return to crime alarmism. *The Crime Report*, November 23. https://thecrimereport.org/2021/11/23/the-danger-of-a-return-to-crime-alarmism/.

Beaudry, Gabrielle, Rongqin Yu, Amanda E. Perry, and Seena Fazel. 2021. Effectiveness of psychological interventions in prison to reduce recidivism: A systematic review and meta-analysis of randomised controlled trials. *Lancet Psychiatry*, 8:759–773.

Blumstein, Alfred, and Joan Petersilia. 1995. Investing in criminal justice research. In *Crime*, edited by James Q. Wilson and Joan Petersilia, 465–487. San Francisco: Institute for Contemporary Studies Press.

Buehler, Emily D. 2021. *Justice expenditures and employment in the United States, 2017*. Washington, DC: Bureau of Justice Statistics.

Carson, E. Ann. 2021. *Prisoners in 2020—Statistical tables*. Washington, DC: Bureau of Justice Statistics.

Clear, Todd R. 2007. *Imprisoning communities: How mass incarceration makes disadvantaged neighborhoods worse*. New York: Oxford University Press.

Cochran, Joshua C., Daniel P. Mears, and William D. Bales. 2014. Assessing the effectiveness of correctional sanctions. *Journal of Quantitative Criminology*, 30:317–347.

Cullen, Francis T. 2005. The twelve people who saved rehabilitation: How the science of criminology made a difference. *Criminology*, 43:1–42.

Cullen, Francis T., and Karen E. Gilbert. 2013. *Reaffirming rehabilitation*. 2nd ed. Waltham, MA: Anderson/Elsevier.

Cullen, Francis T., Cheryl L. Jonson, and Daniel P. Mears. 2017. Reinventing community corrections. *Crime and Justice*, 46:27–93.

Drake, Elizabeth K., and Lauren Knoth-Peterson. 2022. Advancing the evidence-based era: 25-years of lessons learned in Washington State's juvenile justice system. In *The Oxford handbook of evidence-based crime and justice policy*, edited by Brandon C. Welsh, Steven N. Zane, and Daniel P. Mears, 91–116. New York: Oxford University Press.

Durlauf, Steven N. and Daniel S. Nagin. 2011. Imprisonment and crime: Can both be reduced? *Criminology and Public Policy*, 10:9–54.

Farabee, David. 2005. *Rethinking rehabilitation: Why can't we reform our criminals?* Washington, DC: AEI Press.

Feeley, Malcolm. 1979. *The process is the punishment: Handling cases in a lower criminal court*. New York: Russell Sage Foundation.

Feld, Barry. 2019. *The evolution of the juvenile court: Race, politics, and the criminalizing of juvenile justice*. New York: New York University Press.

Forer, Lois G. 1994. *A rage to punish: The unintended consequences of mandatory sentencing*. New York: Norton.

Garland, David. 2001. *The culture of control: Crime and social order in contemporary society*. Chicago: University of Chicago Press.

Garland, David. 2013. The 2012 Sutherland address: Penality and the penal state. *Criminology*, 51:475–517.

Glaze, Lauren E., and Erika Parks. 2012. *Correctional populations in the United States, 2011*. Washington, DC: Bureau of Justice Statistics.

Gottschalk, Marie. 2013. The carceral state and the politics of punishment. In *The Sage handbook of punishment and society*, edited by Jonathan Simon and Richard Sparks, 205–241. Thousand Oaks, CA: SAGE.

Gunderson, Anna. 2022. Who punishes more? Partisanship, punitive policies, and the puzzle of Democratic governors. *Political Research Quarterly*, 75:3–19.

Jeglic, Elizabeth L. and Cynthia Calkins, eds. 2018. *New frontiers in offender treatment: The translation of evidence-based practices to correctional settings.* New York: Springer.

Kyckelhahn, Tracey. 2012. *State corrections expenditures, FY 1982–2010.* Washington, DC: Bureau of Justice Statistics.

Latessa, Edward J., Shelley J. Listwan, and Deborah Koetzle. 2014. *What works (and doesn't) in reducing recidivism.* Waltham, MA: Anderson.

Laub, John H. 2012. Translational criminology. *Translational Criminology* 3:4–5.

Laub, John H. 2021. Moving the National Institute of Justice forward: July 2010 through December 2012. *Journal of Contemporary Criminal Justice*, 37:166–174.

Lipsey, Mark W., and Francis T. Cullen. 2007. The effectiveness of correctional rehabilitation: A review of systematic reviews. *Annual Review of Law and Social Science*, 3:297–320.

Lomax, Lucius. 2004. Who fired Tony Fabelo? The "private" tale behind Perry's veto of the Criminal Justice Policy Council. *Austin Chronicle*, April 30. https://www.austinchronicle.com/news/2004-04-30/208428/.

Lum, Cynthia, and Christopher S. Koper. 2017. *Evidence-based policing: Translating research into practice.* New York: Oxford University Press.

MacKenzie, Doris L. 2006. *What works in corrections: Reducing the criminal activities of offenders and delinquents.* New York: Cambridge University Press.

MacKenzie, Doris L., and David P. Farrington. 2015. Preventing future offending of delinquents and offenders: What have we learned from experiments and meta-analyses? *Journal of Experimental Criminology*, 11:565–595.

Martinson, Robert. 1974. What works? Questions and answers about prison reform. *Public Interest*, 35:22–54.

Mears, Daniel P. 2008. Accountability, efficiency, and effectiveness in corrections: Shining a light on the black box of prison systems. *Criminology and Public Policy*, 7:143–152.

Mears, Daniel P. 2010. *American criminal justice policy: An evaluation approach to increasing accountability and effectiveness.* New York: Cambridge University Press.

Mears, Daniel P. 2013. Supermax prisons: The policy and the evidence. *Criminology and Public Policy*, 12:681–719.

Mears, Daniel P. 2014. The role of information in changing offender behavior, criminal justice system actions, and policy maker decisions. *Criminology and Public Policy*, 13:441–449.

Mears, Daniel P. 2016. Policy evaluation and assessment. In *Advancing criminology and criminal justice policy*, edited by Thomas G. Blomberg, Julie M. Brancale, Kevin M. Beaver, and William D. Bales, 26–39. New York: Routledge.

Mears, Daniel P. 2017. *Out-of-control criminal justice: The systems improvement solution for more safety, justice, accountability, and efficiency.* New York: Cambridge University Press.

Mears, Daniel P. 2019. Creating systems that can improve safety and justice (and why piecemeal change won't work). *Justice Evaluation Journal*, 2:1–17.

Mears, Daniel P. 2022. Bridging the research-policy divide to advance science and policy: The 2022 Bruce Smith, Sr. Award address to the Academy of Criminal Justice Sciences. *Justice Evaluation Journal* 5:163–185.

Mears, Daniel P., and Sarah Bacon. 2009. Improving criminal justice through better decision making: Lessons from the medical system. *Journal of Criminal Justice*, 37:142–154.

Mears, Daniel P., and James C. Barnes. 2010. Toward a systematic foundation for identifying evidence-based criminal justice sanctions and their relative effectiveness. *Journal of Criminal Justice*, 38:702–810.

Mears, Daniel P., and Jeffrey A. Butts. 2008. Using performance monitoring to improve the accountability, operations, and effectiveness of juvenile justice. *Criminal Justice Policy Review*, 19:264–284.

Mears, Daniel P., and Joshua C. Cochran. 2015. *Prisoner reentry in the era of mass incarceration*. Thousand Oaks, CA: SAGE.

Mears, Daniel P., Joshua C. Cochran, William D. Bales, and Avinash S. Bhati. 2016. Recidivism and time served in prison. *Journal of Criminal Law and Criminology*, 106:83–124.

Minton, Todd D., Lauren G. Beatty, and Zhen Zeng. 2021. *Correctional populations in the United States, 2019—Statistical tables*. Washington, DC: Bureau of Justice Statistics.

Nagin, Daniel S., Francis T. Cullen, and Cheryl L. Jonson. 2009. Imprisonment and reoffending. *Crime and Justice*, 38:115–200.

Petersilia, Joan. 1991. Policy relevance and the future of criminology. *Criminology*, 29:1–16.

Petersilia, Joan. 2003. *When prisoners come home: Parole and prisoner reentry*. New York: Oxford University Press.

Rossi, Peter H., Mark W. Lipsey, and Howard E. Freeman. 2004. *Evaluation: A systematic approach*. 7th ed. Thousand Oaks, CA: SAGE.

Sherman, Lawrence W., David P. Farrington, Brandon C. Welsh, and Doris Layton MacKenzie, eds. 2002. *Evidence based crime prevention*. London: Routledge.

Sherman, Lawrence W., Denise C. Gottfredson, Doris L. MacKenzie, John Eck, Peter Reuter, and Shawn Bushway, eds. 1997. *Preventing crime: What works, what doesn't, what's promising*. Washington, DC: Office of Justice Programs.

Shorman, Jonathan, and Jeanne Kuang. 2022. Missouri Gov. Parson will seek harsher sentences to fight violent crime, document says. *Kansas City Star*, January 12. https://www.kansascity.com/news/politics-government/article257217862.html.

Simon, Jonathan. 2007. *Governing through crime*. New York: Oxford University Press.

Taxman, Faye S. 2018. The partially clothed emperor: Evidence-based practices. *Journal of Contemporary Criminal Justice*, 34:97–114.

Texas Sunset Advisory Commission. 1996. *Criminal Justice Policy Council: Sunset staff report*. Austin: Texas Sunset Advisory Commission. https://www.sunset.texas.gov/reviews-and-reports/agencies/criminal-justice-policy-council.

Tonry, Michael. 2007. Determinants of penal policies. *Crime and Justice*, 36:1–48.

Travis, Jeremy, Bruce Western, and Steve Redburn, eds. 2014. *The growth of incarceration in the United States: Exploring causes and consequences*. Washington, DC: National Academies Press.

van der Stouwe, Trudy, Jessica J. Asscher, Geert Jan J. M. Stams, Maja Deković, Peter H. van der Laan. 2014. The effectiveness of Multisystemic Therapy (MST): A meta-analysis. *Clinical Psychology Review*, 34:468–481.

Welsh, Brandon C., Anthony A. Braga, and Gerben J. N. Bruinsma, eds. 2013. *Experimental criminology: Prospects for advancing science and public policy*. New York: Cambridge University Press.

Welsh, Brandon C., and David P. Farrington, eds. 2007. *Preventing crime: What works for children, offenders, victims, and places.* New York: Springer.

Williams, Vanessa. 2016. 1994 crime bill haunts Clinton and Sanders as criminal justice reform rises to top in Democratic contest. *Washington Post*, February 12. https://www.washingtonpost.com/news/post-politics/wp/2016/02/12/1994-crime-bill-haunts-clinton-and-sanders-as-criminal-justice-reform-rises-to-top-in-democratic-contest/.

CHAPTER 30

"BIG DATA" AND EVIDENCE-BASED POLICY AND PRACTICE

The Advantages, Challenges, and Long-Term Potential of Naturally Occurring Data

DANIEL T. O'BRIEN

"Big data" have stormed society in recent years, inspiring hyperbolic prophesies of how they will transform anything and everything. There are also many who do not share this optimism, from those who think the promise is overblown to others who have deep reservations about the merit of the proposed transformations. These debates have occurred in the public square, which is probably preferable to a private conversation among academics, tech entrepreneurs, and a handful of policymakers. But we are consequently faced with competing headlines and buzzwords that mask a highly nuanced middle. To wit, I ask you to consider for a moment, what are "big data"? Not just what some examples might be, but how we define them. Does their size even matter? If not, what about them does? Without an answer to that and related fundamental questions, we cannot identify their strengths and weaknesses, and, per the purpose of this book, how best to leverage them for evidence-based policy and practice.

This chapter aims to demystify, at least partially, big data, with specific attention to its value for evidence-based policy pertaining to crime prevention and law enforcement in local communities. This may seem a narrow application, but it is a popular one, relevant to everyone's daily life. Further, it is an effective vehicle for illustrating the strengths, weaknesses, and potential uses of big data, insights that might easily be extrapolated to other domains. I begin by defining big data, and even suggesting that we might be better off using the less exciting but more precise term "naturally occurring data." I then articulate a series of advantages and challenges these resources pose relative to the types of data that are typically used in research. From there, I present a series of case studies that illustrate each of these advantages and challenges.

For those who like to know the takeaway before they get started (or would rather not wade through an entire chapter to get there), I will say this: Most big data are naturally occurring, meaning they were generated incidentally by digital administrative systems, from government programs to call lines to social media platforms. This makes them large, detailed, and rich in information, often on subjects that could rarely be studied in such scale by intentional data collection efforts. But it also raises questions about potential biases or gaps in their content. As such, the opportunity is great, but the challenges are not to be taken lightly, as we would not want to build evidence-based policies on what amounts to misinterpreted evidence. Nonetheless, such issues are not insurmountable. There is also, lurking in the origins of the data, a special opportunity that is rarely discussed; that is, because the data were generated by an administrative system, they provide a direct window into the operations, impacts, and equitability of that system and any related policies or programs. Herein lies true impact and even a paradigm shift for evidence-based policy. For those who would like to unpack this summary, please read on.

I. Why Are Novel Data Special?

There are two ways to think about novelty: how something new is different from what came before it, and how it enables different opportunities from its predecessors. Much of the discussion around "big data" has centered on the former, as indicated by the name alone. The distinctiveness of big data has been often summarized with "3 V's": volume, or "big"-ness; velocity, or frequent updating, sometimes in real time; and variety, or breadth of content (Laney 2001). Kitchin and McArdle (2016), seeking a more rigorous definition of why big data are so big, concluded that volume is a byproduct of velocity and exhaustivity, or the intent to document the entirety of a particular set of cases. In effect, they replaced variety with exhaustivity, arguing that the proliferation of cases does more to grow a data set than adding more variables. Assessments of "big"-ness are certainly informative and reveal real differences between emergent data sets and their predecessors. Traditional data from surveys, observations, and experiments rarely if ever match the levels of volume, velocity, variety, or exhaustivity attained by administrative records posted on open data portals, social media posts on public platforms, or conditions tracked by sensors. That, however, only tells us about the size of these new data sets, *not* how they are useful or how they might alter data-driven research and policy.

It is not so important that the data are big. Indeed, large data have existed since empires started implementing censuses to count thousands and millions of people a few thousand years ago. Astrophysicists were gathering terabytes upon terabytes of information on distant stars in the 1980s (if not earlier). Instead, what distinguishes many of the novel data sets referenced by this term is that they are "naturally occurring," harvested as the byproduct of some technology-enabled administrative process (e.g., the administration of a police department or court system). I have argued elsewhere about the consequences this has for analytic opportunities (O'Brien 2018), some of which gets a bit technical in terms of database structure and management. Here I want to cut right to the chase and describe what naturally occurring data allow us to do—and where they suffer from limitations.

A. The Advantages

First, and most simply, when a technological system harvests information, the resultant data can capitalize on the spatiotemporal precision afforded by computers, including date-time stamps down to the second and geographic coordinates down to the square meter. This sort of spatiotemporal precision is unprecedented. Researchers have historically sought to convert human-reported addresses and intersections into latitude and longitude through a mixture of automated geocoders and manual error-checking, and rarely have had enough information for it to be useful to identify even the specific date of an event. Similarly, as the data become larger and larger, other information pertaining to a given event or unit of analysis is increasingly detailed—think of the dozens of fields that a 911 dispatcher completes to properly route an emergency responder—and the overall picture depicted by the whole corpus of data gains in resolution. These advances in precision are not unique to naturally occurring data, of course. A researcher conducting original data collection with the requisite resources and foresight could design a computer-aided system for their own purposes. That said, naturally occurring data gain these advantages by default. Meanwhile, it is much harder for researcher-collected data to compete with the analytic precision that arises from exhaustivity.

Second, many administrative systems offer a new vantage point on society that was previously more difficult to access directly—a form of variety that is crucial for asking new questions. In other words, variety of content might not be primarily responsible for the relative size of a data set, but it determines its novelty. For instance, one popular resource over the last decade has been 311 reports requesting nonemergency government services (e.g., graffiti removal, filling potholes), which capture intentional efforts by community members to maintain public infrastructure in their neighborhoods (O'Brien 2018). This important social process was studied by environmental psychologists and criminologists with observational measures decades earlier (Brown and Werner 1985; Taylor 1988), but it always posed a simple limitation: How often would a researcher actually observe someone sweeping a street, picking up trash, or otherwise actively maintaining their community? Another set of examples comes from the proliferation of sensor systems that measure local conditions in real time. These have become popular in environmental science, especially regarding equity and justice. This is because sensors can confirm concerns of air quality, extreme heat, street flooding, and other hazards (e.g., Caubel et al. 2019). The primary use of sensors in criminology is gunshot detection technology (GDT), which uses the sonic signatures to alert police departments to likely shootings, thereby supplementing calls to 911 (Carr and Doleac 2018). Though they differ in various ways, both 311 systems and GDT illustrate how novelty combined with precision opens new lines of research.

Third, we need to think about the implications not of one novel data set but of the confluence of *many* novel data sets. We can best understand this when recognizing that most naturally occurring data come in the form of records that capture events or transactions. Instead of describing units of analysis directly, they might include records that involve a particular unit once, twice, fifty times, or not at all. This grants the researcher extensive flexibility for creating numerous measures that describe the units of analysis in nuanced ways. Thus, our variety is already far greater than it might be traditionally. Further, multiple data sets often describe the same units of analyses—people, addresses, streets, neighborhoods, etc.—meaning we can link them together. Such linkages expand variety even more, creating exponential growth in the number of research questions that might be pursued.

B. The Challenges

Having walked through three major strengths of working with naturally occurring data, we must acknowledge the challenges they present. In fact, we might view each of the three major advantages as having a corresponding limitation. First, precision is powerful, but as many readers will recall from research methods classes, it is not the same thing as accuracy. Data scientists have extended this lesson in recent years, articulating the "big data paradox": by being so large, big data give the illusion of being very certain in their interpretation, when they might instead be remarkably certain about incorrect information (Lazer et al. 2014). How is this possible? It comes down to a question of validity. Whereas naturally occurring data are exhaustive regarding the information that enters the system, they make no claims that what enters the system is complete. Do all crimes make it into a 911 dispatch system? Are all potholes reported through 311? Does Twitter capture all observations and emotions of a population? The answers to these questions are inevitably, "No." Of course, traditional data collection does not capture all relevant information either, but techniques like sampling frames, experimental designs, and weighting algorithms help to mitigate bias. With naturally occurring data, the researcher must wrestle with the inherent biases of the data generation process, which are tied in with the administrative system that generates the data.

Second, novel, nuanced content is exciting, but it is not always clear we know what it means and how it aligns with existing frameworks. Which measures matter? How do we design them? Are they predictive of crime or anything else? There is again a temptation here that data scientists are increasingly warning against. Only a few years ago, a standard solution to this problem was to ask the computer to solve it. Machine learning and artificial intelligence were heralded as absolving us from ever having to develop theoretical models again, as they will identify the multivariate relationships that matter (Anderson 2008). The problem with a computer-directed approach is that the results are often uninterpretable, and thus cannot be translated into generalizable knowledge or evidence-based policies. Put another way, the computers might tell us when a feature in the data predicts crime, but with no information about *why* or what we should do about it. Some in the machine learning world have begun developing "white box" or "glass box" models to counteract these traditional "black box" approaches (Rudin 2019; Wang and Rudin 2015). The alternative is for researchers to roll up their sleeves and get familiar with their data, theorizing about and testing various measures.

Third, when we link data from many sources we can gain a comprehensive, or "360-degree," view of a unit of analysis. While this enables a vast array of research questions, it also raises questions of privacy. Much has been written about the potential to re-identify individuals in anonymized data sets, which becomes more and more possible as additional variables increase the likelihood that unique combinations can be attributed to particular individuals (Sweeney 2002). Similarly for properties and buildings, given enough information an analyst might infer information not contained in the data. For example, New York City discovered that the best way to predict that a business was at risk for closing was to look at whether it had been paying its utility bills on time (Goldsmith and Crawford 2014). Meanwhile, some data collection, like facial recognition software, explicitly targets individual identification. Across these examples, we must consider the tradeoff between the value of the information for the purposes of research and policy and the costs to privacy.

C. The Rest of This Chapter

Whether we use the term "big data" or not, the distinctiveness of naturally occurring data is apparent. But for every strength there is a caveat that must be considered. The data are far more precise than their predecessors, but systematic biases can lead us to overly confident, invalid conclusions. Novel content and variety expand our ways of viewing, understanding, and responding to the world, but we need to be very careful about how we develop the measures that we then incorporate into our science and policy. The vast proliferation of variety across data sets enables an exponential growth in the relationships we can examine and account for, but at the potential risk of privacy.

In this chapter I will concentrate on three classes of naturally occurring data: administrative records generated by government agencies or other institutions, posts to social media platforms and other Internet sites, and sensor systems tracking ambient conditions. The remainder of this chapter presents eight case studies from the use of these types of data for the study and management of crime in local communities, with emphasis on implications for both research and policy. The first six illustrate the three strengths and their corresponding three limitations. The last two move to an additional opportunity I have not yet discussed that is especially pertinent to evidence-based policy and practice. Many of these data sets are generated by the selfsame programs that we might seek to evaluate, refine, or innovate upon. As such, they provide a unique opportunity to see directly into the program itself. Where there is precision in the data, we understand the program more deeply. Where there are biases in the data, we will find biases in the programs. Where we engage with the variety, we learn about the inner workings of the program. Where we discover opportunities and concerns when linking the data with other resources, we reveal the same for the program. How we accomplish this depends on how we navigate the advantages and challenges of the data.

II. Precision Versus Validity

A. Criminology of Place

A basic motivation for urban criminology is the uneven distribution of crime and disorder across neighborhoods (e.g., Sampson, Raudenbush, and Earls 1997; Sampson 2012; Shaw and McKay [1942] 1969). This work has been highly influential, contributing to broader ideas about community dynamics and "neighborhood effects" that have impacted allied fields as well, including public health, sociology, and child development. It has been characterized, however, by the implicit assumption that neighborhoods are homogenous regions and that all places within them have an equal likelihood of experiencing crime and disorder. One could argue that this assumption was in part the result of a methodological limitation: few if any data systems were designed to conduct wholesale assessments of the distribution of crime across all of the streets and addresses of a city. Over the past 30 years or so this has changed with the emergence of a "criminology of place."

Criminology of place started in the late 1980s when two studies in two different cities each demonstrated that ~3% of addresses accounted for 50% of crime events (Pierce, Spaar, and Briggs 1988; Sherman, Gartin, and Buerger 1989). An ensuing body of work has emphasized the importance of "hot spot" street segments as the geographic scale of greatest interest, finding that 4–6% of streets consistently generate 50% of crime events (Andresen and Malleson 2011; Braga, Papachristos, and Hureau 2010; Lee et al. 2017; Weisburd 2015). The initial studies on this subject predated "big data" as we refer to it today, though they relied on crime records and other administrative databases that would now be categorized as big data or naturally occurring data. At that time, however, they would not have been seen that way, and there are important distinctions. The researchers and their policy partners had to clean, organize, and geocode the raw data before conducting any analyses. It is notable that, likely because of this, the early studies examined a single dataset in a single city.

As data systems have improved, however, mapping and analyzing individual incidents of crime and disorder at precise geographical scales has become increasingly efficient, and even embedded in administrative systems. In many cities, for instance, the 911 dispatch system geocodes the reported address when the call is received so that emergency responders can be directed to the correct location. As such, growth of criminology of place has rapidly accelerated, with studies spanning over a dozen cities (e.g., Andresen and Malleson 2011; Braga, Papachristos, and Hureau 2010; Weisburd 2015). Some studies have even examined multiple cities simultaneously (Hipp and Kim 2017) or leveraged indicators of crime and disorder from multiple databases in a single analysis (e.g., 911, crime reports, EMS responses, 311 reports; Hibdon, Telep, and Groff 2017; O'Brien and Winship 2017). Such efforts would have been Sisyphean a mere 15 years ago.

The result—and ongoing product, in all reality—is a robust line of inquiry on the distribution of crime across places. Most famously, Weisburd (2015) has taken the consistent results across cities and data sets to justify a *law of concentration of crime*: that for a given microgeographic unit there is a narrow bandwidth of percentages for a defined cumulative proportion of crime events. There have been longitudinal studies demonstrating that as few as ~2% of street segments being consistently responsible for the bulk of crime in a city over a decade or more, and that these long-term hot spots are largely responsible for citywide crime trends (Braga, Papachristos, and Hureau 2010; Curman, Andresen, and Brantingham 2015; Groff, Weisburd, and Yang 2010). Subsequent studies have also compared the importance of places and neighborhoods in explaining the overall distribution of crime, often finding that both matter, but that places account for more variation (O'Brien and Winship 2017; Schnell, Braga, and Piza 2017; Steenbeek and Weisburd 2016). At the time of this writing, a crucial new direction is to move past comparisons of neighborhoods and places to theoretical and empirical perspectives that integrate them, offering a comprehensive framework for the distribution of crime within a city (Jones and Pridemore 2019; O'Brien and Ciomek 2022). Meanwhile, the continued advancement of geocoding systems is creating greater confidence in the analysis of data at the level of the building or address, introducing an even more granular level to analyses (aka "hotdots" or "problem properties";

O'Brien and Winship 2017; O'Brien et al. 2022a, 2022b)—one that, ironically, was where the field started in the late 1980s when the researchers were geocoding the records themselves.

B. Predictive Policing

Criminology of place has inspired policing innovations that draw on its substantive insights by focusing resources on hotspot streets (Braga, Papachristos, and Hureau 2014) or so-called problem properties (LISC 2019). The same analytic advances that have enabled criminology of place have also produced another policing innovation known as "predictive policing," or the effort to forecast the time and location of crime events based on an extended corpus of data (Pearsall 2010; Ridgeway 2013).[1] The simplest predictive policing algorithms capitalize on the basic premise of criminology of place: crime tends to recur in the same places. In fact, many popular techniques use *only* spatial concentrations of previous crimes to predict future events (e.g., Block and Block 2005; Van Patten, McKeldin-Coner, and Cox 2009). More sophisticated approaches, like risk terrain modeling (RTM), incorporate land use information with historical data to estimate risk levels across places (Caplan and Kennedy 2011; Kennedy, Caplan, and Piza 2011), generating predictions that are consistently more precise than their predecessors (Drawve 2016; Mohler et al. 2011).

Predictive policing is essentially the logical conclusion of CompStat, which was initiated in 1994 to better target police resources on high-need areas, as powered by maximal data precision and volume. It is conceptually attractive for this reason, and there is evidence that the algorithms outperform trained crime analysts, who use similar data to come to manual conclusions (Mohler et al. 2015). As such, it has been championed by major cities like Los Angeles and Santa Cruz, CA, and Chicago, IL, but also less likely participants like Palm Beach County, FL, Memphis, TN, and even Trinidad and Tobago. Despite this popularity, there are multiple concerns about the use of predictive policing. One is the question of implementation and what specific actions police departments or officers should take based on the information the algorithm generates (Ratcliffe et al. 2021). Another is the ethical and legal considerations of acting on a crime that has not yet occurred, including the intersection with existing interpretations of due process and probable cause (Ferguson 2012). The focus here, however, is on a third, more technical issue: What if the algorithms used to generate the predictions are biased in ways that reproduce racial and socioeconomic inequities in enforcement?

Predictive policing is part of a broader trend toward predictive analytics, wherein data, often in conjunction with machine learning or artificial intelligence (AI) techniques, is used to predict events. A major issue in the public conversation about predictive analytics is a more general critique of machine learning and AI that can be summarized as "garbage in, garbage out." That is, if the data going into the decision-making system are biased, the resultant decisions will mirror these imperfections. Predictive policing has become the icon for the dangers of predictive analytics, because of both the nature of the data used and the sensitivity of the decisions they support. It is well established that, in many parts of the United States, a potentially criminal event occurring in a low-income or majority-minority neighborhood is more likely to result in an arrest than the same event occurring in an affluent White neighborhood. As a result, crime records are a racially biased representation of where crimes occur, overemphasizing Black communities. If we use crime records to predict where the next crime might occur and deploy police accordingly, we are perpetuating that same racial bias. This is a major problem, and no one has solved it in the case of predictive policing.

Predictive policing is a prime example of the limitations that face big data–informed, evidence-based policy innovation. The Achilles heel is the data-generation process. In theory, predictive policing is a brilliant idea: use sophisticated models and the geospatial precision of modern crime records to predict future events. In practice, however, it is only as strong as the data themselves, and in this case the data-generation process is corrupted by historical policies. As such, the programs will only be able to reproduce the biases of the past. If someone were to develop a technique for disentangling "true crime rates" from the bias present in crime records while also maintaining the advantages of the data, the story might be different. However, at the time of this writing, no one has achieved that.

III. Measurement: Extracting Signal From Noise

A. Gunshot Detection Technology

Many naturally occurring data sets offer new ways to observe the events and conditions of communities. A striking example comes from sensor networks. These systems consist of multiple "nodes" that contain one or more sensors, each of which captures a specific ambient condition, like pollution, temperature, sunlight, precipitation, or humidity. They are most popular in environmental and climate science and corresponding policy areas and are the centerpiece of "instrumented" neighborhoods (e.g., the Center for Urban Science and Progress's Hudson Yards in New York City) that are designed to be highly efficient and immediately responsive to disturbances (O'Brien and Walton 2016). As such, they would seem to have little relevance to the study of crime, which is concerned with social events and patterns. But there is one aspect of crime that technologists have identified as accessible through sensors: gunshots.

Gunshots generate a loud noise, roughly 150 decibels, or over 250 times the sound of an automobile passing. In theory a microphone could be sufficient to capture such events. It is not quite that simple, however. There are any number of loud sounds that might occur in a community. Loudness is not a sufficient characteristic to differentiate a gunshot from a firework, a car backfire, an HVAC system near the sensor, or even loud music during a block party. This is the classic issue of "signal and noise." Naturally occurring data contain the full corpus of information generated by the environment and captured by the system in question. It is in turn necessary to isolate the specific information desired for a given measurement (i.e., the "signal") from the massive amount of extraneous information (i.e., the "noise"). Thus, a microphone hears all sounds, but algorithms must identify the features that distinguish gunshots from other sounds.

A handful of companies have developed gunshot detection technology (GDT) that they claim identifies specific features that are characteristic of a gunshot. These likely include the duration of the loudness, the speed with which it begins and then dissipates, and the frequencies emitted (i.e., highness and lowness). They claim that they can differentiate them from other loud noises, including, for example, a car backfire (Maher 2007). By installing multiple sound sensors (i.e., microphones and computer chips for processing sound signatures) across a neighborhood, GDT can triangulate the location of a gunshot, generating an objective and precise record of all gunshots within a region.

GDT has grown in popularity in American cities, as it promises to communicate gunshot events more efficiently and reliably to police departments. This trend has been such that a single vendor (ShotSpotter) had deployed sensors in over 200 cities as of this writing. To be certain, GDT systems suffer from some weaknesses, or at least fail to live up to the claims offered by the private companies who build and market them. For instance, though there is evidence that GDT captures more gunshots than 911 calls and crime reports (Carr and Doleac 2018; Irvin-Erickson et al. 2017), these discrepancies are isolated to nighttime hours, largely disappearing throughout the rest of the day (Irvin-Erickson et al. 2017). Further, none of these studies have found variation in the discrepancies between traditional records and GDT across neighborhoods, indicating that the former is still a faithful representation of cross-community rates of violence. Relatedly, Ratcliffe et al. (2019) found that GDT has not increased the number of shootings later confirmed by police, putting the practical relevance of these additionally detected events in doubt.

Though this is a chapter in a book on evidence-based policy and practice, I am going to set aside the shortcomings of GDT in these regards. My focus instead is on its purported successes as a measurement tool. By differentiating the signature of gunshots from other loud sounds, they expose them for both research and policy. In terms of research, Carr and Doleac (2018) used GDT-identified gun shots as a dependent variable when evaluating the effectiveness of Washington, DC's curfew for youth. Meanwhile, Irvin-Erickson et al. (2016) used GDT data in Washington, DC, as one component of a three-city analysis of the impacts of gun violence on economic activity. Even if the precise advantages of GDT as a policy tool are still being assessed, that in and of itself is a manifestation of an ongoing refinement of their inclusion as part of superior evidence-driven policy and practice. That was not possible until the measurement problem was solved. The same lesson might be applied to any naturally occurring data source. Can we convert sound signatures associated with trucks into estimates of heavyweight traffic? Can computer vision be used to turn videos into rates of pedestrians? Can administrative records be reduced to multiple measures of crime and disorder? The list of potential opportunities goes on, suggesting a wealth of new metrics, an idea I will return to in the section on Variety.

B. Social Media Data and Crime

Another form of naturally occurring data comes from social media platforms. These resources have excited many researchers and policymakers with their unique combination of rich textual information, social connectivity between users, and, in many cases, geographic location. Just like sensors, social media data epitomize the need to extract the signal from the noise in a data set that was not designed for the purposes of measurement. There is a massive amount of content, but to measure any given construct requires specifying the relevant features. This dual challenge and opportunity has instigated a variety of lines of research in multiple disciplines. Political scientists have shown how trends in search terms can predict elections with greater efficacy than polls (Beauchamp 2017). Sociologists and psychologists have mapped emotions across space and time using dictionaries that categorize words by their sentiments (e.g., Ritter, Preston, and Hernandez 2014). A team at Yahoo has used Twitter posts to track people's perceptions of the urban landscape by identifying words that were previously rated on how much they reflected good and bad smells and sounds (Aiello et al. 2016; Quercia et al. 2015). Some have also pursued the possibility that social media activity might also predict crime events, though with less success.

The initial studies on social media data and crime have focused on Twitter. There is some evidence that certain patterns, like a drop in tweets in an area (Bendler et al. 2014) or a particular combination of words in tweets (Gerber 2014; Wang, Brown, and, Gerber 2012; Williams, Burnap, and Sloan 2017) are predictive of crime, but these relationships are inconsistent and modest, offering little if any insight beyond historical crime rates. Consequently, an initial assessment would suggest that the new data, while exciting, do not advance our ability to forecast crime. Before this verdict is reached, however, it is important to note that these studies have been few, and instead raise a range of questions about what measures extracted from Twitter posts would be most likely to predict crime. For example, what is the appropriate spatial scale for the relationship between Twitter usage and crime events? Is it a borough in London (avg. pop ≈ 300,000; Williams, Burnap, and Sloan 2017) or a 200-meter square grid in San Francisco (Bendler et al. 2014)? Substantively, Twitter data are so rich that they can generate dozens of different measures, any of which might be tested as a predictor of crime. The simplest approach is to count Twitter posts per unit time in a region. Alternatively, one might ask how many unique individuals (i.e., Twitter accounts) posted something in that time. One might apply machine learning algorithms to textual data to extract "topics," or sets of words that often co-occur (e.g., Wang, Brown, and, Gerber 2012), or could create their own topics based on words of interest (e.g., Williams, Burnap, and Sloan 2017). Even then, which of those topics would we anticipate to presage crime? These are only some of the decisions forced by social media data, and researchers have not yet exhausted the full span of tools necessary to distinguish the signal from the noise.

It is worth noting that these are not the only ways to use social media and Internet data in the study and management of crime in communities. For instance, it has become popular to use such records to measure the ambient population of a community (i.e., the number of people actually present) in place of the residential population to improve crime rate estimation (Hipp et al. 2019; Malleson and Andresen 2015). More recent efforts have started to categorize Twitter users by their estimated home addresses to gain a better understanding of the composition of the ambient population (Tucker et al. 2021). Ethnographers are using the content of social media posts as a window onto neighborhood social dynamics (e.g., Lane 2016). These efforts offer a blueprint—if not some initial insights—that might overcome the current challenges of using social media data for predicting crime in communities.

IV. Variety: The Power and Pitfalls of a 360° View

A. Ecometrics: New Ways to Describe Neighborhoods

Naturally occurring data sets are often composed of thousands (or millions) of individual records that capture a specific event or transaction. Some questions call for the direct analysis of these records, such as the time it takes an officer to arrive on scene, but, more often than not, the value lies in being able to better understand the individuals and communities that are referenced by the records. Naturally occurring data lend themselves well to such aggregations. To illustrate, one can capture variation in crime reports across a city by tabulating them for each census tract or on each street. Such exercises are as old as the earliest studies of crime in communities, but the detail contained in naturally occurring data has greatly expanded the nuance with which such measures can be calculated. One might limit to crime reports of a particular set of types that capture a social process of interest; or compare frequencies during night and day or weekdays and weekends to observe the natural rhythms of crime; or extend the earlier example of officer response time by comparing the average response time for each neighborhood (or the median, or the percent of responses that occurred within 5 minutes, etc.).

In 2015, my colleagues Robert J. Sampson and Christopher Winship and I argued that naturally occurring data could transform the science of *ecometrics*, or measures of the physical and social characteristics of a neighborhood.[2] Ecometrics have most often been derived from resident surveys or in-person audits (i.e., systematic social observation, or SSO) per the methods articulated and pioneered by the Project on Human Development in Chicago Neighborhoods (PHDCN) in the 1990s (Raudenbush and Sampson 1999; Sampson and Raudenbush 1999). The records of naturally occurring data follow a similar logic. Just as each survey or observation reflects a single data point contributing to a composite view of a neighborhood, each administrative record, social media post, or sensor reading captures a discrete event or condition in a space that then contributes to a detailed description of the urban landscape. There are numerous novel data sets that present themselves for the construction of ecometrics, many of which offer measures that have not been accessible through existing methods.

When we articulated the opportunity that naturally occurring data presented for ecometrics, we focused our attention on overcoming weaknesses that are typically absent in intentionally collected research data. Two of the most important have been described in the previous sections: the potential for biases created by the data generation process (i.e., validity) and determining the measures that might be extracted from a data set and isolating the desired content from irrelevant information (i.e., signal vs. noise). For our proof of concept, we measured physical disorder, or "broken windows," a classical measure in criminology (Wilson and Kelling 1982), through the call records of Boston's 311 system. Because these data are designed to direct public works and other city agencies to complete the required work, we had to identify the 33 case types (of 178)[3] that were indicative of physical disorder, which we then organized into two submeasures, *private neglect* and *public denigration*.[4] The final product was a new methodology for measuring multiple dimensions of physical disorder that could be drawn from naturally occurring data, making it far less expensive than a whole-city survey or observational audit.

The dual measure of physical disorder offered by 311 was only the tip of the iceberg. We have since applied our methodology to a wide array of naturally occurring data: social disorder, crime, and medical emergencies from 911 dispatches (O'Brien and Sampson 2015); local investment and new construction through building permits (O'Brien and Montgomery 2015); energy efficiency and valuation through tax assessments (Sheini et al. 2020); rental costs and discrimination from Craigslist postings (Hangen and O'Brien 2022); the prevalence of short-term rentals through Airbnb (Ke, O'Brien, and Heydari 2021);

perceived restaurant quality through Yelp reviews (Chen et al. 2020); and ambient population through Twitter posts (Tucker et al. 2021).

The measures we have derived from the varied types of naturally occurring data have been useful for research on crime and other topics (as evidenced by the citations here), but this is a chapter about evidence-based policy. Of course, papers on predictors of crime, or evidence that increases in Airbnb listings lead to crime in a neighborhood, can inform policy, but I will note two ways that this work has done so more directly. First, the center that has overseen this work, the Boston Area Research Initiative (BARI), maintains the Boston Data Portal, a public platform that makes research-quality data products accessible to multiple levels of data literacy through documented data sets and interactive maps. Since 2015, we have hosted trainings for community-based organizations to access the ecometrics and explore how they might inform planning and advocacy. Second, BARI partnered with Boston Public Schools to build an Opportunity Index composed of the neighborhood-level factors that predicted academic achievement (O'Brien, Hill, and Contreras 2017). Of course, traditional demographic indicators played a major role in the Opportunity Index, but the array of ecometrics available made it more nuanced. These projects illustrate how the diverse measurement opportunities afforded by naturally occurring data can advance not only research but the evidence-based policies and practices that follow.

B. Integrated Data Systems: The Risks of Too Much Linking

People interact with government services in many ways. Schools, transportation, health records, libraries, the criminal justice system, and homeless shelters are just a few examples. Each interaction with public services generates a data record detailing the event, often identifiable at the individual level using information like full name and social security number. All are technically managed by the same entity (the government).[5] Given these circumstances, linking the information in a single database is a few logistical steps away. This is the vision of Integrated Data Systems (IDS), which in their most common form link individual-level information across the multiple Health and Human Services agencies within a given locality.

IDSs have proliferated in recent years. According to Actionable Intelligence for Social Policy (AISP), a national consortium of IDSs based at University of Pennsylvania, they have been established in over 35 states, counties, and cities. Much like the example of ecometrics from naturally occurring data in the previous section, the resultant variety of data is vast and supports a wide array of research questions and applications. In Philadelphia, researchers found that experience with homelessness had long-term impacts on academic performance (Fantuzzo and Perlman 2007). Allegheny County, Pennsylvania, linked the portfolios of social services case workers to school district data to provide real-time alerts on absences to proactively address truancy. Washington State conducted a comprehensive assessment of the well-being of mothers on Temporary Assistance for Needy Families (TANF), spanning housing instability, behavioral health indicators, education levels, and physical health (Patton et al. 2019).

The potential for IDSs is massive. But the potential downfalls are as well. Before I unpack those downfalls, I want to be clear: AISP and the broader population of IDSs *are not* naïve about them. In fact, they might be seen as a blueprint for a carefully considered approach to leveraging big data in the pursuit of evidence-based progress while avoiding data-enabled catastrophe. Let us begin with the sensitivity of a single data system. The use of health records are strictly managed by HIPAA guidelines, and any data breach would be a major scandal. Now, envision how the same concerns multiply when these data sets are combined with education records, criminal justice records, and others, all of which are also highly sensitive. As one IDS director has said to me privately, "If we ever have a breakdown in security, that's the end of the line."

How, then, to manage IDSs? It is not as simple as merging the data and stripping unique identifiers. There would be enough unique combinations of events and characteristics to easily re-identify many individuals (Sweeney 2002). Instead, IDSs have adopted stringent security protocols. Some are post hoc, requiring that all access to the data be strictly vetted and narrowed down to a specific use case. At some IDSs, outside researchers never touch the data; they generate hypotheses and guidelines for testing them and IDS employees conduct the actual analyses. Recent advances in data linkage have allowed for a priori solutions, as well. It is not necessary to have the data from multiple sources exist in linked form at all times. Instead, the technical infrastructure for linking the data and calculating aggregate measures can be activated whenever necessary and limited to the needed content. Thus, a linked data set could be constructed for a particular analysis or could be created just long enough to generate alerts for a reporting system. These and other techniques limit the potential of accidentally revealing a 360° view of a single individual's experiences with government agencies (or, even worse, the experiences of thousands upon thousands of individuals).

The potential relevance to crime and communities should be apparent. Police and court records are often incorporated into IDSs, offering a full view on how people's experiences with the criminal justice system relates to their other experiences and outcomes, including education, homelessness, and health. Some advocates have called on IDSs as a way to track the "cradle-to-career pipeline" (or the more pessimistically named "cradle-to-prison pipeline") and how the accumulated experiences of young people influence their long-term outcomes. Insights from such systems could inform future policing and judicial policies and practices, especially for communities of color and disadvantaged populations. That said, especially with the shortcomings of algorithms for predicting offending and recidivism (Dressel and Farid 2018) and the perceived misuse of gang databases (Johnson 2022), those same advocates are not calling for IDSs to be placed in the hands of police officers. Their variety of information offers great value, but the risks are too great to be brought to bear on such sensitive situations without well-delineated applications.

V. Evaluating Policies through Their Data

Naturally occurring data arise from a computer-aided process or system that is collecting information. We have walked through the advantages and corresponding challenges created by these circumstances. In a sense, the challenges and their solutions amount to isolating the value of the data from the biases, messiness, and vulnerabilities inherent to the system that generated them. Though not incorrect, this perspective misses the additional value that such origins can impart to a data set. *What if we want to know about those biases, messiness, and vulnerabilities?* The data set is a direct window into the program itself, and any insights arising from it will advance our evaluation and refinement of policy. This is not necessarily a groundbreaking perspective, as evaluation research has used programmatic data for a very long time. It is often missed in the discussions about "big" data, however, that many of the "weaknesses" we might lament can also be revelatory for the policies and practices that gave rise to them. I will illustrate this with two somewhat shorter case studies. The first is the use of field interrogation and observation records to evaluate "stop-and-frisk" policies in New York City. Though more traditional in some ways, the data-driven debate highlights some of the dual advantages and challenges created by naturally occurring data. The second describes how 311 systems both enable and document collaboration between public agencies and their constituencies in the maintenance of public spaces and infrastructure. In this latter case, bias in the data was as informative as the content itself.

A. Identifying Racial Bias in "Stop-and-Frisk" Practices

Since at least the Rodney King riots in Los Angeles in 1992, there have been debates in the United States about the extent to which police activity in some jurisdictions is racially biased, with police overtargeting young Black and Latino men. A major flashpoint in this debate has been the strategies inspired by broken windows theory, calling for zero tolerance of any incivilities or potentially criminal behavior (Kelling and Coles 1997; Wilson and Kelling 1982). In practice, this results in police stopping large numbers of individuals that they deem suspicious but who have not in fact committed a crime. This is also known in some cities as a policy of "stop-and-frisk." Most famously, New York City (NYC) has used a stop-and-frisk strategy since the early 1990s, claiming it led to the great drop in crime the city saw at that time.

In 2013, NYC's stop-and-frisk policy was the target of a legal challenge, with plaintiffs arguing that it disproportionately targeted people of color, violating their Fourth Amendment rights (i.e., protection against unreasonable searches). To make their case, they turned to the data. NYC records all stops made by police, known as field interrogation and observation reports (FIOs). These data included information about the acting officer, the age and race of the stopped individual, what actions were undertaken (e.g., stop, frisk, arrest), and the stated justification for the stop. The answer to the question of whether the program was or was not racially biased was hiding in plain sight, documented by the operations of the policy itself. A paper published by Gelman, Fagan, and, Kiss (2007) a few years earlier made the case that more Black and Latino individuals were stopped than would be expected given both the ethnic composition of the city *and* the offending rate within each race.

Gelman et al.'s (2007) conclusions, however, did not lead to an open-and-shut case, as NYC took exception with their benchmarks for defining "disproportionate." As we saw earlier in the chapter, administrative records do not come with readymade guidelines for analysis, and as such many different decisions can be made en route to the design of a single measurement. NYC contracted their own independent audit led by Ridgeway (2007) that used a different benchmark. They argued that "crime-suspect" descriptions—that is, the descriptions of suspects made by private citizens reporting violent crimes—often included race, and that these should be the basis for benchmarking. In other words, if crime-suspect descriptions are biased toward one or more races, one should reasonably assume that police will target their activities toward those groups. Using this technique, they found that Black and Latino men were stopped slightly *less* often than would be expected.

Given two competing interpretations of the same data resulting from distinct definitions "disproportionate," Judge Shira A. Scheindlin of the United States District Court for the Southern District of New York had to determine which case was more compelling. She sided with the plaintiffs, declaring the policy unconstitutional, based on the superior strength of Gelman et al.'s (2007) analysis and what she referred to as the flawed benchmarking strategy of Ridgeway's (2007) NYC-contracted study. She argued that the ethnic composition of arrests was a more acceptable benchmark as crime-suspect descriptions were subject to reporter bias, which is often racially skewed. She also pointed out that the documented justifications for stopping individuals often included highly subjective descriptions like "furtive movements." She maintained that many Black and Latino individuals were being stopped in circumstances in which a White person would not have been, using the stop-and-frisk policy's selfsame data as the primary evidence.

The legal challenge to NYC's stop-and-frisk policy is instructive for the use of naturally occurring data and how it can inform evidence-based policy and practice. The data generated by a policy served as the natural mechanism for evaluating the constitutionality of that policy. It also reminds us of the many decisions that must be made while working with naturally occurring data and how these decisions can lead to varied interpretations, some of which could even directly contradict each other. Rather than ending here, however, and risking the possibility that it might be seen as a stand-alone event, I will end this case study with an epilogue of sorts.

Shortly after the NYC case, the Boston Police Department (BPD) went through a similar debate about its own FIO practices, and again two sets of conclusions were presented to the public. The ACLU of Massachusetts analyzed BPD's FIO data, finding that Black and Latino individuals were stopped three times as often as would be expected based on the racial composition of the city (ACLU 2014). A separate report commissioned by the BPD (and, notably, led by some of the same researchers involved in the Gelman et al. [2007] study that led to Judge Scheindlin's decision in NYC), agreed in concept but tempered the intensity of the ACLU's conclusions (Fagan et al. 2016). They showed that FIOs were primarily targeted toward gang-involved youth and that it was necessary to take into consideration a small number of young individuals who had been stopped many, many times. When accounting for these factors as well as neighborhood crime rates, Black and Latino individuals were more likely to be stopped (and more likely to be frisked after being stopped), and that this bias was driven predominantly by White officers. The point made by the BPD and the authors, though, was that the benchmarking was more rigorous than that presented by the ACLU and gave the BPD and the courts a more realistic understanding of the scope of the problem and its origins, thereby paving the way for a more effective set of interventions. Again, two approaches to a single naturally occurring data set, two sets of interpretations, and a final policy decision based on the body of evidence.

B. 311 Systems and the Collaborative Maintenance of the Urban Commons

I have mentioned 311 systems in passing a few times in this chapter as a source of data on nonemergency issues in neighborhoods, like trash, dilapidation, and graffiti. I have not, however, discussed them as a policy. 311 systems are a relatively recent innovation that proliferated rapidly in the early 2010s, being implemented in over 400 American municipalities by 2015. As much as they promise to make government services more responsive and efficient, they also represent a paradigm shift in how those services are conceived. 311 systems convert the maintenance of public infrastructure and spaces—or what we might refer to as the urban commons—into a collaboration between public agencies and their constituencies. The latter identify and report issues, whereas the former have the authority, equipment, and skills necessary to address them. This is a classic example of coproduction (Ostrom 1996), the same logic that underpins community policing, facilitated in this case by modern technology.

I began studying Boston's 311 system in 2011 in collaboration with the city agencies that had designed and implemented it. We had a debate early on regarding what the data could be used to measure: physical disorder or engagement with government services. Simply put, the issue was that if it was one, it could not be the other. That is, if the reports faithfully represented physical disorder across the city, then the tendency to report issues must be consistent across neighborhoods, meaning there was no variation in engagement. If, however, the reports only reflected engagement, then we must assume that physical disorder and related needs were even across the city. Obviously, neither of these interpretations could possibly be true, and after a neighborhood audit and extended series of analyses, we developed methods for disentangling physical disorder from *custodianship*, or the tendency of a community to report issues in public spaces (O'Brien, Sampson, and Winship 2015).

I entered this project hoping to develop an inexpensive, comprehensive measure of physical disorder based on naturally occurring data, as I described in the section on ecometrics. As the project moved forward, however, it became clear that the real value was the ability to study custodianship. Here was a social process that never had been studied in such detail, with tens of thousands of registered individuals acting to maintain their communities. Further, it was one component of the collaborative relationship that 311 sought to create, and thus crucial to any success that 311 might have in improving neighborhood maintenance. Understanding when and why people reported issues in public spaces was thus necessary to further refining these newly established systems. In terms of criminology of communities, this maintenance was part and parcel of informal social control and the enforcement of norms and expectations for the treatment of public space (Sampson 2012; Shaw and McKay [1942] 1969). As such, the study of 311 could yield immediate conceptual and practical advances.

The work from there has been described at length in a book (O'Brien 2018), but I will summarize it in brief here. Most people reported issues very rarely and predominantly within one to two blocks of their homes (O'Brien 2015). By combining the data with a survey of 311 users we discovered that reporting public issues was motivated primarily by care and concern for the neighborhood, a construct referred to as territoriality in the social psychology literature (O'Brien, Gordon, and, Baldwin-Philippi 2014; O'Brien et al. 2017). We also found parallels between reports of incivilities, like graffiti, and classical definitions of informal social control (O'Brien 2016b). All of these insights were useful to understanding how communities are maintained by their members, but they also explained how 311 systems worked and how they might be designed to work better.

As the work progressed, my colleagues and I, including both researchers and the policymakers responsible for the 311 system, continually observed how territoriality was central to understanding the collaboration that the system created. We decided to probe this further. First, an experiment demonstrated that marketing the system as a way to clean up one's neighborhood was far more effective than exhortations to "Clean Up Boston!" (O'Brien 2016a). Another found that while a smartphone app increased reporting volume, it failed to break the imaginary boundary around one's house. The incorporation of messages from the city agency showing that the work had been completed also increased reporting but did not expand the geographic range, further confirming that individuals were happy to report issues, but only in the spaces they truly cared about (Buell, Porter, and Norton 2021). Recognizing that this could create inequities in maintenance arising from neighborhoods having different levels of custodianship (or at least different levels of comfort and ability in reporting issues to the government), the city has since established new protocols prioritizing issues in neighborhoods that have lower levels of reporting relative to their needs, especially for broken sidewalks (New Urban Mechanics 2020).

I do not want to give the impression that this extended research program is the only work that has been done on 311 systems or with their data. Far from it. For example, legal scholars have evaluated the effects of stop-and-frisk policing on government-community relations (Lerman and Weaver 2014) and sociologists have assessed how the reports might be a channel for ethnic conflict (Legewie and Schaeffer 2016). This versatility reinforces the point of this section and this entire chapter. Naturally occurring data enable many questions, including how to better understand and implement the very policy or program that generated the data. In fact, almost all of those other questions are relevant to that practical set of questions that allow us to pursue superior evidence-based policy.

VI. Conclusions

I hope that you come away from this chapter with three things. First, big data are different, and thus important, for more than just their size. In fact, their true distinction comes instead from being the naturally occurring products of computer-aided processes that were not explicitly intended for research. Second, there are specific advantages and challenges created by these origins that complement each other, and we must be mindful of the challenges while capitalizing on the advantages. Third, if handled properly, naturally occurring data can be a boon for advancing policy, both indirectly through the advancement of research and directly through its incorporation into the evaluation, refinement, and even moment-to-moment operation of our public systems.

I want to end with one final thought. I have repeatedly noted that these data systems were "not intended for research." That is a perfectly reasonable excuse when a resource is truly novel, but after over a decade of "big data," it starts to sound stale and even lazy. Now that we know we are likely to use these resources for research, policy, and practice, we should design our systems accordingly to mitigate some of the challenges before they arise. We can add new variables to data collection, adjust for apparent biases on the fly, and establish norms for use and interpretation of the data. Some of these things are already in development but they are not widespread. Work to date has demonstrated that the value of naturally occurring data for evidence-based policy and practice is both real and nuanced, and we should follow *that* body of evidence to further enhance their impact.

Notes

1. It is worth noting that there have been corollary efforts to take a similar approach for predicting individual perpetrators. See, for example, Saunders, Hunt, and Hollywood 2016; Perry et al. 2013.
2. To be fair, ecometrics can be created for any space, be it a neighborhood, a street, a building, a classroom, or otherwise, as implied by the etymology of the name (*eco-* = space, *-metrics* = measurements).
3. At the time of writing, there are now 220+ case types as the city realized that more nuance was needed to support service delivery.
4. Based both on content and confirmatory factor analysis.
5. Technically these data sets are each held by separate agencies, but as the director of one IDS likes to quip, "If the mayor has to sign both sides of the data use agreement, you don't need a data use agreement."

References

ACLU. 2014. *Black, Brown, and targeted*. Boston, MA: American Civil Liberties Union of Massachusetts.

Aiello, Luca Maria, Rossano Schifanella, Daniele Quercia, and Francesco Aletta. 2016. Chatty maps: Constructing sound maps of urban areas from social media data. *Royal Society Open Science Journal*, 3 (3): 150690.

Anderson, Chris 2008. The end of theory: The data deluge makes the scientific method obsolete. *Wired*, June 23.

Andresen, Martin A., and Nicolas Malleson. 2011. Testing the stability of crime patterns: Implications for theory and policy. *Journal of Research in Crime & Delinquency*, 48 (1): 58–82.

Beauchamp, Nicholas. 2017. Predicting and interpolating state-level polls using Twitter textual data. *American Journal of Political Science*, 61 (2): 490–503.

Bendler, Johannes, Tobias Brandt, Sebastian Wagner, and Dirk Neumann. 2014. Investigating crime-to-twitter relationships in urban environments—facilitating a virtual neighborhood watch. Paper presented at the Twenty-Second European Conference on Information Systems, Tel Aviv, Israel.

Block, Richard, and Carolyn R. Block. 2005. Spatial and temporal analysis of crime (STAC). In *Crimestat III: A spatial statistics program for the analysis of crime incident locations*, edited by Ned Levine, 71.8–77.1. Houston, TX: Ned Levine & Associates.

Braga, Anthony A., Andrew V. Papachristos, and David M. Hureau. 2010. The concentration and stability of gun violence at micro places in Boston, 1980–2008. *Journal of Quantitative Criminology*, 26:33–53.

Braga, Anthony A., Andrew V. Papachristos, and David M. Hureau. 2014. The effects of hot spots policing on crime: An updated systematic review and meta-analysis. *Justice Quarterly*, 31 (4): 633–663.

Brown, Barbara B., and Carol M. Werner. 1985. Social cohesiveness, territoriality and holiday decorations: The influence of cul-de-sacs. *Environment and Behavior*, 17:539–565.

Buell, Ryan W., Ethan Porter, and Michael I. Norton. 2021. Surfacing the submerged state: operational transparency increases trust in and engagement with government. *Manufacturing & Service Operations Management*, 23 (4): 781–802.

Caplan, Joel M., and Leslie W. Kennedy, eds. 2011. *Risk terrain modeling compendium*. Newark, NJ: Rutgers Center on Public Security.

Carr, Jillian B., and Jennifer L. Doleac. 2018. Keep the kids inside? Juvenile curfews and urban gun violence. *Review of Economics and Statistics*, 100 (4): 609–618.

Caubel, Julien J., Troy E. Cados, Chelsea V. Preble, and Thomas W. Kirchstetter. 2019. A distributed network of 100 black carbon sensors for 100 days of air quality monitoring in West Oakland, California. *Environmental Science Technology*, 53 (13): 7564–7573.

Chen, Qiliang, Riley Tucker, Babak Heydari, and Daniel T. O'Brien. 2020. Yelp reviews in Boston, MA. Boston Area Research Initiative (Harvard Dataverse). https://dataverse.harvard.edu/dataset.xhtml?persistentId=doi:10.7910/DVN/DMWCBT.

Curman, Andrea S. N., Martin A. Andresen, and Paul J. Brantingham. 2015. Crime and place: A longitudinal examination of street segment patterns in Vancouver, BC. *Journal of Quantitative Criminology*, 31:127–147.

Drawve, Grant 2016. A metric comparison of predictive hot spot techniques and RTW. *Justice Quarterly*, 33 (3): 369–97.

Dressel, Julia, and Hany Farid. 2018. The accuracy, fairness, and limits of predicting recidivism. *Science Advances*, 4 (1): eaao5580.

Fagan, Jeffrey, Anthony A. Braga, Rod K. Brunson, and April Pattavino. 2016. Stops and stares: Street stops, surveillance, and race in the new policing. *Fordham Urban Law Journal*, 43 (3): 539–614.

Fantuzzo, John, and Staci Perlman. 2007. The unique impact of out-of-home placement and the mediating effects of child maltreatment and homelessness on early school success. *Children and Youth Services Review*, 29:941–960.

Ferguson, Andrew Guthrie 2012. Predictive policing and reasonable suspicion. *Emory Law Journal*, 62:259–325.

Gelman, Andrew, Jeffrey Fagan, and Alex Kiss. 2007. An analysis of the New York City Police Department's "stop-and-frisk" policy in the context of claims of racial bias. *Journal of the American Statistical Association*, 102 (479): 813–23.

Gerber, Matthew S. 2014. Predicting crime using Twitter and kernel density estimation. *Decision Support Systems*, 61:115–25.

Goldsmith, Stephen, and Susan Crawford. 2014. *The responsive city: Engaging communities through data-smart governance*. San Francisco: Jossey-Bass.

Groff, Elizabeth, David Weisburd, and Sue-Ming Yang. 2010. Is it important to examine crime trends at a local "micro" level: A longitudinal analysis of street to street variability in crime trajectories. *Journal of Quantitative Criminology*, 26:7–32.

Hangen, Forrest, and Daniel T. O'Brien. 2022. The choice to discriminate: How source of income discrimination constrains opportunity for housing choice voucher holders. *Urban Affairs Review*, 59 (5): 1601–1625.

Hibdon, Julie, Cody Telep, and Elizabeth Groff. 2017. The concentration and stability of drug activity in Seattle, Washington using police and emergency medical services data. *Journal of Quantitative Criminology*, 33:497–517.

Hipp, John R., and Young-An Kim. 2017. Measuring crime concentration across cities of varying sizes: Complications based on the spatial and temporal scale employed. *Journal of Quantitative Criminology*, 33 (3): 595–632.

Hipp, John R., Christopher Bates, Moshe Lichman, and Padhraic Smyth. 2019. Using social media to measure temporal ambient population: does it help explain local crime rates. *Justice Quarterly*, 36 (4), 718–48.

Irvin-Erickson, Yasemin, Bing Bai, Annie Gurvis, and Edward Mohr. 2016. The effect of gun violence on local economies. Washington, DC: Urban Institute.

Irvin-Erickson, Yasemin, Nancy La Vigne, Ned Levine, Emily Tiry, and Samuel Bieler. 2017. What does gunshot detection technology tell us about gun violence. *Applied Geography*, 86:262–273.

Johnson, Jasmine. 2022. Gang databases: Race and the constitutional failures of contemporary gang policing in New York City. *St. John's Law Review*, 94 (4): 1033–1060.

Jones, Roderick W., and William Alex Pridemore. 2019. Toward an integrated multilevel theory of crime at place: Routine activities, social disorganization, and the law of crime concentration. *Journal of Quantitative Criminology*, 35:543–572.

Ke, Laiyang, Daniel T. O'Brien, and Babak Heydari. 2021. Airbnb and neighborhood crime: The incursion of tourists or the erosion of local social dynamics? *PLoS One*, 16:e0261886.

Kelling, George L., and Catherine M. Coles. 1997. *Fixing broken windows: Restoring order and reducing crime in our communities*. New York: Simon & Schuster.

Kennedy, Leslie W., Joel M. Caplan, and Eric Piza. 2011. Risk clusters, hotspots, and spatial intelligence: Risk terrain modeling as an algorithm for police resource allocation strategies. *Journal of Quantitative Criminology*, 27:339–362.

Kitchin, Rob, and Gavin McArdle. 2016. What makes big data, big data? Exploring the ontological characteristics of 26 datasets. *Big Data & Society*. https://doi.org/10.1177/2053951716631130.

Lane, Jeffrey 2016. The digital street: An ethnographic study of networked street life in Harlem. *American Behavioral Scientist*, 60 (1):43–58.

Laney, Doug. 2001. 3D data management: Controlling data volume, velocity, and variety. Stamford, CT: Meta Group, February 6.

Lazer, David, Ryan Kennedy, Gary King, and Alessandro Vespignani. 2014. The parable of Google Flu: Traps in big data analysis. *Science*, 343:1203–1205.

Lee, YongJei, John E. Eck, SooHyun O, and Natalie N. Martinez. 2017. How concentrated is crime at places? A systematic review from 1970 to 2015. *Crime Science*, 6:6. https://crimesciencejournal.biomedcentral.com/articles/10.1186/s40163-017-0069-x.

Legewie, Joscha, and Merlin Schaeffer. 2016. Contested boundaries: Explaining where ethnoracial diversity provokes neighborhood conflict. *American Journal of Sociology*, 122 (1): 125–61.

Lerman, Amy E., and Vesla Weaver. 2014. Staying out of sight? Concentrated policing and local political action. *Annals of the American Academy of Political and Social Science*, 651:202–219.

LISC (Local Initiatives Support Corporation). 2019. Addressing problem properties and their impacts. New York: LISC. https://www.lisc.org/our-resources/resource/addressing-problem-properties-and-their-impacts/.

Maher, Robert C. 2007. Acoustical characterization of gunshots. In *IEEE SAFE 2007: Workshop on Signal Processing Applications for Public Security and Forensics*, 109–113. Washington, DC: Institute of Electrical and Electronics Engineers.

Malleson, Nick, and Martin A. Andresen. 2015. The impact of using social media data in crime rate calculations: Shifting hot spots and changing spatial patterns. *Cartography and Geographic Information Science*, 42 (2): 112–121.

Mohler, G. O., M.B. Short, P.J. Brantingham, F.P. Schoenberg, and G.E. Tita. 2011. Self-exciting point process modeling of crime. *Journal of the American Statistical Association*, 106 (493): 100–107.

Mohler, G. O., M.B. Short, Sean Malinkowski, Mark Johnson, G.E. Tita, Andrea L. Bertozzi, and P.J. Brantingham. 2015. Randomized controlled field trials of predictive policing. *Journal of American Statistical Association*, 110 (512): 1399–1411.

New Urban Mechanics, City of Boston. 2020. StreetCaster. <https://www.boston.gov/departments/new-urban-mechanics/streetcaster>.

O'Brien, Daniel T. 2015. Custodians and custodianship in urban neighborhoods: A methodology using reports of public issues received by a city's 311 hotline. *Environment and Behavior*, 47:304–327.

O'Brien, Daniel T. 2016a. 311 hotlines, territoriality, and the collaborative maintenance of the urban commons: Examining the intersection of a coproduction policy and evolved human behavior. *Evolutionary Behavioral Sciences*, 10 (2): 123–41.

O'Brien, Daniel T. 2016b. Using small data to interpret big data: 311 reports as individual contributions to informal social control in urban neighborhoods. *Social Science Research*, 59:83–96.

O'Brien, Daniel T. 2018. *The urban commons: How data and technology can rebuild our cities.* Cambridge, MA: Harvard University Press.

O'Brien, Daniel T., and Alexandra Ciomek. 2022. Whence the action? The persistence and aggravation of violent crime at addresses, streets, and neighborhoods. *Journal of Research in Crime & Delinquency*. https://doi.org/10.1177/00224278221112839.

O'Brien, Daniel T., Eric Gordon, and, Jesse Baldwin-Philippi. 2014. Caring about the community, counteracting disorder: 311 reports of public issues as expressions of territoriality. *Journal of Environmental Psychology*, 40:320–330.

O'Brien, Daniel T., Nancy E. Hill, and Mariah Contreras. 2017a. The Opportunity Index: A data-driven tool for countering inequities in Boston Public Schools. Boston: Boston Area Research Initiative.

O'Brien, Daniel T., and Barrett W. Montgomery. 2015. The other side of the broken window: A methodology that translates building permits into an ecometric of investment by community members. *American Journal of Community Psychology*, 55:25–36.

O'Brien, Daniel T., Dietmar Offenhuber, Jessica Baldwin-Philippi, Melissa Sands, and Eric Gordon. 2017. Uncharted territoriality in coproduction: The motivations for 311 reporting. *Journal of Public Administration Research and Theory*, 27:320–335.

O'Brien, Daniel T., Alina Ristea, Forrest Hangen, and Riley Tucker. 2022a. Different places, different problems: profiles of crime and disorder at residential parcels. *Crime Science*, 11:4.

O'Brien, Daniel T., Alina Ristea, Riley Tucker, and Forrest Hangen. 2022b. The emergence and evolution of problematic properties: Onset, persistence, aggravation, and desistance. *Journal of Quantitative Criminology*, 39:625–653.

O'Brien, Daniel, and Robert J. Sampson. 2015. Public and private spheres of neighborhood disorder: Assessing pathways to violence using large-scale digital records. *Journal of Research in Crime and Delinquency*, 52:486–510.

O'Brien, Daniel T., Robert J. Sampson, and Christopher Winship. 2015. Ecometrics in the age of big data: Measuring and assessing "broken windows" using administrative records. *Sociological Methodology*, 45:101–147.

O'Brien, Daniel T., and Christopher Winship. 2017. The gains of greater granularity: The presence and persistence of problem properties in urban neighborhoods. *Journal of Quantitative Criminology*, 33, 649–74.

O'Brien, Miles, and Marsha Walton. 2016. NSF supports "Array of Things" prototype in Chicago. *Science Nation*. https://www1.cs.uchicago.edu/news/nsf-nsf-supports-array-things-prototype-chicago.

Ostrom, Elinor 1996. Crossing the great divide: Coproduction, synergy, and development. *World Development*, 24:1073–1087.

Patton, Deleena, Qinghua Liu, Barbara Lucenko, and Barbara Felver. 2019. The maternal well-being of Washington State's TANF population. Olympia: Washington State Department of Social and Health Services.

Pearsall, Beth 2010. Predictive policing: The future of law enforcement? *National Institute of Justice Journal*, 266:16–19.

Perry, Walter L., Brian McInnis, Carter C. Price, Susan Smith, and John S. Hollywood. 2013. *Predictive policing: The role of crime forecasting in law enforcement operations*. Santa Monica, CA: RAND Corporation.

Pierce, Glenn L., Susan Spaar, and LeBaron R. Briggs. 1988. *The character of police work: Strategic and tactical implications*. Boston: Center for Applied Social Research, Northeastern University.

Quercia, Daniele, Rossano Schifanella, Luca Maria Aiello, and Kate McLean. 2015. Smelly maps: The digital life of urban smellscapes. Paper presented at the 9th International AAAI Conference on Web and Social Media.

Ratcliffe, Jerry H., Matthew Lattanzio, George Kikuchi, and Kevin Thomas. 2019. A partially randomized field experiment on the effect of an acoustic gunshot detection system on police incident reports. *Journal of Experimental Criminology*, 15:67–76.

Ratcliffe, Jerry H., Ralph B. Taylor, Amber Perenzin Askey, Kevin Thomas, John Grasso, Kevin J. Bethel, Ryan Fisher, and Josh Koehnlein. 2021. The Philadelphia predictive policing experiment. *Journal of Experimental Criminology*, 17:15–41.

Raudenbush, Stephen W., and Robert J. Sampson. 1999. Ecometrics: Toward a science of assessing ecological settings, with application to the systematic social observation of neighborhoods. *Sociological Methodology*, 29 (1): 1–41.

Ridgeway, Greg. 2007. Analysis of racial disparities in the New York Police Department's stop, question, and frisk practices. Santa Monica, CA: RAND Corporation.

Ridgeway, Greg. 2013. The pitfalls of prediction. *National Institute of Justice Journal*, 27:34–40.

Ritter, Ryan S., Jesse Lee Preston, and Ivan Hernandez. 2014. Happy tweets: Christians are happier, more socially connected, and less analytical than atheists on Twitter. *Social Psychological and Personality Science*, 5 (2): 243–249.

Rudin, Cynthia 2019. Stop explaining black box machine learning models for high stakes decisions and use interpretable models instead. *Nature Machine Intelligence*, 1:206–215.

Sampson, Robert J. 2012. *Great American city: Chicago and the enduring neighborhood effect*. Chicago: University of Chicago Press.

Sampson, Robert J., and Stephen W. Raudenbush. 1999. Systematic social observation of public spaces: A new look at disorder in urban neighborhoods. *American Journal of Sociology*, 105 (3): 603–651.

Sampson, Robert J., Stephen W. Raudenbush, and Felton Earls 1997. Neighborhoods and violent crime: A multilevel study of collective efficacy. *Science*, 277:918–924.

Saunders, Jessica, Priscillia Hunt, and John S. Hollywood. 2016. Predictions put into practice: A quasi-experimental evaluation of Chicago's predictive policing pilot. *Journal of Experimental Criminology*, 12:347–371.

Schnell, Cory, Anthony A. Braga, and Eric L. Piza. 2017. The influence of community areas, neighborhood clusters, and street segments on the spatial variability of violent crime in Chicago. *Journal of Quantitative Criminology*, 33:469–496.

Shaw, Clifford, and Henry McKay. (1942) 1969. *Juvenile delinquency and urban areas.* Chicago: University of Chicago Press.

Sheini, Saina, Michael Shield, Alina Ristea, and Daniel T. O'Brien. 2020. Property assessment data for Boston, MA v. 2020. Boston Area Research Initiative (Harvard Dataverse). https://dataverse.harvard.edu/dataset.xhtml?persistentId=doi:10.7910/DVN/O2ADLG.

Sherman, Lawrence W., Patrick R. Gartin, and Michael E. Buerger. 1989. Hot spots of predatory crime: Routine activities and the criminology of place. *Criminology*, 27 (1): 27–55.

Steenbeek, Wouter, and David Weisburd. 2016. Where the action is in crime? An examination of variability of crime across different spatial units in The Hague, 2001–2009. *Journal of Quantitative Criminology*, 32 (3): 449–469.

Sweeney, Latanya. 2002. k-anonymity: A model for protecting privacy. *International Journal on Unvertainty, Fuzziness and Knowledge-based Systems*, 10 (5): 557–570.

Taylor, Ralph B. 1988. *Human territorial functioning: An empirical, evolutionary perspective on individual and small group territorial cognitions, behaviors and consequences.* Cambridge: Cambridge University Press.

Tucker, Riley, Daniel T. O'Brien, Alexandra Ciomek, Edgar Castro, Qi Wang, and Nolan Edward Phillips. 2021. Who "tweets" where and when, and how does it help understand crime rates at places? Measuring the presence of tourists and commuters in ambient populations. *Journal of Quantitative Criminology*, 37:333–359.

Van Patten, Isaac T., Jennifer McKeldin-Coner, and Deana Cox. 2009. A microspatial analysis of robbery: Prospective hot spotting in a small city. *Crime Mapping*, 1:7–32.

Wang, Fulton, and Cynthia Rudin. 2015. Falling rule lists. *Proceedings of Artificial Intelligence and Statistics (AISTATS)*, San Diego, CA.

Wang, Xiaofeng, Donald E. Brown, and Matthew S. Gerber. 2012. Spatio-temporal modeling of criminal incidents using geographic, demographic, and Twitter-derived information. *Paper presented at the IEEE International Conference on Intelligence and Security Informatics*, Washington, DC.

Weisburd, David. 2015. The law of crime concentration and the criminology of place. *Criminology*, 53 (2): 133–157.

Williams, Matthew L., Pete Burnap, and Luke Sloan 2017. Crime sensing with big data: The affordances and limitations of using open-source communications to estimate crime patterns. *British Journal of Criminology*, 57:320–340.

Wilson, James Q., and George Kelling. 1982. Broken windows: The police and neighborhood safety. *Atlantic*, 127:29–38.

CHAPTER 31

IMPOSED USE
A New Route to Evidence-Based Policy

STEVEN N. ZANE

ONE of the central questions of evidence-based policy is this: How will policymakers actually *use* the best evidence to inform their decision-making? A field of study called "research utilization," devoted to this question, has identified several routes by which evaluation research can exert influence on policy decisions. As described by Carol Weiss (1998), the four major routes are as follows: instrumental, conceptual, political, and imposed use. Instrumental use involves a direct, linear relationship between research and policy decisions. This is "research as data" (Weiss 1991, 39). With conceptual use, research contributes to policymaker's understanding over time in an indirect, nonlinear fashion. This is "research as ideas" (39). Political use, also known as symbolic use, involves research being used selectively to provide legitimation—to "justify what decision makers want to do anyway" (Weiss, Murphy-Graham, and Birkeland 2005, 13). The fourth category and subject of this chapter—imposed use—involves *legally mandating that decision-makers rely upon the best available research evidence* when making policy decisions, such as funding certain programs or adopting certain practices. Imposed use of evidence-based policy has been growing in recent years (see, e.g., Pew Charitable Trusts 2017), perhaps due to perceived limitations of the first three routes of research influence on policy and a growing interest in the evidence-based paradigm. The application of imposed use in the context of evidence-based crime and justice policy is the primary focus of this chapter.

This chapter begins with a brief description of the research utilization literature and how "imposed use" compares to other forms of research use. Next, the chapter examines how imposed use fits with different conceptions of evidence-based crime and justice policy, and provides examples of imposed use in modern criminal and juvenile justice policymaking. The chapter then turns to a consideration of the limitations of imposed use, including how evidence-based policy is defined and communicated, as well as the role of scientific evidence in the larger, normative context of policymaking. Finally, the chapter concludes with a discussion of the most promising role for imposed use in advancing evidence-based crime and justice policy.

I. Research Utilization

It is often lamented that social scientific research plays too small a role in the policymaking process. Three major obstacles to research influence have been identified: (1) shortcomings attributable to research and researchers, (2) shortcomings attributable to policymakers, and (3) shortcomings involving the links between the research and policy communities (Weiss et al. 2008). To employ an economic metaphor, research shortcomings are "supply-side" problems, since they involve the validity of research findings and how findings are delivered to practitioners and policymakers (such as relevance and external validity). Shortcomings owing to the beliefs, actions, and contexts of policymakers (such as prevailing paradigms, ideology, and short-term political and bureaucratic considerations) are then "demand-side" problems, since the focus is on whether policymakers are interested in using research evidence. The third category of obstacles involves the tenuous links between two independent communities (researchers and policymakers/practitioners) with different interests, values, languages, time frames, and reward systems. The "two community" metaphor dates back to Caplan (1979) and has been described and recognized by many in the evaluation community (see Weiss et al. 2008). Most recently, in the context of evidence-based crime and justice policy, much has been written about "translational criminology" and the need to speak the language of policymakers and politicians (see Blumstein 1997; Tseng 2012; Pesta et al. 2019).

The research utilization literatures provides a helpful framework for thinking through how research evidence comes to be used by policymakers and practitioners. There are four routes to policy influence. First, *instrumental use* of research envisions a direct relationship in which a policymaker asks a question of interest and finds an answer by consulting the scientific evidence (Weiss, Murphy-Graham, and Birkeland 2005). Among social scientists, this sometimes appears to be the implicit expectation for how research will be used. For example: (a) a researcher publishes evidence that program X causes a reduction in social problem Y; (b) policymakers are interested in solving problem Y; (c) policymakers therefore should consult the evidence and adopt program X (Tseng 2012). Yet this model is more of an ideal rather than a real picture of how research influence works (Petersilia 1991), perhaps reflecting the utopian vision of an "evidence-based society, in which informed quantitative reasoning is the dominant modality in public debate, as well as in the decision-making processes of government, business and individuals" (Smith 1996, 367).

When the model of instrumental use was first subjected to examination in the 1970s, it appeared that research actually had little instrumental influence on policy (Deitchman 1976; Knorr 1977; Rich 1977). Instead, research was serving to enlighten policymakers, who slowly changed their perceptions based on generalizations that emerged from research (Weiss, Murphy-Graham, and Birkeland 2005). In contrast to instrumental use—which produces direct, immediate decisions—*conceptual use* produces ideas and understanding indirectly and gradually, and is related to Weiss's (1991, 39) earlier conception of "research as ideas" in contrast to "research as data." This model of use, where research findings percolate and become the new common wisdom over time, more often appears to be how research is actually used (Tseng 2012). For example, Scott and colleagues (2022, 2) note that "theory and scientifically based concepts such as 'trauma-informed' practice or 'developmentally appropriate' treatments" have been "used to shape policies beyond the scope of specific [evidence-based interventions] that are characterized by those attributes."

If instrumental use represents the ideal among researchers, and conceptual use is the more common reality of how research influences policy, the third category—*political use*—represents the model of research utilization that is most often derided. Instead of producing immediate (instrumental) decisions or gradual (conceptual) enlightenment, research is used selectively to support preexisting positions (Weiss, Murphy-Graham, and Birkeland 2005). In studying the decision-making of congressional committees, for example, Weiss (1989, 418) found that congressional staffs turned to the empirical literature to provide "a sense of legitimacy" to their initiatives. This is "research as argument" and will be most influential in high-conflict areas where positions have already been staked out; in particular, the legislative context (Weiss 1991, 39).[1]

The newest addition to the conceptual framework for research utilization is *imposed use*. By requiring policymakers to rely upon findings of evaluation studies, imposed use essentially mandates the instrumental use of research based on funding incentives. Imposed use is not a brand new concept but rather a novel addition to the research utilization lexicon, reflecting that ever-more programs are being required to demonstrate that they are "evidence-based" in order to receive funding (Weiss et al. 2008). Notably, in the past decade there has been an increased emphasis on evidence-based policy—especially in the funding of correctional and juvenile intervention programs. Tying funding to rational use of scientific evidence sends a powerful message to the public that policymakers "are rational," "are holding programs to account," and, most importantly, "their judgments are not arbitrary" (Weiss, Murphy-Graham, and Birkeland 2005, 27). In this climate, it seems likely that imposed use will become increasingly common, possibly even leading to an "age of imposed use" (28).[2]

To return to the earlier economic metaphor, imposed use represents a decidedly demand-side solution to the research utilization dilemma, using legal means to address policymaker and organizational shortcomings. That is, policymakers are *required* to use research evidence—regardless of conflicting paradigms, ideology, timing considerations, or bureaucratic inertia. As such, one obvious limitation is that imposed use does not address the underlying obstacles to the research-policy relationship (Weiss et al. 2008). The dilemma of "two communities" forces us to ask a more fundamental question: What is the proper place for scientific research in the policy context? Does imposed use present a viable solution to this problem? The answer to these questions will of course vary across different policy contexts. For our purposes, the question thus becomes: Does imposed use represent a promising avenue for increasing the application of evidence-based crime and justice policy?

II. Imposed Use and Evidence-Based Policy

A. What Is Evidence-Based Crime and Justice Policy?

In the most general sense, evidence-based policy "involves using research data to shape policy" (Bond 2018, 4). For crime and justice policy, then, an evidence-based approach calls for research evidence to be at center stage in the process of forming rules and guidelines that govern criminal and juvenile justice systems. Much has been written about the growing interest in and application of the evidence-based paradigm in the medical sciences as well as in the social and behavioral sciences (e.g., Millenson 1997, 2021; Sherman 2003). There have also been many milestone developments along the way, including the establishment of the Cochrane Collaboration (in 1993) to advance evidence-based medicine and the Campbell Collaboration (in 2000) to promote an evidence-based approach in education, social welfare, crime and justice, and, most recently, international development. It seems fair to say that in recent years, the notion of evidence-based policy has "rapidly gained cachet" (Yingling and Mallinson 2020, 580).

One can take different perspectives, however, regarding how best to conceive of "evidence-based crime and justice policy." On the one hand, a narrow conception focuses on effectiveness of interventions—specifically in terms of impact evaluations. Here, "rigorous testing of impacts is the heart of the evidence-based enterprise" (Haskins 2018, 12). As Petrosino (2000, 636) puts it: "An evidence-based approach requires that the results of rigorous evaluations be rationally integrated into decisions about interventions by policymakers and practitioners alike." On the other hand, a broader conception focuses on the full evaluation hierarchy of needs, theory, implementation, effectiveness, and cost efficiency (Mears 2010, 2022). Here, "evidence-based" refers to the more general commitment to rational crime and justice policy that is grounded in the best available science (see Mears 2007). According to this broader conception, evidence-based policy requires not only rigorous evaluations of programs, but also "infrastructure that enables the creation, compilation, and analysis of data to inform 'real-time' decisionmaking needs and long-term planning" (Mears 2022, 19).

As an example of the first perspective, the authors of a case study of the Pew-MacArthur Results First initiative have described "the promise of evidence-based policy making" as "achieving materially better outcomes by targeting funds to those interventions that have been shown to be highly effective in achieving desired results" (VanLandingham and Silloway 2016, 546). As an example of the second perspective, Mears (2010) argues that focusing exclusively on program *effectiveness* can miss the forest for the trees, since it is likely that many programs and practices could be abandoned without conducing rigorous (and expensive) impact evaluations:

> The argument for requiring needs, theory, and implementation evaluations of criminal justice policies—especially those that entail large costs—is straightforward: anything less will almost invariably result in a substantial waste of resources. Policies that are not needed may be implemented; policies that lack any coherent theoretical foundation, much less one supported by empirical research, may be adopted; and needed and theoretically grounded policies may be poorly implemented. (249)

While there is certainly much to recommend about this second, broader perspective of evidence-based policy as a general matter, the narrower conception of evidence-based policy as involving outcome-focused goals seems more directly connected to imposed use as a distinct mechanism of research utilization. According to this perspective, an evidence-based approach to crime and justice policy demands that the best available evaluation research be used to assess where, when, and if different interventions reduce crime, as well as helping to establish why an intervention does or does not work. As noted, this mission seems clearly to invoke instrumental rather than conceptual use of research. In this vein, imposed use appears to offer a promising tool for evidence-based crime and justice policy—namely, mandating the instrumental use of evidence-based programs and practices to ensure that policy is rational and effective.

The past decade has witnessed an increased emphasis on evidence-based programs in criminal justice, as "criminal justice agencies have been called upon to demonstrate their effectiveness and efficiency in meeting their goals" (Myers and Spraitz 2011, 136). Examples of government bodies adopting evidence-based programs can be found throughout the criminal justice system, most notably in evidence-based policing (see Lum and Koper 2017; Piza and Welsh 2022), evidence-based juvenile justice programs (see Greenwood 2018; Welsh and Greenwood 2015), and evidence-based corrections (see Duriez et al. 2018; Mears and Barnes 2010). In some cases, this has involved legal requirements to utilize research evidence; that is, imposed use. The next section examines some prominent recent examples of imposed use in criminal and juvenile justice.

B. Examples of Imposed Use in Crime and Justice Policy

According to Pew Charitable Trusts, as of 2017 (the latest data available), 24 states have "developed a framework of laws to support their actions" with respect to evidence-based policymaking in the context of their criminal justice systems (Pew Charitable Trusts 2017, 29). Pew also reports that, as of 2017, 16 states have developed similar legal frameworks for their juvenile justice systems. Although the terminology of "imposed use" is not employed, what the authors refer to as "requiring action through state law" is the essence of imposed use: state laws mandating (or strongly incentivizing) the adoption of evidence-based programs, practices, or policies by criminal or juvenile justice agencies.

As shown in Table 31.1, states can "impose use" of evidence-based programs and practices in a variety of ways. At one end of the spectrum, some states actually *mandate* the use of evidence-based programs within their criminal or juvenile justice systems—or some subset thereof (e.g., Georgia, Florida, Kentucky, Nebraska, Pennsylvania, Tennessee, Vermont). It may be fair to say that this represents the purest example of imposed use: these states simply require that evidence-based programs and practices be utilized in certain contexts. (As can be seen in Table 31.1, this most often involves intervention programs implemented by state correctional or juvenile justice systems.)

Other states have imposed evidence-based programs less directly, requiring that a certain amount of funding must be dedicated to evidence-based programs (e.g., California, Illinois, Oregon, West Virginia). Some states have elected to direct special funding toward evidence-based programs, sometimes in the form of grants (e.g., Kansas, Minnesota, Utah), while others have restricted or eliminated funding for ineffective programs (e.g., North Carolina). Several states require agencies to create inventories of funded programs according to evidence of effectiveness (e.g., Connecticut, Mississippi, Washington), but do not necessarily require the use of evidence-based programs (Pew Charitable Trusts 2015). Additionally, many states *encourage* the use of evidence-based programs and practices in criminal or juvenile justice—without creating legal mandates, funding requirements, or even financial incentives for doing so.[3]

These different methods of imposing use of research evidence involve their own strengths and weaknesses. For example, mandating evidence-based programs presents the simplest and most straightforward approach, but "mandates can fail for a variety of

Table 31.1. Examples of Imposed Use of Evidence-Based Programs or Practices in Criminal and Juvenile Justice

State	Description	Relevant language	Citations
California	In 2009, California established a Board of State and Community Corrections that annually reviews state correctional policies. Among its duties, the board identifies and evaluates programs and recommends funding based on program effectiveness.	"By January 1, 2014, the board shall develop funding allocation policies to ensure that within three years no less than 70 percent of funding for gang and youth violence suppression, intervention, and prevention programs and strategies is used in programs that utilize promising and proven evidence-based principles and practices."	California Penal Code §6027(b)(10) (2020)
Connecticut	As of 2015, the Connecticut Department of Corrections is required to develop program inventories that list all programs and designate whether they are evidence-based.	"Not later than October 1, 2018, and annually thereafter, the Departments of Correction, Children and Families, Mental Health and Addiction Services and Social Services and the Court Support Services Division of the Judicial Branch shall compile a program inventory of each of said agency's programs and shall categorize them as evidence-based, research-based, promising or lacking any evidence."	Connecticut General Statutes §4-68s(a) (2020)
Georgia	As of 2013, the Georgia Department of Juvenile Justice is required to develop polices and regulations that make us of evidence-based programs and practices.	"Services shall be based on evidence based programs or practices and be community centered and responsive to local needs with state and local and public and private entities forming cooperative partnerships that enhance informal support systems for families."	Georgia Code §49-4A-3(b)(3) (2020)
Florida	As of 2019, the Florida Department of Juvenile Justice is required to use evidence-based or "promising" practices for all residential programs.	"For each youth in its care, a residential commitment program shall implement a delinquency intervention model or strategy that is an evidence-based practice, promising practice, a practice with demonstrated effectiveness, or any other intervention approved by the department that addresses a priority need identified for that youth."	Florida Administrative Code §63E-7.105(1)(a) (2020)

State	Description	Citation
Illinois	As of 2020, Illinois requires that funding for evidence-based programs be provided for the majority of persons incarcerated or under local supervision by the Department of Corrections.	"The Department of Corrections shall adopt policies, rules, and regulations that... within 5 years of the adoption, validation, and utilization of the statewide, standardized risk assessment tool result in at least 75% of incarcerated individuals receiving services and programming in accordance with evidence-based practices."	Illinois Compiled Statutes §730-190-10(b)(3)(1) (2020)
Kansas	As of 2016, Kansas created the Juvenile Improvement Fund, which directs all cost savings from reduced reliance on incarceration into funding evidence-based programs and practices for youth.	"There is hereby established in the state treasury the evidence-based programs account of the state general fund, which shall be administered by the department of corrections. All expenditures from the evidence-based programs account of the state general fund shall be for the development and implementation of evidence-based community programs and practices for juvenile offenders, juveniles experiencing mental health crisis and their families by community supervision offices."	Kansas Statutes Annotated §75-52, 164(a) (2020)
Kentucky	In 2011 and 2014, respectively, Kentucky required that state correctional programs and state juvenile justice programs use evidence-based practices (including requiring that 75% of program funding must involve evidence-based practices by 2016).	"In order to increase the effectiveness of treatment and intervention programs funded by the state and provided by the department for inmates, probationers, and parolees, the department shall require that such programs use evidence-based practices." "The Department of Juvenile Justice shall promulgate administrative regulations that shall include:... The provision of treatment for committed and probated children in accordance with evidence-based practices."	Kentucky Revised Statutes §196-111(1) (2022) Kentucky Revised Statutes §15A-0652(2) (2022)
Mississippi	As of 2014, Mississippi has mandated that the Legislative Budget Office and Joint Committee on Performance Evaluation and Expenditure Review assist state agencies, including the Department of Corrections, with cataloguing and categorizing all funded programs based whether they were evidenced-based practices.	"The Legislative Budget Office, the PEER Committee staff, and personnel of each of the agencies required to comply with this section shall review the programs of each agency and shall: (a) Establish an initial inventory of agency programs...; (b) Categorize all agency programs as intervention or nonintervention and all intervention programs as evidence-based, research-based, promising, or other."	Mississippi Code §27-103-159 (3) (2019)

(continued)

Table 31.1. Continued

State	Description	Relevant language	Citations
Nebraska	In 2014, Nebraska established the Director of Juvenile Diversion Programs to direct and oversee evidence-based diversion programs.	"The Director of Juvenile Diversion Programs . . . shall: (a) Provide technical assistance and guidance to juvenile pretrial diversion programs for implementing evidence-based strategies or standardized, replicable practices that have been researched and have demonstrated positive outcomes; . . . (c) Establish baseline program guidelines for juvenile pretrial diversion programs based on evidence-based practices, principles, programs, and research, develop data collection and evaluation protocols, oversee statewide data collection, and generate an annual report on juvenile pretrial diversion programs."	Nebraska Revised Statutes §81-1427 (2022)
North Carolina	As of 2013, North Carolina is required to fund effective correctional and juvenile intervention programs and to discontinue funding of ineffective programs.	"The Division shall fund programs that it determines to be effective in preventing delinquency and recidivism. Programs that have proven to be ineffective shall not be funded."	North Carolina General Statutes §143B-853(a)(1) (2021)
Pennsylvania	In 2012, Pennsylvania established the Juvenile Justice System Enhancement Strategy, which requires juvenile justice agencies to utilize evidence-based practices when possible.	"To achieve the foregoing purposes in a family environment whenever possible, separating the child from parents only when necessary for his welfare, safety or health or in the interests of public safety, by doing all of the following: (i) employing evidence-based practices whenever possible . . ."	Pennsylvania Consolidated Statutes, Title 42, §6301(b)(3) (2021)
Oregon	As of 2011, agencies such as the Oregon Department of Corrections and Oregon Youth Authority must dedicate most of their funding to evidence-based programs.	"An agency shall spend at least 75 percent of state moneys that the agency receives for programs on evidence-based programs."	Oregon Revised Statutes §182.525(1) (2021)
Tennessee	As of 2013, Tennessee requires that all program funding for juvenile justice prevention and treatment must be "evidence-based."	"The department of children's services, and any other state agency that administers funds related to the prevention, treatment or care of delinquent juveniles, shall not expend state funds on any juvenile justice program or program related to the prevention, treatment or care of delinquent juveniles, including any service model or delivery system in any form or by any name, unless the program is evidence-based."	Tennessee Code §37-5-121(b) (2020)

Utah	In 2017, Utah established the Juvenile Justice Reinvestment Restricted Account, reserving funding for evidence-based programs and practices.	"Upon appropriation by the Legislature, the department may expend funds from the account: . . . (b) for nonresidential evidence-based programs and practices in cognitive, behavioral, and family therapy; . . . (d) for infrastructure in nonresidential evidence-based juvenile justice programs, including staffing and transportation."	Utah Code §80-5-302(4) (2022)
Vermont	As of 2013, Vermont required that juvenile justice interventions be based on evidence-based practices.	"In order to accomplish these goals, the [juvenile justice] system should be based on the implementation of data-driven evidence-based practices that offer a broad range of alternatives, such that the degree of intervention is commensurate with the risk of reoffense."	Vermont Statutes Annotated, Title 33 §5101a(b) (2021)
Washington	As of 2012, Washington State requires juvenile justice agencies to substantially increase their use of evidence-based programs based on the inventory methods developed by Washington State Institute for Public Policy (WSIPP) and the evidence-based practice institute at the University of Washington.	"In addition to descriptive definitions, the Washington state institute for public policy and the University of Washington evidence-based practice institute must prepare an inventory of evidence-based, research-based, and promising practices for prevention and intervention services that will be used for the purpose of completing the baseline assessment described in subsection (2) of this section."	Revised Code of Washington §43.20C.005(1)(a) (2021)
West Virginia	As of 2015, West Virginia requires that juvenile justice agencies spend half of community services funding on evidence-based programs.	"By January 1, 2017, the department and the Division of Juvenile Services shall allocate at least fifty percent of all community services funding, . . . either provided directly or by contracted service providers, for the implementation of evidence-based practices."	West Virginia Code § 49-2-1002(b) (2022)
Wisconsin	As of 2005, the Wisconsin Treatment Alternatives and Diversion (TAD) program provides grants to counties to fund evidence-based alternatives to prosecution and incarceration of nonviolent offenders with histories of alcohol and drug abuse.	"The department of justice shall make grants to counties and to tribes to enable them to establish and operate programs . . . that provide alternatives to prosecution and incarceration for criminal offenders who abuse alcohol or other drugs." "A county or tribe shall be eligible for a grant under sub. (2) if all of the following apply: . . . (d) Services provided under the program are consistent with evidence-based practices in substance abuse and mental health treatment"	Wisconsin Statutes §165.95(2) (2020) Wisconsin Statutes §165.95(3) (2020)

reasons: underspecification of the models to be implemented, lack of stakeholder buy-in, lack of accountability for implementation, and inadequate funding ('unfunded mandates')" (Bond 2018, 6). An alternative version of imposed use thus involves prioritizing *funding* for evidence-based programs, which in some cases may also be required to be inventoried. This is a more flexible approach, with the possible downside that "the burden of proof for demonstrating effectiveness of existing or proposed programs is on state agencies," requiring "a sophisticated level of expertise within state agencies" (5).

As can be seen in Table 31.1, imposed use appears to be becoming fairly widespread as a mechanism of research utilization. This might be perceived as a promising sign that more and more policymakers are recognizing the importance of pursuing evidence-based policies in criminal and juvenile justice, such that these statutory requirements reflect a commitment to scientific research informing the policy process. Of course, as the Pew study authors noted, whether there are statutory requirements for evidence-based practices and whether such practices are actually adopted and successfully implemented are two distinct questions. As Greenwood (2018) points out in the context of juvenile justice, the "leading states" in terms of *promoting* evidence-based policy are not necessarily also "leading states" in terms of *using* evidence-based policy.[4] Still, the increased statutory commitment to evidence-based crime and justice policy is noteworthy.

It is also noteworthy that requiring the use of research evidence appears largely limited to two specific contexts: correctional programs and juvenile justice interventions. As we shall see, this makes sense, given that evidence-based policy is most commonly limited to the narrow question of "what works"—that is, evidence of effectiveness (i.e., impact evaluations). Given this understanding, correctional and juvenile justice programs appear to be the most appropriate subjects for imposed use: to the extent that states choose to implement correctional and juvenile justice programs with the goal of reducing recidivism—the narrow conception of evidence-based crime policy—it is reasonable to expect that states would desire to fund effective and cost-efficient programs. The question thus arises: Can imposed use of research evidence be expanded beyond this narrower conception of evidence-based policy? What are the limitations of a more global application of imposed use?

III. Limitations of Imposed Use

A. When *Is* Policy "Evidence-Based"?

The first limitation of imposed use involves the very definition of "evidence-based" programs, practices, and policies. Scott and colleagues (2022, 1) have observed that while statutory mandates for research use have recently increased, "little work has been done to investigate how research evidence can be written into statutory language." Indeed, not every state included in Table 31.1 actually defines the "evidence-based" practices that they require.[5] Among those that *do* provide definitions, most commonly it is quite abstract, such as "policies, procedures, programs, and practices proven by scientific research to reliably produce reductions in recidivism" (Kentucky Revised Statutes §600-020(27); see also Georgia Annotated Code §49-4A-1(7); Illinois Compiled Statutes §730-190(5)(b)(4)). Some states are more specific, such as requiring "multiple randomized control studies or a meta-analysis demonstrating that the program or practice is effective for a specific population or has been rated as effective by a standardized program evaluation tool" (Utah Code §80-5-102(31)). Less common, some states define "evidence-based" to include more than just evidence of effectiveness. For example, Connecticut General Statutes states:

> "Evidence-based" describes a program that (A) incorporates methods demonstrated to be effective for the intended population through scientifically based research, including statistically controlled evaluations or randomized trials; (B) can be implemented with a set of procedures to allow successful replication in the state; (C) achieves sustained, desirable outcomes; and (D) when possible, has been determined to be cost-beneficial. (§4-68r(3))

Despite these exceptions, the general rule is that the legal requirement to employ "evidence-based" practices is somewhat mercurial. As reported by Pew Charitable Trusts (2017, 27), the director of research and statistics at the Pennsylvania Department of Corrections observed that the term *evidence-based* "is thrown around quite loosely within our system . . . in some cases the evidence behind so-called evidence-based programs is quite weak." Importantly, the promise of imposed use assumes high-quality evidence and consensus regarding what the evidence says. Moreover, the potential *political* use of imposed use presents a challenge for evidence-based crime and justice policy.

1. *The Need for High-Quality Evidence*

Mandating the use of high-quality evidence necessarily requires that such evidence exists in the first place. That is, the notion that evidence should drive crime and justice policy assumes that there *is* empirical evidence capable of providing solutions to identified crime problems. Yet while there is a growing push for high-quality evidence demonstrating the causal impact of various programs, practices, and policies, such evidence still remains rather limited. Almost two decades ago, Eskridge (2005, 303) observed:

> We criminologists are somewhat akin to physicians of the 18th century. We have a few ideas, we are making progress; however, we have yet to attain the status of a mature, evidence-based and evidence-driven science. We lack consistent, proven diagnostic instruments; we lack a definitive body of knowledge; and we lack generally consistent treatment modalities. Indeed, we have no criminological thermometers, no criminological computerized axial tomography (CAT) scans, no criminological penicillin. We are using relatively crude instruments, as did the physicians of the 1700s, and largely respond to the crime problem using crude, home-spun, untested remedies, as did the physicians of the 18th century.[6]

Much progress has been made over the subsequent decades, especially in the realm of program evaluation using high-quality research designs in juvenile justice (see, e.g., Elliot et al. 2020; Lipsey 2020; Welsh 2020). Still, there remains important truth to Eskridge's observation. As Mears (2010) observed in the context of calling for a dramatic increase in evaluation research in criminal justice, the state of evidence regarding whether policies are needed, theoretically grounded, properly implemented, effective, and cost-efficient remains rather minimal. This problem is not limited to crime and justice policy. Most social programs in general are simply never evaluated for impact. As Haskins (2018, 36) observes, "When social policy interventions are at last evaluated, they usually turn out to be ineffective. It follows that, to be blunt, we are wasting billions of dollars on ineffective interventions." It is still the case, then, that there are simply not enough high-quality evaluations of criminal and juvenile justice system processing and impact (see Mears 2010, 2017, 2022).

Evidence-based crime and justice policy seems partly motivated by the possibility that imposed use of scientific research will be possible in the future—*once a more comprehensive and reliable evidence base is established*. It may be that intervention programs that are amenable to high-quality evaluations present the most promising avenue for establishing such an evidence base (see, e.g., Elliot et al. 2020). As noted, this is reflected in the major areas where imposed use seems to be taking root: correctional programs and juvenile justice interventions programs aimed at recidivism reduction.

2. *The Need for Consensus on the "Best Evidence"*

Even assuming a more rigorous evidence base in the future, there is need for consensus on what constitutes the best evidence. That is, the research translation problem dictates that the best evidence must be communicated accurately and effectively to policymakers. One of the most common ways of doing so is to provide inventories or lists of evidence-based programs and practices that have passed muster. Still, ensuring that government-mandated inventories of evidence accurately reflect the evidence base is challenging and subject to complications about how we form a consensus regarding what is evidence-based.

When Weiss and colleagues (2008) took a closer look at these lists, they discovered that many of the "promising" and "model" programs identified by rating agencies were based on questionable evidence: "The main reasons for concern are the fact that a program's developers did almost all the evaluations, limited evidence of positive findings, the choice of 'special' sites for study, the use of subgroups rather than the full sample in report of the results, few long-term follow-up studies, and the composition and procedures of the expert panel" (38; see also Gandhi et al. 2007). These concerns have been shared by others who have found lackluster evidence behind many school-based drug prevention programs included on evidence-based lists (Gorman and Conde 2010). As Elliot and colleagues (2020, 1319) argue, "The inconsistency in certification standards is one of the factors that undermines practitioner confidence in the use of registries. . . . We need consensus on a minimum standard for certifying programs and practices as evidence-based and ready for scale-up."

In the juvenile justice context, for example, there is some debate about whether state governments should rely on specific, *proven* evidence-based programs—the "brand-name" approach—or on more general types of evidence-based practices that are, on average, effective—the "generic" approach (Welsh, Rocque, and Greenwood 2014). The brand-name approach identifies model programs that have established a strong evidence base for effectiveness (according to some preestablished criteria; see Fagan and Buchanan 2016). Specifically, only a handful of specific programs have been proven across "multiple well-conducted randomized controlled trials" to reduce recidivism among juvenile offenders. Specifically, these programs are Multisystemic Therapy (MST), Functional Family Therapy (FFT), and Treatment Foster Care Oregon (Elliot et al. 2020, 1319). From this perspective, the best route to increasing evidence-based juvenile justice policy would involve evangelizing these specific programs, with the hopes of them being adopted statewide by most or even all juvenile justice systems.

In response, Lipsey (2020, 1342) notes that "it is simply a fact that few robustly effective model programs for juvenile offenders have been identified and those few have not been widely integrated into juvenile justice practice." As a result, he argues, a broader approach to identifying evidence-based practices (using average effect sizes in meta-analyses of juvenile justice interventions) is more promising if the goal is broad impact. That is, while the model program approach is valuable, it is also quite limited—especially in terms of population impact (Welsh 2020).

As Greenwood (2018) observes, both approaches involve advantages and disadvantages. The model program approach has the advantage of providing local agencies with the "training resources and guidance it will need to successfully adopt the model" (i.e., implementation fidelity) but the disadvantages of "a significant upfront investment in training" and "very little room for local adaptation" (256). As a result, Lipsey (2020) observes that only 7.1% of supervised youth are actually served by model programs. The generic practice approach, in turn, has the advantage of being more "flexible and accommodating to local conditions and resources," but also the disadvantages of "lack of technical assistance, susceptibility to short cuts, and the fact that it has not been adequately evaluated as a strategy for actually improving program outcomes" (Greenwood 2018, 256). With the generic approach, another concern is that the "evidence for practices as effective interventions in the juvenile justice system is too limited for any confident judgment about their utility" (Elliot et al. 2020, 1322).

In short, then, while the model program approach seems more likely to produce positive benefits under ideal conditions, it is also more expensive and inflexible and thus less likely to be adopted in the first place. In the final analysis, it does not seem necessary to choose between these two approaches. As Welsh, Rocque, and Greenwood (2014, 209) note, "[f]ar from seeing this as a problem, state governments have a choice between two rigorous and transparent approaches for advancing evidence-based practice."[7] As a practical matter, it seems unlikely that "model" programs will be adopted and rigorously implemented statewide by every juvenile justice system (Lipsey 2020). Nevertheless, it seems fair to conclude that these proven programs should be adopted whenever they are feasible and appropriate for the particular problem that has been identified by local practitioners and policymakers.[8]

In thinking about imposed use and evidence-based crime and justice policy more generally, each side of this debate carries some important insights. On the one hand, Lipsey (2020) is right to point out that *only* focusing on model programs may greatly limit the adoption of evidence-based juvenile justice interventions. On the other hand, Elliot and colleagues (2020) make the important point that much of our evidence about juvenile justice interventions remains low quality, and that only the highest-quality studies should be considered reliable. As Elliot et al. (2020) point out, many of the studies included in meta-analyses of evidence-based generic practices are lower-quality quasi-experimental studies that provide weak evidence of program effectiveness.[9] It is also true that among inventories of evidence-based programs, the Blueprints model programs requires the most rigorous and well-defined evidentiary requirements for impact evaluations (see Fagan and Buchanan 2016). Still, even Blueprints may sometimes paint an overly rosy picture regarding "proven" programs, many of which have not been evaluated by independent teams and in real-world conditions. This returns us to the dearth of high-quality evaluation evidence in criminal and juvenile justice. More high-quality evidence—that is, impact evaluations with high internal and external validity—is certainly needed in order for imposed use to be a viable strategy for enhancing evidence-based policy.

3. *The Political Application of Imposed Use*

The complications with communicating evidence-based practices to policymakers, and the potential solution via legally mandated inventories of evidence, raises a related potential concern: the political application of imposed use. For example, policymakers may begin to use the "evidence-based" framework to advocate for preestablished programs by exerting influence on the creation of lists of best practice. As others have noted, there are political benefits to describing programs, practices, and policies as evidence-based: "Claiming a policy as evidence-based has legitimizing power and is used to galvanize support for policy agendas" (Yingling and Mallinson 2020, 581). Research even suggests that bills that use a higher number of "evidence keywords" are more likely to advance in the legislative process use (Scott et al. 2022, 7). As Haskins (2018, 10) observes, "[f]ew things are more important to policy-makers . . . than citing reasons why their legislative actions are good for the country. In recent years, claiming that a policy is evidence-based fits this requirement." In such a policy context, there is the risk of the "token use of evidence-based programs" (Scott et al. 2022, 8).

Imposed use may thus simply create another bureaucracy for policymakers and practitioners to navigate, raising the question of whether imposed use actually represents a new form of research use at all—as opposed to a dressed-up, more technocratic version of political use. Especially concerning is that this might produce stagnation and complacency, rather than generate a new and improved evidence base. Specifically, the creation of "best evidence" lists may not encourage policymakers to take evidence more seriously, but instead only creates a legal requirement they must follow.[10] Clear (2010, 6) points out that a major drawback of the evidence-based framework is that it is, "at its core, extraordinarily conservative." In focusing on evidence of effectiveness for existing (and well-established) programs, it could be critiqued as backward-looking rather than innovative.

In sum, the first major limitation of imposed use involves how evidence-based policy is defined and communicated. It can be defined too narrowly—requiring rigorous evidence of impact that we do not possess—as well as too broadly or vaguely—becoming a desirable catchphrase that does not actually constrain the choices of policymakers and practitioners in any meaningful way.

B. When *Should* Policy Be Evidence-Based?

The second limitation of imposed use cuts deeper than the first. Namely, policy decisions involve many inputs, including normative (i.e., nonempirical) considerations. As such, imposed use—even when feasible and not subject to the issues raised thus far—may not always be appropriate. The central assumption of evidence-based policy—that the best possible evidence should be used to guide decision-making—is itself a normative claim. Evidence-based crime and justice policy is, like the evidence-based movement more generally, "ideological in that it supports particular beliefs and values" (Packwood 2002, 267). Specifically, it involves a consequentialist approach to crime policy largely guided by certain foundational values, such as effectiveness and cost-efficiency, which can be easily measured and quantified. While evidence-based crime policy has been compared to, and has some important similarities with, evidence-based medicine (see Sherman 2003), disputed normative considerations are more central to crime policy—a dis-analogy with medicine and public health (Anderson and Burris 2017).

For crime and justice policy, this broader context of competing considerations includes public opinion, conventional wisdom, political issues, resource constraints, special interest group pressures, bureaucratic constraints, ideology, and legal constraints (Welsh and Farrington 2011). It is not always clear that researchers understand this plurality of considerations. Nothing reflects this better than the view that because policymaking is driven by normative considerations, making policy more rational *must* involve replacing normative considerations with social science research (Tseng 2012). For example, criminologists often assume that incarceration has a purely utilitarian function: to deter offenders from future offending and reduce crimes rates. Under this assumption, it could be argued that imprisonment is a "failed program," yet it continues to be used for ideological (and therefore illegitimate) reasons (Eskridge 2005, 305). But other normative considerations, such as justice and fairness, play an equal if not much larger role in public considerations of punishment (Wilson 2011). That is, criminal punishment is more complicated than whether or not incarceration effectively reduces crime (see, e.g., Robinson 2008; von Hirsch 2007).

This does not make normative considerations the enemy of science and evidence. They are simply the pluralistic reality in which social science must operate. It does mean, however, that "research is not a panacea because individual values substantially drive policymakers' decision-making" (Scott et al. 2022, 3). A more nuanced view, then, is that every decision of crime policy is a combination of facts and values. It may be that "evidence-*based* policy" is thus a bit of a misnomer, and that "evidence-*informed* policy" more accurately describes the proper and realistic role of scientific research (Haskins 2018).

A timely example involves policies aimed at reducing gun violence. The first issue with imposed use of evidence-based gun control policy is the lack of high-quality evidence concerning what polices would reduce gun violence. Since evidence of causal impact is difficult to establish without experimental manipulation (Cook and Donahue 2017), the evidence base for specific gun policies is quite weak. The most comprehensive systematic review of gun policies recently concluded that, "there is a surprisingly limited base of rigorous scientific evidence concerning the effects of many commonly discussed gun policies" (Smart et al. 2023, xvi).[11] In this realm of nonexperimental evidence, gun policy researchers disagree about how best to interpret the data, frame the analyses, and draw implications from their findings (see, e.g., Fridel 2021; Kleck 2021).

Even assuming that future research establishes a stronger evidence base, however, such evidence would not necessarily dictate the proper policy response. This is because practical, normative, and legal considerations may ultimately dwarf empirical considerations in the realm of gun policy. For example, imagine that research indicates that the most effective violence prevention strategy would involve drastically reducing the number of guns in private hands. (Given the instrumentality effect, this is not implausible; see Braga et al. 2021). Would this imply that such a policy ought to be imposed? Probably not. First, it is estimated that there are around 300 million guns in private hands, owned by approximately one-third of US households (Cook and Goss 2020). As a practical matter, then, gun prohibition is completely unrealistic (Jacobs 2002). Second, the private ownership of firearms is a constitutionally protected right (see *District of Columbia v. Heller*, 554 U.S. 570 [2008]; *City of Chicago v. McDonald*, 561 U.S. 742 [2010]). It would require enormous public support—enough to pass a constitutional amendment—to be able to implement any meaningful gun prohibition policy. As such, "removing handguns from the American public is just not going to happen, despite the fact that such a policy would definitively result in fewer murders" (Eskridge 2005, 306). That is, gun abolition in the United States is a policy nonstarter—no matter what the evidence indicates. Moreover, this lesson applies to *many* potential gun regulations, not just prohibition. For example, the Supreme Court has most recently held that "may issue" permitting regimes violate the right to bear arms, such that the empirical question as to whether more strict permitting regimes reduce violence—by reducing the number of persons carrying firearms in public—is essentially moot (see *New York State Rifle & Pistol Association v. Bruen*, 597 U.S. ___ [2022]). There remain some questions of gun policy that do not necessarily implicate Second Amendment rights, of course. But some issues are simply off the table due to legal and normative considerations.

In sum, then, it is both inevitable and perfectly reasonable that normative, legal, and practical considerations will often take precedence over scientific evidence. Nevertheless, this in no way implies that research evidence is no longer relevant to policy. Indeed, research evidence is almost *always* relevant to policy, if only to "illuminate the consequences of alternatives in order that people in positions of authority can know what they will get and what they will give up when they select a particular course" (Weiss 1991, 38). This role is not entirely deferential. For one, good science can challenge the empirical assumptions underlying legal and policy decisions. In doing so, science can make normative commitments more transparent.

IV. Discussion

Instrumental use assumes an agreement of *ends* between social science, on the one hand, and policy, on the other. Instrumental use would thus be expected in a pure "evidence-based society," where policy decisions follow directly and immediately from social science research (see Smith 1996). Yet this is not the world we inhabit. We can reformulate the question of imposed use as follows: *When is it appropriate to impose the instrumental use of scientific research into the normative context of policy?*

In an effort to answer this question, Zane and Welsh (2017) propose that it is useful to invoke the heuristic of a traditional "means-ends" framework. Carol Weiss hinted at this same idea. While arguing for evidence-based requirements to enhance rational decision-making, Weiss and colleagues (2008, 44) observed the following:

> [E]valuative evidence is not the only important component of policy making. The ends to which policy and programming are directed are at least as important as the means for getting there. Evidence-based policy assumes that the ends are given, and the issue is to choose the best way to get there. But there are circumstances where appropriate ends are much in contention and ethical and moral considerations must come into play.

In other words, when the ends of policy are at issue, scientific evidence is just one consideration among many within a wider context of normative pluralism. Contrary to this observation, imposed use would involve dictating or compelling policy decisions in a way that may circumvent the larger decision-making process (see Tittle 2004). Imposed use is thus not appropriate to address problems involving deep normative questions about what we value as a society.

Imposed use of research findings is more appropriate, however, when searching for rational and effective means of realizing agreed-upon policy ends. Political directions for crime policy often involve normative considerations that conflict with research evidence. But where the goals of crime policy are clear and agreed upon, imposed use represents a method of publicly supporting instrumental use and making crime policy more rational. Requiring that correctional agencies must adopt evidence-based intervention programs (to the extent they decide to adopt interventions at all), for example, would appear to present such a case.

Since imposed use will not always be appropriate, however, it is also important to conceive better ways for high-quality research to influence the *ends* of crime policy. Where this involves competing normative considerations (e.g., the legislative process), political use often represents how research is utilized. Here, *conceptual use* of research remains possible and important. This is because "politics that has to contend with the results of good science should produce better policy than politics based on poor science or none at all" (Rosenfeld 2000, 616). For instance, it has been observed that while the future of highly value-laden crime policies, such as capital punishment and "three strikes" legislation, are not likely to be dictated by research evidence alone, high-quality evidence still "sharpens the debates and clarifies what the issues really are" (Tonry 2010, 794). As Mears (2022, 2) observes, while most research has "little direct bearing on policy . . . this situation is somewhat offset by the fact that scientific studies sometimes produce insights that may indirectly inform efforts to promote the greater social good."

Indeed, conceptual use actually has important benefits over instrumental use, such as a more lasting effect (Petersilia 1991). Research evidence is typically relevant to policymaking in at least one way: to "illuminate the consequences" of alternative policies and practices (Weiss 1991, 38). While this may not involve the direct and immediate reliance on evidence that is envisioned by imposed use, conceptual use can challenge the empirical assumptions underlying legal and policy decisions. In doing so, science can make normative commitments more transparent: "Research can serve the public good just as effectively when it seeks to enlighten and inform in the interests of generating a wider public debate" (Young et al. 2002, 223). The gun policy example used earlier may again prove illustrative. Rigorous evidence that establishes that certain policies are associated with reduced violence may, over time, begin to matter more than other considerations. Perhaps, over time, a new consensus will form that allows for a possible constitutional amendment that would allow the effective policy to be implemented. That is, it is possible that normative considerations related to crime policy may change over time, influenced by research evidence providing gradual enlightenment rather than immediate guidance. Frustrating for some, this may take generations—but it is not impossible. Scientific research does not determine policy, but it can still have an influence. As Petersilia (2008) observed, researchers thus "have a responsibility to provide *policy relevant* information, but leaders have the responsibility to derive *policy prescriptions*, based on research and other considerations" (354, emphasis in original).

V. Conclusion

Evidence-based crime and justice policy is premised on the idea that that best available research evidence should be at center stage in the policymaking process. But direct, instrumental use of research evidence—in contrast to conceptual or political use—is not common. Imposed use, which mandates the instrumental use of scientific research for public policy, is one possible mechanism for advancing the evidence-based paradigm. This chapter has focused on the role of imposed use in advancing evidence-based crime and justice policy. It would appear that, over the past decade, many states have adopted legal requirements that state agencies utilize evidence-based programs and practices, especially in the realms of correctional and juvenile interventions. On the one hand, this represents a promising commitment to evidence-based crime policy on behalf of the states. On the other hand, one might wonder whether imposed use of evidence-based programs and practices may itself become a kind of political use, especially in a context where (a) few programs and practices have a strong evidence base and (b) there remains disagreement about what should constitute an "evidence-based" program or practice.

Imposed use as it is most currently applied—namely, toward intervention programs with established impact on some desired outcomes (e.g., recidivism)—is thus quite narrow in scope. One alternative might be for states to commit not only to using evidence-based programs and practices, but also to evaluating their entire systems in terms of needs, theory, implementation, outcomes, and cost-efficiency. As Mears (2010, 2017) has suggested, perhaps 5% of all program funding could be dedicated to systems evaluation research.[12] Performance monitoring is broader in scope than imposed use of evidence-based programs, and may be a more fruitful avenue for making sustained improvements to criminal and juvenile justice systems beyond intervention programs (Mears and Butts 2008).

More fundamentally, this chapter has highlighted that normative considerations still drive policymaking, and the proper role for imposed use will involve areas where policy ends are not in dispute. As it turns out, this happens to be where imposed use is most common. For example, imposed use is typically applied in the context of correctional and juvenile interventions programs. In such cases, there is a clear policy goal that has been agreed upon—reduce recidivism. To the extent that a state adopts this policy goal, imposed use represents an appropriate mechanism for ensuring that funded programs are effective and cost-efficient, sending a powerful message to the public that taxpayer-funded programs are being held to account (Weiss, Murphy-Graham, and Birkeland 2005). In other policy areas, however, imposed use will not be appropriate because the ends of policy are in dispute. This should not be viewed as antithetical to evidence-based crime and justice policy, however. Instead, the best available evidence provides the factual basis for democratic policy decisions and "can serve a potentially tempering influence" on inefficient, ineffective, or unnecessary crime policies (Mears 2007, 679). This is the conceptual use of research, and it will likely remain the main pathway by which research influences policy over time.

Finally, as noted by Mears (2022, 2), "there is the simple fact that a great deal of research has little direct bearing on policy. For the development of science, that is not necessarily problematic. Researchers like to generate new knowledge for the sake of it." At the same time that more high-quality evaluation research is needed, it is important to remember that most research will never fall into this category. Instead, it is what Clear (2010, 14) calls "basic research." In addition to imposed use of effective programs, then, it is equally important to produce high-quality basic research that can influence future policy, a "forward-looking evidentiary base for fundamental innovation in justice policy" (Clear 2010, 1). This is the broader sense of evidence-based crime and justice policy that is not limited to impact evaluations. In sum, although imposed use represents a powerful strategy for making the means of agreed-upon policy goals more evidence-based, it is not a panacea and is not without pitfalls. It should be employed carefully and with the above considerations in mind.

Notes

1. It is worth noting that although the research community often laments political use, it is not an inherently inappropriate use of research evidence (see Weiss, Murphy-Graham, and Birkeland 2005). Political use becomes problematic where it involves distortion of research findings or intentional omission of contrary findings.
2. Recently, Natow (2022) observed that political use actually interacts with and possibly conditions other forms of research use, and we might instead envision routes to research utilization such as political-instrumental, political-conceptual, and political-imposed. For example, political-instrumental use "involves using research to address questions and problems that arise within a larger context of using research to advocate for the research user's viewpoint," political-conceptual use "involves actors widely distributing research that favors their policy preferences with the goal that the research will ... change the perspectives of key decision makers on relevant policy issues," and political-imposed use occurs when "the research that is used as a result of [the legal] requirement justifies the policy preference of the research user" (Natow 2022, 707–709).
3. For example, in 2007, Colorado created the Commission on Criminal and Juvenile Justice, which issues annual reports of findings and recommendations regarding criminal justice programs and practices. By law, the commission will "conduct an empirical analysis of and collect evidence-based data on sentencing policies and practices" and "make an annual report of findings and recommendations, including evidence-based analysis and data" (C.R.S. § 16-11.3-103(2)(a–c)). But there is neither a legal *requirement* to utilize evidence-based programs or practices nor is funding of programs or practices conditioned upon such usage. Similar (nonbinding) advisory commissions have also been created in Massachusetts (M.G.L. ch. 6A § 18M), Missouri (M.R.S § 217.147), and New Mexico (N.M.S.A. § 31-28-3). Other states, such as Idaho, require that impact evaluations be conducted for some recidivism reduction programs without necessarily requiring such programs in the first place (e.g., I.S. § 20-216(2)–(3)).
4. For example, South Dakota and Louisiana are the top two states in terms of model program *availability* (per capita), but both are ranked as "below average" according to the Pew study of evidence-based policymaking. Conversely, Utah is considered a top five program in terms of its Pew ranking, but is ranked last among states in terms of model

program availability. Some states, however, do rank highly according to both metrics, most notably Connecticut (Greenwood 2018, 254).

5. For example, while Pennsylvania's "Juvenile Act" requires that juvenile justice agencies employ "evidence-based practices whenever possible" (P. C. S., title 42, §6301(b)(3)), "evidence-based practices" is never defined in the statute.

6. Writing around the same time, Tittle (2004) observed that, "despite what some of my professional colleagues would like to believe, we cannot say with even reasonable certainty what causes crime, we do not know with much assurance whether or under what conditions arresting domestic abusers deters their future misconduct, we do not know whether gun control prevents violence, and we do not even know for sure the extent to which the death penalty curbs capital crime. In every case, there is conflicting evidence. This is not surprising since research is limited, and our data are always incomplete, error prone, and accepted as supporting an argument if it simply shows something 'better than chance.' Indeed, most sociologists are thrilled to explain 25% of the variance in some dependent variable" (1641).

7. No doubt both sides of the debate may resist this compromise position: "The proponents of these two approaches do not exactly see eye to eye regarding their relative merits. The people behind Blueprints will argue that SPEP [Standardized Program Evaluation Protocol] provides communities with an excuse for not adopting the more rigorously evaluated Models that they list on their website. The SPEP folks argue that evaluations of the Blueprint Model Programs usually find much better results when the Model and evaluation are both implemented by the program developer, suggesting that local communities should not expect to achieve the benefits reported in the literature" (Greenwood 2018, 256).

8. One important additional criticism of the model program approach is that while the Blueprints registry requires multiple high-quality studies (i.e., RCTs) showing positive impact, the registry does not require estimates of *average* program effects (Lipsey 2020).

9. As the authors rightly point out, much of what is labeled "quasi-experimental" suffers from relatively low internal validity: "Quasi-experiments can produce unbiased causal inference, but only if they meet the strong ignorability assumption.... This requires that the covariates used in a study capture the true process of selection into treatment that is correlated with the study outcome. However, in actual research practice with QEDs, only regression discontinuity designs have been shown to demonstrably meet this condition" (Elliot et al. 2020, 1312).

10. This may also create more skepticism of "evidence-based policy" by policymakers (see Tittle 2004). As Natow (2022, 712) observes, "Policy actors, aware that research is used for political purposes, may be skeptical of research considered in policymaking. Proponents of evidence-based policy and researchers hoping their work will influence policy should be aware of his skepticism and consider how to cultivate policy actors' confidence in research, such as by educating policymakers on research methods or advocating for more funding to enhance the quality of research."

11. The authors were quick to point out that absence of evidence does not prove evidence of absence: "This does not mean that these policies are ineffective; the policy itself might well be quite effective. Instead, it reflects the absence of scientific study of these policies or methodological shortcomings in the existing literature that limit rigorous understanding of policy effects" (Smart et al. 2023, xvi–xvii).

12. Others have proposed that, more generally, "Congress [should] set aside 2.5 percent of the funds supporting every social program to be devoted to evaluation of the program's impacts" (Haskins 2018, 14). While not the focus of this chapter, the lack of funding of criminal justice evaluation research is an important contributor to the lack of a strong evidence base (Mears 2017).

References

Anderson, Evan, and Scott Burris. 2017. Policing and public health: Not quite the right analogy. *Policing and Society*, 27:300–313.

Blumstein, Alfred. 1997. Interaction of criminological research and public policy. *Journal of Quantitative Criminology*, 12:349–361.

Bond, Gary R. 2018. Evidence-based policy strategies: A typology. *Clinical Psychology: Science and Practice*, 25:e12267.

Braga, Anthony A., Elizabeth Griffiths, Keller Sheppard, and Stephen Douglas. 2021. Firearm instrumentality: Do guns make violent situations more lethal. *Annual Review of Criminology*, 4:147–164.

Caplan, Nathan. 1979. The two-communities theory and knowledge utilization. *American Behavioral Scientist*, 22:459–470.

Clear, Todd R. 2010. Policy and evidence: The challenge to the American Society of Criminology. *Criminology*, 48:1–25.

Cook, Philip J., and John J. Donohue. 2017. Saving lives by regulating guns: Evidence for policy. *Science*, 358:1259–1261.

Cook, Philip J., and Kristin A. Goss. 2020. *The gun debate: What everyone needs to know*. New York: Oxford University Press.

Deitchman, Seymour J. 1976. *The best-laid schemes: A tale of social science research and bureaucracy*. Cambridge, MA: MIT Press.

Duriez, Stephanie A., Carrie Sullivan, Edward J. Latessa, and Lori Brusman Lovins. 2018. The evolution of correctional program assessment in the age of evidence-based practices. *Corrections*, 3:119–136.

Elliott, Delbert S., Pamela R. Buckley, Denise C. Gottfredson, J. David Hawkins, and Patrick H. Tolan. 2020. Evidence-based juvenile justice programs and practices: A critical review. *Criminology & Public Policy*, 19:1305–1328.

Eskridge, Chris W. 2005. The state of the field of criminology. *Journal of Contemporary Criminal Justice*, 21:296–308.

Fagan, Abigail A., and Buchanan, Molly. 2016. What works in crime prevention? Comparison and critical review of three crime prevention registries. *Criminology & Public Policy*, 15:617–649.

Fridel, Emma E. 2021. The futility of shooting down strawmen: A response to Kleck (2020). *Justice Quarterly*, 38:925–941.

Gandhi, Allison Gruner, Erin Murphy-Graham, Anthony Petrosino, Sara Schwartz Chrismer, and Carol H. Weiss. 2007. The devil is in the details: Examining the evidence for "proven" school-based drug abuse prevention programs. *Evaluation Review*, 31:43–74.

Gorman, Dennis M., and Eugenia Conde. 2010. The making of evidence-based practice: The case of project ALERT. *Children & Youth Services Review*, 32:214–222.

Greenwood, Peter W. 2018. Ranking states in their use of evidence-based programs for juvenile offenders: A 20-year progress report. *Berkeley Journal of Criminal Law*, 23:242–260.

Haskins, Ron. 2018. Evidence-based policy: the movement, the goals, the issues, the promise. *ANNALS of the American Academy of Political and Social Science*, 678:8–37.

Jacobs, James B. 2002. *Can gun control work?* New York: Oxford University Press.

Kleck, Gary. 2021. The continuing vitality of flawed research on guns and violence: A comment on Fridel (2020). *Justice Quarterly*, 38:916–924.

Knorr, Karin D. 1977. Policymakers' use of social science knowledge: Symbolic or instrumental? In *Using social research in public policy making*, edited by Carol H. Weiss, 165–182. Lexington, MA: Lexington-Health.

Lipsey, Mark W. 2020. Revisited: Effective use of the large body of research on the effectiveness of programs for juvenile offenders and the failure of the model programs approach. *Criminology & Public Policy*, 19:1329–1345.

Lum, Cynthia, and Christopher Koper. 2021. Evidence-based policing. In *Critical issues in policing: Contemporary readings*, edited by Roger G. Dunham, Geoffrey P. Alpert, and Kyle D. McLean, 65–82. Long Grove, IL: Waveland Press.

Mears, Daniel P. 2007. Towards rational and evidence-based crime policy. *Journal of Criminal Justice*, 35:667–682.

Mears, Daniel P. 2010. *American criminal justice policy: An evaluation approach to increasing accountability and effectiveness*. New York: Cambridge University Press.

Mears, Daniel P. 2017. *Out-of-control criminal justice: The systems improvement solution for more safety, justice, accountability, and efficiency*. New York: Cambridge University Press.

Mears, Daniel P. 2022. Bridging the research-policy divide to advance science and policy: The 2022 Bruce Smith, Sr. Award address to the Academy of Criminal Justice Sciences. *Justice Evaluation Journal*, 5:163–185.

Mears, Daniel P., and James C. Barnes. 2010. Toward a systematic foundation for identifying evidence-based criminal justice sanctions and their relative effectiveness. *Journal of Criminal Justice*, 38:702–710.

Mears, Daniel P., and Jeffrey A. Butts. 2008. Using performance monitoring to improve the accountability, operations, and effectiveness of juvenile justice. *Criminal Justice Policy Review*, 19:264–84.

Millenson, Michael L. 1997. *Demanding medical excellence: Doctors and accountability in the information age*. Chicago: University of Chicago Press.

Millenson, Michael L. 2021. Docs and cops: Origins and ongoing challenges of evidence-based policing. *Cambridge Journal of Evidence-Based Policing*, 5:146–155.

Myers, David L., and Jason D. Spraitz. 2011. Evidence-based crime policy: Enhancing effectiveness through research and evaluation. *Criminal Justice Policy Review*, 22:135–139.

Natow, Rebecca S. 2022. Research use and politics in the federal higher education rulemaking process. *Educational Policy*, 36:689–716.

Packwood, Angela. 2002. Evidence-based policy: Rhetoric and reality. *Social Policy & Society*, 1:267–272.

Pesta, George B., Thomas G. Blomberg, Javier Ramos, and J. W. Ranson. 2019. Translational criminology: Toward best practice. *American Journal of Criminal Justice*, 44:499–518.

Petersilia, Joan. 1991. Policy relevance and the future of criminology. *Criminology*, 29:1–16.

Petersilia, Joan. 2008. Influencing public policy: An embedded criminologist reflects on California prison reform. *Journal of Experimental Criminology*, 4:335–356.

Petrosino, Anthony. 2000. How can we respond effectively to juvenile crime? *Pediatrics*, 105:635–637.
Pew Charitable Trusts. 2015. *Legislating evidence-based policymaking: A look at state laws that support data-driven decision-making*. Philadelphia: Pew Charitable Trusts. http://www.pewtrusts.org/en/research-and-analysis/issue-briefs/2015/03/legislating-evidence-based-policymaking.
Pew Charitable Trusts. 2017. *How states engage in evidence-based policymaking*. Philadelphia: Pew Charitable Trusts. http://www.pewtrusts.org/en/research-and-analysis/reports/2017/01/how-states-engage-in-evidence-based-policymaking.
Piza, Eric L., and Brandon C. Welsh. 2022. Evidence-based policing is here to stay: Innovative research, meaningful practice, and global reach. *Cambridge Journal of Evidence-Based Policing*, 6:42–53.
Rich, Robert F. 1977. Use of social science information by federal bureaucrats: Knowledge for action versus knowledge for understanding. In *Using social research in public policy making*, edited by Carol H. Weiss, 165–182. Lexington, MA: Lexington-Health.
Robinson, Paul H. 2008. Competing conceptions of modern desert: Vengeful, deontological, and empirical. *Cambridge Law Journal*, 67:145–175.
Rosenfeld, Richard. 2000. Tracing the Brady Act's connection with homicide and suicide trends. *Journal of the American Medical Association*, 284:616–618.
Scott, J. Taylor, Sarah Prendergast, Elizabeth Demeusy, Kristina McGuire, and Max Crowley. 2022. Trends and opportunities for bridging prevention science and US federal policy. *Prevention Science*, 23:1333–1342.
Sherman, Lawrence W. 2003. Misleading evidence and evidence-led policy: Making social science more experimental. *Annals of the American Academy of Political and Social Science*, 589:6–19.
Smart, Rosanna, Andrew R. Morral, Rajeev Ramchand, Amanda Charbonneau, Jhacova Williams, Sierra Smucker, Samantha Cherney, and Lea Xenakis. 2023. *The science of gun policy: A critical synthesis of research evidence on the effects of gun policies in the United States*. 3rd ed. Santa Monica, CA: RAND Corporation.
Smith, Adrian F. M. 1996. Mad cows and ecstasy: Chance and choice in an evidence-based society. *Journal of the Royal Statistical Society Series A*, 159:367–383.
Tittle, Charles R. 2004. The arrogance of public sociology. *Social Forces*, 82:1639–1643.
Tonry, Michael. 2010. "Public criminology" and evidence-based policy. *Criminology & Public Policy*, 9:783–797.
Tseng, Vivian. 2012. The uses of research in policy and practice. *Social Policy Report*, 26:1–24.
VanLandingham, Gary, and Torey Silloway. 2016. Bridging the gap between evidence and policy makers: A case study of the Pew-MacArthur Results First initiative. *Public Administration Review*, 76:542–546.
von Hirsch, Andrew. 2007. The "desert" model for sentencing: Its influence, prospects, and alternatives. *Social Research*, 74:413–434.
Weiss, Carol H. 1989. Congressional committees as users of analysis. *Journal of Policy Analysis & Management*, 8:411–431.
Weiss, Carol H. 1991. Policy research as advocacy: Pro and con. *Knowledge & Policy*, 4:37–55.
Weiss, Carol H. 1998. Have we learned anything new about the use of evaluation? *American Journal of Evaluation*, 19:21–33.
Weiss, Carol H., Erin Murphy-Graham, and Sarah Birkeland. 2005. An alternate route to policy influence: How evaluations affect D.A.R.E. *American Journal of Evaluation*, 26:12–30.

Weiss, Carol H., Erin Murphy-Graham, Anthony Petrosino, and Allison G. Gandhi. 2008. The fairy godmother—and her warts: Making the dream of evidence-based policy come true. *American Journal of Evaluation*, 29:29–47.

Welsh, Brandon C. 2020. The case for rigorous comparative research and population impacts in a new era of evidence-based interventions for juvenile offenders. *Criminology & Public Policy*, 19:1347–1354.

Welsh, Brandon C., and David P. Farrington. 2011. Evidence-based crime policy. In *The Oxford handbook of crime and criminal justice*, edited by Michael Tonry, 60–92. New York: Oxford University Press.

Welsh, Brandon C., and Peter W. Greenwood. 2015. Making it happen: State progress in implementing evidence-bed programs for delinquent youth. *Youth Violence and Juvenile Justice*, 13:243–257.

Welsh, Brandon C., Michael Rocque, and Peter W. Greenwood. 2014. Translating research into evidence-based practice in juvenile justice: Brand-name programs, meta-analysis, and key issues. *Journal of Experimental Criminology*, 10:207–225.

Wilson, James Q. 2011. Comment on Durlauf and Nagin. *Criminology & Public Policy*, 10:165–168.

Yingling, Dylan L., and Daniel J. Mallinson. 2020. Explaining variation in evidence-based policy making in the American states. *Evidence & Policy* 16:579–596.

Young, Ken, Deborah Ashby, Annette Boaz, and Lesley Grayson. 2002. Social science and the evidence-based policy movement. *Social Policy & Society*, 1:215–224.

Zane, Steven N., and Brandon C. Welsh. 2018. Toward an "age of imposed use"? Evidence-based crime policy in a law and social science context. *Criminal Justice Policy Review*, 29:280–300.

CHAPTER 32

THE ROLE OF POLICYMAKERS, CRIMINAL JUSTICE ADMINISTRATORS AND PRACTITIONERS, AND CITIZENS IN CREATING, EVALUATING, AND USING EVIDENCE-BASED POLICY

DANIEL P. MEARS AND NATASHA A. FROST

THIS book was developed with three broad goals in mind: (1) to promote new and productive ways to think about evidence-based policy (EBP), viewed as encompassing policies, programs, and practices; (2) to show how high-quality research can contribute to and guide evidence-based policy in the context of juvenile justice, criminal justice, and alternatives to system responses; and (3) to identify strategies that can increase reliance on EBP, and, in particular, on policy that is well designed, implemented, monitored, and evaluated.

In this chapter, we address these goals by focusing on groups who are involved in creating or implementing policy or who are directly affected by it—namely, policymakers, criminal justice administrators and practitioners, and citizens. They all drive policy. They can be instrumental in developing it, shaping its implementation, and evaluating it. And they also can be instrumental in determining which policies to adopt, change, or eliminate.

Although these groups are not researchers, they nonetheless can play a pivotal role in policy through myriad decisions about laws, protocols, rules, interventions, and more. The question, then, is how well they can do so without a strong foundation, or training, in research. We should not expect that everyone have an extensive grounding in research. Yet it is unreasonable to expect that these groups can make informed decisions to advance EBP without an ability to appraise the research on a given topic and to appreciate the types of research relevant to informing specific policy questions or issues. Stated more forcefully, relying on trust in research without at least a minimum threshold of understanding about the strengths and limitations of it does not seem greatly different than relying on personal intuition or ideology.

There is an added consideration—these groups can play a role in *generating* and *evaluating* EBP. They work on the front lines and must make decisions about programs and practices, and some of them experience their effects. For example, when police officers must implement an approach that citizens do not support, the officers—as well as communities—can be affected. Of course, citizens more directly bear the brunt of policy. They, therefore, possess a unique vantage point from which to guide the development, implementation, and evaluation of EBP.

We build on these points to argue that a critical platform for generating EBP and contributing to the more widespread and appropriate use of it is to educate and train policymakers, criminal justice administrators and practitioners, and citizens both in using EBP and in the role of research to identify what counts as EBP. In developing this argument, we draw on and extend our work on how to improve policy (e.g., Frost 2022; Mears 2010, 2017, 2019, 2022).

The chapter is structured as follows. The first section briefly discusses EBP, which includes policies, programs, and practices that are grounded in credible research about policy need, theory, implementation, impacts, and cost-efficiency. The second then asks, and answers, the question: How can EBP be widely and appropriately used without research knowledge among those responsible for implementing it? The third identifies different ways in which policymakers, criminal justice administrators and practitioners, and citizens can play a role in generating, evaluating, and using EBP. The fourth section presents several examples of ways that EBP education and training of these groups might occur and how doing so may improve the generation and use of EBP. We then conclude with a call for investing in education and training in EBP as a way to increase knowledge about EBP and its more widespread and appropriate use.

I. What Is Evidence-Based Policy (EBP)?

EBP can be defined in a wide variety of ways. This section discusses several of them and how and why they matter.

A. Policy That Draws on Scientific Research

As the present volume attests, EBP is grounded in scientific research. Why does that matter? When done well, research can more accurately provide insight into relationships, such as whether and how a given policy (e.g., community policing) influences an outcome (e.g., crime rates). Individual views that we may hold could be accurate. Bias, though, looms large as a potential factor that distorts our understanding. Research can be a corrective to this possibility. As we will argue, it is essential for policymakers, criminal justice administrators and practitioners, and citizens to understand research so that they can contribute to the development, better implementation, and increased and appropriate use of EBP.

What, then, is research? Earlier chapters answer this question (see, e.g., the introductory chapter by Welsh, Zane, and Mears, as well as the chapter by Welsh and Mears, in this volume). We briefly revisit it here to highlight considerations that may be especially important for these stakeholder groups (policymakers, administrators and practitioners, and citizens) to appreciate. Such appreciation can be critical to making more and better requests for research, evaluating claims about the evidence base for policies, and anticipating what may be needed to successfully implement an EBP in their particular jurisdictions or communities.

One answer is that research encompasses a wide range of activities, all of which are unified by various traditions and logic that have accumulated over time and serve to help lead us closer to possible "truth"—that is, truth with a lower-case "t," given that almost all studies provide provisional insights into the world around us (Mears and Cochran 2019). There is a reason that many researchers cautiously describe findings—they know that error can creep in from many different directions, and that only with an accumulation of many studies can we come closer to trusting that some relationship is real, or probable, or that an explanation for the relationship is credible; that is, supported both by logic and empirical research.

As with any vocation in which knowledge and craft come together, the traditions and protocols that arise can be complex. Those that have emerged for science are not perfect. But they arise because a community of scholars has developed tools for accurately apprehending the world as it is, not as we think it works or as we think it should be (Gould 1999).

The complexity involves questions about sampling, data collection, measures, analytic techniques, and more. Studies may vary in the types and amount of sampling or measurement error that attend to them, for example. They also may vary in what outcomes they assess. A rigorous evaluation of a program designed to improve employment, housing, and recidivism outcomes would fall short in its accuracy, and thus usefulness, if it only assessed one of them. There could be good reasons for the omission (data limitations, funding constraints, etc.). Regardless, the study should not be viewed as a definitive basis for assessing effectiveness, given, among other things, a focus on only one relevant outcome. That would be true if hundreds of similar studies identified the same relationship.

Prison program outcome evaluations provide a prime example of this problem. Many evaluations focus exclusively on recidivism. They do so because this information may be more readily available, and it can be difficult to obtain data on housing and employment outcomes among formerly incarcerated populations. That situation, though, can lead to an unbalanced assessment of program effectiveness, much as computing a college grade point average (GPA) based on only one or two classes—rather than of all classes—provides an unbalanced and inaccurate gauge of performance. The problem compounds itself when most studies operate from a similar and inappropriately narrow focus. With time, it can seem that one outcome (e.g., recidivism) matters and others (e.g., employment, housing, family reunification) do not.

There are other important complexities, many of which are directly relevant to making judgments about what counts as an EBP or deciding to adopt one. For example, research might overlook potential unintended policy effects. Studies could well provide exemplary scientific accounts of this or that policy, but they would be limited in not drawing attention to the full range of possible effects. Intensive Supervision Probation (ISP) illustrates the issue. Accumulated evidence indicates that ISP generally offers no post-release recidivism benefit, and studies suggest that ISP may increase the use of incarceration for technical violations, an outcome with substantial cost implications for correctional systems (see, generally, Petersilia 2003; Piehl and LoBuglio 2005; Mears and Cochran 2015). Were the benefits substantial, and these unintended effects trivial, ISP might be a more obvious policy to pursue.

Yet another, and critical, illustration of the complexity that attends to discussions of EBP involves cost-benefit analyses. Even when such analyses have not been formerly undertaken, jurisdictions make cost-benefit calculations implicitly when they support one program over another. For that reason, investing in an EBP ideally entails consideration of the evidence base supporting other policies, programs, and practices, and the relative returns for each. Otherwise, a jurisdiction might invest in some cost-efficient programs that nonetheless indirectly contribute to creation of a portfolio of approaches that collectively is ineffective and inefficient.

The point of these preliminary observations is to highlight that EBP itself flows from research. To understand EBP, then, requires understanding research and what goes into it. Such knowledge can help policymakers, administrators and practitioners, and citizens in making informed decisions about the policies that may be most appropriate, effective, and cost-efficient. As these examples illustrate, understanding and appreciating some important aspects of research, like the importance of assessments that consider all relevant outcomes and unintended harms, does not have to require a great deal of training in research.

B. Policy That Is Based on Research on Five Critical Dimensions

EBP has been defined in different ways, as the present volume attests. Perhaps the most common view is that EBP exists when a particular policy, program, or practice is found to change some outcome in a positive direction. For example, research might show better outcomes among a treatment group versus a control or comparison group. The finding might be viewed as evidence-based if a number of studies that employed rigorous research designs consistently arrived at the same conclusion. It might be argued that the studies must appear in peer-reviewed journals, but, for a variety of reasons, many credible studies exist that do not appear in journals (e.g., studies that fail to find statistically significant findings may encounter challenges getting published). News media accounts obscure this point when they only attend to intriguing study findings from journals. Regardless, as discussed in the introductory chapter (Welsh, Zane, and Mears, this volume), identification of what counts as EBP involves reference to rigorous research studies.

That is simple enough. Even so, there are many questions that we might ask and that underscore the complexity underlying a "treatment works" conclusion. Earlier chapters discussed some of them. For example, and of particular relevance for policymakers, administrators and practitioners, and citizens, how large must an effect be before we view it as evidence-based? A trivial substantive effect, even if statistically significant, would not seem to pass muster. What, though, would? No objective answer exists. Stakeholder groups can make more informed decisions if they directly grapple with this question and appreciate that researchers cannot answer it for them. In addition, how many studies should demonstrate an effect before a policy is given the "evidence-based" stamp of approval? What if the effect sizes vary? What if some studies find a null effect or a harmful effect? Given publication bias, how likely is it that studies with null effects are even discovered? What if the effects seem highly conditional on characteristics of the population being served or on particular community characteristics? What if little rigorous research has been done that assesses the extent to which the policy processes thought to generate the outcomes actually do so? In this case—one that is common—a "black box" evaluation might identify a beneficial effect, but we have no idea which program components gave rise to it.

These and other questions should not offset the importance of rigorous research for identifying evidence-based policy. They simply highlight the challenge that confronts all of science—namely, findings typically raise more questions than they answer, and context matters a great deal. Stakeholder groups can make more informed decisions if they appreciate this fact.

The importance of context is something to which these groups should be especially attuned. It might well be, for example, that a program that many studies have found to be effective may nonetheless produce little beneficial effect for certain groups or areas. Consider a situation where studies of a policing approach exist, but the studies establishing the evidence base always examine urban areas. Whether the effects generalize to rural areas, where the crime problems and their causes may differ in kind or magnitude, would be open to question. At the same time, seemingly small effects in an urban area might amount to a substantively meaningful effect in a rural locale. Context matters.

There is another view of EBP, or, rather, one that takes a broader view. It highlights the centrality of five related policy questions: (1) What is the nature, size, and location of a social problem? (2) Does the policy draw on sound theory to guide its design and to target known causes of the problem? (3) How well implemented is the policy, and what influences implementation? (4) What impacts and unintended harms does the policy have? (5) How cost-efficient is the policy relative to alternatives? As discussed in the introductory chapter (Welsh, Zane, and Mears, this volume), these five types of evaluations form the evaluation hierarchy (Rossi, Lipsey, and Freeman 2004). The hierarchy highlights that we should only fund policies that are needed, based on credible theory, implemented well, produce meaningfully large effects, and are cost-efficient relative to alternatives. Mears (2010) argued that the five types of evaluation can be used to identify evidence-based policy, which would be policy that can satisfactorily address each of these five dimensions (need, theory, implementation, impact, and cost-efficiency).

Our central contention is that the stakeholder groups can contribute to the identification of EBP and more widespread and appropriate use of it if they better understand research. That includes an understanding that EBP can be viewed as encompassing far more than a focus on effectiveness. Why does this broader view of EBP matter for these groups? They focus on or live in areas where numerous laws, programs, practices, and the like are enacted with little clear rationale, and, worse than that, consume substantial resources with little evidence that the polices were needed. From a systems perspective, we want all of these to be as well-grounded in research as possible (Mears 2017). We do not want, for example, a suburban jurisdiction to expend a disproportionate amount of its resources on an EBP that costs a great deal and yet would only serve a small handful of youth, especially when other problems may be far more pressing. If we want more EBP, it is important for these different stakeholder groups to understand what EBP entails and, we would submit, to appreciate the relevance of viewing EBP as requiring credible research on policy need, theory, implementation, impact, and efficiency.

II. How Can EBP Be Widely and Appropriately Used If Policymakers, Criminal Justice Administrators and Practitioners, and Citizens Do Not Have a Strong Foundation in Research?

The question is critical, and the answer to has profound implications for the adoption and appropriate use of EBP. For EBP to become more widespread, groups on the front lines of implementing criminal justice policy must be involved in contributing to and intepreting research.

A. The Short Answer: It Can't

It is difficult to overstate this problem. Widespread and appropriate use of EBP requires that policymakers, administrators and practitioners, and citizens have a strong foundation in research, or at least a well-developed understanding of it. However, these groups all-too-frequently do not have such a foundation. (This problem arises in part from a need for educational systems to improve the research training that they offer students; we discuss this point later in the chapter.) As a result, although these groups may call for EBP, they may not always fully appreciate what that means beyond the idea that at least a few studies found that a particular program reduced crime. A strong foundation in research is relevant not just for policymakers and administrators. Front-line practitioners (e.g., officers and staff as well as directors of intervention and service programs) and citizens cannot effectively promote or advocate for research-based policy without a firm understanding of what goes into research and, thus, EBP.

Collecting more and more information about evidence-based policies does not address this issue. Generating lists of evidence-based policies can be helpful for aiding in decision-making, and helping to orient policy in a more effective direction. It does not, though, address the need for individuals who make policy-relevant decisions to have a foundation in research sufficient to make reasonable and informed judgments about EBP or to appreciate the diverse ways in which evidence might be brought to bear to guide and develop policy. Without such a foundation, they cannot determine whether a given EBP makes sense given unique conditions or operational challenges in their jurisdiction or agency.

There is another important complicating factor—the sheer abundance of information on the Internet can make it difficult to separate the wheat from the chaff. Some information comes from credible sources, some does not. What do we do when flooded with information? Ignore it, or select on sources we most trust. Rather than developing an ability to ask for relevant research and to evaluate the basis for claims about "evidence-based policy," policymakers and administrators may proceed from intuition or ideology, or rely on the judgments of those with whom they most closely work. A better path lies with helping decision-makers, as well as members of the public, understand better how to evaluate EBP and its grounding in research.

The trend in recent decades has been to involve citizens in policy, not just indirectly by how they vote, but also more directly by participating in policy implementation and review processes and by providing information relevant for ensuring accountability (Chari et al. 2017). The involvement in criminal justice is not just through civilian review boards but also through voter referenda (Zimring, Hawkins, and Kamin 2003). Research on evidence-based policing illustrates the continuing influence of this trend—citizens and police work together to identify causes of, and possible solutions to, crime, and to evaluate police practices and responses (Lum and Koper 2021). Citizens can provide critical feedback to the police and to researchers about these issues and what is missed, such as ways to improve policy design and implementation and minimize unintended harms. We will return to this idea, but here mention it to illustrate that research can be a collaborative exercise that enables nonresearchers to become more informed about, and participate in, research.

B. These Groups Are the Ones on the Front Lines of All Aspects of Criminal Justice Policy

It is one thing to produce knowledge about EBP; it is another to understand the on-the-ground reality in cities, counties, police departments, courts, and correctional systems. In some cases, it may be clear as day that a particular policy, program, or practice should be adopted. More likely, though, decision-makers confront a wide range of social problems to address, face numerous competing demands, and must make decisions in the context of limited resources.

Several examples illustrate the point. A police chief likely knows better than most the problems emanating from staffing shortages and insufficient training. Moreover, that same police chief may know better than a researcher what leads to staffing and training problems in the first place. Front-line officers may know best the challenges that they face in their day-to-day work. Those same officers almost certainly know the specific context within which they work better than a researcher. Citizens may know best the extent to which police convey themselves in a professional or respectful manner. Citizens no doubt also know best the consequences of policies targeting their communities and neighborhoods. Court workers—judges, prosecutors, defense attorneys, and so on—have unique insights into how particular laws or programs will be implemented, or what unintended effects they may have. Similarly, those who work in corrections have a direct understanding of numerous operational challenges and problems that shape everyday practice.

In short, these diverse groups hold critical insights relevant for identifying problems and solutions, as well as factors that might affect policy implementation and effectiveness. If researchers ignore or only passingly acknowledge the insights of these groups, they miss opportunities to develop EBP or identify ways to ensure that an EBP is implemented with sufficient fidelity to its design to be effective. Many researchers are optimistic; they want programs to succeed. That can lead to overlooking that quality implementation of a program can quickly recede once a study concludes, and this may happen for reasons that might be readily apparent to those with a boots-on-the-ground understanding of local context. Consider that a new initiative might be staffed by some of an agency's most skilled or experienced personnel. Why? An agency administrator astutely gauges that the program will face substantial implementation challenges and resistance from some groups. As soon as external funding for the program dries up or a study concludes, or a more pressing organizational priority arises, these personnel shift to other areas. The end result? Program implementation quality plummets.

Yet policymaker, criminal justice administrator and practitioner, and citizen voices typically do not feature prominently in accounts of EBP, save to report that they all want more effective policy. Their involvement, though, is critical to identifying a wider range of relevant policies and the conditions under which they may be most effective. Their involvement is critical, too, in helping these groups to appreciate the benefits of EBP and in understanding how to request, evaluate, and appropriately use evidence-based policies. To illustrate this last issue, consider the importance of selecting appropriate individuals for an intervention. Awareness of research on EBP would alert someone to the need to ensure that selection into a given program is undertaken carefully. Matching the "right" individuals to the "right" program increases the chances of success. That axiom is frequently violated, though. Practitioners understandably want to provide programming to those whom they judge to be most likely to succeed, and sometimes want that even though these people may not actually require much, if any, treatment. It is often the researcher's job to explain that assigning low-risk persons to treatment not only undermines the ability to detect a program effect, but also might be harmful (Wilson and Davis 2006; Wilson and Zozula 2011). A better grounding in research would help policymakers and criminal justice administrators and practitioners appreciate these possibilities and, in turn, prioritize screening processes that ensure program placements.

Awareness of the nature of research and its relevance for EBP can have relevance that extends beyond a focus on particular policies or programs. Consider, for example, that criminal justice entails numerous informal decisions, or what amount to everyday practices. These do not necessarily constitute coherent policies or programs, but they nonetheless can greatly affect system effectiveness (Mears and Bacon 2009). For example, prosecutors' or judges' beliefs about who might be more amenable to rehabilitation might influence reliance on diversion. The everyday practice, then, might be to use diversion in a highly patterned manner, with some racial or ethnic groups being more likely to receive diversion. A "researcher sensibility" (Mears and Cochran 2019) would likely lead to a greater likelihood of viewing such practices through an evidence-based lens, one that questions the assumptions that underlie policy and practice and that looks for credible information to support or contradict them. Developing an ability to appreciate how research can be used to evaluate these decisions could go a long way to improving policy.

C. Yet Evaluating and Using EBP Appropriately Are Not Simple Tasks

We cannot expect that these different groups will understand research the way that those trained and experienced in it do. What, then, to do?

Although research can be a complicated undertaking, we would argue that policymakers, criminal justice administrators and practitioners, and citizens can understand critical dimensions that should be considered when creating or evaluating research, or when thinking about using an EBP. The situation is different from what Stephen Jay Gould (1999) referred to as non-overlapping magisteria (NOMA), when describing the idea that science and religion each have unique expertise related to their respective domains. Gould viewed their domain-specific expertise as dictating that they stick to making decisions where that expertise applies, and refraining from crossing over to areas where it does not. That idea may apply well to discussions about religion, but policy is another matter. It constitutes an undertaking that requires accurate information for making appropriate decisions and improving effectiveness and efficiency. Research can produce such information. It is a knowledge-generating enterprise that many people, not just those who undertake it, can understand (Mears and Cochran 2019).

The reality, however, is that some well-meaning policymakers and criminal justice administrators and practitioners (and citizens more so) do not appear to rely much on research. They rely on instinct, intuition, or the judgment of others, and make a decision. We have, then, researchers undertaking work that can be complex and entail many caveats that may be essential to determining whether a policy should be adopted, expanded, or terminated. And we sometimes have decision-makers who do not have sufficient training to evaluate the results in light of the complexity and caveats. That creates a situation rife with room for error and inefficiency. Consider this simple scenario: A jurisdiction hears that Program X is "evidence-based" because it reportedly, based on one moderately rigorous evaluation in another state, is effective. But this program might have been effective in an area where "business as usual" was terrible. If our jurisdiction's "business as usual" practices are quite effective, then Program X will not be likely to create better outcomes. This idea—that the counterfactual condition shapes how one should interpret effects—may be familiar to researchers, but not necessarily to a local criminal justice administrator.

In short, even if we had a long list of evidence-based policies to cover every aspect of criminal justice, decision-maker groups would still benefit from having a "researcher sensibility." It would help them to determine when particular policies might be needed, to evaluate which ones are "evidence-based," to understand what descriptions of "evidence-based" policies mean (given the variability in how the term is used), and to identify contextual factors in an area or agency that might bear on whether or how a policy should be adopted. It would help them, too, to become active participants in identifying needed research and interpreting research results. That is especially important when the results involve these groups' areas or interests. We thus need strategies for helping policymakers, criminal justice administrators and practitioners, and citizens become knowledgeable about research and EBP if we are to have widespread and appropriate use of evidence-based policies.

III. Generating, Evaluating, and Using EBP: The Role of Policymakers, Criminal Justice Administrators and Practitioners, and Citizens

Policymakers, criminal justice administrators and practitioners, and citizens can play at least three roles in relation to EBP: they can help to generate, evaluate, and use it. Each of these activities is briefly described to convey that these decision-maker groups have a critical role to play in producing knowledge about EBP and effectively increasing its use.

A. Generating EBP

Knowledge generation, in general, falls clearly to the researcher community. They receive training in how to conduct studies, they learn about theories and diverse methodologies, and they develop substantive expertise about specific topics or issues. None of that means, though, that creating credible information about the world, including policy, falls solely to this community.

Consider one of the central arguments for qualitative approaches to developing theories and empirical insights—interviewing or observing individuals or groups can lead to insights that researchers would never have identified. Of course, results from qualitative studies may lack generalizability. Perhaps the findings reflect views of an unrepresentative group, for example. That simply means that we need to follow up with studies that allow for testing the generalizability of the findings. (It should be emphasized, for context, that quantitative studies can lack generalizability, too; the findings of even the most sophisticated experiment might not generalize to other places, populations, or times [Feagin, Orum, and Sjoberg 1991].) The point remains—those who live and work in particular organizations or places can have insights about crime and justice, their causes, their solutions, and policy implementation and impacts. The theories and literature on which researchers rely do not magically have these insights.

Top-down approaches to studies ignore this possibility and severely constrain the ability of researchers to generate relevant information. For example, a researcher might obtain funding to evaluate a re-entry program. They focus immediately on recidivism because, well, it seems like such an obvious basis on which to gauge success. What, though, if the program's primary goals include not only recidivism reduction but also success in obtaining housing and employment, reunifying with family, and gaining access to drug and mental health treatment. Criminologists might be forgiven for deprioritizing these outcomes because they typically study crime. However, an evaluation should define success based on a policy's goals (Rossi, Lipsey, and Freeman 2004). A program might not achieve meaningful reductions in recidivism, but may provide other benefits. That matters. A program might be worth pursuing if it achieves no reduction in recidivism but does improve employment and housing outcomes. A top-down approach might miss, too, that these other outcomes might well be critical to reducing recidivism. Knowledge of that possibility could lead to investigation of whether or how intermediate outcomes contribute to other outcomes, as well as to how better to improve the former (Mears 2010).

A bottom-up approach to evaluation would ensure that researchers examined, to the extent possible, not just recidivism but also these other outcomes and the ways in which they may influence one another. A bottom-up approach matters for other reasons. People who work in police departments or the courts or corrections, or live in communities touched by crime or these institutions, may have important insights or ideas about policy theory or design, implementation, likely impacts, and possible harms. Many ideas look good on paper but fall apart in practice. Only under highly controlled conditions can that possibility be minimized. Indeed, that is one reason for the distinction between efficacy and effectiveness studies. The former examine whether an impact might arise under ideal conditions, while the latter examine what will happen in the real world (Mears 2010). Community policing illustrates the point. Citizens might be able to identify places where officers will encounter resistance to this style of policing as well as ways to overcome it. They may also highlight unique causes of crime in their area. And they may identify a policy's unintended harms, such as a reduced willingness to call the police, that a top-down evaluation might miss. In every instance, citizen collaboration with researchers could lead to revisiting a policy's design, creating new policies, and improving implementation and effectiveness. Perspectives from the "ground up" matter.

This idea is captured well by researcher-practitioner partnerships (Pesta et al. 2018; Frost 2022; Piza and Welsh 2022). These entail collaborations that amount to a team-based approach to research. Instead of researchers dictating the framing or focus of a study, they work with practitioners to identify relevant research questions and approaches. For example, police-led science can entail officers leading or participating in creating field experiments (Piza and Welsh 2022). This approach can not only generate knowledge about possible evidence-based policies, but also inculcate a researcher sensibility that extends to and helps to guide thinking about police policy, practice, and decision-making. Embedding researchers in criminal justice agencies achieves a similar goal (Petersilia 2008). It can, for example, help researchers to better understand what kinds of studies may be needed and can be undertaken, and provides a vehicle for disseminating relevant empirical research findings to practitioners.

B. Evaluating EBP

Researchers sometimes get criticized for studying the obvious. Yet the obvious does not always play out the way that people think it will. A host of programs exist that advocates think constitute common sense, but research shows them to be ineffective or highlights that they amount to what Latessa, Listwan, and Koetzle (2014) term "quackery." A simple way to identify such programs? Many of them target none of the known contributors to crime. Observe that one does not have to be a researcher to appreciate that a program that targets none of the known causes of crime would not be a good bet for successfully driving down crime or recidivism (Mears 2010; Cooper and Worrall 2012; Welsh, Zimmerman, and Zane 2018).

A larger issue is that we sometimes end up with research findings that we cannot readily explain, and so we must make assumptions about what produced certain effects. For example, a strength of a well-designed experiment is that we can have greater trust in any identified X-Y relationship. If the drug court participant recidivism rate is lower than that of the control group, we can have greater confidence that the drug court generated that result. What, though, about the drug court did so? The underlying theory for the specialized court might point to deterrence mechanisms (e.g., frequent check-ins with a judge might scare participants from engaging in criminal activity out of fear that they will be caught and sentenced harshly). It also might point to rehabilitative or strain mechanisms (e.g., treatment might reduce drug abuse and, in turn, impulsive acts of crime, or it might reduce the perceived need to steal to support a drug habit, and, in so doing, reduce strain).

An experimental-design study will not always be able to tease out such possibilities (see, e.g., Gottfredson, Najaka, and Kearley 2003). In these cases, relying on information from, say, court actors or treatment group participants might shed light on which mechanisms may have played a role. For example, judges might report that they never implemented the check-ins with much fidelity to the original design. That, then, might suggest that they main effect arose through treatment rather than deterrence mechanisms. Similarly, an effort to mandate prosecution of domestic violence arrests might readily be identified by court actors and victims as having the likely result of slowing down the processing of cases and of creating less trust in or support of the court among individuals who experience domestic violence (Davis, Smith, and Taylor 2003). An experimental design study might not even be worth pursuing if preliminary theoretical and empirical analysis—even if based primarily on informal interviews and observations—shows that the necessary conditions for the policy's effectiveness (e.g., hiring more prosecutors, buy-in from the police, support from domestic violence victims) are not present.

In short, decision-makers from the policy and practice communities, as well as from citizens, can aid in generating ideas about potential policies that are needed or could be effective. They also can help in guiding research evaluations and interpreting results. Collaborative research relationships can leverage these possibilities and help to identify a broader range of evidence-based policies and how to understand when and why they may be more, or less, effective.

C. Using EBP

Another critical aspect of promoting evidence-based policy consists in its use. Researchers can supply information, but that does not necessarily or even frequently inform policy (Laub and Frisch 2016). The reasons vary. It may be that researchers present findings in a confusing manner or use complex terminology (that the researchers themselves may not even fully understand), there may be few structured channels for communicating results to decision-makers, an issue may be highly politicized, and so on.

Whatever the reason, it should be evident that widespread use of EBP requires that decision-makers want it. Many policymakers and other decision-makers may say that they want EBP, or, more generally, policy that "works." That differs, though, from appreciating their own role in helping to create relevant EBP and understanding the opportunities for its use. For example, EBP can entail policy based on credible research information about policy design and implementation. For decision-makers to call for such information, they must understand that EBP includes having relevant and accurate information about the prevalence and causes of a particular problem, as well as similar information about the quality of implementation. Accountability in government includes demonstrating that policy implementation aligns with policy design (Mears 2010). That is important because effective policy requires quality implementation. If decision-makers viewed EBP in this manner, they might be more likely to demand research on all aspects of policy that relate to demonstrating need, credible policy design, full and quality implementation, impacts, and cost-efficiency. Put differently, they can drive demand for EBP.

Policy decision-makers, including citizens, can do more than demand EBP, they can also help to ensure its appropriate use. To do so, however, requires knowledge about research and EBP. For example, just because studies have found that a particular program can produce benefits does not mean that the program will be effective in another place or with a different population. It also does not mean that investing in the program would be indicated more so than investing in policy initiatives that address other problems of potentially greater relevance. Consider prison systems. In the era of mass incarceration, many prison systems suffer from extreme understaffing. In such a context, investing in a program that has been shown to reduce recidivism may not be the best strategy. It might even increase aggregate rates of recidivism by diverting resources from other aspects of prison operations. The importance of staffing to program implementation is an all-too-often overlooked on-the-ground impediment to program effectiveness. Adequate staffing levels within institutions is crucial not only to the effective running of the institution but also to its ability to deploy the programs it seeks to adopt with fidelity. Even where program adoption might make sense from a recidivism reduction perspective, it may make far less sense in a context of extreme understaffing.

Those who work on the front lines of, or experience, the criminal justice system are well-positioned to apply a research perspective to supporting and shaping EBP. They can help determine when it is needed, when it might inadvertently interfere with agency operations, and how best to improve implementation. In some cases, what to do may be obvious. In others, though, a researcher sensibility would provide a foundation for appropriately and effectively using evidence-based policies and programs.

IV. How to Improve EBP Research Education for Policymakers, Criminal Justice Administrators and Practitioners, and Citizens

What can be done to help increase the chances that policymakers, chiefs of police, heads of jail and prison systems, government officials or community organizations focused on criminal justice, and others will be better able to ask for, consume, and use information about evidence-based policy? We offer several recommendations for improving the generation of knowledge about EBP and for its more widespread and appropriate use. Our main contention is simply that efforts to increase knowledge about EBP and its use would benefit from creating more informed demand for it from criminal justice decision-makers and citizens.

A. Improve High School and College Education about Research

One way to proceed is to improve education about research, and to do so from high school through college. At the high school level, students typically never learn anything about social science or policy research. They take math classes and possibly learn about experiments in their biology, chemistry, or physics classes. They might take a statistics course. And they might take a sociology or psychology class where they read about theories and results of studies. Yet they do not once learn about policy research and the many considerations that go into undertaking or evaluating it. This occurs even though most students will face a universe in which an ability to request, evaluate, or use policy research will be essential to informed voting, and an ability to use research more generally will help them with decisions in their personal and professional lives.

It is not much better at the college or university level. Students in the behavioral and social sciences typically must take a research methods *or* a statistics course, even though understanding statistics requires an understanding of research methods, and vice versa. Many undergraduate students dread statistics and put off taking it until their final year, even though understanding statistics earlier would have helped them critically assess research that they read that was presented as evidence. Few will take any additional courses that lead them to develop a researcher sensibility. Students in the humanities and liberal arts typically can avoid research courses entirely. Those in the "hard sciences" do not fare better. Although trained in research, what they learn frequently will not directly extend to the policy research arena. And they may not receive training that helps them to contemplate ways, other than the traditional scientific method, of generating knowledge (Moses and Knutson 2019). Even students in public policy or public administration programs may not always receive much training about how to conduct, request, evaluate, or use research. They instead may learn more about policy creation processes.

Postgraduate programs don't fare much better. Lawyers and medical doctors, for example, typically learn nothing about policy research. Master's degree programs emphasize substantive over methodological coursework. To make matters worse, even doctoral programs in the social sciences do not emphasize policy research, and may dissuade students from pursuing this path. Gaining tenure or being promoted in research-oriented universities typically requires publishing in top peer-reviewed journals. Such journals may not embrace policy-focused studies because of a notion that "pure" science involves a focus on root causes of phenomena, never mind that policy evaluations can lead to theories about such causes (Rossi 1980). This problem shapes graduate education. Within master's and doctoral programs in criminology, there exists a substantial bias toward teaching theories on the causes of crime over theories of system responses to it (Maguire and Duffee 2015). The end result? Faculty pursue scientific questions that do not always or clearly connect to policy, under the logic that it is better to be safe (e.g., tenured) than sorry (e.g., untenured). A related problem that flows from this situation is that students do not learn about collecting or using policy or program data (e.g., correctional system administrative records), or how to communicate results in an accessible manner for a general audience (Petersilia 1991). They also may be socialized to disdain policy research or seemingly "simple" analyses (e.g., percentages or correlations) for more academic or "scholarly" research and more complex analyses.

There is, then, a pressing need to improve the education that all students receive and to help them develop a researcher sensibility. Researchers see the world in a somewhat unique way. They think about samples, ways to measure processes or outcomes, theories that could help anticipate or explain relationships, errors in theory or analytic modeling that might point to the need for caution in interpreting results, and more. One need not have years of training and experience, however, to appreciate the relevance of these considerations. It is a truism to state that the art of many things in life consists in asking better questions. A researcher sensibility can provide a path for students to think about, design, and evaluate policy and the results of research that they read. Unfortunately, educational systems generally do not teach a researcher sensibility; instead, they offer no courses, as is the case in high schools, or they offer courses that teach about dimensions of research, without helping students to develop a sense of how to conduct and evaluate it. That is equivalent to teaching cooking by describing different ingredients, measurement, and techniques, without ever focusing on how one might combine ingredients to create different dishes, or on how chefs develop their ability to do so or to appreciate or appraise their own or others' cooking.

What to do? One solution is to require a policy research course in high school, in college, and in graduate programs. Consider that many high schools emphasize math courses, but push students in the direction of taking algebra, trigonometry, and calculus. Sometimes statistics might be encouraged. They do not, though, require a research course where one might learn about the process of conducting social science and policy-relevant research, the importance of theory (and how to create it) for guiding policy, collecting and analyzing data, presenting results accurately, showcasing limitations, and identifying factors that might influence the generalizability of results. A required course on the research process—in high school and then in college—would address these shortfalls and, ideally, emphasize the "doing" of research (e.g., clarifying research questions, developing theoretical explanations, identifying a relevant sample population, thinking about appropriate measures and analyses). In a perfect world, this course would focus on the most important parts of what traditionally gets covered in a research methods course and in a statistics course, bringing them together in a way that more holistically presents how to do and evaluate research (Mears and Cochran 2019). It would also teach students to use an evaluation hierarchy lens—with an attendant focus on needs, theory, implementation, impact, and cost-efficiency (Rossi, Lipsey, and Freeman 2004)—for conceptualizing and assessing policy. Such a requirement dovetails with national efforts to promote science, technology, engineering, and math (STEM) fields, and to create a workforce capable of thinking creatively about solutions to pressing social problems. Done well, it would lead to individuals who know better how to request, conduct, evaluate, and use research to make better decisions, including appropriately using EBP.

B. Improve Graduate Student Training on EBP Research

Three decades ago, Petersilia (1991) highlighted problems with graduate student training. We discussed several of these problems earlier in the chapter, and they persist to the present day. For example, in many fields, and certainly in criminology and criminal justice, publishing in top journals has become increasingly emphasized. That creates pressure for faculty to "publish or perish," which in turn creates a premium on using extant data sets rather than collecting original data (Kleck, Tark, and Bellows 2006). Students, therefore, have little experiential learning in how to create original data. Policy evaluation courses may not be offered, and numerous other, important course requirements exist; both conditions prevent students from learning how to evaluate policy.

The obvious solution is to emphasize policy research as an important endeavor in its own right (Mears 2022). It can contribute to theory development (Rossi 1980), and so advance scientific knowledge, a primary goal of colleges and universities. It also can lead to identifying new and interesting fields of inquiry. It can result, too, in collaborations with the policy and practice arena in ways that can educate those outside the academy. These collaborations also help researchers to appreciate the contexts and goals of policymakers, criminal justice administrators and practitioners, and citizens. Shifting graduate training in this direction is possible, as can be seen in programs that emphasize experiential learning (Frost 2022).

Recent decades have been witness to calls for translational criminology (Laub and Frisch 2016). That includes efforts to create researcher partnerships that can provide more immediate and relevant information to policy decision-makers and that foster collaboration (Pesta et al. 2018). These efforts can include collaborations among diverse stakeholders. Researchers play a key role, but they do not occupy center stage and are not the only relevant voices. Instead, they work with others to identify relevant questions, possible policy responses, the theoretical logic that might support or argue against particular policies, possible data sources from which to draw or opportunities to create new data, analyses that might be useful, how to interpret results, especially those that may be unexpected or counterintuitive, and so on. Graduate student training on translational criminology thus provides a platform for improving the ability of graduate students to conduct policy-relevant research. It also would educate and train diverse decision-maker groups on the ins and outs of research.

This vision of research—and thus the training that the students might receive—entails a different conceptualization of how research might unfold. Under the traditional view, researchers have all relevant knowledge and arrive to a policy evaluation with everything that they need, except perhaps the data. They then frame the questions, undertake the analyses, and present the findings. An alternative view is to see research as a co-produced undertaking, one where researchers are not the presumptive experts but rather participants in generating knowledge. Seen in this way, all parties contribute to framing the study questions, thinking about relevant questions, and interpreting results. They all, therefore, would share credit in contributing to EBP knowledge. This idea runs counter to the notion that researchers are the sole knowledge producers, but it logically emanates from a collaborative view of research. Nothing about the approach has to mean that researcher expertise on various aspects of research design, measurement, and analysis is diminished. It simply means that many aspects of the research enterprise would be democratized when conducting policy evaluation studies. The take-away for graduate student education would be to view training as emphasizing collaboration that occurs not just across disciplines but also with policymaking, criminal justice administrator and practitioner, and citizen communities. Such training might lead to more relevant knowledge about EBP. It also might increase the likelihood that these groups develop a researcher sensibility that helps to guide their decision-making when they pursue one of any number of careers that involve policy or practice.

C. Create Research and EBP Training Seminars for Policymakers, Criminal Justice Administrators and Practitioners, and Citizens

Many fields and occupations require continuing education courses to be able to maintain employment. A strong case can be made that policymakers and criminal justice administrators should be required to take continuing education courses that emphasize research. These courses could focus not just on the nuts and bolts of research, but also on how to think about it with a researcher sensibility. They would include education and training on how to request relevant research, how to evaluate it, and how to use it. Calling for research on "what works" is easy. Asking for relevant studies on specific aspects of criminal justice—including various existing or proposed policies, programs, or practices—is not. The courses would address this problem by providing participants with examples of ways to think about and evaluate research on different social problems and policies to address them. The courses also would entail exercises that teach about evaluating and using research results, with special attention to caution in assuming that policies will be implemented as designed or that policies that seemingly "work" in one place will "work" as well in another.

Such courses should, in our view, be made freely available to front-line practitioners and the public as well. An educated work force and citizenry can better help guide, inform, and evaluate policy and practice. Not all citizens want to be involved in policy decision-making. Yet many citizens care deeply about their communities and would appreciate having resources that helped them to advocate for policies that would help their communities. Providing such courses could provide a way to help citizens sift through the myriad "facts" and opinions expressed in the news and social media, and possibly make more informed decisions about the policies that they need or that might be effective in their particular community. Public access to such resources could also help citizens, whose tax dollars typically fund interventions, exert constituent pressure when funds are earmarked for approaches that have been shown to have little to no evidence base. In addition, they might be more inclined to demand that policymakers and government officials ground their policies in credible evidence about the need for—and the design, implementation, effectiveness, and efficiency of—them.

A related change that may help is for researchers who seek to advance EBP to look for opportunities to help train policymakers, administrators, and citizens in how to think about it. In university and college settings, publishing in peer-reviewed journals frequently is valued over, and typically at the expense of, undertaking policy-oriented work (Petersilia 1991). That dynamic extends to presentations—discussing research at academic conferences rather than at nonacademic venues can carry much more weight in promotion and tenure decisions. Exceptions certainly exist, and some scholars manage to "hit on all pistons" by undertaking diverse types of research and presenting to a wide range of audiences. In general, though, that appears to constitute the exception rather than the norm.

The simple solution is to push colleges and universities to promote collaborations with policymaker, administrator, and citizen communities, and to encourage presentations to them. Some nonacademic organizations—such as the American Correctional Association (ACA), the International Association of Chiefs of Police (IACP), and the National Association for Civilian Oversight of Law Enforcement (NACOLE)—have annual conferences that would provide structured opportunities for such presentations. With their existing infrastructure of continuing education credit, the conferences of professional associations are also ideal locations for researchers to offer precisely the types of workshops that would help these critical stakeholders develop a researcher sensibility that might facilitate evidence-based policy and decision-making.

D. Embed Policymakers, Criminal Justice Administrators and Practitioners, and Citizens in the Research and EBP Research Evaluation Enterprise

One of the ideas for improving the ability of researchers to assist policymakers and criminal justice administrators in creating or evaluating policy is having them become embedded in agencies or organizations (Petersilia 2008). Doing so enables them to learn the nuances of organizations, the contexts in which they operate, the challenges they face, the types of data that exist, and so on. In some ways, it represents a bottom-up approach. Researchers spend time learning from watching and talking with others rather than having a priori approaches to framing and evaluating particular policies. Embeddedness can help researchers avoid the many pitfalls that can end up compromising research.

A complimentary idea is to have policymakers and agency personnel, along with citizens, become embedded in research activities from the outset. They might spend time with researchers in meetings and participate in the decision-making that goes into conducting a study—how exactly to frame the study questions, identifying potentially relevant literatures to investigate, revisiting study questions after reviewing prior work, exploring possible data sources, thinking about opportunities with and limitations of the data, developing coding rules for certain measures, reviewing preliminary analyses, and so on.

Participating in even just a few such collaborations might help the groups better appreciate what goes into research. It might open their eyes to how research can be used to help inform policy and practice. It also might remove the veil that sometimes exists when researchers discuss findings. Nonresearchers sometimes find the very notion of research opaque. Hands-on involvement could help them discern that, like many activities in life, research is not a mysterious undertaking. Instead, research is a craft, one with protocols that exist for a reason but that also require judgment calls. The involvement could also contribute to a two-way transfer of knowledge and help the stakeholder groups to see that they can play an active role in research. That, in turn, could foster an environment that promotes EBP and promotes the co-creation of knowledge about evidence-based policies and how to improve their use and implementation.

Innovation will be necessary, but there are existing frameworks and mechanisms for citizen involvement in the research enterprise. Some institutions have added civilians to institutional review boards (IRBs); for example, many IRBs have a member representing incarcerated or formerly incarcerated persons. Other institutions have encouraged the use of community advisory boards within research centers and institutes. Effective community advisory boards are involved not just in the oversight of research processes and the dissemination of research findings, but also in problem identification and the co-creation of research agendas. No matter the mechanism, there must be engagement with the community, not simply one-way communication of research to the community. Embedding the different stakeholder groups in the research enterprise constitutes a simple way to enable such engagement to occur.

V. Conclusion

We return to the book's goals and revisit the relevance of focusing on decision-makers—policymakers, criminal justice administrators and practitioners, and citizens—in creating, evaluating, and using EBP. As we have argued, these groups can play a critical role on all of these counts. They can, in turn, contribute to more widespread and appropriate use of EBP.

One goal was to promote new and productive ways to think about EBP. We believe that a focus on policymakers, criminal justice administrators and practitioners, and citizens draws attention to a critical gap in research, and also a missed opportunity to improve knowledge about and use of EBP. Training all students, improving graduate student education, and requiring policy research training for policymakers and criminal justice administrators are, we believe, a productive way to think about EBP. At the least, this focus highlights that producing knowledge about what counts as "evidence-based" policy constitutes only one step toward improving policy. The other part is having decision-makers who can help support this work and evaluate and use it appropriately when making decisions.

A second goal was to show how research can contribute to and guide EBP in the context of juvenile justice, criminal justice, and alternatives to system responses. Here, again, the different decision-maker groups can help in identifying policies that may warrant consideration. They also can help in designing policies, evaluating research results, identifying potential explanations for observed beneficial or harmful effects, and determining when and where particular evidence-based policies may be appropriate and helpful. Put differently, a focus on training these groups on policy research can help them to be able to make more informed decisions and enable them to think about new and different ways to address social problems. To have a researcher sensibility is, in part, to be able to think counterfactually. That forces one to think about exactly what a policy seeks to achieve and what viable alternatives exist.

Finally, a third goal was to identify strategies that can increase reliance on EBP, and, in particular, policy that is well designed, implemented, monitored, and evaluated. Our proposed solution identifies training and researcher-practitioner, as well as researcher-citizen, collaborations as strategies that can contribute to this goal. When key decision-makers understand research—what it is, what it can do, and how to evaluate and use it—they are better positioned to request and rely on it. They would be more likely, in our view, to see research not as an isolated event that sometimes gets used, but rather as an undertaking that should infuse all decision-making. That would lead to a situation where "What works?" is no longer the only question that policymakers or administrators ask. Instead, they would know to ask questions about specific policy goals, what problems it is intended to address, how well the intervention is designed, whether it is suitable for or makes sense in their specific context, and how to ensure that implementation accords with the policy's design. They would be prepared to ask about a policy's potential impacts, both intended and unintended, and, crucially, they would know what research to ask for, and be better able to evaluate its relevance to their specific context.

To improve policy, we need evidence-based approaches that research shows can be effective in improving outcomes. But we need more. We need information about diverse approaches to achieving these outcomes. That way, jurisdictions can choose those that may be most effective for the variety of problems that they face. We also need information about the conditions that must be met for a given approach to be effective. Otherwise, jurisdictions risk adopting policies that may not be effective for their unique contexts. That wastes resources; worse, it diverts resources from where they can be most helpful. Not least, we need a greater reliance on research to inform all aspects of policy, programming, and practice. To get to that place, we need policymakers, criminal justice administrators and practitioners, and citizens who bring a researcher sensibility to the table and who can effectively contribute to and evaluate EBP, and, most important, help to ensure its widespread and appropriate use.

References

Chari, Rayma, Luke J. Matthews, Marjory S. Blumenthal, Amanda F. Edelman, and Therese Jones. 2017. *The promise of community research*. Santa Monica, CA: RAND.

Cooper, Jonathon, and John L. Worrall. 2012. Theorizing criminal justice evaluation and research. *Criminal Justice Review*, 37:384–397.

Davis, Robert C., Barbara E. Smith, and Bruce Taylor. 2003. Increasing the proportion of domestic violence arrests that are prosecuted: A natural experiment in Milwaukee. *Criminology and Public Policy*, 2:263–282.

Feagin, Joe R., Anthony M. Orum, and Gideon Sjoberg, eds. 1991. *A case for the case study*. Chapel Hill: University of North Carolina Press.

Frost, Natasha A. 2022. Research training to advance criminal justice reform. *American Journal of Criminal Justice*, 47:1204–1224.

Gottfredson, Denise C., Stacy S. Najaka, and Brook Kearley. 2003. Effectiveness of drug treatment courts: Evidence from a randomized trial. *Criminology and Public Policy*, 2:171–196.

Gould, Stephen J. 1999. *Rocks of ages: Science and religion in the fullness of life*. New York: Ballantine.

Kleck, Gary, Jongyeon Tark, and Jon J. Bellows. 2006. What methods are most frequently used in research in criminology and criminal justice? *Journal of Criminal Justice*, 34:147–152.

Latessa, Edward J., Shelley J. Listwan, and Deborah Koetzle. 2014. *What works (and doesn't) in reducing recidivism*. Waltham, MA: Anderson.

Laub, John H., and Nicole E. Frisch. 2016. Translational criminology: A new path forward. In *Advancing criminology and criminal justice policy*, edited by Thomas G. Blomberg, Julie M. Brancale, Kevin M. Beaver, and William D. Bales, 52–62. New York: Routledge.

Lum, Cynthia, and Christopher Koper. 2021. Evidence-based policing. In *Critical issues in policing: Contemporary readings*, edited by Roger G. Dunham, Geoffrey P. Alpert, and Kyle D. McLean, 65–82. Long Grove, IL: Waveland Press.

Maguire, Edward, and David Duffee, eds. 2015. *Criminal justice theory: Explaining the nature and behavior of criminal justice*. 2nd ed. New York: Routledge.

Mears, Daniel P. 2010. *American criminal justice policy: An evaluation approach to increasing accountability and effectiveness*. New York: Cambridge University Press.

Mears, Daniel P. 2017. *Out-of-control criminal justice: The systems improvement solution for more safety, justice, accountability, and efficiency*. New York: Cambridge University Press.

Mears, Daniel P. 2019. Creating systems that can improve safety and justice (and why piecemeal change won't work). *Justice Evaluation Journal*, 2:1–17.

Mears, Daniel P. 2022. Bridging the research-policy divide to advance science and policy: The 2022 Bruce Smith, Sr. Award address to the Academy of Criminal Justice Sciences. *Justice Evaluation Journal*, 5:163–185.

Mears, Daniel P., and Sarah Bacon. 2009. Improving criminal justice through better decision making: Lessons from the medical system. *Journal of Criminal Justice*, 37:142–154.

Mears, Daniel P., and Joshua C. Cochran. 2015. *Prisoner reentry in the era of mass incarceration*. Thousand Oaks, CA: SAGE.

Mears, Daniel P., and Joshua C. Cochran. 2019. *Fundamentals of criminological and criminal justice inquiry: The science and art of conducting, evaluating, and using research*. New York: Cambridge University Press.

Moses, Jonathon W., and Torbjørn L. Knutsen. 2019. *Ways of knowing: Competing methodologies in social and political research*. London: Bloomsbury.

Pesta, George B., Thomas G. Blomberg, Javier Ramos, and J. W. Andrew Ranson. 2018. Translational criminology: Toward best practice. *American Journal of Criminal Justice*, 44:499–518.

Petersilia, Joan. 1991. Policy relevance and the future of criminology: The American Society of Criminology 1990 Presidential Address. *Criminology*, 29:1–15.

Petersilia, Joan. 2003. *When prisoners come home: Parole and prisoner reentry*. New York: Oxford University Press.

Petersilia, Joan. 2008. Influencing public policy: An embedded criminologist reflects on California prison reform. *Journal of Experimental Criminology*, 4:335–356.

Piehl, Anne M., and Stefan F. LoBuglio. 2005. Does supervision matter? In *Prisoner reentry and public safety in America*, edited by Jeremy Travis and Christy Visher, 105–138. New York: Cambridge University Press.

Piza, Eric L., and Brandon C. Welsh. 2022. Evidence-based policing is here to stay: Innovative research, meaningful practice, and global reach. *Cambridge Journal of Evidence-Based Policing*, 6:42–53.

Rossi, Peter H. 1980. The presidential address: The challenge and opportunities of applied social research. *American Sociological Review*, 45:889–904.

Rossi, Peter H., Mark W. Lipsey, and Howard E. Freeman. 2004. *Evaluation: A systematic approach*. 7th ed. Thousand Oaks, CA: SAGE.

Welsh, Brandon C., Gregory M. Zimmerman, and Steven N. Zane. 2018. The centrality of theory in modern-day crime prevention: Developments, challenges, and opportunities. *Justice Quarterly*, 35:139–161.

Wilson, James A., and Robert C. Davis. 2006. Good intentions meet hard realities: An evaluation of the Project Greenlight reentry program. *Criminology and Public Policy*, 5:303–338.

Wilson, James A., and Christine Zozula. 2011. Reconsidering the Project Greenlight intervention: Why thinking about risk matters. *NIJ Journal*, 268:10–15.

Zimring, Franklin E., Gordon Hawkins, and Sam Kamin. 2003. *Punishment and democracy: Three strikes and you're out in California*. New York: Oxford University Press.

Index

For the benefit of digital users, indexed terms that span two pages (e.g., 52–53) may, on occasion, appear on only one of those pages.

Tables and figures are indicated by *t* and *f* following the page number

311 systems, 600, 613–14
  Boston's 311 system, 608, 613
Abecedarian Project, 76, 378
academic journals, 206, 339, 491
  academic research, 312–13
  practitioner challenges in accessing academic publications, 40–41
  practitioner receptivity to academic publications, 39–40
ACE Aware Initiative, 517
Achievement Mentoring (program), 451*t*, 453*t*
Actionable Intelligence for Social Policy (AISP), 609–10
action plan, 412–13
Active Implementation, 58–59, 60–61, 66
  criteria for effective innovation based on, 61
  description of, 59
  effective implementation based on, 63
  implementation teams as expert users of, 62–63
  studies using, 69
add-on gun laws/reforms, 558
administrative records/data, 24, 534, 602
  limits of, 611–12
Adolescent Diversion Project, 166, 209*t*, 211*t*
adverse childhood experiences (ACEs), 514
advocacy intervention(s), 497
  for women who experience intimate partner violence, 497
age-based gun restrictions, 569–71
age-crime curve, 23
aggression
  protective factors for, 447
  risk factors for, 446–47
aggression replacement training, 166, 359–60

Washington State Aggression Replacement Training (WSART) program, 91–92
aggressive behavior(s), 403, 445, 446, 451*t*, *See also* aggression
  evidence-based practice (EBP) targeting aggressive behaviors, 456–57
  studies on, 432, 433
Alcoholics/Narcotics Anonymous (AA/NA)
  incarceration-based 12-step programs in the model of, 316
alliance. *See also* Commonwealth Prevention Alliance (CPA)
  parent-therapist, 399–400
  relative importance of working, 399–400
  studies examining influence of therapeutic, 397, 399
American Academy of Child and Adolescent Psychiatry, 358–59
American Correctional Association (ACA), 661
Amlund-Hagen, Kristine, 12–13, 391
Andrews, Donald A., 287, 288
Angulo, Angela G., 13, 444
Anti-Drug Abuse Act of 1988, 311–12
antisocial behavior, 181, 294, 373, 394
  children and adolescents who engage in, 431
  life-course persistent, 392
  peer antisocial behavior, 450
  PMTO program on parent training to address, 395
  as risk factor, 446–47, 457
  school-based interventions targeting risk factors for, 427
  substance use as part of enduring pattern of, 181
  youth programs targeting, 209*t*, 210*t*

anti-fragile legitimacy
  anti-fragile criminal justice agencies, 238
  definition and characteristics of, 238
archival data limitations, 534
Armed and Prohibited Persons System (APPS), 558
arrests, 379, 570f
  after-care program effects on, 293
  concealed handgun permit effects on, 564–65
  developmental and community crime prevention program effects on, 383–84
  disproportionate minority contact in relation to youth, 527–28, 530–31, 533
  domestic violence, 655–56
  ethnic composition of arrests in New York, 612
  gender-responsive drug courts effect on reducing women's, 356
  of high-risk offenders, 438
  made by police officers trained in procedural justice, 234
  as measure of recidivism, 299
  misdemeanor, 255
  NFP effects on, 379
  participation in juvenile drug courts effects on adult, 183–84
  police training that may reduce the use of, 537
  prior, 161
  proactive policing and, 256–57
  race as a predictor of, 184
  reactive, 250
  school resource officers (SROs) and youth, 516
  TC program effects on, 320
Artificial Intelligence (AI), 601
  critiques of machine learning and, 604–5
Askeland, Elisabeth, 12–13, 391
assault weapon ban, 568–69, 569t
  federal, 566f, 567
Association of Chiefs of Police, 339. *See also* International Association of Chiefs of Police
Attention Deficit Hyperactivity Disorder (ADHD)
  PMTO and, 397–98, 402

audience(s), 165, 658, 661
  audience legitimacy, 228–29, 237
  development of policy briefs for several, 519–20
  dissemination tailored to specific, 43, 45
  law enforcement, 254
  legitimacy and, 225, 228, 229
  powerholders and, 225, 227
  practitioner, 341
  third-party, 230

Baglivio, Michael T., 163, 165, 174–75
  on youth interventions guided and RNR model, 162, 164
Balanced and Restorative Justice (BARJ), 128–29
  JJSES framework for achieving mission of, 129f
Baltimore Living Insurance for Ex-Offenders (LIFE) experiment, 329, 331t
basic legitimation expectations (BLEs), 228–29, 232, 237
  definition of, 225
Baumer, Eric
  on disproportionate minority contact, 528–29, 534, 538
  on the modal approach of sentencing research, 530, 531, 538
  on omitted variable bias, 531
Beetham, David
  on audiences, 225
  on legitimate power, 224–25
before-and-after design, 328, 474
  before vs. after treatment impact evaluations, 24–25
Behavior Project (Norway), 392–93
Best Starts for Kids of King County, 84–85
Beyond Trauma (program), 356
bias
  from confounding, 25
  publication, 32
  researcher, 31–32, 34
  selection bias, 101
Big Brothers Big Sisters of America, 211t, 451t, 453t
big data, 15, 599, 609–10, 614
  as naturally occurring, 599, 603
  paradox, 601

black box, 44, 78, 591, 601
  evaluation, 648–49
  of juvenile drug treatment courts, 186–87, 190
Black Family Development in Detroit, 360
Blase, Karen A., 6–7, 58
Blomberg, Thomas A., 152
Blueprints for Healthy Youth Development, 29–30, 127–28, 165, 206–7, 210*t*, 291–92, 297–98, 402, 412–13, 414, 435, 450
Blumstein, Alfred, 588
  on differential treatment, 529
body-worn cameras (BWCs), 234–35, 236, 259, 268
boot camp(s), 291, 293–94, 407
Boston Area Research Initiative (BARI), 609
Boston Police Department, 47, 551, 612
bottom-up approach, 393, 654–55. *See also* top-down approach
Bottoms, Anthony, 9–10, 223
Braga, Anthony
  on embedded criminologist model, 47
  on instrumentality effect, 526–52
  on promoting legitimacy, 231
  on reducing firearm homicides, 555–56
Brief Parent Training (BPT), 394, 400, 401, 403
broken windows theory [also broken windows], 255, 608, 611
Brooklyn Treatment Court, 166
bullying, 125–26, 444, 449
  Olweus Bullying Prevention Program, 429, 451*t*, 453*t*, 456, 457
  perpetration, 446
  in schools, 424, 428–29, 430–31, 432, 433–34
Butts, Jeffrey A., 9, 198

California, 380, 518, 557, 558, 562
  community-based policy in, 517
  diversion initiatives in, 147
  Evidence-Based Clearinghouse, 62
  gun ban (1991), 556
  gun prevalence and homicide in, 553–54
  imposed use of EBPs in, 626*t*
  juvenile drug courts established in, 181–82
  prison reforms, 46–47
  Public Safety Realignment Act, 383
  three-strikes law, 380
Cambridge Study in Delinquency Development, 384
Campbell Collaboration, 12, 46, 270, 290–91, 341, 623–24
  systematic review(s), 46, 253, 293–94, 298
Campbell Crime and Justice Coordinating Group (CJCG), 46
Canada, 468, 474, 553*f*
  drug court research in, 190–91
  evidence-based policing in, 48
  juvenile diversion in, 149
capability approach (also human development approach), 232–33
Case of Place tool, 257–58
Caught in the Crossfire program, 451*t*, 453*t*
causal effect(s), 328, 329, 340
  causal mechanisms, 78, 81–82, 85, 215, 265–66, 270, 339
  causal order, 24–25
  causal relationships, 95, 201, 313–14, 327, 339, 397–98, 553
case management, 100–1, 313–14, 330, 331*t*
  in drug courts, 187
  intensive, 356
  in juvenile probation, 160, 162, 173
  practices, 104
  in victim services, 485–86, 489–90
Centers for Disease Control and Prevention (CDC)
  CTC coalitions funded by, 416–17
  on financial losses stemming from youth violence, 444
  on gun violence, 550, 553
Center for Evidence-Based Crime Policy (CEBCP), 39
Center for Policing Equity, 52–53
Center for Problem-Oriented Policing, 45
Center for Victim Research, 498
Center of Employment Opportunities (CEO), 331*t*
chemical dependency programs, 291, 292
Chief's Council, 119, 121, 130
Child Behavior Checklist (CBCL), 396, 403
Child-Parent Center (CPC) program, 377–78
Children's Advocacy Center Model, 492, 493*t*
Children's Defense Fund, 128

China
    juvenile diversion in, 148
Civil Rights Act of 1964, 513
closed-circuit television (CCTV) video surveillance, 265–66
    CCTV in schools, 425
    CCTV and case clearance, 272–73
    CCTV and crime prevention, 270–75
comorbidity, 8, 119–20
coaching, 62, 63f, 69
    provided by CTC trainers, 412, 413
Cobbina-Dungy, Jennifer, 11–12, 349
Cochran, Joshua C., 15, 580
Cochrane Collaboration, 623–24
cognitive behavioral intervention(s), 129, 129f, 290–91
    cognitive behavioral therapy (CBT), 211t
    Coping Power Program, 433
    for trauma in schools, 211t
    trauma-focused cognitive behavioral therapy, 211t, 493t
collateral consequences of punishment, 11, 326–27
collective efficacy, 213, 410–11
    as protective factor for gun carrying, 449–50
college (and university) education about research, 657–60, 661
Commonwealth Prevention Alliance (CPA), 120, 134
community advisory boards, 662
Community Advocacy Project, 492, 493t
community-based treatment, 168, 214, 291–93, 317–18, 354, 517
    for creating and promoting collective efficacy, 213
    for diverting youth out of the juvenile system, 159, 168
    effectiveness in reducing recidivism, 292
    focused on housing, 355
    focused on mentoring, 30
    focused on substance use/abuse, 292, 319, 382, 383
    for victims of crime, 354, 484
community-based organizations, 84–85, 212–13, 489, 609
community-defined evidence, 80, 83–84, 85

community-oriented policing [also community policing], 232, 247, 249, 251, 255–56, 613, 646, 654–55
Community Juvenile Accountability Act (CJAA), 93–94, 95–96, 109
    CJAA advisory committee, 101–2, 103–4
    CJAA EBPs, 96–97, 99, 100, 101, 102, 105
Community Youth Development Study, 414–16
Communities That Care (CTC), 13, 126–27, 407, 451t, 453t, 460
    benefit-cost analyses on, 379–80
    evaluation in Pennsylvania, 134–35
competency drivers, 62–63, 63f, 65–66
CompStat, 250, 251, 476, 604
conceptual replication, 31
conceptual use utilization, 41–42, 621, 622–23, 624–25, 637, 638
    benefits of, 637–38
conduct disorder, 397–98, 451t
    among children/youth in Norway, 392
confidentiality
    as principle of effective victim services, 487, 489, 491, 499–500
confinement, 28
    in juvenile justice, 92
confounding variables, 25, 269–70, 532
    in quasi-experiments, 313
Connecticut
    use of EBPs in, 626t, 631
consent decree, 235
construct validity, 22, 186, 266
    definition of, 24
contextual factors, 28, 265, 271–72, 403–4, 653
contingent valuation, 384
Continuum of Confidence, 121, 123–24, 123f, 134
control group(s), 164, 339, 556, 557, 655
    in Abecedarian Project, 378
    in Communities That Care (CTC), 415
    in natural experiments, 328
    non-equivalent, 269–70
    in Nurse-Family Partnership (NFP) intervention, 379
    in Perry Preschool program, 377
    propensity score matching for creating equivalent, 272–73

conversion factors, 233
Cook County, Illinois, 357
coordination, 84, 91–92, 108–9
   Coordination of Services (COS), 96
   lack of coordination, 79–80, 590
   of multi-disciplinary personnel involved in juvenile drug courts, 180f
   in victim services, 489, 493t
correctional programs, 148, 298–99, 515–16, 630
   benefits of, 294
   Correctional Program Assessment Inventory, 288
   Correctional Program Checklist evaluations, 296
   evaluations of, 300
   for individuals with particular genetic alleles, 297
   in Kentucky, 626t
   meta-analyses of, 288
   and recidivism, 299, 632
correctional rehabilitation, 287, 297, 300–1
   in the community, 291–92
   effectiveness of particular approaches to, 294, 295
   what does not work in, 293–94
corrupting spots, 477, 478
costs (financial)
   associated with Communities That Care implementation, 415–16
   and benefits of juvenile drug treatment courts, 188
   and benefits of Nurse-Family Partnership program, 381–82
   of correctional rehabilitation, 294
   and cost-efficiency evaluation, 525
   economic costs of crime, 118, 134, 384
   estimation of program, 380
   of Head Start, 378–79
   of imprisonment, 374–75, 381, 383–84, 582, 583–84
   incurred from CCTV, 269, 274, 277
   of "Youth at Home" mentoring program, 212
   prison construction, 382–83
   of re-entry programs, 340
   social costs of gun violence, 550–51, 571
   social costs of RTC laws, 560, 562
cost-benefit analysis
   definition of, 27
   of CCTV, 273–74
   of early prevention programs, 12
   of Perry program, 377
   of Newark CCTV Directed Patrol Strategy, 254
cost-effectiveness, 45, 328, 375
   of California's three-strikes law, 380
   of CCTV, 274–75, 359–60
   of evidence-based prevention programming, 134
   Studies, 27
counseling programs/interventions, 493t
   drug counseling programs, 316, 317
   group counseling programs, 317–18, 321, 322
   incarceration-based group counseling programs, 319–20
   meta-analyses of group counseling programs, 319–20
   one-on-one, 451t
COVID-19 pandemic, 509, 510, 550, 555
   economic and health impacts of, 514
   gun violence during COVID-19 pandemic, 545
   impacts on policing, 259
Creating Lasting Family Connections Fatherhood Program (CLFCFP), 331t
crime-suspect descriptions, 611–12
CrimeSolutions, 167, 209t, 211t
   on CTC effectiveness, 414
   description of, 206–7, 492
   as dissemination strategy, 45, 208
   effective and promising programs in victim services as rated in, 493t
   standards for program effectiveness, 166, 207, 297–98
crime-involved place(s), 472, 477, 478
   comfort spaces as a type of, 476–77, 478
   convergence settings as a type of, 476, 477
   corrupting spots as a type of, 477
   crime sites as a type of, 476
   less visible, 466–67
   within place networks, 475
crime controller(s)
   in place management, 469, 470

crime prevention
   CCTV and, 268, 270–72
   community, 383–84, 385
   CTC's approach to, 411
   developmental, 381, 383–84, 385
   early crime prevention, 385
   in high-crime places, 466
   mental health treatment as a fundamental piece of, 474
   place management as effective, 475
   place-based crime prevention, 466, 475
   police interested in, 476
   situational, 269, 274–75, 277, 474
   technology, 265, 268
crime radiation, 468
crime rates
   before and after enactment of Public Safety Realignment Act, 362
   in cities, 510
   in communities, 509
   fluctuation in, 355–56
   policing in places with low, 247–48
   in states adopting RTC laws, 559
Crime Victims Fund, 486
Crime Victims' Rights Act of 2004, 486
criminal career(s), 313–14
   monetary costs of typical, 384
criminal court(s), 198
   goals of, 201
criminal/prior record
   effects on employment, 350–51, 516
   labeling effects associated with, 327
   as mediator of the relationship between race and punishment outcomes, 532
criminogenic effects, 168–69. *See also* iatrogenic effects
criminogenic needs, 287
   juvenile probation officer training focused on, 173
   risk factors as, 161
   RNR model and, 165, 296
criminology of place, 602–4
   and policing innovations, 604
crossover youth [also dual-system-involved youth], 358
cross-sectional data [also cross-sectional designs], 98–99

causal order issues in, 24–25, 230, 450, 553
cross-sectional designs and the SMS scale, 328
cultural adaptability, 105
   cultural competency and sensitivity in victim services, 490–91
   cultural sensitivity training for reducing DMC, 535, 537
cumulative disadvantage
   empirical evidence on, 108, 170, 528
   social inequality and, 512

data metrics, 518
   gender identity and, 518–19
   race, ethnicity and, 518
Day Reporting Center (DRC), 331*t*
defensive gun use
   evidence on, 562–63
   RTC laws and, 563*f*
delinquency prevention, 7
   JJSES framework and, 129
   programs based and CTC, 409, 418
   psychological approach to, 203
   social developmental model as framework for, 124
delinquency theories, 198–99
   differential association, 205
   individual-level, 202–4
   opportunity theory, 204
   social control, 205
   social disorganization theory, 204
   strain theory, 204
delinquent peers
   as risk factor, 161, 448
dependent youth, 118–19
   definition of, 357
   race and classification of, 357
   services for, 119–20
depression, 312
   advocacy intervention effects on, 497
   COVID-19 pandemic effects on, 510
   Head Start effects on, 378
   NFP program effects on, 379
   victimization effects on, 484
desistance, 330–38
   definition of, 299

desistance-focused rehabilitation, 299–300, 301
  life-course theory and, 410
  research on, 300
  women and, 354–55
deterrence, 51, 655–56
  CCTV and, 272
  decay, 475
  effects of gun laws, 558, 561*t*
  focused, 231–32, 252, 257
  general, 199–200
  incarceration as, 373, 586
  interventions focused on, 586
detoxification
  programs in correctional settings, 315
Detroit's Project Green Light, 271–72. *See also* CCTV
dialectical behavior therapy, 359–60
differential association, 205
differential involvement, 528–29
  DMC and, 521, 535, 537–38
  empirical evidence of, 529, 534
  explanations for, 540–41
differential treatment, 528–29, 539
  data limitations in the study of, 534
  DMC and, 537–38
  effects on inequality, 511
  empirical evidence of, 530–31, 534, 538
  juvenile arrests and, 533
diffusion, 58, 269
  CCTV and, 271–72
  of crime control benefits, 468–69
disciplinary processes in schools, 516–17
discretion
  judicial, 198, 352
  juvenile court prosecutor, 92
  police officer, 146, 148, 247, 248
discrimination, 446, 513
  diversion and racial, 151–52
  interventions aimed at reducing, 52–53
  malevolent and benevolent, 170
  racial, 353, 446–47, 530, 531
  sexual orientation, gender identity and, 518–19
  unintended, 175
  victims of crime and, 490–91
discriminatory policing, 351–52

disorder
  alcohol use, 181
  community, 213
  conduct, 392
  drug use disorder, 311, 315–16
  neighborhood, 448–49, 466, 469, 602–3
  physical, 608–9, 613
  police and, 246, 255
  in schools, 424–25, 437
  substance use, 312
displacement, 144
  area, 267
disproportionality, 170. *See also* discrimination; DMC
  racial and ethnic, 526–27, 528, 531, 540
disproportionate minority contact (DMC), 526–28
  DMC mandate, 170–71, 536–37
  DMC Reduction Cycle, 133*f*
  explanations for, 528–34, 540
  reforms to reduce, 538–42
dissemination, 43, 326, 662. *See also* translational criminology
  in human services, 58
  in Pennsylvania, 117, 120–21
  research on, 39, 59, 416, 519–20
  strategies, 45–46, 48
distributive justice, 228, 234–35, 351
domestic violence, 471, 655–56
  Lautenberg Amendment (1996) effects on, 557
  victim services for victims of, 493*t*
Donohue, John J., 15, 550
dosage, 296, 377, 487
Drake, Elizabeth K., 7–8, 91
drug courts
  adult, 181–82, 185–86
  gender responsive, 356
  juvenile, 179–80, 181–82, 185–86 (*see also* juvenile drug treatment courts)
  juvenile drug court model, 182–83
drug education programs, 317
  in correctional settings, 315–16
drug relapse, 309–10, 314, 321–22
  influence on other criminal activity, 314–15
  interventions aimed at reducing, 320, 321
  and recidivism, 315

Drug Treatment Alternative to Prison
    (DTAP), 331t
drug treatment in correctional settings, 309,
    310, 316
due process, 198
    in criminal courts, 201
    due process revolution, 592–93
    in juvenile justice, 200–1
Duwe, Grant, 291, 293, 296

Early childhood, 76, 82
    EBPs in, 76–77
    education programs, 81
    evaluation studies, 79
    field, 76, 77
    NFP in, 128
    programs, 77, 78, 376–77 (see also
        Head Start)
    RCTs in, 76
    TOCs in, 78, 82
early interventions for children at risk
    program (TIBIR) model, 400, 402
Eck, John, 446
ecometrics, 607–9
economic analysis, 374, 375–76. See also cost-
    benefit analysis
Education and Employment Training (EET),
    96, 105, 331t
education courses about research, 657–59
    college-level, 658
    high-school level, 657–58
educational programs
    in prison, 289–90, 298–99
effect size(s)
    of CBT, 290–91
    of CCTV, 271, 272
    of diversion, 149
    of probation treatment, 292
    weighted mean, 33
effective implementation, 62–63, 65f
    in formula for success, 60, 61, 66
    in human services, 60, 70
effective innovations, 60, 64–65. See also
    formula for success
    active implementation
        attending to, 71
    enabling contexts for, 61, 63–64
    and formula for success, 65f, 66
    in schools, 67

Effective Practices for Community
    Supervision (EPICS), 129
efficacy studies, 28
    internal validity in, 403
efficiency evaluations, 15, 27
embedded criminologist(s), 46–47, 48
    embedded criminologist model, 46–47, 52
embedded researcher(s), 654
    embedded researcher model, 457
employment, 180f, 288
    barriers among justice-involved
        women, 354–55
    effectiveness of employment
        programs, 289–90
    effects of criminal record on, 327, 350–51
    work programs, 96, 105, 289–90, 292, 331t
enabling contexts, 59–60, 63–64
    in formula for success, 60–62, 65f
enduring change, 286
    implications of rehabilitation for, 298–99
Engaging Offenders Families in Reentry
    program, 331t
enlightenment model, 41
    gradual enlightenment, 623, 637–38
evaluation
    designs, 214, 376
    hierarchy, 3, 141, 525, 583, 590–91, 649
    mixed-methods evaluation, 153
    quasi-experiment, 13–207, 214, 341, 416
    RCT, 13, 207, 319–20, 341
    research, 41, 85, 165, 199
evidence-based corrections, 286–87, 625
evidence-based policing, 10, 245, 625
    achieving, 252–53
    challenges of, 259
    creation of societies for, 48
    crime analysts and, 254
    definition of, 252
    facilitation and, 48–49
    institutionalization and, 256
    police technology and, 268
    receptivity and, 255
    translation and, 253
Evidence-Based Policing Hall of Fame, 50, 258
Evidence-Based Policing Matrix, 45, 253
Evidence-Based Policing Playbook, 49, 257
Evidence-based Prevention and Intervention
    Support Center (EPISCenter), 120–21,
    127–28, 129–30, 416

exclusionary discipline, 425–26, 434–35
experiential learning, 258, 659–63
  experiential exercises, 256
  experiential knowledge of practitioners, 236
  experiential therapy, 493t
externalizing behavior
  FFT effects on, 457
  PMTO effects on, 396, 397, 400
  victim service programs targeting, 493t
external validity, 23, 29
  definition of, 270
  establishing, 29, 31–32
extra-legal factors (also extralegal factors), 170
  and juvenile court outcomes, 529, 531–32

facilitation, 44. *See also* translational criminology
  strategies focused on, 48–49
Fagan, Abigail A., 13, 407
family conflict
  interventions focused on, 127–28, 181, 213, 458
Family Integrated Transitions (FIT), 96
family therapy, 206, 208, 209t, 211t, *See also* FFT
  effects on inequality, 514–15
  as juvenile diversion, 168
  youth violence prevention and, 451t
Farrington, David P., 143–44, 270
  on aggression, 446–47
  On Cambridge Study in Delinquent Development, 384
  On creation of national crime prevention strategy, 417
  on early prevention programs, 373
  on Maryland SMS tool, 328
  on prison dog-training programs, 289
  on school interventions, 436
  on SNAP program, 379–80
fatal drug overdose, 314–15, 319
Felson, Marcus, 469, 471, 476
Female Offender Treatment and Employment Program (FOTEP), 356
fidelity, 59
  assessment, 62
field experiments, 655
  Hawaii Opportunity Probation with Enforcement (HOPE) program, 331t

field interrogation and observation reports (FIOS), 611
  Boston Police Department (BPD) FIO practices, 612
Fixsen, Dean L., 6–7, 58
Florida, 46
  DMC in, 526–27
  EBPs in, 166, 352, 626t
  Florida Department of Juvenile Justice, 358–59
  Graham v. Florida, 560 U.S. 48 (2010), 94
  juvenile drug courts, 181–82
  research on risk and needs assessment in, 162, 163, 377
  researcher-policymaker partnership in, 47
Floyd, George, 229, 259
focus group data, 24, 590
Forensic Assertive Community Treatment (FACT), 331t
formula for success, 60–62, 63–64, 65f, 71
  effective implementation in, 62, 63
  enabling contexts in, 64
front-line officers, 651
  front-line powerholders, 236–37
  front-line practitioners, 650, 661
  front-line staff, 171, 172, 173
Frost, Natasha A., 5, 16, 645
Functional Family Therapy (FFT), 209t, 210t, 291–92, 451t, 453t
  costs of, 294
  cost savings of, 96, 294
  description of, 457
  effectiveness of, 457, 514–15
funding [also funders], 76–77, 84
  implementation, 65–66
  LEADS Scholars Program, 48
  NIJ, 52
  from partnerships, 43
  threats in, 79–80

gender
  and effectiveness of TC programs, 320–21
  gender-responsive programming, 184, 356–57
  gender-responsiveness, 360
  gender/sexual minorities, 8, 133
  identity, 490–91, 518–19
  and JDCTCs, 183–84

generalizability, 4, *See also* external validity
  conceptual replication and, 31
  in effectiveness studies, 30–31
  of qualitative studies, 654
  of RCTs, 329
  in victim service evaluation literature, 491
Geographic Information System (GIS), 267
Georgia
  examples of imposed use of EBPs in, 626t
get-tough
  era, 581, 582–83
  policy, 582, 583, 584
  policymakers, 581, 585
Gideon v. Wainwright, 372 U.S. 335 (1963), 515
Glunt, Kristopher T., 5, 117
Gonçalves, Vitor, 8–9, 179
government accountability, 26, 581, 593
  lawmakers emphasizing, 585
  political commitment and calls for, 589
graduate student education, 660, 663
graduate student training
  on EBP research, 659–60
  problems with, 659
  on translational criminology, 660
group-based counseling, 11
  in correctional settings, 315, 317–18, 319–20
  effectiveness of, 321, 322
  in victim services, 485–86
Group Teen Triple-Level 4 program, 451t, 453t
group therapy
  for youth justice, 208, 211t, 215
guardian(s)
  in place management, 469
Guiding Good Choices program, 451t, 453t
gun restrictions [also firearm restrictions], 557
gunshot detection technology (GDT), 600, 605–6
gun violence [also firearm violence]
  during COVID-19 pandemic, 571
  EBPs targeting gun violence, 457–58
  gun carrying, 449–50, 553–54, 559–65
  gun prevalence, 552, 553–55
  homicide, 550, 554f, 555–56, 561t
  interventions for youth, 451t, 456
  reducing, 550

  risk and protective factors for, 450
  in urban settings, 449–50
  victimization, 571

Hawaii Opportunity Probation with Enforcement (HOPE) program, 331t
Hawkins, David J.
  CTC development, 408, 409
  and social development model (SDM), 410
Head Start, 122
  evidence on, 378–79
Heckman, James J., 363, 377, 379
Herold, Tamara D., 13, 466
heterogeneity
  in diversion programs, 147–48
  in JDCTs, 183
  in meta-analysis, 33, 150, 498
  PMTO program and, 398–99
  in re-entry programs, 331t, 340
  in work programs, 289
high-capacity magazine(s), 565
  ban, 565–69, 569t
  California's restrictions on, 562
  restrictions on, 15
high-crime place(s), 252, 466, 468, 469, 470
  place management and crime reductions in, 466, 468–69
homelessness, 313, 513–14
  and drug use disorders, 312
  among females, 313, 355
  and incarceration, 312–13
  and juvenile justice involvement, 106
  long-term impacts of, 609
  and re-entry, 315
homicide(s), 444, 553f, 562, 570
  EBPs' impacts on, 383–84, 458, 558
  gun prevalence and, 553–55
  gun violence and, 510, 551, 552
  international evidence on guns and, 552
  RTC laws and, 561t
  in U.S. states, 553
hot spots
  crime place networks and crime, 13
  EBPs focused on, 257
  hidden crime places in crime, 475–77
  persistent violent, 477–79
  place management and, 466–67, 475, 479

policing, 237, 249–50, 255, 350
    policing studies on, 51, 234
human services, 63–64, 66, 67
    diffusion in, 58
    implementation in, 58–59, 70
Hurricane Katrina, 338

iatrogenic effect(s), 100–1, 167–68, 210–11
    of deterrence-based approaches, 293–94, 301
    of Drug Abuse Resistance Education (D.A.R.E.), 210–11
Illinois
    EBPs in, 626t
    first juvenile court in Cook County, 357
    Illinois Juvenile Court Act (1899), 357
    school interventions in, 430
impacts at scale, 85
implementation
    drivers, 60–61, 63, 63f, 64–65
    evaluation, 26, 38, 525
    failure, 67, 536–37
    science, 59, 60, 65–66, 68
    stages, 60–61, 63, 69
imposed use, 15–16
impulsivity, 183, 431
incarceration-based drug treatment programs, 317–18
    access and availability to, 317
    effectiveness of, 321
    evaluations of, 317–18
    medication-assisted treatment (MAT), 316–17
    residential drug treatment programs, 317
    therapeutic communities, 316
incentives, 6, 432–33, 536
    behavioral reinforcement systems to create, 203
    drug court compliance and, 183, 191
    financial, 50, 592
    imposed use and, 623, 625
    parent training and graduation, 380
    in place management, 478
    as reward for use of research, 44
individual factors, 301, 355–56
    delinquency theories and, 202
individual theories, 202–3. See also delinquency theories

Indonesia's restorative model, 148–49
inequality, 14. See also social inequality
informal diversionary practices, 143
information management systems, 165
    computerized, 300
    used by probation officers, 172–73
input(s)
    CCTV intervention, 274
    intervention, 201
    JDTC implementation, 190
institutionalization, 256
    and evidence-based policing, 252–53, 255–58
    example of, 257–58
    requirements, 258
institutional review board (IRB)
    as innovation, 420
instrumental use, 636, 637, 638
    conceptual utilization for, 41–42
    definition of, 621, 622
instrumentality effect, 551–52, 571
    definition of, 552
intangible costs, 376
integrated data systems (IDS), 615
intelligence-led policing
    definition of, 250
    as evidence-based policing, 251
intensive supervision, 181, 331t
    Intensive Supervision Probation (ISP), 169, 647–48
    meta-analysis on, 293
internal validity, 6, 24–25. See also validity
    as consideration in evaluation research, 22, 214, 270
    in quasi-experiments, 269–70
    in RCTs, 329, 403, 414
    ruling out threats to, 328
    SMS and, 328
International Association of Chiefs of Police (IACP), 40, 661
interpersonal skill building
    EBPs focused on, 209t, 210t, 211t
    for justice-involved youth, 208, 215
interview data, 226. See also focus-group data

John D. and Catherine T. MacArthur Foundation, 128–29

justice-involved women, 353, 356
  research on evidence-based policy for, 356–57
  and victimization, 354–55
Juvenile Drug Treatment Courts (JDTCs)
  effectiveness, 186, 188
  family influences on effectiveness of, 185
  gender and, 183–84
  issues with, 186–87
  race/ethnicity and, 184–85
Juvenile Justice Act of 1977, 93
Juvenile Justice and Delinquency Prevention Act (JJDPA) of 1974
  JJDPA 1998 Amendment, 536
  JJDPA of 2018, 528
  Juvenile Justice Reform Act of 2018, 357–58, 536
Juvenile Justice System Enhancement Strategy (JJSES), 121, 129–30
  JJSES framework, 128–29, 129f
juvenile probation, 8
  EBPs in, 160–67
Juveniles Breaking the Cycle program, 166

Kansas City
  distributive injustice practices in Kansas City, 228
  EBPs in, 458
  imposed use in, 626t
  Kansas City Preventative Patrol Experiment, 247–48
  Pulled Over study in Kansas City, 226
Kentucky
  EBPs in, 626t
Kirk, David S., 11
  on MOVE program, 338–39
  on prisoner re-entry, 326
Knoth-Peterson, Lauren, 7–8, 91
Koper, Christopher S., 10
  on evidence-based policing, 245
  on police technology, 268
  on translational criminology, 38, 49
Kosc, Helen, 11, 326
Kuper, Julie L., 13–14, 484

labeling [also labeling theory], 168, 354
  diversion and risk of, 141

labeling effects, 187–88, 327
language access services, 513
Latessa, Edward J., 1, 48–49
  on CBT programs, 290
  on correctional quackery, 1, 294, 585, 592, 655
Laub, John H.
  on translational criminology, 6, 37, 38, 39, 42, 52, 339, 592, 660
Lautenberg Amendment (1996), 557
Law Enforcement Advancing Data and Science (LEADS) Scholars program, 48
law of crime concentration, 468, 603–4
lawfulness, 52–53
  as concern of legitimacy, 228, 229, 234–35, 259–60
leadership, 173, 175, 258, 456, 535
  drivers, 62–63, 63f, 65f
  implementation and, 171
  institutionalization and, 258
  organizational excellence model and, 44–45
  Pennsylvania state agencies and, 118, 134
  policing and, 247, 248–49
  practitioners and, 48
  systems, 256
  training, 48–49, 256
Learning Together program, 451t, 453t, 456
legitimacy, 9–10
  anti-fragile, 238
  and evidence-based policy, 223
  fragile, 199, 238
  perceptions of, 351, 525
  police, 246, 247, 252
Leslie, Carine E., 13, 444
Lethality Assessment Program Oklahoma, 493t
LGBTQ+ persons [also LGBTQIA+ persons], 417, 518–19
  victimization of, 486, 487, 499
life-course persistent crime, 377
life-course theories, 409–10
  life-course literature, 289
LIFE experiment, 329, 331t
LifeSkills Training program, 211t, 431–32, 451t, 453t
  evaluation of, 436

literature reviews, 21, 31–32, 166–67. *See also* systematic review
Lum, Cynthia, 10
    on evidence-based policing, 245
    on police technology, 268
    on translational criminology, 38, 39–40, 49

machine learning, 601, 607
    in predictive policing, 604–5
mandatory minimum sentencing, 352, 353
Maryland Opportunities through Vouchers Experiment (MOVE), 338, 339
    objective of, 338–39
Maryland Scientific Methods Scale (SMS) [also Scientific Methods Scale], 328, 329
    observational studies and, 338
mass incarceration, 580, 593
    financial burden of, 374–75
    impacts on minoritized individuals, 350
    and inequality, 511
    problems with, 583–84, 656–57
    U.S. investment in, 582, 583, 586
mass shootings, 571–72
    effect of assault weapons ban on, 565–67, 566f, 568f, 568–69, 569t
Martinson, Robert, 286–87, 581. *See also* what works?
Massachusetts
    Department of Mental Health Forensic Transition Team (FTT), 331t
    Youth Screening Instrument-Version 2 (MAYSI-2), 340, 358–59
Masters, Mackenzie, 13–14, 484
matching
    juvenile probation and program, 160, 171
    practitioner training on service, 173
    risk and needs assessment for, 168
    youth needs with services, 164–65
Maternal, Infant, and Childhood Home Visitation (MIECHV) program, 76–77
Matza, David, 205
McCoy, Henrika, 11–12, 349
McKenna, Nicole, 8–9, 179
Mears, Daniel P., 1
    on challenges for diversion, 151–52, 168
    on disproportionality, 170, 528
    on effective policy, 66

on evaluating research and assessing research, 21
on evaluation hierarchy, 51, 525, 590–91, 624
on mass incarceration, 580
mediation analysis, 189
    JDTC model and, 190
    PMTO and, 396
Medication Assisted Treatment (MAT)
    in correctional settings, 316–18, 319, 322
    effectiveness of, 319
Meditation for Female Trauma Intimate Partner Violence Survivors with Co-Occurring Disorders, 493t
Mental, Emotional, and Behavioral (MEB) Interventions
    Spectrum of, 122, 122f, 123, 124, 127–28, 134, 326
mental health, 107, 133–34
    children's, 69, 395–96
    formula for success and outcomes in, 60
    and JDTCs, 185, 188
    justice-involved women and issues of, 353–54
    needs, 128, 146–47, 358, 359
    problems [also mental health disorders], 122, 169, 312, 313
    service use, 358
    treatment, 101–2, 316, 327, 331t
mentoring, 159–60, 208, 360
    community-based mentoring program(s), 30
    programs, 168, 209t, 211t, 212, 213, 451t, 453t
meta-analyses [also meta-analytic review], 24
    WSIPP's, 97–98, 103
Miller v. Alabama, 132 U.S. 2455 (2012), 94
minoritized populations [also minoritized individuals], 11–12, 354
    community-based efforts for, 510, 520
    criminal activity among, 526
    in the criminal legal system, 349–50
Mississippi
    imposed use of EBPs in, 626t
Mitchell, Ojmarrh, 11, 309
mobilization
    community mobilization, 408–9, 410, 457–58

Models for Change Initiative, 128–29
moderation, 189, 190
Moms' Empowerment program, 493t
monetary benefits
  of case clearance, 273
  of CCTV, 277
  of Head Start, 378
  of NFP, 379
  of SNAP, 379–80
monetary sanctions, 515
Monitoring the Future (MTF) study, 180–81
motivation, 318
  in FFT, 457
  as key element for success of substance abuse treatment, 183
motivational interviewing, 100–1, 129, 129f, 161–62, 173
  in intensive probation programs, 169
Moving On program, 356
Moving to Opportunity program, 338–39
Multidimensional Treatment Foster Care-Adolescents, 209t, 211t
multi-site research
  as approach to replication in the field, 31
Multisystemic Therapy (MST), 96, 451t, 453t, 584
  effectiveness of, 185, 514–15
  for juvenile offenders, 123, 166, 209t, 210t, 211t, 359–60, 632–33
  Multisystemic Therapy–Substance Abuse, 166
  Multisystemic Therapy for Problem Sexual Offenders (MST-PSB), 166
Myers, David L., 8, 159

narrative reviews, 23, 31–32
National Academies of Science
  on bullying, 433–34
  on effective policing strategies, 250
National Association for Civilian Oversight of Law Enforcement (NACOLE), 661
National Center for Child Behavioral and Development (NCCBD), 393
National Center for Juvenile Justice (NCJJ), 121
National Center for Victims of Crime, 486, 498

National Center of Excellence in Youth Violence Prevention initiative, 416–17, 450
National Center on Addiction and Substance Abuse
  on substance-involved persons, 312
National Crime Victimization Survey (NCVS), 484
  on self-defense gun use, 562–64, 563f
  on victims of crime and victim services, 486
National Incident-Based Reporting System (NIBRS), 564–65
  data quality of, 571
National Institute of Corrections, 297–98
National Institute of Justice (NIJ)
  budget for criminal justice research, 588
  CrimeSolutions, 297–98, 330, 435, 492
  on limitations of measures of desistance, 299
  on re-entry, 292
  support for EBPs, 48
  on translational criminology, 37, 592
  on victim service programs, 484–85
National Longitudinal Study of Youth, 570
National Organization for Victim Assistance, 486
National Police Foundation, 245, 258
National Research Counci
  public health model of mental health intervention, 433–34
  on RTC laws, 559
  on translational criminology, 50–51
National Rifle Association, 571
National Science Foundation, 52
National Supported Work Demonstration project, 331t
  on effectiveness of work programs, 289
natural experiment, 329
  on DMC, 538
  as high-quality alternative to RCTs, 269
  Hurricane Katrina, 338
  in SMS hierarchy, 328, 329
naturally occurring data, 14. See also big data
  big data and, 598–99
  challenges of working with, 601
  classes of, 602, 606–7

and ecometrics, 607–9
and gunshot detection, 605
for informing evidence-based policy, 612, 614–15
precision of, 600
Nebraska
Nebraska Director of Juvenile Diversion Programs
needs evaluation, 26, 51. *See also* evaluation hierarchy
and DMC, 525, 526
need principle, 161–62. *See also* RNR Model
Netherlands, 338
EBPs for youth violence prevention in, 451t
net-widening, 152, 168–69
as consequence of diversion, 8, 144, 146, 151, 152
Newark CCTV Directed Patrol Strategy, 274
New York
New York Police Department's adoption of BWCs, 236
New York State Rifle & Pistol Association v. Bruen (2022), 551
policing hot spots in, 237
New York City (NYC), 601–2
CompStat model in, 476
restrictions on gun carrying, 559
stop-and-frisk policy, 610–12
New Zealand
EBPs for youth violence prevention in, 451t
evidence-based policing in, 48
juvenile diversion in, 149
nonfatal drug overdoses
MAT participation effects on, 319
nonintervention research, 21
distinguishing intervention versus, 27–28
Non-instrumental use
of research, 41
North Carolina
EBPs in, 626t
North Carolina Assessment of Risk (NCAR), 163
RTC permits effects on crime in, 564–65
Norway, 391
Norwegian Center for Child Behavioral Development (NCCBD), 393
Norwegian Research Council, 391–92

Norwegian Welfare Act, 391–92
null effects (also null results), 648–49
associated with re-entry programs, 293, 331t
associated with research on CCTV, 268, 271
associated with research on diversion, 168–69
associated with research on JDCTs, 188
Nurse-Family Partnership (NFP), 128
effectiveness of, 379, 381–82, 383–84

Obama, Barack, 223, 224, 230
O'Brien, Daniel T., 15, 598
Offender-Focused Policing program, 451t, 453t
Office for Victims of Crime
principles of effective victim services, 487
Office of Justice Programs (OJP), 165, 581
Office of Juvenile Justice and Delinquency Prevention (OJJDP), 170–71, 187, 357–58
CrimeSolutions, 435
endorsement of CTC, 407–8
OJJDP's Comprehensive Strategy Initiative, 408–9, 416
OJJDP's Model Programs Guide, 165
Ogden, Terje, 12–13, 391
Ohio Youth Assessment System (OYAS), 163, 171
omitted variable bias, 328, 531–32, 538
Opportunity Index, 609
opportunity theory, 204
ORCA (organizing space, regulating conduct, control access, and acquiring resources), 470
ORCA functions, 472, 473, 478
as place management, 479
Oregon
EBPs in, 626t
Oregon Social Learning Center, 395
Oregon Youth Assessment System (OYAS), 163
Oregon Youth Authority (OYA), 451t
Parent Management Training–Oregon (PMTO) program, 69, 391, 451t, 453t
Treatment Foster Care Oregon (TFCO), 166
organizational culture, 8, 175, 295
leadership and, 173
organizational excellence model, 44–45

Orts, Kelly, 8, 159
outcome evaluations, 51, 91–92, 95–96. *See also* evaluation hierarchy
outputs, 6, 38, 201, 274
overcontrol bias, 532
Oxford Houses, 331*t*

panel data, 412, 553–55, 559, 564, 567–69
   analysis, 559–60
Parent Group Training (PGT) program, 400, 401
parental monitoring, 394
   effects on gun carrying, 449–50
   effects on substance use, 181
   effects on youth violence, 447, 448
parent training, 380
   brief, 400, 401
   cost-effectiveness of, 380
   for minority groups, 401
   PMTO intervention, 403–4
parental support, 185
parsimony, 80
   in program development, 85
participatory action research (PAR), 46
partnerships, 39–40, 43, 46–47, 416–17
   community, 499
   researcher-community, 83
   researcher-practitioner, 104, 109, 173–74, 519–20, 655
   strategic, 120–21
Paterson, Heather, 12, 373
Payne, Allison A., 13, 424
Peck, Shawn, 8, 117
peer contagion, 168–69
peer effects, 161
peer groups, 125*f*
peer influence, 44, 124, 181, 182, 213
peer relations, 329
Pennsylvania
   Council of Chief Juvenile Probation Officers, 119
   Department of Drug and Alcohol Programs (DDAP), 119, 120–21, 125–26, 127
   Juvenile Court Judges' Commission (JCJC), 118–19

Pennsylvania Commission on Crime and Delinquency (PCCD), 118, 119, 120, 127, 134
Pennsylvania Department of Education (PDE), 120, 134
Pennsylvania Liquor Control Board (PLCB), 119–20, 134
Pennsylvania Youth Survey (PAYS), 125–26
perceived legitimacy, 228, 525
Perry Preschool Project, 76, 377, 381
   effects on U.S. homicide, 383–84
Pesta, George
   on partnerships, 46
   on translational criminology, 38
Petersilia, Joan, 46–47, 588
   on conceptual use, 637–38
   on identifying effective re-entry approaches, 292
Petrosino, Anthony, 1–2
   on developer bias, 297
   on diversion, 150
   on evidence-based approach to crime and justice policy, 624
   on juvenile justice processing, 361–149
   on Scared Straight and other juvenile programs, 293–94
Pew Charitable Trusts, 625, 631
   Pew-MacArthur Results First Initiative, 407, 624
physical disorder, 608–9, 613
Piquero, Alex R.
   on criminal career, 384
   on cumulative disadvantage, 530
   on desistance, 299
   on differential involvement, 540–41
   on racial and ethnic disparities, 170, 526–27, 528–29
Piza, Eric L., 10, 265
place
   definition, 467–68
   pooled place(s), 468
   proximal place(s), 467
placed-based interventions, 266, 474
   place-based patrol, 248
   place-based policing, 257–58
place management, 466
   and crime, 473, 474–75

definition of, 469–73
functions of, 470, 471–73
managers, 469
styles, 473
place network(s), 475, 479
locations, 478
offenders and, 477
Place Network Investigations, 466–67, 475–79
Police Chief Magazine, 48
police-led diversion, 150
police-led science, 655
police legitimacy, 255
studies on, 225, 228–29, 232
police technology, 268, 275–76
police violence, 223, 235
fatal, 238
political use, 621, 623, 637, 638
of imposed use, 631
pooled places, 468
Positive Achievement Change Tool (PACT), 96, 163
Community Positive Achievement Tool (C-PACT), 162
Positive Action program, 451t, 453t
post-traumatic stress disorder (PTSD)
among justice-involved women, 353–54
victimization effects on, 484, 493t
powerholders, 224, 227
and audience(s), 225, 227, 230
in criminal justice, 227, 228
legitimacy and, 229, 230–34
pracademics, 44–45, 47–48, 254
in translational criminology, 48
predictive analytics, 604–5
predictive policing, 604–5
as intelligence-led policing, 250
preschool intellectual enrichment, 385–86
President Biden, 52
Executive Order (EO), 511
President's Commission on Crime (1967), 485
President's Task Force on 21st Century Policing, 223, 259, 351–52, 353
on procedural justice, 224
pretrial detention
in criminal justice, 108, 350
impact of, 512

in juvenile justice, 530
reducing disparities in, 515
pretrial reform, 515–97
preventive patrol, 248. *See also* Kansas City Preventive Patrol Experiment
random, 249
prison-based programs, 288–91, 331t
prison-based drug treatment program, 319, 354
TCs, 321
proactive policing [also proactive patrol], 252, 256–57, 269
CCTV and, 277
problem-oriented policing (POP), 246–47, 257
description of, 249–50
procedural justice, 172, 224
effects on cooperation with police, 230–31
focus of, 232
for generating legitimacy, 228, 230
President's Task Force (2015) on, 224
procedural justice theory (PJT), 224
process evaluation [also implementation evaluation], 38, 525. *See also* evaluation hierarchy
for addressing net-widening issues, 151–52
on Youth Restorative Disposal, 146
Program Evaluation Research Unit at the University of Pittsburgh (Pitt-PERU), 120–21
Project Build program, 166
Project Towards No Drug Abuse program, 451t, 453t
Prolonged Exposure Therapy, 493t
Promoting Alternative Thinking Strategies (PATHS), 211t, 432, 433–34, 435
promoting legitimacy, 231
elements on, 231–32
promotive factors, 162, 447
definition of, 445
propensity score matching, 164
in CCTV research, 269–70, 272–316
proprietary place(s) [also place], 467–68
protective factors, 160–61
CTC system and, 409
validated risk assessment instruments and, 174

psychological theories, 204, 205. *See also* delinquency theories
psychological view of delinquency, 203
Psychotherapies for Victims of Sexual Assault, 493*t*
psychotherapy, 292. *See also* CBT
  in victim services, 492, 493*t*
Pugliese, Katheryne, 9, 198

quackery, 655
  correctional, 1, 294, 585, 592
quality assurance, 62, 96–97, 103, 393
  and implementing RNR, 171–72
  system, 96
  WSIPP's recommendations on, 100
quasi-experimental designs
  propensity score matching, 164
quasi-experimental evaluations, 13, 214, 319–20, 341. *See also* evaluation

racial bias, 52–53, 108, 528–29
  among police officers, 533–34, 604–5, 611–12
  diversity training to reduce, 173
  racial bias amplification, 170
  standardized risk assessments to avoid, 170–71
racial impact legislation, 352
RAND Corporation
  cost-effectiveness of California's three-strikes law, 380
  on EBPs in schools, 66–67
  meta-analyses, 289–90
random assignment, 100, 269
  challenges associated with, 266–67
  in Support Matters program, 331*t*
randomized controlled trials (RCTs), 83–84, 213
  Blueprints and, 207
  CTC, 414
  early childhood field and, 76
  Head Start and, 378
  interventions not amenable to, 206, 214–15
  JDTCs and, 188
  parent training and, 401
  PMTO, 12–13, 391
  procedural justice and, 230–31

re-entry programs and, 292
  SMS and, 328
  TCs and, 291
rational choice, 13, 266
reactive arrests, 249
  reducing, 250
reactive model of policing, 248–49
Reasoning and Rehabilitation program, 290
  effectiveness of, 301
receptivity, 6. *See also* translational criminology
  research on, 39–40, 42, 51
recidivism, 11
  drug court participation and adult, 185–86
  JDTCs effect on juvenile, 184–85
  impact of diversion on, 149–51
  measuring, 106
  rates, 99
  reducing, 52–53, 91–92, 96, 102, 129–30, 162, 164, 167, 168–69, 184
reciprocal relationship, 313–14
Recovery Management Checkups (RMCs), 331*t*
rehabilitation
  community-based rehabilitation programs, 291–93
  correctional treatment and, 9, 287–93, 309
  desistance-focused, 299–300
  juvenile, 99, 514–15
Reintegration of Ex-Offenders (RExO), 331*t*
relative rate index (RRI), 527–28, 527*f*
replication, 23
  for achieving external validity, 21, 29 (*see also* external validity)
  crisis, 341
  meta-analyses and, 270
  study of PMTO, 395–96
REPS (reactors, enablers, promoters, and suppressors), 473, 474
  typology, 473
Research Advisory Committee (RAC), 48
research-based practitioner model, 44–45
research design, 268
  in CCTV evaluations and meta-analysis, 269–70
  in juvenile justice interventions, 631–32
  natural experiment, 269

non-experimental, 162
quasi-experimental, 150
in substance abuse treatment domain, 331t
research utilization, 41, 42, 621, 622–23
efforts to increase, 44–45
imposed use as mechanism of, 624–25, 630
by practitioners and policymakers, 6, 37
studies on, 42
researcher-practitioner partnerships, 46–47.
See also translational criminology
researcher sensibility, 652, 658–59, 660–61
benefits of, 653
and thinking counterfactually, 663
residential change
and criminal recidivism, 338, 339
and successful re-entry, 330
resilient legitimacy, 238
responsivity. *See also* Risk-Need-Responsivity (RNR) Model
responsivity factors, 96, 297
responsivity principle, 100–1, 161–62
restorative justice
JJSES framework and, 129f
in juvenile justice, 128–30
programs, 147–48, 299–300
in schools, 430–31
studies on, 430–31
retribution, 199–200, 583
get-tough era and, 581
right-to-carry (RTC) laws, 559
effects on crime, 559–60, 560f
risk factors, 161
dynamic, 151–52, 153, 161, 162
Risk-Need-Responsivity (RNR) Model, 160, 161–62, 287
effectiveness of, 182
low-risk offenders and, 295
risk principle, 161–62. *See also* Risk-Need-Responsivity (RNR) Model
Rocque, Michael, 10–11, 286
Rodriguez, Nancy, 14, 509
Roman, John K., 9, 198
Roper v. Simmons, 542 U.S. 551 (2005), 94
Ross, Katherine M., 13, 444
Rossi, Peter H., 51
on evaluation hierarchy, 3
routine activity theory, 14

place management and, 472

SafERteens program, 451t, 453t
Safe Streets program, 451t, 453t, 456, 457–58
evaluation of, 458
Safety Net program, 148
sample(s), 23
convenience, 491
non-random, 23–24
random, 23–24
sample size, 24
Sampson, Robert J., 340
on backward causality, 329
on causal revolution, 339
on differential involvement, 529
on naturally occurring data, 608
Sanders, Kaelyn, 14, 349
scaling [also scaling up], 77, 83
definition of, 77
threats to, 78, 79–80
types of scaling, 77
Scared Straight, 293–94
and deterrence, 169
iatrogenic effects of, 124, 293–94
Schindler, Holly S., 7, 76
school(s)
climate, 13, 428, 429, 430–31, 433–34
crime and delinquency, 424–25, 426
discipline, 426, 428
police in, 516
restorative justice in, 430
school resource officer (SRO), 516
security, 425–26
student misbehavior in, 424–25, 430–31
School-based programs
focus of, 427
schoolwide interventions, 427–29, 433–34
school-to-prison pipeline, 358, 360, 426
Schoolwide Positive Behavioral Interventions and Support (SWPBS), 429
second responder program for victims of family violence, 497
selection bias, 101, 532–34
self-control, 127–28, 432
JDTCs and, 183
prison dog-training program effects on, 289

self-defense gun use (SDGU), 555–56, 562–63
  evidence on, 563–64
self-esteem, 161, 202–3, 459
  interventions targeting issues in, 211t, 432
self-legitimacy, 227, 237
  effects of, 228
sensor systems, 600, 602, 608
sentencing guidelines, 93, 171, 359
sex offender treatment program(s), 292
Sexual Assault Nurse Examiner (SANE)
    program, 493t
Sherman, Lawrence W.
  on deterrence decay, 475
  on evidence-based policing, 245, 249, 251
single county authorities (SCA), 117, 119, 120
Smith, Roger S., 8, 117
SNAP® Under 12 Outreach Project, 209t
  cost-benefit analysis of, 380
  social control theories, 205
social development model, 121, 124
social disorganization [also social
    disorganization theory], 204
  CTC and, 409–10
social inequality, 14
  crime, criminal justice and, 510
social media
  and crime, 606–7
  data, 607
social skills training
  individual, 401–2
social theories, 204–5
social learning theories, 203
social learning and interaction (SIL)
    model, 394
  PMTO and, 403
social support programs, 331t
socially significant outcomes, 60–62,
    63, 64–65
  effective implementation and, 64f, 379–80
spatial concentration
  of crime, 511–12
  predictive policing and, 604
Spaw, Roger, 8, 117
Standardized Program Evaluation Protocol
    (SPEP), 120–21
  evaluation of, 167
  JSSES and, 129–30
  predictive validity of, 167

State v. Bassett, 192 Wn.2d 67 (2018), 94
statistical conclusion validity, 21, 22, 268. *See also* validity
statistical significance, 7
  incentivizing, 77
stigma, 351
  associated with a criminal record, 327
strain [also strain theory], 204, 520, 655
Strategic Prevention Framework (SPF), 460
structural factor(s), 91–92, 107, 215
  impact on justice-involved youth, 359
  impact on justice outcomes, 108
structural disadvantage(s), 350, 540–41
Structured Assessment of Violence Risk in
    Youth (SAVRY), 163–64
subcultural theories, 205
Substance Abuse and Mental Health Services
    Administration (SAMHSA), 435, 460
substance use. *See also* Communities That
    Care (CTC)
  disorders, 312, 317, 327, 377
substance use programs, 331t
  medically assisted treatment (MAT) for, 123
  CBT for, 290–91
Sullivan, Christopher J., 8–9, 179
supervision programs. *See also* intensive
    supervision
  meta-analysis of juvenile, 293
Supplemental Nutrition Assistance Program
    (SNAP), 355
Support4Families program, 331t
Support Matters program, 331t
survey data, 24, 226–27, 327, 417
Swansae Bureau, 146, 147, 153
systematic reviews, 4, 12, 24
  Campbell Collaboration, 253, 298
  of CCTV, 268
  of community treatment
    programs, 292
  external validity in large-scale, 270, 403
  of MAT programs, 319
  of place management, 474
  of Scared Straight, 293–94
  WSIPP, 96
systems-level changes, 457, 583

tangible costs, 376
  of CCTV, 274

Tankebe, Justice, 9–10, 223
Technical Assistance Center (TAC), 120–21
Telep, Cody W., 9, 37
Temporary Assistance for Needy Families (TANF), 355, 609
Tennessee
  experiments of NFP in, 379
  imposed use of EBPs in, 625, 626*t*
Texas Criminal Justice Policy Council (CJPC), 592
Therapeutic Approaches for Sexually Abused Children and Adolescents program, 493*t*
therapeutic communities (TCs), 316, 331*t*
  effectiveness of, 291
therapeutic program(s), 169, 211*t*, 213
theories of change (TOC), 78, 80, 82, 85
  community-driven, 81
  definition of, 78
theory evaluation, 26, 51, 525. *See also* evaluation hierarchy
theory failure, 535
  as explanation for DMC, 535, 537–38
third-party policing, 129–30, 249–50
three strikes laws, 637
  in California, 380
Together Helping Reduce Youth Violence for Equity (ThrYve), 451*t*, 453*t*, 456, 458
Tolan, Patrick H., 13, 444
Tonry, Michael, 1, 541, 637
top-down approach, 399–400, 654, 655
training
  as facilitation strategy, 46–47, 48–49, 63*f*
Transitional Aid Research Project (TARP), 329
transition/subsidized job program(s), 331*t*
Transitional Job Reentry Demonstration Program (TJRP), 331*t*
translation, 38–39. *See also* translational criminology
translational criminology, 37, 39–40, 53, 660
  challenge to, 339
  definitions of, 38
translational medicine, 38–39
transparency, 32
trauma
  among incarcerated populations, 327
  among justice-involved women, 353–54
  among justice-involved youth, 41–42, 358, 359
  among victims, 13–14, 361, 486–87, 492
  impacts of, 181
  interventions in schools, 211*t*
Trauma-Focused Treatment for Juveniles and Young Adults with Trauma Symptoms and Externalizing Behaviors, 493*t*
triage model, 142, 146–47
Turanovic, Jillian J., 484

United Kingdom
  CCTV effects on crime in, 271, 274
  diversion in, 143–47
  dominant model of policing in, 247
  intelligence-led policing in, 250
  McPherson Inquiry, 235–36
  punitive turn in England and Wales, 145
  recidivism rates in, 327
  young offenders in, 142–43
United States Department of Education, 61
United States Department of Health and Human Services, 76–77
United States Department of Justice (DOJ), 235, 258, 516
United States Department of Labor (DOL), 329, 516
United States Office of Justice Programs (OJP), 165, 581
United States Supreme Court
  on bail hearings, 515
  on domestic violence, 557
  on gun policy, 551, 555, 571–72, 592–93, 636
  on juvenile law, 94, 200–1
Utah
  imposed use of EBPs in, 626*t*
  Juvenile drug courts in, 181–82
  Juvenile Justice Reinvestment Restricted Account, 626*t*

Validity, 59, 457, 498, 622
  associated with survey data, 24
  construct, 22, 24, 186, 266
  descriptive, 33
  external, 29–31, 270, 340, 403
  internal, 186, 214, 270, 329, 340, 403, 414
  predictive, 163–64, 167, 171
  statistical conclusion, 21, 22, 268
Van Dyke, Melissa K., 58

Vermont
  imposed use of EBPs in, 626t
victim services, 13–14, 484–85
  advocates, 485–86, 488
  programs, 485, 493t
  providers, 488
  trauma-informed, 487, 490
  victim-centered approach to, 490
Victims of Crime Act (VOCA), 484, 486
victimization, 484
  fear of, 424
  justice-involved women and, 354
  occurring in the home, 488
  place management and, 469, 471–72, 473
  rates at school, 424, 426
  school interventions and rates of, 428–29, 433–34, 435
  sexual, 133, 518–19
  social costs of, 384
  studies on bullying and, 429
viewsheds, 267–68, 269
Violent Crime Control Act (1994), 235
vocational training, 331t
  in-prison, 515–16
  programs, 289

Walsh, Colleen S., 13, 444
war on drugs, 184, 311–12, 353
Washington, D.C., 555, 559, 563
Washington State
  Center for Court Research, 104
  juvenile justice system, 91
  Washington State Aggression Replacement Training (WSART) program, 91–92, 96–97, 101, 103, 106, 109, 110, 164–65
  Washington State Institute for Public Policy (WSIPP), 7–8, 91, 95–102
  Washington State Juvenile Court Assessment (WSJCA), 96, 163
  Washington State Legislature, 7–8, 93, 95, 103, 592
Weisburd, David
  on crime distributions across street segments, 467
  on economic data and program evaluations, 294–95
  on focused deterrence, 257
  on law of concentration of crime, 603–4
  on police hot spots, 234

Weiss, Carol
  on promising and model programs, 632
  on research utilization, 621, 623, 636
welfare costs, 377, 381–82
Wellford, Charles F., 340
Welsh, Brandon C., 1, 21
  on CCTV, 271, 275
  on correctional treatment, 294
  on creation of national crime prevention strategy, 417
  on early prevention, 373
  on evaluating research and assessing evidence, 21, 636
  on place management, 474
Welsh, Janet A., 8, 117
what does not work?
  in correctional rehabilitation, 293
  in victim services, 497
  in youth justice, 198, 215
what works?
  in juvenile justice, 167–68
  and translational criminology, 41–44
  in victim services, 484–85, 499
  What Works Centre for Crime Reduction, 45
  What Works in Policing, 37, 45–46, 51
  What Works in Reentry Clearinghouse, 330
William T. Grant Foundation, 52
Wisconsin
  Wisconsin Treatment Alternatives and Diversion (TAD) program, 626t
Women Offender Case Management Model (WOCMM), 356
'Wrap-Around' Service(s) programs, 331t
  employment-focused wrap-around program (Milwaukee), 331t

youth gun carrying
  risk factors for urban, 449
  in urban communities, 449
  youth gun violence, 449, 457–58
Youth Level of Service/Case Management Inventory (YLS/CMI), 129
Youth Justice Board, 145, 146
Youth Justice Liaison and Diversion model, 146–47
Youth Restorative Disposal, 146
youth violence
  economic impacts of, 444

EBPs for youth violence prevention, 451*t*–53*t*, 458
in Norway, 391–92
precedents to, 445
as public health crisis, 444
risk and protective factors for, 446–50
youth violence prevention (YVP) in urban settings, 445, 461

Zane, Steven N., 1
on cumulative disadvantage, 512
on DMC in juvenile justice, 525
on imposed use, 621
Zero-tolerance, 120
Zero-tolerance policies in schools, 426
Zimring, Franklin
on diversion in juvenile court, 142
on outcomes of gun assaults, 526, 552
on reforms to reduce DMC in juvenile justice, 522
on threats to police officers, 555